ENCYCLOPEDIA OF
Race, Ethnicity, and Society

VOLUME 2

ENCYCLOPEDIA OF
Race, Ethnicity, and Society

Richard T. Schaefer *Editor*
DePaul University

A SAGE Reference Publication

SAGE Publications
Los Angeles • London • New Delhi • Singapore

Copyright © 2008 by SAGE Publications, Inc.

All rights reserved. No part of this book may be reproduced or utilized in any form or by any means, electronic or mechanical, including photocopying, recording, or by any information storage and retrieval system, without permission in writing from the publisher.

For information:

SAGE Publications, Inc.
2455 Teller Road
Thousand Oaks, California 91320
E-mail: order@sagepub.com

SAGE Publications Ltd.
1 Oliver's Yard
55 City Road
London EC1Y 1SP
United Kingdom

SAGE Publications India Pvt. Ltd.
B 1/I 1 Mohan Cooperative Industrial Area
Mathura Road, New Delhi 110 044
India

SAGE Publications Asia-Pacific Pte. Ltd.
33 Pekin Street #02-01
Far East Square
Singapore 048763

Printed in the United States of America.

Library of Congress Cataloging-in-Publication Data

Encyclopedia of race, ethnicity, and society/edited by Richard T. Schaefer.
  p. cm.
Includes bibliographical references and index.
ISBN 978-1-4129-2694-2 (cloth)
  1. Racism—Encyclopedias. 2. Race relations—Encyclopedias. 3. Ethnicity—Encyclopedias. I. Schaefer, Richard T.

HT1521.E63 2008
305.8003—dc22   2007042741

This book is printed on acid-free paper.

08 09 10 11   10 9 8 7 6 5 4 3 2 1

Publisher:	Rolf A. Janke
Acquisitions Editor:	Jerry Westby
Developmental Editor:	Diana E. Axelsen
Reference Systems Manager:	Leticia Gutierrez
Production Editor:	Kate Schroeder
Copy Editors:	Carla Freeman, Robin Gold, D. J. Peck
Typesetter:	C&M Digitals (P) Ltd.
Proofreaders:	Scott Oney, Penny Sippel, Dennis Webb
Indexer:	Julie Grayson
Cover Designer:	Candice Harman
Marketing Manager:	Amberlyn Erzinger

Contents

List of Entries *vii*

List of Images *xv*

Reader's Guide *xix*

Entries

Volume 1: A–F

1–518

Volume 2: G–Q

519–1090

Volume 3: R–Z

1091–1430

Appendixes

Appendix A: Data on Race and
Ethnicity in the United States, 1820 to the Present   *1433*

Appendix B: Internet Resources
on Race, Ethnicity, and Society   *1493*

Index   *1499*

List of Entries

Abolitionism: The Movement
Abolitionism: The People
Abortion
Acculturation
Adoption
Affirmative Action in Education
Affirmative Action in the Workplace
Afghan Americans
African Americans
African Americans, Migration of
African American Studies
African American Women and Work
Africans in the United States
Afrocentricity
Aging
Alamo, The
Alaskan Natives, Legislation Concerning
Albanian Americans
Aleuts
Alien Land Acts
American Apartheid
American Dilemma, An
American Indian Movement
American Indians. *See* Native Americans
Americanization
American Jewish Committee
Americans with Disabilities Act
Amish
Anti-Defamation League
Antiracist Education
Anti-Semitism
Apartheid
Apartheid, Laws
Arab Americans
Argentina
Armenian Americans

Asian Americans
Asian Americans, New York City
Asian American Studies
Asian American Studies, Mixed-Heritage
ASPIRA
Assimilation
Assyrian Americans
Asylum
Australia
Australia, Indigenous People
Authoritarian Personality
Aztlán

Back to Africa Movement
Baldwin, James
Balkans
Bangladeshi Americans
Barrio
Belgian Americans
Belize
Bell Curve, The
Bilingual Education
Biomedicine, African Americans and
Birth of a Nation, The
Black Bourgeoisie
Black Cinema
Black Conservatives
Black Elk
Black Enterprise
Blackfeet
Black Intellectuals
Black-Jewish Relations. *See* Jewish-Black Relations: A Historical Perspective; Jewish-Black Relations: The Contemporary Period
Black Marxism. *See* Robinson, Cedric
Black Metropolis

Black Nationalism
Black Panther Party
Black Power
Blockbusting
Blood Quantum
Boas, Franz
"Boat People"
Body Image
Borderlands
Border Patrol
Bosnian Americans
Boycott
Bracero Program
Brain Drain
Brazil
Brazilian Americans
Britain's Irish
Brown Berets
Brown v. Board of Education
Bulgarian Americans
Burakumin
Bureau of Indian Affairs
Burmese Americans. *See* Myanmarese Americans

Cambodian Americans
Canada
Canada, Aboriginal Women
Canada, First Nations
Canadian Americans
Cape Verde
Caribbean
Caribbean Americans
Carmichael, Stokely
Caste
Census, U.S.
Central Americans in the United States
Chávez, César
Cherokee
Cheyenne
Chicago School of Race Relations
Chicano Movement
Child Development
Chin, Vincent
China
Chinatowns
Chinese Americans

Chinese Exclusion Act
Choctaw
Cisneros v. Corpus Christi School District
Citizenship
Civil Disobedience
Civil Religion
Civil Rights Movement
Civil Rights Movement, Women and
Code of the Street
Collins, Patricia Hill
Colombia
Colonialism
Colonias
Color Blindness
Color Line
Community Cohesion
Community Empowerment
Congress of Racial Equality (CORE)
Contact Hypothesis
Cosmopolitanism
Creole
Crime and Race
Criminal Processing
Critical Race Theory
Croatian Americans
Cross-Frontier Contacts
Crown Heights, Brooklyn
Cuba
Cuba: Migration and Demography
Cuban Americans
Cultural Capital
Cultural Relativism
Culture of Poverty
Cypriot Americans
Czech Americans

Danish Americans
Dawes Act of 1887
Death Penalty
Declining Significance of Race, The
Deficit Model of Ethnicity
Deloria, Vine, Jr.
Desi
Deviance and Race
Diaspora
Digital Divide

Dillingham Flaw
Discrimination
Discrimination, Environmental Hazards
Discrimination, Measuring
Discrimination in Housing
Domestic Violence
Domestic Work
Dominican Americans
Dominican Republic
Double Consciousness
Douglass, Frederick
Drake, St. Clair
Dred Scott v. Sandford
Drug Use
Du Bois, William Edward Burghardt
Dutch Americans

East Harlem
Educational Performance and Attainment
Educational Stratification
Egyptian Americans
Emancipation Proclamation
English Americans. *See* United Kingdom, Immigrants and Their Descendants in the United States
English Immersion
Environmental Justice
Equal Employment Opportunity Commission (EEOC)
Estonian Americans
Ethnic Conflict
Ethnic Enclave, Economic Impact of
Ethnic Group
Ethnicity, Negotiating
Ethnic Succession
Ethnocentrism
Ethnonational Minorities
Ethnoviolence
Eugenics
Europe

Familism
Family
Fanon, Frantz
Father Divine Peace Mission Movement
Feminism

Feminism, Black
Feminism, Latina
Filipino Americans
Film, Latino
Finnish Americans
Foreign Students
France
Fraternities and Sororities
Frazier, E. Franklin
French Americans
FUBU Company

Gaming, Native American
Gangs
Gautreaux Decision
Gender and Race, Intersection of
Gender Identity. *See* Lesbian, Gay, Bisexual, and Transgender; Sexuality
Genocide
Gentlemen's Agreement (1907–1908)
Gentrification
Georgian Americans
German Americans
Gerrymandering
Ghetto
Glass Ceiling
Globalization
Global Perspective
Greek Americans
Grutter v. Bollinger
Guatemalan Americans
Guest Workers

Hafu
Haiti
Haitian Americans
Haitian and Cuban Immigration: A Comparison
Haole
Hapa
Harlem
Harlem Renaissance
Hate Crimes
Hate Crimes in Canada
Hawai'i, Race in
Hawaiians
Head Start and Immigrants

Health, Immigrant
Health Disparities
Hernandez v. Texas
Higher Education
Higher Education: Racial Battle Fatigue
Hip-Hop
Hip-Hop and Rap, Women and
Hispanics
Hispanic Versus *Latino*
HIV/AIDS
Hmong Americans
Holocaust
Holocaust Deniers and Revisionists
Homelessness
Homicide
Honduran Americans
Hong Kong
hooks, bell
Hopi
Hourglass Economy
Housing Audits
Huerta, Dolores
Hull House School of Race Relations
Hungarian Americans
Hurricane Katrina
Hutterites

Icelandic Americans
Identity Politics
Illegal Immigration Reform and Immigrant Responsibility Act of 1996
Immigrant Communities
Immigration, Economic Impact of
Immigration, U.S.
Immigration and Gender
Immigration and Nationality Act of 1965
Immigration and Naturalization Service (INS)
Immigration and Race
Immigration Reform and Control Act of 1986
Incarcerated Parents
India
Indian Americans
Indian Child Welfare Act of 1978
Indian Gaming Regulatory Act of 1988
Individuals with Disabilities Education Act of 1990
Indonesian Americans

Informal Economy
Institutional Discrimination
Integration. *See* Resegregation; School Desegregation
Intelligence Tests
Intercultural Communication
Intergroup Relations, Surveying
Intermarriage
Internal Colonialism
Internalized Racism
International Convention on the Elimination of All Forms of Racial Discrimination
Internment Camps
Interracial Friendships
Invisible Man
Iranian Americans
Iraqi Americans
Ireland
Irish Americans
Islamophobia
Issei
Italian Americans

Jackson, Jesse, Sr.
Jamaica
Jamaican Americans
Japan
Japanese American Citizens League
Japanese Americans
Jewish Americans
Jewish-Black Relations: A Historical Perspective
Jewish-Black Relations: The Contemporary Period
Jewry, Black American
Jim Crow
Johnson, Charles S.
Jordanian Americans
Juvenile Justice

Kennewick Man
Kenya
King, Martin Luther, Jr.
Kinship
Kitano, Harry H. L.
Korean Americans
Ku Klux Klan

Kurdish Americans
Kwanzaa

Labeling
Labor Market Segmentation
Labor Unions
Laotian Americans
La Raza
La Raza Unida Party
Latin America, Indigenous People
Latina/o Studies
Latvian Americans
Lebanese Americans
Lee, Spike
Leisure
Lesbian, Gay, Bisexual, and Transgender
Life Expectancy
Lincoln, Abraham
Lithuanian Americans
London Bombings (July 7, 2005)
Loving v. Virginia
Lynching

Machismo
Malcolm X
Mandela, Nelson
Maquiladoras
Marginalization
"Marielitos"
Marshall, Thurgood
Marxism and Racism
McCarran-Walter Act of 1952
Media and Race
Medical Experimentation
Melting Pot
Mennonites
Menominee
Mexican American Legal Defense and Educational Fund (MALDEF)
Mexican Americans
Mexico
Military and Race
Minority/Majority
Minority Rights
Model Minority
Mormons, Race and

Multicultural Education
Multicultural Social Movements
Multiracial Identity
Muslim Americans
Muslims in Canada
Muslims in Europe
Myanmarese Americans

National Association for the Advancement of Colored People (NAACP)
National Congress of American Indians
National Council of La Raza
National Indian Youth Council
National Origins System
National Rainbow Coalition
National Urban League
Nation of Islam
Native American Education
Native American Graves Protection and Repatriation Act of 1990
Native American Health Care
Native American Identity
Native American Identity, Legal Background
Native Americans
Native Americans, Environment and
Nativism
Navajo
Negro League Baseball
Newton, Huey
Nicaraguan Americans
Nigeria
Nigerian Americans
Nikkeijin
Nisei
Northern Ireland, Racism in
Norwegian Americans

Ojibwa
One-Drop Rule
Operation Bootstrap
Operation PUSH
Orientalism

Pachucos/Pachucas
Pacific Islanders
Pakistani Americans

Palestinian Americans
Panamanian Americans
Pan-Asian Identity
Panethnic Identity
Pan-Indianism
Parenting
Park, Robert E.
Parks, Rosa
PATRIOT Act of 2001
Peltier, Leonard
Peoplehood
People of Color
Peru
Peruvian Americans
Peyote
Pipeline
Plessy v. Ferguson
Pluralism
Police
Polish Americans
Political Economy
Popular Culture, Racism and
Portuguese Americans
Prejudice
Prisons
Privilege
Proposition 187
Public Housing
Pueblos
Puerto Rican Americans
Puerto Rican Armed Forces
  of National Liberation (FALN)
Puerto Rican Legal Defense and Education Fund
Puerto Rico

Race
Race, Comparative Perspectives
Race, Declining Significance of. *See Declining Significance of Race, The*
Race, Social Construction of
Race, UNESCO Statements on
Racetalk
Racial Formation
Racial Identity
Racial Identity Development
Racialization

Racial Profiling
Racism
Racism, Aversive
Racism, Cultural
Racism, Types of
Racism, Unintentional
Rainbow Coalition.
  See National Rainbow Coalition
Rap: The Genre
Rap: The Movement
Redlining
Red Power
Refugees
Religion
Religion, African Americans
Religion, Minority
Religious Freedom Restoration Act of 1993
Religious Movements, New
Remittances
Reparations, Slavery
Repatriation of Mexican Americans
Resegregation
Reservation System
Restrictive Covenants
Return Migration
Reverse Discrimination
Rites of Passage
Robbers Cave Experiment
Robinson, Cedric
Robinson, Jackie
Roma
Roman Catholics
Romanian Americans
Russia

Sacred Sites, Native American
Sacred Versus Secular
Salvadoran Americans
Sami
Samoan Americans
Samora, Julian
San Antonio Independent School District v.
  Rodriguez
Sand Creek Massacre
Sansei
Santería

Scapegoats
Schmiedeleut
School Desegregation
School Desegregation, Attitudes Concerning
Science Faculties, Women of Color on
Scottish Americans. *See* United Kingdom, Immigrants and Their Descendants in the United States
Segregation
Self-Fulfilling Prophecy
Separate but Equal
Serbian Americans
Sexual Harassment
Sexuality
Sicilian Americans
Singapore
Sioux
Slavery
Slovak Americans
Slovene Americans
Social Capital
Social Darwinism
Social Distance
Social Inequality
Social Mobility
Social Support
Social Work
South Africa, Republic of
South Americans in the United States
Southern Christian Leadership Conference (SCLC)
Sovereignty, Native American
Spanglish
Spanish Americans
Split Labor Market
Sri Lankan Americans
Stereotypes
Stereotype Threat
Student Nonviolent Coordinating Committee (SNCC)
Sundown Towns
Swedish Americans
Symbolic Ethnicity
Symbolic Religiosity
Syrian Americans

Taiwan
Talented Tenth

Terrorism
Testing
Thai Americans
Third-Generation Principle
Thorpe, Jim
Tibetan Americans
Title IX
Tlingit
Tongan Americans
Tracking
Trail of Broken Treaties
Transnational People
Transracial Adoption
Treaty of Guadalupe Hidalgo (1848)
Trinidad
Truth, Sojourner
Tubman, Harriet
Turkey
Turkish Americans

Ugandan Americans
Ukrainian Americans
Underclass
United Kingdom
United Kingdom, Immigrants and Their Descendants in the United States
United States v. Fordice
Urban League. *See* National Urban League
Urban Legends
Urban Riots
"Us and Them"
U.S. Census. *See* Census, U.S.

Veil
Victim Discounting
Victimization
Vietnamese Americans
Voting Rights

Washington, Booker T.
Washington, Harold
WASP
Water Rights
Wealth Distribution
"Welfare Queen"
Welfare Reform

Wells-Barnett, Ida B.
Welsh Americans. *See* United Kingdom, Immigrants and Their Descendants in the United States
West Indian Americans
"Wetbacks"
White Flight
Whiteness
Whiteness, Measuring
Whiteness and Masculinity
White Privilege
White Racism
White Supremacy Movement
Williams, Fannie Barrier
Wilson, William Julius
Wounded Knee (1890 and 1973)

Xenophobia

Young Lords

Zapatista Rebellion
Zimbabwe
Zionism
Zoot Suit Riots

List of Images

Abolitionism: The People: Harpers Ferry insurrection (photo) *4*
Abortion: Table 1, Estimated Abortion Rate by Poverty Status, According to Race and Ethnicity *7*
Adoption: Family with five adopted, Russian-born children (photo) *10*
Afghanistan (map) *19*
African Americans: Figure 1, Estimated Percent of Blacks in the United States *27*
African American Women and Work: African American women sorting tobacco (photo) *36*
Africans in the United States: Senegalese woman in New York (photo) *38*
Albania (map) *47*
Aleutian Islands (map) *50*
Aleuts: Aleutian child, 1938 (photo) *51*
American Apartheid: Public housing in the Bedford Stuyvesant area of Brooklyn (photo) *55*
Anti-Semitism: *The Eternal Jew* poster (photo) *77*
Argentina (map) *87*
Armenia (map) *89*
Asian Americans: Figure 1, Estimated Percent of Asians in the United States *95*
Assyria (map) *108*
Australia, Indigenous People: June Smith and her work at a Sydney art gallery (photo) *115*
Balkans (map) *129*
Bangladesh (map) *132*
Barrio: Mariachis in East Los Angeles, California (photo) *134*
Belgium (map) *136*
Belize (map) *138*
Birth of a Nation, The: Scene from *The Birth of a Nation* (photo) *150*

Black Conservatives: U.S. Supreme Court Justice Clarence Thomas (photo) *157*
Black Enterprise: Figure 1, Proportion of Employed Black and White College Graduates in Managerial Jobs *162*
Figure 2, Percentage of People Over 24 Who Have Completed College, by Race *163*
Border Patrol: U.S. border with Mexico (photo) *193*
Bosnia-Herzegovina (map) *195*
Brazil (map) *200*
Brazilian men practicing *capoeira* on the beachfront (photo) *201*
Britain's Irish: Figure 1, Irish-born Recorded in Great Britain *207*
Bulgaria (map) *213*
Cambodia (map) *221*
Canada, First Nations: A Haida gift offering to the Tlingit (photo) *231*
Cape Verde (map) *235*
Caribbean Islands (map) *237*
Caste: Hindu children of high caste, Bombay, India (photo) *247*
Central America (map) *252*
Central Americans in the United States: Table 1, Central American Population in the United States *252*
Chávez, César: César Chávez and Coretta Scott King (photo) *256*
Cheyenne: Great Omaha powwow dance of the Cheyenne in Montana (photo) *264*
Child Development: African American grandmother and grandchildren (photo) *275*
China (map) *278*

Chinatowns: Chinese New Year Parade (photo) *282*
Civil Religion: Pledging allegiance to the flag (photo) *303*
Civil Rights Movement: Civil rights march (photo) *305*
Colombia (map) *316*
Contact Hypothesis: Office relations (photo) *330*
Croatia (map) *347*
Cuba (map) *352*
Cuban Americans: Cuban immigrants (photo) *357*
Cyprus (map) *365*
Czech Republic (map) *367*
Danish Americans: Danish Lutheran church, Evan, Minnesota (photo) *370*
Deficit Model of Ethnicity: Cuban exile in Miami (photo) *379*
Denmark (map) *369*
Discrimination: Table 1, Median Income by Race and Gender *393*
Dominican Americans: Dominican Day parade (photo) *409*
Dominican Republic (map) *410*
Douglass, Frederick (photo) *414*
Dred Scott v. Sandford: General parody of the 1860 presidential contest (cartoon) *417*
Drug Use: Table 1, Percentage of Persons Using Drugs in the Past 30 Days, by Age and Race *421*
Du Bois, William Edward Burghardt (photo) *423*
Educational Performance and Attainment: Table 1, Educational Performance and Attainment by Race and Ethnicity *433*
Egypt (map) *438*
El Salvador (map) *1185*
English Immersion: Arab American girl reading (photo) *440*
Estonia (map) *448*
Ethnic Enclaves: Festival in Little Italy (photo) *454*
Eugenics: Buchenwald concentration camp (photo) *472*
Father Divine Peace Movement: Father Divine (photo) *484*
Filipino Americans: Filipino American couple (photo) *494*
Finland (map) *500*
France (map) *506*

Fraternities and Sororities: Sorority members (photo) *510*
Gaming, Native American: Gamblers in Native American casino (photo) *520*
Gentrification: Construction in Harlem (photo) *536*
Georgia (map) *537*
German Americans: German emigrants (engraving) *541*
Germany (map) *540*
Glass Ceiling: Latina executive (photo) *549*
Greece (map) *559*
Guatemala (map) *564*
Haiti (map) *571*
Harlem Renaissance: Langston Hughes (photo) *587*
Hawai'i (map) *599*
Hawai'i, Race in: Table 1, Most Common Racial/Ethnic Groups in Hawai'i *597*
Table 2, Summary Statistics Based on Selected Socioeconomic Indicators by Group *598*
Hawaiians: Figure 1, Native Hawaiian Populations Before and After Western Contact *600*
Higher Education: Fisk University students (photo) *613*
Higher Education: Racial Battle Fatigue: Figure 1, Causes and Stress Reactions to Racial Battle Fatigue *617*
Hispanics: Figure 1, Estimated Percent of Latinos/Hispanics in the United States *626*
Homelessness: Homeless person (photo) *642*
Honduras (map) *647*
Hong Kong (map) *648*
Hungary (map) *662*
Hurricane Katrina: Hurricane Katrina victims (photo) *665*
Iceland (map) *673*
Immigration: Figure 1, Number of New Lawful Permanent Residents *687*
Figure 2, Legal Status of the U.S. Foreign-Born Population *690*
Immigration Reform and Control Act 1986: Illegal immigrants (photo) *702*
India (map) *707*
Indian Americans: Indian American woman (photo) *712*
Indonesia (map) *721*

Intermarriage: Interracial couple with their daughter (photo) *737*

Internment camps: Schoolchildren at Manzanar (photo) *745*

Japanese Americans Fred Korematsu, Minoru Yasui, and Gordon Hirabayashi, at a press conference on January 19, 1983 (photo) *746*

Iran (map) *752*

Iraq (map) *754*

Ireland (map) *755*

Irish Americans: Immigration cartoon *758*

Table 1, Immigration From Ireland to the United States *759*

Italian Americans: Italian neighborhood market (photo) *768*

Italy (map) *767*

Jamaica (map) *775*

Jamaican Americans: Harry Belafonte (photo) *776*

Japan (map) *779*

Kenya (map) *803*

King, Martin Luther, Jr. (photo) *806*

Korea, North and South (map) *812*

Ku Klux Klan: Ku Klux Klan rally (photo) *815*

Laos (map) *827*

Latin America, Indigenous People: Aztec Indian children in Mexico (photo) *834*

Latvia (map) *839*

Lebanon (map) *840*

Lee, Spike: Table 1, Chronology of Films by Spike Lee *842*

Lesbian, Gay, Bisexual, Transgender: Gay rights rally (photo) *847*

Life Expectancy: Figure 1, Life Expectancy at Birth, by Race and Sex *850*

Figure 2, Infant Mortality Rates by Race and Hispanic Origin *851*

Table 1, Ten Leading Causes of Death Among Non-Hispanic Blacks and Non-Hispanic Whites *849*

Lithuania (map) *854*

Loving v. Virginia: Mildred and Richard Loving (photo) *858*

Malcolm X (photo) *865*

Marshall, Thurgood: Official portrait of the 1976 U.S. Supreme Court: Justice Thurgood Marshall (photo) *875*

Medical Experimentation: Tuskegee Syphilis Study (photo) *884*

Mexican Americans: Immigration reform demonstration (photo) *893*

Mexico (map) *898*

Myanmar (map) *929*

Native American Education: Carlisle Indian School physical education class (photo) *945*

Native Americans: Figure 1, American Indian and Alaska Native Household Population by State *965*

Table 1, American Indian and Alaska Native Household Population by Tribal Group *960*

Navajo: Three Navajo women weaving (photo) *971*

Negro League Baseball: Homestead Grays (photo) *973*

The Netherlands (map) *427*

Nicaragua (map) *978*

Nigeria (map) *980*

Norway (map) *991*

Ojibwa: Ojibwa Indian family in a canoe (photo) *996*

One-Drop Rule: Table 1, Percent Reporting Two or More Races by Specified Race *999*

Pacific Islanders: Pacific Island census workers taking a break (photo) *1009*

Table 1, Native Hawaiian and Other Pacific Islander Population *1007*

Pacific Islands (map) *1007*

Pakistan (map) *1010*

Panama (map) *1016*

Parks, Rosa (photo) *1029*

Peru (map) *1040*

Philippines (map) *493*

Poland (map) *1056*

Polish Americans: Polish family working in the fields near Baltimore, Maryland (photo) *1057*

Portugal (map) *1063*

Puerto Rico (map) *1086*

Workers hoeing a tobacco slope in Puerto Rico (photo) *1087*

Racial Profiling: Table 1, Race Differences in Perceptions of Profiling *1112*

Red Power: Sioux tribesmen on Alcatraz (photo) *1130*

Religion, African Americans: Mass at an African American Catholic Church on the South Side of Chicago (photo) *1137*

Roman Catholics: Consecration of St. Patrick's Cathedral (photo) *1171*
Romania (map) *1173*
Russia (map) *1175*
Samoa (map) *1189*
Scapegoats: Men in a Chinese lodging house in San Francisco smoking opium (photo) *1202*
School Desegregation (photo) *1205*
Segregation: Drinking fountain on the county courthouse lawn in Halifax, North Carolina (photo) *1213*
Serbia (map) *1222*
Sicily (map) *1227*
Singapore (map) *1228*
Sioux: Sioux at the White House (sketch) *1232*
Slovakia (map) *1238*
Slovene Americans: Figure 1, Most Important Settlements of Slovene Americans *1243*
Slovenia (map) *1241*
Social Support: Three-generation Asian American family having dinner (photo) *1256*
South Africa, Republic of (map) *1261*
South Americans in the United States:
  Table 1, South American Immigration to the United States *1264*
  Table 2, Characteristics of the Foreign-Born Population From Select Latin American Countries *1266*
Spain (map) *1273*
Sri Lanka (map) *1276*
Sundown Towns: Figure 1, Sundown Counties in Indiana *1284*
Sweden (map) *1286*
Swedish Americans: Bishop Hill Colony (photo) *1287*
Syria (map) *1291*
Taiwan (map) *1293*
Terrorism: Airport security (photo) *1298*
Thai Americans: Ritual of paying respect to the teacher at a Thai American Buddhist temple (photo) *1302*
Thailand (map) *1301*
Thorpe, Jim (photo) *1305*
Title IX: Women's ice hockey game (photo) *1309*
Tlingit: Kaw-Claa (photo) *1311*
  A new chief (photo) *1312*
Tonga (map) *1314*
Trinidad (map) *1326*
  Table 1, Distribution of the Population by Race/Ethnicity in Trinidad *1328*
Truth, Sojourner (photo) *1329*
Turkey (map) *1334*
Uganda (map) *1339*
Ukraine (map) *1341*
United Kingdom (map) *1347*
  Queen Elizabeth II (photo) *1348*
Vietnam (map) *1366*
Vietnamese Americans (photo) *1367*
Wells-Barnett, Ida: Lynching caught on camera (photo) *1389*
West Indies (map) *1391*
White Supremacy Movement: George Lincoln Rockwell (photo) *1409*
Zimbabwe (map) *1425*

Reader's Guide

This list is provided to assist readers in locating entries on related topics. Some entry titles appear in more than one category.

Biographies

Baldwin, James
Black Elk
Boas, Franz
Carmichael, Stokely
Chávez, César
Chin, Vincent
Collins, Patricia Hill
Deloria, Vine, Sr.
Douglass, Frederick
Drake, St. Clair
Du Bois, William Edward Burghardt
Fanon, Frantz
Frazier, E. Franklin
hooks, bell
Huerta, Dolores
Jackson, Jesse, Jr.
Johnson, Charles S.
King, Martin Luther, Jr.
Kitano, Harry H. L.
Lee, Spike
Lincoln, Abraham
Malcolm X
Mandela, Nelson
Marshall, Thurgood
Newton, Huey
Park, Robert E.
Parks, Rosa
Peltier, Leonard
Robinson, Cedric
Robinson, Jackie
Samora, Julian
Thorpe, Jim
Truth, Sojourner
Tubman, Harriet
Washington, Booker T.
Washington, Harold
Wells-Barnett, Ida B.
Williams, Fannie Barrier
Wilson, William Julius

Community and Urban Issues

American Apartheid
Apartheid
Asian Americans, New York City
Barrio
Black Metropolis
Blockbusting
Chicago School of Race Relations
Chinatowns
Code of the Street
Colonialism
Colonias
Community Cohesion
Community Empowerment
Crown Heights, Brooklyn
Culture of Poverty
Discrimination in Housing
East Harlem
Ethnic Enclave, Economic Impact of
Ethnic Succession
Gangs
Gautreaux Decision
Gentrification

Ghetto
Harlem
Homelessness
Housing Audits
Hull House School of Race Relations
Hurricane Katrina
National Urban League
Public Housing
Redlining
Resegregation
School Desegregation
Segregation
Sundown Towns
Urban Riots
White Flight
Zoot Suit Riots

Concepts and Theories

Acculturation
Afrocentricity
Americanization
Anti-Semitism
Assimilation
Asylum
Authoritarian Personality
Aztlán
Barrio
Black Bourgeoisie
Black Nationalism
Black Power
Blockbusting
Blood Quantum
"Boat People"
Body Image
Boycott
Brain Drain
Caste
Chinatowns
Citizenship
Civil Disobedience
Civil Religion
Code of the Street
Colonialism
Colonias
Color Blindness
Color Line
Community Cohesion
Community Empowerment
Contact Hypothesis
Cosmopolitanism
Critical Race Theory
Cultural Capital
Cultural Relativism
Culture of Poverty
Deficit Model of Ethnicity
Desi
Diaspora
Digital Divide
Dillingham Flaw
Double Consciousness
Environmental Justice
Ethnic Enclave, Economic Impact of
Ethnic Group
Ethnicity, Negotiating
Ethnic Succession
Ethnocentrism
Ethnonational Minorities
Ethnoviolence
Eugenics
Familism
Feminism
Feminism, Black
Feminism, Latina
Genocide
Gentrification
Gerrymandering
Ghetto
Glass Ceiling
Globalization
Guest Workers
Hafu
Hapa
Hate Crimes
Hate Crimes in Canada
Higher Education: Racial Battle Fatigue
Hispanic Versus *Latino*
Holocaust
Holocaust Deniers and Revisionists
Homelessness
Hourglass Economy
Housing Audits

Identity Politics
Informal Economy
Intercultural Communication
Internal Colonialism
Internalized Racism
Internment Camps
Invisible Man
Islamophobia
Jim Crow
Kinship
Kwanzaa
Labeling
Labor Market Segmentation
La Raza
Machismo
Marginalization
"Marielitos"
Marxism and Racism
Melting Pot
Minority/Majority
Model Minority
Multiracial Identity
Native American Identity
Nativism
Nikkeijin
Nisei
One-Drop Rule
Orientalism
Pan-Asian Identity
Panethnic Identity
Pan-Indianism
Peoplehood
People of Color
Pipeline
Pluralism
Political Economy
Privilege
Race
Race, Social Construction of
Racetalk
Racial Formation
Racial Identity
Racial Identity Development
Racialization
Racial Profiling
Racism

Racism, Aversive
Racism, Cultural
Racism, Unintentional
Redlining
Red Power
Refugees
Remittances
Resegregation
Restrictive Covenants
Return Migration
Reverse Discrimination
Rites of Passage
Sacred Versus Secular
Sansei
Scapegoats
Segregation
Self-Fulfilling Prophecy
Separate but Equal
Sexual Harassment
Social Capital
Social Darwinism
Social Distance
Sovereignty, Native American
Spanglish
Split Labor Market
Stereotypes
Stereotype Threat
Sundown Towns
Symbolic Ethnicity
Symbolic Religiosity
Talented Tenth
Third-Generation Principle
Tracking
Transnational People
Underclass
Urban Legends
"Us and Them"
Veil
Victim Discounting
Victimization
WASP
"Welfare Queen"
"Wetbacks"
White Flight
Whiteness
White Privilege

White Racism
Xenophobia

Criminal Justice

Apartheid, Laws
Crime and Race
Criminal Processing
Death Penalty
Deviance and Race
Drug Use
Gangs
Hate Crimes
Hate Crimes, Canada
Homicide
Incarcerated Parents
Internment Camps
Jim Crow
Juvenile Justice
Labeling
Lynching
Pachucos/Pachucas
PATRIOT Act of 2001
Police
Prisons
Racial Profiling
Victim Discounting
Victimization

Economics and Stratification

Affirmative Action in the Workplace
Alien Land Acts
Americans with Disabilities Act
Apartheid
Barrio
Black Bourgeoisie
Black Enterprise
Black Power
Boycott
Bracero Program
Brain Drain
Caste
Colonialism
Color Line
Culture of Poverty

Declining Significance of Race, The
Digital Divide
Discrimination
Discrimination, Environmental Hazards
Discrimination, Measuring
Discrimination in Housing
Domestic Work
Double Consciousness
Environmental Justice
Equal Employment Opportunity Commission (EEOC)
FUBU Company
Gaming, Native American
Gentrification
Ghetto
Glass Ceiling
Globalization
Guest Workers
Health Disparities
Homelessness
Hourglass Economy
Indian Gaming Regulatory Act of 1988
Informal Economy
Institutional Discrimination
Internal Colonialism
Labor Market Segmentation
Labor Unions
Maquiladoras
Marxism and Racism
Model Minority
Operation Bootstrap
Political Economy
Public Housing
Redlining
Remittances
Reparations, Slavery
Repatriation of Mexican Americans
Resegregation
Reservation System
Restrictive Covenants
Return Migration
Social Capital
Social Darwinism
Social Inequality
Social Mobility
Split-Labor Market

Talented Tenth
Transnational People
Underclass
Water Rights
Wealth Distribution
"Welfare Queen"
Welfare Reform

Education

Affirmative Action in Education
African American Studies
Afrocentricity
Antiracist Education
Asian American Studies
Asian American Studies, Mixed-Heritage
Bell Curve, The
Bilingual Education
Biomedicine, African Americans and
Black Intellectuals
Brain Drain
Brown v. Board of Education
Chicago School of Race Relations
Child Development
Cisneros v. Corpus Christi School District
Cultural Capital
Digital Divide
Discrimination
Educational Performance and Attainment
Educational Stratification
English Immersion
Fraternities and Sororities
Grutter v. Bollinger
Head Start and Immigrants
Hernandez v. Texas
Higher Education
Higher Education: Racial Battle Fatigue
Hull House School of Race Relations
Individuals with Disabilities Education Act of 1990
Intelligence Tests
Intercultural Communication
Latina/o Studies
Mexican American Legal Defense and Educational Fund (MALDEF)
Model Minority
Multicultural Education

Native American Education
Pipeline
Resegregation
Reverse Discrimination
San Antonio Independent School District v. Rodriguez
School Desegregation
School Desegregation, Attitudes Concerning
Science Faculties, Women of Color on
Segregation
Self-Fulfilling Prophecy
Separate but Equal
Social Capital
Spanglish
Talented Tenth
Testing
Title IX
Tracking
United States v. Fordice

Gender and Family

Abortion
African Americans, Migration of
African American Women and Work
Aging
Body Image
Canada, Aboriginal Women
Child Development
Civil Rights Movement, Women and
Culture of Poverty
Domestic Violence
Domestic Work
Familism
Family
Feminism
Feminism, Black
Feminism, Latina
Gender and Race, Intersection of
Hip-Hop and Rap, Women and
Homelessness
Hull House School of Race Relations
Immigration and Gender
Incarcerated Parents
Indian Child Welfare Act of 1978
Institutional Discrimination

Intermarriage
Kinship
Kwanzaa
Leisure
Lesbian, Gay, Bisexual, and Transgender
Loving v. Virginia
Machismo
Parenting
Rites of Passage
Science Faculties, Women of Color on
Sexual Harassment
Sexuality
Social Support
Social Work
Title IX
Transracial Adoption
Veil
"Welfare Queen"
Welfare Reform
Whiteness and Masculinity

Global Perspectives

Apartheid
Apartheid, Laws
Argentina
Asylum
Australia
Australia, Indigenous People
Back to Africa Monument
Balkans
Belize
Borderlands
Bracero Program
Brain Drain
Brazil
Britain's Irish
Burakumin
Canada
Canada, Aboriginal Women
Canada, First Nations
Cape Verde
Caribbean
Caste
China
Citizenship

Colombia
Colonialism
Cosmopolitanism
Creole
Cross-Frontier Contacts
Cuba
Cuba: Migration and Demography
Diaspora
Dillingham Flaw
Dominican Republic
Ethnic Conflict
Ethnocentrism
Ethnonational Minorities
Europe
Foreign Students
France
Genocide
Globalization
Global Perspectives
Guest Workers
Hafu
Haiti
Hate Crimes in Canada
Hawai'i, Race in
Holocaust
Holocaust Deniers and Revisionists
Hong Kong
India
Intercultural Communication
International Convention on the Elimination of All Forms of Racial Discrimination
Ireland
Jamaica
Japan
Kenya
Latin America, Indigenous People
London Bombing (July 7, 2005)
Maquiladoras
Marxism and Racism
Mexico
Muslims in Canada
Muslims in Europe
Nigeria
Nikkeijin
Northern Island, Racism in
Orientalism

Peru
Puerto Rico
Race, Comparative Perspectives
Race, UNESCO Statements on
Racism
Refugees
Remittances
Roma
Russia
Sami
Santería
Singapore
South Africa, Republic of
Taiwan
Transnational People
Trinidad
Turkey
United Kingdom
Veil
Xenophobia
Zapatista Rebellion
Zimbabwe
Zionism

Health and Social Welfare

Abortion
Adoption
Aging
Americans with Disabilities Act
Biomedicine, African Americans and
Body Image
Census, U.S.
Child Development
Cuba: Migration and Demography
Discrimination, Environmental
Drug Use
Environmental Justice
Eugenics
Familism
Family
Health, Immigrant
Health Disparities
HIV/AIDS
Hurricane Katrina
Indian Child Welfare Act of 1978

Individuals with Disabilities Education Act of 1990
Leisure
Life Expectancy
Medical Experimentation
Native American Health Care
Native Americans, Environment and
Social Support
Social Work
"Welfare Queen"
Welfare Reform

Immigration and Citizenship

Acculturation
Alien Land Acts
Americanization
Assimilation
Asylum
Bilingual Education
"Boat People"
Borderlands
Border Patrol
Brain Drain
Chinese Exclusion Act
Citizenship
Colonialism
Colonias
Cosmopolitanism
Cross-Frontier Contacts
Dawes Act of 1887
Deficit Model of Ethnicity
Diaspora
Dillingham Flaw
Domestic Work
English Immersion
Ethnic Enclave, Economic Impact of
Ethnic Succession
Ethnonational Minorities
Foreign Students
Gentlemen's Agreement (1907–1908)
Guest Workers
Haitian and Cuban Immigrations: A Comparison
Head Start and Immigrants
Health, Immigrant
Illegal Immigration Reform and Immigrant
 Responsibility Act of 1996

Immigrant Communities
Immigration, Economic Impact of
Immigration, U.S.
Immigration and Gender
Immigration and Nationality Act of 1965
Immigration and Naturalization Service (INS)
Immigration and Race
Immigration Reform and Control Act of 1986
"Marielitos"
McCarran-Walter Act of 1952
Minority Rights
National Origins Systems
Operation Bootstrap
PATRIOT Act of 2001
Proposition 187
Refugees
Remittances
Repatriation of Mexican Americans
Return Migration
Symbolic Ethnicity
Third-Generation Principle
Transnational People
Voting Rights
"Wetbacks"
Xenophobia

Legislation, Court Decisions, and Treaties

Alaska Natives, Legislation Concerning
Alien Land Acts
Americans with Disabilities Act
Apartheid, Laws
Blockbusting
Brown v. Board of Education
Bureau of Indian Affairs
Chinese Exclusion Act
Cisneros v. Corpus Christi School District
Dawes Act of 1887
Dillingham Flaw
Dred Scott v. Sandford
Emancipation Proclamation
Gautreaux Decision
Gentlemen's Agreement (1907–1908)
Grutter v. Bollinger
Hernandez v. Texas
Illegal Immigration Reform and Immigrant
    Responsibility Act of 1996
Immigration and Nationality Act of 1965
Immigration Reform and Control Act of 1986
Indian Child Welfare Act of 1978
Indian Gaming and Regulatory Act of 1988
Individuals with Disabilities Education Act of 1990
Loving v. Virginia
McCarran-Walter Act of 1952
Native American Graves Protection and Repatriation
    Act of 1990
Native American Identity, Legal Background
Operation Bootstrap
PATRIOT Act of 2001
Plessy v. Ferguson
Proposition 187
Repatriation of Mexican Americans
*San Antonio Independent School District v.
    Rodriguez*
Separate but Equal
Title IX
Trail of Broken Treaties
Treaty of Guadalupe Hidalgo (1848)
United States v. Fordice
Voting Rights

Media, Sports, and Entertainment

Birth of a Nation, The
Black Cinema
Body Image
Digital Divide
Film, Latino
Harlem Renaissance
Hip-Hop
Hip-Hop and Rap, Women and
Kwanzaa
Leisure
Media and Race
Negro League Baseball
Popular Culture, Racism and
Rap: The Genre
Rap: The Movement

Organizations

American Indian Movement
American Jewish Committee
Anti-Defamation League

ASPIRA
Back to Africa Movement
Black Panther Party
Brown Berets
Bureau of Indian Affairs
Census, U.S.
Chicago Movement
Congress of Racial Equality (CORE)
Father Divine Peace Mission Movement
Fraternities and Sororities
Gangs
Japanese American Citizens League
Ku Klux Klan
Labor Unions
La Raza Unida Party
Mexican American Legal Defense and Educational Fund (MALDEF)
National Association for the Advancement of Colored People (NAACP)
National Congress of American Indians
National Council of La Raza
National Indian Youth Council
National Rainbow Coalition
National Urban League
Nation of Islam
Operation PUSH
Pachucos/Pachucas
Puerto Rican Armed Forces of National Liberation (FALN)
Puerto Rican Legal Defense and Education Fund
Religion, Minority
Southern Christian Leadership Council (SCLC)
Student Nonviolent Coordinating Committee (SNCC)
Young Lords

Prejudice and Discrimination

Affirmative Action in Education
Affirmative Action in the Workplace
American Apartheid
American Dilemma, An
Antiracist Education
Anti-Semitism
Apartheid
Authoritarian Personality
Aztlán
Birth of a Nation, The
Black Metropolis
Body Image
Civil Rights Movement
Civil Rights Movement, Women and
Colonialism
Color Line
Contact Hypothesis
Crime and Race
Critical Race Theory
Deficit Model of Ethnicity
Discrimination
Discrimination, Environmental Hazards
Discrimination, Measuring
Discrimination in Housing
Double Consciousness
Environmental Justice
Ethnic Conflict
Eugenics
Hate Crimes
Hate Crimes in Canada
Health Disparities
Higher Education: Racial Battle Fatigue
Holocaust Deniers and Revisionists
Housing Audits
Immigration and Race
Institutional Discrimination
Intelligence Tests
Intergroup Relations, Surveying
Internal Colonialism
Internalized Racism
International Convention on the Elimination of All Forms of Racial Discrimination
Interracial Friendships
Invisible Man
Jim Crow
Ku Klux Klan
Labeling
Lynching
Marginalization
Marxism and Racism
Medical Experimentation
Military and Race
Minority Rights
Nativism

Orientalism
Popular Culture, Racism and
Prejudice
Privilege
Racialization
Racial Profiling
Racism
Racism, Aversive
Racism, Cultural
Racism, Types of
Racism, Unintentional
Racism, White
Reparations, Slavery
Reverse Discrimination
Robbers Cave Experiment
Scapegoats
Segregation
Self-Fulfilling Prophecy
Slavery
Social Darwinism
Social Distance
Social Inequality
Stereotypes
Stereotype Threat
Sundown Towns
"Us and Them"
"Welfare Queen"
White Supremacy Movement
Whiteness
Whiteness, Measuring
Whiteness and Masculinity
Xenophobia

Public Policy

Abortion
Affirmative Action in Education
Affirmative Action in the Workplace
American Apartheid
American Dilemma, An
Apartheid, Laws
Asylum
Bilingual Education
Black Conservatives
Black Metropolis
Blockbusting

Census, U.S.
Citizenship
Civil Disobedience
Civil Rights Movement
Community Empowerment
Criminal Processing
Death Penalty
Digital Divide
Equal Employment
    Opportunity Commission (EEOC)
Gautreaux Decision
Gerrymandering
Hate Crimes
Health Disparities
Homelessness
Housing Audits
Hurricane Katrina
Intelligence Tests
Juvenile Justice
Ku Klux Klan
Labor Unions
Lynching
Marginalization
Marxism and Racism
Medical Experimentation
Native Americans, Environment and
Nativism
Orientalism
Political Economy
Proposition 187
Public Housing
Racial Profiling
Redlining
Refugees
Reparations, Slavery
Reverse Discrimination
Segregation
Separate but Equal
Self-Fulfilling Prophecy
Sexual Harassment
Slavery
Sovereignty, Native American
Testing
Title IX
Voting Rights
White Supremacy Movement

Racial, Ethnic, and Nationality Groups

Afghan Americans
African Americans
Africans in the United States
Albanian Americans
Aleuts
Amish
Arab Americans
Armenian Americans
Asian Americans
Assyrian Americans
Australia, Indigenous People
Bangladeshi Americans
Belgian Americans
Blackfeet
Bosnian Americans
Brazilian Americans
Britain's Irish
Bulgarian Americans
Burakumin
Cambodian Americans
Canada, First Nations
Canadian Americans
Caribbean Americans
Central Americans in the United States
Cherokee
Cheyenne
Chinese Americans
Choctaw
Creole
Croatian Americans
Cuban Americans
Cypriot Americans
Czech Americans
Danish Americans
Desi
Dominican Americans
Dutch Americans
Egyptian Americans
Estonian Americans
Filipino Americans
Finnish Americans
French Americans
Georgian Americans
German Americans
Greek Americans
Guatemalan Americans
Haitian Americans
Haole
Hawaiians
Hispanics
Hmong Americans
Honduran Americans
Hopi
Hungarian Americans
Hutterites
Icelandic Americans
Indian Americans
Indonesian Americans
Iranian Americans
Iraqi Americans
Irish Americans
Issei
Italian Americans
Jamaican Americans
Japanese Americans
Jewish Americans
Jewry, Black American
Jordanian Americans
Korean Americans
Kurdish Americans
Laotian Americans
Latin America, Indigenous People
Latvian Americans
Lebanese Americans
Lithuanian Americans
Mennonites
Menominee
Mexican Americans
Muslim Americans
Myanmarese Americans
Native Americans
Navajo
Nicaraguan Americans
Nigerian Americans
Nisei
Norwegian Americans
Ojibwa
Pacific Islanders
Pakistani Americans
Palestinian Americans

Panamanian Americans
Peruvian Americans
Polish Americans
Portuguese Americans
Pueblos
Puerto Rican Americans
Roma
Romanian Americans
Salvadoran Americans
Sami
Samoan Americans
Sansei
Schmiedeleut
Serbian Americans
Sicilian Americans
Sioux
Slovak Americans
Slovene Americans
South Americans in the United States
Spanish Americans
Sri Lankan Americans
Swedish Americans
Syrian Americans
Thai Americans
Tibetan Americans
Tlingit
Tongan Americans
Turkish Americans
Ugandan Americans
Ukrainian Americans
United Kingdom, Immigrants and Their Descendants in the United States
Vietnamese Americans
West Indian Americans

Religion

Amish
Civil Religion
Father Divine Peace Mission Movement
Hutterites
Islamophobia
Jewish Americans
Jewry, Black American
Mennonites
Mormons, Race and
Muslim Americans
Muslims in Canada
Muslims in Europe
Nation of Islam
Native American Graves Protection and Repatriation Act of 1990
Peyote
Religion
Religion, African Americans
Religion, Minority
Religious Freedom Restoration Act of 1993
Religious Movements, New
Roman Catholics
Sacred Sites, Native Americans
Sacred Versus Secular
Santería
Schmeideleut
Southern Christian Leadership Council (SCLC)
Symbolic Religiosity
Veil

Sociopolitical Movements and Conflicts

Abolitionism: The Movement
Abolitionism: The People
African Americans, Migration of
Alamo, The
American Indian Movement
ASPIRA
Aztlán
Back to Africa Movement
Black Nationalism
Black Panther Party
Black Power
Boycott
Brown Berets
Chicano Movement
Civil Disobedience
Civil Rights Movement
Civil Rights Movement, Women and
Cross-Frontier Contacts
Crown Heights, Brooklyn
Environmental Justice
Father Divine Peace Mission Movement
Feminism

Feminism, Black
Feminism, Latina
Harlem Renaissance
Jewish-Black Relations:
    A Historical Perspective
Jewish-Black Relations:
    The Contemporary Period
Kennewick Man
Ku Klux Klan
La Raza
La Raza Unida Party
London Bombings (July 7, 2005)
Military and Race
Multicultural Social Movements
Nation of Islam
Puerto Rican Armed Forces of National
    Liberation (FALN)
Red Power
Sand Creek Massacre
Sovereignty, Native American
Terrorism
Trail of Broken Treaties
Voting Rights
Water Rights
White Supremacy Movement
Wounded Knee (1890 and 1973)
Young Lords
Zapatista Rebellion
Zionism
Zoot Suit Riots

Gaming, Native American

Gambling is a part of traditional culture for many North American tribes. Historically, tribes used games as a means of redistributing wealth and circulating possessions within a community. By the late 20th century, there was little wealth to redistribute because the nation's reservations were places of extraordinary poverty. As a result of the federal government's early Indian policies of removal and diminishment of tribal lands, as well as the subsequent development of federal Indian law, tribes had few means of economic development available to them on their reservations. Between one- and two-thirds of reservation Indians lived below the poverty level, and unemployment rates topped 80% in some areas. To survive, tribes have been forced, against the odds, to pursue some form of economic development. Indian gaming—that is, gaming conducted on tribal lands by federally recognized tribes—is the most successful reservation economic development strategy in more than a century and is perhaps the most controversial as well. This entry reviews the history of Indian gaming, the laws that attempt to regulate it, and related issues of business and politics.

Beginning With Bingo

Indian gaming is fundamentally different from most forms of gambling, from church bingo nights to the commercial casinos lining the Las Vegas Strip, because it is conducted by tribal governments as an exercise of their sovereign rights. Tribal sovereignty, a historically rooted doctrine recognizing tribes' inherent rights as independent nations preexisting the United States and its Constitution, is the primary legal and political foundation of federal Indian law and policy and, thus, Indian gaming. Native American tribes have a special status outside as well as within the American federal system, that is, under federal law defined and circumscribed by the historical development of the legal and political doctrine of tribal sovereignty. In essence, the modern legal doctrine means that the United States recognizes tribes as independent sovereign nations, and their location within the boundaries of a state does not subject them to the application of state law, yet they are subject to Congress's asserted plenary power and bound by the trust relationship between the federal government and tribes. Tribes, therefore, have a unique semi-sovereign status under federal law and, accordingly, may be regulated by Congress.

During the late 1970s and early 1980s, a few tribes, notably in California and Florida, opened high-stakes bingo palaces as a means of raising revenue when faced with the Reagan administration's policy of encouraging tribal self-sufficiency and economic development while cutting funding to Indian programs. The strategies available to tribes were limited: Reservation economies had been depressed for a century, in part because of the location and nature of the lands assigned to the tribes by the federal government. Bingo was an attractive option to tribal governments because start-up costs were relatively low, bingo enterprises had a minimal impact on the environment, and the game had potential for high returns on the tribes' investment.

Bingo was legal in California and Florida, as it was in many states at the time, but state law stringently regulated the game through both civil and criminal penalties. Because federal Indian law generally precluded state regulation of tribes, tribal bingo operations frequently did not comply with state gambling laws. As their sole source of government revenue, two tribes—the Cabazon and Morongo Bands of Mission Indians—operated high-stakes bingo halls and a card club on their reservations in Riverside County, California. California law permitted charitable bingo games but restricted the amount of jackpots and the use of gaming profits. The tribes challenged the state's enforcement of its regulations on the tribes' reservations, and the case culminated in the U.S. Supreme Court's landmark 1987 decision in *California v. Cabazon Band of Mission Indians*.

A Crucial Ruling

The *Cabazon* court explained that if California's gambling laws were criminal prohibitions against gambling, the state could enforce them against the tribes under Public Law 280, a federal law that gave California criminal jurisdiction over reservation lands. If, on the other hand, California's gambling laws were civil regulatory laws, the state did not have authority to enforce them against the tribes.

Relying on this "criminal/prohibitory–civil/regulatory" distinction, the Supreme Court examined the state's public policy concerning gambling, noting that California operated a state lottery and permitted pari-mutuel horse race betting, bingo, and card games. The Court concluded that California regulated, rather than prohibited, gambling in general and bingo in particular. Accordingly, because the games did not violate state public policy, Public Law 280 did not grant California authority to regulate the tribes' gaming operations.

As the Supreme Court considered *Cabazon*, states and tribes lobbied Congress to pass legislation governing Indian gaming. States wanted Congress to authorize state regulation of tribal gaming operations, citing the states' interest in preventing the infiltration of organized crime into Indian gaming. Tribes opposed state regulation and lobbied for exclusive tribal regulation. The tribes' position was grounded in preservation of tribal sovereignty generally as well as in protection of Indian gaming as an economic development strategy for tribal governments. In the end, Congress reached a compromise through the Indian Gaming Regulatory Act (IGRA), enacted on October 17, 1988.

Gamblers in Native American casino. *This photo shows gamblers playing on some of the more than 6,000 slot machines at the Mohegan Sun Casino in Uncasville, Connecticut (November 20, 2002). American Indian gaming is subject to a unique and complex federal regulatory system involving layers of federal, state, and tribal regulations. The casino is owned and operated by the Mohegan tribe, which is a sovereign, federally recognized Indian nation. The Mohegan tribe was jointly ruled by the neighboring Pequot tribe until 1637 and was one of the last remaining tribes in southern New England during colonial times.*

Source: Getty Images.

A New Regulatory System

Indian gaming is subject to a unique and complex federal regulatory scheme involving layers of federal, state, and tribal regulations. Through IGRA, Congress established an independent federal regulatory agency, the National Indian Gaming Commission (NIGC); delegated regulatory power to the states; and set the terms for tribal regulation of gaming. One of IGRA's key innovations was to categorize types of gambling and to assign regulatory authority accordingly. Traditional tribal games of chance, or "Class I" games, were left to exclusive tribal jurisdiction. With nearly a decade of tribal experience and relatively few problems, bingo and other "Class II" games would continue to be regulated by the tribes with some federal oversight. Casino-style gambling, however, was seen as potentially a greater regulatory problem than was bingo. To balance competing state and tribal interests in casino gambling, Congress conceived of "tribal–state compacts" in which a state and a tribe would negotiate the regulatory structure for casino-style, or "Class III," gaming on the tribe's reservation.

During the nearly two decades since Congress enacted IGRA, states and tribes alike have challenged the statute's constitutionality and have litigated its murkier provisions. The NIGC and the federal Secretary of the Interior have promulgated extensive and detailed regulations. Accordingly, the law of Indian gaming has grown only more complex since IGRA's passage.

Law is not the only force at play given that Indian gaming has been shaped as much by politics. IGRA necessitates and governs tribal, state, federal, and even local intergovernmental relations. As a practical matter, therefore, IGRA created the terms under which the politics of Indian gaming have played out. Indeed, following the Supreme Court's 1996 invalidation of one of the IGRA's enforcement mechanisms, Indian gaming policy has evolved through political compromise as much as through litigation and law reform.

Throughout the United States, states and tribes have struggled to balance their respective interests in Indian gaming, sometimes working as partners pursuing shared policy goals and other times locking horns in political and legal battles. Tribal–state compact negotiations have expanded to include topics such as relinquishment of tribal treaty rights and revenue-sharing agreements. Whether such provisions are included fairly under IGRA often is overshadowed by the necessity of political compromise. States have been successful in demanding concessions from tribes and, in some cases, in thwarting tribes' efforts to start or expand gaming enterprises, whereas tribes have wielded increasing political clout through state and local elections and voter initiatives based largely on making the case for the economic benefits of Indian gaming to non-Native communities.

A Source of Revenue

Indian gaming has become big business. Generating nearly $23 billion in revenue in 2005, tribal gaming accounts for approximately a quarter of the gambling industry nationwide, and it continues to grow. Across the United States, thirty states are home to more than 400 tribal gaming operations. Not all tribes conduct gaming, of course, and not all tribal casinos are successful financial ventures. Indian gaming encompasses a wide range of reservation casinos, from modest and marginally profitable rural bingo halls to hugely lucrative Las Vegas–style casino–resort complexes near major metropolitan areas. For every tribal gaming facility that earns more than $100 million annually, there are three that generate less than a tenth of that amount, often just enough revenue to keep the casino open and fund a handful of essential public services for tribal members. This diversity complicates the administration of tribal gaming.

The growth of Indian gaming is only part of the ever-expanding legalized gambling industry. Today, Americans can place bets on dog and horse races in forty-three states, buy lottery tickets in forty states, gamble for charity in forty-seven states, and play at commercial casinos in eleven states. All but two states, Utah and Hawai'i, permit some form of gaming.

As states, tribes, and the federal government struggle with regulating a booming industry within the complicated context of tribal sovereignty, Indian gaming raises substantial questions of law and public policy that might not have easy, one-size-fits-all answers. As the industry grows and changes, one conclusion is clear: Indian gaming, perhaps more so than any other legal or political issue facing tribes in the past half-century, is a subject of ever-increasing public policy debate.

Kathryn R. L. Rand

See also Indian Gaming Regulatory Act of 1988; Native Americans; Reservation System

Further Readings

California v. Cabazon Band of Mission Indians, 480 U.S. 202 (1987).

Light, Steven Andrew and Kathryn R. L. Rand. 2005. *Indian Gaming and Tribal Sovereignty: The Casino Compromise.* Lawrence: University Press of Kansas.

Mason, W. Dale. 2000. *Indian Gaming: Tribal Sovereignty and American Politics.* Norman: University of Oklahoma Press.

Pasquaretta, Paul. 2003. *Gambling and Survival in Native North America.* Tucson: University of Arizona Press.

Rand, Kathryn R. L. and Steven Andrew Light. 2006. *Indian Gaming Law and Policy.* Durham, NC: Carolina Academic Press.

Wilkins, David E. 2006. *American Indian Politics and the American Political System.* 2nd ed. Lanham, MD: Rowman & Littlefield.

GANGS

A *gang* is a small group of individuals who bond together for a common purpose, primarily criminal activity. Gangs provide protection for members, a sense of identity, and (most typically) access to the informal illegal underground economy. This entry describes the types of gangs and the nature of gang identification, membership, and recruitment. It also examines structural and individual factors that lead to gang membership, including the impact of immigration and international conflict on gang activity within the United States.

Types of Gangs

Popular culture currently represents gangs as a phenomenon particular to racial/ethnic minorities; however, gangs are not restricted to particular racial or ethnic groups. Gangs vary from outlaw criminal biker gangs, such as the Hell's Angels, Pagans, and Bandidos, to skinhead, youth, prison, ethnic, neighborhood, street, and even occult gangs. Historically the term *gang* was used most frequently to describe a variety of small, loosely organized criminal groups. Currently, the term is frequently used to refer to street gangs who claim neighborhood territories in primarily low-income sections of large cities.

Street gangs are different from organized crime because they usually lack strong ties to economic and political social institutions. A street gang's primary asset is the territory it claims in the form of a series of neighborhood blocks known as its "hood." Street gangs usually involve youth ranging in age from preteens to the thirties. Members generally participate in gangs at four different levels varying from least to most involvement: behavioral emulation, apprenticeship, regular, and hard-core membership. Gangs participate in criminal acts such as the distribution of illegal drugs, home invasion, acts of physical violence, car theft, and extortion. Street gangs position members within territories in such a way as to maximize the distribution of illegal goods and services as well as to monitor authorities. Members communicate verbally as well as by use of hand signals about police and other authorities who might be present.

Gang Identification

Gangs identify themselves primarily through the use of colors, clothing styles, hand symbols, tattoos, and graffiti. All of these symbols are used to communicate to others about gang membership or affiliation, gang conflict, and territory. These identifiers can change over time as clothing styles and colors are adopted by mainstream society. Examples of gang symbols that have been absorbed into mainstream culture include the wearing of bandanas—primarily blue and red—as well as the flipping of hats in various directions. Hand symbols and graffiti are commonly used by gangs to communicate conflicts with rival gangs or specific members within those gangs and have not been absorbed by mainstream culture. For example, "wallbanging," the use of graffiti by gang members to represent affiliation, involves marking over the names of members of rival gangs to communicate that those members are targets. Hand symbols originated from prison gang communications during the 1950s when incarcerated gang members used sign language to communicate between cells. Symbols are an intricate component of modern street gang communication and normally communicate both affiliation and members' ranks.

Gang Membership

Street gangs actively recruit members during school hours and along the main streets that students travel before and after school. In areas where a variety of gangs are operating, the pressure to join a gang is extreme because being nonaffiliated can put an individual in jeopardy. Gang activity pressures youth by creating a general environment of victimization such that individuals join to deter threats of extortion, robbery, and physical violence. Official membership usually occurs after what is known as a "jumping in" ritual that involves the violent beating of a new member. This act secures gang loyalty and provides evidence to the gang that the new member is "tough enough" to endure lifetime membership. The gang mentality facilitates violence and self-mutilation such as branding and cutting skin. Some gangs practice such rituals to show how tough they are, whereas others cite cultural values for mutilation. For example, Southeast Asian gangs believe that one must endure pain to properly repent for sins, and members mutilate themselves in search of atonement for criminal activity and as self-punishment for shaming their families.

Members rise up in gang rank, which loosely mimics military hierarchy, by means of committing criminal acts and serving prison time. The more severe the acts or greater the length of incarceration, the more status an individual gains within the gang. Gangs engage in warfare with other gangs over territory and personal disputes. Violence escalates throughout large urban areas consisting of multiple neighborhoods. Gang warfare has the potential to terrorize local populations and result in the deaths of not only gang rivals and participants but also innocent bystanders. As the parents of gang members move to other neighborhoods in hopes of disassociating their children from violence and gang activity, this relocation actually contributes to an outgrowth of gang activity.

Some nationally recognized gangs include the Crips and Bloods (primarily African American memberships), the Mexican Mafia and Latin Kings (primarily Mexican and Puerto Rican memberships, respectively), the Nazi Low Riders (a White power gang), and the Born to Kill and Tiny Rascal gangs (primarily Vietnamese and Cambodian memberships, respectively).

Racial, Ethnic, and Gender Identity

The majority of gang members are African American or Latino. These groups constitute 79% of gang membership (35% and 44%, respectively). Whites and Asians constitute 20% of American gang membership (14% and 5%, respectively). However, the picture is more complex than it appears.

Gangs are composed of members from the neighborhoods they represent and, as such, are similar in racial/ethnic makeup to those neighborhoods. This is not especially evident to outsiders, who tend to perceive gangs as homogeneous. Gangs not only represent the people of a neighborhood, they also shape and are shaped by individuals constructing racial/ethnic identities. As populations of racial/ethnic minorities grow and ethnic enclaves establish themselves as distinct from one another, gangs split and form separate identities. For example Southeast Asian gangs consisting of primarily Vietnamese members but also including Hmong, Laotian, and Cambodian members have separated into gangs that reflect their distinctly different identities, cultural heritages, and immigration experiences. This is especially true for Latinos who migrated from a host of South American countries and who bitterly oppose merging identities.

Gangs bolster security for marginalized ethnic and racial groups struggling to deal with threats from rival groups, social inequalities, Americanization, and social institutions that fail to meet basic needs. Gangs provide a strong sense of racial/ethnic identity for members and insolate them from societal messages that minimize their status and seek to marginalize them on the basis of their heritage.

Although gangs are overwhelmingly masculine in makeup, a new trend that has emerged over the past 20 years is the increase of independent female gangs that consist of members previously affiliated with male gangs. The largest growing female gangs are among Latinas but also include African Americans and, to a small extent, Whites and Asians.

Explanations for Gang Activity

Gang activity occurs for a variety of reasons, including structural and individual factors such as social inequalities, financial opportunities, identity and status, peer pressure, family dysfunction, protection, personality traits, social disorganization, and acculturation stress. Scholars who focus on individual circumstances contend that a complex combination of personal attributes, including risk-taking behavior and lack of impulse control, are associated with or cause gang activity. It is believed that these personality traits make individuals prime candidates for gang initiation.

Research focusing on agents of socialization such as families and peers reveals that new members' immediate surroundings influence them heavily. According to some criminological theories, criminal acts are thought to be learned behaviors that are reinforced through social interactions. For example, children who associate with delinquent youth or who come from families whose members are in gangs are especially at risk for initiation. In addition, other perspectives assert that significant others who teach positive definitions of gang behavior, such as "killing is okay because it is either you or them," influence the decision making of others by removing moral barriers.

Structural inequalities create pockets in urban areas where residents are underserved with respect to employment opportunities, police protection, educational attainment, and residential mobility. Extreme disparities in the distribution of wealth and income result in unsanitary living conditions for primarily minority urban populations. Many new gang members perceive gangs as a means by which to gain access to financial opportunities not available through legitimate opportunity structures. The criminal justice system, particularly prison, influences gang formation because the hostile environment creates a need for protection. For example, the Mexican Mafia was founded in the California prison system during the 1960s as a response to racism and abuse by prison guards and threats from White gangs, such as the Blue Birds, whose members controlled illegal goods and services behind bars. In addition, the Bloods and Crips formed as a response to physical threats from Whites in close proximity to African American neighborhoods.

Immigration to the United States from countries that are experiencing cultural, social, economic, and political upheavals creates additional stressors to the acculturation process. Policies regulating immigration and deportation have unintended consequences that result in increased gang activity. It is common that immigrants fleeing these circumstances have been traumatized and victimized before and during their journey to the United States. After the passage of the Immigration and Nationality Act of 1965, which abolished national origin quotas, immigration increased dramatically. Those fleeing unstable countries such as Vietnam and other groups from the Southeast Asian peninsula experienced increased acculturation stress as well as social disorganization and isolation. Groups fleeing extreme turmoil, such as those from war-torn countries, make up the most violent and criminally active street gangs. Usually suffering from the psychological trauma of war, as well as from victimization experienced during passage to the United States, recent immigrants are experienced in guerrilla warfare. Their ability to evade police and their success in fighting rival gangs enables them to grow quickly. For example, the Vietnamese Born to Kill (BTK) and El Salvadorian Mara Salvatrucha (MS 13) gangs are considered among the most dangerous street gangs in the United States. In the case of MS 13, deportation has actually spread the gang to El Salvador, where recruitment begins in immigration detention centers and prisons and carries over to the United States on reentry. Immigration policies that regulated the Vietnamese after the Vietnam War, such as the Vietnamese Amerasian Homecoming Act of 1987, created assimilation camps that resulted in the breakdown of cultural and familial relationships, placing youth at high risk for joining street gangs.

Scott Mathers

See also Crime and Race; Deviance and Crime; Drug Use; Ethnic Group; Immigrant Communities; Immigration and Nationality Act of 1965; Informal Economy; Pachucos/Pachucas; Social Inequality; Underclass; Victimization

Further Readings

Chin, Ko-Lin. 1996. *Chinatown Gangs: Extortion, Enterprise, and Ethnicity.* New York: Oxford University Press.
Grenan, Sean, Margie T. Britz, Jeffery Rush, and Thomas Barker. 2000. *Gangs: An International Approach.* Upper Saddle River, NJ: Prentice Hall.
Hagedorn, John M. 1994. "Neighborhoods, Markets, and Gang Drug Organization." *Journal of Research in Crime and Delinquency* 31:264–294.
Long, Patrick Du Phuoc. 1996. *The Dream Shattered: Vietnamese Gangs in America.* Boston, MA: Northeastern University Press.
Montero, Darrell. 1979. "Vietnamese Refugees in America: Toward a Theory of Spontaneous International Migration." *International Migration Review* 13:624–648.
Thrasher, F. M. 1927. *The Gang: A Study of 1,313 Gangs in Chicago.* Chicago, IL: University of Chicago Press.
Whyte, William Foote. 1943. *Street Corner Society.* Chicago, IL: University of Chicago Press.

Gautreaux Decision

The *Gautreaux* decision was a 1976 U.S. Supreme Court consent decree that followed a judicial finding of illegal racial discrimination and segregation in public housing in the city of Chicago. This court order was the result of a suit filed in 1966 by Dorothy Gautreaux against the Chicago Housing Authority and the U.S. Department of Housing and Urban Development (HUD) claiming that they had intentionally selected locations for public housing in poor, racially segregated neighborhoods—the first suit alleging racial discrimination in public housing. In *Hills v. Gautreaux,* the Supreme Court ruled that a remedy extending beyond the city limits of Chicago was permissible because HUD had violated the Constitution and federal laws. This case is important sociologically because, in effect, it resulted in a quasi-social experiment that demonstrated the benefits of moving from an inner-city environment marked by racial segregation and concentrated poverty to suburban locations where employment opportunities and educational quality are significantly better.

The court order required that African Americans in Chicago public housing be offered opportunities to live in private apartments with housing subsidies. Between 1976 and 1998, approximately 7,000 households relocated as a result of the *Gautreaux* decision. Some of the beneficiaries of this court order moved to private apartments in the city of Chicago, whereas others moved to private apartments in the suburbs. The opportunity to move to the suburbs was part of a desegregation remedy that provided rent subsidies to African American families moving to areas within the six-county Chicago metropolitan area that were less than 30% African American. The experiences of these households were studied by James E. Rosenbaum and his colleagues at Northwestern University. These researchers found that, in general, those who moved to the suburban locations fared better in terms of both employment and education. Because the households who relocated elsewhere in the city and those who relocated to the suburbs were otherwise similar in most regards—both groups were public housing residents with similarly low levels of income and education—the differences in outcomes between those who relocated elsewhere in the city and those who moved to the suburbs can be attributed primarily to where they moved. Thus, the study showed that location matters in terms of employment and education outcomes.

With regard to employment, the *Gautreaux* research provides important support for the spatial mismatch hypothesis, which holds that an important reason for high African American unemployment is the disproportionate concentration of African Americans in central cities given that most new job opportunities over the past several decades have been in the suburbs. The *Gautreaux* results show that how close African Americans are to job opportunities geographically affects their employment rates, as predicted by the mismatch hypothesis. Overall, nearly two-thirds of those who relocated to the suburbs were employed after their moves, compared with just half of those who relocated within the city. The effects were most dramatic among the hard-core unemployed—those who had never been employed. Nearly half of those in this group (46%) were employed after moving to the suburbs, compared with just 30% of those who relocated within the city.

These findings suggest that increased opportunities for African Americans to live in suburban areas where job growth is occurring will, in and of itself, lead to reductions in African American unemployment rates. One reason is that African American households are significantly less likely than White households to have access to motor vehicles, so distance from employment is often a more important issue for African Americans than it is for Whites. When Rosenbaum asked the suburban movers how their moves helped them to get jobs, each one mentioned that there were more jobs available in the suburbs. Many also said that they felt freer to leave home to work because they would be less worried about the safety of their children at home compared with when they lived in the city.

The *Gautreaux* experience also suggests that relocation from central cities to affluent, predominantly White suburbs may have significant educational benefits for African American children. In general, Rosenbaum found that the children in African American families that relocated to the suburbs fared better educationally than did the children in those families that remained in the city. Their attitudes toward school were more positive, and just 5% of them dropped out of high school, compared with 20% of those in the city. The grades of students who relocated to the suburbs were the same as those of students who remained in the city, but this likely reflected a higher level of achievement due to higher expectations. A national study of high school sophomores, for example, shows that at a given level of achievement, suburban students are graded roughly a half-point lower than central city students; thus, the grades of the students who relocated to the suburbs probably reflected a higher level of achievement. Perhaps most important, the students who relocated to the suburbs were more likely than those who remained in the city to take a college preparatory curriculum and were more than twice as likely (54% vs. 21%) to attend college after graduation.

The benefits to African American households who relocated to the suburbs as a result of the *Gautreaux* decision also provide support for the argument that the effects of geographically concentrated poverty are greater than the effects of poverty itself. Various researchers have noted that poverty is more geographically concentrated among African Americans than it is among Whites. This occurs for a variety of reasons, and there is debate among researchers about the relative importance of different causes. However, the end result is that African Americans who are poor have significantly more neighbors who are also poor and fewer neighbors who enjoy steady quality employment and financial security. Because of this, social problems become more widespread and the institutions that provide stability in people's lives and provide for day-to-day needs are undermined. If an individual is poor in an area where most others are also poor, it is likely that basic services and the ability to purchase needed goods and services within the neighborhood will be reduced. Role models for regular stable employment will be fewer, and crime and social disruption will be more likely. On the other hand, if an individual is poor in a neighborhood where most others are not poor, things may be quite different. Services, shopping, and job opportunities will be available in the neighborhood, and role models for employment and for seeing the benefits of educational advancement will abound. In other words, location matters. The better outcomes among the *Gautreaux* decision beneficiaries who moved to low-poverty suburban neighborhoods support this conclusion. They began just as poor as those who remained in city neighborhoods with higher poverty rates, but in the end their educational and employment outcomes were better.

Over the years, considerable additional research has been conducted on (a) the longer term outcomes of the *Gautreaux* decision and (b) similar experiments and initiatives elsewhere. Longer term research on families who relocated to the suburbs as a result of the *Gautreaux* decision shows that as long as two decades after they initially relocated to the suburbs, most of the *Gautreaux* families and their children continued to live in suburban areas where crime rates are lower and incomes and educational levels are higher than in the central city neighborhoods they left behind. The program seems to have contributed to racial integration of housing over the long term given that only a minority of those who relocated to the suburbs returned to predominantly African American neighborhoods. However, most do now live in areas with a more even racial mix than the predominantly White areas to which they initially relocated. Although the children in the families who relocated to the suburbs did encounter some racial discrimination and harassment at school in their new neighborhoods, their attitudes toward education improved, their grades remained stable over time, and they interacted with their new middle-class neighbors and classmates as much as those who remained in the city interacted with theirs.

Attempts have been made, with varying success, to apply the findings from the *Gautreaux* case elsewhere. Several cities have undertaken similar programs, and at the national level a relatively small-scale initiative called Move to Opportunity (MTO) was undertaken. MTO sought to provide opportunities for poor households to move from neighborhoods of concentrated poverty to more affluent neighborhoods in five large urban areas. However, unlike *Gautreaux,* MTO did not specifically seek to bring about racial integration, and for the most part it failed to do so, although it did succeed in moving poor families to more socioeconomically diverse areas. In addition, MTO was less successful than *Gautreaux* in getting children into higher achieving schools. Perhaps for these reasons, the effects of MTO on educational achievement appear to have been small, although MTO did succeed in getting people to move to neighborhoods of higher socioeconomic status. These findings suggest that programs seeking to apply the principles of the *Gautreaux* program would be well advised to seek to bring about racial as well as socioeconomic integration and to provide access to areas with high-achieving schools.

John E. Farley

See also American Apartheid; Discrimination in Housing; Educational Performance and Attainment; Housing Audits; Public Housing; Resegregation; Segregation; Social Mobility; Underclass; White Flight

Further Readings

Hills v. Gautreaux, 425 U.S. 284 (1976).

Keels, Micere, Greg J. Duncan, Stephanie DeLuca, Ruby Mendenhall, and James Rosenbaum. 2005. "Fifteen Years Later: Can Residential Mobility Programs Provide a

Long-Term Escape from Neighborhood Segregation, Crime, and Poverty?" *Demography* 42:51–73.

Rosenbaum, James E. 1994. *Housing Mobility Strategies for Changing the Geography of Opportunity.* Evanston, IL: Northwestern University, Institute for Policy Research. Available from http://www .northwestern.edu/ipr/publications/papers/gat96.pdf

Rosenbaum, James E. and Susan J. Popkin. 1991. "Employment and Earnings of Low-Income Blacks Who Move to Middle-Class Suburbs." Pp. 342–356 in *The Urban Underclass,* edited by Christopher Jencks and Paul E. Peterson. Washington, DC: Brookings Institution.

Gender and Race, Intersection of

As forms of oppression and privilege, race, class, and gender "intersect" in people's individual lives, in the cultures and communities of which they are a part, and in the institutions that give structure to their life chances. The notion of intersection highlights the way in which these forms of oppression are bound together, making it impossible to truly understand a race dynamic, for instance, without also considering the influence of gender and class. Focusing on the relationships among race, class, and gender, feminists have developed the empirically grounded theoretical premises that (a) race, class, and gender are social structural locations; (b) structural location shapes perspective; (c) no individual is all-oppressed or all-oppressing; (d) the meanings of race, class, and gender are localized; and (e) race, class, and gender depend on each other; and (f) race, class, and gender mutually constitute each other. These premises are synthesized in this entry.

Structural Locations Rather Than Physical Characteristics

In 1892, classical sociological theorist Anna Julia Cooper wondered which train station restroom would be most appropriate for her to enter—the one "for ladies" or the one "for colored people." Black women's invisibility, still apparent more than 100 years later in the common use of phrases such as "women and minorities," has been the catalyst for the deliberate study of the intersections of race, class, and gender. One of the most fundamental principles race–class–gender scholars have demonstrated is that this invisibility is structural and systematic rather than a result of happenstance. With ideological mortar, race, class, and gender are built as social locations to which individuals are relegated. Much as a dwelling that can be rented in one part of town comes with a garbage disposal, hot water, and air-conditioning, whereas a dwelling across town lacks these amenities, social locations "come with" a variety of (continually varying) advantages and disadvantages that give structure to inhabitants' opportunities to meet their material and emotional needs.

Race, class, and gender, then, are not simply ways of describing people's bodies. Rather, they are organizing principles that maintain differences and separation between groups—between Black men and Latinos, between Asian American women and White men, between working-class and middle-class Arab American women. Focusing on social locations rather than on biology shows that what happens in people's lives is not simply a manifestation of any innate characteristics they may have. Rather, their lives get shaped by the amenities available to people in their social locations. The Civil Rights Movement, the Women's Movement, and the Labor Movement are examples of people working to expand access to those amenities (e.g., voting rights, fair pay) to people who had previously been restricted from them.

According to intersection theorists, those who occupy social locations that provide them with opportunities to express political, economic, and social power may systematically ignore or deliberately deemphasize the conditions attached to the social locations of disadvantaged groups such as the consequences of racism for mothers in the labor market and the disproportionate care work expected of women of color. The lack of attention to issues like these results in laws, policies, literature, history, science, patterns of production, media representation, and other living arrangements structured around the life situations of those in advantageous social locations. This structural invisibility is alternately structural hypervisibility when it meets the interests of those in more powerful social locations such as when Latinas are portrayed as "illegal aliens" or Black men are portrayed as dangerous criminals. These coin sides make up one set of advantages and disadvantages that come with the social locations shaped by the intersections of race, class, and gender.

Locations Shape Perspectives

In her assessment of a society rife with racism and sexism, Cooper argued that Black women, restricted from directly participating in many facets of political, economic, and social life, have a unique perspective that, if heard, would benefit not just Black women but all of society. As caretakers, educators, nurturers, actors, and observers, Black women have been able to see what others have not seen, she argued. Because their structural location has shaped their perspective, Black women's "voices," according to Cooper, are vital for progress in the United States.

Feminist standpoint theorists such as Nancy Hartsock, working from Karl Marx's assertion that the proletariat is positioned to construct a distinctive critical perspective of capitalism, have taken pains to point out that this perspective is not "natural" but rather something that those in oppressive structural locations must struggle to develop. Similarly, some race–class–gender theorists, such as Patricia Hill Collins, have argued against the assertion that Black women's perspective is more accurate than others' because it seems to suggest in an essentialist way that oppression is additive; the more kinds of oppression, the clearer the vision. While we acknowledge the unique vantage point women of color may adopt, we must also recognize that those living at severely disadvantaged structural locations do not necessarily have all-knowing perspectives and may, in fact, be restricted from some forms of knowledge and information. As a theoretical premise, whether disadvantaged structural locations confer blinders on inhabitants or what W. E. B. Du Bois called the "gift of second sight" (or, more likely, both), the way in which people are located structurally affects their experiences and, therefore, shapes the way in which they understand the world. What is needed, according to race–class–gender theorists, is dialogue among those who understand things so differently so that the perspectives of those who have been harmed by the dominant worldview may be heard.

Intertwined Oppressions

Unlike theorists of class who argue that capitalists exploit workers, unlike theorists of race who argue that Whites oppress people of color, and unlike feminists who argue that men dominate women, studies of the intersections of race, class, and gender have demonstrated that relationships among these dimensions do not fall along simple "either/or" hierarchical lines. Being structurally situated in social locations that have been built by the ideologies and material realities of race, class, and gender is sufficiently complex that it would be impossible for any individual in any social location to be either all-oppressed or all-oppressing, scholars of intersection theory assert. Studies of race, class, and gender reveal tangled situations. For example, people who are economically disadvantaged because they face employment discrimination (possibly on the basis of race and gender) may shop at huge discount stores where they can get the best price on shampoo—even though those stores may be exploiting their employees. Thus, they may indirectly become complicit in the exploitation of men and women workers in those stores and around the world.

Collins uses the imagery of a "matrix of domination" to untangle situations like this, charting race–class–gender advantage and disadvantage along the dimensions of personal experience and cultural and institutional contexts. Consistent with the first premise, which focuses us on structural locations rather than on physical or identity categories, this third premise rejects race, class, and gender as dimensions of "who people are" and instead highlights actions and opportunities through which oppression is perpetuated.

Localized Meanings

These situational dynamics reveal a fourth theoretical premise of race–class–gender studies, namely, that meanings and expressions of race, class, and gender are localized. Although many theorists originally focused on the conditions faced by entire "classes" of people—"women," "the proletariat," "Asian Americans"—scholars have more recently problematized these all-encompassing categories as misleadingly homogeneous and divorced from the dynamics of people's everyday lives. They instead encourage investigation of the specific local circumstances under which race, class, and gender are "done" and the particular forms of these dimensions of oppression that are salient within those circumstances.

In studying the localized dimensions of race, class, and gender, scholars have also needed to grapple with people's complicity in their own oppression. Structures may be arranged so that individuals can get local benefits from perpetuating race, class, and gender's "global" logics. Disadvantaged groups may face formidable pressures to accept dominant conceptualizations; indeed, hegemonic forms of power require the cooperation of those who will be most disadvantaged by its exercise, even as this can depend on and result in their internalization of oppressive ideas about themselves. A Black man striving to attain the markers of the middle class, for example, may choose to exclude professional Black women from his pool of potential marriage partners because his image of success includes a wife who subserviently caters to his needs at home. Although this may help to secure his "success" in a local realm (even while it diminishes his household income potential), it serves to maintain ideologies of what is expected of and attractive about women as well as what is deficient about Black men whose wives work for pay. Whether the result of pressure, internalization, choice, or (more likely) a combination of all of these, actions on the local level— actions that make sense or serve individuals' interests within a particular set of conditions—are part of what maintains the larger, dominant, globalized structures of race, class, and gender.

A Relation of Dependence

Is any one of these structures, in any social circumstance, more important than the others? Noteworthy scholars have weighed in on this question. Du Bois argued that "the problem of the twentieth century is the problem of the color-line" (p. 12), Karl Marx and Frederick Engels argued that "the whole history of mankind... has been a history of class struggles" (p. 5), and for Charlotte Perkins Gilman the primary form of inequality is "excessive sex distinction" (p. 52). It is not uncommon to hear scholars talk about how one dimension "trumps" the others as a more salient feature of a particular dynamic.

Among those who find one of these dimensions more important in the organization of social life than the others, most—following the preoccupation of late 20th-century sociology with class analysts such as Marx—begin and end with the assumption that class is primary. However, the fifth premise of race–class–gender theory is that these structures cannot be ranked. Rather, the relationship among race, class, and gender is one of dependence. Karen Hossfeld's research on immigrant women working in Silicon Valley, for example, found that employers make hiring decisions based on racism, chauvinism, and sexism, allowing them to divide, conquer, and control their labor supply. Here, capitalists are able to increase profits because they can oppress people by gender and race; that is, capitalism depends on gender and race. Trying to rank dimensions of oppression reifies them; instead, social analysts must recognize how structures such as race, class, and gender create, shape, depend on, and influence each other.

Mutual Constitution

Structures of oppression do not come together fully formed and engage in sword fights for dominance. Rather, they form within the context of the others. A structure such as race changes and mutates based on the gender and class contexts that surround it, and the task of social scientists is to determine how that happens and what the resulting (constantly shifting) relationships among them are. The language of "mutual constitution" indicates movement, development, change, and time, reminding scholars that the structures of race, class, and gender are processes. How people are categorized according to race, for example, has changed over time based on the relative place of different groups in the economic order. These structures are continually changing (in localized settings), responding to being changed and "constituted," and constituting other forms. So far, efforts at understanding how this occurs have been guided by the notion of structures of oppression such as race, class, and gender as "intersecting."

Ivy Ken

See also Body Image; Civil Rights Movement, Women and; Collins, Patricia Hill; Domestic Violence; Du Bois, William Edward Burghardt; Feminism, Black; Feminism, Latina; Glass Ceiling; hooks, bell; Hull House School of Race Relations; Lesbian, Gay, Bisexual, and Transgender; Marxism and Racism; Sexuality; Social Inequality; Wells-Barnett, Ida B.; Whiteness and Masculinity

Further Readings

Andersen, Margaret. 2005. "Thinking about Women: A Quarter Century's View." *Gender & Society* 19:437–455.

Collins, Patricia Hill. 2000. *Black Feminist Thought: Knowledge, Consciousness, and the Politics of Empowerment.* 2nd ed. New York: Routledge.

De Beauvoir, Simone. [1952] 1989. *The Second Sex,* translated and edited by H. M. Parshley. New York: Alfred A. Knopf.

Du Bois, W. E. B. [1903] 1994. *The Souls of Black Folk.* Avenel, NJ: Gramercy Books.

Gilman, Charlotte Perkins. 1898. *Women and Economics: A Study of the Economic Relation between Men and Women as a Factor in Social Evolution.* Boston, MA: Small, Maynard.

Glenn, Evelyn Nakano. 1999. "The Social Construction and Institutionalization of Gender and Race: An Integrative Framework." Pp. 3–43 in *Revisioning Gender,* edited by Myra Marx Ferree, Judith Lorber, and Beth B. Hess. Thousand Oaks, CA: Sage.

Hartsock, Nancy C. M. 1998. "The Feminist Standpoint Revisited." Pp. 227–248 in *The Feminist Standpoint Revisited and other Essays,* edited by Nancy C. M. Hartsock. Boulder, CO: Westview.

hooks, bell. 1984. *Feminist Theory: From Margin to Center.* Boston, MA: South End.

Hossfeld, Karen. 2007. "Still Small, Foreign, and Female after All These Years: An Update on Immigrant Women Workers in Silicon Valley." Presented at annual meeting of the Pacific Sociological Association, Oakland, CA.

Marx, Karl and Frederick Engels. [1848] 1955. *The Communist Manifesto,* edited by Samuel H. Beer. Arlington Heights, IL: Harland Davidson.

Moraga, Cherríe and Gloria Anzaldúa. 1981. *This Bridge Called My Back: Writings by Radical Women of Color.* New York: Kitchen Table.

West, Candace and Don Zimmerman. 1987. "Doing Gender." *Gender & Society* 1:125–151.

GENDER IDENTITY

See LESBIAN, GAY, BISEXUAL, AND TRANSGENDER; SEXUALITY

GENOCIDE

Article 2 of the 1948 UN Convention on the Prevention and Punishment of Genocide reads,

> In the present Convention, genocide means any of the following acts committed with intent to destroy, in whole or in part, a national, ethnical, racial, or religious group as such: a) Killing members of the group; b) Causing serious bodily or mental harm to members of the group; c) Deliberately inflicting on the group conditions of life calculated to bring about its physical destruction in whole or in part; d) Imposing measures intended to prevent births within the group; e) Forcibly transferring children of the group to another group.

This entry addresses the origins of this definition, criticisms and alternative definitions, examples of genocide, and legal and social responses to genocide.

Origins of Genocide

Polish jurist Raphaël Lemkin is credited as the originator of the term *genocide.* As early as 1933, he showed a prescient understanding of Nazi intentions when he drafted a proposal for penalizing destructive actions taken against minority populations that was presented to the International Conference for the Unification of Penal law in Madrid. Later, as a witness to Nazi aggression against the nations of Europe and specific peoples (e.g., Jews, Roma, Poles, Slavs), Lemkin argued that it was necessary to find a word that could inspire moral condemnation and political action for the world to take seriously this crime that was, at that time, "without a name." After he escaped Nazi-occupied Europe, Lemkin wrote his 1944 book, *Axis Rule in Occupied Europe,* in which he coined the term *genocide,* a combination of *genos* (race, tribe) and *cide* (to kill), for this purpose. With this new word in hand, he directed his efforts toward legal codification so that a clear standard would be in place rather than a hodgepodge of international treaties and agreements that did not speak to the scope or scale of genocidal crimes.

The first formal recognition of Lemkin's new term can be found in the indictment of the major German war criminals by the International Military Tribunal (IMT) at Nuremberg in 1945. However, the IMT did not make significant use of this term in its judgment, and the further codification of genocide as a matter of international law was left to the United Nations. On December 11, 1946, the UN General Assembly passed its first resolution on genocide that compared the crime of genocide, as a denial of group existence, to that of murder, or the denial of individual life. Based on this resolution, the UN's Economic and Social Council was charged with the task of developing a convention on the prevention and punishment of genocide.

Debates among UN member nations ensued. Contentious issues included the groups to be included under the convention, the status of cultural genocide, the meaning of intent, and the challenge of prevention. For example, the Russian representative argued that political groups were too impermanent and unstable to be included under the convention. Likewise, many Western nations opposed the inclusion of cultural genocide, or "ethnocide," under the convention, suggesting that these crimes were of a different order from mass killing.

The end product of these debates was the 1948 UN Convention on the Prevention and Punishment of Genocide. After its passage, attention was turned toward getting nations to sign on to the convention, but otherwise there was little sustained discussion of the subject of genocide during subsequent years.

Criticisms and Alternative Definitions

It was not until the late 1970s and early 1980s that an upsurge in interest in genocide occurred. This was partially the result of increased awareness of the Holocaust; however, it was also sparked by scholarly efforts to conduct comparative research on genocide. Many genocide scholars found the UN convention lacking in several respects. For some, the convention was too exclusive, leaving out political and class-based groups. For others, the convention was too inclusive because it referenced practices deemed to be qualitatively different from mass killing such as the transfer of children from one group to another. Still others found the convention too restrictive in its notion of "intent," which suggests a purposeful formulation of genocidal strategy that, in many cases, is difficult to discern. These and other issues led to attempts to redefine genocide in a manner that would provide both conceptual clarity and comparative flexibility.

For example, Frank Chalk and Kurt Jonassohn, in their 1990 book *The History and Sociology of Genocide,* proposed, "Genocide is a form of one-sided mass killing in which a state or other authority intends to destroy a group, as that group and membership in it are defined by the perpetrator" (p. 23). This definition focuses on instances of mass killing where the target group is unable or unwilling to muster organized military resistance to the genocidal onslaught (so the killing is "one-sided"), thereby excluding wartime cases such as the World War II aerial bombardment of Dresden, Tokyo, Hamburg, and other cities. It also defers the question of what groups might be considered victims of genocide by basing its assessment entirely on the perpetrator's definition of its intended target.

These components of Chalk and Jonassohn's definition have been criticized by other genocide scholars, including Helen Fein, who maintained that the specification of "one-sided mass killings" ignores other forms of attempted biological destruction, such as forced abortions and sterilization, and presents arbitrary grounds for excluding cases (e.g., how much resistance does it take to make a case no longer "one-sided"?). Fein proposed the following definition in a 1990 article:

> Genocide is sustained purposeful action by a perpetrator to physically destroy a collectivity, directly or indirectly, through interdiction of the biological and social reproduction of group members, sustained regardless of the surrender or lack of threat offered by the victim. (p. 24)

In this definition, Fein sought to build on and clarify the UN definition. She did not limit the groups to be considered under the definition to the ascriptive categories of race, ethnicity, and nationhood. Instead, she used the term *collectivity* to refer to all identities that might be constructed or inherited but that nonetheless endure and serve as a source of meaning for group members. She also clarified that genocide is sustained and purposeful action, by which she meant that it consists of multiple acts carried out over a period of time that show, at a minimum, a knowing disregard for the destruction of a collectivity.

Definitional debates continue among sociologists, political scientists, historians, and other genocide studies scholars. Nonetheless, the UN convention has survived as a foundation for all of these subsequent definitions, even if it has seldom seen juridical application.

Examples of Genocide

Genocide is an ancient crime. Events such as the destruction of Melos by Athens in the Peloponnesian War (5th century BC), Rome's assault on Carthage at the end of the Third Punic War (149–46 BC), and the rampages of Genghis Khan's Mongol horsemen during the 13th century are often cited as early examples. The period of colonial expansion and imperialism is also rife with genocidal moments such as in the conquest and colonization of the New World and the subjugation and forced assimilation of Aboriginal peoples—a process that, in many parts off the world, continued into the 20th century. Indeed, the 20th century has come to be known as the "century of genocide." This deadly era began in 1904 when the Herero people of what is now Namibia rose up against their German colonizers, surprising the Germans in a battle that lasted six months until the German government sent in General Luther von Trotha to quell it. Trotha issued an extermination order and, after sealing off all escape routes except those leading to the desert, launched massive artillery attacks against the Herero. Water holes were poisoned so that those fleeing to the desert would perish, and refugees were deprived of sustenance. The Herero population of 80,000 in 1904 was reduced to 15,000 by 1908.

The Armenian genocide is the next widely cited instance of genocide. In April 1915, under the cover of war, the Ottoman government ordered that in all areas outside of the war zones, the Armenians were to be deported from their homes under so-called resettlement programs. Next, approximately 250,000 Armenian soldiers were eliminated to render the Armenian population defenseless. The government then proceeded to round up and kill hundreds of Armenian political, religious, intellectual, and cultural leaders. The rest of the population, composed mainly of the elderly, women, and children, was deported. Along the deportation route, they were attacked by bands of killers and a sizable number of deportees were slaughtered indiscriminately. Others were killed through deliberate starvation, dehydration, and brutalization.

The Nazi extermination campaign against European Jews is often regarded as the paradigmatic case of genocide. Soon after Adolf Hitler and the National Socialists came to power in Germany in 1933, they began to erode the rights of Jewish citizens. But it became clear that denationalization would not be sufficient to appease Hitler's hatred of the Jews and his desire to increase German territory. Gradually, anti-Jewish policies were intensified, moving from pogroms to ghettoization to expulsion. By 1941, mass killings were under way, and it is believed that during the second half of that year Hitler fully committed to the "Final Solution"—the extermination of all Jews. Several concentration camps were transformed into extermination camps with gas chambers and ovens operating to kill and dispose of Jewish lives. The Nazis also subjected other groups to a loss of rights and genocidal action during this period, including Roma and Sinti ("gypsies"), Slavs, Poles, communists, homosexuals, and Jehovah's Witnesses.

Several other cases of genocide have emerged since the Holocaust, and only a sampling can be listed here. In 1971, as a Bengali nationalist movement sought to secede East Pakistan (now Bangladesh) from West Pakistan, and approximately 1.2 million Bengals were killed by West Pakistani forces. In 1972, the Tutsi rulers in Burundi launched a genocidal assault on the majority Hutu population, resulting in nearly 200,000 Hutu deaths. In April 1975, Khmer Rouge forces led by Pol Pot defeated the Lon Nol army and took control of the Cambodian capital, Phnom Penh. Subsequently, they implemented a program of murder, forced labor, and forced relocation against Vietnamese, Cham Muslim and Chinese minorities, religious groups such as the Buddhist monks, the Khmer urban classes, and the Khmer population from the provinces near Vietnam, eventually killing 1.5 million of Cambodia's then population of 8 million. In 1994, in just 100 days, Hutu extremists slaughtered 800,000 to 1,000,000 Tutsis and Hutu moderates in Rwanda while the rest of the world stood by and did nothing to stop the slaughter.

Genocide has continued to trouble the world into the 21st century, as the Darfur region of Sudan has seen murderous attacks on non-Arab inhabitants by the government-sponsored Janjaweed militia and government forces.

Responses to Genocide

In the aftermath of World War II, the Allies confronted the problem of how to deal with National Socialist military aggression and war crimes. It was decided that trials, following the model of Western justice, would be implemented to prosecute the major war criminals. Thus, the IMT at Nuremberg came into existence in 1945. However, this decision was not uncontested at the time; never before had victorious nations sat in judgment on the vanquished, and for some this carried the taint of victor's justice. It is also the case that the twenty-one defendants at Nuremberg were tried for crimes for which there were no well-established legal precedents, resulting in the charge of retroactivity. Finally, the tribunal was viewed to be selective and politicized because it addressed the misdeeds of only defeated nations. The lead prosecutor, Justice Robert H. Jackson, challenged these criticisms in his opening statement, suggesting that whatever the flaws of the tribunal, the crimes of the Nazis were of such a scale that the world could not afford to ignore them, and that the tribunal was a much more rational response to these crimes than the reprisal killings and punitive reparations carried out after previous wars.

Sadly, genocides continued, undeterred by the threat of legal reprisals. Moreover, it would be more than 40 years before the world community would manage another trial of those alleged to have engaged in genocide. In the meantime, the previously mentioned mass atrocities in Burundi, Uganda, Bangladesh, and Cambodia were left unaddressed. It was not until the outbreak of war and "ethnic cleansing" in the former Yugoslavia and the genocide in Rwanda that international tribunals were once again established to deal with genocidal crimes. The International Criminal Tribunal for the Former Yugoslavia came into being through UN Security Council Resolution 827 in 1993 and is located in The Hague, Netherlands. Through its various rulings, it has helped to clarify the UN genocide convention, in particular with respect to specifying the "targets" of genocide. The International Criminal Tribunal for Rwanda (ICTR) was established by the United Nations in 1994 in Arusha, Tanzania, and in the Akayesu case it was the first international tribunal to offer an interpretation of the UN genocide convention. The ICTR also contributed the notion that widespread rape and sexual violence may constitute genocide if they are committed with the objective of destroying a targeted group. Finally, the International Criminal Court was established as a permanent judicial body for contending with major intra- and interstate crimes, such as genocide, through the 1998 Rome Statute.

Other less formal justice options are available to societies dealing with pasts marked by genocide and mass violence. Truth commissions have been used in many Latin America countries, as well as in South Africa, and have more recently been established to work in conjunction with courts in places such as Sierra Leone. There are also a variety of commemorative and reparative techniques employed by countries seeking to deal with unsavory pasts, including apologies, monetary compensation, memorials, museums, and days of remembrance.

Andrew Woolford

See also Armenian Americans; Anti-Semitism; Colonialism; Diaspora; Ethnic Conflict; Ethnoviolence; Global Perspective; Holocaust Holocaust: Deniers and Revisionists; Jewish Americans; Peoplehood; Racism; Roma

Further Readings

Alvarez, Alex. 2001. *Governments, Citizens, and Genocide: A Comparative and Interdisciplinary Approach.* Indianapolis: University of Indiana Press.

Chalk, Frank and Kurt Jonassohn, eds. 1990. *The History and Sociology of Genocide: Analyses and Case Studies.* New Haven, CT: Yale University Press.

Fein, Helen. 1990. "Defining Genocide as a Sociological Concept." *Current Sociology* 38:8–31.

Jones, Adam. 2006. *Genocide: A Comprehensive Introduction.* London: Routledge.

Kuper, Leo. 1981. *Genocide: Its Political Use in the Twentieth Century.* New Haven, CT: Yale University Press.

Minow, Martha. 1998. *Between Vengeance and Forgiveness: Facing Genocide and Mass Violence.* Boston, MA: Beacon.

Power, Samantha. 2002. *"A Problem from Hell": America and the Age of Genocide.* New York: Basic Books.

United Nations. 1948. *United Nations Convention on the Prevention and Punishment of Genocide.* Adopted by Resolution 260(III)A of the UN General Assembly on December 9, 1948. Entry into force: January 12, 1951. New York: United Nations.

GENTLEMEN'S AGREEMENT (1907–1908)

The Gentlemen's Agreement represented a set of six diplomatic notes communicated between the United States and Japan to curtail labor emigration from Japan to the United States. Led by President Theodore Roosevelt, these initiatives were intended to ease increasing tensions between the two countries and to offer a national response to the rising anti-Japanese movement centered in California. On the heels of the Russo–Japanese War and after a wave of anti-Japanese "yellow peril" ordinances in California, the Gentlemen's Agreement arose out of mutual diplomatic needs between the United States and Japan. Consequently, they were informal and shrouded agreements, not entirely revealed to the public until years later, in which Japan voluntarily agreed to restrict its nationals from entering the continental United States. This entry looks at the agreement and its background in both participating countries.

A Series of Notes

On February 24, 1907, the first agreement ended in a Japanese note agreeing to deny passports to laborers planning on entering the United States. Japan also acknowledged the right of the United States to exclude Japanese immigrants holding passports issued for other countries; this would effectively prevent the re-migration to the United States of Japanese laborers from Mexico, Canada, or Hawai'i. Executive Order 589 was signed by Roosevelt on March 14, 1907, excluding from the mainland United States "Japanese or Korean laborers, skilled or unskilled, who had received passports to go to Mexico, Canada, or Hawai'i, and come therefrom."

By February 18, 1908, a final Japanese note was signed, making the Gentlemen's Agreement fully effective. Although this marked the end of new Japanese male labor immigration, the Gentlemen's Agreement launched a new era for Japanese American family formation and unleashed variant forms of anti-Japanese prejudice.

U.S. Background

Understanding the rationale for the Gentlemen's Agreement requires a review of U.S. domestic conditions and of U.S.–Japan relations during the turn of the 20th century. In 1890, there were 2,039 Japanese in the continental United States (0.003% of the population), in contrast to 107,488 Chinese (0.2%). Following the annexation of Hawai'i, according to the 1900 U.S. Census, Japanese Americans represented 0.1% (85,716) of the U.S. population and Chinese Americans represented 0.2%. Moreover, there were thousands of Japanese sojourners who returned to Japan, resulting in low levels of population growth. As one small group struggling like many other immigrants in the U.S. West—Swedes, Italians, Armenians, Punjabis—why were Japanese targeted so intensively, particularly by Whites?

Decades of anti-Chinese fervor had culminated in the Chinese Exclusion Act of 1882, which similarly suspended labor immigration for 10 years; it was renewed and restricted labor entry until after World War II. The labor-organized movement to renew anti-Chinese legislation served to racialize the immigration issue as an "Asiatic" problem. Protests called for the expulsion of all Asians. With the declining Chinese population, the yellow peril—depicted in Hearst publications as hordes of locusts descending on the shores of the Pacific—focused on the Japanese.

The Asiatic Exclusion League, started in San Francisco in 1905 by European immigrant labor leaders, focused on the exclusion of Japanese and Koreans. Its formation marks the start of the anti-Japanese movement. Pressured by the league, the San Francisco School Board decided to segregate Japanese school children in the Oriental School where Chinese children were already confined. Using the San Francisco earthquake's destruction of numerous school buildings as an excuse to reassign the ninety-three Japanese children—25% of them being native born—the board rescinded the segregation order after Roosevelt invited the board to the White House in February 1907 and promised to ask Japan for "voluntary" restriction of new labor immigration. This would be part of the informal negotiations underlying the Gentlemen's Agreement.

Japanese Background

Japanese government officials were alarmed by the rapidly escalating hostilities against their nationals in the United States because for decades they had observed the heightening of anti-Chinese hysteria. Particularly after victory in the Russo–Japanese War, Japan was eager to be viewed as a world power and to be accorded equal status with the European colonizing nations.

By the late 19th century, Japan had already attempted to control those who could emigrate and to monitor their experiences in the United States. Determined not to repeat China's ineffective experience with its overseas population, Japan wanted to enhance its international position by elevating the image and status of its overseas Japanese. Images of Japanese as the "problem" or "peril," leading to anti-Japanese protests, local ordinances, and/or discriminatory immigration policies, were to be avoided at all costs.

Japan's quest for international accolades and national pride contributed to the government's conciliatory and self-controlling posture that paved the way for the Gentlemen's Agreement. The voluntary nature of the agreement signified that it was not meant to restrict the sovereign right of the United States to regulate immigration. For volunteering to limit labor migration to the United States, Japan negotiated that the U.S. would "self-impose not to enact any discriminatory legislation against the Japanese." For American municipal ordinances or national policies to uphold discriminatory treatment of Japanese nationals would be counter to the government's agenda or self-identity as a rising superpower.

Consequently, when the Immigration or National Origins Act of 1924 was passed—effectively ending the Gentlemen's Agreement and barring most East Asians from immigration—the Japanese government felt betrayed. The government had upheld its end of the agreement and completely restricted Japanese labor immigration. Immigration statistics from 1909 to 1923 show that, except for the war period, more

Japanese nationals left the United States than arrived there. For those 15 years, reports from the U.S. commissioner-general of immigration demonstrated that the net increase was 8,681 (578 per year). This pool would include those who were legally allowed to enter through the Gentlemen's Agreement and those exempt groups, including students, merchants, tourists, and government officials.

Although "Japanese" were not named in the 1924 act, it was seen as a Japanese exclusion act because Japan was the only country to be denied even the minimum quota of 100 per year. If the Japanese had been placed on a quota as the Europeans were, fewer than 200 would have been admitted each year given the Japanese population in the United States in 1890. The 1924 act disproportionately affected Asian immigration because all of those "ineligible for American citizenship" would be denied admittance.

Any doubts about the status of Japanese were swept away by the 1922 U.S. Supreme Court case of *Ozawa v. U.S.*, which declared that the Japanese were not eligible for naturalized citizenship. Superseding the Gentlemen's Agreement, the National Origins Act provoked a new low for U.S.–Japan relations, resulting in "hate America" meetings held on "Humiliation Day" (July 1, 1924).

Yvonne M. Lau

See also Chinese Exclusion Acts; Immigration, U.S.; Immigration and Race; Japanese Americans; National Origins System

Further Readings

Inui, Kiyo. 1925. "The Gentlemen's Agreement: How It Has Functioned." *Annals of the American Academy of Political and Social Science* 122:188–198.

O'Brien, David and Stephen Fugita. 1991. *The Japanese American Experience.* Bloomington: Indiana University Press.

Spickard, Paul. 1996. *Japanese Americans.* New York: Twayne.

GENTRIFICATION

The movement of the middle and upper classes into previously lower- and working-class neighborhoods is termed *gentrification.* This movement involves the restoration of derelict housing, revitalization of commercial areas, and a geographic displacement of poorer residents. Although the term *gentrification* is used to describe changes within urban neighborhoods since the 1970s, it has also been applied to the revitalization of small town main streets and older inner-ring suburbs.

Research on gentrification has focused on the role of real estate markets, restructuring of the economy, local politics, and characteristics of the gentrifiers themselves in shaping how, when, and where gentrification occurs. Earlier debates focused on consumption-side versus production-side explanations for gentrification. The consumption-side arguments are that lifestyle, small family size, changing gender roles, high education levels, changes in the workplace, and consumer preferences made city living attractive to a previously suburban middle class. Production-side arguments look to the roles played by changing markets, large institutions, and politics that make it possible for the middle class to live in what were once blighted areas of the city. It is argued that capital investment and revitalization of central business districts (CBDs) and urban waterfront areas could not have succeeded without a significant private subsidy and public government support. The results of revitalized downtowns are areas dedicated to consumption and tourism, a revived business and financial district, and the growth of downtown housing for white-collar workers. Gentrification was such a transformative phenomenon to cities (especially in the United States and Western Europe) during the late 20th century—literally changing the landscape and urban populations—that it is clear that large-scale social processes have helped to shape small-scale residential decisions and neighborhood-level change.

Gentrification is frequently conceptualized as a process. The first wave of gentrifiers to enter a lower- or working-class neighborhood are of the creative class—artists, students, and musicians who are looking for cheap housing and workspace and whose consumer tastes tolerate the grittiness of the area. Urban "pioneers" or "homesteaders" (two popular terms for gentrifiers during the 1970s and 1980s) make investments (sometimes assisted by city subsidies) in older historic areas with the intention of restoring Victorian homes to their original grandeur. After the first wave of in-movers, the city may begin to reinvest in the neighborhood by updating parks, roads, and commercial strips. The real estate market becomes more active, and investors buy property to either rehabilitate or tear down and build again for prospective in-movers.

Construction in Harlem. *A new apartment building was under construction on August 16, 2001, in Harlem, New York City. A small but vocal community in Harlem was upset at the Upper Manhattan Empowerment Zone (UMEZ), claiming that the historically Black community's recent gentrification programs had driven out some local businesses and raised real estate prices on many properties.* Gentrification *refers to the process of the middle and upper classes moving into previously lower- and working-class neighborhoods.*

Source: Getty Images.

As more housing becomes available and commercial areas are revitalized, more middle-class gentrifiers move into the area. Over time, the physical and social landscape changes significantly and a new population moves in to replace an older one.

Whereas earlier research on gentrification processes focused on the gentrifiers themselves, subsequent work has investigated the struggle between newcomers and the original residents of a gentrifying neighborhood over housing and neighborhood resources. The original residents of a gentrifying neighborhood are more likely to be members of a racial or ethnic minority group, members of a lower class, and older than those of the gentrifying class. This results in a clash of interests because property taxes and rents tend to go up as gentrifiers purchase and improve existing housing stock and private reinvestment is made in neighborhood commercial districts. Geographer Neil Smith's study of gentrification in New York City's Lower East Side exemplifies the struggle of working-class and poor residents to defend their neighborhood from change. Smith argued that larger forces such as changes in the political economy—and specifically the local and international real estate market—is what spurs gentrification in neighborhoods. With real estate investments, rental apartment buildings and abandoned squats are redeveloped into luxury condominiums and sold to mostly White and bourgeois consumers. The influx of the new upwardly mobile residents is conceptualized as the "taming of the frontier." In the case of the Lower East Side, the original residents were evicted from their homes but were not given options for relocation. Homelessness and general displacement of poor minority and White residents is the downside of gentrification. Very few studies have been able to document what happens to those who are displaced by neighborhood change. Temporary housing for the displaced, such as tent cities, have become a common sight in highly gentrified cities such as Seattle and San Francisco.

Beyond marketplace forces, the struggle between local politics and community groups is evident in neighborhoods undergoing gentrification. Cities benefit from gentrified neighborhoods in terms of controlling street crime, raising the tax base, and attracting more middle-class residents to invest in city property. The urban political machine rewards redevelopers with building permits, zoning changes, and historic tax credits. Neighborhood change can be highly contested by community groups whose members understand that displacement is the inevitable result of redevelopment. In most large cities, the major players in gentrification are White and middle or upper class (politicians, landlords, redevelopers, and in-movers) and the original residents are a minority. This is evident in the case of West Town in Chicago. Puerto Rican residents organized around the theme of Puerto Rican nationalism and worked in community groups to fight against displacement created by the largely Polish political machine. Studies of local politics and community groups question whether market forces are enough to gentrify a neighborhood and whether gentrification is a one-way process without a struggle from below. Ethnographic evidence shows that the original residents of a neighborhood undergoing gentrification do not simply disappear but rather actively contest neighborhood change. However, what is not clear is whether gentrifiers and original residents can coexist in a neighborhood, side by side, as each block of the city becomes the next frontier to conquer. Future study should focus on the outcome of gentrification and whether racial and class integration of neighborhoods undergoing change is possible.

Meghan Ashlin Rich

See also American Apartheid; Code of the Street; Community Cohesion; Community Empowerment; Discrimination in Housing; *Gautreaux* Decision; Housing Audits; Public Housing; Resegregation; Segregation; Underclass; White Flight

Further Readings

Betancur, John J. 2002. "The Politics of Gentrification: The Case of West Town in Chicago." *Urban Affairs Review* 37:780–814.

Smith, Neil. 1996. *The New Urban Frontier: Gentrification and the Revanchist City.* London: Routledge.

Smith, Neil and Peter Williams, eds. 1986. *Gentrification of the City.* London: Allen & Unwin.

Zukin, Sharon. 1987. "Gentrification: Culture and Capital in the Urban Core." *Annual Review of Sociology* 13:129–147.

GEORGIAN AMERICANS

The first Georgians arrived in the United States during the 1890s to join Buffalo Bill Cody and his Wild West Congress of Rough Riders of the World. However, the four primary waves of immigration from Georgia occurred (a) after Georgia lost its independence in 1921 following a Red Army invasion, (b) after World War II when many captured Georgians serving in the Soviet Army refused to return to the Soviet Union, (c) during the 1980s when Georgian Jews were permitted to leave the Soviet Union, and finally (d) during the 1990s after Georgia regained its independence once more. Although the total population of the Georgian American community is relatively small, some members have made important contributions to U.S. business and culture. This entry describes their country of origin, their immigration history, and the current community.

Georgia Background

The people known as Georgians call themselves *kartvelebi* and call their country *Sakartvelo*. The word *Georgia* probably mutated from the Turkish term for Georgian, *Gurji,* although there are other theories pointing to a Greek or Farsi origin of the word. Georgians speak a language that is part of the southwest (non-Indo-European) Caucasian group of languages. Most Georgians belong to the Georgian Orthodox Church, although there are also a small number of Catholics and Baptists and significant numbers of Georgian Muslims in Achara. Georgia occupies 27,657 square miles (approximately twice the size of Belgium). On its northern border lies the Russian Federation, to the south are Turkey and the Republic of Armenia, and to the west and east are the Black Sea and the Republic of Azerbaijan, respectively.

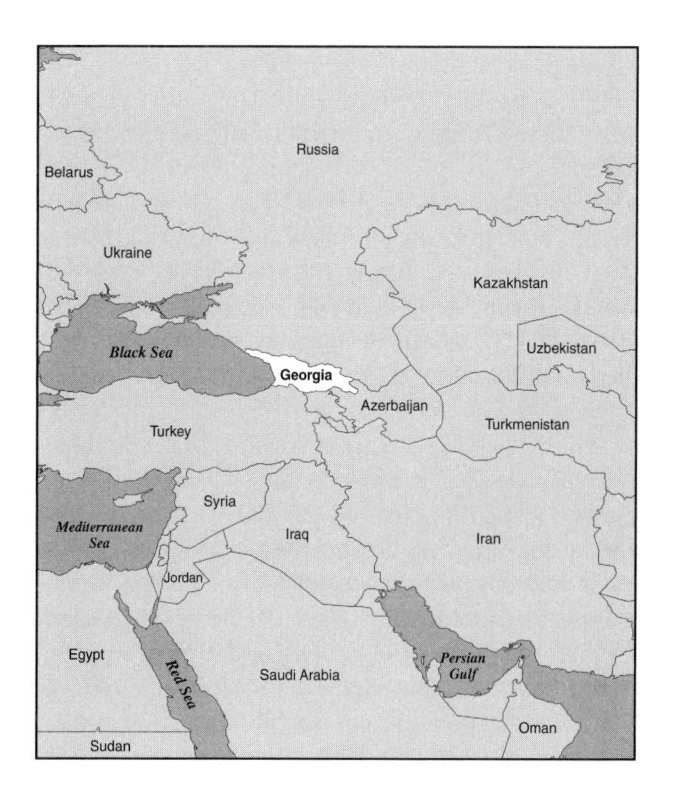

Most Georgian emigrants during the 20th century settled in Russia (the majority), Poland, France, or Germany. Munich and Paris were traditional havens for Georgian political émigrés. Before the 1930s, the vast majority of Georgian political émigrés belonged to the Georgian social democratic movement, which had strong links with European socialist parties in Germany, Belgium, and France. After the invasion of Georgia by the Red Army in February 1921, General Josef Pilsudski, a former socialist and Polish dictator from 1926 to 1935, invited many Georgian emigrants to settle in Poland and train as officers in Polish military academies.

Of all Soviet peoples, the Georgians were the most likely to remain within the boundaries of their republic, but after the collapse of the Soviet Union in December 1991, Georgia experienced a catastrophic economic decline and secessionist wars that led to intensified emigration. Between 1989 and January 2002, the Georgian population declined from 5,456,100 to 4,452,100—a decrease of 16%. The decline was a result of falling birth rates, increased mortality levels, the loss of population in Abkhazia and South Osetia, the out-migration of non-Georgians, and (most significant) the emigration of Georgians in search of work. The official unemployment rate was 13.8% in 2005, and unofficially it was between 30% and 40%. Approximately 40% of Georgia's emigrants during the 1990s ended up in Russia, and 14% ended up in the United States. More of Georgia's national minorities (50.5% vs. 31.0% of Georgians) left for Russia, and more Georgians (19.5% vs. 9.0% of national minorities) left for the United States.

History of Immigration

The first Georgians who came to the United States were a group of fifteen horse riders invited to join Buffalo Bill Cody and his Wild West Congress of Rough Riders of the World during the 1890s. The Ringling Brothers Circus signed up approximately thirty more Georgians after 1900, although they were described as Cossacks. A small number of Georgians seeking to escape military service or attracted by railway construction jobs in California trickled into the United States during the decade before World War I. During the period of Georgian independence (1918–1921), diplomatic links were established with the United States, and Georgia was recognized de jure by the U.S. government.

After the Red Army invasion of Georgia in February 1921, many Georgians fled to Europe, Turkey, and China. During the 1920s, approximately 150 of these exiles, mostly former officers, government officials, and aristocrats, came to the United States. Many were members of Georgian princely families such as the Eristavis and Chavchavadzes. Prince Paul Chavchavadze was married to the niece of Tsar Nicolas II, and Prince Archil Gourielli-Tchkonia was married to Helena Rubenstein, a famous Polish-born perfumier living in the United States.

The next wave of Georgians came after World War II and settled under the terms of the Displaced Persons Act of 1948 and the Refugee Relief Act of 1953. Most of them were former prisoners of war or displaced European citizens. A number of them had been members of the National Committee for the Liberation of Georgia or had been in the Georgian Legion that fought on the German side in the war, hoping to liberate Georgia from Soviet occupation. Many new arrivals had a hard time during these early postwar years. The Tolstoy Foundation and the Church World Service tried to help Georgians find employment. Georgian immigrants from this second wave were, on the whole, less educated than those from the first wave and occupied less prestigious jobs.

The first ten families of Georgian Jews arrived in the United States in 1973 and 1974. Two more larger waves, many from Israel, followed from 1978 to 1980 and during the mid-1980s. They were helped to settle by the Hebrew Immigrant Aid Society and the New York Association for New Americans. Approximately 90% of the 5,000 to 6,000 Georgian Jews in the United States live in the Queens district of New York City. They have built their own synagogue and publish a community newsletter in Georgian, Hebrew, and English. Many of them work in the jewelry trade and have stores on New York's 47th Street.

Besides the post-Soviet immigrants, the Georgian community since 1991 has received a new infusion of students and scholars on exchange programs (there were 1,750 Georgians in U.S. high schools and higher education in 2000) and through the presence of Georgian diplomats and their families in both Washington, D.C., and New York City. Georgians have become geographically scattered during the past decade, but according to figures from the Immigration and Naturalization Service for 1992 through 1995, the vast majority still prefer to settle in either California or New York. In 1995, 27% of legal immigrants from Georgia settled in California and 33% settled in New York.

Today's Community

It is hard to estimate how many Georgians are currently living in the United States. During the pre-Soviet period, Georgian immigrants were classified mostly as Russians, categorized according to their "country of origin." The same pattern continued during the Soviet period. It is only since the collapse of the Soviet Union in 1991 and the creation of an independent Georgian state that Georgians have been recognized by the U.S. government as a separate national category. Adding to the confusion, Georgians made up only 70% of their country's population in 1990. Legalized aliens in the United States since 1991 have been categorized by country of birth, so some immigrants officially classified as Georgian might not consider themselves as such.

The U.S. Census Bureau estimated that there were 10,530 Georgians in the United States in 2000. This does not include the vast illegal community of Georgians who have crossed the Canadian and Mexican borders to find work and the large Georgian Jewish community in Queens. Although Georgian Jews classify themselves as Jewish, they are culturally and linguistically Georgian. Still, the U.S. government figures for the 1990s of 8,000 to 9,000 new Georgian residents represents the largest wave of Georgian legal immigrants in U.S. history. In 2000, Georgian legal residents in the United States had a median age of 36.1 years. In 1999, they had a median household income of $30,640. Approximately 52% had an undergraduate degree or higher, but 23% of families were still below the poverty line.

The number of legal Georgian immigrants in the United States is small because, as subjects of the Russian Empire or citizens of the Soviet Union, emigration was extremely difficult. The rare opportunities for emigration were between 1918 and 1921, a period of Georgian independence; during World War II when some Soviet Georgian prisoners of war made their way to the United States; and during the 1970s when Jews, many of them Georgian, were permitted to emigrate from the Soviet Union as part of the Helsinki agreements. The largest wave came after 1991 when Georgia regained its independence.

Famous Georgians

There have been some great Georgian successes in American cultural and political history. Prince Georges Matchabelli, founder of the Matchabelli perfume group, arrived in New York in 1924, and Alexander Kartveli, designer of the American fighter plane Republic P-47, arrived in 1927. Kartveli helped to establish Republic Aviation, an airplane design company that created the F-84 Thunderjet and many other U.S. fighter planes after World War II.

George Papashvily, an illiterate peasant and sculptor, arrived in the United States in 1920. He described his experiences as a new Georgian immigrant in the book *Anything Can Happen,* published in 1945 and translated into fifteen languages. In 1952, the book was made into a film starring Jose Ferrer and Kim Hunt. The great ballerina and film star Tamara Tumanishvili (Toumanova) made her home in the United States, as did the choreographer George Balanchine (Balanchivadze). General John Shalikashvili, chairman of the Joint Chiefs of Staff from 1993 to 1997, was born in Warsaw in 1936 and was the child of a Georgian contract officer in the Polish army.

Community Life

Georgians in the United States, unlike Armenians, Latvians, and Ukrainians, have never had the numbers or resources to organize a strong political lobby. Georgian immigrants are fiercely loyal to their language, but their children find it hard to retain knowledge of Georgian without community support and Georgian language schools. There are Georgian language programs at a number of universities (e.g., Indiana University, Columbia University, University of Chicago), but these courses serve the academic community. The absence of financial resources is a serious problem: Most Georgians still consider themselves Orthodox Christians but need to use the facilities of the Orthodox Church in North America for their parishes in New York and Washington, D.C., although they have their own priests.

The first Georgian organization in the United States was the Georgian Society founded in San Francisco in 1924. In 1930, the Caucasian Society Alaverdi was formed to unite different Caucasian groups. In 1932, the Georgian Association in the United States was founded. During the 1950s, many of the new emigrants became enthusiastic supporters of U.S. anticommunist policies and formed a number of leagues and parties, including the Georgian–American League, the Georgian National Union, and the American Council for Independent Georgia. The Georgian–American League published a newspaper, the *Voice of Free Georgia,* from 1953 to 1958, and the American Council for Independent Georgia published *Our Path* in 1953. Between 1955 and 1975, the broader and less politicized community was served by the newspaper *Georgian Opinion* (*kartuli azri*). In 1951, Georgians were awarded their own radio section on *Voice of America,* which still functions today.

The Georgian Association in the U.S. which until the 1970s ran a cultural center known as the Georgian House, is the longest serving Georgian organization in the United States. It organizes annual celebrations on St. Nino's Day (January 26) and independence day

(May 26, which marks the Declaration of Independence of the first Georgian Republic in 1918). Two other charitable Georgian associations have been founded since 1991: the American Friends of Georgia (1994) and the Georgian Foundation in California. Both concentrate on humanitarian aid to fight tuberculosis, support orphanages, and distribute food packages for the poor and books for libraries.

The Georgian community in the United States is gradually being linguistically assimilated. Exogamous marriage is common. There is no discrimination or "ghettoization" of Georgians. The strong sense of Georgian kinship and solidarity brings the scattered community together during Georgian national holidays. Georgian Americans are firm supporters of tradition and the family, which has helped the community to survive in the United States. The community has been rejuvenated by its country's independence, the arrival of Georgian diplomats and students, the activity of new associations, and (for younger members) electronic forums.

Stephen Francis Jones

See Appendix A

See also Acculturation; Assimilation; Immigration, U.S.; Russia; Ukrainian Americans

Further Readings

Papashvily, George and Helen Waite Papashvily. 1945. *Anything Can Happen.* New York: Harper.
U.S. Census Bureau. 2000. *Table FBP-1 [Foreign Born Population]: Profile of Selected Demographic and Social Characteristics.* Available from http://www.census.gov/population/www/socdemo/foreign/STP-159-2000tl.html
Wertsman, Vladimir. 1995. "Georgians in America." *Multicultural Review* 4(4):28–53.

GERMAN AMERICANS

Over the course of three and a half centuries, approximately 7 million Germans left their homes to seek better fortunes elsewhere, and although some of them went east into the Russian Empire and some journeyed to Australia, South Africa, and Latin America, the vast majority (more than 90%) aimed for North America; prior to World War I, approximately 90% went to the United States and 2% went to Canada. Since this immigration proceeded on a high level over the whole period, the history of German Americans and the history of the United States are closely interrelated. Major events and developments, such as the settling of the West and the rise of a multiethnic urban culture, are mirrored in their respective histories. This entry looks at that interaction.

The Colonial Period

The period prior to and around the American Revolution, labeled by historians of German America as "before the Great Flood," saw a number of religious dissenters following William Penn's attractive offer of religious freedom and free land for resettlement. The group of "Krefelders," with their leader Franz Daniel Pastorius, arrived in October 1683 to found what came to be known as Germantown. This group nicely provided historians with the material for a foundational myth of German America.

In addition to these religiously motivated settlers, a number of Germans made use of the redemptioner or indentured servant system to have their passage paid for, to work it off over the subsequent couple of years, and then to seek opportunities for settlement. Protective legislation in favor of the redemptioners in

German emigrants. This engraving in Harper's Weekly from November 7, 1874, shows German emigrants embarking on a Hamburg steamer headed for New York. Upon arrival in the United States, these immigrants likely moved to where land was available—first in Pennsylvania and New York and then west into Ohio, Michigan, Wisconsin, Illinois, Iowa, Minnesota, Missouri, and Kansas, and southwest to Texas and California.

Source: Library of Congress, Prints & Photographs Division, LC-USZ62-2054.

some states, and (more so) the entrenchment of African American servitude in America, put an end to this immigration strategy during the 1830s. Regarding the number of people of German-speaking origin (this would include Swiss immigrants) who lived in the colonies around the time of the American Revolution, new research and more refined calculating methods estimate that in 1776 the United States was home to 228.600 people of Swiss and German origin, approximately 11.5% of the White population.

During the American Revolution, young German men were pressed into military service to support the British troops so their ruler could pay off some debt to the British king. Some deserted to join the revolutionaries, some stayed and settled, and some returned home. All of them, however, helped to spread the word about land and opportunities in the New World. It is through these troops that information about the New World disseminated, it has been argued in German historiography.

The Quest for Land

From the 1830s onward, when Germans began to leave Europe in greater numbers, the pull of information about the United States was compounded by the push of deteriorating economic and social conditions, at first in southern and southwestern Germany. During the 1840s and 1850s, the migration fever had reached the middle regions of the country, including the eastern provinces of Mecklenburg. By the 1890s, people living in the northeastern agrarian lands voted with their feet against oppressive political conditions and for an opportunity to carve out a better life for their families.

The demographic transition—that is, a higher birth rate and a lower infant death rate—in conjunction with crop failures, stifled industrial development, declining market value of proto-industrial (textile) production, a resulting lack of employment opportunities, the desire to preserve some independent secure economic status, and some good old *Abendteuerlust*—all of these contributed to the culture of emigration that spread in 19th-century Germany.

People who left Germany during the middle decades of the century had a strong desire to own land, even if it meant working some time as a laborer in the city to earn the money needed to buy land. Thus, settlement occurred where land was available—first in Pennsylvania and New York and then moving west into Ohio, Michigan, Wisconsin, Illinois, Iowa, Minnesota, Missouri, and Kansas, and southwest to Texas and California.

Chain migration—motivated by the desire to live in homogeneous communities based on religion and/or regional origin—influenced the settlement patterns of Germans in the Midwest. The wish to keep the land in the family and to supply every son (and daughter) with a piece of land, as well as the tendency to marry within the ethnic (and religious) group, helped to maintain ethnic identities. Having a critical number of people to support churches and parochial schools and to demand education in German added to the ethnic cohesion, language retention, and continuity of ethnic communities, on the one hand. Adjusting to new farming forms and methods, producing what the market demanded, participating in local politics, and responding to the lure of popular culture for the younger generations contributed to the "Americanization" process, on the other hand. Both trends taken together influenced the culture of the Midwest.

The Urban Experience

Despite the explicit desire to own land—as a status symbol, as a guarantor of social and economic security, as an indicator of continuity and tradition—many Germans settled in cities, thereby participating in the creation of a vibrant ethnically diverse urban culture. New York, Philadelphia, Baltimore, Cincinnati, St. Louis, Chicago, Cleveland, Ann Arbor, Austin, New Orleans, and even San Francisco all housed sizable German ethnic communities. They imposed their distinctive ethnocultural understanding unto the urban landscape and negotiated for a multicultural recognition of their existence and contribution long before multiculturalism became the politically correct paradigm for analyzing immigrant incorporation.

These urban German American communities, however, were never as homogeneous as their agrarian counterparts. Rather, they were divided by religion, regional origin, class, and gender. Looking at an ethnic community in transition in early 20th-century Philadelphia, the categories of Catholic, Lutheran, working-class socialist, and middle-class secular are used to structure the analysis of German Americans and their conversion to "old stock." This concept of religious diversity among Germans may be extended to include Jews as well as any variation of the Anabaptist faiths (Mennonites, Hutterites, and Amish).

Early Jewish immigrants have long been subsumed under the umbrella of German-speaking immigrants, and this may often have been justified due to much interaction and cooperation. However, an independent development toward Jewish community life, in light of religious and spiritual discussion and growing demands for spiritual guidance and charity with incoming Eastern European Jewish immigrants, warrants in-depth and separate analysis.

Germans from many different regional backgrounds, religious denominations, and class affiliations participated in the creation of Chicago's city and cultural landscape. The pioneers arriving in the city, together with the Irish, built the Illinois Michigan Canal during the 1840s. They were soon to be followed by many other immigrants, equipped with a variety of useful skills in the building trades, as bakers and brewers; as cobblers, furniture makers, house movers, printers, and typesetters; as store owners, sales clerks, box makers, and domestic servants. The Germans established churches and parochial schools and spent their leisure time in any number of associations, clubs, and lodges singing, exercising, or celebrating along with the festive German calendar—a carnival in February, picnics and excursions to an out-of-town beer garden in the spring and summer, exercise competitions in the fall, Christmas bazaars, and fancy charity balls in the winter.

They also came together to organize local politics, sometimes along socialist party lines, or they voiced their grievances in the workplace and formed unions. From the 1860s to the 1890s, social, economic, and cultural conditions were able to support class-based and class-divided associational life. Working-class people with socialist leanings organized their leisure time mostly among themselves, competing for attention and public space with "bourgeois" Germans. The latter paraded the streets of Chicago to celebrate the founding of the German Reich, and the former mourned the defeat of the Paris Commune, with both events being interrelated and taking place in 1871. Although in the beer gardens they came together to enjoy beer and coffee or tea on a pleasant Sunday afternoon, the socialists most likely were listening to some uplifting and militant speeches naming and blaming the class enemy. The Haymarket Riot of 1886 in Chicago, with its confrontation between striking workers and police and its aftermath, is the most obvious and best example of the vibrancy of the two German cultures and their interaction with Chicago society. Seven of the eight imprisoned and accused anarchists were immigrants from Germany and active members of the Chicago labor movement. Four were hanged in 1887, and two were pardoned by Governor John P. Altgeld in 1893.

Gender was another diversifier of culture. From the 1880s, a vibrant female public sphere emerged within the German American communities. Women began to organize in auxiliaries in support of the successful male choir or gymnastic group, but eventually they founded their own women's groups to enjoy singing and exercising for girls. In addition, women initiated and funded any number of charity groups and activities, often in support of the community at large such as the old people's home in Harlem near Chicago. Activities in support of these charity efforts brought together many elements of the German community and helped to sustain a sense of ethnic identity. Sometimes women would also meet in promotion of German culture in America and by doing so would venture into some modest feminist activities. German American women rarely supported suffrage endeavors, not necessarily because they opposed women voting but rather because the woman's vote was too closely associated with temperance activities. In their rejection of prohibition, most German Americans united beyond class and gender.

During the 1890s, things began to change. Although up until then most German Americans were securely ensconced in their "German" neighborhoods, reading their newspapers in German (there were 750 publications to choose from in 1900) and attending their respective church services, the sons and daughters became more interested in participating in the emerging consumer and popular culture and the older generation demanded more recognition for their cultural and political contribution to the urban scene. They began to become more active in preserving "Germandom" and started to organize on a national scale.

National Claims

In 1901, the National German–American Alliance, originating in Philadelphia, was formed. At its height in 1907, it attracted a membership of 1.5 million. Although its aim was to speak for all Germans, it was clearly biased toward the urban Protestant middle class. Its goal was to promote the memory of the German American contribution to the development of the United States, to fight prohibition, and (from 1914 onward) to argue for U.S. neutrality. After some national moments of recognition by Theodore Roosevelt and William Taft (e.g., dedication of a Wilhelm von Steuben statue in 1910), the organization disbanded quickly in 1917 after the United States declared war on Germany.

There is a general sense that German American culture finished being a relevant factor in the U.S. urban environment during the 1920s. German Americans, however, continued to have a sizable presence in urban consumer and popular culture, participating in the creation of an "old stock" identity, partly directed against the newcomers and partly in memory of old alliances. Charity efforts in support of the suffering Germany during the mid-1920s gave many German Americans a new respectable opportunity to take up public space and receive public attention. Thus, the paradigm—that World War I put an end to a noticeable German American presence—needs to be reconsidered in light of new scholarship.

The Nazi Period, the War, and the Postwar Years

The Nazi era and the war years of the 1930s and 1940s were marked by a significant migration of refugees from Germany combined with rather restrictive immigration policies that allowed only a select and lucky few to seek asylum in the United States. Whereas Albert Einstein, Thomas Mann, Hanns Eisler, and Bertolt Brecht enjoyed safe havens in Princeton, New Jersey, and in Hollywood, California, others were not admitted. For example, the Jewish passengers aboard the SS *St. Louis* were refused landing permits in 1939 and were required to return to Europe, with many of them ending up in concentration camps.

With the end of World War II in May 1945, many people in Germany wanted nothing more than to emigrate as fast as possible. For those forced laborers, prisoners of war, and concentration camp survivors, a vast resettlement program was put into place and brought approximately 400,000 potential laborers and their families to the United States for resettlement. In addition, some immigrants were invited by the U.S. government, which thought that they might be helpful in facilitating its rocket program. Wernher von Braun and his team were "invited" to come in 1946, first to work in El Paso, Texas, and later to work and live with their families in Huntsville, Alabama. Next to those "distinguished" immigrants were approximately 779,000 "undistinguished" Germans who aimed for a new life in the United States and who received visas during the years 1946 to 1961.

The social, cultural, and economic impact of German immigration during the postwar period, although numerically not insignificant, may be negligible in other respects. In 2005, approximately 9,200 people from Germany, a country estimated to have 82.3 million people in 2007, obtained legal residence in the United States. A shared cold war experience, the impact of U.S. culture on postwar Germany, and the long-standing historical and cultural ties between the two countries make transitions between them fairly easy. This can also be seen in the large number of ongoing academic transnational and transcultural exchanges and migrations between the two countries currently. The traffic almost goes unnoticed.

Christiane Harzig

See Appendix A; Appendix B

See also Acculturation; Amish; Assimilation; Belize; Foreign Students; Holocaust; Hutterites; Immigration, U.S.; Jewish Americans; Mennonites

Further Readings

Adam, Thomas, ed. 2005. *Germany and the Americas: Culture, Politics, and History.* 3 vols. Santa Barbara, CA: ABC–CLIO.

Brinkmann, Tobias. 2002. *Von der Gemeinde zur "Community": Jüdische Einwanderer in Chicago, 1840–1900.* Osnabrück, Germany: Universitätsverlag Rasch.

Conzen, Kathleen N. 2003. *Germans in Minnesota.* St. Paul: Minnesota Historical Society Press.

Freund, Alexander. 2004. *Aufbrüche nach dem Zusammenbruch: Die deutsche Nordamerika-Auswanderung nach dem Zweiten Weltkrieg.* Göttingen, Germany: V&R Unipress.

Grabbe, Hans-Jürgen. 2001. *Vor der großen Flut: Die europäische Migration in die Vereinigten Staaten von Amerika, 1783–1820.* Stuttgart, Germany: Steiner.

Harzig, Christiane. 1991. *Familie, Arbeit, und weibliche Öffentlichkeit in einer Einwanderungsstadt: Deutschamerikanerinnen in Chicago um die Jahrhundertwende.* St. Katharinen, Germany: Scripta Mercaturae.

Holleuffer, Henriette von. 2001. *Zwischen Fremde und Fremde: Displaced Persons in Australien, denn USA, und Kanada, 1946–1952.* Göttingen, Germany: Rasch-Verlag.

Kamphoefner, Walter D. 2006. *Westfalen in der Neuen Welt: Eine Sozialgeschichte der Auswanderung im 19. Jahrhundert.* Göttingen, Germany: V&R Unipress.

Kazal, Russell A. 2003. *Becoming Old Stock: The Paradox of German-American Identity.* Princeton, NJ: Princeton University Press.

Marschalck, Peter. 1973. *Deutsche Überseewanderung in 19. Jahrhundert.* Stuttgart, Germany: Klett.

Pohlmann, Cornelia. 2002. *Die Auswanderung aus dem Herzogtum Braunschweig im Kräftespiel staatlicher Einflußnahme und öffentlicher Resonanz 1720–1897.* Stuttgart, Germany: Steiner.

GERRYMANDERING

Gerrymandering is the drawing of electoral districts, many of which have a highly irregular shape, with the goal of achieving political purposes. At various times, gerrymandering has been used both to exclude and include racial minorities in the electoral processes. The term originates from districts drawn by Governor E. Gerry of Massachusetts early in U.S. history. Their shape was derisively seen as mimicking a salamander and, hence, was called a gerrymander. Gerry was successful in hurting the opposition. In the following election in 1812, the Federalists won only eleven of forty seats in the legislature despite winning a majority of the votes in the state. This entry describes the practice of gerrymandering and its political impact.

How It Works

Gerrymandering is made possible because elections are often held by district, and it is more likely to exist in electoral systems with single-member districts. The U.S. Constitution requires a census every 10 years for the purpose of apportioning seats in the House of Representatives but specifies only that they be elected "as directed by law." During the 1800s, rules were made to elect members of the House of Representatives from districts. Following a disputed election in New Jersey in 1842, an act of Congress stated that districts must determine congressional seats, but Congress was vague on the specifics of how the rule would be enforced.

To get an idea of how the drawing of lines might influence the outcome of elections, consider a square state. Party A is the majority party statewide, and most of its members are concentrated in the northern two-thirds of the state. Party B is the minority party statewide but holds a majority in the southern one-third of the state. If the districts are drawn from north to south, each district will be controlled by Party A. However, drawing the lines east to west will give Party A control of the southern districts.

Three types of gerrymander generally are recognized, and each can affect minorities. In *cracking,* a significant minority population is spread over several districts to dilute its voting strength in any one district. In *stacking,* a large concentration of minority voters are combined with the White population to create districts with a White majority, effectively wasting the minority votes. The final type, *packing,* results in a minority seat, as a large number of minority voters are put in a district that already has many minorities. However, the result is that minority influence in neighboring districts is reduced or eliminated.

Gerrymandering and Race

Before the Civil War, slaves could not vote and freed Blacks were often denied that right. Immediately after the war, African Americans won congressional seats in the South. Following the end of Reconstruction in 1876, however, African American representation diminished as a result of gerrymandering and other tactics such as poll taxes, literacy tests, grandfather clauses, and intimidation. In North Carolina, the congressional lines were drawn to create a district that was overwhelmingly African American, thereby limiting the influence of Blacks in neighboring districts. George H. White, who represented this district, was the last African American of the post-Reconstruction era to hold a congressional seat; his last reelection was in 1898.

Major racial gerrymandering cases have often reached the U.S. Supreme Court. In *Colegrove v. Green* (1946), the Court refused to intervene in a redistricting case in Iowa, arguing that redistricting was a "political thicket" that the courts should avoid. Courts eventually entered the political thicket. In *Gomillon v. Lightfoot* (1960), the Court looked at a redrawing of the city boundaries in Tuskegee, Alabama, that virtually took all of the power away from African Americans voters. The old rectangular boundaries were changed to a twenty-eight-sided figure so that no district had more than 5 of the state's 400 African American voters. The Supreme Court struck down the new irregular city boundaries.

In other cases, the lack of redistricting had an impact on minority voters. During the early 1900s, for example, some states that neither gained nor lost seats did not redraw district lines. With the increase in urbanization over time, some due to the migration of African Americans into cities, old district lines resulted in urban districts having more people than rural districts. The 1920 census was the first one showing more people living in urban areas than in rural areas. If lines were not redrawn by state legislatures, the effect was to give urban areas less influence than they would have had if the district lines were redrawn so that every district in the state had roughly the same population.

By the early 1960s, Tennessee, one of those states with an increasing urban population, had not redrawn its congressional district lines since 1901. Although the state's districts initially had roughly equal population, by the 1960s the urban population was underrepresented. In *Baker v. Carr* (1963), the Supreme Court ruled against the Tennessee district boundaries by interpreting the equal protection clause in the Fourteenth Amendment as saying that there should be "one man, one vote" for congressional elections.

Congress had left the states to decide issues related to state and local elections, and the Supreme Court had a history of not making decisions on districts drawn for elections at the state and local levels. In *Reynolds v. Sims* (1964), however, the Court extended the "one man, one vote" principle to state elections. It interpreted the Fourteenth Amendment to also apply to elections below the national level.

Race and Rules for Redistricting

Additional principles for constructing congressional districts were generated in *Wesberry v. Sanders* (1964). The Supreme Court required "contiguity" and required districts to be "compact." The first principle is that the district should be in one piece so as to avoid the situation where one part of the district is not connected with some other part. The notion of compactness is that all parts of the district should be close together. The ideal case, never seen in practice, is that districts are circles. There is no agreed-on measure for compactness, let alone a minimum standard for compactness, so it can be difficult to show whether or not this preferred characteristic has been satisfied.

An additional principle is "continuity." The idea is that districts should be similar over time so that constituents will be in the same district and will maintain familiarity with the community and their representative. A final criterion is that the district should be drawn consistent with maintaining communities of interest.

With court decisions interpreting the Fourteenth Amendment and the Voting Rights Act of 1965 as stipulating "one person, one vote," district lines drawn during the 1970s and after the 1980 census resulted in a substantial increase in the number of African Americans entering Congress as well as state and local offices.

In the next change, the *Thornburg v. Gingles* (1986) decision, as well as the 1983 Voting Rights Act amendment, introduced rules for drawing lines to create majority–minority districts. Gingles required an affirmative answer to the following three questions for a majority–minority district to be created by state legislative action. Is the minority sufficiently large and geographically compact for a district? Is the minority politically cohesive? Does the White majority vote overwhelmingly as a bloc to enable it to usually defeat the minority's preferred candidate at the polls? An interpretation of the Gingles test was the notion that if it were possible to create a majority–minority district under the Gingles test, it was proper to do so.

The 1990 Census

Another round of redistricting followed the 1990 census. Some of the resulting African American majority districts were clearly compact, most obviously in large urban regions. Three proposed majority–minority districts for congressional seats drew national attention, however, because it was difficult to say they were compact. The three districts were in Georgia, Louisiana, and North Carolina. The North Carolina district had the additional nuance that it could be considered contiguous only because part of it ran along an overpass that connected two pieces of the district.

In *Shaw v. Reno,* the Supreme Court sent the North Carolina districting plan back to the state, ruling that drawing district lines solely for the purpose of creating a majority–minority seat, in absence of other considerations, was not constitutional. Therefore, district lines were redrawn. Republican strategists had hoped that the creation of majority–minority districts would result in the remaining districts in the state becoming more Republican. With the large 1994 Republican victory in the House of Representatives, there was concern that the Republican strategists were correct.

Also, by the middle 1990s, areas that could easily be made into majority–minority districts were identified. This, along with the *Mobile v. Bolen* (1980) case in Alabama stating that it was necessary to show not only racial discrimination but also the intent to discriminate, set a much higher standard for successful challenges. There were few celebrated redistricting cases during the latter half of the decade.

The 2000 Census

The reapportionment of congressional seats following the 2000 census continued a trend shifting seats from northern Frostbelt states to those in the southern Sunbelt. One case was of national interest. In Texas, the congressional lines drawn for the 2002 election resulted in seventeen Democrats and fifteen Republicans being sent to the House of Representatives. Lines were redrawn by a Republican state house for the 2004 elections, this time favoring Republicans and resulting in the election of eleven Democrats and twenty-one Republicans to the House of Representatives, an increase of six Republicans. In 2006, the Supreme Court ruled that it was constitutional to redraw lines a second time after a decennial census but that the lines drawn in Texas were not constitutional because a Hispanic population had been absorbed into another district, thereby reducing Hispanic influence.

Walter W. Hill

See also Discrimination; Ethnic Enclave, Economic Impact of; Pluralism; Voting Rights

Further Readings

Grofman, Bernard. 1990. *Political Gerrymandering and the Courts.* New York: Agathon.

Guinier, Lani. 1994. *The Tyranny of the Majority: Fundamental Fairness in Representative Democracy.* New York: Free Press.

Ghetto

At one time or another, most underprivileged racial/ethnic or religious communities in the United States have been described as a "ghetto." These poverty-stricken communities, in which minorities are typically overrepresented, are deemed "bad neighborhoods" because they suffer disproportionately from social problems such as crime, family disruption, and reliance on government assistance. The use of this loaded term is contextually specific, describing the poorest-of-the-poor Little Italys, shtetls, and Chinatowns at particular periods across the U.S. social landscape. This is mainly because a minority group's association with the ghetto shifts as it collectively experiences upward mobility. In other words, as time passes, what was once a predominantly poor Irish neighborhood slowly becomes a poor Dominican barrio.

The term *ghetto* was originally intended as an anti-Semitic slur describing segregated Jewish communities across Europe during the Middle Ages. The subordination and expulsion of Jews from mainstream society was initially fueled by the spread of Christianity. During the 20th century, the Nazi party reinvigorated anti-Semitism, and many Jews fleeing the Nazi Holocaust were able to escape to the United States. Although the word *ghetto* failed to take root there as a derogatory statement describing Jewish American communities, it has come to denote segregated subordinate communities inhabited by poor Blacks and Hispanics in the United States.

Across time periods and nations, the establishment of ghettos has been driven largely by discrimination and intolerance. Although these factors influenced the emergence of the U.S. ghetto, they were compounded by the rise of the industrial economy, the arrival of millions of minorities and immigrants to

U.S. cities, and metropolitan expansion. Accordingly, these dynamics further complicate our understanding of the U.S. ghetto. This entry looks at the contemporary debate over the creation and sustenance of the U.S. ghetto. It generally addresses (a) the cultural/attitudinal adaptation to inequality, (b) the debate over race versus social class, and (c) policy prescriptions for alleviating social problems in these distressed communities.

The Cultural/Attitudinal Adaptation to Inequality

Ghetto communities have many social problems. However, scholars continue to debate the source—or key cause—of these problems. Is the individual solely to blame for his or her predicament? Or should society accept at least some responsibility for the downtrodden? Survey research has shown that most U.S. residents "blame the individual" for his or her social circumstances. In this regard, they tend to emphasize the choices people make, as well as people's moral character, in explaining why some people achieve their goals while others fall short. This dominant ideology of American individualism clearly explains why the culture of poverty thesis has remained influential.

The culture of poverty theory, first developed by Oscar Lewis, contends that the prolonged experience of poverty has deficits beyond a lack of disposable income. Rather, protracted poverty itself becomes a cultural obstacle to socioeconomic success. This is because destitution gives rise to a pathological set of attitudes and values that block an individual's path to upward mobility. This cultural adaptation to inequality is subsequently instilled in future generations who, like those before them, are likely to grow up in single-parent households, to experience sex at an early age, to lack impulse control, and to be unable to delay gratification or secure long-term employment. In short, this theory asserts that the ghetto was created and sustained by a cycle of intergenerational poverty rooted in defective pathology and culture.

During recent years, even the most liberal social scientists have been forced to confront these oppositional dimensions of ghetto life. For example, an important recent ethnographic study elucidates the "code of the street." This research suggests that alienated young males in the inner city have developed an alternative status system revolving around "violence and respect." Young people residing in these neighborhoods describe kids who are seeking to obtain rewards in mainstream society (e.g., good grades, a college education, a good job) as being raised in "decent families." Conversely, those youth with an oppositional identity, who see themselves as being on the fringes of society, describe themselves as being from "street families."

It is important to note that although many researchers take issue with the implications of pathologically based theory and research, scholars generally no longer challenge the existence of ghetto problems. Meaningfully, however, rather than place the locus solely on ghetto inhabitants, most researchers emphasize the structural roots of ghetto pathology and culture such as residential segregation and unemployment. Although sociologists in particular are not necessarily in agreement about how people adapt to inequality, they nonetheless can be sorted into two competing camps: those who accentuate factors relating to race versus those who emphasize economic factors.

The Debate Over Race Versus Social Class

The contemporary debate over race versus social class addresses the sources and persistence of the U.S. ghetto. In particular, one group of scholars asserts that White Anglo-Saxon Protestants (WASPs), the dominant racial group in U.S. society, purposely use racist tactics to maintain their hegemony. Accordingly, an important means of accomplishing this goal is to residentially segregate Blacks and Hispanics into declining urban areas. On the other hand, another set of thinkers contends that Blacks and Hispanics remain in the ghetto due to structural changes in the U.S. economy. More specifically, these researchers argue that the decline of the manufacturing sector has left many inner-city minorities with few viable prospects for upward social mobility.

Race-based theorists assert that the U.S. ghetto was constructed through a series of intentional decisions by Whites aimed at relegating minorities, Blacks in particular, to debilitating residential areas. Historical studies have shown that Whites have used racial violence, binding legal documents, and other strategic means of preventing Blacks from moving into predominantly White communities. More contemporary research has shown that Whites have undertaken a range of methods to preserve race-based residential inequities, including uneven development (e.g., the improvement of a particular urban area at the expense of another), redlining (e.g., discrimination in mortgage and business lending and in insurance), and the inaccessibility of available funds for community reinvestment. For many scholars, the results of these studies (as well as many others) underscore that the U.S. ghetto was deliberately constructed and conserved for distinctly racial reasons.

Class-based theorists, on the other hand, assert that deindustrialization and shifting opportunity structures explain the creation and sustenance of the ghetto. In this vein, the dynamics of joblessness—not racial antagonisms—take precedence in clarifying why Blacks and Hispanics reside disproportionately in declining urban areas. According to these thinkers, during previous stages of the manufacturing sector, minorities were able to access gainful employment in at least semiskilled and low-level managerial occupations. Since the mid-1960s, however, the shift toward the postindustrial economy required that the vast majority of these factory jobs either be phased out or replaced with low-wage service sector employment or high-status white-collar occupations. As with middle-class Whites, those minorities with a college education and/or specialized knowledge were insulated from the macroeconomic shift. Conversely, those who were unable to keep pace with societal changes experienced downward mobility.

For many scholars, the results of these studies confirm that class has become more important than race in structuring opportunity for minorities. In particular, the growing socioeconomic polarization between poor and middle-class members of racial/ethnic groups, as well as the intergenerational transmission of middle-class status onto succeeding generations of minority families, underscores the importance of class position—not racism—as the source of the U.S. ghetto.

Policy Prescriptions for the Ghetto

Social scientists and policymakers alike are concerned with improving living conditions and opportunities for ghetto residents. Nevertheless, liberal, moderate, and conservative pundits remain in disagreement about how to go about dismantling the U.S. ghetto. Some of the more popular policy prescriptions include the enforcement of federal fair housing legislation and the prosecution of discriminatory practices in housing markets such as redlining and unfair lending practices.

Some less popular strategies include community reinvestment through inner-city "enterprise zones" and gentrification of ghetto areas with special provisions for neighborhood residents to return following area restoration.

Jason Eugene Shelton

See also African Americans; *American Apartheid*; Barrio; Black Metropolis; Code of the Street; Community Empowerment; Culture of Poverty; *Declining Significance of Race, The*; East Harlem; Harlem; Homelessness; Immigrant Communities; Segregation

Further Readings

Anderson, Elijah. 1999. *Code of the Street.* New York: Norton.
Chávez, Linda. 1991. *Out of the Barrio.* New York: Basic Books.
Lewis, Oscar. 1965. *La Vida: A Puerto Rican Family in the Culture of Poverty—San Juan and New York.* New York: Random House.
Massey, Douglas S. and Nancy A. Denton. 1993. *American Apartheid: Segregation and the Making of the Underlass.* Cambridge, MA: Harvard University Press.
Wilson, William Julius. 1987. *The Truly Disadvantaged.* Chicago, IL: University of Chicago Press.

Glass Ceiling

The concept of the *glass ceiling* originated during the middle 1980s to describe the invisible and artificial barriers that have kept women from promotion to upper management and other higher leadership positions in the business world. Most who support the idea that a glass ceiling exists contend that the disadvantages worsen the higher on the corporate ladder women ascend. The barriers are hierarchical in nature and are seemingly impenetrable. This definition originally addressed the difficulties of women to advance but soon evolved to include both male and female racial/ethnic minorities. Women and minorities are significantly represented within the workforce as a whole and even at middle levels of management, but their numbers in senior executive positions remain quite small. Although the 20th century saw many improvements for women and minorities in the business world, advocates for equal rights claim that despite increasing numbers of women and minorities

Latina executive. Although the 20th century saw many improvements for women and minorities in the business world, advocates for equal rights claim that there is still a long way to go. Many upwardly mobile women and men of color face unseen and unspoken barriers as they advance to the upper reaches of management.

Source: iStockphoto.

in top leadership roles in business, there is still a long way to go. There is a belief that both women and minorities continue to face barriers in advancement to positions of leadership in corporations in spite of their much higher overall representation in certain fields and industries. This entry looks at the concept and its social manifestations.

History of a Concept

The phrase *glass ceiling* was first used in 1984 in an *Adweek* profile of Gay Bryant, who at the time was the editor of *Working Woman* magazine. In that profile, she was quoted as saying, "Women have reached a certain point—I call it the glass ceiling . . . in the top of middle management and they're stopping and getting stuck." In 1985, the national chairwoman of the National Organization for Women (NOW) used the phrase in an interview with United Press International, stating that without the women's movement, women would have no chance of moving beyond the glass ceiling. The very next year, in the March 24, 1986, edition of the *Wall Street Journal*, the term was used by both Carol Hymowitz and Timothy Schellhardt (who are frequently credited with first using the term in the media) in their article about the challenges faced by women in the business world.

In a discussion of ascending the corporate ladder, the word *ceiling* implies that there is a limit to how far someone can climb before he or she bumps up against a barrier of some kind. To say that the ceiling is glass suggests that, although it is very real, it is transparent and not obvious to the casual observer. It also implies that what is on the other side is both visible yet inaccessible to those facing it. The term *glass ceiling* is most often applied in business situations where women or minorities believe, either accurately or not, that White men are deeply entrenched in the upper echelons of power and that it is nearly impossible for the women or minorities to break through to that level.

The Department of Labor took the concept seriously in 1991 when it addressed the problem formally, stating that a glass ceiling is made up of "artificial barriers based on attitudinal or organizational bias that prevent qualified individuals from advancing upward in their organization into management-level positions." Senator Robert Dole introduced the Glass Ceiling Act as part of Title II of the Civil Rights Act of 1991. President George H. W. Bush signed the Civil Rights Act of 1991 and established a bipartisan Glass Ceiling Commission composed of twenty-one members. The commission was tasked with forming recommendations on the issue for the president and leaders in the corporate world.

In 1991, Secretary of Labor Lynn Martin completed the Glass Ceiling Initiative Report, which confirmed the existence of the invisible artificial barriers that blocked women and minorities from advancing up the corporate ladder to management- and executive-level positions. Robert Reich, chairperson of the Glass Ceiling Commission, stated that this "ceiling" was a refutation of social justice for a large portion of the population. He also saw it as a problem that has negatively affected American business by hindering some of the most qualified applicants from important positions of power simply because of their race or gender.

The report revealed that although women made up nearly 46% of the total workforce at the time and earned more than half of all master's degrees, 95% of senior-level managers were men and the earnings of female managers accounted for less than 70% of their male manager counterparts. During the decade since the commission's report, things have improved somewhat in that women managers now earn an average of 72% of their male colleagues' salaries.

Male and female minorities were less well represented in management. After the Civil Rights Act of 1954 and the introduction of affirmative action during the mid-1960s, legal barriers to their hiring and promotion were removed, yet their representation in the higher echelons of business was a fraction of their overall presence in the labor force. Some see this as proof of the existence of a split labor market in which racial/ethnic minorities receive lower remuneration than do Whites and are unable to get even entry-level positions in industries that have been long dominated by Whites, White males in particular.

In 1990, the proportion of minorities in top management positions was less than 1%, and their earnings lagged far behind even those of their White female colleagues. Although most scholars of inequality agree that the concept of the glass ceiling refers to the lack of access to the most highly paid corporate positions, many others use this term to describe gender or race discrimination at all levels of the business world. This concept has been adapted to address barriers to women in specific industries such as the *stained glass ceiling* to describe the difficulty women have had in ascending to the highest levels of the ministry, the *grass ceiling* when examining the dearth of women in agriculture-related industries, and the *political glass ceiling* that bemoans the slow pace of women's advances in the political realm. In the world of academia, the combined effects of a glass ceiling and a *maternal wall* are thought to interact to hinder women's advancement in the ivory tower because of choices made in relation to child-bearing and child-rearing responsibilities. Another variation is the *glass cliff,* which refers to a woman in a position that may put her in the precarious position of professional disaster if she fails.

Whereas the aforementioned concepts refer to the difficulties that women and minorities face in making inroads into the higher echelons of male-dominated industries, another concept, the *glass elevator* or *escalator,* refers to the relative ease and rapid advancement that men have in achieving promotions to management in female-dominated industries such as nursing and teaching.

Cracking the Glass Ceiling

Although many continue to insist that the glass ceiling is a real barrier for women and minorities in accessing male-dominated positions in business, others challenge that assertion. They say that the glass ceiling continues to exist primarily because of choices made by women regarding the time they spend on their families that, in the end, limits the time they need to advance in their careers. The cumulative effect of time off for child bearing and child rearing is blamed for women facing lower wages and delayed advancement to the highest positions. Contrary to claims of continuing inequality or discrimination, critics of the glass ceiling concept place the blame for the underrepresentation of women in particular, and of minorities by association, on the individuals themselves and on considerations other than structural or institutional inequality.

Nevertheless, industries such as the investment world have suffered criticism about past sexism, with legal judgments levied against Morgan Stanley and Merrill Lynch for practices deemed to be discriminatory. Recently, the investment industry has made inroads into the recruitment and training of women for top positions in their firms to address their past misdeeds. Changes are slow, however; although women currently represent 33% of the best in the bank analyst classes of business schools, only 25% of newly hired associates in this same industry are women. Only 14% of the top executives in the banking industry are women, and in 2005 one report showed that women make 77 cents for every dollar men make. However, many say that improvement, no matter how small, shows that there are cracks developing in the glass ceiling.

Landmarks in Cracking the Glass Ceiling

In 2004, it was estimated that in the United States, women earned 77 cents for every dollar men earn. Although this is a slight increase from 74 cents during the mid-1990s and is up from 68 cents during the late 1980s, these numbers remain troubling to many proponents of equal rights and equal opportunities. Women and minorities are making inroads into higher echelons of the business world, but their salaries still lag behind those of their male counterparts. Although the overall picture remains discouraging, there are clear examples of individuals who have beaten the odds and made the glass ceiling seem permeable.

In 1962, Harvey C. Russell became the first Black vice president of a Fortune 500 company, PepsiCo. During this very volatile time in U.S. history, the promotion of an African American was very controversial, prompting the Ku Klux Klan to attempt to organize a boycott using handbills informing customers that buying Pepsi products would make Black people rich. PepsiCo has continued to be instrumental in lowering the barriers throughout its history by featuring minorities in their advertising and by not hindering their advancement up the corporate ladder. A recent example was the hiring of Indra Nooyi, the eleventh woman to ascend to the top leadership position in a Fortune 500 company.

Although women in upper management are becoming more visible, they still account for less than 17% of all corporate officer jobs, with women of color accounting for less than 2% of that number. Some notable examples of those pioneers are Carleton Fiorina, who in 1999 became the first female chief executive officer (CEO) of a Fortune 500 company, Hewlett–Packard. Her tenure ended amid controversy in 2006, but her appointment seemed to widen the crack in the glass ceiling that had kept women from the top jobs. Just during the past couple of years, Irene Rosenfeld took over the helm of Kraft Foods and Patricia Woertz became CEO of Archer–Daniels–Midland. Consistently at the top of the Forbes 400 list of richest Americans are those who have moved beyond the barriers whether they be in place due to gender or race. Oprah Winfrey is a self-made success story who not only has moved beyond the glass ceiling of gender and race but also has taken countless others with her. Although women and minorities are still struggling for parity among their primarily White male counterparts, there are definitely examples that challenge the idea that these discriminatory practices are enmeshed in corporate culture.

Karen S. Boyd

See also Affirmative Action in the Workplace; African Americans; Biomedicine, African Americans and; Black Enterprise; Feminism, Black; Feminism, Latina; Gender and Race, Intersection of; Labor Market Segmentation; Science Faculties, Women of Color on; Social Inequality; Social Mobility; Split Labor Market

Further Readings

Blau, Francine D., Mary C. Brinton, and David Grusky, eds. 2006. *The Declining Significance of Gender.* New York: Russell Sage.

Federal Glass Ceiling Commission. 1995. *Good for Business: Making Full Use of the Nation's Resources.* Washington, DC: Government Printing Office.

Hymowitz, Carol and Timothy D. Schellhardt. 1986. "The Glass Ceiling: Why Women Can't Seem to Break the Invisible Barrier That Blocks Them from the Top Jobs." *The Wall Street Journal.*, March 24, 1.

Maume, David J. 2004. "Is the Glass Ceiling a Unique Form of Inequality? Evidence from a Random-Effects Model of Managerial Attainment." *Work and Occupations* 31:250–274.

GLOBALIZATION

Defining *globalization* is difficult. The term has been used both to characterize the development of a globally integrated network of business, trade, science, technology, politics, culture, and everyday life and to describe the results of these processes—a universal awareness and understanding of global relations. Globalization is multidimensional, developing both at the interpersonal level and among nation-states and multinational associations. It builds on existing cross-border ethnic ties and has facilitated the creation of new ties on the basis of ethnic or national bonds. Increasingly, globalization has led to a "compression" of the world. As political boundaries become less relevant, information, goods, services, capital, ideologies, media, and even individuals move more freely across them. Globalization is a historical process that began with trade and migration in the distant past but has recently accelerated as a result of the international spread of capitalism, rationalism, industrial production, and economic liberalism. In this entry, then, the term *globalization* is used to refer to the ongoing growth of interconnections and interdependencies in economics, politics, and culture in which social ties across boundaries have become more regularized and routine.

History of Globalization

Many historians argue that globalization processes have been part of human history since early bands became nomadic. International trade and commerce, migrations, and infusion of cultures from other lands have occurred throughout this history. However, social change in Europe during the 1600s led to the rise of capitalism and, in turn, to the global dominance of European empires by the mid-1800s. During the late 1900s, rapid advances in communication and transportation increased the pace of globalization.

Early Trade and Empires

Trade between city-states and ancient empires was commonplace, albeit geographically limited. During the Early Bronze Age (ca. 3500–2000 BC), the Akkadian Empire dominated Mesopotamia (parts of modern Syria, Iraq, Turkey, and Iran) and engaged in regional trade with nations around the Persian Gulf. Much later, the Mongolian Empire (1206–1405) became the largest contiguous empire in human history. Beginning under Timuchin, or Genghis Khan, and then under later Khans (rulers), the Mongolians unified China and much of Central Asia, extending their empire westward to Europe and southward to the Middle East. They established intercontinental trade routes, which spread cultural influences, goods, and technologies and developed new ties among conquered nations.

Legacies of the Age of Enlightenment

Most scholars of modern globalization, however, see its roots in the expansion of European power through colonization during the 16th century and in ideological revolutions during the Ages of Reason and Enlightenment (17th and 18th centuries). European colonization of the Americas, Africa, and Asia generated global ties among economic markets and helped European cities rise to be capitals of global empires. A period of increased international migration and exchange ensued. Economic, political, and religious conflicts among European power centers eventually led to a series of wars and later to the Peace of Westphalia (1648), which established the fundamental ideologies of the modern nation-state—sovereignty and the right of political self-determination, equality between states, and nonintervention in the internal affairs of other states. These principles became the building blocks of modern nations and international relations and remain integral elements of today's political globalization.

Another important element in the development of globalization stemmed from the Enlightenment—the idea of rationality. Enlightenment philosophers contended that empirical observation and systematic thinking could be applied to social, political, and economic activities to guide optimal decision making. It was proposed that complex systems, such as societies, could be reduced to their fundamental elements and, thus, be better understood. Reductionism and rationality influenced the development of capitalism and scientific positivism and are central aspects of modern economic globalization.

Global Empires

International commerce and trade increased slowly but steadily between 1600 and the late 1800s, due largely to the expansion of merchant capitalism and the establishment of the European global empires. These empires led to the development of interconnected and interdependent systems of trade in goods and peoples. Indentured servants from Europe and Africa were transported to the New World, helping to establish the diverse populace found there today. The African slave trade was an early example of the emerging complex global economy. Slaves, bought from West Africa with Indian textiles, were exchanged for Caribbean sugar and North American cotton and tobacco. These products were then transported to consumers in Europe. Although clearly no longer a part of the global economy, this global trade circuit required complex system of exchange and finance.

During the 1800s, the British Empire became the largest of the European empires, holding more than a quarter of the world's population and land mass. The success of the British Empire may be attributed, in part, to improved transportation technologies, continued economic dominance of former colonies through the Commonwealth, industrialization, and the development of a global marketplace. In particular, the principles of laissez-faire economics, which argued for free market conditions and opposed government intervention, tariffs, and taxation, favored economic globalization. Countries specialized in the production of particular goods, raw materials, or labor skills. The removal of barriers to global trade, increased international migration, reduced tariffs, and reduced transportation costs, attributable to improved technologies such as steamships, resulted in the rapid growth of the interconnection among countries.

The 20th Century

The early 20th century saw a decline in the global ties of the previous century. Protectionist trade practices, international economic recession, and two world wars temporarily slowed globalization. It was not until after World War II that economic relations and technological developments in communications and transportation regained momentum. Much of the postwar increase in economic and political connections has been attributed to the UN Monetary and Financial Conference meeting at Bretton Woods, New Hampshire, in 1944. The meeting established several international economic organizations to encourage rebuilding Europe's infrastructure (e.g., the International Bank for Reconstruction and Development [part of the World Bank]), regularized trade through fixed exchange rates (i.e., the International Monetary Fund), and reduced tariffs and other trade barriers (i.e., the General Agreement on Tariffs and Trade [which became the World Trade Organization in 1995]). These organizations have arguably been successful in expanding capitalism and the laissez-faire economic principles of the 1800s to most of the world.

The Postindustrial Period

The past 40 years have been characterized by ever accelerating growth in international travel, communications, commerce, global governance, and the like. This period, referred to as the Postindustrial Period, has also seen exponential increases in communications, computing, and related technologies as well as a rise of global governance. The increasing number of nation-states, the growing role of the United Nations and other intergovernmental organizations, the growing dominance of transnational corporations, the development of buyer-driven commodity chains, and the influence of international nongovernmental organizations all have played important parts in political and economic globalization. Cultural globalization has been accelerated by consolidation of media outlets into an international oligopoly centered in Europe and the United States. The arrival of a global communications network based on the telephone, the Internet, satellites, and other technologies makes possible close interpersonal ties regardless of geographic location. However, there has also been a significant cultural backlash against "Westernization" in many countries. Globalization, while tangibly raising living standards and improving health and education for many, has also generated extreme economic and social imbalances and increased disparities of wealth and power. The following sections describe today's economic, political, and cultural globalization and summarize the major issues that evoke antiglobalization movements.

Economic Globalization

Neoliberal laissez-faire economic ideologies favoring free trade, free circulation of capital, and freedom to invest anywhere have encouraged the growth of a complex international system of economic interdependence that transcends national borders. Linkages between producer nations and consumer nations have created a single division of labor within a world market with more than 2.5 billion workers. Production is divided between countries with higher skill/higher cost labor and those with lower skill/lower cost labor markets.

These labor characteristics are closely associated with global stratification in which northern countries use their relative market advantage and advanced technologies to maximize profit through low-cost production and natural resource extraction in the global South. As countries are pitted against each other in the global division of labor, they have increasingly relied on the importation of foreign workers to fill the positions that are the most "dangerous, dirty, and difficult." For example, guest workers are imported from the Philippines to work in Japanese and German electronics factories in Taiwan, they come from Sri Lanka to be employed as housemaids and servants for Saudi Arabian families, and they come from Croatia to work in Italian shipyards.

- *Transnational Corporations.* Transnational corporations (TNCs), firms or conglomerates that operate in more than one country, play an influential role in economic globalization. They have benefited greatly from the wage gap between high-income consumer nations and low-income producing nations by relocating production to the latter. Their enormous wealth lets them influence global relations, generate public support, liberalize trade and tariff agreements, limit costly labor and environmental standards, and influence local politicians in many countries. Profits for TNCs have risen at a rate above the increase in the world's gross product. Gross sales of the largest TNCs rival the gross domestic profit of many countries.

- *Global Commodity Chains.* Production in the global economy has changed dramatically from the early days of international trade when finished products, agricultural goods, and natural resources such as iron, timber, and oil dominated international trade. During the industrial period of the mid-20th century, most trade was keyed to manufacturing needs. Natural resources were shipped from low-income countries in the global South to the industrialized North. This "producer-driven" model is less characteristic of today's postindustrial global division of labor. In today's world economy, production begins with research and development of products for the consumer market, which is carried out largely in the North. Manufacturing is then contracted to factories and producers in low-cost labor markets, primarily in developing countries, which may subcontract particularly labor-intensive tasks to even less developed nations. This "buyer-driven" commodity chain maximizes profits by reducing production costs to a minimum. Companies in high-income countries not only save on the cost of labor but also do not need to invest capital in construction or retooling of factories.

- *Export Processing Zones.* To encourage participation in global commodity chains, many countries have created export processing zones (EPZs), where factories may import raw materials and produce export goods without tariffs. This further reduces costs and increases profits. According to the UN International Labour Organization (ILO), in 2006 there were 5,174 EPZs in 116 countries employing nearly 42 million people—roughly a fifth of the global workforce. The majority of those employed in the EPZs are in China, Bangladesh, and maquiladoras (export assembly plants) along the U.S.–Mexican border. Recent technological advances in satellites and international telecommunications are now allowing EPZs to treat information as an exportable commodity, supplying labor to staff call centers and "help desk" computer technical support, tax preparation and accounting, medical transcription, and the like.

- *Development and Structural Adjustment Policies.* Stimulating development in low-income countries has been a major issue in economic globalization. Loans to improve infrastructure and encourage economic growth have been provided by the World Bank and the International Monetary Fund. However, due to mounting debt and default on loans during the 1970s and 1980s, structural adjustment policies (SAPs) have been imposed on debtor nations. The World Bank and the International Monetary Fund are dominated by wealthy nations because votes are allotted on the basis of the funds a country provides. Hence, a few high-income countries are able to dictate lending conditions for the developing countries. The latter must agree to incorporate liberal economic principles of reduced governmental spending, privatization of state-owned industries, reduction in tariffs, and encouragement of foreign investment. Other adjustment policies have included currency devaluation, elimination of government subsidies to local industry, and abolition of minimum wages. The impact of these "austerity measures" has been felt disproportionately by women and the poor. Although resulting in increased profits for TNCs, little if any additional net gain has been generated for low-income countries as new government revenues have gone to pay debts.

Political Globalization

Political globalization has resulted in a complex system of world governance. Nation-states, the primary actors in this system, engage in diplomatic relations partly in the context of regional and global intergovernmental organizations (IGOs). Nation-states and IGOs consult with and are lobbied by TNCs and nongovernmental organizations (NGOs). NGOs in particular have distinct interactions with IGOs, such as the United Nations, where they play an advisory role and also take on activities such as relief, environmental protection, and protection of human rights.

- *Nation-States and Intergovernmental Organizations.* Nation-states engage in international relations to establish trade, maintain boundaries, enforce rules, settle disputes, manage migration, and the like. Most of these tasks were historically accomplished through negotiations among representatives of two or more states. During the past two centuries, however, nation-states have formed large IGOs that are now responsible for many of these tasks. To maintain the sovereignty of nation-states, IGOs operate on principles of intergovernmentalism requiring unanimity among their members before agreements can be finalized. Some IGOs do, however, incorporate elements of supranationalism in which majority rule may force member-states to implement IGO decisions or leave the organization. IGOs may be regional (e.g., European Union) or global (e.g., World Trade Organization). As the number of IGOs has grown and their membership has expanded to include many new nation-states, the structure and organizational characteristics of nation-states have become more similar. This growing isomorphism implies that a normative process, affecting new nation-states, is occurring on a global scale.

- *Nongovernmental Organizations.* NGOs are also important actors in the global political system. These nonprofit, voluntary associations often promote universal norms such as human rights. They lack direct influence over policymaking because they have no vote in IGO decisions, but they have significant influence via lobbying. According to the UN Economic and Social Council (ECOSOC), 2,719 organizations have obtained "consultative" status. Nearly 2,000 of these were formed between 1995 and 2005. Like more recently formed nation-states, there is a great deal of isomorphism in the structure of NGOs. To become eligible for consultative status with the United Nations, for example, an NGO must have a constitution, mechanisms of accountability, and democratic and transparent decision-making processes. In addition to lobbying and playing advisory roles, NGOs conduct research, monitor TNCs and nation-states, and undertake humanitarian relief, emergency services, environmental cleanup, reconstruction, and development.

- *The End of the Nation-State.* Arguably, the power of the nation-state is waning. Although still the major actors in international relations and sovereign within their own territories, countries are increasingly divesting themselves of responsibility for their citizens' welfare. TNCs are taking on former state responsibilities through privatization and corporatization by profiting from providing public goods such as water, health care, agricultural products, and education. At the same time, the dominant corporations in the global economy are using their wealth to gain power by influencing political and social institutions. NGOs, in the roles of both international monitors and providers of relief services, have likewise taken over former state responsibilities, and some claim that IGOs aspire to become supranational regional or global governments with authority over states in a federalist political system.

Cultural Globalization

The ubiquity of chains such as McDonald's and Starbucks, the worldwide recognition of Mickey Mouse and Pokémon, and the fact that *Baywatch* has been broadcast in 148 countries in 32 languages all speak to the concept of globalization of popular culture. This worldwide cultural homogenization is often seen as evidence of cultural imperialism and a result of hegemonic control of media and communication technologies by high-income countries of the North. Increased cultural contact during the past few decades has promoted the conspicuous consumption of fashionable products in the developing world and the fetishism of imported goods in countries of the global North. On the other hand, a counterargument can be made for increasing heterogeneity with the emergence of new hybrid forms of culture that combine elements from the traditions and customs of multiple peoples and, thus, produce new forms of cultural expression.

Cultural Imperialism and Greater Homogeneity

Cultural imperialism occurs when the traditions and way of life of a group of people, whether an ethnic minority or an entire nation, are displaced by those of another. This may be a conscious process in which a dominant group intentionally suppresses another culture by suppressing its language, music, religion, symbols, or other practices. More often, however, it results from global market capitalism's drive to increase profits through rationality, homogeneity, and parsimony.

- *Linguae Francae and Loss of Languages.* The loss of more than 10,000 languages since the beginning of the 17th century is one example of ongoing standardization and homogenization. As global commerce increased and the influence of European empires rose, Spanish, French, German, and English displaced local languages and became the *linguae francae* of diplomacy and trade. Other common international languages have included Mandarin Chinese in Asia, Russian in Central and Eastern Europe, Portuguese and Swahili in parts of Africa, and Arabic in the Middle East and North Africa. By the early 1900s, French was the official language of 41 countries and numerous intergovernmental organizations. Recently, English has become the de facto language of global trade, diplomacy, law, medicine, and technology, although the United Nations recognizes Arabic, Chinese, English, French, Russian, and Spanish as official languages.

- *Media Influence and Media Oligopolies.* The predominance of northern media products—films, television shows, music, news, and advertising—throughout the world, together with the ownership of many of the communication networks, satellites, production companies, news organizations, and telecommunications providers, has ensured a proliferation of Western views and cultural values. Many see global communications as an oligopoly—a market dominated by a few. During the 1980s and 1990s, international media production and distribution became consolidated into a few major media groups based in Europe, the United States, and Japan. These media groups have the ability to socialize, distract, politicize, inform, and mislead individuals around the world. Indeed, in 1980 pressure from developing countries, which felt that their local media were being overrun by Western powers, led the UN Educational, Scientific and Cultural Organization (UNESCO) to commission a study of how to make global media less hegemonic. The report found that media concentration created unequal access to information and the tools of communication. It recommended strategies for more balanced access to media and defense of local sources of information. In late 2005, the Convention on the Protection and Promotion of the Diversity of Cultural Expressions became the first international treaty to protect movies, music, and "other cultural treasures." The United States and Israel were the only two dissenters. At the time of this writing, fifteen states had ratified the agreement.

"Glocalization" and Hybridism

Whereas many view cultural globalization as a process of obliterating traditional cultures, others question the idea of cultural authenticity altogether. Globalization has been under way for centuries, so all existing cultures are products of appropriation and borrowing from one another. The term *glocalization,* originally a marketing concept of adapting goods to a local culture, has been used to describe the phenomenon of the selection of some cultural influences and rejection of others when disparate societies encounter one another. New forms of art, music, theater, food, and other cultural products have resulted.

Antiglobalization Movements

Globalization has been blamed for many social problems of the modern world, and many have criticized standardization, corporatization, and Westernization that accompany economic, political, and cultural globalization. *Antiglobalization* is the term applied to a "movement of movements" that can include traditionalists, nationalists, protectionists, and isolationists as well as environmentalists, internationalists, supranationalists, and social anarchists. In general, antiglobalization movements may be broken down into two categories: particularists and universalists. Universalists are concerned most with concepts and issues that are said to be universal in appeal. These issues transcend societies and include universal human rights, environmental protection, equality for women, eradication of poverty, and reduction of disparities in per capita incomes. Particularism emphasizes protection of one's own group. It calls for greater autonomy, maintenance of traditional values and languages, and the rejection of "foreignness."

Stephen J. Sills

See also Colonialism; Cosmopolitanism; Domestic Work; Environmental Justice; Global Perspective; Immigration and Race; Maquiladoras; Marginalization; Slavery; Zapatista Rebellion

Further Readings

Appadurai, Arjun. 1990. "Disjuncture and Difference in the Global Cultural Economy." *Public Culture* 2(2):1–24.
Barber, Benjamin. 1996. *Jihad vs. McWorld: How Globalism and Tribalism Are Reshaping the World.* New York: Ballantine Books.
Eitzen, D. Stanley and Maxine Baca Zinn. 2006. *Globalization: The Transformation of Social Worlds.* Belmont, CA: Thomson Wadsworth.
Filmer, Deon. 1995. "Estimating the World at Work." World Bank Policy Research Working Paper No. 1488.
Harms, Robert. 2002. *The Diligent: A Voyage through the Worlds of the Slave Trade.* New York: Basic Books.
Huntington, Samuel P. 1996. *The Clash of Civilizations and the Remaking of the World Order.* New York: Touchstone Books.
Lechner, Frank and John Boli, eds. 2004. *The Globalization Reader.* Malden, MA: Blackwell.
Nederveen Pieterse, Jan. 2003. *Globalization and Culture: Global Mélange.* New York: Rowman & Littlefield.
Parenti, Michael. 1995. *Against Empire.* San Francisco, CA: City Lights Books.
Sassen, Saskia. 1999. *Globalization and Its Discontents: Essays on the New Mobility of People and Money.* New York: New Press.
Steger, Manfred B. 2003. *Globalization: A Very Short Introduction.* New York: Oxford University Press.

GLOBAL PERSPECTIVE

Historically, the concepts of *race* and *ethnicity* have been used in different ways by various societies to establish boundaries between groups. The major significance of both race and ethnicity has been economic, political, and social. Recently, the accelerated pace of globalization has been the catalyst for increases in racial/ethnic mobility, diversity, and heterogeneity in many nations; consequently, the importance of both race and ethnicity has increased worldwide. Yet there remains a lack of consensus—within nations as well as across nations—on the definitions of *race* and *ethnicity*. Using a sociohistorical perspective, this entry examines the different ways in which race and ethnicity have been conceptualized and the significance of those differences.

A Sociohistorical Overview

Race and ethnicity function as markers distinguishing one group from another. Language, religion, and skin color can be among the markers of distinction between groups only in societies where these traits are significant. For example, skin color cannot be a marker in societies that have no visible differences in skin color among their subpopulations.

In its earliest uses, the word *race* was used loosely to describe people from different nation-states, for example, the French race. However, during the late 18th century, the English began to use the concept to convey presumed "qualities and degrees of human difference." The concept of race connotes visible physical differences such as skin color, hair texture, and cranium size among groups, differences that are then linked to nonvisible differences such as intelligence, motivation, and morality. These differences not only are passed from one generation to the next but also are believed to be immutable. Starting in the 18th century and continuing to the current time, some scientists have used one or more criteria (e.g., skin color, hair texture, size of cranium) to establish a scientific basis for race; however, these attempts have been unsuccessful. If race were a bona fide scientific category, it would be possible to classify each and every human in one and only one category of a set of categories based on specific criteria. Because this is not the case, there is a consensus among scientists that the biological variation within groups called *races* is often greater than the variation between races.

The word *ethnicity* connotes group boundaries based on factors such as geographic origin, language, religion, and identification. Self-identification is necessary but not sufficient to establish membership in an ethnic group; the group must also recognize an individual as being part of it. Although ethnicity is shaped to some extent by original heritage in terms of factors such as language and religion, ethnicity is also shaped by the economic, political, and social relations between and among groups.

Ethnic groups can be created by the process of panethnogenesis—the formation of a panethnic identity to cope with economic, political, and cultural changes experienced by politically dominated ethnic groups within the confines of a given nation-state. Examples of this phenomenon include American Indians in the United States and the Montagnard (a population of mountaineers) in the Vietnam highlands. Panethnic unity can stem from the creation of a panethnic identity, which in turn results from being treated as one monolithic entity by the dominant group in a given society.

Race and ethnicity are social constructs—that is, products of human perception and classification. The major significance of both race and ethnicity has been economic, political, and social. Historically, the concepts of race and ethnicity have been used in different ways by various societies to establish boundaries between groups.

Race and ethnicity incorporate hierarchies in which one group is used as a baseline against which other groups are compared. Moreover, these hierarchies constitute the structure in which differential treatment of groups occurs. As social constructs, race and ethnicity are not static but rather are changing over time as a result of changes in the human interactions that created them. Meanings of race and ethnicity are dynamic in terms of their significance for a given society and for their socioeconomic and political consequences.

Race and ethnicity are also sociohistorical concepts insofar as their meanings are shaped by the social relations and historical context in which they are embedded. For example, in a given nation-state, the social context determines whether or not color is relevant; color is not essential to any theory of what makes a group of people an ethnic group but is specific to social context.

From a global perspective, three phenomena have significantly affected how race and ethnicity are conceptualized: colonization, decolonization, and globalization.

- *Colonization.* Both race and ethnicity have been the fundamental principles around which most colonized societies were organized; for example, race served as the organizing principle for the United States and South Africa, whereas ethnicity was the organizing principle for Canada and Belgium. Under colonial rule, many European colonies imported labor from outside of the colonies.

- *Decolonization.* World War II heightened sensitivity and concern about race and ethnicity on a global level. Global racism is reinforced by old and new colonialism. Increasing racial/ethnic mobility, diversity, and heterogeneity in many nations heightens the importance of both race and ethnicity. Decolonization, which began at the end of World War II, had a significant impact on the reformulation of ethnic groups insofar as it was the catalyst for the formation of independent states. By 1984, 85 former colonies had become independent states, and in 1990, Micronesia and Namibia gained independence. The boundaries of the new independent states were based on those of the former colonial powers and, consequently, included diverse groups that are regionally based. Moreover, subgroups within these new states included the descendants of the migrant laborers brought to the colonies to work on plantations and in mines; for example, Chinese and Indians were migrant laborers in Asia and the Pacific.

- *Globalization.* The concept of globalization refers to the "connectedness" among nation-states such that events and developments in one nation-state can have profound consequences for one or more of the others. Globalization is characterized by the increased mobility of goods, services, labor, technology, and capital worldwide. Indeed, this unprecedented increase in the mobility of labor worldwide, beginning in the 1980s, had a significant impact on the ethnic composition of many contemporary societies. For example, there has been increasing migration of laborers in Asian nations in the process of industrializing such as Singapore, Korea, Taiwan, Malaysia, and Hong Kong. Similarly, the Middle East imports large numbers of workers from both Asia and North Africa. New technologies—especially telecommunications—have increased the pace of globalization.

Social Science Perspectives

From the inception of sociology as an academic discipline in Great Britain as well as in the United States, race and ethnicity have been major concerns. The conceptualization of race as a social construct was formulated among sociologists during the 1950s and has been elaborated by both empirical and theoretical research.

In both the United States and Great Britain, the theoretical and empirical sociology of race resulted in a bifurcation of the population into Black and White. This is due to important similarities in the sociohistories of the United States and Great Britain, especially the major significance of color as one primary marker distinguishing the former colonizers from the formerly colonized.

Some scholars contend that the sociological study of both race and ethnicity has reflected, and in some cases has reinforced, large-scale sociopolitical changes. One major lesson from World War II concerned the horrific social, political, psychological, and psychic consequences of racism and genocide. After the war, disagreements worldwide concerning the significance— and even the very meanings—of race and ethnicity were heightened by the Civil Rights Movement and Black Power Movement in the United States and the Anti-Apartheid Movement in South Africa.

Major demographic shifts in populations within and between nation-states have been catalysts for sociologists to reexamine the concepts of race and ethnicity and for some nations to reexamine categories for classifying their populations. Other catalysts for reexamining race and ethnicity include major ethnic conflicts such as those between the Rwandan Hutus and the Rwandan Tutsis in Africa and between the Serbians and ethnic Albanians. The impact and ramifications of these conflicts are not limited to national boundaries but rather are global in their consequences.

Since the founding of the UN Educational, Scientific and Cultural Organization (UNESCO) in 1945, race and ethnicity have been major concerns of the organization, as indicated by the fact that over the past 40 years UNESCO has issued several declarations focusing on race and racial prejudice, principles of tolerance, and the importance of international cultural heritage, cultural cooperation, and cultural diversity.

Although the definitions, meanings, and import of race and ethnicity may differ from one nation to another, color, race, and ethnicity remain global concerns. W. E. B. Du Bois's prophecy that the problem of the 20th century was the "color line"—that is, race—can be expanded in terms of both time and scope. In the 21st century, race, ethnicity, and color will continue to be problematic in societies worldwide and, consequently, will be major issues for social science research.

Cheryl B. Leggon

See also Borderlands; Civil Rights Movement; Colonialism; Color Line; Cosmopolitanism; Du Bois, William Edward Burghardt; Ethnic Conflict; Ethnic Group; Ethnoviolence; Globalization; Guest Workers; Hong Kong; Immigration and Race; Panethnic Identity; Race; Race, UNESCO Statements on; Singapore; Social Darwinism; Transnational People

Further Readings

Giordan, Henri. 1994. "Multicultural and Multi-Ethnic Societies." UNESCO, Management of Social Transformations (MOST), Discussion Paper Series No. 1.

Gossett, Thomas. 1997. *Race: The History of an Idea in America.* New York: Oxford University Press.

Inglis, Christine. 1994. "Multiculturalism: New Policy Responses to Diversity." UNESCO, Management of Social Transformations (MOST), Policy Paper No. 4.

Leggon, Cheryl B. 1999. "Race and Ethnicity: A Global Perspective." *Sociological Spectrum* 19:381–385.

Wilson, William Julius. 1973. *Power, Racism, and Privilege.* New York: Free Press.

GREEK AMERICANS

Greek Americans are an ethnic group whose history embraces ancient Hellas (Greece), Byzantine Orthodox Christianity, and the creation of the modern nation of Greece, a country estimated to have a population of 11.2 million people in 2007, during the early part of the 19th century. Since ancient times, Greeks have migrated to foreign lands and established communities, but their nostalgia for their homeland can even be found in Homer's *Odyssey.* Their immigration to the United States began during the late 19th century and peaked again after World War II, providing more than a million members for a community often centered around the Greek Orthodox Church. This entry looks at their history and current situation.

Historical Background

Greece has a glorious history, a span of 4,000 years of continuous presence in Southeastern Europe. Greece is a peninsula in the Mediterranean Sea and the Balkan region. It is the bridge of three continents: Asia to the east, Africa to the south, and Western Europe to the west.

The contributions of ancient Greece are part of the foundation of Western society, from the idea of democracy to the Olympic Games. Greek philosophers such as Plato and Aristotle continue to be widely studied, and the architecture of the period is still admired and copied. Plays by Greek dramatists are often produced on modern stages, and they have also become models for later writers. Ancient Greeks also influenced Western civilization, and indeed world civilization, with their etymology of scientific and medical terms, including the humanities and the social sciences, and thousands of Greek concepts are found in most fields of knowledge. Ancient Greek contributions have a universal and diachronic character. Above all, the Greeks taught us rational thinking and established schools of thought. They were the first to formulate the principles of science and to make an effort to explain the cosmos (universe).

Following the sack of Constantinople by the Ottoman Turks in 1453, a number of Byzantine scholars, known as *logioi,* fled to the West and contributed to the Renaissance.

While Western Europe had its renaissance, reformation, enlightenment, and political and industrial revolutions, Greece as a nation vanished while occupied for 400 years by the Ottoman Empire. The Orthodox Christian faith, the memory of the Ancient Greek legacy, and modern Greek literature kept the Greek identity alive during the long and oppressive

Turkish rule. Southern Greece gained its independence from Ottoman–Turkish rule in 1827, but it took nearly another century for Greece to liberate the rest of its northern territories still occupied by the Ottoman Turkish Empire.

Greek Immigration to the United States

Greek immigration to the United States is, by and large, a 20th-century phenomenon. Although a few Greeks came to the United States during the 18th and 19th centuries, the overwhelming majority of Greek immigrants came to the United States more recently.

Two major waves of Greek immigration can be identified. The early Greek immigration coincided with the second phase of industrial capitalism during the late 19th and early 20th centuries. Greek immigrants joined a tide from Southern and Eastern Europe to the United States. Most early Greek immigrants were single men who did not intend to stay in the United States. In fact, many returned to Greece eventually, and more than 30,000 Greek immigrants volunteered to fight in the Balkan Wars of 1912 and 1913 against the Turks. A number of them remained in Greece. Most early Greek immigrants were poor, had a few skills, and came from the southern agricultural communities and regions of Greece, especially Arcadia and Laconia.

The early Greek immigrants and their children helped their relatives in Greece, especially in the aftermath of World War II. Greece suffered greatly from the ravages of the war and gave the first victory to the Allies on October 28, 1940, by defeating the Italians in the Albanian front. Indeed, it was the Greek victory and resistance to German occupation of Greece that brought respectability to the early Greek immigrants and their children in America.

The late Greek immigration included post–World War II refugees and later immigration under the Immigraton and Nationality Act of 1965. Both families and individuals arrived, many of them with relatives among the early Greek immigrants, who helped them to resettle. A large number of the late Greek immigrants came as international students under the first quota system of 1965. Many of them became professionals, and the majority remained in the United States.

The continued Greek emigration after World War II gave the larger Greek American community a cultural transfusion. Since the mid-1970s, Greek immigration to the United States has almost stopped. Only a few hundred arrive each year as students or relatives of Greek American families.

Although the exact number of Greek Americans is not known, the Greek Orthodox Archdiocese and U.S. Census estimate that between 1.25 million and 3 million identify as Greek Americans or report some Greek and Greek Orthodox ancestry. The majority are second-, third-, or fourth-generation Greek Americans. Although the overwhelming majority of the early Greek immigrants were members of the working class, most Greek Americans today are found in the middle and upper middle classes.

Greek American Community

The most important ethnic institutions that have sustained the Greeks of the diaspora and their children are the church, the Greek school, and the family. Greek Orthodox parishes have been established along with Greek schools and various benevolent societies and organizations. Thus, every Greek American ethnic community is also a spiritual religious community. The church is more than a place of worship; it is the hub around which religious and cultural/secular activities, including Greek language instruction, take place. What the family is for the individual, the church is for the Greek American community.

Merging Secular and Spiritual

For the first two generations, both early- and late-arriving Greek Americans and their children, the secular and spiritual identities were inseparable. For one to be a Greek American, it also meant to be a Greek Orthodox American. However, for the past several years, these identities have been challenged. Some, mostly second- and third-generation descendants of the early Greek Americans, advocate a separation of the Greek secular identity from the Orthodox spiritual/religious identity. An organization known as Orthodox Clergy Laity (OCL), founded in Chicago by a number of second-generation Greek Americans during the 1980s, seeks to establish the American Orthodox Church devoid of its ethnic secular identity.

The Greek Archdiocese lists 543 Greek Orthodox parishes, chapels, and missions; 640 priests; 186 retired priests; and 35 priests with lay vocations. In addition, 20 Orthodox monastic communities are dispersed in different parts of the United States. Most of these parishes have Greek afternoon schools that teach the rudiments of Greek language, religion, history, and culture. In addition, there are 22 full-time parochial schools and six preschools in different Greek American Orthodox communities. There are also a number of private Greek American schools, which are not under the jurisdiction of the Greek Orthodox Archdiocese, Department of Greek Orthodox Education. (Private schools include the Athena Schools founded by Dimitrios Georgakopoulos, the Plato Academy, and the Melegos–Peiraikon School, all three of which are in the Chicago area.)

The Greek Orthodox Archdiocese is the administrative and spiritual organization for the parishes and other religious institutions, including the Hellenic College/Holy Cross School of Theology, the Philoptochos Organization, the Standing Canonical of Orthodox Bishops of America (SCOBA), and religious agencies such as the International Orthodox Christian Charities (IOCC), the Orthodox Christian Mission Center (OCMC), and various other departments of the Archdiocese.

Cultural Groups

Greeks of the diaspora established a plethora of ethnic organizations, federations, associations, benevolent societies, cultural and professional groups, and ethnic media as well as (more recently) a number of foundations, museums, and cultural centers; examples include the Onassis Foundation of New York and the Chicago Hellenic Museum and Cultural Center. The most important ethnic association is the American Hellenic Progressive Association (AHEPA), founded by a group of early Greek immigrants in Atlanta in 1922. Around the same time, the administrative organization of the Greek Orthodox Archdiocese was established in the United States. AHEPA's original purpose was a policy of Americanization; it urged its members to become American citizens.

The American Hellenic Institute Public Affairs Committee is located in Washington, D.C., and was established in the aftermath of the Turkish invasion of Cyprus in 1974. Its main objectives are to work with Congress to monitor legislation affecting Greece and Cyprus. By far, the most important academic professional association is the Modern Greek Studies Association (MGSA), founded by a group of academic professionals in 1968. Its main purpose is to promote modern Greek studies at U.S. universities and colleges. As of 2006, there were thirty-seven modern Greek, Byzantine, and Classics programs at U.S. colleges and universities. In addition, there are a dozen chairs of modern Greek literature or Greek civilization and ten foundations/cultural societies/museums.

Besides these major ethnic Greek American associations and groups, there are a proliferation of federations, organizations, media (print, radio, television, and Internet), and fraternal societies—more than 100 media of all kinds and 30 national and regional federations and organizations. The most important of the Greek American federations are those of Pan-Arcadian, Pan-Cretan, Pan-Macedonian, Pan-Pontian, Pan-Messenian, and Pan-Laconian federations. These federations do not include hundreds of smaller Greek American fraternal and urban village-type societies that were established by the first generation of early and late Greek immigrants.

Another major Greek American organization is the United Hellenic American Congress (UHAC) founded by Greek American industrialist Andrew Athens during the 1980s and located in Chicago. Its main goal is to promote prominent Greek American personalities and those who seek political offices.

The major problem of all these ethnic organizations, federations, and fraternal societies is the replenishment of new members. As the first generations die out, the continuity of these ethnic groups and organizations is problematic.

Educational Projects

More recently, a number of cultural and educational organizations that are regional and national in scope have been established in the Chicago area. One of them is the Paideia Projects, a not-for-profit educational and cultural organization whose main mission is the production and distribution of videos on the multiple contributions to world civilization of ancient Greece, with emphasis on the Golden Age of Pericles of the 5th century BC. *Paideia* means education and learning. Each video deals with a particular theme and topic. This organization was founded by the author of this entry at Northern Illinois University in 2003. At the time of this writing, the Paideia program had produced four videos on the structure of the Athenian city-state and the birth of the first democracy in the West, the origin of freedom, the Greek influence on the U.S. Founding Fathers, and the ancient Greek music. A dozen more videos on different topics and themes are planned. These videos are used as educational aids for classes in the humanities and social sciences.

Three additional educational and cultural initiatives have appeared during the past couple of years in the Chicago area. One is the Pan-Hellenic Scholarship Foundation founded by Chris Tomaras, a first-generation Greek American businessman and benefactor. Another is the Hellenic Academy, an educational institution founded by Demetrios Logothetis, a first-generation Greek American, and the Holy Trinity Greek Orthodox Church and Daily Socrates Greek Orthodox School. The Hellenic Academy is located in Deerfield, Illinois, and is open to all students of Greek Americans.

In the third project, the sister cities of Athens, Greece, and Chicago have agreed to build a classical statue of runners inspired and executed by Theodore Papayannis, the world-famous sculptor of the Athens Polytechnic University. The runners symbolize the diachronic cultural significance of friendship and cooperation between the people of Chicago and the world. The five runners represent the five continents and will be seen by millions of passengers going through O'Hare Airport.

Another recent project linking the Old World and the New World is a Greek American trade and business organization known as the Hermes Expo, which serves as the link between Greek American businesses, products, and services and those of Greece. This trade organization, founded by Paul Kotrotsios, holds an annual international trade show.

George Andrew Kourvetaris

See Appendix A

See also Assimilation; Balkans; Cypriot Americans; Diaspora; Ethnic Enclave, Economic Impact of; Europe; Immigration, U.S.

Further Readings

Georgakas, Dan and Charles Moskos, eds. 1989. "The Greek American Experience" [special issue]. *Journal of the Hellenic Diaspora* 16(1–4).

Georgakas, Dan and Charles Moskos, eds. 1991. *New Directions in Greek American Studies.* New York: Pella.

Karanikas, Alexander. 1981. *Hellenes and Hellions: Modern Greek Characters in American Literature.* Urbana: University of Illinois Press.

Kourvetaris, George A. 1997. *Studies on Greek Americans.* Boulder, CO: East European Monographs. (Distributed by Columbia University)

Moskos, Charles. 1989. *Greek Americans: Struggle and Success.* New Brunswick, NJ: Transaction.

Orfanos, Spyros, ed. 2003. *Reading Greek America: Studies in the Experience of Greeks in the United States.* New York: Pella.

Saloutos, Theodore. 1964. *The Greeks in the United States.* Cambridge, MA: Harvard University Press.

GRUTTER V. BOLLINGER

The U.S. Supreme Court's 2003 decision in *Grutter v. Bollinger* addressed affirmative action in higher education, a practice that has long been the subject of intense controversy. *Grutter* and a companion case, *Gratz v. Bollinger,* involved challenges to the affirmative action admissions policies at the University of Michigan's law school and its undergraduate college, respectively. The Court ruled that the law school's policy was constitutional, whereas the undergraduate college's policy was not, thereby clarifying the conditions under which higher education institutions may implement affirmative action policies. This entry discusses both decisions and their context.

The *Grutter* Case

The plaintiff in *Grutter* was a White female who was denied admission to the University of Michigan's law school. She argued that the admissions policy discriminated against White applicants. At Michigan, applications were evaluated on the basis of factors that included a personal statement, letters of recommendation, the applicant's undergraduate grade point average, and a Law School Admission Test score. Students with the highest grades and test scores were not automatically admitted. A variety of factors were considered, including the race of minority applicants. This was done to promote racial, ethnic, and other forms of diversity so as to ensure that the entering class included students who were members of minority groups that historically had been the victims of discrimination.

The Fourteenth Amendment of the U.S. Constitution guarantees all persons "equal protection of the laws." Cases alleging violations of the equal protection clause of the Fourteenth Amendment may be analyzed under three separate standards of review: rational basis, intermediate scrutiny, and strict scrutiny. Laws or policies that classify on the basis of race are subjected to strict scrutiny, the most exacting of the three standards. Under this standard, classifications based on race must have a "compelling justification," and the means that the government employs must be "narrowly tailored" to achieving the policy's goals. The 1978 decision in *Regents of the University of California v. Bakke* held that affirmative action was constitutional, but the Supreme Court justices did not agree then on the applicable analytical standard. It took 10 years and a dozen Court cases before a majority agreed that strict scrutiny applied to affirmative action programs.

The critical question in *Grutter* was whether diversity was a "compelling" justification. In an opinion authored by Justice Sandra Day O'Connor, the majority held that "the Equal Protection Clause does not prohibit the Law School's narrowly tailored use of race in admissions decisions to further [its] compelling interest in obtaining the educational benefits that flow from a diverse student body." The majority found that classroom diversity "promotes cross-racial understanding, helps to break down racial stereotypes, and enables [students] to better understand persons of different races."

Strict scrutiny's second prong involves the "narrow tailoring" requirement. Previous affirmative action cases suggested several difficult-to-satisfy requirements. First, neutral selection criteria should be explored before resorting to a race-conscious approach. Second, if a university decides that a racial remedy is justified, it must be temporary and flexible. Third, there must be a relationship between any numerical goals for minority representation and the college-bound minority populations in the geographic regions from which students are drawn. Finally, consideration should be given to the impact of the program on nonminority students.

A friend of the court brief submitted by the federal government argued that race-conscious admissions policies could not be implemented without first exploring race-neutral criteria to promote student body diversity. Pointing to minority admissions programs in Texas, California, and Florida, where race-based affirmative action programs were not allowed, the government argued that there were ample race-neutral alternatives to race-based policies that made Michigan's program unnecessary and unconstitutional.

The majority rejected this argument. It found that a "serious, good faith consideration of workable . . . alternatives" must be undertaken but that "narrow tailoring does not require exhaustion of every conceivable . . . alternative." Michigan had considered race-neutral alternatives and determined that they would not have produced the critical mass of minority students that the school desired without sacrificing the institution's academic selectivity.

The majority in *Grutter* considered the effect of Michigan's admissions policy on nonminority students and held that the law school's admissions policy satisfied this requirement. The institution's goal of admitting a "critical mass" of minority students was based on an individualized review of the qualifications of all applicants. A minority candidate's race was merely a "plus" factor among several in the selection process. Nonminority students were not foreclosed from consideration, and a minority applicant's race was not the deciding factor.

The *Gratz* Case

In *Gratz v. Bollinger,* a companion case involving the University of Michigan's undergraduate college, the Supreme Court struck down a different affirmative action program. Applications to the university's College of Literature, Science, and the Arts were evaluated using a "selection index" on which an applicant could score a maximum of 150 points. Under this system, applicants received points based on their high school grade point averages, standardized test scores, the strength of their high schools, in-state residency, alumni relationships, personal essays, personal achievements, and leadership qualities. Under a miscellaneous category, applicants received 20 points based on their membership in an underrepresented racial or ethnic minority group.

The university contended that the large number of applications at the undergraduate level made it impractical to implement the type of individualized consideration that was used in the law school. Rejecting this justification, the majority struck down the policy based on its finding that the policy did not satisfy strict scrutiny's narrow tailoring requirement. It found that the university's policy, which automatically distributed 20 points to minority applicants based solely on race, was not narrowly tailored to achieving the university's legitimate interest in promoting a diverse student body.

Affirmative action policies were designed to increase the representation of minorities in areas of employment, education, and business from which they historically were excluded by generations of racially discriminatory laws and practices. Critics of affirmative action consider it as "reverse discrimination" that is unfair to Whites. The decision in *Grutter* means that colleges and universities can legitimately consider the race of minorities during the admissions process so long as the procedure provides for an individualized consideration of the qualifications of each applicant. The decision in *Gratz,* which struck down the admissions program at Michigan's undergraduate college, represents an example of a process that courts will not approve. The decisions in the Michigan cases confirmed the legitimacy of the affirmative action programs, but the underlying debate will continue.

Leland Ware

See also Affirmative Action in Education; Educational Performance and Attainment; Higher Education; Higher Education: Racial Battle Fatigue; Pipeline

Further Readings

Bowen, William G. and Derek Bok. 1998. *The Shape of the River: Long-Term Consequences of Considering Race in College and University Admissions.* Princeton, NJ: Princeton University Press.

Crenshaw, Kimberle, Neil Gotanda, Garry Peller, and Kendall Thomas. 1996. *Critical Race Theory: The Key Writings That Formed the Movement.* New York: New Press.

Edley, Christopher. 1998. *Not All Black and White: Affirmative Action and American Values.* New York: Farrar, Straus, & Giroux.

Katznelson, Ira. 2005. *When Affirmative Action Was White: An Untold History of Racial Inequality in Twentieth-Century America.* New York: Norton.

Lawrence, Charles R., III and Mari J. Matsuda. 1997. *We Won't Go Back: Making the Case for Affirmative Action.* Boston, MA: Houghton Mifflin.

GUATEMALAN AMERICANS

More than 535,000 people of Guatemalan origin now call the United States home. In adapting to a new life in the United States, they have faced unique obstacles—lingering impacts of intense political repression and poverty, obstacles to obtaining political asylum; and continued gender, racial, and ethnic discrimination even within Latino communities. To overcome these challenges, Guatemalans have formed transnational kinship and social networks enabling them to advance economically in the United States and provide support for family members and communities in Guatemala. This entry discusses their immigration and current situation.

Guatemalans have migrated to the United States through being "pushed" by a combination of negative economic and political conditions in their country of origin and being "pulled" by economic opportunities in the United States. Through the early 1970s, a small number of largely middle-class professional Guatemalans migrated to the United States seeking to improve their economic status. The influx of Guatemalans arriving in the United States increased sharply during the mid-1970s, however, in response to deteriorating economic conditions and deepening political violence in Guatemala.

Much of Guatemala's postindependence economic activity centered on the production of coffee and foreign-controlled banana enclaves. This led to a highly unequal wealth distribution and patterns of landholding in Guatemala. Poverty and social and political exclusion in Guatemala have also been exacerbated by deeply embedded patterns of discrimination against the indigenous Mayans, who make up approximately 40% of Guatemala's population, which was estimated in 2007 to be 13.4 million people.

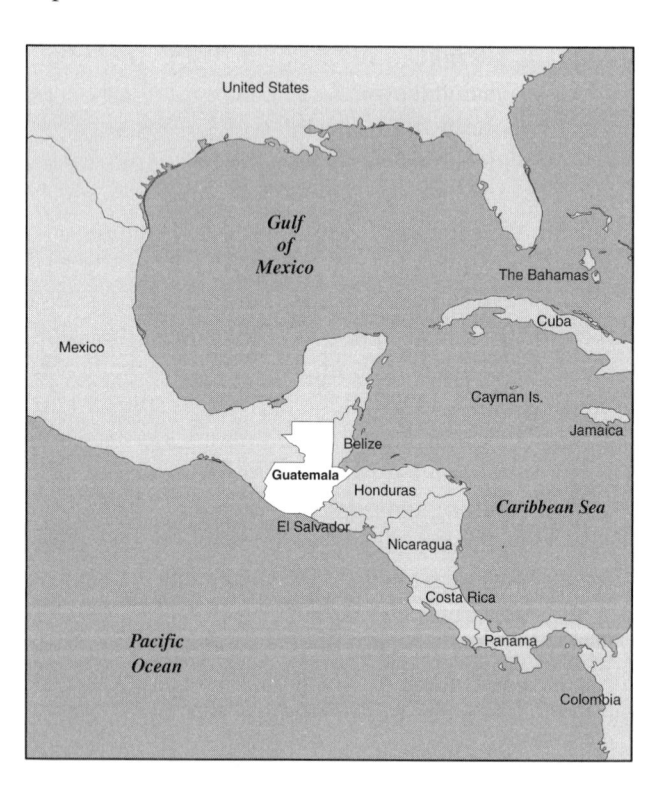

An attempt by President Jacobo Arbenz Guzmán to implement moderate land reform that included the

expropriation of United Fruit Company's banana lands led the United States to support a 1954 military coup against Arbenz. Several decades of military rule and armed conflict between government forces and leftist guerrillas followed. Guatemala's civil war further intensified during the late 1970s, leading to the displacement of an estimated 1 million rural residents. During this period, military forces and death squads linked to the landowning oligarchy targeted Mayan peoples in Guatemala's highlands and political activists with violence. An estimated 200,000 civilians were killed in Guatemala's civil war, which officially ended with the 1996 peace accords. More than 90% of related deaths were attributed to the government and its allies.

During this period, more than 200,000 Guatemalans fled to the United States to escape violence and poverty, becoming the second-largest Central American group in the United States after the Salvadorans. Guatemalans settled in the urban centers of Los Angeles, Chicago, and Houston as well as in rural areas in Florida and the Farm Belt. Although political repression pushed thousands of Guatemalans to flee north, the U.S. government granted political asylum to less than 5% of Guatemalans during the 1980s, classifying them as economic immigrants rather than as political refugees. Through later court settlements and the 1997 Nicaraguan and Central American Relief Act (NACARA), however, a number of these initially undocumented Guatemalans have been able to remain legally in the United States.

Many Guatemalans in the United States have needed to cope with the psychological impacts of past political violence—posttraumatic stress, anxiety, and depression—with only limited access to the support available to recognized political refugee populations. In addition, although Guatemalans have a very high rate of participation in the labor force, they are employed largely in the low-paying service sector. Migrants who arrive illegally also often face the burden of paying off debts accumulated in their journey to the United States. Despite these limitations, Guatemalans sent $584 million in remittances to their families in Guatemala during the early 2000s.

Overall, Guatemalan women have migrated to the United States in greater numbers than have their male counterparts. For some women, migration is a means to escape problems linked to patriarchal family structures such as male infidelity, alcoholism, and domestic violence. Female migrants are often de facto or de jure heads of household and have assumed nontraditional roles as family economic providers in the United States. In the Los Angeles area, gender norms and discrimination have also shaped women's employment options. Most of these women work in garment and electronics factories and as domestic workers. Mayan Guatemalans face additional barriers in work and social life and may be disparaged and hindered within Latino communities because of embedded racial prejudices and Mayan Guatemalans' lack of fluency in Spanish.

One important strategy of Guatemalans to cope with the challenges of life in the United States and to advance economically has been the re-creation of kinship ties and the formation of support networks. Such networks have served dual functions. They address the needs of Guatemalans in the United States and provide economic support for sending communities in Guatemala. In Chicago, Guatemalans formed the Anastasio Tzul Network to provide material support for new arrivals, offer counseling those who suffered torture and violence, and advocate for civil and labor rights. In addition, this group supports health clinics, schools, and infrastructure projects in sending communities in Guatemala. Influenced by Pan-Mayan movements in Guatemala, these kinship and social networks also serve as a space of cultural expression and pride in indigenous values and ways of life. Kanjobal-speaking Mayans, for example, have organized to assert distinct collective identities and practice the indigenous religious customs. These Guatemalans have overcome the legacies of intense political violence, discrimination, and inequality to successfully manage complex transnational identities in the United States.

Lynn Horton

See Appendix A

See also Assimilation; Central Americans in the United States; Cross-Frontier Contacts; Immigration, U.S.; Latin America, Indigenous People; Nicaraguan Americans; Salvadoran Americans

Further Readings

Hamilton, Nora and Norma Stoltz Chinchilla. 2001. *Seeking Community in a Global City: Guatemalans and Salvadorans in Los Angeles.* Philadelphia, PA: Temple University Press.

Hernandez, Romel. 2004. *Immigration from Central America.* Philadelphia, PA: Mason Crest.

Kohpahl, Gabriele. 1998. *Voices of Guatemalan Women in Los Angeles: Understanding Their Immigration.* New York: Garland.

Suro, Roberto. 1999. *Strangers among Us: Latinos' Lives in a Changing America.* New York: Vintage Books.

Zentgraf, Kristine M. 2005. "Why Women Migrate: Salvadoran and Guatemalan Women in Los Angeles." In *Latina/o Los Angeles: Transformations, Communities, and Activism,* edited by Enrique C. Ochoa and Gilda L. Ochoa. Tucson: University of Arizona Press.

GUEST WORKERS

Guest workers are laborers who migrate to other countries for work based on labor importation policies. The durations of their stays are usually limited and temporary. They are usually confined to certain occupations. Whether they are allowed to apply for citizenship depends on the labor and immigration policies of the labor-receiving countries. In contrast, immigrants are people who migrate to other countries for permanent stays. They can immigrate for marriage, employment, or family reunification. Immigrant laborers are workers who migrate to other countries for work and are able to secure permanent residency and eventually citizenship.

Whereas guest workers have been a contentious issue for Western Europe for decades, such as African workers in France and Turkish workers in Germany, the debates concerning guest worker programs have gained increasing momentum in the United States during recent years. This entry examines the current U.S. debate before reviewing the larger history of guest workers. Terms such as *guest workers, contract workers, migrant workers,* and *immigrant workers* are used interchangeably.

Immigration Conflict

On February 25, 2006, tens of thousands of pro-immigration rights advocates and immigrant workers, both documented and undocumented, marched in Los Angeles, Atlanta, and Phoenix. On May 1, 2006, demonstrations took place again in major cities in the United States, drawing millions of immigrant workers and activists demanding the legalization of undocumented workers and the eventual granting of citizenship status. These protests were in response to a bill passed by the House of Representatives that called for restrictive enforcement of immigration regulations. Based on this bill, it would be a felony to work illegally in the United States. The bill also called for more severe punishment of employers of illegal immigrant workers, and it proposed to erect 700 miles of fences along the U.S.–Mexican border.

Lawmakers were at odds with the Bush administration's proposal to create a guest worker program for the estimated 11 million illegal immigrants in the United States. Opponents of this proposal called this an amnesty program that rewarded illegal entry of U.S. borders and weakened the control of borders required for national security. They argued that it had the effect of encouraging illegal immigration.

Although this immigration debate was tied largely to the 2006 midterm election, the issue of whether the United States needs guest workers has been a standing hot topic in the political landscape in the states. The debate is particularly intense this time around because of concern about national security in the aftermath of the September 11, 2001, terrorist attacks. The concern about illegal immigration is not confined to the United States. It has been a concern for European countries as well, including France and Germany. Increasingly, countries in the Middle East, as well as many newly developed countries such as Taiwan, Singapore, and Malaysia, also are facing the dilemma of the control of guest workers.

There are several reasons to oppose the importation of guest workers and the legalization of illegal immigrants. Opponents argue that guest workers take away jobs from Americans, lower average wages, drain social services, inundate public school systems, exploit health care services, engender racial/ethnic conflicts, create a marginalized population in society, and threaten national security. In particular, opponents are concerned about how the legalization of undocumented immigrants will change the demographic landscape of U.S. society.

Supporters for legalizing immigrants' status argue that immigrants take jobs that no (or too few) Americans want, contribute to the national economy by their consumption and paid taxes, and enrich cultural diversity. American society cannot function without the labor of immigrants, both documented and undocumented, they say. In addition, they argue that the United States is a nation of immigrants and that the criminalization of undocumented workers contradicts this tradition.

Labor Migration and Globalization

Labor migration has been an integral part of the globalization process. As the world becomes compressed in terms of time and space, the movement of people across national borders is an inevitable phenomenon. The term *guest workers* has a longer history, however, having become popular after Word War II with the reconstruction of European countries. In different countries, guest workers' entry is usually tied to a contract that delineates terms of employment, job responsibility, working conditions, and government regulations. Depending on the specific regulations of host governments, the contract can be renewable or nonrenewable. The duration of the employment can also lead to the acquisition of permanent status depending on respective governmental regulations. As a result, guest workers sometimes end up becoming permanent residents in some host countries. Due to the restrictive nature of the regulations, guest workers can also, and often do, become illegal immigrants.

Why Workers Migrate

People migrate for work for different reasons. Using a micro-level explanation, it is argued that people migrate overseas for employment because they can earn more money working abroad. Their incentive is a better future. In addition, labor migration is often a family strategy, where members of the family migrate for work to support other family members. In this globalized world, the penetration of mass communication to the developing countries shortens the distance between countries and enables people to imagine possibilities and desire the life enjoyed by people in developed countries.

There are also structural perspectives to explain the movement of people. One theory is based on the neoliberal economic theory of push and pull factors. Push factors include the underdevelopment, unemployment, and underemployment in labor-sending countries, the prevalence of poverty, the lack of social and public services, and the effect of structural adjustment programs. Pull factors include the abundance of job opportunities in host countries, the shortage of labor, the better wages, and the high standards of living.

Another theory contests this neoliberal perspective and focuses on the historical development of colonialism and imperialism. It is argued that migration is driven by the unequal development between labor-sending and labor-receiving nations engendered by colonialism. In a way similar to their extraction of raw materials from the peripheral nations to the metropolis in the world system, the developed nations extract cheap labor from developing nations. Therefore, the preexisting ties between colonial powers and colonies dictate the process of migration. From this perspective, the importation of guest workers is seen as a continual exploitation by the First World over the Third World. It is another form of division of labor in the global system.

In addition to the micro and macro levels of analysis, there is also the meso level of analysis. Scholars have argued that networking accounts for the continual migration of people. This theory argues that networking allows people to gain information and knowledge about migration from return migrants. New guest workers also depend on old migrants to navigate the complexity of the migration process. It is not surprising that people from the same villages and regions often migrate to the same destination of employment.

Other factors account for the massive migration of people across national borders. One is the commercialization of recruitment agencies, which have played an important role in assisting labor migration since the 1970s. Recruitment agencies help to mediate the complexity of migration and deal with state bureaucracy for migrants. Unfortunately, illegal recruitment agencies have also mushroomed to exploit migrants. Another important factor that drives the massive migration of laborers is state policy. Many countries have adopted policies for labor exportation. To gain revenue from remittances, states have encouraged people to migrate to other countries for work. Some countries, such as the Philippines, dictate a particular percentage for remittance. In fact, labor has become a major export product for many countries.

Contemporary Characteristics

There have been several distinctive phenomena concerning guest workers during recent decades. Contrary to the conventional view of guest workers as uneducated and uncivilized, the educational level among recent guest workers may be high. It is particularly true in terms of Filipino workers. Many Filipino workers come from middle-class backgrounds and work as professionals in the Philippines. It is important to note that it is often those with resources, not the poorest, who can migrate overseas.

The second characteristic of contemporary labor migration is the increase of women in the migration process. By the 1980s, migrant women workers constituted the major proportion of the migration population in many countries. The third phenomenon is that women are usually concentrated in certain occupations such as domestic service, entertainment, sex work, and manufacturing. The first three are considered dangerous occupations. Domestic service in particular is the major occupation for women guest workers. This constitutes the gender division of labor. Currently, there are millions of women working as domestic workers all over the world.

The departure of guest workers has had much impact on labor-sending countries. Guest workers' remittances have become the major source of income for many sending countries. As mentioned, labor becomes their main product of export. However, although the remittance from abroad is important, whether it contributes to the development of labor-sending countries is debatable. Most often, the money sent home is used to buy daily necessities, build houses, and establish small businesses rather than being channeled into development projects that have long-term effects. The departure of guest workers, particularly middle-class professionals, also results in the problem of "brain drain." In that sense, labor-sending countries subsidize labor-receiving countries in terms of education, training of skills, and social reproduction.

What is the impact on labor-receiving countries? One of the major advantages for labor-receiving countries is that they are able to exploit the cheap labor for their labor shortage situations. Guest workers are often the most vulnerable group in host societies. Employers do not need to provide guest workers with benefits and/or health insurance. Guest workers are often deprived of civil, political, and socioeconomic rights. They cannot form unions. Although they are often subject to abuse, they often cannot unionize and voice their concerns collectively. For example, women domestics work in isolated households. It is particularly difficult for them to network with one another, not to mention organizing collectively to demand better working conditions.

The entry of guest workers also contributes to racial, ethnic, cultural, and religious conflicts. Guest workers are often deemed as undesirably different and incapable of assimilation. They often face discrimination in the host countries. They often face racism, xenophobia, and prejudice. They do work that no (or too few) natives want to do. However, they become the scapegoats for the unemployment situations in host countries. They contribute to the economies of the host societies, but they are often deemed as lazy and lacking a work ethic. They are said to come to host countries to exploit welfare services. The rhetoric against Mexican workers in the United States is a good example of this prejudice.

Future Outlook

Labor migration will continue to be an important phenomenon in the future. To protect the rights of guest workers, the United Nations has adopted conventions, such as the International Convention on the Protection of the Rights of All Migrant Workers and Members of Their Families, to protect the rights of guest workers. Unfortunately, not enough countries support the convention for it to actually take effect. The protection of guest workers constitutes one major concern for labor migration in the future.

Shu-Ju Ada Cheng

See also Bracero Program; Colonialism; Discrimination; Gender and Race, Intersection of; Globalization; Immigration and Race; Racism; Remittance; Return Migration; Xenophobia

Further Readings

Bartram, David. 2005. *International Labor Migration: Foreign Workers and Public Policy.* New York: Palgrave Macmillan.

Cheng, Shu-Ju Ada. 2006. *Serving the Household and the Nation: Filipina Domestics and the Politics of Identity in Taiwan.* Lanham, MD: Lexington Books.

Gonzalez, Gilbert. 2007. *Guest Workers or Colonized Labor: Mexican Labor Migration to the United States.* New York: Paradigm.

Stalker, Peter. 1999. *Workers without Frontiers: The Impact of Globalization on International Migration.* Boulder, CO: Lynne Rienner.

H

Hafu

Hafu, alternately spelled *Haafu,* means "half" in Japanese, and the word is borrowed from the English. In Japan, *hafu* commonly refers to the child of a Japanese parent and a foreign parent. In this social classification schema, the categories of "Japanese" and "foreign" are dichotomous and conflate citizenship with race, culture, and language. Although *foreign* refers to anyone not Japanese, the dominant racial image of *hafu* is currently people of Japanese and White backgrounds; however, during the postwar period, it also conjured up images of both White and Black mixed-race Japanese. Terminology used to refer to mixed-race Japanese and the mainstream connotation attached to being mixed race in Japan have changed drastically since the postwar period. New terms are beginning to emerge as more politically correct substitutes for *hafu,* although none has yet to be used widely.

Mixed-Race Terminology

In Japanese, *hafu* is used as a noun; this makes sense only in the context of two mutually exclusive social categories (otherwise, it would need to be used as a modifier, e.g., half Japanese, half White). Japanese national identity has been racialized such that most people in Japanese society are seen not only as possessing Japanese citizenship but also as being of "pure Japanese blood" and speaking and acting Japanese. These assumptions, combined with the persistent myth of Japanese homogeneity, have led to a mainstream discourse in which there are unquestionably Japanese people, on the one hand, and everyone else, on the other. Some scholars believe that times are changing in Japan and that conceptions of Japaneseness are becoming more flexible. In this view, the rise in social awareness and social position of *hafu* is a reflection of, or a harbinger of, that change.

In everyday language, *hafu* often refers to phenotype traits; however, depending on the context, it may also mark people based on language abilities, cultural knowledge, and international experience. Although the dominant image does not refer to people who by phenotype blend into mainstream Japanese society (e.g., mixed Chinese, Korean, Thai, Filipino/a), a discussion of national or cultural background often elicits recognition that *hafu* can also be of Asian descent.

The terminology used in Japan to refer to people of mixed racial backgrounds has changed over the years. Opinions differ on the nuances and connotations of each expression; terms clearly change with social and political context and depending on the person. Stephen Murphy-Shigematsu outlined the history of three terms used in Japan/Japanese since the postwar period. *Ainoko* was used during the postwar period to refer to mixed-race children and is the most blatantly derogatory term, used not only in describing humans but also in describing the mixing of animal species. *Konketsuji* literally means "mixed-blood child." This term arose during the postoccupation era as war animosities began to subside and was used as a more politically correct alternative to *ainoko.* Over time, however, the connotations of this word became questioned, and now it is largely interpreted as politically incorrect and offensive. From the 1960s, another image of mixed-race Japanese that was more popular and exotic began to emerge in the media. *Hafu* is currently the most commonly used term, although its connotations are also debatable. The expression is said to have originated with a singing group called the Golden Haafu that was popular during the 1970s.

Several other terms have recently emerged. "Double" (*daburu*) is a new expression that implies a paradigm shift for understanding people of multiple backgrounds. Although not yet heard very often and used more by the parents of mixed-race children than by the individuals themselves, the implication of empowerment through re-articulation is clear; people are not halves of two groups and less than whole, but rather double and twice as much. This may refer not only to having two kinds of racial identities but also to being bilingual and bicultural. In addition, "quarter" (*quotah*) can be heard from time to time and seems to imply that a person is one-fourth Japanese. In some circles in Japan, people use the word "mixed" (*mikkusu*) as well.

Social Implications

The connotations of being mixed race in Japan continue to change. The postwar era provided a particular context for reading race in terms of class and national interests. Mixed-race Japanese during the postwar period were predominantly the children of U.S. military men and lower-class Japanese women. In addition to viewing these children as lower class, most Japanese felt a residual animosity toward the U.S. military, ostensibly influencing how mixed-race children were perceived by mainstream "monoracial" Japanese. Many of these mixed-race children were abandoned and raised as orphans.

In contemporary Japanese society, *hafu* conjures up glamorous images of models and celebrities who are usually White European/American and Japanese. In this way, many young people see mixed-race people as "cool" and "trendy." But these stylish mixed-race Japanese models and celebrities tend to be of Japanese/White backgrounds, and this differs from the postwar period when Japanese/Black mixed-race people were also included; the current use promotes a narrow racial image of mixed-race Japanese people in Japan.

The mainstream popularity of *hafu* in the contemporary era, although certainly superficial, is regarded by many as being correlated with Japan's emphasis on international relations and globalization. In addition, more of the younger generation of mixed-race Japanese have parents who are businesspeople, diplomats, and other upper-class global elites. In this way, the class image of this group has changed. Thus, a group that was previously negatively marginal because of connections to "foreigners" and other countries is now becoming more positively marginal for the same reasons—but still marginal nonetheless.

No matter what term one uses to describe mixed-race Japanese in Japan, there seems to be a shift in their portrayal in the popular media. On television, mixed-race celebrities are becoming more widely noticeable, and many of them were born and raised exclusively in Japan and speak only Japanese. This public portrayal of mixed-race Japanese as not always bilingual or bicultural, with their phenotypes (and family histories) as the only salient markers of their foreignness, leads one to wonder about how this will affect future conceptions of Japaneseness and the boundaries around it.

Although the term is widely used in everyday discourse, there is limited scholarship on *hafu* either empirically or theoretically. Murphy-Shigematsu has defined the academic discourse, having written numerous articles in English on what he calls "multiethnic people" in Japan. With increasing numbers of international and interracial marriages in Japan, the population of *hafu* is also on the rise. It will be interesting to see how the growth of this population might open up possibilities for a third social category in Japan.

Jane H. Yamashiro

See also Asian Americans; Asian American Studies; Hapa; Identity Politics; Intermarriage; Japan; Multiracial Identity; Nikkeijin

Further Readings

Burkhardt, William R. 1983. "Institutional Barriers, Marginality, and Adaptation among the American–Japanese Mixed Bloods in Japan." *Journal of Asian Studies* 42:519–544.

Life, Regge. 1995. *Doubles: Japan and America's Intercultural Children* [video]. Produced and directed by Regge Life.

Murphy-Shigematsu, Stephen. 2000. "Identities of Multiethnic People in Japan." Pp. 196–216 in *Japan and Global Migration: Foreign Workers and the Advent of a Multicultural Society,* edited by M. Douglass and G. S. Roberts. London: Routledge.

Murphy-Shigematsu, Stephen. 2001. "Multiethnic Lives and Monoethnic Myths: American–Japanese Amerasians in Japan." Pp. 207–216 in *The Sum of Our Parts: Mixed Heritage Asian Americans,* edited by T. Williams-Leon and C. L. Nakashima. Philadelphia, PA: Temple University Press.

HAITI

Situated on the island of Hispaniola, Haiti is one of the Caribbean countries visited by Christopher Columbus during the days of early exploration. The island of Hispaniola sits in the North Caribbean Sea and has Cuba, the Bahamas, and Puerto Rico as its neighbors. On the island itself, Haiti shares its eastern border with the Spanish-speaking Dominican Republic. Haitian inhabitants, however, speak Haitian Creole French as an official language. Haiti's major cities are Port-de-Paix, Cap-Haitien, and Gonaives, with Port-au-Prince as the country's capital. Haiti has roughly 8.3 million citizens and had an estimated population of 9 million people in 2007. Haiti has a majority Afro-Caribbean population with 95%. The remaining 5% are mulattos, with less than 1% being Europeans. Haitians currently suffer from a history laden with racial tension, and the majority population is dominated by an antiquated system based on skin color. Looking historically at this phenomenon—the goal of this entry—is helpful to understand the complex dynamics that rule many aspects of Haitian life.

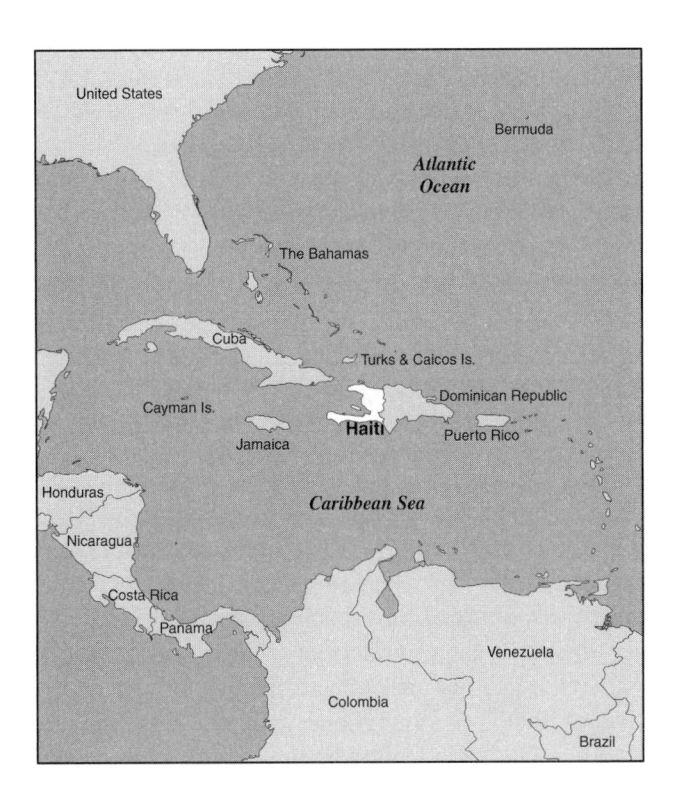

Historical Background

Like the Dominican Republic, Haiti was not a desolate and barren area free of human activity at the time of arrival by Columbus. The Taíno Indians were a Native American group of nomads from the northern areas of the South American continent who eventually settled many of the Caribbean Islands. The Taíno were a relatively peaceful group of natives, unlike the more aggressive Carib Indians, who were known for their thirst for war and territory. The Taíno were experts at fishing and gathering, and although they were numerous during precolonial days, more than 250,000 Taíno had died due to infectious disease and slave labor by the time the explorers had been on the island for two years.

Colonial Times

Exploration and claim to other islands were of a pressing concern to the Europeans, and the Spanish used Hispaniola as a base of operations to execute further Caribbean exploration. During the early and middle parts of the 17th century, French pirates settled the western portion of Hispaniola primarily to serve as a base for looting British and Spanish ships. In an attempt to control pirating in the Caribbean, Spain was forced to recognize the French claim on the western portion of the island. French settlers, assured by new antibuccaneering laws, continued to settle western Hispaniola. Fueled by agricultural profits in coffee and sugar, the French colony of Saint Domingue became one of the richest colonies possessed by the French. By the mid-18th century, Saint Domingue produced 60% of the coffee and 40% of the sugar imported by Britain and France.

Sugar production would push the need for labor and the importation of massive numbers of slaves from Africa and Jamaica, and as was customary with colonies in the Caribbean, the slaves vastly outnumbered the owners. By the dawning of the French Revolution, there were an estimated 500,000 to 700,000 African slaves located on the French portion of Hispaniola alone. The French slave system was particularly cruel and discriminatory, with a variety of restrictive laws passed in Saint Domingue. Most male slaves did not live to childbearing age. At the same time in Europe, France began to undergo revolutionary transformation that recognized people's unalienable rights, particularly those rights of the poor that were suppressed by the upper classes. As word reached the Caribbean colonies, similarities were drawn between France and Saint Domingue, namely, that a fairly large poor population was controlled by a relatively smaller elite.

The Slave Revolt

Racial tension and politics boiled over in 1791, and a slave revolt began. Although the majority of Black Haitians are Christian, customs prior to their arrival in the New World were well entrenched and subsequently interwoven with new religions. Voodoo was a common religion in sub-Saharan Africa, and in Haiti voodoo was used and viewed as a common thread that united African slaves from different countries and languages. With tensions rising among the races, the Haitian leaders, primarily François-Dominique Toussaint Louverture, Georges Biassou, Jeannot, and Boukman (a voodoo priest), used the religion to fanatically rally and engage the impoverished and runaway slaves alike to the cause of rebellion.

The rebellion swept into town after town and visited on the White citizens of Haiti horrific carnage and massacre. On another front, the mulattos, considered as middle class by means of skin color, revolted against the harsh caste system imposed by the ruling French elite. The French quashed the mulatto revolt through the effective recruitment of Black slaves into the French army lured by the promise of freedom. Mulatto involvement signified unrest on a much larger scale.

The Black insurgents seized most of northern Haiti, while outside forces such as the British tried to take advantage of France's weakness. Disease would greatly thin the British army; in addition, the United States, which had an interest in the Louisiana Territory, agreed to help Toussaint and the rebellion provided that Haiti deny the French control of any ports or bases of operation in the future. Under the lead of Toussaint, the English were crushed.

Independence

Despite the victories by insurgents, Hispaniola was not at peace. Napoleon Bonaparte had other plans for the colony. Aided by White colonists and mulattos, the French army recaptured Hispaniola and imprisoned Toussaint. These efforts, however, were not enough to halt forces already in motion. To finance his war, Napoleon was forced to sell the Louisiana Territory, ending true French interest in the area. Cut off from funding and supplies, the remaining French troops on the island were outmaneuvered. By the early 1800s, the last French general had fled Hispaniola.

Due to the fact that Haiti was the first Black republic in history and the only slave colony able to free itself, outside opposition ran high. Trade embargoes were established, and many countries refused to recognize Haiti's independence. On January 1, 1804, Haiti claimed autonomy from the French government, yet the cultural damage had been done. War would permanently instill racial stereotypes and mistrust between the races, and history would show the effects of colonialism to have long-lasting implications for the quality of life of the Haitian people.

C. Centae Richards

See Appendix A
See also Caribbean; Colonialism; Creole; Dominican Americans; Dominican Republic; Haitian Americans; Haitian and Cuban Immigration: A Comparison

Further Readings

Catanese, Anthony V. 1999. *Haiti: Migrations and Diaspora.* Boulder, CO: Westview.

Martínez, Samuel. 1999. "From Hidden Hand to Heavy Hand: Sugar, the State, and Migrant Labor in Haiti and the Dominican Republic." *Latin America Research Review* 34:54–83.

McAlister, Elizabeth. 1999. *Rara! Vodou, Power, and Performance in Haiti and Its Diaspora.* Berkeley: University of California Press.

HAITIAN AMERICANS

Haitians' presence in the United States is not a new phenomenon. As early as 1779, when the United States was consolidating its independence from Great Britain, Haiti—then known as Saint Domingue, the most prosperous of all French colonies—delegated a contingent of slaves under the command of a French military leader named Comte d'Estaing to fight on the side of the U.S. revolutionary forces at Savannah, Georgia. Once the United States became an independent country, migration from Haiti began in earnest.

The first immigrants from Haiti arrived at the end of the 18th century, and since then there has been a continuous, if not always large, stream of arrivals from the island. However, the greatest influx of immigrants, and the one that has drawn the greatest attention, began during the 1960s and 1970s as Haitians fled the dictatorial regime of "Papa Doc" Duvalier. In the United States, the Haitian community has had difficulty in amassing social, economic, and political capital. This entry records the history of Haitian immigration and describes the current community.

Immigration History

The Haitian slaves who fought on the side of the U.S. revolutionary armies did not set roots in the United States. Soon after the end of the hostilities, they were returned to their masters in Saint Domingue. In 1791, at the onset of the Haitian Revolution, thousands of slaves from Saint Domingue were brought to Louisiana, New York, Charleston, and Philadelphia by their French masters to weather the impact of the uprisings and await Napoleon's victory over the insurrectionists. When the Haitian Revolution triumphed in 1804, and as the French colonists finally realized that they would not be returning to Saint Domingue, these immigrant slaves were retained in the United States, still attached to their French masters. Subsequent to the 1863 Emancipation Proclamation, and on being freed at the end of the U.S. Civil War, the Haitian slaves and their progeny became part of the U.S. Black community, adopting an African American identity.

Later, as Haiti was occupied by the United States between 1915 and 1934, small numbers of Haitian intellectuals, artists, poets, and professionals settled in Harlem and, together with their African American counterparts, played significant roles in the Harlem Renaissance movement. A decade or so later, during the economic boom years that followed the end of World War II, Haitian workers (mostly females) were recruited by the U.S. embassy in Port-au-Prince to work in the garment manufacturing industry and in the service sector in cities and communities throughout the United States.

However, it was during the later years of the 1960s, as Haiti was reeling under Duvalier's iron rule, that Haitian migration to the United States began to surge at a very feverish pace to reach its all-time high levels. Duvalier, who ruled Haiti with U.S. consent and support between 1957 and 1971, indiscriminately imprisoned, murdered, and forced into exile many professionals, business people, students, and entrepreneurs—whether or not they were guilty of plotting against his autocratic regime. Other cadre professionals, fearing for their safety and that of their families, left on their own and went abroad in search of political security and improved economic opportunities. In addition, during the late 1960s, international organizations such as the United Nations and the Organization of American States, along with countries such as Canada and France, recruited the remaining Haitian professionals and skilled workers and encouraged them to leave Haiti as well.

The majority of these exiles eventually settled in the United States as refugees and not as immigrants. From their outposts in New York and Miami, they labored assiduously to bring down the regime. In 1971, subsequent to Duvalier's death, Jean-Claude, Duvalier's 19-year-old son, succeeded him as life president. Disheartened by the turn of events in Haiti, the 1960s refugees lost all hopes of returning to their country and began considering themselves as settlers. Taking advantage of the family reunion provision of the 1965 Hart–Celler immigration bill, they proceeded to sponsor their relatives who reunited with them in the United States as immigrants.

By the mid-1970s, the departure of the best educated and qualified cadres began to produce a migratory domino effect that resulted in an urgency to leave. Those Haitians who did not have relatives living in the United States who would sponsor their applications as legal residents came as visitors or students and overstayed their visas. Others who did not have the contacts, resources, and credentials of the preceding groups took to the sea in frail vessels, risking their lives in a difficult and perilous 700-mile journey to reach the United States or the Bahamas. Known as "boat people," during the 1970s and 1980s an estimated 50,000 to 80,000 of these clandestine migrants landed on Florida's beaches alone. By the time the Duvalier regime fell in 1986, Haitians had become one of the largest groups of immigrants from the Caribbean Basin in the United States.

Haitians in the United States

Demographics

Prior to the 1970s, Haitian migration was selective in terms of geographical and class origin. After that, however, the Haitian immigrants came from all of Haiti's regions and social strata. Although at the inception of the Haitian migratory waves of the 1960s most immigrants settled in New York, Miami, or Boston, today sizable Haitian settlements exist throughout the United States. However, the dearth of precise statistical figures makes it difficult to accurately measure the size of the Haitian population in the United States.

The 2000 U.S. Census, the most reliable source of U.S. demographic statistics, reported that 429,848 people living in the United States were born in Haiti and that the combined total of persons who self-described as being of Haitian ancestry was 632,680. These figures are unreliable for many reasons. First and foremost, the numbers do not include most of the undocumented Haitian immigrants who, understandably, have been reticent in volunteering their personal information to the census takers. Also, being proud of their heritage as citizens of the world's first Black independent country born out of the only successful slave revolt in modern times, Haitian immigrants are frustrated by the political and economic morass that stigmatizes their country's image in the U.S. imagination as one of the world's poorest nations. As a result, many conceal their true identity to avoid the ridicule and derision of those with whom they interact. Because of these and many other obstacles, it is impossible to accurately assess the size of the U.S. Haitian population.

Economic Life

Although the U.S. Haitian immigrant population includes a significant number of professionals with high-status positions within its ranks, the number of Haitian immigrants who had completed high school before migrating is low, and lower still is the number who migrated with a college or professional degree. This lack of skills causes many Haitian immigrants to face a difficult economic life in the United States. Whereas in the past unskilled European immigrants found well-paid manufacturing jobs that helped to propel them up the socioeconomic ladder, the situation is completely different today. Nowadays, to maximize their profits, U.S. corporations are outsourcing these jobs to developing economies where salaries are much lower and working conditions are less regulated than they are in the United States.

Also, as late as in the 1960s, government-funded social programs helped immigrants to adapt to their new country. Since the advent of the "Reagan revolution" (referring to Ronald Reagan's presidency during the 1980s), however, these social programs have been dismantled, and today they are being eliminated completely. Consequently, many Haitian immigrants have found it difficult to acquire and develop the necessary skills they need to become socially mobile in the United States. As a result of the combination of these factors, the 2000 census reported that the Haitian unemployment rate and the number of Haitians living below the poverty line were much higher than those of other similar immigrant groups. Correspondingly, the Haitian median income is lower than that of other foreign-born groups.

Political Life

Despite their relatively large numbers, the Haitian immigrants have no significant representation within the U.S. political system. Although a few Haitian politicians have been elected to municipal and state legislative positions in Florida, Massachusetts, and Illinois, the Haitian immigrant populations rely on elected officials from other constituencies to articulate their grievances, represent their needs, speak on their behalf, and protect their interests. This situation is due to the Haitian immigrants' lack of spatial concentration, their cultural singularity, their inability to make alliances with their other ethnic groups, the negative stereotypes that have been associated with them, and their transnationalism.

Social Adaptation

Haitian immigrants are both visible and invisible in the United States. Being of African descent, they are seen as part of the visible minority groups and, therefore, are lumped together with the other Black populations, although Haitians have had historical experiences different from those of the U.S.-native Blacks and share very few cultural traits with them. At the same time, Haitian immigrants are invisible as a distinct Black population with its idiosyncratic and particular historical and cultural characteristics. For example, Haitians' primary language is Haitian Creole, a language that is not well understood and appreciated in the United States. At the same time, it is estimated that 10% of Haitians have a good command of French. These two languages are not very useful to those who speak them in the United States because the few social programs that are still operating are more likely to use Spanish and English, the most widely spoken languages by the majority of new immigrant groups. That linguistic dichotomy further alienates Haitian immigrants from the U.S. mainstream population. Second, the overwhelming majority of Haitian immigrants are accustomed to rural life and not urban life. Third, in addition to being devout Catholics or Protestants, most practice Vodoun, a religion that is branded and stigmatized in the United States.

To further hinder the Haitian immigrants' social conditions in the United States, during the early 1980s the U.S. Centers for Disease Control (CDC) accused Haitians, together with hemophiliacs, heroin addicts, and homosexuals, of being responsible for spreading AIDS in the United States and barred them from giving blood. Although the CDC was later forced to retract its accusation and finally removed Haitians from that list, many U.S. medical organizations and academic journals continue to link Haitian culture with the spread of AIDS in the United States. The persistence of this linkage between Haiti and AIDS has maligned the Haitians' identity, alienating them even further from U.S. mainstream society.

Even Haitian professionals who have migrated with some credentials and resources might not be in a favorable situation to assimilate to U.S. society. Many experience downward social mobility after migrating because U.S. companies often do not accept their Haitian credentials. In addition, they often lack English fluency, are unfamiliar with U.S. cultural norms, and lack proper guidance on how to navigate the U.S. bureaucracy.

However, the second and third generations, along with those who migrated at a very young age, adapt rather well and assimilate more quickly and completely to the normative practices of U.S. society. This often creates serious generational tensions within the Haitian immigrant family. These tensions are exacerbated when these youngsters reject their parents' "Haitian ways," preferring to speak English rather than Creole and/or French and—to the chagrin of many Haitian parents—choosing an African American identity instead of a Haitian identity. However, research has also shown that when these youngsters reach the high school or college level, many reconnect with Haiti as they seek to reclaim their Haitian heritage.

Links With Haiti

Because of these social barriers and prejudices, Haitian immigrants living in the United States have been unsuccessful at entering into cross-ethnic alliances and have not been able to organize ethnic communities of their own in the United States except for Little Haiti in Miami. Instead, most Haitian immigrants, even those who have taken up U.S. nationality, have remained connected with Haiti and continue to consider themselves as part of Haiti while they seek to adapt to their new milieu in their own terms.

In the same vein, in 1995 Haiti reached out to its immigrant populations (also known as the Haitian diaspora)—even those who had acquired foreign citizenship—and officially reincorporated them into the fold of the Haitian population, albeit with very limited rights, as the "Tenth Department" to complement Haiti's nine geographical departments at that time. Together with this designation, a cabinet post was created to institute strong linkages between Haiti and its diaspora.

The Haitian diaspora's longing to reconnect with its homeland population is not hinged solely on nostalgia and sentimental affections, nor is it derived entirely from the immigrants' remembrance of their homeland as an emotional *lieu de memoire*. Rather, the strategy of living in two societies simultaneously, or transnationalism, is also utilitarian because it provides concrete and tangible benefits for Haiti, the sedentary populations, and the immigrant populations. Because of the many ways in which it affects the minds and dispositions of those Haitian immigrants who live transnational lives, the strategy of living simultaneously in two societies can be problematic.

By remaining connected with Haiti, the transnational Haitians have established their homeland as a place where they go to find solace for their personal and social problems. Those who are documented visit Haiti regularly, and this serves to reduce the impacts of racial discrimination, whether perceived or real, that afflict them in the United States.

As for the Haitian state, it pins its hopes on the Haitian immigrants to shoulder some of its responsibilities. Being the sector of the "Haitian community" writ large that comparatively possesses significant social, intellectual, and financial capital, the Haitian immigrants make substantial contributions to their homeland called *remittances*. It is estimated that Haitians living abroad remit more than $1.5 billion per year to their relatives and acquaintances in Haiti. This sum represents five times the money Haiti receives from foreign aid, up to three times the country's budget, and at least 20% of its gross domestic product. In addition to these transfers of cash, Haitian immigrants send ample supplies of provisions and consumer goods of all kinds to their kin, relatives, and friends in Haiti. The multiplier effects of these remittances and transfers of commodities literally keep the Haitian economy afloat.

Moreover, most communities in Haiti are represented abroad by regional organizations or hometown associations created by the immigrants to address the homeland populations' basic survival and infrastructural needs. Through important linkages that these hometown associations establish in Haiti, the immigrants attempt to introduce their native land to modernity, create platforms on which they rely to influence local politics, and help to raise funds for various projects in Haiti. Yet, however well intentioned these initiatives may be, they tend to encourage both the sedentary and immigrant Haitian populations to seek solutions for their problems outside of their residential communities.

Georges Fouron

See Appendix A

See also Birth of a Nation, The; Creole; France; Haiti; Haitian and Cuban Immigration: A Comparison; Immigration, U.S.; Remittances; Slavery

Further Readings

Branson, Susan and Leslie Patrick. 2001. "Étranger dans un Pays Étrange" [Foreigners in a foreign land]. Pp. 193–208 in *The Impact of the Haitian Revolution in the Atlantic World*, edited by David P. Geggus. Columbia: University of South Carolina Press.

Clark, George P. 1980. "The Role of the Haitian Volunteers at Savannah in 1779: An Attempt at an Objective View." *Phylon* 41:356–366.

Farmer, Paul. 1992. *Aids and Accusation: Haiti and the Geography of Blame.* Berkeley: University of California Press.

Fouron, Georges E. and Nina Glick Schiller. 2001. "The Generation of Identity: Redefining the Second Generation within a Transnational Identity." Pp. 58–86 in *Migration, Transnationalization, and Race in a Changing New York*, edited by Héctor R. Cordero-Guzmán, Robert C. Smith, and Ramón Grosfoguel. Philadelphi, PA: Temple University Press.

Glick Schiller, Nina and Georges E. Fouron. 1990. "'Everywhere We Go, We Are in Danger': Ti Manno and the Emergence of a Haitian Transnational Identity." *American Ethnologist* 172:329–347.

Glick Schiller, Nina and Georges E. Fouron. 2001. *Georges Woke up Laughing: Long Distance Nationalism and the Search for Home.* Durham, NC: Duke University Press.

Heinl, Robert Debs and Nancy Gordon Heinl. 1996. *Written in Blood: The Story of the Haitian People.* rev. ed. Lanham, MD: University Press of America.

Konczal, Lisa and Alex Stepick. 2007. "Haiti." Pp. 445–457 in *The New Americans: A Guide to Immigration since 1965*, edited by Mary C. Waters and Reed Ueda. Cambridge, MA: Harvard University Press.

Pierre-Louis, François, Jr. 2004. *Haitians in New York City: Transnationalism and Hometown Associations.* Gainesville: University of Florida Press.

Zephir, Flore. 2001. *Trends in Ethnic Identification among Second-Generation Haitian Immigrants in New York City.* Westport, CT: Bergin & Garvey.

HAITIAN AND CUBAN IMMIGRATION: A COMPARISON

Cuban and Haitian refugees have been both the beneficiaries and the neglected people of U.S. immigration reform. The close proximity of the Caribbean Basin to Florida's shores makes the journey worth the trip for Cubans and Haitians desperate to escape political upheaval and poverty. Miami-Dade County, Florida, is the primary point of entry for Cuba and Haitian exiles, and the reception they have received there has varied from neutral to hostile. Florida's politicians continue to look to the federal government for financial aid and immigration policies to ameliorate these issues. The focus of this entry is the different U.S. responses to the two migration streams. It examines the sociopolitical ramifications of U.S.–Cuban and U.S.–Haitian policies for the immigrants and how the language of immigration reform and the perception of immigration have affected both communities.

A Contrast in Reception

When Cubans first began to flee Fidel Castro's regime in Cuba, the reception in the United States was positive, perhaps related to the fact that helping Cuban refugees could be seen as an anti-communist policy. Later, U.S. administrations set policies that were not always welcoming. However, Cubans arriving in Miami-Dade County have continued to benefit from the perceived cohesive nature of their communities. President George W. Bush, for example, has funded anti-Castro programs such as Radio and

TV Marti and has limited travel and remittances to the island.

Haitian immigrants fleeing the dictatorship of "Papa Doc" Duvalier and his successors have been met with detention in federal holding centers and repatriation. Moreover, the U.S. government intervention into Haitian political instability included sending peacekeepers and military civil affairs units to facilitate the democratization of the small nation-state. The military consultants were there for a limited time and left Haiti in what many Haitian social activists charged was an unstable state. The Bush administration failed to prepare the up-and-coming political leaders for the work of democratizing the island. Those who had been in power with one regime simply changed allegiances and took power within the new regime. Haiti was not seen in the same light as Cuba because Haiti was not considered a communist regime; rather, it was considered an authoritarian government that strategically was of no threat to the United States save for the effects of continued migration.

Haitian and Haitian American social activists have charged the Bush administration with racializing immigration reform to keep Blacks out of the United States. The claims, as stated by the Haitian Coalition in Miami-Dade County, assert that Cubans are fleeing Cuba for the same reasons that Haitians are risking their lives to leave Haiti. Political unrest and the hope of pursuing a better life are the motivators.

The Haitian American Experience

The Haitian community of Miami-Dade County has a population of more than 71,054, according to the 2000 census. The majority speaks French Creole and has been absorbed into the formal economy, accepting low wages and poor work conditions. Those who are here illegally are often actively employed in the informal economy. They work to achieve financial success for themselves and their families and look to contribute to the U.S. economy. Most have made the 600-mile journey through treacherous waters to reach the United States and find employment to provide for their families. Leaving Haiti was an act of desperation; the National Coalition of Haitian Rights asserts that so long as assassinations of dissenters continue in Haiti, emigration will continue to be problematic for the United States.

With the fall of the Duvalier regime and the implementation of democratic elections, participation in the political process of Haiti was expected to reduce the migration stream. However, the mechanisms that kept Duvalier in power—tactics such as torture, murder, and imprisonment—did not end with the new political process. The election of President Jean-Bertrand Aristide with the intervention of the United States did little to stem the tide of migration. More than 70,000 Haitians fled Haiti for the United States in September 1991 when a coup upset the balance of power. The military coup continued the use of force to keep corruption and extortion profitable for those in power.

In 2004, more than 500 Haitian immigrants reached U.S. soil. They were held aboard Coast Guard cutters with minimal opportunity to apply for asylum. Bush responded by announcing that the Haitians would be repatriated and that the international community should work together to facilitate peace in Haiti. The Haitian Refugee Center of Miami-Dade County reports that repatriated Haitians have experienced humiliation, torture, and shunning by their community as a result of their attempts to leave Haiti. In addition, smugglers take advantage of would-be emigrants, demanding thousands of dollars for transport to the Florida coast. Repatriation has left Haitians with little opportunity to obtain employment, and they are dependent on family members for support.

Agents of the Immigration and Naturalization Service (INS) take Haitians in the United States illegally to the Krome Detention Center in Miami-Dade County. They may apply for political asylum and are allowed to plead their cases before INS officials. Most, however, are repatriated to Port-au-Prince.

Immigration from Haiti is not likely to slow. The current population of Haiti is 832,600. More than 38% of the population is under 15 years of age. Young Haitians experience a variety of social strains associated with poverty, presenting the conditions that are the push factors for Haitians to leave the island. Youth are also willing to accept the risk associated with such a dangerous crossing. It is unknown how many Haitians have died in the attempt to make it to the United States.

The United Nations estimates that more than 62% of Haitians are undernourished. It is also projected that the infant mortality rate is 63%. Life expectancy is projected at 52 years. Approximately 34% of Haitians are not expected to reach 40 years of age, and 46% do not have access to improved water sources. These conditions of poverty have created the desperation that is the catalyst for young Haitians to leave the island in search of a better life. Smugglers have used this desperation as an enticement, promising employment and material wealth if they pay the cost to get them to Florida.

The Cuban American Experience

The Cuban and Cuban American community has encountered a different reception from the U.S. government. The first wave of migration from 1959 to 1964 was viewed as a fight for freedom. Castro's regime was vilified as communist, and his alliance with the former Soviet Union strengthened the resolve of U.S. residents that communism was an enemy that should be fought swiftly.

The second major migration from Cuba occurred during 1979 and 1980. The Cuban émigrés were referred to as "Marielitos" based on the port from which they left Cuba. Castro was quick to portray these émigrés as criminals, the mentally ill, and outcasts of society. Through the interviewing of the asylum seekers in the United States, it was discovered that a small percentage were criminals and that many were elderly, ill, or political dissenters. This migration included 100,000 refugees. The federal government, under the administration of President Jimmy Carter, sent in the Coast Guard to stem the wave of émigrés and warned Castro against further action. Although originally detained in Miami's Orange Bowl stadium, many were eventually released into the custody of family members and were absorbed into the Cuban enclave.

The most recent migration wave of Cuban refugees came in 1995, although many still trickle in occasionally. Known as the *Balseros,* the Spanish translation for rafters, Cubans once again took to the seas in hopes of reaching American soil. Those arriving were detained briefly for INS processing. Under the administration of President Bill Clinton, new immigration reform known as the "wet feet/dry feet" policy was enacted. If Cubans or Haitians reached U.S. soil, they would be allowed to apply for asylum. In an agreement with Cuba, the United States would allow applications for 20,000 visas per year. Cuba has limited who can apply for visas, leaving many applicants unable to take advantage of the program.

The wet feet/dry feet policy constructed by the Clinton administration stated that those able to reach U.S. shores would be allowed the opportunity to apply for refugee status. However, with the Coast Guard patrolling the Florida Straits with boats and helicopters, it is a challenge to reach U.S. shores. All Haitians and Cubans found in international waters are repatriated. Interdiction at sea has become a priority due to the increased number of drug and alien smugglers.

Conclusion

The Cuban American community of Miami-Dade County has a population of more than 552,000. Absorption of new arrivals into the community is easier because of the number of Cuban-owned and -operated businesses. The informal economy of the Cuban enclave also facilitates absorption. The Haitian community is much smaller, and social activists contend that the racism and ethnic bias Haitians encounter makes absorption more difficult.

It is unknown how many Haitians and Cubans die in attempting to reach U.S. soil; however, what is clear is that those attempting to leave know the risks they are taking and are willing to risk their lives for better ones. Current immigration reform has not stemmed the tide of those attempting to reach self-exile. Interdiction at sea has only given smugglers the opportunity to take advantage of the desperate. The Haitian and Cuban refugee centers refer to the international water between the United States, Cuba, and Haiti as an international graveyard.

Sandy Alvarez

See Appendix A

See also Asylum; "Boat People"; Cuba; Cuba: Migration and Demography; Cuban Americans; Diaspora; Haiti; Haitian Americans; Immigration, U.S.; Informal Economy

Further Readings

Central Intelligence Agency. 2007. *World Factbook.* Available from https://www.cia.gov/cia/publications/factbook/index.html

Gaines, Jena. 2004. *Haitian Immigration (changing face of North America).* Broomall, PA: Mason Crest.

LaGuerre, Michel S. 2006. *Diasporic Citizenship: Haitian Americans in Transnational America.* New York: Palgrave Macmillan.

McCoy, Terry, William Kennedy, and Arthur Miller. 2003. *Cuba on the Verge of Transition.* New York: Bulfinch Press.

Perez-Hernandez, Julio Cesar and Angelika Taschen. 2006. *Inside Cuba.* Los Angeles, CA: Taschen Press.

Stepick, Alex. 1997. *Pride against Prejudice: Haitians in the United States.* Boston, MA: Allyn & Bacon.

Zephir, Flore. 1996. *Haitian Immigrants in Black America: A Sociological and Sociolinguistic Portrait.* South Hadley, MA: Bergen & Garvey.

Haole

Haole refers to a largely racialized ethnic group in Hawai'i that has significantly shaped the society and direction of the islands. *'Ōlelo Hawai'i,* the Hawaiian language, defines *haole* as either a general foreigner or a White person specifically. It is an often-heard term in Hawai'i, referring to people and things that are not indigenous to the islands. Depending on the context, it can be used as a neutral or pejorative term. Owing to a unique and tangled history, the term provokes strong racial, class, and political associations among Hawai'i residents. Enduring experiences with missionaries, plantation owners, military personnel, and tourists primarily contribute to current notions of haole. This entry looks at the origins of the term, its application to different groups, and its influence today.

Origin of the Term

There is some debate regarding the original meaning of the word *haole.* One popular belief is that the term was first applied to U.S. missionaries who did not exchange breath in the customary fashion when greeting others. Native Hawaiians practice the *honi,* a light pressing of the nose while inhaling each other's *hā* (breath). *Hā* is a symbol of life in Hawaiian culture, and *'ole* means to be without something. The inability of the missionaries to act appropriately caused Hawaiians to say that they were without breath (*hā 'ole*). However, linguists criticize this interpretation, arguing that the pronunciations of *hā'ole* and *haole* are markedly different and would not be easily confused. Still, many people, Native Hawaiians and others, continue to embrace this localized etymology.

On the other hand, ancient *mo'olelo* (native histories) demonstrate that the concept of haole most likely originated prior to the arrival of Westerners to Hawai'i. S. M. Kamakau, an 18th-century Native Hawaiian historian, recorded the oral history of distinguished *kūpuna* (elders of his time). One account, told for generations before the coming of Westerners, mentions the travels of the young chief Paumakuaalonoho'onewa to Kahiki, the land beyond the horizon. When returning from these distant lands, the chief brought back with him foreigners described as *haole*—white-skinned persons with reddish eyes that stare like the *āhole* fish. The fact that the term is linked not only to strange newcomers but also to white-skinned persons in this example may or may not be coincidental.

Haole is routinely used in the Hawaiian kingdom and early censuses to distinguish Native Hawaiians from non-Native Hawaiians. Remarkably, this practice applied to other Pacific Islanders as well, where the categories of "male foreign Polynesians" and "women foreign Polynesians" are listed as *Nā haole kāne Polynesia* and *Nā haole wāhine Polynesia,* respectively. Despite subsequent importation of U.S. ideology and culture, which emphasizes color and race, Native Hawaiians remain interested in connections to ancestors, land, and place.

From an indigenous Hawaiian perspective, people are closely identified with the places and ancestors they come from. The *'āina* (land) is a key component of one's identity and background. When foreigners initially arrived in Hawai'i, whether they were Europeans or other Pacific Islanders, they were most likely treated as *malihini* (newcomers). In contrast, to be *kama'āina* means to be intimately familiar with a place, that is, knowledgeable in both the big and little currents.

Mo'okū'auhau (genealogy) is equally important in determining one's identity, status, and role in Hawaiian society. In some ways, haole are seen as perpetual *malihini.* The term infers that someone is without ancestral connection to the *'āina* and has no *'ohana* (extended family) on which to rely. These sentiments persist today and are consciously woven into the rich fabric of contemporary Native Hawaiian culture.

White People in the Islands

Early Influences

Historically speaking, sustained contact with European and U.S. sailors, tradesmen, and missionaries during the late 18th century drastically changed the composition of Hawaiian society. Massive native depopulation brought about by foreign diseases caused tremendous social upheaval, as did the importation of new religions and the haole concept of private land ownership. During these tumultuous times, haole quickly rose to prominence in the islands through industriousness and intermarriage with native elites or through duplicitous means. From their earliest days in Hawai'i, a handful of White foreigners became members of royal courts and served as advisers to ruling *ali'i* (chiefs). John Young, an Englishman who served Kamehameha I, was given the name Keoni Ana after marrying a high-ranking Hawaiian woman. Through the high status of his English father and Hawaiian mother, his son was later appointed governor of Oʻahu by Kamehameha III.

Haole gained a foothold in Hawaiian society through missionary churches and schools established throughout the islands. The missionaries brought Christianity, but perhaps more compelling to the native populace was their means of reading, writing, and printing. Not long after their arrival in 1820, a large-scale plantation economy emerged that was linked closely to U.S. business and politics. Between 1852 and 1946, thousands of Chinese, Portuguese, Japanese, Korean, Filipino, and other immigrant laborers were contracted to harvest sugar cane, pineapple, and other export crops.

Workers lived in ethnically segregated plantation camps and learned to communicate with each other through Pidgin, a localized Creole language. Nearly all of the plantation owners were haole, many of whom were descendants of well-known missionary families. They became especially wealthy landowners and entrepreneurs capable of influencing the Hawaiʻi kingdom government and the greater public with their vast resources and control of the press. In stark contrast to the haole owners and managers, the laborers and field-hands were predominantly disenfranchised non-Whites.

Political Control

Whereas the missionary and plantation eras saw haole accumulate vast wealth and influence, the overthrow of Queen Liliʻuokalani in 1893 and the illegal annexation of Hawaiʻi in 1898 wrested all remaining political power from the native government. A small contingent of haole businessmen led by Sanford B. Dole were intent on Hawaiʻi becoming a U.S. state and orchestrated the overthrow of the queen with the aid of U.S. military forces. From 1898 to 1959, Whites consolidated their power in what is commonly referred to as the "territorial era" of Hawaiʻi. During this new age, Hawaiian language, tradition, and culture were besieged by an influx of haole ideas, commodities, and practices. The newly dominant U.S. culture promised island residents modernity and enterprise at the wholesale cost of assimilation.

The presence of the U.S. military in Hawaiʻi and cultural clashes between service people and local residents further organize perceptions of haole. From a military standpoint, Hawaiʻi is a strategically positioned staging ground in the heart of the Pacific, roughly midway between North America and Asia. U.S. officers recognized the importance of establishing a Pacific fleet at Pearl Harbor as early as the mid-1800s. Today, the U.S. military controls a great deal of land throughout the islands, and this at times engenders hostility on the part of island residents, Native Hawaiians in particular. In some ways, military personnel are distinctly haole because they often arrive from U.S. states with limited familiarity of island life and culture. Scholars describe the strangeness that haole servicemen and servicewomen experienced during World War II when they were made aware of their position as a White "minority" in Hawaiʻi. More important, beyond the racial differences of most military personnel and island folks are major disparities of cultural values and normative behavior between the groups.

Tourism and Local Residents

The pervasiveness of mass tourism is a profound component of Hawaiian society. Each year, millions of tourists vacation in the islands, and their highly structured encounters with local residents contribute to common perceptions of haole. Anthropologists suggest that the Hawaiʻi visitor industry is a contact zone where haole and locals perform ritualized behavior and form attitudes about one another. Again, from an indigenous Hawaiian perspective, tourists epitomize "haoleness" because they typically stay for short periods of time; they enjoy the benefits of Hawaiʻi without "giving back" in a cultural sense before returning home. A familiar *ōlelo noʻeau* (Native Hawaiian proverb) finds similar behavior in the *Kōlea* bird (golden plovers). These birds seasonally migrate to the islands from Alaska to consume resources and escape a harsh winter, but they never establish lifelong nests.

Given this sociopolitical history, haole as a group are most often contrasted with "locals," composed of any non-White persons raised in Hawaiʻi. Recently, Native Hawaiian and local scholars have written about the formation and implication of local culture and identity. In Marxist terms, haole represent the capitalist and managerial class, whereas locals, as descendants of contract laborers, constitute the proletariat. This sentiment persists today where grassroots efforts against exploitative development often mobilize around a shared pride in localness. Interestingly enough, times have changed such that Whites nowadays trail local Japanese and local Chinese in terms of socioeconomic status and political representation. Critics warn that "local" displaces

Native Hawaiian voice because it reduces indigenous Hawaiians to be simply one of many other ethnic groups in Hawai'i.

Haole Today

Haole, like the label of any ethnic group, masks the diversity of its membership. It is far too easy to stereotype all haole according to a prescriptive set of markers and behavior. The more complicated reality is that *haole* is a socially constructed category based largely on idealized and homogenized views of White foreigners. At the same time, framed by a particular chain of events, these perspectives remain in people's minds as a collective public history and discourse. Precisely because of this, haole are perceived as White wealthy individuals who are set apart from Native Hawaiians and locals due to their shallow roots in the islands and perceived negative behaviors.

The arrival and ascendancy of haole, as a group, is comparatively small when measured against the duration of indigenous Hawaiian occupation and stewardship of the land. Although a highly racialized ethnic group, haole are also culturally conspicuous. The Hawaiian word, *ho'ohaole* means to act like a haole and is applied to individuals who are perceived to be strange, uppity, ignorant, arrogant, or even condescending. Some scholars suggest that there are different types of haole. In particular, it is argued that there is a difference between mainland haole and *kama'āina haole* (sometimes referred to as local haole). The latter category refers to Whites who have lived on the islands for generations, share a love for the land, and act in culturally appropriate ways.

Still, the term *haole* recalls the painful history of Hawai'i and the role many prominent haole played in the forced transformation of Hawaiian society and culture. Modern-day implications of haole provoke overlapping notions of race, class, and politics for island residents. Because haole were the primary agents of past missionary activity and a race/class-organized plantation economy, as well as expansive militarism and tourism, attitudes toward them run deep and continue to manifest in everyday life in Hawai'i. Given this historical framework, there is often little attention paid to the positive value of haole in today's politically charged climate where indigenous Hawaiians' claim to the land is foregrounded.

Brandon C. Ledward

See also Colonialism; Hapa; Hawai'i, Race in; Hawaiians; Native Americans; Pacific Islanders; White Privilege

Further Readings

Fujikane, Candace and John Okamura, eds. 2000. "Asian Settler Colonialism in Hawaii." *Amerasia Journal* 26(2).

Kame'eleihiwa, Lilikalā. 1992. *Native Land and Foreign Desire*. Honolulu, HI: Bishop Museum Press.

Ohnuma, Keiko. 2002. "Local Haole—A Contradiction in Terms? The Dilemma of Being White, Born, and Raised in Hawai'i." *Cultural Values* 6:273–285.

McElrath, Ah Quon. 1999. "Race Relations and the Political Economy in Hawaii." *Social Process in Hawaii* 39:74–84.

Osorio, Jonathan. 2002. *Dismembering Lahui*. Honolulu: University of Hawai'i Press.

Rohrer, Judy. 1997. "Haole Girl: Identity and White Privilege in Hawaii." *Social Process in Hawaii* 38:140–161.

Rohrer, Judy. 2006. "'Got Race?' The Production of Haole and the Distortion of Indigeneity in the Rice Decision." *Contemporary Pacific* 18:1–3.

Silva, Noenoe K. 2004. *Aloha Betrayed*. Durham, NC: Duke University Press.

Whittaker, Elvi. 1986. *The Mainland Haole*. New York: Columbia University Press.

HAPA

The term *hapa* is a Hawaiian word literally translating to portion, mixed, or fragment with no racial inference. However, on the inclusion of Hawai'i as a U.S. territory and the introduction of racial classification during the late 1800s, the term quickly took on racial overtones as a way to identify people of mixed race. Early references to the term *hapa* referred to Hawaiians of mixed Japanese European heritage, but its contemporary use extends to a variety of mixed-race people in Hawai'i and even beyond the island to include Afro-Asians, Latin Asians, Native Asians, and transracial adoptees. This entry describes the evolution of the term and the conflict related to its adoption by mixed-race people outside of Hawai'i.

Definition and Background

Originally a pejorative term, *hapa* referred to the children of mixed Hawaiian Caucasian descent. Its pejorative use dates to the surge in White immigration to Hawai'i that occurred during the 1880s and resulted in intermarriage between the native and Caucasian populations. The Native Hawaiian population's disapproval of these mixed marriages (and, by extension, of the offspring of these unions) stemmed from the White population's role in exploiting and colonizing Hawai'i.

The term *hapa* was later expanded to include all children of mixed Asian heritage after a surge in Asian immigration to the island that occurred during the mid-1880s through 1910 with the recruitment of Chinese, Japanese, Portuguese, Koreans, Puerto Ricans, and Filipinos to work as laborers and the mixed racial/ethnic marriages that arose following this large-scale immigration.

Because of the long history of intermarriage in Hawai'i, the negative aspects associated with biracial or multiracial identification (and the designation of hapa) has largely disappeared. Once an adjective used by group insiders to describe an outsider, it is now a noun or subject (describing an insider); the designation is a source of pride and a link to others in the same insider category. Furthermore, use of the term is no longer limited to those who are part Hawaiian but rather has expanded to include all multiracial/multiethnic Asians as well. Other terms such as *Eurasian, biracial, multiracial, Amerasian, mixed Asian, blasian, hafu,* and *half Asian* are also used to describe those of mixed Asian descent; however, the term *hapa* seems to have resonated most among multiethnic Asians and has been widely adopted. Although it is used by multiethnic/multiracial Asians both in Hawai'i and on the U.S. mainland, the term has different connotations in each place.

Of all the states, Hawai'i has both the highest percentage of Asian and Pacific Islanders (41.6%) and the highest percentage of people who identify themselves in categories of two or more races (21.4% vs. 2.4% in the United States). The long history of racial/ethnic intermixing in Hawai'i has allowed its multiracial populations to inhabit multiple racial/ethnic categories simultaneously. In Hawai'i, the term *hapa* has been normalized to the extent that to be hapa is to be local because so many of the children are of mixed ancestry. The ambiguous hapa identity distinguishes Hawaiian locals from more recent foreign immigrants (nonlocals) to Hawai'i. This is in marked contrast to the mainland United States, where race has historically been socially constructed along a single dimension, thereby forcing those of multiracial heritage to elevate a single racial category at the expense of the other, and where considerable ink has been devoted to the problematic results and consequences of this practice for the multiracial population.

Contested Terrain

Multiracial Hawaiians resent the adoption of the term *hapa* by multiracial Asians on the U.S. mainland who have little knowledge of the historical struggles of the peoples of Hawai'i. From their perspective, the term's use by multiracial Asians is a form of symbolic ethnicity—trendy and ephemeral with only a superficial connection to, and little understanding of, the term's meaning.

Part of the controversy is rooted in the history of Hawai'i and stems from lingering resentment of Hawaiian people over the forced and unlawful overthrow of the Hawaiian monarchy in 1893—an event that was aided and abetted in large part by the United States (and an act that President Bill Clinton formally apologized for in 1993). As a result, Western laws and customs were imposed, including the legal categorization of people by "blood" or heritage in 1900. Hawaiians were "colorized" and quantified along a range from indigenous to (non-White) others, to Whites. This strategy served to limit the number of "native" Hawaiians; the designation was restricted to those who could legally prove their indigenous heritage—something extremely difficult to do in a nation steeped in oral tradition as Hawai'i was. Consequently, indigenous Hawaiians were marginalized socioeconomically, and a decrease in their numbers was nearly ensured given the narrow racial definition that was imposed.

This paved the way for land and asset appropriation by the Western colonizers. Indigenous Hawaiians, or Kanaka Maoli, became minorities in their own homeland, taking on the characteristics of other racial/ethnic minorities in the United States, including high morbidity and mortality rates, poor educational outcomes, and marginalized socioeconomic positions.

The question of who has a valid claim to identity in Hawai'i continues to be a highly contentious and politicized issue, as indicated by the *Rice v. Cayetano* decision by the U.S. Supreme Court in 2000. This decision invalidated the state's limitation to Native Hawaiians (defined as descendants of those inhabiting the Hawaiian Islands in 1778) the eligibility to vote in elections for the Board of Trustees of the Office of Hawaiian Affairs.

With these tensions serving as the backdrop, the widespread adoption of the term *hapa* by multiethnic Asians with little knowledge of the tumultuous history of Hawai'i or of the continuing struggles for identity by indigenous Hawaiians is viewed as reflecting the continuing marginalization and colonization of Hawai'i and its history, people, and culture by groups with more power.

Contemporary Use

The proliferation of the term *hapa* among mainland multiracial Asians and its use in the mass media reflect the term's enduring application and continuing viability, albeit slightly different from its origins. In fact, in many instances, the original Hawaiian roots of the term are not recognized. For example, in her article titled "Mixed-Race Asians Find Pride as Hapas," *Los Angeles Times* staff writer Teresa Watanabe defined *hapas* as all mixed-race Asians. In this article, Watanabe detailed some of the struggles of mixed-race Asians, including the constant questioning of racial/ethnic identification and issues of inclusion and exclusion by the dominant society.

Thus, while Hawaiian hapas see the term as a source of pride, acceptance, inclusion, and desirability, mainland hapas must continuously contend with the mainland's adherence to monoracial categorizations of people such that a multiracial designation remains both suspect and subject to constant question.

Karen Manges Douglas

See also Asian Americans; Asian American Studies; *Hafu*; Hawaiians; Identity Politics; Intermarriage; Multiracial Identity

Further Readings

Halpin, Marianne Maruyama. 2003. *Naming Ourselves: A Participatory Research with Hapa Authors of Japanese Ancestry Writing for Children and Young Adults about Identity.* PhD dissertation, University of San Francisco.

Kan'iaupuni, Shawn Malia and Carolyn A. Liebler. 2005. "Pondering Poi Dog: Place and Racial Identification of Multiracial Native Hawaiians." *Ethnic and Racial Studies* 28:687–721.

Reed, Gay Garland. 2001. "Fastening and Unfastening Identities: Negotiating Identity in Hawaii." *Discourse: Studies in the Cultural Politics of Education* 22:327–339.

Rohrer, Judy. 2006. "'Got Race?' The Production of Haole and the Distortion of Indigeneity in the *Rice* Decision." *Contemporary Pacific* 18(1):1–31.

Watanabe, Teresa. 2006. "Mixed-Race Asians Find Pride as Hapas." *Los Angeles Times*, June 11, B3.

Yoshimi, Jeff. 1997. "Hapas at a Los Angeles High School: Context and Phenomenology." *Amerasia Journal* 23:131–147.

HARLEM

Harlem, a neighborhood in the Manhattan borough of New York City, has long been associated with Black culture. It stretches from the East River to the Hudson River; its northern border is 155th Street, and its southern border is roughly 96th Street. Although Harlem has been home to a multitude of immigrant communities, since the beginning of the 20th century it has been a decidedly Black space. Harlem has been host to jazz, the Harlem Renaissance, poverty, riots, strikes, crime, and influential leaders in the Black community. It is also home to famous landmarks such as the Apollo Theater and Hotel Theresa. Throughout time, Harlem has been one of New York City's most recognized neighborhoods worldwide.

Immigration in Harlem

Harlem, originally a farmland settlement in New Amsterdam known as Nieuw Haarlem, was purchased from the Manhattes tribe during the mid-1600s and settled by Dutch immigrants. In 1626, the first Blacks were brought to Harlem as slaves to labor on Dutch farms. In 1664, the English attacked and seized the property from the Dutch and turned greater New Amsterdam into New York, officially incorporating the village of Harlem. The slave trade grew rapidly under the English, and by 1708 there were thousands of Black slaves living and working in Harlem.

By 1820, there were still only ninety-one White families living in Harlem, and in 1840, after the land was devastated by constant use, many wealthy homeowners sold their land to the city. This led to poor Irish immigrants squatting on the deserted land and establishing shantytowns of living quarters.

Throughout the 19th century, community improvements included the construction of fashionable brownstones and apartment houses and the installation of better sanitation, communications, and lighting. These changes, along with the extension of elevated railroads from New York, encouraged older, White, upper-middle-class immigrant families to move north to Harlem. At that time, the construction of the subway to Harlem was under way; however, due to a delay in completing the project, many houses remained uninhabited, causing real estate prices to fall. Jewish immigrants were attracted to the area and began purchasing properties despite the efforts of landowners to keep them out. Nonetheless, the Jewish population in Harlem reached a peak of 150,000 in 1917. This dominance was short-lived, and by 1930 Jews in the area numbered only approximately 5,000.

Many early Black residents of Harlem were domestic laborers for wealthy White families; however, by 1900 Blacks began migrating to Harlem in record numbers. Landowners were unable to fill properties with White families, so some turned to Black families moving into the area. There was strong resistance from Whites, and organizations bent on denying Blacks residence in Harlem sprang up. One example is the Property Owners Protective Association, which was organized in 1913 and charged that Blacks were destructive and poor tenants who caused real estate values to drop. The movement of Blacks into Harlem continued, however, and as White families deserted the area, landlords surrendered to the inevitable and rented to Black families.

The Harlem Renaissance

Many Blacks from the South, looking for work and community, also joined in the mass migration to Harlem. Black churches in New York were greatly influential in this movement in that they encouraged buying Harlem properties, a possibility for many Blacks because of the World War I boom in wages. Eventually, however, this influx of Blacks faced work shortages as well as exorbitant rents and landlord negligence. These factors contributed to deterioration in living conditions and a death rate of Harlem Blacks that was twice the death rate of Whites. By the 1920s, Harlem was quickly becoming a neighborhood of slums.

The new Harlem community was composed of working-class Blacks who formed a new urban generation. This poverty-stricken community spawned a cultural renaissance of writers and poets such as Claude McKay and Countee Cullen. Others, such as Langston Hughes, provided a historical picture of the Black community. Marcus Garvey also had a great impact in Harlem, preaching racial pride and independence. In addition, the 1920s were considered the Harlem Jazz Age. Although Blacks were producing this new music, many clubs were restricted to White customers only; hence, Harlem was a working community by day but a playground for Whites in the boisterous jazz clubs and bars at night.

Harlem Strikes and Riots

By the late 1930s, the Harlem Renaissance had run its course and Whites were no longer as prevalent a force in the community's nightlife. At the same time, the advent of the Great Depression meant that living conditions in Harlem continued to worsen. In addition, the lack of work in Harlem was exacerbated by large-scale discrimination by White employers who still owned most of the Harlem businesses. During this time, the ceilings and walls of tenements often collapsed. Apartment houses were overcrowded, vermin ridden, and filthy, and most buildings had unsafe stairs, rotted window frames, and severe sanitation problems. Furthermore, most homes had no running water, and many were without electricity. These problems were amplified due to the massive increase in the Black population of Harlem, which rose by more than 600% between 1905 and 1930. In addition, by 1930 approximately 45,000 Puerto Rican immigrants had moved into the area known as East Harlem.

These conditions helped to spark the racially charged Harlem Riot of 1935, which resulted in the arrests of more than seventy Black individuals, injuries to numerous civilians and policemen, and more than 600 broken windows in Harlem. The riot did little to improve the conditions in Harlem; although a few more shopkeepers hired Black workers, they still hired them at the lowest positions and rates of pay. The residents of Harlem participated in political action, but living and work conditions in Harlem failed to improve despite these efforts.

During the 1940s, Harlem was divided into three neighborhoods: Italian Harlem, Spanish Harlem, and Black Harlem. This division mirrored the racial, ethnic, and religious separation present in every borough of New York and contributed to another race-related riot in 1943. This riot was even more costly than the 1935 riot, with at least six Black persons being killed and more than 185 persons being injured. Relative deprivation, blocked opportunity structures, and increased political awareness contributed to both of the early Harlem riots.

By the 1950s, urban renewal projects were under way. These projects ultimately resulted in the forced relocation of Blacks when old buildings were torn down. Because of severe overcrowding, for most the housing situation only became worse. Eventually, there were roughly ten housing developments in Central Harlem housing more than 40,000 of Harlem's 300,000 residents. The rest of those in Harlem lived in older tenement apartment houses built before 1900 or slightly newer brownstone or multidwelling buildings. Few of these housing options were in good repair, and most continued to decline with unabated overcrowding.

Harlem living conditions further deteriorated during the 1960s. Due to the publicity of subpar housing conditions, city and state authorities began to pay attention to the issue but continually failed to follow through on promises. These contradictions led to a series of rent strikes—organized efforts at holding landlords responsible for housing conditions. After years of concerted efforts, including picketing, demonstrations, petitions, and attempts at legal action against landlords as well as countless families being thrown out of their homes for failure to pay rent, Harlem residents gained some ground with legislative measures in support of modifying the conditions of the Harlem ghetto.

Residents of Harlem continued to engage politically, protesting against segregated schools by participating in the great school boycott of 1964, fighting to dismantle discrimination in employment, and protesting for equal rights for Blacks nationwide. After another Harlem riot based on racial issues during the mid-1960s, Malcolm X gained great influence for his nationalist arguments. In addition, by 1966 the Black Panthers were organized in Harlem and agitated for violence in pursuit of change. In 1968, another Harlem riot occurred in response to the assassination of Martin Luther King, Jr. Additional riots in 1995, organized by Black activists against Jewish shop owners on 125th Street, were significantly different from previous riots, with fewer being injured or killed.

Harlem Today

Religious institutions have maintained their importance in Harlem. Today, there are more than 400 churches in the neighborhood, including representation from a variety of religious denominations. Historically, drug use in Harlem has produced high rates of abuse and collateral crime. Heroin was the drug of choice during the 1950s and 1960s, and crack cocaine was the drug of choice during the 1980s; however, after aggressive policing measures initiated during the late 1980s, crime rates in all categories have fallen dramatically. Furthermore, after more than a decade of gentrification, property values in Harlem have skyrocketed and countless new housing units have been developed—improvements that have outpaced the rest of New York since the early 1990s. For these reasons, Harlem today attracts many middle-class Blacks and Whites alike.

Christie A. Sennott

See also African Americans; Discrimination; East Harlem; Ghetto; Harlem Renaissance; Irish Americans; Urban Riots

Further Readings

Anderson, Jervis. 1982. *This Was Harlem: A Cultural Portrait, 1900–1950.* New York: Farrar Straus Giroux.
Brandt, Nat. 1996. *Harlem at War: The Black Experience in WWII.* Syracuse, NY: Syracuse University Press.
Capeci, Dominic J., Jr. 1977. *The Harlem Riot of 1943.* Philadelphia, PA: Temple University Press.
Halliburton, Warren J. and Ernest Kaiser. 1974. *Harlem: A History of Broken Dreams.* Garden City, NY: Zenith Books.
Halstead, Fred. 1966. *Harlem Stirs.* New York: Marzani & Munsell.

Harlem Renaissance

The Harlem Renaissance (1917–1934), originally called the "Negro Renaissance," was a golden age of African American arts. Its mission was to bring about racial renewal through cultural diplomacy. The Renaissance was not just "art for art's sake." That "Negro art" could redraw the public image of "colored" people in the United States was its animating purpose, with the goal of achieving what David Levering Lewis called "civil rights by copyright." Enjoying a "double audience" of Black and White, the Harlem Renaissance was a spectacular success during its heyday. As a public exhibition of African American poetry, prose, drama, art, and music, this valiant effort to remove the masks of racial stereotypes so as to put a new social face on African Americans improved race relations somewhat—a nearly impossible task given the entrenched racial prejudices of the day under the legalized segregation of Jim Crow laws.

Not only did the Harlem Renaissance attract a White patronage and market, the movement instilled a racial pride and nobility among African Americans whose lives it touched. Thus the Harlem Renaissance created a place in the national literary tradition, officially recognized in the "White House Salute to America's Authors" event on March 13, 2002, which paid tribute to "writers of the Harlem Renaissance" who "shaped a rich literary history and became agents of change." Its cultural diplomacy became a cultural legacy. This entry summarizes that era.

The Rise of the Harlem Renaissance

Beginning with the end of World War I in 1917 and concurrent with the Jazz Age, the Harlem Renaissance was made possible in part by powerful social forces effecting sweeping changes across the United States. A mass exodus of an estimated 5 million African Americans from the rural South to the urban North, "The Great Migration" (1915–1960) was described by Harlem Renaissance spokesman Alain Locke (1885–1954) as "a deliberate flight not only from countryside to city, but from mediaeval America to modern." These "shifting crystallizations" in U.S. demography resulted in the rise of a Black middle class in major U.S. cities, particularly in the Northeast. In the midst of this status revolution, one place stood out in particular: Harlem.

Harlem is a large sector of upper Manhattan in New York City—"little more than a note of sharper color in the kaleidoscope of New York," according to Locke. Harlem catalyzed the formation of a distinct racial consciousness that had previously been "a race more in name than in fact" or "more in sentiment than in experience," reflecting a "common condition rather than a common consciousness." The Harlem Renaissance offered African Americans their "first chances for group expression and self-determination." The Harlem Renaissance succeeded in the first objective but failed in the latter one.

Parties played a major role both in Harlem nightlife and in the Renaissance itself, and its official inaugural was a formal banquet. On March 21, 1924, *Opportunity* editor and sociologist Charles S. Johnson invited a group of young writers and artists to a dinner party of the Writers Guild held in the Civic Club, a restaurant on West Twelfth Street near Fifth Avenue in Harlem. The Civic Club was the only "upper-crust" New York nightclub free of color or sex restrictions. The party was called to celebrate Jessie Redmon Fauset's first novel, *There Is Confusion,* and to recognize "a newer school of writers" that included Eric Walrond, Countee Cullen, Langston Hughes, and Gwendolyn Bennett.

After dinner, Paul Kellog, editor of *Survey Graphic* (the premier journal of social work in the United States at the time), approached Johnson with an extraordinary offer, inviting him to assemble and edit literary work from these emergent authors for a special Harlem issue. Wishing to work behind the scenes, however, Johnson passed that invitation on to Locke—who had won national acclaim as the first African American Rhodes Scholar in 1907—asking him to guest edit that special issue of *Survey Graphic*. A week later, the *New York Herald Tribune* proclaimed that Harlem was "on the edge of, if not already in the midst of, what might properly be called a Negro renaissance." Published in March 1925, the special issue titled "Harlem: Mecca of the New Negro" was an instant success. It sold an estimated 42,000 copies in two printings.

The New Negro: African Americans' "First National Book"

Capitalizing on this success, Locke expanded the "Harlem" special issue and in November 1925 recast it as an anthology, *The New Negro: An Interpretation*—the inaugural epochal centerpiece of the New Negro movement and its manifesto and acclaimed as the "first national book" of African Americans. *The New Negro* featured thirty-four contributors, four of whom were White. The volume showcased most of the stellar figures of the Harlem Renaissance who went on to pursue independent literary and artistic careers in their own right. The great W. E. B. Du Bois (1868–1963) crowned the anthology by contributing the final essay. Locke proclaimed *The New Negro* to be "our spiritual Declaration of Independence." Locke figured prominently in the Harlem Renaissance as its principal art critic, promoter, and power broker.

The Artists and Their Legacy

The prime movers of the Harlem Renaissance believed that art held more promise than politics in bringing about a sea of change in U.S. race relations. A more realistic goal was the cultivation of wholesome race pride. The advent of a self-conscious "Negro poetry" by "Negro poets" helped to foster the group consciousness that Locke found to be singularly lacking among African Americans historically yet developing rather suddenly in his generation.

Locke helped to launch the career of Langston Hughes (1902–1967)—widely regarded as the poet laureate of the Harlem Renaissance—whose poems "Let America Be America Again" and "Theme for English B" are frequently anthologized in American literature textbooks. Disinclined to identify himself as a Negro poet, Countee Cullen (1903–1946) published his first volume of poems, *Colors,* in 1925. This volume won the first Harmon Foundation Award in Literature in 1926. A West Indian and British citizen, Claude McKay (1889–1948), contributed the poem "White House" to *The New Negro* anthology. Because of its politically sensitive nature, Locke changed the title of the poem to "White Houses."

In his social protest poem, "To America," McKay personified the United States as a tiger (striped in black and white), racially terrible yet magnificent in its awesome power. Considered to be the "inaugural address" of the Harlem Renaissance and McKay's greatest claim to fame was his military sonnet, "If We Must Die," which appeared in the July issue of *Liberator* during the "Red Summer" of 1919, when race riots swept across twenty-five of the nation's inner cities like a firestorm. The poem took on the power of an anthem; it was reprinted by virtually every leading African American magazine and newspaper. McKay's sonnet surpassed his race when Winston Churchill used "If We Must Die" to rally British soldiers in battles against the Nazis in World War II. As Locke had predicted, Harlem Renaissance poets entered into the canon of mainstream American literature and enriched British culture as well.

The Harlem Renaissance was, to a limited degree, an interracial movement. For instance, in the 1925 "Harlem" issue of *Survey Graphic,* Locke published seven portraits of Harlem folk sketched by German-born Winold Reiss (1886–1953). Carl Van Vechten (1880–1964) was probably the pivotal White promoter

Langston Hughes. *Hughes (1902–1967) is widely regarded as the poet laureate of the Harlem Renaissance. His poems are frequently anthologized in American literature textbooks and have become accepted as central to the nation's literature tradition.*

Source: Library of Congress, Prints & Photographs Division, LC-USZ62-43605.

of the Harlem Renaissance. Patron of Locke, Hughes, Zora Neale Hurston (1891–1960), and others, Charlotte Osgood Mason (1854–1946) was a secret benefactor of major Harlem Renaissance artists and writers. Other influential White patrons included Paul Kellog (1879–1958) and Albert C. Barnes (1872–1951), among others.

Writer Jean Toomer (1894–1967) was a mulatto who could pass for White and ultimately did. In 1923, he published *Cane,* a novel set in Georgia, which Hughes praised as "the finest prose written by a Negro in America" and which Locke hailed as "a brilliant performance." Toomer was a one-book author whose career was abortive for personal reasons. Born of a Danish mother and a West Indian father, Nella Larsen (1893–1963) in 1929 won the Harmon Foundation's Bronze Medal for Literature for her 1928 novel *Quicksand,* which Du Bois praised as "the best piece of fiction that Negro America has produced since the heyday of [Charles] Chesnutt." Although legally Black, Larsen had loyalties to both Blacks and Whites, a theme of racial fusion and confusion explored in *Quicksand,* where the main character, Helga Crane, is a full projection of Larsen herself. In 1930, Larsen became the first Black woman to win a Guggenheim Fellowship.

There are more than 130 published plays by thirty-seven Harlem Renaissance authors. On May 22, 1921, *Shuffle Along* opened at Broadway's David Belasco Theater and became the first musical revue scored and performed by African Americans. In 1929, the Negro Experimental Theatre was founded in February, the Negro Art Theatre was formed in June, and the National Colored Players was established in September.

Acknowledged by some as "the father of Black American art," Aaron Douglas (1899–1979) was recognized by Locke as "the pioneer of the African style among the American Negro artists." In addition to being an illustrator whose work first appeared in the "Harlem" issue of *Survey Graphic* and then in *The New Negro*, Douglas drew on Egyptian and African art and was influenced by cubism, art deco, and art nouveau as well.

These are among the outstanding writers, artists, and performers of the Harlem Renaissance.

The Fall of the Harlem Renaissance

With a mission but without a unifying ideology, the Harlem Renaissance crashed along with the stock market during the early years of the Great Depression, and its failure to effect any real social change was underscored dramatically by the Harlem Riot of 1935. In 1936, Locke wrote an obituary of the Harlem Renaissance: "Eleven brief years ago, Harlem was full of the thrill and ferment of sudden progress and is prosperity; and *Survey Graphic* sounded the tocsin of the emergence of a 'new Negro' and the onset of a 'Negro renaissance.' Today, . . . that same Harlem is prostrate in the grip of the depression and throes of social unrest." Locke had a more sober view on the power of the arts to effect social change: "For there is no cure or saving magic in poetry and art, an emerging generation of talent, or in international prestige and interracial recognition, for unemployment or precarious marginal employment, for high rents, high mortality rates, civic neglect, [and] capitalistic exploitation, on the one hand, and radical exploitation, on the other." The Harlem Renaissance arose during the period of U.S. progressivism, with its faith in the reform of democracy. It was not so much that the Harlem Renaissance failed as it was that the United States failed the Harlem Renaissance.

Christopher George Buck

See also African Americans; *American Dilemma, An*; Discrimination; Du Bois, William Edward Burghardt; Jim Crow; Johnson, Charles S.; Minority Rights; People of Color; Prejudice; Racism; Segregation

Further Readings

Brown, Sterling A. 1996. "*The New Negro* in Literature (1925–1955)." Pp. 203–218 in *Remembering the Harlem Renaissance,* edited by Cary D. Wintz. New York: Garland.

Buck, Christopher. 2005. "Alain Locke: Race Leader, Social Philosopher, Bahá'í Pluralist." *World Order* 36(3):7–36.

Gates, Henry Louis, Jr. 1988. "The Trope of a New Negro and the Reconstruction of the Image of the Black." *Representations* 24:129–155.

Holmes, Eugene C. 1968. "Alain Locke and the New Negro Movement." *Negro American Literature Forum* 2(3):60–68.

Krasner, David. 2002. *A Beautiful Pageant: African American Theatre, Drama, and Performance in the Harlem Renaissance, 1910–1927.* New York: Palgrave Macmillan.

Lewis, David Levering. 1998. *When Harlem Was in Vogue.* New York: Penguin.

Locke, Alain, ed. [1925] 1969. *The New Negro: An Interpretation.* New York: Albert and Charles Boni. (Reprinted with a new preface by Robert Hayden)

Long, Richard A. 1976. "The Genesis of Locke's *The New Negro.*" *Black World* 25(4):14–20.

Nadell, Martha Jane. 2004. *Enter the New Negroes: Images of Race in American Culture.* Cambridge, MA: Harvard University Press.

Spencer, Jon Michael. 1997. *The New Negroes and Their Music: The Success of the Harlem Renaissance.* Knoxville: University of Tennessee Press.

Watts, Eric King. 2002. "African American Ethos and Hermeneutical Rhetoric: An Exploration of Alain Locke's *The New Negro.*" *Quarterly Journal of Speech* 88(1):19–32.

Wintz, Cary D. and Paul Finkelman, eds. 2004. *Encyclopedia of the Harlem Renaissance.* London: Routledge.

HATE CRIMES

Hate crimes or bias crimes are incidents in which the offenders have selected their victims because of their race, ethnicity, national origin, religion, gender, disability, sexual orientation, or other innate characteristics.

These incidents are unlike other crime categories because the offenders target victims largely because of who they are (e.g., African Americans) or because of a group they choose to belong to (e.g., Catholics) rather than because of what has occurred, for example, a protracted incident between neighbors or family members. Like terrorists more generally, these offenders often randomly choose their victims and do not care who they assault or harass so long as they connect the victims to a particular group. Their mission is often to convey a message to an entire group, such as "Leave—your kind isn't wanted in our neighborhood," or to let the group know that they will not tolerate "your behavior." This entry reviews government attempts to address hate crimes, especially in the United States.

U.S. Response

Although crimes motivated by hatred have existed for centuries, there was no push in the United States to distinguish them as a special type of criminal offense until the early 1980s. Advocates from several special interest groups argued, using three general reasons, that hate crimes needed special attention from law enforcement agencies. First, because hate crime offenders target innate characteristics of a group, victims may have greater difficulty in coming to terms with their victimization. Second, some hate crimes appear to have contagious effects on the victim's community that could lead to a backlash against the offender's community. Third, although racially motivated crimes occasionally receive national media attention, most hate crimes are not serious in terms of the penal law and, therefore, will receive only modest police attention. Accordingly, many have argued that, without special law enforcement programs and laws, these incidents will not receive the resources necessary to sanction offenders proportional to the harm they caused to their victims, nor will they significantly deter future perpetrators or satisfactorily address community fears and victim needs.

To address concerns raised by advocates and others, nearly every U.S. state and the federal government have, over the past 30 years, formally addressed hate crimes in one way or another. Yet despite these widespread legislative activities, there is neither a consistent definition for what constitutes a hate crime nor a standard policy for how law enforcement should respond effectively. States legislatures and the federal government do not agree on which groups to include, what activities represent incidents, or what incident attributes are necessary to label a crime as hate motivated.

Federal Activity

For these latter two issues, the U.S. Federal Bureau of Investigation (FBI) recommends that police officers consider several factors when suspecting a hate crime, including whether (a) the victim perceived the offender's actions to have been motivated by bias; (b) there is no other motivation for the incident; (c) the offender has made remarks directed at a protected group; (d) the crime involves the use of offensive symbols, words, or acts that represent a hate group or suggest bias against the victim's group; (e) the incident occurred on a holiday or other day of significance to the victim's or offender's group; and (f) the area's demographic characteristics suggest bias.

As for defining hate crimes, after debating for several years, the U.S. Congress codified, in the Hate Crime Statistics Act of 1990, the first national definition of a hate crime. Although this act did not criminalize any behaviors or expand sanctions for current offenses, Congress required the attorney general to use the FBI's Uniform Crime Reporting Program to collect from local and state law enforcement agencies (but not from federal agencies) data about crimes showing evidence of "prejudice based on race, religion, sexual orientation, or ethnicity, including where appropriate the crimes of murder and non-negligent manslaughter; forcible rape; aggravated assault, simple assault, [or] intimidation; arson; and destruction, damage or vandalism of property." By 2005, 12,417 state and local agencies from forty-nine states and the District of Columbia voluntarily sent information about their hate crimes to the FBI. During the first 10 years of data collection (1992–2001), these agencies collectively reported 78,390 hate crime incidents.

In 1994, Congress again responded to concerns about hate crimes by using the Violent Crime Control and Law Enforcement Act of 1994 to amend the definition, adding disabilities to the list of factors to consider when deciding whether a crime is a hate crime. Within the same act, Congress also added gender as a protected group when it directed the U.S. Sentencing Commission to enhance sentencing for hate crimes. Yet the FBI states that limitations in federal statutes prevent the bureau from investigating crimes motivated by gender, disability, or sexual orientation.

Nevertheless, in 1995 the Sentencing Commission established a sentencing enhancement of a three-level increase for offenses when the court determines, beyond a reasonable doubt, that the offender selected a victim or a victim's property because of the victim's actual or perceived race, color, religion, national origin, ethnicity, gender, disability, or sexual orientation. Thus, at the federal level, hate crimes do not represent separate or distinct crimes but rather are traditional offenses that deserve harsher sanctions when the offenders are motivated, in whole or in part, by their hatred of a protected group.

Differing Definitions

Besides these varied codified definitions, various federal agencies and their sponsored research also define hate crimes somewhat differently. For example, the U.S. Department of Justice's Community Relations Service defines these incidents as "violence of intolerance and bigotry, intended to hurt and intimidate someone because of their race, ethnicity, national origin, religion, sexual orientation, or disability," whereas the Department of Justice's Bureau of Justice Statistics (BJS) states that an "ordinary crime becomes a hate crime when offenders choose a victim because of some characteristic—for example, race, ethnicity, or religion—and provide evidence that hate prompted them to commit the crime."

In 2003, the BJS began collecting data to capture the occurrence of hate crime victimization across the United States. Using its annual National Crime Victimization Survey, the BJS asked respondents whether they suspected that the offenders targeted them because of their race, religion, ethnicity, disability, gender, sexuality, or association with people of certain characteristics or religious beliefs or because of the offenders' perception of their characteristics or religious beliefs. Between July 2000 and December 2003, the BJS reported finding 210,000 hate crime victimizations per year.

Although the decision to include these categories is nearly universal, there was nevertheless some dispute about who should be included, even among those supporting the adoption of hate crime legislation more generally. Some scholars argued that victims belonging to the racial majority should not be considered victims of hate crimes given that legislatures originally conceived hate crime bills to protect minority communities. Thus, some questioned whether laws primarily intended to protect historically victimized groups should also be used to prosecute them for criminal offenses believed to be motivated by hate.

Although the inclusion of racial, ethnic, and religious groups led to some scholarly debates, the movement to include additional groups, such as gays, women, the disabled, and the aged, created widespread substantial and material controversies. Of these categories, the drive toward including sexual orientation probably generated the greatest controversy at all levels of government. For instance, during the late 1980s, for several years Congress could not pass the Hate Crime Statistics Act, largely because of the desire of its sponsors to include sexual orientation. Although the bill eventually passed, the opposition inserted language that explicitly limited the act's authority requiring data collection.

After nearly 20 years, the same issue continues to arise when Congress debates additional hate crime legislation. Some legislatures and advocacy groups argue that inclusion of sexual orientation will only further legitimize an immoral act. Lawmakers also raised these concerns at the state and local levels. For example, a concern that the legislation may also protect child molesters stopped Texas from enhancing penalties for hate crimes. Similarly, a city council repealed its hate crime ordinance after the African American community protested against the inclusion of gays and lesbians in its hate crime legislation. They argued that the inclusion of gays would equate the gay minority status with the struggles of the African American community. Nevertheless, the Anti-Defamation League (ADL) reported that thirty-two states, and in some areas the federal government, specifically included sexual orientation in their legislation by 2006.

State and Local Activities

Besides steps taken at the federal level, nearly every state legislature and many municipalities across the United States have also passed hate crime legislation. The ADL reported that since the states of Washington and Oregon passed their hate crime statutes in 1981, forty-five states and the District of Columbia have enacted some form of legislation codifying bias motivation and intimidation. Forty-four of these states specifically protect race, religion, and ethnicity. Utah, the only state that does not explicitly state any categories, does permit its sentencing judges and Board of Pardons and Parole to consider the "degree to which the offense is likely to incite community unrest or cause members of the community to reasonably fear for their physical safety or to freely exercise or enjoy any right secured by the Constitution or laws of the state or by the Constitution or laws of the United States."

Besides legislative changes, many law enforcement agencies have placed greater importance on attaching hate as a motivation for criminal acts. The Police Executive Research Forum, the Police Foundation, the National Black Police Association, and the National Association of Blacks in Criminal Justice have supported legislation mandating the collection of information on hate crimes. For example, during the 1980s several large U.S. police departments, including those in Boston and New York City, established hate crime investigative units. By 2003, an estimated 8% of the nation's law enforcement agencies reported having a bias crime unit, and only 6% reported having no capacity to address this problem.

Police departments assign these units with the responsibility for investigating incidents that the responding officers believed were motivated by hate, and these units are often given the responsibility for showing that their agencies give priority to these crimes by maintaining links with populations at risk for hate crimes through community meetings and activities. Some prosecutors' offices have likewise established bias crime units consisting of trained investigators who help police or conduct their own investigations.

International Response

Outside of the United States, definitions of and responses to hate crimes also vary geographically. For instance, the United Kingdom's Crime and Disorder Act of 1998, pertaining to England and Wales, states that a racially motivated crime occurs when an offender demonstrates hostility toward the victim based on the victim's membership in a racial group (defined by reference to race, color, nationality, or ethnic or national origin) or when the offense is motivated by hostility toward members of a racial group based on their membership in that group. However, the British Home Office defines a hate crime more broadly as any criminal offense where the victim or any other person perceives that the incident was motivated by prejudice or hate.

Besides Great Britain, many other European countries have some type of hate crime legislation, including Armenia, Austria, Azerbaijan, France, Germany, Italy, Spain, and Sweden. However, besides Europe, North America, and Australia, there is no similarly concerted effort among countries across Africa, Asia, South America, and the Middle East to codify and formally respond to hate-motivated crimes.

Christopher D. Maxwell

See Appendix B

See also Anti-Defamation League; Discrimination; Ethnoviolence; Hate Crimes in Canada; Holocaust; Ku Klux Klan; Lynching; Prejudice; Victim Discounting; White Supremacy Movement; Xenophobia

Further Readings

Jacobs, James B. and Kimberly Potter. 1998. *Hate Crimes: Criminal Law and Identity Politics* (Studies in Crime and Public Policy, edited by Michael Tonry and Norval Morris). New York: Oxford University Press.

Jenness, Valerie and Ryken Grattet. 2001. *Making Hate a Crime: From Social Movement to Law Enforcement*. New York: Russell Sage.

Levin, Jack and Jack McDevitt. 1993. *Hate Crimes: The Rising Tide of Bigotry and Bloodshed*. New York: Plenum.

Maxwell, Christopher and Sheila Royo Maxwell. 1995. *Youth Participation in Hate-Motivated Crimes: Implications for Research and Policy*. Boulder: University of Colorado, Center for the Study and Prevention of Violence.

Shively, Michael. 2005. *Study of Literature and Legislation on Hate Crime in America* [final report submitted to the National Institute of Justice]. Cambridge, MA: Abt Associates.

Wessler, Stephen. 2000. *Addressing Hate Crimes: Six Initiatives That Are Enhancing the Efforts of the Criminal Justice Practitioners* [Bureau of Justice Assistance monograph]. Portland: University of Southern Maine.

HATE CRIMES IN CANADA

Like most other Western nations, Canada has had its share of bias-motivated violence—what is often called crime—throughout history. From the periodic assaults on First Nations communities, to the riotous attacks on Chinese laborers during the 1880s, to the recent spate of anti-Semitic violence in Montreal and Toronto, Canada may be less welcoming than its international image would suggest. This entry considers the racial/ethnic distribution of racially motivated hate crimes and summarizes hate crime legislation in Canada.

Violence and Race/Ethnicity

As seems to be the case in the United States and the United Kingdom, race and/or ethnicity are the most common motivations for hate crimes in Canada, accounting for more than half of all bias-motivated crimes. Moreover, within these broad designations, anti-Semitic violence appears to be most common (typically 25%), followed by anti-Black violence (20%) and violence against those perceived to be Muslim (10%). The latter has become a particular matter of concern in the aftermath of the September 11, 2001, terrorist attacks in the United States.

Black Canadians

Black Canadians make up one of the largest visible minority groups in Canada, and Blacks are the most vulnerable to racially motivated hate crimes, as shown in survey data, federal Uniform Crime Reports data, and victimization data. However, there is virtually no research on their specific experiences as victims of hate crime. Indeed, a report filed following a 2005 symposium on hate and racism in Canada noted the experiences of the Jewish community, Aboriginal peoples, and Muslims, but no specific mention was made of the Black Canadian experience.

The depth of systemic violence against Black Canadians is perhaps best epitomized by the demolition of Africville in Nova Scotia in 1970. Africville was the oldest predominantly Black community in Canada, founded by former Black slaves fleeing the United States in the midst of the American Revolutionary War. Long characterized by extreme poverty and dire living conditions, Africville was nonetheless "home" for hundreds of residents. It represented a safe haven removed from the potential racist attacks that its members confronted outside the community's boundaries. Yet the city of Halifax perceived the community to be a threat, and it was razed by bulldozer with little or no compensation to those who had made their lives there.

First Nations

The preceding extreme case of the razing of Africville is indicative of the disregard that often frames racist actions—including violence—against Black Canadians. Similarly, First Nations people suffer as a result of the devalued status of their humanity. In the infamous "starlight tours," for example, First Nations men have allegedly been picked up by police in the cold of winter and deposited in remote areas to die of exposure.

Aboriginal people become especially vulnerable to victimization when they challenge the mainstream. Specifically, rights claims have triggered hostile and frequently violent reprisals from what might loosely be called an anti-Indian movement. This has been readily apparent in contexts such as the conflict over lobster fishing in the Burnt Church area. Here, Mik'Maq efforts to practice lobster fishing—a right ceded to them by the federal government—were met with violence from lobster fishers and other community members.

First Nations women seem to be at particular risk. A recent Amnesty International report on violence against Canadian First Nations women revealed extensive deaths and disappearances—as many as 500 during the past two decades—of Aboriginal women in Western Canada, and many of these have gone unsolved. The report included another disturbing statistic, namely that Indigenous women between 25 and 44 years of age are thought to be five times more likely to die a violent death as compared with all other women in that age group.

Asian Canadians

As is the case with any broadly defined population, the diverse and uneven patterns of migration associated with Asian Canadians have resulted in a dramatically heterogeneous Asian "community," embracing dozens of Asian identities, including Chinese, Filipino, Laotian, and Taiwanese. Nonetheless, many of these otherwise disparate ethnic groups have shared the common experience of anti-Asian hostility and violence.

It is especially important to understand the historical continuity of violence against Asian Canadians because this history has shaped both how Asians perceive themselves and how they are perceived by others. Successive waves of Asian immigration tended to create corresponding waves of anti-Asian sentiment. Labor leaders, temperance activists, and agricultural interests pressed the government to react to the perceived threats that Asians were thought to represent to employment (e.g., wage deflation), morality (e.g., opium use), and hygiene (e.g., prostitution).

Thus, Asians were subject to extreme forms of violence, including whole-scale assaults on Chinese labor camps. Such violence seemed to be at least tacitly condoned by exclusionary immigration restrictions, which suggested that Asians "did not belong here."

The legacy of such violence remains today; however, contemporary trends are often difficult to document. There is no national audit of anti-Asian violence. The only information comes from the badly flawed Uniform Crime Reports or in sporadic media coverage of individual cases. However, there has recently been increased attention to, and documentation of, violence against one community often associated with South and Southeast Asians in particular—the Muslim community.

Muslim Canadians

Since the 2001 terrorist attacks in New York City and Washington, D.C., ethnic minorities associated with Islam have experienced increased negative attention from the media, police and security forces, and agitated citizenry in most Western countries. In all such countries, there has been a concomitant increase in the extent of anti-Muslim (or "Islamophobic") hate crimes, racial vilification, and discrimination. The Canadian Islamic Congress (CIC) reported a 1600% increase in the annual incidence of anti-Muslim hate crimes reported, albeit from a low base of only 11 cases in the year prior to 2001 to 173 in the subsequent year.

A survey of Canadian Muslims in 2002 by the Council on American–Islamic Relations—Canada (CAIR–CAN) found that 56% of respondents had experienced at least one anti-Muslim incident during the 12 months following September 11, 2001. The same percentage perceived increased media bias against Muslims and Islam. According to the survey, 33% had experienced verbal abuse, 18% had experienced racial profiling, and 16% had experienced workplace discrimination. Clearly, this group has seen a disproportionate increase in victimization. The CIC feared the possibility of more backlash violence following the arrests of seventeen young men related to a planned terrorist attack in Toronto in June 2006. Indeed, within a day of the arrests, a major Toronto mosque was targeted by vandals.

Jewish Canadians

The Jewish community in Canada has also been victimized by crimes against property such as synagogue or cemetery desecrations. During recent years, however, much more interpersonal violence is apparent. In addition, the opening years of the 21st century have been marked by apparent increases in both the quantity and intensity of anti-Semitic violence, largely as a consequence of ongoing hostilities in the Middle East, as well as an apparent resurgence of far right extremist group activity in Canada.

Another disturbing trend is the growth in campus incidents of anti-Semitism. Institutions of higher learning, in particular, have seen an alarming growth in the amount of anti-Semitic violence, vandalism, and leaflet distribution.

Canadian Laws on Hate Crime

Canadian legal provisions revolving around hate crime and related acts are intriguing for their diversity and range. The nation has followed the lead of other Western nations in explicitly legislating against crime motivated by bias. Section 718.2 of the Criminal Code of Canada allows for penalty enhancement where there is "evidence that the offence was motivated by bias, prejudice, or hate based on race, national or ethnic origin, language, color, religion, sex, age, mental or physical disability, sexual orientation, or any other similar factor." Sexual orientation was added to the legislation in 2003, largely as a result of aggressive lobbying by gay rights organizations.

In addition to this legislation, the Criminal Code of Canada also makes reference to the "promotion of genocide" and "incitement to hatred." A unique feature of this legislation is that it explicitly identifies a list of defenses that the accused may attempt to use. These include establishing that the statements were true and expressing or attempting to establish an argument based on a religious opinion. Furthermore, Section 320 of the Criminal Code provides for the seizure and forfeiture of hate propaganda material kept on any premises for distribution or sale. Moreover, in an effort to contain the spread of Internet hate, Section 320.1 (added under the antiterrorism bill in 2001) permits court orders requiring the deletion of hate propaganda from public domain Web sites.

Aside from the standard criminal legislation, Canada also has human rights legislation. People may file a human rights complaint if they believe that their rights, as set out in the Charter of Rights and Freedoms, have been contravened on account of bias. In addition, Section 13(1) of the Canadian Human Rights Act adds a layer of protection against the online dissemination of hate speech in particular.

Although racial/ethnic animosity in Canada has not reached the proportions it has in regions such as the Balkans and Rwanda, Canada has yet to fully realize its promises to the diverse communities that call it home. Hate crimes are a direct threat to the basic principles of Canadian multiculturalism. They represent significant obstacles to the ability or willingness of affected communities to engage in civic culture. However, more systematic research and scholarship in this area is needed to document more concretely both the distribution and dynamics of hate crime. Learning more about the issue enhances the possibility of effective intervention.

Barbara Perry

See also Canada; Canada, Aboriginal Women; Canada, First Nations; Crime and Race; Discrimination; Ethnoviolence; Hate Crimes; Muslims in Canada; Prejudice; Xenophobia

Further Readings

B'nai Brith. 2005. *2004 Audit of Anti-Semitic Incidents.* Toronto, Canada: B'nai Brith.

Council on American–Islamic Relations—Canada. 2002. *Canadian Muslims One Year after 9/11.* Ottawa, Canada: CAIR–CAN.

Janhevich, Derek. 2001. *Hate Crime in Canada: Overview of Issues and Data Sources.* Ottawa: Statistics Canada.

National Secretariat against Hate and Racism Canada. 2006. *Hate Crimes, the Criminal Code, and the Charter of Rights and Freedoms: Report on the October 23, 2005, Symposium.* Prepared by Charles C. Smith Consulting.

Roberts, Julian. 1995. *Disproportionate Harm: Hate Crime in Canada—An Analysis of Recent Statistics.* Working document of the Research, Statistics, and Evaluation Directorate, Canadian Department of Justice.

Silver, Warren, Karen Mihorean, and Andrea Taylor-Butts. 2004. *Hate Crime in Canada.* Ottawa: Statistics Canada.

University of Ontario Institute of Technology, Faculty of Criminology, Justice and Policy Studies. n.d. *Reading Hate: A Clearinghouse of Scholarship on Hate Crime in Canada.* Retrieved from http://criminologyandjustice.uoit.ca/hatecrime

Web Sites

Canadian Islamic Congress: http://www.canadianislamiccongress.com

HAWAI'I, RACE IN

Race both as a concept and in its operationalization are relatively recent introductions in Hawaiian history. Ideas of race did not exist in Hawai'i prior to the arrival of Europeans during the later 18th century. Indeed, it was not really until after Hawai'i was annexed by the United States in 1898 that the first racial categories appeared in an attempt to racially quantify the Hawaiian population. This racialization has had serious consequences as part of the larger experience of colonization, leaving Hawaiians—even those of mixed race—in a disadvantageous position in the land that is their home.

The Introduction of Race

Once European explorers, European and U.S. traders and opportunists, and Protestant, Catholic, and Mormon missionaries "discovered" Hawai'i, they quickly staked their territory. The results were devastating to the Native population on several levels. First, these foreigners, along with their Christianity and capitalism, brought with them a host of diseases—including syphilis, gonorrhea, tuberculosis, smallpox, measles, and leprosy—that killed multitudes of Hawaiians. Censuses conducted by foreign missionaries document the dramatic decline in the local population from 142,050 in 1823 to 39,504 in 1896.

Second, although alien to Hawaiians, racial categorization introduced by Westerners soon became a part of the foreign lexicon in Hawai'i. Indeed, Hawaiians themselves were becoming familiar with Western notions of race and its connection to slavery as early as the 1850s, as documented in missionary-controlled Hawaiian language newspapers. In fact, by the late 1800s, the last reigning king of Hawai'i, King Kalākaua, had requested a racial taxonomy of Hawaiians from E. Arning, a Swedish physician who had been brought in by the Hawaiian government to improve public health. However, although Hawai'i remained under what Andrew Lind referred to as the "trappings of native control," racial categorizations of the Hawaiian population remained outside of the cultural norms and were unpracticed. Instead, Hawaiians classified the foreign population according to the cultural groups to which they belonged—U.S., British, French, Chinese, Japanese, and so on—but not along racial or color lines.

Even the term *haole,* which has become nearly synonymous with Whites or Caucasians, was not a reference to skin color in its early use. This term stems from the Hawaiian words *ha* (meaning "breath") and *ole* (meaning "without") in reference to people who could not speak the Hawaiian language. *Haole* was applied equally to the foreign population—White and Black alike. The term translates to "stranger" and references all non-Hawaiians in Hawai'i regardless of skin color. Moreover, because most of the early visitors to Hawai'i were light-skinned persons with power, *haole* increasingly came to denote exclusively influential and wealthy persons of Northern European and U.S. ancestry.

During the early part of the 20th century, U.S. military personnel further introduced to Hawai'i an element of racial tension once relegated to the U.S. mainland. U.S. servicemen during the World War II period brought their racist attitudes with them to Hawai'i. Derogatory terms applied to racial groups that were minorities on the mainland initiated the new territory into the mainland's brand of racism.

Hawaiian contact with Westerners had lasting impacts on the Native population. For example, tension between the Native Hawaiian population and the military personnel remains today. There continues to be tension between Hawaiians, who face high costs of living, and military personnel, who enjoy many perks (e.g., beach access) not extended to the local population. Another legacy of Western contact with Hawaiians is the near loss of the Native Hawaiian language, which was banned from use in public schools in 1896 by the government of the newly formed Republic of Hawai'i.

The Plantation Economy

Western contact with Hawai'i also led to the establishment of a non-Native economy (plantation based with sugar cane and pineapples as the primary crops) that would supplant and dominate the local subsistence economy based on fish and poi. Although early racial stratification was not manifest in the local population, a racial stratification system separating Whites from non-Whites soon emerged on the large plantations that had been established by foreign agriculturalists and businessmen.

Not unlike the plantation economy of the antibellum South in the United States, the plantation economy of Hawai'i relied on a substantial and reliable labor supply. With the local population declining significantly and reluctant to do plantation work, planters turned to foreign sources—first to China and then elsewhere—to fill their labor needs. By 1884, the Chinese population in Hawai'i (18,254) exceeded the Caucasian population (16,579) and was second only to Hawaiians (40,014).

However, as a form of labor control, planters who did not want to rely on a single race of workers (Chinese) sought alternate labor groups. In this respect, the Portuguese served to diversify the labor pool. Unlike the Chinese, who were largely male and planned to return to China, the Portuguese brought with them a larger proportion of women, thereby inclining them to become permanent settlers.

Japanese labor was also recruited to plantations to replenish the Native population. Japanese labor appealed to planters for a variety of reasons, including cheap passage, their apparent readiness to learn English, the quality of their work, and their thrifty ways. The number of Japanese immigrants increased significantly from 12,610 in 1890 to more than 100,000 (43% of the Hawaiian population) by 1920. However, fears of "yellow peril" incorporating both the Chinese and Japanese sent planters in search of an additional labor supply, and they turned next to the Philippines. Nonexistent in the Hawaiian population in 1900, Filipinos grew to 63,052 (17% of the total Hawaiian population) by 1930.

During a span of 50 years, the demographic composition of Hawai'i had transformed radically. From the emergence of the first significant Chinese population in Hawai'i in 1884 through 1930, the Native Hawaiian population saw itself diminished (from 40,014 in 1884 to 22,636 in 1930) and replaced by "part Hawaiians" (28,224), Caucasians (73,702), Chinese (27,179), Japanese (139,631), and Filipinos (63,052).

The First Census

The demographic transformation of Hawai'i due to the importation of foreign labor by foreign planters had been under way for 20 years when Hawai'i was annexed by the United States in 1898. The racialization of the population of Hawai'i was almost immediate. The 1900 census classified the population by "color," with categories such as "Total White," "Native White," and "Foreign White" appearing for the first time to sort the newly incorporated Hawaiian population. At this time, the term *Negro* was first introduced to document the Black population in Hawai'i. Analysis of the first U.S. Census conducted in Hawai'i confirms the use of skin color to demarcate racial categories. Europeans such as the Portuguese and Spaniards, along with light-skinned mixed-race Hawaiians, were condensed into the broader Caucasian category.

The detailed instructions provided to census enumerators on how to color code the population correctly reveal a dogmatic insistence on separating Whites from non-Whites. These social practices created two new categories of part Hawaiians: "Caucasian Hawaiians" and "Asiatic Hawaiians." Nevertheless, even those who were part Caucasian were to be designated according to the race of the non-Caucasian parent. Equally revealing, delineations from the Hawaiian monarchy period, which distinguished among Caucasians by national origin, largely disappeared—assuming, as Lind noted, a "racial purity" of the Caucasians.

This attention to what might seem minuscule details was neither accidental nor inconsequential. Well before the United States annexed Hawai'i in 1898, Westerners were already dominating much of Hawaiian policy. By 1852, Westerners controlled thousands of acres of prime Hawaiian land and had imposed a Western property rights system on the use of this land. Furthermore, by the early 1800s, Westerners had assumed important political positions on the islands. Indeed, two seats of the five-member Land Commission formed in 1845 were held by Westerners. In addition, strong-armed tactics by leaders in the Missionary party (Western business interests) forced King Kalākaua to relinquish most of the power of the throne in what came to be known as the Bayonet Constitution of 1887. Indeed, his successor, Queen Lili'uokalani, was deposed as a result of her efforts to restore power to the monarchy, and U.S. interests took over in Hawai'i.

Loss of Public Lands

Still at issue today are the million-plus acres of crown lands—public lands that had been set aside for the benefit of the Hawaiian chiefs and people in 1848 but that were ceded (some argue illegally) to the U.S. government on the annexation of Hawai'i in 1898. One of the stated purposes of this land is the betterment of the social conditions of the Native Hawaiians, as called for by the Hawaiian Homes Commission Act of 1920. The act provided for the transfer of approximately 200,000 acres of land to Native Hawaiians, who were defined as descendants with at least one-half blood quantum of individuals inhabiting the Hawaiian Islands prior to 1778. Lessees of this land—those who could prove 50% blood quantum—are entitled to one-fifth of the revenues generated from this land. In 1992, Hawai'i amended this statute so that lessees could designate their spouses or children as successors provided that they could prove at least 25% blood quantum.

At the crux of the arguments over public lands and the revenues generated from them is the issue of entitlement and ownership. Did these lands belong to Native Hawaiians, or are they (and the attendant revenues) simply to help rehabilitate a dying population? Sidestepping the legality of the overthrow of the Hawaiian monarchy, the subsequent annexation of Hawai'i, and the acquisition of the disputed lands, the U.S. government in 1920 decided that the Hawaiian people never had any right or title to these lands. The land served the purpose only of rehabilitating a race of people who the government concluded were in danger of extermination. This is very similar to the position that the British government took with respect to the Aborigines of Australia. Consequently, in Hawai'i, once land and revenues were defined as an entitlement, the setting of boundaries became increasingly important in identifying beneficiaries. In particular, blood quantum definitions prevailed in the proving of one's Hawaiianness.

Although the 1920 act delineated restrictions on the documentation of blood quantum to gain land and benefits for Hawaiians, it extended access of the land to large plantations. Sugar producers won provisions that allowed the leasing of public lands for indefinite periods of time and allowed the removal of other restrictions that had adverse impacts on their operations. At the same time, stronger restrictions—in the form of proving blood quantum—were placed on Hawaiians, making claim to the land and accompanying revenues more difficult. These disparate actions—providing greater access to corporations while limiting access to Hawaiians—served the corporate and plantation interests rather than help to "rehabilitate" Hawaiians, and indeed it deepened the racial divide between Native Hawaiians and others. Thus, the social construction of Hawaiianness as a race was formed in relation to the shift away from their entitlement to the privileging of White property interests.

Entitlement is controlled by placing the burden of proving identity on the Native Hawaiians, whose culture was steeped in an oral tradition. Furthermore, even when the written tradition was introduced, the record keeping was often haphazard, fraught with mistakes, or (in the cases of flood and fire) lost altogether—with the effect being to intensify the actual and continuing violence of the colonization process for the Indigenous population of Hawai'i. The racialized nature of this requirement is brought into focus more sharply when one recognizes that in Hawai'i White people, unlike the Native Hawaiians themselves, have never needed to prove their lineage so as to claim space.

The cumulative effects of these racial politics have been largely negative for the Native Hawaiian population. Native Hawaiians share similar characteristics to other colonized populations, including high unemployment, negative health outcomes, low levels of educational attainment, and high imprisonment rates.

Contemporary Environment

Data from the U.S. Census Bureau's *American Community Survey 2005* (ACS) are used to obtain a portrait of the demography and racial stratification in Hawai'i today. The figures for this part of the analysis are based on the use of statistical weights to obtain population estimates from the ACS sample.

The population of Hawai'i numbered 1,258,528 in 2005. Table 1 shows the ten most common detailed racial/ethnic categories in Hawai'i. At the time of the survey, 54% of the state's population was non-Hispanic White, Japanese, or Filipino. The 68,090 members of the non-Hispanic Hawaiian population constituted approximately 1 of every 19 residents of the state. An additional 32,385 persons were multiracial individuals identifying as non-Hispanic Hawaiian, or White. The other groups comprising the top ten racial/ethnic categories included non-Hispanic Chinese, Korean, and Blacks along with two Hispanic groups (Puerto Ricans and Mexicans).

Hawai'i, however, is the most racially/ethnically diverse state in the United States. Indeed, more than one-fifth (21.3%) of the population of Hawai'i identified with more than one race in 2005. In the nation as a whole, only 1.9% of the population categorized itself as multiracial.

Table 1 Most Common Racial/Ethnic Groups in Hawai'i, 2005

Racial/Ethnic Category	Total	Percentage of Population
Top ten groups		
Non-Hispanic White	282,802	22.5
Non-Hispanic Japanese	201,461	16.0
Non-Hispanic Filipino	188,643	15.0
Non-Hispanic Hawaiian	68,090	5.4
Non-Hispanic Chinese	55,037	4.4
Puerto Rican	37,325	3.0
Mexican	33,406	2.6
Non-Hispanic White and Native Hawaiian	32,385	2.6
Non-Hispanic Korean	25,643	2.0
Non-Hispanic Black	21,614	1.7
Balance		
Non-Hispanic	279,089	22.2
Hispanic	33,033	2.6
Total	1,258,528	100.0

Source: Based on data from U.S. Census Bureau. 2006. *American Community Survey 2005*. Washington, DC: U.S. Census Bureau.

Socioeconomic Indicators

Racial/ethnic groups, especially non-Hispanic Hawaiian single- and multiple-race individuals, are stratified socioeconomically in Hawai'i along three dimensions of socioeconomic status: education (percentage of persons age 25 years or older who are college graduates), occupation (average Duncan Socioeconomic Index for occupations), and poverty (percentage of population with incomes below the poverty threshold). Included in this analysis are eight non-Hispanic groups: Hawaiian, Hawaiian + White, Hawaiian + Other Asian, Hawaiian + White + Other Asian, White (the largest single racial/ethnic category in the state), Japanese, Filipino, and Chinese (the last three are the three largest Asian groups in the state).

Across the three socioeconomic indicators, single-race and multiracial Hawaiians occupy the lower rungs in the socioeconomic hierarchy (see Table 2). For example, only approximately one-sixth to one-eighth of Hawaiians age 25 years or older from these groups have a college diploma. In contrast, more than one-third of Whites, Chinese, and Japanese have this credential. In addition, single-race and multiracial Hawaiians are employed in occupations that have relatively low levels of prestige, although Filipinos work in even less prestigious occupations. In contrast, Japanese, White, and Chinese are employed in the most prestigious jobs. Finally, single-race and multiracial Hawaiians have relatively high levels of poverty along with Chinese. These groups are two to three times more likely to be living in poverty as compared with Japanese, Filipinos, and Whites.

Residential Patterns

Next, the residential patterns of various groups are examined to assess the degree to which they share similar areas where they live. Sociologists commonly use the index of dissimilarity to measure the similarities in geographic residences across racial/ethnic groups. Data from the 2000 Summary File 1 (SF1) are used to assess the residential similarities among three non-Hispanic single-race groups (Hawaiians/Other Pacific Islanders, Whites, and Asians) across the 217 census tracts that comprise the Honolulu Metropolitan Statistical Area (MSA), the largest MSA in Hawai'i. The index of dissimilarity (D) assesses the degree to which members of the three groups of interest share residential space. The D varies from 0 (no segregation—two groups live in the same locations) to 100 (complete segregation—two groups live in completely different areas). The D can be interpreted as the percentage of members of one group that would need to move to achieve the same geographic distribution as the other group.

The results of the analysis show a moderate level of residential segregation between Hawaiians/Other Pacific Islanders and Asians (D = 39.4) but a higher level relative to Whites (D = 48.6).

In sum, the analysis reported here using U.S. census data for 2000 and 2005 indicates that Hawaiians continue to be a relatively small part of the population of the state of Hawai'i despite their Native roots in this land. In addition, Hawaiians continue to fare worse than other major racial groups in the state, including Whites, Japanese, Filipinos, and Chinese. Furthermore, the data show that even Hawaiians who identify with another racial identity do not fare any better than their single-race Hawaiian counterparts. Last, the Hawaiian population remains moderately segregated from Whites and Asian populations. The contemporary racial taxonomy and stratification observed in Hawai'i reflects the historical forces that established the colonization and racialization of Hawai'i and its people.

Karen Manges Douglas and Rogelio Saenz

Table 2 Summary Statistics Based on Selected Socioeconomic Indicators by Group, 2005.

Group	Percentage of Persons Age 25 Years or Older With a College Degree	Average Duncan Socioeconomic Index for Occupations	Percentage of Persons in Poverty
Hawaiian	13.4	37.8	15.4
Hawaiian + White	16.0	38.7	15.6
Hawaiian + Asian	12.7	40.6	13.0
Hawaiian + White + Asian	14.8	39.4	16.2
White	40.7	48.9	7.5
Japanese	33.6	51.5	5.5
Filipino	16.9	32.4	5.9
Chinese	37.5	46.6	16.6

Source: Based on data from U.S. Census Bureau. 2006. *American Community Survey 2005.* Washington, DC: U.S. Census Bureau.

Note: The Duncan Socioeconomic Index assigns a weighted value to the education and income of an occupation ranging from a low of 0 to a high of 97.

See Appendix A; Appendix B

See also Australia, Indigenous People; Colonialism; Filipino Americans; Haole; Hapa; Hawaiians; Internment Camps; Japanese Americans; Pacific Islanders; Race, Social Construction of; Racial Formation

Further Readings

Dominguez, Virginia R. 1998. "Exporting U.S. Concepts of Race: Are There Limits to the U.S. Model?" *Social Research* 65:369–399.

Kauanui, J. Kēhaulani. 1999. "'For Get' Hawaiian Entitlement: Configuration of Land, 'Blood,' and Americanization in the Hawaiian Homes Commission Act of 1921." *Social Text* 59:123–144.

Levy, Neil M. 1975. "Native Hawaiian Land Rights." *California Law Review* 63:848–885.

Lind, Andrew. 1955. *Hawaii's People.* Honolulu: University of Hawai'i Press.

Rohrer, Judy. 2006. "'Got Race?' The Production of Haole and the Distortion of Indigeneity in the Rice Decision." *Contemporary Pacific* 18(1):1–31.

Ruggles, Steven, Matthew Sobek, Trent Alexander, Catherine A. Fitch, Ronald Goeken, Patricia Kelly Hall, Miriam King, and Chad Ronnander. 2004. *Integrated Public Use Microdata Series: Version 3.0* [machine-readable database]. Minneapolis: University of Minnesota (producer and distributor).

Trask, Haunani-Kay. 1991. "Coalition-Building between Natives and Non-Natives." *Stanford Law Review* 43:1197–1213.

U.S. Census Bureau. 2006. *American Community Survey 2005.* Available from http://www.census.gov/acs/www

Warner, Sam L. No'eau. 1999. "*Kuleana:* The Right, Responsibility, and Authority of Indigenous Peoples to Speak and Make Decisions for Themselves in Language and Cultural Revitalization." *Anthropology of Education Quarterly* 30(1):68–93.

HAWAIIANS

Hawaiian refers to an indigenous group of people, *kānaka maoli,* Aboriginal to the Hawaiian archipelago. The first discoverers of the 1,500-mile-long Hawaiian archipelago in the Pacific Ocean, these Polynesians migrated to Hawai'i by sea, using advanced navigation skills long before the Western world discovered the concept of longitude. There, they survived and flourished for hundreds of years prior to Western contact, evolving a complex system of resource management and developing sophisticated knowledge bases and skills to survive on these remote islands with limited resources. Their situation underwent an enormous change after the arrival of Europeans, leaving them a minority in their own homeland, as this entry discusses.

Cosmogonic and religious beliefs of Hawaiians tie the Hawaiian Islands to *kānaka maoli* beginning with creation or *pō* (darkness or obscurity). The islands were born from *Papahānaumoku* (earth mother) and *Wākea* (sky father), who also gave birth to *kalo,* the taro plant and main staple crop of traditional Hawaiians, and ultimately to people. As such, the histories of the land, the gods, the chiefs, and the people are all intertwined with one another and with all other aspects of the universe. In these beginnings, the archipelago is intimately connected to Hawaiians through genealogy, culture, history, and spirituality. The natural elements (land, wind, and rain) and creatures of the islands are considered as primordial ancestors; they are the older relatives of living Hawaiians. Both share an interdependent familial relationship that requires *mālama* (care) and *kia'i* (guardianship) for the older siblings, who in turn provide for the well-being of the younger siblings.

Significant cultural values of the Hawaiian people center on the importance of *'ohana* (family), *aloha 'āina* (love for the land), and *mo'okū'auhau* (genealogy).

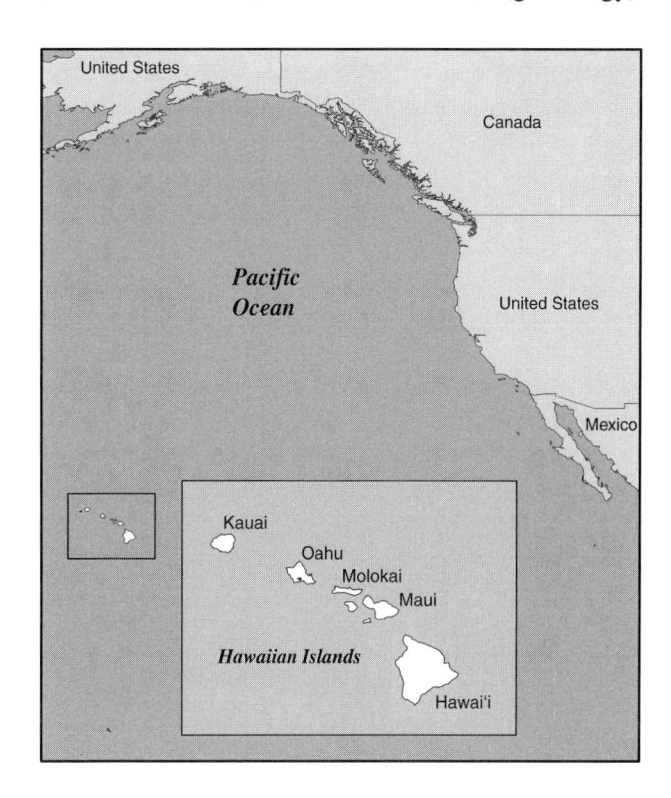

Hawaiians are known for having a deep sense of spirituality and for the special compassion, or *aloha*, that they bring to the world around them, including both animate and inanimate forms of life.

Social Context of Colonization

Historically, the Hawaiian Islands were divided into four chiefdoms until the late 18th century, when King Kamehameha I consolidated them through conquest. United under single rule, the archipelago then modernized rapidly through economic commerce in sugar, pineapple, shipping, and related industries. By the late 19th century, Hawai'i was a fully recognized nation-state with multiple international treaties, including one with the United States.

During the same century, however, several transformations occurred that changed Hawaiian ways and lifestyles drastically. First, Native Hawaiians progressively became a minority in their own homeland. Estimates suggest that the Native population, afflicted by Western disease and (to a much lesser extent) warfare, dropped by at least 90% during the 100 years following Captain Cook's arrival. Figure 1 shows a conservative estimate, whereas other population estimates range as high as 800,000 Hawaiians prior to Western contact. By the end of the century, only approximately 40,000 Aboriginal Hawaiians remained alive. Meanwhile, the immigrant population gained steadily in number, including Whites, who outnumbered Hawaiians by the early 1900s. Today, Native Hawaiians comprise approximately one-fifth of the state population.

Second was the gradual and systematic erosion of indigenous control over the land, primarily through the insertion of Western legal tactics, government, and religion. Gradually, foreigners took more and more control, fully exploiting Hawaiian cultural beliefs in land as collective property. The eventual privatization of land played an important role in the displacement of Hawaiians. From a Hawaiian perspective, it was unfathomable that someone else could deny their rights to place, a precious ancestor, the same land that a family had worked and lived on for generations and generations.

As Hawaiians saw it, they belonged to the land, so they had difficulty in understanding how one could ever own a place, much less sell it like some commodity. Hawaiians regarded the land's true value as the sum of the lives, memories, achievements, and *mana* (spiritual power) of all the generations who had ever

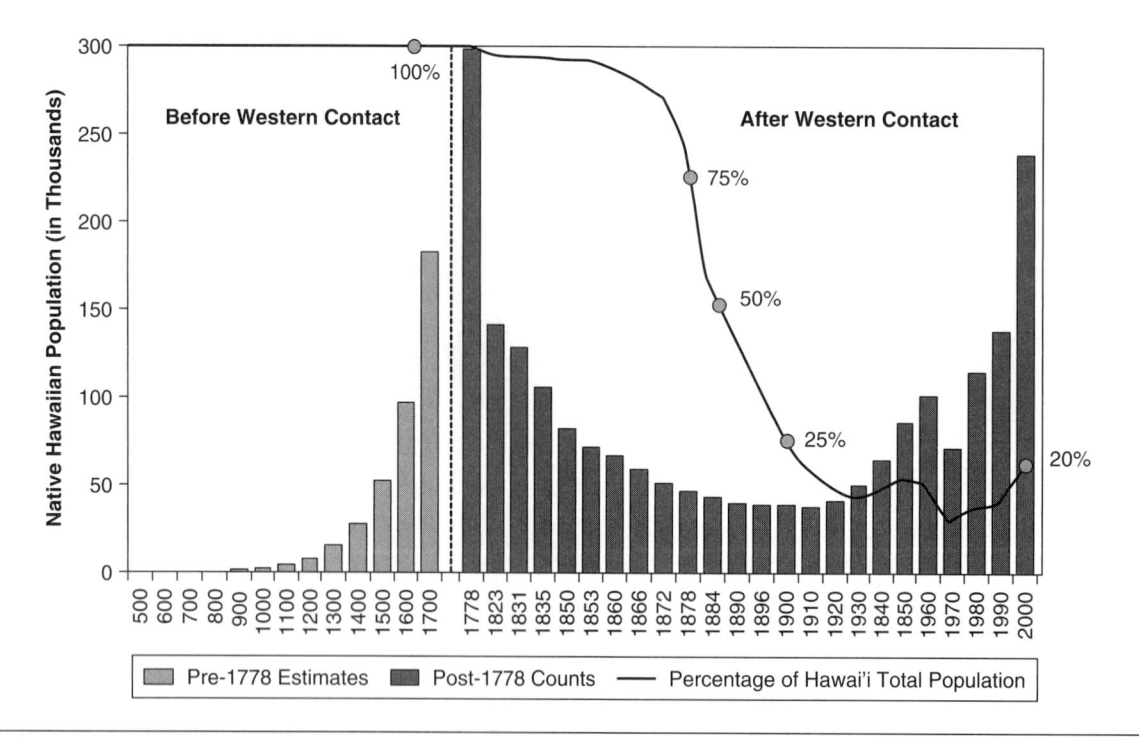

Figure 1 Native Hawaiian Populations Before and After Western Contact

Source: Kana'iaupuni, Shawn Malia, Nolan Malone, and Koren Ishibashi. 2005. *Ka Huaka'i: Native Hawaiian Educational Assessment.* Honolulu, HI: Kamehameha Schools, Pauahi Publications.

dwelled on it. Because most Aboriginals failed to recognize that they needed to formally claim the private ownership of their land under the new system, White foreigners, mostly missionaries and businessmen, rapidly bought up the property where Hawaiians lived and worked, forcing them to move elsewhere in most cases.

These displacing events culminated in 1893, when a small oligopoly of U.S. businessmen and missionary descendants staged a coup d'état, capturing the Hawaiian Queen Lili'uokalani and imprisoning her in the royal palace for eight months with the help of U.S. Marines. The overthrow violated existing treaties and established procedures for annexation. Hawai'i was proclaimed a U.S. territory by Congress via the Newlands Resolution in 1898.

What many do not know is that annexation occurred despite a petition signed by nearly every living Hawaiian at the time (an estimated 38,000 of 40,000) in protest of losing their sovereign nation. In recognition and formal apology by the U.S. government for these actions, U.S. Public Law 103-150, signed in 1993, cites that Indigenous Hawaiians never relinquished claims to their inherent sovereignty as a people or over their lands to the United States. Hawai'i became a state in 1959.

Since statehood, historically high rates of intermarriage and small numbers of full-blooded Hawaiians mean that today's Hawaiians are an almost entirely multiracial population by demographic standards. Nevertheless, more than 400,000 individuals identified themselves as Hawaiian in the 2000 census. The U.S. Census mixes the social issues of racial construction, ethnicity, and culture, and this makes the accurate determination of Indigenous Hawaiians challenging. For example, nearly one-third reported only one race (Hawaiian) despite recent estimates that only 1,000 to 3,000 full-blooded Hawaiians remain alive today. These data indicate the powerful importance of being Hawaiian to the lives of many mixed-race individuals.

Like other indigenous groups, however, Aboriginal Hawaiians face grim prospects in their health, economic, and social well-being. Although assimilation theory would predict that intermarriage brings conformity and improved well-being, analysis of the health and social outcomes for Native Hawaiians tells a different story. For example, by 1990 Native Hawaiian life expectancy at birth continued to be the shortest of all major ethnic groups in the state, where 60% of Native Hawaiians reside today. Life expectancy actually decreased from the average age documented in 1980, whereas other ethnic groups have experienced longer lives and continued increases in life expectancy rates since 1930.

Contested Terrain

A critical area of past and present controversy focuses on the place of Hawaiians in Hawai'i, which is now a U.S. state. Although all other residents of Hawai'i can claim another homeland, this archipelago is the only home of Hawaiians. It is the place that nourishes, replenishes, and sustains the cultural, ancestral, physical, and spiritual existence of the Hawaiian people.

Outside of Hawai'i, a fair amount of confusion also exists on the question of what it means to be Hawaiian. In both the *New Oxford American Dictionary* and *Merriam Webster's Collegiate Dictionary, 10th Edition,* the term *Hawaiian* is defined as "a native *or* inhabitant/resident of Hawaii" (italics added). Both sources list the second definition as "the Polynesian language of the Hawaiians"; this is interesting given that Hawaiians themselves are not necessarily Polynesian according to these definitions. The influential *Associated Press Stylebook,* which is the "journalists' bible," states that all residents of Hawai'i are Hawaiians and only "technically" those who are "natives of Polynesian descent."

Although seemingly innocent enough, the technical issue of Aboriginal Native versus resident has spurred considerable debate in the state of Hawai'i as well as in the continental U.S. Locally, descendants of early European and U.S. missionary families argue that they are just as Hawaiian as the original Polynesian inhabitants of the Hawaiian Islands because their ancestors were part of the Hawaiian kingdom at one point. The confusion is exacerbated by the state's long-standing political rhetoric, which portrays a melting pot paradise composed of racial/ethnic hybrids—with all coexisting harmoniously. This concept traces back to a eugenicist scientific theory prevalent during the 1930s that imagined a "super race" in Hawai'i created by racial fusion. Whether by design or not, treating all residents of Hawai'i as Hawaiian effectively masks the significant marginalization, history, and struggles—not to mention the unique cultural qualities—of *Native* Hawaiians both yesterday and today. It also signifies a dispossession not only of the physical land of Hawai'i but also of its people and their culture.

Naturally, many Hawaiians reject these notions as blatantly colonialist, a negation of the Indigenous Hawaiian culture in favor of a mixed-race assimilated (and cooperative) citizenry. Hawaiians also are keenly aware of the political and economic commoditization of their values and culture by the global tourist industry. One reaction is commemorated by a popular bumper sticker that reads "No Hawaiians, No Aloha." In essence, it protests the co-optation of a venerated cultural value of an existing people while dismissing the existence of the people themselves. Moreover, to avoid being sidestepped as a technicality, Indigenous Hawaiians have needed to adopt the term *Native Hawaiian* (many now use *Kānaka Hawai'i* [the people of Hawai'i]), although the language remains uncontested, Hawaiian (*'ōlelo Hawai'i* [in Hawaiian language]).

What Does the Future Hold?

For more than a century, scholars have written about the end of the Hawaiian people. The plight of this so-called dying race also was depicted in Elizabeth Lindsey's 1995 documentary titled *Then There Were None*. On the one hand, diversity and the threat of cultural assimilation raise questions about the survival of Hawaiians as a distinctive people. Yet today there may be more Hawaiians than at any single point in history.

As more and more Hawaiian scholars enter the discussion about what it means to be Hawaiian, it is quite clear that the answer has little to do with the amount of Hawaiian blood in any individual and has much more to do with genealogy and culture. Native Hawaiians are, therefore, best considered an ethnic group comprising the descendants of the people who had settled the Hawaiian Islands before the first Europeans arrived. Thus, Hawaiians are defined by ancestry, which is an important place of origin in any discussion of Hawaiian identity. The answer, clearly, is that although phenotype (or physical appearance) and lifestyles may adapt to new surroundings and mixes, Native Hawaiian identity continues to thrive uniquely and strongly. It is the continuity of belonging to an ancestral place and people.

Shawn Malia Kana'iaupuni

See Appendix A; Appendix B
See also Colonialism; Haole; Hapa; Hawai'i, Race in; Identity Politics; Pacific Islanders; Race, Social Construction of

Further Readings

Blaisdell, R. Kekuni. 1993. "The Health Status of Kanaka Maoli (indigenous Hawaiians)." *Asian American Pacific Islander Journal of Health* 1(2):116–160.

Halualani, Rona T. 2002. *In the Name of Hawaiians: Native Identities and Cultural Politics.* Minneapolis: University of Minnesota Press.

Kame'eleihiwa, Lilikalā. 1992. *Native Land and Foreign Desires.* Honolulu, HI: Bishop Museum.

Kanahele, George. (1986). *Kū kanaka Stand Tall: A Search for Hawaiian Values.* Honolulu: University of Hawai'i Press.

Kana'iaupuni, Shawn Malia, Nolan Malone, and Koren Ishibashi. 2005. *Ka Huaka'i: 2005 Native Hawaiian Educational Assessment.* Honolulu, HI: Kamehameha Schools, Pauahi Publications.

Kauanui, J. Kēhaulani. 2002. "The Politics of Blood and Sovereignty in Rice v. Cayetano." *Political and Legal Anthropology Review* 25(1):110–128.

Meyer, Manulani. 2003. *Ho'oulu Our Time of Becoming: Hawaiian Epistemology and Early Writings.* Honolulu, HI: Native Books.

Osorio, Jon Kamakawiwoole. 2001. "What Kine Hawaiian Are You? A *Mo'olelo* about Nationhood, Race, History, and the Contemporary Sovereignty Movement in Hawai'i. *Contemporary Pacific: A Journal of Island Affairs* 13:359–379.

Osorio, Jon Kamakawiwoole. 2002. *Dismembering Lāhui: A History of the Hawaiian Nation to 1887.* Honolulu: University of Hawai'i Press.

Pukui, Mary K., E. W. Haertig, and Catharine A. Lee. 1972. *Nānā I ke Kumu* (Look to the source). Vols. 1–2. Honolulu, HI: Queen Liliu'okalani Children's Center.

Silva, Noenoe K. 2004. *Aloha Betrayed: Native Hawaiian Resistance to American Colonialism.* Durham, NC: Duke University Press.

Trask, Haunani-Kay. 1993. *From a Native Daughter: Colonialism and Sovereignty in Hawai'i.* Monroe, ME: Common Courage Press.

HEAD START AND IMMIGRANTS

Head Start is a program that focuses on assisting children from low-income families and was created in 1965, making it the longest running school readiness program. Besides traditional educational skills, it focuses on health, parenting skills, and nutrition. Although it is often considered for its impact on African American and Latino households, the focus here is on its relationship with immigrant households.

Legislative Background

Antipoverty programs were initiated in 1965 as a vehicle to provide the foundation on which the poor could alleviate their suffering and gain a foothold toward achieving self-sufficiency. Federal programs under the umbrella of the Economic Opportunity Initiative (EOPI) included programs such as Head Start, the Community Action Agency, and the Comprehensive Employment and Training Act (CETA). Head Start targeted women and children in low-income communities. Its mission was to provide early childhood intervention to facilitate the transition of poor children to public schools. Open to immigrants and citizens alike, the use of this public service program by women has been pivotal in providing mechanisms for women to escape poverty and access the resources of the larger society.

The prevailing message conveyed to parents urged them to take a prominent role in their children's education and to change their attitude about themselves so that they could present a more positive role model to their children. Parents are strongly encouraged to volunteer in the classroom as a means to reinforce the positive message of learning. Learning is seen to be a lifelong process that does not end when the school day ends. When immigrant parents volunteer, they are active participants in their children's learning process and can continue to stress the importance of education. This message, as conveyed by Head Start staff members, is not only for the children but also for the parents.

Public services such as Head Start, which target poor women and children, attempt to create a means for them to overcome the encumbrance of poverty. In trying to redress poverty, public services have often had the effect of changing family forms. As a part of participating in Head Start programs, parents are required to become involved in program services and policy decisions. This challenge becomes more profound when parents are migrant farmworkers.

Migrant Head Start Programs

Migrant Head Start programs must comply with the same performance standards as do all Head Start programs, and they have the additional challenge of trying to keep migrant parents involved despite the long hours and other challenges consistent with agriculturally based seasonal employment. To address their needs, methods of communication must include multiple options such as visits to migrant camps, personal rather than impersonal written invitations, and interactions with bus drivers and aides. With increased interactions between parents and Head Start workers, several themes became clear to the Head Start researchers.

First, parents have a deep respect for education, and the educators and are hesitant to make any changes. Second, parents who become increasingly involved in the program were demonstrated to be more active in their children's education and encouraged other parents to do so by offering rides to meetings and motivating them. Third, as advocates for their children, parents gain the experience to serve as trainers and advocates for other families. Finally, all of these themes serve to empower the parents toward self-advocacy in other parts of their lives.

Experience in the Head Start program has been illustrated to have beneficial effects for the children and parents alike. The Head Start Bureau asserts that participating in Head Start has an effect long after the involvement has ended. This research includes several longitudinal studies one, three, and five years following children's completion of their Head Start educational experiences. Immigrant parents reported greater attendance in afterschool programs and contact with teachers an average of three times per month. Moreover, parents were more likely to assist their children with different aspects of homework such as asking whether help was needed with reading and arithmetic skills. The Head Start Bureau further contends that this is an indication of parents' self-efficacy increasing with their greater involvement in their children's education through the Head Start program.

Head Start social workers and teaching staff members attempt to accomplish these goals by first encouraging parent participation in the policy changes of their Head Start center through monthly parent meetings and volunteerism in the classroom. Head Start staff members facilitate parents' participation through a variety of workshops and training in the basic skills of participating in meetings; they learn how to use Robert's Rules of Order, how to contact and engage public officials, and what their rights are when dealing with their local public school.

Moreover, Head Start parents foster a working relationship within the community through activism and communication with their neighborhood community developers in target areas. These objectives are considered particularly important for immigrant women, who are just beginning to learn how to navigate their new environment. Moreover, mothers are more likely to attend parent meetings, complete the needs assessment, and take part in parent trainings. These objectives can be instrumental in assisting with the assimilation processes for immigrant women. In addition, Head Start makes a concerted effort to promote cultural sensitivity and to facilitate the transition process for immigrant families.

Contacts with the parents of Head Start children are typically done in the language of the parents, using bilingual teachers or interpreters whether the language is Arabic or Spanish. Bilingualism is a critical component of Head Start nationally. Classrooms themselves have bilingual and sometimes multilingual labels, materials, and books. For example, one might see plastic (play) food of rice and beans rather than a hamburger and fries.

Head Start as a public service program assists women in developing and increasing their social network. By concentrating efforts on young mothers, Head Start initiates the creation of social networks that will assist in developing contacts with other mothers for common goals such as fund raising for their children's centers, promoting safety campaigns for their children's general welfare, and engaging in community activism for their family's well-being to enhance the quality of life in their neighborhood.

Due to the limited resources that many immigrant families have available, public services such as Head Start are often vital for their economic survival. Head Start is a federally funded program that provides early preschool as a means of preparing 3- to 5-year-olds for the rigors of elementary school.

Through an intensive interview and needs assessment process, social workers are able to work with Head Start families to target goals to better the lives of their children as well as the lives of other family members. The services may include English as a second language classes for immigrant families, self-advocacy training, computer training, GED classes, and parenting classes.

The focus of Head Start is to involve families in self-advocacy. An important objective is for parents not only to become more actively involved in their children's education but also to increase the level of participation in their community. Training workshops are also available in multiple languages to better serve immigrant parents.

The education and training received by mothers of children in the Head Start program can be interpreted as enhancements of their self-esteem, whereas the workshops designed to increase their self-confidence aim to foster their building of social networks. Immigrant parents who are involved in Head Start are more likely to advocate for their children when they leave Head Start and enter the larger public school system.

The increasing numbers of Head Start parents furthering their own educational attainment levels as well as finding employment within the Head Start system that their children attended can demonstrate the lasting effects of Head Start on immigrant families.

Sandy Alvarez

See also Assimilation; Bilingual Education; Child Development; Cuban Americans; Educational Performance and Attainment; Educational Stratification; Immigrant Communities; Pipeline

Further Readings

Head Start Bureau. 2005. *Head Start Program Performance Standards and Other Regulations.* Washington, DC: Government Printing Office.
Peters, Barbara. 1998. *The Head Start Mother: Low-Income Mothers' Empowerment through Participation.* New York: Routledge.
Schorr, Lisbeth B., Edward Zigler, and Sally J. Styfco, eds. 2004. *The Head Start Debates.* Baltimore, MD: Brookes.
Vinovskis, Maris A. 2005. *The Birth of Head Start: Preschool Education Policies in the Kennedy and Johnson Administrations.* Chicago, IL: University of Chicago Press.
Zigler, Edward and Susan Muenchow. 1994. *Head Start: The Inside Story of America's Most Successful Educational Experiment.* New York: Basic Books.

HEALTH, IMMIGRANT

The foreign-born population of the United States has continued to grow at a fast rate, increasing from 4.7% of the total population in 1970 to 11.7% in 2003. During a similar peak period of immigration during the early 1900s, the majority of immigrants were from Southern and Eastern European countries. Today, the sources of immigration are more diverse, with the greatest percentage being from Latin America (53.3%) and Asia (25.0%) and only 13.7% now coming from Europe. Breaking down the Latin American group, 10.1% of all U.S. immigrants are from the Caribbean,

36.9% are from Central America, and 6.3% are from South America. As the immigrant population grows, it is becoming increasingly important for health care workers and policymakers to know about the health outcomes and status of this changing racial/ethnic demographics.

Unfortunately, there have been some major impediments to learning about the needs and conditions of health among the foreign-born U.S. population. First of all, there have been inconsistencies with the very definition of *immigrant* used in various research methodologies. More specifically, some research has maintained that once an individual enters the United States as an immigrant, he or she maintains that status indefinitely. Other research has limited the definition of immigrant to include only those who immigrated during the past five years. Some research makes no distinction between immigrant and refugee status, further conflating the definitional issues. Second, some immigrant subgroups are difficult to study. For example, undocumented immigrants have their own health status concerns, but this can be a group whose members are reluctant to speak with researchers. Others have serious language limitations, meaning that they may be excluded from certain studies; thus, the health needs and concerns of an extremely vulnerable population may be ignored. Third, much of the research done on various racial/ethnic groups often does not make a distinction between native-born and foreign-born status. This has been the case particularly for Latinos and Asians. Finally, research instruments have often been created and then used for different groups, making the assumption that what is acceptable in one immigrant community will work in another.

Nevertheless, there are several useful resources for information on the health status and outcome of various immigrant groups. Two in particular are the *Journal of Immigrant and Minority Health* and "advance data" papers from Vital and Health Statistics, a division of the U.S. Department of Health and Human Services, National Center for Health Statistics. These two resources are responsible for filling the gap in existing immigrant health knowledge. Much of this research centers on a comparison of health statistics for the native-born population with those for the foreign-born population. This entry focuses on a general discussion of immigrant health status as compared with that of the native-born population and examines three immigrant subgroups more specifically.

General Immigrant Health Status

Overall, most research indicates that the foreign-born population has significant advantages in terms of various health measures. Although the foreign-born population is poorer, less likely to have a high school diploma, and less likely to have access to health care than is the native-born population, they still appear to maintain a better overall health status than the U.S.-born population. In particular, nearly all immigrant groups are less likely to be obese, experience fewer symptoms of physical distress, are underrepresented in all major disease groups (e.g., HIV/AIDS, cancer, heart disease), and have lower levels of smoking and hypertension. More specifically, native-born adults are 50% more likely to be obese than are the foreign-born adults and are three times more likely to be smokers. Overall, most recent foreign-born persons are healthier than native-born persons, and even immigrants who have lived in the United States for 10 years are healthier overall than native-born U.S. residents. However, the longer immigrants remain in the United States, the closer their health status becomes to that of the native-born population. For example, in terms of obesity, although recent immigrants are on average 2% to 5% lower on the body mass index (BMI) than are native-born U.S. residents, this gap closes within 10 to 15 years.

Several factors may explain the more positive health outcomes of the immigrant population. First of all, in general, the foreign-born adult population is younger than the native-born adult population, The only group this does not hold true for are White immigrant adults, who have a higher proportion of elderly persons (over 65 years) than do U.S.-born White adults. Second, the phenomenon known as the "healthy immigrant" effect tells us that selectivity among those who migrate means that those who leave their country tend to be healthier than those who stay behind. Finally, certain behavioral, cultural, and lifestyle differences may help to account for the more positive health outcomes among the foreign-born population.

Several issues, however, may have a negative effect on the health status of the foreign-born population. First of all, the foreign-born population is much more likely to be uninsured than is the native-born population, resulting in an overuse and need of emergency and walk-in health services. In addition, often because of the lack of health insurance, immigrants are much more likely to lack a usual source of care, with frequency of visits to a doctor's office being much higher among the native-born population than among the foreign-born population. Consistent with this, the longer immigrants remain in the United States, the more likely they are to adopt a regular source of care rather than use emergency or walk-in services. Related to the concerns of lack of health insurance and regular care is the fact that immigrants, because of the Welfare Act of 1996, are unable to receive any benefits under federal means-tested programs, including medical benefits programs, for the first five years they are in the United States. This greatly reduces their ability to seek medical assistance on a more regular basis. Finally, some studies have looked at injury rates among immigrant groups and found that some immigrant groups, particularly Hispanics, are overrepresented among homicide deaths.

Immigrant Subgroup Populations

Hispanic Immigrants

Studies have shown that there are differences not only between the foreign-born Hispanic population and the native-born Hispanic population but also between different segments of the Hispanic immigrant population. For example, Cuban immigrants and Mexican immigrants are significantly different in terms of sociodemographic characteristics. In particular, Cuban immigrants have tended to be more highly educated and less likely to live in poverty than have Mexican immigrants. Overall, however, the Hispanic immigrant population has larger families than does the native-born U.S. population, a third of Hispanic immigrants live in poverty, they are more likely to be undocumented than any other immigrant subgroup, and they have lower levels of education and English proficiency.

For all immigrant groups, Hispanic immigrants are also least likely to have access to health insurance or a usual source of health care. Hispanics immigrants have higher morbidity for infectious diseases, such as tuberculosis, meningitis, and AIDS, than do native-born White U.S. residents, but consistent with other immigrant groups, Hispanics have lower levels of heart disease and cancer. Nonetheless, Hispanic immigrants still have better health than do U.S.-born Hispanics.

In terms of recognizing the long-term effects of living in the United States on the health status of immigrant populations, among the foreign born, Hispanics are more likely to become obese the longer they live in the United States. In addition, their rates of hypertension and cardiovascular disease increase significantly the longer they remain in the United States. As a group, a significant portion of the Hispanic population lives in lower socioeconomic conditions, and this can foster inadequate living conditions and lack of adequate hygiene. In particular, seasonal migrant workers suffer a high rate of work-related injuries and ailments, especially hazardous work conditions, poor nutrition, and lack of health care access.

Black Immigrants

Overall, native-born U.S. residents rate their own health slightly more positively than do foreign-born immigrants. However, Black immigrants are the one exception to this. Among Black immigrant adults, those who have been in the United States longer than five years rate their health less positively than do those who are more recent immigrants. Even more important, Black immigrants have much higher rates of positive health status than do native-born Black U.S. residents. In particular, they are less likely to be smokers or to be obese, and they are much less likely to have symptoms of psychological distress. In essence, the longer Black immigrants live in the United States, the less likely they are to be in excellent or good health.

Several demographic factors are likely to account for the differences between foreign-born Blacks and native-born Blacks. First of all, Black immigrants have a smaller percentage of children and elderly (over 65 years) than do native-born Blacks. Second, Black immigrants have higher levels of educational attainment, are more likely to be employed, and are less likely to be living in poverty. Finally, it is likely that the "healthy immigrant" effect is in place for Black immigrants, with those with health problems being least likely to migrate.

Asian Immigrants

More than any other immigrant group population, the Asian foreign-born immigrants differ with regard to their subpopulations. Vietnamese and Korean foreign-born immigrants have lower rates of positive health self-assessment than do Chinese, Japanese, and Filipino foreign-born immigrants. In addition, a higher percentage of Korean immigrant adults are smokers as compared with Chinese and Asian Indian immigrant adults. However, Asian immigrants are more likely than Hispanic and Black immigrants to have access to health insurance, although among Asian subgroups Koreans are least likely to have health insurance. For all immigrant groups (Hispanic, Black, White, and Asian), Asians are the least likely to report serious psychological distress. Overall, Asian immigrants are healthier than native-born Asian Americans. They are less likely to be obese and have lower levels of hypertension, lower rates of most cancers, and fewer risk factors for chronic diseases.

Again, highlighting differences among Asian immigrant subgroup populations, Asian Indian immigrants are at greater risk for morbidity and mortality from heart disease and diabetes than are other immigrant groups and native-born populations. One possible reason for this has to do with lower levels of physical activity as well as higher fat and lower fiber diets among many Asian Indian groups. These factors have contributed to the higher risks for obesity and non-insulin-dependent diabetes among Asian Indian immigrants the longer they reside in the United States.

Some of the reasons for the differences in health status and health outcome among Asian foreign-born immigrants are related to migration history and circumstances under which individuals migrated. In particular, the sociodemographic differences among the Asian subpopulations affect their English language proficiency, poverty levels, and educational attainment. In turn, these factors affect their health behaviors, access to care, and knowledge of health-supportive services. Japanese immigrants are much more likely to have graduated from high school and to have higher income rates than are Vietnamese and Hmong immigrant adults. This is often reflected in the fact that Southeast Asians have higher levels of smoking, parasitic infections, and tuberculosis rates than do Japanese, Korean, and Chinese immigrants.

Conclusion

A medical exam is required for all documented immigrants and refugees who enter the United States. Grounds for exclusion are based on communicable diseases, which would certainly affect the numbers of unhealthy immigrants living in the United States. Immigrants tend to be in better overall health than their native-born U.S. counterparts. Unfortunately, the more acculturated immigrants become, the more their health deteriorates.

Beth Merenstein

See also Biomedicine, African Americans and; Cambodian Americans; Health Disparities; HIV/AIDS; Medical Experimentation

Further Readings

Dey, Achintya N. and Jacqueline Wilson Lucas. 2006. *Physical and Mental Health Characteristics of U.S.- and Foreign-Born Adults: United States, 1998–2003* (Advance Data from Vital and Health Statistics, No. 369). Hyattsville, MD: National Center for Health Statistics.

Hamilton, Hayley. 2005. *Health and Behavior among Immigrant Youth.* New York: LFB Scholarly Publications.

Kramer, Elizabeth, Susan Ivey, and Yu-Wen Ying, eds. 1999. *Immigrant Women's Health: Problems and Solutions.* San Francisco, CA: Jossey–Bass.

Loue, Sana, ed. 1998. *Handbook of Immigrant Health.* New York: Plenum.

Mahoney, Annette. 2004. *The Health and Well-Being of Caribbean Immigrants in the U.S.* Binghamton, NY: Haworth.

HEALTH DISPARITIES

Disparities in health related to various demographic factors have been documented since data have been collected in the United States. Recently, interest in a working definition for health disparity has sparked attention among researchers and policymakers. Most dictionaries agree that the term *disparities* can be defined as inequality, difference, or something markedly distinct in quality or characteristics. In the United States, disparities may be associated with characteristics such as race/ethnicity, socioeconomic position (SEP), gender, access to health care, and geographic region or area of residence. The main health disparities are associated with race/ethnicity, characteristics that confer advantages and disadvantages to members of one racial/ethnic group over others. This entry discusses the history behind the definitions of health disparities in the United States, the health disparities of interest, the potential causes of health disparities, and the importance of reducing or eliminating health disparities for society as a whole.

Developing Definitions

Definitions of health disparities in the United States can be traced as far back as 1985, when the Secretary's Task Force on Black and Minority Health of the Department of Health and Human Services raised awareness of the health differences between minority groups and the White majority population in the country. The task force was a group of experts formed by the U.S. government to examine minority health problems comprehensively. It uses excess deaths as the primary indicator of a disparity and defines *excess deaths* as "the difference between the number of deaths actually observed in a minority group and the number of deaths that would have occurred in that group if the minority group experienced the same death rates for each age and sex as the White population."

The task force report was motivated by the release of the Department of Health and Human Services report, *Health, United States 1983,* in 1984. Although this report was the eighth of its kind on the health status of the nation, it was the first report to go beyond the Black/White dichotomy by presenting health status information according to ethnicity, namely for Hispanics and non-Hispanics. Moreover, information on Mexican Americans, Puerto Ricans, and Cubans was included whenever the data were available. This report underscored that although the health of the overall population had improved significantly, Blacks and other minority groups were experiencing a disproportionate burden of disease and death.

This differential between minority and majority in disease and death continued into the next decade, as underscored by *Healthy People 2000: National Health Promotion and Disease Prevention Objectives* in September 1990 and by *Healthy People 2010* in January 2000—nearly 10 years later. These reports suggest that the health status of U.S. residents has been improving over time but that this improvement has been unequal across groups. In fact, because of this unequal improvement among groups of the population, the differences between racial/ethnic and socioeconomic groups have increased over time. These differences led to one of the two overarching goals of *Healthy People 2010,* namely, "to eliminate health disparities among segments of the population, including differences that occur by gender, race/ethnicity, education or income, disability, geographic location, or sexual orientation."

The National Institutes of Health (NIH) included a definition of health disparities in its draft for the *Strategic Research Plan to Reduce and Ultimately Eliminate Health Disparities.* The 2005 plan, which started in 2000, defined health disparities as "differences in the incidence, prevalence, mortality, and burden of diseases and other adverse health conditions that exist among specific groups in the United States. Research on health disparities related to socioeconomic status also is encompassed in this definition." Each institute within the NIH has adopted this definition with a focus on its disease orientation.

The Institute of Medicine (IOM) also proposed a definition for health disparities with a focus on health care in 2002. Specifically, the IOM defined health disparities as "racial or ethnic differences in the quality of health care that are not due to access-related factors or clinical needs, preferences, and appropriateness of intervention."

In summary, these definitions, taken together, underscore the differences in disease occurrence and death between and among groups associated with race/ethnicity, socioeconomic position, access to health care, geographic region or area of residence, gender, and age. These differences between and among groups is usually associated with a disproportionate burden of disease and death for one group over another. Finally, despite these definitions of health disparities and the importance of their monitoring over time, the use of a standardized definition of health disparities that fits all possible differences between and among groups in the U.S. population is still to come.

The Record on Disparities

The best-documented health disparities in the United States are those across racial/ethnic groups. Specifically, minority groups exhibit a higher burden of morbidity and mortality (with a few exceptions) than does the White majority. For example, in 2002, African Americans exhibited higher age-adjusted mortality rates for seven of the ten leading causes of death. These disparities have existed in the United States since data have been collected, and in fact the gap has remained the same. For example, in the case of infant mortality, although the absolute difference between African Americans and Whites has decreased during the past 50 years from 43.9% for Blacks and 26.8% for Whites (in 1950) to 13.5% for Blacks and 5.7% for Whites (in 2000–2002), the Black/White ratio has increased over time (1.6 in 1950 vs. 2.4 in 2000–2002). Thus, race was and remains a strong predictor of health disparities in the United States.

Because race/ethnicity channel people into opportunities (or lack thereof) that can either promote or deteriorate health, other disparities related directly or indirectly to racial/ethnic health disparities have been documented, including SEP, gender, geographic region or area of residence, access to quality health care, and age. Evidence suggests that individuals with low SEP and without access to quality health care exhibit worse health outcomes than do those with high SEP and access to quality health care regardless of their insurance status.

The evidence on gender, area of residence, and age is more condition specific. For example, all-cause mortality rates and the prevalence of diabetes and hypertension are higher among men than among women. Moreover, some health-related behaviors are more common in urban settings (e.g., illicit drugs such as opiates and cocaine), whereas others are more common in rural settings (e.g., cigarette smoking among adolescents and adults). These existing disparities due to a particular characteristic (e.g., SEP, racial/ethnic group, area of residence) could cluster additively and/or synergistically across different groups. For example, low-income African American adults without health insurance living in an urban setting will exhibit worse health status than will high-income African American adults with access to health care. Moreover, evidence suggests that people without health insurance are more likely to receive emergency care as their health service and, thus, lack continuity of health care.

In summary, the understanding and elimination of health disparities represents a multidimensional process intertwined across different characteristics of individuals and the environment in which they live and interact.

Causes of Health Disparities

The major contributors to racial/ethnic health disparities are racial discrimination, residential segregation, socioeconomic position, and access to quality health care. Racial discrimination has recently emerged as an important risk factor for health—one that is differentially distributed across racial/ethnic groups and may contribute to elevated health risks for African Americans. For example, recent research reveals that a substantial proportion of African Americans experience racial discrimination, and there is evidence that racial discrimination is adversely related to multiple indicators of health status, including self-rated physical and mental health, blood pressure, and other cardiovascular outcomes.

Racial Discrimination

Although the extant evidence on racial discrimination and health focuses on African Americans, research suggests that the health of other racial/ethnic groups (e.g., Hispanics) also could be affected by racial discrimination. For instance, although research on racial discrimination and health outcomes among Hispanics is scant, the evidence suggests that Hispanics' mental health may be associated with racial discrimination. Specifically, as with African Americans, several studies suggest an association between self-reported perceived discrimination (based on skin color or race) and mental health among Mexican Americans, Puerto Ricans, and Dominicans. These studies found that self-reported perceived discrimination was associated with worse mental health (as measured by depressive symptoms).

Racial discrimination manifests itself not only at the personal level but also at the institutional level. Residential segregation is an example of the latter. Residential segregation was recently described as a fundamental cause of racial disparities in health. Residential segregation creates disparate physical and social environments between minority groups and Whites. Although residential segregation has been higher for African Americans, other ethnic subgroups also are experiencing residential segregation. The differential in the social environment associated with residential segregation leads to restricted access to education and employment opportunities. This restricted access to economic resources has implications for socioeconomic mobility among African Americans and other minority groups. This constraint in social mobility could further translate into conditions detrimental to health. Moreover, the physical environment also could be affected by residential segregation. Specifically, segregated areas are more likely to have elevated exposure to noxious pollutants and allergens that may adversely affect the health of the residents of the area.

Residential Segregation

The social characteristics of segregated areas can lead to the adoption of healthy or unhealthy behaviors. Evidence suggests that segregated areas tend to lack recreational facilities and to be less safe than more racially/ethnically diverse communities, and these are characteristics associated with physical inactivity. Moreover, these areas are heavily targeted by the tobacco and alcohol industries. These products act as buffers for the stress generated by living in disadvantaged and deprived environments. Thus, people in disadvantaged neighborhoods are more likely to smoke cigarettes and drink alcohol so as to relieve stress. Finally, research shows that segregated areas are less likely to have stores and supermarkets stocked with fresh fruits and vegetables than are less segregated or racially/ethnically mixed areas, and this also may contribute to health disparities.

Health care also is affected by residential segregation. In fact, one of the stronger predictors of hospital closures during the 1980s was the percentage of African Americans in the census tracts where hospitals were located. Research has shown that pharmacies in minority neighborhoods are less likely to carry adequate medication for severe pain than are those in more racially/ethnically diverse neighborhoods.

Although evidence for the association between residential segregation and health in other racial/ethnic groups is in its infancy, evidence suggests that Hispanics, specifically Puerto Ricans, experience high levels of segregation. Interestingly, segregation tends to affect the health of all their residents independent of their race/ethnicity. For example, Whites living in segregated areas have been found to exhibit higher mortality rates than those of their counterparts in low-segregated areas. Thus, the deleterious effects of residential segregation on health, although not well understood, deserve attention.

In summary, racial discrimination at the individual and institutional levels, as manifested by residential segregation, has implications for most of the disparities of interest in the United States such as racial/ethnic, SEP, and geographic region or area of residence.

Reducing or Eliminating Disparities

Whereas in the United Kingdom and other countries the terms *inequality* and *inequity* are commonly used when referring to differences in health, the United States has adopted the term *health disparities* for the same purpose. When making the distinction in the use of these terms, it is important to underscore the intrinsic sense of fairness and equity embedded in inequality and/or inequity on health. However, this same sense might not be found when using health disparity. For example, disparities across racial/ethnic and socioeconomic groups have been documented with regard to obesity, the prevalence of which has been increasing gradually throughout the past century and sharply during the past two decades. This pattern has been consistent across all age groups. However, minority and low-income children and adolescents represent the highest proportion of the prevalence.

The extent to which people are obese is a shared responsibility of individual choice and the food environment in which they live. Thus, the following questions need to be asked. What proportion of obese people freely choose to be obese? What is the excess of obesity in the population attributable to living in a particular environment? Who is responsible for the latter? Such questions highlight the debate between personal choice and societal responsibility. This debate raises the issues of fairness and equity, leading to how unacceptable health disparities are and how disparities in the environment may affect everyone sharing the same social milieu.

Thus, the fabric of society determines and shapes disparities in health for disadvantaged groups, namely racial/ethnic or socioeconomic groups, and may have "spillover" to other groups sharing the same environment independent of their racial/ethnic or socioeconomic group memberships. Thus, if the causes of health disparities are social, reducing and eventually eliminating them requires raising awareness of the social determinants of health disparities among the people with power to change the health policy agenda from an individual model to a population health approach. This approach will lead to improving the health of the entire population and, eventually, to eliminating health disparities.

Luisa N. Borrell

See also Biomedicine, African Americans and; Discrimination; Discrimination, Environmental Hazards; Educational Performance and Attainment; Ethnic Group; Health, Immigrant; HIV/AIDS; Medical Experimentation; Native American Health Care; Race; Racism; Segregation; Social Inequality; "Us and Them"

Further Readings

Braveman, Paula. 2006. "Health Disparities and Health Equity: Concepts and Measurement." *Annual Review of Public Health* 27:167–194.

Carter-Pokras, Olivia and Claudia Baquet. 2002. "What Is a 'Health Disparity'?" *Public Health Reports* 117:426–434.

National Institutes of Health. 2005. *NIH Strategic Research to Reduce and Ultimately Eliminate Health Disparities.* Available from http://www.nih.gov/about/hd/strategicplan.pdf

Smedley, Brian D., Adrienne Y. Stith, and Alan R. Nelson, eds. 2002. *Unequal Treatment: Confronting Racial and Ethnic Disparities in Health Care.* Washington, DC: National Academies Press.

U.S. Department of Health and Human Services. 1985. *Report of the Secretary's Task Force on Black and Minority Health,* vol. 1: *Executive Summary.* Washington, DC: Government Printing Office.

U.S. Department of Health and Human Services. 1991. *Healthy People 2000: National Health Promotion and Disease Prevention Objectives for the Nation.* Washington, DC: Public Health Service.

U.S. Department of Health and Human Services. 2000. *Healthy People 2010: Understanding and Improving Health.* 2nd ed. Washington, DC: Government Printing Office.

Williams, David R. and Chiquita Collins. 2001. "Racial Residential Segregation: A Fundamental Cause of Racial Disparities in Health." *Public Health Reports* 116:404–416.

HERNANDEZ V. TEXAS

The U.S. Supreme Court decision in *Hernandez v. Texas* in 1954 grew from the most pedestrian roots— a drunken barroom brawl and a club-footed murder suspect. At the time, the courts were so hostile that Mexicans were not called for juries, and rural towns in Texas were often so inhospitable that the lawyers trying a murder case could not safely find housing in the county seat. The state of Texas had fewer than two dozen Mexican American lawyers in active practice when the crime was committed and had no true legal services network to assist in trying such complex cases. Into this milieu came four lawyers determined to test the idea that Mexican American defendants tried on criminal charges should be entitled to a "jury of their peers," including other Mexican Americans. This entry describes the case, the Supreme Court decision, and its impact.

The Murder Trial

On August 4, 1951, 24-year-old service station attendant Pedro (Pete) Hernandez shot and killed tenant farmer Joe Espinosa during a fight at Chinco Sanchez's Tavern, Sprung's Grocery, Edna, Jackson County, Texas. Within 24 hours, Hernandez was indicted by an all-White grand jury and petit jury panel for murder. On August 8, he was denied bail. During this period of time, John Herrera and James deAnda of Houston were retained as counsel for Hernandez, although Jackson County was well over an hour's trip by highway from their offices. In September, San Antonio attorneys Gustavo Garcia and Carlos Cadena joined the defense team.

On October 4, 1951, the district court refused to quash the Hernandez indictment, not unexpectedly, and deAnda sent his research materials on jury composition to Cadena, who drafted the brief, edited for Jackson County demographics. Between October 8 and 11, Hernandez was tried by an all-White jury, and at the end of the trial he was convicted of murder. On October 11, he was sentenced to life imprisonment. On June 18, 1952, the Texas Court of Criminal Appeals affirmed the judgment, and on October 22, that court refused a rehearing on the jury selection issue.

A variety of factors came together and persuaded the attorneys that they should take the case to the next level, the U.S. Supreme Court, although no Mexican American lawyer had ever pleaded a case before the Supreme Court. They had taken notice of the bathroom signage in the Jackson County Courthouse—the bathroom door read, "Colored Men" and "Hombres Aqui"—and knew that the government attorneys had noticed, and they vowed to include those facts at trial and in their briefs.

Supreme Court Appeal

By the end of the year 1952, the attorneys had made the collective decision to appeal the case beyond the state, and their patience and preparation were rewarded when on October 12, 1953, certiorari was granted for the case to be heard. At approximately the same time, the Supreme Court also granted cert on the well-known school desegregation cases, which had been consolidated and styled *Brown v. Board of Education* and which were being reargued after the death of Chief Justice Fred Vinson. Attention was focused on that set of cases, which had been carefully selected and prepared for the final assault on segregation.

To an extent, the *Hernandez* case flew under the radar, not attracting the massive attention accorded *Brown* and the Legal Defense Fund's long-standing and meticulous agenda. On January 11, 1954, Garcia and Cadena argued the *Hernandez* case. In what was unprecedented at the time, Garcia was given 12 minutes more than was usually allowed for oral arguments because of considerable questioning by the justices. Two weeks later, *Brown* was argued before the same Court by Thurgood Marshall with a much larger audience and international attention devoted to his efforts.

On May 3, 1954, Justice Earl Warren delivered the unanimous opinion of the Supreme Court, overturning the trial result and the Texas Court of Criminal Appeals decision on the jury issue. As a result, Texas juries needed to be reconstituted to select Mexican American jurors along with other Texas jurors, although this was met with considerable foot dragging in many jurisdictions. On November 15, the second trial was held, with Garcia arguing the case. With a jury that included two Mexican American women, Hernandez was again found guilty and was sentenced to 20 years.

Aftermath

Five years later, all of the parties had moved on to other matters. Cadena became the first Mexican American law professor, joining the St. Mary's University law faculty in San Antonio, and then became city attorney. Herrera and deAnda returned to their practice in Houston, and deAnda was appointed to the federal bench in 1959. Garcia fell on hard times but maintained his practice in San Antonio and other cities, including Houston, for a short time as he partnered with Herrera during the late 1950s.

Apparently concerned about his former client, in 1960 Garcia tracked down the whereabouts of Hernandez, who was still serving his term. He lobbied the state parole authorities and organized efforts to write letters on behalf of Hernandez. He succeeded on June 7, 1960, when Hernandez was recommended for parole by the Texas Board of Pardons and Paroles. The next day, he was paroled and released by order of Governor Price Daniel. On June 3, 1964, Garcia was found dead of natural causes on a San Antonio market bench, where he had been unnoticed for several hours. Hernandez's fate is even more obscure, and if he has died, he did so without public notice of his passing.

Before the *Hernandez v. Texas* case, there had been efforts to diversify juries, reaching back at least to the trial of Gregorio Cortez in 1901. In addition, there would be later efforts to strike down unrepresentative juries, including efforts by the legendary Oscar Zeta Acosta in Los Angeles during the 1960s. By 2005, there was still clear evidence that Latino participation in the Texas jury system was substantially unrepresentative of the growing population. But in a brief and shining moment in 1954, Mexican American lawyers prevailed in a system that accorded their community no legal status and no respect. Through sheer tenacity, brilliance, and some luck, they showed that it is possible to tilt against windmills and to slay the dragon.

Michael A. Olivas

See also Brown Berets; *Brown v. Board of Education*; Crime and Race; Criminal Processing; Mexican Americans

Further Readings

Brown v. Board of Education, 347 U.S. 483, 1954.
Hernandez v. Texas, 347 U.S. 475, 1954.
Olivas, Michael A., ed. 2006. *"Colored Men" and "Hombres Aqui":* Hernandez v. Texas *and the Emergence of Mexican American Lawyering.* Houston, TX: Arte Publico Press.

HIGHER EDUCATION

Higher education is a central variable that affects people's ability to gain upward social mobility in U.S. society. Hence, exploring past and present cultural beliefs, policies and laws are important for understanding experiences of minorities in higher education. It is also crucial to understand the changes within higher education that have increased minority enrollment, diversified curriculum, and altered campus climates.

Early Steps

Inequities in minority access to higher education have existed throughout the history of U.S. society. Education of Blacks was barred at all levels during the years of slavery. Yet in the northern states, abolitionist groups created colleges for the education of Blacks who were free or runaway slaves. The first of these was Cheney University, founded in 1837. Cheney and the other colleges founded during this era are recognized as the first historically Black colleges and universities (HBCUs).

After the abolition of slavery, the United States embraced policies to segregate Black and White students in the school system. In the 1896 case *Plessy v. Ferguson,* the U.S. Supreme Court set a precedent for separate but equal education. Although the institutions

Fisk University students. *The junior normal class of Fisk University, Nashville, Tennessee, is shown seated on steps outside of building in the early 1900s. Since its conception in 1866, Fisk University has a long history as an educational institution and has trained a large number of important leaders in the Civil Rights Movement.*

Source: Library of Congress, Prints & Photographs Division, LC-USZ62-112357.

for Black students were theoretically supposed to be of equivalent quality, the small number of existing Black colleges severely lacked critical educational resources.

Nearly 60 years later, the legal segregation of schools was officially ended in 1954 when the Supreme Court ruled in *Brown v. Board of Education* that the segregation of schools based on race had led to unequal opportunities for Black students at all levels of education. Also, during this era, the U.S. government instituted the G.I. Bill, which provided college financial assistance for veterans of all races. Although the G.I. Bill did not fully address issues of Black college student enrollment, this educational funding was an important tool for Black veterans to access higher education.

Affirmative Action

Brown v. Board of Education eradicated blatant segregation, and the G.I. Bill provided financial assistance, but inequities in minority college enrollment continued. During the 1960s, affirmative action was instituted as a tool to increase the numbers of minorities on college campuses.

Affirmative action for college admissions is a contentious issue for many reasons, and the courts continue to debate its use. The application of obvious quota systems in college admissions, ensuring that a given number of applicants will be of a specific race, is one area of debate. *Regents of the University of California v. Bakke* in 1978 was one of the most notable cases debating quotas. Allan Bakke, a White applicant, had twice applied to the medical school program at the University of California, Davis, and had twice been denied entrance. The medical school used different evaluation procedures for White and minority candidates. In addition, the school reserved a specific number of seats for minority students. In its decision, the U.S. Supreme Court ruled that the use of race in college admissions is acceptable, but the Court also prohibited strict quotas intended to ensure minority enrollment.

Two decades later, in 1997, two crucial cases were filed against the University of Michigan. In *Gratz v. Bollinger*, Jennifer Gratz alleged that unlawful preference was given to minorities in the University of Michigan's undergraduate admissions. The university used a 150-point system to evaluate student qualifications. Of 150 points, 20 were given specifically for minority status. The Supreme Court determined that the university's use of points designed for race in its freshman admissions policy was a violation of the Equal Protection Clause and violated the intent of affirmative action.

But the outcome was different in the second lawsuit against the university. *Grutter v. Bollinger* alleged that the university gave unlawful preference to minorities in University of Michigan Law School admissions. In this case, the Supreme Court ruled in favor of the university. The Court asserted that the University of Michigan's law school admissions policy is designed to ensure that applicants are evaluated based on individual criteria and that race is not a defining component of this evaluation.

Racial Inequities in Higher Education

U.S. policies of minority inclusion have increased the numbers of minority students in colleges across the country. During the 1960s, only approximately 8% of

Whites and 3% of Blacks were graduates of four-year colleges. Since then, college completion rates have increased for all races in the United States. Yet the 2000 U.S. Census reported that Whites and Asian Americans had higher rates of college completion in comparison with Black and Hispanic Americans. Only 18% of Black Americans age 25 years or older had a bachelor's, master's, doctorate, or other professional degree. The proportion of Hispanic Americans with postsecondary degrees was even lower at 12%. In comparison, 28% of White Americans and 49% of Asian Americans in this same age group held college credentials.

Although college completion for minorities is increasing, there are some disparities along the lines of institution type, area of study, level of degree, and sex. Many minority students are concentrated at community colleges. The American Association of Community Colleges reports that community colleges enroll 45% of all Black undergraduates and 55% of all Hispanic undergraduates. These figures are strongly related to the lower cost of tuition at two-year colleges, making these institutions more accessible to minorities. The higher percentage of minority attendance at community colleges is a concern, however, because an associate's degree does not provide credentials or earning power equivalent to that of a bachelor's degree.

In addition, the percentages of racial minorities remain low in critical areas of education such as math and science. The importance of including minorities in these areas of study has been recognized, and efforts are being made by agencies such as the National Science Foundation to increase enrollment of racial minorities in science programs.

Race is also an issue when exploring levels of degrees earned. The National Center for Education Statistics reports that for all bachelor's degrees earned in 2002–2003, African Americans accounted for approximately 9% and Hispanic Americans accounted for approximately 6%. The percentages of minority graduates decreases with advanced degrees. At the doctoral level, only approximately 5% of PhDs are awarded to African Americans and approximately 5% are awarded to Hispanic Americans.

College attendance rates also vary by sex category. This is most notable among African Americans. There is a significantly larger percentage of African American women enrolled in college as compared with African American men. The 2000 U.S. Census reported that approximately 44% of all 18- and 19-year-old Black females attended college, whereas only 28% of all 18- and 19-year-old Black males were enrolled in higher education.

Increased numbers of minorities in higher education is important because graduation from college continues to be a crucial tool for enhancing economic and social standing. Black Americans with a bachelor's degree earn approximately $36,000 per year, which is roughly $10,000 more than the earnings of Black Americans with only a high school diploma. Although college graduation is enhancing the economic status of minorities, their bachelor's degree does not ensure the same earnings as does a bachelor's degree earned by White graduates. On average, Whites with a four-year college degree earn $45,000 per year. In comparison, Blacks and Hispanics with a bachelor's degree earn $9,000 and $10,000 less, respectively.

Accessibility of higher education for the economically challenged is becoming more difficult. Most college funding comes from the state level, and the amount of available state funds for higher education has decreased. To offset this, colleges and universities are placing the burden on students by raising tuition. On average, college tuition is rising by 5% to 8% annually. The tuition hikes are moving at a rate faster than the growth in family income, so college tuition requires a greater share of household earnings. This shift is a significant burden for minority students and their families, who on average have lower incomes. To assist with tuition increases, the federal government has expanded its student loan programs. Student loans open more opportunities for minority students, yet these graduates will need to shoulder the burden of debt after their graduation.

It is important to note that the experiences of minorities in higher education vary by race. Although considered a minority group, Asian Americans have much better success in higher education even compared with White Americans. One factor is that average median income is higher for Asian Americans, helping their families to pay college tuition. In comparison, because of lower than average incomes, African Americans and Hispanic Americans suffer more severely as a result of tuition increases. Also, cultural differences may enhance the significance of postsecondary degrees for Asian Americans. Asian American families are often more supportive of educational attainment for their younger generations.

All areas of higher education are affected by racial inequities. According to the U.S. Department of Education, National Center for Education Statistics, minorities currently constitute less than 15% of total college and university faculty members. Many minority faculty members are concentrated at the community college level, with fewer working at the university level. But efforts are being made to increase minority faculty members because they are important for creating a diverse college environment, and many minority faculty members have made significant contributions to restructuring college curricula and creating new pedagogies.

Cultural Pluralism and Multiculturalism in Higher Education

Within higher education, historically Black colleges and tribal colleges were designed specifically to address the postsecondary educational needs of minorities. Cheney University, founded in 1837, is recognized as the first HBCU. The first tribal college, Navajo Community College (currently called Diné College), was started in 1968. In the United States, there are currently 32 federally recognized tribal colleges and universities and 106 HBCUs.

Rather than isolating the minority experience, many people are contending that the racial landscape of the entire system of higher education must become more multicultural. During the 1960s and 1970s, minority scholars and students began to highlight how postsecondary institutions and college curricula created Anglocentric campuses that were biased in defining what constitutes history and knowledge. As a result, multiculturalism was infused throughout higher education curricula. Many postsecondary institutions are now embracing majors, minors, certificates, and individual courses that focus on groups such as African Americans, Asian Americans, and Latin Americans. These programs and courses move the curriculum away from Anglocentric perspectives and provide students with different lenses for exploring college course material and wider social life.

Outside of the classroom, minority students face many other challenges in their experiences in higher education. Racially diverse and inclusive campus climates continue to be a concern. Institutional use of minorities for sports mascots remains a source of racial tension. Some believe that the use of humans as mascots creates discriminatory campus climates, whereas others believe that these mascots are simply images used to increase school spirit.

To improve retention of minority students, many campuses are instituting measures to enhance diversity. Many schools have developed requirements that students of all races take diversity courses for graduation. Also, colleges have created offices of minority student affairs to assist students in their transition to and success in college. Recently, the National Campus Diversity Project researched minority inclusion in higher education and identified the most successful tools for achieving diverse and inclusive college campuses. To support and retain minority students, the report recommended funding for diversity programs, transformation of curriculum, academic support programs for minority students, and continual assessment of campus climate.

Laura Chambers

See also Affirmative Action in Education; African American Studies; Asian American Studies; Biomedicine, African Americans and; Educational Performance and Attainment; Educational Stratification; Fraternities and Sororities; *Grutter v. Bollinger*; Latina/o Studies; Higher Education: Racial Battle Fatigue; Model Minority; Native American Education; Pipeline; Pluralism; *United States v. Fordice*

Further Readings

Freire, Paulo. 2000. *Pedagogy of the Oppressed.* New York: Continuum International.

Giroux, Henry A. and Susan Searls Giroux. 2004. *Take Back Higher Education: Race, Youth, and the Crisis of Democracy in the Post-Civil Rights Era.* New York: Palgrave Macmillan.

hooks, bell. 1994. *Teaching to Transgress.* New York: Routledge.

Howell, Annie and Frank Tuitt. 2003. *Race and Higher Education: Rethinking Pedagogy in Diverse College Classrooms.* Cambridge, MA: Harvard Education.

Williams, John B. 1997. *Race Discrimination in Public Higher Education: Interpreting Federal Civil Rights Enforcement, 1964–1996.* Westport, CT.: Praeger Paperback.

Yamane, David. 2001. *Student Movements for Multiculturalism: Challenging the Curricular Color Line in Higher Education.* Baltimore, MD: Johns Hopkins University Press.

HIGHER EDUCATION: RACIAL BATTLE FATIGUE

Contemporary multiracial and multiethnic institutions of higher education are indeed microcosms of the broader U.S. society, which is still undergoing profound sociopolitical and demographic restructuring from predominantly and historically White to unprecedented levels of racial/ethnic diversity within its institutions, schools, and communities.

The system of legal segregation in the United States that was institutionalized in the 1896 *Plessy v. Ferguson* case ensured that most colleges and universities remained essentially all-White until the 1960s. During the latter half of the 1960s, unprecedented numbers of African American students gained admittance to historically White campuses under the impetus of both nonviolent protests in the South and more violent urban unrest in the North. Equally important in the demographic change from all-White to increasing numbers of racially/ethnically underrepresented students was the U.S. Supreme Court case of *Brown v. Board of Education* in 1954.

Social scientists often refer to the *Brown* case for its impact on racial/ethnic "integration" and "inclusion," but it also represents a theoretical paradox. Although *Brown* had a significant impact in breaking down racial segregation, it did not always have an impact on negative racial ideologies and reactions among White students and faculty members about the presence of Blacks and other people of color. As a result, today's historically White campus racial culture may nevertheless include an ideology of reactionary racism toward people of color that promotes *Plessy*-like environments on post-*Brown* campuses.

Among students of color, the ongoing impact of subtle and overt discrimination may create a kind of racial battle fatigue. This entry describes campus race relations in this context.

Understanding Student Perceptions

Student perceptions of the institutional environment are influenced by interconnected factors—an institution's historical legacy of exclusion, its numerical representation of underrepresented racial/ethnic groups within the institution, and the racist behaviors and psychological climate observed inside and outside of the classroom. The historical legacy of inclusion/exclusion involves resistance to desegregation, the mission of the institution, the policies that are in place, and the rituals and traditions that have benefited White students prior to and since the arrival of students of color.

Despite the increasing numbers of students of color in historically White colleges and universities, the administration, faculty, and student body remain predominantly White. The numerical representation of students of color is one factor that continues to fuel stereotypes and racist ideologies among some White students and faculty members, creating the psychological and behavioral dimensions of the institutional environment.

The psychological dimension considers the individual views of group relations, the college's overall responses to diversity, the perceptions of discrimination or racial conflict, and the attitudes toward different racial/ethnic backgrounds. In contrast, the behavioral dimension of the institutional climate considers (a) the actual ways in which social interaction occurs, (b) the interaction between and among students from various racial/ethnic backgrounds, and (c) the temperament of intergroup relations on campus.

Both these psychological and behavioral dimensions are of primary importance. On today's college campuses, the complex racial ideologies that students from diverse ethnic groups bring with them and the cross-ethnic conflicts associated with such ideologies can erode campus race relations and a sense of community. Although many believe that race and ethnicity are no longer relevant—the color-blind viewpoint—campuses are nevertheless witnessing a growth of reactionary racism among some White students. Reactionary racism is a negative reactionary sentiment that social changes demanded by people of color have "gone too far." This racial ideology shapes the campus racial environment along with the various racial microaggressions and discrimination that students of color may face inside and outside of the classroom.

Racial microaggressions include racial slights, recurrent indignities and irritations, unfair treatment, stigmatization, hypersurveillance, contentious classrooms, and personal threats or attacks on a student's well-being. As a result of chronic racial microaggressions, many people of color perceive the campus environment as extremely stressful, exhausting, and diminishing to their sense of control, comfort, and meaning while eliciting feelings of loss, ambiguity, strain, frustration, and injustice. When racially oppressed groups are in situations where they experience environmental stressors as mundane events, the ramifications are as much psychological and emotional as they are physiological. Therefore, the most common aspect of campus race relations for students of color, according to Chester Pierce, is one of mundane, extreme environmental stress, which creates the conditions that lead to racial battle fatigue.

Understanding Racial Battle Fatigue

Racial battle fatigue addresses the physiological, psychological, and behavioral strain exacted on racially marginalized and stigmatized groups and the amount of energy they expend coping with and fighting against racism. To be sure, the historically White campus is just one of the many lingering environmental conditions that produce racial battle fatigue for far too many people of color. Racial battle fatigue has three major stress responses: (a) psychosocial, (b) physiological, and (c) behavioral. These responses are not separate but rather intertwined; it is now widely recognized that personalities, emotions, and thoughts both reflect and influence physical condition. Among many interesting manifestations of this recognition is understanding the adverse effects of extreme emotional disturbances. Put in the vernacular, stress can make people sick, and a critical shift in medicine has been the recognition that many of the damaging diseases of slow accumulation can be either caused or made far worse by race-related stress. This kind of stress response may be linked to the mundane, extreme racial microaggressions found in the campus racial climate.

The conditions that cause psychological racial battle fatigue can range from frustration to fear, and the body may respond to racial insults as if it were under a physical attack. Therefore, racial microaggressions found in the campus racial climate may be physiologically coded as violent attacks or acts of aggression. Very few clinicians or campus counselors are trained to appropriately recognize the sources that lead many students of color to display a range of physiological conditions such as constant headaches and frequent illness.

Psychological Stress Responses

Examples

Frustration, defensiveness, apathy, irritability, sudden changes in mood, shock, anger, disappointment, resentment, anxiety, worry, disbelief, disappointment, helplessness, hopelessness, and fear.

Physiological Stress Responses

Examples

Headaches, grinding teeth, clenched jaws, chest pain, shortness of breath, pounding heart, high blood pressure, muscle aches, indigestion, gastric distress, constipation or diarrhea, increased perspiration, intestinal problems, hives, rashes, sleep disturbance, fatigue, insomnia, and frequent illness.

Racial Microaggressions

Behavioral Stress Responses

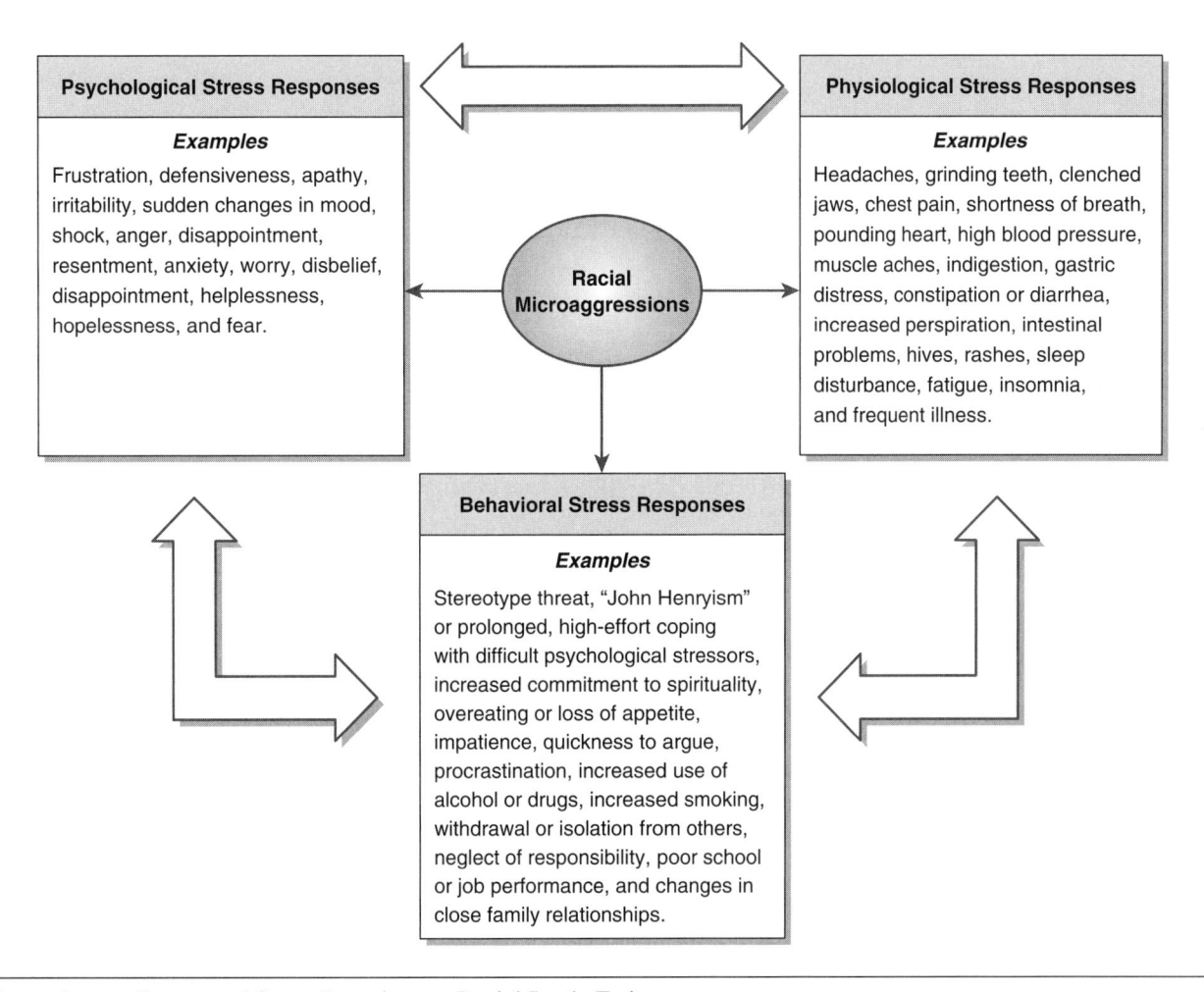

Examples

Stereotype threat, "John Henryism" or prolonged, high-effort coping with difficult psychological stressors, increased commitment to spirituality, overeating or loss of appetite, impatience, quickness to argue, procrastination, increased use of alcohol or drugs, increased smoking, withdrawal or isolation from others, neglect of responsibility, poor school or job performance, and changes in close family relationships.

Figure 1 Causes and Stress Reactions to Racial Battle Fatigue

Microaggressive insults can diminish self-confidence, drain personal and family coping resources, suppress the body's immune system, and deflect important time and energy away from what students of color are really in higher education to do—to achieve academically and professionally. How postsecondary institutions, and the United States in general, choose to address this racial dilemma during the 21st century will determine how the current racial crisis in higher education, and in the society at large, will be handled.

William A. Smith

See also Brown v. Board of Education; Color Blindness; Discrimination; Educational Performance and Attainment; Educational Stratification; Fraternities and Sororities; Higher Education; Institutional Discrimination; Model Minority; Native American Education; Pipeline; *Plessy v. Ferguson*; Prejudice

Further Readings

Anderson, James D. 1998. *The Education of Blacks in the South, 1860–1935.* Chapel Hill: University of North Carolina Press.

Anderson, James D. 2002. "Race in American Higher Education: Historical Perspectives on Current Conditions." Pp. 3–22 in *The Racial Crisis in American Higher Education: Continuing Challenges to the Twenty-First Century,* edited by W. A. Smith, P. G. Altbach, and K. Lomotey. Albany: State University of New York Press.

Bobo, Lawrence and James R. Kluegel. 1993. "Opposition to Race-Targeting: Self-Interest, Stratification Ideology, or Prejudice?" *American Sociological Review* 58:443–464.

Bowman, Phillip J. and William A. Smith. 2002. "Racial Ideology in the Campus Community: Emerging Cross-Ethnic Differences and Challenges." Pp. 103–120 in *The Racial Crisis in American Higher Education: Continuing Challenges to the Twenty-First Century,* edited by W. A. Smith, P. G. Altbach, and K. Lomotey. Albany: State University of New York Press.

Hurtado, Sylvia. 2002. "Creating a Climate of Inclusion: Understanding Latina/o College Students. Pp. 121–136 in *The Racial Crisis in American Higher Education: Continuing Challenges to the Twenty-First Century,* edited by W. A. Smith, P. G. Altbach, and K. Lomotey. Albany: State University of New York Press.

Pierce, Chester. 1975. "The Mundane Extreme Environment and Its Effect on Learning." In *Learning Disabilities: Issues and Recommendations for Research,* edited by S. G. Brainard. Washington, DC: U.S. Department of Health, Education, and Welfare, National Institute of Education.

Pierce, Chester M. 1995. "Stress Analogs of Racism and Sexism: Terrorism, Torture, and Disaster." Pp. 277–293 in *Mental Health, Racism, and Sexism,* edited by C. V. Willie, P. P. Rieker, B. M. Kramer, and B. S. Brown. Pittsburgh, PA: University of Pittsburgh Press.

Smith, William A. 1998. "Gender and Racial/Ethnic Differences in the Affirmative Action Attitudes of U.S. College Students." *Journal of Negro Education* 67(1):1–22.

Smith, William A. 2004. "Black Faculty Coping with Racial Battle Fatigue: The Campus Racial Climate in a Post-Civil Rights Era. Pp. 171–190 in *A Long Way to Go: Conversations about Race by African American Faculty and Graduate Students,* edited by D. Cleveland. New York: Peter Lang.

Smith, William A. Forthcoming. "Campus Wide Climate: Implications for African American Students." In *A Handbook of African American Education,* edited by L. Tillman. Thousand Oaks, CA: Sage.

Smith, William A. Forthcoming. "Racial Ideology and Affirmative Action Support in a Diverse College Student Population." *Journal of Negro Education.*

Smith, William A. Forthcoming. "Toward an Understanding of Black Misandric Microaggressions and Racial Battle Fatigue in Historically White Institutions. In *The State of the African American Male in Michigan: A Courageous Conversation,* edited by V. C. Polite. Ann Arbor: University of Michigan Press.

HIP-HOP

Hip-hop started in the Bronx, New York, as a genre of music based on "DJ-ing," "B-boying," graffiti writing, and "MC-ing." Over time, hip-hop artists addressed concerns pertinent to inner-city inhabitants such as urban poverty and racism in the form of police brutality and racial profiling. Despite its potential for empowerment and emancipation, there are several criticisms leveled against the genre, with the main ones being that it glorifies violence and is sexist and misogynistic. Although these are legitimate critiques, in general hip-hop music and culture offer marginalized and oppressed individuals the space to tell their sometimes horrific stories about urban life, often demonized or unrecognized by mainstream society. This entry looks at the history of the genre.

The Bronx

Hip-hop originated in the South Bronx during the 1970s. At this time, in the Bronx as well as in major cities across the nation, deindustrialization and urban renewal were having a negative impact. Manufacturing jobs during the 1950s and 1960s were low skilled and did not require a postsecondary degree; in addition, they paid well and afforded residents a working- and middle-class lifestyle. However, with deindustrialization, companies were taking factories out of urban areas and moving them to other countries, such as Mexico and India, where cheaper labor could be hired. This produced high rates of joblessness; in the South Bronx alone, 600,000 manufacturing jobs were lost, with unemployment reaching 40% overall and youth unemployment ranging between 60% and 80%.

At the same time, various urban renewal and slum clearance programs that harmed inner-city individuals were implemented. Robert Moses, an urban developer, led the charge for reenvisioning the Bronx. He created the Cross-Bronx Expressway, which allowed travelers to drive from the suburbs of New Jersey through the Bronx and Manhattan to the suburbs of Queens. However, the building of this road displaced 60,000 Bronx residents. Without any say, their homes were torn down and residents were forced to move into public housing developments in the South Bronx.

Many of these apartment buildings were run by slumlords who profited from the residents by withholding heat and water as well as other services. Some scholars note that multiple landlords engaged in chicanery by hiring thugs to destroy buildings so that they could collect on the insurance. Due to the destruction of property, state and federal authorities took the view that the residents in these areas did not want to maintain their neighborhoods. Subsequently, a decrease in social services occurred. This, in turn, exacerbated the marginalization felt by inner-city inhabitants.

The alienation and growing lack of trust for authorities further pushed some individuals, especially young males, to join gangs. Although violent and prone to engage in illegal activities such as theft, robbery, and drug selling, gangs appealed to disenfranchised youth because they offered them a sanctuary. Ostensibly, gangs were "families" that accepted the downtrodden and poverty stricken and understood their plight. Those who did not have the strength to fight for themselves could become gang affiliated and instantly have ten or twelve other individuals who protected them and came to their aid when necessary. Moreover, in many cases gangs provided food, shelter, and income for displaced urban residents. These are the conditions in which hip-hop formed as a music and a culture.

Characteristics and Topics

Two Bronx natives and hip-hop pioneers, Afrika Bambaataa and Kool Herc, were credited with coining the term *hip-hop*. Bambaataa is a former gang member who transitioned into music as an alternative to the violence propagated by gangs. Kool Herc took an intense interest in music when he was a young teen, eventually becoming a disc jockey. Both artists fused various genres of music, such as disco, rhythm and blues, and soul, to create a new eclectic sound that became hip-hop. Influenced by these two individuals, hip-hop was created based on DJ-ing, B-boying, graffiti writing, and MC-ing. Rather than engage in illegal or gang-related activities, some urban youth turned to hip-hop activities as outlets, although involvement was viewed as deviant, oppositional, or illegal by those in the mainstream.

During its early years, DJ-ing involved the scratching, mixing, and sampling of different kinds of music on a turntable with the intent of generating a fun atmosphere and exciting a crowd at a house or block party. There were often metaphorical battles or contests between DJs where each one would demonstrate his or her innovative turntable skills. Usually at parties, many youth engaged in highly competitive and aggressive stylized dancing known as B-boying, also called breakdancing. This type of dance consisted of elaborate footwork, head spins, bouncing around, and the pivoting, twisting, and contorting of one's body. There were also contests between B-boys, some of whom were gang affiliated, to see who could breakdance the best. Winners often obtained money and also garnered respect from their opponents and peers. Youth were often able to resolve their tensions through breakdancing rather than violence.

Another way of gaining attention and respect from peers was through graffiti writing. Graffiti is an ornate, often flamboyant, and ostentatious kind of spray painting where individuals simply write their names or create elaborate murals on buildings, trains, or the pavement. Often, graffiti was used to mark territory, challenge another graffiti artist, or pay respect to someone who died. However, local and city police did not see breakdancing and graffiti as forms of dance or art. Rather, in the case of breakdancing, police officers often thought that youth were engaging in violent gang-related battles. Graffiti was viewed as a costly nuisance that further stained communities that were already an eyesore. Thus, ordinances were passed against large numbers of teenagers congregating on the streets, and other laws made graffiti writing illegal. Breakdancing and graffiti were punishable by fines or imprisonment at the extreme.

The most prominent and well-known aspect of hip-hop is MC-ing, also called rapping. Rappers can be thought of as griots, or storytellers, who discuss a multitude of themes, ideas, beliefs, or happenings via rhyme. Since hip-hop's inception, rappers rhymed about the poor conditions in their communities. Early hip-hop groups, such as Grand Master Flash and the Furious Five, articulated their disgust with their rundown environments and poverty-stricken conditions in the Bronx. Grand Master Flash's song, "The Message," epitomizes urban alienation and marginalization and voices the concerns of an ignored population. The group discussed how ill equipped school systems, burned-down and abandoned buildings, rampant crime, and nonexistent social services pushed them "to the edge." This song opened the floodgates for other rappers who discussed living in the ghetto; rappers became the voices and role models for the young, poor, and oppressed minority populations residing in inner cities across the nation.

Along with poverty, many rappers also discussed racism in the form of police brutality in their communities. According to many artists, common urban residents, along with graffiti artists and B-boys, were viewed as potential gang members or criminals who were treated with disrespect, beaten, or killed for merely being Latinos or Blacks. A plethora of artists wrote songs that accused police officers of behaviors worse than those of gangs, including unprovoked beatings and shootings. They argued that officers exercised indiscriminate mistreatment of minority populations without making an effort to discern decent upstanding individuals from criminals. Indeed, according to some hip-hop artists, racial profiling—the targeting of a certain group based strictly on the color of their skin—originated with poor police–civilian interactions in inner cities. Highly controversial songs, such as "F*** the Police" by the rap group N.W.A., exposed the realities of the tumultuous relationship between minorities and law enforcement.

Criticisms of the Genre

Although hip-hop artists are the mouthpieces for disaffected urban residents, they are not above criticism. Some proponents and many opponents of hip-hop argue that these artists, in painting the grim and dark realities of inner-city life, glorify the violence that takes place in these areas. Multiple artists detail in their songs how they shoot, maim, or kill other individuals. Often, these putative actions are not in self-defense; rather, the violence occurs because an individual is disrespected. Indeed, the top-selling rappers over the past several years—DMX, Eminem, and 50 Cent—all have songs that graphically and explicitly discuss killing other men who have "dissed" them. In promotional ads for his compact discs (CDs), 50 Cent wears a bulletproof Kevlar vest, signaling that he is protected if competitors attempt to shoot him.

Violence does exist in urban areas but tends to be exaggerated in rap music. Yet to young listeners, or individuals not familiar with inner cities, the messages that these songs convey may be taken as reality—precisely the criticism of hip-hop. Many rappers create a facade of brutality and violent behavior. Instead of speaking against violent activity, some artists promote it for record sales.

Another criticism of hip-hop is that rap lyrics tend to be sexist, in some cases verging on misogyny. Although there were undertones of sexism in rap lyrics during its infancy, it took a potent, more explicitly antifemale slant during the late 1980s and early 1990s with the inception of "gangsta rap" and groups such as Too Short, N.W.A., and Snoop Doggy Dogg. These artists' lyrics objectified, demeaned, belittled, and expressed utter contempt for women. Rappers frequently used derogatory words such as *bitch* and *ho* to describe women. Several female rappers provided rebuttals to these types of characterizations of women, but arguably their voices were lost when compared with the sea of male artists who wrote these kinds of songs.

By the mid-1990s, depictions of women took a turn for the worse in the lyrics of artists such as Eminem. On several of his CDs, Eminem presents skits where he kills the mother of his child. He also has several songs where he raps about this act—dumping her dead body in the backseat of his car—and other foul misdeeds directed toward other women. Although Eminem never performed this behavior, this song and others like it are misogynistic; there is a clear unadulterated fear of women that manifests itself as assaults against them.

Chuck D of the group Public Enemy called hip-hop/rap the CNN of the Black community (referring to the Cable News Network). It emerged in the Bronx during a time when there were high rates of unemployment due to a loss of manufacturing jobs, increasing crime manifested via gang activity, and growing substandard housing. These structural factors created communities on the brink of destruction. However, many urban residents turned to the aforementioned elements of hip-hop culture to escape their dire conditions and express their concerns. Several aspects of the music are indeed negative, although in many instances they are exaggerations. With hip-hop being one of the top-selling musical forms over the past three decades, becoming a billion-dollar cottage industry, it is clear that violence, rebelliousness, and irreverence for authority and mainstream norms sell.

Hip-hop has allowed those who do not live in urban areas to become voyeurs by hearing about hard times but not experiencing them. Simultaneously, it allows inner-city individuals to tell their stories—sometimes true to life, sometimes hyperbole. Currently, hip-hop has become a global pop cultural form, allowing oppressed and marginalized individuals from across the world, such as France and South Africa, to tell their own stories. And it all started in the Bronx.

Matthew Oware

See also Crime and Race; FUBU Company; Ghetto; Hip-Hop and Rap, Women and; Jamaican Americans; Parks, Rosa; Racial Profiling; Rap: The Genre; Rap: The Movement

Further Readings

Chang, Jeff. 2005. *Can't Stop, Won't Stop: A History of the Hip-Hop Generation.* New York: St. Martin's.

hooks, bell. 1994. "Gangsta Culture–Sexism and Misogyny: Who Will Take the Rap?" Pp. 115–124 in *Outlaw Culture: Resisting Representations,* edited by bell hooks. New York: Routledge.

Kelley, Robin. 1996. "Kickin' Reality, Kickin' Ballistics: Gangsta Rap and Postindustrial Los Angeles." Pp. 117–158 in *Dropping Science: Critical Essays on Rap Music and Hip Hop Culture,* edited by W. E. Perkins. Philadelphia, PA: Temple University Press.

Kitwana, Bakari. 2002. *The Hip Hop Generation: Young Blacks and the Crisis in African American Culture.* New York: Basic Books.

Rose, Tricia. 1994. *Black Noise: Rap Music and Black Culture in Contemporary America.* Hanover, NH: Wesleyan University Press.

HIP-HOP AND RAP, WOMEN AND

Hip-hop is defined as a culture and lifestyle that originally emerged out of Black, Latino, and Caribbean working-class youth cultures of the postindustrial urban milieu of the South Bronx, New York, during the mid-1970s. This entry looks at the involvement of women as hip-hop and rap artists and discusses charges of misogyny and women's responses.

The Basics of Hip-Hop

The original elements of the culture are the DJ, the emcee, breakdancing, graffiti art, and beatboxing. These elements emerged as a means of vocalizing what S. Craig Watkins calls the "ghettocentric" reality of the urban space. Early influences on hip-hop culture included spoken word poetry, which comes out of the Black Power and Black Pride social movements; reggae music, which was brought to New York by Jamaican immigrant youth; and the rhythm and blues (R&B), jazz, soul, and funk music of the baby-boomer generation. Hip-hop culture is distinct in that, from its origins, it has encompassed a cross-section of class, race, ethnicity, gender, sexual preference, nation origin, and age subjectivities. For example, Kool DJ Herc, one of the founding fathers of hip-hop, noted that without the presence of Puerto Rican and Dominican youth, breakdancing (or "B-boying"/"B-girling") would have been a dying urban-cultural art form.

Hip-hop scholars point out that although the bridging of the original elements into a self-defined culture called *hip-hop* emerged in the South Bronx, it is important to recognize the diverse origin stories of hip-hop cultures as they surfaced throughout urban centers across the United States. Yet these original elements are constant across space and time. KRS-One, one of the pioneering emcees who perfected the art of political rap, extended the elements to include street knowledge, street entrepreneurship, street fashion, and street language. By virtue of commercialization and mass popularity, in particular "rap music" (the delivery of lyrics or poetry by the emcee over a mixed track by the DJ), hip-hop culture has expanded into the broader culture industry that includes television, film, literature, fashion, and advertising.

The culture has been criticized for its presumed glorification of violence, sex, and drugs and for promoting a heightened sense of homophobia and misogyny. The adoration of deviant lifestyles is not limited to hip-hop but rather is part of a larger cultural discourse on U.S. society that emerges across musical genres. In particular, gendered norms of masculinity promote violence and the denigration of conflicting genders and sexual orientations (e.g., women, gays) as a means of reifying what it means to be a man in U.S. culture.

In an analysis of more than 400 rap songs defined as "gangsta rap" (the subgenre of rap music with the presumed overrepresentation of violence and misogyny), sociologist Charis E. Kubrin found that misogyny is not as prevalent within this subgenre as is alleged and that the violence presented is often contextualized within gang culture or as a means of denigrating other men for the purpose of uplifting one's manhood.

Women as Contributors

Within the scope of gender representation in hip-hop, women have been contributors to the culture from its inception. The emergence of strong female (primarily Black) voices in hip-hop coincides with the rap music surfacing in mainstream popular music. The first female emcees, DJs, and rapping crews emerged during the late 1970s and included the Mercedes Ladies and the Zulu Queens. The first females to record an album were Dimples D. and Sha-Rock and the Funky Four Plus One More. Although Sha-Rock was one of the architects of the beatbox sound, it was Roxanne Shante who became the first queen of rap, as noted by historian Tricia Rose.

The lyrical style of female emcees is captured in what were known as "answer records" (songs that responded to male-initiated attacks or beefs). Answer records became a battle of the sexes over lyrical form, mirroring a quasi-heterosexual courtship between male and female emcees. In 1985, Shante's "Roxanne's Revenge" was recorded as a response to UTFO's classic rap song "Roxanne Roxanne". In her answer to UTFO's elusive censure of a young woman's negative reaction to male sexual advances, Shante exuded a level of confidence and braggadocio in lyrical style and security in maintaining a young girl's (she was 13 years old when she recorded the track) ability to resist the negative banter of young men. The mass appeal of Shante laid the foundation for the reception of rappers such as Salt-N-Pepa, M. C. Lyte, Queen Latifah, and Monie Love as well as female DJs and producers such as DJ Mocha, Spinderella, Missy "Misdemeanor" Elliott, DJ Jazzy J, DJ Icey Ice, and Lauryn Hill.

Female hip-hop artists face exclusionary contests, including the battle for representation, positive imagery, and access to the hip-hop game and the process through which artists negotiate the music industry (including obtaining management, recording contracts, and getting album promotions and distribution), while maintaining credibility among the hip-hop connoisseurs who purchase their albums. The increased number of Black female voices in rap music allows a legion of representations of Black female experiences, particularly within independent or underground rap music and other aspects of hip-hop culture. Female emcees and DJs are overrepresented in the underground. Women have a strong presence in all aspects of hip-hop culture, from the production of music, graffiti art, and breakdancing to what many refer to as hip-hop activism or the use of hip-hop culture to promote social justice and educational reforms in urban communities.

Depiction of Women

In its conception, hip-hop music spoke to and for young urban males and was, as noted by rapper, author, and hip-hop journalist Chuck D., the CNN of the ghetto (referring to the Cable News Network). As the music industry increased its interest in signing rap artists during the 1980s, female emcees were often forced to conform to a B-boy persona, which represented a lyrical style, dress, vernacular, and hard attitude adopted by male emcees. Nelson George argued that young male consumers, irrespective of race, do not validate female rappers. This illustrates the grave paradox between the hypersexualized imagery of women by male rappers and what is expected of female emcees to gain legitimacy.

The primary method of gatekeeping that limits access for female rappers is the construction of a hip-hop lexicon that negatively categorizes women as *hoes, skeezers, chickenheads, hoochies, bitches,* and *pigeons*—with each term laced with stereotypes of female economic self-interest, lack of self-worth, and sexual availability. These contemporary urban depictions of Black women are reminiscent of the sapphire and jezebel imagery that defined Black women on the basis of ignorance and sexual prowess, respectively, adversely affecting the avenues for women to get into the hip-hop game.

The other aspect of rap music that aids in the representation of women is the music video. Music videos have the potential to construct narratives based on the persona of the artist and the fabricated visualization of symbols. This visual medium provides the possibility of mass appeal for an artist. Particularly with the command of an eminent video director and the increased popularity of music video programming on cable television, a video has the ability to create instant, but temporary, stardom.

The competition among women for visibility is blatant, particularly on videos of male rappers who are surrounded by scantily clad women—hence the terms *video hoe* and *video girl*. Critics argue that these videos promote negative depictions of Black women, sustaining traditional definitions of Black female sexual availability to men. Sexually explicit lyrics and video imagery sustain negative archetypes and glorify materialism at the expense of Black female sexuality.

Hip-Hop Feminism

Cultural critics such as Joan Morgan caution against attacks that do not take into account the personal responsibility of Black women for their individual agency and complacency. Commentary on Black female rappers often falls short of understanding the complexities of Black male and female relations. Morgan calls for the creation of a hip-hop feminism that articulates the intersections of race and gender to locate the particular spaces within hip-hop occupied by Black women. The complexities of sexism produce an environment in which women are torn between battling male rappers over their misogynist lyrics and tackling outside forces of domination that threaten the existence of hip-hop.

Rose inferred two positions that typify the connection of Black female emcees to this discourse. The first position considers female rappers as feminists who publicly combat sexism in hip-hop and speak out against the misogynist overtones of certain male rappers. The second position regards the lyrics of female rappers as counternarratives on women's experience in hip-hop that serve to indirectly dispute the mischaracterization of women's role in hip-hop. These positions create a polar effect that places both Black male and Black female rappers at conflicting ends of a dichotomous debate, creating hostile relations within the hip-hop community.

Gendered power relations, coupled with attempts by dominant media sources to co-opt the critiques of female emcees as a means of censuring Black male rappers, further silence the voices of Black female rappers by consistently judging them based on the standards for male rappers. Female emcees speak to the larger institutional systems of racial and gender oppression that affect young Black women. Their lyrical discourse is not restricted to the sexist exclusions of the hip-hop community but rather encompasses more complex societal forces that manifest in the music. Rose referred to this as the "hidden politics" of hip-hop music that encapsulates concerns over public access to community resources and the construction of Black expression. For Black female rappers, this translates into a discourse on the production of sexism within hip-hop as a manifestation of the larger society and not a vacuous examination of the sexism in the industry exclusively.

Rap emcee, activist, and author Sister Souljah argued that women need to overcome their competitive nature first before a feminist collective can be established. She urged women to come together to discuss sexism in the industry and come up with a plan of action to improve the representation of women in hip-hop. The foremothers of sexually explicit rap, including Oaktown 357, B.W.P., and H.W.A., discussed the power of sex and sexual expression; however, these female rappers and their progeny, including Lil' Kim, Foxy Brown, Solé, and Eve, do not suggest the use of sex as a means of advancing one's career; rather, they suggest the use of sex as a mode of personal fulfillment and self-awareness. The existence of a strong female presence in hip-hop that displays diverse images of self-defined Black female sexuality is part of a larger social discourse on breaking down institutional and psychological systems of oppression and eliminating barriers to Black female visibility and collectivity.

Mako Fitts

See also Feminism, Black; Hip-Hop; Rap: The Genre; Rap: The Movement

Further Readings

Chang, Jeff. 2005. *Can't Stop, Won't Stop: A History of the Hip-Hop Generation*. New York: St. Martin's.

Forman, Murray and Mark Anthony Neal, eds. 2004. *That's the Joint! The Hip-Hop Studies Reader*. New York: Routledge.

George, Nelson. 1996. *Hip Hop America*. New York: Penguin.

Kitwana, Bakari. 2003. *The Hip Hop Generation: Young Blacks and the Crisis of African American Culture*. New York: Basic Civitas Books.

Kubrin, Charis E. 2005. "Gangstas, Thugs, and Hustlas: Identity and the Code of the Street in Rap Music." *Social Problems* 52:360–378.

Morgan, Joan. 1999. *When Chickenheads Come Home to Roost: A Hip-Hop Feminist Breaks It Down*. New York: Touchstone.

Pough, Gwendolyn D. 2004. *Check It while You Wreck It: Black Womanhood, Hip Hop Culture, and the Public Sphere.* Boston, MA: Northeastern University Press.

Rose, Tricia. 1994. *Black Noise: Rap Music and Black Culture in Contemporary America.* Hanover, NH: Wesleyan University Press.

Watkins, S. Craig. 2006. *Hip Hop Matters: Politics, Pop Culture, and the Struggle for the Soul of a Movement.* Boston, MA: Beacon.

HISPANICS

During the early 20th century, the U.S. government adopted the panethnic term *Hispanic* to describe descendants from Latin America, the Caribbean, and other Spanish-speaking countries, territories, and colonies. Hispanics, or Latinos, represent the largest ethnic minority group in the United States, making up approximately 12.5% of the current population. Since its incorporation into the U.S. Census, *Hispanic* has become a highly debated, problematic, and politicized term. The main arguments against the term stress its panethnic emphasis, which oversimplifies the variety of differences among people who represent a multitude of Spanish-speaking nationalities and which also ignores ethnically distinct residential settlement patterns of different national groups in the four main regions of the United States. Others point out that the term emphasizes the Iberian Spanish heritage and excludes the Amerindian, African, and Asian roots of a panethnic group whose members can be of any race. It represents the largest multiracial contingency of any group worldwide.

Government Definition

Hispanic is a panethnic minority group identifier and category; the term is derived primarily from Spain, whereas the group includes the intermixing of African, Indigenous, Asian, and other European peoples. In general, a person of Latin American descent whose country of origin was a former colony of Spain is identified as Hispanic by the U.S. government. The federal government traditionally uses the term as an ethnic category rather than a racial category for statistical purposes because members of this group may come from any racial background. Sociologist Alejandro Portes noted that the term reflects a denationalized identification with racial/ethnic minorities in the United States and self-conscious differences in relation to the White Anglo population.

The term *Hispanic* has been employed by the U.S. government at least since the 1920s. Sociologist Clara Rodriguez found that between 1940 and 1970, the classification of Hispanic has fluctuated in the U.S. Census because of racial classifications and, more important, because of cultural criteria such as language (1940), surname (1950 and 1960), and origin (1970). During the 1970s, the U.S. Census institutionalized it as a category for all populations from any Spanish-speaking country of the Caribbean, Central or South America, or Spain, and a common category became standardized and widespread on a national basis.

The 1980s appeared to be the defining decade for U.S. Census and its use of the term *Hispanic.* For the 1980 census, people were finally able to identify themselves either as of Spanish-speaking origin or descent or as one of the specific Latin American nationalities. With these new categorical options, the number of people who categorized themselves as Hispanic increased by more than 50%. During the 1990s, the term came to represent the highlighted commonalities of a panethnic consciousness. The arbitrary nature of the label, however, started to become problematic for census use. In particular, many persons of Latin American or Spanish origin continued to select "some other race" to best describe themselves. Nationality was the defining category for many people of Latin American or Spanish descent, where more people chose to identify specifically as El Salvadoran or Dominican, for example, rather than merely as Hispanic.

In 1993, a proposal was issued to the U.S. government to include "Hispanic" specifically as a racial category. If approved, all persons identified as Hispanics would become one race. In previous attempts, the proposal was strongly denied. However, the 1993 proposal was seriously considered due to the shifting demographic and social changes taking place nationwide as more people emigrated to the United States from Latin America, particularly from Mexico. Making "Hispanic" a racial category on the census would help to reduce the number of persons choosing the "other race" category. One of the key findings from the government studies was that people who are identified as Hispanic will still choose more than one category even when instructed not to do so. Eventually, the proposal was dismissed and "Hispanic" was not incorporated as a racial category.

Changes were instituted, however. The term *Latino* appeared on the census form for the first time in 2000.

The option to select more than one race on the census form was also introduced in 2000, and this allowed those who were designated as Hispanic to identify their ethnicity and their racially mixed backgrounds without needing to delineate their race(s) for their ethnicity and vice versa.

In 2003, the U.S. Census issued a statement, "Guidance on the Presentation and Comparison of Race and Hispanic Origin Data." Recognizing that some researchers and government agencies use the term *Hispanic* to describe a separate racial category, the census bureau issued the explanation for how the term is used in government census data. Principally, the issued statement confirmed that *race* and *Hispanic origin* are two separate concepts in the federal statistical system. Furthermore, *Hispanic* can be used to describe people of any race, people in each race group may be either Hispanic or not Hispanic, and people have two attributes for the purposes of the census: their race(s) and whether or not they are Hispanic. The issued statement emphasized the concern for "overlapping" and subsequent reporting errors. The statement specified that the overlap of race and Hispanic origin is the main comparability issue, the "more than one race" option increases possible numbers and overlapping groups, the complete cross-tabulation of race and Hispanic origin data is problematic, and comparability of data on race and Hispanic origin is affected by several other factors.

The term *Hispanic* not only is a government-issued panethnic term in its own right but also is a highly loaded social label that conjures debates, invokes political awareness, serves as a divisive internal tool pitting one nationality against or in comparison with another, and confirms the assertion that race, as operationalized in the United States, is indeed a social construction that is ever changing to meet the perceptions of societal needs.

Population

Hispanics comprise the fastest growing ethnic minority group in the United States, making up approximately 12.5% of the current population broken down as follows: 7.5% of Mexican origin, 1.2% Puerto Ricans, and 0.4% Cubans, with "other Hispanics" comprising the remainder. The median age of all Hispanics is 27 years. Comparatively high Hispanic fertility rates and substantially increased rates of immigration from Latin America, especially from Mexico, are likely to sustain Hispanic population growth.

By 2015, the Hispanic population in the United States is expected to reach 44 million, and some demographers calculate that the Hispanic population is already at 40 million. This estimate does not include or account for approximately 12 million legally undocumented persons predominantly of Mexican or Central American origin who currently work and reside in the United States. By 2050, there are expected to be 81 million Hispanics, of either legal or undocumented status, living in the United States. With this projected estimate, Hispanics will account for more than one-quarter of the total U.S. population—the largest panethnic group.

Panethnicity

Himilce Novas proposed that as a label, *Hispanic* combines second-generation natives and their offspring, foreigners, and political refugees under one ethnic umbrella. Yet the Hispanic category includes representatives from more than 20 nations. *Hispanic* is a panethnic term and includes people whose ancestors hail from Argentina, Bolivia, Chile, Colombia, Costa Rica, Cuba, the Dominican Republic, Ecuador, El Salvador, Guatemala, Honduras, Mexico, Nicaragua, Panama, Paraguay, Peru, Puerto Rico, Uruguay, or Venezuela. The U.S. Census Bureau also includes Spanish Americans whose ancestry is directly from Spain, although this group is also referred to as European, or White, by other governmental agencies and research organizations. The term *Hispanic* has helped the panethnic group to obtain political clout and encourages government representatives to see Hispanics as a viable voting bloc.

Differential Residential Settlement Patterns

To refer to Spanish-speaking people as a single ethnic category is misleading because it obscures the diversity of historical, cultural, and geographic backgrounds among them. The various ethnic groups also differ substantially in their socioeconomic status and their regional distribution in the United States. The diverse settlement patterns and immigration experiences of Mexicans, Puerto Ricans, Cubans, and other Hispanic groups have created distinct subpopulations with discernible demographic and economic characteristics across the United States. Many subpopulations of Hispanics develop and transform residential communities into barrios or ethnic neighborhoods.

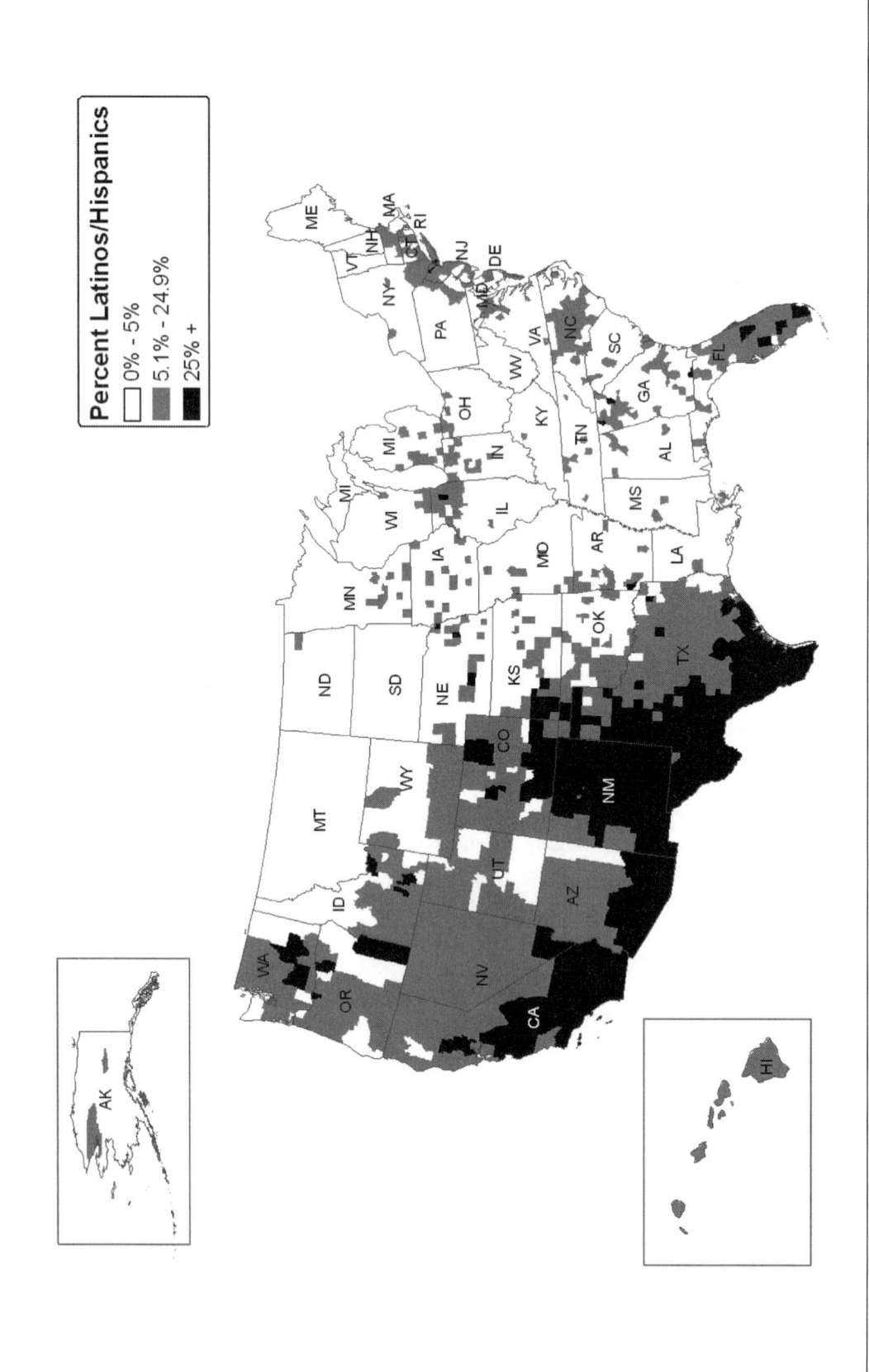

Figure 1 Estimated Percent of Latinos/Hispanics in the United States in 2003.

Source: Developed by Egan Urban Center, DePaul University, Chicago, from U.S. Census data, *County Population Estimates by Age, Sex, Race, and Hispanic Origin*, July 1, 2005; used by permission.

Regionally, more than three-quarters of Hispanics live in the western or southern sections of the United States. Half of all Hispanics live in just two states: California and Texas. Sorted by national background, Mexicans reside predominantly in the West, whereas the majority of Puerto Ricans and Dominicans reside in the Northeast and the majority of Cubans reside in the South, particularly in South Florida. Central and South Americans reside predominantly on the West Coast, particularly in California, or in the Northeast and the Mid-Atlantic region, particularly in Washington, D.C., and northern Virginia.

Hispanic ethnic enclaves and the Spanish language thrive in different regions of the country, and the different nationalities bring a different kind of Hispanic "experience" to each of the respective areas. Placing all Latin American and Spanish-speaking groups under one ethnic label masks the distinct residential distributions and subsequent life opportunities presented to various national groups, and this in turn will affect the socioeconomic status of these particular groups.

The *Hispanic* Problem

In Latin America, people do not refer to themselves as Hispanic. National identity takes precedence. Many Americans prefer the term *Latino* when describing those of Latin American, Amerindian, African, or Asian descent. Many persons are colonial minorities, such as Black Hispanics and others from the Spanish-speaking Caribbean Islands, whereas some have direct European lineage, such as Argentines and other South American nationalities. Some believe that placing various nationalities into one generic group, whether in the United States or in Latin America, blurs the colonial model. They argue that the systematic oppression and racist experiences many members of these colonized groups routinely encounter are ignored through the panethnic use.

Various modes of incorporation and the assimilation patterns of different groups into mainstream U.S. society are consolidated by the term *Hispanic*. All of the nuances of citizenship, refugees and asylum seekers, and pigmentocracy within Spanish-speaking nations are lost.

Some see the term *Hispanic* as translating to "His PANIC," and they argue that this is an overt racial epithet. Suzanne Oboler called *Hispanic* a historical term that draws attention to the European colonial past while diverting attention away from the long-standing historical assertion of U.S. domination and control over Latin America as well as Latin Americans in the United States. Some believe that it places a premium on *White* over *Black*. Others see it as offensive to conglomerate people into one group without taking the specific racial, ethnic, and political dimensions into account. Hispanics come to represent a multiracial ethnic group where the label appears to require modification. However, the historical and bureaucratized roots of the term run deep.

Judith A. Perez

See Appendix A; Appendix B

See also Aztlán; Barrio; Borderlands; Brazilian Americans; Central Americans in the United States; Cuban Americans; Dominican Americans; Feminism, Latina; Film, Latino; *Hispanic* Versus *Latino*; Honduran Americans; *La Raza*; Mexican Americans; Panamanian Americans; Panethnic Identity; Peruvian Americans; Puerto Rican Americans; Salvadoran Americans; South Americans in the United States; Spanglish

Further Readings

Bean, Frank D. and Marta Tienda. 1987. *The "Hispanic" Population of the United States.* New York: Russell Sage.

Davila, Arlene. 2001. *Latinos Inc.: The Marketing and Making of a People.* Berkeley: University of California Press.

Morin, Jose-Luis. 2005. *Latino/a Rights and Justice in the United States: Perspectives and Approaches.* Durham, NC: Carolina Academic Press.

Novas, Himilce. 1998. *Everything You Need to Know about Latino History.* rev. ed. New York: Plume/Penguin Books.

Oboler, Suzanne. 1995. *Ethnic Labels, Latinos Lives: Identity and the Politics of Representation in the United States.* Minneapolis: University of Minnesota Press.

Portes, Alejandro and Ruben G. Rumbaut. 2001. *Legacies: The Story of the Immigrant Second Generation.* Berkeley: University of California Press.

Rodriguez, Clara E. 2000. *Changing Race: Latinos, the Census, and the History of Ethnicity in the United States.* New York: New York University Press.

Yetman, Norman R. 1999. *Majority and Minority: The Dynamics of Race and Ethnicity in American Life.* 6th ed. Boston, MA: Allyn & Bacon.

HISPANIC VERSUS LATINO

Contemporary literature in the social and behavioral sciences generally uses one of two labels to refer to individuals who trace their ethnic background to one of the Spanish- or Portuguese-speaking countries of the Americas: *Hispanics* or *Latinos.* Nevertheless, there is controversy regarding not only the appropriateness of each label but also the denotative accuracy and overall usefulness of the labels. Overall, there is consensus on the fact that some individuals, particularly those who have recently migrated and even those who belong to the second generation, often use a label related to their national origin (e.g., Mexican, Salvadoran) or a compound label (e.g., Cuban American, Mexican American) rather than a more general label, be it *Hispanic* or *Latino.* This entry looks at the discussion of these labels.

About the Term *Hispanic*

The English word *Hispanic* has a confusing etymological history. On the one hand, it is assumed to be a derivation of the Latin word *Hispanicus,* which was used to identify residents of ancient Hispania or today's Iberian peninsula (Spain, Portugal, and Andorra). On the other hand, its Spanish equivalent (*Hispanoamericanos* or Hispanic Americans) is a word used in Spain to identify those individuals born in the Spanish-speaking countries of the Americas, although this same word is seldom used in Latin America.

Probably the first generalized use of the term *Hispanic* occurred in 1977 when the U.S. Office of Management and Budget printed a directive indicating that the term should be used to denote individuals who trace their cultural origin to Mexico, Puerto Rico, Cuba, Central or South America, or "other Spanish culture or origin," regardless of the person's race. In practice, this label replaced older and inaccurate labels frequently used in the literature such as *Spanish, Spanish speaking,* and *Spanish surnamed.*

In general, *Hispanic* is considered to be a comprehensive label covering persons of Mexican, Puerto Rican, Cuban, or Central or South American background. Criticisms of the label have been numerous. First is the fact that the label was imposed by an agency of the U.S. government rather than freely chosen by members of the group. Second is the argument that the label overemphasizes the contributions of Spain to Latin American cultures, ignoring the important role played by Indigenous cultures as well as the African traditions brought to the Americas by slaves.

A third criticism, and one that is relevant to all ethnic/racial labels, refers to the fact that *Hispanic* blurs intragroup differences that respond to heritage or national origin, generational history, and reasons for migration.

As such, the label *Hispanic* includes those individuals who trace at least part of their heritage to Spain or Portugal (e.g., immigrants from Latin America, Puerto Ricans, immigrants from Spain) as well as individuals who have lived in the United States for many generations (e.g., those whose ancestors lived in the Southwest before the land was ceded by Mexico to the United States). Another criticism leveled against the label *Hispanic* is that it stigmatizes the population by ignoring social class and national origin variables.

About the Term *Latino*

The label *Latino* has been proposed as a way to correct the problems inherent in the use of *Hispanic* and to more accurately reflect the political, geographical, and historical links between U.S. Hispanics and Latin American countries. *Latino* also is perceived to be a culturally and racially neutral label. Unfortunately, as an ethnic label, it is also fraught with problems.

First, *Latino* has at times been defined using geographical markers rather than sociocultural characteristics. As such, the label *Latino* has been used to denote individuals who trace their background to any of the nations south of the Rio Grande regardless of their cultural heritage. This approach encompasses Spanish-speaking countries (e.g., Mexico, Puerto Rico, Colombia, Argentina) as well as Brazil (a Portuguese-speaking nation) and sometimes English-speaking countries such as Belize, Jamaica, and the Virgin Islands. Another limitation of this label is the fact that etymologically, it could include individuals who trace their cultural heritage to any of the cultures heavily influenced by European Roman/Latin influences, that is, Latin American countries as well as France, Italy, Romania, Spain, and Portugal.

Limiting the use of the label *Latino* is the fact that despite grammatical rules in Spanish that render masculine adjectives nongendered when referring to more than one person, it could be perceived to be a sexist term. The use of *Latino/a* is cumbersome, particularly when using plural forms (Latinos/as), and slashed terms have become less frequent in contemporary writing in English. The more recent use of the "at" symbol to denote gender inclusiveness (Latin@s) seems contrived and is difficult to pronounce. The label also lends itself to further confusion when some publications and dictionaries use *Latino* to denote a resident of Latin America. Finally, the use of this term in the social and biobehavioral sciences could become a problem when establishing the comparability of samples defined as *Latino* and national statistics that have been collected by government agencies using *Hispanic* as the label of choice.

Other labels have been used to denote Hispanics or Latinos as a group, including *Chicano* and *Raza*. Often, these labels have been used as political statements or before *Hispanic* and *Latino* gained wide acceptance. The label *Chicano* has sometimes been used in the social science literature to refer to Hispanics inappropriately when its etymology limits it to individuals of Mexican background. The label *Raza* may trace its roots to Mexico's early 1900s when José Vasconcelos, a leading scholar of the time, proclaimed Indians and mestizos as members of *La Raza Cósmica* (the cosmic race) as a way to recognize and highlight the achievements of early Mexican civilizations. Although *Raza* has been used and supported by a number of individuals, it has gained little acceptance in the literature because it shares with *Chicano* the same limitation of not properly addressing all Latinos.

As with many ethnic labels, it is possible that during the next few years either *Latino* or *Hispanic* will fall into disuse or that an alternative label may emerge. What seems certain is that in practice, both labels are often used interchangeably, although it is recognized that they are labels of convenience that mask much intragroup variability and that either word might not be the label of choice of members of the ethnic group.

Gerardo Marin

See also Ethnic Group; Hispanics; *La Raza*; Race; Racial Formation; Racial Identity

Further Readings

Marin, Gerardo and Barbara VanOss Marin. 1991. *Research with Hispanic Populations*. Newbury Park, CA: Sage.

Treviño, Fernando M. 1987. "Standardized Terminology for Hispanic Populations." *American Journal of Public Health* 77:69–72.

HIV/AIDS

HIV/AIDS is a viral disease of the autoimmune system that was first identified during the 1980s and has since led to more than 25 million deaths worldwide. In the United States, HIV/AIDS has been most prevalent among men who are homosexually active. In addition, the class composition of racial/ethnic communities, associated with reduced access to heath care and prevention information, may be responsible for the larger prevalence of HIV/AIDS there. This entry briefly reviews information about the disease before taking a closer look at how the disease affects various racial/ethnic communities in the United States.

About the Disease

On June 5, 1981, Michael Gottlieb and his colleagues at the University of California, Los Angeles, published an article titled "Pneumocystis Pneumonia—Los Angeles" in the *Morbidity and Mortality Weekly Report*, a publication of the Centers for Disease Control and Prevention (CDC), chronicling the experiences of five homosexually active men treated for *Pneumocystis carinii* at three different hospitals in the greater Los Angeles area. This article, now believed to be the first article documenting acquired immune deficiency syndrome (AIDS) in the United States, noted that *Pneumocystis pneumonia* is almost exclusively limited to severely immunosuppressed patients and hinted at the possibility of a virus acquired through homosexual contact that might negatively affect the immune system.

By August of the same year, the CDC reported 108 cases of the new disease in the United States. Because all of the early reported cases were found among homosexually active men, it was originally given the name gay-related immune deficiency (GRID). However, as early as 1982, the CDC began receiving reports of GRID in people who were not homosexually active, particularly injection drug users and people who had undergone blood transfusions for various reasons, most noticeably hemophilia. In addition, reported cases of AIDS began surfacing in other nations, many among largely heterosexually active populations. Shortly thereafter, the condition started to be referred to as AIDS to reflect the reality that it was not limited to homosexual transmission.

Today, it is understood that AIDS is caused by the human immunodeficiency virus (HIV), a retrovirus that attacks the cells of the immune system and is transmitted through direct contact at the mucus membrane or the bloodstream with HIV-infected body fluids such as blood, semen, vaginal fluid, and breast milk. The three major modes of transmission for HIV are sexual contact with an HIV-positive individual, exposure to infected bodily fluids such as through injection drug use or blood transfusions, and mother-to-child transmissions. Although saliva does contain trace amounts of HIV, it is now understood that infection from saliva is virtually impossible.

Course of the Disease

In many cases, initial HIV infection is followed immediately by a short period of high HIV viremia with flu-like symptoms. However, during this period, a diagnosis of acute infection is missed due to the absence of HIV antibodies. Following this brief period, HIV infection is marked by a latent period characterized by an absence of symptoms, a period that lasts 9 to 10 years. Following the latent period, the infection progresses to early HIV infection and then AIDS. Without antiretroviral therapy, the median survival time following progression to AIDS is slightly more than 9 months. However, multiple other factors also influence disease progression; some individuals never progress beyond the latent period, even without antiretroviral therapy. Although current treatments have lengthened the progression time from HIV infection to AIDS and the time from AIDS to death, currently there is no cure.

By damaging and/or destroying the cells of the immune system, HIV interferes with the functioning of the immune system, and this makes HIV-infected individuals more susceptible to opportunistic infections and hinders the immune system's natural ability to fight various tumors that can lead to cancer and infections by various viruses, bacteria, fungi, and parasites that can lead to illnesses such as pneumonia.

Many factors also contribute to HIV transmission, including the type of sexual activity, the presence of other sexually transmitted diseases, and the progression of the disease in the HIV-positive partner. Currently, proper use of male latex condoms has been demonstrated to be the single most effective strategy for preventing HIV transmission during sexual contact. If used correctly, latex condoms can virtually eliminate the risk of transmission. Although HIV transmission from blood transfusions is extremely low in the developed world, the World Health Organization (WHO) estimates that much of the world does not have access to a safe, uncontaminated blood supply. As such, HIV transmission from blood transfusions accounts for up to 10% of new HIV infections worldwide each year. For injection drug users, not sharing needles and other drug paraphernalia can lead to decreased risk of HIV transmission. The risk of transmission during pregnancy, labor, and delivery can be reduced from 25% to less than 1% by antiretroviral therapy and caesarean childbirth.

The Pandemic

During the 25 years since the first reported cases of AIDS, it has grown to become a global pandemic. Currently, it is estimated that more than 40 million people are living with HIV/AIDS around the world, with the largest numbers in sub-Saharan Africa, where it is believed to have originated. In 2005, the WHO estimated that there were more than 4 million new cases of HIV/AIDS around the globe. To date, more than 25 million people around the world have died from AIDS-related complications. The CDC also estimates that more than half of the people infected with HIV are unaware of their status due to limited testing.

By the end of 2003, an estimated 1,039,000 to 1,185,000 people in the United States were living with AIDS, and the CDC estimates that more than 40,000 people in the country are diagnosed with HIV/AIDS each year.

Treatment

Although there is currently no cure for HIV/AIDS, many advances in treatment have been made within the past 25 years. The most widely used treatment is highly active antiretroviral therapy (HAART), which consists of a combination of at least three drugs from at least two types of antiretroviral agents, normally referred to as a "cocktail." HAART and treatments intended to limit opportunistic infections have prolonged the lives of those living with HIV/AIDS in much of the industrialized world. Although international efforts are slowly making progress, most people living with HIV/AIDS around the globe have little access to such treatments.

HIV/AIDS and Race

The Asian American Community

Although reported cases of HIV/AIDS among Asian Pacific Islander (API) Americans is comparatively low, with APIs making up less than 1% of the estimated cases of people living with AIDS in the United States, there is concern regarding gay API men. Recent studies with gay API men show rates of unsafe sex that parallel or surpass those of even the most "at risk" group, signaling the potential for a large future outbreak of HIV/AIDS within this subgroup of APIs. In addition, there is reason to believe that the overall number of API people with HIV/AIDS may be larger than reported due to both underreporting and misclassification of APIs. Among API men, 65% of the diagnosed cases of HIV/AIDS between 2001 and 2004 involved men who had sex with men; this is a larger percentage of men who have sex with men than in any other ethnic group.

Among API men who were diagnosed with HIV between 2001 and 2004, 18% contracted the disease through heterosexual contact, 65% through homosexual contact, 13% through injection drug use, and 3% through combined homosexual contact and injection drug use. In 2004, women accounted for 22% of HIV diagnoses. Among API women, heterosexual contact accounted for 79% of diagnosed HIV cases and injection drug use accounted for 16% of cases during the 2001–2004 interval.

The heterogeneity of the API community in the United States has made prevention efforts with this group difficult. Among those who are categorized as API by the U.S. Census, there are more than three dozen different ethnic groups who speak more than 100 different languages and dialects. Because immigrants with multiple cultural and linguistic characteristics still make up the majority of APIs, tailoring prevention messages to this group has been difficult.

More important, many API communities in the United States have been conservative about issues of sexual behavior, further hindering prevention efforts. Adding to the problem is that language and cultural barriers also prevent many APIs from using health care and prevention services. For example, a smaller percentage of HIV-positive APIs use HIV case management services and other related HIV services than do Whites.

HIV/AIDS in the Native American and Alaska Native Community

Native Americans and Alaska Natives accounted for 0.5% of all HIV/AIDS diagnoses in 2004 while making up slightly less than 2% of the total U.S. population. Although the absolute number of Native Americans and Alaska Natives who were diagnosed with HIV/AIDS is relatively small, Native Americans and Alaska Natives were ranked third in rates of AIDS diagnoses, behind only African Americans and Hispanics.

Among Native Americans and Alaska Native men diagnosed with HIV between 2001 and 2004, 61% contracted the disease through male-to-male sexual contact, 14% through injection drug use, 12% through heterosexual contact, and 11% through combined male-to-male sexual contact and injection drug use. In 2004, women accounted for 29% of the HIV diagnoses among Native Americans and Alaska Natives. Among Native American and Alaska Native women, heterosexual contact accounted for 69% of the diagnosed HIV cases and injection drug use accounted for 29% of cases between 2001 and 2004.

Scholar Irene Vernon addressed the specific problem of HIV/AIDS within Native American populations, most notably by pointing out that given the relative isolation of Native American groups on reservations and the small population size, HIV/AIDS has the potential of devastating Native groups if the risk is not adequately addressed. As such, it is not surprising that many Native American HIV/AIDS activists equate AIDS with smallpox, which wiped out much of the Native population centuries ago.

Because there are 562 federally recognized Native American and Alaska Native tribes whose members have different cultural views and beliefs, tailoring intervention programs with Native Americans and Alaska Natives has been difficult. Also problematic has been the fact that the poverty rate for Native Americans and Alaska Natives is nearly twice the national average, with nearly one in four Native Americans and Alaska Natives living below the federal poverty line. More important, their socioeconomic status also hinders access to adequate health care, including health-promoting information, and this may increase their risk of contracting HIV.

HIV/AIDS in the Hispanic Community

Although Hispanics make up roughly 14% of the U.S. population, they accounted for slightly more than 20% of AIDS cases diagnosed in 2004. Like APIs, the group categorized as Hispanic by the U.S. Census includes people with vastly different cultural backgrounds. As such, it is difficult to speak of a Hispanic culture outside of the common shared language of Spanish. In fact, studies of HIV/AIDS risk behaviors differ by country of origin. For example, according to the CDC, the highest risk factor for those of Puerto Rican origin is injection drug use, whereas the highest risk factor for those of Mexican origin is sex between men.

Among Hispanic men who were diagnosed with HIV between 2001 and 2004, 59% contracted the disease through male-to-male sexual contact, 19% through injection drug use, 17% through heterosexual contact, and 4% through combined male-to-male sexual contact and injection drug use. Hispanic women accounted for 23% of HIV diagnoses between 2001 and 2004. Among them, 73% contracted HIV through heterosexual contact and 23% contracted the disease through injection drug use.

Prevention efforts in Hispanic communities are also hindered by the low socioeconomic status of those most likely to be at risk among this group. According to recent research, a large number of Hispanic men who have sex with men had annual incomes far below the federal poverty line. Low socioeconomic status hinders access to adequate health care, as it does among Native Americans and Alaska Natives.

The African American Community

Although African Americans make up slightly more than 12% of the U.S. population, they accounted for nearly half of all new HIV/AIDS diagnoses in the country in 2004, making HIV/AIDS a serious health crisis for this group. According to the CDC, HIV/AIDS was among the top three causes of death for African American men between 25 and 54 years of age and among the top four causes of death for African American women in the same age group. In addition, in 2005, 73% of infants perinatally infected with HIV were African Americans. The epidemic seems to be particularly dire for younger African Americans given that 61% of those under 25 years of age who were diagnosed with HIV between 2001 and 2004 were African Americans. In fact, in 2004, the CDC estimated that the rate of AIDS diagnoses for African Americans was ten times the rate for Whites and nearly three times the rate for Hispanics, the next highest group. For African American women in particular, the rate of diagnosis was twenty-three times the rate for White women.

Among African American men diagnosed with HIV between 2001 and 2004, 49% contracted the virus through male-to-male sexual contact, 25% through heterosexual contact, 19% through injection drug use, and 5% through male-to-male sexual contact and injection drug use. For African Americans, women accounted for 38% of the diagnosed HIV cases between 2001 and 2004; this is the largest percentage of women with diagnosed cases in any racial/ethnic group. Among women, 78% contracted HIV through heterosexual sexual contact and 19% contracted the disease through injection drug use. In addition, recent attention has been paid to the problem of former prison inmates who engaged in homosexual activity while in prison and then engage in heterosexual activity once they are released.

The problem of HIV/AIDS in the African American community is further compounded by high rates of other sexually transmitted diseases. According to the CDC, African Americans were approximately nineteen times more likely than Whites to have gonorrhea and six times more likely to have syphilis. The presence of other sexually transmitted diseases can increase the chance of contracting HIV by as much as 500%. Likewise, those who are HIV positive and also have other sexually transmitted diseases are much more likely to infect others.

Like Hispanics and Native Americans, the class composition of African Americans also contributes to the spread of HIV/AIDS within this community. Currently, nearly a quarter of African Americans live below the federal poverty line. Given these socioeconomic constraints, a much smaller percentage of African Americans have access to quality health care and prevention education than do Whites.

General Characteristics

Despite the differences among racial/ethnic groups, the primary mode of infection continues to be between men who have sex with men. In addition, the percentage of transmissions attributed to male-to-male sexual contact may actually be higher given the cultural and societal norms regarding male homosexual behavior for all ethnic groups. As such, men who contract HIV through male-to-male sexual contact may be underreporting or may be attributing the transmission to other causes. Within communities of color, there may be strong social pressures for gay men to remain in the closet. In fact, at least among African American men, recent research suggests that a significantly larger percentage of men who have sex with men also engage in heterosexual contact with women than is the case among White men. Among Hispanic men, the cultural concept of machismo may lead to more risky behavior among men who have sex with men.

Among women, it is clear that the primary mode of infection is through sexual contact with men who are HIV positive. Nonetheless, the class composition of most minority communities hinders access to quality health care as well as prevention education for both men and women.

Although it has long been suspected that homophobia within ethnic communities may affect sexual behavior indirectly, leading to higher rates of HIV infection among men of color who have sex with men, recent studies have indicated that racism found within the larger gay community may also contribute to the rising rates of HIV infection among men of color who have sex with men. According to this view, racial marginalization in the gay community works in similar ways to stigmatize men of color as gay men are stigmatized in ethnic communities, thereby increasing the practice of unsafe sex among men of color who have sex with men.

Chong-suk Han and Scott E. Rutledge

See also African Americans; Asian Americans; Gender and Race, Intersection of; Health, Immigrant; Health Disparities; Hispanics; Medical Experimentation; National Urban League; Native Americans; Scapegoating

Further Readings

Diaz, Rafael. 1997. *Latino Gay Men and HIV.* New York: Routledge.
Hogan, Katie. 2001. *Women Take Care: Gender, Race, and the Culture of AIDS.* Ithaca, NY: Cornell University Press.
Levenson, Jacob. 2004. *The Secret Epidemic: The Story of AIDS and Black America.* New York: Pantheon.
Vernon, Irene. 2001. *Killing Us Quietly: Native Americans and HIV/AIDS.* Lincoln: University of Nebraska Press.

Hmong Americans

Hmong Americans constitute one of the most sizable Asian ethnic communities in the Upper Midwest and in some regions of the South and the West. This entry briefly discusses the history of Hmong Americans in the United States while also providing information about demographics of the community, sources of internal community diversity, and Hmong American socioeconomic and political advancement over time.

Immigration Patterns

The Hmong people are a stateless ethnic group whose origins go back at least 3,000 years in China. In Asia, Hmong live in southwestern China, Thailand, Burma, Laos, and northern Vietnam, where they moved during the 19th century following persecution in China. The first Hmong migration of notable size to the United States began with the fall of Saigon and Laos to communist forces in 1975. Many Hmong had worked with pro-American, anti-communist forces during the conflicts in Vietnam and Laos. As a result, they were subject to violence and retribution in Laos. Many Hmong escaped Laos to Thailand, where they were incarcerated in refugee camps.

From the late 1970s to the mid-1990s, large numbers of Hmong refugees were resettled in the United States. The peak was 1980, when 27,000 Hmong refugees were admitted. From 1981 to 1986, the number of Hmong refugees slowed to a few thousand per year, but admissions picked up again between 1987 and 1994, when approximately 56,000 Hmong refugees were accepted. After 1994, Hmong refugee admissions slowed to a trickle as most of the Thai camps were by now empty, with the remaining Hmong repatriated to Laos or moving to Wat Tham Krabok in Thailand, where thousands of Hmong were given shelter by Thai Buddhist monks beginning in the early to mid-1990s, prior to an official resettlement program of more than 15,000 Hmong from the Wat to the United States during the 2004–2006 period. Hmong immigration based on family reunification has remained low over the years, especially compared with that of other Southeast Asian ethnic groups.

Where did the Hmong settle? With the first wave that arrived during the late 1970s and early 1980s, voluntary resettlement agencies consciously tried to disperse the Hmong around the country in a number of locales. At that time, sizable Hmong populations could also be found in eastern cities such as Providence (Rhode Island) and Philadelphia; in midwestern cities such as Chicago, Des Moines (Iowa), and Kansas City; and in western cities such as Denver, Missoula (Montana), Tulsa (Oklahoma), and Salt Lake City (Utah).

This strategy, however, proved to be unsuccessful in many instances. For example, during the early 1980s, several thousand Hmong were settled in a poor, predominantly African American neighborhood in west Philadelphia, where they encountered considerable hostility and violence. Most of the Hmong moved out within a few years. Also, many wished to be reunited with family and clan members and to be near cultural ritualists (shamans and marriage and funeral ceremony facilitators) from the traditional Hmong religion. These factors led to a massive shift of the Hmong population during the mid- to late 1980s to central California cities such as Fresno, Stockton, and Merced and, to a lesser extent, to Minnesota and Wisconsin. By 1990, Fresno and Central Valley cities such as Sacramento, Stockton, and Merced were the center of Hmong American community life. Census figures show that by far the largest Hmong population at this time was found in California, followed by Minnesota, Wisconsin, Michigan, and Colorado. The 1990 census counted 94,439 Hmong Americans across the United States.

During the 1990s, the Hmong moved again, away from the West and toward the Midwest and the South. This shift was epitomized by the emergence of St. Paul (Minnesota) as the unofficial Hmong American capital, taking over from Fresno. According to estimates of the U.S. Census Bureau's *American Community Survey 2005* (ACS), 52% of Hmong Americans now live in the Midwest—mostly in Minnesota, Wisconsin, and Michigan—compared with 41% in 1990. Meanwhile, the proportion of Hmong in the western states fell to 40% from 55% in 1990, according to the 2005 estimates. In 2005, just under nine of every ten Hmong living in the West lived in California, with much smaller communities found in Colorado, Oregon, Washington, and Alaska. In 2005, the Hmong population estimated by the ACS to reside in the northeastern states remained very small at less than 1%. In 2005, approximately 7% of the Hmong were estimated to live in the South, an impressive increase from just 1.3% in 1990. This movement was focused within a few states such as North Carolina, South Carolina, Florida, Arkansas, and Oklahoma.

The midsection of the United States—Arkansas, Missouri, and Oklahoma—has seen an impressive increase in Hmong population since 2000 as a secondary migration of Hmong from other states to get into the chicken farming industry, and to return to a more rural and agrarian lifestyle, has occurred. Some Hmong have done well in this new field of work, but numerous newspaper articles in 2006 documented the bankruptcies and very difficult economic circumstances experienced by some Hmong families from other parts of the country who were sold chicken farming properties in this region during the past several years.

By 2000, there were 169,428 Hmong in the United States, representing a nearly 90% increase in the population since 1990. In 2005, the ACS estimated the U.S. Hmong population at 183,265. Many agree, however, that these figures probably represent significant undercounts, and the numbers do not reflect the more than 15,000 Laotian–Hmong refugees resettled in the United States from Wat Tham Krabok in Thailand during the 2004–2006 period. Most of these Hmong refugee newcomers were resettled in California, Minnesota, and Wisconsin.

According to the 2000 census data, the "Twin Cities" of Minneapolis–St. Paul claimed 40,707 Hmong residents. Second was Fresno with 22,456. After Fresno, the largest Hmong populations in the United States were found in the Sacramento–Yolo (California), Milwaukee–Racine (Wisconsin), and Merced (California) areas. Why did Minneapolis–St. Paul emerge as the new Hmong American capital? The opportunity to make a better life seems to be at the heart of things, with the perception of lower-cost housing, educational opportunities, and the existence of a large institutionally complete ethnic enclave being prime motivating factors for migration from California and other parts of the country. In the Twin Cities area, most Hmong live in St. Paul, which also hosts an annual New Year's celebration and a summer sports tournament that attracts thousands of Hmong to visit from around the United States.

Contemporary Social Patterns

A recent community directory provides listings of thirteen Hmong community organizations and thirty-nine Hmong religious congregations in the Minneapolis–St. Paul area. Whereas many Hmong in California's Central Valley have taken up their old occupations of farming, many of those in Minnesota have found jobs working in factories. But there is a substantial emerging class of Hmong small business owners—many of them congregated near St. Paul's University Avenue, also known for its Vietnamese businesses—and college-educated Hmong professionals going into fields such as law, medicine, and nonprofit management. In the Twin Cities, Hmong are opening restaurants serving Lao or Thai cuisine, although traditional Hmong dishes are available on request.

The Hmong came to the United States less prepared for the modern capitalistic society of their new home than did most other immigrant groups. Most had been farmers in their native country and did not graduate from high school or the equivalent. Nearly all Hmong also first came to the United States as refugees. As a result, many Hmong families, when they first arrived, were forced to go on public assistance. In 1999, the median household income of Hmong Americans was $31,934 compared with $41,994 among all U.S. households. This, however, represented a significant advance from 1989, when the median Hmong household income was approximately $11,000. Just over one-third (34.9%) of Hmong families lived below the poverty line in 1999, according to census data. However, the poverty level among Hmong American families was nearly cut in half over the 1990s given that 67.1% of Hmong lived below the poverty line in 1989.

In 1990, only 15% of Hmong owned their homes. Similar to the income-related statistics, housing data from the 2000 census show considerable upward socioeconomic movement as many Hmong had settled into stable or more lucrative jobs over the 1990s. In 2000, 40% of all Hmong Americans owned their homes; however, the national figures were brought down by the very large Hmong population residing in California. The 2000 census data show that whereas Hmong home ownership was still low in California at approximately 18%, it was well above 50% in states such as Minnesota, Wisconsin, Michigan, and North Carolina.

In terms of job distribution, the largest proportion of Hmong American adults worked in manufacturing jobs (38.6%), according to 2000 census data; this compared with 14.0% of all U.S. adults who were employed in manufacturing. In 2000, Hmong American adults in the workforce exhibited smaller concentrations in the broad industrial classifications of education, health, and social services (14.5%); arts, entertainment, recreation, and accommodations (10.8%); and retail (10.0%). In a few states such as Michigan (restaurant ownership) and Washington (the flower industry), Hmong Americans have formed occupational niches similar to those well documented over time among other U.S. ethnic groups in the social science literature.

Traditionally, the Hmong have favored large families with many children. Some of this can be explained by the Hmong's traditional farming roots and the high infant mortality rate in Laos and Southeast Asia. As a result, 2000 census figures show that Hmong households averaged more than 6.0 persons per house or apartment in Minnesota and Wisconsin, as compared with approximately 2.5 persons among the entire U.S. population. This helps to explain the huge U.S. population growth between 1990 and 2000 despite the decline in refugee admissions after 1994. The large number of Hmong children also makes the population very youthful. At least half of the Hmong in California, Minnesota, Wisconsin, North Carolina, and Michigan were under 18 years of age in 2000, as compared with roughly a quarter among the general population.

The Hmong are a fairly tight-knit group; many community leaders are old clan leaders or politicians from Laos or are their descendants and relatives. For instance, the Hmong general Vang Pao, who commanded the Hmong forces fighting against the communist North Vietnamese, remains a political leader for many Hmong in the United States. After escaping Laos, Vang Pao moved to Orange County, California, and helped to found a Hmong organization, Lao Family Community, which has branches nationwide, many of them run by people close to Vang Pao or his relatives.

Still, there is a new generation of Hmong leaders emerging. They are young, well educated, and not necessarily willing to be as beholden to old loyalties based on clan affiliation. Cleaved along this generational divide, the younger leaders support the reform of aspects of Hmong culture that may clash with U.S. norms. For instance, Hmong women's groups have campaigned against polygamy and domestic violence. Other leaders are trying to tackle the increasing number of Hmong youth being lured into gangs—an unfortunate side effect of assimilation into the U.S. youth culture.

Indeed, it is very important to realize that there is considerable diversity in the Hmong American community. Sources of diversity include, but are not limited to, clan affiliation (there are 18 Hmong clans in the United States), religion, dialect (Green Hmong vs. White Hmong), age and time of arrival in the United States, veteran versus nonveteran status, gender, and socioeconomic status along with social class. Different social groups in the Hmong community have held contrasting views related to important community issues over the years, including the perceived importance of maintaining Hmong cultural traditions such as the traditional Hmong marriage and funeral ceremonies. Another issue of debate that has divided the Hmong American community is the question of whether the United States should establish a closer economic relationship with the government of Laos.

The majority of Hmong in the United States still practice the traditional Hmong religion, a form of animism that involves the worship of numerous spirits, including those of ancestors, and incorporates shamanism. A growing number of Hmong Americans have become Christians. The largest Hmong American Christian denomination is the evangelical Christian Missionary Alliance church, which has been sending missions to work with Hmong in China and Southeast Asia since the early 20th century. In cities with sizable Hmong populations, Hmong churches from a variety of Protestant denominations can also be found. In St. Paul and a few of the largest Hmong communities, there are also Hmong Catholic churches.

The United States' first Hmong public official elected to serve in state government, a young female lawyer named Mee Moua, was elected to the Minnesota State Senate in 2002 and was quickly followed by Cy Thao, an artist, who was elected to the Minnesota House of Representatives the same year and was subsequently reelected in 2004. Hmong Americans have also been elected to the school boards in St. Paul, Fresno, and several Wisconsin cities. In Eau Claire (Wisconsin) and Omaha (Nebraska), Hmong Americans have been elected to the city councils.

Hmong Americans certainly have faced a number of challenges as a historically stateless minority community, most of whom arrived in the United States as refugees. On occasion, they have also faced prejudice and discrimination as a cultural minority in the United States. Through education, socioeconomic gains, community cohesion, and political empowerment, they are moving toward a brighter future.

Mark Pfeifer

See Appendix A; Appendix B
See also Acculturation; Asian Americans; Assimilation; Laotian Americans

Further Readings

Hein, Jeremy. 2006. *Ethnic Origins: The Adaptation of Cambodian and Hmong Refugees in Four American Cities.* New York: Russell Sage.

Moua, Mai Neng, ed. 2002. *Bamboo among the Oaks: Contemporary Writing by Hmong Americans.* St. Paul: Minnesota Historical Society.

Omoto, Susan. 2002. *Hmong Milestones in America: Citizens in a New World.* Evanston, IL: John Gordon Burke.

Tapp, Nicholas, Jean Michaud, Christian Culas, and Gary Yia Lee, eds. 2004. *Hmong/Miao in Asia.* Seattle: University of Washington Press.

Yang, Kou. 2001. "The Hmong in America: Twenty Five Years after the U.S. Secret War in Laos." *Journal of Asian American Studies* 4:165–174.

Web Sites

Hmong Studies Resource Center: http://www.hmongstudies.org

HOLOCAUST

Although the word has a more generalized meaning, the term *Holocaust* is commonly used today to denote the systematic persecution and mass murder that Nazi Germany perpetrated against European Jewry during World War II. Based on an ideology of racial superiority, the Nazi leadership under Adolf Hitler launched a program of mass killings aimed at a variety of people considered to be undesirable but focused on the extermination of European Jews. This entry summarizes the facts of the Holocaust and briefly examines issues related to the events, including the ensuing debates and lasting moral and political influence.

Political and Ideological Background

Nazi ideology rejected the values of egalitarianism and the Enlightenment, replacing them with a hierarchy based on "racial value." The Nazis saw the world populated by various races with greater or lesser value. At the top was the "Nordic" or "Aryan" race (blond hair and blue eyes), embodied in the German people, which was alleged to have been the most creative and politically and militarily capable throughout history. Individual people also possessed higher or lower racial value measurable by their bodily features. Consequently, the Nazis sought to increase procreation of those of the "highest value." A mix of the "races" through intermarriage was considered to be detrimental, leading to a nation's decadence and decline.

The pronounced Nazi belief in the inequality among people led to the justification of suppressing "lower races" and forcing them into perpetual servitude. According to the Nazis, eternal struggle between races and peoples, resulting in a "survival of the fittest," was a law of nature. Non-nation-state-based groups, such as Jews and so-called "Gypsies," were considered to be particularly pernicious. Indeed, the Jewish people were seen as the antipode and eternal enemy of the Aryans. Heinrich Himmler, chief of Nazi Germany's police, the Nazi Party vanguard SS, and one of the major perpetrators of the Holocaust, described "world Jewry" as intrinsically opposed to a racial hierarchy and, thus, having inspired Christianity, Freemasonry, the Enlightenment, the French Revolution, liberal capitalism, and Bolshevism—all based on some concept of equality among people.

Within the state, the Nazis said that individual rights had no importance; only the overall interest of the "people" was important. What this consisted of was decided by a nation's leader, Hitler in the case of Nazi Germany. Linked to the concept of an overarching common good was the notion of the "health" of a nation, which was considered to be endangered by people with hereditary diseases or with disabilities and "nonproductive elements" such as criminals, prostitutes, and people refusing to work. Politically, Nazi ideology was antidemocratic, authoritarian, and violently opposed to the political working-class movement. Industrialization was considered to be dangerous because of the attendant social problems; in its stead, a return to a romanticized agrarian life was proposed. Because Germany did not possess the amount of land needed for a return to agrarianism, Hitler proposed the conquest of land in Eastern Europe (the quest for *Lebensraum*), which implied an attack on neighboring countries.

Both the racist and political convictions of the Nazis were based on views discussed since the late 19th century in Europe and even outside of it. During the period between the two world wars, fascist movements and regimes sprang up all over Europe and a number of countries turned from democracies to authoritarian systems. Thus, the Nazis were part of a larger political trend within Europe. In Germany, resentment over the sanctions imposed by the Versailles Treaty at the end of World War I, along with mass unemployment and massive economic problems, increased the antagonism toward the democratic system of the interwar Weimar Republic that was already prevalent among right-wing circles. The right wing was pitted against a strong left-wing movement (socialist and communist), which led to increasing political violence and further instability. The Nazi political platform appealed to Germans by its promises of stability, strong rule by a strong leader, and economic recovery, whereas the extent of the appeal of anti-Semitism is debatable.

History of the Holocaust: 1933 to 1939

After Hitler was appointed German chancellor by President Paul von Hindenburg on January 30, 1933 (contrary to an often-held belief, the Nazi Party never won a majority in an open election), his government started to implement the Nazis' political and ideological aims. One of the most important legal tools allowed police to arrest and incarcerate anybody without legal recourse (so-called "protective custody"). Using this power, the Nazis filled newly created concentration camps, initially mainly with members of the Communist and Social Democrat parties.

A boycott of Jewish businesses in Berlin in 1933 gave a first signal to the German Jewish community that the Nazis were determined to put their racist ideology into practice. Acts of anti-Jewish violence were committed throughout Germany during the following years. The population of Germany was systematically segregated. Germans needed to provide proof of Aryan descent (interestingly, this shows that it was not self-evident to which race a person belonged). Two laws passed in 1935—called "Nuremberg Laws" because they were issued at the Nuremberg Nazi Party rally—further cemented the segregation of Germans from Jewish Germans. Marriage and sexual relationships were banned, and Jews and members of other "alien races," such as Gypsies, lost their citizenship. An avalanche of laws and decrees (roughly 2,000) forced Jewish Germans out of most jobs and severely limited their ability to earn a living and live a normal life.

Nazi policy during this period aimed at forcing Jewish Germans out of Germany. However, those willing to emigrate had great difficulty in finding countries that would admit them. The government also stripped them of their assets before they could leave. But the majority of German Jews, and Austrian Jews after the annexation of Austria in 1938, managed to flee. A pogrom in November 1938 (often referred to as *Reichskristallnacht*) showed the imminent danger to those who had been reluctant to emigrate. Exploiting the murder of a German diplomat by a young Jewish man in Paris, the Nazis organized the burning of synagogues as well as attacks on Jewish businesses and homes, and they sent a large number of Jewish Germans into concentration camps.

History of the Holocaust: World War II Period

Germany's attack on Poland on September 1, 1939, triggered the outbreak of World War II. The war marked a new stage. During the war, and especially in Eastern Europe, Nazi Germany implemented the full range of its radical ideological aims. The first scene of atrocities was Poland. Mass executions decimated Polish elites, large-scale ethnic cleansing occurred, and population transfers took place between the western part of Poland, annexed to Germany, and the eastern part under German administration. Discriminatory laws against Poles and Jews were issued; here, for the first time, Jews needed to wear the "Yellow Star" of David. In Germany proper, wearing a star became mandatory two years later in 1941. In Poland, the first ghettos were established and the Jewish population was forced into them.

In Germany, the Nazis also moved to mass murder. The targeted victim group was disabled inmates of mental institutions (mainly not Jewish), who were "without value," according to Nazi ideology. From 1939 to 1941, at six mental institutions in Germany and Austria, patients were killed with gas. This is the first example of mass gassing; many of the perpetrators of this crime later staffed the death camps in Poland.

The attack on the Soviet Union in 1941 marked the pinnacle of Hitler's ideological aims—a total war against "Judeo-Bolshevism" that he hoped would lead to the destruction of this main ideological opponent and to the conquest of land for future German settlement. The Slavic population was considered to be expendable or consigned to a life of serfdom. The Jewish population was targeted for mass murder. On the heels of the German army, mobile task forces consisting of members of the "Security Police and SD" advanced. At first, they conducted large-scale executions of the Communist leadership and the male Jewish population. This soon escalated into the mass murder of the Jewish population in total.

No direct order exists, but according to the majority of scholars, this shift to full-blown genocide took place during the summer or fall of 1941. The lack of a final order cannot be interpreted as proof that Hitler was not aware of what was happening or that the genocide itself did not happen, as revisionists sometimes suggest. There is ample indication in contemporary documents that Hitler was at the center of Holocaust decision making, even as local power holders showed considerable initiative in implementing the mass murder as speedily and efficiently as they could. Mass murder was first committed by shooting. Later, the Security Police developed mobile gas vans as a more efficient way. As in Germany before, the mentally ill were included in the murder actions. In the occupied territories, the Nazis implemented the full range of measures to create a "racially and socially cleansed" country; apart from Jews, Roma (Gypsies), and Communists, so-called "asocials" (e.g., common criminals, prostitutes, "work-shy elements"), who in Germany had been sent to camps, were simply killed in the East. The Holocaust in the Soviet Union was perpetrated by killing actions on-site, although much of the Jewish population was forced into ghettos until several waves of murder actions had been completed. How the war radicalized matters became apparent in 1941 in Serbia, where the German army command murdered the male Jewish population as an act of retaliation against partisan activities. In most countries occupied by Germany or allied with it, the genocide unfolded in a set manner: The Jewish population was segregated from others, marked, forced into ghettos of constantly diminishing size, robbed of their valuables, subjected to forced labor, and finally deported into death camps.

The protocol of the so-called *Wannsee Konferenz* (taking place on January 20, 1942, and aimed at organizing cooperation among various German government departments participating in the genocide) shows that the Jewish population of all European countries was the final target of the genocide. The success of the genocidal plan depended on the local political situation, the extent of local collaboration with the Germans, the strength of resistance movements, and the possibility that persecuted Jews could hide.

Around 1942, labor shortages led to a shift in German policies; additional laborers were required for the German war effort. Whereas in 1941–1942 the majority of an estimated 3.3 million Soviet prisoners of war (POWs) were starved to death in POW camps, during the following years roughly 7.5 million people (mainly Poles, Ukrainians, and Russians, including POWs) were deported to Germany to perform forced labor. Concentration camp inmates, including Jews, were slave laborers at production sites. However, this did not mean that the goal of the destruction of European Jewry had been abandoned; it only meant that their work capacity should be exploited before their death. For this purpose, deportees into camps were subjected to "selections"; stronger people were selected for work, whereas the weak, the old, and children went straight to the gas chambers.

Of the six death camps, four (Chelmno, Belzec, Sobibor, and Treblinka) were just killing facilities, whereas Auschwitz and Majdanek served the dual purposes of incarcerating and killing victims. Auschwitz, for instance, contained three complexes: Auschwitz–Stammlager, where opponents from all ethnic backgrounds were imprisoned; Auschwitz–Birkenau, where Jewish victims and a large number of Gypsies were routinely killed in gas chambers; and Auschwitz–Buna, which was a slave labor site for the chemical industry.

The headquarters of the Security Police (RSHA) played a leading role in the overall organization of the genocide, including the deportations into death camps. In addition, the police, other German government departments, the civil occupation administration, and the German army participated in the Holocaust; indeed, all parts of German government and society were involved. The priority that the Nazi leadership gave to the destruction of European Jewry is illustrated by the fact that, in 1944, resources that would have been crucial for the war effort were instead used to deport Jews from Greece and Hungary to their deaths in Auschwitz. At the same time, the Security Police attempted to cover their tracks by disinterring corpses from mass graves and burning them. The surviving Jewish camp inmates were forced to retreat with the German forces. The horrendous conditions during these "death marches" took another high toll in Jewish lives—just as liberation seemed to be close.

Historical Debates

The total number of victims of the Holocaust is estimated to range between 5 million and 6 million. Scholars have estimated that 100,000 to 300,000 Jews survived camps and ghettos. However, in the recent discussions about compensation for slave labor, much higher numbers of survivors have been suggested. A scholarly assessment of these figures has not yet taken place.

An ongoing debate concerns the extent of involvement and culpability of Germans in the Holocaust. Over the past two decades, detailed studies have shown the participation of a widening range of German organizations in the mass murder. However, no consensus has been reached about the degree of involvement, ideological commitment, and overall contribution of, for instance, the German army. Also under discussion is how to evaluate the culpability of participation—collaborators in the Holocaust can range from police officers with command responsibilities to engine drivers of deportation trains—and to what extent the German population, or the non-German population in occupied countries, supported the mass murder or simply knew about it. Although the Holocaust was declared "top secret," a lot of information was publicly available.

Another hotly debated issue concerns whether the Holocaust should be considered a "unique" event. One side argues that this was an unprecedented event in world history and that Jewish suffering was unique. On the other side, it is said that "uniqueness" is not a useful category because all historical events are unique by themselves but also comparable to others. In addition, it is said that the assumption of uniqueness all too often leads to the denigration of the suffering of other victims of Nazi Germany.

The Holocaust had an enormous moral and political impact on the second half of the 20th century, leading to the establishment of legal principles and standards in the protection of human rights. To begin, the International Tribunal in Nuremberg sat in judgment of the Nazi leadership and developed notions of "crimes against humanity" and war crimes. This led to the 1948 "Genocide Convention," which introduced the term *genocide* and its definition, and (most recently) to the 1998 "Rome Statute," which established an international criminal court.

The Holocaust and Nazi history have also been used to justify political crimes. Communist leaders, for instance, used the struggle against Nazi Germany to legitimize Soviet rule and expansionism. In the Western world, where references to the Nazis and the Holocaust abound, Holocaust imagery has been pressed into the service of nearly any imaginable concern, from abortion to animal rights. Nazism and the Holocaust are also used to support power politics that is not in agreement with international and humanitarian law, as has been noticeable, for instance, in the United States during recent years.

Ruth Bettina Birn

See also African Americans; Anti-Semitism; Eugenics; Genocide; Holocaust Deniers and Revisionists; Jewish Americans; Roma; Social Darwinism

Further Readings

Browning, Christopher. 1992. *Ordinary Men: Reserve Police Battalion 101 and the Final Solution in Poland.* New York: HarperCollins.

Enzyklopädie des Holocaust. 1993. *Die Verfolgung und Ermordung der europäischen Juden.* Munich, Germany: Piper.

Friedlander, Henry. 1995. *The Origins of Nazi Genocide: From Euthanasia to the Final Solution.* Chapel Hill: University of North Carolina Press.

Friedländer, Saul. 1997. *Nazi Germany and the Jews: The Years of Persecution, 1933–1939.* New York: HarperCollins.

Hilberg, Raul. 1961. *The Destruction of the European Jews.* New York: Quadrangle Books.

Krausnick, Helmut, Hans Buchheim, Martin Brozat, and Hans-Adolf Jacobsen. 1968. *Anatomy of the SS-State.* New York: Walker.

Holocaust Deniers and Revisionists

The Holocaust, the extermination of Europe's Jews and other stigmatized groups during World War II, is one of the most thoroughly documented events of the 20th century, but this does not prevent some from either significantly downplaying the event or even denying it occurred, as this entry summarizes.

Revisionism Versus Denial

Ordinarily, revisionism means a reinterpretation of history. This goes on all the time. Interpreting history is an acceptable form of research. However, when such revisionism means the denial or the obvious skewing of a historical fact, this passes beyond the category of commonly accepted social scientific research and becomes outright lies and distortions. The European death camps were still smoldering when some people began to argue that they did not exist or that, if they did exist, only a small number of people died in them; some said that the ovens were used to bake bread or that most Jews died from disease and not from genocidal intent.

Actual denial of the Holocaust has become a growing problem in Holocaust historiography, and takes many forms. The most egregious form took place in the fall of 2006 when Iranian President Mahmoud Ahmadinejad hosted an international conference on Holocaust denial in Tehran that welcomed hundreds of foreigners, including Orthodox Jews from New York and Israel, Ukrainians, Americans, Europeans, and others from around the world.

Claims of Holocaust Denials

"There Were No Gas Chambers"

This allegation can often be traced to the writings of Arthur Butz, a Northwestern University engineering professor. His work, *The Hoax of the Twentieth Century,* is based largely on the fact that Butz could not find the name of one prisoner on the list of Auschwitz prisoners—that of Vrba Rosenberg, who wrote an eyewitness account called *I Cannot Forgive* that was published in 1946. As it turns out, Vrba was an adopted name and the author was listed in the Auschwitz rolls under his original name, Walter Rosenberg.

"The Concentration Camps Were Not so Bad"

Ernst Zundel, a denier in Toronto, Canada, has testified at trials that many camps had all "the luxuries of a country club," with dance halls, orchestras, recreational facilities, sauna baths, and other amenities. True, there were showers for inmates, and there was an orchestra that played in the morning when prisoners went to work and again in the afternoon when they returned. But these were simply ruses to help camouflage the fact that the "work" in these camps was meant to lead eventually to the deaths of the prisoners.

"Hitler Was a 'Man of Peace'"

According to proponents of this view, the Allied air raids on Dresden and the German postwar population transfer from territory ceded to Poland to the West were more brutal than the punishment that was "allegedly" imposed on the Jews in the gas chambers. Harry Elmer Barnes, a prominent historian during the 1930s and 1940s, and people such as Austin App, Robert Faurisson, and David Irving share this opinion. Irving, in fact, devoted an entire book to the bombing of Dresden. These deniers typically overlook the massive German bombing of Rotterdam, Warsaw, Coventry, and London.

"Anne Frank's Diary Was a Hoax"

Even the memoirs of young children are targets of deniers. There are many versions of this denial—that the memoirs were forgeries; that Anne Frank's father, Otto, had plenty of time to forge a diary and make a fast buck; and that the diary was not even written by a young girl. Rather, the book was supposedly written by a Jewish author, Meyer Levin, and Anne's father after the war. First, Otto Frank had neither the time nor the talent to create a teenager's diary and had no idea that his daughter's private thoughts might be publishable. In fact, he was reluctant to publish the book and several publishing houses rejected the manuscript, thinking that it would not sell very well.

The Meyer Levin scandal is complex and fascinating. The principal source of this claim was David Irving of Great Britain. Levin, a successful novelist, praised the diary and tried to interest producers in his own adaptations of the diary for stage and film. He failed, and the diary was adapted for the stage by Albert Hackett and Frances Goodrich with the title *The Diary of Anne Frank*. It enjoyed a long Broadway run, won the Pulitzer Prize in 1956 for the best play of the year, and was later adapted as a successful film. Levin, meanwhile, sued the playwrights as well as the Broadway producers for breach of contract and plagiarism. They brought Otto Frank into the case, and he eventually settled out of court, paying Levin $15,000 in return for dropping all further claims. Levin's own theatrical version of the diary was staged in Tel Aviv in 1966 and has been attempted in smaller venues during the past 40 years.

Why Denial?

The major question that goes begging is . . . why? Why do people deny the Holocaust and its participants? There is not enough space in this entry to go into the psychological factors that explain deniers. Many are failed academics or writers who are attempting to make a mark with radical ideas and some are Nazi ideologues. They truly believe in Hitler's ideas and want a world like his to be brought to fruition.

Other deniers are anti-Zionists. Still others, even if not politically inclined about the State of Israel, publish writings that feed into general anti-Semitic thought. For example, contemporary Web sites of Ku Klux Klan organizations either directly reference or repeat without citation material from Holocaust deniers and revisionists. The idea seems to be that if revisionists and deniers can weaken the case for the Holocaust, they can weaken Israel's position in the world and eventually destroy the country.

Jack Nusan Porter

See also Anti-Semitism; Genocide; Holocaust; Jewish Americans; Ku Klux Klan; Victim Discounting

Further Readings

Evans, Richard J. 2001. *Lying about Hitler: History, Holocaust, and the David Irving Trial.* New York: Basic Books.
Irving, David. 1977. *Hitler's War.* New York: Viking.
Julius, Anthony. 2007. "Irving v. Lipstadt." Pp. 30–32 in *Encyclopedia Judaica.* 2nd ed., vol. 10. New York: Macmillan.
Kuttner, Paul. 1996. *The Holocaust: Hoax or History? The Book of Answers to Those Who Deny the Holocaust.* New York: Dawnwood.
Lipstadt, Deborah E. 1993. *Denying the Holocaust.* New York: Free Press.
Lipstadt, Deborah E. 2005. *History on Trial: My Day in Court with a Holocaust Denier.* New York: Harper Perennial.
Stern, Kenneth S. 1993. *Holocaust Denial.* New York: American Jewish Committee.

HOMELESSNESS

Homelessness is a national and global problem driven by poverty and the cost of housing. As housing costs increase and wages remain flat, the working and nonworking poor have become either homeless or at risk for homelessness. Although there are many explanations of why people are homeless—mental illness, declines in public assistance, domestic violence, and addiction—it is commonly agreed that homelessness and poverty are inextricably linked. When people are poor, they must make difficult choices because limited resources cover only some of their basic necessities. Often housing, which absorbs a high proportion of income, must be dropped.

Two factors account for increasing poverty: eroding employment opportunities for large segments of the workforce and the declining value and availability of public assistance. This interpretation of homelessness as poverty frames the issue as one of race, class, and ethnicity based on examination of the demographics of homelessness. Homelessness also appears to be increasingly related to ruptures in relationships between social institutions and the society of citizens as well as between the society of citizens and the poor. Glenn Drover and Patrick Kerans noted the failure of institutions to face extreme poverty in a situation where poor and homeless persons were rapidly marginalized from the society of citizens.

Who Is Homeless?

Demographic groups that are more likely to experience poverty are also more likely to experience homelessness. They are also more likely to be minority groups. In 2003, 12.7% of the U.S. population, or 37 million people, lived in poverty. This overall poverty rate more than doubles for racial/ethnic minorities. Latinos/as have had poverty rates at or exceeding 20% for many years, and the poverty rate for African Americans is 22.2%. The most recent homeless demographic data on age, race, gender, and ethnicity are summarized here.

Age

In 2001, children under 18 years of age accounted for 39% of the population, with 43% of those were under 5 years of age. The National Law Center on Homelessness and Poverty reported that 25% of homeless were 25 to 34 years of age and that 6% were 55 to 64.

Gender

Most studies have found that single homeless adults are more likely to be male than female. In 2005, a survey by the U.S. Conference of Mayors found that single men comprised 43% of the homeless population, whereas single women comprised 17%.

Families

The number of families experiencing homelessness is rising. The National Alliance to End Homelessness found that one-half of the homeless population is composed of families (mothers with children). The National Coalition for the Homeless and the U.S. Conference of Mayors reported that families with children comprise 33% of the homeless population. On either count, it is apparent that the number of homeless families with children is large. Notably, it has increased significantly over the past decade.

Ethnicity

Like the total U.S. population, the ethnic makeup of homeless populations varies according to geographic location. In any area, however, minority groups comprise the largest number of homeless people. The U.S. Conference of Mayors found that the majority of the homeless population in twenty cities involved minorities of color. People experiencing homelessness in rural areas were more likely to be White, and homelessness among Native Americans and migrant workers was more generally a rural phenomenon.

Homeless person. Homelessness and poverty are inextricably linked. As housing costs increase and wages remain flat, the working and nonworking poor have become either homeless or at-risk for homelessness. Although African Americans constitute about 12% of the U.S. population, they make up nearly 40% of the homeless population.

Source: Morguefile.

The demographic data offer a partial understanding of the relationship among race, class, gender, ethnicity, and homelessness. It is possible to view homeless people as a subclass among the poor. In many respects, the characteristics of homeless people resemble those of housed poor people. There are, however, some significant differences. Homeless people have incomes that are far less than half of the official poverty level. Only one-half of homeless people have a high school degree. Just as they are marginally attached to the labor force, they also have thinner support networks. They are slightly younger and tend to be from racial/ethnic minority groups. Their rate of experience with foster care is greater, and they are more likely to have had a mother with drug problems than are housed poor people.

Poverty and homelessness are far more concentrated in cities, especially the mega-cities where the poorest and richest classes compete for space. Roughly half of the world's population lives in cities, and it is anticipated that this number will grow to 75% by 2050. In the United States, the National League of Cities reported that increasing numbers of poor people live in neighborhoods where at least 40% of the residents are below the official poverty level.

In most important respects, homeless people are not appreciably different from poor housed families living in urban environments. They are a subclass of poor people who, for one reason or another, have lost housing and cannot get back into the housing market.

Social Citizenship and Homelessness

Social policy analysts consistently explain that the number of claimants to social insurance and public assistance has grown beyond the public capacity to serve all of them. The restricted access to the labor force, housing, and public assistance that drives marginal people to homelessness suggests that the society of citizens has grown to such an extent that institutions have difficulty in responding adequately to the many claimants. Globally, homelessness has been transformed from a problem that affects mostly individuals to one that involves a kaleidoscope of economically marginal people among whom there are ethnic and cultural differences. The combination of events leading to homelessness varies with each life story up to the extreme limit when the homeless person renounces his or her citizenship rights and begins to perceive himself or herself as out of the society of citizens with diminished or nonexistent rights to claims making.

Linking homelessness with poverty poses several important issues of social relationships among the homeless, citizens, and institutions. Even the most advanced welfare nations favor workers, whose claims to social rights hold the greatest legitimacy based on their past and present attachment to the workforce. As more homeless people fall out of the workforce, their social and civil claims diminish despite their citizenship. They then need to compete in a large and growing arena of claims makers who have established moral justification for their claims against institutions. Among these are the retired, the disabled, those uprooted by political forces and natural disasters, and other groups of marginalized people.

The exponential growth of claims making has rendered homeless people, or those at risk for homelessness, as a less important class than other priority populations that capture public sentiment such as displaced refugees from the former Soviet Union and victims of Hurricane Katrina. In one perspective, homeless single adults—largely minority group members—have become the new "undeserving poor" among competing claims makers.

The structural dynamics in postmodern society have fundamentally altered the social contract between governing institutions and citizens and between citizens and marginalized poor people. Homelessness can be seen as a major consequence of these changes.

The ultimate question facing global urban societies is as follows: What is the nature of the social contract among institutions, the society of citizens, and the poor? Due to declining resources and altered public sentiment, post–World War II social contracts have been rejected to various degrees. This has occurred in the midst of dramatic social and economic changes in which the polarization of wealth, class, poverty, and opportunity is framed against the backdrop of increasing claims making and entitlement. Because the poorest members of society have lost credibility among the constellation of claimants, some social thinkers see the need to create new paradigms for meting out social justice.

The growing debate about the morality, ethics, and institutional arrangements for addressing inequality is central to the 21st century. On one side are those who have serious concerns that the inequality explosion is undermining global politics and the quality of life. They see the globalization of homelessness in urban centers as a reminder of the social polarization that characterizes the society of citizens.

One potential direction for change lies in making the claims of nonworkers more legitimized in the claims-making process. Other social thinkers believe that the changing socioeconomic demographics require a redesigned housing supply and built environment to accommodate housing needs and respond to social isolation. Another concern is that the human environment requires more formal social supports to augment the numerous formal and informal systems of support currently operating. Others suggest that self-help, mutual aid, and microdevelopment strategies are essential strategies for change.

At the level of the relationship between institutions and the society of citizens, some social thinkers call for increased recognition of the equality of claimants. At the level of the relationship between the society of citizens and the poor, they see the need to remedy the lack of interventions that address homeless people. The postindustrial economies have shaped new normative social systems that feature conflicting and competing cultures. The challenge is to create a social and built environment that supports the coexistence of mainstream and marginal citizens at global and local levels.

Madeleine R. Stoner

See also Social Inequality; Underclass; Wealth Distribution; "Welfare Queen"; Welfare Reform

Further Readings

De Bernart, M. 1994. "The Reality and Culture of Homelessness in the Post-modern City." Presented at the 13th World Congress of Sociology, Bielefeld, Germany.

Drover, Glenn and Patrick Kerans, eds. 1998. *New Approaches to Welfare Theory.* Aldershot, UK: Edward Elgar.

Fantasia, Rick and Maurice Isserman. 2004. *Homelessness: A Sourcebook.* New York: Facts on File.

National Coalition for the Homeless. 2006. *Who Is Homeless?* Washington, DC: Author.

Stoner, Madeleine R. 2002. "The Globalization of Urban Homelessness." In *From Chicago to LA: Making Sense of Urban Theory,* edited by M. J. Dear. Thousand Oaks, CA: Sage.

U.S. Department of Agriculture, Rural and Community Development. 1996. *Rural Homelessness: Focusing on the Needs of the Rural Homeless.* Washington, DC: U.S. Department of Agriculture.

Web Sites

National Alliance to End Homelessness: http://www.naeh.org
National Law Center on Homelessness and Poverty: http://www.nlchp.org
U.S. Conference of Mayors: http://www.usmayors.org

HOMICIDE

Homicide rates in the United States differ substantially by race and ethnicity. According to data for the year 2004, which provide a snapshot of the prevalence of homicide during an era of relatively low homicide rates, the national homicide offending rate for Blacks was 24.1 per 100,000 Blacks, as compared with a rate for Whites of 3.65 per 100,000 Whites. This nearly sevenfold difference has been fairly characteristic of the discrepancy between Whites and Blacks for several decades. Until the mid- to late 1980s, social science research on race-specific homicide rates was sparse. Some have attributed this to, among other things, a fear among social scientists of being labeled racist. However, during the 1990s, a virtual explosion of race-specific homicide research occurred, considerably advancing scientific understanding of the significant underlying social problems suggested by this massive chasm between racial groups.

African American Communities

At its core, the discrepancy may be attributable to the fact that substantial segments of the Black population live in socioeconomic contexts that are considerably more disadvantaged than those for even the poorest Whites. The problems of social dislocation experienced by many urban Black populations have been well documented by social scientists for several decades now, and the alarmingly high rates of poverty, family distress and breakdown, unemployment, and violence are well known. The literature on urban Black violence has revealed, with a high degree of consistency, that the overlap of these social problems, coupled with the residential segregation of Blacks from Whites, more advantaged groups, and mainstream institutions of social mobility, has a robust association with the urban Black homicide rate.

Much of this empirical research relies conceptually on William Julius Wilson's research on the most disadvantaged segments of the urban Black population and two important concepts he coined: social isolation and concentration effects. The disadvantaged urban Black population in the United States emerged from the throes of industrial restructuring during the 1960s and 1970s, which also enhanced the movement of more prosperous middle-class Blacks out of central-city neighborhoods and into peripheral areas of urban ghettos and into suburban enclaves. The evaporation of high-quality, low-skilled jobs and the growth of service sectors of the economy ravaged the employment prospects of significant segments of the urban Black population. This created a "spatial mismatch" between the supply of low-skilled workers and the demand for high-paying, low-skilled factory work, ultimately elevating poverty and unemployment. In addition, much of the stable Black middle class moved out of central cities. Credited with sustaining local businesses, providing a network connection for displaced workers, and serving as the leaders of civic affairs, this out-migration initiated a decline in local noneconomic civic and social institutions. Those left behind constituted the socially isolated casualties of industrial restructuring who lacked contact with both members of middle-class society and the institutions of social mobility that make middle-class attainment a reality. Over time, the high rates of poverty, unemployment, family breakdown, welfare dependence, and the like led to concentration effects—subtle adaptations to an extremely alienating existence that involve the partial inversion of mainstream middle-class norms and values to more realistically reflect the day-to-day existence of the socially isolated. The intensive concentration of structural disadvantage may also compromise the level of collective efficacy within social units or their ability to activate social networks to address social problems collectively. One pernicious by-product of this whole process is high levels of violence.

Elijah Anderson, in his influential book *Code of the Street,* documented one important way in which cultural adaptations to extreme structural deprivation manifest themselves. The "code of the street" refers primarily to a set of behavioral regulations governing interpersonal interaction and communication among those living in the crumbling urban cores of many U.S. cities. The code essentially prescribes the use of violence or the threat of violence for many minor and trivial breaches of others' personal space, reputation, or public status. Violence in this context is not only a means to resolve disputes but also a way to shore up reputations and gain status in a milieu where conventional routes to status are severely circumscribed. While widely adhering to the main foundations of the "American dream," material wealth, and status, the severely disadvantaged live in communities where the conventional institutional routes to such forms of success are substantially inoperative. Participation in the drug culture or just spending unstructured time on the streets elevates the likelihood of subscribing to the code to secure at least a small grasp of the widely sought-after status and respect. Many public arenas, especially those catering to young people and teenagers, become staging areas where the dramaturgy of street life and the code play themselves out.

Other Minority Communities

Although the large bulk of race- and ethnicity-specific crime-related research has focused on the Black–White difference, it is useful to contrast these groups with what little is known about Latino, American Indian, and Asian homicide. For these groups, directly comparable yearly estimations for homicide rates are difficult to come by due to the nature of reporting practices. However, using several different data sources helps to round out the picture.

Latinos are the largest ethnic minority group in the United States and are the subject of much public concern over a potential link between immigration and violence. One study, using homicide victimization data for Latinos (treating them as a homogeneous group), reported Latino homicide rates per 100,000 of 16.0 in 1985, 18.6 in 1991, and 12.4 in 1996. Thus, these figures place Latinos' ranking as higher than that of Whites but lower than that of Blacks. Available research indicates that, despite compelling conceptual arguments and much public attention to the matter, there is little evidence that immigration is associated with higher rates of homicide for this group; if anything it may be associated with lower rates of homicide among Latinos. Research also finds that Latino homicide is driven by relative deprivation and structural conditions but that Latino homicide rates are not as high as those for Blacks because of the higher levels of labor market involvement, and thus social capital, that Latino communities maintain.

Although reliable empirical data are more difficult to come by for American Indians, the available evidence from the past 25 years or so indicates that on average American Indian homicide rates are higher than White homicide rates but significantly lower than Black homicide rates. One study from 1980 to 1984 provided a national-level American Indian homicide rate of 9.6 per 100,000, whereas another reported that the Native American homicide arrest rate from 1987 to 1992 was between 5 and 7 per 100,000. A later government report estimated the homicide rate from 1992 to 1996 to average approximately 7 per 100,000. A 2004 Uniform Crime Report estimate enumerated 102 American Indian/Alaska Native arrests for murder and nonnegligent manslaughter, accounting for 1.1% of the total number of murder and nonnegligent manslaughter arrests. As these numbers reveal, the statistically rare nature of homicide for this group makes it difficult to infer much about the nature and extent of homicide among this group.

One prominent study describes a set of social circumstances and processes for American Indians that closely parallel descriptions of Black social life in the United States. Thus, social disorganization and economic deprivation, a cultural tolerance for violence, and a generalized sense of culture conflict and powerlessness associated with minority status all are integral to a comprehensive understanding of American Indian homicide. The only notable feature that seems to be more important for the American Indian experience than for other groups is the very high rate at which alcohol is involved in American Indian violence.

Involvement in homicide among the Asian population is a vastly understudied topic in the United States. The Asian population, much like the Latino and American Indian populations, is unevenly distributed geographically and so national violence figures are not particularly helpful. For example, in 2004 the Uniform Crime Reports data indicated that Asian Pacific Islanders accounted for 117 homicide arrests or 1.2% of the total number of national arrests. Analyzing data from cities where Asians constitute a significant proportion of the population is helpful. One study using this strategy compared the Asian homicide victimization rate in San Diego with the rates for all cities with at least 1 million people and with the total rate for San Diego. The study found that Asian homicide rates were well below both of these contrast categories but that the temporal trends were nearly identical in terms of the high and low periods, suggesting that the basic social and cultural causes of homicide for Asians are similar to those described for the other racial/ethnic groups discussed in this entry.

Matthew R. Lee

See also African Americans; Asian Americans; Code of the Street; Community Cohesion; Crime and Race; Death Penalty; Victim Discounting; Victimization; Wilson, William Julius

Further Readings

Anderson, Elijah. 1999. *Code of the Street: Decency, Violence, and the Moral Life of the Inner City.* New York: Norton.

Bachman, Ronet. 1992. *Death and Violence on the Reservation: Homicide, Family Violence, and Suicide in American Indian Populations.* New York: Auburn House.

Greenfeld, Lawrence A. and Steven K. Smith. 1999. *American Indians and Crime.* Washington, DC: U.S. Department of Justice.

Martinez, Ramiro, Jr. 2002. *Latino Homicide: Immigration, Violence, and Community.* New York: Routledge.

Martinez, Ramiro, Jr. and Matthew R. Lee. 2000. "On Immigration and Crime." Pp. 485–524 in *Criminal Justice 2000: The Changing Nature of Crime,* edited by Gary LaFree. Washington, DC: National Institute of Justice.

Sampson, Robert J., Stephen Raudenbush, and Felton Earls. 1997. "Neighborhoods and Violent Crime: A Multilevel Study of Collective Efficacy." *Science* 277:918–924.

Silverman, Robert A. 1996. "Patterns of Native American Crime." Pp. 58–74 in *Native Americans, Crime, and Justice,* edited by Marianne O. Nielsen and Robert A. Silverman. Boulder, CO: Westview.

Wilson, William Julius. 1987. *The Truly Disadvantaged: The Inner City, the Underclass, and Public Policy.* Chicago, IL: University of Chicago Press.

Honduran Americans

In response to poverty and natural disaster in their country of origin, an estimated 315,000 Honduran migrants have arrived in the United States seeking to build a new life. Hondurans form the third-largest group of Central Americans in the United States. They have employed a variety of strategies to improve their economic status and maintain community and family ties.

Honduras, a nation estimated in 2007 to have 7.1 million people, avoided the civil warfare that devastated its Central American neighbors during the 1970s and 1980s. Structural inequalities and deep poverty, however, have been persistent facets of Honduran nationhood. The Honduran economy has historically centered on the export of coffee and bananas and has been highly dependent on U.S. capital. During the early 20th century, U.S. banana companies owned most of the land in northern Honduras and were powerful political and economic actors. Links to the United States further deepened during the 1980s when Honduras became a staging ground for U.S. counterinsurgency operations in the region. Such cultural and economic penetration of the United States was an important factor that primed migration to the United States. In addition, although civilian rule was restored to Honduras in 1982, human rights abuses persisted and contributed to out-migration.

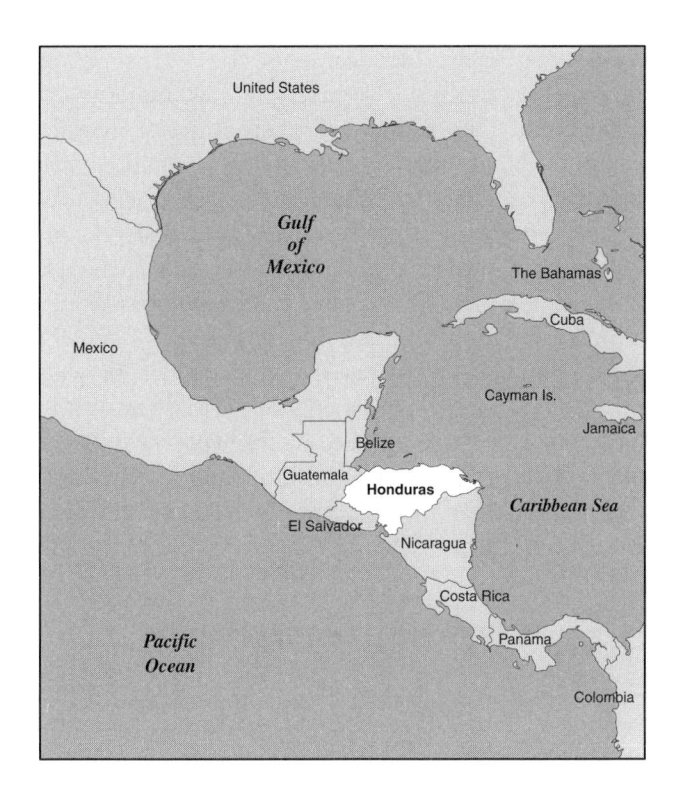

Most scholars believe, however, that the great majority of Hondurans have migrated to the United States for economic reasons, forming important communities in the Bronx, New York, Houston, Texas, and elsewhere. Estimates rank Honduras as the fifth-largest sending country of undocumented migrants with 138,000 in the United States. Honduras is one of the poorest countries in the Western Hemisphere, and more than half of Hondurans live below the poverty line. The poor of Honduras received a further blow in 1998 when Hurricane Mitch struck. More than 7,000 people were killed and 1 million were left homeless. Economic damage totaled $3 billion, and numerous jobs were lost. Following Hurricane Mitch, the U.S. government extended temporary protected status to many of the Hondurans who had entered the United States illegally but could not easily return to their country of origin because of the devastating impact of the hurricane.

Arriving in the United States, Hondurans have sought employment in factories, agriculture, the hospitality and care industries, and commercial cleaning. Upward economic mobility of Hondurans in the United States is closely linked to their means of incorporation into the economy, legal status, caretaking responsibilities, and levels of formal education and English. In addition, structural inequalities often trap migrants in low-skilled, low-wage jobs. Employment of Hondurans is also characterized by unstable work hours, migration-related debt, job insecurity, and conflicts with family obligations. Patriarchal household norms further limit women's job opportunities.

Despite these obstacles, Hondurans continue to strive and are able to send approximately $1 billion as remittances back to their country of origin, providing 15% of Honduras's gross domestic product. Honduran family and social structures have been strained by separation of parents and children and by competition for scarce resources. However, women in particular have formed networks for economic, domestic, and emotional support. Hondurans remain hopeful that they will be able to build a better life for themselves and their children in the United States.

Lynn Horton

See Appendix A
See also Central Americans in the United States; Hispanics; Immigrant Communities; Immigration, U.S.; Remittances

Further Readings

Hernandez, Romel. 2004. *Immigration from Central America.* Philadelphia, PA: Mason Crest.

Miyares, Inés M. 2006. "Central Americans: Legal Status and Settledness." In *Contemporary Ethnic Geographies in America,* edited by Inés M. Miyares and Christopher A. Airriess. Boulder, CO: Rowman & Littlefield.

Schmalzbauer, Leah. 2005. *Striving and Surviving: A Daily Analysis of Honduran Transnational Families.* New York: Routledge.

Suro, Roberto. 1999. *Strangers among Us: Latinos' Lives in a Changing America.* New York: Vintage Books.

HONG KONG

Hong Kong is located on the south China coast near the Pearl River Delta, a region of China with a long history of foreign trade. Hong Kong was a British colony from 1842 until 1997 and is now a special administrative region (HKSAR) of the People's

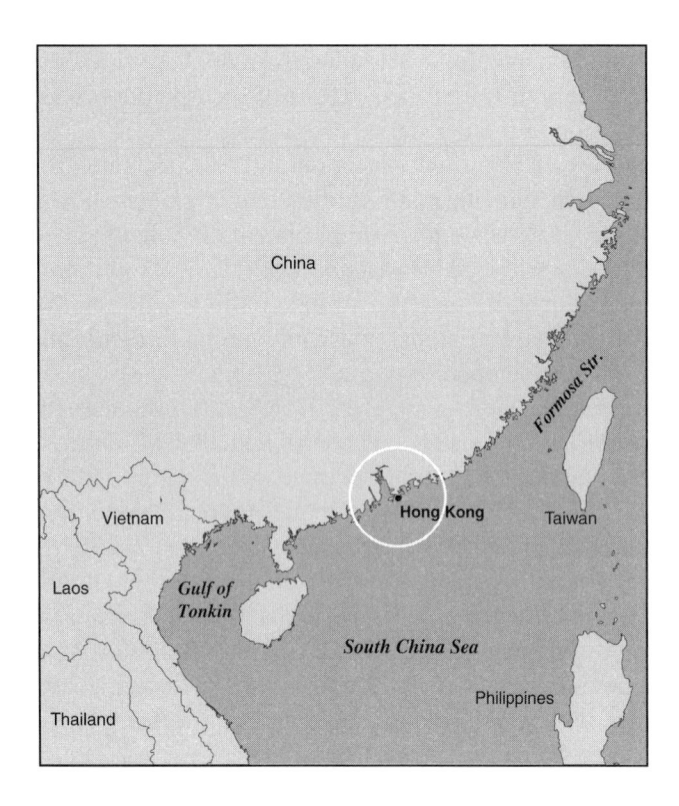

Republic of China (PRC) with an estimated 2007 population of 6.9 million people. The legal framework of the HKSAR grants Hong Kong a degree of independence from the legislation of the PRC as the "one country, two systems" formula implies. Given its colonial and trading history, Hong Kong has long been a place of exchange between people of various races and ethnicities. This entry examines the history of Hong Kong from the perspective of issues related to the situation of various racial/ethnic groups over time.

A Colonial Past

Disagreement over the exchange of silver and opium between China and Britain led to the First Opium War in China that lasted from 1839 to 1842. One of the conditions imposed by Britain on China was that Hong Kong became a British colony in 1842. The trade that Hong Kong attracted as a British port encouraged immigration, mostly of individuals from neighboring Guangdong Province in China but also from other parts of China, Asia, and the West. From the early 1950s, Hong Kong's population increased rapidly, supporting its development into one of East Asia's prime manufacturing, financial, and service centers. After the introduction of economic reforms in the PRC in 1978, many of Hong Kong's industries moved to Guangdong Province.

Cantonese-speaking residents from Guangdong Province have always formed the vast majority of Hong Kong's population. Chinese minority ethnic groups include the Fujianese, the Hakka, the Shanghainese, and the Teochew. Cantonese is widely spoken among all groups of Chinese residents in Hong Kong who also adopted, to various extents, other elements from Cantonese culture. Siu-lun Wong, in *Emigrant Entrepreneurs: Shanghai Industrialists in Hong Kong,* observed that many Shanghainese who migrated to Hong Kong during the second half of the 20th century were highly skilled and established themselves as prosperous and influential individuals. Members of other Chinese minorities, however, often held less prominent positions.

A Change of Sovereignty

Except for its final years, the British colonial administration in Hong Kong provided Chinese residents with few political rights and social benefits. Benjamin K. P. Leung, in *Perspectives on Hong Kong Society,* suggested that a "national identity" of Chinese residents in Hong Kong—that is, an identity that sees its interests as being different from the aims of the colonial government—only became widespread among Chinese residents during the 1970s when the colonial administration increased its accountability for the provision of housing, transport, and education. The preceding anti-imperialist movements in China, Leung observed, did not result in a widespread politicization of Chinese residents in Hong Kong.

Significant identity changes in Hong Kong's Chinese population stem from the fact that in 1984 Britain ceded to the request of the PRC to make Hong Kong part of China in 1997. This decision raised the question among the Chinese population of Hong Kong as to what it meant to be Chinese and gave rise to discussion on the relations among ethnicity, nationality, and governance. Britain's determination to increase the level of democracy during the final years of its rule had a strong impact on this discussion, namely by defining Hong Kong's way of life as democratic. The prospect of unification with the PRC, on the other hand, led to requests for more patriotic education in Hong Kong, especially for the younger Hong Kong–born Chinese residents.

Siu-kai Lau and Hsin-chi Kuan, in *The Ethos of the Hong Kong Chinese,* suggested that the Chinese population in Hong Kong during the late 1980s could be distinguished according to whether people saw themselves as rooted in "Hong Kong" or in "China." Individuals who identified themselves as "Hongkongese" (being mostly younger, well educated, professional, and/or wealthier residents), rather than as "Chinese," thought that Hong Kong was significantly different from the PRC. Unlike individuals with a Chinese identity, those with a Hong Kong identity were likely to consider migrating to other countries in view of the unification with the PRC. The authors did not correlate Hongkongese and Chinese with other Chinese ethnic characteristics.

Transnational Migration

The suppression of student protests in Beijing's Tiananmen Square in 1989 increased fears in Hong Kong about possible restrictions on civil liberties after 1997. An unknown but significant number of Hong Kong Chinese residents began investigating the likelihood of obtaining the right of abode in another nation as an "insurance policy." Britain did not welcome the immigration of Hong Kong residents. Since the 1960s, Britain's concern over potentially large numbers of immigrants from its various dependent territories has led to restrictions on who could obtain the right of abode in Britain. Of Hong Kong's population, only 50,000 heads of households (both Chinese and non-Chinese) were granted British citizenship in 1990. Reportedly, these individuals were selected on the basis of their business and professional qualifications.

Meanwhile, large numbers of mostly middle-class Chinese residents (approximately a half-million) have started to migrate to Australia, Canada, Singapore, and other places. However, Hong Kong's economic opportunities, problems with integration in other nations, and the relatively smooth establishment of the HKSAR motivated a very high percentage of those who had migrated abroad to return to the SAR. The question that researchers are now investigating is whether these returnees are inclined to remain in Hong Kong. David Ley and Audrey Kobayashi's article, "Back to Hong Kong: Return Migration or Transnational Sojourn," suggested that Hong Kong Chinese residents with the right of abode in Canada are likely to plan future residence in either of the two places according to different stages in their life circle. Return migrants in Hong Kong often value the education their children acquired while residing abroad, yet they also report difficulties with readjustment, and some express regrets that the time they spent abroad had made them miss out on opportunities in Hong Kong.

When it comes to the ease with which residents in Hong Kong can gain citizenship in different nations, Barry Sautman, in a chapter in *Re-making Citizenship in Hong Kong,* stressed that Chinese residents have advantages when compared with non-Chinese residents. Chinese residents who became citizens of the PRC in 1997 are entitled to retain citizenship in other nations and to obtain HKSAR passports. Non-Chinese individuals, even if they were born in the HKSAR, are entitled to apply only for permanent residency but not for HKSAR passports (although there have been exceptions).

"Ethnic Minorities" Today

Approximately 5% of Hong Kong's population, counted as 6,994,500 residents in the provisional census for 2006, is non-Chinese. The 2001 census refers to non-Chinese residents as "ethnic minorities" and includes among the largest groups 142,556 Filipinos, 50,494 Indonesians, 19,441 individuals of mixed races (of whom 16,587 are partially Chinese), 18,909 British, 18,543 Indians, 14,342 Thais, 14,180 Japanese, 12,564 Nepalese, and 11,017 Pakistanis. The majority of the residents from the Philippines, Indonesia, and Thailand are female domestic helpers working on temporary contracts. Many Indians work in import and export businesses, whereas a number of the Pakistanis are laborers. Most Westerners work in white-collar occupations or have their own businesses.

Most families of non-Chinese residents have not stayed in Hong Kong over several generations. Yet some of Hong Kong's most prosperous families, such as the Hotungs, are of Eurasian origin. Being familiar with several cultures helped Eurasians, including the Hotungs, to work as *compradors* that mediated between the colonial firms, which they represented, and the Chinese merchants. The "local boy" identity is another example of the hybrid ethnicity of an interracial group. Local boys (and girls) are the descendants of male Muslim immigrants from South Asia who married Chinese women. They have retained elements of their Islamic culture and have strongly assimilated into Cantonese culture.

During colonial times, the British administration favored individuals from South Asia to work in certain occupations in Hong Kong. The Royal Hong

Kong Police recruited Sikhs and Muslims in north India to serve as constables. Parsis were given liquor licenses to trade in the British possessions in the East, and Sindhis owned chains of provision stores that catered to the British garrisons in several Asian port cities. Using ties with coethnics was common among most ethnic groups in Hong Kong to establish businesses and engage in trade, and this solidified their shared ethnicity. This characteristic is still prevalent among some ethnic groups in Hong Kong. For example, Jain diamond traders rely on coethnic networks to buy diamonds, and insider positions in these networks require shared family links and participation in shared religious activities.

However, for poor non-Chinese ethnic groups, a high degree of adaptation to Cantonese culture was often necessary to earn a living. For example, since 1997 a high degree of assimilation to Cantonese culture is expected from ethnic minority children whose parents cannot afford the high fees of the international schools. They need to succeed in public primary and secondary schools, which teach them in the Cantonese language, but often the children are unable to compete.

Action on Inequality

Since the establishment of the HKSAR, members of non-Chinese minorities, civil society organizations, and international chambers of commerce have voiced more demands for anti-racial discrimination legislation. Hong Kong signed the International Convention on All Forms of Racial Discrimination in 1969, but the colonial framework hindered legislation. Recent surveys of Hong Kong residents of South Asian origin show that the large majority reports discrimination, notably vilification and unequal access to employment. Reports of violent attacks, however, are rare.

Chinese public opinion during the initial years of the HKSAR included a strong element that was against anti-racial discrimination legislation. Such voices considered Hong Kong to be a "Chinese city" and were not concerned about non-Chinese residents. Reports of tragedies that allegedly resulted from discrimination against non-Chinese individuals in hospitals, along with the plight of ethnic minority children in Hong Kong public schools, have worked toward wider support for the legislation. After 10 years of debate, the draft of Hong Kong's anti-racial discrimination law was unveiled in November 2006, addressing discrimination in employment, education, club membership, and the provision of goods and services.

The proposed law was criticized for its exemptions, especially in the language policies in Hong Kong's public schools, which are not obliged to help non-Cantonese-speaking pupils to learn Cantonese. This exemption prevents many ethnic minority children from competing on an equal basis with Cantonese-speaking children. Moreover, insisting on Cantonese proficiency is also a hidden means of allowing schools to exclude pupils with a darker skin color on the grounds that this would supposedly diminish the schools' reputations.

The question of whether discrimination against newer immigrants from mainland China should or should not be covered by the law was debated extensively during the years preceding the drafting of the law. Kuah Khun Eng, in a chapter in *Hong Kong in China: The Challenges of Transition,* examined the unfavorable treatment of new immigrants from mainland China in Hong Kong, including the plight of children who live in the PRC and who have a Chinese parent who is a permanent resident in the HKSAR. These children have the right to live in Hong Kong. An estimated 66,000 children were expected to immigrate after July 1, 1997, and Hong Kong established a quota system for daily immigration from mainland China in response. Introducing this quota meant that many of these children were expected to wait for up to two years in mainland China before being united with family members in Hong Kong. Children of non-Chinese residents usually receive permission to immigrate within a few weeks. However, given that the Hong Kong government considers Chinese residents in Hong Kong and in mainland China to share the same (Han) ethnicity, the proposed anti-racial discrimination legislation cannot cover new immigrants from mainland China.

Caroline Plüss

See Appendix A
See also Australia; China; Chinatowns; Chinese Americans; Colonialism; Diaspora; Globalization; Singapore

Further Readings

Das, Rup Narayan. 1990. "A Nationality Issue: Ethnic Indians in Hong Kong." Pp. 147–157 in *The Other Hong Kong Report 1990,* edited by Richard Y. C. Wong and Joseph Y. S. Cheng. Hong Kong: Chinese University Press.

Guldin, Gergory Elliot. 1980. *Overseas at Home: The Fujianese of Hong Kong.* Ann Arbor, MI: University Microfilms International.

Hamilton, Gary, ed. 1999. *Cosmopolitan Capitalists: Hong Kong and the Chinese Diaspora at the End of the Twentieth Century.* Seattle: University of Washington Press.

Ku, Agnes and Ngai Pun, eds. 2004. *Re-making Citizenship in Hong Kong: Community, Nation, and the Global City.* London: Routledge.

Ku, Hok Bun, Chan Kam Wah, Chan Wai Ling, and Lee Wai Yee. 2003. *A Research Report for the Life Experiences of Pakistanis in Hong Kong.* Hong Kong: Hong Kong Polytechnic University, Centre for Social Policy Studies.

Lau, Siu-kai and Hsin-chi Kuan. 1988. *The Ethos of the Hong Kong Chinese.* Hong Kong: Chinese University Press.

Leung, Benjamin K. P. 1996. *Perspectives on Hong Kong Society.* Hong Kong: Oxford University Press.

Ley, David and Audrey Kobayashi. 2005. "Back to Hong Kong: Return Migration or Transnational Sojourn." *Global Networks* 5(2):111–127.

Loper, Kelley. 2004. *Race and Equality: A Study of Ethnic Minorities in Hong Kong's Education System—Project Report and Analysis.* Hong Kong: University of Hong Kong, Centre for Comparative and Public Law.

Plüss, Caroline. 2005. "Constructing Globalised Ethnicity: Migrants from India in Hong Kong." *International Sociology* 20:203–226.

Richburg, Keith B. 2003. "Hong Kong Crusaders against Racism Gain Little Support, Even from Victims." Pp. 350–352 in *Racism: A Global Reader,* edited by Kevil Reilly, Stephen Kaufman, and Angela Bodino. Armonk, NY: M. E. Sharpe.

Wang, Gungwu and John Wong, eds. 1999. *Hong Kong in China: The Challenges of Transition.* Singapore: Times Academic Press.

Wong, Siu-lun. 1988. *Emigrant Entrepreneurs: Shanghai Industrialists in Hong Kong.* Hong Kong: Oxford University Press.

HOOKS, BELL (1952–)

bell hooks is a scholar, a writer, and an activist who has made various contributions to both feminist and antiracist scholarship and theorizing. A self-identified feminist, she has used her work to engage topics such as feminist theory, White supremacy, capitalism, and postmodernism. She has been especially instrumental in challenging the classist and racist assumptions of mainstream second-wave feminism as well as the sexist biases in the Black Civil Rights Movement.

hooks's work has illustrated the ways in which both the mainstream feminist movement and the Black civil rights movement marginalized the interests of Black women. Her first book, *Ain't I a Woman* (1981), focused in particular on the assumptions of these social movements in regard to Black women. In this work, which she first began writing at 19 years of age, she explored how Black women were placed in particularly precarious positions during slavery because of the intersecting oppressions of racism and sexism that affected their lives. She also articulated specific manifestations of racism in the women's movement and Black women's relationship to feminism.

hooks's body of work as a whole has influenced the ideologies and directions of feminist movements, urging a broadly defined feminist agenda with the task of leading movements of resistance against sexism, racism, and classism. Her later piece, *Feminist Theory, Margin to Center,* continued to urge feminists to rethink issues of race, class, violence, work, and families under the guise of a more inclusive feminist ideology.

About Her Life

bell hooks was born Gloria Jean Watkins in Kentucky in 1952. She was one of seven children, with five sisters and one brother. She later adopted the name bell hooks as a writing pseudonym and then began using it for lectures as well. The name is a family name and belonged to her great-grandmother on her mother's side. In her essay, "To Gloria, Who She Is: On Using a Pseudonym," she explained how taking on this name was a strategy of empowerment that enabled her to find her own voice. hooks received a bachelor's degree in English from Stanford University in 1973, and three years later she received her master's in English from the University of Wisconsin–Madison. She later obtained her doctorate from the University of California, Santa Cruz, where she wrote her dissertation on the work of Pulitzer Prize–winning writer Toni Morrison.

hooks has taught at various institutions of higher education, including the University of California, Santa Cruz; San Francisco State University; Yale University; Oberlin College; and the City College of New York, where she held the position of distinguished professor of English. She currently holds a position as distinguished writer-in-residence at Berea College in Berea, Kentucky.

hooks's pedagogical work has received a significant amount of attention, and she has written extensively on feminist and antiracist pedagogy and overall how education can be a holistic and liberating experience for students and teachers alike. She has cited Paulo Freire and Thich Nhat Hanh as two major influences on her pedagogical work.

Her Writings

hooks has published more than thirty books throughout her career, including *Yearning: Race, Gender, and Cultural Politics; Black Looks: Race and Representation; Sisters of the Yam: Black Women and Self-Recovery; Teaching to Transgress: Education as the Practice of Freedom; Bone Black: Memories of Girlhood; Reel to Real: Race, Sex, and Class at the Movies; Wounds of Passion: A Writing Life; The Will to Change: Men, Masculinity, and Love;* and *Feminism Is for Everybody: Passionate Politics.* These works address topics such as feminism, love, self-esteem, masculinity, racism, film, and the writing process.

hooks has also participated in various collaborations, with perhaps the most famous of these being *Breaking Bread: Insurgent Black Intellectual Life*, which is composed of a series of dialogues, interviews, and essays written by her and Cornel West, another prominent African American intellectual. Other collaborations include *Daughters of the Dust* (written with Julie Dash and Toni Cade Bambara) and *Homegrown: Engaged Cultural Criticism* (written with Amalia Mesa-Bains). She is also the author of four children's books: *Skin Again, Happy to Be Nappy, Be Boy Buzz,* and *Homemade Love*. She has also published two works of poetry: an early chapbook titled *And There We Wept* and a later book titled *A Women's Mourning Song*.

hooks has also produced various works of cultural criticism focusing on films such as *Mad Max, Crooklyn,* and *Do the Right Thing*. Her pieces of cultural criticism interrogate the politics of gendered and raced representation and issues of commodification. The body and breadth of hooks's work reflect a lifetime commitment to feminist and antiracist scholarly production and activism. Her work is widely read in various humanities and social science courses, among others.

Amanda Moras

See also African American Studies; African American Women and Work; Black Intellectuals; Body Image; Civil Rights Movement, Women and; Feminism; Feminism, Black; Gender and Race, Intersection of; Internal Colonialism; White Racism

Further Readings

Florence, Namulundah. 1998. *bell hooks' Engaged Pedagogy: A Transgressive Education for Critical Consciousness* (Critical Studies in Education and Culture Series). Westport, CT: Bergin & Garvey.

hooks, bell. 1984. *Feminist Theory from Margin to Center.* Boston, MA: South End Press.

hooks, bell. 1989. *Talking Back: Thinking Feminist, Thinking Black.* Boston, MA: South End Press.

HOPI

The Hopi people, with a population of 10,000 to 12,000, though not a large tribal group, have lived in the area they now occupy for more than 1,000 years. One of their villages, Oraibi, is one of the oldest, if not the oldest, continuously occupied communities in the United States. The Hopi people are considered the westernmost branch of the Pueblos. The Hopi's separation from the other Pueblos as well as their being completely surrounded for centuries by the Navajos has led the Hopi to often be considered apart from the other Pueblos while recognizing their cultural ties. One significant exception to similarities in lifestyle is that the Hopi are the only Pueblo people to speak a language in the Uto-Aztecan language family. This entry will include an overview of Hopi history and the contemporary life focusing on the Hopi reservation.

The ancestors of the Hopi, the name said to mean virtuous or peaceful people, are referred to as the Anasazi (although Hopi prefer to call them Hisat-Sinom). The Hopi have been and continue to be dry-farming agricultural people, since early 500 AD in their current area in northeast Arizona. Living in conditions challenging to most agricultural practices, the Hopi, like the Anasazi people before them, became proficient in the farming of corn and other vegetables.

Basketry emerged as another staple of Hopi culture and has progressed to be a source of revenue as the artistry of this craft has become recognized. In the early 1900s, collectors also became interest in *titu* (pl. *tithu*), the dolls with Hopi spiritual representations given to their girls. This craft evolved into the carving of cottonwood root katsinas (or kachinas) that came to be sold in roadside stands along what was then Highway 66 as a means of economic support during the Great Depression. Contemporary katsinas take many forms and often depart radically from the *titu* tradition. Silversmithing with the pattern of overlaying, distinctive from the Navajo and Zuni styles, with inlaid stones, began in earnest in 1949, when returning veterans used the G.I. Bill to become trained in this craft.

The settlement of the last thousand years is viewed by the Hopi as actually the fourth creation of life, which began deep below the surface of today's earth, with the first three preceding lives or worlds ending in destruction. These earlier times are regarded as times when the people denied the plan of the Creator and thus are not truly part of the Hopi Way. The faithful during these earlier times were protected underground with the Ant People. According to Hopi legend, the Ant People resided underground and deprived themselves of food, which explains why today's ants are so small around the waist. The kivas of today, square-walled private rooms used for religious rituals by all Pueblo people, are considered representations of these anthills.

The Hopi's first contact with Europeans came with Spaniards dispatched by Francisco Coronado in 1540. Some villages had violent encounters whereas others had more peaceful relationships. Compared with other Pueblos, the Hopi have had by far the least Spanish influence, which again contributes to the Hopi's somewhat distinctive character. Franciscan missionaries began settling in 1629 and erecting churches. These encounters were particularly brutal, with attacks on both sides. Despite violent periods, the relative isolation of the homeland compared with other Southwest Indians allowed the Hopi to largely preserve their culture and traditions.

The Hopi have always been a matrilineal, matrilocal society in which women form the basis of family social organization. The women are the backbone of everyday Hopi society, overseeing the household and owning property. The husband's real home is said to be with his mother's family because his responsibilities to her continue, yet while married, he lives with his wife, her sisters, her mother, and, if living, her grandmother, along with their respective husbands. Despite the matrilineal family traditions, men serve as the ritual leaders of each village and are expected to provide role models through hard work, humility, and good spiritual thoughts.

The traditional Hopi way of life was threatened in more modern times when the Navajo moved into the area settled by the Hopi from New Mexico in the early 1800s. Though the Navajo tended to occupy the area only in the winter, their movement of large herds of sheep, goats, and cattle led to overgrazing on the mesa. The rough boundaries of the Hopi reservation as outlined in 1882 included only a small fraction of the land they regarded as theirs and that of their ancestors. Further complicating the Hopi–Navajo dispute was the federal government's wish to distance itself from this contentious situation. The Bureau of Indian Affairs further complicated the friction by creating a "joint use area" between the two official reservations of the Hopi and Navajo.

The assimilationist stance of the Bureau of Indian Affairs became evident as Hopi village autonomy was ignored and government schools were built that met during Hopi ceremonial occasions but were closed for Sundays and other Christian holidays. Resistant to this refusal to recognize their traditions, some Hopi kept their children from school, only to have troops in 1890 forcibly round up 104 children and take them to the school.

Contributing to the push to assimilation was the arrival of Mormon and Mennonite missionaries. As was often true of religious outreach activities, the tolerance for tribal people's spirituality varied tremendously by historical period and the individual approach taken by mission leaders. By the 1920s, permanent homes were constructed by the Navajo in the northern Black Mesa, land viewed by the Hopi as theirs. Further complicating the situation was the presence of the Peabody Coal Company that began strip-mining operations on land leased to both the Navajo and Hopi beginning in 1968. This economic development expanded into the largest coal strip-mining operation in the world. The Hopi people, reflecting the development-ecology divisions in larger U.S. society, have often been divided over the opportunities and challenges such as economic development poses. These tensions regarding land and economics and, in the view of many traditional people, alleged violations of mining on sacred lands have led to continuing disputes with the Navajo and the Bureau of Indian Affairs that were still being resolved in the 21st century.

Today, the Hopi largely live on the Hopi Reservation on the Black Mesa. The mesa rises 1,000 feet or more above the grasslands and is regarded by the Hopi as the center of the universe. Hopi off the reservation live primarily in Arizona or California.

The Hopi are a traditional people who still recognize the individual autonomy of each village, although the Hopi Tribal Council is recognized as the official governing body. The Hopi people take residency in one of their twelve villages on the reservation seriously, and such residency forms a membership requirement in addition to blood quantum. Disputes arise about the authenticity of being Hopi if one works off the reservation and, at times, lives outside their village.

Although the Hopi continue to be somewhat more isolated than many tribal people or other Pueblos, they are increasingly influenced by and interact with other cultures, either by choice or through economic pressure. Younger Hopi people today listen to the message of the katsina without any thought of outsiders but also adjust by interacting in varying degrees with larger society as they seek to support themselves economically. In a real sense, this is what they have been doing for 5 centuries.

Richard T. Schaefer

See Appendix A

See also Assimilation; Blood Quantum; Bureau of Indian Affairs; Environmental Justice; Native American Education: Native American Health Care; Native Americans; Native Americans, Environment and; Navajo; Pueblos

Further Readings

Bureau of Indian Affairs. 1972. *Indians of Arizona.* Washington, DC: U.S. Government Printing Office.

Griffin-Pierce, Trady. 2000. *Native Peoples of the Southwest.* Albuquerque: University of New Mexico Press.

Havens, Bill. 2007. "Every Hopi Comes Home Again." *Indian Country Today* (April 16):A3.

Kelly, Shannon. 2007. "Black Mesa, Arizona." Retrieved September 29, 2007, from http://cpluhna.nau.edu/Places/black_mesa.htm

National Park Service. 2997. "Old Oraibi." Retrieved September 30, 2007, from http://tps.cr.nps.gov/nhl/detail.cfm?ResourceId=100&ResourceType=District

Northern Arizona University. 2007. "Hopi." Retrieved September 27, 2007, from http://cpluhna.nau.edu/People/hopi.htm

Rohn, Arthur H. and William M. Ferguson. 2006. *Puebloan Ruins of the Southwest.* Albuquerque: University of New Mexico Press.

Hourglass Economy

An economic paradox has been at play and growing in the United States for more than a third of a century—a race to the top of the economy by the rich and the powerful, a slide to the bottom of the economy by low-wage workers and the poor, and a gradual shrinkage of the middle class. The low-wage class is populated primarily by members of racial/ethnic minorities as well as by many of the new immigrants.

The net result is that the United States is experiencing its greatest economic inequality since the era of the robber barons some hundred years ago. This, in turn, fuels another economic paradox. The United States, unchallenged as the richest country in the world, has the greatest relative economic inequality of any developed country in the world, as described in this entry.

How It Happened

The *hourglass economy* is a metaphor suggesting the economic shape of the U.S. labor force resulting from the extreme economic equality that began during the early 1970s in the country and continues to the present day. The hallmark of this economic change is a bifurcated labor force taking the shape of an hourglass, where a large number of workers at the top of the hourglass have well-paying jobs, another large number of workers at the bottom have poor-paying jobs, and a small number of workers at the neck of the hourglass constitute what's left of the middle class. Three distinctions need to be made to locate the conception of hourglass within the context of economic inequality.

Growing Inequality

An analysis of the rise, fall, and rise again in economic inequality in the United States for the past 100 years shows that for a quarter-century before World War II, the income share of total national wages for the top 10% of wage earners (the top decile) ranged between 40% and 47%. Come the "Great Compression"—the period between the late 1930s and the early 1970s—that share shrunk to a low of 30%. A major shift in the allocation of economic gains during the early 1970s resulted in the raising of the ceiling and a lowering of the floor for the U.S. labor force, with the few getting a great deal more and the many getting a great deal less. At that point, inequality accelerated markedly, and by the late 1990s it had reached pre–World War II robber baron levels.

Bifurcation of Wealth

David Ellwood, a Harvard University economist, added another dimension to the analysis of economic inequality—the bifurcation of income and wealth. He examined the percentage change in the earnings of different percentile groups of full-year, full-time male workers from 1961 to 2000, using 1961 as the base year. There were three key statistical groups in the crosshairs of his analysis: (a) rich wage earners at the 90th and 75th percentiles of the income hierarchy, (b) poor wage earners at the 25th and 10th percentiles, and (c) "the middle" wage earners at the 50th percentile.

All three groups had relatively equal income growth from 1961 to the early 1970s. Then income divergence began, somewhat slowly at first and then accelerating markedly from 1975 onward. The character of the divergence is just as dramatic as its magnitude. The poor had the same percentage growth as the rich until the early 1970s. Then their real wage earning actually began to decline until around 1995. The rich saw their percentage of income start growing in 1961 and experienced few declines up to the present time. The net result was the rise of economic bifurcation—an extreme difference in the percentage of income growth between the "haves" and the "have lesses" and also the rise of an extreme absolute dollar difference. So, as the gap between middle-income America and high-income America (the top 1%) grows, that same gap for racial/ethnic minority groups has exploded.

The Birth of the Hourglass

Job growth prior to the 1990s was either "golden" as in the 1960s—when high-paying jobs grew most and low-paying jobs grew least—or relatively equal for all. The decade of the 1990s, however, represented a significant departure from this trend. New jobs took the shape of an asymmetric, top-heavy hourglass that exhibited strong growth at the top tier of the employment structure, moderately strong growth at the bottom tier, and especially weak growth in the middle.

Analysis of the changing occupational wage structure—and the morphing of the economy into the shape of an hourglass—indicated that the experience of workers generally conforms to the hourglass metaphor. New jobs generated during the middle and late 1990s (1994–2000) took the shape of an asymmetric, top-heavy hourglass that exhibited strong growth at the top tier of the employment structure, moderately strong growth at the bottom tier, and especially weak growth in the middle. The good news is that a larger number of above middle-income jobs than below middle-income jobs were added to the labor force (55.9% vs. 38.2%). The bad news is that these data represent the first evidence of two trends: the economic bifurcation of the labor force and the dramatic shrinking of middle-income jobs.

The projected occupational growth in the labor force for the period between 2000 and 2014 also takes a bottom-heavy hourglass shape, with a continued shrinking of middle-income jobs; thus, a continued economic bifurcation of the labor force is consistent with the known hourglass growth trend of the 1990s and reflects a 20-year trend of the labor force morphing into an hourglass economy.

Why It Happened

One source of economic inequality is sociopolitical in origin. These factors include exceptionally generous tax breaks for the wealthy, runaway executive and chief executive officer salaries and stock options, significant increases in worker productivity and corporate and business profits with little or no commensurate raises in the wages of workers, the declining economic and political power of labor unions, the stagnation of the minimum wage, and increases in the "premium" for a college degree.

A second source of economic inequality is the rise of structural factors in a postindustrial, high-technology information society that resulted in an hourglass economy. Three characteristics of the new economy have implications for the changing structure of economic rewards for the labor force: (a) the assignment of investment and development resources to information technology and service industries, (b) a shift—radical in some instances—in the number and kind of occupations considered as core to the new economy, and (c) a reallocation of the economic rewards provided for occupations in the new economy.

The compact in U.S. society has always been hard work in return for achieving the "American dream." The rise of an hourglass economy, however, results in a system where no amount of hard work facilitates social mobility and economic parity and low-wage workers are in danger of becoming a permanent underclass. Therefore, as the new high-technology service economy replaces an industrial economy, the United States faces the possible rise of a permanently bifurcated labor force characterized by extreme economic inequality with a shrunken middle class. If this new structure replaces the classic U.S. ideal of an egalitarian middle-class society, there will be not only economic consequences but also political and social consequences.

John Koval

See also Ethnic Enclave, Economic Impact of; Immigration, U.S.; Informal Economy; Underclass; Wealth Distribution

Further Readings

Bean, Frank D. and B. Lindsay Lowell. 2003. "Immigrant Employment and Mobility Opportunities in California." *State of California Labor* 3:87–117.

Ellwood, David. 2002. *Grow Faster Together or Grow Slowly Apart.* Washington, DC: Aspen Institute.

Hecker, Daniel E. 2005. "Occupational Employment Projections to 2014." *Monthly Labor Review,* November.

Massey, Douglas H. and Deborah S. Hirst. 1998. "From Escalator to Hourglass: Changes in the U.S. Occupational Wage Structure 1949–1989." *Social Science Research* 27:51–71.

Milkman, Ruth and Rachel E. Dwyer. 2002. "Growing Apart: The 'New Economy' and Job Polarization in California, 1992–2000." *State of California Labor* 2:3–31.

Piketty, Thomas and Emannuel Saez. 2001. *Income Inequality in the United States.* Cambridge, MA: National Bureau of Economic Research.

Wright, Erik Olin and Rachel Dwyer. 2003. "The Patterns of Job Expansion in the USA: A Comparison of the 1960s and 1990s." *Socio-Economic Review* 1:289–325.

HOUSING AUDITS

During the past decade, nationally representative surveys of the general public reveal that the majority of U.S. residents endorse principles of equal access to housing, believing that people should be able to live where they want, based on what they can afford, regardless of their race/ethnicity. Indeed, the Fair Housing Act of 1968 prohibits discrimination in the U.S. housing rental and sales markets based on one's race or color, religion, sex, national origin, familial status, or disability. Unfortunately, past and recent housing audits, which are experimental tests of housing discrimination, reveal that discrimination and lack of equal access to all sales and rental markets persist as a reality in U.S. society, especially for minorities. This is important because many race scholars argue that housing discrimination plays a pivotal role in the maintenance and perpetuation of residential segregation in U.S. society.

Historically, housing audits have been used by fair housing groups as a systematic experimental method of testing for and uncovering discrimination in rental and sales markets based on sex, familial status, and race/ethnicity and national origin. During the past 30 years or so, the U.S. federal government has also used large-scale national housing audits to detect levels of racial/ethnic discrimination and to analyze trends across time. To provide a comprehensive overview of housing audits, this entry explains the housing audit methodology, summarizes findings from major national housing audits in the United States, and discusses limitations of the housing audit methodology. Fair housing groups, scholars, and government agencies rely most heavily on the housing audit methodology to uncover racial/ethnic discrimination; thus, that is the explicit focus of this entry.

Methods and History

Racial housing audits are experimental in design, characterized by the quantitative comparison of matched testers' (or auditors') experiences in the housing market. Most often, multiple teams of two racially distinct, but similarly situated, individuals (one minority and one White) are sent into the housing market in an attempt to acquire housing from a random sample of ads placed online and in newspapers. The testers, aside from their racial/ethnic status, are assigned similar identities and characteristics (e.g., same credit score, same income, same education). Testers complete detailed questionnaires following their experiences, and the data are then compiled and analyzed to determine whether minority and White testers were treated differently. Hence, with efforts to control for social and human capital characteristics, such tests have served as an effective way to uncover discrimination.

Beginning in 1977, the Department of Housing and Urban Development (HUD) launched the Housing Market Practices Survey (HMPS), which conducted 3,264 tests in forty metropolitan areas. The study provided evidence of significant discrimination against

Blacks in sales and rental markets. The results of the HMPS played a role in the passage of the 1988 amendment to the Fair Housing Act and demonstrated the need for a second national study, The Housing Discrimination Study, which was launched in 1989 and covered twenty-five metropolitan areas. A comparison of the two nationwide studies demonstrated that discrimination had not decreased between 1977 and 1989.

In 2000, HUD launched a third national housing audit, with initial analyses revealing that African Americans and Hispanics continue to face significant discriminatory barriers when searching for a home to rent or buy. However, rates of overall discrimination may have decreased somewhat between 1989 and 2000, with the exception of "racial steering"—a realtor suggesting more or less desirable alternatives based on the race of the client—of African Americans and limitations in the financing opportunities and access to rental units for Hispanics. Some scholars argue that declines in housing discrimination revealed in the 2000 HUD audit may be the result of a shift in the prevailing forms of housing discrimination used by landlords, realtors, and others in the housing market. In other words, actors in U.S. housing markets may have become more privy to the illegal forms and consequences of exclusion according to fair housing laws and, thus, have turned to more covert and subtle forms of discrimination not revealed through the audit methodology.

Since the original study, numerous other housing market audit studies have also been conducted in individual cities. These local-level audits, like national studies, reveal that most Blacks and Hispanics encounter discrimination revolving around housing availability and access to the housing sales and rental markets.

Audit research suggests that discrimination may be more intense in integrated neighborhoods than in segregated neighborhoods and that racial steering is a common mechanism. Black and Hispanic home buyers can expect to encounter approximately one act of discrimination every time they interact with a real estate broker. Furthermore, there appears to be widespread discrimination by landlords, including making fewer offers of rental assistance and showing fewer units to minority auditors. Similar evidence is reported from recent scholarly analyses of rental inquiries by phone and interactions with mortgage lenders and homeowners insurance agents.

Limitations of Housing Audits

Clearly, the audit methodology is a useful method for assessing levels of discrimination faced by potential residents. There are, however, obvious disadvantages. Some argue that testers are predisposed to find discrimination and that testers' characteristics (e.g., work experience, education) may influence the test itself. Audit studies are also constrained by the sampling frame (e.g., units advertised in major metropolitan newspapers or on the Internet) and might not be as useful for studying complex transactions, transactions involving interaction at later stages of the housing acquisition process, and cases involving adverse impact rather than disparate treatment. Finally, audit studies seldom consider discriminatory processes, behaviors, and practices that minorities may experience once actually housed, including differential treatment, coercion, harassment, and intimidation. It is important to note that all of these are illegal forms of discrimination as defined by the Fair Housing Act.

Although the audit methodology clearly remains a useful tool in uncovering and measuring current levels of discrimination in U.S. housing markets, a sole reliance on this method provides only a limited understanding of housing discrimination given that this methodology, by design, cannot capture all forms of illegal housing discrimination.

Diana Leilani Karafin

See also Discrimination; Discrimination in Housing; *Gautreaux* Decision; Public Housing; Segregation

Further Readings

Galster, George C. 1990. "Racial Steering by Real Estate Agents: Mechanisms and Motives." *Review of Black Political Economy* 19(Summer):39–63.

Massey, Douglas. 2005. "Racial Discrimination in Housing: A Moving Target." *Social Problems* 52:148–151.

Massey, Douglas and Garvey Lundy. 2001. "Use of Black English and Racial Discrimination in Urban Housing Markets: New Methods and Findings." *Urban Affairs Review* 36:452–469.

Ondrich, Jan, Alex Stricker, and John Yinger. 1999. "Do Landlords Discriminate? The Incidence and Causes of Racial Discrimination in Rental Housing Markets." *Journal of Housing Economics* 8:185–204.

Ross, Stephen L. and Margery A. Turner. 2005. "Housing Discrimination in Metropolitan America: Explaining

Changes between 1989 and 2000." *Social Problems* 52:152–180.

Yinger, John Milton. 1995. *Closed Doors, Opportunities Lost: The Continuing Costs of Housing Discrimination.* New York: Russell Sage.

HUERTA, DOLORES C. (1930–)

Dolores C. Huerta was raised in a family of activists, followed the family tradition throughout her long and active life, and continues to act on issues important to Mexican Americans. Known as an important advocate for *La Raza,* probably her best-known activism was her work with farmworkers and cofounding the United Farm Workers (UFW) union with César Chávez. Her activism began before the UFW and has continued since with other causes that benefit the rights of farm laborers as well as women and immigrants. The establishment and protection of the rights of those Huerta perceives to be without a voice in the United States continues to be her mission in life. This entry describes her life and work.

Her Early History

Huerta was born to Juan Fernandez and Alicia Chávez Fernandez on April 10, 1930, during the Great Depression, in Dawson, a small mining town in the northern part of New Mexico. She met challenges early in life. When she was three years old, her parents divorced and she moved with her mother and two brothers to Stockton, California. Huerta's mother, after remarrying and having two more daughters, eventually pulled herself out of her own personal financial depression and was able to buy both a restaurant and a small twenty-room hotel, which Huerta and her two brothers helped her to run. Although physically separated from her father, Huerta maintained contact with him and was inspired by his rise from coal miner and farm laborer to labor organizer as well as by his acquisition of a college degree. He went on to hold office as a state legislator in New Mexico, where he worked to enact laws that protect laborers.

Huerta drew inspiration from the success of both her parents, and after graduating from high school she went on to attend Delta College of the University of the Pacific. Although there is some debate over whether she actually graduated, she went on to teach grammar school for a short time. Many of the students she taught were from families of farmworkers, and she expressed her frustration in seeing children come into her classroom without decent shoes or enough to eat. Huerta believed that she could do more by working with the farm workers to organize than by teaching their children.

Leaving teaching, she became a founding member of the Stockton chapter of the Community Service Organization (CSO), a grassroots organization that was founded to battle segregation, lead voter registration drives, and fight to enact new legislation that affected Mexican Americans. Through this organization, Huerta saw firsthand the problems that the migrant farmworkers faced, and this inspired her to organize and found the Agricultural Workers Association (AWA) in 1960.

Through her work with the CSO, she lobbied in Sacramento for both voting and driver's license examinations in Spanish and in Washington, D.C., for an end to the Bracero program, a temporary contract labor program between the United States and Mexico. Through her work with the CSO, she met César Chávez. Both recognized the need to organize farmworkers, and when they were unable to convince others in the CSO to take on this task, they both resigned in 1962. Huerta moved with her seven children to Delano, California, to be near Chávez and his family, and together they formed the National Farm Workers Association (NFWA). This organization was formed in response to the lack of support from the union leadership to the idea of organizing farmworkers comprised primarily of Filipinos and Latinos. Working with the Agricultural Workers Organizing Committee (AWOC), they organized a grape strike that, over the course of five years, had more than 5,000 grape workers who walked out on their jobs and worked successfully toward the first contract between a wine company and its workers in U.S. history. This event garnered national attention and heralded the merger of the AWOC and the NFWA into the United Farm Workers Organizing Committee (UFWOC), which officially became UFW, AFL–CIO after the success of the strike.

UFW and Beyond

Huerta negotiated the contract between the farmworkers and the Schenley Wine Company, the first time that farmworkers made up the negotiating committee for a collective bargaining agreement with an agricultural corporation. This was only the first of many successes for Huerta and the organizing committees.

She worked with laborers not only in the grape industry but also in the vegetable industry, and she organized a second boycott in reaction to violence that resulted in the deaths of several farmworkers. This East Coast boycott of grapes, lettuce, and Gallo wines brought together community workers, student protesters, peace groups, religious groups, Hispanic associations, and feminists to fight for the rights of farmworkers.

In 1975, then California Governor Jerry Brown signed the Agricultural Labor Relations Act, which legally allowed farmworkers to form a union that could negotiate with farm owners for better wages and working conditions. Huerta worked for more than three decades with her friend Chávez, and together they achieved many notable milestones for the rights of farmworkers and programs that helped to make their working and living conditions more humane. They founded the Robert F. Kennedy Medical Plan, the Farm Workers Credit Union, and the National Farm Workers Service Center to provide affordable housing and a Spanish language radio communications network. Huerta has lobbied for unemployment insurance for farm laborers and against guest worker programs, including the recent effort by President George W. Bush. She equates the program with indentured servitude, allowing people to work at subsistence wages yet denying them the opportunity for citizenship.

Other Notable Accomplishments

In addition to her efforts for farmworkers, Huerta has used her voice and influence with other issues that are important to her. She has fought for the rights of women as well and has served on the boards of the Feminist Majority Foundation, Democratic Socialists of America, Fairness and Accuracy in Media (FAIR), the Center for Voting and Democracy, and Latinas for Choice. She has received many honors through the years, including the Outstanding Labor Leader Award (by the California State Senate), the Ellis Island Medal of Freedom Award, the Consumers' Union Trumpeter's Award, and the Robert Baldwin Medal of Liberty Award (by the American Civil Liberties Union), as well as several honorary doctoral degrees.

Karen S. Boyd

See also Chávez, César; Guest Workers; La Raza; Mexican Americans; Minority Rights

Further Readings

Ferris, Susan, Ricardo Sandoval, and Diana Hembree, eds. 1998. *The Fight in the Fields: César Chávez and the Farmworkers Movement.* Orlando, FL: Harvest/HBJ Book.

Garcia, Richard A. 1993. "Woman, Organizer, Symbol." *California History* 72:56–71.

HULL HOUSE SCHOOL OF RACE RELATIONS

The Hull House School of Race Relations was a vital exciting world of scholarship and political activism that brought together Black and White Chicago residents from 1892 to 1935. Anchored at Hull House and the University of Chicago, the school embraced men and women of several racial/ethnic groups and various disciplines, many of them articulate and powerful. Together, they developed and espoused a U.S. theory uniting liberal values and a belief in a rational public with a cooperative, nurturing, and liberating model of the self, the other, and the community. The perspective was based on the historical ideas and commitments of abolitionists and Abraham Lincoln. Its proponents believed that education and democracy were significant mechanisms to organize and improve society, especially the relations between Black and White Americans. Among accomplishments of the Hull House School was the founding of the National Association for the Advancement of Colored People (NAACP) and the National Urban League, along with their notable Chicago branches. The school's influence, however, extended to other institutions as well, including social settlements, churches, newspapers, journals, and voluntary associations in Chicago. This entry describes the theoretical foundation of the Hull House School and briefly summarizes its key members and main accomplishments.

Epistemology

Looking at social behavior and conduct, proponents of the Hull House School argued that race relations could be changed because human behavior was flexible, learned, and capable of social reconstruction. Although they believed in cultural pluralism, they also believed that the individual develops a mind, intelligence, and the ability to take the role of the other—abilities that generate a self that learns organized attitudes of the community toward social situations. These attitudes form perspectives emerging from the group and the "generalized other." People sharing the same neighborhood and community develop shared experience, which proponents saw as the greatest of human goods. The self emerges from others and is not in conflict with others unless it is taught to be in conflict, in this view.

According to the Hull House School, the self emerges in a society that is "racialized" or fundamentally divided into ethnic and racial/ethnic groups. As a result, the natural unity of the world is sundered. Proponents held that the modern world was White dominated and defined; thus, Whites controlled public life (especially the legal system and business), the definition of rationality, and the community. The state should provide a good education for children and youth along with minimum housing, health care, and food, proponents said. In their view, Fabian socialism was an ideal format for developing a responsive public and eradicating the color line from all public policy.

The Hull House School saw women and African Americans as the primary sources for social change. These groups would become a fulcrum for redefining the larger social situation of the White world, proponents believed. The Hull House School felt that the ability to change society was based on a reflexive understanding of the unity of society. People can act to change public life by using their political commitment to law and the state, combined with their cooperative worldview, to implement the goals of democracy. In other words, people—especially women and African Americans—can take the role of the other as well as the role of the oppressed other, proponents said. Women and African Americans can understand being limited in public rights because they exist behind the "veil" of racial and gender discrimination and are limited both structurally and systematically, albeit in distinct historical and cultural ways.

Women and African Americans could be leaders in a "new social consciousness" based on a commitment to end the legacy of slavery, according to the Hull House School. Proponents saw signs of this awakening consciousness in the integration of the objective with the subjective and in the cooperative relations between Whites and Blacks. They saw this new consciousness as being organized through activities involving civil rights, vocational education, pacifism, labor, social science, and women.

According to this perspective, women learn folk wisdom and share a culture based in the myths of African and other oral cultural traditions, and they are responsible for passing along this folk knowledge. Women and African Americans learn to cherish the good in others and in life. Because they do not see the world the same way as White men do, they are well suited to change existing institutions. In the Hull House view, women have the special role of helping to create and distribute food, a consumer role that can be used to change industry. By extending the model of home and family to the larger racial situation, women engage in what the Hull House School called "civic housekeeping."

The Hull House School assigned to African American women a special role arising from their unique cultural heritage reflecting African values, myths, and culture. Seeing their children suffer from racial discrimination, African American women were obliged to speak out against lynching, to organize through women's clubs, and to preserve a historical legacy. It was thought that African American women had more egalitarian marriages than did women from European ethnic groups.

Through being more productive economically and making better choices in the marketplace and the community, women and African Americans could be empowered to reunite the White and Black communities, proponents of the Hull House School believed. New perspectives on race relations, prejudice, and segregation could be developed through the use of rational facts, alternate attitudes, new legislation, new social situations, and changed economics. Proponents saw this happening through the development of working hypotheses that could enter social situations and change them. Some of the specific working hypotheses adopted by the Hull House School were the elimination of lynching, opposition to corruption in the criminal justice system, the demand for equal and qualified education at all levels, and statistical documentation of Jim Crow inequalities.

As Hull House School proponents saw it, social inequality for women followed the patterns found in inequalities of class and race. Democracy emerges from equality in politics, economics, and interaction, whereas inequality emerges from a distinct perspective, history, community, and structure of the self. Therefore, social change must articulate and respond to cultural differences. The Hull House School espoused a return to the abolitionist model to generate a new conscience opposing racial hatred, linking its members to a wider social movement called the "new abolitionism."

Although many people and writings about race relations took sides in the debate between Booker T. Washington, who supported vocational education and acceptance of Jim Crow inequality, and W. E. B. Du Bois, who supported Black colleges and fighting for political and civil rights, supporters of the Hull House School included both of these men and their worldviews. Thus, this third perspective developed by the school—a new conscience against an ancient evil—combined interracial cooperation, refused to choose between Washington and Du Bois, and enacted radical opposition against racism. It has remained largely unknown, misinterpreted, and/or misunderstood in the study of race relations in Chicago or in the nation generally.

The Hull House School model of nonviolence emerged from the ideas of William Lloyd Garrison, Leo Tolstoy, and Mahatma Gandhi. It was the intellectual and practical forerunner of many ideas and practices underlying the modern Civil Rights Movement, especially as developed and led by Martin Luther King, Jr.

The School in Action

Members of the Hull House School became founders of the NAACP and its Chicago branch as well as of the Urban League and its Chicago branch. These groups worked for African American rights and opportunities because of their belief in democratic law and basic human rights regarding housing, employment, food, education, and free speech. These two organizations employed many of the concepts developed in the Hull House School.

In addition, members organized and promoted voluntary associations that worked to implement these and other working hypotheses also founded by Hull House sociologists such as the American Civil Liberties Union (ACLU) and the Women's International League for Peace and Freedom. They worked in biracial social settlements and African American social settlements as well. Disagreements on working hypotheses were anticipated within the model, and these debates and differences were viewed as signs of its responsiveness, strength, and flexibility.

The role of the Hull House School in the founding of the NAACP and its Chicago branch is a seriously neglected but important component in U.S. race relations. The founding of the National Urban League and its Chicago branch is recognized as an important step in U.S. race relations, but the work of the Hull House School in this organization has been neglected. The earliest years of both organizations—roughly between 1909 and 1925—are connected directly to the Hull House School.

Members of the Hull House School

The roots of the Hull House School can be found in the works of Jane Addams, John Dewey, W. E. B. Du Bois, George Herbert Mead, W. I. Thomas, Charlotte Perkins Gilman, Jessie Taft, Fannie Barrier Williams, and Ida B. Wells-Barnett. Other important members were Hull House residents or visitors and/or faculty or students at the University of Chicago between 1892 and 1920. They included Edith Abbott, Emily Greene Balch, Sophonisba Breckinridge, Katherine Bement Davis, Loraine Richardson Green, Elizabeth Ross Haynes, George E. Haynes, Florence Kelley, Frances Kellor, Julia Lathrop, Mary E. MacDowell, Annie Marion MacLean, Anna Garlin Spencer, Marion Talbot, William English Walling, Richard Wright, Jr., and Ella Flagg Young.

Mary Jo Deegan

See also Chicago School of Race Relations; Civil Rights Movement; Du Bois, William Edward Burghardt; King, Martin Luther, Jr.; Williams, Fannie Barrier

Further Readings

Addams, Jane. 1910. *Twenty Years at Hull-House.* New York: Macmillan.

Addams, Jane. 1912. *A New Conscience and an Ancient Evil.* New York: Macmillan.

Deegan, Mary Jo. 2002. *Race, Hull-House, and the University of Chicago: A New Conscience against Ancient Evil.* Westport, CT: Greenwood.

Dewey, John. 1899. *School and Society.* Chicago, IL: University of Chicago Press.

Du Bois, W. E. B. 1903. *Souls of Black Folk.* Chicago, IL: A. C. McClurg.

Du Bois, W. E. B. 1920. *Darkwater: Voices from within the Veil.* New York: Harcourt Brace.

Mead, George H. 1899. "Working Hypotheses for Social Reform." *American Journal of Sociology* 5:369–371.

Mead, George H. 1934. *Mind, Self, and Society,* introduced and edited by Charles Morris. Chicago, IL: University of Chicago Press.

Reed, Christopher Robert. 1997. *The Chicago NAACP and the Rise of Black Professional Leadership, 1910–1966.* Bloomington: Indiana University Press.

Strickland, Arrarh E. 1966. *History of the Chicago Urban League.* Urbana: University of Illinois Press.

Wells-Barnett, Ida B. 1970. *Crusade for Justice: The Autobiography of Ida B. Wells,* edited by Alfreda M. Duster. Chicago, IL: University of Chicago Press.

Williams, Fannie Barrier. 2002. *The New Woman of Color: The Collected Writings of Fannie Barrier Williams,* introduced and edited by Mary Jo Deegan. DeKalb: University of Northern Illinois Press.

HUNGARIAN AMERICANS

Although never one of the largest ethnic groups in the United States, by the early 20th century, only Budapest could claim to have a larger population of Hungarians than the city of Cleveland, Ohio. Even so, Hungarian Americans did not constitute the largest ethnic majority in the city. While the mines and steel mills of West Virginia and Pennsylvania recruited and attracted the agricultural workers from Hungary who made up the largest wave of emigrants, between 1870 and 1920, the industries in Cleveland drew workers to the heart of America.

Migrations to other cities from Cleveland occurred by the turn of the 20th century. Hungarians from the mines and mills wandered the United States, continually searching for better pay. The "Hunkies," as U.S. residents and fellow workers derogatorily knew them, were the most mobile ethnic cohort in the country. Although thousands of Hungarians wandered back and forth across the Atlantic and within the United States, Cleveland remained the existential Hungarian American city; it serves as a model for the Hungarian American experience, according to Julianna Puskás. Other locales, such as the Delray enclave of Detroit, Michigan, and the Birmingham neighborhood in Toledo, Ohio, offer their own local manifestations of Hungarian American ethnicity, having drawn their early settlers from Cleveland.

Today, Hungarian American ethnicity combines the remnants of the old ethnic enclaves with an awareness of identity that has reemerged since the 1970s. New and often younger leaders of ethnic associations have emerged to guide and challenge the Hungarian Americans of the 21st century. Hungary was estimated in 2007 to have a population of 10.1 million people. This entry describes their history in the United States and their current situation.

An Immigration History

Tidal Wave, 1870–1920

More than 3.5 million immigrants arrived in the United States from Hungary during this period. Mostly economically distressed agricultural workers, they sought work in the mines and factories of an increasingly industrialized United States. The coal mines in Pennsylvania and West Virginia, as well as the steel mills, claimed the lives of many Hungarians, but they continued to come. Relatives and friends from various villages in Hungary would arrive together, or would follow others, forming links in the chains of migration.

Those who arrived during this 50-year period hoped to make enough money, as quickly as possible, so that they could return to Hungary, buy some land, and return to farming. Hungarians tended to migrate back and forth across the Atlantic more than did other immigrants. Single men, or married men who had left their families behind, lived together in boarding houses (*burdos gazda* or *burdosházak*) run by Hungarian women, usually wives or widows of fellow countrymen. The Hungarian immigrants, however, tended to move more readily than others; seeing themselves as temporary workers in the United States, they continually sought better opportunities despite the discrimination they faced nearly everywhere they went.

The industries in Cleveland, and by the 1910s the automobile industry in Detroit, drew the Hungarians from the mines and mills of the East. However, Hungarians continued to find employment in New Jersey factories (e.g., textile, rubber, wire, cigar, chemical, paper), and the textile industries especially attracted female workers. Bridgeport, Connecticut, claimed the third-largest Hungarian population in the pre–World War I United States. With its active Hungarian American community, this city played a significant role in laying the foundation for several national organizations.

Cleveland claimed more Hungarian Americans than did any other city in the United States by the early 20th century. Two settlements, or ethnic enclaves, developed: the west side, or Lorain Road community, made up of skilled craftsmen from Hungary who lived among German and Czechoslovakian immigrants in the neighborhood; and (b) the more homogeneous ethnic neighborhood on the east side, the Buckeye Road community, composed of former agricultural workers, the Magyars. The National Malleable Casting Company proved to be the biggest draw for the Magyar workers. Once this company expanded to Toledo and Detroit during the late 1800s, it transferred workers to these locales, resulting in the establishment of Hungarian American communities there. In all locales, Hungarian (Magyar) language newspapers, fraternal associations, and churches (Catholic and Protestant) represented the ethnic makeup of the communities despite members' transient nature.

The Treaty of Trianon (1920) and Its Effects

World War I cut off contact with Hungary. Furthermore, the Treaty of Trianon, resulting in the partition of the homeland, forever changed the future of Hungarian migrants. The country to which they had hoped to return no longer existed. Hungarian minorities now found themselves in newly created nations—Yugoslavia, Romania, and Czechoslovakia. Faced with postwar inflation, unemployment, and discrimination in Europe, more Hungarians decided to emigrate; those caught in the United States during World War I decided to remain in the country. After 1920, an unprecedented number of Hungarian Americans began to buy homes and settle down in one location. With their Hungarian language newspapers (*Szabadság* and *Amerikai Magyar Népszava*) and their associations, they turned to becoming Americans; however, in their neighborhoods, in their religion, and in their cultural outlook, they maintained their Hungarianness through Magyar language maintenance, folkways, and food.

Post–World War II: The Displaced Persons and '56-ers

Not only were the second and third generations seeking an identity of their own, often refuting the Hungarianness of their parents and grandparents, but with the arrival of refugees from postwar Europe, an identity crisis of sorts developed for many Hungarian Americans. One Hungarian language newspaper began production of a bilingual version, titled *Young Hungarian American,* to provide a broader ethnic perspective, at least for the U.S.-born generations. The "displaced persons" who arrived during the post–World War II years did not fit comfortably into the Hungarian American neighborhoods. Coming from a different socioeconomic class from those who had established the ethnic neighborhoods, the "DPs," as they would be called, tended to avoid the ethnic enclaves. Never quite comfortable in the Hungarian American communities, and never quite welcomed elsewhere, they established their own Hungarian America modeled on a Hungary that had been extinguished in postwar Europe but in a U.S. setting. Hungarian heritage became all important to them, and the Hungarian Scouts in Exile, centered in Garfield, New Jersey, during the 1950s, offered the means by which their remembered Hungarian ways could be passed on to the next generation.

The Hungarians who fled after the Revolution of 1956 against the communist regime, the '56-ers or Freedom Fighters as they would be known, presented a new wrinkle for a coherent Hungarian American identity. Although these refugees would find the established Hungarian American communities to be extremely helpful in offering aid, especially in the form of housing and employment opportunities, the paternalistic attitude of such communities and the U.S. government, as well as the youth of most '56-ers and their familiarity with U.S. culture, caused many of this group of immigrants to merge more easily into the host culture as they often shunned their ethnic heritage. There would, however, be exceptions to the pattern. Perhaps the distinct differences of the welcoming Hungarian American community played a factor.

By the 1960s, the decline in Hungarian language newspapers, urban flight, distancing DPs, and disinterested '56-ers contributed to the decline and dissolution of the Hungarian American neighborhoods. Although a reemergence of interest in ethnic identities appeared during the 1970s, contemporary ethnicity took place outside of the old neighborhoods.

Contemporary Communities

Hungarian Americans seemed to never stay in one place. Extremely migratory, particularly when compared with other ethnic groups, their pattern of mobility has changed during recent decades. According to a sampling by Sandor Vegh of records from the century-old fraternal insurance society, the Hungarian Reformed Federation of America, contemporary Hungarian Americans move at a rate lower than the national average. Although still heavily concentrated in the states of Ohio, New York, Pennsylvania, New Jersey, California, and Michigan, all but the latter two states have lost more Hungarian Americans than they have gained since the 1960s. Florida tends to be a recipient of the largest numbers as retirees move to that state. California continues to attract those in the professional ranks as they move away from the old industrial communities of the East and Midwest.

As more and more move out of the old neighborhoods, the traditional ethnic communities are quickly dissolving. There are some neighborhoods that have attempted to maintain a semblance of Hungarian American ethnicity through churches, organizations, and culture clubs, although many of the older generations (pre-'56ers) maintain that locale (the old neighborhood) is the key to being a "real" Hungarian.

Manifestations of Hungarianness take on various forms—festivals such as the *Betlehemes játék* Christmas plays, folkways such as dances and handcrafts, and particularly foodways such as the ritual of *sutni saluna* (backyard bacon roasting) and *kolbaza* stuffing in a church basement in Toledo and the making of *csiga* (rolled) noodles in Detroit. These manifestations, however, are not Hungarian so much as they are products of Hungarian ways and remembrances shaped by U.S. experiences.

Less than 1% of the total population claimed a Hungarian identifier on a recent U.S. Census. However, the establishment of new national organizations and ethnic religious institutions suggests a new and vital interest in ethnic identity. Examples include the Washington, D.C.-based Kossuth House Social Club (in 1997) and Hungarian American Foundation (in 2003); the regionally based Hungarian American Cultural Center (HACC) in Taylor, Michigan, and the Hungarian Reformed Church in Allen Park, Michigan; the local Birmingham (Toledo) Center Cultural Center and Calvin United Church of Christ, where at least one service a week is held in Hungarian, embroidery classes meet, Magyar dancers practice, and *kolbaza* is handmade once a year.

The success of self-proclaimed Hungarian Americans is evident. According to the 2000 U.S. Census records, more Hungarian Americans owned their homes than rented. In addition, their median household and family incomes were, on average, $10,000 to $13,000 higher than those of the general population. Unlike those who came before them, they have moved beyond the discrimination and prejudices that, more often than not, held them to a socioeconomic status barely above that of African Americans during the late 19th and early 20th centuries.

Kay J. Blalock

See Appendix A
See also Acculturation; Assimilation; Immigration, U.S.; Nativism; Refugees; Symbolic Ethnicity

Further Readings

Barden, Thomas E. and John Ahern, eds. 2002. *Hungarian American Toledo: Life and Times in Toledo's Birmingham Neighborhood.* Toledo, OH: University of Toledo, Urban Affairs Center.

Huseby-Darvas, Éva V. 2002. *Hungarians in Michigan.* East Lansing: Michigan State University Press.

Papp, Susan M. 1981. *Hungarian Americans and Their Communities of Cleveland.* Cleveland, OH: Cleveland State University Press.

Puskás, Julianna. 2000. *Ties That Bind, Ties That Divide: 100 Years of Hungarian Experience in the United States,* translated by Zora Ludwig. New York: Holmes & Meier.

Vardy, Steven Béla. 1985. *The Hungarian-Americans.* Boston, MA: Twayne.

Web Sites

Hungarian America Foundation:
http://www.hungarianamerica.com

Hurricane Katrina

Hurricane Katrina, a Category 3 hurricane, made landfall south of Buras in Plaquemides Parish, Louisiana, during the early hours of August 29, 2005. Four days earlier, it had made landfall as a Category 1 hurricane north of Miami, Florida. It affected an area of 108,456 square miles in Florida, Louisiana, Mississippi, Alabama, and Tennessee. In New Orleans, the levees at the 17th Street Canal, the London Avenue Canal, and the Industrial Canal breached, flooding the city. The social impacts associated with the storm surge and flooding caused by Katrina were truly catastrophic—more than 1,800 dead, thousands injured and missing, close to 700,000 left homeless, approximately 800,000 displaced throughout the United States, with total damages estimated at $34.4 billion. Particularly noteworthy, and not lost on the international audience watching the media, was the particularly devastating impact this disaster had on the poor and people of color.

On August 28, New Orleans Mayor C. Ray Nagin ordered the forced evacuation of the city, and more than 1 million people left. However, approximately 150,000 people, most of them poor, minorities, and the elderly, could not leave the city and were the main category of victims caused by the flooding in the city. The general poverty rate in all storm-damaged areas was 20.7% (and approximately 30.0% for children)—much higher than the national average of 12.4%. In affected areas of Louisiana, the poverty rate was 21.4%. The labor force participation for men 25 to 64 years of age was 77% as compared with 82% nationwide; for male youth, it was 55% as compared with 65% nationwide. Particularly vulnerable were disabled elderly minority populations; approximately 48% of all persons age 65

Hurricane Katrina victims. More than 140 evacuees from New Orleans, victims of flooding caused by Hurricane Katrina, fly to Austin, Texas, in a cargo plane (August 2005). There, they were given food, fresh water, and a place to sleep. Hurricane Katrina's impact on minority populations in many respects coincides with literature established in the social sciences regarding disasters, which suggests several ways that racial, ethnicity, and socioeconomic status shape the experiences of at-risk populations and disaster victims.

Source: U.S. Air Force photo by Neil Senkowski.

years or older living in Katrina-affected areas reported having disabilities. In sum, the population victimized by Katrina had much vulnerability that rendered them less capable of responding to and recovering from the effects of the storm.

The challenge produced by Katrina is a matter of national interest not only because of the sheer catastrophic scale of its immediate and short-range effects but also because, like no other previous disaster, it illustrated the failure of the current public administration to manage emergencies and the lingering effect and power of social stratification and cultural practices in increasing the risks of disasters. It also mocked the often-repeated mantra heard after the terrorist attacks of September 11, 2001, that the newly created U.S. Department of Homeland Security (DHS) had improved the security of the country. Katrina and its aftermath generated a great deal of soul searching. Most of it reflected a technical, tactical approach to the enormous problems that Katrina uncovered rather than a strategic assessment of what needs to change in the society and culture of the United States to mitigate the effects of hazards and to increase the resilience of the institutions of the society.

Post-Katrina Reports and Commissions

Four after-action government reports have been published, each with its own set of recommendations and emphases. The White House Report examined how future events of this kind will be handled. It concluded that the current system of homeland security failed to handle catastrophic events appropriately, the unified management of the national response was inadequate, command-and-control in the federal government was defective, there is a need to train organizations in the incident command system, and there was widespread ignorance of the plans and insufficient regional planning and coordination.

The House of Representatives Report offered criticisms of the response to Hurricane Katrina, identifying ten major failures in the response. The Senate Report analyzed the response in New Orleans and the problems that need to be corrected in the future. It identified factors that contributed to the failure of the response effort, including that long-term recurrent warnings about New Orleans's vulnerability to floods were ignored and government officials were unable to act decisively and wisely during the crisis, failing to provide effective leadership. The Senate report also included a set of basic recommendations, among them to abolish the Federal Emergency Management Agency (FEMA) and replace it with the National Preparedness and Response Authority, to give enhanced powers to the new agency, to enhance regional operations to improve coordination and supervise regional assets, to build a super-operations government center to enhance awareness and management of interagency coordination in disasters, and to encourage renewed commitment to the principles of the emergency management system.

The General Accounting Office report, a brief precursor to a longer report still being written in 2007, discussed the future of FEMA, the federal involvement in rebuilding the Gulf Coast region, and the appropriateness of using a risk-management scheme to determine investment allocation in disaster mitigation efforts.

Independent agencies, including the National Council of La Raza (NCLR), Oxfam America, and the Center on Budget and Policy Priorities, have also issued reports, focusing on the fate of minorities and the poor in the aftermath of the storm. The NCLR examined the special needs of Latino populations in the Gulf Coast region and the lack of planning for them by FEMA and other governmental organizations involved in response. According to the NCLR, eligibility criteria for FEMA-administered benefits lacked clarity, access to FEMA shelters was not made available to all immigrants, warnings often did not reach many people who did not know the English language, and undocumented immigrants were not given assurances that they would not be apprehended if they asked for help, thereby increasing their suffering and privations. The NCLR report offered cogent criticisms of the way in which the American Red Cross and other voluntary organizations served the Latino populations affected by Katrina.

Oxfam America examined the housing reconstruction and recovery of the Gulf Coast and found that poor households were being left out of the disaster recovery efforts. It urged officials to make sure that the tax dollars for reconstruction will reach all people in need, particularly the poorest segments of the communities. It encouraged them to target for special attention low-income homeowners and renters to receive federal funds recently approved by the U.S. Congress for the reconstruction of the region to rebuild, repair, and rehabilitate their homes. It also urged officials to facilitate home ownership of poor people victimized by Katrina and to finance mitigation efforts in their building projects.

A similar concern with housing discrimination of low-income people was reflected in the report by the Center on Budget and Policy Priorities, which focused on the need to provide rental assistance to disaster victims and to help owners repair their properties. It urged restoration of the pre-hurricane supply of federally subsidized housing and suggested that a share of the rebuilt private housing should be made available to poor people.

Impact on Minorities

Hurricane Katrina's impact on minority populations in many respects coincides with knowledge established in the social sciences about disasters. The literature on disasters suggests a number of ways in which race, ethnicity, and socioeconomic status shape the experiences of at-risk populations and disaster victims. Ethnic groups within the U.S. population differ from the White majority in their levels of disaster awareness and preparedness as well as in the sources they access to obtain disaster information and what information sources they consider to be credible, this research concludes. Ethnicity has been shown to influence a wide range of behavior in actual disaster situations, including the receipt of disaster warnings, decision making with respect to warning response, emergency evacuation, and postdisaster sheltering patterns. Poverty and ethnicity are typically associated with living in substandard housing and in the types of dwellings that are vulnerable to disaster damage, often resulting in greater rates of disaster-induced homelessness among minority populations than among the White majority.

Even though minority communities may well be at greater risk in disaster situations, with some notable exceptions, community-based organizations that serve and represent minority communities are not well linked with community-wide disaster loss reduction and preparedness efforts. Studies also indicate that when disasters strike, minority status can affect both awareness of available services and the ability to receive disaster assistance. There is evidence to suggest that residents of minority communities receive less in the way of disaster assistance and insurance reimbursements following disasters, even for comparable levels of loss and disruption, compared with residents of predominantly White communities.

Rules associated with formal disaster assistance programs tend to penalize lower income minority group households with extended families as well as families who are forced to "double up" so as to make housing more affordable.

Immigration-related concerns may also affect the manner in which minority group members respond following disasters; for example, they may avoid using disaster services due to fear of possible deportation. Examples abound of problems that have developed following disasters because official agencies have failed to take into account patterns of cultural adaptation to disasters such as the tendency for immigrants from Mexico and Central America to prefer to shelter outdoors, rather than in officially designated indoor shelters, following earthquakes. Official shelters set up for disaster victims often provide food that is culturally inappropriate for members of minority communities, and printed information on disaster services might not be available in languages people can understand. Some states, such as California, have moved to make noncitizens ineligible for all but emergency postdisaster aid. Many members of non-English-speaking minorities find it difficult to complete applications for some disaster aid such as the forms required for Small Business Administration disaster loans.

Dealing with bureaucratic requirements is even more daunting for those whose first language is not English or who have limited English language skills. In a more general sense, those who are not fully acculturated into U.S. society and who lack various kinds of social and cultural capital often have difficulty in navigating the bureaucratic requirements associated with the receipt of disaster aid, just as they have problems in other areas of service delivery. Despite the aforementioned findings that examine the relationship between race/ethnicity and disaster preparedness and response, it is still the case that the impact of disasters on racial/ethnic minority groups in the United States has been insufficiently examined and that much more needs to be done to establish a more reliable knowledge base and extend it to other questions that have not been studied so far.

Long-Term Strategies

Most of what has been written about Hurricane Katrina fails to address strategic long-term questions centered on the structural features of society and how changing them might mitigate the disastrous effects of future hazards. The emphasis seems to be on the centralization of power—what government officials and government systems do or fail to do—and not on the efforts of civil society and regional, more localized approaches, and the emphasis seems to be on command-and-control and not on the loosely coordinated and yet very effective efforts of private organizations, volunteers, citizens, and philanthropists who have always been present in response, reconstruction, and recovery in the aftermath of disasters and who are very effective actors in these processes. This is particularly ironic in the case of Katrina, for it has been the loose network of churches and religious communities that have acted quietly, shown effective charity, and brought about worthwhile assistance to the people of the Gulf Coast.

Few reports ask what the proper responsibilities of government should be when faced with and are at risk for a catastrophe. Rather, the prevailing weight of culture is to expect the government to solve all problems—a faulty hope in need of correction, as Katrina and other disasters have shown. An area of useful exploration might be how the federal, state, and local governments might assist in the formation of—and help to energize, train, and integrate into the formal emergency management systems of the society—networks of volunteer organizations that would adopt the mitigation and resilience perspective and could help to bring about cultural change to maximize sustainability and the resilience of institutions. Particularly appropriate in light of Katrina is to ask what needs to happen so that African American communities faced with catastrophic risk can self-organize for mutual help, protection, and development.

Benigno E. Aguirre

See also African Americans; Discrimination; Discrimination in Housing; Health Disparities; Medical Experimentation; Sundown Towns; "Welfare Queen"

Further Readings

Aguirre, Benigno E., Walter A. Anderson, Sam Balandran, Brian E. Peters, and H. Max White. 1991. *Saragosa, Texas Tornado May 22, 1987: An Evaluation of the Warning System.* Washington, DC: National Academy of Sciences.

Center on Budget and Policy Priorities. 2006. *Housing Needs of Many Low-Income Hurricane Evacuees Are Not Being Adequately Addressed.* Washington, DC: Center on Budget and Policy Priorities.

Gabe, Thomas, Gene Falk, Maggie McCarty, and Virginia W. Mason. 2005. *Hurricane Katrina: Social Demographic Characteristics of the Impacted Areas.* Washington, DC: Library of Congress Congressional Research Service.

Kent, Joshua. 2006. *2005 Louisiana Hurricane Impact Atlas.* Baton Rouge: Louisiana Geographic Information Center. Retrieved from http://lagic.lsu.edu/hurricanes.htm

Muniz, Brenda. 2006. *In the Eyes of the Storm: How the Government and Private Response to Hurricane Katrina Failed Latinos.* Washington, DC: National Council of La Raza.

Oxfam America. 2006. *Recovering States? The Gulf Coast Six Months after the Storms.* Washington, DC: Oxfam America.

Peacock, Walter Gillis, Betty Hearn Morrow, and Hugh Gladwin, eds. 1997. *Hurricane Andrew: Ethnicity, Gender, and the Sociology of Disasters.* London: Routledge.

Phillips, Brenda D., Lisa Garza, and David M. Neal. 1994. "Intergroup Relations in Disasters: Service Delivery Barriers after Hurricane Andrew." *Journal of Intergroup Relations* 21:18–27.

U.S. Department of Transportation. 2006. *Report to Congress on Catastrophic Hurricane Evacuation Plan Evaluation.* Retrieved from http://www.fhwa.dot.gov/reports/hurricanevacuation

HUTTERITES

The Hutterites of North America are the oldest successful communal group on the continent. Started in 1528 in Europe, the community continues to thrive today, with a distinctive language, dress, and social practices, including a rejection of private property. This entry describes the history and current situation of one of the more colorful ethnic groups in the United States and Canada.

European Roots

The Hutterite story began in 1525 in Switzerland during the Protestant Reformation when a group of radical reformers called for a cleaner break from Catholic traditions. They refused to baptize their babies, raised questions about the mass, scorned the use of images, and criticized the morality of church officials. Known as

Anabaptists (meaning rebaptizers), these radical reformers argued that only adults who had made a voluntary decision to become Christians should be baptized.

Convinced that "true" Christians must reject private property, the Hutterites formed in 1528 as a distinct Anabaptist group. Faced with bitter persecution, torture, and execution, they fled to safe havens in Moravia in present-day Austria. Jacob Hutter, an Anabaptist pastor from whom the Hutterites took their name, advocated sharing material goods as described in the Bible.

The early years of Hutterite history were filled with frequent migration and persecution. Many members faced cruel means of torture—beheading, burning, branding, drowning, and starvation in dungeons. Against incredible odds, the Hutterites survived. In 1770 they moved to Russia, and during the 1870s they immigrated to the United States.

New World Communities

The Hutterites have enjoyed remarkable growth since they arrived in the United States during the 1870s. The original immigrants have multiplied to more than 460 colonies. Persecuted for being conscientious objectors during World War I, many Hutterites moved to Canada. Currently, approximately three-fourths of the colonies are found in several Canadian provinces; the others live primarily in South Dakota and Montana. Hutterite adults and children in both countries number more than 45,000. They are organized into four subgroups: *Dariusleut, Lehrerleut,* and two groups of *Schmiedeleut.*

The four branches share many common beliefs, but they have separate leaders and function as independent groups. Members of the three *leuts* rarely intermarry. Although there is much diversity within each group, the *Lehrerleut* tend to be the most traditional. The *Schmiedeleut,* on the other hand, are the most progressive in their use of technology and interaction with the outside world.

Hutterites live in large agricultural colonies segregated from the larger society. Colony buildings, clustered like a small village on several thousand acres of land, are often hidden from major highways. A typical colony will have approximately ninety adults and children. Rural settings insulate colonists somewhat from the outside world, leading one Hutterite to conclude, "We have our own little country." Although outside salespeople and suppliers visit colonies regularly, they are physically cloistered from the outside world. Their agricultural and business operations are linked to the economy of the region, but residential segregation insulates colonists from daily interaction with outsiders. Nearby colonies often help each other with special projects that require extra labor, and they join together for weddings and funerals, but the world of the local colony is *the* world of the typical Hutterite. Without access to television and other mass media, life revolves around the cares of fewer than a hundred kindred souls.

The colony lives as an extended family—eating meals together in a common dining hall and sharing laundry facilities. Each family has an apartment with a coffee area, living room, bathroom, and bedrooms. Long barrack-like houses with several apartments, the common dining hall, and the church building provide the main living facilities. The average family has five or six children.

Hutterites speak an Austrian dialect called *Hutterisch.* They use an archaic form of High German in sermons and other religious writings; however, young people learn English in schools in the colony that are typically operated by local public school districts. Their dialect is peppered with many words from the countries of their European sojourn. The dialect enables them to converse directly, as it were, with their religious ancestors, who are much closer to them in spirit than are their English neighbors. Language, a key component of their ethnicity, marks the boundaries between sacred and secular and between pious and profane.

Life in the Colony

Hutterite culture emphasizes three core values: sharing material goods, surrendering self-will for communal well-being, and maintaining social separation from the outside world. Communal property, the hallmark of Hutterite culture, distinguishes Hutterites from other Anabaptist groups such as the Mennonites and the Amish. For the Hutterites, private property symbolizes selfishness and greed, which they believe breed many other evils.

Communal Property

Sharing material goods, in Hutterite eyes, is the highest form of Christian love. They seek to follow the example of the early church described in the Book of Acts, where members of the church reportedly had all things in common. At baptism, members relinquish any claim to colony property. Those who abandon colony life may take only the clothes they are wearing and a few personal items as they embark into the larger world.

Apart from a few personal items—clothes, knickknacks, dishes, books, and the like—individual Hutterites do not own private property. Everyone works without pay. Some colonies provide a monthly allowance of $5 to $10 for personal effects, but others do not. In some colonies, parents receive $20 for each child to buy Christmas gifts. Individuals receive an allotment of clothing from the colony manager roughly once per year. A family may have a few personal belongings as well as some furniture, but the larger household items are owned by the colony.

The colony is a legal corporation that buys and sells products, often in large quantities, on the public market and with other colonies. The corporation pays taxes and owns the title to land and equipment. Colonies are somewhat self-sufficient with their own gardens, orchards, poultry, and cattle as well as their own shoemakers, tailors, and electricians. Nevertheless, many supplies and equipment are purchased from outside distributors. Bartering of furniture, toys, vegetables, clothing, and antiques sometimes occurs within colonies, between colonies, and between colonists and outsiders.

Modern Ways

Although they reject many worldly values, Hutterites have no scruples about tapping worldly technology to boost farm productivity. Colony-owned trucks and vans haul supplies, products, and people. Huge tractors pull a full array of modern equipment across the vast stretches of colony land.

Colonies vary in their mix of agricultural enterprises, but a typical colony might have 1,000 hogs and 50,000 turkeys and might farm some 5,000 to 10,000 acres of land. A growing number of colonies operate flourishing businesses as well. During recent years, some colonies have established sizable industries related to wood, metal, stainless steel, feed, and other manufacturing operations that sell products outside of the colony.

Computers track management records and control equipment for farming and business operations. Each colony also has large shops that specialize in woodworking, plumbing, electrical, and mechanical expertise to support the colony operations. New buildings are constructed, equipped, and repaired by colony members. Most colony kitchens are fully automated with electric ovens, mixers, and freezers. Although tradition dictates many religious and social norms, modern technology is widely embraced for farming and household operations.

Remaining Apart

Hutterite conflicts with civil authorities from the 20th century onward have flared up over land use, taxes, education, military service, and social security. The discord is often fueled by the rapid growth of Hutterite colonies. When new colonies form, they frequently disturb surrounding rural communities. Several colonies, each with several thousand acres of land, can have a dramatic impact on land prices, school systems, and local consumer markets. Thus, Hutterites sometimes face protests from citizen groups and business organizations when they prepare to plant new colonies.

The Hutterite strategy for separation is rather simple—establish colonies in isolated rural areas beyond the reach of urban vices. By controlling the use of vehicles and monitoring who enters and leaves the colony, Hutterites are able to regulate interaction with outsiders. Members traveling outside a colony are often accompanied by another member, providing a mobile system of social control. Non-Hutterites often visit colonies to conduct business, and some Hutterite leaders participate in agricultural organizations.

Separation from the world is also maintained with taboos on television and other forms of mass media. Despite the traditional taboos, some progressive colonies have televisions in their schools to watch educational videos and broadcasts. Colonists often read farm magazines or newspapers, but the average member does not read national news magazines, at least not on a regular basis. Entertainment outside the colony is forbidden.

By regulating exposure to outside media, the colony limits contact with outsiders and filters contaminating influences. Hutterites believe that easy access to ungodly values would undermine their entire way of life. They do tap the services of outside professionals, veterinarians, medical doctors, dentists, lawyers, bankers, and accountants. Most babies, for example, are born in hospitals. Nevertheless, in all of these contacts, Hutterites are cautious not to interact too closely with the outside world.

The Hutterite "experiment" has endured for nearly 500 years. Hutterites' strong ethnicity, social control, and social isolation have enabled them to resist assimilation into mainstream society and the acculturation of individualistic values. But in their eyes, communalism is not just an interesting social experiment; it is a sincere attempt to practice Christian teachings that lead to eternal life.

Donald Kraybill

See also Amish; Ethnic Enclave, Economic Impact of; Mennonites; Religion, Minority; Schmiedeleut

Further Readings

Hostetler, John A. 1997. *Hutterite Society.* Baltimore, MD: Johns Hopkins University Press.

Hutterian Brethren, trans. 1987–1998. *Chronicle of the Hutterian Brethren* (Vols. 1–2). Rifton, NY: Plough.

Kraybill, Donald B. and Carl Desportes Bowman. 2001. *On the Backroad to Heaven: Old Order Hutterites, Mennonites, Amish, and Brethren.* Baltimore, MD: Johns Hopkins University Press.

Kraybill, Donald B. and C. Nelson Hostetter. 2001. *Anabaptist World USA.* Scottdale, PA: Herald Press.

Packull, Werner O. 1995. *Hutterite Beginnings: Communitarian Experiments during the Reformation.* Baltimore, MD: Johns Hopkins University Press.

Icelandic Americans

Iceland, a country with an estimated population of .3 million people in 2007, is one of the world's largest islands and the least densely populated nation in Europe, thanks partly to its historic isolation and its rather inhospitable volcanic and glacial interior. Emigration from Iceland to North America has also significantly contributed to this characteristic. The latest available U.S. Census Bureau statistics list slightly more than 75,000 people who identify themselves as Icelandic in all of North America (United States and Canada combined), but this is not one homogenous group. Rather, Icelandic Americans arrived here in three distinct waves: The first took place between 1870 and 1890, the second between 1950 and 1970, and a third is currently taking place. Distinguishing between these three phases better illustrates the current configuration of the loose Icelandic American ethnic identity. But despite their differences, and despite the ease with which Icelanders have assimilated into the dominant White Anglo-Saxon Protestant (WASP) ethnicity (as Scandinavians and Lutherans), members of each immigrant wave have maintained links to their Icelandic heritage. This entry recounts the immigration history of Icelandic Americans and describes the current community.

1870s to 1890s Emigration

The first emigration of Icelanders took place in the 1870s and continued into the 1890s. Faced with a series of particularly cold winters, and spurred by a significant volcanic eruption in Northern Iceland in 1874, Icelandic fisherman and farmers from small communities scattered along the Icelandic coast were tempted to emigrate. Like all Icelanders, they were literate people who cherished their mother tongue, so they wished to settle near one another in the New World. Advance teams scouted potential areas in Canada (Nova Scotia and Kinmount, Ontario) and the northern extreme of the midwestern United States (Milwaukee and Washington Island, Wisconsin), where several dozen Icelandic families settled.

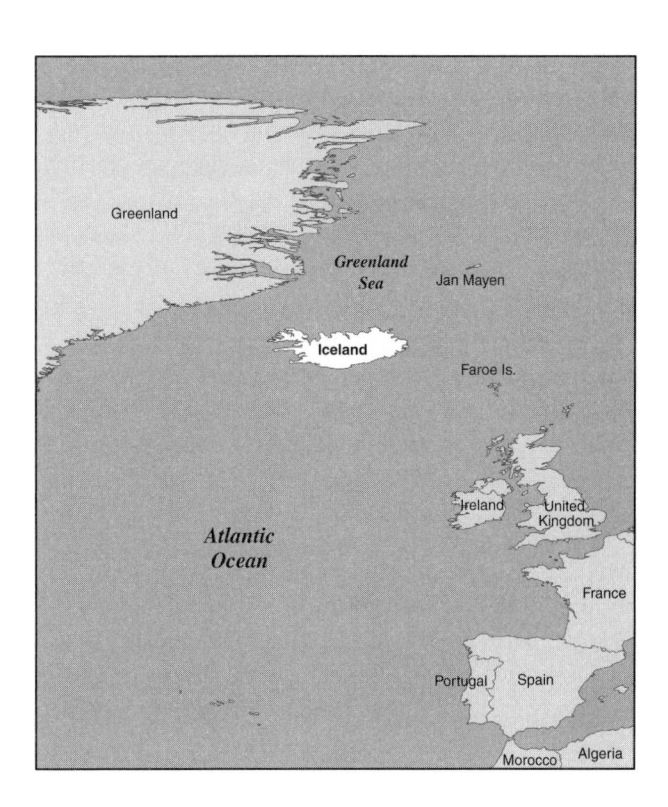

"New Iceland" Canada

In 1875, negotiations with the Canadian government secured land along an 80-kilometer stretch of Lake Winnipeg for an Icelandic colony, dubbed "New Iceland." This became the destination of choice for Icelandic immigrants, including 1,200 who came to Canada in 1876. Because the Canadian government was eager for European settlers in the newly opened Manitoba province, Icelanders were granted exclusive homesteading rights and a separate constitution. Most Icelanders who had settled elsewhere in Canada and the United States relocated here during that period.

These immigrants were primarily fishermen and livestock farmers, with limited experience growing grains or other produce, and they faced considerable hardships in New Iceland. The fishing conditions on Lake Winnipeg were quite different from ocean fishing in the North Atlantic, and locust plights and smallpox outbreaks caused significant loss of life. Nevertheless, the community held on, eventually numbering 1,500. In 1886, a newspaper was founded that is still in print under the title *Logberg-Heimskringla*. Several churches were established, and Icelandic was spoken by most residents until the 1950s. Although New Iceland eventually integrated into the Manitoba provincial jurisdiction, the towns in Manitoba bearing Icelandic names, such as the former capitol Gimli, demonstrate a distinct Icelandic identity through festivals celebrating Icelandic history, businesses with Icelandic names, a senior center catering to Icelandic speakers, and statues and other landmarks referencing Icelandic heritage. Winnipeg also has a sizable Icelandic population, and the University of Manitoba has the only Icelandic Department in North America. In the 2001 Canadian census, more than 26,000 Manitobans self-identified as Icelandic.

Pembina County, North Dakota

During the early rough years of the New Iceland colony, some Icelanders decided to seek better prospects in the United States. There were already a few Icelanders in Wisconsin and Minnesota, but an enthusiastic younger pastor encouraged his followers to immigrate to the northeastern corner of North Dakota. The towns of Mountain, Beaulieu, Akra, Cavalier, Thingvalla, Gardar, and Park in what is now Pembina County all had Icelandic founding families, and their descendants today number about 3,000. This does not include numerous descendants who integrated into the existing large Norwegian community, mostly through intermarriage. Today, the Icelandic community in this area has its own church, where guest pastors occasionally still preach in Icelandic, and they have an annual "Icelandic Celebration" in August.

From the settlements in Manitoba and North Dakota, later generations spread further west, establishing small communities in Saskatchewan, British Columbia, Utah, and Washington. Though geographically dispersed, the descendants of the 1870–1890 immigrants share familial connections that foster a real sense of an Icelandic American community stretching across the U.S.–Canadian border. The Icelandic National League of North America, which has a large annual meeting, works especially hard to give this disparate group a sense of cohesion. Web sites advertising annual events, such as Icelandic Days in Gimli, also encourage extended families to gather, keeping the connection to Iceland alive.

1950s to 1970s Immigration

Later immigrants to North American had a significantly different reason for leaving and a significantly different experience. In 1950, a North Atlantic Treaty Organization (NATO) base was established in Iceland (which lacks its own military), staffed by the U.S. Navy. Along with this strategic relationship came new business, social, educational, and cultural links between the United States and Iceland. Some immigration to the United States occurred when Icelandic businesspeople and their families moved here to take advantage of this new relationship. Emigration also resulted, quite naturally, from the presence of many young U.S. service members in Iceland, some of whom took home Icelandic wives.

Between 1950 and 1970, more than 2,000 of these so-called cold war brides immigrated to the United States, settled permanently in various areas, had families, and took on U.S. citizenship. But they did not simply abandon their links to Iceland: Some taught their children Icelandic, and others frequently took their children to visit extended family in Iceland. They also formed social clubs with one another in urban areas such as Los Angeles, Atlanta, Miami, Kansas City, Boston, and Seattle, organizing events on Icelandic Independence Day (June 17th), at Christmas, and in February (to observe an Old Icelandic festival called Thorablot). Because the members of these associations have a more immediate link to Iceland, their sense of their Icelandic identity is noticeably distinct from that of the descendants of the 1870–1890 immigrants.

Present Day

Since the 1990s, Iceland has enjoyed considerable economic prosperity. This has led fewer families to emigrate, but it has also meant that better educated and more affluent young people are eager to explore other opportunities, because Iceland has limited postsecondary educational facilities. Presently, there are more than 3,000 Icelandic nationals in the United States, many of whom are students or former students who have remained after finding suitable jobs in the United States. This last wave has its own reason for being in the United States, the closest link to Iceland, and a rather ad-hoc social network. But they do sometimes join existing Icelandic associations, giving these clubs new vibrancy.

Icelandic Americans are an interesting ethnicity in that there are few external forces contributing to their sense of identity. Lacking "visible" ethnic identity markers (they descend from blue-eyed, blond-haired Vikings) or a distinguishing religious affiliation (Iceland is a Protestant country), Icelandic immigrants have faced few prejudices. Their language has been preserved only in the most concentrated settlement in Manitoba and is dying out with the younger generation. Icelandic naming conventions, which are unusual (Icelanders do not have family names) and hard for English speakers to pronounce, were usually simplified by immigrants upon arrival in North America.

Despite this ease of assimilation, Icelandic Americans work to maintain a sense of their Icelandic heritage. Various associations, social clubs, publications, and annual celebrations have all done their part to create a feeling of community—if not necessarily a strong ethnic identity—among the dispersed and disparate populations that constitute Icelandic Americans. The Icelandic government also actively and financially supports the maintenance of this identity. An oft-repeated phrase in Iceland is that there are as many people of Icelandic descent living in North America as in Iceland, a sentiment not entirely supported by the statistics (Iceland's present population is almost 300,000). However, the census figure of 75,000 Icelanders in North America probably does not reflect the total Icelandic genetic heritage because third- or fourth-generation descendants may no longer self-identify as Icelandic. Guðjon Arngrimsson estimated in his study of the first wave of Icelandic immigration that its descendant population, broadly defined, would number at least 200,000 people.

No matter what the exact figures are, in a nation as small and interconnected as Iceland, each emigrant is keenly felt as a loss. The Icelandic government therefore sponsors efforts such as the Snorri Program, which provides grants for descendants to come learn Icelandic, as a way to maintain links with this extended population. Icelandic companies (especially Icelandair) cater to all of these groups as a single market, one interested in its Icelandic heritage, thus contributing to a sense of a shared identity. So although each of these three groups has different historical circumstances that brought them to North America and their own internal social networks, all have reason to think of Iceland as their homeland.

Elisabeth I. Ward

See Appendix A
See also Assimilation; Canada; Immigrant Communities

Further Readings

Arngrimsson, Guðjon. 1997. *Nyja Island: Saga of the Journey to New Iceland.* Translated by Robert Christie. Winnipeg, ON, CA: Turnstone Press. (Originally published Reykjavik: Mal og Menning, 1997).

IDENTITY POLITICS

Identity politics—sometimes referred to as the politics of recognition—represents both a practical politics and an analytical tool. As a practical politics, identity politics is associated with the emergence of the varied self-conscious counter-hegemonic social movements arising since the 1960s in particular—for example, the women's movement, and the Black Civil Rights Movement. Thus, it can be understood to refer to interactions in which individuals relate to others with reference to the group membership of the actors concerned. As an analytical tool or theoretical construct, identity politics is intended to provide a framework for critical analyses that foreground the histories and patterns of oppression experienced by minority groups. Hence, the experiential and theoretical become linked: Activism oriented around recognition and valuation of long stigmatized and disadvantaged collectives both inform and are informed by a concomitant discourse on injustice. In both respects, the notion of identity politics has also become a particularly volatile point of debate within the scholarship on difference. This entry examines identity politics and several critiques of these movements and perspectives.

Shifting U.S. Identities

The counter-hegemonic movements that have emerged in celebration of diverse identities since the 1960s challenged the traditional primacy and privilege of Whiteness and of masculinist heterosexuality. The "national identity" has undergone dramatic change during the past 2 decades. Immigration patterns have reshaped the demographics of the United States, so that by 2050, it is estimated that Whites will represent a mathematical minority of the population. With numerical strength has come political expression. Beginning with the Black and Native American civil rights movements of the 1960s, racial and ethnic minority groups, as well as women and sexualized minority groups, have mobilized, demanding a place and a voice that represents their identity. They are "in America's face." The United States is now in the midst of a cultural shift as identity politics challenges the historical correlation of American-ness with Whiteness, maleness, and heterosexuality.

What these movements have shared has been a commitment to the equal valuation and treatment of all social groups. Minority groups and women have asserted claims to freedom from discrimination, to group autonomy, to inclusion, and to participation, that is, to the status of American. Such an approach challenged long-standing and deeply embedded ideologies and practices that consciously sought to devalue "otherness"—Jim Crow laws, job segregation, and sodomy legislation, for example. Actors assert the claim to inclusion and recognition in the broader society on the basis of these stigmatized identities, but explicitly as "different" rather than as "same."

The experiences of these increasingly vocal counter-hegemonic movements have inspired a corresponding scholarship on the politics of identity that similarly privileges identities grounded in difference. Theoretically, those engaged in a politics of difference challenge the principles of liberal democracy that reify the equal universal citizen. Such long-standing doctrines are said to deny and occlude the reality of exclusion and oppression experienced by those who are not represented by the fictional citizen: Those who are not White, heterosexual, Christian males. Those lying outside these rigid boundaries—by virtue of their group membership—have limited and uneven access to power and resources on all levels of society. Yet the object of mobilization should not be to gain an "equal" footing, according to the counter-hegemonic viewpoint; this leads only to assimilation and the *loss* of discrete identities. On the contrary, emancipatory politics, from this perspective, must concern itself with the recognition and celebration of difference.

A Range of Critiques

Both the politics and philosophy of identity have come under fire. Ironically, both the left and the right are critical of identity politics for their potential, if not actualized tendency, to lead to balkanization. Arthur Schlesinger has been among the most vocal in his resistance to what he refers to as the "cult of ethnicity." He claims that the politics of identity "exaggerates differences, intensifies resentments and antagonisms, drives ever deeper the awful wedges between races and nationalities." Nancy Fraser lays the blame for such devastating ethnic conflicts as the Rwandan genocide and ethnic cleansing in the Balkans squarely at the feet of identity politics. Writing specifically of hate crime, James Jacobs and Kimberly Potter contend that "legislating hate" reinforces the tendency of people to think of themselves as members of affected identity groups, which subsequently contributes to the balkanization of U.S. society, rather than its unification.

Martha Minow succinctly identifies three further interrelated limitations of identity politics. First among these is the tendency toward essentializing identity. This refers to the common tendency to reduce individuals simply to members of a single identifiable group. As such, they are presumed to represent "the group." Critics respond that although individuals within a group may share some traits, they will certainly differ on others. Are all Black people representative of "the group?" All Muslims? All women? Surely not, argue the critics. Such a view of identity is monolithic and carries on as if all individual members of a group had the same perceptions, experiences, and interests.

In a related vein, identity politics is often criticized for its failure to account for the intersectionalities that characterize identity. Each individual occupies multiple identity positions, which may be more or less salient depending on context. Moreover, these positions may reinforce or contradict one another. A woman who is also White is privileged by virtue of the latter, but relatively disadvantaged by the former. Each person occupies a racial, a gender, a religious, and a sexual place, among others. Each of these heuristically distinct aspects of identity is shaped by its intersections at the point of contact with the others. Images and expected gender roles, for example, are conditioned by race. Kimberle Crenshaw highlights the significance of intersectionality in her analysis of violence against women of color. In this context, Black women and White women experience male violence differently. Similarly, Black women and Black men understand the dynamics of male violence against women in distinct ways.

Minow finally draws attention to the fluidity of the "boundaries" that define identity—both cross-culturally and temporally. Who gets to define group inclusion? Blood quantum laws defining tribal membership of Native Americans may have little in common with who *self*-identifies as Native American, or with what tribe they associate. Moreover, definitions of race, gender, sexuality, and other related categories shift over time. There was a time when the Irish, the Italians, and the Polish, for example, were not considered White. Today, their "belongingness" goes without question. "Identity" is unstable. It is subject to ongoing challenges and redefinition—sometimes by subordinate groups, sometimes by dominant groups. Consequently, to tie a philosophy or practice of politics to the complex notion of identity is akin to walking on shifting sand.

Another set of critiques comes from what might be seen as traditional Marxist approaches. These take identity politics to task for the overreliance on the cultural rather than material roots of oppression. The claim, from this perspective, is that an emphasis on representation, recognition, and cultural worth distracts attention from the structural roots of these phenomena. In short, these critics argue, a politics that seeks only to alter the misrepresentations and cultural value of diverse groups will fail to eliminate the roots of oppression because such efforts have no effect on the structural and institutional dimensions of injustice.

The forgoing criticisms not withstanding, identity politics has been a vital driving force behind progressive social change during the last half century. There can be no denying that the self-conscious social movements of the late 20th century have had a profound impact on popular imagery, on the nature of democratic practice, and on the (re)distribution of resources. Yet, as Fraser reminds us, alongside the emancipatory potential of identity politics, we have also witnessed the ways in which it can contribute to provocative divisions across racial, ethnic, and religious lines. What is needed, then, is not the wholesale rejection of the logic of identity politics but, rather, a way of connecting—through coalitions, for example—reified social identities to one another based on parallel histories and experiences.

Barbara Perry

See also Civil Rights Movement; Cosmopolitanism; Ethnicity, Negotiating; Minority/Majority; Minority Rights; Multicultural Social Movements; People of Color; Racial Identity; Racialization

Further Readings

Crenshaw, Kimberle. 1991. Mapping the Margins: Intersectionality, Identity Politics, and Violence against Women of Color. *Stanford Law Review* 43(July):1241–1299.

Fraser, Nancy. 2003. "Social Justice in the Age of Identity Politics" In *Redistribution or Recognition? A Political-Philosophical Exchange,* edited by N. Fraser and A. Honneth. New York: Verso.

Jacobs, James and Kimberly Potter. 1998. *Hate Crimes: Criminal Law and Identity Politics.* New York: Oxford University Press.

Lipsitz, George. 1998. *The Possessive Investment in Whiteness: How White People Profit from Identity Politics.* Philadelphia, PA: Temple University Press.

Minow, Martha. 1997. *Not Only for Myself: Identity, Politics and the Law.* New York: New Press.

Schlesinger, Arthur M., Jr. 1992. *The Disuniting of America: Reflections on a Multicultural Society.* New York: Norton.

Taylor, Charles. 1992. *Multiculturalism and the Politics of Recognition.* Princeton, NJ: Princeton University Press.

Young, Iris Marion. 1990. *Justice and the Politics of Difference.* Princeton, NJ: Princeton University Press.

ILLEGAL IMMIGRATION REFORM AND IMMIGRANT RESPONSIBILITY ACT OF 1996

President Bill Clinton signed the Illegal Immigration Reform and Immigrant Responsibility Act (IIRIRA) on September 30, 1996, while expressing concern about its more draconian provisions. This act contained five major sections: (1) improvements to border control, facilitation of legal entry, and interior enforcement; (2) enhanced enforcement and penalties against alien smuggling and document fraud; (3) inspection, apprehension, detention, adjudication, and removal of inadmissible and deportable aliens; (4) enforcement of restrictions against employment; and (5) restrictions on benefits for aliens. The act continued a tradition of strengthening enforcement, particularly at the U.S.–Mexico border.

Four elements of the bill had a particularly negative impact on new immigrants or political asylum applicants. First, the classification of "aggravated felonies," for which a permanent resident alien could be deported, was expanded and made retroactive with only limited options for relief. Second, the process of deportation became one of "removal" in which undocumented immigrants apprehended near ports of entry lost due process rights, including judicial consideration of an appeal. Third, refugees were no longer to be voluntarily released pending a return court date. Instead, most were to be detained. Fourth, access to welfare benefits and certain social services for legal permanent aliens were withdrawn in conjunction with the Welfare Reform Act of 1996. The IIRIRA also specified that sponsors of aliens coming to the United States had to guarantee support. All these measures were passed by a Congress dealing with a negative public reaction to new immigrants, particularly the stereotypical idea that immigrants come to the United States to receive welfare benefits, and negative opinion about allowing individuals who entered without documents to stay in the United States. These elements are reviewed in more detail in this entry.

Aggravated Felonies as Grounds for Removal

An aggravated felony is a crime classified as of sufficient severity to warrant deportation of a noncitizen. IIRIRA is the most recent in a series of legislative acts aimed at deporting criminal aliens. Aggravated felonies were first designated in the 1988 Anti-Drug Abuse Act, which included murder, drug trafficking, and firearms trafficking as grounds for removal. Next, the Immigration Act of 1990 specified that violent crimes resulting in sentences of more than 5 years were aggravated felonies.

After the first attack on the World Trade Center and the Oklahoma City bombing, the Antiterrorism and Effective Death Penalty Act (AEDPA) was passed in 1996, 5 months before the IIRIRA. The AEDPA expanded existing aggravated felonies to include gambling, transport for purpose of prostitution, alien smuggling, and passport or other document fraud. It created the aggravated felony designation for obstructing justice, perjury, bribery, commercial bribery, forgery, counterfeiting, and vehicle trafficking convictions with sentences of 5 years or more. The IIRIRA was passed in this climate of crackdowns on criminal aliens and the beginning of more stringent efforts to stop terrorism.

IIRIRA significantly expanded the definition of aggravated felonies for which an immigrant could be deported. Fifty new categories of crime, including shoplifting and driving while intoxicated, were added to prior aggravated felonies. Any noncitizens, including permanent resident aliens, were made subject to collateral penalties that affect immigration status. These penalties include removal from the United States and a lifetime ban on having legal status to be in the United States. An immigrant convicted of an aggravated felony is unable to plead on the basis of good moral character or any basis for cancellation of deportation. This collateral penalty has had a major impact on noncitizens because it was applied retroactively. In other words, an immigrant could have committed a crime many years ago and served time for it; if the Immigration and Customs Enforcement (ICE) unit became aware of this record, the immigrant could still be deported. In fact, thousands of immigrants have been designated as "criminal aliens" and deported because of a previously committed aggravated felony or on being released from prison after having served time for such an offense.

In legal tests of this legislation, individuals have asked that prior convictions be vacated and that they be retried because they were not legally advised that deportation would be a consequence of their guilty pleas. As a result, some individuals have been permitted to stay in the United States. In 2001, the U.S. Supreme Court, in *INS v. St. Cyr*, ruled that permanent resident aliens who pleaded guilty to crimes before IIRIRA do not have to be automatically deported and can undertake judicial review under prior exemptions.

Denial of Access to Judicial Review

The second major IIRIRA change was the creation of a process called "expedited removal" in place of traditional deportation procedures. This eliminated access to a lawyer and judicial review for most undocumented entry cases. The Immigration and Naturalization Service (INS, the predecessor of ICE) was given the authority to detain and then deport individuals without a court procedure. This has a strong impact on undocumented immigrants because it also specified that individuals could be barred from entering the country for as long as 10 years depending on the amount of time they were present in the United States.

There are two exceptions to removal. First, refugees applying for asylum are permitted to have an interview to determine a credible fear of persecution. If an asylum officer does not find in favor of the refugees, they are to be deported unless they appeal their case, which requires a judicial review. Second, cancellation of removal requires being present for 10 years or more, evidence of good moral character, not having been convicted of a serious crime, and evidence of extreme hardship for a citizen or permanent resident spouse, parent, or child. This is limited to 4,000 cases per year. Except for refugees, limits were placed on judicial review to the effect that individuals could not appeal INS or lower court decisions. At the time the IIRIRA was passed, it applied to individuals apprehended at ports of entry such as the U.S.–Mexico border. As a result, most individuals convicted of aggravated felonies and undocumented entrants who did not make it into the U.S. interior were denied the recourse to due process of law that is granted to citizens.

Refugee Detention

International law specifies that applicants for political asylum and refugees should be released into the general population before appearing for a court hearing. Because many applicants were not presenting themselves for a court hearing, IIRIRA significantly changed the asylum process. Refugees were to be detained and then removed if they could not make a case for credible fear of persecution. Detained asylum-seekers who are deemed deportable can ask for judicial review of their cases. One significant problem is that asylum-seekers have been sent to overcrowded INS detention centers or jails and prisons without any certainty of when their case will be tried. Once in detention, they are treated the same as prisoners, including uniforms, shackling, disciplinary use of isolation, and verbal and physical abuse. Some individuals have been in detention for years because they have been denied asylum, and they can only appeal once a year.

Since September 11, 2001, ICE has been uniformly detaining all asylum-seekers and basically treating them as criminals. The International Covenant on Civil and Political Rights Article 10(1) specifies that detainees should be treated with dignity. The system of federal detention and the actual jails and prisons in which asylees are kept do not meet this criterion.

Provision of Support

The fourth major change in IIRIRA concerned the provision for public benefits and for providing affidavits of support for admitting immigrants to ensure that they would not become public charges. Both the IIRIRA and the Welfare Reform Act of 1996 were combined to exclude noncitizens from receiving public benefits such as food stamps and Supplemental Security Income.

The IIRIRA specifically applied to new entrants, who require an affidavit of support from an individual who agrees to be responsible for financially supporting them. The change specifies that a sponsor must support an alien at 125% of poverty level income and that the alien must not receive means-tested public benefits or the sponsor or the individual sponsor could be sued. In addition, sponsorship is restricted to U.S. citizens or permanent resident aliens residing in the United States. Sponsors are required to support immigrants until they have naturalized or been employed for at least 10 years in a job providing social security payments. Following the passage of IIRIRA, steps have been taken to restore federal benefits to permanent resident aliens.

Judith Ann Warner

See Appendix A
See also Asylum; Crime and Race; Immigration, U.S.; Immigration and Naturalization Service; PATRIOT Act of 2001; Refugees; Welfare Reform

Further Readings

Dow, Mark. 2004. *American Gulag: Inside U.S. Immigration Prisons.* Berkeley: University of California Press.
McDermid, Lea. 2001. "Deportation Is Different: Non-Citizens and Ineffective Assistance of Counsel." *California Law Review* 89:741–778.
U.S. Commission on Immigration Reform. 1997. *Impact of Federal Welfare Reform on Immigrants. Final Report.* Washington, DC: U.S. Government Printing Office.

Welch, Michael. 2001. *Detained: Immigration Laws and the Expanding I.N.S. Jail Complex.* Philadelphia, PA: Temple University Press,

Welch, Michael. 2003. "Ironies of Social Control and the Criminalization of Immigrants." *Crime, Law and Social Change* 39:319–337.

IMMIGRANT COMMUNITIES

The policies, practices, performances, possibilities, and prejudices related to U.S. immigration have been and continue to be some of the most hotly contested issues within the public sphere. Indeed, the implications of immigration for community life in the United States have been discussed and debated since the beginning of this democracy. Leaders such as Benjamin Franklin considered the costs and benefits of immigration for colonial communities, noting a particular concern about the ability of immigrants to assimilate into public life. To this day, the influx of immigrants into the United States continues to challenge and enrich traditional notions of the U.S. society as a "melting pot" of many ethnic subcommunities. Consequently, many have questioned the figurative fit of this metaphor, preferring instead to imagine the movements of immigrant communities in terms of tributaries that eventually meet to form a single larger body or a tapestry in which the single threads that represent individual communities remain distinct as they combine to create the larger fabric of society.

Many scholars have argued that the late 20th century is a moment of great historical significance for immigration to the United States. During the last 35 years, the number of immigrants to this country has more than tripled. More important, contemporary immigration largely originates from developing countries. These new immigrants bring with them a host of cultural and social practices largely unfamiliar to people in mainstream Western culture. Modern immigrants often work hard to maintain connections, both literal and symbolic, to their countries of origin, modifying traditional notions of assimilation and enculturation. In short, this recent wave of immigration is changing the composition of U.S. communities and raising new issues related to social and racial intolerance, patterns of community integration, and civic participation. This entry begins by considering the current nature of U.S. immigration and the fundamental nature of community. Issues specifically related to immigrant communities are discussed, including (a) their indicators and composition; (b) their roles, responsibilities, and functions; (c) reasons why some fear strong immigrant communities; and (d) the impact of declining or resilient communities.

The Nature of U.S. Immigration

Anxiety regarding immigration into the United States has increased in recent years. Today, there are more than 130 million migrants worldwide, and the foreign-born population in United States has increased to approximately 30 million. As in previous historical moments, today's immigrants often face ambivalence and acrimony from the broader mainstream society. This situation is further complicated because, as a result of the 1965 immigration act, the countries from which people are migrating to the United States are generally less economically advanced. This has led to the mistaken perception among many U.S. citizens that the immigrants themselves are generally poor and uneducated. In reality, this is often not the case. Many immigrants come with advanced degrees and professional skills and are able to find opportunities that will lead them to successfully negotiate mainstream culture.

Immigrants and their families leave their countries of origin for the United States for a wide variety of reasons. In addition to immigrants who seek educational, entrepreneurial, and professional gains, there are labor migrants, refugees, and asylum seekers. Many are motivated to consider leaving their countries of origin because liberalized provisions allow them to immigrate. Others do so to close gaps between actual and expected socioeconomic status. In other cases, desperate poverty and unemployment motivate immigrants. Most often, individuals immigrate for a combination of reasons.

For most, the potential benefits of immigrating to the United States are enticing. However, the process of immigration is often stressful and may have high emotional as well as economic costs. For example, the process frequently destabilizes family life. Data from the Harvard Immigration Project suggest the immigrant journeys are a multiphase process, resulting in intricate patterns of family fragmentation and reunification. Children often are left behind or sent ahead and expected to live in the care of relatives. In many cases, considerable time may pass before families are reassembled. This also tends to undermine parental authority and family cohesion. A common fear expressed by immigrant parents is that they will lose their children to the new culture.

Previously, acculturation or assimilation was assumed to have overwhelmingly positive consequences for immigrants' economic progress and psychological well-being. Acculturation, the first step of the adaptation process, is defined by different patterns of learning the language and culture of the host country. Assimilation, the final stage of the process, is defined as the process by which people who do not have a common cultural heritage come to share the same body of opinions, traditions, and allegiances. These concepts advance the notion of straight-line movement into the social and economic mainstream, accompanied by the loss of original language and culture.

Today, many scholars argue that contemporary immigration has significantly complicated these models. Immigration today comprises a diverse set of arrival and return patterns, socioeconomic backgrounds, and ways of adapting to U.S. society. That is, theories coined in earlier immigrant contexts—theories that argue for the notion of uniform assimilation as a precondition for social and economic advancement—are increasingly implausible. Some scholars argue that this type of assimilation never happened at all. Rather, the melting pot myth emerged from the need to pressure immigrants into the White Anglo-Saxon Protestant cultural mainstream. In reality, immigrant groups are constantly re-created by new experiences, even after profound language, custom, and culture losses.

Beyond this, patterns of assimilation usually depict an upwardly mobile journey; that is, the longer immigrants stay in the United States, the better they do in school, health, and income. However, several scholars have argued that social and economic divisions are creating new patterns of entrance into U.S. culture. Factors such as education, race, ethnicity, and socioeconomic status all shape immigrants' experiences in the United States. Consequently, today some immigrants, such as those from South Asia, are climbing the socioeconomic ladder at rates never before seen in U.S. history. Others, however, are denied a place in the opportunity structure, creating what some have termed a "rainbow underclass."

Indeed, for some immigrant groups, length of residency in United States is associated with declining goals, health, and school achievement. For example, a National Research Council (NRC) study revealed the length of time an immigrant youth lives in the United States is positively associated with a decline in overall physical and psychological health. Those who had been here longer were more likely to engage in risky behaviors such as substance abuse, unprotected sex, and delinquency, as well as suffer from phobias and antisocial personality disorders. In attempting to explain these findings, the study noted that less acculturated immigrants are least likely to be exposed to these practices and are under the influence of stronger family ties, social controls, and traditional values associated with their cultural heritage.

Thus, the best way of dealing with these challenges seems to be balancing the process of acculturation with a reaffirmation of primary social ties within the ethnic community. For example, a study of native-born Mexican Americans found that a strong sense of cultural heritage was positively related to mental health and social well-being. In addition, studies have shown that children who have parents who remain authority figures while encouraging strong ties to an immigrant community will be best able to embrace the widest range of opportunities. Thus, acculturation is not a simple solution to the challenges of immigration.

Community and Immigration

Many scholars note that immigrants depend on community networks to ease the pains of culture shock and aid in the development of new social connections and friendship networks. Community can be understood as a social system composed of institutional, organizational, occupational, friendship, and kinship relations. A community is also understood to represent the images and identities that people hold about it. Some scholars even argue that members of a human community not only live together but also feel and think together. Consequently, community involves a common identity and a common way of life. Interestingly, others argue that community is not created merely from shared common characteristics or a common situation. Indeed, even racial distinctions do not necessarily lead to communal relationships. From this perspective, communal relationships are based on a sense of solidarity and mutual orientation growing from emotional and traditional connections among the participants.

Ethnic communities may also be the neighborhoods and primary social environments in which many immigrants interact. In general, characteristics that indicate the existence of an immigrant community of this kind include clear geographical areas inhabited by the immigrant group, a common language, a common historical and cultural heritage, common interests, and businesses and community leadership expressing an ethnic lifestyle. Yet, immigrant communities, which outsiders often see as tightly organized, may not be characterized by a unity of thought, action, and way of life. Some scholars have noted that internal division may help to maintain ethnic consciousness. That is, immigrants may share a common set of values, cultural heritage, or national identity, but not think and act alike.

Scholars have provided a variety of arguments to explain how these communities are created. Many contend that work opportunities are the primary reasons immigrant communities arise. Other scholars focus more closely upon immigration laws and their effect upon patterns of settlement. Scholars even argue that social support in the form of basic institutions leads to community, as migrants bring their theaters, groceries, restaurants, hotels, formal and informal support organizations, and regional societies. This effectively creates communities that reflect, in many ways, those they left behind. Immigrant community connections help individuals preserve and adapt their old-world culture among strangers through the continuation of traditions, festivals, and institutions.

And yet, these immigrant communities are also living entities that continue to grow and diversify over time. Scholars who take this approach seek to alter the traditional view that ethnic communities comprise homogeneous, static populations trapped in a defined area. Additionally, immigrants from the same country of origin who settle in different areas of the United States create communities that have distinctive features. For example, early in their creation, midwestern communities of Mexican Americans tended to be less diverse than are those in the Southwest. These immigrant communities comprised primarily of young males from lower economic agricultural backgrounds, who originated from Mesa Central, especially Michoacán, Jalisco, Guanajuato, and Mexico City.

Lack of Community Connection

When there is no community connection, immigrants face a host of problems and lose several valuable resources that contribute to economic success and psychological health. They often are denied a voice or presence in economic and political arenas and are cut off from valuable resources that can help to regulate the pace of acculturation. Problems may arise if parents struggle alone with new social and cultural expectations and are unable to maintain social control of their children. In particular, role reversal can occur when first-generation parents are unable to cope with the outside environment because they do not have personal resources or community support and must depend on their children to negotiate issues involving the mainstream culture.

Others assert that the absence of immigrant communities means the loss of a social safety net. Immigrant communities provide recent arrivals with networks of interaction, assistance, and intervention, as well as access to capital, protected markets, and pools of labor. Some scholars express concern that this type of safety net can easily deteriorate as immigrants and their children assimilate and become more like mainstream U.S. residents; their patterns of social mobility become similar to those of the rest of the population. However, other scholars note that the descendants of late 19th-century and early 20th-century immigrants, particularly those coming from the Mediterranean and non-European countries, continue to remain concentrated in particular geographic locations. Beyond this, when members of an ethnic group change locations, they are likely to go where their own group is already plentiful; thus, when an ethnic group moves en masse, it often reconnects in another region.

Fear of Strong Ethnic Communities

Despite the important long-term contributions immigrant communities have made in U.S. culture, some people have expressed concern over their potential strength. In some cases, nativism grows from nationalistic movements. These groups tend to rally around issues of job competition and the nature of "being an American," and their rhetoric focuses on the potential of "alien invasions" and the preservation of "our" nation. Some groups argue that immigration constitutes an attack on "U.S. sovereignty." In addition, some believe immigrant groups will irrevocably alter U.S. culture and foster the alienation of certain ethnic groups.

Immigrants who are minorities in race, culture, and language are often the focus of degrading stereotypes and judged to be incompatible with modern U.S. culture and less deserving of the U.S. dream. These fears certainly found public voice in recent debates over immigration law and its reform. Suggestions, for example, have been made to use electrified "super-fencing" on the Mexican border to keep out illegal immigrants. Moreover, to date, thirty states have passed fifty-seven laws prohibiting undocumented individuals from receiving social services. The National Conference of State Legislatures notes that in 2005, almost 500 immigration measures were introduced. In 2006, more than forty-four bills were enacted. Some scholars contend that the response of immigrant communities to these nativist fears has been one of passive endurance rather than active opposition. However, the hundreds of thousands of protesters that participated in the "national day of action" rallies in April 2006 provide evidence to the contrary and illustrate the many ways immigrant communities have taken an active concern in promoting the just treatment of documented and undocumented immigrants in the United States.

Scholars studying issues relating to immigration and community have indicated a need to consider how contemporary patterns of immigration are influencing the formation of new types of communities. In addition, many have argued that rather than looking for indicators of difference, researchers should examine how groups of immigrants who display profound differences find ways in which to bond together within a community. In this same vein, it also would seem important to further consider how different immigrant communities interact with one another and with the mainstream society.

Christine Garlough

See Appendix A

See also Assimilation; Barrio; Chinatowns; *Colonias;* Community Cohesion; Community Empowerment; Ethnic Enclave, Economic Impact of; Ethnic Group; Gentrification; Ghetto; Immigration, U.S.; Melting Pot; Social Mobility

Further Readings

Capps, Randy. 2006. *Immigration and Child and Family Policy.* Washington, DC: Urban Institute.

Dasgupta, S. 1989. *On the Trail of an Uncertain Dream: Indian Immigrant Experiences in the U.S.* New York: AMS Press.

Garlough, Christine 2002. "The Rhetoric of Culture: Shaping Indian-American Identities Through Grassroots Community Education." Unpublished PhD dissertation, University of Minnesota, Minneapolis, Minnesota.

Granatir, June. 1991. "Staying Together: Chain Migration and Patterns of Slovak Settlement in Pittsburgh Prior to World War I." In *Emigration and Immigration,* edited by G. Pozzetta. New York: Garland.

Kritz, Mary. 2004. *Immigration and a Changing America.* New York: Russell Sage Foundation.

Navarro, Armando. 1998. *The Cristal Experience: A Chicano Struggle for Community Control.* Madison: University of Wisconsin Press.

Portes, Alejandro and Rubén. Rumbaut. 1996. *Immigrant America: A Portrait.* Berkeley: University of California Press.

Sanchez Korrol, Virginia. 1983. *From Colonia to Community: The History of Puerto Ricans in New York City 1917–1948.* Westport, CT: Greenwood Press.

Suárez-Orozco, Carola and Marcelo Suárez-Orozco. 2001. *Children of Immigration.* Cambridge, MA: Harvard University Press.

Vega, William, George Warheit, Joanne Buhl-Auth, and Kenneth Meinhardt. 1985. "Mental Health Issues in the Hispanic Community: The Prevalence of Psychological Distress." Pp. 30–47 in *Stress and Hispanic Mental Health,* edited by W. Vega and M. Manual. Rockville, MD: National Institute of Mental Health.

IMMIGRATION, ECONOMIC IMPACT OF

The United States has always been the land of immigrants, from the arrival of English settlers at the beginning of the 17th century to the present day, and from the beginning, immigrants have had a powerful economic impact. The Irish, Germans, Italians, Jews, Polish, Russians, and others played important roles in the development of the new nation. The agricultural needs of the Southwest and the construction of the transcontinental railroad and mining industries drew many Chinese and other Asian immigrants to the United States in the middle of the 19th century. These immigrants provided cheap labor for growing U.S. industry and created diverse communities in previously undeveloped areas in the Midwest and the Southwest.

The beginning of the 20th century saw the tremendous growth of manufacturing industry in the United States, attracting many immigrants from Southern and Eastern Europe. Eastern Europeans also established several dozen garment industries in various industrial cities, reflecting their diverse professional experience from the old country. One study noted that the credit for the development of garment industry in New York must be given to Eastern European Jews because 60% were employed in those industries by 1900. The important role these immigrants played in the local economy is illustrated by the fact that there were 1,000 garment factories in New York City in 1880; by 1910, their number increased to almost 11,000 and made New York the largest clothing manufacturing center at the time.

The most recent immigrants to the United States are from Asian and Latin American countries. Asians consist of several distinct groups from East and Southeast Asia, with diverse cultural norms and values. Today, the largest groups are Chinese, Filipino, Asian Indians, Pakistani, Japanese, Koreans, and Vietnamese. These non-Europeans have something in common with the Europeans who came before them: They all want to fulfill their U.S. dream and to live in peace and prosperity. Spread throughout the country, immigrants are gaining economic stability by getting jobs and education, so they can enjoy a better life for themselves and their families. This entry looks at the economic impact of immigration and how that is related to current debates about immigration.

Economic Effects of Immigration

Asians and Latinos are among the fastest-growing ethnic groups in the United States. As indicated in the U.S. Census 2000, most Latinos and Asians are relatively young when they come to the United States with 45% between the ages of 25 and 44, whereas 27% of U.S.-born residents fall in that age range. These immigrants are young, so they are also productive and have a successful and healthy impact on the U.S. economy.

Alex Stepick, an anthropologist studying race relations in Miami, observed that young Haitian immigrants in Miami schools tend to have a positive outlook for the future. They feel superior to and typically outperform American Blacks in academics. Another study observed the same optimism among many immigrants in New York and other cities. These immigrants are ambitious youth and have strong faith in opportunities and success. Scholars argue that the younger adult immigrants are, the greater likelihood of their net contribution in taxes because the younger immigrants have longer working lives to contribute to tax and social security payments.

Educational and Professional Achievements

The educational and professional achievements of these immigrants also influence their impact. Compared with the past, a much higher proportion of today's immigrants, particularly Asians, come to the United States with advanced academic credentials. The results from the Current Population Survey 2003 indicate that among Asians as a group, 45% had completed college. In comparison, only 27% of U.S.–born Whites had completed college. The college completion rate for Latin Americans was 11%, much lower than that of natives and Asians.

The high level of educational skills among Asians contributes to their success in the labor market, which in turn, helps the United States economy grow. The data further indicate that 37% of Asians had median earnings of $50,000 or higher in 2003, whereas 30% of U.S.-born Whites had reached this income level. The study also shows that Asians have higher levels of professional employment than any other group. For example, 33% of Asians have professional and technical occupations, compared with only 21% of U.S.-born Whites.

Although Asians represent only a small percentage of the total U.S. population, their higher educational and professional skills as a group have gained the attention of the U.S. public and media. For instance, studies indicate that these immigrants provide professionals in the field of science, engineering, and high-tech industries and helped the United States to maintain its global image in the fields. These facts advance the notion that these immigrants have added much more to the society than they have taken in benefits and that their presence in the country is beneficial. Their services in the health care, high-tech, and service sector, their attainment in education, and their focus on upward mobility provides a rich ethnic diversity to this country and thus makes enormous economic contribution to United States society.

Poverty Rates

Among immigrant groups, the poverty rate is lowest among Asians; only 11% of Asians are below poverty level in comparison with 11.5% of the U.S.-born population. The low poverty level among this group suggests that these immigrants do not impose a burden on United States taxpayers by their use of social and public services.

In this regard, however, it is important to note that all Asians are not alike. Vietnamese and other Southeast immigrants earn substantially less and have less education than many other Asian groups. For example, the median income for Vietnamese and Cambodians was much less than that for Chinese and Asian Indians, who rank among the highest income earners in 2003. Also, in education, only 20% Vietnamese and 9% Cambodians completed college graduation, which is far less than other Asian groups mentioned earlier.

Also, the poverty rates for these groups are much higher compared with Asian Indians and Chinese. This shows that several Asian groups are doing well and outperform Whites on many measures of socioeconomic achievement, whereas other Asian groups perform poorly on social economic indicator, further contributing to their problems of adjustment into U.S. society.

Job Categories

Among today's immigrants are engineers, computer scientists, teachers, academics, and health workers. They are hired by U.S. professional institutions such as hospitals, high-tech companies, and colleges and universities and thus are well represented in the U.S. labor force. These immigrants tend to reduce labor shortages that might otherwise occur. The more qualified the immigrants are, the more likely they are to get highly paid jobs, and, consequently, their net contribution in taxes grows. Thus, their fair contribution to the social security system contributes to U.S. prosperity.

In the agriculture and labor intensive industries such as construction, food preparation, and manufacturing, many businesses believe that restricting immigration would disrupt the U.S. economy. Many unskilled immigrants contribute their human capital in labor intensive industries where the pay is low, the benefits are nonexistent, and the working conditions are harsh. Mayor Larry Nelson, a Republican from Yuma, Arizona, says that he once believed the border should be closed entirely, but responsibility for his community's economy has changed his mind. With more jobs than workers in the United States, he says, without immigration the economy would "come to a screeching halt." According to one study, the post-1965 immigrant groups who arrived without much education or capital sought employment in the declining occupations and industries that the U.S.-born were leaving as well as in the growing low-wage service and retail industries that Whites would not enter.

Immigrant Entrepreneurs

Regarding business operation, scholars have observed that middle-class Asians and Latinos come to the United States with the specific objectives of investing their small funds. Although not as well educated, they moved into the small business sector such as grocery, restaurant, construction, and laundry service. They do not mind working long hours and are ardent supporters of the free enterprise system. The Current Population Survey indicates that Latinos and Asians owned 2.7 million non-farm U.S. businesses in 2002, employed 3.7 million people, and generated $548 billion in business revenues.

Thus, the success of immigrant business has an important impact on the U.S. economy. Beyond the self-employment of Asian and Latino immigrants, immigrant business also provides jobs and services for other U.S. residents. These jobs would not exist if the immigrants were not here. These immigrants are consumers as well as workers. They raise the demand for goods and services where they reside, as well as the supply of labor, and are more likely to take risks to start and expand enterprise.

According to one study, many Korean and Chinese immigrants engage in labor-intensive small businesses to avoid low-paying jobs. They succeed by relying on kinship networks and are therefore able to draw on a larger capital and employee base. Another study argues that California can be prosperous with high levels of recent immigrations. In attempting to explain this, the study notes that Asians and Latinos—accounting for 80% of all U.S. immigrants—form natural connections to fast-growing Pacific Rim and Latin U.S. economies, thus expanding California's trade with those regions.

Current Immigration Debates

Given the ongoing processes of chain migration, family reunification, and liberal immigration and emigration policies, the influx of immigrants from all over the world is likely to continue in the near future.

The constant growth of Latino and Asian communities has led to some opposition to current immigration as well as to concern about the ability of the nation to absorb so many immigrants. U.S. residents have also expressed concern about culturally different newcomers: Muslims, Asians, Arabs, or Latinos. Some perceive particular groups as a threat to national security, but other U.S. residents are apprehensive about the new immigrants' possible integration, believing such an eventuality would somehow undermine the "purity" of the U.S. character.

Illegal immigration is also an issue. Many U.S. residents believe that illegal immigrants are a burden on taxpayers' money and can be a security threat. Others argue that this charge is preposterous because illegal immigrants could not take advantage of welfare benefits without fear of being apprehended and deported. The issue of illegal immigrants, however, is a matter of concern to the U.S. policymakers. Although U.S. laws are against illegal immigrants, many U.S. residents depend on the work of illegal immigrants. Recent studies show that most U.S. people believe that for the safety and security of this country, controlling illegal immigration should be given a top priority.

Today, there is a rising fear about continuous immigration from non-European countries. A recent poll that the Pew Research Center carried out shows that 61% of U.S. residents believe that immigrants take more in public benefits such as education and health care than they contribute with their taxes, but only 31% argue that immigrants contribute more in social benefits with their taxes.

Against this concern stands a long record in which earlier generations of U.S. residents were successfully integrated into the mainstream. Isbister argued that at a time when many U.S. residents are calling for controlling immigration, the positive side of continued immigration to the United States needs attention. He also argued that immigration helps the United States economy grow and make United States strong as well as benefits the immigrants themselves.

Unless the United States takes strong actions to reduce immigration, the U.S. Census 2000 predicts that by the year 2050, Latinos will be the second-largest ethnic group after Whites, with African Americans and Asians third and fourth in the line. These different cultures, religions, and ideologies are likely to mean socioeconomic changes in U.S. society and lifestyle.

Navid Ghani

See Appendix A

See also Assimilation; Bilingual Education; Citizenship; Cultural Capital; Ethnicity, Negotiating; Hourglass Economy; Immigration, U.S.; Informal Economy; Model Minority; Remittances; Social Capital

Further Readings

Geis, Sonia. 2005. "Shortage of Immigrant Workers Alarms Growers in West." Washingtonpost.com. Retrieved November 22, 2005, from http://www.washingtonpost.com/wp-dyn/content/article/2005/11/21/AR2005112101357.html

Isbister, John. 1996. *Immigration Debate: Remaking America.* West Hartford, CT: Kumarian Press.

Marger, N. Martin. 2006. *Race and Ethnic Relations: American and Global Perspectives.* Belmont, CA: Thompson/Wadsworth.

Martin, L. Philip. 1994. "The United States: Benign Neglect Toward Immigration." In *Controlling Immigration. A Global Perspective,* edited by W. A. Cornelius, P. L. Martin, and J. F. Hollifield. Stanford, CA: Stanford University Press.

Muller, Thomas. 1993. *Immigrants and the American City.* New York: New York University Press.

Pew Research Center. 2006. *Polling the Nations: 2006.* Available from http://www.orspub.com

Portes, Alejandro and Rubén G. Rumbaut. 1996. *Immigrant America.* 2nd ed. Berkeley: University of California Press.

Sanjek, Roger. 1998. *The Future of Us All: Race and Neighborhood Politics in New York City.* Ithaca, NY: Cornell University Press.

Stepick, Alex, Guillermo Grenier, Max Castro, and Marvin Dunn. 2003. *This Land Is Our Land: Immigrants and Power in Miami.* Berkeley: University of California Press.

U.S. Census Bureau. 2000. *Current Population Survey.* 2000.

U.S. Census Bureau. 2003. *Current Population Survey.* 2003.

IMMIGRATION, U.S.

Immigration, the entry and settlement of persons born in another nation-state, has played an important role in shaping the population and culture of the United States since the nation's founding. The country has experienced three large waves of immigration following the first arrival of Europeans, and is currently in the midst of a fourth. This entry reviews the history of immigration and examines past and present policies governing the arrival of people from other countries.

The Record

The first immigration wave included the original settlers of the U.S. colonies beginning in the 17th century and continuing into the 18th century, consisting mainly of British, Scots, Scotch Irish, Germans, and people from the Netherlands, France, and Spain. Servants and slaves from Africa were also brought coercively to the continent during this period. The second wave began in 1820 and consisted mostly of German, British, and Irish migrants who furthered the westward expansion of the country's settlements.

The third wave, from about 1880 until 1914, included settlers first from Northern and Western Europe, and then from Southern and Eastern Europe. Alongside these European waves, Chinese laborers were recruited from the late 1840s until the 1880s to work in Hawai'i and California and to build the railroads of the West. Following the Chinese Exclusion Act of 1882, Japanese and Filipino workers took their place until the 1907 "Gentlemen's Agreement" between the United States and Japan ended migration from Japan. Mexican immigrants entered without restriction, and came in growing numbers, particularly after 1880.

The United States is now experiencing a fourth wave of immigration. About 14 million immigrants, legal and illegal, came to the country during the 1990s—more than in any previous decade. Unlike previous flows, the most recent immigrants have hailed from Asia, particularly China, India, and the Philippines, and from Latin America, primarily Mexico. Demographers estimate that more than 15 million immigrants will have entered by 2010. However, despite these large flows, the share of foreign-born persons living in the United States is not as high as it was at the beginning of the 20th century, about 12% currently compared with 15% earlier (see Figure 1).

Past Immigration Policy

The orientation of U.S. immigration policy has passed through several phases. During the first hundred years following the country's founding, immigration was

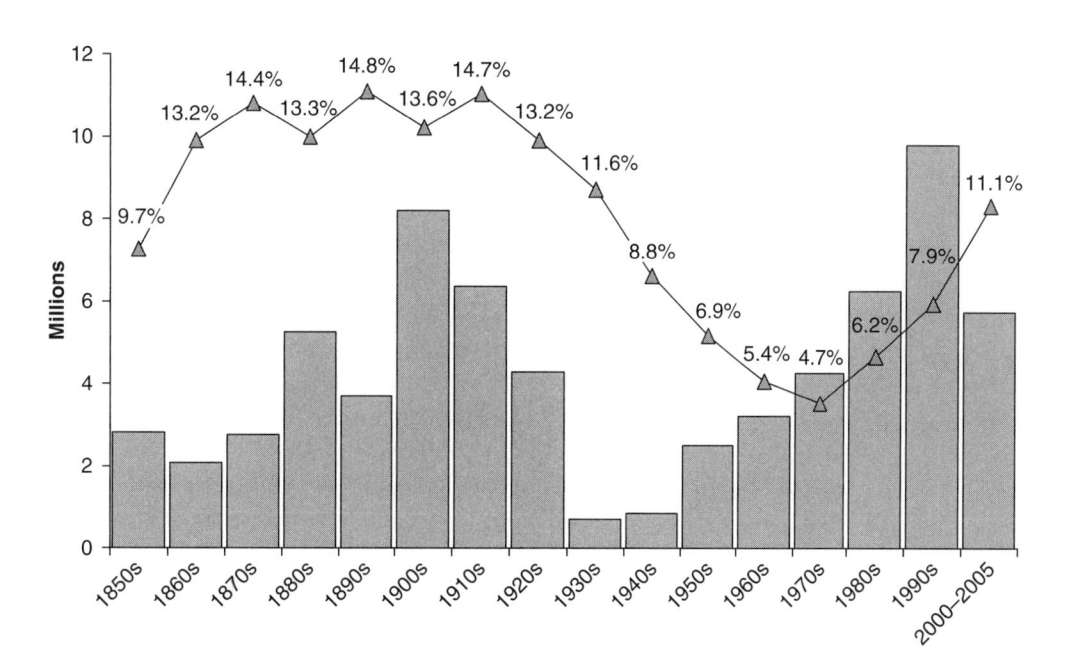

Figure 1 Number of New Lawful Permanent Residents by Decade and Foreign-Born Share of U.S. Population, 1850s to 2000s

Sources: U.S. Department of Homeland Security, *Yearbook of Immigration Statistics:* 2005, Table 1 (Washington, DC: Office of Immigration Statistics, 2006); Campbell J. Gibson and Emily Lennon, "Historical Census Statistics on the Foreign-Born Population of the United States: 1850–1990," Population Division Working Paper No. 29 (Washington, DC: U.S. Census Bureau, February 1999); U.S. Census 2000.

Notes: Percentages show foreign-born share of the total U.S. population in the year of the decennial census, so 1850s data show 2.8 million new lawful permanent residents between 1850 and 1859, with the foreign-born share of the U.S. population at 9.7% in 1850. Although the foreign-born made up 11.1% of the U.S. population in 2000, that share grew to 12% by 2005.

quite unrestricted, and both the government and private groups actively recruited new migrants. Immigration did not require any admissions tests or fees. However, some limited bars to admission were enacted following the Civil War, first blocking convicts and prostitutes and later paupers and "mental defectives" from entry.

The government established an admissions test in 1917, which required immigrants older than 16 to prove literacy in at least one language. The Immigration Act of 1924 further limited entry by establishing a national origins quota system, which set caps on migration from any given country based on the percentage of U.S. residents who traced their heritage to that country. This arrangement clearly favored immigration from the Northern and Western European countries that had sent the largest numbers in the past. Immigrants were also required to have a sponsor in the United States. The Immigration and Nationality Act (INA) of 1952 generally continued this quota system, with only minor modifications. No special category for entrance by refugees was established until the Displaced Persons Act of 1948, which was followed by the Refugee Relief Act of 1953.

The quota system was finally overhauled by 1965 amendments to the INA that equalized treatment of all immigrants from the Eastern Hemisphere through the establishment of a 20,000 per-country limit. Migration from individual countries in the Western Hemisphere was not capped, though the hemisphere as a whole was subject to a cap. The revised laws allocated the most visas to family members of U.S. citizens and permanent residents. As a result, immigration levels increased substantially, and immigration flows shifted from mainly European origins to large-scale immigration from Asian and Latin American countries.

Furthermore, levels of unauthorized immigration began to grow, as would-be immigrants from Europe and particularly from Mexico found that insufficient permanent visas were available to permit their entry. Mexican workers had lost a primary legal migration stream with the end of the Bracero program, which had allowed entry by temporary agricultural workers from 1942 through 1964. In addition, the 20,000 per-country cap as applied to Mexico in 1976 allowed only half as many visas as Mexican migrants had previously used.

The next revision of permanent immigration preference categories came in the Immigration Act of 1990. The act shifted the emphasis of immigration quotas toward employment-based migration, more than doubling the number of annual employment-based visas and setting aside most of these visas for highly educated workers. It also established the Diversity Visa program for persons from countries with low levels of immigration to the United States.

Beginning in 1940, the administration of immigration law, including the adjudication of applications for temporary and permanent immigration and enforcement of immigration laws, had been the responsibility of the Immigration and Naturalization Service, under the Department of Justice. Following the creation of the Department of Homeland Security (DHS) in 2002, immigration responsibilities were transferred to Immigration and Customs Enforcement (ICE), U.S. Citizenship and Immigration Services (USCIS), and Customs and Border Protection (CBP), all within DHS.

The Current Immigration System

Permanent Immigration

The current immigration system remains largely that set by the 1990 law. Most visas for permanent immigration are allocated according to per-country and preference category caps. Uncapped visas are also available for the immediate family, including spouses, minor children, and parents of U.S. citizens age 21 or older, and for certain other humanitarian and assorted special visa categories.

Each year, 226,000 visas are reserved for family-sponsored preference categories. These visas are divided among four family preference categories, reserving the largest number for spouses, minor children, and unmarried adult children of lawful permanent residents. Employment-based visas are limited at 140,000 a year, with most allocated to skilled and highly skilled workers. Each country of the world is limited to no more than 7% of the visas allocated under any given family or employment-based preference category.

Nonimmigrant System

The nonimmigrant (temporary) immigration system offers visas for limited entry to the United States for specific purposes. There are more than seventy classes of nonimmigrant admissions including, for example, temporary visits for business or tourism, work visas, student visas, religious workers, intracompany transferees, diplomats, and representatives of international organizations.

The number of nonimmigrants entering each year is not capped, although specific nonimmigrant visas do have numerical limitations; this applies to the H-1B visa for those with a bachelor's or higher degree to work in "specialty occupations" and the H-2B visa for workers in other than agricultural occupations, among others. Temporary visas allow widely differing lengths of stay in the United States. For example, visitors on transit visas are authorized to stay for only a number of hours, but H-1B holders may enter for 3 years, renewable once for a total of 6 years. Individual athletes on P-1 visas may enter for as long as two 5-year periods. Persons on many temporary worker visas can adjust to permanent resident status, including E visas for treaty traders, H-1B visas for specialty occupations, L visas for intracompany transferees, and O-1 visas for individuals with extraordinary ability in science, art, business, or athletics.

Humanitarian Immigration

In addition to the temporary and permanent immigration systems, humanitarian entries as asylum seekers or refugees constitute a third path of entry into the United States. In this area, people are granted protection if they can demonstrate they are unable or unwilling to return to their home country because of persecution, or well-founded fear of persecution, based on their race, religion, nationality, membership in a particular social group, or political opinion. This requirement is adapted from international law set by the 1951 United Nations Convention Relating to the Status of Refugees and amended by the 1967 Protocol Relating to the Status of Refugees. Refugees and asylum seekers are eligible to apply for lawful permanent immigrant status after one year in the United States.

Normally, refugees apply for resettlement and are interviewed while outside the country they fled following the outbreak of armed conflict, violence, persecution, human rights violations, or other circumstances in their home country. In contrast, asylum seekers apply for protection upon entry to or after entering the United States (as long as it is within 1 year of arrival).

Each year since the passage of the Refugee Act of 1980, the president has consulted with Congress to determine the number of refugees who could be admitted to the United States for the coming fiscal year. The level fluctuates depending on world events and estimates of the size of the refugee population worldwide. The cap on refugee resettlement has varied since 1980 between a high of 231,000 in fiscal year (FY) 1980 and a low of 67,000 in FY 1986. Refugee admissions have been capped at 70,000 since FY 2002, though regional allocations have shifted during these years. The number of persons granted asylum in a given year is not limited.

In FY 2005, 25,257 people were granted asylum. Numbers of persons granted asylum grew significantly between FY 1991 and FY 2001, but have dropped in each year since then. About 53,800 refugees were admitted to the United States in FY 2005, which was substantially under the 70,000 ceiling. Refugee admissions have reached historic lows following the implementation of new policies after the terrorist attacks of September 11, 2001.

Unauthorized Immigration

A fourth stream of immigration includes those who enter without authorization or violate the terms of a temporary visa. According to demographer Jeffrey Passel, the number of unauthorized immigrants living in the United States is 11 to 12 million, more than double the number 20 years ago. He estimates that the size of the unauthorized population is growing by about 500,000 a year. About two-thirds of the unauthorized population have been in the United States for 10 years or less, and 40% have been in the country only 5 years or less.

About 40% to 50% of unauthorized immigrants entered on legal temporary visas and remained beyond the terms of the visa, and the rest crossed the U.S. border illegally. As a result of these high levels of unauthorized immigration in recent years, by 2005, almost a third of the foreign-born persons in the country were unauthorized immigrants (see Figure 2). Immigrants from Latin America (particularly Mexico but also Guatemala, Honduras, and El Salvador) compose the largest numbers of unauthorized immigrants.

Trends in U.S. Immigration

The level of immigration to the United States has been increasing substantially during the past decade, with growing numbers of temporary, permanent, and unauthorized immigrants. An average of almost 1 million people have gained permanent resident status during each of the past 5 years, and the unauthorized immigrant population has grown by an estimated 500,000

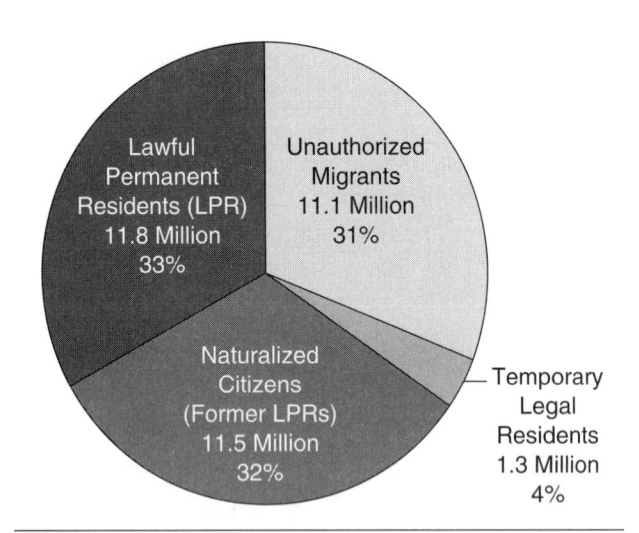

Figure 2 Legal Status of the U.S. Foreign-Born Population, 2005

Source: Jeffrey S. Passel, "The Size and Characteristics of the Unauthorized Migrant Population in the U.S." (Washington, DC: Pew Hispanic Center, March 2006).

Note: Although the unauthorized population was estimated at 11.1 million in 2005, the estimate for 2006 is 11.5 to 12 million.

per year. The majority (64%) of legal permanent immigrants over recent years have been family-based immigrants. Only a small share of permanent immigrants are workers: Employment-based immigrants made up only 17% of all immigrants, but more than half of those employment-based immigrants were spouses and minor children, rather than the workers themselves. About 11% of lawful permanent residents during this period were adjusting from refugee, asylum seeker, or another humanitarian status.

U.S. immigration flows are shaped by the existence of substantial backlogs in both the employment- and family-based permanent immigration streams. Employment-based permanent visas are delayed by backlogs for workers from some countries and for some skill levels, and most workers must wait for often-lengthy labor certification processes, intended to protect the wages, working conditions, and job opportunities of U.S. workers. Low-skill workers face another barrier to entry because of the very low number (5,000) of visas available each year for workers with low educational levels. In the family-based permanent immigration system, backlogs for certain categories can stretch to 14 or even 23 years.

As a result of backlogs, many workers of all skill levels as well as other would-be immigrants work their way around the permanent entry system. High-skill workers and their employers increasingly turn to temporary work visas to facilitate faster entry. Nearly two-thirds of those gaining lawful permanent resident status in recent years were already in the country, often on a temporary visa, and were adjusting their status. Among employment-based immigrants, that share was 80%. Congress has facilitated this process by creating increasing categories and subcategories of temporary visas to allow skilled workers to enter the country. Many of these visas now allow adjustment to permanent status. Low-skilled workers often turn to illegal means of entry by crossing the border without authorization or overstaying the terms of a legal temporary visa.

Within the overall trend of increasing immigration from Asia and Latin America, migrants' origins vary somewhat by mode of entry. For example, the main countries of origin for lawful permanent residents in recent years have been Mexico, India, China, the Philippines, Vietnam, El Salvador, and the Dominican Republic. The largest numbers of temporary workers in 2005, in contrast, were from India, Mexico, the United Kingdom, Japan, and Canada. Tourist and business travelers arrived in largest numbers from the United Kingdom, Mexico, Japan, Germany, and France. Foreign students were most likely to arrive from Asia, with more than half of student admissions in 2005 coming from South Korea, Japan, India, Taiwan, China, and Canada. About 56% of the unauthorized immigrants currently living in the country are estimated to have come from Mexico, 22% from other parts of Latin America, 13% from Asia, 6% from Europe or Canada, and about 3% from Africa and other areas. Asylum seekers in recent years have come from China, Colombia, Haiti, and Venezuela. The main countries of origin of new refugees in FY 2005 were Somalia, Laos, Cuba, Russia, and Liberia.

The traditional states of settlement for the largest numbers of immigrants—California, New York, Florida, Texas, and New Jersey—continued to receive the largest absolute numbers of permanent, temporary, and unauthorized migrants in recent years. However, states experiencing the fastest growth in the size of their foreign-born populations in the last 10 to 15 years have included many states for whom immigration is a new phenomenon, including North and South Carolina, Georgia, New Hampshire, Tennessee, Nevada, Arkansas, and Delaware.

As growing migration flows, and particularly growing populations of unauthorized immigrants, reach new communities, state and local legislators have faced real challenges and costs. Immigration was the subject of more than 500 bills in state legislatures around the country during 2006, including measures to limit government services to unauthorized immigrants and prevent employers from hiring workers who lack authorization to work in the country. Both the Senate and House of Representatives passed immigration-related legislation in 2006 after much debate, but ultimately, only a provision requiring a fence became law. Immigration promises to remain a pressing topic of policy debates as the country decides how immigration fits into national values and the country's demographic and economic future.

Julia Gelatt

See Appendix A; Appendix B
See also Alien Land Acts; "Boat People"; Borderlands; Border Patrol; Bracero Program; Chinese Exclusion Act; Citizenship; Dillingham Flaw; Gentlemen's Agreement (1907–1908); Guest Workers; Illegal Immigration Reform and Immigrant Responsibility Act of 1996; Immigration and Nationality Act of 1965; Immigration and Naturalization Service (INS); Immigration Reform and Control Act of 1986; "Marielitos"; McCarran-Walter Act of 1952; National Origins System; Refugees; Remittances; Return Migration; "Wetbacks"

Further Readings

Daniels, Roger. 1990. *Coming to America: A History of Immigration and Ethnicity in American Life.* New York: HarperCollins.

Martin, Philip and Elizabeth Midgley. 2003. "Immigration: Shaping and Reshaping America." *Population Bulletin* 58:3–44.

Meissner, Doris, Deborah W. Meyers, Demetrios G. Papademetriou, and Michael Fix. 2006. *Immigration and America's Future: A New Chapter.* Washington, DC: Migration Policy Institute.

Ong Hing, Bill. 2004. *Defining America Through Immigration Policy.* Philadelphia, PA: Temple University Press.

Passel, Jeffrey S. 2006. "Size and Characteristics of the Unauthorized Migrant Population in the U.S." Research Report. Washington, DC: Pew Hispanic Center. Available from http://pewhispanic.org/files/reports/61.pdf

Patrick, Erin. "The U.S. Refugee Resettlement Program." *The Migration Information Source.* Washington, DC: The Migration Policy Institute. Retrieved November 13, 2006, from http://www.migrationinformation.org/USFocus/display.cfm?ID=229

U.S. Department of Homeland Security. 2006. *Yearbook of Immigration Statistics*: 2005. Washington, DC: Office of Immigration Statistics.

Williams, Mary E., ed. 2004. *Immigration: Opposing Viewpoints.* San Diego, CA: Greenhaven Press.

IMMIGRATION AND GENDER

According to the Social Science Research Council's Working Group on Gender and Migration, gender structures identities, practices, and institutions of immigration. Considering immigration with gender also is a way of understanding migration from the historically neglected perspective of women. Many racial and ethnic communities in the United States and throughout the world are shaped by changing constructions of gender and family in countries of ancestry, origin, and destination. Thus, a gendered perspective sheds light on social institutions such as migrant families, networks, and employment. The study of gender through migration also demonstrates that gender roles are not fixed in racial and ethnic communities; rather, masculinity and femininity shift over time and in different places. This entry discusses the contemporary feminization of migration related to globalization processes, offers an overview of the field of gender and migration studies, and discusses important arenas and debates on the role of families and households in immigration, the impacts of migration on gender relations and women's power, and gender and transnationalism.

Feminization of Migration and Migration Studies

Historically, much of the understanding of migration was drawn from male experiences presented as normative rather than as relating specifically to one gender. Migration was understood through a male perspective because of the predominance of male labor migration in history, assumptions that women and children migrate to follow male breadwinners, researchers' tendency to interview only heads of households, and the early domination of men in social science research. An assumption that the male migration experience was the norm masked both the ways that migration is shaped by gender and the distinctive experiences of women migrants.

Since the 1970s, there has been a significant shift toward gendering an understanding of migration. This change was produced by the entry of more women into migration research, the growth of feminist and gender studies, and the feminization of migration, which refers to the increase in the proportion of migrants who are women. According to UN estimates, approximately 50% of all global migrants are women. The feminization of migration also refers to the growing role of women migrants as family wage-earners; workers in gendered industries such as domestic service, entertainment, and sex work; and providers of hard currency for ailing Third World economies.

Women, Gender, and Migration

There are two ways to understand the field of gender and migration, and they complement and stand in tension with each another. A focus on women and migration reveals the historically neglected experiences of women as they differ from those of men, as well as gives voice to migrant women. On the other hand, a gendered perspective examines the ways that migration processes, institutions, and identities are structured by gender. In addition to incorporating women's lives, this strand analyzes the ways that femininity and masculinity structure and are transformed by migration. It also includes nonconforming gender expressions and sexuality. For example, people who demonstrate same-gender desires and behaviors may migrate because of their sexual orientation or related persecution. Yet, being gay or lesbian was legal grounds for exclusion from immigration to the United States until the 1990s.

Looking at migration through a gendered lens offers many insights. Citizenship law has historically been gendered, and women's citizenship has often been tied to their husbands' status. Migration networks are gendered; women often migrate, find work, and socialize in the United States through distinctive networks compared with their male counterparts. Gender shapes the decisions that people make about when and how to cross borders. In Mexican communities, migration to the United States may be part of a male rite of passage passed on over generations. Although women are more likely to migrate to flee violent or abusive family situations, they are also highly vulnerable to sexual assault and exploitation during the process of unauthorized border-crossing. Today, both women and men are recruited as labor migrants. However, migrant labor is structured by race, ethnicity, and gender. Employers believe that women of certain races and ethnic backgrounds are suited to different employment than are their male counterparts. Women are more vulnerable than men to trafficking for sexual and domestic servitude.

Key Themes: Family, Power, and Transnationalism

Gender structures migration at multiple levels, including the individual, family, community, nation, and transnational arenas. Gender also shapes a variety of key institutions in the lives of migrants, such as laws of immigration and immigrant incorporation, migrant politics, and the labor force. Key areas where a gendered perspective sheds important light on migration and migrants' lives are family and household dynamics, power, and transnational processes. Historically, many researchers believed that people migrated based on unified family decisions that weighed the costs and benefits of migration to household income and resources. A gendered perspective has demonstrated that families may be divided about migration. Migration may benefit or harm different family members in distinct ways, and related decisions often reflect gendered power and influence.

For example, many young women migrate to urban or border regions within their countries of origin to labor in export-processing zones, or migrate across borders to perform domestic work. Demand for their labor is generated by employers who perceive them as vulnerable and docile workers. The behavior of young women migrants may be a source of family debate and dissention; this includes how much of their earnings will be sent to support their families, how they dress, and what activities they engage in after work hours. Families, communities, and even national economies have become increasingly dependent on the remittances of women migrants as a source of family sustenance and foreign exchange.

Another important question is how gendered power shifts and transforms with migration. Early feminist research on women's migration stressed the importance of women's entry into the paid labor force in immigrant-receiving countries and its positive impacts on their power in the household. Also, when men migrate for work alone and bring their spouses and children later, gendered dynamics in the household may be disrupted because women have been running family affairs in the country of origin during their husbands' absence. Likewise, men may learn to perform new domestic tasks in the receiving country during their wives' absence. This optimism about women migrants' power is tempered when the focus shifts to the stress of family separation across borders, the racialized abuse and exploitation of women migrants in the workplace, and the loss of women's family support and social networks upon migration. Social isolation, racism, and challenges to male migrants' masculinity all contribute to domestic violence in the receiving society.

Early discussions of transnational identities, institutions, and processes also tended to celebrate the ability of migrants to maintain attachments to both countries of origin and reception. However, transnational institutions and processes, such as leadership in hometown associations, appear to be infused with power inequalities of gender, race, and class. Researchers will continue to examine the gendering of identities, processes, and institutions of migration at multiple scales and in various arenas.

Hinda Seif

See Appendix A; Appendix B

See also Body Image; Bracero Program; Domestic Work; Feminism; Gender and Race, Intersection of; Guest Workers; Immigrant Communities; Immigration, U.S.; Remittances; Transnational People

Further Readings

Bhabha, Jacqueline. 1996. "Embodied Rights: Gender Persecution, State Sovereignty, and Refugees." *Public Culture* 9:3–32.

Ehrenreich, Barbara and Arlie R. Hochschild, eds. 2003. *Global Woman: Nannies, Maids, and Sex Workers in the New Economy.* New York: Metropolitan Books.

Gabaccia, Donna, Katharine Donato, Jennifer Holdaway, Martin Manalansan, and Patricia Pessar, eds. 2006. "Special Journal Issue: Gender and Migration Revisited." *International Migration Review* 40.

Hondagneu-Sotelo, Pierrette, ed. 2003. *Gender and U.S. Immigration: Contemporary Trends.* Berkeley: University of California Press.

Louie, Miriam Ching Yoon. 2001. *Sweatshop Warriors: Immigrant Women Workers Take on the Global Economy.* Cambridge, MA: South End Press.

Luibhéid, Eithne and Lionel Cantu, eds. 2005. *Queer Migrations: Sexuality, U.S. Citizenship, and Border Crossings.* Minneapolis: University of Minnesota Press.

Oishi, Nana. 2005. *Women in Motion: Globalization, State Policies, and Labor Migration in Asia.* Stanford, CA: Stanford University Press.

Parrenas, Rhacel Salazar. 2001. *Servants of Globalization: Women, Migration, and Domestic Work.* Stanford, CA: Stanford University Press.

Sassen, Saskia. 1998. "Toward a Feminist Analytic of the Global Economy." Pp. 81–110 in *Globalization and Its Discontents: Essays on the New Mobility of People and Money,* edited by S. Sassen. New York: New Press.

Web Sites

Social Science Research Council, Migration: http://www.ssrc.org/program_areas/migration

IMMIGRATION AND NATIONALITY ACT OF 1965

The Immigration and Nationality Act of 1965 changed the racial and ethnic landscape of the United States drastically by eliminating the quotas placed on the number of immigrants from non-European countries who would be allowed entry into the United States. The passage of this act brought about an enormous change in the sources of new immigration, compared with the previous U.S. experience. This entry will briefly review immigration law, look at the context of the 1965 act, and discuss how it changed the racial and ethnic make-up of the United States.

The Race-Based Record

Race and ethnicity have historically been significant factors in U.S. immigration. Over the years, several laws and policies have prevented immigration from some countries while welcoming immigrants from other places, most notably Western Europe. The Alien Act of 1798, however, reflected a popular fear that Irish immigrants (a once-racialized group in the United States) would rise up against the government, granting the president the authority to deport any alien considered dangerous, including during times of peace. The National Origins Act of 1924 barred immigration from Eastern Europe. The 1924 legislation also halted immigration from Asia, part of a stream of laws and policies restricting entry of people from Asia. Asian immigrants, particularly the Chinese and

Japanese, have a long history of fluctuating inclusion and exclusion into this country.

The Chinese Exclusion Act of 1882 prohibited the immigration of Chinese laborers and the naturalization of Chinese in the United States, and the Scott Act of 1888 prohibited any immigration of Chinese into the United States. Scholars note that the Chinese were drawn to the United States to work as cheap labor, then faced extreme prejudice and racism through political and social exclusion. Chinese men were not allowed to bring their wives and children to the United States, nor were they legally permitted to date or marry White women. The War Brides Act of 1945, however, allowed U.S. veterans to bring their foreign wives and children home with them, increasing the number of Chinese (and other Asian) immigrants to the United States.

Anti-Japanese sentiments were high in the United States during the early part of the 20th century as well. Along with the National Origins Act of 1924, which prohibited immigration from several Asian countries including Japan, Executive Order 9066 legalized the internment of Japanese immigrants and Japanese Americans during World War II because they were seen as threats to the security of the United States. Arabs and South Asians were also denied citizenship in the United States because citizenship was a right that only "free" White men enjoyed under the U.S. Naturalization Act of 1790. Thus, legally, Asian Americans were excluded from privileges and rights, such as citizenship and entry into the United States, because of the color of their skin.

Tide of Change

The McCarran-Walter Immigration and Nationality Act of 1952 changed several portions of the National Origins Act of 1924, allowing limited immigration from Asian countries. The real change came in 1965, however, when the United States was promoting the ideals of democracy and freedom in response to what was perceived then as the threat of communism. Racial tension in the United States was also high, and the Civil Rights Movement had picked up momentum during the late 1950s and early 1960s. The United States found itself trying to rebut the accusations that its laws and policies toward people of color, from Jim Crow segregation laws to the National Origins Act of 1924, were antithetical to the ideology of freedom and democracy that the United States had promoted globally since World War II. Scholars see this as a relevant context in which the passage of the Civil Rights Act of 1964 paved the way for the passage of the Immigration and Nationality Act of 1965, which attempted to make immigration from all countries, European and non-European, more equitable.

As a result of this law, the rate of immigration to the United States has greatly increased, and the nature of immigration has changed, with more people of color coming to the United States. This act opened U.S. borders to 170,000 immigrants from the Eastern hemisphere, with no more than 20,000 per country, and 120,000 immigrants from the Western hemisphere. Immigrants from Asia, South Asia, and Middle Eastern countries came in large numbers to the United States. This altered the nation's racial and ethnic composition and its religious make-up because more Muslims and Hindus migrated.

Race and ethnicity scholars argue that this act has changed the United States from a biracial to a triracial society, one that is not simply White and Black but includes a wide range of people of color from various ethnic backgrounds such as South Asian, Asian, and Latino. The skin tone, class, and reasons for migrating to the United States have affected how these new immigrants have fared in the United States. For example, the model minority myth, originating in the 1960s, holds that the success of certain Asian ethnic groups in the United States was the result of their hard work and diligence. This stereotype was used to promote the idea that some cultures encourage hard work and success, which inevitably leads to class mobility, whereas less desirable cultures inhibit this type of progress. The myth also minimizes the struggles of some Asian Americans, ignoring the contextual situation of each immigrant group and personal characteristics such as wealth and education. Scholars found that Chinese immigrants, shortly after the Immigration Act of 1965, were predominantly educated professionals, which gave them an economic advantage in the United States. By comparison, most Vietnamese immigrants at this time lacked the same educational credentials and so were relegated to a different class with different opportunities. Thus, the model minority myth masks the real reasons for success of some immigrant groups over others.

Sociologists, especially those who study race and ethnicity and immigration, are currently looking at how the assimilation process for post-1965 immigrants differs from the experiences of previous

European immigrants. Some scholars argue that comparing the assimilation of White European immigrants with that of Asian immigrants is necessary to reveal the role that racism and discrimination play in predicting rates of acculturation and success in the United States. Further research is needed on the effect of the Immigration and Nationality Act of 1965 on the racial and ethnic composition of the United States and on the subsequent impact on society. Research might also foster a better understanding of the racialized treatment of these new immigrants and how their background affects interracial relationships.

Saher Farooq Selod

See Appendix A

See also Alien Land Acts; Asian Americans; Assimilation; Border Patrol; Chinese Exclusion Act; Citizenship; Dillingham Flaw; Gentlemen's Agreement (1907–1908); Guest Workers; Illegal Immigration Reform and Immigrant Responsibility Act of 1996; Immigration and Naturalization Service (INS); Immigration Reform and Control Act of 1986; "Marielitos"; McCarran-Walter Act of 1952; Muslim Americans; National Origins System; Refugees; "Wetbacks"

Further Readings

Espiritu, Yen Le. 1992. *Asian American Panethnicity: Bridging Institutions and Identities.* Philadelphia, PA: Temple University Press.

Leonard, Karen Isaksen. 2003. *Muslims in the United States: The State of Research.* New York: Russell Sage Foundation.

Portes, Alejandro and Rubén G. Rumbaut. 2006. *Immigrant America: A Portrait.* 3rd ed. Berkeley: University of California Press.

Takaki, Ronald. 1994. *From Different Shores: Perspectives on Race and Ethnicity in America.* Oxford, UK: Oxford University Press.

IMMIGRATION AND NATURALIZATION SERVICE (INS)

The Immigration and Naturalization Service (INS) was among the more enduring bureaucratic attempts to manage the entry of the foreign-born into the United States through a single agency. With a mandate to administer U.S. immigration laws, the INS was responsible for determining the admissibility of new entrants, removing and preventing the entry of those not authorized to be in the United States, and processing the applications for citizenship, permanent residence, work authorization, and other such benefits to which applicants were legally entitled. This entry reviews the development of the INS, describing key functions and mandates as well as its shifting institutional location.

History

The Immigration and Naturalization Service, as most current readers know it, dates to 1940, when it was transferred to the Justice Department by President Franklin D. Roosevelt as a national security measure during World War II. Previously, however, the immigration service had been housed in the Labor Department, the State Department, the Treasury Department, and the Commerce Department.

When the Congress first established a commissioner of immigration in 1864, it placed the responsibilities in the State Department and specified a relatively narrow mandate of protecting new immigrants from fraud and overseeing their transportation to their final destination. In 1891, Congress consolidated federal control over the regulation of immigration and designated a superintendent of immigration within the Treasury Department, although states maintained responsibility for inspections of new arrivals and naturalization procedures.

With a growing focus on enforcing laws regarding foreign contract labor, the Bureau of Immigration was transferred in 1903 to the newly created Department of Commerce and Labor. It was renamed the Bureau of Immigration and Naturalization 3 years later. However, in 1913, the Department of Commerce and Labor was subdivided, with the immigration responsibilities moving into the Labor Department but split into two bureaus. Twenty years later, the bureaus were recombined into the Immigration and Naturalization Service, which was transferred into the Justice Department in 1940, where it remained until 2003.

Overview of Functions

The principal law implemented and enforced by the INS has been the Immigration and Nationality Act (INA) of 1952, as modified by 1965 amendments and other subsequent legislation. For instance, the Immigration Reform and Control Act of 1986 (IRCA) provided amnesty for 2.5 million illegal immigrants residing in the United States. It also authorized, for the first time in U.S. history, sanctions upon employers who knowingly hired unauthorized workers. Similarly, the Illegal Immigration Reform and Immigrant Responsibility Act of 1996 (IIRIRA) charged the INS with developing pilot programs for employment verification and mechanisms to track the entry and exit of foreign travelers. Furthermore, the IIRIRA mandated the detention of criminal aliens and broadened the scope of those who could be deported, applying the new standards retroactively. Both laws imposed significant implementation burdens on the agency and necessitated a shifting of internal priorities and resources to meet the new mandates.

As the agency responsible for regulating the flow of immigrants into the United States, INS was charged with a dual mission—service and enforcement. The service side of INS included adjudicating petitions for legal permanent status, citizenship, and refugee and asylum status; issuing work authorization and other documents; regulating the admission of temporary visitors including tourists, foreign students, and guest workers; and administering naturalization tests and ceremonies. Enforcement functions included inspecting arrivals at ports of entry to determine citizenship and admissibility; preventing and apprehending unauthorized entrants between ports; detaining and removing criminal aliens and others without lawful status in the United States; and investigating illegal hiring, smuggling, and document and benefit fraud.

By its very nature, the immigration function is a crosscutting one, encompassing a range of policy issues that include foreign policy, economic policy, education policy, law enforcement, and tensions over state and federal roles. The broad array of responsibilities is paperwork-intensive and laden with complex and seemingly contradictory missions that reflect the ambivalence of the U.S. Congress and the U.S. public regarding immigration-related issues. Moreover, the agency's actions affect the lives of large numbers of individuals, including U.S. citizens and legal residents, as well as the foreign-born and foreign perceptions of the United States.

To provide a sense of the scale of INS responsibilities at the beginning of the 21st century, the INS handled 510.6 million inspections at air, land, and sea ports of entry and admitted more that 32 million non-immigrants in fiscal year (FY) 2001, according to the 2002 *Statistical Yearbook of the Immigration and Naturalization Service*. It also issued 1.06 million green cards and naturalized more than 600,000 individuals. In the same year, the agency received 7.9 million applications of all types, completed more than 7 million applications, and faced a pending caseload of 4.8 million. Furthermore, the INS was responsible for nearly 1.3 million apprehensions at U.S. borders, formally removed more than 177,000 individuals from the United States, and completed almost 90,000 criminal investigations.

These achievements were accomplished with a budget that was nearing $5 billion in FY 2001 and with approximately 32,000 full-time employees in headquarters, three regions, and thirty-three district offices around the country. Of the full-time employees, three-quarters were considered enforcement personnel, the largest group of which was Border Patrol agents. This was significant growth from earlier INS budgets. In the fiscal year before IRCA, the INS appropriation had been a mere $1 billion.

Any discussion of the INS, however, must note that a variety of immigration-related functions, including policymaking, have been housed outside the INS. For instance, the State Department is responsible for making determinations about visa eligibility overseas and issuing such visas at U.S. consulates. Similarly, the Labor Department certifies the need for foreign workers, the Department of Health and Human Services resettles refugees brought to the United States, and the immigration courts are housed in the Justice Department.

Structural Change

The notion of a centralized federal agency to manage the flow of immigrants into the United States has been critiqued and tweaked ever since it arose in the middle of the 19th century. Within a few decades, the commissioner general of the Bureau of Immigration was expressing frustrations regarding inadequate records and statistics, unclear responsibilities, and insufficient means to enforce the immigration regulations, sentiments likely shared by all twenty-six immigration commissioners. Internal restructurings of the INS have veered from decentralization of services in the regions in 1954 to centralization of management and operations in 1991, and then back to restoration of some field office authority and management responsibilities in 1994, culminating with a never-implemented 2001 internal reorganization plan that was overtaken by events.

Among the more recent external reports that addressed the structure of the immigration function were those produced by independent government commissions. For instance, the 1981 Select Commission on Immigration and Refugee Policy recommended separating the INS's service and enforcement functions and upgrading the level of the INS commissioner within the Justice Department. The Commission for the Study of Migration and Cooperative Economic Development in 1990 proposed creation of an independent Agency for Migration Affairs to centralize and raise the profile of the immigration and refugee issues found across various cabinet agencies. In 1997, the U.S. Commission on Immigration Reform recommended in its final report eliminating the INS and parceling out of its immigration-related functions to the Justice Department and State Department, citing mission overload, overlap with other agencies, and a desire for better delivery of both better service and enforcement functions. The U.S. Commission on National Security/21st Century concluded in its February 2001 final report that significant changes were required in the U.S. national security apparatus and urged creation of a cabinet-level National Homeland Security Agency that would include the Border Patrol, along with the Coast Guard, Customs Service, and the Federal Emergency Management Agency (FEMA).

Despite the repeated efforts at modifying and reshuffling the immigration function during the last century, the problems and challenges remained startlingly similar, particularly relating to agency capacity and clarity of mandate, as have the solutions of separation or consolidation. Ultimately, the placement of the immigration function has reflected shifting policy goals and political priorities, as well as the broader global environment.

Repercussions of September 11 for the INS

The attacks of September 11, 2001, were devastating to the country as a whole. For the INS, though, the attacks signaled the beginning of the end, as post-event reviews indicated that some of the hijackers had petitions pending before the agency, which were later approved, and that the hijackers had been inspected and admitted by officers upon arrival into the country. Combined with the frustration with the INS's performance, which had been mounting throughout the 1990s, and the growing scale and importance of the immigration function (the 1990s was the single largest decade of immigration in U.S. history in absolute numbers), these public failures obliterated any remaining confidence in the agency's capacity or support for the agency's existence.

In the aftermath of the attacks, proposals emanated from the White House Office of Homeland Security to combine aspects of the border enforcement functions; from the House of Representatives and the Senate to dismantle the INS and move its functions directly into the Justice Department (though the proposals differed with regard to leadership structure and policy coordination); and from the Senate to establish a new cabinet-level Department of National Homeland Security incorporating many existing law enforcement and inspection duties. Ultimately, the White House quietly developed a broader second plan that to some extent drew upon elements of previous proposals and studies, and President George W. Bush announced his proposal for a permanent cabinet-level Department of Homeland Security (DHS) in June 2002. He signed the resulting Homeland Security Act (PL 107–296) in November 2002.

The DHS combined 180,000 personnel and elements of twenty-two agencies (including the INS, the Coast Guard, the Customs Service, and FEMA), becoming operational January 1, 2003. On March 1, 2003, the INS was formally abolished; its functions and authorities were transferred into DHS. The principal immigration-related responsibilities were placed into three separate divisions: U.S. Citizenship and Immigration Services (USCIS), the Bureau of Immigration and Customs Enforcement (ICE), and the Bureau of Customs and Border Protection (CBP).

Deborah W. Meyers

See Appendix A

See also Border Patrol; Citizenship; Illegal Immigration Reform and Immigrant Responsibility Act of 1996; Immigration, U.S.; Immigration and Nationality Act of 1965; Immigration Reform and Control Act of 1986

Further Readings

Papademetriou, Demetrios G. and Deborah Waller Meyers. 2002. "Reconcilable Differences? An Evaluation of Current INS Restructuring Proposals." Migration Policy Institute. Available from http://www.migrationpolicy.org/files/200206_PB.pdf

Papademetriou, Demetrios G., T. Alexander Aleinikoff, and Deborah Waller Meyers. 1998. *Reorganizing the U.S. Immigration Function: Toward a New Framework for Accountability.* Washington, DC: Carnegie Endowment for International Peace.

Seghetti, Lisa M. 2002. "Immigration and Naturalization Service: Restructuring Proposals in the 107th Congress." Congressional Research Service. Available from http://fpc.state.gov/documents/organization/16174.pdf

Smith, Marian L. 1998. "Overview of INS History." In *A Historical Guide to the U.S. Government,* edited by G. T. Kurian. New York: Oxford University Press.

Transactional Records Access Clearinghouse (TRAC). 2002. "DHS at Work: INS History." Retrieved from http://trac.syr.edu/tracins/findings/aboutINS/insHistory.html

U.S. Citizenship and Immigration Services. 2006. "History, Genealogy, and Education." Available from http://www.uscis.gov/portal/site/uscis

U.S. Immigration and Naturalization Service. 2002. *Statistical Yearbook of the Immigration and Naturalization Service.* Washington, DC: U.S. Government Printing Office. Available from http://www.dhs.gov/ximgtn/statistics/publications/archive.shtm#2

IMMIGRATION AND RACE

At a key moment in *The Good Shepherd,* the 2006 film about the birth of the Central Intelligence Agency (CIA), agent Edward Wilson (played by Matt Damon) pays a visit to the Mafia boss Joseph Palmi (Joe Pesci). As they sit down to discuss their common "problem" of Fidel Castro's Cuba, Wilson insinuates to Palmi that he will be deported to Italy if he refuses to cooperate with the CIA. Clearly insulted, Palmi retorts, "You're not going to deport anyone. I've lived in this country since I was two months old." Palmi then questions Wilson, "Tell me something. We Italians got family and the Church. The Irish got the old country. The Jews got their tradition. Hell, even the Blacks got their music. But, what have *you people* got?" Perfectly calm and deadly serious, Wilson (a Yale graduate and member of Yale's secret society, Skull and Bones) responds, "We've got the United States of America. The rest of you are just visiting."

The preceding pointed exchange captures with dramatic precision the mid-century assumptions about the way that immigration and race are linked in U.S. history. Though often celebrated as an idyllic "melting pot" or mythic "mosaic" of racial equality and ethnic tolerance, the history of race and ethnic relations in the United States is actually one of struggle for inclusion as full and equal members by a series of immigrant and racial "minorities"—often thought of as immigrant outsiders "just visiting." Ironically, one "ethnic" or "racial" group never directly named during the above exchange, who Palmi refers to as, "you people" (White Anglo-Saxon Protestants or WASPs), is the very group that founded the United States as a nation and established itself as the charter group atop a surprisingly resilient, if still evolving and increasingly complex ethnoracial hierarchy.

More ironic still is that this fictionalized exchange between a "blue-blooded" representative of the U.S. "mainstream" and an Italian American (both of whom would be defined as "White" today) took place *before* 1965, the year that heralded the arrival on U.S. shores of a massive new wave of non-European and largely non-White immigrants from all across the world. Given their large numbers and unprecedented racial diversity, the arrival of this most recent wave of immigrants has challenged long-established notions of race and ethnicity in the United States. This group has also tested as never before the nation's ongoing effort to balance the assimilation of immigrants with respect for their racial and ethnic pluralism. In short, what is at stake is the United States's definition of itself as "a nation of immigrants." This entry looks at immigration through the lens of race.

The U.S. Ethnoracial Hierarchy

Racial and ethnic relations can follow several distinct patterns, including assimilation, pluralism, multiculturalism, segregation, slavery, and even genocide. Although the history of the United States has been dominated by an ambivalent balance between assimilation and pluralism often celebrated as the U.S. "melting pot," at different times it has included each of these other patterns—especially with reference to the reception and treatment of those defined as non-White. Furthermore, changes in racial and ethnic relations in the United States have often come about because of changes in immigration, as well as because of direct moral or legal challenges to the status quo. For example, who could be defined as "White" or as an "American" was gradually expanded between 1850 and 1950 as two massive waves of non-Anglo immigrants from northwest Europe (Germans and Irish) and southwest Europe (Italians and Jews) added their distinctive cultures, languages, religions, and colors to the melting pot. Also, as a result of the Civil Rights Movement, African Americans gained protection from legal discrimination for the first time despite having been members of the U.S. mosaic for more than 400 years. Finally, how an ethnic group enters U.S. society (voluntary immigration versus involuntary immigration: conquest, slavery, or annexation) directly affects its subsequent place in the U.S. ethnoracial hierarchy and, thus, the overall pattern of race and ethnic relations in the country.

The more than 230-year history of the United States has witnessed the transformation of a fairly homogenous group of thirteen British colonies into the world's most wealthy, powerful, and, arguably, most ethnically diverse society. Immigration to the United States can be divided into five different "waves": The colonial period (1607–1775), the early republic (1776–1839), the "old immigration" of the mid-19th century (1840–1879), the "new immigration" of the turn of the century (1880–1924, followed by a forty-year lull), and the contemporary immigration of today, which began in 1965. Each successive wave of immigration has added new groups (races, ethnicities, languages, religions, etc.) in larger numbers, gradually modifying, if not fundamentally altering, the U.S. ethnoracial hierarchy first established by the British colonists.

Although the colonial period witnessed the establishment of the ethnic dominance of a charter group of White, English-speaking, Anglo-Saxon Protestants (WASPs), the years of the early republic saw an expansion of the racial and ethnic profile of the nation to include European immigrants from a wider array of national, ethnic, linguistic, religious, and "racial" groups, the most prominent of whom were fellow Northern Europeans such as the Germans, French, Dutch, and Swedes. Still, before 1840, most new immigrants to the United States hailed from northwestern Europe and shared similar racial and ethnic backgrounds, as well as similar motivations for immigrating. Of course, from the earliest days of the British colonies, many other, non-White or non-European racial and ethnic groups were already present in North America, and their contribution to the U.S. mosaic has frequently been either overlooked or deliberately suppressed. Most prominent among these groups are Native Americans, Hispanic Americans, and African Americans, each of whom initially joined the U.S. union involuntarily—either through conquest, annexation, or slavery.

Starting in 1840, the size and diversity of the U.S. population began the first of three major expansions that would transform the ethnoracial make up of the nation. Between 1840 and 1880, political and economic upheaval in Europe led to the arrival of hundreds-of-thousands of German and Irish immigrants. An even more massive and diverse flow of newcomers began in 1880 and lasted until the early 1920s, largely made up of Southern Italians and Eastern European Jews. Although the differences of such immigrants are unremarkable in retrospect, these newcomers were routinely met with hostility at the time because of their perceived linguistic, religious, and "racial" distinctiveness. Many early German immigrants were Jewish, and nearly all of the Irish were unskilled Catholics of peasant origins fleeing poverty and famine at home. Likewise, pseudo-scientific racial theories of the era held that "swarthy" peoples of Mediterranean, Slavic, and Semitic stock were racially inferior to those of northwestern Anglo and Alpine origins.

Establishing a much repeated pattern, these newcomers sought protection and political power by forming ethnic enclaves across the nation, especially in immigrant-rich cities like New York and Chicago. Ironically, when banding together in immigrant neighborhoods or forming ethnic businesses, these immigrants were subsequently blamed for their supposedly inherent "clannishness," "miserliness," and refusal to assimilate to U.S. values and culture. The early 1920s saw the passage of a series of laws restricting new immigration on the basis of national origin quotas to halt the immigration of more of these "unassimilable" southwestern Europeans. Not fully revoked until 1965, these laws purposely favored Europeans of "Anglo" and "Alpine" origins over others because admission quotas were based on the profile of the U.S. population in 1890. These restrictive laws followed previous ones aimed at eliminating "Orientals" from the United States. For example, Chinese immigration was frozen by the Chinese Exclusion Act of 1882 and the Japanese were kept out after the passage of the so-called Gentlemen's Agreement in 1907.

Race and Ethnicity Since 1965

The McCarran-Walter Act of 1952 and the subsequent epoch-making passage of the Immigration and

Nationality Act of 1965 (also known as the Hart-Celler Act) began a fundamental shift in U.S. ethnic and racial composition, repealing previous race-based restrictions and national origins quotas that had favored immigrants from northwest Europe and making family reunification the basic principle of U.S. immigration law. These changes led to a fundamental, if largely unintended, shift in the numbers, national origins, and racial and ethnic background of subsequent immigrants. As a result, large numbers of non-White immigrants from the developing world began to come to the United States for the first time, led by Mexicans, Filipinos, Chinese, Koreans, Dominicans, Cubans, and Vietnamese. Although the 1970 census counted just 9.6 million immigrants in the nation, by 2000 that number had risen to 28.4 million (constituting just over 10% of the population). Additionally, Latin American, Caribbean, and Asian immigration grew rapidly after 1965, coming to supplant more traditional European immigrant flows. For example, whereas between 1900 and 1965, 75% of all immigrants came from Europe, since 1968, 62% of new immigrants have come from Latin America, the Caribbean, or Asia.

This shift has begun to significantly alter the ethnic and racial profile of the United States. Between 1945 and 1995, the White proportion of the U.S. population fell from 87% to 75%, whereas Hispanics (admittedly not a racial category) increased their presence from 2.5% to 10.2% (reaching 12.5% by 2000). At the same time, the entire Hispanic population of the United States (including the U.S.-born children of Latin American immigrants) reached 35.3 million in 2000. Thus, the Hispanics in the United States (12.5%) in 2000 surpassed the number of African Americans (34.7 million or 12.3%) for the first time.

By 2002, the population of the United States had reached more than 281 million persons. Official census categories (as modified in 2000) allow respondents to self-identify into one (or more) of a number of racial and ethnic groups. Although 75% (211.5 million) of respondents self-identified as White, another 12.3% (34.7 million) respondents identified as Black/African American. Asians stood at 3.6% (10.2 million) of the population followed by American Indians who made up just 1.1% (2.9 million). Interestingly, another 7.9% (22.2 million) respondents refused to choose any of the above four racial categories, choosing "some other race" or mixed race instead. Most of these respondents were Hispanics (who can be of any race). That is, of the 35.3 million Hispanics in the United States, 48% (17 million) identified themselves as White, and another 42% (15 million) marked "some other race."

To its credit, the U.S. Census Bureau has recognized that racial and ethnic definitions and categories are somewhat arbitrary because they have changed in the past and are likely to change in the future. The bureau has also recognized the socially constructed nature of race as a concept, allowing people to self-identify as one or more races. Furthermore, the race categories include *both racial* and *national-origin groups*. Many new immigrants feel that U.S. racial and ethnic labels tend to oversimplify the richness and complexity of their cultural origins and attempt to resist having a racial category imposed on them. Some groups, such as Jews and Italians, see their ethnicity as a symbolic or situational identity that can be emphasized or discarded at will, but others such as West Indians tend to experience it as an unavoidable liability given the persistence of the U.S. color line. Still others attempt to escape this forced choice dilemma by proudly asserting their national, linguistic, or cultural distinctiveness while adopting U.S. cultural norms to achieve socioeconomic mobility.

Race and U.S. Nativism

As new immigration has increasingly affected U.S. economic and cultural patterns, the beginning of the 21st century has witnessed a resurgence of the age-old immigration-assimilation debate with a concomitant rise of U.S. nativism. Contentious debates have emerged for a major overhaul of the immigration system, including increased border security, employer sanctions, legalization, and a guest-worker proposal. The Republican Party is split between economic liberals who favor cheap and energetic immigrant labor and social conservatives who seek to safeguard U.S. national identity against what is perceived as a growing cultural (and racial) onslaught against the U.S. mainstream. In short, the United States faces a dilemma regarding the economic benefits that new immigrants bring and the sociocultural accommodations that welcoming newcomers will require. U.S. residents seem to agree that the nation needs immigrants economically but are undecided as to whether they want them as friends and neighbors.

Harvard political scientist Samuel P. Huntington has voiced the concerns of many social and economic conservatives by arguing that Latino immigration in general and Mexican immigration in particular threatens to divide the United States into two peoples, two cultures, and two languages. He distinguishes today's Latino immigrants from past groups by arguing that they have not assimilated and instead have begun to form potentially divisive political and linguistic enclaves across the country. Moreover, Huntington believes that Latinos have rejected the very Anglo-Protestant values that built the American dream. Finally, he lists six ways that Mexican immigration in particular is unique and troubling: Latinos come from a nation in direct proximity to the United States, they come in unprecedented numbers, they include a very high proportion of undocumented immigrants, their impact is concentrated in particular regions, they show no signs of diminishing, and they justify their arrival with reference to historical claims to parts of the U.S. Southwest.

In response to Huntington's alarm, one-time neoconservative Francis Fukuyama has questioned the need for such a "Hispanic panic." Specifically, Fukuyama counters Huntington's claim that immigrants do not respect U.S. values by pointing out that the United States actually benefits from these new immigrants' deep belief in values of religion and family. More importantly, new Latino and other immigrants are distinguished from most U.S. residents by their adherence to what Fukuyama considers the true U.S. religion: hard work. Finally, Fukuyama indicates that a more serious threat to U.S. culture arises from the nation's own internal contradictions rather than from the "wrong" foreign values of supposedly unassimilable immigrants. Indeed, for Fukuyama, if Latino immigrants present a threat at all, it is that of their assimilating the "wrong" U.S. values of laziness, disrespect for authority, and other gangland attitudes after becoming trapped in poor schools and taking on the hopelessness and resentment of the U.S. inner city.

Conclusion

Although the United States is today one of the world's most successful, peaceful, and prosperous multiethnic societies, for most of U.S. history, full and equal membership was restricted to White Protestant males of European descent. Although some immigrant and ethnic groups have been able to assimilate effortlessly, those who did not fit into the WASP mold have had to force their way into the mainstream, sometimes at the price of losing their cultural distinctiveness. Still others have sought to preserve their ethnic identity and maintain the dense community ties that often accompany it as a way to achieve economic independence. Finally, there have always been those immigrants who consistently experience rejection in their efforts to become full members of the U.S. mainstream. For some of these groups, such rejection can breed resentment and lead to the formation of an oppositional ethnic subculture where success in the mainstream is stigmatized as an ethnic betrayal. This last struggle has been characteristic of some Native Americans, African Americans, and Latinos (especially Puerto Ricans). However, the history of race and ethnic relations in the United States reminds us that at different times and in different contexts, other immigrant groups as diverse as the Irish, Chinese, Japanese, Jews, and Italians have each had to struggle against the U.S. ethnoracial hierarchy for equal access to the opportunity promised in the American Dream.

Ted Henken and Melinda Brahimi

See Appendix A

See also Americanization; Assimilation; Census, U.S.; Chinese Exclusion Act; Genocide; Gentlemen's Agreement (1907–1908); Immigration, U.S.; Immigration and Nationality Act of 1965; Melting Pot; Nativism; Pluralism; Police; Segregation; Slavery; Social Movements; Symbolic Ethnicity; WASP

Further Readings

Alba, Richard D. and Victor Nee. 2003. *Remaking the American Mainstream: Assimilation and Contemporary Immigration.* Cambridge, MA: Harvard University Press.

Bailey, Benjamin. 2001. "Dominican-American Ethnic/Racial Identities and United States Social Categories," *International Migration Review* 35(3).

Gans, Herbert J. 2007. "Ethnic and Racial Identity." In *The New Americans: A Guide to Immigrants Since 1965*, edited by M. C. Waters and R. Ueda with H. B. Marrow. Cambridge, MA: Harvard University Press.

Glazer, Nathan and Daniel P. Moynihan. [1963] 1970. *Beyond the Melting Pot: The Negroes, Puerto Ricans, Jews, Italians, and Irish of New York City.* 2nd ed. Cambridge, MA: MIT Press.

Gordon, Milton M. 1964. *Assimilation in American Life: The Role of Race, Religion, and National Origins.* New York: Oxford University Press.

Grieco, Elizabeth M. and Rachel C. Cassidy. 2001. "Overview of Race and Hispanic Origin," Census 2000 Brief. Washington, DC: U.S. Census Bureau.

Huntington, Samuel P. 2004. *Who Are We? The Challenges to America's National Identity.* New York: Simon & Schuster.

Jacobsen, Matthew Frye. 1998. *Whiteness of a Different Color: European Immigrants and the Alchemy of Race.* Cambridge, MA: Harvard University Press.

Office of Management and Budget. "Revisions to the Standards for the Classification of Federal Data on Race and Ethnicity," Federal Register Notice. Retrieved October 30, 1997, from http://factfinder.census.gov/home/en/epss/glossary_r.html

Perlmann, Joel and Mary C. Waters, eds. 2002. *The New Race Question: How the Census Counts Multiracial Individuals.* New York: Russell Sage Foundation.

Portes, Alejandro. 2000. "An Enduring Vision: The Melting Pot That Did Happen." *International Migration Review* 34:243–79.

Portes, Alejandro and Rubén G. Rumbaut. 2001. "Not Everyone Is Chosen: Segmented Assimilation and Its Determinants." In *Legacies: The Story of the Immigrant Second Generation.* Berkeley: University of California Press.

Roediger, David. 1990. *The Wages of Whiteness: Race and The Making of the American Working Class.* Revised ed. New York: Verso.

IMMIGRATION REFORM AND CONTROL ACT OF 1986

The Immigration Reform and Control Act of 1986, also recognized by its acronym IRCA, is one of the most comprehensive and significant immigration reform bills of the 20th century, even though it failed to meet its intended goals in the long term. In a three-tiered attempt to reduce the flow of undocumented immigration into the United States, IRCA provided amnesty and legal U.S. citizenship to approximately 3 million immigrants who were living and working in the United States. This entry looks at the context of the act, its implementation, and reasons for its lack of success.

The Historic Need for Workers

Historically, the United States has looked to other countries to provide labor for U.S. industries. In 1864, when the first comprehensive federal immigration bill was passed, its intent was to encourage immigration and provide workers to meet production needs during the Civil War. At the time, the United States was experiencing an inflow of about 1 million immigrants annually, and this was seen as positive and beneficial for the U.S. economy.

Because of the close proximity to their homeland, Mexicans were seen as a more desirable source of labor than Europeans because it was felt that Mexicans could easily return home when the need for labor ceased. Through the mid-1900s, Mexicans were encouraged to migrate to the United States and were even excluded from required literacy exams and quota restrictions to gain entrance to the United States. In 1942, the United States and Mexico launched the Bracero Program, which legally brought thousands of Mexican laborers to the United States to work. Though the program claims responsibility for bringing more than 5 million Mexican workers to the United States during the 24 years the program was in existence, it acted as a catalyst for many more undocumented immigrants to cross the border illegally.

The Bracero Program was officially stopped in 1964, but ending the program did not diminish the labor needs, so many of the Mexican laborers stayed and continued to work in the United States, albeit illegally. By the 1970s, nativist sentiments proliferated, and some blamed immigrants for everything that was wrong with society. In this environment, work began on immigration legislation that would eventually become the Immigration and Reform Control Act. Although the bill is written to address immigrants in

Illegal immigrants. Mexican nationals apprehended while illegally crossing the U.S.–Mexican border wait in a holding area at the Brownfield Customs and Border Patrol (CBP) processing center in Otay Mesa, California, on March 6, 2006. Mexican nationals caught illegally crossing the border are sent back to Mexico and classified as "voluntarily returned" without any charges filed if there are no outstanding criminal cases against them on record. The U.S. government estimates that 11 to 12 million illegal immigrants reside in the United States as of 2007.

Source: Getty Images.

general, the focus is on undocumented Mexican immigrants, as evidenced by the attention to the U.S.–Mexico border and provisions for agricultural workers, who were predominantly Mexican laborers.

After many attempts and variations of bills to address immigration, amnesty, and employer sanctions for more than 10 years, the House and Senate finally compromised on a bill. The Immigration Reform and Control Act had several monikers during its lengthy creation process, including the Simpson-Mazzoli Act and the Simpson-Rodino Act.

Implementing IRCA

In its final rendition, IRCA called for increased border enforcements, introduced sanctions against employers who willingly hired undocumented workers, and granted amnesty to immigrants who had been living in the United States continuously since January 1982. In addition, legalization was available for undocumented workers through the Special Agriculture Workers (SAW) program. The SAW program applied to laborers who had worked in U.S. agriculture for a minimum of ninety days between May 1985 and May 1986.

In the amnesty provision of the bill, workers were given one year of amnesty during which documents could be presented to prove continued residency in the United States. This proof of residency led to regularization and, ultimately, full citizenship in the United States. Many undocumented workers did not become legal citizens because of disqualification (because of lack of continuity in residence or employment for the previous 4 years), failure to produce the required documents to prove continuous residency or employment, or inability to understand the process well enough to participate. Socially, this process caused demographic splitting among extended families when some family members gained legal citizenship and others within the family did not.

Lack of Success

History has shown that IRCA was not successful in its intent. With the enactment of IRCA, the United States experienced a decrease in immigration numbers, but by 1989, immigration was on an upsurge. The continued influx of immigrants can be linked to the fact that the bill addressed the pull factors of employment, which is why many undocumented immigrants risk crossing the border illegally, but it did not address the push factors, namely, what is pushing them away from their homeland.

Policymakers theorized that employer sanctions would deter the hiring of undocumented workers, which in turn would decrease the number of illegal immigrants coming to the United States. In practice, the government was unwilling to allocate funds to monitor employer violations, and sanctions were not enforced; consequently, employers kept hiring undocumented workers. Even in cases where violators were caught, fines were rarely assessed for the infractions. There was no incentive to stop hiring undocumented workers, and access to cheap labor was a greater incentive to business owners.

Although many employers continued to hire undocumented workers, many others refused to hire anyone who looked Latino rather than risk hiring someone illegally. This presumed ethnicity generated increased discrimination that extended beyond the employment arena.

An unintended result of the IRCA was a burgeoning and lucrative business for smugglers, who saw an opportunity to expand their illegal business beyond drugs and weapons to include human trafficking. Individuals wanting to cross the border but lacking the proper documentation often employed *coyotes* to guide illegal passage across the border. With the promise of increased security at the border and more scrutinizing of documents by employers, smugglers found a market for full-package deals, which consist of transportation across the border, false documents, and job connections. Reduced to commodity status, individuals are inhumanely packed and transported in trucks and vans across the border, stashed in drop houses for undetermined periods, often held for ransom, and run the risk of being the prize at the heart of deadly battles between smugglers.

Alma Alvarez-Smith

See Appendix A
See also Border Patrol; Bracero Program; Citizenship; Guest Workers; Immigration, U.S.; Nativism

Further Readings

Calavita, Kitty. 1993. "The Contradictions of Immigration Lawmaking: The Immigration Reform and Control Act of 1986." Pp. 229–260 in *Making Law: The State, the Law, and Structural Contradictions,* edited by W. J. Chambliss and M. S. Zatz. Bloomington: Indiana University Press.

Krauss, Erich with Alex Pacheco. 2004. *On the Line: Inside the U.S. Border Patrol.* New York: Kensington.

Meyer, Michael C., William L. Sherman, and Susan M. Deeds. 1999. *The Course of Mexican History.* New York: Oxford University Press.

INCARCERATED PARENTS

The United States has the largest incarcerated population in the world, and this number continues to grow with unprecedented increases in women's incarceration, disproportionate imprisonment rates for women and men of color, and high recidivism rates. Most of these 2.2 million incarcerated U.S. residents are parents—mothers and fathers held in U.S. jails and prisons who typically have one or more children under the age of 18. Today, Black Americans are more than six times more likely to be incarcerated than are Whites; Latinos are more than twice as likely. These vast racial disparities suggest that current U.S. imprisonment has direct and severe consequences for families and communities of color. It is estimated that if contemporary sentencing and incarceration trends remain stable, 2.4 million children will have a parent behind bars in 2007—most of them will be children of color. This entry addresses the experiences of incarcerated parents and their children, focusing on their demographic profiles, the challenges faced in keeping families intact during incarceration, and the implications of U.S. criminal justice and social policies that negatively affect incarcerated parents, their children, and families.

Demographic Profile

More than half of those incarcerated in state and federal prisons have children. According to a 2000 Bureau of Justice Statistics (BJS) special report, "Incarcerated Parents and their Children," nearly two-thirds of women incarcerated in state prisons were mothers to minor children; more than half of all men incarcerated in state prisons were fathers. At the federal level, similar percentages of women and men were parents—approximately six in ten. About half of all incarcerated parents in state prisons were Black, 29% White, and 19% Latino. In federal prisons, Blacks and Latinos made up nearly three-quarters of the parents; 22% were White.

Most (about 60%) parents in both state and federal prisons were less than 35 years old. Most parents in state (70%) and federal (55%) prisons did not have high school diplomas. About half of parents in state prisons had never married; parents, however, were much more likely to have been married than were inmates without children. Incarcerated parents have young children—more than one-fifth were younger than age 5.

Many incarcerated parents lived with their children at the time of their offense. For fathers in state prisons, the children's mothers provide care (in 90% of the cases). However, for the increasing number of mothers being incarcerated, only 28% report that their children go to live with their fathers. Maternal grandmothers (53%), followed by other relatives (26%), are the most likely to become primary caregivers for children with incarcerated mothers. Still, approximately 8% to 10% of children of incarcerated mothers and 2% to 5% of children of incarcerated fathers enter the foster care system. Many parents' ties to their children will be severed forever while they are incarcerated.

Incarcerated Fathers

Scholars have argued that the criminal justice system has estranged Black men from their families—particularly from their children. Most incarcerated parents are fathers of color, reflecting the gendered and racial nature of the incarcerated population. Many marital relationships end during imprisonment, and relationships with children and children's mothers are often strained during this time. These strains are financial, emotional, and social. In many cases, employed fathers may have been the primary source of income for their families.

Incarcerated Mothers

Women's rates of incarceration have skyrocketed during the past 2 decades. The affects of a mother's incarceration are often thought to be more disruptive because mothers are often their children's primary caregiver. Indeed, incarcerated mothers often have a difficult time maintaining meaningful relationships with their children and often report missing their children as one of the most difficult aspects of their imprisonment. Many incarcerated mothers report being homeless in the year before their offense, reflecting their tenuous economic situations. Overall, incarcerated mothers' offending should be understood in the context of drug use and a lack of viable economic skills.

Children of Incarcerated Parents

Children of incarcerated parents have been identified as the "hidden population" most seriously harmed collaterally by incarceration. In 1999, there were nearly 1.5 million children with at least one incarcerated parent, an increase of 500,000 children since 1991. The overrepresentation of incarcerated parents of color spells racial disparities among their children as well. Black children are nearly nine times more likely than White children to have a parent in prison; children of Latino or Hispanic descent are three times more likely. According to the 2000 BJS report, 7% of Black children, 3% of Latino children, and less than 1% of White children had at least one parent incarcerated.

Coupled with issues of poverty, instability, and a lack of social support, children with incarcerated parents face myriad emotional, behavioral, and psychological developmental problems. Given that most children of incarcerated parents live in poverty before, during, and after a parent's incarceration, parental incarceration is thought to deliver a final blow to already vulnerable families. Incarceration affects children's physical care and custody, and caregivers are placed in a precarious role in meeting the unique emotional, social, and economic needs of children.

Children often experience shame and stigma from having an incarcerated parent—a significant number of them actually witnessed their parent's arrest. Children often have difficulty in maintaining privacy while navigating educational and community settings. They may experience trouble at school and exhibit signs of withdrawal, concentration problems, and poor school performance. Given current criminal justice trends that leave millions of children parentless, the future consequences of mass incarceration remain unseen.

Staying in Touch

Visitation

More than half of all parents in prison have not seen their children since their incarceration. Visitation is significantly hindered because women on average are incarcerated 160 miles from their children, and men are on average 100 miles away. One-third of federally sentenced women are more than 500 miles away from their children and families. Trying to maintain contact through visitation poses a significant financial burden on families that try to do so. Travel to prisons hundreds of miles away requires time off from work, transportation, meals, overnight lodging if necessary, or child care.

Maintaining contact between family members—particularly between parents and children—is not a free endeavor. Collect calls from prison are the most expensive type of phone calls in the United States. Despite this, maintaining familial relationships during incarceration has significant positive outcomes for incarcerated persons, families, and children.

Reentry

When incarcerated parents return from prison, they are faced with strained familial relationships, limited employment opportunities, and increased housing difficulties. Depending on how much children understand of their parent's absence and the level of contact throughout their parent's sentence, reunions may be markedly difficult. Children may be wary of reconnecting with parents who have been absent for lengthy periods.

Yet, the scholarly research in this area is clear: Family support during and after incarceration can make the transition from prison to home much smoother. Social support during and after incarceration is thought to lower recidivism rates, disrupt intergenerational patterns of incarceration, and lower the economic costs to taxpayers by mitigating the social and emotional affects of incarceration, providing a link to the "outside world" and assisting with community transition.

Implications of Policies

Although strengthening families has long been touted as a goal of U.S. social policy, current criminal justice policies appears at odds, given what is known about the disruptive nature of incarceration on families. Further, the gendered implications of such policies have been ignored, and families and women are disproportionately punished as a result. Public policy changes in drug policy, welfare reform, public housing, and reunification with children are key areas for scholars to address in understanding the affects of mass incarceration on families.

The war on drugs has stiffened criminal justice sentencing through mandatory minimum sentencing and "three strikes" laws, affecting both women and men. The emphasis on incarceration, rather than on treatment, helps explain why so many poor women and women of color enter the criminal justice system—they are more likely than men to commit drug offenses. Drug offenses account for half the increase in rates of women's incarceration from 1986 to 1995; the number of women incarcerated for drug offenses rose nearly 900% in this period. Given the vast racial disparities in arrest, conviction, and imprisonment rates among both women and men of color compared with Whites, the war on drugs has filled prisons—particularly at the federal level—with parents who have been overwhelmingly convicted of drug offenses.

Relatedly, Section 115 of the 1996 Welfare Reform Act mandated that persons convicted of a state or federal felony offense involving the use or sale of drugs would be banned from receiving Temporary Assistance for Needy Families (TANF) for the course of their lives. This ban disproportionately affects Black and Latina women and their children, given their greater likelihood of criminal justice supervision as a result of racial disparities in drug enforcement and sentencing. In addition, Black and Latina women are more susceptible to poverty and disproportionately represented among those in need of cash assistance and food stamps provided by TANF.

Also in 1996, the federal government passed the "One Strike Initiative," which authorizes public housing authorities to obtain the criminal background records of all adult applicants and tenants. In some areas, these investigations are required for all public housing authorities, Section 8 providers, and additional federally assisted housing programs. Women and men found guilty of even one drug conviction can be denied housing under this initiative, making the search for affordable housing for poor families and families of color even more impossible.

Lastly, the Adoption and Safe Families Act of 1997 (AFSA) disproportionately affects incarcerated parents in terminating parental rights once a child has been in foster care for 15 or more months of the past 22 months. Given that parents serve lengthy sentences spanning several years, those who do not have established long-term caregivers for their children are at most risk for losing them forever. Coupled with foster care policies that provide less financial aid to relatives who are caregivers than to nonrelatives, this increases the risk of terminating parental rights. Racial disparities within the foster care system indicate that Black children remain in foster care longer, move within foster care more often, and receive less desirable placements, further suggesting that Black families with incarcerated parents are vulnerable to state intervention that is much more disruptive when compared with White families.

Several authors and scholars have argued that current criminal justice policies will have long-lasting affects that will affect communities of color for several generations. This era of criminal justice sentencing affects both families of color directly via racial disparities and removing family members from households, but also indirectly. The billions of dollars devoted to mass incarceration have placed fiscal pressure on state budgets; these funds could be devoted to education, health care, and other social service provisions to help the most vulnerable U.S. families. Without drastic reforms to current criminal justice and social policies hinged on punishment reforms, incarcerated parents—and their children—will continue to suffer in trying to maintain their families.

Danielle Dirks

See also Crime and Race; Criminal Processing; Family; Juvenile Justice; Prisons

Further Readings

Braman, Donald. 2004. *Doing Time on the Outside: Incarceration and Family Life in Urban America.* Ann Arbor: University of Michigan Press.

Bureau of Justice Statistics. 2000. "Incarcerated Parents and Their Children." Washington, DC: Bureau of Justice Statistics. Available from http://www.ojp.usdoj.gov/bjs/pub/pdf/iptc.pdf

Johnston, Denise and Katherine Gabel, eds. 1995. *Children of Incarcerated Parents.* New York: Lexington Books.

Othello, Harris and R. Robin Miller, eds. 2003. *Impacts of Incarceration on the African American Family.* New Brunswick, NJ: Transaction.

Patillo, Mary, David F. Weiman, and Bruce Western, eds. 2004. *Imprisoning America: The Social Effects of Mass Incarceration.* New York: Russell Sage Foundation.

Travis, Jeremy and Michelle Waul, eds. 2004. *Prisoners Once Removed: The Impact of Incarceration and Reentry on Children, Families, and Communities.* Washington, DC: Urban Institute Press.

INDIA

The inhabitants of India, estimated in 2007 to number at 1.1 billion, have ancient roots in diversity. Applying a U.S. racial/ethnic framework is difficult in a country with different salient identifying characteristics. Instead, we can draw parallels between U.S. race/ethnicity and Indian group differences based on religion, caste or tribal affiliation, language/region, and skin color. This entry looks at how these differences affect Indian society, where the people are predominantly Hindu, rural-dwelling, and economically underprivileged.

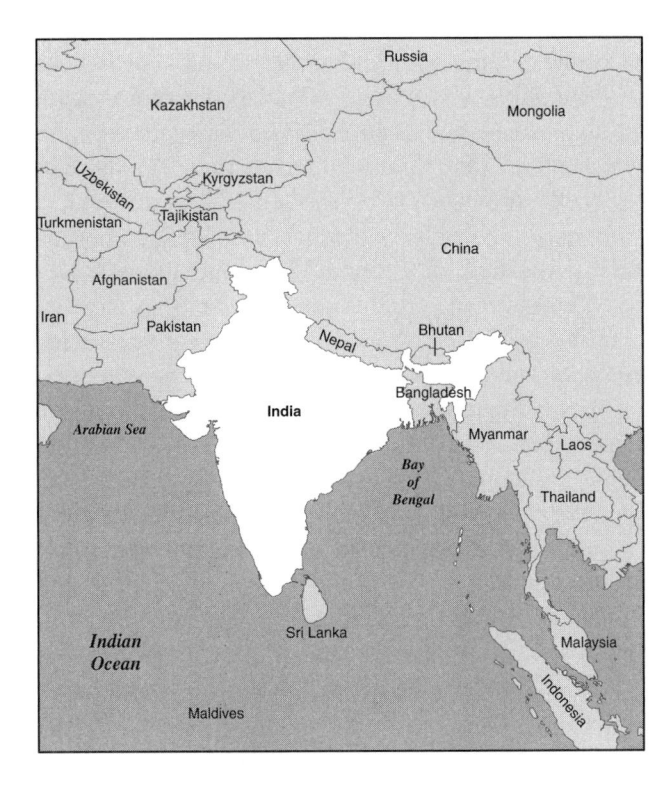

Religious Differences

Muslim Minorities

When outsiders consider ethnic conflict in India, they think of Hindu-Muslim violence. Yet, Hindus and Muslims coexisted for centuries. Muslims conquerors swept into India 1,500 years ago. Although some rulers forced subjects to convert, others were religiously tolerant, allowing intermarriage and promoting Hindus in their courts. By the early 1800s, Muslim princes were overtaken by British forces. Disdain for the British prompted Muslims to avoid all things Western. With the independence movement, Muslim leaders pushing for their own territory began to be seen as outsiders. The 1947 partition separating India and Pakistan at independence left 1 million Muslims dead and 14 million homeless as Muslims left India and non-Muslims left Pakistan. The number of Muslims in the civil service dropped, and Indian Muslims became politically aloof.

Like Hindus, Muslims are predominantly rural. Though there has been controversy for decades that Muslims have high birth-rates, these accounts are exaggerated. Muslims are currently 13.4% of the population. There is virtually no intermarriage with other groups. Many women wear full purdah and are guarded from contact with outsiders. No formal caste system separates Muslims from one another, and they have close-knit communities, especially in cities. Though cities were originally more integrated, separate neighborhoods formed in the 1930s, driven by political groups concentrating support. Today, villages see more social interaction between groups because Muslims are not separated into ethnic enclaves. Violence rarely erupts against Muslims in rural areas; most cases occur in cities where Muslims are more visible and clustered together.

Muslims tend to be less educated (with a 59% literacy rate compared with 65% for the nation) and have fewer economic resources than average. A lack of specific means to advance through "reservations" (as affirmative action is known there) or scholarships leaves few opportunities for upward mobility. Divisions within the Muslim community impede political power. Those few Muslim candidates who are successful are often sponsored by Hindu parties and have difficulty advocating for their religious constituency. Muslims are still distrusted in India by some wary Hindus, who believe their true allegiance is to Pakistan.

The Christian Community

Christianity may have come to India before spreading through Europe. It thrived along the west coast in the 15th and 16th centuries through forced conversions by Portuguese colonists. Conversions grew steadily during British rule but dropped afterward. Protestantism and Catholicism drew low-caste Hindus hoping to escape deplorable social conditions. Many converts lived within Christian compounds to avoid being shunned by disapproving villagers.

Missionaries brought not only religion but also Westernization to India, especially through British-style education. Christian schools attracted Hindus, Parsis, and other elites who wanted to learn English and gain upward mobility. With the Great Depression in the 1930s and World War II in the 1940s, Christianity went into decline, as fewer funds and greater travel restrictions thwarted missionary efforts.

Today, 2.3% of India is Christian; most of them marry other Christians, avoid involvement in politics, and interact with other Indians at work. Most are low-income, with jobs as industrial or service workers in cities and farmers and milk workers in villages. However, they also have an 80% literacy rate, which provides Christians with better outcomes for education, economic class, and urban living than other Indians.

The Powerful Sikhs

Though forming only 2% of the population, Sikhs have considerable influence, especially within Punjab. Sikhs are perhaps the most conspicuous minority, with unshorn hair and beards. Sikhism began in the late 15th century with Guru Nanak, who urged followers to strive for salvation without reliance on Brahman priests or worship of idols. He recognized the holiness within all people, regardless of caste, and the values in everyday life, not simply ceremonial rituals. Both Hindus and Muslims were drawn to his teachings. Sikhism fused religion and politics early on; persecution from Muslim rulers threatened by Sikhs' growing numbers solidified their militarism. Their renown for valor served them well under British rule; a significant percentage of the British colonial army consisted of Sikhs. During drought and famine in Punjab in the 1920s, Sikhs emigrated abroad for better opportunities.

During partition, Punjab saw indescribable violence with Sikhs and Hindus unified against Muslims. During this time, approximately 6 million Hindus left newly created Pakistan, and 6.5 million Muslims left India for Pakistan. Sikhs were caught in the middle, with half of their homeland in Pakistan and half in India. Most remained in India, but some moved north and others joined compatriots abroad. Sikhs also advocated for their own state, which eventually resulted in predominantly Hindu Haryana splitting from Sikh and Hindu Punjab in 1966. Many Sikhs align themselves with the Hindu-based Congress Party, though remaining an internally cohesive community resisting assimilation.

Sikh military prowess gained them considerable stature within India. They have a higher economic standing than average and slightly higher literacy rate (69%). The majority are farmers who have contributed greatly to economic conditions. They are well represented in the government of Punjab and nationally—as evidenced by current Sikh Prime Minister Manmohan Singh—though discrimination against them continues, especially in the South. This has led some community leaders to push for an independent Sikh nation.

Buddhism Returns

Buddhism originated in India around 500 BC with Siddhartha Gautama, called "Buddha," meaning "enlightened one." Although today fewer than 1% of Indians are Buddhist, the religion flourished from the 7th through the 12th centuries. The Ajanta Caves in Maharashtra offer murals and sculptures of Buddha dating back more than 2,000 years. Buddhist art from that time has also been discovered from the Western Deccan to Orissa in the East and South in Andhra Pradesh.

Although many Hindus see Buddha as an incarnation of their God Vishnu, Buddhists were persecuted by Hindus and Muslims alike. For these and other reasons, Buddhism went into decline and by the 13th century had almost no institutional structure within India. Buddhist monks traveled to Southeast Asia, China, Korea, and Japan spreading teachings. Recent resurgence of Buddhism in India is largely the result of migrations from Tibet and Myanmar (Burma) and conversions from tribal groups and Scheduled Castes, including a mass conversion of thousands in 1956. With a 72% literacy rate, Buddhists are more educated than the average Indian. Most tend to be clustered in the northern states and Maharashtra.

The Moral Jains

Jains, most of whom live in the north, account for less than 1% of Indians. Jainism reaches back 2,500 years and holds among its major tenets *ahimsa* or non-violence. Jains reject the rigid Hindu caste system. Rather than performing sacrifices or praying to deities, they revere past teachers called *tirthankaras* who found liberation through moral living. Jain influence in society predates Indian independence and British occupation; many were favorites of early rulers. They also suffered discrimination, especially in southern India.

Today, Jains are significantly more assimilated than are other religious minorities. They have no separate forms of dress or language; they have also adopted many cultural and institutional features of Hinduism. Overall, Jains occupy superior status in Indian society based on significantly higher educational attainment with a full 94% literacy rate, acquired affluence through self-employment in business, and urban dwelling.

The Parsi Elite

Though the Zoroastrian or Parsi population of India had dwindled to less than 70,000, they remain an elite group. With ancestors who arrived in Gujarat 1,300 years ago after persecution in Persia, the Parsis share national identity and language with locals but maintain separate cultural and religious traditions. Parsis pray to their god Ahura Mazda and seek to live honest and charitable lives to attain heaven. They are the most educated group, with a 98% literacy rate, and are highly urban, with 96% living in cities (especially Mumbai) compared with the national average of 27%. A tradition of entrepreneurship has also led to great economic success.

Caste and Tribal Affiliation

The caste system that applies to the 80.5% Hindu population creates additional cleavages. Divided into four groups determined by birth and virtually impossible to change, each category of Hindus corresponds to traditional occupational niches through generations. Thus, Brahmans top the hierarchy as the priestly/scholarly class, and Kshatriyas historically served as military and secular rulers. Vaisyas represent the merchant class, and Sudras are the workers. Hindus believe that one's caste is a result of fate or *karma,* that one's actions in past lives result in one's position now; the hope is that through obedience and faith in this life, the next life may be better. Thus, most low-caste Hindus dutifully act according to custom to improve their next life. Though there are some marital, occupational, and other distinctions between each caste, the major cleavage separates all four upper castes from the "Scheduled Castes."

The Scheduled Castes

The 18.2% of Indians constituting the "Scheduled Castes" (SCs)—also known as "Untouchables," "Harijans," or "Dalits"—have always occupied the bottom rungs of society. Although some place SCs within the Sudra caste, they are generally considered outside the caste system altogether. Most SCs continue to work in jobs considered impure for Hindus, including leather-making, tending funeral pyres, and cleaning waste. However, constitutional guarantees that reserve certain percentages of university and government seats for SCs have increased in prominence. Some have sought to escape caste stigma through participation in the military or religious conversion. Discrimination against SCs continues despite antidiscrimination legislation.

Recently, SCs have grown more political, resisting ongoing oppression benefiting upper castes. Most live in rural areas, relegated to the outskirts rather than within village boundaries. Because SCs have been subordinated and restricted to menial positions for centuries, they remain segregated. Almost all marry within the group; literacy rates remain extremely low—in some districts less than 2%.

The Scheduled Tribes

In addition to the religious groups previously discussed are the 8.2% making up the Scheduled Tribes (STs). Many of their social, economic, and cultural differences are based on geographic concentration and isolation. Most live in rural areas, especially the mountainous, hilly, or forested regions of northern India, and many have limited contact with outsiders. Each tribe is separate, with distinct religions, languages, and traditions. The economic life of STs centers on hunting, fishing, and slash-and-burn agriculture, though specific constitutional reservations for university admission and government service have increased education and employment. Literacy and school attendance rates are extremely low, except for areas near Christian missionary schools. Thus, STs remain toward the bottom of the socioeconomic structure.

Other Backward Classes

The Indian constitution provides for special measures to promote the "Other Backward Classes" (OBCs) along with SCs and STs. Because no explicit definition was provided, the Mandal Commission was convened to make this determination. Released in 1980, the report said that 52% of the population was OBCs deserving of special protections and promotions, including reservations for university admission, government positions, and vocational training programs.

Language/Region and Skin Color

In addition to the earlier-mentioned diversity, India is also divided by linguistic groups representing many different regions. There are eighteen official languages in addition to thousands of dialects. The tribal groups alone have some 700 hundred dialects among them.

A strong resistance to internal migration has sustained linguistic diversity and affected skin color. Though some mistakenly believe skin color indicates caste, it is more an indication of regional origination—with lighter tones in the north and darker hues in the south. Some offer this as proof of an "Aryan invasion" from the north that conquered Dravidian locals, though this history has been widely challenged. With British rule and ongoing significant migration abroad, Indians came to have even more of a preference for light skin and the divisions are more pronounced.

Indians are separated into diverse groups. Some of these are clearly hierarchical (i.e., Brahmans have higher social standing than SCs), though not all minorities are oppressed (i.e., Parsis are elites). Also, those in the "minority" nationally may be the majority within a state, and vice versa.

Meera E. Deo

See Appendix A; Appendix B

See also Bangladeshi Americans; Caste; Foreign Students; Indian Americans; Muslim Americans; Pakistani Americans; Roma

Further Readings

Kashyap, Subbhash C. 1998. "Ethnicity and Constitutional Reforms in India." In *Ethnicity and Constitutional Reform in South Asia,* edited by Iftekharuzzaman. Colombo, Sri Lanka: Regional Centre for Strategic Studies.

Muzumdar, Sucheta. 1989. "Race and Racism: South Asians in the U.S." In *Frontiers of Asian American Studies,* edited by G. M. Nomura, R. Endo, S. H. Sumida, and R. C. Leong. Pullman: Washington State University Press.

Prashad, Vijay. 2000. *The Karma of Brown Folk.* Minneapolis: University of Minnesota Press.

Robb, Peter (ed). 1995. *The Concept of Race in South Asia.* New Delhi, India: Oxford University Press.

Schermerhorn, Richard Alonzo. 1978. *Ethnic Plurality in India.* Tucson: University of Arizona Press.

Varney, Ashutosh. 2001. "Ethnic Conflict and Civil Society: India and Beyond." *World Politics* 53:362–398.

Web Sites

Census India 2001: http://www.censusindia.gov.in

Indian Americans

Indian American communities have been forming since the mid-19th century, when the first of the Punjabi laborers arrived on the U.S. West Coast. Early photographs and written descriptions of these migrants, who worked in lumber mills, railroad yards, and farm fields, often called forth a sense of the exotic that served the xenophobic and nationalistic agendas of the time. Some argue that not much has changed in this respect. In the media, from popular television shows such as *The Simpsons* to news programs like *Fox News,* representations of Indian Americans and their communities are often oversimplified and reduced to a single signifier, such as the turban or a heavy accent. Such figures both inform and confound the ability to ascertain what constitutes Indian American communities and how their unity and diversity can be understood.

Indeed, the multiple ways of being Indian American have much to do with the diversity of India itself. The population of India is more than a billion people, the second highest population in the world after China and nearly one-sixth of the planet's population. It is the world's largest democracy, with twenty-three official languages, and more than 1,000 dialects spoken. Within the nation's twenty-eight states, there exists a rich variety of regional and tribal cultures, in addition to a wide array of religious affiliations such as Buddhism, Christianity, Hinduism, Jainism, Judaism, Islam, Sikhism, and Zoroastrianism, to name but a few.

Consequently, the Indian American community exhibits a notable degree of variance in worldviews and lifestyles. This diversity is both a source of strength and frustration, for although many individuals share common goals of promoting a politically or culturally unified sense of "Indian-ness," conflicts regarding issues such as communalism or caste continue. Members of the Indian American diaspora also must negotiate this complex set of identities with the wide range of values, beliefs, and practices they find within U.S. culture. Moreover, their community identities also are understood through a history of race and ethnic relations in the United States. Consequently, membership in this diaspora implies a state of multiplicity and an affiliation with many different and contextually shifting identifications.

Most generally, this entry considers the difficult questions of who might be named an Indian American and how Indian American communities have been constituted. In each section, issues specifically related to Indian American communities will be discussed, including (a) historical immigration patterns, (b) changing immigration law, (c) community identity building and maintenance, and (d) current community concerns.

History of Indian American Immigration

Indians' movements around the globe began long before colonialism. However, it was through colonialism that various modes of migration developed their contemporary character. The abolition of slavery in Britain in 1833 caused labor shortages in agricultural activities and sugar production. Consequently, from 1830 through 1920, indentured labor in Burma, Mauritius, Ceylon, Malaya, and Natal became an option for Indians facing overpopulation and few employment opportunities at home.

The first wave of Indian immigration to the United States occurred in the mid 1800s, and by 1899, more than 2,000 Indians were forming communities on the West Coast. Most of these initial migrants were male Sikh Punjabi; the remainder included immigrants from Gujarat and Bengal. Significantly, at the time, only a handful of Indian women made the journey. Most of the male immigrants came from rural areas in India and found work on farms, ranches, lumber camps, and railroads. In addition, a small number of individuals sought refuge as political refugees or arrived to pursue educational opportunities.

During this time, Indian immigrants became an integral part of the expanding Pacific economy, so much so that their hard labor and acceptance of low wages began to attract unwanted attention. Like many other non-European migrant workers, the Indian Americans began to be the target of racist and xenophobic groups. For example, in 1907, a group calling itself the Asian Exclusion League began to press lawmakers to oppose immigration from Asia. This led to violent anti-Hindu riots in Washington, California, and Oregon that were organized to drive out "cheap labor."

In 1907, growing out of this burgeoning movement, the Bellingham, Washington, riots occurred. During this unrest, 500 individuals in Bellingham destroyed property and injured Indian American community members, until the police, unable to control the mobs, agreed to hold the 200 Indian Americans in the city hall "for their protection." Days later, members of this Indian American community fled the city, taking with them only what they could carry; many chose to return to India. Anti-Asian pressure continued to grow, and in 1917, the "Asiatic-Barred Zone" was enacted, restricting immigration from India. Soon, frustrated by xenophobic laws, prohibitions on land ownership, everyday racism, and the denial of citizenship, more than 3,000 Indians returned to India.

Changing Immigration Law

In 1924, a national origin quota system was put into place, further restricting immigration from India. Consequently, Indian immigration to the United States during the first half of the 20th century diminished dramatically. Indeed, until 1952 lawmakers continued to create restrictions on citizenship based on race. These laws did not go unchallenged, however.

For instance, in 1923, a crucial confrontation occurred when Bhagat Singh Thind applied for naturalization. Thind had immigrated to the United States in 1913, enrolled as a student at the University of California–Berkeley, and served in the U.S. Army during World War I, receiving an honorable discharge. His appeal for citizenship was denied and eventually his case was taken to the U.S. Supreme Court. After much waiting and deliberating, the outcome of *U.S. v. Bhagat Singh* was disappointing. The court ruled that Indians were ineligible for naturalization because they were not "White" in the ways that "White" was understood in the United States. Indeed, not until 1946 did immigration law eventually permit the naturalization of Indians, establishing a quota of 100 immigrants a year.

In 1965, years of discriminatory immigration legislation were repealed with the U.S. Immigration and Nationality Act. This act allowed as many as 20,000 individuals to immigrate from India annually and began what was later to be labeled the *brain drain*. This term referenced the highly select group of migrants from China, the Philippines, Great Britain, India, and Taiwan who were encouraged to apply. These individuals were extremely well educated and possessed skills in specific sought-after professions such as medicine or engineering. Most Indian immigration to the

United States occurred from 1966 to 1977, and unlike the past, these immigrants often brought their families as well. This group of newcomers contained 25,000 medical doctors, 20,000 scientists with PhDs, and 40,000 engineers.

After 1965, members of the Indian American diaspora began the difficult process of negotiating their degree of assimilation. Although most had held positions of importance in their home country, they often found that respect for their skills, education, or personal background did not outweigh the prejudice fueled by the social designation of "Third World migrant." And even as the category of "Asian American" disrupted Black-White binaries of race, most Indian American community members disagreed strongly with being categorized as Asian Americans, citing deep and important differences between Chinese, Japanese, Korean, and Indian culture, to name but a few. Together, they struggled through the 1970s to create the category "Indian American" in the U.S. Census. In 1975, their efforts resulted in individuals of Asian Indian descent being re-designated as White by the director of Federal Contract Compliance. In addition, in 1977, the Census Bureau reclassified Indian immigrants to Asian Indian, which still holds.

During the same period, the Indian government also worked to create the category of nonresident Indian (NRI) in an effort to repatriate investment from abroad. Through this designation, the Indian migrant is viewed as an Indian national living abroad. This strategy of naming establishes a continuing relationship to India. As such, this person is given benefits not typically offered, such as the right to own property in India, as well as the ability to profess duel political loyalties. This option made immigration to the United States much more appealing for many potential Indian migrants.

As a result of these opportunities in the 1970s, Indian American communities grew in the 1980s to more than 300,000. In 1990, the U.S. Census Bureau reported that the population was more than 800,000, and the most recent census, performed in 2000, indicates that there are now 1,678,765 individuals. During this time, progressive activists began using the term *South Asian* to support their sense that individuals from similar geographical areas would be best served by forgoing historical divisions and creating a unified political identity in the United States.

Within this framework, Indian Americans constituted a small portion of a larger community of South Asian Americans that included people from Bangladesh, Maldive Islands, Nepal, Pakistan, Bhutan, and Sri Lanka. Although many applauded this political move, others in the community expressed a strong desire to mobilize their ethnicity by adopting "Indian American" as a primary self-descriptor. For these individuals, reference to this ethnicity served as a way of distinguishing themselves from other Asian immigrants—recognizing a specific set of identities in terms of culture, language, and history—and also aided in downplaying their own racialization.

Because immigration from India has been heavily weighted toward university-educated professionals, their economic success has been remarkable during the last 2 decades. In 1990, the median household income of Indian immigrants was $48,320. This was $18,000 higher than the median for the U.S. population, and $20,000 more than the figure for foreign-born individuals, even though almost 60% of these immigrants had been in the United States 10 years or less. Moreover, immigrants from India within the last 2 decades have contributed to the diversity of the South Asian population by including larger numbers of working-class families, as well as H-1B visa holders, and international students.

Indian American woman. *A woman of South Asian descent shops in a store with a white-skinned mannequin wearing South Asian women's clothing in the New York City immigrant hub of Jackson Heights in the borough of Queens in New York City. Indian Americans are the largest segment of the growing number of South Asians who have immigrated to the United States.*

Source: Aurora/Getty Images.

Negotiating Identity

Today, like other Asian groups, South Asian communities continue to comprise primarily foreign-born individuals who are naturalizing in significant numbers. Although most of these immigrants tend to create large communities in major metropolitan areas, the 2000 U.S. Census data also reveals that South Asians are settling in large numbers in less urban areas within the United States. Many of these immigrants choose to negotiate their new environs through the maintenance of particular Indian values, beliefs, and practices. This choice challenges mainstream U.S. notions of ethnicity such as assimilability and foregrounds the complexities of identity politics.

Rather than behaving and believing in ways that support traditional conceptions of the U.S. "melting pot," Indian Americans enact multiple identities, in terms of language, regional culture, ethnicity, religion, and nation. As members of this diaspora negotiate multiple lived categories, they also are simultaneously engaging U.S. public life and democratic culture. In this complex space, Indian American communities continue to develop.

For example, for many their identity refers not so much to national affiliation as to an elaborate network of regional culture, dialect, and social custom. This fragmentation, of course, is not surprising, given that India was composed of separate different princely states before and during British colonization and did not become a nation until a little more than 50 years ago. Indeed, India is still developing a sense of what it means to be "Indian." Most individuals connect much more closely with regional or religious identities rather than with a national loyalty. Given this, it is relatively easy to understand how adopting an Indian American identity might be challenging for some immigrants, particularly those in the first generation.

Such a regional identity often is supported in larger, urban environments where the population of immigrants tends to be dense. In these contexts, smaller subgroups, such as the Bengalis or Gujaratis, identify based on a regional dialect spoken at home or regional customs practiced. Relatives who have arrived more recently may reinforce these cultural distinctions and re-inject local practices. This does not mean that Indian American communities have little cohesion. Loyalties to an Indian homeland unite this diverse group on many levels, providing a collective sense of identity. But like all groups, they must struggle against their own discrepancies, differences that must be resolved if the group is to be viable.

For these reasons, the answer to the question, "Who are you?" is markedly negotiable for many Indian Americans. While in a group of other Indians, a person might identify regionally, as a Gujarati. On the other hand, while at work, surrounded by non-Indians, a person might choose to label as Indian, Indian American, Asian American, Asian, or just American. Strategic with their responses, the answer often depends on who is asking the question and why.

In the absence of the cultural environment available in India, exposing children to important aspects of their Indian heritage poses challenges for Indian American parents. Some choose to make frequent trips back to India to expose their children to local practices and traditions. Most families actively try to take advantage of the growing commercial success of Indian markets, restaurants, and clothing. Indeed, in recent years, thanks to celebrities such as Madonna and Goldie Hawn, Indian fashions (saris and churidars), jewelry (belly chains), and body art (mendhi), have found a market with both U.S. and Indian American youths. Beyond this, increasingly, the Indian American community is using the Internet to sell and buy Indian goods. Another means by which children can become more mindful of their Indian heritage is to participate in organizations such as the Indian Association of America or weekend ethnic schools. Of course, these attempts to encourage children to recognize their Indian heritage may go unheeded in favor of more mainstream affiliations. This first generation born in the United States faces many challenges in connecting to a "homeland" they may have never seen. Yet, in creatively appropriating and re-appropriating diverse cultural forms to meet everyday needs and address political exigencies, this group exhibits the important ways in which traditions are also dynamic and can work in ways that can support social and cultural change.

Contemporary Community Issues

Despite diversity within Indian American community groups, these immigrants share many common problems. The most pressing include hate crimes, racial profiling, immigration policies, educational inequity, and poverty. The United States is currently struggling with its identity as a "country of immigration." During the late 1980s into the 1990s, when the foreign-born population reached 20 million (nearly 8% of the total population), anti-immigration sentiment rose among U.S. citizens.

For instance, in 1987, Navraze Mody was murdered in a "dotbusting" hate crime spree in New Jersey; a practice in which Indian Americans were visually identified by a *bindi* (a red dot traditionally worn on the forehead of married Hindu women) and then verbally or physically assaulted. In the aftermath of the September 11, 2001, attacks on the World Trade Center in New York City and the Pentagon in Washington, D.C., anti-immigrant sentiment has grown stronger, with large proportions of the populations indicating that they fear certain immigrant groups, such as those from South Asia, and favor polices that restrict or curtail immigration from these countries. Some argue that this rising intolerance may not simply be a function of the attacks but, instead, is linked to the fact that the new influx of immigrants is often not European in origin; rather, they are commonly non-White and from developing countries. Others argue that the tragic events of September 11, 2001, have sharply increased suspicion and prejudice toward South Asian immigrants in a manner that recalls the marked backlash felt by East Asians following the Japanese attack on Pearl Harbor.

Given this social and political climate, a handful of grassroots advocacy groups have formed around the country to help Indian Americans unite and increase their influence through active civic and political engagement. The continued efforts of groups such as these, as well as the commitment of socially engaged artists, performers, and writers, have great potential to increase understanding and forge connections between Indian American communities, the broader Indian diaspora across the globe, and U.S. mainstream society.

Christine Lynn Garlough

See Appendix A; Appendix B
See also Assimilation; Cross-Frontier Contacts; *Desi;* Ethnicity, Negotiating; Foreign Students; Hate Crimes; Immigrant Communities; Immigration, U.S.; India; Melting Pot; Panethnic Identity; Rites of Passage

Further Readings

Backburn, Robin. 1988. *The Overthrow of Colonial Slavery, 1776–1848.* London: Verso.

Hall, Stuart. 1996. *Stuart Hall: Critical Dialogues in Cultural Studies,* edited by D. Morely and K.-H. Chen. London: Routledge.

Jensen, Joan. 1988. *Passage from India: Asian Indian Immigrants in North America.* New Haven, CT: Yale University Press.

Shukla, Sandhya. 2003. *India Abroad: Diasporic Cultures of Postwar America and England.* Princeton, NJ: Princeton University Press.

Tinker, Hugh. 1993. *The New System of Slavery: The Export of Indian Labor Overseas, 1830–1920.* London: Hansib.

Varma, Premdatta. 1995. *Indian Immigrants in USA: Struggle for Equality.* New Delhi, India: Heritage.

Indian Child Welfare Act of 1978

Perhaps the most significant threat to the continuing existence of Native American tribes as culturally distinct, self-governing nations has been the forced removal of American Indian children from tribal communities into boarding schools and non-Indian homes. Although both an explicit tactic by federal and state governments to foster the assimilation of Native Americans into mainstream society and the result of well-meaning social workers who lack knowledge about tribal cultures, the removal of American Indian children from the reservations has resulted in the disruption of traditional family life and has hindered the transmission of tribal values, customs, and languages to future generations of Native American people.

In the 1970s, after decades of failed assimilation policies that left Native American communities culturally and politically fragmented, tribes began to achieve moderate levels of success in winning recognition of their sovereign rights to exclusively govern their reservations and their members without interference from the states. Tribes argued that a crucial part of this sovereign authority was the ability to protect their most valuable cultural resources, their children, from being taken away and raised in ways that are incompatible with tribal cultural values. As these arguments were consistent with the federal government's post-assimilation era policy of tribal self-determination, Congress responded with the enactment of the Indian Child Welfare Act (ICWA) in 1978. Specifically acknowledging the importance of protecting the stability and security of Native American tribes and further asserting that it is in the best interest of Native American children to be raised in culturally relevant settings, ICWA implemented sweeping jurisdictional and substantive requirements for all child placement proceedings involving American Indian children. Although not immune from controversy, ICWA's implications for tribal and state authority regarding the welfare of American Indian children have been considerable. Indeed, many assert that ICWA is one of the most significant pieces of legislation dealing with Native Americans that has ever been passed. This entry describes the legislation, its context, and its consequences.

The Removal of American Indian Children Before 1978

The forced removal of Native American children from their tribal communities goes back to the late 1800s and coincides with the beginning of the reservation era, which was marked by the end of tribal military resistance to U.S. expansion. At this time, American Indian children were removed to non-Indian controlled boarding schools as part of the federal government's policy of assimilation. By separating Native children from their traditional communities and prohibiting them from speaking their native languages, dressing in tribal attire, or practicing their traditional religions, while teaching them the norms and customs of Anglo American society, it was believed that educators could "kill the Indian, but save the man."

The consequences of the boarding school experiment were devastating for the children as well as the tribes. Children suffered emotional and psychological trauma from being separated from their families and forced to adopt lifestyles that were unfamiliar and inconsistent with their traditional customs, and it was not uncommon to hear of physical, sexual, and emotional abuses occurring at these schools. Tribes lost generations of members to boarding schools who, after graduating, either returned to their reservations lacking the cultural knowledge and tribal identities required for reintegration back into the community or, more often, moved away from the tribes and started lives elsewhere. American Indian boarding schools were most active in the late 1800s to mid-1900s, although many continued to operate in the decades that followed. As late as 1971, 17% of American Indian children were still being removed to boarding schools operated by the Bureau of Indian Affairs or by non-Indian religious organizations.

In many ways, the adoption of American Indian children into non-Indian homes is ideologically linked to the boarding school experiment. Both endeavors represent the failure of state and federal institutions to recognize and respect native practices of child rearing; they also demonstrate the paternalistic belief that American Indian children are better off raised by non-Indian parents in mainstream cultural settings, rather than by members of their own tribe. Whereas the removal of children to boarding schools was often the result of official assimilationist policies, the adoption of Native American children into non-Indian families has more generally resulted from the actions of well-meaning, but culturally insensitive, state social workers who fail to understand tribal family customs.

Because of disproportionate rates of alcoholism and poverty on the reservations, many American Indian children are born into broken homes and raised outside of their nuclear families. Although reliance upon extended families for child rearing is consistent with the traditional, communally focused, customs of many native communities, such practices are regularly deemed unorthodox and flawed by non-Indian child welfare agents. As a result, many more Native American children are removed from their families on allegations of neglect and emotional mistreatment than are non-Native children.

Non-Indian biases against tribal child-rearing practices are further reflected in the more general trends of American Indian child placements in the decades before the passage of ICWA. For example, in 1969, 85% of all Native American children who were adopted or placed in foster homes were living in non-Indian households. In states with larger Native American populations, the ratios of adoptions for American Indian children versus non-Indian children were staggeringly high, reaching ten-to-one in Wyoming, and five-to-one in Maine, Wisconsin, Washington, the Dakotas, and Utah.

ICWA and Its Implications

ICWA was passed in 1978 as part of a string of legislation purporting to give greater power to Native American tribes in governing their own people, controlling their land bases, and protecting vital aspects of tribal culture. As a general matter, the 1970s marked a shift from federal policies of assimilation to greater acknowledgment of tribal sovereignty and self-determination. Specifically, ICWA was enacted to reverse the historic trends of tribal cultural breakdown that had resulted from the forced removal of generations of American Indian children from their communities. It sought these objectives by articulating jurisdictional requirements and placement priorities for all cases involving the adoption or foster placement of Native American children in ways favorable to tribes.

ICWA recognizes the exclusive jurisdiction of tribal courts in all placement cases involving American Indian children who reside on the reservation and requires the immediate transfer of such cases from state court to tribal court where the appropriate motions are raised. Under ICWA, an "Indian child" is defined as a minor who is a member of, or eligible for membership in, the tribe and who is the biological child of a member. Where state courts retain jurisdiction, such as in cases where American Indian children reside off the reservation, American Indian tribes are permitted to intervene in the proceedings and the courts must adhere to specific preference requirements for placing American Indian children in adoptive or foster homes. Barring good cause to the contrary, preferences for adopting American Indian children should go, first, to members of the Indian child's extended family; second, to other members of the child's tribe; and third, to other American Indian families.

Although Congress intended ICWA to provide clear guidelines for the adoption and foster placement of American Indian children, the application of the law by state courts has been anything but uniform. For example, some states have interpreted the "good cause" exception to the application of the placement preferences and transfer requirements as an invitation to determine whether placement with an American Indian family is in the best interest of the child. This contravenes a foundational purpose of ICWA, however, which is to uphold native practices of child rearing and remove such practices from the scrutiny of state courts and child welfare workers that lack the cultural knowledge to make such judgments.

Other state courts have carved out a judicial exception to the application of ICWA where an American Indian child is not being immediately removed from an "existing Indian family," even though no such exception is written into the act itself. Although amendments to ICWA were proposed in 2003 to clarify the act by explicitly rejecting the "existing Indian family exception," the amendments were never passed.

Notwithstanding these inconsistencies, the consequences of the act have been mainly positive. The application of ICWA has helped prevent the future removal of American Indian children from tribal communities and has strengthened the autonomy of tribal governments and courts, educated state courts and child welfare workers on matters of tribal sovereignty and the importance of upholding tribal cultural value systems, and encouraged increased cooperation between tribes and the states over issues of child welfare.

Julia Miller Cantzler

See also Adoption; Assimilation; Child Development; Native American Health Care; Native American Identity; Native Americans; Sovereignty, Native American

Further Readings

Adams, David Wallace. 1995. *Education for Extinction: American Indians and the Boarding School Experience, 1875–1928.* Lawrence: University of Kansas Press.

Bensen, Robert. 2001. *Children of the Dragonfly: Native American Voices on Child Custody and Education.* Tucson: University of Arizona Press.

Garner, Suzanne. 1993. "The Indian Child Welfare Act: A Review." *Wicazo Sa Review* 9(1):47–51.

Harjo, Susan Shown. 1993. "The American Indian Experience." Pp. 199–207 in *Family Ethnicity: Strength in Diversity,* edited by H. P. McAdoo. Newbury Park, CA: Sage.

Jones, B. J. 1995. *The Indian Child Welfare Act Handbook: A Legal Guide to the Custody and Adoption of Native American Children.* Chicago, IL: American Bar Association.

INDIAN GAMING REGULATORY ACT OF 1988

The Indian Gaming Regulatory Act or IGRA (Public Law 100–497), passed by Congress in 1988, established a federal statutory basis and regulatory framework for governing the operation of gaming by federally recognized American Indian tribes. This entry describes the legal evolution of gaming as tribal revenue-earning activity and summarizes the law's content.

History and Background

The first federally recognized tribe to operate a high-stakes gaming facility was the Seminole Tribe of Florida. The state of Florida tried to shut down the tribe's bingo parlor, arguing that under Public Law 280, the state had criminal jurisdiction over the tribe's lands and the tribe was operating a facility that did not comply with a number of state laws. The U.S. Court of Appeals in the 1979 case of *Seminole Tribe of Florida v. Florida* found that because the state generally allowed charitable bingo, the regulation of the industry fell under civil jurisdiction, which the state did not have on the reservation's lands.

In the 1980s, tribal government-sponsored gaming operations began to spread throughout Indian Country, and by 1988, more than 100 tribes were operating bingo halls. Many states attempted to restrict or stop tribal gaming operations on the grounds that they violated state gaming laws and under significant pressure from the non-Indian gaming industry, which feared competition. State interests also voiced concerns that the lack of federal regulation of the industry would lead to an increase in organized crime and social problems associated with gambling. States were also concerned about their inability to tax gaming on American Indian reservations.

In 1987, the U.S. Supreme Court ruled on the ability of tribes to operate gaming facilities on their lands independent of state regulation. In *California v. Cabazon Band of Mission Indians,* the Court ruled six to three in favor of the Cabazon, asserting that Public Law 280 did not grant the state of California the jurisdiction to regulate activities on American Indian reservations if they were not completely illegal under state criminal laws. This meant that if a state prohibited gambling but allowed some form of gaming for charitable organizations, state lotteries, or otherwise, as regulated under civil law, American Indian tribes could engage in those forms of gaming free of state control. If, however, the state completely criminally prohibited gaming, then tribes in the state could not engage in that activity.

The *California v. Cabazon* decision ultimately led states and Nevada gaming interests to seek federal legislation to limit and control tribal gaming and to give states some regulatory authority over it. The Indian Gaming Regulatory Act, which was passed a year later, was Congress's response, relying on the principles put forth by the *Cabazon* case. With this legislation, Congress tried to achieve a balance between the right of tribes to be generally free of state jurisdiction and the interest of states in regulating gaming activities. States have a voice in setting the scope and extent of tribal gaming, and the tribes keep regulatory authority over certain kinds of gaming. Neither the states nor the tribes were pleased. Tribes wanted to continue operating according to the *Cabazon* decision and did not welcome any form of state involvement. States felt their role was too limited and worried that the act exposed them to possible lawsuits.

What IGRA Says

As stated in the Declaration of Policy or Section 2702 of IGRA, the purpose of the act is threefold:

1. To provide a statutory basis for the operation of gaming by American Indian tribes as a means of promoting tribal economic development, self-sufficiency, and strong tribal governments;

2. To provide a statutory basis for the regulation of gaming by an American Indian tribe adequate to shield it from organized crime and other corrupting influences, to ensure that the American Indian tribe is the primary beneficiary of the gaming operation, and to assure that gaming is conducted fairly and honestly by both the operator and players; and

3. To declare that the establishment of independent Federal regulatory authority for gaming on American Indian lands, the establishment of Federal standards for gaming on Indian lands, and the establishment of a National Indian Gaming Commission are necessary to meet congressional concerns regarding gaming and to protect such gaming as a means of generating tribal revenue.

Regulations Affecting Tribes

For a tribe to operate gaming facilities under IGRA, it must be a federally recognized tribe. This means that it must be a tribe, band, nation, or other organized group or community of American Indians that is recognized as eligible by the secretary of the interior for the special programs and services provided by the U.S. government to American Indians and as possessing powers of self-government. Federal recognition can be a result of historical continued existence, executive order, congressional legislation, or the Department of the Interior's federal acknowledgement process.

IGRA requires that American Indian gaming occur on Indian lands. These include land within the boundaries of a reservation as well as lands held in trust or restricted status by the U.S. government on behalf of a tribe or individual, over which a tribe has jurisdiction and exercises governmental power. Tribes operating gaming facilities off-reservation on non-Indian lands are subject to the laws of the state where the facility is located. A tribe's lands can only be conferred as federally entrusted lands by an act of Congress, a court decision or settlement, or, most commonly, through an application through the U.S. Department of Interior.

Tribes may also operate casinos on lands acquired after the enactment of the IGRA, subject to certain restrictions and exceptions as set forth in Section 2719 of the act. To do so, the secretary of the interior must consult with the tribe and appropriate state and local officials, including officials of other nearby American Indian tribes, to determine that a gaming establishment on newly acquired lands would be in the best interest of the tribe and its members and would not be detrimental to the surrounding community; the governor of the state in which the gaming activity is to be conducted must concur in the secretary's determination. Gaming facilities may also be opened on lands that are taken into trust as part of a settlement of a land claim or through the restoration of lands through the federal acknowledgement or other federal recognition process. IGRA does not require that a tribe operate a casino within the borders of the state in which the tribe is based.

Key Provisions

Under IGRA, gambling operations are divided into three categories with varying levels of tribal, state, or federal regulation. Balancing state and tribal interests, IGRA generally requires that states and tribes enter into compacts to authorize the types of gambling commonly associated with tribal casinos today—such as slot machines—when state law permits similar gambling operations in any other context. The act permits casino operations on American Indian lands, which it defines as (1) reservation lands, (2) lands held in trust by the United States for benefit of an American Indian tribe or individual, or (3) certain specified lands over which an Indian tribe exercises governmental power. The act requires states to negotiate with tribes that request the opportunity to enter into a compact. The IGRA establishes the National Indian Gaming Commission within the U.S. Department of the Interior as a body to limit organized crime and corruption, ensure that tribes benefit from gambling revenues, and enforce the honesty and fairness of certain tribal gambling operations.

The regulatory framework established under IGRA divides gaming into three classes:

- *Class I gaming* is defined by IGRA to include social games played solely for prizes of minimal value or traditional forms of Indian gaming engaged in by individuals as a part of, or in connection with, tribal ceremonies or celebrations. The operation and regulation of Class I gaming activities is within the exclusive jurisdiction of the tribe on its lands.

- *Class II gaming* includes bingo, pull tabs, lotto, punch boards, tip jars, instant bingo, other games similar to bingo, and card games played exclusively against other players rather than against the house. Class II gaming is allowed if these games are authorized or not explicitly prohibited by the state in which the tribal operation is located. Class II gaming does not include banking card games (including baccarat and blackjack), electronic or electromechanical facsimiles of any game of chance, or slot machines of any kind. Class II gaming is permitted as long as the state in which the tribe's lands are located permits such gaming for any purpose by any person, organization, or entity.

Although states almost always heavily regulate and restrict such games, many of those state restrictions do not apply to the tribe. For example, although Class II card games must be played in conformity with state laws and regulations on hours of operation and limitations on wager or pot sizes, state limits do not apply to bingo at a tribal reservation facility. Before a tribe can operate Class II gaming, it must also authorize a tribal resolution or ordinance that is approved by the National Indian Gaming Commission. Regulation of Class II games is thus within the jurisdiction of the tribes, but subject to oversight by the Gaming Commission.

- *Class III gaming* includes all forms of gaming that are not classified as Class I or II games. These include slot machines, blackjack, craps, roulette, and other games that are commonly operated by Nevada or Atlantic City casinos. The Gaming Commission's Office of General Counsel reviews games on request by a tribe or a game developer and issues advisory opinions about whether they are Class II or Class III. Class III gaming is the most important type of gaming for tribal gaming enterprises.

Tribes may use the revenues generated by their Class II and III gaming enterprises only for purposes designated in the IGRA. According to IGRA, these revenues are not to be used for purposes other than the following:

- To fund tribal government operations or programs
- To provide for the general welfare of the American Indian tribe and its members
- To promote tribal economic development
- To donate to charitable organizations
- To help fund operations of local government agencies

Once these obligations have been met, a tribe may petition the secretary of the interior to approve a revenue allocation plan under which the tribe may make per capita payments to individual tribal members. Approximately one-third of the tribes engaged in class II and III gaming distribute per capita payments to their members. The size of these payments varies considerably from tribe to tribe, depending on the profitability of the gaming enterprises.

Angela Ann Gonzales and Melanie Stansbury

See also Bureau of Indian Affairs; Gaming, Native American; Native Americans

Further Readings

Anders, Gary C. 1998. "Indian Gaming: Financial and Regulatory Issues" *Annals of the American Academy of Political and Social Sciences* 556:98–108.

Cornell, Stephen, Joseph Kalt, Matthew Krepps, and Jonathan Taylor. 1998. *American Indian Gaming Policy and its Socio-Economic Effects. Report to the National Gambling Impact Study Commission.* Cambridge, MA: Economics Resource Group.

Eadington, William R. 1990. *Indian Gaming and the Law.* Las Vegas: University of Nevada Press.

Manson, Dale. 2000. *Indian Gaming: Tribal Sovereignty and American Politics.* Norman: University of Oklahoma Press.

INDIVIDUALS WITH DISABILITIES EDUCATION ACT OF 1990

The Individuals with Disabilities Education Act (IDEA) of 1990 was enacted to decrease the overrepresentation of minorities in special education, which had occurred previously within public education. In reality, however, it has failed at its legislative intent and become a gateway for introducing school-age minorities, more specifically, Black males, into special education at rates disproportionate to those of their White counterparts. This entry looks at the law, its application, and its impact.

The Law and Its Context

The reauthorized IDEA was enacted into law by President George W. Bush on December 3, 2004, to strengthen IDEA of 1990, which was derived from the federal policy, Education for All Handicapped Children Act. The original intent and continued responsibility of the acts is to provide all students with special needs access to a "free and appropriate" public education, to protect the rights of parents and their school age children, to assist state and local education agencies in educating students with disabilities, and to assess and ensure that state and local education agencies are successful in providing a quality education within a least restrictive environment (LRE) for all children with disabilities.

Before these enactments, 1 million children with special needs were segregated from the mainstream classrooms of public schools, and more than 4 million did not receive the educational assistance necessary to access the opportunities offered by the U.S. public school system. The original 1975 act also enabled the federal government to enforce the equal protection clause for families and students. This clause bars state and local agencies from excluding and misclassifying students with special needs.

Was the original intent of protecting families and students through IDEA successful? Many in the field of education would answer No. The question has been raised, to how and why an act such as IDEA, which was implemented to protect all children, could allow for the overrepresentation of racial minorities, especially Black and Latino children, in special education.

In 1992, according to the Office of Civil Rights, elementary and secondary schools reported that Black males accounted for only 8% of total school enrollment nationally but more than twice that percentage in the categories of Educable Mentally Retarded, Severely Emotionally Disturbed, and Trainable Mentally Retarded. In certain school districts, enrollment in special education for Black students was almost 50% higher than their representation in the districts as a whole. In addition, the *Chicago Tribune* discussed how Black pupils were 2.9 times more likely to be labeled with a disability than were Whites. Wealthier school areas were more likely to place Black children in special education by labeling them mentally impaired.

Special education students are still kept apart from regular education students within the United States. Such findings raise concern about potential biases in assigning children of color to special groups, particularly in light of findings demonstrating that advocates for special education students, within and outside of government, have allowed for the continuation of policies that foster inequality and segregation.

The Impact of Racism

To understand how this phenomenon occurs, one must realize and understand that the construction of IDEA rests on the notion that race does not influence the identification of students. Furthermore, IDEA is founded on trust for those who evaluate and work with students with disabilities. Current beliefs among many Whites—that race and discrimination are not everyday fundamental aspects of racially marginalized children's lives—contribute to misrecognition of the covert effects of racism and discrimination that occur as a result of the unanalyzed socialization experiences of special education workers.

The premise of IDEA and those within education who feel that racism is not a factor within the determinant classification of students ignore the subtle acts of discrimination toward minority students, especially Blacks, that later become detrimental variables in determining the presence of a disability. Moreover, those who enacted IDEA did not consider that some teachers, especially White teachers, may operate on stereotypes, social distance, racism, biased research, and ignorance of community norms of the minority children with whom they work.

In combination with the failure to acknowledge and validate a particular child's culture and race, these tendencies have a negative impact on the population of school children of color with whom teachers are working. In addition, aside from the fact that race was never factored into the construction of IDEA, the criteria for defining disabilities, such as speech/language, emotional, and specific learning disabilities, have been highly criticized for vagueness and as invalid testing procedures.

Classification of Students

IDEA has helped many students with special needs and their parents. In the face of its explicit mandates against misclassification on the grounds of race, however, it still introduces minority children to special education at unrepresentative rates. What holes exist to allow misclassification of minority students?

The numerical increase in incoming college freshmen who have been diagnosed with disabilities covered under IDEA is one sign of potential problems. The definitions, broadness of terms, and inconsistent application of the policy from state to state and school district to school district because of the broad language of IDEA have allowed for a significant increase in learning disabilities diagnoses.

Another reason that the current language of IDEA may have a negative effect on minorities is that the law is based on a system from which they were originally excluded. Numerous studies illustrate that assigning a disproportionately high number of minority students to special education serves as a form of discipline and control in public schools. Disproportionate numbers of Black students are assigned to special education programs, a phenomenon that predates IDEA and continues. Research shows that this results from a complex system that schools unconsciously and consciously employ in an effort to impede the academic success of minority students.

By means of labeling, minority students who do not readily comply are easily grouped into a circle of minorities plagued with an inferior and tracked curriculum and decreasing educational expectations by school staff. This in turn reduces the achievement level of labeled students. In addition, this segregation of special education students also encourages labeling and stereotyping of people with disabilities, a disservice to Black and other pupils of color.

Terrence Fitzgerald

See also Americans with Disabilities Act; Educational Performance and Attainment; Institutional Discrimination; Labeling; Pipeline; Racism; School Desegregation, Attitudes Concerning; Stereotypes; Tracking

Further Readings

Barnes, Colin. 1991. *Disabled People in Britain and Discrimination: A Case for Anti-Discrimination Legislation.* London: Hurst.

Barton, Len and Sally Tomlinson. 1984. *Special Education and Social Interest.* London: Croom Helm.

Delpit, Lisa. 1995. *Other People's Children: Cultural Conflict in the Classroom.* New York: New Press.

Fitzgerald, Terrence. 2006. "Control, Punish, and Conquer: U.S. Public Schools' Attempts to Control Black Males. *Challenge: Journal of Research on African American Men* 12:38–53.

Glennon, Theresa. 1995. "Race, Education, and the Construction of a Disabled Class." *Wisconsin Law Review:*1237–1339.

Irvine, Jacqueline. 1990. *Black Students and School Failure: Policies, Practices, and Prescriptions.* New York: Greenwood Press.

Jarvinen, D. and R. Sprague. 1995. "Using Actors to Screen Minority Children for ADHD: An Examination of Items Bias." *Journal of Psychoeducational Assessment: ADHD Special:*173–183.

Lawrence-Lightfoot, Sara. 1978. *Worlds Apart: Relationships Between Families and Schools.* New York: Basic Books.

Pressman, Roger. 1993. "A Comprehensive Approach to the Issue of Disparate Special Education Placement Rates of African American and National-Origin Minority Youths." *Clearinghouse* 27:322–332.

Skrtic, Thomas. 1991. *Behind Special Education: A Critical Analysis of Professional Culture and School Organization.* Denver, CO: Love.

Turnbull, Rud and Ann Turnbull. 1998. *Free Appropriate Public Education: The Law and Children with Disabilities.* Denver, CO: Love.

Zirkel, Perry A. 2001. "Sorting Out Which Students Have Learning Disabilities." *Phi Delta Kappan:* 639–641.

INDONESIAN AMERICANS

Most Indonesians are recent migrants, arriving after passage of the 1965 Hart-Celler Act, and they share social and cultural characteristics of people in their homeland. Racial, ethnic, and religious differences and intergroup relations are important because of the cultural diversity in Indonesia and events in Indonesia relating to these differences that encouraged migration, as described in this entry.

Indonesia's Diversity

Indonesia has about 8,000 inhabited islands and an estimated population of 231.6 million people as of 2007. Some 200 culturally diverse ethnic groups range in population from several thousands to tens of millions, most with homelands within Indonesia in which they represent the dominant culture. Islam, Christianity, Hinduism, Buddhism, and local supernatural traditions are found there. Indonesia has the largest Muslim population of any nation, with about 90% of its people said to be Muslim. Some ethnic groups mostly follow one faith (for example, Acehnese are Muslim; Batak, Protestant; Florenese, Catholic; Balinese, Hindu.) Others, such as the populous Javanese, have various faiths.

Colonial Influences

The archipelago experienced Dutch influence beginning in the 17th century. In the 19th century, the Netherlands-Indies government was formed, and by the beginning of the 20th century extended control over what is now the Republic of Indonesia. British scholar J. S. Furnivall described the Netherlands Indies as a plural society, two or more social orders living side by side without mingling. These social orders were racially stratified: Dutch at the top, Chinese and other "foreign Asiatics" in the middle, and Indonesians on the bottom. The Dutch led government, big businesses, and professions. Chinese became economic mediators between urban and rural economic sectors. Indigenous Peoples were primarily farmers but increasingly came to cities during the 20th century.

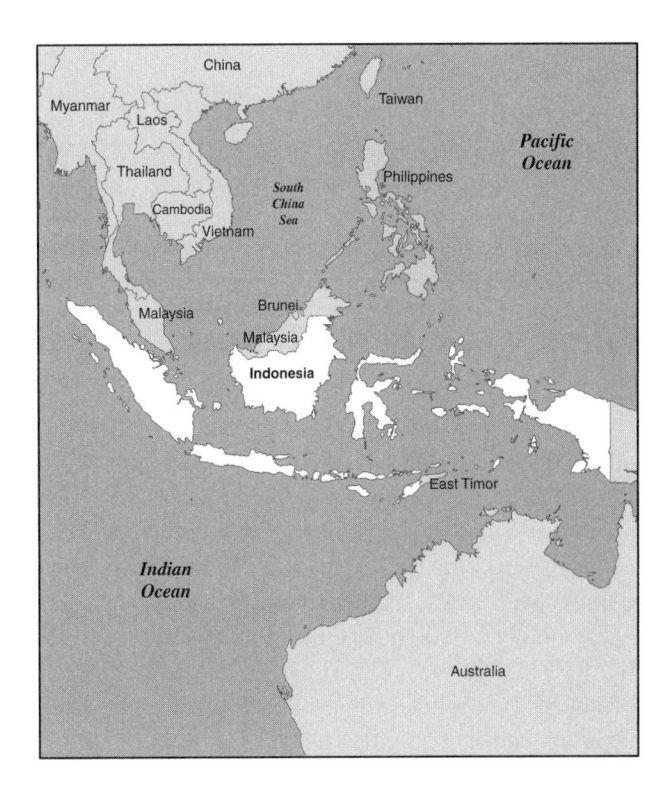

The three races had relatively exclusive lives and legal rights and followed dress codes and modes of respect. Conventional separation between the races led to the growth of two interstitial categories of people, Indo-Europeans (or Indo) and Peranakan. The Indo were the offspring of wives or concubines of Dutch and local women. The Peranakan were the offspring of Chinese men with local women. Neither the Indos nor the Peranakan was socially well accepted by the other three races. Indos did serve in Dutch governmental, military, and business activities and gained Dutch citizenship. Peranakan were mainly in commerce and professions. Over time, each group developed a subculture that included dress, arts, newspapers, and organizations.

The New Nation

A nationalist movement grew from about 1912 through the end of the Japanese occupation in 1945 when its leaders declared independence. Revolution arose in Java and some other islands as the Dutch tried unsuccessfully to reassert control between 1945 and 1949. Indonesia became a nation in 1950 with the motto, "Unity in Diversity." Indigenous people became citizens and others could choose citizenship, and Indonesian (based on Malay, a long-time lingua franca) became the national language. Local languages were used only in the first three grades of rural schools, and their indigenous literatures were no longer published. Indonesian served government, media, education, and business, but local languages remained used in homes and other settings.

Ethnic cultures and regional loyalties were downplayed under the regimes of President Sukarno (the "Old Order") and Suharto (the "New Order) from 1950 to 1998, because of concerns about the nation's fragility. Both regimes supported a unitary form of government with power and finances centered in the capital, Jakarta. After the downfall of Suharto in 1998, new efforts grew for "reformation" that included democracy, popular elections, and decentralization. The 2000 census of Indonesia became the first since 1930 to measure distributions of ethnicity and religion.

Indonesian Migrants to the United States

The first major migrants from Indonesia were Indos who came following independence. Many Indos, who held Dutch citizenship and faced an unfriendly Indonesian populace, moved to The Netherlands and then, after the Refugee Acts were passed by the U.S. Congress between 1953 and 1962, about 30,000 came to the United States, mainly to southern California. By 1973, another 30,000 had come, sponsored by relatives. In 1972, in Azusa, California, Indo Seventh Day Adventists (and a few Indonesian Adventists, including the Batak pastor) bought a church. By the early 1980s, many Indonesians had come and joined the church, and conflicts arose between them and the Indos. Many Indos then withdrew to other churches and began assimilation to White U.S. society.

Migrants and Their Churches

By the time of the 2000 U.S. Census, some 35,000 to 50,000 Indonesians were in the country. About half reside in California, and more than half of those are in southern California, primarily in the Los Angeles and San Bernardino areas. This is the largest concentration of Indonesians in the country. Two major groupings emerged there: Indonesian Chinese (mostly Peranakan and Christian) and indigenous ethnic groups that were predominantly Christian such as Minahasans, Bataks, Ambonese, and Florenese. About 60% are estimated to be Chinese Indonesians, and most of the rest are from the Christian groups. Members of Muslim groups are more likely to be transient students, government officials, and business representatives.

These groups migrated for different, but related, reasons. Chinese in Indonesia were classified as citizens of foreign descent and were subject to restrictions on participation in government employment and higher education. There were also regulations governing public celebrations, the use of temples, and public display of written Chinese characters. The Chinese were forced to do business and to reside in urban areas, to develop private universities, and to seek employment and education abroad for family members. In the United States, Chinese Indonesians use their business experience advantageously as do certain groups such as Minahasans and Bataks. In recent decades, violence in Indonesia against Chinese and against Chinese and Indonesian Christians led many people to migrate.

In the United States, Indonesians are among minority "people of color" (though in Los Angeles that racial category has gained parity in numbers with White Americans.). Ironically, in the United States, the cultural character of Indonesian Chinese as essentially Indonesian comes to the fore, but their links to other Chinese migrants are few. In many ways, Indonesian Chinese and indigenous migrants become socially closer than they would have been in Indonesia. Most Chinese speak Indonesian in the home, churches, and other contexts. Few speak or are literate in Chinese, and in Indonesia, many had become Christian.

In southern California, for example, which has more Asian migrants than any other region of the country, there are few relationships between ethnic Chinese from places such as Indonesia, Vietnam, Taiwan, or China. They differ in national background experiences, Chinese dialects, and facility in English, which leads them to remain socially with migrants from the same country. Indonesian consular personnel, who work with migrants to perpetuate cultural ties and who are not Chinese, remain closer to Indonesian Chinese in the United States than they would be in Indonesia. Los Angeles consular officials are mostly Muslim and sponsor weekly prayer and Koran reading sessions at the consulate, but they maintain close ties with Christian church groups, whether Chinese or indigenous ones, despite increasing conflict between Muslims and Christians in Indonesia.

Religious conflict in Indonesia also has led some members of Christian ethnic groups to migrate, and though Christians are a small minority in Indonesia, they are a majority among migrants to the United States. In southern California, for example, Protestant congregations have grown from two in 1975 to about fifty in 2005. Religion and ethnicity may be associated. For example, the Batak Protestant Christian Church is found now in several places in the United States. Its members are all Bataks, and their language may be used in church. Not all Bataks belong to this church. Some are prominent Seventh Day Adventists. Adventist congregations may have a majority of Bataks or Minahasans, but others are more ethnically mixed. People commonly join denominations to which they belonged in Indonesia, but others may be drawn to new churches. Many Chinese in Indonesia are Baptist, and the second Indonesian church in the Los Angeles area was Baptist. Its founding minister and most of its congregation are Chinese.

Indonesian migrants are still relatively few, even in southern California, so members of different ethnic groups are more likely to meet in church there than in Indonesia. Churches may help bridge ethnic differences in some cases, but may deter bridging in others. Also, one Indonesian leader in Los Angeles, Emile Mailangkay, has noted that the proliferation of Indonesian congregations there can bring about unhealthy divisions in an Indonesian community that otherwise benefits from unity.

Ethnic and Regional Associations

In the late 1960s in Los Angeles, the Union of People of Indonesian Origin was formed. The union was an umbrella for all Indonesians, as its name implies, but its membership was largely Chinese Indonesian and remains so. Later, the organization Maesa was formed in Los Angeles (the word *maesa* means "united" in the Minahasan language of North Sulawesi). Its celebrations are attended by as many as 500 people and include music and dance from the North Sulawesi region.

The Batak Community of California Club was established in the 1980s to assist Batak people and provide social activities. This club has another name in the Batak language that means "Descendants of Sri Raja Batak in California" (which refers to lineal descent from a mythical ancestor, Sri Raja Batak). Both Maesa and this club, like the earlier union, reflect the tendency to form broad ethnic or regional organizations in the early days of migration when population is small. As numbers increase, other organizations may grow along lines appropriate to ethnic group cultures. North Sulawesi migrants have formed subregional homeland associations, called *rukun*, whereas Batak have formed associations of patrilineal clans (*marga*).

Maesa, for example, held a U.S. Labor Day picnic near Los Angeles in 1997, at which its chairperson urged unity among those from the same ethnic homeland: "We are all Minahasans, and all Indonesians." At the same picnic, also urging unity, were leaders of two *rukun* groups—one for people from the northern peninsula of North Sulawesi, another for people from the Lake Tondano region. Both are dedicated to preserving their local subcultures in Los Angeles, and there is even an umbrella association of *rukun* groups, Homeland Associations of California. Such groups proliferate as their numbers allow whereas Maesa serves a broader regional constituency and has expanded to other U.S. cities.

The Batak Club's role has declined somewhat because of the growth of associations of clans that are central to Batak culture and that manage life cycle rituals and social support for their members. The first Batak clan association in the United States, the Organization of the Descendants of Raja Sonak Malela's Daughters and Sons in California, was formed in southern California in 1997. It consists of four named clans that descend from a common ancestor, Raja Sonak Malela. Others have followed.

"Unity in Diversity"

Indonesian migrants gain support from their ethnic and religious identities and associations. They must adapt to racial minority status, and Chinese Indonesians experience stress from having been a racial minority in Indonesia and then becoming one in the United States. These migrants share a problem faced by all of their compatriots in Indonesia: how to achieve and maintain a sense of community while holding to primordial identities that provide social and other supports. Indonesians in the United States can achieve greater intergroup harmony because the forces that threaten relations between ethnic, racial, and religious groups in Indonesia—economic competition, land rights, political power, and religious animosity—are muted or absent among them in their new home.

Clark E. Cunningham

See Appendix A

See also Asian Americans; Chinese Americans; Community Cohesion; Ethnic Group; Religion

Further Readings

Cunningham, Clark E. 1997. "Indonesians." Pp. 433–438 in *American Immigrant Cultures: Builders of a Nation*, vol. 1, edited by D. Levinson and M. Ember. New York: Macmillan Reference USA.

Cunningham, Clark E. 2007. "Unity and Diversity Among Indonesian Migrants to the United States." Chapter 6 in *Emerging Voices: The Experiences of the Under Represented Asian Americans*, edited by H. Ling. Brunswick, NJ: Rutgers University Press.

Furnivall, John Sydenham. 1938. *Netherlands India.* Cambridge, UK: Cambridge University Press.

Furnivall, John Sydenham. 1956. *Colonial Policy and Practice.* New York: New York University Press/

Klinken, Gerry van. 2003. "Ethnicity in Indonesia." In *Ethnicity in Asia*, edited by C. Mackerras. London: Routledge Curzon.

INFORMAL ECONOMY

The concept of *informal economy* was first used in academia by a British anthropologist, Keith Hart, who was astonished by the busy traders in the streets and markets of Accra, Ghana. He had not seen anything like this in England, and for lack of a better way to present his findings, he referred to this as the "urban informal sector." His research, begun in 1971, was published in 1973 in the *Journal of Modern African Studies*. During the same period, the International Labor Organization (ILO) undertook a major study in Kenya where researchers tested the concept of the informal sector. That study, published in 1972, became an influential document globally; researchers could now affix a label to the many trades and occupations that were previously left undefined in academia. In 2002, the ILO added a modified definition distinguishing between "decent and indecent work."

Initially, most of the informal economic activities were associated with Third World cities. Indeed, most of the literature on the informal sector was from Latin American, Asian, and African cities. In the late 1980s, Alejandro Portes and Manuel Castells focused on industrialized cities of Europe and North America, showing that various entrepreneurial activities in these places fit the same label as those in the cities of the non-industrialized nations. This entry examines phenomena of both informal economic activities in developing nations and industrialized countries.

Definition

The informal economy can be defined as all those economic activities that operate without state regulation. Most of these businesses also tend not to pay taxes and usually operate in zones that are not meant for them, hence, they experienced frequent harassment by local or national police. Informal economic activities are usually considered legitimate but may be seen as illegal, depending on where the operation is taking place; for example, a food seller in a main downtown street who is not licensed to be on that street—the food is legitimate, but selling it in this location is illegal. Researchers on the informal economy have tended to distinguish between the legitimate and illegitimate economic activities. The former activities are seen as legitimate in society but may be considered illegal by government authorities mainly because of zones where they operate. Illegitimate economic activities involve the so-called "Black market": drug selling and trafficking, money laundering, and prostitution (adult and children, human trafficking). Though some researchers may view illegitimate activities as part of the informal economy, many believe these activities border on criminality. When the concept of informal economy is used, especially in Africa, most people think of the legitimate rather than the illegitimate activities.

Another defining character of the informal economy is entrepreneurship. Most of those involved in the informal economy are entrepreneurs to the core because they have to come up with their own business ideas and figure out how to fund those ideas. Work in the informal economy is not like a formal job where people present their credentials to become employed. To earn a living in the cities, especially in the Third World, many people have had to be innovative, driven by their acumen and entrepreneurship. In turn, this has made the informal economy grow and expand, particularly in all Third World cities, where it has become the main employer of the majority of the urban dwellers.

Key Issues

Gender and the Informal Economy

Just as the larger society features gender differentials, so does the informal economy. A large percentage of women earn a living from various informal economic activities (various forms of trade, for example, cooked food selling, vegetable and fruit selling, hair dressing, being maids, etc.). What is notable is that the women tend to occupy the lower ranks of the informal economic activities. The city authorities in various countries also tend to harass the women's economic activities much more than those of the men.

The men may be involved in more lucrative economic activities such as car mechanics, metal artisan drum selling, and carpentry. The additional harassment may be because women are not in a position to interact closely with male police officers as the men do and are therefore more vulnerable. Women, however, continue to play a big role in the informal economy. For example, the 2006 Nobel Prize went to the Grameen Bank of Bangladesh, the world's largest bank for poor people, and its founder, Muhammad Yunus. Most of its borrowers are women.

Informal Economy and (Urban) Governance

One of the current and future challenges especially in Third World cities is how to govern in such a way that the laws and rules will allow for the formal and informal economies to coexist. Given much evidence that has been shown in the last 30 years about the importance of the informal economy, policies and programs should bring the informal economy (which is itself part of the city economy and, by extension, part of the national economy) more into the fold of legitimacy so that it is subjected to little or no harassment. Licensing and moderate tax systems could help those involved to feel more confidence and to expand their business.

Informal Economy and Social Networks (Urbanization)

Social networks have been part of the mortar that drives the growth of the informal economy and in turn continues to expand the process of urbanization especially in Third World cities. The movement of people from rural to urban areas has continued to grow, with support for new arrivals coming from social networks (friends, relatives, people from the same rural region, people of the same religion). People do not move to towns blindly; neither do they just bump into an economic activity to operate in the city. Indeed, the informal economy is not easy to enter without the right contacts because it is competitive; even getting the right information about where to start a new business can be challenging without social networks.

This is another area in which women tend to be at a disadvantage because men tend to have more helpful social networks, especially for start-up capital. Getting the money to start a business is a problem for most informal economy entrepreneurs. The hope of engaging in an informal economic activity continues to be a "major pull" to the cities for the youth, both men and women, and this has been contributing to the ever-expanding urbanization in Third World regions, especially in Africa.

Kinuthia Macharia

See also Ethnic Enclave, Economic Impact of; Gender and Race, Intersection of; Wealth Distribution

Further Readings

Hart, Keith, 1973. "Informal Income Opportunities and Urban Employment in Ghana." *Journal of Modern African Studies* 11:61–89.

International Labor Organization. 1972. *Employment, Incomes and Employment: A Strategy for Increasing Productive Employment in Kenya.* Geneva, Switzerland: ILO.

International Labor Organization. 2002. *Decent Work and the Informal Economy,* 90th Session, International Labor Conference, 2002, Geneva, International Labor Organization (ILO).

Macharia, Kinuthia, 1997. *Social and Political Dynamics of the Informal Economy in African Cities: Nairobi and Harare.* Lanham, MD: University Press of America.

Portes, Alejandro, Manuel Castells, and Lauren Benton, eds. 1989. *The Informal Economy: Studies in Advanced and Less Developed Countries.* Baltimore, MD: Johns Hopkins University Press.

INSTITUTIONAL DISCRIMINATION

Discrimination is the negative treatment of one individual or group by another individual or group based upon some characteristic of that group, such as gender, race or ethnicity, or age because of a belief that the characteristic justifies such negative treatment. *Institutional discrimination* occurs when that negative or unfair treatment takes place at or is performed by an institution as a result not of individual belief but as a result of the structure, organization, or practices of that institution. Scholars, policymakers, and members of the general population have struggled with the effects and significance of racial and ethnic discrimination in the multiethnic, multiracial U.S. society, one that is based on equality and, in theory, praises and accepts differences, yet so often accepts and at times promotes both individual and institutional discrimination.

As described in this entry, institutional discrimination may be more difficult to detect than individual discrimination and is certainly more difficult to address precisely because it requires a review or analysis of the practices, policies, and structure of what are often complex and multilayered bodies: institutions. These institutions may be public, such as governments or government agencies, schools, or public universities, or they may be private, such as businesses, private colleges or universities, corporations, or media outlets.

Racism and Institutional Discrimination

Individual discrimination is an almost natural result or outgrowth of racism, which is the belief that one group of people is inherently superior to another. When a person has such a belief concerning members of another race, and sometimes another ethnic group, that belief makes the person feel justified in pursuing negative, often harmful acts that others see as discrimination. In the case of institutional discrimination, the negative or harmful behavior may not be the result of individual racism or of the beliefs of individuals currently involved with the institution; nevertheless, the negative impact is felt by members of the race or ethnic group affected.

The Housing Case

When the Federal Housing Administration (FHA) preferred to guarantee home mortgages in "stable" neighborhoods or for newer homes, as was the case as early as the 1940s, it practiced institutional discrimination. Blacks were far more likely than Whites to live in less stable neighborhoods because of both a lack of money and individual discrimination, which limited their housing choices and their employment opportunities. Further, Blacks were far less likely than were Whites to be able to afford to purchase newer homes because of a significant degree of discrimination in the labor market at that time. As a result, Blacks were far less likely than were Whites to receive the FHA guarantees. This all had a negative impact on their housing options and choices and ultimately on the neighborhoods in which they lived.

Although the U.S. government had guidelines for the FHA that clearly indicated a preference for supporting single-race neighborhoods, the practice of supporting mortgage lending for newer homes or in "stable" neighborhoods was institutional discrimination. It may or may not have been the result of the racism or beliefs of any individual connected to the FHA at that time. Indeed, it may have been just a wise business decision, given that newer homes and homes in more stable neighborhoods are better investments.

Still, Blacks felt the effects disproportionately, and to end the discrimination, the practices, policies, and priorities of the institution had to be changed. Because individuals involved with the institution may well claim that they have no negative feelings toward, ideas about, or feelings of superiority regarding Blacks, those changes would be somewhat more difficult to effect.

The Education Case

If a university has a policy of legacy admissions—that is, an admissions policy that favors the children of alumni of that institution—that university could be seen as engaging in institutional discrimination because it is making a decision on the basis of a variable other than merit, the accepted standard for admission. Also, Blacks and members of some ethnic groups are less likely to be related to alumni because many colleges and universities systematically excluded Blacks until the 1960s.

This does not mean or suggest that someone in the university administration or the admissions office desires to discriminate against Blacks and therefore devised the policy to do so. Indeed, it may be the case that no one even considered race or ethnicity when deciding upon the policy. Rather, it may have resulted from efforts by alumni to have their children favored in the admissions process, or from a belief by administrators that such a policy helped build tradition, something highly prized on college campuses. Still, the negative effects are felt by Blacks and by members of ethnic groups whose parents may have been denied admission or had their admission limited for reasons other than merit.

Reverse Discrimination

During the past 20 years or so, a heated debate among scholars, policymakers, and politicians has taken place regarding what is often referred to as reverse discrimination. *Reverse discrimination* tends to be defined as practices and policies of institutions that discriminate in favor of Blacks, members of various non-White ethnic groups, and in some cases women. Critics argue that such practices and policies grew out of what may have been well-intentioned efforts by institutions to either ensure that they no longer discriminated against Blacks or members of certain ethnic groups or to compensate for past discrimination. Some universities, for example, acknowledge that they had in the past systematically failed to admit qualified Black students solely because of their race. In an effort to make up for this discrimination, they devised plans to admit more Blacks than might have been admitted via the normal admissions process.

Other universities were less concerned with past acts of discrimination than with whether their current policies had a negative impact on the admission of Blacks or members of certain ethnic groups, including and especially Latinos. The belief is that Blacks and Latinos are just as intelligent, just as capable as Whites of being admitted to universities, and just as capable of doing well in those universities as Whites, but the admissions numbers suggest that they have not been admitted in numbers proportionate to their numbers in the society or among college-age students. To some, the numbers alone suggest institutional discrimination and require adjustments by the institutions to either guard against current institutional discrimination or to make up for past discrimination.

The same arguments hold for non-educational institutions as well. Latinos and Blacks have argued that they should be represented in all areas and at all levels of institutional life in numbers reflecting their presence in the society. According to this argument, if Blacks are one-third of the population of a city, then they should represent one-third of the workforce of that city, especially in public life, given that public institutions have a special obligation, according to this argument and many court cases, to avoid racial discrimination. Many Blacks and Latinos then believe that if Blacks or Latinos are one-third of the population of a city, then they should be one-third of the police officers, one-third of the firefighters, and one-third of the teachers, assuming that enough Latinos or Blacks want those positions. If they are not, according to this argument, then those institutions—the fire department, the police department, and the school system—are guilty of institutional discrimination.

Given that there are often many more Blacks or other underrepresented minorities who want to be admitted to a university or hired by a city than the available positions will allow, some Whites may have to be denied admission or not hired to achieve the goal of diversifying the workforce or the university. Some see this as discrimination against those Whites, or reverse discrimination because they are being denied based almost solely because of their race. For a variety of reasons including attendance at elementary and high schools that often fail to properly prepare their students, some Blacks and Latinos find themselves ill prepared for some standardized tests. Given that such tests often serve as the gatekeepers to certain jobs and for admission to most colleges and universities many see them as inherently discriminatory, and suggest that institutions that use them are guilty of institutional discrimination because they use screening devices that systematically and unfairly limit the opportunities for Blacks and some Latinos.

Whites, for reasons that can be debated almost forever, tend to perform better on the standardized tests that are used by various institutions to determine who is hired and who is admitted. Because some Whites are denied admission or are not hired whereas some Blacks and Latinos are admitted or hired with what are seen as lower grades or lower test scores, some suggest that those Whites are being discriminated against. If, however, both institutional and individual discrimination can be traced at some point to racism, as most scholars suggest, then reverse discrimination is unlikely, for it is unlikely that anyone in this society believes or has believed that Blacks or Latinos are inherently superior to Whites.

Still, practices such as affirmative action, which is a policy that requires institutions, often voluntarily, though sometimes by law, to take positive, affirmative steps to ensure that racial, ethnic, or gender discrimination does not take place in institutions, are seen by many Whites, and some Blacks, as reverse discrimination, or policies that favor Blacks, no matter how good the initial reason or laudable the goals, to the detriment of Whites. Some Blacks also suggest that such policies actually harm Blacks more than they help because they suggest that Blacks require help to be hired or admitted, and this suggests that Blacks are inferior.

Discrimination Against Businesses

Institutions hire a host of private companies to perform many tasks. They hire building companies to build schools or libraries. They hire consultants. They hire contractors to build bridges, or to supply food to cafeterias. Often, the decision to hire is a function of public bidding, and those bids must meet often complex criteria. On many occasions, the work requires that the company be a large company because the job is very large. However, in the past in the United States, institutions had a host of practices and policies that restricted the growth of companies owned by Blacks and some by Latinos more recently. If lenders would not lend to Black-owned companies, or institutions did not in the past award contracts to Latino-owned companies even though the bidding was to be open to all qualified bidders, then those companies owned by members of certain racial or ethnic groups could not get much business and therefore could not grow.

If an institution now requires that the bidders for certain jobs or contracts be large because the job, such as building a large building or highway, is large, then Black and Latino companies will be at a disadvantage mostly because of practices and policies employed by institutions long ago. They were denied the opportunity to grow because they were owned by members of a racial group or ethnic group that was not favored, and then denied the opportunity to obtain the contract because they could not grow. It may be that one person years ago practiced individual discrimination and ensured that members of certain racial or ethnic groups were favored but others were excluded. Today, however, the discrimination is institutional because it is based not on the concerns of an individual, but on the requirements for the contract, which systematically limits the opportunities for small companies, and many Black and Latino companies had no choice but to be small.

If an institution decides to structure the bidding process so that those companies owned by members of groups that had experienced this institutional discrimination in the past have a better opportunity to win the bid, then some suggest that that institution is engaging in reverse discrimination because it now has policies and practices that may favor companies owned by members of groups discriminated against in the past over companies owned by members of a group favored or discriminated in favor of in the past. Others see this as only a fair response to past discrimination by institutions, and a safeguard against continued institutional discrimination.

In the end, this is not an academic debate as much as a power struggle. Many Whites do not want to concede their superior position in this society that they often believe that they have earned, whereas many Blacks and Latinos believe that they deserve more power because of past discrimination, and because of their numbers in the society. Institutional discrimination was one of the factors that limited that power and the opportunities that typically go along with power. As the global economy continues to limit various opportunities in vast parts of the United States, the debate is likely to become even more heated. Fewer opportunities means more competition, and the numbers of Blacks and members of various ethnic groups clamoring for less discrimination by the institutions involved with those opportunities is growing.

William Alfred Sampson

See also Affirmative Action in Education; Affirmative Action in the Workplace; Carmichael, Stokely; Critical Race Theory; Discrimination; Discrimination in Housing; Northern Ireland, Racism in; Racism; Reverse Discrimination

Further Readings

Banks, William M. 1996. *Black Intellectuals: Race and Responsibility in American Life.* New York. Norton.

Barone-Jeanquart, S. and Uma Sekaran. 1996. "Institutional Racism: An Empirical Study." *Journal of Social Psychology* 136:477–448.

Bielby, William. 1987. "Modern Prejudice and Institutional Barriers to Equal Employment Opportunities for Minorities." *Journal of Social Issues* 43:79–84.

Fredrickson, George M. 2002. *Racism: A Short History*. Princeton, NJ: Princeton University Press.

Jalata, Asafa. 2002. "Revisiting the Black Struggle: Lessons for the 21st Century." *Journal of Black Studies* 33(1):86–116.

McWhorter, John. 2000. *Losing the Race*. New York: Free Press.

Merton, Robert. 1968. *Social Theory and Social Structure*. New York: Free Press.

INTEGRATION

See RESEGREGATION; SCHOOL DESEGREGATION, ATTITUDES CONCERNING

INTELLIGENCE TESTS

Intelligence tests are widely used in modern industrialized societies to measure various kinds of mental abilities. Some people argue that their results may reveal cultural differences by race and class rather than underlying intelligence. This entry briefly describes the origins of the most famous of these instruments and looks more generally at what the tests attempt to measure and why their results are sometimes challenged.

Early Tests

Serious scientific concern with human intelligence and its causes and consequences began somewhat independently in England and France in the middle of the 19th century. In England, Sir Francis Galton attacked the problem by characterizing the accomplishments of highly talented individuals, but he failed to provide any reliable and valid measurement instruments (mental ability tests).

The Stanford-Binet Test

In France, Alfred Binet developed the first true intelligence tests in response to requests from the French Ministry of Instruction to provide reliable diagnosis of mental ability levels in children considered subnormal. Binet's famous test was made up of a number of different measures of mental ability (now called subtests), and some were incorporated into the Stanford-Binet (S-B), which was made famous by Louis Terman when IQ tests were introduced into the United States at the beginning of the 20th century. The current S-B is in its fifth edition (S-B5) and a brief description of the ten subtests can be found at the publisher's Web site http://www.riverpub.com/products/sb5/details.html.

The WAIS for Adults

The S-B was initially constructed to measure intelligence in children and did not measure intelligence in adults adequately. Consequently, in the late 1930s, David Wechsler, a clinical psychologist working with patients in the Bellevue hospital in New York City, developed the Wechsler-Bellevue Scale of Intelligence, which in 1955 morphed into the Wechsler Adult Intelligence Scales (WAIS). The WAIS is now in its third edition (WAIS-III). A version of the WAIS for children is called the Wechsler Intelligence Scale for Children (WISC, now in its fourth edition).

Like the S-B and the WAIS, intelligence tests have generally been developed for practical purposes: to aid educators, clinical psychologists, military recruiters, employment services, and so on. Apart from these famous IQ tests, numerous intelligence tests and specialized measures of mental ability are available. The Buros Institute of Mental Measurements provides reviews of nearly 4,000 tests. The Educational Testing Service has a test collection of more than 25,000 instruments and other mental measurement devices.

What Tests Measure

Employing modern factor analytic methods, all mental ability tests are positively correlated because they share a broad common factor called g, after the work of the English Psychologist Charles Spearman; g is the underlying theoretical construct most intelligence tests are trying to approximate with their IQ score. Of course, g is not the only mental ability; it is simply the broadest one. According to Carroll, there are about ten other broad mental ability factors and numerous narrow abilities.

A typical intelligence test like the WAIS-III or the S-B5 is made up of a group of specific mental ability tests that are believed to provide a good assessment of the theoretical construct, "human intelligence" or g. Consequently, it is often argued, particularly by those who dislike intelligence tests, that intelligence is whatever an intelligence test measures. The explicit implication is that every intelligence test measures something different, sometimes a little different and sometimes a lot different. It turns out that this argument is incorrect. Most authors of intelligence test batteries were correct in their assertion that a reasonably broad sample of mental ability tests give a good approximation to the general factor or g and that the g in one battery is highly related to the g in another battery.

Intelligence is taken to be a general mental capacity that, among other things, involves the ability to reason, plan, solve problems, think abstractly, comprehend complex ideas, learn quickly, and learn from experience. This general mental capacity is known to be influenced significantly by both genetic and environmental factors. Tests that have revealed differences among racial and ethnic groups also differ in these factors. Although the tests have generally been shown to be reliable and valid in many different groups, they have still been challenged. Some critics of intelligence tests argue that the tests evaluate experiences that are not shared by all racial and ethnic groups; rather, they test the experiences of the privileged. The explanation of group differences in general mental capacity, including gender differences, continues to be controversial.

Thomas J. Bouchard, Jr.

See also Bell Curve, The; Educational Performance and Attainment; Eugenics; Labeling; Pipeline; Self-Fulfilling Prophecy; Social Inequality; Social Mobility; Tracking

Further Readings

Carroll, John B. 1993. *Human Cognitive Abilities: A Survey of Factor-Analytic Studies.* New York: Cambridge University Press.

Flynn, James R. 2007. *What Is Intelligence?* Cambridge, UK: Cambridge University Press.

Gottfredson, Linda S. 1997. "Editorial: Mainstream Science on Intelligence: An Editorial with 52 Signatories, History, and Bibliography." *Intelligence* 24:13–24.

Johnson, W., T. J. Bouchard, Jr., R. F. Krueger, M. McGue, and I. I. Gottesman. 2004. "Just One *g:* Consistent Results from Three Test Batteries." *Intelligence* 32:95–107.

Johnson, W., J. te Nijenhuis, and T. J. Bouchard, Jr. 2007. "Replication of the Hierarchical Visual-Perceptual-Image Rotation Model in de Wolff and Buiten's 1963 Battery of 46 Tests of Mental Ability." *Intelligence* 35:69–81.

Kuncel, N. R. and S. A. Hezlett. 2007. "Standardized Tests Predict Graduate Students' Success." *Science* 315:1080–1081, and references therein as well as replies and refutations.

Schmidt, F. L. and J. E. Hunter. 2004. "General Mental Ability in the World of Work: Occupational Attainment and Job Performance." *Journal of Personality and Social Psychology* 86:162–173.

INTERCULTURAL COMMUNICATION

Intercultural communication is communication among people from two or more cultures. It exists in contexts such as traveling, immigration, business transactions, diplomatic negotiations, and multicultural or multinational corporations. The increased diversity in the United States and globalization in the world has made intercultural communication an indispensable part of everyday life. On a daily basis, people may meet and need to communicate with someone from a different race, ethnic group, or nation, someone who may have a different set of values, beliefs, norms, habits, and practices. When these differences are not accepted, tolerated, and appreciated, culture shock and cultural clash often take place, causing misunderstandings, stereotypes, prejudice, and even conflict and violence. Thus, many scholars agree that it is imperative to learn about other cultures, for the self-benefits and for world peace. This entry outlines the history of intercultural communication studies in the United States, major approaches in intercultural communication studies, and major theoretical frameworks that have guided the discipline.

History of Studies

Intercultural communication studies in the United States began after World War II when the U.S. government established the Foreign Service Institutes (FSI) to prepare business personnel and foreign diplomats working overseas. The FSI offered courses on language variations and nonverbal communication such as the use of voice, gesture, time, and space across cultures. The focus was on skill development and cultural sensitivity training. Culture was narrowly defined in terms of nationality, and being aware of the cultural differences between nations was considered essential to effective communication. This stage was characterized by an interdisciplinary approach to the study of culture and communication. Edward T. Hall, an anthropologist, is regarded as a pioneer of intercultural communication studies in the United States. Today's diversity training programs at workplaces exemplify this training-based model to intercultural education.

From the 1960s to 1980s, the United States experienced an influx of immigrants and sojourners from overseas. To help immigrants adjust to the new culture, some scholars developed models of cultural patterns and provided ways to develop knowledge, attitudes, and skills for effective and appropriate communication in intercultural communication settings. In this period, training, cultural-general knowledge, mindfulness, and individual competency were emphasized. The burden of adjustment was placed on immigrants or sojourners, and the best outcome was believed to be assimilation into the U.S. mainstream culture.

Beginning in the 1990s, some scholars began to challenge the competence-centered approach to intercultural communication studies. These scholars asserted that the previous models overlooked the role of history and power in shaping interracial, interethnic, and international relations. Scholars critically evaluated how the impact of language and media from the dominant group functioned to stereotype, marginalize, oppress, and dehumanize submerged groups; examined the identity development of multicultural individuals and their diasporic experiences; provided communication strategies to empower marginalized groups; and criticized what they saw as cultural imperialism couched in the name of globalization. Today, intercultural communication has expanded its studies from international cultures to include race, gender, ethnicity, sexual orientation, aging, and persons with disability.

Approaches to Communication

Three approaches in intercultural communication studies have been applied and engaged by scholars: the social science approach, the interpretive approach, and the critical approach. The social science approach is generated from the fields of psychology and sociology. It looks at culture as a measurable entity from which communication behavior of a people can be described and predicted. Scholars using this approach gather data by surveys and questionnaires, in what is known as quantitative methodology. The approach assumes that culture is a determining variable that influences communication behavior.

For example, using the construct of individualistic and collectivistic cultures, scholars have predicted communication differences in the manner and frequency with which people use polite language, the degree of directness and indirectness in asking questions, and the emphasis on face or clarity in conversations among people of different cultures. Although the social science approach has been helpful in generating knowledge of culture and communication, it has been criticized for making broad generalizations about cultures and being insensitive to the native people under study.

The interpretive approach is rooted in the disciplines of ethnography and anthropology. In contrast to the social science approach, the interpretive approach treats culture as being created and maintained through communication and assumes that human behavior cannot be predicted and that people's perception of the world is subjective. This approach employs the methods of interviews, field studies, and participant observation.

The goal of this approach is not to predict communication behavior but, rather, to describe and understand it. This approach has been used by scholars to study culture and communication in specific contexts or of a particular group of people in depth. The approach examines how the use of core symbols, rituals, and discursive practices communicate, enact, preserve, or construct a culture, how communicative practices are related to cultural norms, and how meanings are interpreted based on specific contexts and cultural orientations. A lack of a comparative focus and potential bias in the interpretation of other cultures are considered limitations of this approach.

The critical approach in intercultural communication studies emphasizes how historical, political, and social contexts affect the outcome of communication in shaping perception, identity, and power relations. Critical scholars are influenced by philosophical orientations of cultural studies, postcolonialism, and postmodernism. The purpose of the critical approach is not to describe, understand, and predict culture and communication, but to critique and make changes in discursive practices that perpetuate and reinforce social injustices, discursive oppression, and human alienation.

Scholars using this approach consider culture as a site of struggle that is filled with contestation of meanings and negotiation of identities related to historical contexts and power relations. The study of cultures, for critical scholars, is to raise consciousness among, give voice to, and provide strategies for marginalized individuals to resist oppression and empower themselves. The data scholars use are typically textual materials such as speeches, magazine advertisements, narratives, media messages and images, and Internet exchanges. This approach is often used by scholars in the study of race, gender, class, and the Third World population, where voices may be muted or deemed worthless by dominant cultures. Though this approach has its strength in providing a macro perspective and critical analyses, some scholars consider it as missing a face-to-face interaction with the members of a certain culture and lacking guidelines for improving intercultural competency.

Major Theories

Theories on Value Orientation

Early intercultural communication scholars were interested in understanding cultural differences as a way to raise cultural sensitivity and improve effective communication. To do so, they have identified different value orientations. For example, cultures are described as having different perceptions of human nature, having different time orientations, and exhibiting different kinds of relationships with nature and among people.

Further, cultures have been classified as individualistic or collectivistic cultures, with the former placing individual interests above the group's and the latter sacrificing the individual interests for the sake of the group. Cultures are also divided into high- or low-context cultures. High-context cultures are believed to value social relationships, use an indirect communication style, and think in spiral fashion. Low-context cultures are supposed to value individual autonomy, use a direct communication style, and think in a linear manner.

These contrasting frameworks on cultural value orientations have been criticized as too simplistic, creating overgeneralizations and reinforcing stereotypes. In response, some scholars have created the cultural synergy model, recognizing that a successful intercultural communication must be based on a collaborative effort of people with different value orientations to achieve a common goal. The model assumes that participants in an intercultural communication mutually negotiate their cultural differences, making efforts to adapt to each other's cultural values and practices.

Theories on Process

Another group of theories on intercultural communication describe the process and challenges an individual faces in intercultural situations. The most popular ones are the anxiety and uncertainty management theory, the communication accommodation theory, and the intercultural adaptation theory. The anxiety and uncertainty management theory assumes that the challenges of intercultural encounters consist of anxiety and uncertainty about the new culture. The goal of intercultural communication is to seek information to reduce ambiguity, anxiety, and uncertainty. People with strong self-esteem, flexible attitudes, and cognitive complexity are better able to manage anxiety, reduce uncertainty, and explain and predict others' behavior.

The communication accommodation theory describes three communication processes in intercultural situations concerning the use of language: convergence, divergence, and maintenance. *Convergence* is characterized by adapting one's speech behavior to the intercultural partner to show solidarity and seek approval. *Divergence* refers to choosing a different speech behavior from the intercultural partner as a way to show one's own cultural pride and emphasize the cultural differences. *Maintenance* is the type of communication in which one sustains his or her own speech behavior without considering the other person. In intercultural encounters, individuals strategically choose one of the styles over others depending on the contexts and the person's self-perceived identity.

The intercultural adaptation model discusses the process of culture shock by sojourners in four stages: honeymoon, crisis, adjustment, and biculturalism. The honeymoon period is characterized by the person's fascination with and excitement about the new culture at the initial stage. The crisis period takes place when the person begins to experience confusion, frustration, and hostility on a daily basis because of cultural clash. At this stage, the person may exhibit behavior of cultural superiority or severe depression. With time and effort, the person will gradually adapt to new ways of thinking and behaving in the new culture (the third stage). Moreover, the person will think more positively about the new culture and communicate more effectively in the host culture. In the final stage of biculturalism, the person has become comfortable and appreciative of the new culture and has developed a dual cultural identity.

Other scholars believe that intercultural adaptation is not a linear process and may not end with biculturalism in all cases. Rather, adaptation may manifest in four different outcomes: assimilation, separation, integration, and marginalization. *Assimilation* refers to those individuals who choose or are pressured to adapt to the new culture and in the process abandon their own original culture and language. *Separation* is to retain one's original culture and separate oneself from the new culture by choice. However, separation can become a forced segregation when the government imposes it through laws and policies. *Integration* shows the individual's attempts to combine one's original culture with the host culture. *Marginalization* describes individuals who do not feel they are accepted by either the host culture or their own original culture; this may be caused either by the government's policy, societal attitudes, or personal perception. All these models deal with intercultural relationships and address the immigrants and sojourners with an objective of raising intercultural awareness, helping to understand the process, and cultivating intercultural competency for both those coming to a new culture and members of the host society.

Theories on Impact

In recent years, some intercultural communication scholars have used critical frameworks to analyze intercultural communication process in terms of power relations. One of the frameworks is the theory of Whiteness, which asserts that White people in the United States have enjoyed unearned privileges and their norms have become the standard, thus creating racism, discrimination, social injustice, and discursive oppression toward people of color. To reach effective and ethical intercultural communication, this perspective holds, White people must be aware of and unpack their privileges, and the society must provide environments for multiples voices.

An example of this is described in the co-cultural theory. In the communication between dominant groups and nondominant groups, the dominant group will use language that supports its dominant perception and practice whereas members of nondominant groups find themselves operating in a communication system that does not represent their experiences and values. Thus, they will face a dilemma of conforming to or resisting the dominant ways of communicating.

In the international arena, scholars have turned to the notions of cultural imperialism developed in 1920s in the critique of popular culture, especially U.S. domination of the resources and media market in the world and its implications on intercultural communication. These scholars believe that people are informed about other cultures from popular media and cultural products. Often, the media representations of other cultures are problematic, contributing to misconceptions and stereotypes of other cultures.

In short, understanding theories and practices of intercultural communication is an important part of multicultural literacy. Scholars have taken diverse approaches and different perspectives in the studies of cultures and how cultures interact. Challenges remain for achieving social equality and harmony among people of different cultures and groups.

Xing Lu

See also Acculturation; Assimilation; Cultural Relativism; Ethnicity, Negotiating; Intergroup Relations, Racetalk; Surveying; Spanglish

Further Readings

Gonzalez, Alberto, Marsha Houston, and Victoria Chen. 2004. *Our Voices: Essays in Culture, Ethnicity, and Communication*. 4th ed. Los Angeles, CA: Roxbury.

Gudykunst, William B. and Young Yun Kim. 1992. *Readings on Communicating with Strangers*. New York: McGraw-Hill.

Hall, Edward T. and Mildred Reed Hall. 1987. *Understanding Cultural Differences*. Yarmouth, ME: Intercultural Press.

Kluckholn, Clyde and Fred Strodbeck. 1961. *Variations in Value Orientation*. Evanston, IL: Row, Peterson.

Hofstede, Gert H. 1980. "National Cultures in Four Dimensions." *International Studies of Management and Organization*, 13:46–74.

Martin, Judith N. and Thomas K. Nakayama. 2007. *Intercultural Communication in Contexts*. 4th ed. Boston, MA: McGraw-Hill.

Orbe, Mark P. 1998. *Constructing Co-Cultural Theory: An Explication of Culture, Power, and Communication*. Thousand Oaks, CA: Sage.

Tomlinson, John 1991. *Cultural Imperialism*. Baltimore, MD: Johns Hopkins University Press.

INTERGROUP RELATIONS, SURVEYING

The National Conference for Community and Justice (NCCJ), called the National Conference of Christians and Jews when it was established in 1927, is one of the nation's first intergroup relations organizations dedicated to opposing bias, bigotry, prejudice, and intergroup conflict. As part of this mission, the NCCJ has commissioned a series of telephone surveys on intergroup relations known as Taking America's Pulse I, II, and III (TAP-I, TAP-II, TAP-III). Data from TAP-II and TAP-III are available from the Roper Center for Public Opinion Research at the University of Connecticut. The surveys provide a snapshot of changing perceptions of relationships among groups varying by race/ethnicity, age, gender, class, and sexual preference. This entry describes the surveys and summarizes the findings.

The Survey Process

TAP-I, carried out in 1993 by Louis Harris and Associates, interviewed 2,755 adults living in the United States. TAP-II, conducted in 2000 by Princeton Survey Research Associates, interviewed 2,584 U.S. adults. Oversamples of Blacks, Hispanics, and Asians were drawn in TAP-II, yielding interviews with 995 non-Hispanic Whites, 709 non-Hispanic Blacks, 572 Hispanics (who can be of any race), 198 Asians, and 100 of other or mixed races. TAP-III, conducted in 2005 by Princeton Survey Research Associates, surveyed 2,558 adult U.S. residents. As in 2000, there were oversamples of Asians, Blacks, and Hispanics. Of the total sample, 942 were non-Hispanic Whites, 677 non-Hispanic Blacks, 630 Hispanics, 200 Asians, and 109 of other and mixed races.

The TAP surveys have greater depth and wider coverage than most studies of intergroup relations. First, by repeating many items over time, the TAP surveys examine changes in intergroup relations. Second, by oversampling major minority groups, they are able to consider not only what the majority thinks of various minorities, but also how the minorities view both the majority and each other. Third, the TAP surveys are particularly comprehensive in the wide range of groups covered. These include races and ethnicities, which form the core of most studies of intergroup relations, and religions, socioeconomic groups, age groups, sexual orientations, and gender. Finally, the surveys cover many topics, including both attitudes, such as judgments on group influence, intergroup harmony, closeness, and level of discrimination, and behaviors such as intergroup contact and personal experiences of discrimination.

Survey Results

Among key results from the TAP surveys are the following: The public realizes that intergroup relations need much improvement. A small plurality (58%) say they are not satisfied with the current state of intergroup relations, and 75% of participants acknowledge that the country as a whole has serious group tensions. Although most people see intergroup conflict as a problem, most do not view it as a top priority; rather, they believe the problem largely occurs elsewhere in the country and is not part of their daily lives.

The inventories of social groups in general indicate that many are neither thought of nor treated equally. First, there is a definite pecking order in social groups; for example, many people say they are unfamiliar with Muslims and atheists or that they don't feel close to other groups, such as gays and lesbians, atheists, and Muslims. Only 10% to 12% of U.S. residents felt close or very close to Muslims and atheists. Second, most U.S. residents acknowledge that all groups except Whites suffer a great deal or some discrimination; some, such as Muslims, gays and Lesbians, and the poor, are viewed as especially subject to discrimination. Third, a plurality believes that American Indians, Blacks, the elderly, Hispanics, women, and the disabled have less influence than they should have. Fourth, although intergroup contact is high for many groups, a few groups, such as Muslims, atheists, and American Indians, have rather limited contact with other U.S. residents. Finally, intergroup relations go well beyond race relations. Although races and ethnicities are important groups, they are only one set of groups along with social classes, genders, age groups, and others that make up U.S. society.

Differences by Race/Ethnicity

Evidence of social inequalities also appear for races and ethnicities. First, participants say that intergroup harmony between some groups (e.g., Asians and Whites) is higher but much lower for others (e.g., Whites and Blacks; Blacks and Asians). Second, in the areas of education, health, management promotions, equal justice, police treatment, and media coverage, a plurality recognizes that the four main minority races/ethnicities have notably less opportunity than Whites have. On average, about 45% to 47% believe that Blacks and Hispanics have equal opportunity with that of Whites. Asians are deemed to be better off, with 59% of participants seeing their opportunities as on a par with Whites. Third, the life satisfaction of Blacks and, to a lesser extent, Hispanics, is seen as much lower than that of Whites and Asians.

Fourth, interracial/ethnic contact is fairly limited. Although most non-Whites have contact with Whites as friends, neighbors, co-congregants, and coworkers, contact by outsiders with minority groups is much more restricted. For example, most non-Blacks have contact with Blacks only as friends. In each of the types of contact surveyed, most non-Hispanics, non-Asians, and non–American Indians lack contact with those respective groups. Thus, intergroup contact is limited and often restricted to just a few roles (e.g., as employee, but not as supervisor, neighbor, or friend).

Fifth, actual experiences of unfair treatment because of race/ethnicity are fairly common, according to participant reports. In a given month, 9.5% of Whites, 21% of Hispanics, 22.5% of Asians, and 32% of Blacks said they experienced discrimination at least once. These reports provide stark testimony that racial and ethnic discrimination remains a common feature of everyday life for many. Finally, when asked about race relations, 36% of U.S. residents still find acceptable the separate but equal model of *Plessy v. Ferguson,* which the Supreme Court overturned as an acceptable legal standard in *Brown v. the Board of Education* in 1954.

The differences in views of tensions, discrimination, intergroup harmony, and other aspects of intergroup relations are magnified when the points of view of Whites, Blacks, Asians, and Hispanics are compared. Compared with Blacks and Hispanics, Whites see a much more benign intergroup landscape with less tension and discrimination and more opportunity. Blacks have the most negative view, finding much more inequality and conflict and wanting to do the most about the problem. Asians and Hispanics generally have an intermediate outlook on issues such as level of inequality and group conflict, but Asians see even less discrimination existing against many groups than Whites perceive.

Differences by Region, Income, and Age

Similarly, just as races and ethnic groups have their own distinct point of view on intergroup relations, important differences show up across regions, community types, educational and income levels, and age cohorts. Every region has a unique perspective shaped by its own history and the relative prominence of the various races and ethnicities within its communities. Differences also exist across community types with rural residents tending to show less support for intergroup equality than those in metropolitan areas show.

Education works in opposing ways. Racial and ethnic minorities are underrepresented in the college-educated group, and Whites in that group are less likely to know disadvantaged minorities. On the other hand, more education tends to expand intergroup contacts and to make people more sympathetic toward intergroup equality. This tends to lead to either the least or best educated being the most likely to recognize intergroup disparities and support efforts to improve intergroup relations.

The other stratification variable, income, shows less notable differences. Higher earners are more distant from the socioeconomically disadvantaged (the poor and people on welfare) and closer to relatively successful minority groups (e.g., Asians and Jews). Opinions about immigrants are mixed. Compared with low earners, the high earners are more supportive of immigration restrictions but have much more positive views of the contributions that immigrants have made. Older generations are most likely to support the traditional, separate-but-equal doctrine and to be reluctant to accept emergent groups such as gays and Lesbians, atheists, and immigrants, but they often feel closer to many other groups—by race, ethnicity, religion, and class—than the younger generation does. The youngest generation is most concerned about intergroup relations and is most likely to see groups as lacking enough influence, but participants in this age group do not perceive especially high levels of discrimination. The youngest generation is also closest to emergent social groups such as gays and Lesbians and atheists. The differences across cohorts are particularly important because cohort turnover means that society will move toward the viewpoints of the younger, emerging cohorts over time.

Interesting Linkages

The clustering of group evaluations indicates that each group has a distinctive, social profile. The same groups do not consistently link together across dimensions, and the clusters often do not form simple and clean categories such as races or religions. However, social classes do tend to distinguish themselves from racial, religious, and ethnic groups and usually cluster together. Also, newer, emergent groups such as gays and Lesbians, atheists, and sometimes recent immigrant groups tend to be linked by how others view them.

Most intergroup attitudes and behaviors are associated with each other in expected ways. Of particular note is the connection between contact with other racial and ethnic groups and greater concern over intergroup relations. More contact is associated with more feelings of closeness, more perception of discrimination, more perception of groups as lacking enough influence, more support for intergroup equality and integration, and less negative views of immigrants.

Most measures of attitudes toward and behaviors concerning intergroup relations show improvement during the last decade, and this progress comes on top of similar gains during the last half-century. For example, feeling close to Blacks was an experience reported by 38% of participants in 1996 and 56% in 2005. Among Blacks, personal experiences of racial discrimination at work during the last month fell from 21% in 1997 to 11% in 2005, and the judgment that Blacks have too much influence dropped from 20% in 1996 to 10% in 2005. The changes are more of the slow-and-steady type, rather than representing breakthroughs or dramatic surges, but because they have generally been in the same direction over time, notable shifts have often occurred.

There is, however, much room for further change. As the large increase in those perceiving a great deal of discrimination against Muslims (from 11% to 35% between 2000 and 2006, before and after the September 11, 2001, terrorist attacks) indicates, events can intrude to stall or reverse improvements in intergroup relations.

Tom W. Smith

See also Brown v. Board of Education; Color Blindness; Contact Hypothesis; Discrimination; Intercultural Communication; Interracial Friendships; Muslim Americans; *Plessy v. Ferguson;* Prejudice; Racetalk

Further Readings

Smith, Tom W. 1998. "Intergroup Relations in Contemporary America: An Overview of Survey Research." In *Intergroup Relations in the United States: Research Perspectives,* edited by W. Winborne and R. Cohen. New York: National Conference of Christians and Jews (NCCJ).

Smith, Tom W. 2000. *Taking America's Pulse II: NCCJ's 2000 Survey of Intergroup Relations in the United States.* New York: National Conference of Christians and Jews (NCCJ).

Smith, Tom W. 2006. *Taking America's Pulse III: Intergroup Relations in Contemporary America.* New York: National Conference of Christians and Jews (NCCJ).

INTERMARRIAGE

Family systems reproduce race by insisting upon endogamy, or marriage within the group. Racial intermarriage, the opposite of endogamy, tends to undermine racial barriers. In any society in which race is important, racial intermarriage will be a focus of legal, social, and political interest. The United States has been a society deeply divided by race from its beginning, as a nation in which slavery was practiced, so the issue of intermarriage has always been important in the United States. This entry describes the history of policy on intermarriage and its wider impact.

The Racial Caste System

Before the civil war, most Blacks in the United States were slaves. Although there had always been some sexual relationships between White (male) slaveowners and Black (female) slaves, White society worked diligently to make these relationships invisible. White U.S. society adopted what was called the "one-drop rule," which meant that anyone with as much as "one drop" of non-White blood could not be considered White. By legal definition, if a White slave master made a Black slave pregnant, her child was Black (because of the "one-drop rule") and a slave as well. Formal marriage was generally not possible between slaves (because slaves had no legal standing), and therefore formal marriage between free Whites and slaves was impossible.

One irony of the one-drop rule was that it was created to clarify racial distinctions, but the rule left White racial status always vulnerable. The discovery of some previously unknown brown or dark ancestor (or even an ancestor who was remembered by someone as dark) would rob all descendants of their Whiteness and therefore of their property and their rights.

With the emancipation of the slaves at the end of the Civil War, White society was suddenly confronted with Blacks as legal equals, at least in theory. White elites professed a horror at the possibility of social mixing on an equal footing with Blacks, and the deepest horror was preserved for the most intimate type of mixing, intermarriage. In the 1864 presidential election, while the Civil War was still raging, proslavery newspaper editors in New York promulgated a hoax implying that Abraham Lincoln and the abolitionists in the North were secretly hoping to marry Blacks to Whites on a mass scale. The proslavery hoax coined the term *miscegenation* for racial intermixing and intermarriage, and such was the fear of intermarriage that White voters in the North had largely abandoned Lincoln's reelection campaign until battlefield victories ensured his reelection.

Interracial couple with their daughter. During the 20th century, several changes occurred that made intermarriage more acceptable and common, undermining the racial caste system of the United States. In addition, the U.S. Supreme Court in Loving v. Virginia (1967) overturned state laws that prohibited marriage across racial lines. Today, many interracial families live in culturally diverse neighborhoods where they find greater acceptability for interracial households.

Source: Ronnie Comeau/iStockphoto.

Whites feared racial intermarriage for several reasons. First, a White person who married a Black person was throwing his or her lot in with Black society in more than just a symbolic way. Such a gesture was sure to be a blow to the social standing of the White person's family (raising questions about whether they were really White after all), so families worked diligently to ensure that their children understood that interracial marriage was taboo. Second, interracial marriage created the possibility that Black descendants could inherit property from White families. Third, 19th-century intellectual justifications for racial differences emphasized the theory that Blacks and Whites were different biological species, a theory that implied that an interracial couple could not reproduce, or that the offspring of a Black-White union would necessarily be weak of mind and body. Although there was plenty of evidence that Blacks and Whites had reproduced successfully, the informality of liaisons during slavery allowed that evidence to be overlooked.

Interracial marriages were such a threat to the racial order that in the aftermath of the Civil War, many states hurried to pass laws making interracial marriage illegal, and these laws were commonly referred to as antimiscegenation laws. The state laws against interracial marriage varied in which groups were prohibited from marrying which other groups, but every such law prohibited Blacks from marrying Whites.

Intermarriage in 20th-Century Law

The 20th century brought several changes that made intermarriage more acceptable and common and that undermined the racial caste system of the United States. The first great Black migration North, around the time of World War I, brought several million Blacks into Northern states, which had never had laws against racial intermarriage, partly because these Northern states had never had many Black residents. Residential segregation grew in the North as Black neighborhoods and ghettos grew, and as Whites found ways to limit their social exposure to Blacks.

Racial intermarriage between Blacks and Whites did not begin to increase in the United States until after

World War II, with the fastest rise coming after 1960. During World War II, the United States mobilized its entire society to fight fascism. The atrocities of Nazi Germany discredited ideas of White biological superiority, which had been used to justify anti-intermarriage laws and other discriminatory legislation.

In the aftermath of World War II, citizens challenged the anti-intermarriage laws in state courts. In 1948, in *Perez v. Sharpe,* the California Supreme Court was the first court to strike down its state anti-intermarriage law as unconstitutional. A dozen states followed California's lead and retired their laws against racial intermarriage, but several other states, mostly the states of the old Confederacy, strengthened their anti-intermarriage laws as a way of demonstrating their fealty to the old racial caste system and their discomfort with Black demands for civil rights.

In 1967, in *Loving v. Virginia,* the U.S. Supreme Court unanimously declared that all the remaining state laws and state constitutional provisions that prohibited intermarriage by race were unconstitutional, and therefore unenforceable. The anti-intermarriage laws remained on the books, unenforced, for decades until the last of the laws was finally rescinded by a popular referendum in Alabama in 2000. The narrowness of the referendum (with a substantial proportion of Whites casting ballots in favor of allowing the unconstitutional and unenforceable anti-intermarriage law to remain on the books) demonstrated that even decades after *Loving,* White discomfort with racial intermarriage remained strong in some parts of the United States.

Classic Research About Intermarriage

Ruby Jo Reeves Kennedy was the first researcher in the United States to make a careful study of historical data on intermarriage trends. Kennedy used marriage license data from New Haven, Connecticut, to support an argument that the United States was not a single melting pot into which all ethnic groups were poured and mixed but, rather, a triple melting pot with strong religious divisions between Catholics, Protestants, and Jews. Kennedy's vision of a religiously divided society has been influential, even though her own data tables belied her conclusions. Of Kennedy's original sample of more than 9,000 marriage records from New Haven between 1870 and 1940, there were hundreds of religious intermarriages, but only five marriages between Whites and Blacks.

Racial intermarriage had never been illegal in Connecticut, but Kennedy's data showed (and subsequent analyses of census data have reconfirmed) that racial intermarriage was rare in the past even where it was legal. The small number of racial intermarriages precluded analysis, so Kennedy ignored the issue of race and focused on religious intermarriage. Because the U.S. Census and other official federal surveys have generally not included questions on religion, meaning that newer data are not easily available, Kennedy's work on religious intermarriage and the triple melting pot continues to be influential (the March 1957 Current Population Survey did include several questions on religion, but the individual level data were never released to the public).

Milton Gordon's extended essay on *Assimilation in American Life* is another pioneering and often-cited work about intermarriage. Gordon argued that widespread intermarriage between an immigrant group (and their descendents) and the dominant native group was both a powerful force for greater assimilation and a sure sign that the final stages of assimilation had already taken place. Gordon was impressed with how the early 20th-century immigrants, chiefly Southern and Eastern European immigrants, had managed to assimilate into U.S. society, and specifically into White U.S. society. The Poles, Italians, and Greeks (among others) had faced a great deal of discrimination in the United States when they first arrived, but somehow over three generations, they managed to become integral parts of the dominant White ethnic group. Gordon reasoned that frequent intermarriage between the early 20th-century immigrant groups (such as Italians, Poles, and Greeks) and the already established White ethnic groups (English, Germans, Irish) was a clear sign that Southern and Eastern European national groups had assimilated into White America.

Hannah Arendt's essay "Reflections on Little Rock" is a final and rather controversial statement about the important place of intermarriage rights within the pantheon of civil rights. Arendt's essay was written in the aftermath of the forced integration of public schools in Little Rock, Arkansas, in 1957. Arendt argued that the civil rights establishment was wrong to force the issue of integration (and its inevitable backlash) upon children, who were in no way responsible for racial segregation in the first place. In Arendt's view, the right to marry the person of one's choice was a more fundamental human right than the right to attend a racially integrated school.

The Civil Rights Movement in the 1950s and the 1960s saw school integration and economic issues such as the elimination of workplace discrimination as much more important issues to tackle than anti-intermarriage laws. The reasoning of civil rights leaders was that all children attend school, and nearly all adults work at some point, but the number of individuals who were affected by bans on racial intermarriage was thought to be so small as to make the issue of anti-intermarriage laws one of secondary importance. In addition, White hostility toward intermarriage was thought to be so virulent that civil rights leaders feared that a White backlash against intermarriage could possibly overwhelm civil rights gains in other areas such as workplace and school integration.

Arendt's position and the debate about the place of intermarriage rights among all human rights are both increasingly relevant in the early 21st century as the United States grapples with the politically charged issue of same-gender marriage. In the legal debates about same-gender marriage, interracial marriage and specifically the *Loving* decision are the key precedents. Although the legality of racial intermarriage was conclusively decided in 1967 in the *Loving* case, the meaning of marriage rights and the openness or exclusiveness of state-defined marriage rights remain an important issue.

Michael J. Rosenfeld

See also Blood Quantum; Caste; Civil Rights Movement; *Hafu*; Hapa; Interracial Friendships; *Loving v. Virginia*; Nikkeijin; One-Drop Rule

Further Readings

Arendt, Hannah. 1959. "Reflections on Little Rock." *Dissent* 6:45–56.

Davis, F. James. 1991. *Who Is Black? One Nation's Definition.* University Park: Pennsylvania State University Press.

Gordon, Milton. 1964. *Assimilation in American Life: The Role of Race, Religion, and National Origin.* New York: Oxford University Press.

Gould, Stephen Jay. 1996. *The Mismeasure of Man.* New York: Norton.

Heer, David. 1980. "Intermarriage." Pp. 513–521 in *Harvard Encyclopedia of American Ethnic Groups,* edited by S. Thernstrom, A. Orlov, and O. Handlin. Cambridge, MA: Belknap Press.

Kalmijn, Matthijs. 1998. "Intermarriage and Homogamy: Causes, Patterns, Trends." *Annual Review of Sociology* 24:395–421.

Kaplan, Sidney. 1949. "The Miscegenation Issue in the Election of 1864." *Journal of Negro History* 34:274–343.

Kennedy, Ruby Jo Reeves. 1944. "Single or Triple Melting Pot? Intermarriage Trends in New Haven, 1870–1940." *American Journal of Sociology* 49:331–339.

Moran, Rachel. 2001. *Interracial Intimacy: The Regulation of Race and Romance.* Chicago, IL: University of Chicago Press.

Romano, Renee C. 2003. *Race Mixing: Black-White Marriage in Postwar America.* Cambridge, MA: Harvard University Press.

Rosenfeld, Michael J. 2007. *The Age of Independence: Interracial Unions, Same-Sex Unions, and the Changing American Family.* Cambridge, MA: Harvard University Press.

Spickard, Paul. 1989. *Mixed Blood: Intermarriage and Ethnic Identity in Twentieth-Century America.* Madison: University of Wisconsin Press.

Wallenstein, Peter. 2002. *Tell the Court I Love My Wife: Race, Marriage and Law—An American History.* New York: Palgrave Macmillan.

INTERNAL COLONIALISM

Internal colonialism, a theory on race, came into popularity during the Civil Rights Movement and is used by Black activists to explain White and Black relations in the United States. Internal colonialism exemplifies a form of exploitation and disinvestment in minority racial and ethnic communities by a dominant race in the same nation. This term has also been used by Chicano activists in the United States, borrowing from Latin American theories of exploitation, and in other nations where it describes relations of domination and subordination among diverse races and ethnicities. Although this term has its critics, it is still used to explain systems of domination within regions based on racial and ethnic differences. This entry describes the concept and its use both in the United States and around the world.

Internal Colonialism in the United States

Traditional colonialism is conceptualized as political and economic domination by a nation over a region beyond its geographic border; those colonized are often of a different race and culture, and their land, labor, and other resources are mined for profit by the colonizer. As well, sociocultural dominance may occur with the colonizer imposing its own values, language, beliefs, and customs on the subordinated populations. Often, a formalized structure is implemented to ensure the continued subjugation of a colonized people. Internal colonialism reflects economic, political, and cultural domination of a subordinate population within its nation's borders by another group, based upon racial and ethnic differences leading to economic, political, and social exploitation.

Usage During the Civil Rights Era

The term *internal colonialism* grew from multiple sources, primarily the discussion of White and Black relations during the U.S. Civil Rights Movement. The Civil Rights era was a time of wide public discussion about the social, political, and economic abuses of Blacks, including examination of historical abuses. Works about the oppression of Blacks, such as Kenneth Clark's *Dark Ghetto* (1965) and Stokely Carmichael's *Black Power* (1967), framed the experiences of minorities as being similar to those of colonized groups, with the latter book providing the first detailed discussion of internal colonialism of Blacks in the United States.

Black activists found internal colonialism to be a proper theory to explain the oppression they encountered in the United States. Such thinkers viewed similarities between the oppression of U.S. Blacks and relationships of African nations with their White European colonizers. Internal colonialism was used to explain the geographic, economic, political, and social isolation of Blacks from larger institutions. Continued lack of resources in urban areas predominantly inhabited by Blacks fueled the use of this theory, reinforcing the idea of historical processes that exploit the lives of minorities. The subordination of Blacks began to be understood in structural terms, whereas previous race theories focused on purported psychological or cultural inferiorities among people of color. This emphasis on institutions of oppression led to acceptance of such terms as *internal colonialism*, which became adopted as an expression of dominance and exploitation of Blacks by Whites in the United States.

Latin American Theories

The term *internal colonialism* also has its roots in Latin American theories explaining economic relations. The scholarly discussion of economic exploitation in Latin America influenced discourse on U.S.-based race relations. Historically, nations in both Europe and North America have exploited Latin American countries for various resources. However, an internal form of exploitation also occurred, dictated by race; relations between dominant races and subordinated Indians in places such as Mexico and Peru became classified as internal colonialism. These systems of disinvestment in Latin America were then extrapolated and used to describe the lack of power of Blacks in the United States during the Civil Rights period.

In addition, Chicano activists at the time used *internal colonialism* to highlight their perceptions of living in dependent and politically powerless communities in the United States. From economics to education, the lives of Chicanos were seen as impeded by their status as a subordinate group in the United States. The use of the term *internal colonialism* was a way to conceptualize exploitation, as well as a mechanism to center grievances, helping to formulate and mobilize discontent with a lack of privilege in the United States for racial and ethnic minorities.

Critiques of Internal Colonialism

Critics of the use of the term *internal colonialism* claim that it imprecisely labels the experiences of racial and ethnic minorities in the United States. Scholars have highlighted several aspects of Black domination that are at odds with the term *internal colonialism*. Unlike traditional colonialism, Blacks in the United States are not a numerical majority of insiders dominated by a minority of outsiders; Whites did not settle in land that was primarily Black; also, the geographical separation of colony and mother country is not a component of Black oppression.

Such terms as *colonization* were promoted by race scholar Robert Blauner to represent the process in which the daily life of a minority group is controlled by an outside race, ethnicity, or group. In his view, colonized Americans have less freedom than ethnic immigrants do, and Blacks are unique in the extent to which their segregation is controlled by socioeconomic and political forces from outside the community. Whites perform administrative functions within Black communities while residing outside of them geographically, conveying the reality that Blacks have little impact structurally in their own neighborhoods.

Geographic segregation remains a factor in the United States, where a lack of resources impedes social advancement, leading to lower quality of life in racially homogenous communities for lower socioeconomic status Blacks.

The concept of internal colonialism has also been criticized in its application to the experiences of Mexican Americans with Whites, and more diverse conceptions of colonization have been offered. U.S. society first engaged in relations with Mexicans through invasion, whereas with Blacks, capitalist motives promoted the idea of importing people into a framework of domination. To some, the relations between Whites and Mexicans may fit more traditional conceptions of colonialism.

Scholars such as Joan Moore, however, argue for a multiple understandings of colonialism among Mexican Americans. In examining three diverse regions in the United States (New Mexico, Texas, and California), Moore found varied experiences of domination among Mexican Americans. In New Mexico, once part of a Spanish colony, an institution of formal colonization and informal controls carried over in U.S. occupancy of the region; Mexican elites retained power and political control for many years under White rule. In contrast, Texas experienced a history of violence and conflict as White domination in local communities limited the political power of Mexicans; this was seen as conflict colonialism. In California, Mexicans have historically been barred from political power and exploited for their labor, leading to an economic colonialism that secures their lowered status in the state. Such factors as history, geography, and social, economic, and political relations affect the use and interpretation of the term *colonialism* when applied to racial and ethnic minorities.

The theory of internal colonialism has lost its primacy in the lives of Blacks and Chicanos searching for a tool to mobilize actors to achieve social mobility in the United States. Nevertheless, institutionalized patterns of segregation, disinvestment, and oppression are still recognized as key elements of racial relations between subordinate and dominant groups. Structural constraints that led to the adoption of internal colonialism as tool to rally support for movement actions in the Civil Rights era are still prevalent.

Global Issues of Internal Colonialism

Globally, the concept of internal colonialism has become a tool used to describe dominant and subordinate race relations. The political, economic, and social relationships between Aboriginal peoples in Canada and the wider Canadian society have been viewed through the lens of internal colonialism. The colonization process, for example, is seen as lowering the academic performance of Aboriginal students, leading to the underdevelopment of their society. Internal colonialism has also been used to explain how lack of education in Australia affects mobility of Aborigines. *Internal colonialism* is still used to describe institutionalized exploitation and oppression of racial minorities by dominant groups within the same geographic context.

Manuel R. Torres

See also African Americans; Chicano Movement; Civil Rights Movement; Colonialism; Critical Race Theory; Marxism and Racism; Sami

Further Readings

Blauner, Robert. 1972. *Racial Oppression in America.* New York: Harper & Row.

Carmichael, Stokely and Charles Hamilton. 1967. *Black Power: The Politics of Liberation in America.* New York: Vintage Books.

Clark, Kenneth. 1965. *Dark Ghetto.* New York: Harper & Row.

Gonzalez Casanova, Pablo. 1965. "Internal Colonialism and National Developments." *Studies in Comparative International Development* 4:27–37.

Gutierrez, Ramon A. 2004. "Internal Colonialism: An American Theory of Race." *Du Bois Review* 1(2):281–295.

Moore, Joan. 1970. "Colonialism: The Case of Mexican Americans" *Social Problems,* 17(4):463–472.

INTERNALIZED RACISM

When members of racially oppressed groups accept as true the derogatory myths and identities imposed upon them by the dominant group, it is said that they have internalized the racism of the larger society. Although internalized racial oppression is an important feature of racism often discussed among antiracist activists, novelists, and filmmakers, such as Malcolm X, Toni Morrison, and Spike Lee, there has been only a scattering of empirical research on the topic. This may be the result of a widespread tendency to misconstrue internalized racism as reflecting some personal failing among those who experience internalized racism rather than as a structural problem imposed on them. This entry looks at how internalized racism operates.

Internalizing Oppression

All systems of inequality generate conditions encouraging the subjugated to accept their subordinated position and adopt the negative images and beliefs attached to their identity by the dominant group. One example is racial identities, which are socially constructed from power relations. These socially defined characteristics are often presented as flowing naturally from "real" biological differences. Ideologies that legitimize and normalize inequality and intimate the inferiority of people of color and the superiority of Whites are thus woven into the fabric of commonsense knowledge, where they are easily absorbed by all members of society, including people of color.

Cloaked in normalcy, these derogatory myths may be adopted by people of color without their conscious awareness of doing so. This aspect of internalized racism is often likened to the impact of colonial oppression on the colonized and referred to as *mental colonization*. When people of color are socialized to accept racial inequality and their subordinated position within the racial hierarchy, they pose less of a threat to the power and privilege of Whites.

Internalized racism is not the result of any inherent personal deficiencies, frailties, or moral shortcomings, nor is it a consequence of psychological make-up or cultural beliefs. Most important, internalized racism is not a cause or source of racism. Rather, it is an outcome of racial oppression, which is never total. In White-dominated societies, people of color may devise strategies of resistance, disruption, subversion, and rebellion. By studying the subtle forms that internalized racism can take and raising awareness about them, people of color can further develop ways to resist the internalization of racial oppression.

Several forms of internalized racial oppression are discussed in the limited amount of literature on the topic. One form is evident when the people of color respond to their denigrated racial status by distancing themselves from their racial group in an attempt to be seen as more like Whites. To avoid the stigmatized racial status, people of color may assume traits and characteristics associated with Whites, denigrate members of their group for not behaving more like Whites or for being "too ethnic," and avoid association with their racial group. By reiterating a belief in the inferiority of their own racial group—and the superiority of Whites—they reinforce rather than challenge the system of racial inequality.

Another example of internalized racism is the skin-tone bias or "colorism" within the Black American community. Higher status, greater beauty, and desirability are attributed to those Blacks with lighter skin tone and straight hair while the darker-skinned and nappy-haired are more likely to suffer discrimination and denigration from members of their own racial group. Colorism has its roots in slavery and continues to be propped up by the beauty standards of the dominant society, which defines White European American features as more attractive than the racialized features of non-Whites. This encourages non-Whites to view their own racialized features with displeasure, contributing to high rates of cosmetic surgery among non-Whites, particularly non-White females, who alter racialized features to more closely resemble those associated with European Americans.

Many perceive that the pop singer Michael Jackson used some of his many cosmetic surgeries to acquire a more White-like appearance. Common forms of cosmetic surgeries among African and Asian Americans include nose jobs to narrow flared nostrils and raise the bridge. The most popular cosmetic surgery among Asian American women is a double eyelid procedure, which creates an extra fold of skin and widens the appearance of the eyes. Those who undergo such procedures do so to enhance their social prestige by conforming more closely to definitions of beauty that emphasize Whiteness. As these examples highlight, internalized racial oppression is an adaptive response to the experiences of racism.

Karen D. Pyke

See also Body Image; Color Blindness; hooks, bell; Lee, Spike; Media and Race; Prejudice; Racism

Further Readings

hooks, bell. 2003. *Rock My Soul: Black People and Self-Esteem.* New York: Atria.

Kaw, Eugenia. 1993. "Medicalization of Racial Features: Asian American Women and Cosmetic Surgery." *Medical Anthropology Quarterly* 7:74–89.

Osajima, Keith. 1993. "The Hidden Injuries of Race." Pp. 81–91 in *Bearing Dreams, Shaping Visions: Asian Pacific American Perspectives*, edited by L. Revilla,

G. Nomura, S. Wong, and S. Hune. Pullman: Washington State University Press.

Pyke, Karen and Tran Dang. 2003. "'FOB' and 'Whitewashed': Identity and Internalized Racism Among Second Generation Asian Americans." *Qualitative Sociology* 26:147–172.

Russell, Kathy, Midge Wilson, and Ronald Hall. 1991. *The Color Complex*. New York: Harcourt Brace Jovanovich.

INTERNATIONAL CONVENTION ON THE ELIMINATION OF ALL FORMS OF RACIAL DISCRIMINATION

In 1965, the United Nations General Assembly adopted the International Convention on the Elimination of All Forms of Racial Discrimination (hereinafter ICERD). By 2006, 170 of the 192 UN member states had become parties to this treaty. At the time of its drafting, it was a remarkable innovation, the outcome of moves that started in 1960 when attacks on synagogues and Jewish burial grounds in Germany gave rise to fears of a rise in neo-Nazism. When international remedial action by the United Nations was proposed, newly independent African states, with their eyes on Southern Africa, argued for a convention against racial discrimination. This entry examines the treaty, its implementation, and its future prospects.

What It Says

The ICERD was the first human rights convention to include a provision by which the actions of state parties were to be monitored to see whether they were fulfilling the obligations they had undertaken. It obliged them to report every 2 years on their implementation of the convention and provided for the examination of their reports by an independent expert committee, which was to report the results of its examination to the UN General Assembly.

According to Article 1 of the convention, "The term 'racial discrimination' shall mean any distinction, exclusion, restriction or preference based on race, colour, descent, or national or ethnic origin which has the purpose or effect of nullifying or impairing the recognition, enjoyment or exercise, on an equal footing, of human rights in the political, economic, social, cultural or any other field of public life." The differentiation of purpose and effect means that both direct and indirect discrimination (or disparate treatment and disparate effect) are covered. Distinctions made by states between citizens and noncitizens are exempted from the definition, as are measures of affirmative action as long as they are not maintained after their objectives have been fulfilled.

Articles 2 through 7 condemn racial segregation and define the obligations of state parties: to make incitement to racial hatred a punishable offence, to provide protections, to compensate victims, and to combat racial prejudices by educational and other means.

Implementation

Those who negotiated its drafting did not expect many states to ratify the convention, yet the number of states becoming parties to it has steadily risen: from 41 in 1970 to 107 in 1980 and 129 in 1990. The United States became the 141st in 1994, though its ratification was subject to extensive reservations. Many states display an ambivalent attitude to this and other human rights treaties. Although states hope to put pressure on certain other states to secure adequate protections for racial minorities, they may not want to expose their own policies and actions to unfriendly criticism.

State reports are examined by the Committee on the Elimination of Racial Discrimination (CERD), composed of eighteen experts elected by the state parties. From its first meeting in 1970 through to 1988, its work was influenced by the tensions of the cold war between East and West. Its activities were seen in some quarters as an adjunct to the decolonization movement at the United Nations. CERD found that many governments did not appreciate the extent of the obligations they had assumed by becoming parties to the treaty. For example, in several Latin American countries, citizens could vote only if they understood the Spanish language. CERD held that the less favorable treatment of those who spoke indigenous languages constituted racial discrimination and persuaded these states to amend their laws. In this period, members interpreted the convention as allowing them to receive information from state parties only, and they expressed only their individual opinions on state party compliance.

With the ending of the cold war, CERD members were able to agree on concluding observations expressing a collective opinion of state implementation of treaty obligations. CERD members started to take note of information received from nongovernmental sources and to use it as a basis for questions put to state representatives in oral dialogue. CERD introduced new measures to review implementation of the ICERD in respect of states that failed to submit reports and to follow up its recommendations to see whether they had been implemented by states. CERD agreed to procedures for issuing early warning about potentially dangerous situations and for outlining the urgent action that should be undertaken. For example, having received credible information alleging that the U.S. government was not protecting the traditional land rights of the Western Shoshone Indigenous Peoples, and having tried to expedite submission of the overdue report of that government, CERD in 2006 issued a decision expressing its concerns and listing the kinds of action required if the United States were to meet its treaty obligations in respect of the Shoshone.

The ICERD, by its Article 14, was also the first UN human rights treaty to include a provision whereby a state party could agree to a procedure for individual complaints. By 2005, forty-six states had made the declaration allowing their citizens to petition CERD if they claimed that their governments had not protected their rights as set out in the convention. CERD considers such complaints, and the responses of the governments in question, in private session. In some cases, it has found the complaints to be justified. On occasion, the government has then recompensed the aggrieved person and taken action to prevent any recurrence.

Prospects

Despite signs that CERD has been gaining authority, especially with the newer and smaller states, there are occasional disagreements. The government of India denies that its policies relating to caste distinctions come under its treaty obligations, whereas CERD, referring to the use of the word *descent* in Article 1, has affirmed "the situation of the scheduled castes falls within the scope of the Convention." The government of Mauritania has protested vigorously about CERD's statement, "It remains concerned about information on the persistence of slavery-like practices, which constitute serious instances of discrimination based on descent." After CERD reviewed Australia's implementation of its obligations toward its Aboriginal population, the attorney-general of that country, in a press statement, declared, "The Committee's comments are an insult to Australia." CERD gave no ground, but reaffirmed its criticisms. If a dispute about the application of the convention were serious enough, the UN General Assembly or Security Council could refer it to the International Court of Justice for an advisory opinion.

The Third World Conference Against Racism in 2001 concluded, "We affirm that universal adherence to and full implementation of the International Convention on the Elimination of All Forms of Racial Discrimination are of paramount importance for promoting equality and non-discrimination in the world." CERD has helped develop application of the convention as the primary expression of international law in its field by agreeing on general recommendations about such matters as racial segregation and the rights of particular groups, notably Indigenous Peoples, the Roma, and noncitizens. CERD operates under restrictive conditions, meeting for only six weeks of the year, and its members serve without salary.

The UN High Commissioner for Human Rights has published proposals for unifying the activities of the seven human rights treaty bodies (covering economic rights, civil rights, race, torture, and the rights of women, children, and migrant workers) and for improving their funding. However, it is doubtful whether UN member states are yet ready for any significant improvement in the international oversight of actions of theirs that they see as expressions of their national sovereignty.

More about the text of the convention, the list of state parties, and CERD's reports and observations can be found on the Web site of the Office of the UN High Commissioner for Human Rights (http://www.unhchr.ch).

Michael Banton

See also Australia, Indigenous People; Discrimination; Minority Rights; Roma

Further Readings

Banton, M. 1996. *International Action against Racial Discrimination.* Oxford, UK: Clarendon Press.

Banton, M. 2002. *The International Politics of Race.* Oxford, UK: Polity Press.

INTERNMENT CAMPS

On February 19, 1942, President Franklin D. Roosevelt signed Executive Order 9066, which allowed military authorities to exclude "any or all persons" from areas they designated as a military or exclusion zone. On February 25, 1942, this order was used to begin excluding people of Japanese ancestry from the entire Pacific Coast. Thus, almost 120,000 Japanese Americans who lived in California, western Oregon, western Washington, and southern Arizona were removed from their homes in the largest forced relocation of U.S. citizens in U.S. history. Some residents of German and Italian descent also were arrested on an individual basis and interned when deemed to be security risks.

Idaho Governor Chase Clark stated before a Congressional committee in February 1942 that Japanese Americans would be welcome in Idaho only if they were in "concentration camps under military guard." This statement has often been discussed as the precursor to the establishment of internment camps for Japanese Americans. Executive Order 9095 created the Office of the Alien Property Custodian, allowing the government to take control of Japanese Americans' assets and property. President Roosevelt signed Executive Order 9102 on March 18, 1942, which established the War Relocation Authority (WRA) that eventually oversaw the administration of the internment camps. This entry describes the system and impact of internment camps.

The WRA System

Assembly centers were initially established by the WRA as temporary facilities to assemble and organize evacuated residents before transporting them to *relocation centers*. Relocation centers were camps that were established outside established exclusion zones. The terms *relocation centers* and *internment camps* are often used interchangeably. The WRA also established a *segregation center* at Tule Lake, California, for evacuees identified as security risks and their families. Some also refer to relocation centers as *detention camps* or *concentration camps*.

Japanese Americans were incarcerated in nine internment camps and one segregation center. The first internment camp was established at Manzanar, California, and opened on March 21, 1942. The following internment camps were subsequently established in 1942: Poston (Colorado River), Arizona; Tule Lake, California; Gila River, Arizona; Minidoka, Idaho; Heart Mountain, Wyoming; Amache (Granada), Colorado; Topaz, Utah; Rohwer, Arkansas; and Jerome, Arkansas. In September 1943, the Tule Lake, California, internment camp was transformed into a camp for "dissenters" based on evacuees responses to a loyalty questionnaire. The first camp closed was Jerome,

Schoolchildren at Manzanar. *This 1943 photograph by Ansel Adams shows schoolchildren at the Manzanar War Relocation Center, California, one of ten camps where Japanese American citizens and resident Japanese aliens were interned during World War II. Starting in the 1960s, many Sanseis (third-generation Japanese Americans, the children of Nisei) became involved in the Civil Rights Movement and began the "Redress Movement," in an effort to obtain an apology and reparations from the federal government for the interment at Manzanar and elsewhere. In 1980, Congress established a commission to study the matter and finally in 1988, President Ronald Reagan signed the Civil Liberties Act of 1988, which provided redress of $20,000 for each surviving detainee.*

Source: Library of Congress, Prints & Photographs Division, LC-DIG-ppprs-00354.

Japanese Americans Fred Korematsu (left), Minoru Yasui (center), and Gordon Hirabayashi, at a press conference on January 19, 1983. During World War II, U.S. citizens of Japanese descent living on the West Coast were first ordered to submit to a curfew and then were relocated to desert internment camps under the provisions of Executive Order 9066. The order was based on a military report by Lt. Gen. J. L. DeWitt stating that there was a danger of espionage by persons of Japanese ancestry. According to the report, all Japanese Americans should be evacuated from the West Coast "out of military necessity" because there was no way to determine which were dangerous. Korematsu, Yasui, and Hirabayashi refused to comply and challenged the constitutionality of the measures. The U.S. Supreme Court first upheld the curfew in 1943 in Hirabayashi v. United States *(320 U.S. 81)* and then the internment in 1944 in Korematsu v. United States *(323 U.S. 214.)* Forty years later, researchers discovered evidence that the Department of Justice had suppressed and altered portions of DeWitt's report at the time of the Supreme Court cases. These actions removed his racially biased statements against all people of Japanese ancestry and his acknowledgment that there was no known threat by these Japanese Americans.

On the basis of the newly discovered information, the U.S. District Court ruled in 1984 that Korematsu's conviction was invalid, and in 1987, the U.S. Court of Appeals for the Ninth Circuit invalidated Hirabayashi's. The U.S. government did not appeal either decision to the Supreme Court. Because the subsequent decisions came from lower courts rather than the Supreme Court itself, these wartime decisions still stand, though now in disgrace. The ruling in Korematsu that military urgency can justify measures such as internment remains effective.

In recognition of Korematsu's work for civil rights, he was awarded the Presidential Medal of Freedom in 1998. In 2003, an amicus brief was filed on Korematsu's behalf in two cases that challenged the constitutionality of detentions at Guantanamo Bay as part of the U.S. "War on Terror."

Korematsu died in 2005. Hirabayashi's nephew, Lane Rho Hirabayashi, holds the first appointment as the George and Sakaye Aratani Professor of Japanese American Internment, Redress, and Community in the Asian American Studies department at the University of California, Los Angeles.

Source: Bettmann/CORBIS.

Arkansas, on June 30, 1944, when all inmates were transferred to Rohwer, Arkansas, which was the last camp to be closed on November 30, 1945.

Internal Conditions. WRA reports acknowledged that Japanese Americans were housed in barracks covered in tar paper without plumbing or cooking facilities of any kind. Some evacuees themselves were required to build the barracks in which they lived. Evacuees had to use unpartitioned toilets or outhouses in temperatures ranging from 35 degrees below zero in the winter to 115 degrees in the summer. They slept on cots and received 45 cents per day for food rations. Most families did not have clothing appropriate for the climates in which the internment camps were located and were not provided with clothing.

Two small internment camps were established in Hawai'i, which had declared martial law. However, because of the large population of Japanese Americans in Hawai'i, the U.S. government realized that interning all people of Japanese ancestry in Hawai'i would result in the destruction of Hawai'i's economy.

Military Recruitment and Dissenters. Many young men in the internment camps were drafted into the military. On January 14, 1944, the military draft for *Nisei* (Japanese Americans born of immigrant parents) was restored. Although many volunteered for the draft, there also were many resisters. Some at the Heart Mountain camp organized the Fair Play Committee to support draft resistance. Other soldiers refused to participate in combat training to protest the treatment of their families in the internment camps. Many of the resisters or dissenters were arrested, convicted, and imprisoned before finally being pardoned.

Japanese Americans drafted from internment camps and from Hawai'i were assigned to one of three major units, the 100th Infantry Battalion, the 442nd Regimental Combat Team, and the Military Intelligence Service. In 1944, the 100th became a part of the 442nd and, to date, is the most highly decorated military unit in U.S. history.

Economic Impact. All internees suffered significant property losses. Some estimate it to be around $6 billion. Although the U.S. government promised to store large items such as furniture, if boxed and labeled properly, the security of this property was not promised, and most Japanese Americans did not have their belongings returned to them. A few farmers were able to find non-Japanese Americans who agreed to tend to their farms, but most property owners were forced to sell their farms and homes at huge losses.

Reparations

Starting in the 1960s, many *Sanseis* (third-generation Japanese Americans, the children of Nisei) became involved in the Civil Rights Movement and began the "Redress Movement" in an effort to obtain an apology and reparations from the federal government. In 1980, Congress established a commission to study the matter. The commission's report in 1983 condemned the internment as unjust, asserting that it was the result of racism rather than military necessity. In 1988, President Ronald Reagan signed the Civil Liberties Act of 1988, which provided redress of $20,000 for each surviving detainee, totaling more than $1.25 billion. The first nine redress payments were made in October 1990.

Gayle Y. Iwamasa

See Appendix B
See also Asian Americans; Civil Disobedience; Issei; Japanese American Citizens League; Japanese Americans; Military and Race; Nisei

Further Readings

Children of the Camps: PBS Documentary. 1999.
Nagata, Donna K. 1993. *Legacy of Injustice: Exploring the Cross-Generational Impact of the Japanese American Internment.* New York: Plenum Press.
Tateishi, John, ed. 1999. *And Justice for All: An Oral History of the Japanese American Detention Camps.* Seattle: University of Washington Press.
Weglyn, Michi Nishiura. 1996. *Years of Infamy: The Untold Story of America's Concentration Camps.* Updated ed. Seattle: University of Washington Press.
Yamamoto, Eric K., Margaret Chon, Carol L. Izumi, Jerry Kang, and Frank H. Wu. 2001. *Race, Rights and Reparation: Law and the Japanese American Internment.* Gaithersburg, NY: Aspen Law & Business.

Web Sites

Densho: The Japanese American Legacy Project: http://www.densho.org
Internment Archives: http://www.internmentarchives.com
Of Civil Wrongs and Rights: The Fred Korematsu Story (by Eric Paul Fornier): http://www.pbs.org/pov/pov2001/ofcivilwrongsandrights/index.html

Interracial Friendships

Interracial friendships provide a context of equality in which intergroup differences may be addressed to reduce prejudice and conflict. Measures of the extent of interracial friendships also reflect the state of race relations in a society, capturing the positive feelings between group members rather than the negative sentiment so often emphasized in studies of racial attitudes. When friendships cut across racial lines, they represent a form of bonding capital and a form of bridging capital.

A sizable body of research finds that having interracial friendships is associated with reduced prejudice and greater social competence for both children and adults. Unfortunately, interracial friendships tend to be shorter lived and less intimate than same-race friendships unless the cross-race friend is one of several rather than an isolated cross-race friend. This entry reviews social science research on interracial friendships in the United States, including the observed benefits, recent trends, historical context, measurement issues, and factors that help initiate and maintain interracial friendships.

Historical Context

Historically, interracial friendships were virtually unknown from the U.S. Revolution to the 1830s, partly because of Enlightenment beliefs in hierarchy and order. Even the early abolitionist societies excluded Blacks as members. John Stauffer has shown that this mind-set began to shift in the 1840s as the abolitionist movement gained momentum and moral might. A "golden age" of interracial friendship took place from the 1840s to the 1860s, a period when radical abolitionists, both Black and White, joined forces to defeat slavery. Interracial friendships flowered as activists of all racial groups embraced the idea of a perfect society.

This window was not repeated soon, as interracial friendships in both life and literature faded into insignificance before reemerging after World War II. Interracial friendship lost much of the prestige it once possessed. According to Stauffer, the waning of interracial friendship as an inspired ideal coincided with a dramatic rise in overt racism and racial oppression.

Prevalence and Benefits

Recent Trends

The bulk of research has focused on Black-White friendships. The estimated prevalence of interracial friendship in the United States varies by study. A closer look suggests that both real changes over time and differences in methodological approach may underlie this variation. A recent longitudinal study using consistent measures by Steven Tuch, Lee Sigelman, and Jason MacDonald found that African Americans increased their friendships with Whites in the late 1970s and early 1980s, but decreased such friendships in the early 1990s until the percentage in 1995 was basically equivalent to the percentage in 1975. The various cross-sectional estimates from other studies paint a more inconsistent picture of interracial friendships, although research concurs that there have been consistent increases in interracial acquaintances over time.

How friendship is measured is also an important source of variability, with results varying by how the relationship is defined, whether specific friendship nominations were required, and the number and pool of people from which friends can be considered. For example, a 1998 study by the National Opinion Research Center at the University of Chicago found that when White respondents were asked "Are any of your friends that you feel close to Black?," 42% of Whites said yes. However, when asked to give the names of friends they felt close to before identifying their race, only 6% of Whites listed a close friend of a different race or ethnicity. Overall, real variation over time, aspects of methodology, and normative pressure on respondents to emphasize interracial friendships may affect the variability and accuracy of estimates.

Benefits

Studies of both children and adults suggest that cross-race friendships increase positive intergroup relations for members of both majority and minority groups. For children, having one or more interracial friendships is associated with greater social competency and multicultural sensitivity. The positive effects of these friendships for children transcend intergroup attitudes to also influence social skills and achievement aspirations. Even observing positive intergroup friendships among children's fellow in-group members appears to benefit intergroup relations. For adults, interracial friendships have been most commonly linked to decreased prejudice. Thomas Pettigrew and Linda Tropp's meta-analysis of studies of intergroup contact revealed that having an interracial friendship was associated with less prejudicial attitudes in thirty-nine studies. Similar to children, even the knowledge among adults that another in-group member has an out-group friendship is associated with more positive out-group beliefs.

Influencing Factors

A sizable body of research has sought to identify what factors influence interracial friendships. Empirical work has considered the number of opportunities for contact, the quality of contact, characteristics of the environments that groups share, characteristics of individuals, and the level of family and parental support for interracial friendships.

Several studies support the opportunity hypothesis, which suggests that the prevalence of interracial friendships is a function of the number of opportunities to initiate cross-race versus same-race friendships. For children and adolescents, demographically diverse classrooms have had the most success in increasing the prevalence of interracial friendships. A recent study by Ted Mouw and Barbara Entwisle suggests that about a third of friendship segregation by race is attributable to residential segregation, with segregation across schools more important than within them. Among adults, Jennifer Chatman and coauthors found that employees in racially diverse business organizations had more interracial friendships. Michael Emerson, Rachel Kimbro, and George Yancey also found that adults who have lived in multiethnic neighborhoods or attended interracial schools were more likely to have racially diverse friendships and social networks. Maureen Hallinan and Steven Smith found little support for a competing hypothesis that minorities isolate themselves from the majority when there are many opportunities for contact because they feel socially threatened. One caveat of the opportunity hypothesis is that racial diversity has been found to be less effective in fostering interracial friendships in large classrooms because a suitably large pool of same-race peers remain, making it unnecessary for students to make the effort to cross racial boundaries to form friendships. Thus, although opportunity is clearly important, it is by itself insufficient for initiating interracial friendships.

In addition, several studies have hypothesized that optimal conditions for contact must be present for demographic diversity to blossom into interracial friendships. Supporting this hypothesis, research with children and adults has found that environments and situations that emphasize cooperation, team culture, and collective reward systems tend to foster more interracial friendships. For example, Robert Slavin and Robert Cooper observed that changing school structure from traditional to cooperative learning programs increases children's formation of cross-race friendships, as well as friendship quality. Chatman and colleagues found that corporate environments that emphasized organizational membership and rewarded team achievement instead of individual achievement increased interracial interaction among adults and reduced the salience of race and ethnic categories.

Individual characteristics such as personality, friendliness, gender, social competence, multicultural sensitivity, and shared interests may influence interracial friendships. Friendlier and more popular school children are more likely to report cross-race friends. In addition, students were much more likely to have same-gender interracial friendships than opposite-gender interracial friendships. Social competence and multicultural sensitivity is believed to be both a cause and a consequence of having interracial friendships. Grace Kao and Kara Joyner found that shared activities are important, with cross-race friends reporting fewer shared activities than did same-race friends.

The level of support and engagement of family and parents may influence the initiating and retaining of interracial friendships. Worry about family reactions to interracial relationships may deter individuals from making interracial friendships. One study found that African American parents knew more of their children's cross-race friends than did White parents, and African American parents reported feeling closer to their children's other-race friends than to same-race friends, whereas White parents reported closer relationships with their children's same-race friends than with different race friends.

Brent Berry

See also Contact Hypothesis; Intergroup Relations, Surveying; Interracial Marriage; Melting Pot; Prejudice; Robber's Cave Experiment; Segregation

Further Readings

Chatman, Jennifer A., Jeffrey T. Polzer, Sigal G. Barsade, and Margaret A. Neale. 1998. "Being Different Yet Feeling Similar: The Influence of Demographic Composition and Organizational Culture on Work Processes and Outcomes." *Administrative Science Quarterly* 43:749–780.

Clark, M. L. and Marla Ayers. 1992. "Friendship Similarity During Early Adolescence: Gender and Racial Patterns." *Journal of Psychology* 126:393–405.

Emerson, Michael O., Rachel T. Kimbro, and George Yancey. 2002. "Contact Theory Extended: The Effects of Prior Racial Contact on Current Social Ties." *Social Science Quarterly* 83:745–761.

Hallinan, Maureen T. and Steven S. Smith. 1985. "The Effects of Classroom Racial Composition on Students' Interracial Friendliness." *Social Psychology Quarterly* 48:3–16.

Kao, Grace and Kara Joyner. 2004. "Do Race and Ethnicity Matter Among Friends? Activities Among Interracial, Interethnic, and Intraethnic Adolescent Friends." *Sociological Quarterly* 45:557–574.

Mouw, Ted and Barbara Entwisle. 2006. "Residential Segregation and Interracial Friendship in Schools." *American Journal of Sociology* 112:394–441.

Pettigrew, Thomas F. and Linda R. Tropp. 2003. "A Meta-Analytic Test of Intergroup Contact Theory." *Journal of Personality and Social Psychology* 90:751–783.

Slavin, Robert E. and Robert Cooper. 1999. "Improving Intergroup Relations: Lessons Learned from Cooperative Learning Programs." *Journal of Social Issues* 55:647–633.

Stauffer, John. 2002. *The Black Hearts of Men: Radical Abolitionists and the Transformation of Race.* Cambridge, MA: Harvard University Press.

Tuch, Steven A., Lee Sigelman, and Jason A. MacDonald. 1999. "Trends: Race Relations and American Youth, 1976–1995." *Public Opinion Quarterly* 63:109–148.

INVISIBLE MAN

Published in 1952, Ralph Ellison's novel *Invisible Man* chronicles the trials of a young, Black man making his way from Oklahoma to an all-Black college in the South, and finally settling in New York City. The work made Ellison a leading spokesperson on race relations in the United States because he criticized institutionalized racism and indicted White philanthropy, which often supported segregation and racial biases. The novel also drew attention to economic and social inequalities caused by centuries of racism. Ellison's targets included White philanthropists and members of the Communist Party of the United States (CPUSA) as well as some Black leaders who competed for White patronage. Consequently, both Black and White critics accused the novelist of anticommunism, militancy, and self-hate. This entry summarizes the work, its relation to Ellison's experiences, and its impact.

Section I: Education

Generally, scholars laud the first section of the novel for exposing the tenacity of racism and the fragile nature of race relations during the mid-20th century. The main character, the Narrator, receives a college scholarship from a local fraternal organization. At the award ceremony, he learns that the town's White civic and business leaders expect what Ellison terms a "Battle Royal." The Narrator and several young Black men must box until one man is left standing. Throughout the match, the White men yell racial epithets at the fighters. The interest of White philanthropists in racial progress contrasts with their vulgar language and confuses the young man. He is reminded of his grandfather's deathbed advice to resist racism and defy racists at every opportunity.

Although not autobiographical, the novel relates experiences similar to those of Ellison and his friends. Ellison spent his youth in Oklahoma City, aware of racial tensions throughout the state. When Ellison was seven, one of the deadliest attacks on a Black community occurred: the Tulsa Race Riot of 1921. His interactions with Whites and observations of racism stayed with him as he matured. In 1933, Ellison left his hometown for the Tuskegee Institute in Alabama. In the novel, the Narrator attends a southern, all-Black technical school, much like Tuskegee, established by "the Founder," a Black educator, and supported by White philanthropy. Ellison exposes the dichotomy of a segregated institute, created for and by Blacks and financially dependent on White money. Ellison uses the characters of Mr. Norton, a northern White philanthropist, and Dr. Bledsoe, the school's Black president, to indict this paternalistic system.

At school, the Narrator becomes aware of the dysfunctional relationship between Black leaders and White philanthropists. While escorting Mr. Norton around campus, the Narrator inadvertently allows the benefactor to meet the seamier population living near the school. Consequently, the young man is expelled. The school's president explains that running the university is a game in which he must appease Whites to keep the school funded. Dr. Bledsoe warns the Narrator never to tell Whites the truth or let them know what he is thinking.

Section 2: Life in the City

Forced to leave school, the Narrator moves to New York City, where he encounters more ambiguities in relationships between White and Black social activists and reformers. This section of the novel created controversy among some scholars who saw it as an attack on communism and Black leaders. After learning that Dr. Bledsoe sabotaged his attempts to find employment, the Narrator becomes an unwilling participant in a medical experiment and an unwitting strikebreaker, and he witnesses racism in a labor union. Unemployed and out of options, he joins the Brotherhood, a thinly veiled cover for the CPUSA. The Narrator is invited to be a spokesman for his race. He learns that the Brotherhood hopes to end racial and class inequality. However, the young man encounters racial chauvinism, prejudice, and ignorance among the White membership. Additionally, Black members who willingly sacrifice each other for recognition by their White comrades mortify him. Ultimately, members of the Brotherhood undermine him for his popularity and he leaves.

Some critics believe that Ellison depicted the Brotherhood negatively to insulate himself from the anticommunist hysteria of the Second Red Scare. Although he never officially joined the party, like the Narrator, Ellison left Tuskegee in 1936 and moved to New York City where he spent time among members of the CPUSA, including Langston Hughes, Louise Thompson, and Richard Wright. Although some critics accused Ellison of fabricating overt racism within the party, many of the Narrator's experiences in this section of the novel mimic those of the novelist and his friends during the 1930s. In truth, Ellison and many other Black Americans abandoned the party by the end of World War II because the communists misunderstood the connection between racial and economic inequality.

Upon leaving the Brotherhood, the Narrator becomes involved in a race riot and reassesses his role as a political activist. When he encounters Mr. Norton, who fails to recognize the young man, the Narrator imposes self-exile and vows to follow his grandfather's advice and use his writing to expose the ambiguities found in relationships between the races. Like the Narrator, Ellison's writing asks some difficult questions, for example: At what point does the Black beneficiary become equal to the White benefactor?

Invisible Man exposed many harsh realities concerning the place of Black Americans in the mid-20th century United States. It is a work of social protest, chastising White paternalism and chauvinism and calling attention to the marginalization of social and economic classes in society. At the time of its publication in 1952, it awoke many to consider the nature of race relations and contributed to a growing interest in Black Nationalism and independence from Whites in civil rights organizations. Today, its significance lies in its usefulness in understanding the extent of the frustration among Black intellectuals and leaders in White-dominated society.

Amy E. Carreiro

See also Black Intellectuals; Black Nationalism; Discrimination; Double Consciousness; Labor Unions; Marginalization; Marxism and Racism; Medical Experimentation

Further Readings

Jackson, Lawrence. 2002. *Ralph Ellison: The Emergence of Genius.* New York: Wiley.
Nadel, Alan, ed. 1988. *Invisible Criticism: Ralph Ellison and the American Canon.* Iowa City: University of Iowa Press.
O'Meally, Robert G. 1988. *The Craft of Ralph Ellison.* New York: Cambridge University Press.
Schor, Edith 1993. *Visible Ellison: A Study of Ralph Ellison's Fiction.* Westport, CT: Greenwood Press.

Iranian Americans

Following a wave of immigration from Iran, which was estimated to have a population of 71.2 million people in 2007, during the last quarter of the 20th century, Iranian Americans have emerged as a substantial ethnic community in the United States. Although Iranian Americans are drawn from the several ethnic and religious groups of Iran, a set of shared experiences have reinforced a specifically Iranian identity and strengthened shared cultural traditions. The Iranian American community has simultaneously undergone processes of assimilation to the dominant U.S. culture and strengthening of a specifically Iranian ethnic identity. This entry briefly reviews Iranian immigration and then focuses on the ethnic, religious, and economic characteristics of the Iranian American community, its political issues, and its adaptation to the new home country.

Immigration History

Iranian immigration dates back to the late 19th century, including a group of Iranians in the Iranian

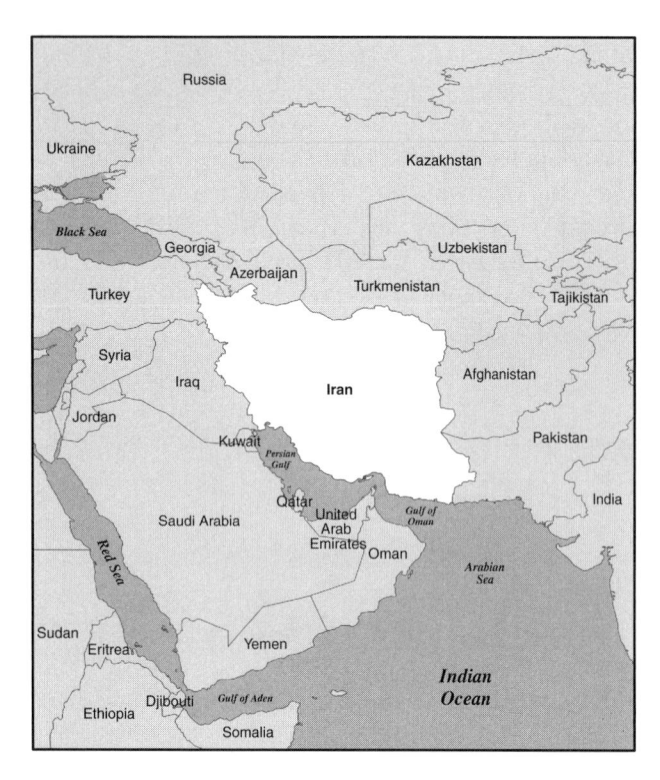

Exhibition of the 1893 World's Columbian Exposition in Chicago. Through the first half of the 20th century, the number of new Iranians entering the United States numbered several hundred annually. More substantial numbers of Iranians did not enter until the late 1960s and early 1970s. Iran was rapidly industrializing during this period, and a growing professional class in Iran was seeking education and professional opportunities outside Iran.

The political turmoil preceding the Iranian Revolution of 1979 sparked a mass exodus of Iranians to locations in Western Europe and the United States. The Iranian Revolution played a major role in shaping the subsequent relationship between Iranian Americans, the nation of Iran, and their host society of the United States and was the direct cause of many immigrants' departure for the United States. As such, the Iranian Revolution remains a powerful memory for most Iranian Americans and continues to influence the construction of their ethnic identity.

Community Characteristics

The 2004 American Communities Survey reports a population of 341,979 who identify their primary ancestry as Iranian. This figure is likely an underestimate of the true size of the Iranian American population because it reports only those Iranian Americans who choose to volunteer information on ancestry and who also choose "Iranian" as their primary ancestry. Competing estimates of the population vary, with some estimates as high as 1 million Iranian Americans.

Iranian Americans live in nearly every state, but specific states and metropolitan regions are host to large Iranian American communities. California contains the largest number of Iranian Americans; more than half of all Iranian Americans live in California, including more than 100,000 in greater Los Angeles alone. The Los Angeles community represents the single largest concentration of Iranian Americans, who are one of the more visible ethnic communities in that city. Virginia, Texas, and New York are also host to sizable Iranian American communities, each with a population greater than 10,000.

Ethnicity

The modern nation of Iran is composed of multiple ethnic and religious groups. The predominant ethnic group is Persian, composing over half of the population of Iran. Persian culture plays a dominant role in the construction of Iranian identity through the use of Persian language (Farsi) and the importance of traditional Persian customs, holidays, music, and literature. Yet, Iran also contains many other ethnic groups, such as Azeris, Kurds, and Arabs, which collectively constitute more than a third of the population of Iran.

Although the ethnic composition of Iran is known, the precise ethnic makeup of the Iranian American population is more difficult to ascertain because of shortcomings in how information on ethnicity, nationality, and race are collected in the United States. Although the Iranian American community has a diverse ethnic composition, some scholars argue that the ethnic differences among Iranian Americans have become less pronounced as Iranian Americans coalesce around a common diasporic experience and shared cultural traditions. Thus, although many non-Persian Iranian Americans may construct part of their ethnic identity from their non-Persian ethnic heritage, it does not lead to a division within the Iranian American community.

Religious Affiliation

The dominant religious group of Iran is Shi'a Muslim, containing nine of ten Iranians; other groups include Sunni Muslims, Zoroastrians, Jews, Christians, and Baha'is. Although most Iranian Americans are Shi'a Muslim, the level of religiosity varies widely. For some, devout practice of Islam has continued or even increased with migration to the United States. As Georges Sabagh and Mehdi Bozorgmehr have argued, however, the Iranian American community has a strong secular character, in which ethnic identity functions independently of religious identity. This is partly because of the higher levels of migration from Iran for those who had low levels of religiosity and a higher social class standing, leading to an Iranian American community with a lower level of religiosity than Iranian society has.

Economic Status

That Iranian immigration is selective and immigrants are mostly of a higher social class, along with the traditional emphasis on education and upward mobility, has led to an ethnic community that has been economically successful on average. The median household income of Iranian Americans was $58,912 in 1999, which was substantially greater than the national median household income of $41,994. Iranian Americans have also attained a high level of education, with 28% of Iranian Americans over age 25 having a master's degree or higher, including the 12% with a professional or doctorate degree. In contrast, 9% of all U.S. residents over age 25 have a master's degree, including 3% with a professional or doctorate degree. The emphasis on education and professional careers is also visible in the disproportionately high number of Iranian Americans who work in the fields of medicine and science, including a large number of physicians and engineers.

The economic success of many Iranian Americans illustrates their effort to assimilate to the mainstream. Yet, and seemingly paradoxically, Iranian Americans maintain a strong connection to traditional cultural practices. Nilou Mostofi makes sense of this paradox by emphasizing the strong division of social space for Iranian Americans between the public space and the private or familial space. Although this division exists even for Iranians in Iran, for Iranian Americans, this division allows for the strengthening of ethnic identity concurrent with assimilation to mainstream society. In the public sphere, Iranians have assimilated to mainstream U.S. society in social mobility and the strong identification with U.S. ideals of freedom, individuality, secularism, and civic nationalism. Yet, in the private sphere of the home and in community gatherings, Iranian Americans reinforce their ethnic identity through the practice of Iranian culture and specifically those Iranian traditions that predate the introduction of Islam to Iran. This is most evident in the continuing significance of Nowruz, the Persian New Year, as an important holiday for Iranian Americans that also helps to reinforce a sense of Iranian American identity and community.

Political Issues

The turbulent political relationship between the United States and Iran has influenced the relationship of Iranian Americans with their host society. Although Iran was closely allied with the United States before the Iranian Revolution of 1979, U.S. support for the regime of Shah Mohammad Reza Pahlavi embittered many of those Iranian Americans who favored democratic ideals and were opposed to the Shah. The Iran-Iraq war (1980–1988), which led to at least half a million Iranian deaths, was a painful event for Iranian Americans, many of whom had close ties to Iran. U.S. support for Iraq during the war created contradictory feelings among Iranian Americans, many of whom were strongly in favor of the U.S. political system yet opposed to U.S. foreign policy.

The Iranian Revolution introduced a new government that was hostile to the United States, and the student takeover of the U.S. embassy and the following hostage crisis from 1979 to 1981 led to a pronounced change of U.S. popular opinion from ignorance or apathy toward Iran and Iranian Americans to antipathy and even hostility. Popular attitude toward Iranian Americans was also affected following the terrorist attacks of September 11, 2001, as many Iranian Americans reported experiencing a rise in hostility toward anyone perceived to be of a Muslim background. Though these events have led to a degree of tension between Iranian Americans and the mainstream U.S. society, they have led neither to a significant exclusion of Iranian Americans from society nor toward the construction of an Iranian American identity in opposition to the host society.

The experience of Iranian Americans, as members of a relatively new ethnic community in the United States, is one of both assimilation to mainstream society and the simultaneous reinforcement of a specifically Iranian ethnic identity. For many Iranian Americans, this process is not contradictory but, rather, results in an identity that is at once Iranian and American, reinforced and validated through the shared experiences of the Iranian American community.

Bijan Warner

See Appendix A

See also Assyrian Americans; Diaspora; Ethnicity, Negotiating; Immigration, Economic Impact of; Muslim Americans

Further Readings

Kelley, Ron, ed. 1993. *Irangeles: Iranians in Los Angeles.* Berkeley: University of California Press.

Mostofi, Nilou. 2003. "Who We Are: The Perplexity of Iranian-American Identity." *Sociological Quarterly* 44(4):681–703.

Sabagh, Georges and Mehdi Bozorgmehr. 1994. "Secular Immigrants: Religiosity and Ethnicity Among Iranian Muslims in Los Angeles." Pp. 445–473 in *Muslim Communities in North America,* edited by Y. Y. Haddad and J. I. Smith. Albany: State University of New York Press.

Sullivan, Zohreh T. 2001. *Exiled Memories: Stories of Iranian Diaspora.* Philadelphia, PA: Temple University Press.

U.S. Census Bureau. 2005. American Community Survey 2004. Available from http://www.census.gov/acs/www

IRAQI AMERICANS

Iraqi Americans are the immigrants and their descendants from Iraq, a country of 29.0 million, as of 2007 estimates. Iraqi Americans represent one of the many diverse groups of the Arab nation, which includes those from Algeria, Bahrain, Egypt, Jordan, Kuwait, Lebanon, Libya, Morocco, Oman, Palestine, the Republic of Yemen, Qatar, Saudi Arabia, Syria, Tunisia, and the United Arab Emirates, and of who speak the Arabic language. According to the 2000 census, there were 89,890 people born in Iraq resident in the United States, of whom 50.7% are citizens. This entry will look at recent immigration from Iraq to the United States and the emerging picture of Iraqi refugees.

The Iraqi Diaspora

The large waves of emigration from Iraq that began with the Saddam Hussein regime have continued. This is referred to as the Iraqi Diaspora, and destinations include many other countries besides the United States. Between 1989 and 2001, a little more than 49,000 Iraqis immigrated to the United States. Many entered as refugees or were granted refugee status after entering. According to the Bureau of Citizenship and Immigration Services (formerly a part of the Immigration and Naturalization Service), 25,710 Iraqi-born immigrants were naturalized between 1991 and 2001.

Many assume that the immigration of Arabs decreased immediately after September 11, 2001. However, the number of immigrants who entered or became legal permanent residents stayed level, though the number of non-immigrants who were issued visas and admitted to the United States as tourists, students, or temporary workers did decrease. There was about a 70% decrease in the number of tourist and business visas issued to individuals from Gulf countries.

According to the U.S. Census Bureau American Community Survey, there were 37,728 people of Iraqi national origin in the United States in 2005. In geographic distribution, the top five states were Michigan, California, Illinois, New York, and Pennsylvania. The largest population of Iraqi Americans can be found in Detroit. According to the 2000 census, 50.1% speak English less than "very well." Their median family income was $41,179 compared with $50,890 for the nation as a whole.

Among famous Iraqi Americans are Heather Raffo, playwright and actress; TIMZ (Tommy Hanna), rapper; Eliott Yamin, singer; Chris Kattan, actor; Stephan Smith, singer, songwriter, and musician; and Zainab Salbi, cofounder and president of Women for Women International.

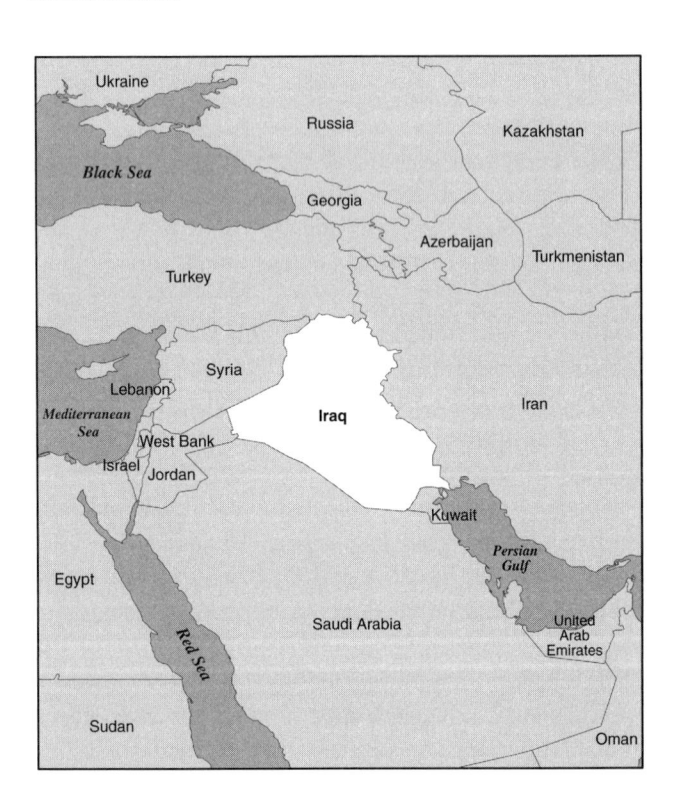

Iraqi Refugees

The number of Iraqis granted refugee status averaged 2,000 to 3,000 annually in the years leading up to the Iraq War, and then less than 500 in 2002 and less than 300 annually beginning in 2003 during the subsequent occupation. Numbers granted asylum status similarly declined.

With U.S. presence in Iraq continuing, many Iraqis who have aided the U.S.-led mission have increasingly sought refuge in the West. Advocates on their behalf have sought policies similar to those in the aftermath of the Vietnam War when President Gerald Ford authorized the admission to the United States of more than 131,000 South Vietnamese refugees. Observers wonder whether, even if a level of stability is achieved in Iraq, some of the individuals most closely associated with the United States might be put at risk with the departure of U.S. troops.

As a more long-term policy is debated, the United States has struggled to respond to the growing number of refugees (more than 8,000 by mid-2007) seeking to flee sectarian fighting within Iraq. Depending on the occupation outcome and U.S. resettlement polices, the Iraqi American community could potentially experience a major transformation in the coming years.

Jennifer M. Klein

See Appendix A
See also Arab Americans; Assimilation; Assyrian Americans; Diaspora; Immigrant Communities; Immigration, U.S.; Kurdish Americans; Muslim Americans; Refugees; Symbolic Ethnicity

Further Readings

Ajabi, Fouad. 2006. *The Foreigner's Gift: The Americans, the Arabs, and the Iraqis in Iraq.* New York: Free Press.

Cooper, Helene. 2007. "U.S. Officials Admit Delays in Issuing Visas to Iraqis." *New York Times,* July 28, p. A10.

Department of Homeland Security. 2006. *Yearbook of Immigration Statistics*: 2005. Washington, DC: Office of Immigration Statistics. Available from http://www.dhs.gov/ximgtn/statistics/publications/yearbook.shtm

Samhan, Helen Hatab. 1999. "Not Quite White: Race Classification and the Arab-American Experience." In *Arabs in America: Building a New Future*, edited by M. W. Suleiman. Philadelphia, PA: Temple University Press.

Tripp, Charles. 2000. *A History of Iraq.* Cambridge, MA: Cambridge University Press.

U.S. Census Bureau. 2004. *Profile of Demographic and Social Characteristics: 2000. People Born in Iraq.* Available from http://www.census.gov/population/www/socdemo/foreign/STP-159-2000tl.html

U.S. Census Bureau. 2006. American Community Survey 2005. Available from http://www.census.gov/acs/www

IRELAND

Ireland, estimated to have a population of 4.1 million people in 2007, is a particularly interesting case for ethnic and racial studies scholars because of its history of colonization, struggle for independence, and recent economic growth. Studying Ireland's complex ethnic and racial landscape may help scholars understand the processes of changing conceptions of race and ethnicity. This entry discusses the history, religion, language, and politics, all of them important factors in understanding race and ethnicity in Ireland—and elsewhere.

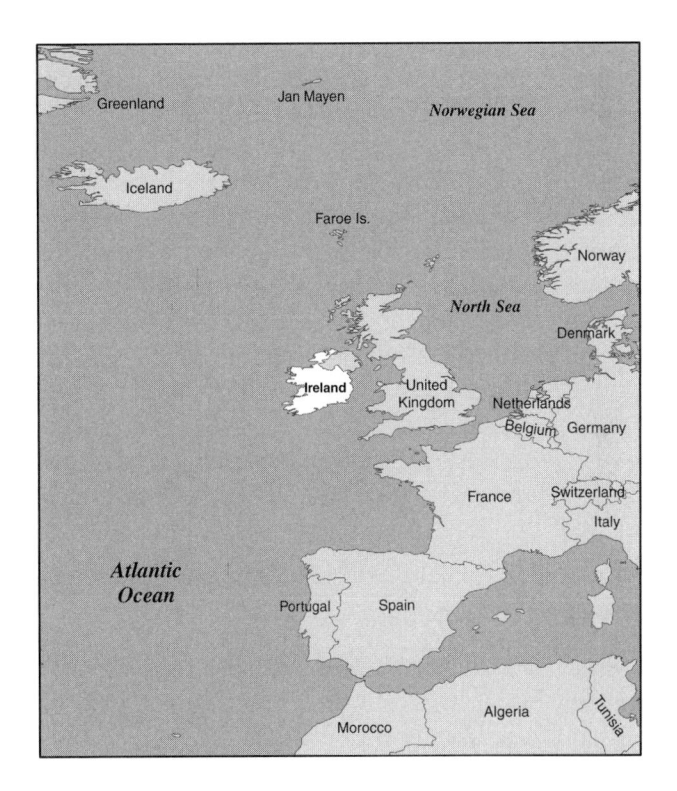

The English in Ireland

The island of Ireland was settled by many different groups of people, including Celts, Gaels, Vikings, Normans, and English. As with any nation, the Irish are not a primordial group but a socially constructed nationality.

Norman settlers (later known as the Old English) arrived in Ireland in the 12th century and established themselves in Dublin and its surrounding area, which became known as the Pale. English rule of Ireland effectively began in 1601, with Hugh O'Neill's loss at the battle of Kinsale. Less clear is when the negative image of the Irish emerged, but they suffered degradation and stereotyping at the hands of the English. This negative identity was partly associated with Catholicism, which the then-Protestant English viewed as papistry and ignorance.

The Role of Religion

Since the time of St. Patrick in the 5th century, Ireland has been largely Catholic. Religion played a significant role in constituting an ethnic Irish identity, partly because it helped differentiate Irish from English. However, the English negative image of the Irish was not solely associated with religion; apparent differences from the English were used to create the Irish as "others." High taxes and English economic and political favoritism of the New English planters resulted in economic hardship for the majority in Ireland.

In an effort to establish firm control in Ireland, extend their influence "beyond the Pale," and settle Ireland with loyal English, the English established many laws favoring New English and Protestants. Examples include recusancy fines, the Act for the Settling of Ireland, the Penals Laws, and restricting Parliament to Protestants only. Although their rule had created the impoverished situation of the Irish, the English viewed the unemployed, poor, and powerless Irish as deserving their lot because of laziness, stupidity, and backwardness, which helped to rationalize English rule.

The Role of Language

Like Catholicism, the Irish language also helped to constitute the Irish as a distinct ethnic group. Official business was usually conducted in English, and the favoritism of the New English settlers effectively eliminated the Irish-speaking ruling class. As a result, Irish language lost cultural respect while it remained a vernacular, particularly in rural areas. Irish language and names came to symbolize resistance to English rule and loyalty to the Irish independence effort. In the path to independence, Irish language helped unite opposition to English rule.

The Gaelic League was established in 1893 and, though originally apolitical, increased Irish ethnic pride and helped organize opposition to colonial occupation. Thus, Irish language helped construct both Irish identity and the nation-state. The role of Irish language in the political and cultural creation of Ireland is reflected in the 1937 constitution, which prioritizes Irish as the first official language. A national language is associated with a people, whereas an official language is related to a state. The constitution deemphasizes English, recognizing it as a second official language or another language (in the Irish version of the constitution). Referencing Irish as the national and official language links the language with Irish people and the Irish state.

The Great Potato Famine (1845–1849), and other terrible suffering under English political economic control, caused mass emigration of Irish language speakers and further reduced the vibrancy of the Irish language. However, the suffering also strengthened Irish identity and resistance to English rule. Irish emigrants—in the United States, for example—contributed financially and emotionally to the independence effort. The suffering of the famine produced a strong icon to rally around and remains a powerful symbol in Irish history and identity.

An Independent State

The struggle for independence required changing the negative stereotypes of Irishness into a positive self-image. In the 19th century, Gaelic revival of Irish culture—including athletics, language, literature, and history—helped produce a positive Irish identity and nationalistic pride. The Gaelic Athletic Association (1884) and the Gaelic League preceded the formation of Sinn Féin, an Irish nationalist party established in the early 20th century, now committed inter alia to a united Ireland free of English rule in Northern Ireland.

The Gaelic revival helped establish Irishness as a strong and positive identity around which to organize politically. Ireland gained independence from England in 1921, but required a strong Irish identity to do so, which alienated those perceived as different, including non-Catholics, Irish Travellers, and immigrants. The partitioning of the island, with the English maintaining control of Northern Ireland, led to continued efforts to nationalize the entire island and strong nationalistic sentiment evidenced in the goals of Sinn Féin and the Irish Republican Army.

Conflict in the North

Irish ethnicity has played a large part in the conflicts in Northern Ireland. Unionists are mainly Protestants favoring continued British control of Northern Ireland, and Nationalists are mainly Catholics preferring Irish control. The strength of the conflicts has fluctuated, but strong feelings are held on both sides because ethnic identity is so closely involved in these politics. The continued struggle forces those living there to choose a side and strengthens religious, ethnic, and national identity.

The conflict in Northern Ireland has also indirectly affected the ethnic and racial landscape in the Republic of Ireland through the 1998 Good Friday Agreement (GFA), which is sensitive to identity and represents a historic step toward peace in Northern Ireland. It emphasized inclusion and equality with a constitutional amendment that anyone born on the island of Ireland is entitled to Irish citizenship. Previously, birth on the island also qualified one for Irish citizenship, but before the 1999 constitutional ratification of the GFA, this qualification for citizenship was only based on law and could have been changed without a national referendum.

The GFA might indicate an inclusive society. However, just 6 years later, on June 11, 2004, almost 80% of those who voted in the citizenship referendum approved changing the citizenship requirement from birth on the island (*jus soli*) to hereditary (*jus sanguinis*). Since January 1, 2005, the constitutional requirement for citizenship at birth is a parent (or grandparent) with Irish citizenship. The strong Irish identity, which aided the independence effort, was originally largely anti-British. This citizenship referendum indicates that the strong Irish identity has now resulted in closure and exclusion of those not considered Irish; Irish identity was previously largely oppositional and is now exclusive.

Economic Growth and Racism

The result of the citizenship referendum is surprising because it coincides with tremendous economic growth, which is usually associated with low racial and ethnic conflict. Despite unprecedented economic growth from the early 1990s and gaining the label "the Celtic Tiger," racism has been apparent in Ireland, as experienced by asylum seekers, for example. This apparent contradiction might be partially explained by the extremely uneven distribution of the economic prosperity, with many seeing no economic improvement in their lives.

The history of Irish suffering, though cruel and inhumane, may now fuel nationalism and a sense of entitlement to participate in the economic prosperity. When many fail to participate, they may scapegoat recent immigrants, those who do not appear to belong, and those who are supposedly costing them tax money. Asylum seekers are not permitted to work legally and are largely perceived to be a drain on the economy. Politicians scapegoat them to avoid blame for economic disparity and suggest that asylum seekers are only fleeing their homes in search of a better economic life. The long-evident racist treatment of Irish Travellers also remains despite economic success. Meanwhile, return migrants receive a relatively friendly welcome.

The ethnic and racial landscape in Ireland is complex, with strong internal and external conflicts. There has been change over time in some respects (e.g., the recent citizenship referendum), but remarkable stability in other areas (e.g., anti-Traveller sentiment and conflict with Protestants). Conflicts along ethnic, religious, national, and racial lines all exist in Ireland, making it an important site for research to understand various forms of exclusion and their processes of change. Antiracism campaigns (such as the National Consultative Committee on Racism and Interculturalism) are active and may provide other countries with effective strategies to combat racism.

Emily Rauscher

See Appendix A
See also Britain's Irish; Colonialism; Ethnic Conflict; Irish Americans; Northern Ireland, Racism in

Further Readings

Allen, Kieran. 2000. *The Celtic Tiger: The Myth of Social Partnership in Ireland.* Manchester, UK: Manchester University Press.

Foster, R. F. 1988. *Modern Ireland: 1600–1972.* London: Penguin Books.

Ignatiev, Noel. 1995. *How the Irish Became White.* New York: Routledge.

Kirby, Peadar. 2002. *The Celtic Tiger in Distress: Growth with Inequality in Ireland.* New York: Palgrave.

Lentin, Ronit and Robbie McVeigh. 2002. *Racism and Antiracism in Ireland.* Belfast, Ireland: Beyond the Pale.

MacSharry, Ray and Padraic White. 2000. *The Making of the Celtic Tiger: The Inside Story of Ireland's Boom Economy.* Cork, Ireland: Mercier Press.

O'Hearn, Denis. 1998. *Inside the Celtic Tiger: The Irish Economy and the Asian Model.* London: Pluto Press.

IRISH AMERICANS

The Irish presence in the United States stretches back to the 1600s and reflects a diversity based on time of entry, settlement area, and religion. Irish Americans have been visible positively, as playing a central role in U.S. life; however, like many other immigrant groups, they also been victimized at certain historical periods. The Irish were the first immigrant group to encounter prolonged organized resistance. Strengthened by continued immigration and facility with the English language, and building on strong community and family networks and on familiarity with representative politics, Irish Americans became an integral part of the United States, as described in this entry.

Irish Immigration Before 1845

Protestants dominated early Irish immigration to the colonies even though these Presbyterians from Ireland of Scotch descent accounted for only one of ten, at most one of seven, of the island of Ireland's residents in the 18th century. Motivating the early immigrants was the lure of free land in North America, a sharp contrast to Ireland where more and more tenants had to compete for land. Powerful Irish property owners took full advantage by squeezing more and more profits, making migration to colonial America attractive.

The Roman Catholics among the early immigrants were a diverse group. Some were extensions of the privileged classes seeking to prosper even more. Protestant settlers of all national backgrounds united in their hatred of Catholicism. In most of the colonies, Catholics could not practice their faith openly and either struggled inwardly or converted to Anglicanism. Other Roman Catholics, and some Protestants, came as an alternative to prison or after signing articles of indenture that bound them to labor for periods customarily of 3 to 5 but sometimes as long as 7 years.

The U.S. Revolution temporarily stopped the flow of immigration; soon, however, deteriorating economic conditions in Ireland spurred even greater movement to North

Immigration cartoon (circa 1882). Reflecting the prejudices and stereotypes of the time, Thomas Nast's cartoon depicts Irish and Chinese immigration to the United States, showing "Fritz" and "Pat" seated at table talking. Fritz to Pat: "If the Yankee congress can keep the yellow man out, what is to hinder them from calling us green and keeping us out too?"

Source: Library of Congress, Prints & Photographs Division, LC-USZ61-2195.

America. British officials, by making passage to the newly formed republic of the United States expensive, diverted many immigrants to British North America (Canada). Yet a significant number continued to come to the United States, and although still primarily Protestant, they represented a broader spectrum of Ireland both economically and geographically.

Many mistakenly overlook this early immigration and see Irish immigration as beginning during the Great Famine. Yet, the Irish were the largest group after the English among immigrants during the colonial period. The historical emphasis on the famine immigrants is understandable given the role it played in Ireland and its impetus for the massive transfer of population from Ireland to the United States.

The Famine Years

In 1845, a fungus wiped out the potato crop of Ireland, as well as much of Western Europe and even the coastal United States. Potatoes were particularly central to the lives of the Irish, and the devastating starvation did not begin to recede until 1851. Mortality was high especially among the poor and in the more agricultural areas of the island. To escape catastrophe, some 2 million fled. Most went to England, but many continued on to the United States. From 1841 through 1890, more than 3.2 million Irish arrived in the United States.

This new migration from the old country was much more likely to consist of families than of single men. This arrival of entire households and extended kinship networks increased significantly the rapid formation of Irish social organizations in the United States. This large influx of immigrants led to the creation of ethnic neighborhoods, complete with parochial schools and parish churches that served as focal points. Fraternal organizations such as the Ancient Order of Hibernians, corner saloons, local political organizations, and Irish Nationalist groups seeking the ouster of Britain from Ireland rounded out neighborhood social life.

Already sick and weak, many migrants died while crossing the Atlantic. Upon arrival, some stayed in New York, but most moved on to other coastal cities. Some traveled inland, but for most Irish, in contrast with English and German immigrants, the railroad tickets to midwestern cities were just too expensive, so the East Coast was typically the final destination.

Later Irish immigrants would follow others westward, attracted by the California Gold Rush of the late 1840s or the emergence of new commercial trading points such as Chicago in the 1860s. Another draw was employment as laborers in the difficult and often dangerous work of building the transcontinental railroad that finally linked the East and West coasts in 1869.

Even in the best of times, the lives of the famine Irish would have been challenging in the United States, but they arrived at a difficult time. Nativist—that is, anti-Catholic and anti-immigrant—movements were already emerging and being embraced by politicians.

From independence until around 1820, little evidence appeared of the anti-Catholic sentiment of colonial days, but the cry against Roman Catholicism grew as Irish immigration increased. Prominent citizens encouraged hatred of these new arrivals. Samuel F. B. Morse, inventor of the telegraph and an accomplished painter, wrote a strongly worded anti-Catholic work in 1834 titled *A Foreign Conspiracy Against the Liberties of the United States*. Morse felt that the Irish were

Table 1 Immigration from Ireland to the United States

Decade	Number in 000s
1820s	50.7
1830s	207.4
1840s	780.7
1850s	914.1
1860s	435.8
1870s	436.9
1880s	655.5
1890s	388.4
1900s	339.0
1910s	141.1
1920s	211.2
1930s	10.9
1940s	19.8
1950s	48.4
1960s	33.0
1970s	11.5
1980s	31.9
1990s	57.0
2001–2004	5.5

Source: Department of Homeland Security. *Yearbook of Immigration Statistics*: 2004. Washington, DC: Office of Immigration Statistics, 2006. Table 2.

Note: Immigration after 1925 from Northern Ireland included with United Kingdom.

shamefully illiterate and deserved no respect. In the mind of the prejudiced people, the Irish were particularly unwelcome because they were Catholic. Many readily believed Morse's warning that the pope planned to move the Vatican to the Mississippi River Valley.

This antagonism was not limited to harsh words. From 1834 to 1854, mob violence against Catholics across the country led to death, the burning of a Boston convent, the destruction of a Catholic church and the homes of Catholics, and the use of Marines and state militia to bring peace to U.S. cities as far west as St. Louis.

In retrospect, the reception given to the Irish is not difficult to understand. Many immigrated after the potato crop failure and famine in Ireland. They fled not so much to a better life as from almost certain death. The Irish Catholics brought with them a celibate clergy, who struck the New England aristocracy as strange and reawakened old religious hatreds. According to the dominant Whites, the Irish were worse than Blacks, because unlike the slaves and even freed Blacks who "knew their place," the Irish did not suffer their maltreatment in silence. Employers balanced minorities by judiciously mixing immigrant groups to prevent unified action by the laborers. For the most part, nativist efforts only led the foreign born to emphasize their ties to Europe.

By the 1850s, nativism became an open political movement pledged to vote only for "native" Americans, to fight Catholicism, and to demand a 21-year naturalization period. Party members were instructed to divulge nothing about their program and to say that they knew nothing about it. As a result, they came to be called the Know-Nothings. Although the Know-Nothings soon vanished, the anti-alien mentality survived and occasionally became formally organized into such societies as the Ku Klux Klan in the 1860s and the anti-Catholic American Protective Association in the 1890s. Revivals of anti-Catholicism continued well into the 20th century.

Mostly of peasant backgrounds, the arriving Irish were ill-prepared to compete successfully for jobs in the city. Their children found it much easier, improving their occupational status over that of their fathers as well as experiencing upward mobility in their own lifetimes.

Becoming White

Ireland had a long antislavery tradition including practices that prohibited Irish trade in English slaves. In 1841, some 60,000 Irish signed a document known as the Irish Address in 1841, which urged Irish Americans to join the abolitionist movement in the United States. Many Irish Americans already opposed to slavery applauded the appeal, but they were soon drowned out by fellow immigrants who denounced or questioned the authenticity of the petition.

The Irish immigrants, subjected to derision and menial jobs, sought to separate themselves from the even lower classes, particularly Black Americans and especially slaves. The Irish were not truly "White" during the antebellum period because the Irish as a group were seen as inferior by Whites. Irish character was rigidly cast in negative racial typology. Though the shared experiences of oppression could have led Irish Americans to ally with Black Americans, instead they grasped for "Whiteness" at the margins of their life in the United States. Direct competition between the two groups was uncommon. In 1855, for example, Irish immigrants made up 87% of New York City's unskilled laborers, but free Blacks accounted for only 3%.

In 1863, the Union government implemented a national conscription law requiring able-bodied men between the ages of 20 and 45 to fight in the Civil War. Men could avoid service by presenting an acceptable substitute or paying $300. Irish Americans, already experiencing heavy losses in the war, had grown tired of it. Opposition to conscription was widespread but especially visible in Boston and New York City. The opposition grew violent in New York City with participants, mostly poor Irish Americans, striking out first against symbols of the government and then targeting African American organizations and even individual Blacks. The vandalism and violence were aimed at those even weaker than the working-class Irish who resented "a rich man's war and a poor man's fight." The "Draft Riots of 1863," as they came to be called, violently showed the dilemma many Irish Americans felt in fighting for the freedom of their Negro competitors in the labor market. Eventually the rioters were quelled with the dispatch of troops fresh from Gettysburg, including Irish American soldiers.

As Irish immigration continued in the latter part of the 19th century until the Irish gained independence from British crown in 1921, Irish immigrants began to see themselves favorably and as superior to the initial waves of Italian, Polish, and Slovak Roman Catholic immigrants. More frequently, Irish Americans began to assume leadership positions in politics and labor unions. Still, loyalty to the church played a major role.

By 1910, the priesthood was the professional occupation of choice for second-generation men. Irish women were more likely than were their German and English immigrant counterparts to become schoolteachers. In time, the occupational profile of Irish Americans diversified, and they began to experience slow advancement. They were gradually welcomed into the White working class as their identity as "White" overcame their status as "immigrant."

With mobility came social class distinctions within Irish America. As the immigrants and their children began to move into the more affluent urban areas, they were derogatorily referred to as the "lace-curtain Irish." The lower-class Irish immigrants they left behind, meanwhile, were referred to as the "shanty Irish." But as immigration from Ireland slowed and upward mobility quickened, fewer and fewer Irish qualified as the poor cousins of their predecessors.

In the 1950s, as in the 19th century, economic hard times in Ireland spurred immigration to the United States. However, a cap of 2,000 immigrants from any one European country led to the sporadic influx of illegal immigrants from the Republic of Ireland. Congressional action in 1987 included a provision that resulted in another 16,000 visas for Irish immigrants. This recent experience with immigration controls led several national and local Irish American organizations to stand with those in 2006 who protested for procedures to allow illegal immigrants in the United States to apply for citizenship.

The most visible components of Irish American life, such as schooling and work, had their roots in the 20th century. Extended formal schooling was stressed, and young people were encouraged to enter professions, especially the law. The Irish, with their heritage of the long struggle for political independence in Ireland, comprehended the essentials of representative government. Politics and civic employment opportunities such as law enforcement became a critical path to both influence and upward mobility. This pattern has continued to the present. Indeed, of the 345 firefighters who perished in the September 11, 2001, attacks on New York City's World Trade Center, 145 were members of the Emerald Society, the fire department's Irish American fraternal group.

For the Irish American man, the priesthood was viewed as a desirable and respected occupation. Furthermore, Irish Americans played a leadership role in the Roman Catholic Church in the United States. The Irish dominance persisted long after other ethnic groups swelled the ranks of the faithful.

Contemporary Irish Americans

In the 2000 census, people identifying as Irish accounted for 30.5 million people—second only to those claiming German ancestry. This represented a decline of more than 8.2 million from the number of people self-identifying as Irish in 1990, a product of assimilation rather than of out-migration.

Contemporary Irish immigration is relatively slight, accounting for perhaps 1 of 1,000 legal arrivals today compared with more than a third of all immigrants in the 1840s and 1850s. About 202,000 people in the United States were born in Ireland—comparable to the numbers of Portuguese born in the United States. Today's Irish American typically enjoys the symbolic ethnicity of food, dance, and music. Gaelic language instruction is offered in fewer than thirty colleges. Visibility as a collective ethnic group is greatest with the annual St. Patrick's Day celebrations when everyone seems to be Irish, and there is occasional fervent nationalism aimed at curtailing Great Britain's role in Northern Ireland. Some stereotypes remain concerning excessive drinking, despite available data indicating that alcoholism rates are no higher and sometimes lower among people of Irish ancestry compared with descendants of other European immigrant groups.

St. Patrick's Day celebrations offer an example of how ethnic identity evolves over time. The Feast of St. Patrick has a long history but the public celebrations with parties, concerts, and parades originated in the United States and were exported to Ireland in the latter part of the 20th century.

Well-known Irish Americans span society, including the celebrity chef Bobby Flay, actor Philip Seymour Hoffman, comedian Conan O'Brien, and author Frank McCourt, as well as the political dynasties of the Kennedys in Massachusetts and the Daleys in Chicago. But, reflecting growing intermarriage, Irish America also includes singer Mariah Carey, whose mother is Irish and whose father is African American and Venezuelan.

Irish Americans are firmly anchored in contemporary United States society. Some members keep a more vigilant eye on their past roots or on contemporary events in Ireland and Northern Ireland, but in everyday life, most people of Irish ancestry move through social life with ease and little conscious thought of their ethnic roots.

Richard T. Schaefer

See Appendix A; Appendix B
See also Assimilation; Britain's Irish; Harlem; Ireland; Nativism; Stereotypes; Symbolic Ethnicity; Whiteness

Further Readings

Fallows, Marjorie R. 1979. *Irish Americans: Identity and Assimilation.* Englewood Cliffs, NJ: Prentice Hall.

Greeley, Andrew M. 1981. *The Irish Americans: The Rise to Money and Power.* New York: Warner Books.

Ignatiev, Noel. 1995. *How the Irish Became White.* New York: Routledge.

Lee, J. J. and Marion R. Casey. 2006. *Making the Irish American.* New York: New York University Press.

Meagher, Timothy J. 2005. *The Columbia Guide to Irish American History.* New York: Columbia University Press.

Roediger, David. 1994. *Towards the Abolition of Whiteness.* London: Verso.

ISLAMOPHOBIA

The term *Islamophobia* is a neologism dating from the early 1990s, constructed by analogy with terms such as *agoraphobia, xenophobia,* and *homophobia.* Islamophobia denotes a range of negative feelings toward Muslims and their religion, from generalized bigotry, intolerance, and prejudice on the one hand to a morbid dread and hatred on the other. It may manifest itself in an equally broad range of negative actions and responses, including discrimination against Muslims, social exclusion, verbal and physical harassment, hate crimes, attacks on mosques, and vilification of Islam in the media. The history and current manifestations are described in this entry.

Background

Islamophobia has been described as "a new name to an old phenomenon." Its roots can be traced to early Christian and Jewish polemic against Islam, as well as to more recent theories such as the clash of civilizations thesis. Western involvement in Muslim lands, from the Crusades to the widespread colonization in the 17th and 18th centuries and the more recent political interventions in Afghanistan, Iraq, and elsewhere, has created a climate in which hostility toward Islam can thrive. In the postcommunist era, Islam can be seen as being drawn into the vacuum created by the absence of an "Other" for the West.

The media have fed this hostility in two ways: First, the religion of Islam is often presented as inflexible, barbaric, and so stuck in the past that it is not worth engaging seriously with it as an ideology. Second, particularly in the aftermath of the September 11, 2001, attacks, Muslims have often been stereotyped as aggressive, uncompromising, potential terrorists. The outcome of this sustained targeting in the media and elsewhere is that hostility against Muslims and their religion has become normalized.

Several organizations have been set up in the West in recent years with the specific goal of challenging Islamophobia, including the Forum Against Islamophobia and Racism in the United Kingdom and the Collectif Contre l'Islamophobie en France. Public awareness of Islamophobia in the United Kingdom was increased with the publication in 1997 of a report by the Commission on British Muslims and Islamophobia (an offshoot of the Runnymede Trust) entitled *Islamophobia: A Challenge for Us All.* This report defined *Islamophobia* as "unfounded hostility towards Islam and therefore fear or dislike of all or most Muslims" and recommended sixty ways of challenging and combating its effects. A follow-up report in 2004, entitled *Islamophobia: Issues, Challenges and Action,* highlighted the lack of progress in challenging and changing attitudes and discriminatory behavior, and argued that the situation would only be improved through a combination of recognizing Muslim identities in official statistics and the legal system, ensuring equality in employment, changing attitudes through education, encouraging community cohesion in multiethnic neighborhoods, and developing more ethical approaches to the coverage of Muslim issues in the media. The term *Islamophobia* has quickly come into general use throughout the Western world, from Europe to the United States and Australia, and Middle Eastern politicians and scholars increasingly use it to describe a growing sense of alienation between Islam and the West.

Manifestations

Four main kinds of Islamophobia can be identified. The first of these is *pre-reflective personal*

Islamophobia. This involves prejudice and discrimination against Muslims simply because they have different beliefs and values and is embodied in the phrase, "Why can't they be more like us?" Such prejudice may have deep roots, which some psychologists consider fundamental to human personality, including motivational dispositions such as rejection, aggression, dominance, and superiority, and the tendency to feel fear, insecurity, and suspicion in the presence of people who are perceived as strange, foreign, or unfamiliar. It may also be related to ignorance of Muslim beliefs and values, which may leave people open to an uncritical acceptance of myths about Islam.

From these roots, Islamophobic attitudes can easily develop that are extremely difficult to change by argument or the presentation of facts. The attitudes may be kept hidden or expressed openly and may be directed toward all Muslims or toward an individual because he or she is Muslim. The attitudes are likely to be expressed in hostile behavior that includes blaming all Muslims for terrorist attacks, defacing mosques and Muslim graves, and ripping the *hijabs* from women's heads, along with rudeness, threats, verbal abuse, spitting, bullying, attacks on property, violence, and murder. Islamophobia also includes the avoidance of social contact with Muslims (even to the extent of refusing to fly in the same aircraft as a Muslim) and discrimination against them in employment, housing, and other areas of social contact. There is strong evidence to suggest that the less dramatic manifestations of pre-reflective personal Islamophobia form part of the everyday experience of many Muslims in the West and that its more dramatic manifestations are commonly perceived as real threats.

The second form of Islamophobia is *post-reflective personal Islamophobia.* In this form, the hostile attitudes and behavior are more conscious and intentional. Prejudice and discrimination against Muslims are justified by the claim that Islamic values are inferior to the liberal values of the West. Islamic education is dismissed as indoctrination, and evidence of the inferiority of Islamic values is found in the "fanatical" Muslim protests against freedom of speech (for example, against *The Satanic Verses* or the Danish Jyllands-Posten cartoons that depicted the Prophet Muhammad as a terrorist) and the "oppression" of Muslim women symbolized in the *hijab* and the burqa. Journalists have often led this righteous crusade, legitimizing and giving credibility to hatred and prejudice against Islam, and these attitudes are further reinforced through the exaggerated stereotypes of Muslims in films such as *The Siege, Aladdin,* and *Raiders of the Lost Ark.*

The third kind is *institutional Islamophobia.* This occurs where certain practices that disadvantage Muslims in the West are built into social institutions and structures, and no attempt is made to remove them as long as the balance of power lies in the hands of non-Muslims. The practices may be existing ones or new policies, but the key factor is that they ignore the needs and wishes of Muslims. An example is dress codes that are not necessary for health and safety reasons but that put Muslims in a position where they are expected to act in a way that contravenes the requirements of their faith. Other examples might be setting public examinations on important Islamic festivals like *Eid al-Fitr* or *Eid al-Adha,* denying opportunities for Muslim workers to pray at the workplace in accordance with the requirements of their faith, or insisting that no sacred texts other than the Bible can be used when witnesses are sworn in for testimony in court. The assumption in the West that all religions are like Christianity may also result in institutionalized practices that disadvantage Muslims, especially assumptions that faith is a matter of individual choice and that individuals should be free to interpret their faith in the light of their own understanding.

The fourth kind is *political Islamophobia.* Politicians have frequently played on Islamophobic attitudes to increase their popularity. Policies such as the banning of conspicuous religious symbols in schools in France have also been condemned as Islamophobic, especially when they have led to the expulsion of girls wearing Muslim headscarves from school. Attempts to counter the threat of terrorism in the aftermath of the September 11th attacks have had a disproportionate impact on the lives of Muslims in the West: Muslims are more likely than other groups to be stopped by the police, to be targeted in antiterrorist raids, to be accused of not being fully committed to citizenship in the West, and to be spied on in universities and other institutions as potential terrorist suspects.

Political Islamophobia is the most controversial of the four kinds because politicians can always claim that they are representing the views of their constituents and also because the line is not always clear between the legitimate self-protection of a country from terrorist attacks and the illegitimate targeting and harassment of an entire religious group because of the activities of a tiny minority within that group.

However, some scholars have concluded that the whole concept of Islamophobia is controversial, and have dismissed it as a myth or a form of intellectual blackmail. They argue that the term is unhelpful in the complex context of Muslim minorities in the West because the onus is on Muslims themselves to adopt the dominant public values of the society in which they live. These scholars claim that the term *Islamophobia* is being used to deflect and silence legitimate critical scrutiny of Islam and its values. From this view, the Danish cartoons should not be considered as Islamophobic, but as an example of a long-standing Western tradition of satire, and raising issues such as wearing the veil as a matter for debate is not Islamophobic but, rather, a necessary approach in a liberal, multicultural society. Claiming that Islamophobia is responsible for the low achievement of Muslim students is also dismissed as an excuse; students should accept responsibility for their own levels of achievement.

Though the term may sometimes be misapplied to anything that Muslims do not like, fear, hatred, and prejudice toward Muslims are widespread in the contemporary Western world, and treating these views and emotional responses as natural or as necessarily the fault of the Muslims themselves (because they refuse to change their own beliefs and values) is not a helpful response. States and organizations that claim to base their practices on justice, equality, and freedom must be willing to review policies and procedures to avoid discrimination against, and promote equal opportunities for, Muslims and to ensure that harassment and hostility are not part of the daily experience of Muslims living in the West.

J. Mark Halstead

See also France; Intergroup Relations, Surveying; Muslim Americans; Muslims in Canada; Muslims in Europe; Prejudice; Racism, Cultural; Religion, Minority; Veil

Further Readings

Allen, Chris and Jorgen Nielsen. 2002. *Summary Report on Islamophobia in the EU After 11 September 2001.* Vienna, Austria: European Union Monitoring Centre on Racism and Xenophobia.

Bhatia, Amir 2003. *The Fight Against Anti-Semitism and Islamophobia: Bringing Communities Together.* Brussels, Belgium: EU Directorate-General for Employment and Social Affairs.

Commission on British Muslims and Islamophobia. 1997. *Islamophobia: A Challenge for Us All.* London: Runnymede Trust.

Commission on British Muslims and Islamophobia. 2004. *Islamophobia: Issues, Challenges and Action.* Stoke-on-Trent, UK: Trentham Books.

Vertovec, Steven. 2002. "Islamophobia and Muslim Recognition in Britain." In *Muslims in the West,* edited by Y. Y. Haddah. New York: Oxford University Press.

Issei

First-generation Japanese immigrants/emigrants are called *Issei,* literally, "first generation" in Japanese. In the United States, the term typically refers to the migrants from Japan who entered Hawai'i and the U.S. mainland between 1868 and 1924. Official migration began on a large scale following the enactment of the Chinese Exclusion Act and an agreement between the Japanese government and the Hawaiian monarchy; it officially ended with the passage of the 1924 Immigration Act.

Most emigrants to Hawai'i were from farming families in rural areas of southwestern Japan, in particular Hiroshima, Yamaguchi, Kumamoto, Fukuoka, and later, Okinawa prefectures. Japanese who migrated to the United States after World War II are included as Issei but sometimes referred to more specifically as *Shin-Issei* or "new (postwar) Japanese" to distinguish between the major prewar and postwar waves of Japanese migration. As with other first-generation immigrant groups, understandings of Issei in the United States have changed with shifts in scholarship on race and ethnicity. This entry looks at immigration patterns, points out the differences between Issei in Hawai'i and on the U.S. mainland, and summarizes trends in research on the Issei.

Patterns of Migration

Official Japanese migration to what is now the United States actually began to a place that was not part of the United States at the time: the Kingdom, Republic, and later, U.S. territory of Hawai'i. Between 1885 and 1894, there were three different periods of migration from Japan, according to Alan Moriyama. From 1885 to 1894, married couples and single men emigrated as government-sponsored contract laborers to work primarily on sugar cane plantations. From 1894 to 1908, migrant sponsorship shifted from the Japanese government to private emigration companies based in Japan. Finally, between 1908 and 1924 was a period of primarily "independent" emigration, meaning most people were not sponsored by the government or private emigration companies and, instead, had the support of relatives already in the United States.

Meanwhile, patterns of migration to the U.S. mainland are generally divided into two major periods, according to Yuji Ichioka. From 1885 to 1907, migrants were mostly single male *dekasegi* (sojourners) who took on wage labor in mining, lumber, canneries, and agriculture. In large cities such as San Francisco, Portland, and Seattle, they often worked as "schoolboys," attending school while also working as domestic servants. The passage of the 1907–1908 Gentlemen's Agreement marked the end of prewar labor migration from Japan to the United States. From 1908 to 1924, more settled immigrant communities began to develop around urban centers and farming areas. After Hawai'i became a U.S. territory in 1900, thousands of laborers left the islands for the mainland, presumably to escape the harsh plantation conditions and to access the relatively higher wages available on the West Coast.

Issei women are probably best known as "picture brides." This refers to the practice of arranged marriage between women in Japan (and Korea) and their countrymen living in Hawai'i and on the U.S. mainland. In most cases, the wives had seen only pictures of their husbands before meeting them upon arrival in the United States. Picture bride migration peaked between 1908 and 1924 and enabled the formation of Japanese (and Okinawan in Hawai'i) communities based on the development of families and women's additional paid and unpaid labor.

Four major patterns of migration explain how Japanese migrants ended up in the United States. First, some went to the Kingdom of Hawai'i, settled there, and Hawai'i itself became part of the United States. Most people in this group came from poorer farming backgrounds. Second, some emigrants went directly to the U.S. mainland. This group tended to come from slightly higher class backgrounds compared with the first group. Third, some people migrated to Hawai'i then saved money for the passage to the U.S. mainland and made a second domestic migration after Hawai'i became a U.S. territory. Finally, a smaller number of Japanese went to Canada or Mexico, then crossed the border to the United States.

U.S. Mainland Versus Hawai'i: Differences

Issei experiences and identities have been shaped by different social histories and demographics in Hawai'i and on the U.S. mainland.

Starting in 1900, Okinawans also began migrating to Hawai'i and eventually their numbers became the largest. Okinawa had been an independent kingdom until it became a prefecture of Japan in 1879. Some Okinawans also went to the U.S. mainland, but their numbers remain most concentrated in Hawai'i, where they represent a large proportion of the Japanese American population today. In contrast to the U.S. mainland, where they are commonly subsumed as Japanese, in Hawai'i, Okinawan ethnic identity was shaped by plantation experiences and persists, possibly because of their large numbers; Okinawans have distinct cultural and linguistic differences from other Japanese and a history of discrimination by *Naichi* (mainland Japanese).

Perhaps the most significant difference occurred during World War II. People of Japanese ancestry experienced a mass removal and internment by the U.S. government, but this did not occur in Hawai'i. In the islands, Japanese priests, schoolteachers, and other community leaders were incarcerated at Honouliuli and Sand Island camps on O'ahu and in U.S. mainland camps, but most Japanese Americans in Hawai'i were not interned, ostensibly because of their large population and their significance for the territory's economy.

Developments in Scholarship on Issei

Frameworks for conceptualizing and discussing Issei have shifted in recent years. In earlier periods, Issei were studied primarily in terms of their lives in the United States—within what might be called a U.S. ethnic studies framework. This type of research largely assumed that migration was unidirectional and stressed the rightful inclusion of Issei as Americans regardless of citizenship (for which they were ineligible until the McCarran-Walter Act of 1952). It focused on their experiences as immigrants who left their homelands, families, and former lives to start new ones in the United States. More recent scholarship, however, takes a more transnational or global approach, looking beyond Issei experiences in the U.S. domestic context to examine ways in which they continued to be influenced by Japan, the country they supposedly left behind. This perspective re-situates Issei as living more multifaceted lives with complicated and multiple allegiances that were not based only in the United States.

This shift can be explained by the convergence of several factors. First, a growing awareness and condemnation of Japanese American internment history in mainstream U.S. discourse is changing the way that Japanese Americans as a whole can be, and are being, discussed. Possibilities are opening up to talk about Issei identifications in more complex ways. Instead of dwelling on bifurcated loyalties to either the United States or Japan, discussions can move on to other issues and don't need to linger on proving the "Americanness" of U.S. residents of Japanese ancestry. Earlier scholars undoubtedly avoided this kind of framework because of the previous need to emphasize the Americanness of Japanese immigrants. The transnational perspective is quite controversial, given the propaganda and discourse that justified the internment of Issei and their U.S.-born children based on continued ties to Japan that supposedly posed a military threat.

This discursive shift reflects similar trends in Asian U.S. studies, immigration studies, and racial and ethnic studies. This understanding of the world as more interconnected than previously imagined is affecting the way that contemporary studies are being conducted and the ways in which we understand history.

Another contributory factor is the increasing amount of bilingual research being conducted. In addition to studies that previously examined English language documents by and about Issei, a growing body of scholarship also accesses documents in Japanese by and about Issei. Accessing these additional documents is leading to new understandings of Issei lifestyles and attitudes.

Scholars producing work on Issei are coming from increasingly diverse backgrounds. More and more scholars in and from Japan are contributing to the body of knowledge about Japanese immigrants/emigrants. Most work on Issei in the United States was originally conducted by people greatly influenced by the politics of ethnic studies programs; that, too, is changing. Broader interpretations of Issei and other Asian American histories and experiences are leading to what some are calling the denationalization and depoliticization of the field.

Finally, Issei experiences are being examined not only in the context of other immigration histories in the U.S. context, but also in relation to other Japanese emigrants and as part of a larger Japanese diaspora. Increasing interaction between ethnic Japanese communities and scholars in Brazil, Peru, Argentina, Bolivia, Cuba, Canada, and Mexico, among other countries, is resulting in more of this type of research from a more global perspective. Through comparisons of Issei experiences in North and South American countries, for example, the different ways in which each government shaped the racial (and ethnic) formation of Japanese immigrants and their communities is being better understood.

Jane H. Yamashiro

See also Chinese Exclusion Act; Gentlemen's Agreement (1907–1908); Haole; Hawai'i, Race in; Hawaiians; Internment Camps; Japan; Japanese Americans; Nisei

Further Readings

Azuma, Eiichiro. 2005. *Between Two Empires: Race, History, and Transnationalism in Japanese America.* New York: Oxford University Press.

Glenn, Evelyn Nakano. 1986. *Issei, Nisei, War Bride: Three Generations of Japanese American Women in Domestic Service.* Philadelphia, PA: Temple University Press.

Hirabayashi, Lane Ryo, Akemi Kikumura-Yano, and James A. Hirabayashi, eds. 2002. *New Worlds, New Lives: Globalization and People of Japanese Descent in the Americas and from Latin America in Japan.* Stanford, CA: Stanford University Press.

Ichioka, Yuji. 1988. *The Issei: The World of the First Generation Japanese Immigrants 1885–1924.* New York: Free Press.

Kikumura, Akemi. 1992. *Issei Pioneers: Hawaii and the Mainland, 1885–1924.* Los Angeles, CA: Japanese American National Museum.

Kimura, Yukiko. 1988. *Issei: Japanese Immigrants in Hawaii.* Honolulu: University of Hawai'i Press.

Moriyama, Alan Takeo. 1985. *Imingaisha: Japanese Emigration Companies and Hawaii.* Honolulu: University of Hawai'i Press.

Italian Americans

Nearly 16 million strong, Italian Americans are often identified with the tide of poor immigrants who arrived in the early 20th century and built cohesive communities in large cities. Italians, however, were coming to this continent before the United States existed as an independent nation: among them, explorers, artists, and educators. This entry explores the full range of the Italian presence in the United States, with a particular focus on how the immigrant community related to the mainstream culture during more than a century.

The Early Years

The presence of Italians in what would become the United States begins with explorers and adventurers who journeyed here almost 5 centuries before Italy itself united and became a modern nation. Included among them were such important early explorers as Cristoforo Colombo (Columbus), Giovanni Cabotto (John Cabot), Amerigo Vespucci, and Giovanni de Verrazano, all of whom explored and charted the new land. Enrico de Tonti, together with French explorer Robert La Salle, was the first European to explore the Mississippi River in 1682. The two of them canoed from the Illinois River to the Mississippi Delta, negotiating peace treaties with many local tribes that allowed French settlement throughout the vast Mississippi Valley, later acquired by the United States through the Louisiana Purchase in 1803.

Long before the English colonies came into existence, missionaries such as Father Marcos da Nizza explored Arizona in 1539. Father Eusebio Chino, who arrived in 1681, spent almost 30 years in the U.S. Southwest, exploring and mapping while founding settlements in the region and helping to develop its cattle industry.

In the early years of the thirteen English colonies, Italian artisans were often invited to bring their needed skills to the fledgling new settlements. As early as 1621, they were in Jamestown, manufacturing glass beads for British authorities to use as currency to trade with the Indigenous Peoples. In Georgia colony, Italians brought their raw silk production expertise to build a silk industry. Along with many other nationalities, Italians migrated to Maryland colony, which welcomed Catholics in a religiously intolerant age, and there they obtained land to begin their lives anew.

Much has been written about Filippo Mazzei—a physician originally from Tuscany with a strong interest in agricultural science—who influenced the writings and farming of his neighbor, Thomas Jefferson. Mazzei's own writings, which Jefferson helped translate and publish, spoke of all men being equal, an idea and phrase that Jefferson used in the Declaration of Independence. In the Revolutionary War, fifty Italians—including two officers—joined the ranks of the Continental Army, and two regiments of volunteers were recruited in Italy to come fight for the cause of U.S. independence.

The 19th Century

Most of the 14,000 Italians who came to the United States between the Revolutionary War and the Civil War were skilled artisans, artists, educators, musicians, or political refugees, rather than the mostly unskilled peasants who would come later. A prime example is Constantino Brumidi, both an artist and political refugee, who arrived in 1852 and spent the next 25 years decorating the Capitol building. Painting monumental frescoes in its rotunda, he became known as the "Michelangelo of the U.S. Capitol Building." Another example is an 1850 arrival from Florence, Antonio Meucci, who invented the first primitive version of the telephone 26 years before Alexander Graham Bell.

When the Civil War broke out, hundreds of Italian-born men living in the South joined the Confederate Army, and thousands in the North joined the Union army. Among the 100 Italian Union officers, three were generals: Enrico Fardello, Eduardo Ferraro, and

Francis Spinola. Ferraro commanded an all-Black combat division, and Spinola headed four regiments of Italian troops recruited from the New York region. Another Italian, Lt. Col. Luigi Palma di Cesnola, distinguished himself in battle and later became the first director of New York's Metropolitan Museum of Art.

Throughout the 19th century, some parallels and relationships existed between Italians and Blacks. In some pre–Civil War southern localities, futile efforts were made to replace Black slaves with Italian workers. In other areas, Southerners barred Italian children from White schools because of their dark complexions. In 1899, five Sicilian storekeepers were hanged in Tallulah, Louisiana, for the crime of treating Black customers the same as Whites.

The Great Migration

Of the more than 5.4 million Italians who have come to the United States throughout its history (as compared to an estimated Italian population of 59.3 million people as of 2007), 80% came between 1880 and 1920. This statistic is misleading, however, because one-fourth or more returned home. Although many skilled workers and professionals continued to arrive from Italy, most Italian immigrants during this period were peasants fleeing abject poverty and economic disaster in the harsh *Mezzogiorno* east and south of Rome. Many of these were those who engaged in "shuttle migration," males arriving with the intention of staying just long enough to earn sufficient money for dowries or land before returning home.

Most of these Italian newcomers, whether sojourners or those who chose to put down roots in their adopted country, came from rural areas and were thus ill prepared for employment in an industrial nation. As a result, some labored in low-status, low-paying manual jobs as railroad laborers, miners, and dock workers. In construction, others dug ditches, laid sewer pipes, and built roads, subways, and buildings in urban areas. Still others worked in the factories and mills, with new ones continually opening as the country evolved into an industrial giant.

Earning poor wages as part of the unskilled labor force, the new Italian immigrants moved into run-down residential areas vacated by earlier arrivals, whose children and grandchildren had moved up the socioeconomic ladder. Settling in urban enclaves in cities both large and small—many of which had included Italian residents since at least the mid-19th century—the new arrivals re-created in miniature the land they had left behind. Among the most prominent of these "Little Italys" were the North End of Boston, the Mulberry District in New York City's Lower East Side, the Near West Side of central Chicago, and San Francisco's North Beach district. Often, families from the same village lived together in the same tenement.

Quickly, these easily recognized, often overcrowded territorial neighborhoods with their everyday ethnicity developed a strong social network that eased the Italians' adjustment to a new society. Parallel social institutions—their own

Italian neighborhood market. This market, photographed between 1900 and 1910, is on Mulberry Street in New York. The Mulberry District on New York City's Lower East Side was a prominent "Little Italy." These centers of Italian American life were typically overcrowded territorial neighborhoods. These cities within cities with their everyday ethnicity developed a strong social network that eased the Italians' adjustment to a new society. Parallel social institutions—their own churches, social clubs and organizations, stores, newspapers, and a vibrant street life—generated a familiar lifestyle for these urban villagers, even as they struggled to overcome poverty.

Source: Library of Congress, Prints & Photographs Division, LC-D418-9350.

churches (perhaps built in an Italian architectural style), social clubs and organizations, stores, newspapers, and a vibrant street life—generated a familiar lifestyle for these urban villagers, even as they struggled to overcome poverty and eke out an existence.

Societal Hostility

With a booming chain migration pattern of new arrivals joining family and friends (more than 1 million Italians came between 1901 and 1910), the public became increasingly aware of their presence, stereotyping this "swarm" of immigrants as possessing objectionable traits incompatible with U.S. society. When an Italian got into trouble, newspaper headlines often magnified the event and stressed the offender's nationality. Italians, like Jews, found certain occupations, fraternities, clubs, and organizations closed to them, and restrictive covenants excluded them from certain areas of the city and suburbs. The now extensive Italian American population—together with the sizable numbers from other parts of Central, Southern, and Eastern Europe—prompted demands to control immigration, which led to restrictive legislation in 1921, tightened even further by additional legislation in 1924.

The growing resentment against the presence of so many dark-haired, dark-complexioned Catholics occasionally erupted in violence and even killings. Several Italians were lynched in West Virginia in 1891. That same year, when ten Sicilians were acquitted by a jury of having killed the New Orleans police chief, an angry mob that included many of the city's leading citizens stormed the prison and brutally executed the prisoners, adding an eleventh victim who had been serving a minor sentence for a petty crime. Four years later, coal miners and other residents of a southern Colorado town murdered six Italians. In 1896, three Italians were torn from a jail in Hahnsville, Louisiana, and hanged. In a southern Illinois mining town, after a street brawl in 1914 that left one Italian and two native-born U.S. citizens dead, a lynch mob hanged the only survivor, an Italian, seemingly with the approval of the town's mayor. A few months later, another Italian was lynched in a nearby town after being arrested on suspicion of conspiracy to murder a mining supervisor, even though there was no evidence to substantiate the charge.

In Massachusetts, Nicola Sacco and Bartolomeo Vanzetti—an immigrant shoe-factory worker and a poor fish peddler—were charged with and convicted of robbery and murder in 1920. The prosecutor insulted immigrant Italian defense witnesses and appealed to the prejudices of a bigoted judge and jury. Despite someone else's later confession and other potentially exonerating evidence, the seven-year appeals fight failed to win these men retrial or acquittal; they were executed in 1927. Fifty years later, Massachusetts Governor Michael Dukakis exonerated them. Although debate continues regarding their guilt or innocence, all agree that prevailing anti-immigrant sentiments prevented their receiving a fair trial.

Social Patterns

In adapting to life in the United States, Italians continued to rely primarily on their extended families (*la famiglia*). Relatives were their principal focus of social life, and they usually regarded non-Italians as outsiders, rarely developing true interethnic friendships. Moreover, they did not encourage individual achievement, which was a U.S. tradition. More important were family honor, group stability, and social cohesion and cooperation. Each member of the family was expected to contribute to the economic well-being of the family unit.

In the old country, absentee landowners had commonly exploited Italian tenant farmers, as priests and educators silently supported this inequitable system, rarely welcoming peasant children in the schools. Landowner resistance to the political unification of Italy, which finally occurred in 1871, further increased the hardships of tenant farmers and small landholders. Consequently, Italian immigrants generally mistrusted priests and educated people.

In the United States, as in Italy, the common people—especially males—had little involvement with the church. In the early 20th century, for the most part, Irish priests staffed the churches in the Italian immigrant neighborhoods. These priests typically practiced—at least as the Italians perceived—a strange and harsh form of Catholicism, thus making them less receptive to clergy for whom they felt no affinity. In turn, the Irish priests had little empathy for the extensive veneration of the Madonna and local saints that the Italians displayed.

Similarly, Italian newcomers regarded education as having only limited practical value. Their children thus typically attended school for just as long as the law demanded and then, under their parents' encouragement, went to work to increase the family income.

A few families did not follow this pattern, but most second-generation Italian Americans who attended college did so against the wishes of their families.

Furthermore, the outside world was one of deprivation and exploitation. Not only did their employers exploit them with low wages for long hours under harsh working conditions, but often so did one of their own—the *padrone* or agent who acted as their representative in the labor market. Seeking help from elsewhere was unlikely, for Italians were reluctant to approach the non-Italians who ran the social agencies and the political machines. Surrounded by strangeness, the immigrants tried to retain the self-sufficiency of the family circle as much as they could. They also founded a number of community organizations that supported this circle, keeping away from the outside world whenever possible.

Social Mobility

Upward mobility occurred more slowly for the Italians than for many other groups arriving in the United States at about the same time, such as the Greeks, Armenians, and Jews. Contributing to this outcome were the Italians' retreatist lifestyle, disdain for education, negative stereotyping, and overt dominant-group hostility, protracted by the continuing flow of new Italian immigrants. Sheltered within their ethnic communities, the Italians gradually adapted to industrial society. They joined the working class and encouraged their children to do likewise as soon as they were able.

Second-generation adults, although drawn to *la via nuova*—"the new way"—through schools, movies, and other cultural influences, still adhered to a social structure centered on the extended family. Expected to contribute to the family's support early in life, they followed their parents into working-class occupations without benefit of the advanced education necessary to secure higher-status jobs. More Americanized than their parents, who retained much of their language and customs, the second generation experienced marginality, caught between the routines and demands of their parents and the organized ways of their ethnic life, on the one hand, and the attraction of life in the larger society, despite its prejudices against them. In this strain between the two generations, those who did not remain long in the Little Italys assimilated much more quickly. Some even changed their names and religion to accelerate the process.

Today, the picture has changed. Third- and fourth-generation Italian Americans have greatly improved their educational levels, although they remain behind other non-Italian Whites in graduate education. Nevertheless, their high school dropout rate has significantly declined since the 1980s, and the proportion getting a college education significantly increased. No longer a minority group, most have achieved economic, political, and social power; they are mostly middle class and well represented in the professional fields.

Intermarriage, or marital assimilation, is a primary indicator of structural assimilation, the last phase of minority-group mainstreaming. Exogamy among Italian Americans, especially among those three and four generations removed from the old country, exceeds 40%, which is similar to that of most European American groups. As structural assimilation proceeds, Italian Americans, like other Whites of European ancestry, are experiencing "a twilight of ethnicity." Various expressions of symbolic ethnicity continue—*bocce* leagues, festivals, and organizations celebrating Italian heritage, foods, and Italian studies programs, for example—but everyday ethnicity, language preservation, and minority group status are fading quickly. Moreover, Italian Americans take pride in the past and present achievements of individuals of Italian ancestry who have excelled and gained wide recognition in academics, the arts, athletics, business, government, literature, the military, and science.

Italian Americans still find themselves the target of prejudicial accusations about their allegedly prominent role in criminal activities, however, a stereotype perpetuated in films and television. Despite their progressing assimilation, the perception about members of this group as potential criminals or as part of the Mafia-connection stereotype persists. This especially haunts politicians of Italian descent, undermines voters' trust in them, and thus limits their political success in non-Italian settings.

The 2000 U.S. Census identified 15.9 million people (5.8% of the total U.S. population) claiming Italian ancestry. States with the highest proportions of Italian Americans were Rhode Island and Connecticut (20%), New Jersey (18%), New York (15%), Massachusetts (14%), Alabama (11%), and New Mexico (8%). In addition, other states with populations of 500,000 or more Italian Americans included California, Florida, Illinois, Ohio, and Pennsylvania.

Vincent N. Parrillo

See Appendix A

See also Americanization; Ethnic Conflict; Immigrant Communities; National Origins System; Sicilian Americans; Stereotypes; Xenophobia

Further Readings

Alba, Richard. 1985. *Italian Americans: Into the Twilight of Ethnicity.* Upper Saddle River, NJ: Prentice Hall.

LaGumina, Salvatore, Frank J. Cavaioli, Salvatore Primeggia, and Joseph A. Varacalli, eds. 1999. *The Italian American Experience: An Encyclopedia.* New York: Garland.

Mangione, Jerre and Ben Morreale. 1993. *La Storia: Five Centuries of the Italian American Experience.* New York: HarperCollins.

Sensi-Isolani, Paola Alessandra and Anthony Julian Tamburri, eds. 2001. *Italian Americans: A Retrospective on the Twentieth Century.* Chicago Heights, IL: American Italian Historical Association.

J

JACKSON, JESSE, SR. (1941–)

Like Rosa Parks, Ralph Abernathy, and Martin Luther King, Jr., Jesse Jackson is associated with the U.S. Civil Rights Movement by many. He was part of the circle around King and was present when King was assassinated. During the 1970s and 1980s, Jackson's efforts sought to expand on the legal accomplishments of the movement, seeking economic parity for all of the disenfranchised people in the United States, not just African Americans. He founded Operation PUSH with this goal, and he also established the National Rainbow Coalition to encourage electoral participation; the two organizations are now merged. Jackson also ran for president unsuccessfully in 1984 and 1988. This entry describes his life and impact.

Family and Education

Jesse Louis (Robinson) Jackson was born October 8, 1941, in Greenville, South Carolina, to Helen Burns and Noah Robinson. In 1943, his mother married Charles Jackson, who adopted him in 1957.

Jackson graduated from Sterling High School in 1959 and used a football scholarship to attend the University of Illinois. After an unsuccessful year, Jackson transferred to North Carolina Agricultural and Technical State University (A&T) in Greensboro. While at A&T, he became student body president and a member of the Congress of Racial Equality (CORE). Jackson graduated in 1964 with a degree in sociology and enrolled at the Chicago Theological Seminary (CTS).

In 1962, he married Jacqueline Brown; they have five children. In 2001, Jackson admitted to an extramarital relationship that had resulted in the birth of a daughter in May 1999.

Civil Rights Movement Leadership

Operation Breadbasket

In 1965, after watching the brutal attacks on civil rights activists in Selma, Alabama, on television, Jackson organized a trip there. Quickly introducing himself to the Southern Christian Leadership Conference (SCLC) directors—including Ralph Abernathy and Martin Luther King, Jr.—he asked for a job. Later that day, he adopted a "staff" role, even taking the podium during a series of speeches. Although his actions surprised and disconcerted many on the SCLC staff, Abernathy was impressed.

After two days in Selma, Jackson returned to Chicago and, despite not having been hired by SCLC, began organizing Black ministers on behalf of the organization's economic arm, Operation Breadbasket. Breadbasket's "selective patronage" model organized local ministers to encourage White business owners with large Black customer bases to hire Blacks and invest in the Black community. After 6 months—and despite skepticism by King—Abernathy hired Jackson as the head of Operation Breadbasket in Chicago. Afterward, Jackson withdrew from CTS. He was ordained in 1968 but later received his master of divinity degree from CTS in 2000.

The Breadbasket group—dogmatically led by Jackson—was successful: 3,000 jobs and more than

$20 million were added to the south side of Chicago in 2 years. In 1967, King named Jackson Breadbasket's national director, with fifteen affiliates. Meanwhile, Jackson built a large and loyal following among Breadbasket members in Chicago. During weekly meetings, Jackson's "I Am Somebody," call-and-response refrain was popular:

> I am—Somebody!—
>
> I may be poor—But I am—Somebody!—
>
> I may be uneducated—But I am—Somebody!—
>
> I may be unskilled—But I am—Somebody!—
>
> I may be on dope—I may have lost hope—
>
> But I am—Somebody!—
>
> I am—Black!—Beautiful!—Proud!—
>
> I must be respected!—I must be protected!—
>
> I am—God's child!—
>
> What time is it?—(*Nation Time!*)—
>
> What time is it?—(*Nation Time!*)—
>
> All right—look out! . . .

In 1969, without SCLC approval, Jackson organized the Black Expo, a weeklong business and entertainment fair held in Chicago. In 1971, board members learned that that year's EXPO was not an SCLC-sponsored event. As a result, Jackson left the organization and began Operation People United to Save (later Serve) Humanity (PUSH).

Operation PUSH

Using Breadbasket resources, staff, and business model, Operation PUSH enjoyed immediate success. During this period, Jackson authored his "kingdom theory" (which reads more like a manifesto), describing how Blacks can exert the absolute "authority of kings" and control *every* aspect of the numerous economies that influence their lives: employment, banking, and politics. Subsequently, Jackson began constructing a "Marshall Plan" for Blacks, negotiating hiring and partnership "covenants" with various corporate giants. He also developed the *PUSH for Excellence* program, aimed at increasing the number of Black students graduating from high school.

The Political Arena

The National Rainbow Coalition

In 1984, to encourage minorities to vote, Jackson announced his bid for the U.S. presidency. Based in Washington, D.C., the goal of the National Rainbow Coalition was a "progressive, Black-led, multiracial, anti-corporate, and anti-imperialist movement that took an electoral form." The result was the registration of more than 1 million new voters, and it secured 3.5 million primary election votes. Although the campaign was deemed a political success for Jackson and the Democratic Party, it drained resources from Operation PUSH and brought its financial practices and solvency into question. During the election, Jackson was quoted making anti-Semitic remarks in an interview. Although he admitted the blunder and apologized, the backlash dashed his presidential hopes.

In 1988, Jackson again ran for president. This time, an additional 2 million new voters registered, and he received 7 million votes. Despite his tremendous popularity and his hopes for the vice presidential candidacy, he was not selected.

Rainbow/PUSH Coalition

In 1996, Jackson announced that PUSH and the National Rainbow Coalition would merge to form the Rainbow/PUSH Coalition (RPC). Headquartered in Chicago, its goal was to continue the selective patronage model. RPC's *Wall Street Project* works at increasing the numbers of Blacks on corporate boards of directors and seeks to strengthen Black companies by offering ongoing business and capital investment workshops.

Glynis Christine

See also Boycott; Civil Rights Movement; King, Martin Luther, Jr.; National Rainbow Coalition; Operation PUSH; Southern Christian Leadership Conference

Further Readings

Abernathy, Ralph David. 1989. *And the Walls Came Tumbling Down.* New York: Harper & Row.

Frady, Marshall. 1996. *Jesse: The Life and Pilgrimage of Jesse Jackson.* New York: Random House.

Johnson, Ollie A., III and Karin L. Stanford, eds. 2002. *Black Political Organizations in the Post-Civil Rights Era.* New Brunswick, NJ: Rutgers University Press.

Reynolds, Barbara A. 1985. *Jesse Jackson: America's David.* Washington, DC: JFJ Associates.

Timmerman, Kenneth R. 2002. *Shakedown: Exposing the Real Jesse Jackson.* Washington, DC: Regnery.

Web Sites

Rainbow/PUSH Coalition: http://www.rainbowpush.org

Jamaica

Jamaica is an island country rich in cultural history located in the Caribbean Sea basin just south of Cuba, east of the Yucatán Peninsula, and due West of Haiti. Jamaica, which enjoys a subtropical climate year round, is separated into a number of provinces called "parishes" where its approximately 2.7 million people live according to 2007 estimates. Its chief exports are bauxite and aluminum, yet it also exports sugar, citrus, and bananas. The culture of Jamaica is a multifaceted phenomenon involving the convergence of African, Native American, and European history and lineage. Human inhabitation began with the Native American Arawak tribe, then transitioned to Spanish control briefly, and then to the British, who ruled the colony for 300 years before its independence in 1962. This entry looks at that history.

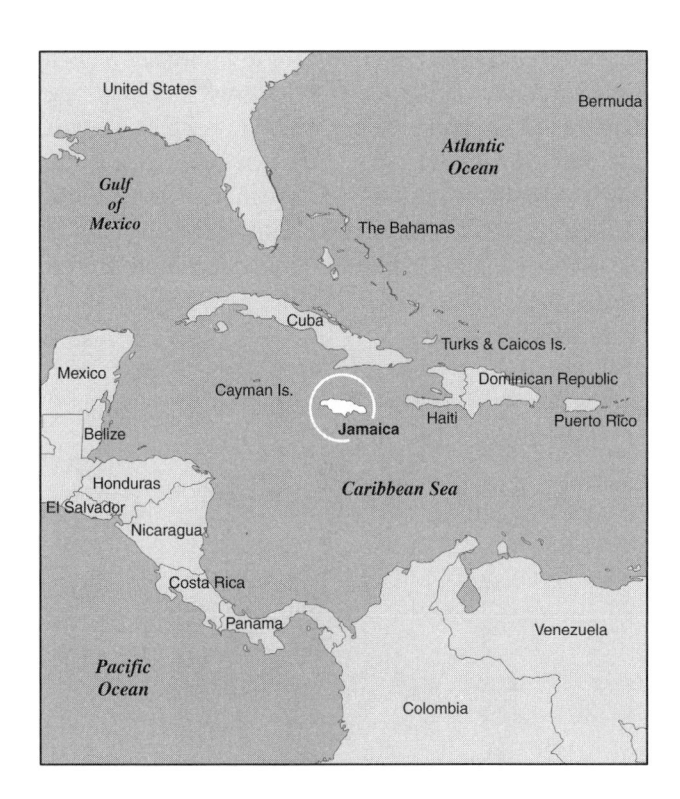

The Arawaks

The history of Jamaica begins with the Arawak Indians of Jamaica, who lived in prosperity in Jamaica until the 15th century. The Arawak, Native Americans originating in the Andes Mountains, settled many Caribbean islands off the coastal countries of South America. There is some debate about whether the Taíno Indians also inhabited the island. The natives were skilled in hunting and trapping, and maintained complex social structures, economy, and politics. Their contributions to society include the hammock and tobacco.

The arrival of the Europeans marked the end of Arawak prosperity because the natives were enslaved and ultimately decimated by disease. By the late 15th century, smallpox had so diminished the island's Arawak population that demand for labor rose, and consequently the first Black slaves were brought to Jamaica around 1517. From that time, Jamaica became one of the largest importers of slave labor into the New World.

The European Colonists

Christopher Columbus, an Italian explorer contracted by the Spanish, arrived at Jamaica during his second voyage to the West Indies in 1494. The Spanish took control of what was then an underdeveloped island. The Spanish colonial economy relied on ship repair and buccaneering and as a result was constantly subjected to pirate attacks. In 1655, the Spanish were displaced by the British, and Jamaica began slave importation and sugar production in earnest.

Jamaica's coastline and rolling hills were deemed highly fertile land, and the British began to export citrus in addition to sugar and bananas. During the late 17th and most of the 18th centuries, the British called Jamaica the Jewel of the Empire, as Jamaican exports generated by slave labor on sugar plantations increased England's profitability margins. The Caribbean climate and the island's strategic location were important contributing factors that led to its rise as one of the prized Crown Colonies of England during the colonial period. Today, the European proportion of the population is at 0.2%

The African Creoles

Because of the large amounts of labor required for sugar production during colonial times, the African population of Jamaica was a solid majority of 90.1%. By 1807, more than 600,000 Africans had been brought to the island, most of them purchased through the transatlantic trade routes that originated in forts on the Gold Coast of Africa, the Bight of Benin, Lonango, Melimba, and Cape Benda. In Jamaica, the Africans were taught skilled labor trades such as masonry, shipbuilding, and plantation maintenance. Many slaves did not stay in Jamaica but were shipped to other colonial islands such as Antigua or Trinidad, or as far as the United States. High amounts of labor required to work the sugar fields demanded a slave population many times larger than the number of colonists. In 1790, for example, the number of English colonists on the island was 23,000, whereas the number of slaves was 256,000, roughly 11 slaves to 1 English settler. This uneven ratio was the root of slave revolts that were a colonial reality in Jamaica.

Additionally, the Maroons, former slaves freed under Spanish rule before the arrival of the British, were a continual threat to the English. These former slaves lived in the mountainous interior of the island and still enjoy some autonomy from formal government. Many of the Maroon community still keep their African traditions because they are a relatively isolated group. World wide, Afro-Jamaicans have made significant contributions, from the philosophical musings of Marcus Garvey, the major contributor of Rastafarianism, to the musical political movements of reggae. The creoles have a rich dance culture ranging from the religious African tradition to the social hybrid Euro-Creole dances such as the Jonkunnu.

Other Ethnic Groups

After the abolition of the slave trade, the sugar and citrus markets needed cheap labor. During the next 50 years, the East Indian and the Chinese migrated to the Caribbean islands looking for work. Today, the East Asians in general control much of the grocery and convenience store businesses in Jamaica. The East Indian and the Chinese are represented in the island's population at 1.3% and 0.2 %, respectively. The remaining percentage of the population is a mixture of races and other nationalities, and is composed of roughly 7.5% other minorities, including African, Scottish, Portuguese, and Lebanese (.02%).

C. Centae Richards

See Appendix A
See also Caribbean; Colonialism; Creole; Diaspora; Nigeria; United Kingdom

Further Readings:

Butler, Kathleen Mary. 1995. *The Economics of Emancipation: Jamaica & Barbados, 1823–1843.* Chapel Hill: University of North Carolina Press.

Higman, Barry W. 1995. *Slave Population and Economy in Jamaica, 1807–1834.* Kingston, Jamaica: University of the West Indies Press.

Statistical Institute of Jamaica. 2001. *Population Census 2001 Jamaica Volume 1 Country Report.* Kingston, Jamaica: Government of Jamaica.

JAMAICAN AMERICANS

Settled primarily along the East Coast, Jamaican Americans constitute a significant segment of the immigrant Black population and have migrated to the United States for more than 100 years. This ongoing migration adds dynamism to the community, constantly circulating culture between the former country and the Caribbean. Transnationalism, along with the cultural and social capital characteristic of the group, partially frames their adaptation to U.S. society, but race is probably most significant in this respect. Like African Americans, Jamaican Americans face racial discrimination but operate instead from a Jamaican frame of reference that often tries to minimize racism. The contradictions between this outlook and their negative racial experiences in the United States complicate assimilation for immigrants, but the second and later generations assimilate more easily into the African American community. This entry provides an overview of Jamaican immigration to the United States

Harry Belafonte. *Jamaican American singer and actor Belafonte is shown speaking at an equal rights rally that marked the sixth anniversary of the U.S. Supreme Court decision in* Brown v. Board of Education of Topeka.

Source: Library of Congress, Prints & Photographs Division, LC-USZC2-5807.

and of Jamaican American culture. It also explores the way in which race and racism shape the relationship between Jamaican and African Americans.

Demographics

Like other British West Indians, Jamaicans migrate at high rates, spurred by Jamaica's economic underdevelopment, elevated levels of unemployment, and culturally entrenched traditions promoting migration. First manifesting itself in the mid-1900s, these traditions originally spread Jamaicans throughout the circum-Caribbean. The United States became a favored destination in the 20th century, however, and Jamaicans migrated to the United States in three waves: 1900s to the beginning of the Great Depression, the mid-1940s to the 1950s, and post-1965 to the present. Typically, they have outnumbered other British West Indian immigrants. For instance, Department of Homeland Security data show that 18,346 migrated in 2005, which ranked them fourteenth among all immigrants. Guyana, the next largest source of British West Indians, sent 9,318. Most Jamaicans (35%) settle among other British West Indians in the New York City metropolitan area, but Florida—especially the southern region—draws almost as many (30%). The rest reside in such favored locations as Bridgeport and Hartford, Connecticut; Newark, New Jersey; Baltimore, Maryland; and Atlanta, Georgia. Occupationally, they concentrate mostly in service industries, particularly women who, for cultural and financial reasons, find employment in health care particularly appealing. A sizable proportion of the population (19%) also finds employment as managers and professionals.

Culture and Assimilation

Jamaican culture intermingles with that of other British West Indians because a history of colonialism bequeathed to that Caribbean zone a common language, institutions, and pastimes. Nevertheless, a peculiar Jamaican element stands out, often being taken by U.S. society as representative of the whole group. Ska and Reggae music and Rastafarianism are especially noteworthy in this respect because their infiltration into U.S. culture has made what was once exotic now commonplace. The popularity of Jamaican resorts such as Montego Bay and Negril among U.S. tourists has added to the allure of Jamaican culture. Among Jamaican Americans, the culture is constantly reinforced through frequent back-and-forth travel.

The resulting cultural consciousness, enhanced even more by the growing Jamaican American population, has created semi-autonomous, mixed Jamaican–West Indian enclaves that somewhat retard assimilation into the African American population. This assimilation is viewed as natural because most Jamaicans are of African ancestry, and anti-Black racism blocks the full absorption of both groups into U.S. society. But immigration-related factors, political dynamics in areas settled by Jamaicans and other West Indians, and sociohistorical differences between Jamaica and the United States make Jamaicans' assimilation into the African American population bumpy rather than automatic. This occurs because these factors often orient Jamaican Americans inwardly rather than outwardly toward the larger Black community.

Specifically, Jamaican Americans' ever-increasing numbers enhance feelings of in-group solidarity (ethnicity) by allowing them, and West Indians in general, to replicate many aspects of West Indian life—such as religion, voluntary organizations, informal banking networks, and cuisine—in areas of concentrated settlement. Parts of New York City—such as Crown Heights and East Flatbush—are typical in these respects, and the large West Indian, not just Jamaican, presence has served as a magnet for ethnic and non-ethnic politicians seeking to tap into and magnify the West Indian vote. The ethnic feelings underlying these dynamics build on an immigrant mentality among West Indians that emphasizes economic and social mobility to validate the decision to migrate.

Behind all this is a British West Indian cultural tendency to de-emphasize race in those societies despite centuries of slavery and colonialism. Although historically deep, racism in British West Indians societies was less institutionalized, and those societies changed more quickly to allow for Black political prominence. Moreover, the reality of majority Black populations—allied with nation-building ideologies promoting multiculturalism and complex ways of viewing race—effectively removes race as a day-to-day issue for many modern-day Jamaicans (although the issue remains salient on other levels). Typically, they express greater worry over entrenched economic problems.

In contrast with these dynamics, Jamaican Americans experience racism that is typical for Blacks in the United States, and this contends with their ethnic consciousness, while helping to shape their assimilation into the African American population. Importantly,

Jamaicans' acquaintance with African American culture is long-standing, stemming historically from frequent travel and from the popularity of Black music, which inspired the birth of reggae. U.S. racism tightens these nascent bonds, forging a common Black voice on a wide range of issues. In recent years, police mistreatment of Blacks in core settlement areas has often produced such unity.

This and other issues manifest themselves politically, where Jamaican Americans are as likely as are African Americans to vote Democratic. Residential segregation is crucial in tightening bonds between the two groups because in many cases "Jamaican/West Indian" neighborhoods are essentially segregated Black neighborhoods with high concentrations of West Indians. Such proximity promotes friendships and alliances of all sorts between Jamaican Americans and African Americans, even though first-generation Jamaican Americans continue to maintain an ethnic consciousness.

U.S. birth attenuates this consciousness in the second generation but immigrant Jamaican parents often encourage its maintenance, believing that it facilitates social mobility. Although this view remains contested, it is more certain that second and later generation Jamaican Americans are creating a hybrid culture as they interact, intimately, with African Americans. Though many expressions of this melding exist, music is, perhaps, the most significant because of its importance to Black culture. Stylistically, "Dancehall and Rastafarian" reggae owes much to hip-hop, but an early 1970s version of reggae—"Toasting" (where performers talked over beats)—contributed to the development of hip-hop in New York City. Consequently, some early hip-hop celebrities—for example, Busta Rhymes, Shinehead, and Biggie Smalls—were of Jamaican ancestry. Trends such as these indicate that in coming years, second-generation Jamaican Americans will increasingly merge with the African American population in the large, East Coast metropoles where Jamaicans have resided for more than a century.

Milton Vickerman

See Appendix A

See also African Americans; Assimilation; Caribbean Americans; Crown Heights, Brooklyn; Cultural Capital; Hip-Hop; Immigration, U.S.; Jamaica; Social Capital; West Indian Americans

Further Readings

Bashi, Vilna. 2007. *Survival of the Knitted.* Stanford, CA: Stanford University Press.

Bryce-Laporte, Roy. 1972. "Black Immigrants: The Experience of Invisibility and Inequality." *Journal of Black Studies* 3(1):29–56.

Foner, Nancy. 2001. *Islands in the City.* Berkeley: University of California Press.

Kasinitz, Philip. 1992. *Caribbean New York.* Ithaca, NY: Cornell University Press.

Kasinitz, Philip, John Mollenkopf, and Mary Waters. 2002. "Becoming American/Becoming New Yorkers: Immigrant Incorporation in a Majority Minority City." *International Migration Review* 36(4, Winter):1005–1019.

Model, Suzanne. 1995. "West Indian Prosperity: Fact of Fiction?" *Social Problems* 42(4, November):525–552.

Palmer, Ransford W. 1995. *Pilgrims from the Sun.* New York: Twayne.

Sutton, Constance and Elsa Chaney. 1984. *Caribbean Life in New York City: Sociocultural Dimensions.* New York: Center for Migration Studies.

Vickerman, Milton. 1999. *Crosscurrents.* New York: Oxford University Press.

Waters, Mary. 1999. *Black Identities.* Cambridge, MA: Harvard University Press.

JAPAN

Japan, a country with an estimated 2007 population of 127.7 million people, has long been seen as a racially and ethnically homogeneous nation; however, many scholars argue that Japan has actually been a multiethnic, rather than a mono-ethnic, society. The continuing influx of foreign workers since the 1970s has brought visible changes to Japan—changes that, concomitantly, have shed light on the ethnic minorities that have long been present, but invisible, in Japan.

In a population of 1.9 million foreign residents in 2002, the largest group consisted of Koreans, many of whom have been in Japan for generations; they are labeled "foreigners" (*Zainichi* Koreans) even when born or raised in Japan. The second largest group of foreign residents, *Nikkeijin,* includes second- and third-generation Japanese who were born and raised mainly in Brazil and Peru. Most of them came to Japan in the 1990s and have been employed largely as unskilled contract workers. Other foreign residents include service and unskilled workers who entered from the Philippines, Thailand, China, South Korea, India, and Bangladesh after the late 1980s. Many have been employed in jobs often shunned by the Japanese, with low pay and little job security. And what may be less well understood outside Japan is that, even among Japanese nationals, there are different ethnic groups: the Ainu, Okinawan, and *Burakumin* people. All these groups have challenged Japan's monoethnic ideology and have raised serious questions about citizenship and multiculturalism: For example, how can Japan provide them with civil and social rights and lessen pervasive discrimination against them? This entry discusses those questions.

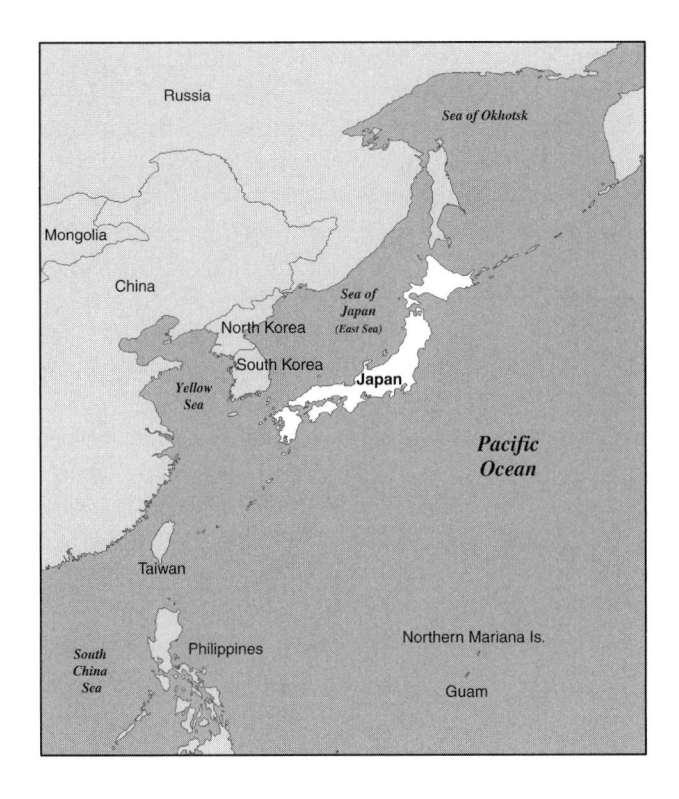

Ethnic Minorities in Japan

Zainichi *Koreans*

The largest contingent of foreign residents in Japan is Koreans (635,422 in 2002); they are the product of the nation's colonial legacy. Japan's colonization of Korea between 1910 and 1945 brought approximately 2 million Koreans into Japan by the end of World War II. With the defeat of Japan in 1945, Koreans were deprived of their Japanese nationality and voting rights. The Alien Registration Law, enacted in 1952, ensured that resident Koreans would be regarded as foreigners. Japan only conferred citizenship through bloodlines and naturalization, and excluded non-nationals. Throughout the postwar period, Korean Japanese continued to be treated with contempt. Many resident Koreans hid their backgrounds from ethnic Japanese for fear of discrimination, passing as Japanese in their public lives. Since the late 1980s, however, Japan has loosened restrictions on naturalization, and a large number of resident Koreans have become naturalized.

Nikkeijin

The *Nikkeijin* population, typically consisting of second- and third-generation Japanese who were born and raised mainly in Brazil and Peru, increased in the 1990s. These individuals are Japanese by blood but categorized as "foreigners" because of their foreign birth. The population increased after 1990 because, in that year, the Japanese government revised the Immigration Control and Refugee Recognition Act, providing new long-term visas exclusively for the descendants of Japanese emigrants. The legal admission of *Nikkeijin* to Japan was a critical step, designed to prevent illegal immigration from other Asian countries and to meet a labor shortage in small-scale factories. Many *Nikkei*-Brazilians were trained in professions before coming to Japan, but most of them could only find positions as contract laborers upon their arrival. Although the *Nikkeijin* bloodline was seen as a critical asset in the ability of these individuals to assimilate into Japanese society, most did not speak Japanese fluently and experienced blatant prejudice and discrimination in the workplace.

Filipino Women

Of the 1.9 million registered foreigners recorded in 2002, Filipinos constitute the third largest group of migrant women, following Koreans and Chinese. Intermarriage between Filipino women and Japanese men has increased rapidly since the 1980s; in fact, Filipino women account for the highest number of foreign wives in Japan, followed by Korean women, Chinese women, and Thai women. This situation resulted from a shortage of women in rural areas in the 1970s; Japanese local governments promoted marriage with Filipino women, and Filipino brides started arriving in the 1980s. At the same time, many

Filipino women, most of whom were provided with "entertainer visas," started working as dancers and hostesses in Japan. These women have encountered economic and emotional exploitation at the hands of Filipino and Japanese brokers and have been denied basic legal protections, making them vulnerable to victimization by the sex industry. In 2004, the Japanese government adopted the Action Plan for Measures to Combat Trafficking in Persons, which, for the first time, criminalized trafficking in persons to enhance the protection of these women's rights.

Ainu, Okinawan, and Burakumin

Much like the *Zainichi* Korean and Chinese, the Ainu and Okinawan peoples were also the products of colonialization. Japan annexed Hokkaido in 1873, imposing an assimilation policy on the "backward" Ainu people. The government assigned Japanese names to the Ainu and encouraged intermarriage with ethnic Japanese. Through the post–World War II period, many Ainu were economically deprived and discriminated against in the workplace, in marriage, and in the schools. Beginning in the late 1960s, activists and organizations such as the *Utari Kyokai* organization campaigned for a policy of *Kyosei:* coexistence or multiculturalism, in a society free from racial discrimination. More recently, in 1997, the Ainu Cultural Promotion Act (CPA) was introduced to enhance the public recognition of Ainu as a distinct group with a non-Japanese cultural identity.

Okinawa, an island group to the south of Japan, also became part of the Japanese Empire in the 1870s, providing sugar and coal to the nation. Like the Ainu, Okinawans were often seen as primitive and inferior and were thus treated as second-class citizens. After Japan's defeat in World War II, Okinawa was occupied by the United States. The U.S. occupation fostered anti-U.S. sentiment and a desire to return to Japan, further complicating the local Okinawans' ethnic identities.

Although the *Burakumin* people are often characterized as having the same ethnicity as ethnic Japanese, scholars categorize the *Burakumin* as a distinct ethnic group because of its distinct shared culture and history of exclusion. For many years, the *Burakumin* people were seen as a breed apart from mainstream Japanese, consigned to living in particular assigned villages and to working in the leather and funerary industries. Many among them were poor, homeless, and even handicapped. The Japanese government abolished the caste system in 1871 in its efforts to convert Japan into a modern nation-state. Yet the *Burakumin* saw few benefits; they still held the worst jobs, lived in inferior housing, and suffered poverty and social stigmatization. With emancipation, they even lost their occupational monopoly on leatherwork and their tax exemption for their low status. Many decades later, legislation passed in 1969, 1982, and 1987 provided funds to improve the living conditions of the *Burakumin.*

Multiculturalism in Japan

Many point out the increasing voices of multiculturalism and the coexistence of diverse ethnic groups as positive changes in Japan. Yet questions remain about how the idea of multiculturalism can translate into the political and social empowerment of previously ignored or oppressed ethnic groups. It is not clear whether making ethnic minorities culturally visible will transform the hierarchical or colonial view of the ethnic Japanese as being superior to the other groups. Furthermore, some argue that Japan's policies regarding the citizenship of minority groups or multiculturalism derive mainly from political pressures from foreign countries such as the United States, or from the United Nations' human rights agenda, rather than from within its own society. Although social awareness of multiethnic cultures and a pragmatic acceptance of ethnic minorities have become much more common in public, xenophobic reactions toward ethnic minority groups seem to remain strong. Plans for multicultural education have been much discussed, yet most remain far from implementation.

Kumiko Nemoto

See Appendix A
See also Burakumin; Colonialism; Foreign Students; Hapa; Hawai'i, Race in; Japanese Americans; Nikkeijin; Race; Racism; Xenophobia

Further Readings

Douglass, Mike and Glenda S. Roberts, ed. 2000. *Japan and Global Migration: Foreign Workers and the Advent of a Multicultural Society.* London: Routledge.

Ito, Ruri. 2005. "Crafting Migrant Women's Citizenship in Japan: Taking 'Family' as a Vantage Point." *International Journal of Japanese Sociology* 14:52–69.

Lie, John. 2001. *Multiethnic Japan.* Cambridge, MA: Harvard University Press.

Morris-Suzuki, Tessa. 1998. *Re-inventing Japan: Time, Space, Nation.* Armonk, NY: M. E. Sharpe.

Takamichi, Kajita, ed. 2001. *Kokusaika to Aidentiti (Internationalization and Identity).* Kyoto, Japan: Minerva Shobo.

Weiner, Michael, ed. 1997. *Japan's Minorities: The Illusion of Homogeneity.* London: RoutledgeCurzon.

Weiner, Michael, ed. 2004. *Race, Ethnicity and Migration in Modern Japan* (Routledge Library of Modern Japan). London: RoutledgeCurzon.

Weiner, Myron and Tadashi Hanami, eds. 1998. *Temporary Workers or Future Citizens? Japanese and U.S. Migration Policies.* London: Macmillan.

JAPANESE AMERICAN CITIZENS LEAGUE

The Japanese American Citizens League (JACL) was established in 1929 in California, initially to address discrimination against individuals of Japanese ancestry residing in the United States. JACL is the oldest and largest Asian American civil rights organization in the country. The JACL's current mission is to focus on securing and maintaining the civil and human rights of Japanese Americans and others who experience injustice. It has 113 chapters and 8 regional districts composed of more than 24,000 members. The JACL national office is located in San Francisco, with regional offices located in Los Angeles, Seattle, Chicago, and Washington, D.C. This entry describes the development of the JACL.

At the time the JACL was founded, Japanese Americans in California faced numerous and significant limitations in human rights, as well as the actions of organizations such as the Japanese Exclusion League, founded for the sole purpose of ridding California of residents of Japanese ancestry, including U.S. citizens. At the time of JACL's formation, more than 100 statutes in California limited the rights of anyone of Japanese ancestry. Other nongovernmental organizations such as the Grande Association and Sons of the Golden West lobbied the state legislature and Congress to limit the rights of Japanese Americans.

Following the Japanese attack on Pearl Harbor during World War II, JACL leaders found themselves confronting the U.S. government, which subsequently decided to exclude and imprison all Japanese Americans on the U.S. West Coast. During the war, the JACL fought for the right of Japanese Americans to serve in the U.S. military, which led to the formation of the well-known 100th Infantry Battalion/442nd Regimental Combat Team, the most highly decorated military unit in U.S. military history. Following World War II, the JACL began working on a series of legislative efforts to obtain rights for Japanese Americans.

In 1946, the JACL began work to repeal California's Alien Land Law, which prohibited Japanese immigrants from owning land. In 1949, the JACL began efforts to allow Japanese immigrants to become naturalized U.S. citizens. The JACL also reportedly played a large role in the initiation of the McCarran-Walter Act, which afforded women more rights to participate in politics, as well as the passing of the 1964 Civil Rights Act. During the 1970s and 1980s, the JACL participated in the Redress Movement, which sought reparations from the U.S. government for the imprisonment and loss of property suffered by Japanese Americans interned during World War II. The 10-year effort to obtain redress resulted in the passage of the Civil Liberties Act in 1988, which provided monetary compensation and a formal apology from the U.S. government to Japanese Americans who were interned during World War II.

Although a major focus of the JACL remains the rights of Japanese Americans, the JACL has expanded its focus to include the welfare of any who experience social injustice, Asian Americans in particular. Among its responsibilities, the JACL now pays attention to the well-being of all Asian Americans, particularly new immigrants, who may be least able to protect themselves from social injustice. This broadening focus began in the early 1980s when Vincent Chin, a Chinese American man, was murdered by two Caucasian men in Detroit because they thought he was of Japanese ancestry, and they attributed the decline of the U.S. auto industry and the economy of Detroit to competition with the Japanese. Chin's murder made it apparent that those who hold racist and discriminatory attitudes toward Japanese Americans often generalized their bigoted attitudes to other Asian Americans and people of color.

Recently, the JACL underwent a strategic planning process to reevaluate its mission and develop a plan for the next century. This culminated in an internal report, Vision 2000, which articulated the JACL's plan for education, community empowerment, capacity building, and protecting the rights of Asian Americans and those who may be disadvantaged. Additionally, the JACL recognizes that the United States has undergone significant changes since September 11, 2001, and that its own work has been affected by issues involving national security and civil liberties. Continuing changes in the composition of society in race, ethnicity, and age also continue to be challenges. Thus, the JACL has developed a Program for Action Committee, whose recommendations set the objectives for each biennium. The most recent recommendations of the committee focus on the following areas: membership, youth, finance, planning and development, operations, and public affairs.

Further information about JACL's activities may be found on its Web site, which includes JACL press releases, and Web pages on anti-hate, educational activities and resources, leadership development activities, JACL events, and resources and links. JACL also publishes the biweekly *Pacific Citizen*, which is also available online on JACL's Web site.

Gayle Y. Iwamasa

See Appendix A; Appendix B
See also Chin, Vincent; Internment Camps; Japanese Americans; McCarran-Walter Act; Nisei

Further Readings

Takezawa, Yasuko. 1995. *Breaking the Silence: Redress and Japanese American Ethnicity.* Ithaca, NY: Cornell University Press.

Web Sites

Japanese American Citizens League: http://www.jacl.org

JAPANESE AMERICANS

Japanese Americans are residents or citizens of the United States whose ancestry is Japanese or Okinawan. Okinawa, formerly an independent nation, was annexed by Japan in the late 19th century. Japanese Americans constitute one of the earliest Asian American ethnic groups in the United States, along with Chinese Americans. Japanese Americans were among the three largest Asian American groups in the United States until the 1990s. Since then, in addition to Chinese Americans and Filipinos, the populations of Asian Indians, Vietnamese Americans, and Korean Americans have surpassed the population of Japanese Americans, which now compose the sixth largest group. Historically, Japanese Americans have experienced hatred, bigotry, discrimination, and institutionalized racism by the U.S. government, including the unconstitutional internment of Japanese Americans living on the West Coast during World War II. Later, Japanese Americans were included among the "model minorities," a term, although seemingly flattering, that divides Japanese Americans from other minority groups and stereotypes Japanese Americans. This entry discusses Japanese Immigration to the United States, the effects of World War II, Japanese American farming, and issues facing contemporary Japanese Americans.

Japanese Immigration to the United States

The Japanese first began immigrating to the United States in the mid-19th century, following political, cultural, and social changes resulting from the Meiji Restoration in 1868. Further, Japanese laborers were recruited by many business owners following the Chinese Exclusion Act of 1882 to replace the no longer available Chinese laborers. In the 1890s, young Japanese men were recruited to provide labor for Hawaiian sugarcane and pineapple plantations, as well as to work on California fruit and produce farms. In the early 1900s, the Japanese who had come to the United States had begun to lease land and sharecrop. However, in 1907, the so-called Gentlemen's Agreement was established between the United States and Japan, which stated that Japan would stop issuing passports for new laborers. This occurred because of White farmers' and landowners' concerns about Japanese competition. In 1908, Japanese women, mostly picture brides, were allowed to enter the United States. As a result, the population of Japanese Americans began growing, and these women began giving birth to U.S. citizens. In 1913, the California Alien Land Law was enacted, banning those of Japanese ancestry from purchasing land. This act was initiated by Whites who were threatened by the increasingly successful independent Japanese farmers. This act was followed by the U.S. Immigration Act of 1924, which banned immigration from Japan. Given the previous immigration patterns and the prohibition of new immigrants, Japanese Americans born after 1924 were by definition Japanese Americans and U.S. citizens. The bans on immigration produced well-defined generations within the Japanese American community. Issei were the immigrant generation, followed by the Nisei, who were their U.S.-born children.

Japanese American activism to address the continual racism and discrimination faced by Japanese Americans began in the early part of the 20th century. The Japanese American Citizens League (JACL) was founded in 1929 in California to address discrimination against individuals of Japanese ancestry.

The Effects of World War II

Following the December 7, 1941, Japanese attack on Pearl Harbor, President Franklin D. Roosevelt signed Executive Order 9066, demanding that those of Japanese ancestry residing on the West Coast be "excluded" from areas deemed military or exclusion zones. The order was signed on February 19, 1942; 6 days later, the order was implemented, and nearly 120,000 U.S. citizens of Japanese descent were forced to leave their homes and belongings and taken to internment camps. Each family was allowed only two suitcases of belongings. Subsequently, Executive Order 9095 was implemented to allow the U.S. government to take control of the property and assets of Japanese Americans in internment camps. Much of this property was never returned once the internment camps were closed.

Japanese Americans were incarcerated in nine camps and one segregation center located in mostly desolate areas. The segregation center was established for individuals identified as "dissenters" and their families. The last camp to close was at Rohwer, Arkansas, on November 30, 1945. Although an initial attempt was made to intern Japanese Americans in Hawai'i, the U.S. government realized that it was not economically feasible to incarcerate all the people of Japanese descent in Hawai'i. Following their release, many Japanese Americans returned to the West Coast to rebuild their lives. Some returned to family businesses such as grocery stores and farming, and some Japanese American communities were reestablished. Others, who were not able to recover their property, went elsewhere to find work and housing, in cities such as Chicago and New York. Following their release, many Japanese Americans faced continued racism and discrimination in finding housing and employment, even those who were educated and had served in the U.S. military.

During the war, through the assistance of the JACL, some of those interned fought for the right to serve in the U.S. military. As a result, the all-Japanese American 100th Battalion and the 442nd Regimental Combat Team were formed. This combined unit is the highest decorated military unit in U.S. history. These brave individuals are memorialized in Washington, D.C., at the National Japanese American Memorial.

The Redress Movement to obtain an apology and reparations from the U.S. government for the unconstitutional incarceration of Japanese Americans during World War II was initiated by Sanseis, third-generation Japanese Americans. Many of these individuals were young children of the Nisei who were interned. After several decades of efforts, President Ronald Reagan signed the Civil Liberties Act in 1988, which provided redress of $20,000 to each surviving detainee. The first payments were made in October 1990.

Japanese American Farming

Japanese Americans have contributed significantly to the agriculture on the West Coast of the United States since the Issei first immigrated. Upon arrival in the United States, the Japanese immigrants introduced sophisticated irrigation techniques that allowed for the cultivation of crops on previously unusable lands, thus leading to successful production. As indicated previously, many White land owners and farmers were concerned about competition by these successful Japanese and Japanese American farmers, resulting in many laws and acts to squelch the competition. Although many of the immigrants who began farming independently were successful in the early part of the 20th century, many of them lost their farms during the internment, when the U.S. government confiscated much of their property. However, some Japanese Americans remain involved in the agriculture industry today, particularly in Southern California, where some Japanese American family farms continue to exist.

Contemporary Japanese Americans
Generations and Communities

Japanese Americans have special names for their generational groups. The Issei are the first generation, born in Japan or Okinawa. Nisei are the second generation, born U.S. citizens. Sansei are the third generation, *Yonsei* is the fourth generation, and *Gosei* is the fifth generation. Japanese American sociologists coined the term *Nikkei* to encompass all Japanese Americans across the generations. The term *Kibei* refers to those who are born in the United States, but who are chiefly educated in Japan. These individuals often returned to the United States as adults, but have vastly different experiences than the Nisei.

Currently, Japanese Americans constitute the sixth largest Asian American group in the United States. The states with the largest numbers of Japanese Americans are California, Hawai'i, Washington, and New York. Each year, although approximately 7,000 new immigrants arrive from Japan, net immigration of Japanese to the United States hovers around zero because some older Japanese Americans immigrate to their ancestral homeland each year. Many Japanese Americans live in communities with established Japanese American neighborhoods, such as those found in Northern and Southern California and Seattle, Washington.

One issue facing the Japanese American community is the high rate of out-marriage. This has resulted in the dispersion of Japanese Americans as well as an increase in the number of biracial Japanese Americans. Some are concerned that continuation of this trend will result in the demise of an actual "Japanese American community" and the loss of Japanese and Japanese American traditions among young Japanese Americans, particularly those who live in areas that are less apt to have Japanese American activities. Further evidence of increasing diversity is that older Japanese Americans (i.e., age 65 years and older) are now composed of many different groups. For example, some Issei are still alive, but now Nisei and even some Sansei are included in the category of older adult. Additionally, many U.S. military servicemen stationed in Japan during World War II who had married Japanese women brought their wives to the United States when they returned home. These women have vastly different cultural values and experiences, not to mention differences in language and food preference, compared with Japanese American older adults who have higher generational status.

Language Issues

Many Issei and Nisei speak Japanese or Okinawan in addition to English. However, later generations of Japanese Americans speak primarily English, and may learn Japanese as a second language. One exception is in Hawai'i, where *Nikkei* comprise about 20% of the population; thus, Japanese is more apt to be spoken, written, and studied by many residents of Hawai'i, including those not of Japanese descent. Japanese women who met and married U.S. military personnel still tend to speak Japanese and very little English even though they might live in areas where few people speak Japanese.

Education

Japanese and Japanese American culture emphasizes and values education of its youth. Often as a result, Japanese Americans do well in academics, exceeding national averages in many different subject areas. This has resulted in stereotyping of Japanese Americans and in assumptions that Japanese Americans are skilled only in areas of science and math, rather than in areas such as social sciences and humanities. Further, because of their academic strengths as well as the influence of the "model minority" stereotype, Japanese Americans are often not eligible for scholarships or Affirmative Active programs, and are sometimes even assailed as being co-conspirators with the dominant group against other ethnic minority groups.

Spirituality and Celebrations

Japanese Americans practice a full range of religions, including Christianity, various forms of Buddhism, and Shinto. In Japan, the practice of Buddhism and Shintoism were ingrained in values and traditions. Although a large number of Japanese Americans continue to practice Buddhism in some form, these practices have a decidedly Japanese American flavor rather than a traditional Japanese one. For example, in many Japanese American communities, the annual Obon Festival in July or August, where the spirits of deceased ancestors are celebrated, is much more of a family celebration rather than a solemn religious event. These festivals often occur at local Japanese American community centers and involve food, obon dancing, carnival games, and other forms of family entertainment. They provide opportunities for families to gather with other Japanese American families and enjoy historical and cultural practices and traditions.

In areas where large groups of Japanese Americans live, they may have their own Christian churches, which may even offer some services in Japanese. In other areas of the United States, however, Japanese American Christians tend to attend churches in predominantly White communities. On the West Coast, many Japanese American community centers were established after the internment. These community centers provided people with a place to celebrate and experience their heritage in a positive and uplifting manner. Many community centers are located next to or near Japanese American churches and temples and often collaborate on events. Activities such as Japanese language school, sports teams for youth, and older adult day services are provided by such centers.

Many Japanese American celebrations tend to focus more on community-building than on religious foundations. Although many invoke aspects of Japanese traditions and influence, such as Cherry Blossom festivals and Taiko Drumming Festivals, some are Japanese American specific such as Nisei Week in Los Angeles.

Acculturation and Ethnic Identity

Contemporary Japanese Americans are vastly diverse in their level of acculturation—that is, the degree to which they value, live by, and interact in the dominant society, and the strength of their ethnic identity—their sense of themselves as Japanese Americans. This is not surprising given that this group comprises individuals across many different generational levels with vastly different experiences. For example, some Japanese Americans clearly recall their experiences being interned during World War II, but the youngest Japanese Americans, who may be biracial, might have no knowledge or understanding of the internment. Some Japanese Americans are recent immigrants, but others have U.S. family histories that date back to the 1800s. Many Japanese Americans are used to living and functioning in predominantly White environments such as neighborhoods, schools, and industry, and have become accustomed to being one of few ethnic minorities. Some of these individuals may not often reflect on their ethnicity, but others are much more active in their interest in and desire to learn more about the Japanese American experience.

Gayle Y. Iwamasa

See Appendix A; Appendix B
See also Acculturation; Alien Land Acts; Asian Americans; Asian American Studies; Hawai'i, Race in; Immigration, U.S.; Internment Camps; Issei; Japanese American Citizens League; Model Minority; Nikkeijin; Nisei; Pacific Islanders

Further Readings

Daniels, Roger. 1993. *Prisoners Without Trial: Japanese Americans in World War II*. New York: Hill and Wang.
Fugita, Stephen S. and David J. O'Brien. 1991. *Japanese American Ethnicity: The Persistence of Community*. Seattle: University of Washington Press.
Hohri, William. 1988. *Repairing America: An Account of the Movement for Japanese American Redress*. Pullman: Washington State University Press.
Kimura, Yukiko. 1988. *Issei: Japanese Immigrants in Hawaii*. Honolulu: University of Hawai'i Press.
Matsumoto, Valerie. 1993. *Farming the Home Place: A Japanese American Community in California, 1919–1982*. Ithaca, NY: Cornell University Press.
Nakano, Mei. 1990. *Japanese American Women: Three Generations, 1890–1990*. Berkeley, CA: National Japanese American Historical Society.
Takagi, Dana 1994. "Japanese American Families." In *Minority Families in the United States: A Multicultural Perspective,* edited by R. L. Taylor. Englewood Cliffs, NJ: Prentice Hall.
Weglyn, Michi. 1976. *Years of Infamy: The Untold Story of America's Concentration Camps*. New York: Morrow.

Web Sites

Discover Nikkei: http://www.discovernikkei.org
Japanese American National Museum: http://www.janm.org
Japanese American Citizens League: http://www.jacl.org
National Japanese American Historical Society: http://www.njahs.org
National Japanese American Memorial Foundation: http://www.njamf.com
Nikkei Federation: http://www.nikkeifederation.org

JEWISH AMERICANS

American Jewry is among the most complex groups in the United States. Although there are only about 4 million to 7 million Jews out of 300 million U.S. residents, that is, between 1% and 2% of the population, they make up a vastly disproportionate number of people in politics, the arts, academia, national media (movies, TV, radio), law, and medicine. Thus, they are in a position to influence though not control a great deal of public debate. The actual figures of U.S. Jewry are difficult to ascertain because one can only rely on surveys; the census does not collect data on religion or offer "Jewish" as an ethnic identity.

Based on available estimates, the United States has the largest Jewish population in the world, with 46% of the world's Jewish population living in the United States. Jewish Americans play a prominent role in the worldwide Jewish community, as well as in the United States. The nation with the second-largest Jewish population, Israel, is the only one in which Jews are in the majority, accounting for 81% of the population, compared with less than 2% in the United States.

This entry offers an overview of Jewish identification, immigration history, and their current situation in the United States.

Racial, Ethnic, or Religious Group?

The issue of what makes a Jew is more than a scholarly question; in Israel, it figures in policy matters. The Israel Law of Return defines who is a Jew and extends Israeli citizenship to all Jews. Currently, the law recognizes all converts to the faith, but pressure has grown recently to limit citizenship to those whose conversions were performed by Orthodox rabbis. Although the change would have little practical impact, symbolically this pressure shows the tension and lack of consensus, even among Jews, regarding who is a Jew.

The definition of race used here is fairly explicit. The Jewish people are not physically differentiated from non-Jews. Many people believe they can tell a Jew from a non-Jew, but actual distinguishing physical traits are absent. The wide range of variation among Jews makes it inaccurate to speak of a Jewish race in a physical sense. Jews today come from all areas of the world and carry a variety of physical features. Most Jewish Americans are descended from Northern and Eastern Europeans and have the appearance of Nordic and Alpine people. Many others carry Mediterranean traits that make them indistinguishable from Spanish or Italian Catholics. Many Jews reside in North Africa, and although North African Jews are not significantly represented in the United States, many people would view them as a racial minority, Black.

To define Jews by religion seems the obvious answer because there are Judaic religious beliefs, holidays, and rituals. But these beliefs and practices do not distinguish all Jews from non-Jews. To be a Jewish American does not mean that one is affiliated with one of the three religious groups: the Orthodox, the Reform, and the Conservative. A large segment of adult Jewish Americans, more than a third, do not participate in religious services or even belong, however tenuously, to a temple or synagogue. They have not converted to Christianity, however, nor have they ceased to think of themselves as Jews. Jewish religious beliefs and the history of religious practices remain significant legacies for all Jews today, however secularized their everyday behavior. In a 1998 survey, half of all Jews felt that a "shared history or culture," much more than religion, defined what it means to be Jewish.

The trend for some time, especially in the United States, has been toward a condition called Judaization, the lessening importance of Judaism as a religion and the substitution of cultural traditions as the ties that bind Jews. Depending on one's definition, Judaization has caused some Jews to become so assimilated in the United States that traditional Jews no longer consider them acceptable spouses.

Jewish identity is ethnic. Jews share cultural traits, rather than physical features or uniform religious beliefs. The level of this cultural identity differs. Just as some Apaches may be more acculturated than others, the degree of assimilation varies among Jewish people. Judaization may base identity on such things as eating traditional Jewish foods, telling Jewish jokes, and wearing the Star of David. For others, this cultural identity may be the sense of a common history of centuries of persecution. For still others, it may be an unimportant identification. They say, "I am a Jew," just as they say, "I am a resident of California."

Immigration Patterns

The first Jews came to the Americas in late August or early September of 1654, to New Amsterdam, a Dutch colony in what is today New York. Twenty-three arrived from the Recife, also a Dutch colony, in northeastern Brazil. A few generations earlier, however, their families had lived in Spain and Portugal. These Iberian Jews were known as Sephardim (*Sepharad* in Hebrew means "Spain"). Under Muslim rule, they were a large, prosperous, and close-knit community. But the Golden Age of Jews living in Spain ended in 1492, and Jews were forced to convert to Christianity. Thousands fled all over the world, including to Brazil, and from there, a few came to the United States. These Sephardic Jews became known as the "grandees," the most elite of all Jews.

The second wave of Jews to arrive in the United States comprised the German Jews. They also came seeking freedom from the revolutions in Europe. The height of their immigration was from 1820 to 1880. A distinct third wave, from 1880 to 1924, came from Russia and Eastern European countries. From 1924 to 1945, because of immigration quotas, the Depression, and World War II, immigration slowed down, with only small numbers allowed to leave Nazi Germany. However, after the Shoah and the establishment of the State of Israel in 1948, numerous refugees from Europe, the Middle East (another type of Sephardic immigration), and later thousands from the former Soviet Union enlarged and broadened the Jewish community of the United States.

Assimilation and Intermarriage

One of the major threats and challenges to Jewish Americans has been intermarriage. An early study in the 1960s shocked the community: Intermarriage was 17% and rising. Today, the figure is greater than 50%. This has led to alarm but it has also led to a renewed tolerance and acceptance of non-Jewish partners. Some even delight in the process, seeing it as a means of enlarging and broadening the community.

For many in the Jewish community, intermarriage is viewed as a social problem. Intermarriage makes a decrease in the size of the Jewish community in the United States more likely. In marriages that occurred in the 1970s, more than 70% of Jews married Jews or people who converted to Judaism. In marriages since 1996, that proportion has dropped to 53%. This trend means that U.S. Jews today are just as likely to marry a Gentile as a Jew. For many, religion is a non-issue; neither parent practices religious rituals. Two-thirds of the children of these Jewish-Gentile marriages are not raised as Jews.

Many Jewish Americans respond that intermarriage is inevitable and the Jewish community must build on whatever links the intermarried couple may still have with a Jewish ethnic culture. There are many programs throughout the United States to help Gentile spouses of Jews feel welcome so that the faith will not lose them both. Yet other Jews feel that such efforts may be sending a dangerous signal that intermarriage is inevitable. Therefore, it is not surprising to see that probably more than any other ethnic or religious group, organizations within the Jewish community commission research on the trends in intermarriage

Organizational Life

The Jewish American community has a vast array of organizations for such a small community. They are religious and secular, defense and artistic, schools, colleges, seminaries, and community centers. No organization, secular or religious, represents all U.S. Jews, but there are more than 300 nationwide organizations.

Among the most significant are the United Jewish Appeal (UJA), the American Jewish Committee, the American Jewish Congress, and B'nai B'rith. The UJA was founded in 1939 and serves as a fund-raising organization for humanitarian causes. Recently, Israel has received the largest share of the funds collected. The American Jewish Committee (founded in 1906) and the American Jewish Congress (1918) work toward the similar purpose of improving Jewish-Gentile relations. B'nai B'rith (Sons of the Covenant) was founded in 1843 and claims 500,000 members in forty nations. It promotes cultural and social programs and, through its Anti-Defamation League, monitors and fights anti-Semitism and hate crimes directed at other groups.

Besides the national groups, many community-based organizations are active. Some local organizations, such as social and business clubs, were founded because the existing groups barred Jews from membership. The U.S. Supreme Court has consistently ruled that private social organizations such as country clubs and business clubs may discriminate against Jews or any other ethnic or racial group. Jewish community centers are also prominent local organizations. To Gentiles, the synagogue is the most visible symbol of the Jewish presence at the community level. However, the Jewish community center is an important focus of local activity. In many Jewish neighborhoods throughout the United States, it is the center of secular activity. Hospitals, nurseries, homes for the elderly, and child care agencies are only a few of the community-level activities sponsored by Jewish Americans.

Politics

U.S. Jews, along with Blacks, have been the mainstay of the Democratic Party and of liberal, as well as left-liberal, politics in U.S. life. Though this is substantively still true, a powerful shift since the 1980s, the Reagan years, have shifted the Jewish community to the right. This shift has not simply found expression in support of Republicans but more seriously, in a small but vocal group support by Jewish right-wingers, both religious and secular, for such issues as immigration, Muslim influence in the United States, anti-Semitism, and support for Israel. These right-wing groups include The David Project, the American Israel Public Affairs Committee (AIPAC), the American Zionism Organization, the American Jewish Congress (which was once liberal), the Agudat Yisroel orthodox groups, and many others. Although Jews still vote liberal, most of them are not affiliated with the Jewish community; those affiliated tend to be more reactionary and conservative. This shift during the past 25 years has become a major challenge for the Jewish community and the general U.S. community.

Religion in the Future

Jewish identity and participation in the Jewish religion are not the same. Many U.S. residents consider themselves Jewish and are considered Jewish by others even though they have never participated in Jewish religious life. The available data indicate that 57% of U.S. Jews are affiliated with a synagogue or temple, but only 10% view participation in religious worship as extremely important. Even in Israel, only 30% of Jews are religiously observant. Nevertheless, the presence of a religious tradition, which for some represents symbolic religiosity, is an important tie among Jews, even secular Jews.

The era of the one Jewish leader, especially a religious one, that all could admire and follow has long been over. The Jewish community is splintered and shattered into many factions. There is no one person or organization to lead. Furthermore, the latest surveys and studies showed some shocking conclusions: The fastest growing Jewish group in the United States was Reform Jews, 29%, often considered the most "assimilated," whereas the group with the greatest loss of members was Conservative Jews, down to 32%, and the Orthodox, which many thought was the fastest growing group, actually had only a slight increase to 19% of U.S. Jews. Reconstructionism and other "Jewish renewal" groups grew faster than the Orthodox, but still emerged at about 2% to 4%. Other important determinants of Judaism included day school attendance, summer camps, and trips to Israel. These factors are crucial in determining one's future Jewish identity.

Jack Nusan Porter

See Appendix A; Appendix B

See also Americanization; American Jewish Committee; Anti-Defamation League; Anti-Semitism; Argentina; Assimilation; Diaspora; Holocaust; Holocaust Deniers and Revisionists; Intermarriage; Jewish-Black Relations: A Historical Perspective; Jewish-Black Relations: The Contemporary Period; Jewry, Black American; Ku Klux Klan; Racialization; Stereotypes; Symbolic Religiosity; Zionism

Further Readings:

American Jewish Committee. 2002. *2001 Annual Survey of American Jewish Opinion.* New York: AJC.

American Jewish Committee. 2005. *2005 Annual Survey of American Jewish Opinion.* New York: AJC.

Diner, Hasia R. 2003. *A New Promised Land: A History of Jews in America.* New York: Oxford University Press.

Feldberg, Michael. 2005. *Three Hundred and Fifty Years: An Album of American Jewish Memory.* New York: American Jewish Historical Society and the American Jewish Archives.

Finklestein, Norman H. *Forged in Freedom: Shaping the Jewish-American Experience,* Philadelphia, PA: Jewish Publication Society, 2002.

Gans, Herbert J. 1956. "American Jewry: Present and Future." *Commentary* (May 21):424–425.

Los Angeles Times Poll. 1998. *American and Israeli Jews.* Los Angeles: Los Angeles Times and Yedioth Ahronoth.

Porter, Jack Nusan, ed. 1980. *The Sociology of American Jewry: A Critical Anthology.* 2nd rev. ed. Lanham, MD: University Press of America.

Rosenthal, Steven T. 2001. *Irreconcilable Differences? The Waning of the American Jewish Love Affair with Israel.* Hanover, VT: Brandeis University Press.

Ruggiero, Adriane, ed. 2006. *The Jews.* Detroit: Greenhaven Press.

Ukeles, Jacob B., Ron Miller, and Pearl Beck. 2006. *Young Jewish Adults in the United States Today: Harbingers of the American Jewish Community of Tomorrow?* New York: American Jewish Committee.

JEWISH-BLACK RELATIONS: A HISTORICAL PERSPECTIVE

African Americans have been in the United States for several hundred years—often arriving involuntarily—whereas Jewish Americans are more recent and voluntary arrivals to the United States, arriving in large numbers only within the last 120 years. Nonetheless, these two groups have a strong history that at times has been supportive but full of conflict and disagreement at other times. At times, there have been charges of Black anti-Semitism and Jewish racism. At other times, similarities in their experiences as groups have been highlighted, with oppression and lack of acceptance by the dominant majority the most salient. The reality is that all of this is true. This entry focuses on a chronological review of that history, beginning with the pre-20th century period, then moving on to the 1900s through 1960s, and ending with an exploration of the relationship through 1970.

Before the 20th Century

Historically, Black leaders often pointed to the experiences of Hebrews in bondage in ancient Egypt as being similar to their own experiences under slavery and then under Jim Crow discrimination. In addition, some Blacks have presented themselves as actual descendents of the tribes of Israel.

Although the number of Jews in the United States rose dramatically during the peak years of immigration from 1880 through 1924, a small number of mainly German Jewish immigrants were living in the United States during slavery. There have been arguments about the role these few Jews played in both the slave trade and in slavery itself. What historians generally agree on is that Jews did play various although limited roles in the African slave trade.

Few Jews owned plantations mainly because Jews in the old country of Europe were not allowed to own land and, therefore, fulfilled roles as merchants or peddlers. In keeping with this tradition in their new country, Southern Jews tended to fill these same positions, living in more urban areas. Nonetheless, there were some Jewish plantation and slaveowners, though the numbers pale in comparison with the larger White population. Overall, Jewish relations to slaves in the South differed little from those of non-Jews in the South.

As more Jews began entering the United States in the 1850s fleeing persecution and seeking economic and social freedom, the Jewish abolitionist participation in the United States began to emerge. Sharing certain political and ideological leanings, this group helped create the Reform Judaism movement, which largely believed that all humans should be treated equally. The Jewish abolitionists arose from this movement.

By the late 1800s, as more and more immigrants arrived in the United States, Black Americans had a keen awareness that the newcomers were given special treatment whereas Blacks were still being treated as second-class citizens. However, the general population often did not include Jews in the favored group, feeling that Jews were often as discriminated against as they were. Further, the Black press, as well as various Black leaders, frequently pointed to Jews as examples and role models for Black economic success and social behavior. Most especially, Black leaders pointed to Jewish solidarity as a successful model for Blacks to adopt. At this time, some Black leaders began to see the potential for collaboration with Jews in achieving social acceptance and for financial assistance from Jews for Black causes. Two such leaders were Booker T. Washington and W. E. B. Du Bois.

Booker T. Washington firmly believed that to succeed in the United States and be fully accepted, African Americans needed to work hard together to gain full access to all that the United States had to offer. In making this argument, Washington believed that Blacks should look to Jews as examples of what Blacks could do. Washington also actively sought Jewish financial support for various Black causes, particularly for educational institutions.

Another major African American leader, W. E. B. Du Bois, also welcomed Jewish support of Black causes and organizations. Du Bois invited Jewish participation in the National Association for the Advancement of Colored People (NAACP), which he founded, and he even helped a Jewish man win election as president of the NAACP. In particular, during the years of World War II, Du Bois consistently compared what Hitler was doing to the Jews in Germany with what the United States had done to African Americans.

1900 Through 1970

From 1890 to 1924, thousands of Jews streamed into the United States. Mainly from Russia and other areas of Eastern Europe, these new Jewish immigrants were different from the mostly German Jews already living in the United States. These newer Jews came into contact with African Americans in two ways. First, many of the new immigrants primarily stayed in the North, and as Blacks began migrating north in massive numbers during and after World War I, they often moved into neighborhoods that were predominantly Jewish. Second, some Jews went south to try to make a living, often owning small stores or managing larger factories. Contact in both of these ways had a lasting impact on the relations between Blacks and Jews.

Leo Frank: The Lynching of a Jew

Between 1900 and World War I, more than a thousand Blacks had been lynched in the South. In 1915, Leo Frank, a White Jewish manager of a factory, was accused of killing a young White girl. After a guilty verdict was returned but before he could be sentenced, a White mob stormed the jail where Frank was being held and hung him. The trial itself had rested on the word of one witness, a Black janitor. To Jews everywhere, Frank's lynching highlighted how much they had in common with Blacks; Jews felt they were not seen as White, but as a separate race altogether.

Frank's lynching actually made many in the Black press angrier. Essentially, they questioned why there was now so much outrage over a White man being lynched when hundreds of Blacks had been lynched and ignored. For Jews, Frank's lynching highlighted their similarities with Blacks; for Blacks, it highlighted their own continued lower-class status in society.

Blacks Move North

Although Blacks continued to use Jews as role models for success as outsiders in the United States, their relations became more strained as Blacks moved north into urban areas. For Blacks, the move often meant Jewish property managers, Jewish shop owners, and employment as servants in Jewish homes. Often filling what has been referred to as the "middleman position," Jews were often self-employed, owning the small retail shops frequented by Black residents. Although many interactions between the groups were positive, there were problematic exchanges that often became overcharged, leaving both sides with a negative view of the other. Nonetheless, by the end of the 1940s, Black and Jewish groups were joining in efforts to benefit one another. As their agencies and organizations began to realize, protecting the rights of one minority group meant protecting the rights of all. Many of the issues raised by Black civil rights leaders were the same problems being faced by U.S. Jews, including being rejected by U.S. centers of power. Furthermore, the Jewish tradition meant a commitment to human rights and equality, and being racist was seen as being "un-Jewish."

Jewish involvement in civil rights causes has often included financial support of various Black organizations. In particular, wealthy Jews made significant contributions to support the NAACP, as well as contributions to various Black educational institutions, such as Howard and Fisk universities. Working-class Jewish immigrants in unions often believed, contrary at times to the racist practices of the larger national unions, that Blacks should be unionized as well. One of the most famous of these unions, the International Ladies Garment Workers Union, had a significant Jewish leadership that extended full union benefits to Blacks and was a militant promoter of Black civil rights.

By the end of the 1950s and throughout the 1960s, Black organizations in the North and South grew less accommodating and more radical in their attempts to achieve equality. For example, the Student Nonviolent Coordinating Committee (SNCC) eventually asked all Whites to leave their organization. As Blacks began pushing to take control of their own movements and make more demands of White establishment, some Jews began to feel Blacks were asking for too much too quickly.

Nowhere was this more evident than in the 1968 Ocean Hill–Brownsville Teachers' Strike in New York City, a situation many believe was the beginning of the disintegration of positive Black-Jewish relationships. Increasingly, Blacks and Puerto Ricans had entered previously Jewish neighborhoods, yet the school boards continued to reflect the previous Jewish population. Unhappy with the educational situation, the community attempted to take control of the schools, resulting in more than 350 teachers going on strike. Although 50% of the replacement teachers were Jewish, the teacher's union (United Federation of Teachers) continued to have a predominantly Jewish leadership, which resisted the efforts of the local community. Although the Ocean Hill–Brownsville community control experiment was eventually eliminated, relations between the two groups were never the same.

Beth Frankel Merenstein

See also African Americans; Anti-Semitism; Du Bois, William Edward Burghardt; Jackson, Jesse, Sr.; Jewish Americans; Jewish-Black Relations: The Contemporary Period; Lynching; Washington, Booker T.

Further Readings

Adams, Maurianne and John Bracey, eds. 1999. *Strangers and Neighbors: Relations Between Blacks and Jews in the United States.* Amherst: University of Massachusetts Press.

Berman, Paul, ed. 1994. *Blacks and Jews: Alliances and Arguments.* New York: Delacorte.

Diner, Hasia. 1977. *In the Almost Promised Land: American Jews and Blacks, 1915–1935.* Westport, CT: Greenwood Press.

Pritchett, Wendell. 2002. *Brownsville, Brooklyn: Blacks, Jews, and the Changing Face of the Ghetto.* Chicago, IL: University of Chicago Press.

JEWISH-BLACK RELATIONS: THE CONTEMPORARY PERIOD

Throughout U.S. history, the relationship between Blacks and Jews has been complex and sometimes volatile, marked by periods of collaboration and troubled by episodes of conflict and contention. Perhaps because from the beginning both groups were considered outsiders by the White Christian majority, Jewish perceptions of similarities between White racism and anti-Semitism led to organized efforts to aid African American's struggles to eliminate racism. Yet, as some observers have pointed out, if those efforts were motivated chiefly by altruism, they were also based to some degree on self-interest.

To the extent that Jews, as White European Americans, had always been accorded somewhat higher status than Blacks in U.S. society, the relationship between the two groups could not be one of collaboration between true equals. Accordingly, Blacks have sometimes viewed Jews as allies and at other times as exploiters, though usually as different from other Whites. Even at the peak of their relationship, during the Civil Rights Movement of the 1950s and 1960s when Jews and Blacks worked together to achieve racial equality, considerable ambiguity, sometimes leading to hostility, existed about what was perceived as Jews' own role in maintaining inequality. Contemporary relations remain fraught with ambiguity as class and cultural conflict have increased and as contemporary national and international events have highlighted group differences, as this entry shows.

Urban Competition and Conflict

Northern urban Jews have often lived in close contact with African Americans, but at different status levels, and maintained unequal hiring and renting practices. Jews' intermediary status allowed some to profit from Blacks' earnings, resulting in unequal contact and thus fostering anti-Jewish sentiment within the Black community. Local Jewish merchants offered credit and a wide variety of goods, but also fixed prices. Similarly, many Jewish landowners rented to Blacks, but some among them were notorious for overcharging Black renters and not keeping appliances, heat, and electricity in their buildings in clean and working order. Those Jewish merchants and owners who exploited Blacks were a minority of the Jewish population, and many other Jews had no problems living side-by-side with Blacks in integrated neighborhoods. However, systematic exploitation by a minority left a deep impact on Blacks' consciousness of Jews.

As U.S. Jews improved their material condition, many came to interpret racial difference through a lens of liberalism that placed responsibility for success on group prowess and ambition rather than on a recognition of the existence of structural inequalities. Believing that success for Blacks would come with their willingness to integrate and conform to mainstream U.S. society, even as Jews refused to wholly do so, resulted in cultural strife, notably during the Ocean Hill–Brownsville conflict of 1968 to 1971.

Nationally, Jews' status improved relative to Blacks' throughout the postwar period, creating and exacerbating class-based and cultural differences. As Jews assimilated, they tended to acquire the attitudes of the dominant culture, further distancing themselves from the Black community. Some educated Jews, embracing neoconservatism, began to oppose affirmative action policies that had significantly aided Blacks and better positioned them to compete in universities and for jobs. Moving into power positions in business and politics, Jews could not necessarily be relied on to assist Blacks in gaining access to or a step up on the economic ladder.

Contemporary Cleavages

Contemporary national and international events have highlighted the growing divergence between the two groups. For example, activists promoted ideological links to other oppressed peoples, such as Palestinians in the Israeli-occupied West Bank, precipitating another fissure in Jews' and Blacks' relationship. In August 1991, a Black youth was accidentally struck and killed in Crown Heights, Brooklyn, by a car driven by an Orthodox Jew; in retaliation, a Jewish religious school student was stabbed to death. These highly publicized events generated increased alienation between the two communities and continue to loom large in the collective histories of both groups

Some argue that Jews' alleged indifference to Black inequality constitutes a particular betrayal and abandonment of civil rights ideologies, given Jews' earlier arguments of their linked fates. A growing conservative Republican Jewish population, opposed to civil rights legislation, suggests that assimilated Jews have become more like their non-Jewish counterparts with regard to racial attitudes. Inaction and inattention by Jews concerning Blacks' contemporary social, political, and economic condition is seen as perpetuating the racial hierarchy and status quo.

Contemporary research suggests that although Blacks see Jews as different from other Whites, Blacks are ambivalent and unsure of Jews' allegiances. Recent studies find Blacks have higher rates of anti-Semitism than do Whites, because of both contemporary antagonisms and collective memories of Jewish exploitation of Blacks. Because of this history, many Blacks no longer consign fellow-victim or minority status to Jews.

Black-Jewish relations remain complex. Though contemporary scholars within each community have attempted to bridge the gap between the groups, alliances remain fragile. Different perceptions of the specific policies needed to support Black advancement and Jews' higher status relative to Blacks in the U.S. racial hierarchy remain formidable barriers to collaboration. Nevertheless, organizations such as the Southern Poverty Law Center and the Anti-Defamation League of B'nai B'rith continue to unite Jews and Blacks seeking to eliminate racism and anti-Semitism.

Melissa F. Weiner

See also Anti-Defamation League; Anti-Semitism; Civil Rights Movement; Crown Heights, Brooklyn; Jewish Americans; Jewish-Black Relations: A Historical Perspective; White Racism

Further Readings

Adams, Maurianne and John H. Bracey, eds. (2000). *Strangers and Neighbors: Relations Between Blacks and Jews in the United States.* Amherst: University of Massachusetts Press.

Berman, Paul, ed. (1994). *Blacks and Jews: Alliances and Arguments.* New York: Delacorte.

Franklin, V. P., Nancy L. Grant, Harold M. Kletnick, and Genna Rae McNeil, eds. (1998). *African Americans and Jews in the Twentieth Century: Studies in Convergence and Conflict.* Columbia: University of Missouri Press.

Greenberg, Cheryl Lynn. 2006. *Troubling the Waters: Black-Jewish Relations in the American Century.* Princeton, NJ: Princeton University Press.

Marx, Gary T. 1967. *Protest and Prejudice: A Study of Belief in the Black Community.* New York: Harper & Row.

Salzman, Jack and Cornell West, eds. 1997. *Struggles in the Promised Land: Toward a History of Black-Jewish Relations in the United States.* New York: Oxford University Press.

Sniderman, Paul M. and Thomas Piazza. 2002. *Black Pride and Black Prejudice.* Princeton, NJ: Princeton University Press.

JEWRY, BLACK AMERICAN

Although some African Americans belong to traditional Jewish congregations, there also exists a separate African American Jewry, one of the many variants of Judaism and one with a long history in the United States. Although numbers have been debated, there is some consensus that Black American Jewry may consist of between 100,000 and 260,000 members. Some in mainstream Judaism may believe that Black Jewry is at odds with how Judaism should be practiced, but many African American Jews have also rejected features of European Jewry, asserting their right to define and practice Judaism while incorporating many features of their historical and cultural background as long as they remain true to Jewish religious law. In this manner, Black American Jewry seeks to validate its version of Judaism in the same spirit with which similar validations have been made regarding the uniqueness of Ethiopian Jewry, Yemenite Jewry, and Moroccan Jewry. This entry summarizes the history and current status of African American Jewry.

Beginnings

Many believe the Judaic presence in African American religious life can be traced to the exile and diaspora that followed the destruction of the Temple in Jerusalem in 70 CE; this resulted in the dispersion of many Jews to many parts of Africa. Hence, African and African American Judaism are deeply rooted in some of the legends, folk tales, and uncertainties surrounding the Ten Lost Tribes of Israel and the more than 2,500-year history of Ethiopian Jewry (Beta Israel).

It may be difficult to unravel all of ancient Judaism's history, but what is verifiable is the historical identification of Black Americans with Ancient Israel and the Hebrew people. In 18th and 19th centuries, in speeches and sermons, and especially in the spirituals, suffering African Americans poured out their grief, joy, and their longing for freedom as they too imagined themselves marching forward to their Promised Land. They viewed their persecution, enslavement, exile, and emancipation as paths that would follow the path of the suffering Hebrews. This identification with the Ancient Israelites also included the idea of having been selected like the Israelites as the Chosen People who were, like the Hebrews, in search of their Promised Land, which would be a return to Africa, though the double meaning of the term would also mean Heaven.

Though fragmentary data indicate some Hebraic ideas and practices within African American religious practices in the early and mid-19th century, the earliest record of formal institutional Judaic practices occurred in 1886 with the formation of the first Black Jewish sect, the Church of the Living God, the Pillar Ground of Truth for all Nations, founded by F. S. Cherry in Chattanooga, Tennessee. This was followed by The Church of God and Saints of Christ, organized by William S. Crowdy in Lawrence, Kansas, in 1896.

Though both groups contained elements of Christian teachings, they introduced ideas and practices that served as foundations for subsequent African American Jewish groups: that Blacks were the true descendants of the ancient Hebrew people and that Europeans had usurped the original meaning and intent of the Hebrew scripture to elevate themselves over others and therefore claim to be the sole inheritors and interpreters of the scripture and Jewish life. Crowdy's Jewish sect was the first among many groups that followed his lead to initiate circumcision rites, observe the Shabbat on Saturday, wear the yarmulke, and observe Pesach and kosher.

The next major development in African American Jewry was the congregation B'nai Abraham founded by Rabbi Arnold Ford, musical director for Marcus Garvey's Universal Negro Improvement Association, and the Commandment Keepers Congregation, one of the largest African American Jewish synagogues, founded in Harlem by Rabbi Wentworth Arthur Matthew. Rabbi Matthew was born in Africa and raised in the West Indies. He elevated the importance of Africa and Ethiopian Jewry for Black Jews in the United States, therefore creating the link that validated legitimate Black claims to authentic Judaism, one that he asserted was much older than the European claims to Judaism. He was also the first African American Jewish rabbi to create a rabbinical college, the Ethiopian Hebrew Rabbinical College, and until his death ordained dozens of men into the rabbinate.

These early attempts to validate Judaism as a natural, and true, religion for African Americans also often included the proviso that indeed African Americans were the "original" and "true" Hebrews. Efforts to forge a Black Jewish presence would take the form of a rejection of Christianity, indictment of the Christian West's role in the international slave trade, the enslavement of Blacks in the United States, and the European colonization of Africa. Establishment of a Judaic presence was rooted in a deeply felt belief by many Black Jewish sect founders that African people had been robbed of their rights and dignity by Christianity. Therefore, only an intense sense of nationalism and pride, and the restoration of Black dignity, which they believed always existed in Africans and African Americans within some parts of their Jewish past, would rescue the group.

Today's Practice

A review of African American Jewry today reveals a variety of names—Hebrew Israelites, Israelites, Black Hebrews, Ethiopian Hebrews, or Black Jews; what is clear is the absence of any doctrine related to Christianity. African American Jewish congregations observe the High Holy Days, and many might recognize, but not observe, the minor holidays; some observe kashrut; some have separate seating for males and females; and many have choirs with drums and other non-Western musical instruments that are played during the service.

Despite these similarities, there are differences and variations in some ritual practices between European American Jewry and African American Jewry. Whereas the two largest U.S. Jewish mainstream denominations (the Conservative and Reform movements) orient themselves culturally to Yiddish, Yiddishkeit, and the Holocaust, African American Jewry focuses largely on Africa, the history of the Black struggle in the United States, and Black leaders who have waged the battle for Black freedom, such as Harriet Tubman, Frederick Douglass, Marcus Garvey,

W. E. B. Du Bois, Booker T. Washington, and Martin Luther King, Jr. Many African American Jews believe that contemporary European Jewry simply reflects the infusion of long-standing European cultural habits and values rather than *Halachah,* Jewish law based on the Torah. Some African American synagogues reflect and depict the cultural life and history of African Americans, choosing to have special days honoring Black leaders and celebrating Emancipation Proclamation Day and Juneteenth, and other important highlights of the African American experience. For example, during Pesach, rice, and kosher foods such as corn bread, collard greens, and yams may be served, and "Let My People Go"; "We Shall Overcome"; and the Black National Anthem, "Lift Every Voice and Sing"; and other songs may be sung.

Thousands of African American Jews belong to the four mainstream Jewish denominations, the Conservative, Reform, Orthodox, and Reconstruction movements, though most of them are likely members of the Conservative and Reform movements. Many became Jews through conversion, and many are or were the children of at least one and sometimes two Jewish parents.

One of the greatest hurdles confronting African American Jewry is the deeply held view by many—Jews and non-Jews alike, and European American and African American—that Judaism is a religion for and by Europeans. For this reason, many Jews may be surprised when told of the existence of large numbers of African American Jews. Subtle forms of rejection and racism may be directed toward African American Jews, especially if it is believed that their form of Judaism does not fit the European American model and paradigm. Likewise, African American Jews may encounter suspicion from other Blacks, who may view Black Judaism as a betrayal of their historical Christianity, because they, too, may see Judaism as a European religion. There is a double irony here, because Christianity in the modern era has taken on the paraphernalia of being largely a European religion.

Some of the problems African American Jews face parallel many of the problems of mainstream European American Jewry: Quite often the non-Jewish world knows and hears so little about Judaism from its adherents, and there are historical reasons why this has been the case. Just as most White Christians don't know much about Jewish Americans, most Black Christians know little about African American Jewry.

Thus, African American Jews may experience what W. E. B. Du Bois called "double consciousness" and what this author calls "dual marginality." Both terms can suggest paradoxes surrounding Jews in the United States, but for African American Jews, the setting can be labeled a "triple paradox" in that they are a minority religious group located within another group that is also a minority group in the society. To offset their feeling of being outsiders and what they believe to be structural barriers that hinder their sense of being Jews, several organizations have been created to provide a venue for discussion, creativity, and the probing of their Judaism: The Alliance for Black Jews, Ayecha Resource Organization, and the Pan-African Jewish Alliance. The latter group attempts to include Jews on every continent.

The various ways of practicing Judaism inevitably raise the larger question, "Who is a Jew?" This issue is currently at the center of an intense debate between the Reform, Conservative, and Orthodox religious leadership in Israel, just as it is often an issue in many U.S. Jewish synagogues and communities. Ari Goldman puts the question within larger Jewish contexts when he notes four important points germane to the question of who is a Jew and what constitutes Jewishness. These points serve as an important epilogue to the discussion and analysis of African American Jewry: (1) There was never one true, divinely approved way of "being Jewish"; (2) Judaism has always been a work-in-progress; (3) Jews in the United States and elsewhere "do" Judaism in eccentric, idiosyncratic ways; and (4) Jews respond to the large "table" of Jewish practices, teachings, memories, texts, art, and relationships and are creating a Judaism that makes sense to them.

Rutledge M. Dennis

See also Double Consciousness; Du Bois, William Edward Burghardt; Emancipation Proclamation; Holocaust; Jewish Americans; Marginalization; Pluralism

Further Readings

Azoulay, Katya Gibel. 1997. *Black, Jewish, and Interracial.* Durham, NC: Duke University Press.
Berman, Paul. 1994. *Blacks and Jews.* New York: Delacorte.
Chireau, Yvonne and N. Deutsch eds. 2000. *Black Zion.* New York: Oxford University Press.
Cohen, David, ed. 1989. *Jews in America.* San Francisco, CA: Collier.

Landing, James. 2002. *Black Judaism.* Durham, NC: Carolina Academic Press.

Lester, Julius, 1988. *Lovesong: Becoming a Jew.* New York: Arcade.

JIM CROW

Jim Crow refers to the laws and customs present in the United States, typically in the former states of the Confederacy, that prescribed a segregated society and kept Black people in a subservient position in everyday life. The term is taken from a song, "Jump Jim Crow," which was performed in minstrel shows by White singers in Blackface. The character Jim Crow was a rural Black man who was poorly dressed. This entry describes the history of Jim Crow laws in the United States.

Following the Civil War and the end of Reconstruction in 1876 and lasting until the Civil Rights Act of 1964, different states, particularly in the South, enacted various laws to enforce racial segregation between Whites and Blacks. Jim Crow laws reflected the racial ideology that Whites were superior to Blacks and any forms of integration would destroy the purity of the White race.

During the Progressive era, Jim Crow laws were broadened to the federal level. Although Jim Crow laws were tightly enforced, there were challenges. In 1896, a Black man named Homer Plessy was convicted in Louisiana for riding in a Whites-only railway car. Plessy appealed to the U.S. Supreme Court, which upheld the Louisiana decision. The "separate but equal" doctrine was thus established.

The actual nature of Jim Crow practices was limited only by the imagination of Whites who wanted to keep Blacks separate from—and not necessarily equal to— themselves. In many places, Blacks and Whites attended separate schools, and there were often separate facilities, including restrooms and water fountains, for Blacks and Whites in public places. In Louisiana, the law prohibited renting housing to someone of African ancestry if the housing was partially occupied by Whites. In Georgia, there were separate restaurants for Blacks and Whites. Throughout the South, Blacks and Whites could not legally marry. Some signs said, "No dogs, Negroes, and mulattos." In many places, a Black man could not extend his hand to a White man, have any contact with White women, or curse White people.

Jim Crow laws were gradually dismantled after World War II. In the 1950s, the National Association for the Advancement of Colored People (NAACP) attempted to end the segregation on buses and trains. In 1950, the Supreme Court declared that the University of Texas must admit Herman Sweatt, an African American, to the law school on the ground that the state should provide equal education for him. The Supreme Court finally declared the segregation of the railway unconstitutional in 1952. In 1954, in *Brown v. Board of Education,* the U.S. Supreme Court declared the segregation of educational system unconstitutional. Despite the Court's decision, segregation continued in some states. Congress passed the Civil Rights Act in 1964 when Lyndon Baines Johnson was the president. This act made racial segregation illegal. Although Jim Crow law is a de jure system of segregation; the de facto segregation of races continues in some places today.

Shu-Ju Ada Cheng

See also African Americans; Civil Disobedience; Civil Rights Movement; Discrimination; National Association for the Advancement of Colored People; *Plessy v. Ferguson;* Racism; Racism, Types of; Sundown Towns

Further Readings

Klarman, Michael J. 2006. *From Jim Crow to Civil Rights: The Supreme Court and the Struggle for Racial Equality.* Oxford, UK: Oxford University Press.

Upchurch, Thomas Adams. 2004. *Legislating Racism: The Billion Dollar Congress and the Birth of Jim Crow.* Lexington: University Press of Kentucky.

Woodward, C. Vann. 2001. *The Strange Career of Jim Crow.* Commemorative ed., afterword by William S. McFeely. New York: Oxford University Press.

Wormser, Richard. 2004. *The Rise and Fall of Jim Crow.* New York: St. Martin's.

JOHNSON, CHARLES S. (1893–1956)

Charles S. Johnson used social science methodology to systematically seek to understand the impact of race on the social and personal challenges of African Americans. His personal experiences with racial discrimination, from childhood on, shaped his intellectual curiosity about human relations, and after a close call on his life during the Chicago riots of the 1920s, Johnson's career in race relations began. After receiving the PhB in 1917 from the University of Chicago, he began to study the societal conditions that shaped the hatred manifested in the race riots, and he served on the Chicago Race Commission. He became the national director of research for the Urban League. As founder and editor of the Urban League's *Opportunity: A Journal of Negro Life,* Johnson provided a vehicle for under-recognized artisans such as Langston Hughes, Countee Cullen, and Aaron Douglas. This entry describes Johnson's career.

Johnson was a scholar, a researcher, and a policymaker, but perhaps one of his greatest skills was in the role of convener. He convened a group of African America's most talented artists, writers, poets, and musicians, which blossomed into one of the most productive intellectual and cultural movements—the Harlem Renaissance. In 1924, he convened a grand dinner seeking philanthropic donations to establish literary awards for the under-recognized stars of the Harlem Renaissance. Later, at Fisk University, Johnson attracted Black intellectuals such as Arna Bontemps, E. Franklin Frazier, James Weldon Johnson, and Horace Mann to ultimately create a new intellectual renaissance at Fisk University. Johnson went on to convene teams of researchers to form the Fisk Race Relations Department and study race relations across the global diaspora.

Johnson's research, using the survey method combined with a case study approach, provided a voice to the oppressed and disenfranchised. Scholarly works such as *Shadow of the Plantation, Growing Up in the Black Belt: Negro Youth in the Rural South,* and *Patterns of Negro Segregation* became landmark studies that provided an understanding of the impact of segregation on the American Negro. Beginning in 1944, he convened annual Race Relations Institutes where Thurgood Marshall, Martin Luther King, Jr., and many White activists came together in desegregated spaces in the midst of the segregated South.

Within the intellectual oasis that he helped to shape at Fisk University, Johnson built a rigorous research infrastructure that rivaled the best of the majority White institutions. His academic training at Chicago under the direction of Robert E. Park had provided a theoretical underpinning that served as the foundation of Johnson's race relations model. The Fisk Race Relations Institute provided leadership to the field of race relations.

Over the objection of W. E. B. Du Bois, the board hired Johnson as the first African American President of Fisk University. His mentor and former teacher, Robert E. Park, retired from University of Chicago and finished his academic career working alongside Johnson at Fisk. As Fisk University president, Johnson continued to attract substantial funding for Fisk and to develop innovative academic programs such as the Basic College for talented young teenagers who matriculated at Fisk University in their mid-teens. Johnson continued to balance his research with his growing administrative duties in service to Fisk. He served, in addition, as consultant to the United Nations.

Johnson was criticized for his relationship with his White philanthropic contacts as well as for his diplomatic demeanor. His groundbreaking research paradigm was well respected within academic circles, even though Johnson would become less well known than some contemporaries. Still, he touched the social sciences and shaped policies on race relations within educational systems, the Armed Forces, and regional, national, and international policies.

Although Johnson did not live to see the fulfillment of the Civil Rights Movement, his work laid the blueprint for policy development addressing racial discrimination and segregation. Known as the sideline activist, Johnson used research as a tool to shape policy that would improve race relations. His action research—and his study of urban, rural, Southern, and Northern America, as well as racial patterns and practices in other countries—provided the basis for disenfranchised groups to gain a voice in the face of segregation. Johnson, who struggled in his later years with migraine headaches, succumbed on a trip by train to a Fisk board of trustees meeting in New York in 1956.

Sheila Renee Peters

See also Chicago School of Race Relations; Du Bois, William Edward Burghardt; Frazier, E. Franklin; Harlem Renaissance; Jim Crow; Marshall, Thurgood; Park, Robert E.

Further Readings

Gilpin, Patrick J. and Marybeth Gasman. 2003. *Charles S. Johnson: Leadership Beyond the Veil in the Age of Jim Crow.* Albany: State University of New York Press.

Johnson, Charles S. 1934. *Shadow of the Plantation.* Chicago, IL: University of Chicago Press.

Johnson, Charles S. 1941. *Growing Up in the Black Belt*. New York: American Council on Education.

Johnson, Charles S. 1943. *Patterns of Negro Segregation*. New York: Harper Brothers.

Robbins, Richard. 1996. *Sidelines Activist: Charles S. Johnson and the Struggle for Civil Rights*. Jackson: University Press of Mississippi.

JORDANIAN AMERICANS

Jordanian Americans are the immigrants from Jordan, a kingdom of 5.7 million in 2007, and their descendants. Jordanian Americans represent one of the many diverse groups of the Arab nations—including Algeria, Bahrain, Egypt, Iraq, Kuwait, Lebanon, Libya, Morocco, Oman, Palestine, the Republic of Yemen, Qatar, Saudi Arabia, Syria, Tunisia, and the United Arab Emirates. Jordan, as an independent nation, is relatively young. However, the land it now occupies (about 35,000 square miles, bordered by Israel to the west, Syria to the north, Iraq to the northeast, and Saudi Arabia to the east and the south) has been inhabited for thousands of years, and historically, under great conflict.

According to the 2000 U.S. Census, 46,795 people born in Jordan were resident in the United States, of whom 60.1% were citizens. This entry will look at the background of immigration from Jordan to the United States and the contemporary picture of Jordanian Americans.

Immigration Patterns

Since 1850, Arabs have been migrating to the United States, but Jordanian immigration began after World War II. According to census statistics, during the 1950s, about 5,000 Jordanians immigrated to the United States. The number of Jordanian immigrants doubled to about 11,000 in the 1960s and continually increased, reaching about 25,000 in the 1970s. This mass increase was mainly because of conflict with other Arab nations. About 2,900 Jordanians immigrated annually during the 1980s. However, an estimated 42,755 arrived during the 1990s.

Contemporary Community

In recent years, people from Jordan have sought permanent residency and completed the naturalization process to become citizens. From 1997 through 2006, about 3,700 Jordanians immigrated to the United States annually. At least 2,400 Jordanian Americans have become naturalized citizens annually beginning with 1997.

According to the U.S. Census Bureau 2005 American Community Survey, there were 45,113 of Jordanian national origin in the United States in 2005. In geographic distribution, the top five states were California, Illinois, Ohio, New Jersey, and New York. Because Jordanians are at or have not reached third generation, many are not well "Americanized." Therefore, Jordanian immigrants find comfort in settling into areas and neighborhoods that have already been established. Additionally, immigrants may face a language barrier. According to the 2000 census, 45.9% speak English less than "very well." Their median family income was $45,532 compared with $50,890 for the nation as a whole. Of those Jordan-born present here in 2000, 27% had entered the country before 2000.

Jennifer M. Klein

See Appendix A; Appendix B
See also Arab Americans; Assimilation; Immigrant Communities; Immigration, U.S.; Islamophobia; Muslim Americans; Refugees

Further Readings

Department of Homeland Security. 2007. *Yearbook of Immigration Statistics*: 2006. Washington, DC: Office of Immigration Statistics. Available from http://www.dhs.gov/ximgtn/statistics/publications/yearbook.shtm

Horani, Albert. 1991. *A History of the Arab Peoples*. Cambridge, MA: Warner Books.

Metz, Helen Chapin. 1991. *Jordan, A Country Study*. Washington, DC: Federal Research Division, Library of Congress.

Satloff, Robert B. 1986. *Troubles on the East Bank: Challenges to the Domestic Stability of Jordan*. New York: Praeger, 1986.

U.S. Census Bureau. 2004. *Profile of Demographic and Social Characteristics: 2000. People Born in Jordan*. Available from http://www.census.gov/population/www/socdemo/foreign/STP-159-2000tl.html

U.S. Census Bureau. 2006. *American Community Survey 2005*. Washington, DC: Author. Available from http://www.census.gov/acs/www

Juvenile Justice

The U.S. juvenile justice system has evolved considerably over the years, moving from informal discipline during the colonial era to more formal systems of social control—police, courts, corrections—in the 19th and 20th centuries. However, a number of themes and trends have remained essentially unchanged, as this entry shows. Juvenile justice institutions have focused their attention on lower-class children, particularly African Americans and the progeny of immigrants: the "dangerous classes." Juvenile reformatories and courts, as well as newer innovations, have attempted to instill in lower-class offenders the habits of order, discipline, and self-control, fitting them into their "proper place" in the economic, political, social, cultural, and legal order. There has always been a wide disparity between the promise and practice of U.S. juvenile justice: Rehabilitation and social control have both been elusive goals.

Colonial America: Managing Troublesome Children

Crime and delinquency were not serious problems during the colonial era. Colonial towns and villages were, as legal historian Lawrence Friedman concisely puts it, small and homogeneous "tight little islands." The attention of the early colonists was focused on survival: building shelters, planting crops, maintaining security against Indian attacks. The colonists were intimately familiar with neighbors and kept them, as well as their own children, under close surveillance. Juvenile misbehavior and serious adult crime—for example, murder, rape, and robbery—were secondary concerns.

Colonial criminal justice systems were small and informal, and there was no need for separate juvenile justice systems. Sheriffs, marshals, or constables—the title varied by colony—served as the chief law enforcement officers. Some colonies, following the example of England, used the night watch system: Citizens took turns patrolling the streets at night. The structure of court systems and the content of penal codes were also colony-specific. In some colonies, especially in the 17th century, religious congregations served as courts. Other colonies, following the example of England, adopted state-based judiciaries. But these court systems, much like the night watch, were staffed by amateurs. Adult criminals and juvenile offenders were processed through the same system of justice, but juveniles received more lenient punishments. Throughout the colonial period, parents and family members were the first line of defense against juvenile misbehavior.

Colonies also developed unique systems of punishment. Prisons and juvenile reformatories, both costly post-Revolution inventions, did not exist. Instead, adult criminals and juvenile offenders were subjected to a variety of colony- and case-specific forms of discipline. Minor offenders issued apologies, paid fines or restitution, wore badges of dishonor—for example, the letter "D" for drunkenness—or served time in the stocks. More serious offenses merited whipping. Some colonies built small jails or lockups to hold offenders for brief periods of incarceration. Criminals might be forced to serve apprenticeships. In extreme cases, they were banished from the community. Colonial punishments were generally based on the notion of reintegrative shaming: public humiliation followed by reintegration back into the community.

The death penalty was prescribed for the most serious offenses. Juvenile offenders were not exempt from capital punishment. In 1642, 16-year-old Thomas Graunger, a servant, was executed in Massachusetts for bestiality—specifically, sodomizing a horse, cow, and chicken. In 1722, 17-year-old William Battin, an indentured servant, was executed in Pennsylvania for arson and murder. In 1786, 12-year-old Hannah Ocuish was hung for stoning and strangling a young child. However, capital punishment was rarely used for adult or juvenile offenders.

19th Century: The Juvenile Reformatory Movement

The end of the U.S. Revolution set the stage for a variety of extraordinary political, economic, and legal transformations. The ratification of the Constitution and Bill of Rights laid the foundation for the rise of democracy, as well as new legal rights and legal institutions. The introduction of capitalism transformed the economic system, including production, distribution, and consumption and exchange networks. During the 19th century, the United States became a world economic and political power.

The arrival of millions of immigrants sparked economic growth and laid the foundation for the rise of big cities. But economic bounty came with a cost. Old U.S. residents, who traced their roots to England, viewed the new immigrants—Irish immigrants early in the century and later Germans, Italians, and Russians—as biologically, psychologically, socially, culturally, and morally inferior. Xenophobia and class conflict intensified. The emancipation of millions of Black slaves in 1865 exacerbated U.S. anxieties, particularly in the South. Rising city-related social problems—crime, delinquency, drinking, and immorality—convinced many U.S. residents that immigrants and Blacks were virtually social dynamite. Armageddon, from this perspective, was at hand.

New strategies of social control were needed to maintain social order. Formal police departments replaced the inefficient night watch system and neighbor surveillance. New laws were written to define the limits of acceptable behavior and control the "dangerous classes." Courts became more formal, and amateur part-time judges were replaced with trained lawyers. Prisons were opened to punish and deter adult criminal offenders. Put simply, 19th-century U.S. residents introduced more complex state-specific criminal justice systems to tame, train, and discipline the criminal classes.

U.S. residents in the 19th century were also concerned with increases in juvenile misbehavior, particularly in urban areas. The opening of the New York House of Refuge, the nation's first juvenile reformatory, on January 1, 1825, was a pivotal event in the history of the U.S. criminal justice system. This marked the birth of a separate juvenile justice system in the United States. Juvenile offenders would no longer—except in extreme cases—be committed to adult prisons. More importantly, the New York House of Refuge, in theory, provided children with kindly treatment and benevolent reform. A carefully crafted regimen of reform—education, labor, religion, classification, and post-release supervision (indenture and later parole)—was to steer youthful lower-class offenders away from the temptations of the city and prepare them to become respectable citizens.

The New York House of Refuge was hailed as a new model for saving criminally inclined and troublesome children. Other states followed New York's example. The opening of the Boston House of Reformation in 1826 and the Philadelphia House of Refuge in 1828 set the stage for the birth of the juvenile reformatory movement. By 1857, thirteen reformatories had opened in the United States. By 1876, fifty-one were in operation. Nineteenth-century reformers believed that they had found the magical elixir for juvenile crime and misbehavior.

There was, however, a much darker side to 19th-century juvenile reformatories. These institutions were, in fact, miniature prisons. Beyond that, reformatories employed four versions of "treatment" and "reform." White males received the most intense academic education and vocational training and were prepared to take their place in society as obedient lower-class workers. White females, the second priority, received training aimed at making them domestics and good wives and mothers of the next generation of lower-class workers. Black boys were denied vocational and academic skills and were prepared to assume their "proper place" in the economic order: obedient lower-class laborers. Black girls were stigmatized by race and gender. Reformatory regimens prepared them for the lowest domestic duties. Ultimately, they would raise and train the next generation of "nigger workers." Race, ethnicity, gender, religion, and social class were, then, key driving forces behind the "rehabilitation" of 19th-century juvenile offenders.

Modern Juvenile Justice: The Rediscovery of Punishment

In the 20th and 21st centuries, the United States has been marked by increasing urbanization, new waves of immigration, more industrialization, new economic relations, technological innovations (e.g., electricity, telephone, automobile, computers and the Internet) and increasing civil liberties for African Americans and women—in short, a march toward modernity. But concerns with juvenile misbehavior remain unchanged.

Modern juvenile justice history can be divided into two distinct eras. The period from 1899 through the 1960s was dominated by a new legal innovation, the juvenile court, which was aimed at rehabilitation. The period from the 1970s into the 21st century has been marked by the introduction of more complex forms of juvenile social control structured around a recycled goal: punishment. However, the issues of race, ethnicity, gender, and social class have continued to shape the aims, operation, and evolution of the U.S. juvenile justice system.

The opening of the nation's first juvenile courts in 1899 in Denver and Chicago was, perhaps, the single most important event in the history of juvenile justice. Juvenile courts were introduced to remove youthful offenders and troubled children from adult courts and, in theory, provide them with kindly reform. Legal rights for children were, then, not necessary. Children who appeared in juvenile courts did not have the right to an attorney. There was no jury. Juveniles did not have the right to notification of the charges against them or the right to confront their accusers or call witnesses on their behalf. Courts proceedings were under the direct control of the judge. The judge asked questions, weighed evidence, decided guilt and innocence, and meted out sentences—a model that remained essentially unchallenged and unchanged into the late 1960s.

Historians have discovered, however, that early juvenile courts failed to achieve many of their stated goals. Decisions made by judges were often arbitrary and capricious. Traditional levels of proof required in adult court—guilt beyond a reasonable doubt—were not employed. As a result, juveniles were sometimes sent to reformatories even though the charges against them were unproven. Complicating matters, dependent, neglected, and incorrigible children could be sent to juvenile reformatories with hardened delinquents, including murderers. From the turn of the century into the 1960s, the decisions of juvenile court judges often reflected prevailing racist, nativist, and sexist views. Juvenile courts, like reformatories, were aimed at human refuse management.

The shroud of secrecy surrounding the U.S. juvenile justice system was unceremoniously lifted in the 1960s and 1970s. The U.S. Supreme Court, ruling for the first time in history on a juvenile justice case, declared in 1966 that there was a wide disparity between the promise and practice of the juvenile court system. The Court issued a series of rulings in the late 1960s and early 1970s that afforded juveniles many of the same legal rights as adults, with the exception of the right to a jury trial. The findings of the President's Commission on Law Enforcement and the Administration of Justice (1967), a major governmental investigation of adult and juvenile justice, also raised questions about the alleged benevolent impact of juvenile courts and reformatories. Research by academic criminologists, an emerging discipline, provided historical and empirical evidence to buttress these concerns.

The juvenile justice system was radically transformed in the late 1960s and early 1970s. States created separate legal procedures in juvenile court for delinquents and status offenders (dependent, neglected, and incorrigible children), and the federal government mandated that status offenders and delinquents not be incarcerated together in juvenile reformatories. Overt forms of racism and discrimination were prohibited. Diversion programs were introduced to keep children out of juvenile court. Community-based corrections programs were expanded to keep juveniles out of reformatories. Some states actually closed their reformatories to avoid the abuses of the past. In short, the U.S. juvenile justice system attempted to fulfill its historical mission: treatment and reform.

The movement to help, treat and reform juveniles was, however, short-lived. The rise of the conservative movement in the late 1970s, culminating in the election of Ronald Reagan as president in 1980, marked the introduction of a new approach to juvenile justice. Juveniles, much like adults, were increasingly regarded as free, rational, and hedonistic actors who needed and deserved punishment. During the last 2 decades of the 20th century, the juvenile justice system moved in a new direction. States have introduced boot camps and reopened reformatories. "Softhearted" diversion- and community-based corrections programs have been terminated. Chronic juvenile offenders have been transferred back to adult courts and given long, mandatory sentences aimed at punishment, deterrence, and incapacitation.

America's new dangerous classes—poor, uneducated, city-raised Blacks, Hispanics, and "White trash"—are still being prepared to assume their "proper place" in the economic, political, social, cultural, and legal order. One could conclude that with the return of punishment, modern U.S. juvenile justice has "progressed" into the 18th century.

Alexander W. Pisciotta

See also African Americans; Crime and Race; Criminal Processing; Drug Use; Gangs; Pachucos/Pachucas; Xenophobia

Further Readings

Friedman, Lawrence M. 1994. *Crime and Punishment in American History.* New York: Basic Books.

Mennel, Robert M. 1973. *Thorns and Thistles: Juvenile Delinquents in the United States, 1825–1940.* Hanover, NH: University Press of New England.

Pisciotta, Alexander W. 1994. *Benevolent Repression: Social Control and the American Reformatory-Prison Movement.* New York: New York University Press.

Platt, Anthony M. 1977. *The Child Savers: The Invention of Delinquency.* 2nd ed. Chicago, IL: University of Chicago Press.

Schlossman, Steven L. 1977. *Love and the American Delinquent: The Theory and Practice of "Progressive" Juvenile Justice, 1825–1920.* Chicago, IL: University of Chicago Press.

Streib, Victor L. 1987. *Death Penalty for Juveniles.* Bloomington: Indiana University Press.

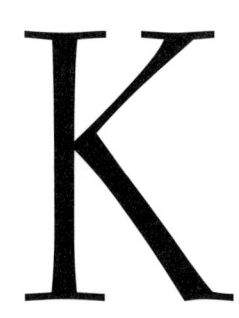

KENNEWICK MAN

Kennewick Man is the appellation bestowed upon the prehistoric human remains of an individual discovered in the Columbia River at its confluence with the Snake River, near Kennewick, Washington, during the summer of 1996. A legal battle ensued between the scientific community and the Native American community as to whether the bones should be studied or buried.

Discovery and Disputed Claims

Kennewick Man's near-complete skeleton had washed into the riverbed from a nearby eroding bank. The remains were examined by Dr. James Chatters, a local anthropologist, who initially described the morphology of the bones as that of a Caucasian middle-aged male. Although Chatters initially considered the skeleton to be that of an early pioneer, a stone spearpoint lodged in the pelvis caused Chatters to order further analysis, which revealed an age of over 9,000 years.

Because the skeleton was discovered in a navigable waterway, it came under the jurisdiction of the U.S. Army Corps of Engineers, a federal agency subject to federal laws and regulations. Upon announcement of the find, several Native American tribes laid claim to the bones on the basis of shared ancestry, under the Native American Graves Protection and Repatriation Act of 1990 (NAGPRA). This federal law allows for a claim of repatriation of Native American remains to affiliated tribes. Among the many bases for such a claim is a showing that the claimant tribes historically occupied the area in which the remains were found.

Because of the age and location of the Kennewick Man, the Corps decided that the claimant tribes were indeed affiliated with the remains and so repatriation for reburial at an undisclosed location would be proper. The claimant tribes included the Yakima Nation, the Nez Perce, and the Confederated Tribes of the Umatilla Indian Reservation.

Before the Corps could return the remains, however, a group of eight forensic scientists filed suit in federal court disputing whether the skeleton was indeed Native American. They sought an injunction of the repatriation of Kennewick Man until they could first study the bones. Ancient human remains of the age of Kennewick Man are very rare in North America, and paleoanthropologists consider them to be source material that opens a window into prehistory on the continent. From the perspective of the scientific community, the loss of even one of these scarce skeletons to a secret burial place is tantamount to losing a critical volume that completes a larger collection telling the vital story of the human narrative.

Obversely, the Native American community places a larger emphasis on continuity of respect for the dead and the undisrupted spiritual narrative of the tribe. Moreover, many Native American religions and faiths are based on tenets holding that they were the original people of this continent and have always been here. Thus, ancient human remains discovered in North America are by definition Native American and should be considered revered ancestors of present-day Native Americans. Scientific discoveries proving that non-Native-American peoples might have predated Native Americans in the Western Hemisphere would run directly counter to such beliefs. The views of

Native Americans are given far greater legal weight in NAGPRA than those of the scientific community. Consequently, a strict application of the law would have resulted in repatriation and reburial.

Legal Resolution of Kennewick Man's Case

The federal case erupted into a media frenzy as a dramatic tug-of-war ensued between scientists and Native Americans. Because Kennewick Man exhibited morphology quite distinct from what Native Americans typically exhibit, news reports began to provocatively ask what a person with Caucasoid, as opposed to more-Asian features, was doing in North America before the Native Americans. That, in turn, drew a third claim from a group of Norse pagans, based on the presumed White racial features of the bones. However, only the Native American claim was defended by the federal government against the plaintiff scientists in district court, which eventually ruled that Kennewick Man could be studied because the tribes claiming the remains could not be proved lineal descendants. The Department of Interior had previously found Kennewick Man to be culturally affiliated with the claimant tribes.

The 9th Circuit Court of Appeals in San Francisco upheld the lower court's decision, ruling that the government's finding of cultural affiliation was tenuous and unproven. Judge Ronald Gould wrote, "No cognizable link exits between Kennewick Man and modern Columbia Plateau Indians." Subsequent rulings and approved study plans enabled the plaintiff scientists to begin their long-awaited study of the remains.

Kennewick Man is housed at the University of Washington's Burke Museum, in Seattle. Studies on the bones continue to be carried out. Recent discoveries include that he did not physically resemble the Native Americans of that location or time, that the stone spearpoint in his pelvis was not the cause of death (it had healed over), and that he was buried by other humans with his feet facing downstream and his head elevated five degrees to face the eastern rising sun.

Leaders of the Yakima Nation remain dismayed that Kennewick Man is being studied by scientists. Nevertheless, an appeal to the U.S. Supreme Court has been ruled out so as not to risk extending the negative precedent on NAGPRA's interpretation with regard to prehistoric human remains to the rest of the country. Other claims by Native American groups to repatriate prehistoric human remains are ongoing, such as that by Great Basin Intertribal NAGPRA coalition to secure the 10,000-year-old "Spirit Cave Man," discovered outside Reno, Nevada, in the 1940s. Although this discovery is within the 9th Circuit, it is unclear whether the facts will require the district court to strictly follow the Kennewick Man precedent.

Further legal battles are likely to ensue in the courts until NAGPRA is adequately amended to either specifically allow or disallow scientific study of particularly ancient human remains that do not exhibit physical features of modern-day Native Americans.

Michael J. Kelly

See also Blood Quantum; Bureau of Indian Affairs; Native American Graves Protection and Repatriation Act of 1990; Native Americans

Further Readings

Bonnichsen v. United States, 357 F.3d 962 (9th Cir. 2004).
Chatters, James C. 2001. *Ancient Encounters: Kennewick Man and the First Americans.* New York: Simon & Schuster.
Kelly, Michael J. 1999. "A Skeleton in the Legal Closet: The Discovery of 'Kennewick Man' Crystalizes the Debate over Federal Law Governing Disposal of Ancient Human Remains." *University of Hawai'i Law Review* 21(1):41–72.
Thomas, David Hurst. 2000. *Skull Wars: Kennewick Man, Archaeology, and the Battle for Native American Identity.* New York: Basic Books.

Kenya

Kenya is a nation of 36.9 million people, according to 2007 estimates, and is located on the east coast of Africa. Its neighbors to the north include the Horn countries of Sudan, Ethiopia, and Somalia. To the south is the Republic of Tanzania, and to the west is Uganda, with the Indian Ocean to the east. The country has temperate climates, except along the coast and also to the north where the environment is more one of semidesert vegetation, dry, and generally hot. In the Central Highlands and the Rift Valley are located some of the most fertile lands. This entry discusses the history of Kenya and current political, economic, and social conditions.

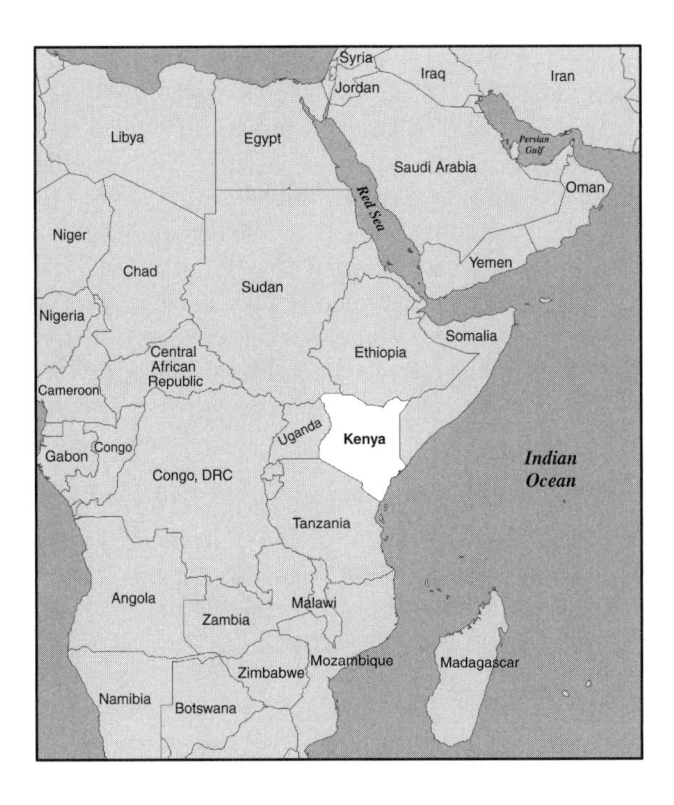

Colonial Background

The first British came to Kenya in 1890 under the flagship of the Imperial British East African Company, and administrators as well as missionaries followed. Settler farmers also started occupying some of the most fertile land in Kenya (30% of the most fertile land was occupied by British settlers). Kenya became a British colony in 1920, and the British settlers decided Kenya was to be their home forever and had no intentions of leaving the country. They appropriated for themselves the most fertile lands, often referred to as the "White Highlands." Africans could not own land in this exclusive area, and they existed only as workers or squatters.

The most affected ethnic group in the land issue was the Kikuyu of Central Highlands of the Kiambu, Nyeri, and Murang'a districts. Their population had been growing in numbers, and when the British came, the Kikuyu was the largest ethnic group and continues to be—to date, numbering about 7 million, or one-fifth of Kenya's total population of 30 million people. The Kikuyu were forced to live in crowded situations in the Central Province. They were also forced to work as cheap labor for the White settlers. Taxes were imposed in the colony and Western culture was introduced, and the Africans were forced, for example, through Christianity, to abandon many of their cultural traditions.

Many Kenya tribes felt deprived of their land, and the Kikuyu were the most agitated group, mainly because they were in close proximity to the land settled by the British. They were politically astute and started organizing political groups as early as the 1920s under the auspices of the Kikuyu Central Association (KCA). In 1928, they sent one of their own, Jomo Kenyatta, to England to present to the King and the Home Office their grievances, especially related to their "stolen land" and racial discrimination in their own country.

Such grievances went unattended, and this led to the violent movement, called the Mau Mau War, from 1952 through 1956. This was guerrilla-like war, where the majority of Kikuyu, Meru, and Embu youth went to the forests of Nyandarua and Mt. Kenya to fight against the British authorities, who firmly governed the country. While there is no unanimous agreement as to whether the British left and gave Kenya independence because of the violent Mau Mau, most agree that the Mau Mau disrupted peace and stability in Kenya. The movement also instilled fear in the settlers and disrupted their farming; they started to have second thoughts about making Kenya their permanent home. The colony also started being a liability, and the Home Office back in London had grown tired of subsidizing the Kenya colonial government.

Thus, the Mau Mau movement accelerated Kenya's road to independence, which came in 1963. The first Kenya president was Jomo Kenyatta, who had been jailed for 7 years, having been accused of leading the Mau Mau movement against the Kenya Europeans and the colonial government.

Current Situation

Politics/Government

Kenyatta died in 1978, and his vice president, Daniel Arap Moi, took over. By the 1980s and 1990s, he had become a tyrannical dictator, clinging to power with all his might. In 1992, constitutional reforms in Kenya limited an individual to holding the presidency for two 5-year terms. In 2002, Moi was forced to give up power. His anointed successor, Uhuru Kenyatta, the son of the first president, was defeated at the polls. That also saw the end of KANU (Kenya African National Union), the ruling party since independence in 1963.

President Mwai Kibaki, the current president, took over on December 31, 2002. He is about to finish his first 5-year term, and he has already declared that he will be contesting again when the elections are called in December 2007.

The Economy

Kenya's economy is based mainly on agriculture. The primary cash crops are tea, coffee, pyrethrum, livestock, and dairy products. Tourism has also been a major foreign income earner and is second to agriculture. The first 10 years after independence saw a booming economy, growing at about 5%. The Moi years, especially the 1980s and 1990s, saw a declining economy in Kenya; and, in the late 1990s, there was negative growth. Corruption was at its highest level with scandals like "Goldenberg" (a scheme hatched by government officials to siphon out money under the pretext that Kenya was to export gold—which it does not mine).

The economy has been improving since the new government came to power in December 2002. While the formal economy has not been performing well, the informal economy, especially in the large and medium-sized towns, has been booming and indeed is the mainstay of the Kenyan economy besides agriculture and tourism. More people are today employed in the informal economy than in the formal economy (60% and 40%, respectively).

Society

Before the coming of the British in the late 1800s, Kenya was inhabited by over forty ethnic groups. Along the coast, in the towns of Mombasa, Malindi, and Lamu, there had been a long association with outsiders, mainly Portuguese and Arabs, who fought regularly for the control of the coastal towns, especially Mombasa. In the interior were a number of ethnic groups who interacted with each other, sometimes on a friendly basis and at other times at war. The Kikuyu and the Maasai were such an example, sometimes warring and sometimes experiencing friendly relations, for example, involving intermarriage. In western Kenya, the Luo and the Luhya as well as the Kalenjins also had such relations.

Today, there are at least forty-two different ethnic groups in Kenya. While they have generally coexisted and do speak a unifying national language, Kiswahili, there have been politically motivated animosities, especially in the Rift Valley. There were tribal clashes during the Moi regime, especially between the Kalenjin (Moi's group) and the Kikuyu, and especially in Nakuru district. Conflict also occurred between the Maasai and the Kikuyu and between the Nandi and the Luhya and the Nandi and the Luo.

Social class formation has been a continuing problem in Kenya, where the gap between the rich and the poor has continued to widen. This has led to various types of crime, especially carjacking, violent robbery, and ordinary thuggery. Social justice and equality will remain a challenge in Kenya and will have to be addressed through sound policies and programs.

Kinuthia Macharia

See Appendix A

See also Africans in the United States; Colonialism; Diaspora; HIV/AIDS; Informal Economy

Further Readings

Kinuthia Macharia and Muigai Kanyua. 2006. *The Social Context of the Mau Mau Movement (1952–1960)*. Lanham, MD: University Press of America.

Republic of Kenya. 1999. *Kenya Population Census*. Nairobi, Kenya: Government Press.

KING, MARTIN LUTHER, JR. (1929–1968)

The Reverend Martin Luther King, Jr., was one of the most significant U.S. figures of the 20th century, not just for Black America, but for the entire nation. Leader of the Southern Christian Leadership Conference (SCLC), advocate of nonviolent resistance, and an eloquent spokesman for the Civil Rights Movement, King set events and ideas in motion that were to shape the country, as shown in this entry.

Early Years

The great civil rights proponent was born with the name Michael Luther King, Jr., just before noon on Tuesday, January 15, 1929, at the King family's home at 501 Auburn Avenue in northeast Atlanta, Georgia, in the house that belonged to the parents of his "Mother Dear." His father was Michael Luther King, Sr., the prominent pastor of Ebenezer Baptist Church, and his mother was Alberta Williams King, a musician.

Young Michael was the second of their three children. In 1937, when Michael was 8 years old, his father changed his own name, and, by extension, the name of his son, to Martin Luther King, Sr., in honor of the great Protestant reformer Martin Luther.

By the standards of the day, the King family was comfortably middle class, and, by all accounts, young Martin's childhood was no different from that of other middle-class Black children of the 1930s. The expectations the Reverend and Mrs. King had for the King children reflected the temperament and values of the middle class. The Reverend King, Sr., was the well-respected patriarch of the extended King family, some of whom were part of the King household. Together, they provided all of the instrumental (food, clothing, and shelter) and expressive (love, identity, and security) functions that are expected of stable, strong families.

King's early years were "normal," with the usual high jinks of youth. He played with two White boys whose parents owned a store in the Sweet Auburn Avenue neighborhood. His father's sense of the injustices and indignities Blacks suffered during his early years was reflected in his apparent decision to try to shelter his children from racial discrimination. The young King's first realization of racial discrimination came when the parents of his White childhood playmates stopped their children from playing with him because he was a "Negro." The memory of this loss remained with him for the rest of his life.

The religious values and sense of justice espoused by the King family formed the foundation of the young King's vision of a better world. He joined Ebenezer Baptist Church, where his father was the pastor, on May 1, 1936, and his father, his family, and his church were the greatest influences on his development. His father, a graduate of Morehouse College, in Atlanta, was an exceptional preacher who believed that the minister and the church should be committed to the social and spiritual uplifting of Black people.

Education

Martin Luther King, Jr., attended Atlanta public schools. His high school friends gave him the nickname "Tweeds" because of his penchant for good clothes, especially those made from tweed cloth. In 1944, at the end of eleventh grade and at the age of 15, King enrolled as a freshman at Morehouse College. On his admission to and matriculation at Morehouse, Dr. Benjamin E. Mays, sixth president of the college, said that no one could have predicted King's future. He was a typical college student, concerned about his appearance and dating the young women at nearby Spelman College, a school for Black women. After flirting with the idea of a professional career in medicine or law, he majored in sociology at Morehouse.

At Morehouse College, King came under the powerful influence of Dr. Mays. Dr. Mays was a scholar-activist and a renowned preacher in his own right, and he instilled the call to service in the men of Morehouse during the 27 years that he led the college. King was one of "Benny's Boys," as Morehouse graduates who studied at the college under the leadership of Dr. Mays often called themselves.

Although King was a member of a family of preachers when he entered Morehouse, he had not decided on a career in the pulpit, and by this time he had taken a nonliteral interpretation of the scriptures. King began to consider a future in the ministry during a religion course that he took under the tutelage of George D. Kelsey, a professor of religion at Morehouse. With his father's approval, King preached his trial sermon at Ebenezer, on February 25, 1948, less than 4 months before he graduated from Morehouse.

After completing the requirements for the bachelor's degree in sociology at Morehouse in 1948, King continued his studies at Crozer Theology Seminary, in Chester, Pennsylvania. At Crozer, he embraced the "evangelical liberalism" of Dr. George W. Davis. Davis introduced King to the ideas of Walter Rauschenbusch, the principal exponent of the early 20th-century Social Gospel movement. He also studied the communist theories of Karl Marx and the theological perspectives of Reinhold Niebuhr. The most valuable experience that King had at Crozer may have been social rather than intellectual, as this was the first time that he had lived in an integrated social setting for any length of time.

Whereas King did not have a stellar academic career at Morehouse, he graduated at the top of his class at Crozer in 1951. He continued his academic career at Boston University, in Massachusetts, where he finished the doctorate in June 1955. His dissertation was titled "A Comparison of the Conceptions of God in the Thinking of Paul Tillich and Henry Nelson Wieman."

Before he completed the requirements for the PhD, King married Coretta Scott, the daughter of Obie and Bernice Scott, of Marion, Alabama. She had studied music at Antioch College, in Yellow Springs, Ohio, and was studying at the New England Conservatory of Music when King met her. The marriage was strong, and the couple would come to symbolize the movement.

Before he completed his dissertation, King accepted the call to become the pastor of historic Dexter Avenue Baptist Church, in Montgomery, Alabama. So, in 1955, Martin and Coretta moved to Montgomery, a city that prided itself on being the "Cradle of the Confederacy." Over the years, Dr. and Mrs. King became the parents of Yolanda Denise, Martin Luther III, Dexter Scott, and Bernice Albertine.

Civil Rights Movement

On December 1, 1955, Mrs. Rosa Parks, a seamstress at the Montgomery Fair Department Store, refused to give up her seat to a White man in the segregated section on a city bus, sparking the successful Montgomery bus boycott. King emerged as the leader and voice of the Montgomery Improvement Association, which helped to prosecute the struggle against racial discrimination on the city's buses. Jo Anne Robinson and the Women's Political Council were also pivotal to the successful outcome of the struggle.

King devoted the remainder of his life to the cause of civil rights for Blacks and justice for mankind. To facilitate his crusade, he and other religious leaders formed the SCLC in 1957. The headquarters were first located in Montgomery but were soon moved to Atlanta, Georgia, where SCLC occupied permanent offices on Auburn Avenue, two blocks west of King's birthplace. King was SCLC's first president and held that office until his assassination in 1968.

As the African American Civil Rights Movement escalated with the sit-down protest events by four college freshmen from North Carolina A & T College, King was arrested with college students protesting the discriminatory policies and practices of Rich's Department Store in Atlanta. His arrest and incarceration in the DeKalb County Jail and the Reidsville, Georgia, State Prison, and the intercession by Robert F. Kennedy, the brother of presidential candidate John F. Kennedy, were major events in the civil rights struggle. King's credibility among activists was made stronger by his arrest and resolve in the face of untold dangers.

In 1963, King made two important philosophical contributions to the Black struggle for freedom in America. The first was his powerful "Letter from Birmingham City Jail," written during his arrest and incarceration on Good Friday, April 12, 1963. The letter became his most systematic explanation of civil disobedience. He bluntly warned of a "frightening racial nightmare" if Blacks surrendered to bitterness and racial hatred.

A little more than 4 months later, on August 28, 1963, King gave his "I Have A Dream" speech, one of the most famous speeches of the 20th century, at the March on Washington for Freedom and Jobs. In January 1964, *Time* magazine named him "Man of the Year." Dr. King's persuasive explanation for the Black Civil Rights Movement and the other tragic events of 1963—the murder of Medgar Evers, the bombing of the Sixteenth Street Baptist Church, and the assassination of President John F. Kennedy—provided the impetus and context for passage of the civil rights bill. The Civil Rights Act was signed into law by President Lyndon B. Johnson, on July 2, 1964. Dr. King was awarded the Nobel Prize for Peace in Oslo, Norway, on December 10, 1964.

Martin Luther King, Jr. King, president of the Southern Christian Leadership Conference, is shown speaking at the Civil Rights March on Washington, D.C., on August 28, 1963. King delivered his "I Have a Dream Speech" on this occasion. He was just 34 at the time.

Source: National Archives.

Black Consciousness

With the establishment of the Civil Rights Act of 1964, King and his fellow crusaders in the struggle for freedom turned their attention to voting rights. After a successful campaign to get the U.S. Congress to eradicate the obstacles to voting for U.S. citizens, which included the March from Selma to Montgomery, the voting rights bill was passed, and President Johnson signed it into law on August 6, 1965. With the creation of the Civil Rights Act of 1964 and the Voting Rights Act of 1965, many civil rights protesters became "civil rights testers."

But the winds of Black consciousness were changing, and Willie Ricks (Mukasa) gave the rallying cry for "Black Power" at the James Meredith March in Mississippi, in June 1966. Stokely Carmichael began the popular use of the slogan when he screamed it from the back of a flatbed truck at a voters' registration rally in Greenwood, Mississippi, in 1966. King, ever conscious of the tenor and temperament of his time, began to shift the focus of SCLC in the struggle for freedom and justice.

In 1967, he published *Where Do We Go from Here: Chaos or Community?* and devoted a chapter to a discussion of "Black Power," He saw Black Power as "a cry of disappointment," as "a call to Black people to amass the political and economic strength to achieve their legitimate goals," and as "a psychological call to manhood." As a counterpoint to the tenets of Black Power as he had come to understand them, toward the end of 1967 King began planning the Poor People's Campaign. By this time, he had also begun to speak out against the Vietnam War.

King called for "a radical restructuring of the architecture of American society," but he did not live to see the realization of his "Beloved Community," where Blacks and Whites of all social strata would join together for their salvation. According to Crane Brinton's *The Anatomy of Revolution,* in the first stage of a revolution, writers and other intellectuals criticize existing conditions. King's message can be seen as part of this stage.

In the second stage, there is widespread dissatisfaction, including riots and assassinations. In 1967, King led a march of thousands on the United Nations headquarters in New York City to protest the War in Vietnam. In the summer of that year, riots occurred in many northern cities. Several attempts had been made to kill King over the 12-plus years he was directly involved in the Black struggle for freedom, including the stabbing by Izola Ware Curry in New York City, on September 17, 1958. Late in the afternoon of April 4, 1968, an assassin succeeded.

King's death came while he was in Memphis, Tennessee, leading a march in support of striking Black sanitation workers, a demonstration of his belief that Blacks of all social strata must join together for their salvation. He was shot to death as he stood on the balcony of the Lorraine Hotel, and James Earl Ray was charged with and convicted of his murder. King's funeral was held at Ebenezer Baptist Church, in Atlanta, and thousands attended a memorial service at Morehouse College, his beloved alma mater. His body was borne to the Morehouse campus by a mule-drawn wagon.

King's body was first interred in the Southview Cemetery in southeast Atlanta, but later, he was entombed at the King Memorial site on Auburn Avenue, one block south of his birthplace and adjacent to the historic Ebenezer Baptist Church. His epitaph, "Free at last, free at last, thank God Almighty I'm free at last," is recited by people of all races and ages around the world. On November 20, 2006, Coretta Scott King's body was entombed beside her husband. Her epitaph resonates in so many ways: "And now abide faith, hope, love, these three; but the greatest of these is love." 1 Cor. 13:13.

Marcellus C. Barksdale

See also African Americans; African American Studies; Black Power; Boycott; Carmichael, Stokely; Civil Rights Movement; Civil Rights Movement, Women and; Parks, Rosa; Religion, African Americans; Segregation; Southern Christian Leadership Conference (SCLC)

Further Readings

Branch, Taylor. 1988. *Parting the Waters: America in the King Years, 1954–63.* New York: Simon & Schuster.

Branch, Taylor. 1998. *Pillar of Fire: America in the King Years, 1963–65.* New York: Simon & Schuster.

Branch, Taylor. 2006. *At Canaan's Edge: America in the King Years, 1965–68.* New York: Simon & Schuster.

Fairclough, Adam. 1995. *Martin Luther King, Jr.* Athens: University of Georgia Press.

Farris, Christine King. 2003. *My Brother Martin: A Sister Remembers Growing Up with the Rev. Dr. Martin Luther King, Jr.* New York: Aladdin Paperbacks.

Forman, James. 1985. *The Making of Black Revolutionaries.* Seattle: University of Washington Press.

Garrow, David J. 1988. *Bearing the Cross: Martin Luther King, Jr., and the Southern Christian Leadership Conference.* New York: Vintage Books.

King, Coretta Scott. 1970. *My Life with Martin Luther King, Jr.* New York: Avon Books.

King, Martin Luther, Jr. 1968. *Where Do We Go from Here: Chaos or Community?* Boston, MA: Beacon Press.

Mays, Benjamin E. 1971. *Born to Rebel: An Autobiography.* New York: Scribner's.

KINSHIP

Kinship is the relation of a group of persons of common ancestry and in some instances others who have been adopted formally or informally into the family. Although the degree of kinship varies across different groups, it plays an important role for all racial and ethnic groups in the United States. Although the definition of family and kin has changed throughout U.S. history, kinship still plays a defining role in the function of familial groups, especially ethnic and racial minority families. This entry examines kinship historically and currently for the major racial and ethnic groups in the United States.

Notions of kinship vary considerably across both settings and minority groups. The term *kinship* is sometimes used to include only people related by common ancestry, or "blood." Other times, it is used in a broader sense, in which a whole group shares kinship. At still other times, it includes those with whom one feels closeness. These latter uses are reflected in the related concepts of Confucian filial piety and the Christian concept of charity toward others. In all of these uses, individuals may be expected to forgo their own wants and needs for needs of the larger group.

Kinship, then, is the tie formed through familial relationships or larger group relationships that bring economic, emotional, or other support. Family kinship connotes a tie that is sufficiently strong that the kin group is expected to help members when needed. Hence, this expectation explains why some people, especially in immigrant groups, are immediately integrated into a family structure that provides economic and social well-being. Kinship relations also help new immigrants while they establish themselves in their new countries. Kin give important advice and emotional support. To some, these ties may be the only defining relationships they have. These helps are expected and often provided without request. Thus, kinship is key to group identity and even survival.

Classically, kinship units provided sustenance for all of the members of the group. Members had a duty to provide for the survival of their extended families. Some argue that kinship historically was defined only as it related to human reproduction and biological relatedness. With the change from a traditional, agricultural-based society into a more modern one, the view of kinship ties broadened. The unit of kinship remained the ancestral family but was now viewed as providing emotional support as well as sustenance. During industrialization, kinship became more limited for European Americans, with a focus on the nuclear family instead of the extended family. Minority families have often relied on extended family to compensate for grinding poverty and as a source of emotional support. Thus, these families have tended to retain larger family ties that provide financial, social, and emotional support.

Kinship for African Americans began immediately as they arrived here as indentured servants and, for most, as slaves. Though often from different groups in Africa, they melded together as a community, albeit a suppressed one. Kinship played a vital role in the emotional health of slaves in their transition from African freedom to American slavery. Plantation slaves were related by blood or marriage. For example, it is estimated that slaves on the Good Hope Plantation of South Carolina from 1835 to 1856 were related by "blood" to 28% of the other slaves. Geographic isolation and oppression often made for tight communities of related slaves. As slaves were bought and sold, the kinship ties were reduced, but a sense of a larger kinship of all slaves emerged. Evidence of kinship among the African American community continued after slavery, as numerous ex-slaves traveled long distances to find family members from whom they had been separated.

African American kinship declined in the 20th century, as families became more nuclear and less extended. Kinship ties were further reduced in the African American community by the mass movement of many to urban areas and to the North. Whereas approximately 90% of African Americans lived in the South at the turn of the 20th century, only about half lived there by midcentury. Though kinship relations were often maintained, the ties were not as complex and close because kin did not live close by.

Nevertheless, kinship ties of African Americans remain strong today, with African American grandparents playing a crucial role in child rearing and supervision.

According to reports from the 2000 census, 51.7% of African American grandparents had grandchildren living with them, with neither parent present. The grandparents have prime responsibility for these grandchildren. Often, grandparents become the guardians because the parents are in prison, on drugs, or financially unable to care for their own children. Grandmothers are the main guardians for their grandchildren, with 64% of coresident grandparents being women. Guardianship of the grandchildren is a clear result of kinship ties. Regardless of how they may feel about the responsibility of child rearing again, grandparents prefer to raise and provide for their kin rather than have them in the state foster care system. These kinship relations also foster better opportunities for the children and parents to see one another. Kinship relations among African Americans are also strong because they band together for support against racism.

Hispanics in the United States today are composed of quite separate and distinct groups based on country of origin. The majority of Hispanics in the United States are of Mexican ancestry, but the term *Hispanic* includes large groups of Puerto Ricans, both in Puerto Rico itself and in the continental United States; Cuban Americans; and people from a variety of other South American countries. All have a strong sense of kinship identity.

Kinship ties are especially prevalent within immigrant groups and often result in "chain migration." Newly arrived immigrants needing housing, food, and help finding employment usually move to locations where previous immigrants have settled.

Another major component of Hispanic kinship is *compadrazgo*, the creation of godparents through ceremonial rituals. *Compadrazgo* began with the invasion of Europeans, who brought war and disease to the indigenous groups. Other natives became substitute parents or godparents to many orphaned children. These rituals can include baptism, communion, or the inclusion of a best man or woman at a marriage. Godparents became de facto members of the family. If birthparents are unable to provide for the children, the godparents assume full responsibility. Godparents also play an important function as role models for the children. Some argue that the economic functions of *compadrazgo* are diminishing but that it is still a vital source of emotional support.

Among Asian Americans, kinship ties tend to be strong in part because of the experience of immigration but also in part because of the traditional ethic of filial piety: love, respect, and obedience to one's parents and ancestors. As with other groups historically and Hispanic immigrants in the 20th century, new immigrants from Asia need support while settling. Typically, Asian families have strong expectations about care of kin. After acculturation, kinship ties remain intact.

Indigenous groups in the Americas often had small societies that were highly endogamous, with a high sense of kinship. Native American kinship includes extended family and nonkin, as among other minority groups. Historically, nonkin formally became family members through rituals that conferred upon them the obligations and responsibilities of family and kin. The allotment policies and later the relocation policies of the U.S. government had the potential to substantially reduce the kinship ties of Native American groups. Though most Native Americans today live in urban areas, they often retain strong kinship ties and identity with tribal affiliations.

In sum, most Americans have kinship ties. The strength and type of ties vary, however, among the various racial or ethnic groups in the United States. Recent immigration, group size, and historical and cultural factors are some of the influences that affect the type and strength of kinship ties found in various groups.

Robyn J. Barrus and Cardell K. Jacobson

See also Community Cohesion; Ethnic Group; Familism; Family; Immigration, U.S.; Peoplehood

Further Readings

Carsten, Janet. 2004. *After Kinship.* New York: Cambridge University Press.
Franklin, Sarah and Susan McKinnon. 2001. *Relative Values: Reconfiguring Kinship Studies.* Durham, NC: Duke University Press.
Parkin, Robert and Linda Stone. 2004. *Kinship and Family: An Anthropological Reader.* Malden, MA: Blackwell.
Pasternak, Burton, Carol R. Ember, and Melvin Ember. 1997. *Sex, Gender, and Kinship: A Cross-Cultural Perspective.* Upper Saddle River, NJ: Prentice Hall.
Rawick, George P. 1972. *From Sundown to Sunup: The Making of the Black Community.* Westport, CT: Greenwood.
Schneider, David Murray. 1980. *American Kinship: A Cultural Account.* Chicago, IL: University of Chicago Press.

Stone, Linda. 1997. *Kinship and Gender: An Introduction.* Boulder, CO: Westview Press.

U.S. Census. 2003. *Grandparents Living with Grandchildren: 2000.* Available from http://www.census.gov/prod/2003 pubs/c2kbr-31.pdf

KITANO, HARRY H. L. (1926–2002)

Harry H. L. Kitano was a pioneer in the development of cross-cultural and multicultural literature in the social sciences and the field of Asian American studies, applying a broad spectrum of sociological and behavioral science theories to enhance the understanding of intergroup and intragroup dynamics. His work explored cross-cultural interactions and illuminated the historical experiences and cultural contexts of various ethnic groups within the United States, with an emphasis on Asian American populations and the Japanese American population in particular.

Internment Camp Experience

Born in San Francisco to immigrant parents, Kitano was raised in a family-owned hotel in Chinatown. In 1942, in the wake of Japan's attack on Pearl Harbor, the federal government's mandatory relocation of all persons of Japanese descent on the West Coast forced Kitano's family into the Topaz concentration camp, in Utah, where he completed high school as the class valedictorian. In 1997, he served as keynote speaker for the graduation ceremony, at which he was awarded the high school diploma denied him by his incarceration.

In 1945, Kitano moved to Milwaukee, where his talent as a trombone player led to his being hired by an African American jazz band. Due to prejudices and hostility toward persons of Japanese descent at the time, the band leader hired him on the condition that he assume a Chinese American identity while touring with the band, dubbing him "Harry Lee" (the initials "H. L." represent this nom de guerre).

Education and Scholarship

Returning to California, Kitano continued his education at the University of California, Berkeley, earning a BA in 1948, an MSW in 1951, and a PhD in 1958. His dissertation, *The Child Care Center: A Study of the Interaction Among One-Parent Children, Parents, and School* (1963), resulted in his first major publication. The sociological analysis in his 1969 book, *Japanese Americans: The Evolution of a Subculture,* was the first scholarly study of Japanese Americans from their earliest immigration in the 19th century to post–World War II. He published the well-regarded *American Racism: Exploration of the Nature of Prejudice* (1970) (with Roger Daniels) and, shortly thereafter, *Race Relations* (1974), which became an important text in universities across the nation, into its fifth edition. He authored over 150 books and articles, including such major works as *The Japanese Americans* (1987), *Asian Americans: Emerging Minorities* (1988, 1995, 2001, with Roger Daniels), and *Generations and Identity: The Japanese Americans* (1993). His articles in academic journals were based on his empirical research in a number of areas, including interracial marriages, juvenile delinquency, mental health, and alcohol abuse among various Asian American populations.

The impact of Kitano's wartime relocation experience is reflected in his scholarly work, most notably in two of his books: *Japanese Americans: From Relocation to Redress* (1986, 1991, with Roger Daniels and Sandra Taylor) and *Achieving the Impossible Dream: How Japanese Americans Obtained Redress* (1999, with Mitchell Maki and S. Megan Berthold). The latter chronicles and presents a theoretical structure for understanding the decades-long struggle and development of the movement and multiple forces that led to the passage of the Civil Liberties Act of 1988, which provided redress to survivors of the Japanese American incarceration during World War II. Securing a grant from the trust fund established by this act, Kitano served as the driving force for a historic 3-day conference, "Voices of Japanese American Redress," held at UCLA. The presentations and group discussions brought together for the first time the diverse segments of those involved in the redress movement across time, including scholars, political activists, legislators, and individuals from the community, to discuss the process and its effects. His work and life had come full circle to a satisfying culmination.

Kitano was deeply committed to his academic career at UCLA, which spanned 4 decades. He was a full professor, with a joint appointment in the departments of Social Welfare and Sociology. As professor emeritus after his retirement in 1995, he continued his scholarship and his service in various positions within the university, including acting chair of the Department of Social Welfare (1997–1998). Throughout his career, he held a number of influential positions within UCLA and other academic institutions, including acting director of the Asian American Study Center (1971–1972, 1988–1989), Academic Affirmative Action Officer (1977–1982), codirector of the UCLA Alcohol Research Center (1979–1981), and visiting professor at universities in Hawai'i, Japan, and England.

Dr. Kitano was recognized for his contributions both within the university and the broader community. He was appointed the first incumbent of the endowed chair in Japanese American Studies at UCLA, the only academic chair of its kind in an American university. The Japanese American Citizens League (JACL) presented him with honors on three separate occasions: Nisei of the Biennium, Nikkei of the Year, and the JACL Pacific Southwest District Annual Award; the Los Angeles County Human Relations Commission honored him as Outstanding Volunteer. He was a member of numerous governmental and community boards and commissions over the years, including the Board of Visitors, Equal Opportunity Management Institute, U.S. Department of Defense (chair); the Advisory Committee of the Columbia University Minority Leadership Project; the Los Angeles Police Department Advisory Committee; the Skirball Institute of American Values; and the Japanese American National Museum.

An important part of Kitano's legacy is his influence as an outstanding teacher and generous mentor for decades of students, junior and aspiring academics, and colleagues. He served as an important role model, in particular, for academics of color, demonstrating that legitimate scholarly endeavors could focus on one's community, as these communities were an integral, significant, and equal part of the American fabric, and that one's personal experience as a member of this population brings a unique perspective critical to an accurate understanding of the cultural context.

Diane de Anda and Roger Daniels

See also Asian Americans; Asian American Studies; Internment Camps; Issei; Japanese Americans; Japanese American Citizens League; Nisei

Further Readings

Kitano, Harry H. L. 1963. *The Child Care Center: A Study of the Interaction among One-Parent Children, Parents, and School.* Berkeley: University of California Press.

Kitano, Harry H. L. 1993. *Generations and Identity: The Japanese American.* Needham Heights, MA: Ginn Press.

Kitano, Harry H. L. 1995. *Japanese Americans: The Evolution of a Subculture.* 4th ed. Englewood Cliffs, NJ: Prentice Hall.

Kitano, Harry H. L. 1997. *Race Relations.* 5th ed. Englewood Cliffs, NJ: Prentice Hall.

Kitano, Harry H. L. and Roger Daniels. 1970. *American Racism: Exploration of the Nature of Prejudice.* Englewood Cliffs, NJ: Prentice Hall.

Kitano, Harry H. L. and Roger Daniels. 2001. *Asian Americans: Emerging Minorities.* 3rd ed. Englewood Cliffs, NJ: Prentice Hall.

Kitano, Harry H. L., Roger Daniels, and Sandra Taylor, eds. [1986] 1991. *Japanese Americans: From Relocation to Redress.* Seattle: University of Washington Press.

Kitano, Harry H. L., Mitchell Maki, and S. Megan Berthold. 1999. *Achieving the Impossible Dream: How Japanese Americans Obtained Redress.* Urbana: University of Illinois Press.

KOREAN AMERICANS

Korean Americans commemorated the centennial of their immigration to the United States in 2003. The fifth-largest ethnic group within a heterogeneous Asian Pacific Islander American (AAPI) population, Korean Americans numbered over 1.2 million in the 2000 census. Despite this long history in the United States, more than three-fourths of Korean Americans are foreign-born, reflecting a historical legacy of exclusionary immigration and citizenship laws aimed at Asians and continued significance of contemporary immigration policies and social, economic, and political conditions in South Korea (a nation of 48.5 million people according to 2007 estimates) and the United States.

Popular media accounts and scholarly research have often focused on Korean Americans and their high rates of entrepreneurship. Korean Americans exhibit the highest rate of self-employment among all racial/ethnic groups in the United States. First-generation immigrants, in particular, unable to find jobs commensurate with premigration education levels and occupations, have used self-employment as a vehicle to pursue economic stability and upward mobility for themselves and their children.

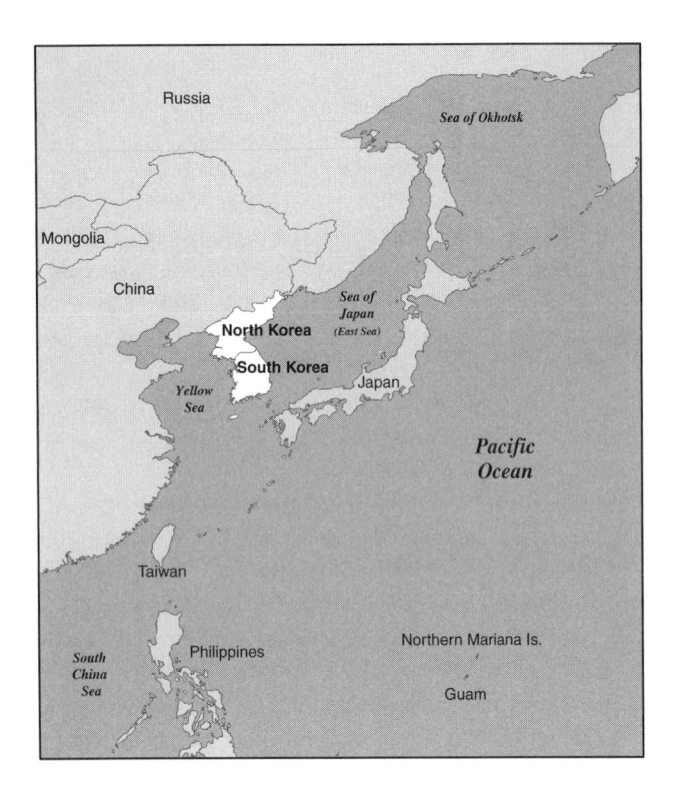

Yet, in 1992, Korean Americans realized that this pursuit of the "American Dream" cannot happen in a political vacuum; Korean Americans realized their political invisibility in the wake of the 1992 Los Angeles civil unrest, a multiethnic disturbance with the highest death toll and financial costs in U.S. history. The psychological and economic devastation of *Sa-I-Gu*, or "4–2–9," served as a catalyst for political awakening for Korean Americans in Los Angeles and elsewhere.

Often portrayed as monolithic and culturally/linguistically homogeneous, Korean Americans include descendants of those who landed in Hawai'i in 1903, as well as diasporic citizens who have arrived from China, Brazil, Russia, Argentina, and South Korea in the last decade. They represent a range of socioeconomic, multiracial, and political ideology backgrounds and are a vibrant part of contemporary United States, while reworking transnational kinship, ethnic, and institutional ties in the age of globalization, as this entry shows.

U.S. Immigration

Korean immigration to the United States can be divided into three different waves. A handful of Koreans came to the United States before the turn of the 20th century as students and ginseng merchants. About 7,000 Koreans, about 90% men, migrated between 1903 and 1905 as contract laborers to work in the sugar cane fields of Hawai'i and the farmlands along the West Coast of the United States. Sugar plantation owners, working with American missionaries in Korea, recruited Koreans as strike breakers to replace Japanese workers who were demanding higher wages; the Korean government abruptly ended emigration in response to pressure from Japan, which declared Korea its protectorate in 1905.

Approximately 1,000 Korean "picture brides" arrived between 1910 and 1924 to join—or in some cases, meet for the first time—their husbands, under a provision of the Gentlemen's Agreement between Japan and the United States, which categorized Koreans as Japanese nationals. These women played a pivotal role in the early Korean communities as they raised families, contributed to household income, provided social services, and actively promoted and organized the Korean independence movement. Many first-wave immigrants were also Protestant Christians seeking to escape persecution under Japanese colonial rule; upon arrival, they organized churches to cope with harsh immigrant life as well as passionately engage in the Korean independence movement, the primary concern of most Koreans at this time.

The early Korean community worked with students and political exiles, a small but significant part of first-wave arrivals, to gain international support for Korean liberation. They organized around political leaders such as So Chae-pil (Philip Jaisohn), Ahn Chang Ho, Pak Yong-man, and Syngman Rhee, who advocated different and often divisive approaches to achieving independence. After the passage of the Immigration Act of 1924, Koreans and other Asians, categorized as "aliens ineligible for citizenship," were barred from migrating to the United States.

Postwar Years

After Korea gained its independence from Japan in 1945, the United States more directly intervened in the political and economic affairs of Korea as a strategic means to contain communism centered in the Soviet Union, resulting in its heavy military involvement during the Korean War (1950–1953). A second wave of Korean immigrants came to the United States between the 1950s and mid-1960s, including about 18,000 wartime brides, orphans, and students. The military brides and orphans, who tended to come from impoverished backgrounds, married or were adopted by non-Koreans and settled throughout the United States. Those who entered as students tended to be men from elite families.

Most Korean immigrants arrived after the passage of the Immigration Act of 1965, a product of the Civil Rights Movement and post–World War II international relations. It abolished the racial quotas that had effectively excluded most Asian immigration for decades. Due to the historical legacy of exclusionary policies, the wartime brides and students who entered the United States between the 1950s and early 1960s played a critical role in the establishment of the third-wave Korean immigration due to their ability to sponsor their family members.

After 1965

Most Koreans tended to emigrate through occupational preferences of the Immigration Act of 1965. The changes in U.S. immigration policies followed changes in South Korean emigration policies, such as the 1962 Overseas Emigration Law. The third wave, responding to economic, political, cultural, and military relations between South Korea and the United States, tended to be from urban, middle-class backgrounds, seeking educational, occupational, and economic opportunities, along with other foreign-educated and trained post-1965 immigrants sent to work in underserved areas of the United States.

After U.S. immigration laws were amended in the 1970s to restrict occupational admissions, Koreans have entered largely through family reunification preferences. Recent immigrants represent a greater spectrum of education and occupational backgrounds that more accurately reflects the South Korean general population. Throughout the 1970s, more than 30,000 Koreans migrated to the United States each year; Korean immigration peaked in the late 1980s, but new immigrants continue to arrive.

Contemporary Communities

Like a majority of AAPI groups, Koreans tend to live in the western U.S. region, in particular the states of Hawai'i and California, with the largest concentration living in the Los Angeles/Riverside/Orange County metropolitan area in Southern California. Ethnic enclaves such as Koreatown in Los Angeles (now with local "satellite" locations) receive much attention as the cultural, social, and economic centers for all things Korean, and they are continuously reinvented and revitalized by newly arrived immigrants. However, Koreans are more geographically dispersed than most AAPI groups; according to the 2000 census, 44% of Koreans live in the West, 2% in the Northeast, 21% in the South, and 12% in the Midwest. About 80% of Korean Americans live in suburbs and central cities of large metropolitan areas.

A large percentage of those immigrating after 1965 have experienced downward mobility and language barriers in accessing work, regardless of education levels and premigration occupations. For many first-generation Koreans, the church is a sanctuary from the everyday experience of racism and linguistic and cultural barriers; it is a place to interact with other Koreans. Korean immigrant churches were established as community centers as early as 1903 and continue to be a community force and institution for more than two-thirds of the population. As one of the strongest and accessible social institutions for first-generation Koreans, the church provides critical social networks, support, and ways of obtaining meaningful social status in the United States.

Among the second generation, Korean American ministry involvement has provided not only spiritual support for young Korean Americans (especially within a college campus setting) but also opportunities to share familiar struggles and experiences and ways to cope not only with marginalization but also with bicultural and intergenerational conflicts. In addition, second-generation Korean Americans engage in social, political, and civic participation through churches and faith communities in the United States.

Korean American Families

For many Korean immigrants, the adolescent years of their U.S.-born and/or raised children are a turbulent time exacerbated by cultural and language differences; at the same time, the children of immigrant parents observe and appreciate the difficulties their parents face in the dominant society, in particular in the workplace. In response, children are driven by a combination of self-motivation and parental pressure to do well in school, as education is seen as a path to economic and career opportunities.

According to Jamie Lew, many Korean immigrant parents are informed by their experience with the highly competitive South Korean educational system, even though they may not know how to navigate through the U.S. system. As a result, they often seek out special college preparation courses or private tutors for their children to make up for their lack of knowledge in hopes that this might increase their children's chances for admission to an elite university, as a strategy for collective socioeconomic mobility.

An emerging issue is the caretaking of aging post-1965 immigrants who make up the majority of the Korean American population. Second-generation Korean Americans, adult children of their first-generation parents, face structural, cultural, and intergenerational issues not only when it comes to child rearing but also in caring for aging parents. *Filial piety,* a central aspect of Confucianism that continues to shape Korean and Korean American societies, can be defined as the expression of responsibility, respect, sacrifice, and family harmony that regulates children's attitudes and behavior toward family-based support. Older Koreans as well as their children must negotiate different traditions and expectations in the contemporary United States. With increasing acculturation and adaptation, these ideals of filial piety may or may not resonate with subsequent generations.

Korean American families and communities are also increasingly racially and ethnically heterogeneous. In 2000, more than 12% of Koreans were racially and/or ethnically mixed. Many of the more than 200,000 military brides and Korean adoptees (and their families and extended kin) have consciously created communities that challenge dominant notions of Korean, American, and Korean American identities. These emerging generations will continue to negotiate and expand aspects of Korean/Korean American culture, history, traditions, and identity as individuals, families, and communities.

National Citizens, Global Citizens

Even as the first wave of Korean immigrants in Hawai'i and California rallied around the Korean national independence movement, Korean immigrants and their U.S.-born children have demonstrated that they are here to stay. Contemporary immigrants have largely arrived with a positive outlook and a firm belief in the pursuit (and attainability) of the "American dream" as a result of the strong U.S. military, economic, political, and cultural presence and influence in Korea since the 1940s.

Scholars and media coverage have focused on the hard work and sacrifices of the first-generation immigrants to establish communities and economic stability for themselves and their children. But many Korean Americans continue to struggle; the high rates of ethnic entrepreneurship, for example, may be one reason why in California, Koreans have one of the lowest rates of health insurance coverage, a situation that could significantly impact their emotional and financial well-being.

Events such as *Sa-I-Gu* have served to remind Korean Americans that regardless of socioeconomic status and generation, they need to think and act beyond ethnic solidarity and economic mobility. While they maintain contact with the dynamic South Korean society and transform their ethnic and cultural identities, Korean Americans are increasingly entering diverse professions and creating alliances for political and economic empowerment that serve themselves and other members in the multiethnic, multiracial, and multilingual U.S. society.

Barbara Kim and Grace J. Yoo

See Appendix A

See also Asian Americans; Ethnicity, Negotiating; Foreign Students; Immigrant Communities; Model Minority; Pan-Asian Identity

Further Readings

Chang, Edward Taehan, ed. 2003–2004. "What Does It Mean to be Korean Today?" Special issue. *Amerasia Journal* (29)3: xix-xxvi. Los Angeles: UCLA Asian American Studies Center.

Chin, Soo-Young. 1999. *Doing What Had to Be Done: The Life Narrative of Dora Yum Kim.* Philadelphia, PA: Temple University Press.

Lee, Mary Paik. 1990. *Quiet Odyssey: A Pioneer Korean Woman in America.* Berkeley: University of California Press.

Lew, Jamie. 2006. *Asian Americans in Class: Charting the Achievement Gap among Korean American Youth.* New York: Teachers College Press.

Park, Kyeyoung. 1997. *The Korean American Dream: Immigrants and Small Businesses in New York City.* Ithaca, NY: Cornell University Press.

Park, Lisa Sun-Yee. 2005. *Consuming Citizenship: Children of Asian Immigrant Entrepreneurs.* Palo Alto, CA: Stanford University Press.

Yoon, In Jin. 1997. *On My Own: Korean Businesses and Race Relations in America.* Chicago, IL: University of Chicago Press.

Ku Klux Klan

Although the Ku Klux Klan (KKK) is often treated as a unitary organization, it is more accurately a collection of ideologically linked symbols appropriated by groups that have gained influence and popularity in varied places and times. From its earliest incarnation, the Klan has been synonymous with the promotion of White supremacy, often through terrorist or otherwise violent means. This entry will discuss the history and significance of the Klan and its activities.

The first wave of KKK activity swept across the South soon after the Civil War, with hundreds of chapters, or "dens," engaging in thousands of violent acts against Black and Unionist enemies. During the 1920s, the Klan reemerged across the nation, recruiting millions of members—including a significant number of elites and professionals—to their political program, which incorporated anti-immigrant, anti-Catholic, anti-Semitic, and anti-communist elements into its traditional White supremacist agenda. And in response to 1960s civil rights activity, a variety of newly established KKK organizations recruited tens of thousands of members throughout the South. Klan adherents committed many of the most brutal and infamous acts of racial violence of the era, including the murder of four teenage girls in the 1963 bombing of a Birmingham church, the killing of three civil rights workers during the 1964 Mississippi Freedom Summer campaign, and the fatal shooting of a Michigan woman during a 1965 protest march in Alabama. Various incarnations of the Klan have continued to mobilize since, though in small numbers and without significant impact on mainstream political processes.

Origins

The origins of the KKK had less to do with purpose than circumstance. Conceived initially as a fraternal organization for its own members' amusement, the Klan was formed in 1866 by a small group of young Confederate veterans in Pulaski, Tennessee. These founders established much of the Klan's enduring iconography, including its elaborate initiation rituals, complex slates of offices, and long robes topped with conical hoods. The group's name drew upon the Greek word for "circle," *kuklos,* supplemented, for alliterative purposes, by the word *klan.*

In Pulaski, a community beset by pervasive lawlessness following the Civil War, the group's fraternal aims were superseded by new members' desire to restore order. In the Reconstruction-era context, in which many White Southerners feared political, economic, and social upheaval engineered by newly freed Blacks and their Republican allies, such calls referred not only to reducing criminality but also to a reassertion of the White supremacist culture that had defined the antebellum status quo. An 1867 meeting in Nashville reorganized the Klan, placing it in the hands of several prominent Confederate officers, including General Nathan Bedford Forrest, who became the group's first and only "Grand Wizard," or national leader.

Forrest and his associates proceeded to recruit extensively, mobilizing many Confederate veterans throughout the South as local leaders. With the added assistance of newspapers supportive of Southern Democrats and their causes, the KKK grew significantly throughout 1868. The Klan's appeal was greatest where Democrats could pose an effective challenge to "radical" Republican political institutions. Along with similar vigilante groups, such as the Order of Pale Faces and the Knights of the White Camellia, the group quickly became known for its efforts to violently intimidate Black community leaders

Ku Klux Klan rally. *The Grand Dragon of the Michigan Ku Klux Klan (left) addresses the crowd as another Klan member looks on during a Klan rally on August 21, 1999, in downtown Cleveland. This rally was part of the Klan's effort to spread its message of segregation, hate, and intolerance toward African Americans, gays, and Jews.*

Source: AFP/Getty Images.

and the "carpetbaggers" (i.e., Northerners who settled in the South during this period) and the "scalawags" (i.e., White Southern Republicans) who supported them. During Reconstruction, KKK adherents committed literally thousands of criminal acts, ranging from arson to severe beatings, shootings, and lynchings; it was not unusual for a single Southern county to witness 100 Klan-perpetrated "outrages" over the course of a year.

While this violence had a pervasive logic—to consolidate support for White supremacy—it also occurred in the absence of significant regional or national coordination. Despite their nominal ties to the overall KKK organization, local Klan "dens" were largely autonomous and increasingly engaged in unregulated terrorist activity. In reaction, Grand Wizard Forrest issued a largely unsuccessful order to curtail members' actions in 1869. Mounting public outrage against the Klan's vigilante-style atrocities led to the passage by the U.S. Congress of the Enforcement Act in 1870 and the Ku Klux Klan Act in 1871, as well as to subsequent federal government investigations. Hundreds of Klan members were arrested as a result of these measures, and despite the fact that relatively few were ultimately prosecuted, such actions resulted in a drastic downturn in Klan-related violence during the 1870s.

Revival of the KKK

With the fall of Republican control and the end of Reconstruction in 1877, the KKK had all but disappeared. But the group's legacy endured in the occasional rise of Klan-like groups and, more significantly, as a romanticized ideal. The Klan's image as heroic defenders of the White South became increasingly resonant, furthered by the popular Thomas Dixon novel, *The Clansman,* the basis of the epic D. W. Griffith film, *The Birth of a Nation.*

William J. Simmons, a failed minister and salesman, had long dreamed of reviving the KKK, and, in 1915, the high-profile release of Griffith's film provided an ideal opportunity to do so. Shortly before the movie's Atlanta opening, he gathered a handful of sympathetic fraternal types and led them up nearby Stone Mountain for the KKK's official refounding. Following a scene in Dixon's novel, the ceremony featured the Klan's first cross burning.

Simmons's KKK grew rather slowly at first, claiming a membership of several thousand Georgia and Alabama residents by 1920. That year, in an effort to bolster the group's appeal, Simmons hired professional marketers Edward Clarke and Elizabeth Tyler to build the organization. Clarke and Tyler commissioned hundreds of Klan recruiting agents, who emphasized the group's focus on racial purity, Protestantism, and patriotic "100% Americanism." In a nation beset by post–World War II nativist tendencies, along with racial and labor strife, an agricultural crisis, and the start of Prohibition, these appeals resonated with many White Americans, who perceived the Klan to be the solution to a variety of political, economic, and moral ailments.

Within the year, Klan membership took off, reaching 85,000 in 1921 and somewhere between 3 and 5 million by 1925. Unlike the Reconstruction-era KKK, chapters were not confined to rural communities or to the South. Membership reached six digits in many states across the nation, with tens of thousands joining in cities such as Chicago, Detroit, and Denver. While the Klan was an exclusively male organization, a parallel group, the Women of the Ku Klux Klan, recruited tens of thousands of women into its ranks. Far from marginal individuals, Klan adherents came from both white- and blue-collar sectors and frequently included prominent community leaders.

The Klan accumulated considerable political influence, and scores of Klansmen were elected or appointed to local and state offices. While vigilantism at times remained associated with the organization, such violence was often subsumed by the Klan's populist civic character. Chapters often had ties to a range of fraternal and church groups and sometimes organized around issues such as law enforcement and good schools. These emphases have caused some historians to suggest that racism was not primary to the 1920s Klan, though the intersection of class and race issues in many localities aligned the KKK's civic efforts with its overarching White supremacist—and anti-immigrant, anti-communist, anti-Jew, and anti-Catholic—agenda.

The Klan began to lose momentum after 1925, as the organization became plagued by leadership crises and moral and financial scandal. Unlike the Reconstruction-era KKK, Simmons's outfit was highly centralized, profiting tremendously from initiation fees and the sale of regalia and other Klan-related products. As early as 1923, issues of financial control created rifts within the Klan's leadership. Paired with Klan politicians' general inability to live up to their rhetoric, increasingly pervasive charges of financial and moral corruption contributed to a sharp decline in membership. By the end of the 1920s, the KKK had almost entirely lost its support base and political influence. What remained of the organization was officially disbanded in 1944 after the Internal Revenue Service filed a lien for unpaid back taxes.

The Civil Rights Era and After

The first of many independent Klan organizations emerged soon after, when Atlanta obstetrician Samuel Green organized a Stone Mountain cross burning to introduce his Association of Georgia Klans. By 1954, when the Supreme Court's school desegregation decision provided impetus for the segregationist cause, there were at least eight self-styled Klan organizations competing for adherents across the South. Much of this activity ultimately consolidated into the United Klans of America (UKA), headed by Alabama-based Robert Shelton. By the mid-1960s, the UKA had more than 20,000 members, spread over nearly 400 chapters in seventeen states.

Though the UKA never achieved the broad national appeal of Simmons's Klan, it did retain a similar public character, building support through nightly rallies and cross burnings across the South, as well as periodic parades featuring members in full regalia. Despite considerable opposition from community elites and the media, the UKA's hard-line response to federal desegregation efforts drew hundreds, and sometimes thousands, of supporters to each of its rallies. The group's militant core was also responsible for much, though not all, of the violence that befell civil rights workers across the South. During the 1964 Freedom Summer voter registration campaign, three civil rights workers were killed in Neshoba County, Mississippi, by members of the Mississippi White Knights, a highly secretive and militant group that competed with Shelton's UKA for members in that state.

In response, the FBI began infiltrating various KKK organizations, as well as actively disrupting their activities through a formal counterintelligence program (COINTELPRO). These efforts, alongside various internal struggles and quickly receding hopes for the resuscitation of Jim-Crow-style segregation, contributed to the Klan's significant decline by the late 1960s. The UKA continued on with only a small fraction of its peak membership until the 1980s. In 1981, in reaction to the killing of a White police officer, two UKA members abducted at random and then lynched Michael Donald, a 19-year-old Black man, in Mobile, Alabama. Five years later, a landmark civil suit sponsored by the Southern Poverty Law Center resulted in a $7 million settlement against the UKA, which officially put the group out of business.

Various self-declared Klan organizations have emerged since, sometimes in partnership with neo-Nazis and other factions of the far right. In a few instances, such as the 1979 killing of five Communist Workers Party members in Greensboro, North Carolina, and a 1991 gubernatorial bid by former Klansman David Duke, adherents have gained national attention, though their organizations have never come close to approaching the size or influence of the Klan's three previous waves.

David Cunningham

See also Anti-Semitism; Civil Rights Movement; Jim Crow; Lynching; Racism; Voting Rights; White Supremacy Movement

Further Readings

Blee, Kathleen M. 1991. *Women of the Klan: Racism and Gender in the 1920s.* Berkeley: University of California Press.

Chalmers, David M. 1981. *Hooded Americanism: The History of the Ku Klux Klan.* New York: New Viewpoints.

Lay, Shawn, ed. 1992. *The Invisible Empire in the West: Toward a New Historical Appraisal of the Ku Klux Klan of the 1920s.* Urbana: University of Illinois Press.

Trelease, Allen W. 1971. *White Terror: The Ku Klux Conspiracy and Southern Reconstruction.* Baton Rouge: Louisiana State University Press.

U.S. House of Representatives, Committee on Un-American Activities. 1967. *The Present-Day Ku Klux Klan Movement.* 90th Congress, 1st Session. Washington, DC: Author.

Kurdish Americans

The Kurds are a nomadic, distinct, and global group without an autonomous or politically recognized homeland. Estimates of the Kurdish population range from 5 to 26 million. The Kurds are an ethnic group without a nation. In this respect, they have a similar status to that of Jews, the Roma (Gypsies), and Assyrians. Kurds are typically Sunni Muslims but are not Arabs and are culturally closer to Persians (Iranians). This entry clarifies who the Kurds are and discusses their settlement patterns in the United States.

Kurds typically speak Kurmanji and the language of their home country (such as Arabic among Iraqi

Kurds). Kurds have distinct gender roles, with men serving as the heads of families. Although Islamic, Kurdish women are less restricted than many Muslims; they do not wear veils, feel free to associate with men who are not family members, and may occupy political office, for example.

"Kurdistan," is the name commonly given to the territory between the mountain areas of Iran, Iraq, Syria, and Turkey, which the Kurds claim as their homeland. Because their region is subdivided among four countries, the Kurds who live in each region have varying types of relationships with the governments. For instance, Kurds in Iraq refer to the region as "Iraqi Kurdistan," which is administered by the Kurdistan Regional Government; it is, in other words, a state within a state. Most recently, Iraqi Kurdistan has been strengthening bonds with the United States and promoting business and travel to their region. On the other hand, the region of "Turkish Kurdistan" has no unified administrative identity, and the Turkish state even rejects the use of the term *Kurdistan* to describe it.

Kurdish history is filled with struggle, conflict, destruction, and displacement. War and persecution often fuel constant movement and migration of their people. Although major concentrations of Kurds live in Iran, Iraq, Turkey, and Syria, a large diaspora community exists outside the Middle East.

Prior to 1970, very few Kurds were documented as living in the United States. During the 2-year period between 1975 and 1977, however, the number of Kurdish immigrants, mostly refugees, rose to about 350 per year. Across the world at this time, thousands more fled from Iraq to Iran after a failed Kurdish revolution. In addition, during the Iran/Iraq War (1980–1988), 60,000 Kurds fled from Iraq to Turkey. Their plight captured global attention during this time. While many stayed in refugee camps or were forced to return to Iraq, a "safe haven" for Kurds was created in Iraq in 1991. As of 2007, Kurds make up 20% of Iraq's population.

Some of the estimated 1.5 million Kurdish refugees worldwide have resettled in North America as a result of an international humanitarian relief effort; about 40,000 Kurds live in the United States. Kurdish communities can be found in Nashville, Tennessee; San Diego, California; and Washington, D.C. Changes in immigration practices after the attacks on September 11, 2001, have posed challenges for those seeking citizenship, as well as those wanting to return home.

Given the recency of their arrival and instability in the Middle East, the small Kurdish American community is vigilant about the treatment of Kurds worldwide, especially in Middle East, and many look toward a future with a truly independent Kurdistan.

Jennifer M. Klein

See Appendix A

See also Assimilation; Diaspora; Immigrant Communities; Immigration U.S.; Iranian Americans; Iraqi Americans; Islamophobia; Minority/Majority; Muslim Americans; Refugees; Syrian Americans; Turkish Americans

Further Readings

Chandrasekaran, Rajiv. 2007. "Kurds Cultivating Their Own Bonds with U.S." *Washington Post,* April 23, p. A01. Retrieved from http://www.washingtonpost.com/wp-dyn/content/article/2007/04/22/AR2007042201568.html

Jabar, Faleh A. and Hosham Dawod, eds. *The Kurds.* 2006. Berkeley, CA: SAQI.

McDowall, David. 1996. *A Modern History of the Kurds.* New York: I. B. Tauris.

McKiernan, Kevin. 2006. *The Kurds: A People in Search of Their Homeland.* New York: St. Martin's Press.

Wahlbeck, Osten. 1999. *Kurdish Diasporas: A Comparative Study of Kurdish Refugee Communities.* London: Macmillan Press.

Kwanzaa

Kwanzaa is a 7-day African American and pan-African holiday that celebrates family, community, and culture. It begins on December 26 and continues through January 1. Based on ancient African first-fruits harvest celebrations, its name is derived from the Swahili phrase *matunda ya kwanza,* which literally means "first fruits." This entry recalls the history and describes current celebration.

Historical Background

The celebrations of first-fruits harvests are recorded from the earliest African history and have various names depending upon the language of the society in which they are observed. Examples of such festivals are *Pert-en-Min* in ancient Egypt, *Umkhozi* in Zululand, *Incwala* in Swaziland, *Odwira* in Ashantiland, and *Odu Ijesu* in Yorubaland.

Dr. Maulana Karenga, an activist scholar and now professor of Black Studies at California State University, Long Beach, created the U.S. Kwanzaa celebration in 1966 in the midst of the Black Freedom Movement. Kwanzaa was created to reaffirm African Americans' rootedness in African culture, to bring Africans together to reinforce the bonds between them, to meditate on the expansive meaning of being African in the world, and to introduce and reaffirm the importance of communitarian African values, especially the *Nguzo Saba* (The Seven Principles).

Kwanzaa was first celebrated in the context of the cultural and social change organization Us (us, African people), which Karenga chairs, and then in the country as a whole. However, Kwanzaa soon developed into an international pan-African holiday, now involving over 30 million celebrants throughout the world African community.

Meaning and Celebration

The meaning and activities of Kwanzaa are rooted in and organized around the *Nguzo Saba* (The Seven Principles), also developed by Maulana Karenga. These principles are directed toward cultivating practices that reaffirm and strengthen family, community, and culture. They are *Umoja* (Unity), *Kujichagulia* (Self-Determination), *Ujima* (Collective Work and Responsibility), *Ujamaa* (Cooperative Economics), *Nia* (Purpose), *Kuumba* (Creativity), and *Imani* (Faith). In fact, one of the reasons Kwanzaa is 7 days is to dedicate a day to the discussion and modeling of each principle by those who celebrate Kwanzaa.

In addition, Kwanzaa is organized around five fundamental kinds of activities rooted in the practices of ancient African harvest celebrations: (1) the ingathering of the people to reinforce the bonds between them, especially those of family, community, and culture; (2) special reverence for the Creator and creation in gratitude for the bountifulness and goodness of the earth and with a self-conscious commitment to preserve and protect it; (3) commemoration of the past, in fulfillment of the obligation to remember and honor the ancestors and to reaffirm the fundamental mission and meaning of African history (i.e., to constantly bring good into the world); (4) recommitment to the highest African cultural, ethical, and spiritual values that bring forth the best of what it means to be African and human; and (5) celebration of the Good—the good of family, community, and culture; of work, struggle, and life; and of the wonder of the world and all in it.

Kwanzaa has seven basic symbols and two supplementary ones. Each symbol represents views and values rooted in African culture and contributive to the reaffirmation and strengthening of family, community, and culture. The seven basic symbols are the *mazao* (crops), symbolizing African harvest celebrations and the rewards of productive and collective labor; *mkeka* (mat), symbolizing tradition and history and therefore the foundation on which to build; *kinara* (candleholder), symbolizing ancestral roots, the parent people, Continental Africans; *mishumaa saba* (the seven candles), symbolizing the *Nguzo Saba,* the Seven Principles; *muhindi* (corn), symbolizing children and the future of African people they embody; *kikombe cha umoja* (unity cup), symbolizing the foundational principle and practice of unity, which makes all else possible; and *zawadi* (gifts), symbolizing the labor and love of parents and the commitments made and kept by the children. The two supplemental symbols are a representation of the *Nguzo Saba* and the *bendera* (flag), containing three colors: black, red, and green. These colors, respectively, symbolize African people, their social struggle, and the promise and future that come from the struggle.

Kwanzaa activities are numerous and varied, directed toward reaffirmation and strengthening of family, community, and culture. Moreover, daily activities are organized around discussion, dramatization, and modeling of the principles through conduct, recitation, reading, narrative, performance, libation, sharing meals, and candlelighting. Most often at the evening meal, family members light one of the seven candles each night to focus on the principles. This ritual is called "lifting up the light that lasts" and symbolizes lifting up and upholding the *Nguzo Saba* and all the other life-affirming and enduring principles that reaffirm the good of life, enrich human relations, and support human flourishing. As each candle is lit, the person lighting the candle explains the meaning of the particular principle of the day to her or him. Also, a narrative from Black history or a poem might be told or recited to illustrate the principle.

A central and culminating event is the gathering of the community on December 31 for an African *karamu* (feast), featuring libation to the ancestors and ceremonies honoring elders, narratives, poetry, music, dance, and other performances to celebrate the goodness of life, relationships, and cultural grounding. The last day of Kwanzaa, January 1, called *Siku ya Taamuli* (The Day of Meditation), is dedicated to self-assessment and recommitment to the *Nguzo Saba* as well as other African values that reaffirm commitment to human rights and dignity, family and community well-being and flourishing, environmental protection and preservation, and human solidarity. To conduct this self-assessment, each person is to ask and answer three questions: Who am I? Am I really who I am? Am I all I ought to be?

This represents measuring oneself in the mirror of the best of African culture and history and recommitting oneself to standards and practices of human excellence that reflect this. Through this practice and throughout Kwanzaa, the people reaffirm the values and life lessons of the ancestors; strengthen commitments to family, community, and culture; and thus create the context for the ongoing creation, harvesting, and sharing good in the world.

Maulana Karenga

See Appendix B

See also African Americans; Afrocentricity; Black Nationalism; Multicultural Education; Symbolic Ethnicity

Further Readings

Karenga, Maulana. 1998. *Kwanzaa: A Celebration of Family, Community, and Culture.* Los Angeles, CA: University of Sankore Press.

Web Sites

Official Kwanzaa Web Site: http://www.officialkwanzaawebsite.org

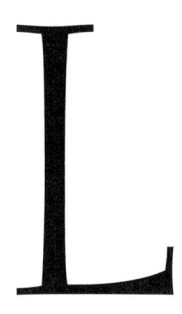

LABELING

Labeling is a concept introduced by sociologist Howard Becker during the 1950s in an attempt to explain why certain people are viewed as deviant while others who engage in the same behavior are not. Although not initially applied to issues of race, ethnicity, and gender, labeling has become widely used in these social contexts. This entry defines the term and discusses its impact.

Definition

According to labeling, a child who misbehaves might be considered and treated as delinquent if she or he comes from the "wrong kind of family," whereas another child who commits the same sort of misbehavior might be given another chance before being punished if she or he comes from a middle-class family. Using this formulation, observers of racial/ethnic relations observe that the behavior of members of different groups is labeled depending on the relative power that these groups are able to exert in society. For example, in the scrutiny of the media in the aftermath of Hurricane Katrina in 2005, many contended that Black people seen taking items from abandoned stores were labeled by reporters as "looters," whereas Whites engaged in the same apparent behavior were seen as "survivors" or "scavengers."

The labeling perspective directs attention to the role that negative stereotypes play in race and ethnicity. Stereotypes are unreliable generalizations about all members of a group that do not take individual differences into account. The "warrior" image of Native American (American Indian) people is perpetuated by the frequent use of tribal names or even terms such as *Indians* and *Redskins* as sports team mascots.

However, this labeling is not limited to racial/ethnic groups. For instance, age can be used to exclude a person from an activity in which he or she is qualified to engage. Groups are subjected to stereotypes and discrimination in such a way that their treatment resembles that of social minorities. Social prejudice exists toward ex-convicts, gamblers, alcoholics, lesbians, gays, prostitutes, people with AIDS, and people with disabilities, to name a few.

Labeling can also be positive, as in the *model minority* notion that often characterizes Asian Americans as being very successful and intelligent and, significantly, as not causing trouble or asking for any special allowances. Even positive labeling has negative consequences, for in this case some Asian American adolescents may feel undue pressure to succeed by society's standards and may see failure even in modest accomplishments. Furthermore, by relishing the alleged success of the model minority, society seems to reassure itself that racism is disappearing if not gone entirely.

Labeling points out that stereotypes, when applied by people in power, can have negative consequences for people or groups identified falsely. A crucial aspect of the relationship between dominant and subordinate groups is the prerogative of the dominant group to define society's values. U.S. sociologist William I. Thomas, an early critic of racial and gender discrimination, saw that the "definition of the situation" could mold the personality of the individual. In other words, Thomas observed that people respond not only to the objective features of a situation (or person) but also to the meaning these features have for them. So, for example, someone out walking alone who sees a young Black man approaching may perceive the situation differently if the oncoming person were an older woman. In this manner, people can create false images or stereotypes that become real in their social consequences.

Impact of Stereotypes

In certain situations, people may respond to negative stereotypes and act on them, with the result that false definitions become accurate. That is known as a *self-fulfilling prophecy*. A person or group described as having particular characteristics begins to display the very traits attributed to the person or group. Thus, a minority child may be defined by teachers as a troublemaker, and this in turn may encourage the student to repeat the behavior or to believe that it is useless to try to stem antisocial behavior. Society may come to "blame the victim" for unacceptable actions and not enter into any reexamination that society's structure may bring about unfavorable results or behavior.

Self-fulfilling prophecies can be devastating for minority groups. Such groups often find that they are allowed to hold only low-paying jobs with little prestige or opportunity for advancement. The rationale of the dominant society may be that minority people lack the ability to perform in more important and lucrative positions. Training to become scientists, executives, or physicians is denied to many individuals in subordinate groups, who are then locked into society's inferior jobs. As a result, the false definition becomes real. The subordinate groups have become inferior because they were defined at the start as inferior and, therefore, were prevented from achieving the levels attained by the majority.

Because of this vicious cycle, talented people in subordinate groups may come to see the worlds of entertainment and professional sports as their only hope for achieving wealth and fame. Thus, it is no accident that successive waves of Irish, Jewish, Italian, African American, and Hispanic performers and athletes have made their mark on culture in the United States. Unfortunately, these very successes may convince the dominant group that its original stereotypes were valid—that these are the only areas of society in which members of subordinate groups can excel. Furthermore, athletics and the arts are highly competitive areas. For every LeBron James or Jennifer Lopez who "makes it," many more will end up disappointed.

Richard T. Schaefer

See also Deviance and Crime; Hurricane Katrina; Marginalization; "Marielitos"; Model Minority; Prejudice; Racial Profiling; Self-Fulfilling Prophecy; Stereotypes; "Welfare Queen"

Further Readings

Becker, Howard S. 1963. *The Outsiders: Studies in the Sociology of Deviance*. New York: Free Press.
Ryan, William. 1976. *Blaming the Victim*. Rev. ed. New York: Random House.
Thomas, William Isaac. 1923. *The Unadjusted Girl*. Boston, MA: Little, Brown.

LABOR MARKET SEGMENTATION

Throughout U.S. labor history, peoples of color have been disproportionately tracked and channeled into secondary or periphery sectors of the labor market. Although federal legislation, such as the Civil Rights Act of 1964, has been central in addressing racially discriminatory employment practices and policies, U.S. Census data continually show an overpopulation of racial/ethnic minorities in occupations or firms associated with the service sector and manual labor. As a consequence, underrepresented minorities have generally had a lower socioeconomic status, fewer occupational choices, and less social mobility—relative to White non-Hispanic populations—throughout U.S. history. This entry discusses the concept of labor markets and the process by which work and workers in the United States become racially segmented within this economic and sociopolitical construct.

The Significance of Labor Markets

Labor markets are social and economic constructs that organize the process by which labor—or, in the Marxian context, one's *labor power*—is purchased and sold. This socioeconomic exchange exists between the laborer (who may be defined as an individual who must sell his or her labor or labor power to capitalists as a means of earning wages) and the employer (who owns the means of production specific to a given labor market or occupational niche). According to the writings of early labor market scholars such as Richard Edwards, Michael Reich, and David Gordon, a labor market functions as the socioeconomic context through which various institutions merge to govern and determine the interactions between the laborer and the employer.

Within the published scholarship on the labor market process, two leading schools of thought emerge. A more conservative and orthodox economic argument posits that the labor market is composed of various key actors who enter into a competitive labor market with varying levels of human and skill capital. The market is seen as an imperfect yet efficient system that best organizes the labor process, the production and cost of goods and services, the wages of laborers, and the profits of employers or corporations. At the core of this system is the Western economic principle of supply and demand, which is perceived as being pivotal to the organizing of every aspect of the labor market process.

A more radical perspective about the labor market process also exists within the published scholarship. This perspective is grounded in the Marxist tradition and, therefore, begins with the fundamental assumption that the labor market process seeks only to generate or accumulate profits for capitalists. The ability of capitalists to accumulate profits is linked to the structure of the labor market, which creates a system of wage laborers whose well-being and survival are dependent on their ability to sell their labor or labor power to those who own the means of production. Because of this inequitable arrangement, the labor market's most important, if not its most central, function is to maintain a hierarchical relationship between laborers and employers, on the one hand, and to legitimize a stratified distribution of resources, power, and opportunities among all workers, on the other.

Although the exchange of labor power for wages—or various occupational rewards—is a defining and underlying process associated with labor markets, this interchange often occurs in a context that is undetectable or constantly being redefined. In other words, a labor market is also a series of interlocking and invisible boundaries. A boundary can be defined as a physical construct that marks a territory and, subsequently, restricts or regulates the movement both within and outside its parameters. As it relates back to the concept of labor markets, the idea of boundary can also function as a metaphor for how labor markets exist. Regardless of the work performed, most laborers find themselves bound to specific work sites, workspaces, or geographical regions, thereby demarcating a physical characteristic or boundary of labor markets.

However, a boundary need not always be physically present to restrict or regulate an individual's mobility. Even when a boundary is invisible, it is capable of distinguishing space, establishing who may and may not occupy that space, and reifying the idea of the marked "other" through means of differentiation, devaluation, and discrimination. Although the regulation and division of labor and capital are fundamental socioeconomic characteristics of any labor market, labor markets are also distinguishable by the marked and unmarked boundaries that underlie the fragmentation and segmentation of work and workers across their varying sectors.

The Segmentation of Labor Markets

The process of labor market segmentation is widely recognized as a distinct marker of the age of Western industrialization. As Western societies began to transition from a more agrarian and feudal-based mode of economic production and social arrangements to a worker-based society grounded in industrial labor and manufacturing, there was the increased homogenization and centralization of the Western labor force. Western industrialization is at the core of the labor market process given both the formation of wage labor and the emergence of extremely routinized or specialized occupations.

For Michael Piore and other early dual economy theorists, the rise of the industrial age created the need for increased differentiation of labor within labor markets. Most dual economy theorists identify four labor market characteristics when conceptualizing the polarized and bifurcated nature of the industrial labor market: the stability of occupations within a given sector, the wages earned, the level of skill and human capital required for employment, and the odds of upward mobility within an occupational niche. The dual economy argument assumes that the structure of the labor market is organized into two fairly distinct labor market sectors: the primary sector and the secondary sector. The primary sector (or center) firms are seen as consisting of highly prestigious, competitive, and stable occupations or firms within a given labor market.

The secondary sector (or periphery) firms are defined by a socioeconomic arrangement that is often less prestigious, constantly in flux, and lacking the degree of upward mobility associated with the primary sector.

Dual economy theorists developed a theoretical framework by which to assess the complex structure of the industrial labor market. Such structures, moreover, are pivotal in shaping the conditions and manner in which various "classes" of workers must labor. Furthermore, the division of labor that underlies this dual economy is inextricably linked to the durability of larger forms of social (e.g., race, ethnicity) and economic inequalities.

Race and the Segmentation of Labor

The uneven distribution of various racial/ethnic groups across and within sectors of the labor market can be best understood with a historical and sociopolitical assessment of labor in the United States. The racialized division of labor has been a central phenomenon throughout the evolution of labor in the United States. As the institution of chattel slavery took root in the Americas, so did sociopolitical systems and cultural norms that were fundamental in creating and legitimizing the positioning of racial/ethnic groups into race-specific forms of labor. At its most basic level, the institution of chattel slavery identified the racialized boundaries of work and occupations in a preindustrial United States. This peculiar institution also set in motion legal policies and sociocultural practices that shaped the racial/ethnic composition of labor during the rise of the industrial era in the early waves of immigration to the United States.

As the United States transitioned into an industrial era marked in part by the ascendancy of a more federally centralized economy and a more urban, manufacturing-based workforce, the racialization of work or the racialized division of labor became increasingly intense and severe. This intensification was largely the result of two interconnected and colinear socioeconomic phenomena. The first half of the 20th century can be characterized by an increased demand for manual labor in the booming urban labor market sectors in the Northeast and Midwest. This demand for labor was addressed largely by an expanding labor force with significant variations in its racial/ethnic, citizenship, sex, and skill composition. Although this supply of labor was essential to meeting the enormous demand for (manual) labor in these industrial centers, the demands for increased economic resources and prestigious occupational positions by increasingly non-White populations—which also included "White" ethnic groups from non–Western European countries—threatened a hegemonic racial structure that emerged during the preindustrial era in the United States.

As noted by early race scholars such as W. E. B. Du Bois, Anna Julia Cooper, and Oliver Cox as well as by more contemporary (critical) race scholars such as Jacqueline Jones, George Lipsitz, and David Roediger, the racialized distribution of workers across stratified sectors of the labor market is grounded in the preservation of whiteness and the maintenance of White privilege and supremacy. To that end, federal, state, and local labor policies during the late 19th century and at the turn of the 20th century reinforced the privileged occupational status of White men—especially those who had high socioeconomic status, were Protestant, were U.S. citizens, and were affiliated with organized labor. As for the majority of women and non-White peoples, the emergence of Jim Crow labor policies further positioned them in what critical labor scholars such as Teresa Amott, Julie Matthaei, Jacqueline Jones, and Donald Tomaskovic-Devey described as a legacy of race/sex segregated, substandard, and highly devalued labor conditions.

Conclusions

The distribution of workers across sectors of the U.S. labor market remains both a stratified and segmented process. Classic arguments concerning labor market segmentation have been a hallmark of the early scholarship on social stratification and occupations in the United States. At the core of this body of literature are three fundamental arguments. First, it is widely assumed that occupations are distinguished by distinct and stratified sectors of the labor market. This division of labor is seen as emanating from the increased specialization of labor during the rise of both industrialization and advanced capitalism. Second, the distinction between these labor sectors is often characterized by the inequitable distribution of job rewards and the social demographics of their respective labor force. Finally, theories of labor market segmentation often argue that mobility both between labor sectors and among occupations within a labor sector is highly constrained and credentialed in the primary sector, whereas mobility in the secondary sector is more tenuous. For critical labor market theorists, the structure of the labor market is racialized or race specific, and, as a consequence, it is responsible for maintaining the subordinate status of racial/ethnic minorities in society.

Gary Kinte Perry

See also Affirmative Action in the Workplace; *Declining Significance of Race, The;* Racism; Social Mobility; Split Labor Market; White Privilege

Further Readings

Amott, Teresa and Julie Matthaei. 1991. *Race, Gender, and Work: A Multicultural Economic History of Women in the United States.* Boston, MA: South End Press.

Brewer, Rose, Cecilia Conrad, and Mary King. 2002. "The Complexities and Potential of Theorizing Gender, Caste, Race, and Class." *Feminist Economics* 8(2):3–18.

Browne, Irene, ed. 1999. *Latinas and African American Women at Work: Race, Gender, and Economic Inequality.* New York: Russell Sage.

Cohn, Samuel. 2000. *Race and Gender Discrimination at Work.* Boulder, CO: Westview.

Gordon, David, Richard Edwards, and Michael Reich. 1982. *Segmented Work, Divided Workers: The Historical Transformation of Labor in the United States.* London: Cambridge University Press.

Jones, Jacqueline. 1985. *Labor of Love, Labor of Sorrow: Black Women, Work, and the Family, from Slavery to the Present.* New York: Vintage Books.

Piore, Michael. 1975. "Notes for a Theory of Labor Market Stratification." Pp. 125–150 in *Labor Market Segmentation,* edited by Richard Edwards, Michael Reich, and David Gordon. Lexington, MA: D. C. Heath.

Reich, Michael, David Gordon, and Richard Edwards. 1973. "A Theory of Labor Market Segmentation." *American Economic Review* 63:359–365.

Tomaskovic-Devey, Donald. 1993. *Gender and Racial Inequality at Work: The Sources and Consequences of Job Segregation.* Ithaca, NY: ILR Press.

Wilkinson, Doris. 1991. "The Segmented Labor Market and African American Women from 1890–1960: A Social History Interpretation." *Research in Race and Ethnic Relations* 6:85–104.

Labor Unions

Labor unions are organizations formed or joined by workers to represent them at their workplaces and negotiate with employers over wages, hours, and conditions of employment. Labor unions are bargaining agents with legal rights to sign collective bargaining agreements. When impasses are reached in bargaining, unions pressure employers to offer better terms by mobilizing their members to withdraw from work, that is, to go on strike. This entry deals with the activities and structures of labor unions and their representation of minority and immigrant workers.

Union Activities, Structures, and Governance

Aside from collective bargaining with employers, unions organize nonunion workers and engage in political action. Unions organize when they recruit new members, and they ask employers to recognize them as bargaining agents. Under the certification procedures of the federal and state labor boards (judicial agencies that enforce labor laws), a union can gain certification as a bargaining agent by proving, usually in a secret-ballot election, that it is supported by a majority of employees at the workplace.

Unions engage in political action by endorsing candidates and contributing to their election campaigns, encouraging members to help get out the vote for endorsed candidates on Election Day, and lobbying for legislation that is pro-worker or pro-union (e.g., favoring higher minimum wages, favoring protections against employment discrimination, favoring stronger penalties against employer misconduct during union organizing). Historically, unions have overwhelmingly supported candidates and policies of the Democratic Party because they believe that this party values the economic concerns of workers and their families. However, unions do not affiliate with any party formally. Their political creed is simple—to reward their friends and punish their enemies.

Labor unions are among the most diverse organizations in the U.S. society. There is no typical union. There are 60 national and international unions (international unions have some members in Canada) as well as 2,000 to 3,000 regional or companywide unions. Eight national unions have more than 500,000 members each, whereas another eight national unions have fewer than 10,000 members each. Regional and companywide unions usually have fewer than 1,000 members each. Some unions represent mostly government workers (e.g., American Federation of State, County, and Municipal Employees), others confine themselves to the private sector (e.g., United Food and Commercial

Workers), and still others organize both government and private employees (e.g., Communications Workers). Some unions are exclusive, restricting membership to a particular occupation (e.g., Screen Actors Guild, Airline Pilots Association, Major League Baseball Players Association), whereas others will represent any worker in any occupation or industry (e.g., Teamsters, Service Employees). Most unions represent workers in their core industry (e.g., automobile manufacturing for United Auto Workers), a few related industries (e.g., farm and construction equipment), or some miscellaneous groups of workers (e.g., educational workers and maintenance workers).

Unions are administered at their national headquarters, but collective bargaining and organizing are often carried out by union locals individually or through councils of locals. Local size can range from a dozen workers to several thousand workers, and the local can be for a particular shop, office, or factory or for all of a union's members in a geographic area. There are approximately 33,000 union locals.

Labor unions are self-governing organizations with their own constitutions, elected officers, and conventions. Union constitutions have clauses specifying how members run for office or vote in officer elections, when and why conventions are held, and how membership dues are increased. Because unions should act as a voice for their members, they are expected to be run democratically. Union officers should be responsive to the will of the members, negotiating for what members want and letting them participate in running the union. Officers should be challenged in elections and voted out if they become autocratic.

Most unions affiliate with labor federations that coordinate their political and organizing activities and restrict rival organizing. The principal federation is the AFL-CIO (American Federation of Labor–Congress of Industrial Organizations), which was established in 1955 and has 53 affiliated unions with 9 million members. An alternative federation, Change to Win (7 affiliated unions with 6 million members) was formed in 2005 by officers of AFL-CIO affiliates who were dissatisfied with the federation's apparent inability to revive union growth.

Union Decline

There has been a severe and continuing decline in union membership. Since 1980, unions have lost 4.4 million members. Membership losses are the result of intense employer opposition, the time-consuming and expensive certification election process used by unions for organizing, and the inability or unwillingness of most unions to devote sufficient financial resources and staff for large-scale organizing.

Union density—the percentage of the labor force in unions—fell from 23% in 1980 to 13% in 2005. The proportion of private nongovernmental workers in unions dropped to approximately 8%. It is widely believed that it would be extremely difficult to reverse membership losses because the organizing task is so difficult and expensive. As employment declines at unionized firms, primarily because of globalization and the movement of production overseas, unions must offset membership losses through extensive new organizing. Unions need to organize roughly a half-million new members each year to offset losses. They must organize a million new members each year to raise union density by 1 percentage point. Because it costs unions nearly $2,000 to recruit each new member, unions would need to allocate one-third of their operating budgets to organizing merely to offset membership losses. Most unions devote approximately 5% of their budgets to organizing (the rest is used for bargaining and political activities), and only 250,000 workers are organized each year.

Minority and Immigrant Workers in Unions

The unionization rates are 11% for White workers, 15% for African American workers, 11% for Asian workers, and 10% for Hispanic workers. Unions have had a mixed relationship with minority and immigrant workers. Many early unions gave in to the wishes of their White members by ignoring or segregating African American and/or Asian workers or blocking them from entry into skilled and higher paying jobs. For example, in southern paper mills, there were often separate union locals for White and African American workers. African American workers were excluded from the best jobs and membership in most unions in the railroad and construction industries. The first union label (a symbol indicating that a product is union made) appeared in an 1872 union boycott of cigars made by nonunion Chinese workers.

But there have also been numerous positive cases. In the garment industry, unions were a powerful force for the assimilation of Eastern European Jews and Italian immigrants a century ago as well as for the assimilation of Mexican and Asian immigrants during recent decades. During the early years of the

20th century, the Industrial Workers of the World, a radical union, gained great notoriety for its skill in organizing diverse groups of immigrant workers at textile mills and mobilizing them for strikes; for example, in a 1912 strike in Lawrence, Massachusetts, the union led a group of 25,000 textile workers representing 25 different nationalities. During recent decades, the Hospital Workers Union has organized extensively among African American, Puerto Rican, and Filipina/o health care workers in large cities. The United Food and Commercial Workers organized low-paid minority workers at meatpacking plants and grocery chains, whereas the Service Employees International Union organized immigrant janitorial workers in urban areas. The United Farm Workers Union, founded by César Chávez, has always considered itself to be more of a social movement for the working poor than a traditional labor union, and it has organized extensively among Mexican American agricultural workers.

Unions now recognize that minority and immigrant workers are most in need of unionization to protect against job loss, substandard wages and working conditions, and arbitrary employer conduct. For example, unions from the AFL-CIO and Change to Win are forming alliances with advocacy groups ranging from associations of day laborers (many are minorities and immigrants) to community associations of Asian workers in the garment industry. The labor federations and their affiliated unions are prominent in demonstrations for the rights of undocumented immigrants, for universal health care, and for higher minimum wages.

Most unions now place a high priority on organizing minority and immigrant workers in their plans for revival. They consider such organizing vital if they are to present themselves as the voice of all workers and their families. Union leaders recognize that the only alternative to organizing and representing minority and immigrant workers is that of further decline.

Gary Chaison

See also African Americans; Assimilation; Chávez, César; Chinese Americans; Discrimination; Huerta, Dolores; Immigration, Economic Impact of; Jewish Americans; Mexican Americans; Ukrainian Americans

Further Readings

Chaison, Gary. 2006. *Unions in America.* Thousand Oaks, CA: Sage.
Chaison, Gary and Barbara Bigelow. 2002. *Unions and Legitimacy.* Ithaca, NY: Cornell University Press.
Milkman, Ruth and Kim Voss, eds. 2004. *Rebuilding Labor: Organizing and Organizers in the New Union Movement.* Ithaca, NY: Cornell University Press.
Ness, Immanuel. 2005. *Immigrants, Unions, and the New U.S. Labor Market.* Philadelphia, PA: Temple University Press.
Tait, Vanessa. 2005. *Poor Workers' Unions: Rebuilding Labor from Below.* Cambridge, MA: South End Press.
Wheeler, Hoyt. 2002. *The Future of the American Labor Movement.* New York: Cambridge University Press.

LAOTIAN AMERICANS

Laotian Americans' recent immigration has contributed to the heterogeneity of Asian American communities and the diversity of U.S. society. They arrived mostly as refugees, and thus the difficulties in their transition from life in an agricultural country to life in an industrialized one have placed Laotian Americans among the most disadvantaged of population groups. This entry briefly explores the nature of the contexts surrounding the experiences of Laotian Americans—their ethnically diverse population; their process of settlement, adjustment, and acculturation; their traditional values and culture; and the lives of Laotian Americans today.

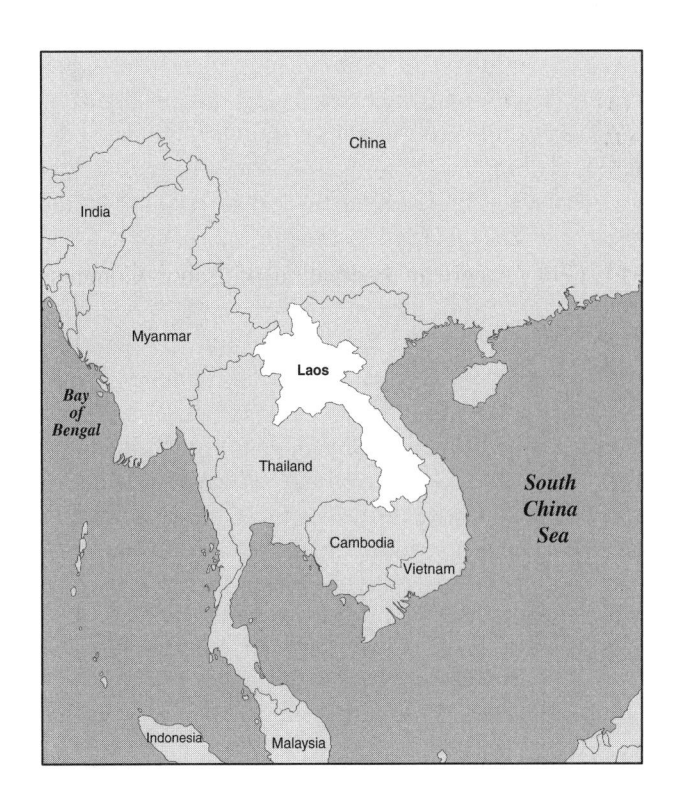

History of Laos

Laos is an underdeveloped country and home to an estimated 5.9 million people, as of 2007, who mostly practice subsistence agriculture. A mountainous country landlocked by Vietnam, Cambodia, Thailand, Myanmar (Burma), and China, it is home to an ethnically diverse population. Laos traces its history to the Kingdom of Lan Xang (or "Land of a Million Elephants"), which existed from the 14th to 18th centuries. The country has been ruled by competing monarchies and foreign powers such as Thailand, Japan, and France.

In 1954, Laos gained full independence with the end of France's colonial rule of Indochina; however, years of civil war ensued, and in 1975 the communist Pathet Lao regime took control of the country. Consequently, many Laotians sought refuge in neighboring Thailand and other countries, where they were placed in refugee camps. Through resettlement programs, many Laotians gained entry to the United States as refugees. Today, Lao People's Democratic Republic is founded as a socialist multiethnic nation.

Migration and Settlement

Laotian Americans' ethnic makeup is diverse, with ethnic groups that have their own distinct languages, beliefs, and cultural traditions. The three major subgroups are named after their traditional residence patterns: the lowlanders (Lao Loum, also referred to as Lao), the midlanders (Lao Theung), and the highlanders (Lao Soung). The lowlanders are the largest of the many ethnic groups and are linguistically and ethnically close to neighboring Thailand. The midlanders are considered to be of Austro-Asiatic (Mon-Khmer) origin and are regarded as the original inhabitants of Laos. They have the greatest cultural and linguistic differences, with groups including the Kmhmu, Lamet, Katang, Makong, Loven, and Lawae. The highlanders are considered an ethnic minority group and include the Hmong, Mien, Akha, and Lahu—all linguistically different. Indigenous to southern China, they migrated 200 years ago to escape Chinese oppression and have resided in the highlands of Laos as subsistence farmers practicing slash-and-burn cultivation. For the purpose of this entry, Laotian Americans include all people with roots in Laos, including Hmong Americans. However, statistics presented in this entry exclude Hmong Americans because data reported by the U.S. Census Bureau are separate for them.

Due to changes in immigration laws, the number of Asian Americans has increased greatly since the 1960s. The Indochina Migration and Refugee Assistance Act of 1975 opened the gate for the flow of migration of refugees from Vietnam, Cambodia, and Laos. Laotians were predominantly part of the second wave of refugees, who tended to be farmers and villagers and to be less educated and poorer than the first-wave immigrants. From 1979 to 1981, they arrived in great numbers—approximately 105,000.

Resettlement continued throughout the late 1980s and early 1990s, totaling more than 230,000 Laotians. This resettlement was also due to the U.S. family unification program, which allowed refugees already in the United States to sponsor their relatives. Many were resettled all over the country to prevent formation of ethnic enclaves and to minimize their impact on local communities. However, most were originally settled in California, and many later resettled in Minnesota, Texas, Wisconsin, and Washington because of the large Laotian American communities, job availability, lenient eligibility requirements for public assistance, and higher public assistance benefit levels in those states.

Today, most Laotian Americans live in large metropolitan areas in California, especially in the Central Valley (Sacramento, Stockton, and Fresno), San Diego, and San Francisco Bay areas. They have also formed large communities in Texas, Minnesota, Wisconsin, and Washington. Other communities are located in North Carolina, Georgia, Kansas, Illinois, Tennessee, Oregon, Ohio, Iowa, Florida, and Pennsylvania. According to the U.S. Census Bureau's *American Community Survey,* there are approximately 227,000 Laotian Americans who reported one or more ethnic designations.

Most Laotians are either one-and-one-half-generation Americans (individuals who immigrated to the United States before their early teens) or second-generation Americans. They account for 1.7% of the Asian American population in total. As a group, Laotian Americans are a young population, and in 1990 their median age was 20.4 years. According to the Immigration and Naturalization Service, approximately 84,000 Laotian Americans are naturalized as U.S. citizens. To date, as many as 31% of households are linguistically isolated.

Religion

The values, cultures, and religions of Laotians vary by their subgroups. Most Laotian Americans adhere to Theravada Buddhism, and the temple (*wat*) serves as an important center for spiritual, social, and cultural needs of the community. A significant number of Laotian Americans have been converted to Christianity owing to the influence of early Western missionaries and have established Lao churches, which also serve as community centers. Animist religions, shamans, and spirit practitioners are seen among some Laotian Americans, who believe that inanimate objects and natural phenomena have souls. Despite different faiths, Laotian Americans come together during the Lao New Year (Pi Mai) in mid-April, funerals, and the traditional Baci-Sou Khuan ceremony.

The traditional Baci-Sou Khuan ceremony is celebrated to maintain the balance of good relationships between individuals and their neighbors. Laotians continue to respect the spirits and believe that in each person there are thirty-two spirits that are linked to cause health, happiness, and prosperity. A lack of any of these spirits can cause depression, illness, and disease in an individual. The purpose of the ceremony is to promote recovery of the individual by calling back the spirits that have left a person's body. The ceremony is performed by an elder male, usually one who is respected in the community. During the ceremony, an offering plate of food and the tying of cotton strings around the wrist of the person for whom the ceremony is being held represent a blessing by the well-wisher.

Family and Kinship

Many Laotian Americans have retained values and traditions brought with them from their homeland. The family relationships are arranged in a nuclear family, and extended families often live in the same house or within close proximity for social and financial support. The attachment to the family, home, and community is seen as a stable and integrated whole of Laotian Americans' traditional values. Women are important decision makers within the household and manage the family's finances. The husband or oldest male heads the home and family, and elders are given great respect. Laotian American children are expected to respect and care for their parents.

The changing dynamics of family have created tensions in the home. Although women are gaining independence and joining the workforce to contribute financially to the family's income, one-and-one-half- and second-generation Laotian Americans are acquiring power in the family by learning English and becoming familiar with U.S. society and culture. They are called on as translators or interpreters for family interactions outside of the home. Inevitably, some traditional parental authority over one's children is lost with this role reversal as children undertake adult responsibilities.

Process of Adjustment

As second-wave refugees, most Laotians started their lives in the United States in poverty and were dependent on the U.S. welfare system. However, the community has built its own organizations and social programs throughout metropolitan centers to provide a variety of services, including job training and placement, youth services, English-language tutoring, citizenship classes, health care services, and psychological counseling. Compared with other Southeast Asian ethnic groups, Laotians have the highest percentage of people on public assistance, with one of every three Laotians living below the poverty line and receiving government assistance income. They remain one of the poorest Asian ethnic groups in the United States, with a poverty rate of approximately 19.1% and a median per capita income of less than $12,000.

Furthermore, according to the 2000 U.S. Census, 22.7% of Laotians age 25 years or older in the United States had no formal schooling, 50.5% graduated from high school, 26% had some college, and 7.6% held a bachelor's degree or higher. As noted earlier, lack of formal education among Laotian immigrants is attributable to their agrarian background, with little or no access to schools.

It is difficult to predict the future course of Laotian Americans' assimilation and acculturation given that they are recent members of U.S. society. However, one-and-one-half- and second-generation Laotian Americans are seeking educational attainment and immigrant adaptation by maintaining a positive outlook to attain self-reliance. They are a dynamic and rapidly growing community, creating visibility through education and becoming active participants as students, professionals, and community leaders.

Davorn Sisavath

See Appendix A
See also Acculturation; Asian Americans; Assimilation; Hmong Americans; Immigration, U.S.; Refugees

Further Readings

Bankston, Carl L. 1995. "Who Are the Laotian Americans?" Pp. 131–142 in *The Asian American Almanac,* edited by Susan Gall and Irene Natividad. Detroit, MI: Gale Research.

Caplan, Nathan, John K. Whitmore, and Marcella H. Choy. 1989. *The Boat People and Achievement in America: A Study of Family Life and Cultural Values.* Ann Arbor: University of Michigan Press.

Haines, David W., ed. 1989. *Refugees as Immigrants: Cambodians, Laotians, and Vietnamese in America.* Totowa, NJ: Rowman & Littlefield.

Hein, Jeremy. 1995. *From Vietnam, Laos, and Cambodia: A Refugee Experience in the United States.* New York: Twayne.

Kunstadter, Peter, ed. 1967. *Southeast Asian Tribes, Minorities, and Nations.* Vol. 1. Princeton, NJ: Princeton University Press.

Mansfield, Stephen. 1997. *Culture Shock! A Guide to Customs and Etiquette: Laos.* Portland, OR: Graphic Arts Center.

Ngaosyvathn, Mayoury. 1990. "Individual Soul, National Identity: The Baci-Sou Khuan of the Lao." *Journal of Social Issues in Southeast Asia* 5:283–307.

Proudfoot, Robert. 1990. *Even the Birds Don't Sound the Same Here: The Laotian Refugees Search for Heart in American Culture.* New York: Peter Lang.

Rumbaut, Ruben G. 1995. "A Legacy of War: Refugees from Vietnam, Laos, and Cambodia." Pp. 315–333 in *Origins and Destinies: Immigration, Race, and Ethnicity in America,* edited by Ruben Rumbaut and Silvia Pedraza. Belmont, CA: Wadsworth.

Tenhula, John. 1991. *Voices from Southeast Asia: The Refugee Experience in the United States.* New York: Holmes & Meier.

LA RAZA

La Raza translates literally to "the race," but a more accurate or colloquial translation is "the people." The term *la raza cósmica* (the cosmic race) was coined by Mexican scholar and politician José Vasconcelos to refer to the mixing of the races and, consequently, to the birth of a new race, *latinoamericanos* (Latin Americans). According to Vasconcelos, over time various races mix with one another to form a new type of human.

La Raza was used sparingly prior to the 1960s, but during the 1960s political activists, especially Chicano movement activists, used the term increasingly to refer to themselves and other people of Latin American descent who shared the cultural and political legacies of Spanish conquest and colonialism and U.S. imperialism and internal colonialism. The term is similar to the panethnic terms *Latino* and *Hispanic* insofar as all three refer to the same group, although *raza* has been used, and continues to be used, more narrowly by some to refer solely to people of Mexican descent. The term retains some of the racial significance associated with Vasconcelos's use of the term in that it captures the "mestizo" character of Latinos—a people of indigenous, African, and European descent.

Criticized by some as a term that promotes separatism or even racism, La Raza was employed, and continues to be employed, by political and community activists principally to promote political unity and cultural pride among Latinas/os. La Raza harkens back to and acknowledges the contributions of advanced pre-Columbian civilizations to the Americas and the indigenous roots of present-day Latinas/os, or *la raza.* The concept places as much importance on these indigenous and African roots as it does on the European roots of Latin Americans, thereby celebrating, rather than denigrating, the mixed origins and identity of Latinas/os in the United States. It is a form of "Brown pride," similar to the "Black is beautiful" slogan of the Black Power movement in the United States, and like the Black Power slogan, it has been used to mobilize people into collective action. A common placard among protesters reads *El Pueblo Unido, Jamas Sera Vencido* ("The People United Will Never Be Defeated"). Often *La Raza Unida* is substituted for *El Pueblo Unido.*

Columbus Day is celebrated on the second Monday in October in the United States, but *El Dia de la Raza,* either combined with or in place of Columbus Day, is celebrated on October 12 in most of Latin America, principally as a celebration of the birth of a new people, or *raza,* and not as a tribute to the explorer. The history of the conquest or "discovery" and the subsequent centuries of exploitation and bloodshed are well known, and for this reason many Latin Americans and Latinas/os in the United States do not celebrate Columbus Day as a day of discovery. For many indigenous people, it is a day of mourning. Millions of their ancestors were slaughtered or died from diseases borne by the European conquerors. But despite this history and distortions of this history, Latin Americans and Latinas/os are a product of that history, and they and their cultures reflect the fusing of these populations. This is what is celebrated on *El Dia de la Raza.*

A number of organizations have adopted *raza* in their names, including the National Council of La Raza, the largest Latino civil rights and advocacy organization in the United States. Ethnic studies departments and community centers have adopted *La Raza* in their names, and in 1970 the La Raza Unida party was created to give a stronger political voice to Chicanas/os in the United States. The party enjoyed limited success in challenging the two major parties, but it instilled ethnic pride and promoted political activism in the Chicano community. The term and what it embodies contributed to a renaissance in Chicano and Latino art, theater, and literature, and it continues to inspire a sense of unity and purpose among many Latinos.

Héctor L. Delgado

See also Alamo, The; Black Power; Chicano Movement; Hispanics; La Raza Unida Party; Latin America, Indigenous People; Latina/o Studies; Panethnic Identity

Further Readings

Gonzales, Manuel G. 1999. *Mexicanos: A History of Mexicans in the United States.* Bloomington: Indiana University Press.

Muñoz, Carlos, Jr. 1989. *Youth, Identity, and Power: The Chicano Movement.* London: Verso.

Vasconcelos, José. 1997. *The Cosmic Race/La Raza Cósmica,* translated by Didier T. Jaén. Baltimore, MD: Johns Hopkins University Press.

La Raza Unida Party

The La Raza Unida party was founded in Crystal City, Texas, located in the southeastern portion of the state approximately forty miles from the Mexico–Texas border. This locale and the emergence of the party played an important role in the long struggle of Chicanas/os (persons of Mexican origin) against racism, discrimination, and inequality, as shown in this entry.

Crystal City Background

The roots of Crystal City extend back to 1884, when the first artesian well was discovered in the area. During the early part of the 20th century, Whites migrated to the region and transformed the economy from ranching to farming. The native Mexican-origin population became essential to the development of farming in the region. Thus, White farmers, despite their deep animosities toward Mexicans, saw them as a limitless source of cheap labor. With the proliferation of farming, Mexicans—who where clearly marked as a subordinate racial group—continued to migrate to Crystal City so that by 1930 Crystal City's population was majority Mexican.

Even though Mexican Americans constituted the overwhelming majority of Crystal City residents, Whites had controlled the city—its political and educational systems—since its inception. However, in the early 1960s, this Texas town witnessed a complete turnover from an all-White to an all–Mexican American city council. The 56-year White leadership ended when five Mexican Americans, known as *Los Cinco,* won in 1963. Their sweeping victory was fueled by the long history of discrimination and oppression in Crystal City.

Jose Angel Gutierrez, a nineteen-year-old Crystal City high school student at the time, later founded La Raza Unida Party. Although many claimed there was no discrimination, he says, one had only to look around to know the truth. *Los Cinco*'s reign was short-lived and struggled against many challenges, including retaliation from the entrenched power structure. Nonetheless, although Whites regained power, the success of *Los Cinco* aided in the formation of the political consciousness of the Mexican Americans of Crystal City.

The Chicano Movement

During the 1960s, a significant social change took place in U.S. politics. The Civil Rights Movement stimulated similar activities in the United States, including the Chicano movement. The goals of the movement included ethnic pride, autonomy, and the improvement of the standing of the Chicano community. It was during this era that the terms *Chicano* and *Chicana,* which connote a cultural identity of pride associated with the group's indigenous roots, were popularized. Events surrounding the Chicano movement provided the social and political context for the rise of the La Raza Unida party.

Crystal City and its native son, Gutierrez, took center stage in the development of the party and the building of Chicana/o political muscle. Even though Chicanas/os comprised 85% of the population of the city, they did not hold political or school administration offices after the short-lived victory of *Los Cinco.* Young Chicanas/os faced similar treatment within the schools. For example, custom dictated that the high school's cheerleading squad be made up of four White females and one Chicana, a rule established by the

White power structure. When a qualified Chicana was bypassed in favor of two less qualified White girls, the student body clearly saw the system of discrimination that Chicana/o students were forced to endure. Given the increasing political consciousness of Chicanas/os in the community, many students and parents took their grievances to the school board. The group was assisted by Gutierrez, who was now the president of the Mexican American Youth Organization (MAYO) at St. Mary's University in San Antonio, Texas.

The group achieved some temporary progress, but tensions rose with a "grandfather clause" that limited the competition for homecoming queen to those who had at least one parent who had graduated from Crystal City High School, a policy that clearly disadvantaged Chicanas/os. Severita Lara, a student, was suspended when she distributed flyers pointing out the injustice of this policy. With the help of Gutierrez, the aggrieved students got their parents to join in the revolt.

The school board claimed that allegations of discrimination were unfounded and dismissed the Chicano group's request for an end to such practices. Then the aggrieved students replicated what had been done in Elsa, Texas, in 1968—the "walkout." Students and parents united to execute these walkout protests. The students employed these peaceful actions to address the public school system's injustices. On the first day, 500 students marched, and by the second day, one-third of the student body was absent from school. The school board eventually gave in to the students' demands for equality.

From this mobilization, Gutierrez went on to form the La Raza Unida party and become one of the major figures of the Chicano movement in the country.

The Party and Its Legacy

The La Raza Unida party was established on January 17, 1972, in Crystal City. Chicanas/os were dissatisfied with the Democratic and Republican parties; La Raza Unida was a third party—one that represented the interests of the Chicano community. The party achieved significant successes in Crystal City and other selected communities of south Texas, with chapters emerging in numerous other states as well.

During the early 1970s, La Raza Unida party members won political offices, including representation on school boards. The party ran Ramsey Muniz as its candidate in the 1972 Texas gubernatorial election. Although Muniz did not win, he received a significant number of votes that nearly cost Democrats the election. Chicanas were also crucial to the development of the political party. For example, Alma Canales, from Edinburg, Texas, was nominated to run for lieutenant governor of the state in 1972. The high point for the party occurred at its first national convention in September 1972 in El Paso, Texas.

Toward the middle and end of the 1970s, as the national political pendulum swung to the right, the La Raza Unida party was challenged with internal conflicts and began to fragmentize. In 1978, the party lost its legal status by failing to receive the required 2% of the total vote in that year's gubernatorial election. Nonetheless, the party had confronted the power structure and left an important legacy—the social and political awareness of the racial oppression of Chicanas/os.

Carlos Siordia and Rogelio Saenz

See also Chicano Movement; *La Raza;* Mexican Americans; Voting Rights

Further Readings

Barrera, James B. 2004. "The 1968 Edcouch–Elsa High School Walkout: Chicano Student Activism in a South Texas Community." *Aztlán* 29:93–122.

Chávez, Ernesto. 2002. *Mi Raza Primero! Nationalism, Identity, and Insurgency in the Chicano Movement.* Berkeley: University of California Press.

Garcia, Ignacio M. 1989. *United We Win: The Rise and Fall of La Raza Unida Party.* Tucson: University of Arizona, Mexican American Studies Research Center.

Goodwyn, Larry. 1963. "Los Cinco Candidatos." *Texas Observer,* April 18, pp. 3–9.

Gutierrez, Jose Angel. 1999. *The Making of a Chicano Militant: Lessons from Cristal.* Madison: University of Wisconsin Press.

Gutierrez, Jose Angel and Rebecca E. Deen. 2000. "Chicanas in Texas Politics." Occasional Paper No. 66, Julian Samora Research Institute, Michigan State University.

Handbook of Texas Online. 2007. *Raza Unida Party.* Austin: University of Texas at Austin. Retrieved from http://www.tsha.utexas.edu/handbook/online/articles/RR/war1.html

Marquez, Benjamin and Rodolfo Espino. 2002. "The Origins and Impact of Mexican American Support for Third-Party Candidates: The Case of La Raza Unida in the 1972 Texas Gubernatorial Election." Presented at the annual meeting of the American Political Science Association, Boston.

Muñoz, Carlos. 1989. *Youth, Identity, Power: The Chicano Movement.* New York: Verso Books.

Navarro, Armando. 2000. *La Raza Unida Party: A Chicano Challenge to the U.S. Two-Party Dictatorship.* Philadelphia: Temple University Press.

Rivera, George, Jr. 1972. "Nosotros Venceremos: Chicano Consciousness and Change Strategies." *Journal of Applied Behavioral Science* 8:56–71.

Shockley, John S. 1974. *Chicano Revolt in a Texas Town.* Notre Dame, IN: Notre Dame University Press.

Trujillo, Armando. 2005. "Politics, School Philosophy, and Language Policy: The Case of Crystal City Schools." *Educational Policy* 19:621–654.

LATIN AMERICA, INDIGENOUS PEOPLE

The terms *indigenous, native,* and *Indian* emerge from the colonial experience but at the same time are very much a part of modernity and postmodernity. On their arrival in Latin America, conquering European forces of the 16th through 20th centuries imposed this single identity on vastly diverse groups of peoples with their own histories, practices, problems, and conflicts. Even today, the term *Maya,* referring to descendants of preconquest populations throughout much of contemporary southern Mexico, Guatemala, Honduras, El Salvador, and Belize, incorporates no less than twelve distinct groups, many with mutually indistinguishable languages. Since conquest, the meanings inherent in the *indigenous* moniker have been heavily weighted through multiple forms of actions, policies, and dialogues, although always under conditions of domination by groups of European descent.

During the past 20 years, massive popular mobilizations indicate that the indigenous populations of Latin America are acquiring the full rights of citizenship, parallel to the accomplishments of the 1960s Civil Rights Movement in the United States. These new mobilizations, based significantly on indigenous identity and rights, emerged from populations long regarded as heavily subjugated and politically marginal. Where did these mass movements come from? How are they changing society? How is this related to the larger changes of globalization? This entry outlines the historic struggles over the meaning of *indigenous* to address these contemporary questions.

The European Conquest

At the time of conquest, the most high-profile groups were the Mixtec (Aztecs) of central Mexico and the Tawantinsuyo (Incas) of the central Andes. These groups are particularly famous because they had recently engaged in local conquest and had established empires of their own. Although many argue that the Aztec Empire was in precipitous decline by the time Hernando Cortez and his small cavalry arrived, the ability of the small invading Spanish fleet to quickly overcome these battle-hardened peoples derived in no small part from the ruling strategy of the Aztecs. By creating discord and animosity between conquered groups, the Aztecs dominated but also created bitter local enemies willing to unite under an invading force with the vastly superior military technology of horses, steel, and gunpowder.

In 1532, Francisco Pizarro followed Cortez's example, uniting parts of an Andean population highly divided by a civil war most likely precipitated by the spread of European diseases. Both conquerors seated themselves at the head of the defeated empire, using their positions to indulge their seemingly unquenchable gold lust. In the genocidal violence that followed initial contact, the Spanish tried to repeat this strategy of placing themselves in the most advantageous position of already existing social structures so as to extract the maximum amount of labor and resources from the native populations.

Beyond superior technology, however, the Catholic Spaniards needed to morally justify their conquering actions to themselves. Notions of universal human equality were then emerging out of the European Enlightenment, which seemingly contradicted the bloody actions and policies of the new colonies, a point made by some European dissenters of the time such as Bartolomé de las Casas. To address this predicament, Europeans ruled that all natives were subhuman and, therefore, needed the enlightened guidance of European masters. For this reason, many journals of conquistadores show the Spanish praising God after they have mercilessly slaughtered the entire population of an indigenous village.

By royal decree, natives faced a choice of either converting to Christianity or being put to the sword even if they did not understand the language in which the proclamation was read or its terms. This supposed indigenous "biological inferiority" (to use current parlance) has informed social relations in Latin America ever since, with natives incorporated into the various states as wards to be looked after rather than as citizens with full rights and the ability to participate in creating and enforcing the institutions and laws that govern them.

Aztec Indian children in Mexico (1910). The term Aztec, originally associated with the migrant Mexica, is today used as a collective term that is applied to all the peoples linked to these founders by trade, custom, religion, and language. During the past 20 years, massive popular mobilizations indicate that many of the indigenous populations throughout Latin America are acquiring the full rights of citizenship, parallel to the accomplishments of the 1960s Civil Rights Movement in the United States.

Source: Library of Congress, Prints & Photographs Division, LC-USZ62-9967.

The Conquered Groups

The native populations were highly diverse in their cultural practices and forms of social organization. Indeed, prior to conquest, the Incas had never successfully overcome the groups in the lowland jungle areas and regarded them as uncivilized. The major groups of this time—the Incas, Aztecs, and Mayas—had created vast cities, many of which rivaled or even surpassed those in Europe in terms of the differentiation and specialization of activities of the populace. Much of the population of these empires, however, lived in villages of distinct ethnic origins over which the dominant group ruled through acts of colonization and theocratic sway. Prior to conquest, many vast city-states had emerged through agricultural domestication and centralized religion and later declined through the twin processes of warfare and natural resource depletion. Tiwanaku in contemporary Bolivia, Teotihuacán in Mexico, Tikal in Guatemala, and Huari in Peru are but a few examples.

Large populations also lived throughout the vast territories of the Americas. Swidden (slash-and-burn) agriculture was widely practiced throughout the Amazon basin and other lowland jungle areas. Human settlements tended to be much less centralized under these conditions, with families rotating their fields and homes over large territories of land, across long periods of time. Jungle areas proved to be particularly resilient to Spanish conquest, with horses and cannons having difficulty in engaging a population scattered through forests and not predisposed to exploitation through already belonging to an empire or a federation. But the European hunger for wealth seemed to be an inexhaustible resource, driving the colonizing forces into most corners of the New World.

Paternalistic European rule was redolent with strife and conflict. The drive to extract resources and native labor reduced the indigenous populations by approximately 97%, with this "great dying" representing the most genocidal period on the planet. From its nadir during the 18th century, the population levels of the Americas did not recover until the second half of the 20th century. Native groups continually attempted to resist these policies, generally forced to choose between the extremes of "weapons of the weak" and militaristic uprisings. Many millenarian cults, such as Taki Onqoy in Peru, envisioned an "inevitable" disappearance of Europeans, providing practitioners with an alternative framework around which to organize their lives. Uprisings were also common, ranging from highly localized scuffles against draconian overlords to near revolutionary movements sweeping up large territories. Some of the more famous of these include Tupac Amaru and Tupac Katari in late-18th-century Peru and Bolivia and the Caste War in 19th-century Yucatan, Mexico.

Native discontent frequently focused on land in terms of who controlled it and how it was controlled. Since conquest, people of European descent have dominated through a system of "indirect rule" in which local overlords have been granted authoritarian powers in exchange for managing local discontent. These state proxies have largely governed through mixing patronage with sowing divisions. Rather than quelling local restiveness, these overlords used the resources they controlled to redirect discontent against other partsof the indigenous populations. In this way, natives remained divided against themselves, beholden to powerful patrons, and the overall situation remained highly volatile. Natives almost always immediately directed their militancy against these local strongman figures, particularly in their hoarding of land resources or their ability to circumscribe native control. Larger movements tended to be based on these same grievances writ large such as the globally minded Zapatistas, whose primary complaints focused on local despots.

Recent Movements

The processes of conquest and colonization continued overtly until the independence movements at the beginning of the 19th century. Indeed, Europeans did not bring to heel the more recalcitrant populations, such as the Mapuche and the Apache, until the 20th century. Government reforms starting in the mid-20th century were intended to alter the land-based system of patronage by redistributing land to the native populations (although this did not occur in all countries). Many of these changes, however, were embedded in assimilationist policies. The state granted lands to native peoples based on their use of the land as small-scale farmers (peasants) rather than on their ancestral claims. State officials deliberately changed legal categories from "native" to "peasant." Although they saw the former as "racist," their actions ironically stripped indigenous groups of their legal claims to the lands their peoples had historically controlled; the indigenous groups were peasants—not natives—and so had no patrimonial claims.

The racism of previous centuries persisted through these policies, with natives still seen as a barrier to progress and needing to be assimilated so as to achieve "modernization." Furthermore, Indigenous Peoples generally did not achieve citizenship through these policies but rather acquired a new patron in the form of the state and its bureaucrats. These reforms, however, were generally responses to widespread popular mobilizations through which subaltern populations acquired rich experiences in networking and political action.

At least by the 1980s, however, marginalized groups throughout the Americas began mobilizing for various forms of inclusive citizenship based on the central assertion of the validity of native cultures. As this entry has shown, such practices were not vestiges from preconquest times but rather customs that had been reformed and reshaped as "indigenous" during the previous centuries. These movements generally demand different forms of control over their ancestral land, much of which has been stripped from them. Whereas groups such as the Zapatistas in Mexico demand nearly total autonomous control, other groups, such as COCEI (Coalición Obrero Campesino Estudiantil del Istmo) in Oaxaca are willing to undertake power-sharing agreements.

The policies of neoliberal globalization prove to be particularly threatening to native peoples, opening their resource base to exploitation by multinational corporations while removing traditional protections such as corporate rights to lands. These threats have helped to spur much of the population to nationwide mobilizations, aided considerably by the abilities to network nationally and internationally. At the same time, however, neoliberalism's embrace of multiculturalism also threatens to diffuse native demands by recognizing their cultural claims but not their economic claims; dominant groups generally no longer view native cultures as barriers to modernization but condemn redress of historic wrongs as "reverse racism." In addition, the parallels between indigenous calls for autonomy and neoliberalism's emphasis on political decentralization have tended to weaken indigenous calls for economic redistribution in favor of regressive market-based policies aided by the power of transnational organizations (e.g., the World Bank, Chevron) coupled with the long history of localized authoritarianism. As such, native movements have suffered a serious weakening and realignment, and the prospect for inclusive citizenship remains elusive.

Arthur Scarritt

See Appendix A; Appendix B
See also Belize; Colonialism; Internal Colonialism; Mexico; Native Americans; Peru; Zapatista Rebellion

Further Readings

Hale, Charles R. 2006. *Mas Que un Indio.* Santa Fe, NM: School of American Research Press.

Nelson, Diane. 1999. *A Finger in the Wound.* Berkeley: University of California Press.

Postero, Nancy Grey and Leon Zamosc. 2004. *The Struggle for Indigenous Rights in Latin America.* Portland, OR: Sussex Academic Press.

Wolf, Eric R. 1982. *Europe and the People without History.* Berkeley: University of California Press.

Yashar, Deborah J. 2005. *Contesting Citizenship in Latin America.* New York: Cambridge University Press.

Latina/o Studies

Latina/o Studies typically refers to Latina/o Studies programs in educational institutions, but it can also refer to a body of knowledge on and alternative approaches to the study of Latinos and Latinas in the United States. Although Latina/o Studies as a body of knowledge is more than a century old, Latina/o Studies *programs* are of a more recent vintage. Latina/o Studies can refer to programs focusing on Latinos and Latinas broadly or collectively to more specific programs such as Chicana/o Studies, Puerto Rican Studies, Dominican Studies, Cuban Studies, and Central American Studies. All of these programs were created only within the past 40 years. This entry looks at research about Latinos and Latinas and at academic programs that help to enlarge and disseminate this body of knowledge.

Research and Writing

It is difficult to pinpoint the exact age of Latino Studies. If we include memoirs from the Mexican–American War and the second half of the 19th century, for example, Chicano Studies is roughly 150 years old. During the early 1900s, labor economist Paul Taylor conducted research on Mexican Americans in the Southwest and other locales, including Chicago, where Robert Redfield, the noted anthropologist, conducted fieldwork on Mexican *colonias* during the 1920s. The work of Mexican archaeologist Manuel Gamio during the 1930s on the migration to and work in the United States by Mexican immigrants also contributed to this nascent body of research, as did the work of folklorist Aurelio Espinosa, Jr. in New Mexico and Colorado during the first half of the 20th century. George I. Sánchez made important contributions, both as a scholar and as an activist, in the area of Mexican Americans and education.

Sociologist Julian Samora conducted pioneering work in Mexican American Studies and participated in the creation of the Mexican American Legal Defense and Educational Fund (MALDEF) and the Southwest Voter Registration and Education Project. As a professor at Notre Dame University, he created the Mexican Border Studies Project and mentored generations of Latino graduate students. He wrote several books, but perhaps the best known is his classic *Los Mojados: The Wetback Story*. The Julian Samora Research Institute at Michigan State University was named in his honor.

Perhaps no scholar is linked more closely to the genesis of Chicano or Mexican American Studies than Américo Paredes, an English and anthropology professor at the University of Texas at Austin. His contributions to the Latino Studies literature, including his groundbreaking book *With His Pistol in His Hand: A Border Ballad and Its Hero,* and to the creation of Latino Studies programs were enormous. He cofounded the Center for Intercultural Studies of Folklore and Ethnomusicology in 1967 and fought to create a Mexican American Studies program at the University of Texas at Austin a few years later.

Other trailblazers in the creation and development of Chicano Studies included Rodolfo Acuña, Juan Gómez-Quiñones, Jesús Chavarria, Tomás Rivera, and Luis Leal. Other Latino Studies programs had their own trailblazers, including Frank Bonilla and Juan Flores in Puerto Rican Studies; Ruth Behar, Lisandro Perez, Alejandro Portes, Silvia Pedraza, and Eliana Rivero in Cuban Studies; and Silvio Torres-Saillant, Ramona Hernández, Sherri Grasmuck, and Patricia R. Pessar in Dominican Studies.

Although the road for women into scholarly circles was difficult to travel because of a long history of sexism in the academy and Latino communities, today women are among the top scholars in Latino Studies and other disciplines. In addition to the women already mentioned, these scholars include Marta Tienda, Vicki Ruiz, Ruth Zambrana, Beatriz Pesquera, Adela de la Torre, Edna Acosta-Belen, Norma Alarcon, Denise Segura, Sandra Cisneros, and Judith Ortiz Cofer.

Latino Studies is interdisciplinary in its approach to the study of Latinas/os in the United States. Latino Studies scholars study virtually every facet of Latino life and experience. The individuals mentioned in this entry represent many disciplines, including sociology, history, anthropology, political science, the arts, and literature. Latino Studies, of course, has the widest breadth of all these programs, but even programs that focus on a particular group (e.g., Mexican American Studies) typically compare "their" group not only with other Latinos but also with other minority groups and the majority population.

This body of knowledge, beginning early in the 20th century, contributed to the movement that eventually gave birth to academic programs in Latino Studies. Interest in Latino Studies is not confined solely to Latina/o scholars and students. Non-Latino scholars have made important contributions to this literature, and growing numbers of graduate students who are not Latino are drawn to the study of Latinos in the United States.

Academic Programs

The earliest Latino Studies programs were born from political struggles on college campuses during the 1960s as a response to Latino students' demands for a curriculum that recognized their history and culture, increases in Latino student enrollments and retention, and the hiring of Latino faculty members and administrators. Latino Studies programs sought to fill a gap left by traditional disciplines that, in the opinion of Latino Studies scholars and students, either ignored or misrepresented the histories and cultures of Mexican Americans, Puerto Ricans, Central Americans, and other Latino groups in the United States. These programs did this principally with faculty members who offered courses specifically on these groups and wrote books and published articles in journals on Latinos in the United States.

Some of these scholars established journals in Latino Studies, including *Aztlán: A Journal of Chicano Studies* and *Centro: Journal of the Center for Puerto Rican Studies,* usually in response to traditional journals' reluctance or refusal to publish articles submitted by Latino scholars. Today, articles on Latinos can be found in most mainstream academic journals, and books on Latinos are published by most of the major publishing houses.

Chicano/Mexican American Studies

The first Chicano Studies program was established at California State University, Los Angeles, in 1968 after sustained pressure by Chicano students, but especially by the United Mexican American Students (UMAS). A year later, a Chicano Studies department was established at California State University, Northridge (at the time it was called San Fernando Valley State College) after heated confrontations between protesters and the institution's administration. Others followed.

Today there are Chicano or Mexican American Studies programs or departments in many states, including Minnesota, Wisconsin, and Michigan. Most Chicano Studies programs, however, are found in the Southwest, where the bulk of the Chicano or Mexican American population resides. Key events in the creation and proliferation of Chicano Studies were the Denver Youth Conference in Denver, Colorado, and a conference in Santa Barbara, California, in 1969. At the Santa Barbara conference, a document, *El Plan de Santa Bárbara* (as it became known), called for, among other things, the creation of Chicano Studies programs with both academic and community foci.

Chicano Studies has evolved over the years in response to both internal and external challenges and debates. Internally, there have been epistemological debates and challenges by Chicana feminists to the male-centric character of the new discipline. Most Chicano and Latino Studies programs now have both female and male faculty members, who offer courses and write on the experiences of Chicanas/Latinas and on the role of gender in virtually every facet of Latino life. Externally, many in the academy challenged the legitimacy of the new discipline, charging that it was more political than academic in character, and often tried to prevent the creation of new programs or to undermine existing ones.

Chicano Studies weathered these and other storms, some of which still rage on, and today is credited, both directly and indirectly, for contributing new approaches to the study of and knowledge about Latinos, the fastest growing population in the United States; increasing the number of Chicana/o and Latina/o faculty members, administrators, and students on college campuses; and helping to train scores of Latina/o scholars, intellectuals, and professionals.

Puerto Rican Studies Programs

Most Puerto Rican Studies programs and departments are located in the northeastern part of the United States. In 1969, the Board of Higher Education of the City University of New York (CUNY), in response to student and community demands, announced its support for Black and Puerto Rican Studies programs. Programs were created in the CUNY system and eventually in adjoining states and the Midwest. These programs focus principally on the Puerto Rican diaspora but on Puerto Rico as well given that Puerto Ricans on the island are U.S. citizens and have been since 1917.

Furthermore, an understanding of the Puerto Rican experience in the United States requires knowledge of the island and the relationship between the island and the continental United States. The political status of the island is an issue at the heart of many discussions, both academic and nonacademic, on the island and in the continental United States.

Puerto Rican Studies programs offer courses on other Latino groups, such as Dominicans, Mexicans, and Cubans, in response to significant demographic changes in the Latino population in the Northeast. One of the oldest programs in the CUNY system changed its name to the Department of Latin American and Hispanic Caribbean Studies. Puerto Rican/Latino Studies is a "sequence" in Hunter College's (CUNY) Department of Africana and Puerto Rican/Latino Studies and includes the study of Puerto Rico, the Dominican Republic, and Cuba specifically, and the Caribbean generally, in addition to the study of Puerto Ricans in the continental United States.

In fact, a number of institutions have moved toward syntheses of Latino and Latin American Studies. In addition to Puerto Rican Studies departments, several research centers or institutes were created. The best known and oldest of these is El Centro de Estudios Puertorriqueños, located on the Hunter College campus. The center's mission is to collect and preserve archival and library resources about the history and culture of Puerto Ricans and to produce and disseminate interdisciplinary research about the experiences of Puerto Ricans in the diaspora, linking scholarly inquiry to social action. The center collaborates and participates in exchange programs with scholars and institutions in Puerto Rico and other Latin American countries.

Cuban, Dominican, and Central American Studies Programs

Although Puerto Rican, Chicano, and Latino Studies programs often include the study of Cubans, Dominicans, and Central Americans in the United States, these groups have formed separate programs as well. Cuban Studies programs, sometimes housed in Latin American and Caribbean Studies programs, were created to study Cuban politics and the Cuban exile to and presence in the United States. Cuban Studies programs are offered at several institutions, including the Institute of Cuban and Cuban American Studies at the University of Miami and the Cuban and Caribbean Studies Institute at Tulane University.

The Center for Cuban Studies in New York City is one of the oldest programs in the United States. The center was created in 1972 by scholars, writers, and other professionals who wanted to improve relations between the United States and Cuba. The scholarly journal *Cuban Studies* was founded in 1970 and since 1985 has been published in English and Spanish by the University of Pittsburgh Press.

Dominican Studies and Central American Studies are the newest programs. In 2000, California State University, Northridge, created the first Central American Studies program and minor. The Chicano Studies department and the Central American United Student Association (CAUSA) played important roles in the creation of the program, which focuses on Central Americans in the United States and the relationship between the United States and Central American countries. Half of the Central American population in the United States lives in the Los Angeles area.

Another rapidly growing segment of the Latino population is Dominicans. In 2004, CUNY instituted a bachelor of arts degree program in Dominican Studies, and in 1994 it had already established the Dominican Studies Institute (DSI) as a research unit of the institution. The Council of Dominican Educators group played the most important part in the creation of the institute, but the Dominican community played an important role as well. The institute, in turn, maintains close ties with the Dominican community, whose population will surpass—if it has not already surpassed—that of the Puerto Rican community in New York City.

Although resistance to Latino Studies programs persists, it is more muted than it was during the early years of these programs. These are young programs by academic standards, but they have managed to carve out niches in their home institutions, and many have finally been accepted in the academy. On many campuses, faculty members hold joint appointments in traditional departments and Latino Studies programs. The rapid growth and economic importance of Latino populations in the United States have given a boost to these programs and departments, as evidenced by the new programs and the growing number of scholars from a wide range of fields studying these groups. The current and future impact of Latinos on the economy, education, and politics requires serious study, and Latino Studies programs are likely to take the lead.

Héctor L. Delgado

See also Central Americans in the United States; Chicano Movement; Cuban Americans; Dominican Americans; *La Raza;* Mexican Americans; Puerto Rican Americans; Samora, Julian

Further Readings

Butler, Johnnella E., ed. 2001. *Color-Line to Borderlands: The Matrix of American Ethnic Studies.* Seattle: University of Washington Press.

Cabán, Pedro. 1998. "The New Synthesis of Latin American and Latino Studies." Pp. 195–216 in *Borderless Borders: U.S. Latinos, Latin Americans, and the Paradox of Interdependence,* edited by Frank Bonilla, Edwin Meléndez, Rebecca Morales, and Maria de los Angeles Torres. Philadelphia, PA: Temple University Press.

De la Torre, Adela and Beatriz M. Pesquera, eds. 1993. *Building with Our Hands: New Directions in Chicana Studies.* Berkeley: University of California Press.

Flores, Juan. 2003. "Latino Studies: New Contexts, New Concepts." In *Critical Latin American and Latino Studies,* edited by Juan Poblete. Minneapolis: University of Minnesota Press.

Muñoz, Carlos, Jr. 1984. "The Development of Chicano Studies, 1968–1981." In *Chicano Studies: A Multidisciplinary Approach,* edited by Eugene E. García, Francisco Lomelí, and Isidro D. Ortiz. New York: Columbia University, Teachers College Press.

Torres-Saillant, Silvio and Ramona Hernández. 1998. *The Dominican-Americans.* Westport, CT: Greenwood.

LATVIAN AMERICANS

Latvian Americans are the immigrants and their descendants from Latvia, a country of 2.3 million as of 2007 estimates. According to the 2000 census, there were 27,230 people born in Latvia residing in the United States; of these, 73.2% were citizens. This entry describes the background of immigration from Latvia to the United States and the contemporary picture of Latvian Americans.

Immigration Patterns

Latvian immigration can be divided into two distinct groups: those who arrived in the United States before World War II and those who arrived after the war. The first group, often referred to as the "Old Latvians," began to be documented in the 1850 census. According to census data for that year, there were 3,160 Latvians in the United States, although Lithuanians were included in this group in census data because they spoke a similar language. Half a century later, the number of Latvians residing in the United States was 4,309, most of whom were sailors, artisans, missionaries, laborers, and craftsmen.

In the aftermath of the Russian Revolution of 1905, approximately 5,000 Latvians immigrated. Their reason for migrating was mainly political, and immigrants included many well-educated socialist and nationalist leaders. Due to World War I, the Immigration Act of 1924, and the Great Depression, migration to the United States slowed during the period between world wars. In addition, when Latvia gained independence in 1918, several hundred Latvians returned to their home country. Only 4,669 Latvians arrived between the years 1920 and 1939.

Census data indicate that more than 40,000 Latvians arrived between 1939 and 1951, with the majority arriving after 1945. Many of these immigrants arrived in the United States as refugees and displaced persons who were fleeing Nazi and Soviet suppression. This second group of Latvian immigrants often referred to themselves as living in exile and as having a great desire to return to Latvia. However, since the collapse of the Soviet Union in 1991, which reestablished Latvia's independence, very few have undertaken return migration and many have made the United States their permanent home.

Contemporary Community

During recent years, people from Latvia have sought permanent residency and refugee status and have completed the naturalization process to become citizens.

From 1997 to 2006, approximately 6,100 Latvians immigrated to the United States. An additional 600 refugees arrived between 1999 and 2006. Approximately 325 Latvian Americans have become naturalized citizens annually beginning in 1997.

According to the U.S. Census Bureau's *American Community Survey 2005*, there were 63,867 people of Latvian national origin in the United States in 2005. In terms of geographic distribution, the top five states were California, New York, Michigan, Florida, and New Jersey. According to the 2000 census, more than 75% spoke a language other than English at home. Their median family income was $55,209, as compared with $50,890 for the nation as a whole.

Jennifer M. Klein

See Appendix A

See also Acculturation; Assimilation; Deficit Model of Ethnicity; Europe; Immigrant Communities; Immigration, U.S.; Refugees; Return Migration; Symbolic Ethnicity

Further Readings

Department of Homeland Security. 2007. *Yearbook of Immigration Statistics: 2006.* Washington, DC: Office of Immigration Statistics. Available from http://www.dhs.gov/ximgtn/statistics/publications/yearbook.shtm

Neimanis, George J. 1997. *The Collapse of the Soviet Empire: A View from Riga.* Westport, CT: Praeger.

Plakans, Andrejs. 1995. *The Latvians: A Short History.* Stanford, CA: Stanford University, Hoover Institution Press.

U.S. Census Bureau. 2004. *Profile of Demographic and Social Characteristics: 2000. People Born in Latvia.* Available from http://www.census.gov/population/www/socdemo/foreign/STP-159-2000tl.html

U.S. Census Bureau. 2006. *American Community Survey 2005.* Available from http://www.census.gov/acs/www

LEBANESE AMERICANS

Lebanese Americans are immigrants from Lebanon, a country of 3.9 million people as of 2007, as well as their descendants. Lebanese Americans represent one of the many diverse groups of the Arab nations, including Algeria, Bahrain, Egypt, Iraq, Jordan, Kuwait, Libya, Morocco, Oman, Palestine, the People's Democratic Republic of Yemen, Qatar, Saudi Arabia, Syria, Tunisia, the United Arab Emirates, and the Yemen Arab Republic. According to the 2000 census, there were 105,910 people born in Lebanon residing in the United States; of these, 67.7% were citizens. This entry looks at the background of immigration from Lebanon to the United States and the contemporary picture of Lebanese Americans.

Immigration Patterns

Arabs have been migrating to the United States since 1850. However, early Lebanese immigrants were categorized together with Syrian immigrants. Therefore, accurate records and statistics are difficult to obtain. The first wave peaked in 1914 with 9,023 people immigrating; however, immigration fluctuated greatly through the 1920s. Many were drawn to the United States because of economic opportunities. The years between 1870 and 1918 were quite significant because Lebanon lost a quarter of its population to emigration. The Immigration Act of 1924 primarily ended all immigration from Lebanon during the years it was in force.

Most Lebanese arrived during the first wave. However, the end of the Arab–Israeli war in 1967 sparked the second wave of immigration. In addition, the civil war between Muslims and Christians that lasted from 1975 to 1991 created a mass exodus from Lebanon during those years. The new immigrants carried with them a strong Arab identity, or "Arab consciousness," with their Islamic and political traditions.

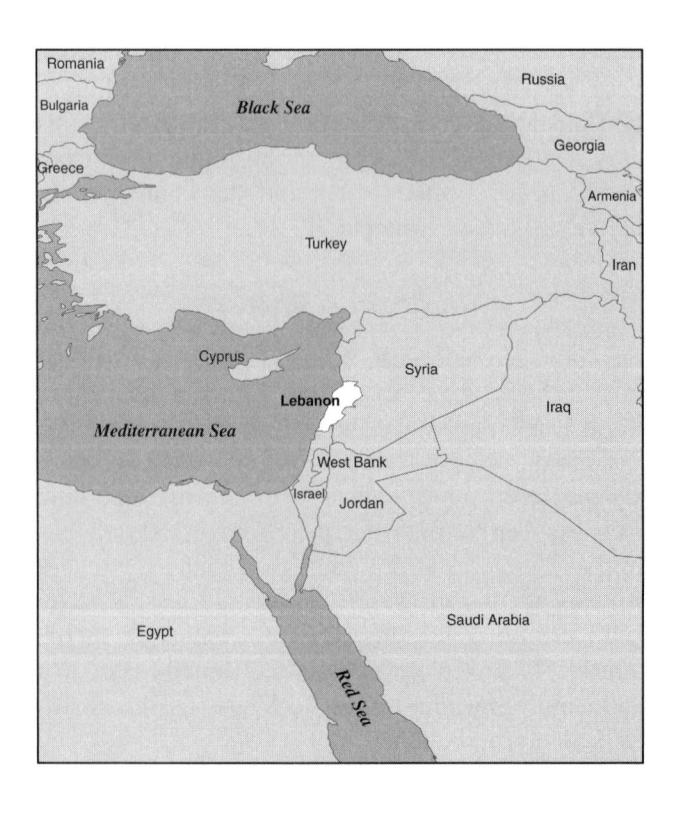

These immigrants were better educated than their predecessors and helped to revive their customs and culture in Lebanese communities in the United States.

Contemporary Community

During recent years, people from Lebanon have sought permanent residency status and have completed the naturalization process to become citizens. From 1997 to 2006, approximately 3,700 Lebanese immigrated to the United States annually. At least 3,400 Lebanese Americans have become naturalized citizens annually beginning in 1997.

According to the U.S. Census Bureau's *American Community Survey 2005*, there were 363,015 people of Lebanese national origin in the United States in 2005. Large Lebanese communities can be found in the Northeast and Midwest. Detroit has the largest Lebanese community. In terms of geographic distribution, the top five states are Michigan, California, Florida, Massachusetts, and New York. According to the 2000 census, 32.4% spoke English less than "very well." Their median family income was $54,798, as compared with $50,890 for the nation as a whole. Of those Lebanese-born individuals present in the United States in 2000, 20% had entered the country prior to 2000.

Americans of Lebanese descent have made many contributions to entertainment and politics. Among famous actors of Lebanese descent are Danny Thomas and his daughter Marlo. Other famous Americans of Lebanese descent include Frank Zappa, musician; Paul Orfalea, founder of Kinko's; and John Elway, professional football star quarterback. James Abourezk was the first Lebanese American to serve in the U.S. Senate (1974–1980) and founded the American Arab Anti-discrimination Committee.

Jennifer M. Klein

See Appendix A

See also Arab Americans; Assimilation; Deficit Model of Ethnicity; Immigrant Communities; Immigration, U.S.; Islamophobia; Muslim Americans; Refugees; Symbolic Ethnicity

Further Readings

Department of Homeland Security. 2007. *Yearbook of Immigration Statistics:* 2006. Washington, DC: Office of Immigration Statistics. Available from http://www.dhs.gov/ximgtn/statistics/publications/yearbook.shtm

Horani, Albert. 1991. *A History of the Arab Peoples.* Cambridge, MA: Warner Books.

Kayal, Philip M. 1975. *The Syrian–Lebanese in America: A Study in Religion and Assimilation.* New York: Twayne.

Khater, Akram Fouad. 2001. *Inventing Home: Emigration, Gender, and the Middle Class in Lebanon, 1870–1920.* Berkeley: University of California Press.

U.S. Census Bureau. 2004. *Profile of Demographic and Social Characteristics: 2000. People Born in Lebanon.* Available from http://www.census.gov/population/www/socdemo/foreign/STP-159-2000tl.html

U.S. Census Bureau. 2006. *American Community Survey 2005.* Available from http://www.census.gov/acs/www

LEE, SPIKE (1957–)

Spike Lee has used the art of film to entertain, tell stories, and—at his most compelling—provoke the viewer to think about society. To date, Lee's body of work includes twenty films completed between 1986 and 2006. Although the genres of his films vary from comedy and satire to drama and documentary, consistent themes of race, class, ethnicity, gender, and the inequalities arising from these social categories have emerged to make him one of the leading provocateurs of U.S. cinema. This entry provides a brief biography of Lee and discusses the impact of his films and their role in reflecting U.S. race and ethnic relations.

Beginnings

Raised in Brooklyn, New York, Lee was exposed to ethnic diversity throughout his childhood given the multiculturalism of his neighborhoods and schools. He has characterized his childhood and growing up in these communities as enriching and as raising his awareness of race and ethnic relations. Occasionally, Lee and his family would experience the effects of racist attitudes. For example, on the first day of moving into the Cobble Hill section of Brooklyn, his family was called "nigger." However, most of his interactions and relationships cultivated with Jews, Italians, Puerto Ricans, and Blacks were not filled with conflict; rather, they were felt to be mutually rewarding.

Many early experiences shaped Lee's interest in becoming a filmmaker. His father, a jazz musician, exposed him to ideas and to the process of creating one's voice through art. His mother, a teacher, encouraged constant exposure to the arts through attending the theater and museums. Later, Spike graduated from

Morehouse College with a bachelor of arts degree in mass communication and went on to graduate from the New York University (NYU) Film School with a master of fine arts degree.

Authentic Representations of African Americans

In 1986, the year Lee debuted as a filmmaker, there was still a dearth of diverse images and representations of African Americans. His first three films, *She's Gotta Have It, School Daze,* and *Do the Right Thing,* signaled a departure from the blaxploitation genre that had dominated films portraying Blacks since the early 1970s. Blaxploitation films gave Black filmmakers and actors opportunities to work; however, the films were a hyperbole of urban ghetto life, with characters depicted as hypersexual and hyperviolent. Overwhelmingly, stereotypes of African Americans were reinforced, as were those of Whites.

Lee's films deviated from the formula of blaxploitation and sought to depict African Americans in their everyday lives. Moreover, he used his films as a platform to wrestle with the ways in which race and racism shape people's identities and interpersonal relationships. In a sense, Lee returned to the roots of cinema initiated by filmmaker Oscar Micheaux, who in 1919 became the first African American to make a film. Lee has credited Micheaux as one of his most significant influences and as a model of how to address race and challenge stereotypes in film.

In addition, all of Lee's films have tapped into a social consciousness to reflect the relevant social and political issues of the times. His first student film, *The Last Hustle in Brooklyn,* captured images of people looting during the New York City power blackout of 1977. At NYU, his student film *The Answer* nearly got him dismissed from the program for challenging D. W. Griffith's 1915 film *The Birth of a Nation.* In *The Answer,* Lee selected some of the most degrading images of how African Americans were depicted to demonstrate how stereotypes about African Americans were perpetuated. In challenging the status quo and the iconic work of Griffith, Lee provoked controversy by addressing issues of racism. His later films continued to push the status quo by addressing a range of taboo topics, from intragroup racism, interracial relationships, and ethnic relations to retelling U.S. history in the form of historical dramas and documentaries.

His Films

Lee's body of work includes more than films; however, his films have garnered the most attention and raised the most controversy. At times, Lee has been criticized for exploiting the issue of race and even of reinforcing stereotypes, especially of ethnic groups such as Jews and Italians. Although a discussion of all of Lee's films is beyond the scope of this entry, several of them warrant discussion here.

School Daze, Do the Right Thing, and *Jungle Fever* are films that most prominently feature aspects of race and ethnic relations. *School Daze* grapples with the complexity of identity and how belonging to a marginalized ethnic group shapes one's identity. In so doing, Lee brought to light how African Americans have been affected by internalized racism and have struggled with the historical legacy of racism that privileges light skin color and straight hair. He called for African Americans to resist this form of racism and "wake up," as the protagonist challenges the audience to do at the end of the film.

Do the Right Thing captures the tension that results when an outside ethnic group benefits economically

Table 1 Chronology of Films by Spike Lee

Film	Date of Release
She's Gotta Have It	August 20, 1986
School Daze	February 12, 1988
Do the Right Thing	June 30, 1989
Mo' Better Blues	August 3, 1990
Jungle Fever	June 7, 1990
Malcolm X	November 18, 1992
Crooklyn	May 13, 1994
Clockers	September 11, 1995
Girl 6	March 22, 1996
Get on the Bus	October 16, 1996
4 Little Girls	October 16, 1997
He Got Game	May 1, 1998
Summer of Sam	July 2, 1999
The Original Kings of Comedy	September 18, 2000
Bamboozled	November 11, 2000
Jim Brown: All American	March 22, 2002
25th Hour	December 16, 2002
She Hate Me	December 29, 2004
Inside Man	March 24, 2006
When the Levees Broke	August 29, 2006
Lovers & Haters	September 16, 2007

from an African American community. The pizza restaurant owned by an Italian American serves as a catalyst to ignite the sense of powerlessness that results from racial inequality. The character Radio Raheem symbolizes the frustration and anger triggered by racism. As in *Jungle Fever,* where the viewer observes how a fictional Italian American family responds to an interracial dating relationship, *Do the Right Thing* purports to show how members of other ethnic groups construct beliefs about race.

Finally, each of the later films *Malcolm X, Get on the Bus,* and *Bamboozled,* as well as each of the documentaries *4 Little Girls* and *When the Levees Broke,* reflects some historical event, wrestles with a political or societal issue of the day, and seeks to give voice to a story that was silenced or perhaps underrepresented. This body of work might be considered Lee's most compelling in that these films focus on the multiple faces of oppression and the intersection of race, class, geography, and gender.

As Lee continues to make films, he also continues to challenge the viewer to reflect on issues of race and ethnic relations. As a filmmaker, he has garnered critical acclaim and received mainstream success; the film *Inside Man* opened successfully at the box office and was overwhelmingly supported by a major studio company. Continually faced with the struggle to secure financing for his films, Lee seems to persist and sustain his work by seeking and taking on alternative and independent projects.

Tracey Lewis-Elligan

See also African Americans; Black Cinema; Black Intellectuals; Internalized Racism; Malcolm X; Stereotypes

Further Readings

Bowser, Pearl, Jane Gains, and Charles Musser. 2001. *Oscar Micheaux and His Circle: African American Filmmaking and Race Cinema of the Silent Era.* Bloomington: Indiana University Press.

hooks, bell. 1996. *Reel to Real: Race, Sex, and Class at the Movies.* London: Routledge.

Lee, Spike and Kaleem Aftab. 2005. *That's My Story and I'm Sticking to It.* New York: Norton.

Lee, Spike and Nelson George. 1987. *Spike Lee's Gotta Have It: Inside Guerrilla Filmmaking.* New York: Simon & Schuster.

Lee, Spike and Ralph Riley. 1997. *Best Seat in the House: A Basketball Memoir.* New York: Crowne.

Micheaux, Oscar. 1994. *The Conquest: The Story of a Negro Pioneer.* Lincoln: University of Nebraska Press.

Leisure

The sociological analysis of leisure is a valuable window through which to view issues of race and ethnicity. All leisure behavior is learned, and the norms, attitudes, values, and beliefs that govern leisure involvement are learned through the process of socialization. Precisely what norms, attitudes, values, and beliefs people learn are often shaped by their racial/ethnic identity. Like all of the major social institutions (the educational system, the criminal justice system, and government), leisure is embedded within the larger society, and as such all of the elements of that society are evident. In leisure, one can find privilege and stigma, equality and stratification, benevolence and selfishness. However, unlike interactions with most other social institutions, leisure involvement is freely determined. And because there is more freedom regarding what people do (and how they choose to do it), those decisions are more revelatory of what people perceive is their true identity.

Leisure is a notoriously difficult concept to define. Much like the terms *race* and *ethnicity,* most people have a general understanding of what *leisure* is but have a hard time in articulating an exact definition. In theory, a complete definition of leisure combines three different but related concepts: (a) leisure as residual time, (b) leisure as activity, and (c) leisure as a state of mind. However, in practice, researchers typically operationalize leisure, referencing only one of these concepts. How one chooses to define leisure is especially important when examining leisure in the context of race and ethnicity because the choice that researchers make has consequences for whether or not leisure differences are revealed and what the extent of those differences may be. This entry looks at leisure from each of these perspectives, as well as related research, with a particular focus on race and ethnicity.

Leisure as Residual Time

The first conception of leisure, as residual time (also as discretionary or unobligated time), is commonly used by researchers trying to determine how much leisure time people have and by researchers employing "time diaries" as a primary methodological tool. In this instance, leisure is whatever people choose to do in the time that is left over after work (occupation), personal maintenance (e.g., sleeping, eating, bathing), and the other chores of daily living (e.g., cooking, cleaning) have been accomplished. It does not matter whether the activity is active or passive or whether the motivation for that activity is primarily intrinsic or extrinsic; so long as the activity occurs during residual time, it is designated as *leisure.*

These studies generally report that members of racial/ethnic minority groups have less available leisure time than do Whites, although such differences are usually conflated with social class differences. For example, people with lower status occupations accrue less vacation time than do people with higher status occupations, and they often need to work longer hours or multiple jobs to make ends meet. Historically speaking, members of racial/ethnic minority groups are overrepresented in lower status occupations, have been less able to take early retirement, and have higher rates of unemployment. All of these factors result in less available leisure time.

The definition of leisure as unobligated time is somewhat problematic because, for most people, the obligations of daily living are never fully completed. Yet people still experience leisure. Many people combine leisure with compulsory or work-related activities (multitasking) that make mutually exclusive categorizations difficult. For example, how does one classify time spent folding laundry while watching television or time spent washing dishes while listening to music? Similarly, a dinner out with friends or business associates typically involves more than just consuming the basic calories required for sustenance, so how does one properly portion the time spent? How one chooses to classify residual time can greatly affect the determination of how much leisure time is available.

Leisure as Activities

The second conception of leisure is as an activity. Following this line of thinking, researchers compile a finite list of leisure activities (e.g., dancing, watching television, knitting, snorkeling, playing softball, working crossword puzzles) and then ask people to list the activities in which they participate. Whoever acknowledges participating in one of the predetermined activities has engaged in leisure. This definition is most commonly used by researchers seeking to measure leisure involvement; whether participation in selected activities is increasing or decreasing; or whether certain groups differ in their respective rates of participation.

Such studies reveal that African Americans and Latinos, when compared with Whites, prefer home-based and family- or group-oriented leisure activities. Also, African Americans and Latinos are less likely to participate in "high-culture" leisure activities (e.g., visiting art museums, attending operas or symphony concerts) and are less likely to be involved in outdoor resource-based leisure (e.g., hiking, camping), water-based recreation (e.g., swimming, boating, snorkeling), and winter sports (e.g., skiing, snowshoeing, sledding). Finally, minority group members are less likely than Whites to be involved in "extreme" leisure (e.g., skydiving, bungee jumping, mountain climbing).

Much of the research of this type has focused on Black–White differences and has been informed by two broad theoretical traditions: the marginality perspective and the ethnicity perspective. The marginality perspective attributes leisure differences to the history of socioeconomic disparity between the races—stating, in essence, that racial difference are really social class differences. Proponents of this perspective argue that the dominant group (Whites) has historically had larger discretionary income and greater access to recreational facilities and other public goods, resulting in a broad set of leisure opportunities from which to choose.

Conversely, socioeconomic discrimination has prevented people in marginalized groups from developing an appreciation for expensive or high-culture leisure activities, and even if they do have a desire for such leisure activities, they lack the resources to engage in them. The ethnicity or subculture perspective offers a cultural explanation for intergroup differences. It states that an identifiable set of Black leisure activities stems from a distinctive Black subculture. In other words, Black Americans have culturally based values and tastes that are different from those of White Americans, and those subcultural values result in alternative leisure choices. Although there may be overlap between the two races regarding some activities, ethnic differences lead Blacks to prefer some leisure pursuits in which Whites do not engage and to reject other activities that Whites embrace. This perspective is often applied post hoc after observing leisure differences that cannot be explained by socioeconomic factors, and proponents rarely outline what ethnic or cultural values are responsible for leisure differences or how they influence leisure involvement.

Like the previous view of leisure, the conception of leisure as an activity is also problematic. First of all, it is difficult to compile an exhaustive list of activities on which everyone agrees. For example, some people consider only active pursuits as leisure and so would not include activities such as napping, reading, and watching television. Some may discount hedonistic or antisocial activities (e.g., drinking alcohol, using recreational drugs, gambling), whereas others may fail to consider socially beneficial or altruistic behavior (e.g., volunteering). Finally, some activities that most people would consider to be leisure might not be perceived as such by people whose involvement is primarily one of obligation, remuneration, or other extrinsic motivations. For example, the survey question "Have you played basketball during the past week?" may have a different meaning for suburban Whites than for urban Blacks.

There is some research suggesting that members of racial/ethnic minorities are more likely than Whites to value leisure activities for the potential extrinsic benefits. Some young African Americans may see playing sports or making music as the only real chance they have for economic success—an attitude that could conflict with their freedom to participate.

Leisure as Attitude

That brings us to the third and final conception—leisure as an attitude or state of mind—which hinges entirely on the motivation. In this view, leisure is conceptualized as behavior that is intrinsically motivated—something done for its own sake, free from coercion and without the promise of external rewards. Whereas the first conception focuses on *when* (during discretionary time) and the second conception focuses on *what* (a set list of activities), this perspective focuses on *how*. Leisure is carefree behavior performed with a sense of freedom and enjoyment regardless of what the activity is or when it is performed.

In fact, some people are able to turn tasks deemed by others to be unpleasant responsibilities into opportunities for leisure by internalizing the activities and redefining them as chances for creative self-expression and satisfaction. One person's dreaded chore or obligation (e.g., gardening, cooking) may be another person's prized form of relaxation or amusement. For most people, intrinsic motivation is the true essence of leisure, and although this definition has high validity, from a research perspective it has low reliability. It is difficult to compare results when attitudes regarding a potential leisure activity vary from person to person (and from day to day). That is why few researchers tend to operationalize leisure in this way.

Regardless of the exact definition chosen, members of racial/ethnic minorities tend to have less leisure than do members of the dominant group. As stated earlier, members of minority groups have historically been underrepresented in high-status occupations, so they have fewer resources available to them to spend on leisure. Similarly, because of historical discrimination, the menu of leisure activities from which members of racial/ethnic minority groups may select is not as broad or varied as that from which members of the dominant group may select.

For example, in many parts of the United States, African Americans are still rarely observed on golf courses, on tennis courts, or in the audiences at classical music concerts. Although leisure activities are freely chosen, that freedom is more restricted for some groups than for others. Members of minority groups are more likely than Whites to report the presence of barriers or constraints to leisure participation. As noted earlier, in some cases lack of participation can be attributed to social class differences, but it is naive to assume that race does not also play a part. In some instances, overt discrimination or the threat of physical harm may serve as an obstacle to participation. In other cases, the barrier may be something more subtle such as the uneasy feeling of being the only dark face among a sea of Whites at Carnegie Hall. Either way, leisure opportunities for minorities are narrowed.

Derek Martin

See also Cultural Capital; Media and Race; Negro League Baseball; Popular Culture, Racism and

Further Readings

Bradshaw, Tom. 1998. *1997 Survey of Public Participation in the Arts: Summary Report.* Washington, DC: National Endowment for the Arts.

Falk, John H. 1998. "Visitors: Who Does, Who Doesn't, and Why." *Museum News,* March/April, pp. 38–43.

Floyd, Myron F. 1998. "Getting beyond Marginality and Ethnicity: The Challenge for Race and Ethnic Studies in Leisure Research." *Journal of Leisure Research* 30:3–22.

Gartner, William C. and David W. Lime, eds. 2000. *Trends in Outdoor Recreation, Leisure, and Tourism.* New York: CABI.

Martin, Derek Christopher. 2004. "Apartheid in the Great Outdoors: American Advertising and the Reproduction of a Racialized Outdoor Leisure Identity." *Journal of Leisure Research* 36:513–535.

Philipp, Steven F. 2000. "Race and the Pursuit of Happiness." *Journal of Leisure Research* 32:121–124.

Robinson, John P. and Geoffrey Godbey. 1997. *Time for Life: The Surprising Ways Americans Use Their Time.* University Park: Pennsylvania State University Press.

Schor, Juliet B. 1991. *The Overworked American: The Unexpected Decline of Leisure.* New York: Basic Books.

Veal, Anthony J. 1992. "Definitions of Leisure and Recreation." *Australian Journal of Recreation and Leisure* 2(4):44–52.

Washburne, Randel F. 1978. "Black Under-participation in Wildland Recreation: Alternative Explanations." *Leisure Sciences* 1:175–189.

Lesbian, Gay, Bisexual, and Transgender

The phrase *lesbian, gay, bisexual, and transgender* (LGBT) refers to members of a community of people marginalized by sexuality and gender. The acronym LGBT itself owes its existence to decades of identity politics and organizing. Ethnoracial minorities who are LGBT face specific issues where sexuality, gender, and their experience as people of color intertwine, and LGBT categories are infused with racial readings not often discussed. This entry consists of two sections; the first discusses the historical relationship between these categories, and the second addresses specific aspects that relate to ethnoracial groups, LGBT identity, and community organizing.

Historical Overview

In general, social scientists, service providers, and even lawmakers are beginning to make a distinction between gay, lesbian, and bisexual as a type of *sexual orientation* (along with heterosexual and, as some people would argue, asexual) and transgender and transsexual as specifically referring to one's own sense of *gender identity* (or a rupture from the basic categories of male and female imposed on all social beings at birth as man and woman and based primarily on genitalia). In mainstream U.S. society, however, conflations among sex, gender, and sexuality continue to be made in reading lesbian, gay, bisexual, and transgender/transsexual people as members of the same group.

The language of much community organizing during the past 15 years or so has employed the terms *lesbian, gay, bisexual,* and *transgender* (or *transgendered*) and only sometimes names *transsexuality* explicitly. Transgender as a category often refers to an action against gender-binary impositions, and *transsexual* is much more specific to a move from one gender construct to another. In addition, the use of *transexual*—with one *s*—was coined by Riki Anne Wilchins to denote a different relationship to a transgender person's experience; the term *transsexual*—with double *ss*—is historically tied to the psychiatric, medicalized, and surgically based experience that tended to define and regulate transsexuality.

Although of some utility, the application of broad community labels such as *gay and lesbian; gay, lesbian, and bisexual;* or *gay, lesbian, bisexual, and transgender/transsexual* is problematic because these categories of identity did not come together without continual experiences of social discrimination and bias, sometimes including violence, for instance, the constant sexism faced by many lesbian and bisexual women in the Castro neighborhood of San Francisco when it was becoming a primarily gay male neighborhood during the 1970s and the frequent invisibility of bisexual and transgender people even though current social movement leaders and organizations often name or list "bisexual" and "transgender" as part of their titles. The use of the acronym LGBT is much more recent in identity politics and community organizing. Organizing among same-sex male- and same-sex female-bodied individuals, which only emerged with some political significance during the 1950s, took place separately as organizations such as the Daughters of Bilitis and the Mattachine Society erupted. Organizing for "gay" rights was first gay, then gay and lesbian, and co-ed organizing began during the 1970s with the former National Gay Task Force becoming the National Gay and Lesbian Task Force. Bisexuality is seldom mentioned, although in much theorizing, as well as in organizing since perhaps the 1980s, bisexuality is attached to "gay and lesbian," often to counter accusations of atypical gender presentation by gays and lesbians—attempting to produce gender-normative men and women with nonhegemonic sexualities.

Transsexuality was mentioned in relationship to the psychiatric and medical establishments and only began to be linked explicitly to lesbian, gay, and bisexual nomenclatures later on. Transgender is a 1990s term, as argued by writers such as David Valentine. From this brief historical outline of "gay," "lesbian," "bisexual," and "transgender/transsexual" as newly emerged identity markers, it should be clear that decades of struggles to this level of organizing and inclusiveness did not just come about "naturally." Many activists and scholars alike, however, use the acronym LGBT without much consideration to where sex/gender/desire intersect with these identities.

Racial Aspects of LGBT Identity and Organizing

Racial/ethnic minorities and immigrants in U.S. society who are LGBT experience not only those challenges that White LGBT people experience but also the legal, institutional, and social barriers to people of color and immigrants. For instance, during recent decades requests for political asylum on the basis of a person's sexual orientation or gender identity have become increasingly common in applications to stay in the United States. There are structural differences to understanding LGBT communities of color; in the United States, a certain hegemonic way of being LGBT is often imposed without a racial reading of whiteness noticeably imposing it. Whiteness fuses with gayness in ways that have unfortunate results for people of color. For instance, the relationship of Black and Latino sexuality in contemporary portrayals has solidified notions of how communities of color are homophobic; how men of color are often "closeted" and cannot identify as gay, remaining (as commonly stated) on the "down low"; and how machismo is perceived to be an element that affects only Latino culture. Similarly, whereas Black and Latino men are hypersexualized, Asian men tend to be desexualized or effeminized. These structural readings make it much more feasible to read whiteness as an ideal basis for gayness (although this is rarely noticed) and to read communities of color as more homophobic. And because communities of color are highly affected by issues such as HIV/AIDS, a simple justification is made to link and establish homophobia as the basis for such high incidence.

LGBT people of color have historically been involved in community organizing and activism on various fronts. Writers such as Audre Lorde, bell hooks, Cherríe Moraga, and Gloria Anzaldúa have discussed the relationship of being women of color and managing their own sexuality as such. Many community organizing centers in the United States, for example, organizations such as the Austin Latina/o Lesbian and Gay Organization in Texas and the Audre Lorde Project in New York City, use the experience of being both LGBT and people of color as an active platform to mobilize. In sum, both racial status and sexual status are active components of their organizing and activism. (Note, however, that in many instances the placement of LGBT people of color's racial status as secondary by mainstream LGBT people tends to be accompanied by that general group's sense of tolerance

Gay rights rally. Tina and Melissa Lesley-Fox of Portland, Oregon, holding their 13-month-old daughter Amelia at a rally for gay rights at the Oregon State Capitol in Salem on March 7, 2007. The rally was being held to support the Oregon Equality Act, a statewide nondiscrimination bill that would prohibit discrimination in housing, employment, and public accommodation on the basis of sexual orientation, and the Oregon Family Fairness Act, a relationship recognition civil unions bill that would extend to same-sex couples benefits, protections, and responsibilities similar to those afforded to opposite-sex couples through marriage.

Source: Getty Images.

toward racial minorities in the LGBT communities; interracial dating is often understood to be proof of such lack of bias toward LGBT people of color.)

Gender and sexuality are also complex categories through which LGBT people understand their experiences. Although no reductionist approach should be used to juxtapose Whites' and people of color's experiences with these categories, it is important to mention how terms such as *two-spirited, same-gender loving, family,* and *de ambiente* (Spanish for "from the crowd") are used by various communities of color to identify their behavior, attraction, or belonging to an LGBT community (or to a community at large but with some specific recognition). Lesbians and lesbians of color are particularly affected by the erasure of gender and gendered experiences within studies of LGBT communities because much funding, attention, and literature respond to male-identified individuals who are members of LGBT communities—more so when speaking of African American or Latino men. Lesbians also experience a set of erasures when their sexuality is highlighted; commonalities between them and heterosexual and bisexual women concerning harassment, experiencing sexism and developing tools to respond to it, and histories of abuse and trauma tend not to be foregrounded.

In sum, LGBT communities comprise a variety of experiences. LGBT identities are often framed through the lens of whiteness even when seldom noticed. LGBT people of color experience additional barriers toward social acceptance in society. And although LGBT is used as a coalitional term, it does not mean that all communities are represented equally—or treated equally—within such coalition movements.

Salvador Vidal-Ortiz

See also Civil Rights Movement; Discrimination; Immigrant Communities; Immigration, U.S.; Machismo; People of Color; Privilege; Sexuality

Further Readings

Fung, Richard. 2001. "Looking for My Penis: The Eroticized Asian in Gay Video Porn." Pp. 515–525 in *Men's Lives*, 5th ed., edited by Michael S. Kimmel and Michael A. Messner. Needham Heights, MA: Allyn & Bacon.

Guzmán, Manolo. 2006. *Gay Hegemony/Latino Homosexualities*. New York: Routledge.

Hidalgo, Hilda, ed. 1995. *Lesbians of Color: Social and Human Services*. New York: Harrington Park Press.

Luibhéid, Eithne and Lionel Cantú, Jr., eds. 2005. *Queer Migrations: Sexuality, U.S. Citizenship, and Border Crossings*. Minneapolis: University of Minnesota Press.

Mukherjea, Ananya and Salvador Vidal-Ortiz. 2006. "Studying HIV Risk in Vulnerable Communities: Methodological and Reporting Shortcomings in the Young Men's Study in New York City." *The Qualitative Report* 11:393–416.

Rodríguez-Rust, Paula. 2000. *Bisexuality in the United States: A Social Science Reader*. New York: Columbia University Press.

Somerville, Siobhan. 2000. *Queering the Color Line: Race and the Invention of Homosexuality in American Culture*. Durham, NC: Duke University Press.

Valentine, David. 2003. "'I Went to Bed with My Own Kind Once': The Erasure of Desire in the Name of Identity." *Language & Communication* 23:123–138.

Wilchins, Riki Anne. 1997. *Read My Lips: Sexual Subversion and the End of Gender*. Ithaca, NY: Firebrand Books.

LIFE EXPECTANCY

Life expectancy, broadly defined as the number of years an individual can expect to live, is widely regarded as one of the most powerful indicators of the overall health of a society as well as the health of specific subpopulations within a society. In the United States today, Blacks have a significantly lower life expectancy than do their White, Asian, and Hispanic counterparts, with Blacks living roughly 7 fewer years than Whites. This gap is due largely to Blacks' high infant mortality rate, which is more than twice that of Whites. Multiple factors contribute to race disparities in life expectancy, including socioeconomic resources, lifestyle and health behaviors, social environment, and access to and quality of health care services. This entry describes the methods used to calculate life expectancy and document racial differences in life expectancy throughout the 20th and 21st centuries in the United States. It describes the social factors that influence life expectancy and reviews current debates about the relative strengths of these purported influences. Finally, it discusses ways in which policies and public health practices may help to close the race gap in life expectancy.

Defining Life Expectancy

Life expectancy is a statistical projection of the length of an individual's life. Specifically, it is an estimate of the average number of additional years a person can expect to live if the age-specific death rates for a given year prevail for the rest of his or her life. It is a hypothetical measure because it is based on current death rates, yet actual death rates change over the course of a person's life. Consequently, each person's life expectancy changes as he or she ages. Demographers typically calculate two different life expectancy measures: (a) life expectancy at birth, or the number of years a new baby born in a given year can expect to live, and (b) one's life expectancy at age *n*, or the number of additional years an individual who is *n* years old can expect to live.

Life expectancy at birth does not simply equal life expectancy at age *n* plus *n* years because age-specific life expectancy is selective. That is, individuals who have survived the potentially dangerous years of infancy and childhood are more likely to have an extended life span than is the average member of their birth cohort. For example, life expectancy at birth for a given cohort may be 75 years, yet 75-year-olds in that birth cohort probably can expect to live another 10 years. Life expectancy at birth is lower than life expectancy at 75 years of age because it includes in its calculations those babies who went on to die during infancy, adolescence, or young adulthood. These young ages at death reduce the average life span for members of that birth cohort.

Life expectancies vary widely across nations and within nations by race, ethnicity, and social class. In developing nations, high infant mortality rates contribute to low life expectancies. For instance, life expectancy at birth in Malawi was approximately 46 years in 2006. In contrast, life expectancy at birth in Japan topped 80 years. In addition, life expectancy is affected heavily by "crisis" mortalities that affect large numbers of young persons such as wars and epidemics. For example, life expectancies in many sub-Saharan African nations during the early 21st century range from 35 to 40 years, reflecting high rates of AIDS in nations such as Botswana and Swaziland and reflecting warfare in Sierra Leone and Angola.

Race Differences in Life Expectancy in the United States

In the United States today, the leading causes of death for Blacks and Whites are similar. The top three causes of death (heart disease, cancer, and stroke) and seven of the ten leading causes of death are the same for both groups (Table 1). However, Blacks generally die younger than do Whites, and the racial gap in mortality has widened during the past 2 decades. According to the National Center for Health Statistics, White women outlive Black women by roughly 5 years, with life expectancies at

Table 1 Ten Leading Causes of Death Among Non-Hispanic Blacks and Non-Hispanic Whites in the United States, 2002

	Non-Hispanic Blacks		*Non-Hispanic Whites*	
Rank	Cause of Death	Percentage	Cause of Death	Percentage
1	Heart disease	26.8	Heart disease	29.2
2	Cancer	21.6	Cancer	23.1
3	Stroke	6.5	Stroke	6.7
4	Diabetes	4.4	Chronic lower respiratory disease	5.7
5	Unintentional injury	4.3	Unintentional injury	4.1
6	Homicide	2.8	Influenza and pneumonia	2.8
7	Chronic lower respiratory disease	2.7	Alzheimer's disease	2.7
8	HIV/AIDS	2.7	Diabetes	2.6
9	Nephritis	2.6	Nephritis	1.5
10	Septicemia	2.1	Suicide	1.3
	All others	23.5	All others	20.2
Total		100		100

Source: National Vital Statistics System. 2005. "Deaths: Leading Causes for 2002." *National Vital Statistics Reports,* March 7, Tables E and F.

birth of 80.3 and 75.6 years, respectively (Figure 1). For men, the gap is even more pronounced; in 2003, White men's life expectancy at birth was 75.3 years as compared with just 69.0 years for Black men. During the first half of the 20th century, all U.S. residents experienced tremendous gains in life expectancy and the race gap nearly halved from 15 to 8 years between 1900 and 1950. The gap narrowed again during the 1970s and 1980s, yet it has widened over the past 2 decades.

The narrowing disparity during the 1970s and 1980s is attributed to four factors. First, racial differences in smoking declined during that time. Second, Blacks experienced a large reduction in the prevalence of hypertension, especially among men. Third, with the passage of Medicare and Medicaid programs in 1965, Blacks gained greater access to health care. Finally, racial differences in income declined slightly during the 1970s and early 1980s; however, progress has since stalled and, in some cases, reversed. A 2005 study by former U.S. Surgeon General David Satcher found that the racial gap in mortality increased during the late 1980s and 1990s for infants and for men age 35 years or older. This retrenchment is due largely to the AIDS epidemic and deaths from violence (particularly homicides related to drugs), both of which increased during the 1990s.

Infant and Late-Life Mortality

A further analysis of the race gap in mortality reveals that it is most pronounced at the beginning of life, particularly during infancy. The gap narrows, and actually reverses according to some scholars, during old age. Infant mortality rates can be calculated in three ways. First, overall infant mortality rates refer to the number of deaths of infants under 1 year old per 1,000 live births during a given year. Second, neonatal mortality rates reflect deaths of infants under 28 days old per 1,000 live births. Third, postneonatal mortality refers to deaths of infants between 28 days and 1 year of age per 1,000 live births. Regardless of the measure used, Black infant mortality rates are roughly twice those of Whites today, whereas White, Asian, and Hispanic rates are roughly comparable. Native American rates are slightly higher than those of Whites yet lower than those of Blacks.

Perhaps the most disheartening pattern is that the race gap in infant mortality has remained large and stable for the past 5 decades. Figure 2 shows infant mortality rates by race and Hispanic ethnicity from 1940 to 2003 (rates for Hispanics were first calculated in 1985). Although infant mortality rates were nearly halved between 1940 and 1950, dropping from 74 to 43 for Blacks and from 43 to 27 for Whites, the racial gap has narrowed only slightly. The high infant mortality rate among Blacks in the United States is the single largest contributor to the overall life expectancy gap and also contributes to the fact that the United States is currently ranked 28th worldwide in its infant mortality rate.

Infant deaths are due primarily to congenital abnormalities, preterm or low birth weights, sudden infant death syndrome (SIDS), problems related to pregnancy complications, and respiratory distress syndrome. However, each of these risk factors affects infants born into ethnic minority families far more than those born into White families, with Blacks being the most severely affected. Maternal health behaviors such as smoking, substance use, poor nutrition, lack of or delay in receiving prenatal care, medical problems, and chronic illness (particularly maternal diabetes) have been cited as the primary contributors to the high infant mortality rates in the Black community.

Although Blacks are disadvantaged relative to Whites during infancy and adulthood, some demographers argue that the race gap in life expectancy

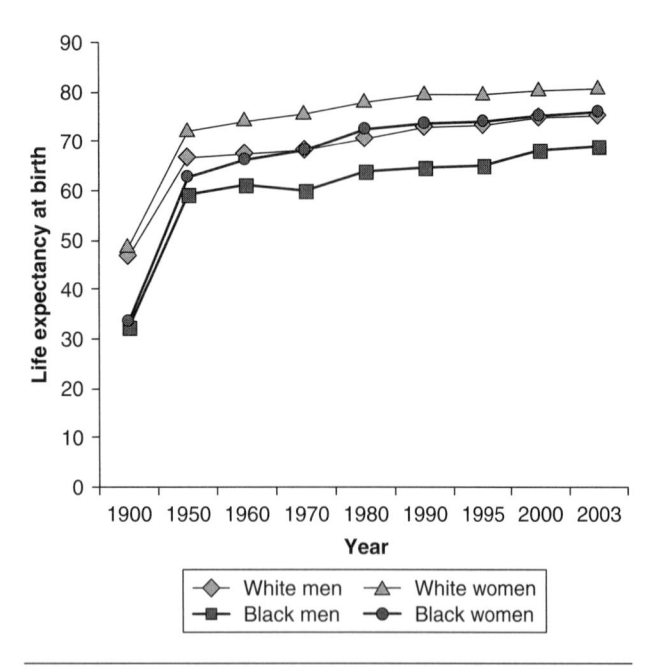

Figure 1 Life Expectancy at Birth, by Race and Sex, United States, 1900–2003

Source: National Center for Health Statistics. 2006. "United States Life Tables, 2003." *National Vital Statistics Reports,* April 19, Table 12.

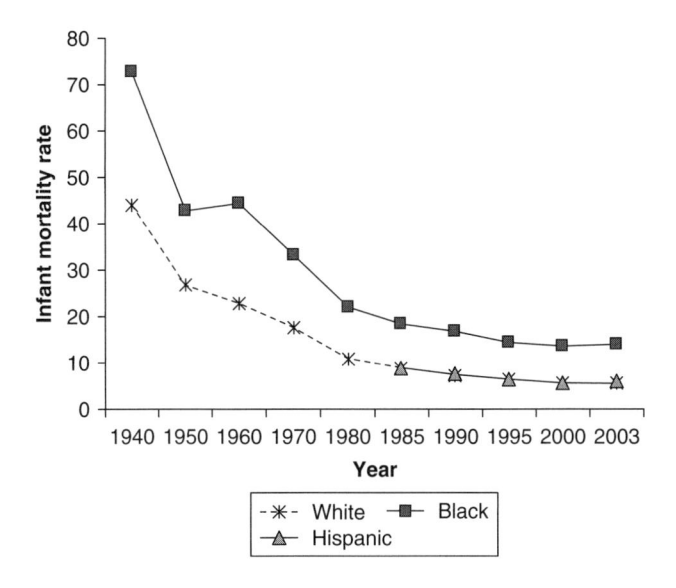

Figure 2 Infant Mortality Rates (Deaths of Infants Under 1 Year of Age) per 1,000 Live Births, by Race and Hispanic Origin, 1960–2003

Source: National Center for Health Statistics. 2006. *Health, United States, 2006* (Table 22). Washington, DC: Government Printing Office.

actually reverses among the "oldest-old" (persons age 85 years or older). To date, evidence for the "race crossover" effect is equivocal. Some propose that Blacks who have managed to withstand and survive the environmental stresses of their younger years may have a survival advantage or "hardiness" that destines them to live especially long lives. However, others counter that the apparent crossover reflects age over-reporting among older Blacks, for whom advanced age is a source of pride and respect.

Unpacking the Race Gap in Life Expectancy

Racial/ethnic differences in life expectancy are not unique to the United States. Among countries with reliable data, demographers have documented that in the early 21st century, Whites have a higher life expectancy than do First Nations people in Canada, whereas Parsis in India and Jews in Israel have higher life expectancies than do members of minority ethnic groups. Policymakers and practitioners must recognize the specific sources of mortality differentials if they hope to develop effective strategies for reducing such gaps. Four explanations are widely accepted for these discrepancies in the United States and elsewhere: socioeconomic factors (e.g., education, employment stability, job quality, income), lifestyle and health behaviors (e.g., nutrition, physical activity, diet, smoking, substance use), social environment (e.g., neighborhood and work conditions, discrimination, social integration, stress), and access to and quality of health care services (e.g., quality of local hospitals and clinics, treatment by health care professionals, access to early screening and vaccinations). On each of these dimensions, Blacks are disadvantaged relative to Whites in the United States, and these disparities in social and personal resources contribute to the life expectancy gap.

Scholars disagree, however, about the relative importance of these influences. Although social epidemiologists emphasize socioeconomic resources as a powerful influence on life span, some researchers point to the "Hispanic paradox" as evidence that economic disadvantage does not necessarily portend a shortened life span. Hispanics, like Blacks, have lower levels of education and income than do Whites, yet they enjoy life expectancies and infant mortality rates on a par with those of Whites. This pattern is attributed, in part, to the hardiness of Hispanics—particularly Mexicans—who migrate to the United States, but it is also attributed to the healthy diets, greater reliance on breast-feeding infants, low levels of smoking and drinking, and extensive social networks and strong family ties maintained by recent Mexican immigrants. Adherents to the Hispanic paradox perspective focus on targeting health behaviors as a strategy for reducing the race gap in life expectancy.

Experts also disagree about the influence of genetics. Although some racial/ethnic groups have a heightened risk of specific illnesses, such as sickle-cell anemia among African Americans and Tay-Sachs disease among Ashkenazi Jews, social scientists generally believe that such illnesses are not pervasive enough to explain overall racial differences in life expectancy. During recent years, many scholars have turned their attention away from individual-level risk factors, such as health behaviors and genetics, and instead have focused on social relationships that influence health and, ultimately, mortality. Recent research documents that racial discrimination is associated with elevated blood pressure, whereas neighborhood characteristics, including the availability of goods and services and the social integration and stability of neighborhoods, affect the health, health behaviors, and mortality of the residents.

Policymakers also increasingly recognize the role of community, socioeconomic resources, and access to care as powerful influences on health and longevity. *Healthy People 2010,* a policy statement developed by the U.S. Department of Health and Human Services, has as its top two objectives "to increase quality and years of healthy life" and "to eliminate health disparities." The strategies proposed for achieving these aims encompass "improving health, education, housing, labor, justice, transportation, agriculture, and the environment." Ultimately, the elimination of economic and social disparities on the basis of race may be the most effective way to alleviate racial disparities in health and longevity.

Deborah Carr and Alena Singleton

See also African Americans; Discrimination; Health Disparities; HIV/AIDS; Social Inequality

Further Readings

Goodman, Alan H. 2000. "Why Genes Don't Count (for Racial Differences in Health)." *American Journal of Public Health* 90:1699–1702.

Institute of Medicine. 2003. *Unequal Treatment: Confronting Racial and Ethnic Disparities in Health Care.* Washington, DC: National Academy Press.

Johnson, Nan. 2000. "The Racial Crossover in Comorbidity, Disability, and Mortality." *Demography* 3:267–283.

Palloni, Alberto and Elizabeth Arias. 2004. "Paradox Lost: Explaining the Hispanic Adult Mortality Advantage." *Demography* 41:385–416.

Pearce, Neil and George Davey Smith. 2003. "Is Social Capital the Key to Inequalities in Health?" *American Journal of Public Health* 93:122–129.

Rogers, Richard, Robert A. Hummer, and Charles B. Nam. 1999. *Living and Dying in the USA: Behavioral, Health, and Social Differentials of Adult Mortality.* San Diego, CA: Academic Press.

U.S. Department of Health and Human Services. 2000. *Healthy People 2010: Understanding and Improving Health.* Washington, DC: Author.

Wise, Paul H. 2003. "The Anatomy of a Disparity in Infant Mortality." *Annual Review of Public Health* 24:341–362.

LINCOLN, ABRAHAM (1809–1865)

Abraham Lincoln was the 16th president of the United States (1861–1865). Previously, he had been in the Illinois legislature (1834–1842) and the U.S. House of Representatives (1847–1849). He was an unsuccessful U.S. Senate candidate in 1855 and 1858, losing the latter race to Stephen A. Douglas.

Views on Slavery

Lincoln's views on slavery were consistent but complex. His father had moved the family from Kentucky to Indiana partly to avoid association with slave society. During his 20s, Lincoln transported goods on a flatboat to New Orleans, where he observed the slave markets and reportedly expressed revulsion at slavery. As a member of the Illinois legislature, he refused to sign a resolution condemning abolitionists for encouraging slave revolts; he endorsed another resolution that, although critical of abolitionists, noted that the system of slavery was founded on injustice and bad policy. Yet in his early public career, Lincoln did not give prominence to the issue. In speeches such as the 1838 Lyceum Address and the 1842 Temperance Society Address, he referred to slavery only elliptically and by analogy. As a lawyer, he defended a master seeking to reclaim a fugitive slave as well as a fugitive claiming his freedom.

Lincoln's antislavery convictions were aroused by the passage of the Kansas–Nebraska Act of 1854. Until then, he said, public opinion was that the founders had placed slavery on the path to extinction. So long as that was the case, its continued existence could be tolerated as a matter of necessity. But the Kansas–Nebraska Act opened the possibility of perpetual slavery. Lincoln made opposition to slavery's extension the centerpiece of his political creed, and it became the organizing principle of the new Republican Party. He believed that slavery must either expand or die, so containing it would be the first step toward its demise. He considered this to be a conservative position, returning to the approach of the founders.

For Lincoln, the fundamental evil of slavery was that it denied slaves the fruits of their labor, and secondarily, it was inconsistent with self-government. To the argument that slaves in the South were treated better than wage earners in the North, he responded that slavery precluded upward mobility, whereas northern wage earners might become self-employed merchants or capitalists. He defended the right to strike on the grounds that one retained control over one's labor. Frequently, he maintained that any system holding that one person was entitled to rule another person placed liberty for all at risk. Lincoln was not insensitive to the plight of the slaves, but neither their wretched condition nor the brutality of their owners furnished the principal grounds of his opposition.

Although opposed to slavery, Lincoln was not an abolitionist. His preferred solution was colonization—the simultaneous voluntary emancipation and deportation of slaves. Despite evidence of the infeasibility of colonization and the lack of enthusiasm for it, he continued to advocate it as late as 1862.

Even if he had not shared dominant U.S. views about race, Lincoln believed that he was legally precluded from doing anything about slavery where it already existed. Slavery was recognized—albeit implicitly—in the U.S. Constitution. It was a matter over which each state was sovereign. The Constitution also recognized the obligation to return fugitive slaves to their masters. Lincoln thought that he was bound by these compromises as much as by any other provisions of the Constitution. Accordingly, he frequently disclaimed any intent to interfere with slavery in the southern states. As president-elect, he indicated that he would be willing to accept a proposed constitutional amendment irrevocably guaranteeing protection of slavery where it already existed. Believing that this protection was already implicit in the Constitution, he did not object to making it explicit.

The Civil War

At the outset of the Civil War, Lincoln believed that the war was not about slavery but rather about preservation of the Union. This judgment was partly a matter of constitutional principle and partly a practical necessity to keep the slaveholding border states from seceding. Lincoln twice revoked emancipation orders issued by commanders in the field. He did not vigorously enforce the First and Second Confiscation Acts, which declared slaves as contraband that could be seized from rebellious owners. Replying to a newspaper editorial by Horace Greeley urging emancipation, Lincoln said that his goal was to save the Union, not to protect or destroy slavery.

Yet the course of the war radicalized Lincoln's thought. He had heard the argument, first developed by John Quincy Adams, that the president's war powers were sufficient to overcome normal constraints against emancipation. Under stress of military defeats, he came to recognize that slavery's survival aided the Confederate cause by releasing owners for military service, bolstering the South psychologically and depriving the North of a source of manpower. Moreover, Northern failure to crush the rebellion and the lack of an overriding moral issue increased the risk that Britain and France would extend diplomatic recognition to the Confederacy. For these reasons, after the Union success in the Battle of Antietam, Lincoln issued the Emancipation Proclamation. Some critics have chastised him for issuing a proclamation that he could not enforce given that it applied only to areas in rebellion. But Lincoln had justified emancipation as a war measure, so that was the extent of his constitutional power. Furthermore, he recognized that the proclamation was a signal that, as Union troops advanced on the ground, emancipation would follow. This signal, in turn, created a powerful incentive for slaves to desert their masters and escape behind Union lines. Still, the authority of the proclamation might expire with the end of the war. To guarantee slavery's demise, a constitutional amendment would be needed. Radical Republicans in Congress had proposed the Thirteenth Amendment, and Lincoln endorsed it in 1864.

Views on Race Relations

Lincoln's views about race relations were more convoluted than his opposition to slavery. For most of his career, abolitionism was outside of the political mainstream. Abolitionists who championed social and political equality of the races were particularly derided. It was advantageous for Lincoln's political opponents to insist that he secretly was an abolitionist regardless of what he might say publicly. His "House Divided" speech, in which he predicted that the nation would become all slave or all free, was seen as a reluctant confession of abolitionism. To blunt these attacks, Lincoln vigorously disclaimed any belief in social and political equality. His strongest statement came in the fourth debate with Douglas, where he announced that he opposed permitting Blacks to vote, to serve on juries, or to intermarry with Whites and that he favored the White race having the superior position. Lincoln's harshest critics today cite this passage as evidence of racism, whereas his defenders allege that it was a necessary adaptation to the realities of Illinois politics. Even as he denied social and political equality, however, Lincoln firmly maintained that Blacks and Whites were equal in the right to enjoy the fruits of their own labor, and this was the meaning he attributed to the phrase "the pursuit of happiness" in the Declaration of Independence.

In personal relationships, Lincoln did not display racial prejudice. He befriended Frederick Douglass, who had escaped slavery and become a prominent abolitionist speaker and writer, and invited him to the White House. He also invited a delegation of African American clergymen, although his purpose was to seek their support for colonization. Once he admitted Black soldiers into the Union Army, he opposed their discriminatory assignments and pay. Moreover, the experience of war began to modify his view of race. Impressed by the performance of Black soldiers and by their heroism, he thought that their valor called for additional recognition beyond emancipation. Accordingly, in describing his reconstruction plan, Lincoln proposed—without insisting—that educated Blacks, as well as those who fought in the Union army, be permitted to vote. Interestingly, Lincoln did not advance this proposal until what would become the final speech of his life. At the time, his reconstruction proposals were being criticized by congressional radicals who considered them to be too lenient. Meanwhile, it is likely that Black suffrage would have been anathema to conservatives. As it was, the Fifteenth Amendment was not added to the Constitution until 1870.

Lincoln was neither the principled abolitionist implied by the stereotype of the "Great Emancipator" nor the committed racist implied by the application of 21st-century moral standards. He was a politician attempting to address slavery and race within the arena of practical politics, the venue in which he believed that effective action was possible.

David Zarefsky

See also Abolitionism: The People; Douglass, Frederick; *Dred Scott v. Sandford;* Emancipation Proclamation; Slavery

Further Readings

Donald, David Herbert. 1995. *Lincoln.* New York: Simon & Schuster.
Fehrenbacher, Don E. 1962. *Prelude to Greatness: Lincoln in the 1850s.* Stanford, CA: Stanford University Press.
Miller, William Lee. 2002. *Lincoln's Virtues: An Ethical Biography.* New York: Alfred A. Knopf.
Paludan, Phillip Shaw. 1994. *The Presidency of Abraham Lincoln.* Lawrence: University Press of Kansas.
Zarefsky, David. 1990. *Lincoln, Douglas, and Slavery: In the Crucible of Public Debate.* Chicago, IL: University of Chicago Press.

LITHUANIAN AMERICANS

Lithuania, a nation roughly the size of West Virginia and having an estimated 2007 population of 3.4 million people, is located in northeastern Europe, between Russia and Latvia and bordered by the Baltic Sea. The first Lithuanian Americans who immigrated to the United States, around the beginning of the 20th century, were economic immigrants. Like most other immigrant groups of that period, they were concerned mostly with assimilating into U.S. society. Those who did retain an ethnic identity or who later constructed one were generally more concerned with expressing their ethnic heritage than with political events in Lithuania. These turn-of-the-century emigrants differed from those Lithuanians who left their country after it was incorporated into the Soviet Union in 1940. The latter, a distinct group who were convinced that someday they would return to their homeland, believed that they, as part of a diaspora, had a mission to keep alive the ideals of an independent Lithuania and to work toward restoring Lithuanian independence. Consequently, they were not as eager to assimilate into U.S. society as were earlier immigrants, and they formed their own ethnic enclaves separate from non-Lithuanian Americans as well as from earlier Lithuanian immigrants. These émigrés had the additional problem of trying to educate their children to be Lithuanian while living in the United States. Gradually, however, many of the émigrés or their descendants adopted an ethnic identity more consistent with that of the Lithuanian ethnic population. Since the independence of Lithuania from the Soviet Union in 1990, there has been additional immigration to the United States, primarily for economic reasons.

Waves of Immigration

The differences between the first two waves of Lithuanian immigrants to the United States, however, are greater than simply having disparate reasons for emigrating. The first wave of immigrants were derived primarily from the peasant population and arrived before the U.S. immigration restrictions of 1924. The second wave, composed primarily of skilled and educated individuals, immigrated under the U.S. Displaced Persons Act of 1948, following World War II and Lithuania's incorporation into the Soviet Union. (World War I and the restrictive immigration laws of the 1920s had severely limited Lithuanian immigration between the two waves.) These two groups ultimately formed very different conceptions of themselves as Lithuanian Americans. They had different relationships with their homeland, had different socioeconomic backgrounds, and arrived during different eras in U.S. history. Studying the two distinct waves, therefore, is useful for understanding the factors that produce variations in the processes of ethnic identity and ethnic mobilization.

The first wave of Lithuanian immigration to the United States, beginning in the 1880s, was a response to the abolition of serfdom; compulsory military service introduced by the Russian czar in 1874; religious, political, and national oppression by Russia; and famine in Lithuania. Many Lithuanians, of course, believed that the "American dream" of wealth and a better life was awaiting them in the United States. The movement to the United States grew through the 1880s and peaked during the late 1890s and early 1900s. Information about Lithuanian immigration before 1899 is not available because incoming Lithuanians were not registered as Lithuanians but instead were counted as Poles, Russians, or Germans. The 16-year period following the start of registration of Lithuanians by the U.S. Immigration Service shows a constant stream of Lithuanian immigration to the United States. In all, approximately a quarter-million Lithuanians immigrated to the United States. The peak years within that time frame were 1907, 1910, 1913, and 1914. The majority of the immigrants settled in urban industrial centers, especially in Chicago and in northeastern states such as New York and Pennsylvania.

Lithuanian immigrants soon formed social, economic, and cultural organizations to help themselves adapt to their new home yet still retain ties with the old one. Frequently, immigrants from the first wave had no particularly strong attachment to Lithuania because they saw themselves more as part of a village or family than as citizens of a nation-state. Often, they settled in Lithuanian–Polish neighborhoods and spoke more Polish than Lithuanian. Many Lithuanian Americans were proud to belong to a group whose members could easily assimilate into U.S. society. Although U.S. immigration from Lithuania was never completely stopped by the changes in U.S. immigration laws, a sharp decline in the numbers of more recent immigrants meant that Lithuanian American identity would be deprived of a revitalizing influence.

Leaders back in Lithuania, on the other hand, were quite concerned about the Americanization and assimilation of Lithuanian immigrants, especially around the turn of the 20th century when Lithuania was mobilizing for independence from Russia. Not all Lithuanian immigrants, however, became entirely assimilated. Some formulated a national identity after they had settled in the United States. For example, in 1893 they were rallied to the cause of their homeland when police and Cossack troops were used against Lithuanian demonstrators who were protesting the close of their Catholic Church and convent. The Lithuanian press in the United States also contributed to the creation of a Lithuanian identity by keeping Lithuanian immigrants informed about events in their homeland and the struggles for its independence. Still, they gradually came to consider themselves 100% American and saw the advantages of their lives in the New World.

According to U.S. Census figures from 1910 to 1990, however, the numbers of Lithuanian Americans born in Lithuania have declined steadily since 1930 because the older waves of Lithuanian immigrants died off at a faster rate than they could be replaced by new arrivals. Only in the data from 1950 to 1990 can one see the impact of the refugee wave of immigration in increased numbers of Americans of Lithuanian heritage.

When it became clear that Lithuanian occupation was not a temporary situation, many Lithuanians petitioned to relocate to the United States. However, the nationality quota was only 384 Lithuanians per year and thousands wished to immigrate. In 1948, Congress passed the Displaced Persons Act, which ultimately led to the immigration of approximately 36,000 Lithuanians.

These émigrés had a tremendous impact on Lithuanian civic and cultural organizations that had already been formed by members of the first Lithuanian migration by renewing their interest in their ethnicity. One could argue that Lithuanians who immigrated before 1924 and those who immigrated under the Displaced Persons Act of 1948 (émigrés) formulated their ethnic identities differently. In a sense, the Lithuanian Americans whose grandparents and great-grandparents had immigrated to the United States during the preindependence years relied on a more flexible set of standards for ethnic behavior, whereas the émigrés believed that ethnicity was a fixed phenomenon tied to their homeland. For example, Lithuanian American ethnics accept as "Lithuanian" even those who do not speak Lithuanian, whereas Lithuanian American émigrés place great importance on maintaining the mother tongue. As a result, the émigrés have accused the earlier immigrants of not exhibiting the proper feelings of *Lietuvybe* (Lithuanianness). Lithuanian Americans whose ancestors had immigrated to the United States voluntarily in search of better economic opportunities or to escape poor conditions in Lithuania often did not understand the concerns of the émigrés.

However, the variations were not simply because of generational differences. The depth of the émigrés' nationalist sentiments was also created by their experiences in the displaced persons camps. People's past lives and careers may have been lost, but they were still Lithuanians. Despite the strength of the Lithuanian identity of the émigrés, soon they faced the same problems of identity maintenance with their children as the ethnic Lithuanian Americans had faced. They also had the additional burden of dealing with their grief and guilt over the loss of their country. Thus, the exiles were caught between two worlds; they were not like the Lithuanians they left behind, and their children would not experience the same grief and guilt as they did.

This does not mean that third- and fourth-generation Lithuanian Americans—the descendants of the first wave of Lithuanian immigration—have no ethnic identity; on the contrary, it simply signifies that they changed their ethnic identity to fit current needs and circumstances. The refugee community, for example, is characterized by the use of language as a boundary marker. This is due to the belief that if there is to be any hope for a return to Lithuania, language must be retained at all costs. On the other hand, the retention or learning of Lithuanian cultural aspects, such as knowledge of foods and folk dances, is a marker of Lithuanian ethnic identification for ethnics because they do not expect to return to Lithuania permanently. Jewelry specific to the region, such as Baltic amber, is another easily identifiable cultural marker for both ethnics and émigrés. The maintenance of ethnic identity, therefore, has a variety of expressions among Lithuanian Americans. The differences, however, can result in misunderstanding and tensions between the groups.

Contemporary Lithuanian Americans

Lithuanian Americans today are still a relatively small ethnic group. In 1990, there were 842,209 Lithuanian Americans living in the United States, according to the U.S. Census; of these, 30,344 were foreign-born and 811,865 were born in the United States. The total number in 1990 was up from the 1980 figure of 742,776. The five states with the largest populations of Lithuanian Americans in both 1980 and 1990 (in descending order) were Illinois, Pennsylvania, New York, Massachusetts, and California.

In general, the percentage of the 1990 Lithuanian American population in each state was the same as, or similar to, that in 1980. There were, however, a few notable exceptions. Traditional strongholds such as Illinois and Pennsylvania experienced a decline in the percentage of Lithuanian Americans (15.1% to 13.9% for Illinois and 14.3% to 12.4% for Pennsylvania). Florida, however, experienced an increase in its percentage of Lithuanian Americans from 1980 to 1990 (3.8% to 5.3%). This was attributed to Lithuanian American retirees moving from the northeast to Florida and other sunnier climes. Since 1990, there has been an 18.7% decline in the Lithuanian American population. The current immigration has not been enough to offset the deaths of older Lithuanian Americans from the first waves. It remains to be seen how these three very different groups, some with lived experiences of communism, interact and blend together in the United States.

Mary E. Kelly

See Appendix A
See also Americanization; Assimilation; Ethnic Enclave, Economic Impact of; Immigration, U.S.; Polish Americans; Symbolic Ethnicity

Further Readings

Ališauskas, Arūnas. 1980. "Lithuanians." Pp. 665–676 in *Harvard Encyclopedia of Ethnic Groups,* edited by S. Thernstrom. Cambridge, MA: Harvard University Press.

Baškauskas, Liucija. 1981. "The Lithuanian Refugee Experience and Grief." *Immigration and Migration Review* 15:276–291.

Baškauskas, Liucija. 1985. *An Urban Enclave.* New York: AMS Press.

Budreckis, Algirdas M., ed. 1976. *The Lithuanians in America, 1651–1975.* Bobbs Ferry, NY: Oceana.

Gedmintas, Aleksandras. 1989. *An Interesting Bit of Identity.* New York: AMS Press.

Jonitis, Peter. 1985. *Acculturation of the Lithuanians of Chester, Pennsylvania.* New York: AMS Press.

Kelly, Mary E. 2006. *Born Again Lithuanians.* Unpublished doctoral dissertation, University of Kansas.

Kučas, Antanas. 1975. *Lithuanians in America.* Boston, MA: Encyclopedia Lituanica.

Roucek, Joseph Slabey. 1978. "General Characterizations of Lithuanian Immigrants." Pp. 46–60 in *Lithuanians in the United States,* edited by Leo J. Aliunas. San Francisco, CA: R&E Research Associates.

Senn, Alfred Erich and Alfonsas Eidintas. 1987. "Lithuanian Immigrants in America and the Lithuanian National Movement before 1914." *Journal of American Ethnic History* 6(2):5–19.

London Bombings (July 7, 2005)

The London bombings of July 7, 2005, killed 52 people and injured nearly 800, and four British-born Muslims were identified as the perpetrators. The coordinated attacks were aimed at the London transport system, with explosions both on a bus and underground. This entry describes the events and their aftermath, with particular attention paid to their racial, ethnic, and religious social contexts.

On July 6, 2005, London was awarded the Summer Olympic Games for 2012. Within 24 hours of that announcement, the jubilant mood in the English capital would swing from euphoria to complete terror. The first bomb exploded at 8:50 a.m. on a Piccadilly Line train traveling south from King's Cross station to Russell Square. Here 26 people and the bomber were killed, and nearly 350 people were injured. At the same time, another bomb exploded in a Circle Line train traveling from the Liverpool Street station to Aldgate. Here 7 people and the bomber were killed, and more than 150 people were injured. Yet again, at 8:50 a.m., a third device exploded on another Circle Line train that was traveling between Edgware Road Station and Paddington. Here 6 people and the bomber were killed, and more than 150 people were injured. Finally, at 9:47 a.m., a bomb tore apart the back of a No. 30 double-decker bus at the junction of Tavistock Square and Upper Woburn Place. Here 13 people and the bomber were killed, and more than 110 people were injured.

The planning of the operation was simple, the operation did not cost much, and little expertise was needed to turn the materials into bombs. The suicide bombers, on the morning of July 7, had driven separately down from Yorkshire and met in Luton, north of London, where they took a train south to Kings Cross and then went their separate ways on the London transport network.

The aftermath of the bombings quickly brought increased scrutiny for both the Muslim and Arab communities of the United Kingdom. Indeed, the notion of "homegrown terrorists" seemed to take on a renewed ethnic tone. One of the most pertinent questions that the *Report of the Official Account of the Bombings* asked was the following: Why did the terrorist attackers do it?

Mohammad Sifique Khan, the 30-year-old Edgware Road bomber, had a university education and had also been a teaching assistant and youth worker. Shehzad Tanweer, the 22-year-old Aldgate bomber, also had received a university education and was working for his father, who was looking to set him up in business. Hasib Mir Hussain, the 18-year-old Tavistock Square bomber, was not a high academic achiever but still studied an advanced business program in college. Germaine Lindsay, the 19-year-old Russell Square bomber, was bright, successful academically at school, and good at sports. All of the bombers were British-born Muslims.

Socially, Khan, Tanweer, and Hussain met around the mosques, youth clubs, gyms, and Islamic bookshop in Beeston, Yorkshire, in the north of England. Lindsay was the outsider but had met Khan through Islamic networks in the Huddersfield and Dewsbury areas of Yorkshire. The official report described Khan as a leading figure and a mentor to many in his local area.

Khan's video statement, which was first broadcast on the *Al Jazeera* network on September 1, 2005, provided insights into his motivations. Khan suggested, "Until we feel security, you will be our targets. And until you stop the bombing, gassing, imprisonment, and torture of my people, we will not stop this fight." The official report highlighted that Khan's last will and testament focused on the importance of martyrdom as supreme evidence of religious commitment. This links with similar attacks by suicide bombers—the fierce opposition to perceived injustices by the West against Muslims in countries such as Iraq and Afghanistan and a resulting desire for martyrdom.

The group involved in the bombings was integrated into British society, and this meant that detecting people with similar goals would be difficult. The general public became more suspicious of its native Arab and Muslim populations.

Terrorist attacks are nothing new to Londoners, nor have they been without an ethnic context before. The Irish Republican Army (IRA) attacked London on several occasions; in 1993, one bomb explosion ripped apart the NatWest Tower in central London. However, the IRA would send coded telephone messages as a warning. The terrorists of July 7 attacked without any such warning. This fact alone increased tension in a society where terror seems, in the 21st century, to constantly reside just under the surface.

Perhaps due to an increase in security measures, some subsequent attacks were prevented, most notably on July 21, 2005, with the halting of four attempted bombings, three of which were again aimed at underground trains and one of which was aimed at a bus. However, on June 29, 2007, unexploded car bombs were discovered in London, and a day later two men drove a car loaded with gas canisters into barriers at the Glasgow airport. No one was killed in these attacks, which appeared to be related.

A current issue that concerns security forces in the West is how to gain insider information on ethnic immigrant communities without infringing on immigrant rights. The British government has called for continuous national preparedness involving the public, private, and voluntary sectors at all levels across the United Kingdom against the continuing possibilities of future attacks.

Richard Race

See also Europe; Immigrant Communities; Islamophobia; Muslim Americans; Northern Ireland, Racism in; Racial Profiling; Terrorism; United Kingdom

Further Readings

Gove, Michael. 2006. *Celsius 7/7*. London: Wiedenfeld & Nicolson.

U.K. Home Office. 2006. *Addressing Lessons from the Emergency Response to the 7th July 2005 London Bombings: What We Learned and What We Are Doing about It*. Retrieved from http://security.homeoffice.gov.uk/news-publications/publication-search/general/lessons-learned?view=Binary

U.K. House of Commons. 2006. *Report of the Official Account of the Bombings in London on 7th July 2005*. London: Her Majesty's Stationery Office. Available from http://news.bbc.co.uk/1/shared/bsp/hi/pdfs/11_05_06_narrative.pdf

LOVING V. VIRGINIA

The *Loving v. Virginia* (1967) U.S. Supreme Court decision, which rendered antimiscegenation laws unconstitutional, was the final element in a series of civil rights legislative and judicial actions that dismantled legalized segregation in the United States. The plaintiffs—Mildred Delores Jeter, of mixed African American and (Rappahannock) Indian ancestry, and her White fiancé, Richard Perry Loving, both of Central Point, Virginia—were married in Washington, D.C., on June 2, 1958. The Lovings returned to Central Point and resided with Mildred's parents while Richard worked to build a new house for his pregnant bride. On July 11, 1958, as the Lovings lay asleep in bed, the sheriff, accompanied by two additional law enforcement officers, burst into the couple's bedroom and arrested them for the felony of miscegenation. Two separate

Mildred and Richard Loving. *Married couple Mildred and Richard Loving answer questions at a press conference the day after the U.S. Supreme Court ruled in their favor in Loving v. Virginia (June 13, 1967). The Court, in a unanimous decision, overturned Virginia's antimiscegenation statute, which had resulted in the Lovings' arrests shortly after their 1958 marriage.*

Source: Time & Life Pictures/Getty Images.

warrants along with an indictment were issued for Richard Loving and Mildred Jeter, respectively.

The Lovings were in violation of Virginia's 1924 Act to Preserve Racial Integrity, a law passed during the apex of the American eugenics movement, which promoted ideals of racial purity. The racial integrity act was the culmination of Virginia's three-centuries-long obsession with racial purity, as demonstrated by the earliest statutes recorded by the legislature of the Virginia Colony dating back to 1630. From the colonial era until the end of the 19th century, the Virginia General Assembly enacted no fewer than forty statutes against mixed marriages. Despite such laws, interracial liaisons persisted. Hence, Virginia's 1924 act, forbidding intermarriage between Blacks and Whites, served to tighten any loopholes in previously enacted legislation and to stiffen the penalty for those who violated the law. Prior to 1930, however, several multiracial couples, who were denied marriage licenses by vital statistics clerks, successfully sued in the Virginia courts, claiming in each case that the spouse in question was not Black but rather American Indian. Mildred Loving, whose Central Point community was composed of people of mixed Black, White, and Indian ancestry, laid claim to an exclusive Native American identity as indicated on her District of Columbia marriage license. Nevertheless, as a result of earlier challenges to the racial integrity act, the Virginia General Assembly in 1930 enacted legislation that recognized as Indian only those residing on reservations. All others, even those of unquestionable Indian ancestry, were classified as Negro and forbidden to marry Whites. Hence, Mildred Loving's claim to an exclusive Indian identity did not exempt her from the racial integrity law.

Miscegenation was a felony, and the penalty for violation was a year in the penitentiary. On January 6, 1959, Judge Leon M. Bazile suspended the sentence provided that the couple leave the state and not return as husband and wife for 25 years. The Lovings immediately moved to Washington, D.C. In 1963, they petitioned the Virginia Supreme Court to vacate the 1959 judgment and to set aside their sentence. Bazile, who had handed down the earlier decision, denied the motion, stating that God had not intended for the races to mix. The couple returned to the District of Columbia and wrote a letter to Robert Kennedy, then U.S. attorney general, requesting his assistance. The Attorney General's Office forwarded the letter to the American Civil Liberties Union (ACLU). Bernard Cohen, a young lawyer who at the time was doing pro bono work for the ACLU, took the case. Another lawyer, Philip J. Hirschkof, signed on as cocounsel when he joined the Cohen firm. Both men were aware that the case was destined for the U.S. Supreme Court, but two earlier attempts to overturn state antimiscegenation laws, in the cases of *Naim v. Naim* (1955) and *McLaughlin v. Florida* (1964), caused the lawyers to question whether the High Court was ready to take such a drastic measure.

The *Naim* case involved Ham Say Naim, a Chinese sailor, and his White wife, Ruby Elaine Naim of Virginia, whom he had married in North Carolina. Whereas Virginia held that Whites could marry only Whites, North Carolina restricted only White–Black marriages. The couple returned to Virginia and lived for a time in Norfolk but later separated. Ruby Naim petitioned the Virginia court to grant her an annulment on the grounds that her husband had committed adultery; however, if the court refused to grant her petition on that ground, she requested that the petition be granted based on Virginia's antimiscegenation law. Ruby Naim's petition was granted. Ham Say Naim challenged the decision in the Virginia Supreme Court on the grounds that the lower court decision violated his rights under the Fourteenth Amendment. Nevertheless, as it did for the Lovings, whose lawyers would use the same argument 10 years later before the U.S. Supreme Court, the Virginia Supreme Court ruled unanimously against Ham Say Naim. Yet unlike for *Loving,* the U.S. Supreme Court refused to hear the *Naim* case. Subsequently, in the 1964 U.S. Supreme Court case of *McLaughlin v. Florida* in which a White woman and a Black man were arrested for unlawful cohabitation, the Supreme Court justices, although not overturning antimiscegenation laws, voted unanimously to overturn the couple's conviction, rendering it unlawful for states to prohibit people from living together on the basis of race.

When the justices agreed to hear the *Loving* case on December 12, 1966, twenty of the thirty-one states that had once enforced antimiscegenation laws had repealed them. However, eleven states, all in the South, remained steadfast in their position against mixed-race marriages. Both sides for the *Loving v. Virginia* case presented their arguments on April 10, 1967. On June 12, 1967, the High Court handed down its decision. It overturned the Lovings' conviction and declared antimiscegenation laws unconstitutional.

Arica L. Coleman

See also Ethnicity, Negotiating; Eugenics; Intermarriage; Multiracial Identity; One-Drop Rule; Racial Formation

Further Readings

Coleman, Arica L. 2006. "'Tell the Court I Love My Indian Wife': Interrogating Race and Identity in *Loving v. Virginia*." *Souls: A Critical Journal of Black Politics, Culture, and Society* 8(1):67–80.

Loving v. Virginia, 388 U.S. 1 (1967).

McLaughlin v. Florida, 379 U.S. 184 (1964).

Naim v. Naim, 197 Va. 80 (1955).

Newbeck, Phyl. 2004. *Virginia Hasn't Always Been for Lovers: Interracial Marriage Bans and the Case of Loving v. Virginia*. Carbondale: Southern Illinois University Press.

Wallenstein, Peter. 2002. *Tell the Court I Love My Wife: Race, Marriage, and Law—An American History*. New York: Palgrave Macmillan.

LYNCHING

Any historical account of the United States must note the violence associated with race relations. An important part of understanding this history lies with examining lynching and its violent impact on U.S. society and discourse. Recently, the definition of lynching, the historical accounts of its victims, and the reasons and motivations for lynching have been examined closely to shed more light on this disturbing component of U.S. history. The late-18th-century definition of lynching as nonlethal flogging, tarring and feathering, and running people out of town began with Colonel Charles Lynch, a justice of the peace in Virginia and creator of an informal court system of "lynch mobs" to deal with Tories and suspected horse thieves in the county. During the following century, lynch mobs were formed as an expression of Whites' fears of Black uprisings or slave insurrections, increasingly with lethal consequences. The definition later changed to the extralegal murder of individuals and groups of people by a mob of two or more persons.

Lynching Documented

In 1882, Tuskegee University began keeping records of lynchings in the United States. Tuskegee's first director of records, sociologist Monroe Work, and subsequent generations of Tuskegee librarians and students maintained newspaper and magazine reports of lynchings. This record, published annually from 1882 to 1962, became an important contributor to public attention to this phenomenon. From 1882 to 1885, the number of Whites lynched outnumbered the number of Blacks lynched. After the year 1886, the number of Blacks lynched always exceeded the number of Whites lynched. Through 1944, Tuskegee recorded 3,417 lynchings of Blacks, meaning that, on average, a Black person was murdered by a White mob nearly once a week, every week, during this time period. Although lynchings declined after 1944, it was not until 1952 that a year passed without a single recorded lynching. It is important to note that these records indicate only the number of documented lynchings and that many lynchings occurred without public record.

Reconstruction and Mob Violence

In the Reconstruction era South, lynching of Blacks was used, especially by the Ku Klux Klan, in an effort to reverse the social changes brought on by federal occupation. With the development of the Black Codes, and later the Jim Crow laws, a rise in African American lynchings in the South occurred. Lynching was a means to intimidate, degrade, and control Black people and to soothe the tensions of Whites throughout the southern and border states from Reconstruction to the mid-20th century.

Lynching was an illegal act because it denied a suspect due process under the law. Thus, the information that due process generated (including lawyers' arguments, sworn testimony, and evidence) was not available to assist in understanding the instigating deed and in weighing guilt or innocence. In many cases, if a person was charged with a particular crime, the details of the actual incident would become obscured or falsified. If an individual was being detained by criminal justice authorities, an incensed vigilante mob would form and demand that law officials release the prisoner to the crowd. The law officials either easily acquiesced or surrendered the prisoner through force. Once the mob had obtained the prisoner, a crowd would gather—sometimes up to several thousand people—and the act of the lynching would occur. Many scholars note that lynchings were highly ritualized spectacles.

Advocacy Against Lynching

Rather than viewing lynching as a frenzied abnormality, historians during recent years have sought to understand it as a tradition, a systematized reign of terror that was used to maintain the power that Whites had over Blacks, a way to keep Blacks fearful and to forestall Black progress. Owing chiefly to advocacy by the National Association for the Advancement of Colored People (NAACP) and by several key figures from the early 20th century, including antilynching activist Ida B. Wells, Congress began to create laws to abolish the practice of lynching.

The United States still suffers from the legacy of lynching. Many opponents of the death penalty cite its historical roots in lynchings. In 1998, a Black man, James Byrd, Jr., was lynched in Jasper, Texas. The killers placed a chain around his neck, and Byrd was dragged for three miles behind a truck before his remains were deposited in front of a Black cemetery. The White men who murdered Byrd were later charged and convicted of a hate crime.

Troy Harden

See also Death Penalty; Homicide; Jewish-Black Relations: A Historical Perspective Jim Crow; Ku Klux Klan; Racism; Wells-Barnett, Ida B.

Further Readings

Allen, James. 2000. *Without Sanctuary: Lynching Photography in America.* Santa Fe, NM: Twin Palms.

Dray, Philip. 2002. *At the Hands of Persons Unknown: The Lynching of Black America.* New York: Random House.

Pfeifer, Michael J. 2004. *Rough Justice: Lynching and American Society, 1874–1947.* Chicago, IL: University of Illinois Press.

Tolnay, Stewart E. and E. M. Beck. 1992. *A Festival of Violence: An Analysis of Southern Lynchings, 1882–1930.* Urbana: University of Illinois Press.

M

Machismo

The term *machismo* has been used in a variety of ways to mean different, sometimes contradictory things. It is typically associated with Latin American men as an imputation of negative character traits related to masculinity. The *American Heritage Dictionary* defines *machismo* as a strong or exaggerated sense of masculinity stressing attributes such as physical courage, virility, domination of women, aggressiveness, and an exaggerated sense of strength and toughness. The *Diccionario de la Real Academia Española,* 21st edition, defines machismo as "an arrogant *(prepotencia)* attitude by men towards women."

Machismo—the idea of being macho—appears to be embedded in matters pertaining to the roles, statuses, rights, responsibilities, influence, and moral positions of men as they relate to women. The principal characteristics of machismo are exaggerated aggressiveness and intransigence in male-to-male relationships and arrogance and sexual aggression in male-to-female relationships. In a broader cultural context, machismo may be associated with male chauvinism, which the *Oxford Dictionary* defines as male prejudice against women and the regarding of women as inferior to men.

Whether the notion of machismo originated in Latino culture is debatable. Some social scientists argue that the term was coined by ethnographers studying Latino cultures and then became part of the Latino lexicon. At any rate, while the male attributes associated with machismo are universal, the term in the popular as well as the scholarly literature is often explicitly connected with Latino culture.

According to the *Dictionary of Mexican Cultural Code Words, machismo* means (a) rejecting so-called feminine characteristics, such as unselfishness and kindness; (b) being willing to lie; (c) being suspicious and jealous; and (d) being willing to fight or even to kill to protect an image of manliness. Proof of being a man, in this definition, includes dominating the family, having sexual relations with anyone one chooses, and never showing one's real feelings. Jerry Tello, cofounder of the National Compadres Network in the United States, says that this negative—and typically American—view of machismo is uninformed. According to Tello, a true man in Latin America is someone who carries respect, responsibility, and honor. This latter notion of machismo harks back to pre-Columbian times, when to be a man meant respecting sacred things and people, including women. Such a man was considered in that cultural tradition to be an *hombre noble*—an honorable man.

In most societies, female and male roles are considered complementary; in Hispanic cultures, machismo refers to essentially male or masculine attributes and behaviors, while *hembrismo* pertains to matters feminine. Some writers note that just as machismo may be seen as an exaggerated sense of masculinity, hembrismo is the feminine quality of being excessively submissive and subservient to men. The two concepts must be considered in concert.

It is evident that there are contradictions within the range of matters that pertain to machismo. Definitions of machismo may be placed on a grid, where one axis represents "self-confidence" and the intersecting axis represents "self-doubt." On the former axis are attributes such as honor, shame, formality, and respect.

The self-doubt axis comprises characteristics pertinent to inferiority and insecurity. Thus, where males feel that they are not in control regarding power relationships and matters involving prestige, they put on a façade of "in your face" masculinity to obscure any possible personal shortcomings. The popular conception of machismo tends to consider only the self-doubt axis, and discussions of machismo consequently exaggerate the negative attributes of machismo.

Naturally, intense male feelings of superiority ensure that a man holds a traditional view of the role of women: A woman's place is in the home. This traditional patriarchal view of the role of women seems inextricably bound up in the treatment of women by men around the world. However, to equate machismo with patriarchy would be a disservice to the cultural context in which machismo must be understood. Some writers in the Latin American context expressly relate machismo to the domestic situation: Women are of the home *(la mujer es de la casa),* and men are of the street *(el hombre es de la calle).* Whereas women are thought of by macho men as destined to be domestic, men expect—and are expected—to have little, if anything, to do with the household; their role, aside from fathering progeny, is to be in the public domain only.

While expectations with respect to machismo are not held exclusively by males, the male perspective is unique to those of the masculine gender. In addition to a gendered perspective, there is evidence that social class and educational level impinge upon how one views machismo. A 1999 Colombian study demonstrates that for the 7,035 consumers sampled, there was a positive correlation between agreement with the statement "A woman's place is at home" and the respondent's sex, age, social class, and educational level. Male respondents were more likely than females to agree. Similarly, older respondents, those who had not completed primary school, and those in the lowest socioeconomic categories were more likely to agree with the statement than those who were younger, those with relatively higher levels of formal education, and those at the higher socioeconomic levels.

Many would argue that failure to promote and ensure equal rights for women contributes to the deleterious effects of machismo. In certain Latin American countries, such as Nicaragua, wife beating and abandonment are accepted as normal, and only recently have there been systemic or even grassroots initiatives undertaken to educate men about the disastrous effects of domestic violence.

The status of women globally can be seen as a direct result of macho attitudes. Certainly, many Latin American feminist writers identify machismo as the cause of sexual inequality. As an indication of this phenomenon, the United Nations Department of Public Information reports that worldwide, up to 50% of women experience some degree of domestic violence during marriage. Many more are the victims of rape, both domestically and when rape is used as a weapon of war. From such statistics, it is evident that an excessive expression of male power and privilege has a corresponding indication of low status, inferiority, and powerlessness among women.

Peter Doell

See also Barrio; Central Americans in the United States; Domestic Violence; Film, Latino; Gender and Race, Intersection of; Hispanics; Latina/o Studies

Further Readings

Boye, Lagayette de Mente. 1996. *NTC's Dictionary of Mexican Cultural Code Words.* Chicago, IL: NTC Publishing Group.

Brusco, Elizabeth E. 1995. *The Reformation of Machismo: Evangelical Conversion and Gender in Colombia.* Austin: University of Texas Press.

De La Torre, Miguel. 1999. "Beyond Machismo: A Cuban Case Study." *Annual of the Society of Christian Ethics* 19:213–233.

Jensen, Evelyn E. 1987. *The Hispanic Perspective of the Ideal Woman.* Ann Arbor, MI: UMI Dissertation Information Service.

Malcolm X (1925–1965)

Malcolm X was an African American political leader whose dynamic speaking ability, keen intellect, and fiery persona catapulted him to the forefront of the Black Nationalist Movement of the 1950s and 1960s. In the early phase of his career, his analysis of the links between religion and racial oppression made him a lightning rod for controversy. Closely linked to his shifts in ideology, however, was his private pursuit of truth—the wellspring of radical

Malcolm X. *Black Nationalist and Muslim leader Malcolm X (1925–1965) talks with to a woman inside Temple 7, a Halal restaurant that serves food permissible under Islamic law. The restaurant, patronized by Black Muslims, is situated on Lenox Avenue and 116th Street in the Harlem section of New York. A portrait of Elijah Muhammad, founder of the Nation of Islam, appears on the back wall of the restaurant.*

Source: Getty Images.

character transformations throughout his life. Author of a best-selling autobiography and, by the time of his death, an internationally famous figure, he was assassinated in New York City in 1965. This entry focuses on the three phases of Malcolm X's adult life: his days as a small-time street hustler and drug addict, his religious conversion and public leadership of the Nation of Islam, and his analytical shift away from biological arguments about White racism toward a more global and structural understanding of intergroup relations. While Malcolm X was not directly involved with the Civil Rights Movement, his combative perspective strongly influenced militant factions in the struggle for racial equality. Consequently, to this day, Malcolm X remains revered for his assertion that Black progress must occur "by any means necessary."

Malcolm Little

Malcolm X was born Malcolm Little, on May 19, 1925, in Omaha, Nebraska. Soon after his birth, Malcolm's family relocated near Lansing, Michigan. His father, Earl Little, was a Baptist preacher and member of Marcus Garvey's Universal Negro Improvement Association (UNIA). This allegiance, as well as his speaking out against racial injustice, led to his violent death at the hands of White supremacists. Unable to cope with this loss and its aftermath, Malcolm's mother, Louise, was subsequently committed to a mental institution.

Malcolm and his siblings were sent to live in foster homes. Despite his family's circumstances, he continued to excel in school, remaining near the top of his eighth-grade class. In his autobiography, Malcolm described an incident in which his favorite teacher asked him whether he had considered his occupational future. After Malcolm divulged that he was interested in the legal profession, the teacher told him that becoming a lawyer was not a "realistic goal for a nigger" (*Autobiography of Malcolm X*, p. 36). Malcolm dropped out of school soon after this unfortunate interaction.

Detroit Red

Malcolm divided his adolescent and early adult years between Boston and New York City. During this time, he became fascinated with urban Black life; the cosmopolitan culture sharply contrasted with the small-town environment of his youth. Malcolm became a hipster, frequenting nightclubs and emulating the latest trends. His superior dancing and social skills earned him a favorable reputation. He developed a network of Black underworld associates and pursued relationships with White women. Although interracial intimacy was taboo in mainstream society, in urban Black society it was a mark of high status.

Malcolm's loose associations with the underworld soon evolved into structured criminal activity. He went from working odd jobs and abusing drugs to organizing illegal hustles such as drug dealing, gambling, prostitution, and armed robbery. He soon earned the nickname "Detroit Red" because of his Michigan familial roots and fair-skinned complexion. In 1946, at age 21, Malcolm was sentenced to 8 to 10 years in prison for orchestrating a string of burglaries.

Minister Malcolm

While serving his prison term, Malcolm was informed that many of siblings had converted from Christianity to the Nation of Islam (NOI). His brother, Reginald, had hoped that Malcolm would join along with them. During a prison visit, he proselytized Malcolm with an account of how God appeared on earth in the form of a Black man, the Honorable Elijah Muhammad, who had come to uplift the Black condition by defeating the devil—the American White man.

Malcolm was taken aback by this theology. He carefully considered this information for several weeks, reflecting on his family's history and his involvement in the underworld. He soon joined the NOI, which he now believed was the "natural religion for the Black man" (*Autobiography of Malcolm X,* p. 155). For the remainder of his prison term, Malcolm wrote to Elijah Muhammad daily and studied religious doctrine and world history so relentlessly that his eyesight suffered. His tutelage under Elijah Muhammad was much more than mentorship. Malcolm came to believe that Muhammad was a supernatural being who possessed the "power of the sun" (*Autobiography of Malcolm X,* p. 212).

In 1952, Malcolm was paroled after serving nearly 7 years of his sentence. After meeting Elijah Muhammad in person, he changed his name from Malcolm Little to Malcolm X. This change, which was customary for NOI members, symbolized the Black man's unknown African identity. Within months, Malcolm X was named an assistant minister of the Detroit mosque. His efforts helped triple the local membership.

Muhammad soon declared Malcolm X the NOI's national spokesman and charged him with increasing membership in major metropolitan centers, including New York City, Philadelphia, Los Angeles, and Atlanta. His efforts helped the group's following swell from less than 1,000 members in the early 1950s to over 30,000 within 10 years.

Malcolm X and the NOI were becoming nationally known. Mike Wallace, a noted television news journalist, broadcast an exposé of the NOI entitled "The Hate That Hate Produced." The general public in the United States would now become familiar with Malcolm X's arguments that Christianity was a "White man's religion," that Blacks and Whites could not coexist equally, and that the Black community suffered from deep-seated racial self-hatred. The *New York Times* reported that by 1963, Malcolm X was the second most sought-after public speaker in the United States.

By this same year, however, problems emerged within the NOI. Malcolm X discovered that Muhammad had committed adultery, fathering several children with women within the NOI. He warned several of his closest confidants about Muhammad's indiscretions. Some of these members considered Malcolm's investigation and dispersal of information an act of treason.

By November 22, 1963, Malcolm X's leadership within the NOI had become tenuous. His direct disregard for Muhammad's order to not publicly comment on the assassination of President John F. Kennedy brought group tensions to a boiling point.

Malcolm X's statement that the president's death was symptomatic of the "chickens coming home to roost" outraged the general public. Consequently, Muhammad stripped Malcolm X of his authority for 90 days. It was made known that his authority would not be restored unless Malcolm X submitted to Muhammad's leadership.

On March 8, 1964, Malcolm X publicly announced his break with the Nation of Islam. It was during this tumultuous period that he realized "after twelve years of never thinking for as much as five minutes about myself, I became able finally to muster the nerve, and the strength, to start facing the facts, to think for myself" (*Autobiography of Malcolm X,* p. 306). He soon converted to orthodox Islam and announced the establishment of his own Islamic temple, Muslim Mosque, Inc.

El-Hajj Malik El-Shabazz

As required by the tenets of his new faith, Malcolm X soon commenced his *Hajj,* or pilgrimage, to the holy city of Mecca, Saudi Arabia. This excursion proved to be a fundamental, life-changing experience. In this Islamic capital, Malcolm X reported experiencing the "true meaning of brotherhood" (*Autobiography of Malcolm X,* p. 362) with Muslims from all over the world. These believers, whose backgrounds crossed a range of racial/ethnic groups and nationalities, welcomed him in ways he had never previously experienced. This appreciation inspired an ideological transformation within Malcolm X; he came to realize that the American White man was not inherently evil, but rather a victim, just as Blacks were, of an oppressive social structure that fostered racial discord.

During this trip, Malcolm X traveled extensively throughout Africa and the Middle East, meeting with

Arab dignitaries and African politicians. These experiences broadened his beliefs about religion, politics, and the need for building alliances with oppressed people across the globe.

Upon his return to the United States, Malcolm X announced that he had changed his name to El-Hajj Malik El-Shabazz. This name change was consistent with his more traditional Sunni Islamic beliefs. He also made known his intent to establish the Organization of Afro-American Unity (OAAU), an interfaith nonpartisan group aimed at advancing human rights.

Soon after making these statements, Malcolm X was asked by a White man if they could shake hands. Malcolm responded, "I don't mind shaking hands with human beings. Are you one?" (*Autobiography of Malcolm X,* p. 363). He now lamented that he once told a young White coed that there was nothing she could do to help his cause. Instead, he believed that Blacks and Whites could work together, although independently, toward the promotion of human rights.

Unfortunately, Malcolm X was unable to follow through with much of his new agenda. On February 21, 1965, he was assassinated while giving a speech at the Audubon Ballroom, in New York City. He was 39 years old. Although some scholars theorize that several organizations were involved in his death, all three of the men prosecuted for his murder were members of the NOI. Further information about his assassination and records of the FBI's investigation of Malcolm X are available on the Federal Bureau of Investigation Web site.

Jason Eugene Shelton and Jeffrey C. Johnson

See Appendix B

See also Baldwin, James; Black Nationalism; Black Power; Muslim Americans; Nation of Islam

Further Readings

Malcolm X, with Alex Haley. 1964. *The Autobiography of Malcolm X.* New York: Ballantine.

Malcolm X, with George Breitman. 1965. *Malcolm X Speaks: Selected Speeches and Statements.* New York: Merit Publishers and Betty Shabazz.

McCartney, John. 1992. *Black Power Ideologies.* Philadelphia, PA: Temple University Press.

Sales, William. 1994. *From Civil Rights to Black Liberation: Malcolm X and the Organization of Afro-American Unity.* Boston, MA: South End Press.

Web Sites

Federal Bureau of Investigation Web Site, information on Malcolm X: http://foia.fbi.gov/foiaindex/malcolmx.htm

Official Web Site of Malcolm X (maintained by the Estate of Malcolm X): http://www.cmgworldwide.com/historic/malcolm/about/index.php

MANDELA, NELSON (1918–)

Born in a small, rural village in racially segregated South Africa, Rolihlahla Nelson Mandela, lawyer and political activist, attained international recognition for his commitment to social justice. For many, he has come to personify the struggle against racial oppression in the modern world. Released from prison in February 1990, after 27 years behind bars, Mandela led the African National Congress in the negotiations that led to South Africa's first democratic elections and served as his country's first democratically elected president, from 1994 to 1999. He was awarded the Nobel Peace Prize in 1993.

Mandela's life has entailed, to quote the title of his autobiography, "a long walk to freedom." When his father, a hereditary chief, died, Mandela was taken into the care of a much more senior chief. From him, Mandela learned that a great chief is able to keep together all of his people, whether traditionalist or reformist, conservative or liberal. Mandela's schooling was completed at Methodist mission schools. In 1939, he moved on to the South African Native College at Fort Hare, then the only Black university in South Africa and thus the key institution forming the new Black South African intellectual and professional elite. Despite being generally apolitical, he was expelled after challenging the university's principal. In 1941, he migrated to the fast-growing "City of Gold," Johannesburg, where he was employed as a night watchman. Mandela soon moved to a legal firm and began to study law. He was slowly drawn into circles of political activists around the African National Congress (ANC) and the Communist Party of South Africa.

The ANC had been formed in 1912, just after the establishment of the Union of South Africa. The early ANC was dominated by a mission-educated, Anglophile, professional African elite, whose goal was neither to resist colonization nor to transform it, but rather to achieve full political and economic assimilation into colonial society. But instead of making progress toward a common nonracial society, the ANC spent its first 3 decades in unsuccessful opposition to deepening racial segregation and discrimination. It generally failed to build strong support and was often overshadowed by more ephemeral millenarian movements. The Communist Party has also spent much of its short life since 1920 applying inappropriate policies dictated from Moscow.

In 1944, Mandela joined with other young activists, including Walter Sisulu, Oliver Tambo, and Anton Lembede, in forming the ANC Youth League. The young radicals espoused an anticolonial African nationalism and were generally hostile to the Communist Party, which they saw as dominated by White and Indian activists and importing foreign ideas. In 1949, the Youth League effectively seized power in the ANC, with Sisulu becoming Secretary-General and Mandela soon being persuaded to become the national executive. In 1950, Mandela was elected president of the Youth League.

The Youth Leaguers quickly radicalized the ANC and pushed it toward greater militancy. Mandela's attitude to both multiracial politics and communism shifted from hostility to support (although Mandela never joined the Communist Party), and he soon emerged as a champion of direct action. In 1952, he was prominent in the ANC-led Defiance Campaign (against "unjust laws"), which resulted in the ANC's membership rising to 100,000. In 1953, Mandela designed the M-Plan (the M standing for Mandela) for rebuilding the ANC's organization. In addition to his political work, Mandela, with Oliver Tambo, ran a legal practice in Johannesburg.

In 1955, Mandela and 155 others were charged with treason. The mammoth treason trial was concluded only in 1961, with the acquittal of all accused. In the meantime, South African politics had been transformed. The ANC's co-operation with White, Indian, and colored activists, especially Communists, had resulted in a split and the formation of the rival Pan-Africanist Congress (PAC). In 1960, both the ANC and the PAC proposed new defiance campaigns focused on the "passes" that governed where African people were allowed to live and work. At Sharpeville, the police fired on a large crowd of Black protesters in a PAC-organized demonstration, killing sixty. In Cape Town, a massive march into the city center was defused only with promises that were soon broken. The state banned the ANC and PAC, detained activists, and forcefully tried to regain control. When the Treason Trial ended, therefore, Mandela immediately went into hiding.

Faced with their apparent inability to achieve change through nonviolent action, the ANC and other organizations turned to sabotage. Mandela was given the task of forming the ANC's armed wing, called *Umkhonto we Sizwe* (Spear of the Nation). The campaign was aimed at infrastructural, not human, targets and at sabotage, rather than terrorism. In 1962, soon after returning from a trip around much of newly independent Africa as well as Europe, Mandela was arrested and convicted of minor crimes. The following year, together with other senior leaders of the ANC and Umkhonto we Sizwe, Mandela was put on trial for the much more serious crime of sabotage. Mandela used the trial as an opportunity to promote the ANC's message. Asked to plead, he declared that "it is not I, but the government, that should be in the dock." Speaking in his own defense, and facing a possible death penalty, Mandela made what was probably his most famous speech: "During my lifetime, I have dedicated myself to this struggle of the African people. I have fought against White domination, and I have fought against Black domination. I have cherished the ideal of a democratic and free society in which all persons live together in harmony with equal opportunities. It is an ideal which I hope to live for and achieve. But if needs be, it is an ideal for which I am prepared to die." Mandela and his coaccused were convicted and sentenced to life imprisonment.

Mandela spent the following 25 years out of sight in jail, first on Robben Island (just off Cape Town) and later at prisons on the mainland. Robben Island was a harsh environment. Prisoners were subjected to hard labor in the lime quarry, poor food, and routine brutality from warders. Visits and reading materials were strictly controlled. When Mandela's oldest son died in a car crash, he was refused permission to attend the funeral. Prisoners ran their own political education programs and debated strategies and tactics.

Meanwhile, South African society and politics were changing rapidly. In the 1940s and 1950s, South Africa was still a largely rural society. Most Black people in urban areas had been born and raised in the countryside and retained a rural orientation in many respects. Several of the laws singled out as unjust in the 1952 defiance campaign affected the countryside alone. Despite restrictions on education and urbanization, a new generation of urban-born and -schooled

Black adolescents grew up, reaching high school in the 1970s. At the same time, semiskilled (and later skilled) occupations were opening up to Black workers. These changes provided fertile conditions for the emergence of protests in township schools—notably in Soweto and elsewhere in 1976 and 1977—and the emergence of trade unions among Black workers. Repression and exile had diminished the ANC's stature, however, and anti-apartheid protesters lacked a clear identity.

From the late 1970s, the ANC resumed its premier role, and with it Mandela became reestablished as an international as well as national icon. After 1976, militant and politicized young people left the country, joined the ANC in exile, and revived Umkhonto we Sizwe. In 1983, pro-ANC organizations inside South Africa joined together to form a United Democratic Front (UDF), with the initial objective of opposing the apartheid state's constitutional reforms (which sought to co-opt colored and Indian South Africans into support for a reformed version of apartheid). The UDF became the vehicle for the reestablishment of the ANC's hegemony in anti-apartheid politics inside South Africa. When, in 1984 and 1985, protests erupted in Black townships across the country, the UDF was given the much broader task of coordinating internal opposition to apartheid. Both inside and outside the country, demands grew that Mandela should be released from jail.

Faced with escalating protest, the South African government offered to release Mandela in 1985, on the condition that he would renounce violence. Mandela replied that it was the government that should renounce violence. He could and would not renounce violence until the people of South Africa had their freedom. The South African government recognized the necessity of dealing with Mandela. Soon after his rejection of their conditional offer of release, the Minister of Justice opened an informal conversation with Mandela (as well as with the exiled ANC leadership). Mandela's negotiations worried many of his colleagues in jail and exile, but the ANC's varied leaders converged around support for a transitional deal: In broad terms, if the government unbanned the ANC and other organizations, released political leaders, and committed to negotiations, then the ANC would suspend the armed struggle.

Following his release from prison in 1990, Mandela immediately assumed de facto leadership of the ANC. Over the following decade—as president-in-waiting and then, from 1994, as elected president—he did not take the leading role in negotiations or policymaking, but rather focused his efforts on racial reconciliation and nation building. His leadership style was that of the people's chief of his childhood: Listen and unite. Mandela was the ideal antidote to the racialized divisions of apartheid. He was less well suited to the challenges of tackling poverty that required hard policy choices.

Tall and heavily built (Mandela was an enthusiastic amateur boxer in his 20s) but a reluctant convert to violence, Mandela was an ideal icon for the global struggle against racism. His story is, as one of his biographers, Anthony Sampson, wrote, a story of "the triumph of the human spirit, the return of the lost leader."

Jeremy Seekings

See also Apartheid; Apartheid, Laws; South Africa, Republic of

Further Readings

Buntman, Francine. 2003. *Robben Island and Prisoner Resistance to Apartheid.* Cambridge, UK: Cambridge University Press.

Lodge, Tom. 1983. *Black Politics in South Africa since 1945.* London: Longman.

Lodge, Tom. 2006. *Mandela: A Critical Life.* Oxford, UK: Oxford University Press.

Mandela, Nelson. 1995. *A Long Walk to Freedom.* New York: Little, Brown.

Sampson, Anthony. 1999. *Mandela: The Authorised Biography.* London: HarperCollins.

Seekings, Jeremy. 2000. *The UDF: A History of the United Democratic Front in South Africa, 1983–1991.* Cape Town, South Africa: David Philip.

Walshe, Peter. 1970. *The Rise of African Nationalism in South Africa.* London: C. Hurst.

MAQUILADORAS

Introduced in the mid-1960s, *maquiladoras* are assembly plants that are located in Mexico and owned by foreign companies. These outsourcing mechanisms of globalization generate 40% of Mexico's exports and are the single most important factor in the Mexican economy. Maquiladoras have changed the geographic landscape and socioeconomic conditions of the U.S.–Mexico border region.

In the maquiladora industry, components, including machinery and nonprecious metals, are transported to Mexico duty-free, where labor-intensive assembly is performed by a low-paid Mexican labor force, and the finished product is then returned to the country of origin. In accordance with sections 806.30 and 807.00 of the U.S. tariff schedule, finished products that are transported back to the United States are taxed only on the value-added cost. Although many countries participate in the maquiladora industry, the United States enjoys the next-door-neighbor advantage of doing business with minimal transportation activity and expense.

Maquiladora businesses are also known as in-bond plants and twin plants. *In-bond* refers to the in-bond industry, in which components are brought into the country under bonded status, the finished product cannot be sold in Mexico, and reexporting of the product is required. The reexporting requirement was lifted in 1983, first allowing 20% of finished products to be sold within Mexico, and later increasing this allowance to 50% in 1989.

The term *twin plant* refers to the sets of twin cities on either side of the U.S.–Mexico border, where most of the maquiladoras operate. While the assembly work is done in Mexico, the administrative work, including capital and development, remains in the country of origin. Mexican foreign-investment laws limit foreign investors to minority ownership, but maquiladoras are exempt from these laws, permitting headquarters and ownership to reside outside of Mexico. The twin cities hosting maquiladoras are Mexicali, Baja California/Calexico, California; Nogales, Sonora/Nogales, Texas; Matamoros, Tamaulipas/Brownsville, Texas; Ciudad Juarez, Chihuahua/El Paso, Texas; Nuevo Laredo, Nuevo Leon/Laredo, Texas; Reynosa, Tamaulipas/McAllen, Texas; and Piedras Negras, Coahuila/Eagle Pass, Texas.

The term *maquiladora* comes from the Spanish word *maquila,* which is used in reference to the grinding of grain. When someone takes grain to the miller for grinding, the miller keeps a small portion of the resulting flour as payment for the grinding. That small portion is known as a maquila. In the scenario of maquiladoras, when foreign companies bring components to Mexico for assembly, the wages paid for the labor are, in essence, the maquila.

The maquiladora industry was part of the 1965 Border Industrialization Program (BIP), which was intended to raise the standard of living in the border regions.

The maquiladora program was expected to generate foreign exchange for Mexico by stimulating the manufacturing sector, create linkages with the national economy in the interior of Mexico, encourage technical transfer, and create new jobs and provide employment for displaced *braceros* returning from the United States. (Braceros were Mexican laborers who participated in the guest worker Bracero Program, in effect in the United States between 1942 and 1964.)

Maquiladoras host numerous and varied businesses, such as food packing, electronics, apparel, auto parts, furniture, toys, television sets, refrigerators, and computer keyboards, to name a few. Some of the companies represented include RCA, GE, Sylvania, Motorola, Zenith, Sony, and Samsonite. The industry, which began in 1965 with twelve plants and 3,000 employees, saw a 14% annual job growth rate between 1978 and 1993. By 2001, the industry had peaked, with 3,763 plants and 1.3 million employees. Originally confined to the border region, maquiladoras expanded into the interior of Mexico after 1972.

Maquiladoras are typically housed in industrial parks that provide utilities such as electricity, water, and natural gas; amenities such as phone and data lines and satellite; and conveniences such as access to transportation and low-cost housing for employees. Professional services such as legal, fiscal, customs, and banking often draw companies to industrial parks, while support from public and private sectors, cooperation from customs officials, and interest from the academic community and labor force can draw companies into regions.

While maquiladoras have increased purchasing power in Mexico and been instrumental in producing managers and technical professionals, the industry has also encountered issues and concerns, including institutionalized sexual discrimination and uncontrolled environmental pollution.

In its infancy, the industry perceived female workers as more passive and less likely to unionize, possessing higher levels of manual dexterity with small components, and demonstrating more patience with tedious, repetitive work. Given these characteristics, many companies preferred to hire female employees. Unfortunately, the predominantly female workforce was managed almost exclusively by males, creating an environment ripe for extortion of sexual favors and firing (or not hiring) pregnant women. A 1998 complaint filed with the U.S. Labor Department reported that pregnancy tests were administered at maquiladoras in an effort to weed out pregnant applicants.

With the tremendous growth in the number of plants, the border region has experienced an increasingly scarce water supply, air pollution caused by fugitive emissions from industrial processes and unpaved roads, and industrial waste released into the municipal drainage system without pretreatment. Lack of legal integration between the two countries, unclear laws, and lax enforcement help explain why only 12% of the companies have complied with hazardous material regulations. Exacerbating the environmental problem is the fact that Mexico's infrastructure has not kept pace with the growth. In 1997, Mexico only had two fully operational treatment, storage, and disposal (TSD) sites, prompting companies to rely on alternative solutions for disposal of hazardous waste.

The maquiladora industry has created an economic interdependence between the United States and Mexico due to U.S. reliance on low-paid Mexican labor to make a profit and Mexico's dependence on the vitality of the U.S. economy. At the same time, the border twin cities have developed complementarity and unexpected bonds resulting from shared experiences.

Alma Alvarez-Smith

See also Borderlands; Bracero Program; *Colonias;* Environmental Justice; Globalization; Mexico

Further Readings

Candelaria, Cordelia C. 2004. "Maquiladora." Pp. 516–517 in *Encyclopedia of Latino Popular Culture,* edited by C. C. Candelaria, A. J. Aldama, and P. J. Garcia. Westport, CT: Greenwood Press.

Lorey, David E. 1999. *The U.S.–Mexican Border in the Twentieth Century: A History of Economic and Social Transformation.* Wilmington, DE: Scholarly Resources.

Wilson, Patricia A. 1992. *Exports and Local Development: Mexico's New Maquiladoras.* Austin: University of Texas Press.

MARGINALIZATION

Marginalization is the singling out of a specific group on the basis of some social demographic characteristic that is negatively viewed by a dominant group or class who, through institutionalized and informal practices, exclude the unwanted from social, economic, and political realms of the larger society. During the colonial period, attributions of inferiority based on phenotype or the physical appearance of the Indigenous Peoples supported the manipulation of people of color for the economic and social benefit of European nation-states, which also profited greatly by the enslavement of African people. The parallel development of the notion of "whiteness" through such ideologies as Social Darwinism allowed Europeans to legitimize beliefs about phenotype as a rationale for restricting the freedom of those identified as non-White throughout the world. This entry looks briefly at some historical and contemporary examples of marginalization.

U.S immigration history provides an example of how phenotype, culture, and historical context affect rates of exclusion. Rates of assimilation for contemporary immigrants underscore the racial, social, and economic differences between late-19th- and early-20th-century European immigrants and post-1965 Asian, Latino, and West Indian immigrants. Although Jews, Italians, and Irish were initially discriminated against, these early immigrants and their successive generations were able to advance due to social and economic opportunities in the industrial sector, as well as through the establishment of ethnic enclaves. In addition, these European immigrants were able to become "White," allowing for many to assimilate fully into society.

In contrast, post-1965 U.S. immigrants have often been non-Whites who come into a society where they may face discrimination based upon their physical appearance, although public debates on the issue are phrased in terms of issues relating to skills, education, and English literacy. Even second-generation immigrants from this cadre may have become marginalized on the basis of skin color, lack of social resources within their families, and their proximity to impoverished urban neighborhoods.

Marginalization in European countries, such as Italy and Spain, is sanctioned through laws and policies that prohibit the inclusion of immigrant workers, keeping them marginalized as a ready pool of labor for low-wage positions that natives will not perform. These immigrants (Asian, Latin American, and sub-Saharan African) in Europe are often denied permanent residence and cannot become full citizens. The construction of the immigrant as the "other" in Europe and the marginalization of immigrants in the United States keep these populations on the fringes of society. Immigration globally often serves to benefit the political and economic interests of the host country, while emigrants are kept from mobility.

Issues of marginalization in U.S. society are also evident in the legal system. Such political campaigns as the "war on drugs" have had a grossly negative impact on people of color in the United States. The rate of incarceration for African American minority populations in the United States is generally higher than that for Whites. Such differences are often attributed to the greater severity of criminal histories and racial bias in prosecution and sentencing, especially for drug sentences. Such racial bias in the U.S. criminal justice system is evident in David Jacobs and Jason Carmichael's analysis of death penalty sentencing. They discovered that those states with the greatest economic inequality and the largest African American populations retained the use of the death penalty. Such racial disparities highlight how non-Whites experience greater likelihood of loss of freedom. The removal from society or punishment of certain groups based upon phenotype is a common occurrence cross-nationally: For example, race has been correlated with higher incarceration rates of Aboriginals in Australia.

The marginalization of racial and ethnic minorities has an impact on later generations' social, political, and economic mobility. Current studies on wealth as a source of stratification highlight how historical processes widen the discrepancy in social and economic capital between African Americans and Whites in the United States. Racially biased acts, such as discrimination against African American veterans obtaining federal housing loans after World War II and the practice of residential segregation, have limited the accumulation of capital among minorities, preventing the purchase of a home, a key facet of economic stability. Wealth derived primarily from homeownership acts as a safety net for hard times. In addition, inherited wealth perpetuates inequality, with many more Whites than Blacks passing along wealth.

As W. E. B. Du Bois stated in *The Souls of Black Folk*, the problem of modernity is that of the "color line," referring to a widespread system of social stratification based on skin color. While a variety of factors contribute to social stratification, skin color remains a relevant factor in the 21st century.

Manuel R. Torres

See also *American Apartheid;* Australia, Indigenous People; Color Line; Discrimination; Double Consciousness; Drug Use; Du Bois, William Edward Burghardt; Labeling; Racialization; Racial Profiling; Social Capital; Social Darwinism

Further Readings

Calavita, Kitty. 2005. *Immigrants at the Margins: Law, Race, and Exclusion in Southern Europe.* Cambridge, UK: Cambridge University Press.

DuBois, W. E. B. 1903. *The Souls of Black Folk.* Chicago, IL: A. C. McClurg.

Feagin, Joe. 2000. *Racist America.* New York: Routledge.

Hogg, Russell. 2001. "Penalty and Modes of Regulating Indigenous Peoples in Australia." *Punishment & Society* 3:355–379.

Jacobs, David and Jason T. Carmichael. 2002. "The Sociology of the Death Penalty: A Pooled Time-Series Analysis." *American Sociological Review* 67:109–131.

Massey, Douglas S. and Nancy A. Denton. 1993. *American Apartheid: Segregation and the Making of the Underclass.* Cambridge, MA: Harvard University Press.

Mauer, Marc. 1999. *Race to Incarcerate.* New York: New Press.

Portes, Alejandro, Patricia Fernandez-Kelly, and William Haller. 2005. "Segmented Assimilation on the Ground: The New Second Generation in Early Adulthood." *Ethnic and Racial Studies* 28:1000–1040.

Shapiro, Thomas M. 2004. *The Hidden Cost of Being African American.* New York: Oxford University Press.

"Marielitos"

"Marielitos" was the blanket label applied to the 125,000 Cubans who arrived in the United States during a Cuban-government-sanctioned boatlift from Mariel, Cuba, in 1980. The label, which literally means "little person from Mariel," was coined by the established anti-Castro, Cuban American community in South Florida as a way to distance itself from those the Cuban government and Cuban President Fidel Castro had labeled as "social deviants" and "scum." These characterizations were not only unfair, but inaccurate, since the overwhelming majority of those who arrived in the boatlift were just as honest, hardworking, and enterprising as their predecessors, as this entry shows.

The biggest differences between the recent arrivals and the previous Cuban exodus were race and class. The Cuban community established in South Florida was predominantly White (91%) and came mainly from the upper and middle classes in prerevolutionary Cuba. The Mariel entrants were more racially mixed, and most were classified as working class and poor upon arrival. However, despite the label and class and racial discrimination, most Marielitos made a relatively smooth transition to the economic and social life of Cuban Miami.

The Cuban Excludables

As the Mariel entrants continued adjusting to life in the United States—and many became successful in business, education, the arts, and other professions—the "Marielito" stigma was applied almost exclusively to a group of 2,746 boatlift participants who were classified as "excludable" by the U.S. Immigration and Naturalization Service (INS) and detained upon arrival in the United States. The main reason for their exclusion and detention was the fact that most had committed crimes in Cuba and therefore had to be kept in captivity until they completed their sentences in U.S. prisons or were deemed admissible to the country by a U.S. court.

The detention of this group stirred a major controversy and created a legal dilemma for the U.S. government, since (a) they had been invited to the United States by President Carter, who allowed the boatlift to continue for 5 months; (b) they were imprisoned for crimes committed in a foreign country, a country that the United States did not even recognize; (c) they were detained indefinitely, without specific charges; (d) prison conditions were considered "deplorable" and "shameful" by national and international human rights groups; and (e) they were denied a speedy trial by a jury of their peers. Even worse, most were never charged nor tried in the United States.

The detention, exclusion, and treatment of this group represented a sharp reversal in the traditional "open arms" U.S. immigration policy of welcoming and admitting virtually all Cuban migrants as political refugees. Cubans are also privileged by the Cuban Adjustment Act of 1966, which allows Cubans entering the United States, by any means, the right to permanent resident status 1 year and 1 day after their arrival. The Mariel detainees, however, were not protected by the act, since they were never officially admitted to the United States.

A Question of Human Rights

The U.S. government justified the extreme measures taken against the detainees by claiming that it had been overwhelmed by the more than 125,000 Cubans who arrived during the Mariel boatlift and because it feared that Castro had intentionally sent hardened criminals on the boatlift to export Cuba's crime problems to the United States. Although there was some truth to the latter, 98% of all boatlift entrants were hardworking, law-abiding citizens. The harsh treatment of the detainees and their detention without trial, however, represented a gross violation of U.S. civil rights and universal human rights.

Political and civil rights groups like the American Civil Liberties Union (ACLU), the Coalition to Support Cuban Detainees (CSCD), and the Cuban-American National Foundation (CANF), among others, advocated for the prisoners' rights through litigation and public pressure but had little success. The failure of these efforts indicated that the Cuban exile community was losing political clout in Washington, at least on immigration issues, as the detainees lingered in prison without charge and without trial. It was not until 1984 that the U.S. and Cuban governments agreed on a plan to repatriate all Mariel entrants who had been detained since 1980. Unfortunately, the agreement was short-lived when Cuba suspended the deportation to protest the Reagan administration's creation of Radio Martí, a U.S.-government-funded radio station dedicated to transmitting propaganda programs to Cuba.

The Mariel boatlift and detainees controversy came at a time when the United States was confronted by more than 1 million asylum seekers from Haiti, Nicaragua, El Salvador, Honduras, and Guatemala. Although most of these people were trying to escape and survive political repression and war in their home countries and had legitimate cases by humanitarian standards, the INS ruled on their cases according to U.S. foreign policy priorities in the sending country, not the humanitarian merits of the case. For example, most Salvadorans were denied political asylum, since they were escaping the violence and repression of a government supported by the United States. On the other hand, Nicaraguans escaping the leftist Sandinista government (1979–1990), which the United States was trying to overthrow, were welcomed as political exiles.

Political Impact

The detention and exclusion of Mariel entrants and the double standard used by the INS to grant and deny asylum had significant political repercussions for both the Carter and Reagan administrations. Many analysts agree that the Mariel boatlift and the way it was handled was one of the main causes for President Jimmy Carter's failure to win reelection in 1980. Faced with 125,000 asylum seekers from socialist Cuba and 50,000 Haitians fleeing from a pro-U.S. government, the Carter administration created a vague migratory status: "Cuban-Haitian Entrant: Status Pending." The new category helped cover the policy contradiction but did not solve the status issue.

Likewise, the Reagan administration faced a major crisis when the Cuban detainees rioted to protest the reactivation of the 1984 Cuba-U.S. immigration agreement. Frustrated by their seemingly endless prison terms and faced with the possibility of being deported to Cuba, the prisoners staged riots in the two prisons holding the largest numbers of Mariel detainees. The November 1987 riots in the Oakdale, Louisiana, Detention Center and the Atlanta Penitentiary lasted 10 days and left a toll of one detainee killed and more than a dozen injured. The rioters also burned five prison buildings and caused more than $20 million in property damage.

Almost 30 years after the boatlift, the detainees' situation may soon be resolved. In 2006, the U.S. Supreme Court ruled that federal law prohibits open-ended detention of Cubans who entered the United States during the boatlift and who, despite crimes later committed, cannot be held indefinitely. Thus, the nearly 800 Mariel "excludables" who remain imprisoned in the United States may soon be tried and many, if not all, released. The ruling also provides new hope for Haitian asylum seekers, who, like the Cubans, live in an indefinite state of limbo and are still seeking asylum in South Florida.

The Supreme Court ruling was a major victory for Mariel entrants, and although Cubans are still arriving illegally in South Florida in large numbers, as a result of a U.S.-Cuba migratory agreement, most are almost immediately deported back to Cuba. There, the U.S. government guarantees them an opportunity to apply for a U.S. entry visa, without the Cuban government's interference. The agreement was an attempt by both governments to eliminate the illegal human traffic in the Florida Straits.

Félix Masud-Piloto

See also "Boat People"; Crime and Race; Cuba: Migration and Demography; Cuban Americans; Nicaraguan Americans; Refugees; Salvadoran Americans

Further Readings

Grenier, Guillermo J. and Alex Stepick III, eds. 1992. *Miami Now: Immigration, Ethnicity, and Social Change.* Gainesville: University Press of Florida.

Hamn, Mark S. 1995. *The Abandoned Ones: The Imprisonment and Uprising of the Mariel Boat People.* Boston, MA: Northeastern University Press.

Larzelere, Alex. 1988. *Castro's Ploy–America's Dilemma: The 1980 Cuban Boatlift.* Washington, DC: National Defense University Press.

Masud-Piloto, Félix. 1996. *From Welcomed Exiles to Illegal Immigrants: Cuban Migration to the U.S., 1959–1995.* Lanham, MD: Rowman & Littlefield.

Porte, Alejandro and Robert L. Bach. 1985. *Latin Journey: Cuban and Mexican Immigrants in the United States.* Berkeley: University of California Press.

MARSHALL, THURGOOD (1908–1993)

Thurgood Marshall was the first African American justice to serve on the U.S. Supreme Court, appointed in 1967. He had been a successful civil rights lawyer, winning twenty-nine of thirty-two cases he argued before the Court, including *Brown v. Board of Education* in 1954. In an earlier federal appointment, nominated by President John F. Kennedy and confirmed after fiery Senate debates, Marshall served from 1961 to 1965 as a judge on the U.S. Court of Appeals for the Second Circuit. Subsequently, President Lyndon B. Johnson appointed Marshall as solicitor general of the United States in 1965, a position in which he served until 1967, when President Johnson named him as Associate Justice to the U.S. Supreme Court. An African American had never before held any of these positions. This entry describes Marshall's life and achievements.

Early Years

Born in Baltimore, Maryland, on July 2, 1908, to William and Norma Williams Marshall, the future justice attended local racially segregated elementary and secondary schools. After graduating from Douglass High School in 1925, he attended Lincoln University in Chester County, Pennsylvania. At that time, Lincoln was a college for African American men.

Official portrait of the 1976 U.S. Supreme Court: Justice Thurgood Marshall. Besides being a lifelong advocate for civil rights, Marshall strongly supported free speech, stood firmly against use of the death penalty, and was a defender of a woman's right to an abortion.

Source: Public domain.

Marshall met many Black men who would assume leadership roles throughout the nation. He was a member of the varsity debating team, which faced off on various topics with interracial and international opponents.

Marshall married Vivian G. Burey in 1929, and, upon his graduation in 1930, he decided to pursue a law degree. He thought about attending the University of Maryland law school, but it was not open to African American students at that time. Instead, he attended Howard University law school, where he met his mentor, the law school dean, Charles Hamilton Houston, an accomplished Harvard law school graduate. Howard was a coeducational university open to all qualified students but attended primarily by African Americans. Many African American law students who argued and analyzed their civil rights cases at the law school later went on to become the vanguard in the Civil Rights Movement.

With the NAACP

Marshall graduated at the top of his class, passed the bar exam, and practiced law in Baltimore from 1933 to 1937. In 1934, he became counsel for the Baltimore branch of the National Association for the Advancement of Colored People (NAACP), and, from 1936 to 1938, he was assistant to the special counsel for the NAACP. His former dean, Charles Houston, held the special counsel position. Marshall and Houston traveled all over the racially segregated South offering legal aid to African Americans who could not afford to hire their own lawyers to protect their rights. The NAACP, a rights organization founded in 1909, worked tirelessly to restore the rights guaranteed to African Americans by the U.S. Constitution, especially the Thirteenth, Fourteenth, and Fifteenth Amendments. These amendments were passed after the Civil War in an attempt to establish civil rights for 6 million newly emancipated Blacks.

One of Marshall's early successes as an NAACP lawyer was a case against segregation policies at the University of Maryland. In the NAACP's efforts to desegregate the university's graduate and professional schools, Houston and Marshall filed a case before the Maryland Court of Appeals on behalf of an African American law school applicant named Donald Gaines Murray. They won, and Murray was admitted in 1936. When Houston retired 2 years after Marshall's appointment as his assistant, Marshall succeeded him as the NAACP's chief legal officer. In 1939, Marshall was admitted to practice before the Supreme Court.

Marshall was the founding director of the NAACP Legal Defense and Educational Fund, which was established in 1940, after the U.S. Treasury Department refused to grant tax-exempt status to the NAACP. The fund's purpose was to raise money to finance the organization's legal fights against discrimination and to fund other programs that were eligible for tax-deductible contributions. Marshall served as counsel and director of the fund from 1940 to 1961.

During that time, Marshall was responsible for scores of legal actions to secure full citizenship rights for African Americans. The fund's records at the Library of Congress document Marshall's grueling travel and meeting schedule as well as his acute sense of humor even in the face of threats from Whites and the distrust and fear of southern Blacks he was trying to help. His work focused on voting privileges, justice in criminal proceedings, and the equalization of the funds granted for public education throughout the United States.

The NAACP awarded Marshall its coveted Spingarn Medal in 1946. The citation he received described his unrelenting efforts to ensure equitable treatment of African Americans by leading the courts to overturn laws discriminating against African Americans in travel, labor, education, military service, public accommodations, and other areas of life in the United States. The NAACP particularly cited his leadership in the Texas all-White primary election case, which the organization's leadership felt would have greater influence than other cases in ending racial disenfranchisement in America. Sometimes Marshall's office worked on as many as 400 cases at a time.

Marshall's long and successful career as a trial attorney culminated with the 1954 U.S. Supreme Court decision in *Brown v. Board of Education of Topeka*. When Marshall and the other NAACP lawyers presented their arguments in *Brown*, they used cases relating to segregated schools in various parts of the United States so that the "separate but equal" doctrine could be challenged in a variety of settings around the country. The court actually heard the case twice before ruling unanimously that separate schools were inherently unequal. This was the NAACP's key victory in the legal battle to dismantle segregation in the United States.

Marshall's first wife died in 1955, and he married Cecilia A. Suyat in the same year. They had two sons, John and Thurgood, Jr.

On the Federal Bench

Marshall's federal career began in 1961, when he was appointed by President Kennedy to be a federal judge in the Second District Court of Appeals in New York City. From this point on in his career, Marshall could no longer focus on civil rights issues. He had to make decisions about whatever case came before him in court. Despite the fact that he was no longer in his area of specialty, the Supreme Court did not overturn any of his decisions. In 1965, President Johnson appointed Marshall as Solicitor General of the United States. Of the nineteen cases he tried, he won fourteen. Outside of the courtroom during the 1960s, Marshall traveled to Kenya, Tanzania, and Uganda as a representative of the State Department.

In his official capacity as a Supreme Court justice, Marshall tried to ensure that the civil rights gained for African Americans and other minority groups would be secure. He was also a tenacious advocate for the rights of women and affirmative action. He wanted judicial remedies to be securely in place so that the hard-won civil rights gains would not be lost. His opinion files at the Library of Congress generally document Marshall's many concurrences with the liberal majority position of the court during the early years of his tenure on the court and an increasing number of his dissents as the court's position changed when Presidents Nixon, Reagan, and George H. W. Bush appointed conservative judges to the court. Marshall's opinions reflect his strong advocacy for the rights of minority and disadvantaged individuals, his arguments for First Amendment rights, and his support for the rights of criminal defendants, including arguments in almost 200 cases against capital punishment as a cruel and unusual form of punishment.

After serving on the United States Supreme Court for 24 years, Justice Thurgood Marshall announced his retirement in the fall of 1991 because of ill health. He died on January 24, 1993. In an editorial in the *Washington Post* on January 31, one of his biographers, Juan Williams, said Marshall was "a man who led a team that skillfully deployed the Constitution in an unprecedented way: to dismantle the world of 'separate but equal.' Little attention is paid to the man who loved the law and legal argument, who would arrange long moot court sessions to prepare for any day in court. Largely forgotten is the brilliant advocate of free speech, the man who along with Justice William Brennan stood firmly against use of the death penalty, the fierce defender of a woman's right to an abortion."

Debra Newman Ham

See also Brown v. Board of Education; Civil Rights Movement; National Association for the Advancement of Colored People (NAACP); Segregation; Separate but Equal

Further Readings

Greenberg, Jack. 1994. *Crusaders in the Courts: How a Dedicated Band of Lawyers Fought for the Civil Rights Revolution.* New York: Basic Books.

Kluger, Richard. 1963. *Simple Justice: The History of* Brown v. Board of Education *and Black America's Struggle for Equality.* New York: Knopf.

Rowan, Carl. 1993. *Dream Makers, Dream Breakers: The World of Justice Thurgood Marshall.* Boston, MA: Little, Brown.

Thurgood Marshall Papers. n.d. Washington, DC: Library of Congress.

Williams, Juan. 1998. *Thurgood Marshall, American Revolutionary.* New York: Times Books.

Marxism and Racism

Marxists argue that it is impossible to discuss racism without also considering the economic context in which that racism exists. In the United States, that means capitalism and its accompanying class exploitation. Racial oppression, it is argued, has always been an integral part of U.S. economic and political history. That being said, there are at least two general approaches taken by Marxists who study racism. The first, *traditional Marxism,* sees class as the fundamental or primary source of oppression, with racism being an important but secondary issue. The second approach, *race-sensitive Marxism,* argues that both race and class are primary sources of oppression. What follows is an outline of the major points within each of the two approaches.

Traditional Marxism

Traditional Marxists argue that the class oppression that is part of capitalism affects both White workers and workers of color. While all workers are exploited by capitalists, they argue, workers of color are "super-exploited." In other words, while capitalists make profits from the labor of White workers, they make larger profits from workers of color due to race-segregated labor markets and unequal pay for the same work. The degree of exploitation of workers of color and White workers is viewed as a difference in degree rather than a difference in kind.

In this view, people of color are also seen as part of the "reserve labor force" that is necessary to the smooth functioning of capitalism. In periods of economic expansion when more workers are needed (i.e., World War II), people of color are pulled into jobs they can't usually obtain. During periods of contraction, they are pushed out of these jobs.

It is in the interests of the working class to become class conscious, say traditional Marxists. This means that workers of all races and cultures will understand that their common class interests (exploitation by capitalists) are more important than any differences they may have in terms of race, ethnicity, religion, or culture. It is in the interests of the capitalists, on the other hand, to keep the working class divided.

Racism is one of the ways that the working class remains divided. The ideological and attitudinal aspect of racism (stereotypes, prejudice, political beliefs) make workers believe that workers of other races, rather than capitalists, are their enemies. Whites and people of color will fight each other rather than uniting against the capitalists. This is sometimes called "false consciousness." Sometimes, capitalists purposely try to use race to divide workers, such as by using Blacks as strikebreakers in a predominantly White workplace. Most of the time, however, the free-floating culture of racism causes workers to think in racial rather than class terms. Traditional Marxists tend to be suspicious of Nationalist movements among people of color (e.g., Black Power during the 1960s and 1970s), since this could further divide the working class.

In analyzing social phenomena like racism, traditional Marxists always ask the question "Who wins and who loses?" White capitalists clearly benefit from racism, and workers of color clearly lose out.

As for White workers, Marxists say that they lose more than they gain from racism. Although they have short-term benefits (e.g., better housing, jobs, pay, education), they are ultimately hurt by their continual exploitation by the capitalists. They would be better off uniting with workers of color against the capitalists.

Capitalists of color, according to traditional Marxists, also lose more than they gain. Although they can make profits off the labor of workers of any race, their businesses are often small and marginal, and they are at the mercy of the more powerful White capitalists. However, traditional Marxists are more interested in organizing workers of color than in building a strong business class among people of color.

The expectation of traditional Marxists is that once capitalism is replaced by socialism, the material base of racism is removed. All that remains is to address some of the residual attitudes, cultural stereotypes, and behavior patterns that no longer fit the new economic conditions.

Race-Sensitive Marxism

The militant social movements in the Black and Latino communities during the 1960s and 1970s gave rise to a more race-sensitive Marxism, which argued that both race and class are fundamental sources of oppression. While people in these movements would agree with much of traditional Marxism, they would argue that racial oppression has a life of its own that goes beyond issues of class.

The prejudiced attitudes and discriminatory behavior of White workers are seen as more than just false consciousness. White workers are seen to gain real material benefits from being the privileged group in society. While they are still exploited by White capitalists, they also share some of their racial privilege in terms of better jobs, higher social status, and more political power than workers of color. Prejudice and stereotypes are seen as part of a racist ideology that justifies and protects White privilege.

This also has implications for postcapitalist society, since White workers would still have real advantages over workers of color. Their better education, for example, means that they would be more likely than workers of color to qualify for better jobs, even in a socialist society. Creating racial equality in a socialist society would be a long-term process that involves more than just changing residual prejudiced attitudes.

Several all-Black political organizations have articulated race-sensitive Marxism. The Black Workers Congress had some success in organizing Black autoworkers in Detroit in the 1970s by seeing both the companies and the liberal, predominantly White United Auto Workers Union as their enemies. The Black Panther Party for Self-Defense focused on organizing poor Black communities around issues of police brutality and political oppression in the late 1960s and early 1970s. Although both groups were Black, they were willing to work in coalition with White Marxists who supported their principles.

Race-sensitive Marxists are also concerned about the globalization of capitalism. Immigrants of color come to the United States from poor countries in search of jobs and compete with native-born workers of color for low-paying jobs. This, in turn, has caused animosity between White workers and immigrants as well as between native-born workers of color and immigrant workers of the same race. In the view of race-sensitive Marxists, the predominantly White capitalists continue to make profits from the labor of native-born and immigrant workers of all races.

Fred L. Pincus

See also Black Nationalism; Black Panther Party; Chicano Movement; Color Line; Privilege; Social Mobility

Further Readings

Geschwender, James A. 1978. *Racial Stratification in America.* Dubuque, IA: Wm. C. Brown.

Marable, Manning. 2000. *How Capitalism Underdeveloped Black America.* Cambridge, MA: South End Press.

McCarran-Walter Act of 1952

The McCarran-Walter Act, also called the Immigration and Nationality Act of 1952, was meant to systematize immigration to the United States. This act is noted for establishing trends in immigration policy that were expanded in later congressional legislation. The most liberal change was the opening of the United States to immigrants of all races and ethnicities. Other trends included establishing immigration preferences based on skill or family preference and the keeping of systematic documentation of aliens. The act was an expression of national sovereignty because it established social boundaries as to who could enter, and it finally recognized a need for political alliances with other nations through inclusion of their immigrants. This entry looks at its historical context and impact.

Historical Context

The two World Wars of the 20th century had a definite impact on shaping immigration policy. World War I did not overturn a U.S. policy of isolationism and resulted in a rejection of immigration through limited quotas established by the Johnson-Reed Act of 1924. This was because of a U.S. reaction to the conflict in Europe as based on racial and ethnic quarrels. In contrast, World War II prompted the internationalization of the United States and an understanding that the United States had made alliances with nations of varied races and ethnicities. In world opinion, Hitler's policy of racial eugenics had been destructive, and the fact that the United States barred certain races from immigration was rendered suspect.

In this period, immigration was recognized as germane to foreign policy, and those in favor of changing the rules wanted to recognize foreign alliances and show compassion for a common humanity. It was thought that increased immigration would offset the global cold war rivalry with the Soviet bloc, so that ideology rather than race was seen to define America's enemies. Opening up immigration was recognized as an international position that would maintain goodwill and provide labor.

Power was increasingly felt to be based on moral authority, which could not rest on discrimination. It was felt that U.S. power should be based on foreign alliances with countries of other races who could provide manpower and economic markets for U.S. goods. It seemed hypocritical to condemn imperialism and colonialism and yet retain a racist immigration policy. The McCarran-Walter bill was sold as an anti-Nazi weapon to undermine the idea of racial superiority and inferiority.

Quotas Replace Exclusion

The McCarran-Reed Act of 1952 maintained the eastern hemisphere quota system of the Johnson-Reed Act of 1924, with a cap of 154,667 based on percentages of the population in the 1920 census. The difference was that it allowed for immigrants of all races and ethnicities to enter within the quota. As a result, the racist national origins principle of the Johnson-Reed Act of 1924 remained in place only to the extent that the quota system prevented individuals of national origins with low representation from having a substantial immigration quota. Quotas for this act were based on one-sixth of 1% of individuals of a given national origin enumerated in the 1920 census, with a minimum quota of 100. A major change was the end of exclusion for Asians. The law added twelve new quota areas in Southeast Asia and the Arab Gulf, referred to as the "Asia-Pacific triangle," and assigned a maximum quota of 2,000.

Special-Preference Immigrants

The Immigration and Nationality Act of 1952 introduced the principle of admitting "special preference" immigrants in professions or with skills considered useful. It paired this concept with an emphasis on reuniting citizens and permanent resident aliens with their relatives. First preference was given to aliens with special skills who had spouses and children (50%). Second preference was parents of U.S. citizens (30%). Third preference was for spouses and children of resident aliens (30%). Fourth preference was for additional relatives of U.S. citizens (25%, with use of slots not taken under other preferences). Finally, any remaining unused slots were to be used without preference. In either category or within quotas, gender discrimination was eliminated. In addition, the number of relatives admitted could be above the quota limits. Unlimited entrance was given to husbands of U.S. citizens.

The Alien Registration System

It should be noted that individuals were supposed to officially enter with documents. A significant practice established at this time was the alien address report system. It required aliens to file papers each year specifying their address, which would be kept in a central system.

This paperwork proviso became an issue, as the Mexican "Bracero" guest worker program had been under way since 1944 and many growers had started giving work to undocumented entrants under a lower pay scale. In reaction, the U.S. government began stigmatizing undocumented Mexican workers as "illegal aliens" and launched "Operation Wetback" in 1954. Operation Wetback involved a roundup of undocumented Mexicans and caused tensions between Mexico and the United States. These tensions continue today due to quotas for Mexico and current policies requiring documentation whereby mutual violation by employers and workers results in negative public opinion about undocumented Mexican immigration.

Other Exclusionary Criteria

Another element of the 1952 act was the ideological exclusion of communists because of the cold war, a provision that has been described as racist, xenophobic, and destructive of foreign policy efforts. The legislation tightened deportation procedures, especially for "communist subversives." An unexpected impact of the bill was that a formerly racially identified group, the Chinese, became excluded because China was a communist nation. Racial outcasts, in effect, became ideological outcasts. Previously, southern Europeans were racially identified with very restricted quotas, but despite fascism in Italy during World War II, they became recognized as refugees from communism. Their country quotas, however, were not raised until passage of a new system under the Immigration and Nationality Act of 1965 (Hart-Cellar Act).

Other categories of individual exclusion under provisions of this legislation included drug addicts, fraud attempters, polygamists, homosexuals, and "subversives," a category that included communists. Although the act made the point that no individual was excluded from citizenship, in practice, many individuals were excluded based on this act and prior legislation prohibiting persons who were considered physically or mentally defective or diseased, likely to become public charges, or considered to be characterized by "moral turpitude," otherwise referred to as criminality.

Isolationism Versus Internationalism

In the early 1950s, members of Congress who wanted to preserve U.S. isolationism and those who wanted a more liberal immigration bill opposed the act. Internationalists wanted to expand America's relations with other nations through barring racial exclusion in order to extend America's power base and adopt a policy of cold war alliances. Isolationists viewed all immigrants as potential subversives. Internationalists saw the strength of immigrants. A divided Congress passed a compromise bill, and President Harry Truman vetoed it. Truman thought that immigration policy impacted foreign policy by indicating national attitudes toward particular racial and ethnic groups and that this bill was insufficiently liberalized.

The Congress disagreed with Truman and overrode his veto. As a result, the McCarran-Walter Act continued the U.S. policy of isolationism. The legislation changed the United States from thinking in racial terms to thinking in terms of ideological issues. This legislation strengthened the boundary between citizens and aliens and still impacts debate about immigration policy today. The United States continues today to debate who belongs and who doesn't in a new context of national security, as well as terms of the economic impact immigration has on the United States.

Immigration policy is connected to how the United States is perceived in the world. The McCarran-Walter Act was substantially criticized for using the national origins principle to regulate quotas. Although the act had a liberal principle, removal of race or ethnicity as a basis for barring people from immigrating to the United States, the retention of the national origins quota system was more likely to restrict potential southeastern Europeans than individuals from northwestern Europe. As a result, race and ethnicity remained a source of bias because of retention of lower quotas for countries without a major presence in the U.S. population in 1920.

These quotas were not removed until the very liberal Immigration and Nationality Act was passed in 1965. Under the 1965 act, national origin, race, or ancestry would no longer be criteria for immigration to the United States, and Eastern Hemispheric quotas were equalized. In addition, Western Hemispheric quotas were created and equalized. The McCarran-Walter Act began but did not fully realize a trend toward liberalization of immigration by elimination of racial criteria, a trend that is reflected in the current cultural diversity of U.S. society. Nevertheless, the conservative distinction between citizen, alien, and the undocumented continues today and remains a source of controversy about immigrants and how to legally admit individuals.

Judith Ann Warner

See also Alien Land Acts; Bracero Program; Discrimination; Europe; Gender and Race, Intersection of; Immigration, U.S.; Immigration and Nationality Act of 1965; National Origins System

Further Readings

Grebler, Leo, Joan W. Moore, and Ralph C. Guzman. 1970. *The Mexican American People.* New York: Free Press.

Reimers, David M. 1985. *Still the Golden Door.* New York: Columbia University Press.

Shanks, Cheryl. 2001. *Immigration and the Politics of National Sovereignty.* Ann Arbor: University of Michigan Press.

MEDIA AND RACE

For most of its history, U.S. television has been predominantly White—not simply in the faces it has portrayed but also in its support of White cultural norms. Until the 1990s, White media bias went largely unexamined. This entry discusses media portrayals of race, examines critical theories of media and race, and reviews the findings of cognitive research in this area. Because Asian Americans, Native Americans, and Latinos have, for the majority of U.S. television history, been noticeable primarily for their absence, most of the discussion here deals with media portrayals of African Americans.

Concerns about the influence of electronic media on U.S. race relations predated television, and the roots of those concerns go back to depictions of

Blacks in Western popular culture since the 17th century. In many respects, television simply extended and recycled these earlier popular forms. However, television's arrival in the late 1940s coincided with growing hopes among African Americans for greater inclusion in U.S. society. Television, it was hoped, could help speed that inclusion. The medium's capacity to expose viewers to supposedly unmediated reality helped stoke the belief that it would correct the distortions of earlier media. Moreover, its widespread adoption, with nearly 90% of homes possessing a set by the end of the 1950s, meant that realistic images of African Americans could be beamed into almost every U.S. household.

Given these high hopes, many African Americans were indignant about early fiction series starring African Americans. The now infamous *Amos 'n' Andy,* for instance, came under fire from the National Association for the Advancement of Colored People (NAACP), which passed a resolution criticizing the show at its 1951 convention. The NAACP's objections continue to shape research and thinking about media and race today. Eight of the NAACP's twelve objections addressed the lack of diverse African American characters and their reliance on received caricatures, including charges that "every character . . . is either a clown or a crook" and "Negroes are shown as dodging work of any kind." The remaining four objections dealt with the perceived impact of these televisual characterizations on White viewers. "*Amos 'n' Andy* on television is worse than on radio because it is a *picture*, . . . not merely a story in words. . . . Millions of White children learn about Negroes for the fist time by seeing *Amos 'n' Andy.*" These related yet distinct concerns—about the diversity of African American portrayals and the impact of such portrayals on viewers' attitudes—spawned distinct research traditions in media and race.

Concerns about diversity of African American portrayals were initially limited to distinctions between positive and negative images, with researchers chronicling disparities between portrayals of African American life and its realities. Under the influence of cultural studies, feminist theory, and African American literary theory, critical media scholars began moving beyond questions of positive and negative characters to examine how television as an aesthetic medium, encompassing settings, narratives, and generic classifications as well as characters, participates in ideological struggles over race.

Contemporary critical research on media and race addresses three main areas: the role that African American audience members play in reinterpreting and reproducing the ideologies of popular television texts; the impact of network decline, globalization, and channel multiplication on African American portrayals; and revisionist histories of African American television, often looking at how African American creative workers actively shaped representational strategies.

The NAACP's concerns about *Amos 'n' Andy*'s influence on audience perceptions of African Americans led to social scientific research into the effects of televised imagery on individuals. This research generally employed a pretest–stimulus–post-test model, in which participants were first probed on their racial attitudes, then exposed to stereotyped material, then probed again on their racial attitudes. Typically, this research exposed White participants to stereotyped African American imagery, but research on African American subjects as well as Native American and Asian American stereotypes has also been conducted. This research design was prey to increasing social pressures against espousing racist attitudes, which plagued responses in both the pre- and post-tests. Moreover, little evidence existed that any attitudinal changes were more than the momentary effects of the artificial research conditions.

Current cognitive research tries to bypass these problems by distinguishing between implicit and explicit racial bias and limiting its focus to implicit biases. The large, ongoing Project Implicit measures participants' automatic responses to combinations of ideas and images in an effort to uncover participants' positive and negative associations of skin color. Cognitive research on media and race assumes that in the aggregate, African Americans are portrayed in the media as an undesirable out-group, that the consequence of these portrayals is that a majority of Americans of all races have internalized the equation of blackness with undesirability, and that these basic cognitive schemas then serve to underwrite higher-order discriminatory attitudes, as reflected, for example, in housing segregation.

Cognitive research does not generally distinguish between fictional and nonfictional television because it views both as visual stimuli that either accurately or inaccurately represent the social world. Nevertheless, these researchers share with some critical scholars an interest in story *frames,* or received ways of constructing news stories. Research on story frames has examined which types of frames recur in stories about race, the ways in which journalistic practices encourage racially discriminatory frames, and the effects of frames on viewers' racial attitudes. Some critical researchers, however, go beyond story frames, analyzing such topics as the ways in which the visual power of television journalism helped civil rights politics in the late 1950s, while civil rights protests legitimated television journalism as a news source that showed the violence of the protests more vividly than newspapers or radio.

Both cognitive and critical theories of media and race have also been applied to non-Black minority groups. For cognitive researchers, implicit bias measurements work equally well for all races and demonstrate that non-White groups are, in the aggregate, more associated with out-group status than are Whites. For critical scholars, questions of diversity of portrayal and the ideological struggle over the meanings of race have also been asked about non-Black minorities. Articles and books have chronicled conventional stereotypes of Latinos, Arabs, Asians, and Native Americans in popular television, as well as the continued privileging of White supremacist story frames in news reports of these minorities.

Since the 1990s, a number of critical media scholars have explored the media's role in perpetuating and challenging White privilege. This research tends to take one of two approaches: The first set of approaches examines the discursive processes whereby whiteness naturalizes contemporary racial hierarchies in the United States, especially through strategies of invisibility and naturalizing. The second set of approaches examines White audiences and the ways in which they negotiate their identities as racially privileged members of society through media texts. Research has shown, for instance, that *The Cosby Show* encouraged White viewers to believe that the only reason for African American poverty in the 1980s was lack of motivation.

The current increase in specialty minority channels due to cable and satellite television raises questions that confound traditional assumptions of both cognitive and critical research on media and race. Scholars in both traditions have typically relied on prime-time network programming as a barometer of racial attitudes, but the accelerating decline in network prime-time viewership has drawn that practice into question. In many ways, the total television output available to U.S. audiences today defies accurate description. Latinos now have access to dozens of channels of programming from Latin American and U.S. Latino sources. While Asian Americans and Native Americans have fared less well than Latinos, specialty channels devoted to Asian Americans have begun to appear. Likewise, Internet Protocol Television allows viewers worldwide to watch streaming video on their television sets, promising to further increase accessibility to nondomestic minority programming, while also decreasing start-up costs for new minority channels. Some researchers question whether this increased segmentation by race undermines racial tolerance, while others insist that it allows for more complex imaginings of racial difference. Yet others point out that the political economy of these specialty channels tends to limit program diversity to middle- and upper-class cultural values regardless of race.

One final area of inquiry that has received only scant scholarly attention involves the question of television production and ownership. Most such research has been carried out by political interest groups such as the NAACP and the National Council of La Raza. In general, this research confirms that minority participation in television production is minimal and concentrated in the less prestigious jobs. Meanwhile, the Federal Communications Commission's removal of caps on the number of broadcasting outlets a single entity can own has diminished minority-owned broadcast stations. In the cable arena, Black Entertainment Television (BET), founded by African American businessman Robert Johnson, was sold to media giant Viacom in 2000, although the impact of the sale on BET's programming has been debated. Some critical research has begun to explore the link between political/economic changes and portrayals of race, but more research of this type is needed.

Timothy Havens

See also Birth of a Nation, The; Black Cinema; Crime and Race; Digital Divide; Film, Latino; Hip-Hop; Japanese American Citizens League; Lee, Spike; Leisure; Model Minority; Multiracial Identity; Rap: The Genre; Rap: The Movement; Stereotypes; Urban Legends

Further Readings

Dates, Jeanette and William Barlow. 1983. *Split Image: African Americans in the Mass Media.* Washington, DC: Howard University Press.

Dyer, Richard. 1997. *White.* London and New York: Routledge.

Entman, Robert M. and Andrew Rojecki. 2000. *The Black Image in the White Mind: Media and Race in America.* Chicago, IL: University of Chicago Press.

Fiske, John. 1986. *Media Matters: Race and Gender in U.S. Politics.* Rev. ed. Chicago, IL: University of Chicago Press.

Gandy, Oscar. 1998. *Communication and Race.* London: Arnold.

Gray, Herman. 2004. *Watching Race: Television and the Struggle for Blackness.* Minneapolis: University of Minnesota Press.

Hamamoto, Darrell Y. 1994. *Monitored Peril: Asian Americans and the Politics of TV Representation.* Minneapolis: University of Minnesota Press.

hooks, bell. 1992. *Black Looks: Race and Representation.* Boston, MA: South End Press.

Jhally, Sut and Justin Lewis. 1992. *Enlightened Racism: The Cosby Show, Audiences, and the Myth of the American Dream.* Boulder, CO: Westview Press.

MacDonald, J. Fred. 1992. *Blacks and White TV: Afro-Americans in Television since 1948.* 2nd ed. Chicago, IL: Nelson-Hall.

Rodriguez, Clara E. 1997. *Latin Looks: Images of Latinas and Latinos in the U.S. Media.* Boulder, CO: Westview Press.

Shohat, Ella and Robert Stam. 1994. *Unthinking Eurocentrism: Multiculturalism and the Media.* New York and London: Routledge.

Smith-Shomade, Beretta. 2007. *Pimpin' Ain't Easy: Selling Black Entertainment Television.* London and New York: Routledge.

Torres, Sasha, ed. 1998. *Living Color: Race and Television in the United States.* Durham, NC: Duke University Press.

Zook, Kristal Brent. 1999. *Color by Fox: The Fox Network and the Revolution in Black Television.* Minneapolis: University of Minnesota Press.

Medical Experimentation

Medical experimentation is the use of human subjects to evaluate, test, and monitor the effects of medical treatments and practices on the human body. Researchers have long relied on medical experimentation as a means to advance scientific knowledge in treating myriad diseases and conditions. Historically, however, it has been chiefly members of ethnic minorities and socially marginalized groups who have been used in such experiments. This has had profound implications for medical ethics generally and for the way in which members of these groups have constructed meaning and interacted with the medical establishment and government-sponsored research. This entry reviews the nature of medical experimentation and uses three case examples to illustrate how ethnic minorities and the socially marginalized have been used in medical experimentation and research.

At its best, medical experimentation adheres to rigorous research protocols that serve to protect human subjects. For example, in the United States, before any prescription drug is made available for mass consumption, pharmaceutical companies are required by the U.S. Food and Drug Administration to conduct clinical trials of the drug's efficacy and safety. This typically involves recruiting individuals who will participate in a study to evaluate the effects of the drug. Participants are randomly assigned to either a group that will receive the drug or a group that will receive a placebo. The effects of the drug, including health consequences and side effects, are monitored. If its effectiveness is high and the associated risks are relatively low (for example, the drug is highly effective in reducing the presence of a disease and death is unlikely to occur from taking it), the drug has a high probability of making it to the market.

This example reflects the ideal form of medical experimentation: All human subjects who participate in medical experimentation are informed of the purpose, methods, and risks of the experimentation, and subjects must give their consent to participate. This is known as *informed consent.* Ultimately, the benefits of the experimentation for the advance of science should outweigh any potential human costs or risks.

Unfortunately, these conditions have not always been met, and, moreover, society's most vulnerable and marginalized have been used to advance the agenda of science and industry. It can be argued that medical experimentation reflects the stratification of society and reinforces the inequality of groups. Consequently, members of marginalized groups such as African Americans, Jews, the poor, children, people with mental illness, and the prison population have been exploited and used to test myriad conditions on the human body. Moreover, researchers conducting medical experimentation have not always adhered to the practice of soliciting informed consent from participants and, at worst, have used deception and coercion to exploit participants as human subjects. The use of such methods has sometimes resulted in extreme harm to participants—including suffering and death.

Historical Cases

Prior to World War II, little attention was given to safeguarding human rights in medical research and experimentation. Three of the most well-known cases that violated human rights are recognized as the Tuskegee Syphilis Study, conducted on African American men in the United States; the Nazi experiments conducted on Jews in concentration camps in Germany; and the Willowbrook School Study, conducted on children with disabilities in the United States.

Tuskegee Syphilis Study

Over a 40-year period, the U.S. Public Health Service conducted the Tuskegee Syphilis Study (1932–1972) to evaluate the progression of syphilis. The purpose of the study was to determine the effect of syphilis on the human body if left untreated. Deceptive tactics were used in the study. First, African American males who were infected with the disease were recruited as participants, but information about their diagnosis was withheld: The men—rural, poor, and mostly illiterate—were deliberately not told they had syphilis. Second, even after penicillin became available, the men were denied any treatment for syphilis. Instead, the men were told, disingenuously, that they were being treated for an illness that physicians called "bad blood."

The Tuskegee Syphilis Study reflects the intersection of race and class inequality. Members of a minority population were exploited, while the larger society benefited from the findings of the experimentation. Not until 1997 did President Clinton offer a public apology to the community and families who were victims of the abuse.

Nazi Experiments

Some of the most egregious medical experimentation was performed on Jewish inmates at concentration camps in Dachau, Sachsenhausen, and Auschwitz during the German Nazi regime. The physician Joseph Mengele is notorious for having conducted some of the most inhumane studies on twins and dwarfs. According to documented accounts from Holocaust survivors and hearings on war crimes, victims were used as involuntary subjects in experiments involving hypothermia, injection of infectious diseases, and amputations, to name only a few of the experiments conducted. These experiments were justified, it was later explained, as a means to improve society for the dominant group, or what the Nazi regime referred to as the "superior race."

Willowbrook School Study

The Willowbrook School Study (1963–1966) used children with mental disabilities to investigate viral hepatitis. Willowbrook, located in Staten Island, New York, was a state institution for children with mental disabilities. For children to be admitted to the institution, their parents had to consent to allow them to participate in the study. As in the Tuskegee study, a deceptive approach was used. Parents were told their children would receive a vaccination for hepatitis. Instead children were deliberately infected with hepatitis, and inoculations against the virus were then tested.

Tuskegee Syphilis Study. *Dr. David Albritton is shown drawing blood from an unidentified individual for the notorious Tuskegee Syphilis Study (1930s). The purpose of the study was to determine the effect of syphilis on the human body if left untreated.*

Source: National Archives and Records Administration, Southeast Region.

Reform of Medical Experimentation

To safeguard against these unethical practices, the scientific community has established guidelines to protect human rights. Today, two of the most widely instituted guidelines followed by medical researchers include the Nuremberg Code and the Declaration of Helsinki. The overall objective of these guidelines was established to protect human subjects in medical research and to minimize the risk of exploitation and abuse of individuals.

The Nuremberg Code was established in 1947 as a result of the Nuremberg Trials of Nazi war criminals following the end of World War II; it laid the foundation to ensure that individuals have rights in medical research. Among the core principles of the Nuremberg Code, it is held that individuals must be voluntary participants in research, they cannot be coerced into medical experimentation, informed consent must be granted, and the benefits of the experiment must outweigh the risks of participation.

Similarly, the Declaration of Helsinki was established in 1964 by the World Medical Association to provide ethical standards for how physicians should interact with patients when conducting medical research. The declaration echoed the principles outlined in the Nuremberg Code, such as ensuring that medical experimentation be voluntary, informed consent be granted, and the benefits of the research outweigh the risks. In addition, it specified guidelines for medical research and experimentation to further protect human subjects in research. These include protecting the privacy and confidentiality of participants, establishing a research protocol by the researcher, establishing a review of the research protocol by an independent committee, and protecting children and other vulnerable populations by soliciting their assent. The Declaration of Helsinki has been adopted by most institutions that conduct any kind of research with individuals. Most universities, research institutions, and hospitals have developed an independent committee, or institutional review board, which requires all research with humans to be approved and monitored.

Reform in medical experimentation has been helpful in establishing protocols to protect human rights in medical research; however, violations of human rights persist, especially with marginalized groups. For example, as recently as 2001, the pharmaceutical company Pfizer was sued for conducting clinical trials of a drug for tuberculosis with African children. It is alleged that the experimentation was conducted without informed consent and that participation in the study was not voluntary.

Tracey Lewis-Elligan

See also African Americans; Eugenics; Holocaust; Holocaust Deniers and Revisionists; Scapegoats; Social Inequality

Further Readings

Caplan, Arthur L. 1992. *When Medicine Went Mad: Bioethics and the Holocaust.* Totowa, NJ: Humana.
Jones, James H. 1993. *Bad Blood: The Tuskegee Syphilis Experiment.* New York: Free Press.
Jonsen, Albert R., Robert M. Veatch, and Leroy Walters. 1998. *Source Book in Bioethics: A Documentary History.* Washington, DC: Georgetown University Press.
Lewin, Tamor. 2001. "Families Sue Pfizer on Test of Antibiotic." *New York Times,* August 30, Business Section p. 1.

MELTING POT

Few social metaphors have dominated American thought as pervasively as that of the melting pot—a key symbol for the United States. A melting pot is, literally, a vessel in which metals or other materials are melted and mixed; this metaphor compares America's sundry racial, ethnic, and religious groups to foundry-type metals that are transmuted, in the crucible of the American experience, into social gold. This entry charts the origins and ideological trajectory of this defining idea and that of its rival, cultural pluralism.

The verbal trope of *melting* as a code for Americanness can be traced to J. Hector St. John de Crèvecoeur (1735–1813), author of *Letters From an American Farmer* (1782). Here, he likened "Americans" to individuals from all nations being "melted" into a new race. As a full-blown descriptor of the United States, however, the term *melting pot* made its dramatic debut in Israel Zangwill's (1864–1926) play, *The Melting-Pot,* which opened in Washington, D.C., in October 1908.

The play's protagonist is David Quixano, a young Jewish immigrant bent on composing the great American symphony. The visionary Quixano heralds America as "God's Crucible, the great Melting-Pot" where "the Great Alchemist" (God) "melts and fuses" those who hail from "all nations and races" in coming to her shores. This prophetic exaltation of America soon captured the public's imagination in New York, when in 1909, it was performed 136 times to popular acclaim, despite critical disdain.

This mythic image of America has had its share of demythologizers. The melting pot is perhaps defined more sharply by its detractors than by its proponents. Indeed, social reality in the United States has arguably belied the myth. The melting pot, for one thing, excluded African Americans. Proverbially, it was "the pot calling the kettle black," in that Jim Crow segregation was the polar opposite of Quixano's vision of integration. Among the most detailed and well-documented cultural histories of the initial reception of *The Melting-Pot* and its subsequent impact is that of Philip Gleason, who concluded that among intellectuals, the real challenger to the symbol of the melting pot is the concept of cultural pluralism.

Cultural Pluralism

Over time, the trope of the melting pot became tarnished, for it threatened to gradually destroy diversity, not preserve it. Ironically, a year before the image of the melting pot was popularized by Zangwill, the term *cultural pluralism* was coined and later, in 1915, was used to criticize Zangwill's gilded metaphor. Horace Kallen (1882–1974), a Jewish pragmatist philosopher, invented the term in 1907 at Oxford University, after refusing to attend a Thanksgiving dinner with Rhodes Scholars from the South because they had excluded Alain Locke (1885–1954), who earlier that year had won national acclaim as the first African American Rhodes Scholar.

In his most famous essay, "Democracy Versus the Melting Pot" (1915), Kallen had already subjected Zangwill's conceit to a searing critique. Yet it was not until 1924 that the term *cultural pluralism*—antipode of the melting pot—first appeared in print. Kallen defined cultural pluralism as the view that democracy is an essential prerequisite to culture and asserted that culture can be and sometimes is a fine flowering of democracy, as illustrated by U.S. history. The countermetaphor that Kallen proposed is that of the *philharmonic,* in which American civilization may be seen to embody the cooperative harmonies of European civilization—a multiplicity, but unified in a sort of orchestration of humanity in which every type of instrument contributes to the symphony that is civilization.

Among other critics of the melting pot, Randolph Bourne, John Dewey, and Isaac B. Berkson, author of the 1920 book *Theories of Americanization,* figured prominently, as well as Alain Locke himself. Like Kallen, Locke called into question the assimilationist paradigm of the melting pot. In one lecture, Locke reportedly characterized America not as a melting pot, but as a crucible for enrichment. In a speech titled "The Negro Renaissance," held in Chicago at the Women's City Club and reported in the *Chicago Defender,* Locke advocated the continuing development of African American culture, rejecting both Zangwill's "melting pot" and Kallen's "symphony of civilization" in favor of a Bahá'í-inspired vision of "unity through diversity," where cross-fertilization is made possible only when cultural identity is preserved and intergroup reciprocity encouraged. Yet Locke conceded that ultimately the races would, in the distant future, disappear. Beyond Kallen's own formulation of cultural pluralism, Christopher Buck showed how Locke enfolds cultural pluralism into a multidimensional theory of democracy.

To be fair, the melting pot concept continued (and continues) to have its proponents, such as Arthur M. Schlesinger, Sr., who listed the melting pot as among America's ten great contributions to civilization. Rather than one or the other, perhaps both or neither of the concepts will embody the hope and enthusiasm they once did.

Beyond the Melting Pot

The idea of the melting pot held sway among many U.S. sociologists until the 1950s and 1960s. The publication of *Beyond the Melting Pot* in 1963 was a watershed event that overturned the metaphor by sheer force of sociological analysis. While the rhetoric of the melting pot was still in play as a patriotic ideal, social reality in the United States was a thing apart. Chronicling the ethnic and religious cleavages of New York City at midcentury, Nathan Glazer and Daniel Moynihan's sociology remains a classic work, although subsequent waves of immigration have altered New York's racial, ethnic, and religious landscape so considerably that the dream of cultural pluralism was as unlikely as any hope of a melting pot.

Assimilation operated on immigrant groups in different ways to change them but still make them identifiable. This finding suggests that the reality of U.S. society is in equipoise between the ideals of the melting pot and cultural pluralism and that the future course of U.S. civilization may be difficult to chart with precision. An overarching American ideology may be one thing, but a sociological theory—especially one with explanatory power and predictive potential—remains elusive.

The melting pot, and its rival, cultural pluralism, are by no means the only theories of Americanization—or of minority socialization in the North American context generally. Added to Zangwill's assimilationist paradigm and to Kallen's and Locke's pluralist models are the sovereigntist examples of Quèbec and *Nunavut* ("our land," in the Inuktitut language). Generally, an overarching policy of multiculturalism, officially adopted in 1971, both informs and structures Canada (with English and French as its two official languages).

Canada offers its official brand of multiculturalism expressed in the trope of the *cultural mosaic*—which may be thought of as a kind of "tossed salad" of ethnic, racial, and religious minorities. Somewhat anachronistically, perhaps, Canadians contrast their social model of the mosaic with the American ideal of the melting pot. While this alternative Canadian paradigm has its appeal, its critics can still show the dominance of the founding British and French cultures and argue that successive Québécois referenda have come dangerously close to sundering Canada as a nation.

The huge Aboriginal Canadian land claim settlement that led to the redrawing of the map of Canada in the formation of the territory of Nunavut in 1999 illustrates Kallen's model in the extreme. Furthermore, too great an emphasis on multiculturalism (which is the modern progeny of Kallen's and Locke's cultural pluralisms) can lead to hyphenated identities and ultimately to "ethnic ghettoization." To make matters worse, that not-so-well-hidden prejudice known as "polite racism" continues to vitiate Canada's multicultural ideals such that its model—just like Canada's nationalized health care system—affords neither an easier nor a readier solution for North Americans south of the forty-eighth parallel.

One of the most thought-provoking recent reflections is Werner Sollors's chapter on "Melting Pots" in his book, *Beyond Ethnicity: Consent and Descent in American Culture;* he argues that ethnicity is nothing more than a key metaphor, a typological rhetoric that serves as social symbolism for defining a group (rather than a nation). This is somewhat akin to Alain Locke's theory of race as a social construct, arguing that "race" is far more socially than biologically determined and that race consciousness, like individual personality, is always in flux in an ongoing process of "transvaluation."

Among contemporary advocates, Michael Barone, senior writer at *U.S. News & World Report,* expresses renewed support for the old social paradigm in *The New Americans: How the Melting Pot Can Work Again.* (Space does not permit a survey of other contemporary examples.) Social metaphors, such as the melting pot, are condensed paradigms: constellations of competing American values collapsed into symbolic slogans. All of these—from Walt Whitman's "orbicular" vision of American democracy, to Zangwill's "melting-pot," to Kallen's "symphony of civilization," to Locke's "unity through diversity" (and "the New Negro"), to the Canadian "mosaic," and to everything in between—shows how identity politics is not only highly topical, but intrinsically tropic. In the fusioning crucible of Zangwill's melting pot, a more unifying vision of America may someday emerge.

Christopher George Buck

See also African Americans; Assimilation; Canada, First Nations; Civil Religion; Cosmopolitanism; Cultural Relativism; Culture of Poverty; *Desi;* Identity Politics; Internalized Racism; Jewish Americans; Jim Crow; Marginalization; Minority/Majority; Multicultural Social Movements; Nativism; Pluralism; Race; Race, Social Construction of

Further Readings

Barone, Michael. 2006. *The New Americans: How the Melting Pot Can Work Again.* Washington, DC: Regnery.

Buck, Christopher. 2005. *Alain Locke: Faith and Philosophy.* Los Angeles, CA: Kalimát Press.

Crèvecoeur, J. Hector St. John de. [1782] 1999. *Letters from an American Farmer,* edited by S. Manning. Oxford, UK: Oxford University Press.

Glazer, Nathan and Daniel Moynihan. 1970. *Beyond the Melting Pot: The Negroes, Puerto Ricans, Jews, Italians, and Irish of New York City.* 2nd ed. Cambridge, MA: MIT Press.

Gleason, Philip. 1964. "The Melting Pot: Symbol of Fusion or Confusion?" *American Quarterly* 16(1):20–46.

Kallen, Horace M. 1915. "Democracy versus the Melting Pot." *Nation* 100, February, pp. 18–25. Reprinted 1996, pp. 67–92 in *Theories of Ethnicity: A Classical Reader,* edited by Werner Sollors. New York: New York University Press.

Kallen, Horace M. 1924. *Culture and Democracy in the United States: Studies in the Group Psychology of the American People.* New York: Boni & Liveright. Reprinted 1977, New Brunswick, NJ: Transaction.

Kraus, Joe. 1999. "How *The Melting Pot* Stirred America: The Reception of Zangwill's Play and Theater's Role in the American Assimilation Experience." *MELUS* 24(3):3–19.

Sollors, Werner. 1980. "A Defense of the Melting Pot." Pp. 181–214 in *The American Identity: Fusion and Fragmentation,* edited by R. Kroes. Amsterdam, The Netherlands: Amerika Instituut.

Sollors, Werner. 1986. "A Critique of Pure Pluralism." Pp. 250–279 in *Reconstructing American Literary History,* edited by S. Bercovitch. Cambridge, MA: Harvard University Press.

Sollors, Werner. 1986. *Beyond Ethnicity: Consent and Descent in American Culture.* New York: Oxford University Press.

Szuberla, Guy. 1995. "Zangwill's *The Melting-Pot* Plays Chicago." *MELUS* 20(3):3–20.

Zangwill, Israel. 1909. *The Melting-Pot Drama in Four Acts.* New York: Macmillan. Reprinted 2005, Whitefish, MT: Kessinger.

MENNONITES

Mennonites, members of a Protestant group that originated in the 16th-century Anabaptist movement in Europe, migrated to North America in several waves that began in 1683 and continued into the mid-20th century. Differences in ethnicity, history, and convictions have produced some thirty different Mennonite groups in the United States. Some Mennonites have a Swiss-German lineage, while others come from Dutch-Russian stock. Sizable numbers of Asian, Latino, and African American members also add color to the ethnic mosaic. Mennonites in Los Angeles and Philadelphia, for example, worship in nearly a dozen languages. The different immigrant groups exude distinctive cultural, historical, and theological flavors. All of these factors create a complicated but fascinating story of ethnicity.

History

The Mennonite story began in 1525, in Zurich, Switzerland, when a group of young radicals secretly baptized each other. In 16th-century Europe, baptizing an adult was a defiant act of civil disobedience—a capital crime that could lead to execution. The young reformers were soon nicknamed "Anabaptists," meaning "rebaptizers," because they had already been baptized as infants in the Catholic Church. They refused to baptize their babies, raised questions about the mass, scorned the use of images, and criticized the morality of church officials. The Anabaptist refusal to baptize infants, swear oaths of allegiance, or follow the dictates of established tradition incensed political and religious authorities.

Leaders of the new movement were promptly arrested, imprisoned, and banned from several cities and regions. Within 4 months of the first rebaptism, the first Anabaptist was killed for sedition, and the "heretics" began to flee for their lives. Meetings were often held secretly and in secluded places to avoid detection. Thousands of Anabaptists were imprisoned, tortured, branded, burned, and drowned. Nevertheless, Anabaptism mushroomed in many areas of Europe. Stories of the harsh persecution can be found in the *Martyrs Mirror,* a book of some 1,100 pages, which chronicles the bloody carnage.

Anabaptism surfaced in the Netherlands about 1530. Menno Simons, a Dutch Catholic priest, had growing sympathies for Anabaptist convictions. He joined the movement in 1536 and soon became a leader and writer with a sizable following. As early as 1545, some followers of Menno were called "Mennists," and, by 1550, they were the dominant group of Anabaptists in North Germany and Holland. Anabaptists in other areas soon carried the Mennonite name as they migrated to Prussia, Russia, and, eventually, North America.

Swiss and South German Mennonites settled in Pennsylvania throughout the 18th century and soon became known as outstanding farmers. They gradually moved westward and southward with the frontier, settling in Maryland, Virginia, Ohio, Indiana, Illinois, and other states, as well as in Ontario, Canada. Mennonites with Dutch-Russian roots came in later waves of immigration in the 1870s and settled in the Great Plains, the far West, and Canada.

Old Order, Transitional, and Assimilated Mennonites

In terms of assimilation into U.S. society, there are three broad types of Mennonites: Old Order (10%), transitional (20%), and assimilated (70%). On the traditional end, the Old Order groups preserve and perpetuate many older Mennonite customs. At the other end of the spectrum are assimilated Mennonites, who have absorbed mainstream values in the United States related to dress, technology, and lifestyle. In the middle are the conservative groups that are in transition. They drive cars but still wear plain clothing and embrace conservative standards and church practices.

After the Civil War, tradition-minded Mennonites began resisting certain innovations that were creeping into the Mennonite Church. Those who clung to traditional ways were eventually identified as Old Order Mennonites. The Old Order movement that emerged between 1872 and 1901 protested the acceptance of Sunday school, evening services, revival meetings, the use of English in worship, the foreign missions movement, higher education, and other aspects of U.S. culture that were beginning to influence Mennonite life. The rural, separatist Old Orders have preserved some of the earlier forms of Mennonite ethnicity and religious practices.

Old Order Mennonites can be sorted into two types—those who drive automobiles and those who do not. The two largest Old Order groups are the car-driving Horning Mennonites and the Wenger Mennonites, who use horse-and-buggy transportation. Most of the Old Order groups have Swiss-German roots. The Wenger Mennonites speak the Pennsylvania German dialect, but most other Mennonites, apart from recent Asian and Hispanic immigrants, speak English.

The conservative, transitional churches are largely rural, but many of their members no longer farm. Although they dress plainly, ordain lay ministers, and emphasize separation from the world, they have few restrictions on technology for agriculture or business purposes. Homes are equipped with telephones and electricity. Virtually all of the transitional Mennonite groups forbid television, and many have a taboo on the radio and computers. They are less likely to pursue higher education, engage in professional occupations, participate in politics, or advocate for social justice. They embody the historic Mennonite standards of nonresistance (pacifism) and separation from the world, and they will excommunicate members who do not uphold conservative standards. These groups strongly detest divorce as well as the ordination of women—practices that have become acceptable among many assimilated Mennonite groups.

The two major assimilated denominational bodies are the Mennonite Brethren (23,000) and the Mennonite Church USA (110,000), which was formed in 2002, when the former Mennonite Church and General Conference Mennonite Church merged into one body. The two ethnic immigrant streams of the 18th-century Swiss-German and Dutch-Russian have shaped this denomination. However, with recent immigrants, the current Mennonite Church USA is sprinkled with many strains of ethnicity, race, nationality, and language. Some rural congregations still embody a traditional outlook in religious practice and cultural lifestyle. Other congregations in Chicago, Los Angeles, and New York, as well as in many suburban areas, are quite cosmopolitan. Some follow informal patterns of worship; others are more formal; and still others have a charismatic flavor. The ethnic mix is growing as well. White persons of German ancestry still dominate the formal church structures, but growing numbers of Latinos, African Americans, Asians, and people from a variety of ethnic backgrounds participate in the church. Recognized bodies within the Mennonite Church USA represent African Americans, Hispanics, Hmong, Lao, Native Americans, and Vietnamese.

Members of some of the congregations of the former General Conference Mennonite Church were German-speaking immigrants who had come to the United States and Canada from Poland, Prussia, and Russia in the 1870s. Many of these new immigrants settled in the midwestern and central states, especially in Kansas. Compared with the Mennonite Church prior to the merger in 2002, the General Conference Mennonite Church had a stronger Dutch-Russian flavor, flourished more in the central states, and granted more autonomy to local congregations. The General Conference Church never developed distinctive patterns of plain dress like the Mennonite Church did. In some regions of the country, the General Conference Church assimilated into U.S. culture more quickly than the Mennonite Church did in the first half of the 20th century; but in some communities, General Conference Mennonites spoke German longer. Nevertheless, the Mennonite Church, at least before World War II, was generally more separatist in many regions of the country.

The Mennonite Brethren are the other large assimilated group. Some 10,000 Mennonite and Hutterite immigrants came to the United States in the 1870s and 1880s from Prussia and Russia. Russian Mennonite farmers, along with other Russian immigrants, brought a hardy and productive variety of "red" wheat with them to the prairie states. Numerous historical, geographical, cultural, and theological differences hindered the new immigrants from easily fraternizing with the earlier Amish and Mennonite immigrants of Swiss-German stock.

Some of the Prussian and Russian Mennonites joined the General Conference Mennonite Church, and others formed the Mennonite Brethren Church. Members of this group trace their roots back to renewal movements among Mennonites in Russia in the 1860s. In the 1880s and 1890s, Mennonite Brethren immigrants established congregations in Kansas, Nebraska, and the Dakotas. Eventually, the Mennonite Brethren moved westward to California, a stronghold of the denomination today that claims more than a third of their congregations. Many Mennonite Brethren also settled in Canada, and by the end of the 20th century, over half of their membership was residing north of the U.S. border.

Cultural, regional, ethnic, and theological differences crisscross the American Mennonite landscape in the early 21st century. With some thirty distinct subgroups, descendants of the followers of Menno Simons can be found singing in Chinese, English, Pennsylvania German, Spanish, and Vietnamese. Some drive horse-drawn carriages on back roads, while others drive their Corollas and BMWs on metropolitan freeways. Some wear plain dress, and others sport designer clothing. Some manufacture computer software, and others prohibit the use of it. Ethnic identity is most crystallized among the Old Orders and transitional groups, whose distinctive clothing sets them apart from mainstream culture. Assimilated Mennonites, on the other hand, have few external symbols of ethnicity, but values such as pacifism, community, and international service shape their sense of Mennonite identity.

Donald B. Kraybill

See also Amish; Belize; German Americans; Hutterites; Schmiedeleut

Further Readings

Kraybill, Donald B. and C. Nelson Hostetter. 2001. *Anabaptist World USA*. Scottdale, PA: Herald Press.

Kraybill, Donald B. and James P. Hurd. 2006. *Horse and Buggy Mennonites: Hoofbeats of Humility in a Postmodern World*. University Park: Pennsylvania State University Press.

The Mennonite Encyclopedia: A Comprehensive Reference Work on the Anabaptist-Mennonite Movement. 1955–1990. Scottdale, PA: Mennonite Publishing House/Herald Press.

The Mennonite Experience in America, 4 vols. 1985–1996. Scottdale, PA: Herald Press.

Nolt, Steven and Harry Loewen. 1996. *Through Fire and Water: An Overview of Mennonite History*. Scottdale, PA: Herald Press.

Scott, Stephen E. 1996. *An Introduction to Old Order and Conservative Mennonite Groups*. Intercourse, PA: Good Books.

Web Sites

Global Anabaptist Mennonite Encyclopedia Online: http://www.gameo.org

MENOMINEE

The Menominee Tribe are a small, federally recognized tribe of Native Americans who still reside in their ancestral homeland in northern Wisconsin. The Menominee are from the Algonquian linguistic group and are present-day Wisconsin's oldest continuous inhabitants, with a 10,000-year history of living in the Great Lakes and Green Bay area.

Once reduced to only 2,221 in 1937 and 3,700 in 1957, the current total tribal enrollment is 7,200 people, with approximately half (3,400) living on the reservation and the rest living in other locations, including cities and suburbs. The ancestral land base of the Menominee comprised 9.5 million acres (including areas of present-day Minnesota, Illinois, and Michigan's Upper Peninsula) and was reduced to the reservation of 235,000 acres in the Treaty of 1854. The reservation is heavily forested (223,500 acres), with the largest single tract of virgin timberland in Wisconsin. The Menominee are a self-governing, sovereign nation and are internationally renowned for their forestry and natural resource management.

The struggle of most racial and ethnic minority groups in the United States has been to gain a place in the so-called melting pot of American society. For the Menominee and other indigenous people, however, the struggle has been, and continues to be, to preserve their ancestral lands, natural resources, political sovereignty, and distinct culture. Throughout their long history, the Menominee have proven themselves to be highly resilient and adaptive to many threats, including disease, warfare, colonization, and radical cultural change.

History and European Contact

The Menominee (also spelled *Menomini*) called themselves *Mamaceqtwa* ("The People") and were given the name Menominee (meaning "wild-rice gatherers") by neighboring tribes. The French explorers and missionaries called them *Folles Avoines,* or "wild-oats people." The Menominee gathered wild rice as a staple of their diet, which also consisted of fish, game, and cultivated beans, corn, and squash. The oral history and creation story of the tribe originates at the mouth of the present-day Menominee River, and unlike other tribes, the Menominee have no migration story. They are part of the widely diverse Woodland cultural grouping (beginning in 1,000 BC), and although some archaeologists have asserted that they may be descendants of the Mississippian mound-building cultures on account of the abundance of mounds in the area, this conflicts with the tribal history. Tribal history mentions the presence of a separate mound-building people in the area who either migrated elsewhere or were absorbed into the Menominee or other local tribes. The tribe was organized into various bands consisting of the five clans: Eagle, Bear, Moose, Crane, and Wolf.

The Menominee's first European contact was with French explorer Jean Nicolet (1634). During the period of early European contact and colonization, the area was dominated by the French (1630–1760), and, in 1671, the French annexed the Great Lakes region, and all tribes were declared French subjects. The Menominee became very successful in the fur trade; however, contact with French explorers, traders, and missionaries greatly reduced the tribe's population through epidemics of smallpox, cholera, and measles. Their success in the fur trade changed the economic focus of the tribe, and the frequent raids by the Iroquois (1600–1800) created a further reliance on trade with Europeans for weapons and ammunition. Unlike other Great Lakes tribes of similar size who disappeared, the Menominee also survived additional threats from large and powerful tribes, such as the Fox Sauk, the Ojibwas, and the Huron. As colonization progressed, the tribe faced new threats to its existence from the newly formed United States.

Missionaries and Religion

One of the threats to Menominee culture has been the freedom to practice and preserve the traditional tribal religion. Like all indigenous people, the Menominee had their own ancient spiritual practices and beliefs at the time of European contact. During the early 1600s, the Jesuits entered Menominee territory along with other tribes from the East. The Jesuits were unsuccessful and left the region by the 1680s. The Franciscans, however, were much more successful at converting the Menominee to Christianity. They entered the region in 1831, and, by 1855, it is estimated that over half of the population was Roman Catholic.

In 1883, the U.S. government passed the Major Indian Crimes Act that made the practice of traditional religions a federal offense. This forced the remaining Menominee practicing the traditional religion to go underground. The Indian Civil Rights Act of 1968 returned religious freedom to Native people but was not enforced until 1978.

Many traditional beliefs and practices have survived into contemporary times. Understandably, those who practice or have knowledge of traditional spiritual practices (such as the Big Drum Society) are secretive and protective of these traditions. On the reservation today, there are not only a large number of Roman Catholics but also Presbyterians and members of the Assemblies of God and the Native American Church.

Threats to the Language

The Menominee language is a melodic Algonquian language. It is, however, an endangered language. Despite renewed interest and numerous efforts to teach and preserve it, it is estimated that there are only 39 fluent speakers remaining. For the Menominee and other Native people, language is a central element of tribal identity and cultural survival.

The key components in the preservation of culture and language are economic success, a strong tribal government, and control over the educational system. A prosperous tribe has the resources for preserving language and culture. A strong tribal government ensures control over these resources and control over the educational system that allows for the early transmission of language and cultural values. Despite threats to all of these areas, the Menominee's success in attaining all three of these leaves room for optimism.

Economic Success: A Double-Edged Sword

Just as they became successful in the fur trade, the Menominee later achieved success through the timber industry. In the state of Wisconsin during the 1800s, the so-called pine barons had thoroughly exploited the timber outside of the reservation boundaries. Utilizing their natural resources allowed the Menominee to achieve a great deal of economic success, and they opened their own lumber mill in 1872—only 18 years after the establishment of the reservation. Forestry and the timber industry became the central component of the Menominee tribe, and it remains so today. The logging museum on the reservation hosts the largest collection of logging artifacts in the world.

Despite their ability to achieve early economic independence and success through their pioneering work at sustainable forest management, the Menominee faced numerous continued threats through various U.S. policies and legislation. It was the strength of various leaders that allowed the Menominee to survive. For example, the General Allotment (Dawes) Act of 1887 posed a serious threat to the Menominee; however, they refused to participate. Because of this, they were able to retain their reservation lands for at least another three generations. Attempts by the U.S. government to relocate the tribe to Minnesota were successfully staved off by Chief Oshkosh.

The "Termination Policy," in which the U.S. government sought to end its obligations to and protection of sovereign Native nations, proved to be catastrophic for the Menominee. The U.S. government used the Menominee's success with building an economic base and infrastructure (such as the first tribally owned and operated clinic, law enforcement, judicial, and educational systems) to justify termination. In 1954, the Menominee Termination Act was signed into law by President Eisenhower, which started a downward economic spiral and turned one of the most successful Native nations into one of the most impoverished. In addition, the tribe lost thousands of acres of its reservation.

The Menominee fought back against termination in the 1960s and early 1970s, spurred on by the other civil rights movements, such as the American Indian Movement (AIM). Leaders and activists such as Ada Deer formed DRUMS (Determination of Rights for Menominee Shareholders) to draw national attention and media coverage to the plight of the Menominee. In 1971, the Menominee March for Justice, from Keshena to Madison, drew further attention to the problems created by termination. Finally, in 1973, President Nixon signed the Menominee Restoration Act, ending the termination era and reestablishing the original reservation boundaries.

The Menominee Nation today is in many ways a model for other Native nations. They have a strong tribal government consisting of a tribally elected, nine-member legislative branch and a judicial branch consisting of a lower and a supreme court. In addition to the lumber industry (now Menominee Tribal Enterprises), there is a tribally owned and operated casino and tourism bureau. The tribal clinic, opened in 1977, is the first tribally owned and operated health care facility. The tribe runs its own schools, and in 1987 founded the College of the Menominee Nation, offering higher education to both tribal members and students from surrounding communities off the reservation. The tribe has demonstrated that it can not only survive but, in many ways, thrive.

Arieahn Matamonasa-Bennett

See Appendix A

See also American Indian Movement; Assimilation; Blood Quantum; Bureau of Indian Affairs; Dawes Act of 1887; Native Americans; Reservation System; Trail of Broken Treaties

Further Readings

Davis, Thomas. 2000. *Sustaining the Forest, the People, and the Spirit.* New York: State University of New York Press.

Keesing, Felix M. 1987. *The Menomini Indians of Wisconsin: A Study of Three Centuries of Cultural Contact and Change.* Madison: University of Wisconsin Press.

Spindler, George and Louise Spindler. 1984. *Dreamers with Power: The Menominee.* Prospect Heights, IL: Waveland Press.

Web Sites

Case Study: Menominee Tribal Enterprises: http://www.menominee.edu/sdi/csstdy.htm

Menominee Indian Tribe of Wisconsin: http://www.menominee-nsn.gov

Menominee Tribal Clinic: http://www.mtclinic.net/history.htm

Mexican American Legal Defense and Educational Fund (MALDEF)

The Mexican American Legal Defense and Educational Fund, also known by its acronym, MALDEF, is a nonprofit organization that has been providing Latinos with legal assistance and advocacy since its inception in 1968. In addition to litigation, MALDEF empowers Latinos through educational outreach programs that build skills and train individuals to participate in their communities as leaders and advocates.

Modeled after the National Association for the Advancement of Colored People Legal Defense Fund

(NAACPLDF), MALDEF was established in 1968, in San Antonio, Texas. Under the tutelage of Jack Greenberg, director of the NAACPLDF, Pete Tijerina, a civil rights attorney and the first executive director of MALDEF, launched the organization with a $2.2 million grant from the Ford Foundation. The grant was secured on the conditions that the money would be spent in five states (Arizona, Texas, California, New Mexico, and Colorado) over 5 years to conduct civil rights legal work for Mexican Americans and that $250,000 would be distributed through scholarships for Chicano students pursuing an education in law and legal studies.

The organization is headquartered in Los Angeles and maintains regional offices in Atlanta, San Antonio, Chicago, Sacramento, and Washington, D.C., and a program office in Houston. MALDEF is governed by a board of thirty-five directors, made up of leaders from throughout the public and private sectors, government, and law firms. The focus of MALDEF's mission is to safeguard the civil rights of Latinos through the fostering of sound public policy, programs, and laws and to expand the opportunities for Latinos to participate as positive contributors to society. This mission is accomplished by implementing activities that are grounded in litigation and legal assistance or training and leadership development. MALDEF efforts are concentrated in six areas, including employment, education, political access, public resource equity issues, immigration, and language.

MALDEF's Employment Economic Development Department houses the Employment and Equal Opportunity Program, which addresses workplace discrimination, cases involving unfair and inhumane labor practices, and the need to protect employee rights. Many of the court cases that have passed through this department pertain to equal opportunity issues, hiring practices, discriminatory practices, and the right to work.

Education is a large part of the mission for MALDEF, and one of the busiest departments is the Community Education and Leadership Development (CELD) department, where programs are promoted to keep community members informed so they can be strong, knowledgeable advocates. One key program in this department is the Parent School Partnership (PSP) program, which provides parents with information and skills to advocate for their children to receive a quality education. This 16-week training program teaches parents about curriculum, partnerships, parent rights and responsibilities, and leadership skills. Another major program in this department, the Leadership Development Program, provides midcareer professionals with leadership skills and knowledge, preparing them to take leadership roles on boards and commissions that set policy at the local, state, and national levels. The education department also instructs the Latino community on the electoral and legislative processes, voter rights, and civil rights issues, such as redistricting and census adjustments.

In the Fair Share and Equal Access Department, the primary work occurs in the Public Resource Equity Program, ensuring that Latinos are receiving an equitable share of public resources. Another aspect of equitable distribution pertains to access, so MALDEF works to eliminate language barriers and protect the rights of individuals who have a limited proficiency in the English language.

MALDEF's work in the area of immigration has grown as immigrant communities continue to expand and spread across the nation. In addition to addressing issues of denied education, fair housing, and language access, MALDEF's Immigrant's Rights Program has produced materials to assist immigrants in adjusting to their new homeland and devotes time to monitoring

Immigration reform demonstration. *On May 1, 2007, in Detroit, Michigan, thousands marched for immigration reform and to stop deportations in southwest Detroit, a heavily Hispanic neighborhood.*

Source: © Jim West/The Image Works.

proposed legislation on the federal and state levels and attending hearings that could impact immigrants.

From the time MALDEF opened its doors for business in 1968, the organization has been inundated with cases dealing with injustices like school segregation, racial discrimination, and employment abuses. Today, the cases continue to pour in, and many of the concerns remain the same, although additional issues have been added, such as police brutality, immigration, and voting rights abuses. Over the years, MALDEF has been involved with many precedent-setting cases.

Some examples of the types of cases MALDEF fights on behalf of the Latino community include *Ramirez v. Desert Community College District*, in which the college refused to promote Ramirez to supervisor because he did not have a high school diploma, yet they expected him to participate in the interviewing of candidates and to train the new supervisor. MALDEF challenged these actions as discriminatory. In *Velez v. Lindow*, a landlord's policy of not renting to monolingual Spanish-speaking tenants was challenged under the umbrella of unfair housing practices. MALDEF argued that Latinos are disproportionately affected when federal housing laws are violated. In *Guevara v. City of Norcross, Georgia*, a minister faced criminal charges when he posted signs inviting the community to religious services. The signs were in Spanish and deemed in violation of a city ordinance that restricts sign display to English. MALDEF argued that the city ordinance violates the First and Fourteenth Amendments, and the criminal charges were dismissed. In *Rodriguez v. Malloy*, MALDEF challenged the right of the Immigration and Naturalization Service (INS) to invade a person's home without a warrant.

The work MALDEF does to protect the basic rights of Latinos serves to protect everyone, because when a community suffers from or allows unjust treatment such as discriminatory practices, voting rights violations, and direct violations of constitutional rights to occur, it is not an individual violation, but a violation against society. MALDEF provides an invaluable and much-needed service to the Latino community through their legal and advocacy work, collaborations with state, local, and federal agencies, and contributing to the education of the community.

Alma Alvarez-Smith

See also Hispanics; Mexican Americans; Minority Rights; Proposition 187; School Desegregation; Voting Rights

Further Readings

Alvarez-Smith, Alma. 2004. "MALDEF." Pp. 508–509 in *Encyclopedia of Latino Popular Culture,* edited by C. C. Candelaria, A. J. Aldama, and P. J. Garcia. Westport, CT: Greenwood Press.

Magaña, Lisa. 2005. *Mexican Americans and the Politics of Diversity.* Tucson: University of Arizona Press.

Web Sites

Mexican American Legal Defense and Educational Fund: http://www.maldef.org

MEXICAN AMERICANS

Mexican Americans are U.S.-born citizens of Mexican descent and represent the fastest-growing ethnic group in the United States. An overview of key historical events in this group's history and contemporary social and cultural characteristics illustrates the important role that this group has played in American history.

Mexican Americans use a variety of ethnic self-identification terms, including Hispanic, Hispano, Mexican, Mexicano, Latino, and Chicano. These vary with history, geographical region, and age; many Mexican Americans use all or some of these terms interchangeably. The U.S. Census Bureau uses *Hispanic* as an umbrella term that includes Mexicans, Cubans, Puerto Ricans, and other groups from Latin and South America. In 2005, there were approximately 40,425,000 Hispanics in the United States representing 14% of the total population. Mexican Americans numbered approximately 26,630,000 and made up 65% of the total Hispanic population.

Historical Overview

The historical legacy of Mexican Americans begins with the history of the Spanish conquest of the New World. With colonization, the Spanish intermixed with the native population and produced a *Mestizaje*, the blending of races, cultures, and society between Spaniards and the indigenous groups of the Western Hemisphere. Like other parts of Spanish America, Mexico established its independence from Spain in 1825 with a national territory that reached into what is now the American Southwest. The U.S. doctrine of manifest destiny culminated in the Mexican American War of 1846–1848. With Mexico's defeat, the United States annexed the Southwest and, in so doing, gained nearly 80,000 Mexican Americans. Their descendants and future waves of Mexican immigrants, particularly during the Mexican Revolution of 1910, changed the social fabric of American society.

Throughout the 20th century, the Mexican American population has confronted serious obstacles that have jeopardized their rights as U.S. citizens. During the Great Depression, the U.S. government engaged in widespread deportation of Mexican immigrants and Mexican Americans who were mistaken for foreign-born Mexicans. The belief that Mexicans were taking jobs away from U.S. citizens combined with hostile and xenophobic public sentiments against Mexican Americans. The U.S. government implemented the policy of repatriation of almost a half million of the estimated 3 million Mexicans and Mexican Americans living in the United States between 1929 and 1939. For Mexican Americans, as native-born citizens, this policy represented a violation of their civil rights.

Despite the mass deportations, Mexican Americans engaged in several important strikes in the Southwest. The San Joaquin, California, cotton strike of 1933 (considered a precursor to the workers' strike against the grape industry led by labor activist Cesar Chavez in the early 1960s) began as a response to low wages and poor working and living conditions. Mexican immigrants and Mexican Americans joined together and walked off their work in the cotton fields. A series of violent confrontations involving the owners and the police eventually led to mediation and the end of the strike, but tensions between cotton workers, the owners, and the police continued for years. In San Antonio, Texas, pecan shellers, mostly women, went on strike in 1938 to protest their low wages and the conditions on the shelling assembly lines. With the help of organizers such as Emma Tenayuca, approximately 12,000 workers joined together in the Texas Pecan Shelling Workers Union. The strike broke out in violence and resulted in the arrest of 6,000 union members. The settlement of the strike brought few benefits for the workers, who were gradually displaced with the mechanization of the industry. Labor activism continues to the present date.

With the entrance of the United States into World War II, the U.S. government encouraged Mexican immigration to the United States to fill labor shortages produced by the war. The Bracero Program (*brazo* is Spanish for "arm") represented an agreement between the United States and Mexico to guarantee a steady supply of workers. An estimated quarter of a million braceros worked in the agricultural fields and war industries. Although the Bracero Program stipulated that the workers would return to Mexico at the conclusion of the war, large numbers of Mexican immigrants stayed in the United States, creating new Mexican communities throughout the Southwest and also in the Midwest, where they had worked on building railroads. Their U.S.-born children, the second generation, increased the Mexican American population, with subsequent generations making this the largest Hispanic group in the United States. Despite the end of the Bracero Program, the rate of Mexican immigration, both documented and undocumented, continues to increase. Mexican immigration remains a national issue because the constant flow of Mexican immigration has always contributed to population increases among this ethnic group.

World War II produced major changes within Mexican American communities. Due to the growth of the U.S.-born population of Mexicans living in the United States, World War II, unlike World War I, led to the participation of approximately 300,000 Mexican Americans in the armed forces. Their service exposed them to life in different parts of the country and the world. Mexican Americans became the most decorated ethnic group. They returned to their communities with new experiences and outlooks. Having fought in a war to end the horrors of genocide, Mexican American veterans, more so than Mexican immigrants, were appalled when they experienced prejudice and discrimination. In some cities, ordinances and informal practices barred Mexican Americans from swimming pools, eating establishments, theaters, and public bathrooms. The case of Felix Longoria represented one of the most tragic examples of such discrimination. Longoria was a Mexican American soldier who was killed in the Pacific, and when his body was returned to Texas for burial, his widow could not find a chapel that would hold services for him, because he was Mexican. Ultimately, U.S. Senator Lyndon B. Johnson of Texas intervened and had Longoria buried in Arlington National Cemetery.

As a response to such episodes of discrimination, Mexican Americans, many of whom had reached middle-class status due to the G.I. Bill that provided veterans with low-interest loans for homes and college educations, started numerous civic organizations.

The League of United Latin American Citizens (LULAC), founded in Texas in 1929, rose to prominence in the post–World War II period through its attempts to gain full citizenship rights for Mexican Americans. LULAC spearheaded the fight to end school segregation and other forms of discrimination in the legal system, business, and politics. The Mexican American Political Association (MAPA) was founded in California in 1959 as a nonpartisan lobby group whose major goal was to pressure politicians to address problems facing their communities. MAPA also sought to increase the number of Mexican American elected officials. Congressman Edward R. Roybal, from California's 25th District, and Congressman Henry B. Gonzalez, from Texas's 20th District, emerged as key Mexican American national political figures.

The climate of social protest of the 1960s produced changes among Mexican Americans, particularly among the youth. Referring to their protest movement as "El Moviemiento," Mexican American students adopted the ethnic self-identification term *Chicano* or *Chicana,* a controversial label that had been used as early as the late 19th century by Anglos as a derogatory name for Mexicans and Mexican Americans. The term *Chicano* became a symbol of nationalism and ethnic pride for Chicano students who mobilized to fight against all forms of discrimination, particularly educational inequity. Chicano student groups emerged throughout the United States and organized marches, boycotts, and conferences. Their movement also joined the anti–Vietnam War protest movement that culminated in the National Chicano Anti-war Moratorium held in East Los Angeles on August 29, 1970, with over 20,000 demonstrators. The noted Chicano international journalist Ruben Salazar was killed by the police under suspicious circumstances and became an icon of the Chicano movement's fight against social injustice. César Chávez's farmworker movement developed during this time and included lettuce and grape strikes and boycotts. The United Farm Workers Union, started in 1962 in Delano, California, brought the plight of the farmworkers, largely Mexican Americans, to the national and international scene. The union won many labor strikes, and their efforts resulted in the passage of laws to protect farmworkers.

A Chicano renaissance in the arts, literature, drama, and music emerged with strongly nationalistic overtones. A Chicana feminist movement developed within the Chicano movement to address the issue of sexism and homophobia within the ranks of Chicano activists whose political agendas ignored the specific injustices experienced by Chicanas within the movement's organizations and the larger U.S. society. Chicanas formed both parallel and separatist organizations to advance their feminist agendas, which were frequently met with hostility. Mexican Americans in Texas formed a political party called La Raza Unida Party (LRUP) (the United People Party) in 1970 to harness Mexican American voters into an independent third party. Their greatest electoral victory came in Crystal City, Texas, when Mexican American LRUP candidates won every seat on the city council; for the first time, Mexican Americans to controlled an entire city government. LRUP gained widespread support throughout the Southwest, achieving various degrees of success, but, by the late 1970s, it declined with the waning of protest politics. With the decline of the social protest movements of the 1960s and early 1970s, Mexican Americans turned to other political venues. Organizations such as the Southwest Voter Registration Office worked within Mexican American communities to register voters in an attempt to harness the group into an ethnic voting bloc.

Mexican American Politicians

During the 1980s, Mexican American politicians, both Democrat and Republican, turned to mainstream politics and won major political offices. Democrats and Republicans now make regular efforts to campaign in cities with large Mexican American populations. The political careers of Henry Cisneros and Gloria Molina serve as examples of Mexican Americans who have succeeded in making inroads into U.S. politics.

Henry Cisneros (1947–) became one of the two Mexican Americans to be elected mayor of a major city in the United States. He was mayor of San Antonio, Texas, in 1981, and served until 1989, when he completed his fourth term. Cisneros also became the first Hispanic and Mexican American to be appointed as a cabinet member. He served as U.S. Secretary of Housing and Urban Development under President Bill Clinton. Prior to his election as mayor, Cisneros had achieved a distinguished record in politics. He gained political experience working with the Washington, D.C., National League of Cities, and as a White House Fellow. In 1974, he was elected to San

Antonio's city council and served two terms. Then, as mayor, Cisneros aimed to develop the city into a major metropolis by attracting tourism and high-tech businesses and other businesses. He worked to increase the political clout of Mexican Americans in San Antonio. Owing to his son's serious illness, he did not run for a fifth term and started his own business.

As U.S. secretary of housing and urban development under President Bill Clinton, Cisneros addressed issues such as racial segregation in housing and supported reform measures of federal housing policies. In 1999, Cisneros became a controversial political figure when, during the regular investigation conducted for all cabinet appointees, he pleaded guilty to a misdemeanor for lying to the FBI about his payments to a former mistress. (Clinton pardoned Cisneros in 2001.) Univision Communications, the largest Spanish-language broadcasting company, named him president, and he continues to work with several nonprofit groups, particularly those that deal specifically with Mexican American communities.

Gloria Molina (1948–), a native of Los Angeles, made Mexican American history in 1991 when she was elected to the Los Angeles County Board of Supervisors, becoming the first Mexican American and woman to be elected to this position. This victory represented one of the most significant political developments for Mexican Americans. Molina started her political activism as a Chicano student activist during her undergraduate years at East Los Angeles City College and later worked as a volunteer in Robert F. Kennedy's 1968 presidential campaign. After completing college, Molina became active in various Mexican American community organizations and dedicated herself to such community issues as health care, education, and housing. She founded and was elected the first president of the *Comisión Femenil de Los Angeles* (Women's Council of Los Angeles), an organization that developed social services programs for Mexican American women. Molina's early political involvement in Los Angeles involved the establishment of Hispanic American Democrats and a chapter of the National Association of Latino Elected and Appointed Officials (NALEO). She also worked on the political campaigns of several California politicians, and, in 1976, President Jimmy Carter appointed her to a position in the Department of Health, Education, and Welfare. In 1982, Molina won in an election for the California Assembly. *Time* magazine named Gloria Molina one of the Democratic Party's "Ten Rising Stars" in 1996. She served as one of the four vice-chairs of the Democratic National Committee. In 2006, *Hispanic Business* magazine named Molina as Hispanic Businesswoman of the Year, and, in 1992, she received the prestigious Aztec Eagle Award from the Mexican government, the highest honor given to a foreigner.

Demographic Overview

An overview of some of the major demographics identifies several issues facing Mexican Americans. They have always been the largest group within the total Hispanic population and continue to live primarily in the Southwest. Among Hispanic groups, Mexicans have the lowest percentage of persons with at least a high school diploma and of persons who have attained at least a bachelor's degree. The percentage of Mexican Americans without a high school diploma is alarming, with rates averaging close to 45%, or almost three times that of the national figure. Mexican Americans rank fourth among seven of all Hispanic groups in family income. Their poverty rates have remained steady over the last 20 years; almost 25% fall below the poverty level, a rate twice that of the total population. As with other groups, female-headed households with children have the highest poverty levels. Women are clustered in service and sales occupations, while men are concentrated in construction and transportation. Although the number of middle-class Mexican Americans is growing, the general population continues to be slow in improving its socioeconomic status. The impact of Mexican immigration, both documented and undocumented, on U.S.-born Mexicans continues to be a major social and public policy issue. The effect of immigration on occupations and income is a subject of debate and ongoing research, with some studies stressing a positive impact on the native-born population and others emphasizing the negative, although most studies identify both positive and negative effects.

Artistic Contributions

Mexican Americans have contributed to the wealth of U.S. artistic diversity that has been described as part of the "Latinization" in the nation's music, art, theater, literature, and other forms of artistic expression. Although these artists may focus on universal themes, themes rooted in Mexican culture, such as the group's indigenous cultural heritage, permeate their works. Their cultural expressions have been greatly affected by their experiences as a historically marginalized group. Novelists such as Tomas Rivera and Francisco Jimenez draw on their family experiences as farmworkers. Sandra Cisneros documents her urban life in a working-class, second-generation family. The paintings of Yolanda Lopez and Rupert Garcia document the political issues their communities have faced, particularly during the Chicano movement. The popular singer Selena, whose life was cut short when she was killed by a troubled associate, contributed to the development of Tejano music, a male-dominated genre. Many more Mexican American artists are shaping U.S. popular culture, and a younger generation is emerging.

Alma M. Garcia

See Appendix A; Appendix B
See also Bracero Program; *Colonias;* Hispanics; Latina/o Studies; Mexican American Legal Defense and Educational Fund (MALDEF); Mexico; Pachucos/Pachucas; Samora, Julian; Treaty of Guadalupe Hidalgo (1848); "Wetbacks"

Further Readings

Garcia, Alma M. 2004. *Narratives of Mexican American Women: Emergent Identities of the Second Generation.* Walnut Creek, CA: Altamira Press.

Meier, Matt and Margo Gutierrez. 2003. *The Mexican American Experience: An Encyclopedia.* Westport, CT: Greenwood Press.

Meier, Matt and Feliciano Rivera. 1981. *Dictionary of Mexican American History.* Westport, CT: Greenwood Press.

MEXICO

Mexico, the country that lies just to the south of the United States, had an estimated population of 106.5 million people in 2007. In Mexico, there has been a tendency to define and study Indigenous Peoples in terms of ethnicity, Blacks in terms of race and racism, and *mestizos* (the mixed population) as embodying the national identity. In the last 2 decades, however, there has been a move toward understanding how the category of *Indian* became important in the construction of discourses of race and how this group is fundamentally part of the nation. Conversely, there is an interest in looking at how Blacks have been able to reproduce their own cultural distinctiveness through time, even if they are physically indistiguishable from other mestizos or Indigenous Peoples. While the national identity has been the object of countless debates and reflections since the independence of Mexico, today, it is of interest to rethink and redefine the idea of the mestizo nation from a pluricultural perspective that includes all the different cultures that make up the society.

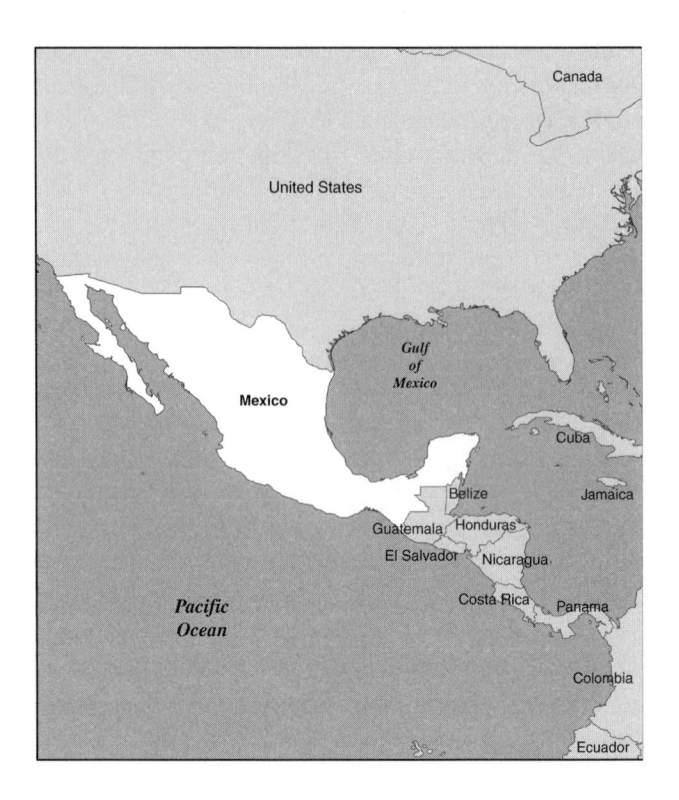

"Indians" in the 16th Century

As the Spanish conquerors began to explore and settle in what was then called "New Spain" during the 16th century, many of the Indigenous Peoples they encountered fell under their influence and power. The main objective of the conquerors was to encroach upon the lands, exploit labor, and gain tribute, as prescribed in the Crown *encomiendas,* or trusteeship, they had been granted over the Indigenous Peoples. In return for this right, the *encomenderos* were required to indoctrinate and protect the Indigenous Peoples, while also maintaining military control on behalf of the Crown.

This system facilitated the enslavement of Indigenous Peoples at the same time that it also fostered the demise of the population. In the first decades after the conquest, the indigenous population decreased significantly due to genocide, diseases and epidemics, forced labor and abuse, and famines. This prompted the Crown to abolish the *encomienda* and replace it with the *repartimiento* system, by which the conquerors could organize and use for a period of time the labor of Indigenous Peoples in agriculture, mining, construction, public works, and shipbuilding.

The Spanish conquerors moved and concentrated Indigenous Peoples in *reducciones de indios,* that is, Indian reductions or towns, to facilitate their control, exploitation, and evangelization. The ownership system in these reductions was communal, and the land and resources could not be transferred to others. While the idea of collective ownership of the land was an integral part of indigenous society before the conquest, the Indian community that developed from this system became heavily constrained by legislation, a situation that has remained, albeit with different conditions, until today.

The "Indian" identity, thus, became an administrative category under which the vast cultural diversity that existed among Indigenous Peoples was reduced and subsumed. However, this administrative category gave Indians an institutionalized position that Blacks did not have. Nevertheless, the Indian communities, especially their lands, have been the object of continuous attacks throughout Mexico's history.

In 1542, the slavery of Indigenous Peoples was outlawed in the Spanish colonies, but their exploitation and abuse did not diminish. The mistreatment and population demise of Indigenous Peoples became an object of controversy between Fray Bartolomé de Las Casas and Juan Ginés de Sepúlveda in the Valladolid Debate (1550–1551). Las Casas argued that Indians were free humans and that Africans should replace their labor; Sepúlveda, instead, claimed that Indians were natural slaves and their conquest a "just war."

Although many other missionaries concerned with the mistreatment of Indigenous Peoples were able to convince the Crown to establish special protections for them, in fact, their actions also helped consolidate the status of Indigenous Peoples as minors incapable of self-governance. This status has had everlasting effects and changed very little with the independence of Mexico or after the Mexican Revolution.

The Spaniards brought Africans, called Blacks, as slaves to New Spain beginning with the conquest. They used their free labor in mining, agriculture, and domestic service. As the indigenous population declined, Africans replaced them. However, as the Black population grew because of new arrivals and intermarriage, some slaves were able to mount rebellions and escape. The rebellious slaves were called *cimarrones.* They were able to form communities with other slaves who had escaped the harsh conditions in plantations and mines and also with freed slaves. These communities were called *palenques.* The first free African community in the Americas was founded in the Atlantic coastal region in the 1570s, but it was not recognized as such until 1630.

Race and Ethnicity in the Colonial Period

During the colonial period, dual images of the Indians and Africans coexisted. The Africans were considered both infidels and Christians, and the Indians were seen as both pagan savages and innocent native beings. This ambivalence justified the status of both groups, but it also influenced social relations and interactions with the Spaniards. Africans were "justly" enslaved because they were "infidel," that is, not Christian, but the enslavement was a temporary condition, and they could potentially become free. The Indians had to be reformed and protected, but exploited as well. While the authorities tried to keep these three different groups separate as distinct social strata, their social interaction and mixing was very significant from the beginning of the colonial period.

Indigenous Peoples moved into urban areas, whereas Spaniards and the *criollos* (Spaniards born in America) settled in rural areas, usually by usurping land. While these last two groups were able to consolidate their power and authority outside of the cities, the Indigenous Peoples continued to be dependent laborers. Furthermore, the move to the cities and the *latifundios* (great landholdings) weakened their ties with the Indian community, which was and still is an important source of their identity. This resulted in the loss of status and privileges in the Indian community. Their sexual and spatial mixing with Spaniards as well as the interchange of cultural elements resulted in the rise of the mestizos as an important, and eventually dominant, social group; because of their mixed heritage, mestizos held a better social status than Indians and Blacks.

Although the Spaniards and Creoles tried to regulate marriages among the social groups, Blacks also mixed sexually, spatially, and culturally with Indigenous Peoples, mestizos, Spaniards, and Creoles. In the social stratification, their offspring were recognized as mixed people. All the social groups were classified and stratified in a system of *castas* that developed throughout the colonial period as the mixing continued. While Spaniards, Indians, and Blacks all had specific status and different positions in the system of privilege, the status and position of the various *castas* was more indeterminate. For these middle strata, color and descent were important bases for determining status but were not definitive factors. Occupation and other socioeconomic criteria also played important roles in the status of the various *castas*. By the 18th century, there were a vast number of labels to classify people; however, only five basic terms were ordinarily used: *Black, Indian, mulatto, mestizo,* and *Spanish.*

In New Spain, there was no strict idea of race (something that continued in Mexico). The Indians that had lost their connections with their communities and had adopted different cultural elements could "pass" and be considered mestizos. The same applied to Blacks and *castas*. Rather, the factor that distinguished the various social groups was their *calidad;* this concept of "quality" was related to an idea of blood as conferring status, but there were also other elements, such as occupation and marriage, that could have the effect of *blanqueamiento* (whitening) on people and influence their upward social mobility. However, those considered Indians and Blacks, especially those enslaved, had a more difficult time moving up in the social stratification as their culture and *calidad* were submitted to constant devaluation.

Mexican Independence (1810) to the Revolution (1910)

Black communities in the 19th century were concentrated in the central coastal zones and had maintained close interaction with indigenous and mestizo populations over the years. The majority of Blacks and other mixed peoples of African descent who lived in the cities and towns had become integrated into the rest of society. Several of them fought together with Creoles and mestizos for the independence of Mexico. Blacks had a very important role in the abolition of slavery in Mexico after its independence in 1821. For example, Vicente Guerrero, a mulatto leader, emancipated slaves during his presidency in 1829.

Over the course of the century, some Black Seminoles and descendants of slaves who escaped the sugarcane farms in the United States settled in Northern Mexico. Slave hunters and slaveowners often threatened to cross the Mexican border and, on some occasions, tried without success to pressure the Mexican government to return Blacks to slavery. In 1857, taking a stance regarding slavery in the United States, Mexico declared that any slave who set foot on its territory would become free.

During the ethnic conflicts of the 19th century, several Blacks and *castas* participated in various peasant movements, sometimes in conjunction with Indigenous Peoples. At the end of that century, some of the Blacks working in the oil refineries of Tampico established a branch of Marcus Garvey's Universal Negro Improvement Association and also rose in arms along with other peasants and workers during the Mexican Revolution. However, during the next 2 centuries, while the idea of an "Indian problem" put indigenous issues in the social, economic, political, and cultural agendas of the nation-state, the absence of a discourse regarding a "Black problem" as it existed in other Latin American countries contributed to Blacks' invisibility and further marginalization.

Mexico's search for a national identity in the 19th century was influenced by liberalism and theories about human difference and heredity. As Mexico sought to modernize the countryside under the liberal ideas of equality and freedom of the citizenry, the status and legal position of the Indians, as well as their lands and communities, came under attack. Together with this, a proposal emerged in the national imagination that the mestizo represented the quintessential Mexican identity and the solution to Mexico's social and economic problems. In order to achieve the ideals of prosperity and progress, an agrarian reform freed large portions of "unused" lands and labor for the market. Thus, the special protection of the Indians ended. The idea was to convert the Indians into citizens who owned small plots of land. Over time, the agrarian reform failed due to the opposition of the clergy, the large *latifundios,* and the Indian communities.

Ethnic conflicts increased significantly in the 19th century due to the attacks on indigenous lands and identity. Most of the indigenous and *castas* rebellions in this time included both land and ethnic claims, among others, as these were seen as interrelated and essential elements of the indigenous communities. The absence of a strong state presence and racial prejudices (which marked these conflicts as a battle between the "civilized White people" and the "indigenous barbarians") fostered intensified violence in these rebellions. But it also allowed an alliance between peasant mestizos and Indigenous Peoples that was important in the Mexican Revolution of 1910.

Postrevolutionary Mexico

The Constitution of 1917, in Article 27, restored the *ejido* system by which Indian and mestizo peasant villages were given land to be held in common; it could not be sold. In this system, the land was owned by the state but could be used by the villagers in usufruct. The land distribution reached its climax during the presidency of Lázaro Cárdenas in the late 1930s. Yet in the new ideology of the agrarian reform, there were few provisions for improving the living conditions of peasants and Indians.

During the revolution, indigenous cultures were celebrated as the true soul of the nation, and a great interest in rescuing what was called the "glorious indigenous past" emerged. Nevertheless, it was also widely believed that the only way to rescue Indigenous Peoples from poverty and marginalization was to integrate them fully into the socioeconomic dynamics of the country. The Mexican state developed an official ideology, called *indigenismo*, to tackle this issue and incorporate the Indians into society, and the Instituto Nacional Indigenista was established to carry out this policy. This was also an ideology espoused by the clergy, academia, and civil society. This postrevolutionary ideology underwent many changes throughout the century, reflecting socioeconomic and political interests but also the consolidation of an indigenous movement in Mexico.

Early *indigenista* ideology of the 1930s and 1940s viewed the ethnicity of Indigenous Peoples as a problem because it did not allow them to fully integrate into the national society. Thus, racial and ethnic relations and identifications were not the object of study or address. The study of Afro-Mexicans, their contributions to the cultural mix of the nation, and their distinctiveness in the 1940s was the exception. These studies, however, were very few. When, in the 1950s and 1960s, the study of ethnic relations became important, indigenous communities were seen as coherent harmonious wholes characterized by interdependency, and total cultural assimilation was seen as unnecessary or even negative. Yet the idea that indigenous communities could improve only by modernizing remained imperative.

By the 1970s, important critiques of *indigenismo* began to challenge this idea. Studies at this time argued that the exploitation and marginalization of Indigenous Peoples was a condition of capitalist development and that their apparent isolation and discrimination was the result of the expansion of dominant society. Two important realizations that came out of this period were (1) that that the label *Indian* was a tool used to indicate and ascribe an inferior status vis-à-vis the mestizos and thus justify this group's exploitation and (2) that despite continuous interethnic relations and *indigenista* projects, indigenous ethnic identities survived and maintained their cultural distinctiveness.

Indigenous movements strengthened in the 1970s with the organization of various conferences and congresses to discuss indigenous issues. These movements voiced their claims and at the same time denounced the system that oppressed them. For the most part, the movements remained local and regional. One of the most significant movements was that of the Worker-Peasant-Student-Coalition of the Isthmus of Tehuantepec (COCEI), in the state of Oaxaca. The COCEI used an ethnic banner in its mobilizations, which was significant, as other movements of the time prioritized socioeconomic demands. In the 1980s, they were able to win twice in electoral politics but were then repressed violently. At this time, many scholars began continuous advocacy work on behalf of Indigenous Peoples, arguing that they had to participate in their own ethnodevelopment as well as in national politics.

The proposition that Mexico's cultural diversity had to be recognized and fully embraced became an important political issue in the 1990s. It not only challenged the idea that Mexico was a mestizo nation but also pointed out the need to protect legally the cultural diversity existing in its territory. In 1992, as a result of indigenous mobilization against the celebration of the quincentenary of the "discovery" of America, the work of anthropologists, and political opening, Article 4 of the Constitution was reformed to recognize Mexico as a pluricultural nation. Other reforms recognized the juridical personality of the indigenous community and a limited right to autonomy and self-determination.

These constitutional reforms have energized an important debate in Mexico about the place of Indigenous Peoples in society. However, at the same time that constitutional recognition was given to the indigenous community, Article 27 was also reformed as part of the neoliberal agenda of the Mexican state, ending the protection of the *ejido* system. Today, this lack of legal protection presents a great challenge to Indigenous Peoples' rights to land and territory.

In response to the neoliberal agenda of the Mexican state, another important movement appeared on the national scene in 1994: the Zapatista Army of

National Liberation (EZLN). This movement has dominated indigenous–state relations since then, at the same time that it has achieved international recognition and solidarity. The EZLN has been able to maintain in the national agenda the issue of indigenous rights. Today, there has also been a slow but growing consciousness within the communities of Afro-Mexicans about their heritage.

In sum, most people in Mexico consider themselves to be mestizos, or peoples of mixed cultural and biological descent. Although discriminated against and marginalized and despite continuous efforts to assimilate them, Indigenous Peoples have been important in the imagination of the colonial and the national spaces in Mexico. As Mexico consolidated its self-image as a mestizo nation, the Indigenous Peoples have concurrently resisted and struggled for their recognition as distinct peoples.

Blacks or Afro-Mexicans have had a different place in society. While their enslavement and distinctiveness conferred on them a separate status during colonial times, after the abolishment of slavery in 1829, Blacks were made invisible in the making of a national identity and were marginalized in the social, economic, political, and cultural life of the nation. Blacks are imagined to have become an undistinguishable part of the mixed population. Afro-Mexicans have yet to create a movement for their cultural recognition and rights at the national level.

Sylvia Escárcega

See Appendix A

See also Borderlands; Bracero Program; Colonialism; Ethnic Conflict; Identity Politics; Latin America, Indigenous People; Maquiladoras; Marginalization; Mexican Americans; Mexico; Treaty of Guadalupe Hidalgo (1848); "Wetbacks"; Zapatista Rebellion

Further Readings

Hernández Cuevas, Marco Polo. 2004. *African Mexicans and the Discourse on Modern Nation.* Lanham, MD: University Press of America.
Joseph, Gilbert M. and Timothy J. Henderson, eds. 2002. *The Mexico Reader: History, Culture, Politics.* Durham, NC: Duke University Press.
Levi, Jerome M. 2002. "A New Dawn or a Cycle Restored? Regional Dynamics and Cultural Politics in Indigenous Mexico, 1978–2001." Pp. 3–49 in *The Politics of Ethnicity: Indigenous Peoples in Latin American States,* edited by D. Maybury-Lewis. Cambridge, MA: Harvard University Press.

MacLachlan, Colin and Jaime E. Rodríguez. 1980. *The Forging of the Cosmic Race: A Reinterpretation of Colonial Mexico.* Berkeley: University of California Press.
Tresierra, Julio C. "Mexico: Indigenous Peoples and the Nation-State." Pp. 187–210 in *Indigenous Peoples and Democracy in Latin America,* edited by D. L. Van Cott. New York: St. Martin's Press.
Wade, Peter. 1997. *Race and Ethnicity in Latin America.* London: Pluto Press.

MILITARY AND RACE

African Americans, as well as Whites, have always fought in America's wars. In more recent eras, other peoples of color also have fought in this nation of immigrants. This entry examines the history of this participation, some of the racial issues in the military services, and current trends in participation.

Colonial Period

During colonial times, African Americans participated in the military services, including the early engagements at Lexington, Concord, and Bunker Hill. The Revolutionary War was unusual in that African Americans sometimes fought alongside Whites, sometimes as free men and sometimes as indentured men or even as slaves. The British offered emancipation for any slaves who joined them, though, like the Americans, they were reluctant to recruit many African Americans; they, too, had their racial prejudices. Military commissions as early as 1775 recommended the exclusion of African Americans from military service, but military necessities resulted in both covert and overt enlistments. The lower South, in particular, strongly resisted arming African American slaves. The service of African Americans in the Revolutionary War was one of the contributing factors to the abolition of slavery in the northeastern states.

The issue of whether African Americans should be part of the military services simmered for several decades, even as the United States was engaged in wars with England in 1812 and with Mexico from 1846 to 1848 and the nation debated the role of slavery before the Civil War. At least 3,000 African Americans reportedly participated in the Mexican American War in de facto integrated units, despite the official policy of exclusion. Following the U.S. victory and annexation of territory, many Mexicans became Americans without relocating, as a result of the changed national boundary. Likewise, numerous Native American groups and their territories eventually became part of the United States as a result of American-Indian wars, though most Native Americans were not given the right to vote until the 20th century.

Civil War

During the Civil War, neither the South nor the North initially enlisted African Americans, free or slave, in the armed services. Nevertheless, many volunteered. The law at the time restricted militia duty to White males; the regular army had a policy of not enlisting African Americans. Further, the policy of the Lincoln administration at the beginning of the Civil War, not wanting to disaffect the border states, was to return all fugitive slaves to their masters. Some states in the South began to use free men of color both as soldiers and in support services. As the war wore on, and particularly after the Emancipation Proclamation, in January 1863, the North used African Americans as soldiers. Almost all in both the North and the South served in segregated units. The implementation of the Conscription Act became another major step toward abolition of slavery and the granting of citizenship for African Americans.

World Wars I and II

Segregated units remained the norm during subsequent wars through most of World War II. This included the brief conflict with Spain in 1898 and World War I, where an estimated 380,000 African Americans served. Senior officers for these units were always White. Between World Wars I and II, the army adopted a quota system that kept the number of Blacks in the Army proportionate to the total population. More than a million African Americans served in World War II, which was about 10% of the total military personnel and roughly their proportion in the population.

Several ironies and inconsistencies exist with regard to race and ethnicity in World War II. First, while the United States was at war with Japan, Japanese nationals and Japanese Americans were placed in internment camps in the interior of the United States. While some argued that they were potential spies for Japan, the military itself never considered them as such. Further, the largest concentration of Japanese Americans was on the Islands of Hawai'i, where America was first attacked and probably the most vulnerable territory of the United States. Yet those on the islands were never interned. Later, young men from among the internees were recruited and served with honor in the European theater.

African Americans also served with honor during World War II, usually in segregated units. Of particular note were the Tuskegee Airmen, trained at Tuskegee, Alabama. Training began there even before the outbreak of World War II, in July 1941. Commissions were awarded from 1942 through 1946, and 994 pilots graduated at Tuskegee Army Air Field, eventually receiving commissions and pilot wings. Many were highly decorated for their service in the war.

The general tradition of segregation in the military services prevailed until conditions in World War II necessitated the combination of units. In 1945, Secretary of War Robert P. Patterson appointed a commission to study the issues surrounding segregation in the services. A presidential commission appointed in 1947 recommended desegregation. Official desegregation of the military services began after World War II, in 1948, when President Harry Truman signed Executive Order No. 9981, which stated, "It is hereby declared to be the policy of the President that there shall be equality of treatment and opportunity for all persons in the armed services without regard to race, color, religion, or national origin."

The order also established the President's Committee on Equality of Treatment and Opportunity in the Armed Services. Some army staff officers resisted the desegregation order so that some parts of the military services were not desegregated until 1951. In late 1953, the Army announced that 95% of African American soldiers were serving in integrated units. Integration of the leadership was much slower, however, and racial hostility increased over the course of the Vietnam War. Only in the 1980s, after the increase in the number of African American military leaders and the change to an all-volunteer army, did race relations improve in the military services.

Military Services Today

Today, the military services are generally recognized as one of the best examples of integration in U.S. society. Fully integrated military services were characteristic of the Persian Gulf War of 1990 to 1991 and the Iraqi War begun in 2003. While cultural norms and prejudice are part of the nexus of segregation in the larger society, these forces are greatly mitigated in the military services. The military emphasizes nonprejudicial, nondiscriminatory treatment of other groups. Because military service requires reliance on other soldiers in times of battle, the services emphasize equality of treatment. To track problems, the services survey members about their perceptions on intergroup relations. The result is that Blacks and Whites commingle and socialize together by choice, and they carry out their military duties together, with little display of racial animosity.

Further, rates of intergroup marriage are higher in the military services than in the country as a whole. The educational differences between Whites, Blacks, and Hispanics are lower in the services than they are in the country as a whole. Thus, even though the U.S. military services are highly structured and hierarchical, they provide an environment that is characterized by heterogeneity and egalitarianism within ranks, a substantially different environment than exists in the larger society.

Percentages of racial and ethnic groups in the military services and trends in them are available from a variety of sources, including each of the services. Total numbers and percentages are available from the Department of Defense and from each of the services with offices of demographics. In 2003, the Department of Defense reported that 35.8% of the active duty members of the military services identified themselves as a minority (African American, Hispanic American, Native American, Alaskan American, Asian American, Pacific Islander, or multiracial). From 1990 to 2003, the number of officers who identified themselves as a minority increased from 9.1% to 20.2%; and the number of enlisted personnel increased from 28.2% to 38.7%. The overall percentage of self-identified minorities in the Reserves and National Guard was somewhat lower, at 30.1% (compared with the 35.8% among the enlisted).

These numbers are further delineated by racial and ethnic groups. Self-identified African Americans were 19.1%, Hispanic Americans 9.0%, Asian Americans (including Pacific Islanders) 4.1%, and Native American/Alaskan Natives 1.2%. Two-tenths of 1% identified as multiracial. African Americans (12.3% of the national population in the 2000 census) were overrepresented in the military services, while Hispanics (12.5% of the population) and Asians (3.6% of the population) were underrepresented. Native populations were about equal to their percentage in the total population.

The total percentage of minorities is higher in the army (40.7%) and slightly higher in the navy (38.6%), slightly lower in the Marine Corps (32.7%), and substantially lower in the air force (27.7%). Interestingly, minorities in the air force are more likely than those in the other services to be officers. The percentage of officers among minorities serving in the military nearly doubled from 1990 to 2003. Likewise, the percentage of minority officers in the Reserves and National Guard roughly doubled from 1990 to 2003, but the overall numbers of both minority officers and enlisted personnel are lower than in the regular forces, and they are much closer to the percentages of minorities in the national population. African Americans are somewhat overrepresented, while Hispanic and Asian Americans are underrepresented among the Reserves.

African Americans remain underrepresented among casualties in the Iraqi War. Through November 5, 2005, African Americans represented about 17% of the force in Iraq yet accounted for 11% of deaths. On the other hand, Whites accounted for 67% of the force and suffered 74% of deaths. The corresponding numbers for Hispanics were 9% and 11%.

These casualty rates likely reflect the occupational choices made by the racial and ethnic groups in the services. For example, African American youth choose to serve in support occupations such as the health care field, which tend to feature valuable job training over bonuses or education incentives.

The South produces 41% of all recruits (compared with 36% of the 18- to 24-year-old population). The Northeast generates 14% of new recruits, whereas the region has 18% of the 18- to 24-year-old population. The West and North Central regions produce 21% and 24% of new recruits, whereas they have 24% and 23%, respectively, of the 18- to 24-year-old population.

Currently, the army has the highest number of minorities, and the air force has the lowest. In 2005, just over 39% of the active army members were minorities, and 40.9% of the Reserves were minorities. The percentage of minorities in the Reserves is lower (26.0%). The number of African Americans in the army has been declining (from 22% in 2000 to 13.5% in 2005), while the number of Hispanics has been increasing (from 6.5% to 11.7%) in the same time period. The number of officers has remained more stable (10.2% African Americans and 5.5% Hispanics in 2005). The number of Asians on active duty was 4.0% in 2005.

Minority women, especially Black women, are overrepresented in the military services, and they are more likely than minority men to serve. White women represent only about 50% of all women in the services.

Cardell K. Jacobson

See also Discrimination; Internment Camps; People of Color; Prejudice; Racism; Segregation

Further Readings

Berry, Mary Frances. 1977. *Military Necessity and Civil Rights Policy: Black Citizenship and the Constitution, 1861–1868.* Port Washington, NY: Kennikat Press.

Jacobson, Cardell K. and Tim B. Heaton. 2003. "Intergroup Marriage and United States Military Service." *Journal of Political and Military Sociology* 31:1–22.

Moskos, Charles C. and John Sibley Butler. 1996. *All That We Can Be: Black Leadership and Racial Integration the Army Way.* New York: Basic Books.

U.S. Department of Defense. N.d. *Armed Forces Equal Opportunity Survey, 1996–97.* Retrieved from http://www.defenselink.mil/prhome/e096exsum.html

U.S. Department of Defense. N.d. *Demographics Profile of the Military: 2003.* Retrieved from http://www.militaryhomefront.dod.mil/dav/lsn/LSN/BINARY_RESOURCE/BINARY_CONTENT/1869841.swf

MINORITY/MAJORITY

The related concepts of *minority* and *majority* denote inequalities in social, political, and economic power. Both terms originate in ideas of democratic government, where it is assumed that the majority should rule. This view of political authority has its origins in the idea of popular sovereignty. As defined, for example, in the 1789 "Declaration of the Rights of Man and the Citizen," the doctrine of popular sovereignty asserts that the principle of sovereignty rests essentially in the nation and therefore all authority must emanate from the nation expressly.

Yet, as Ivor Jennings famously pointed out, this formulation still leaves open the necessity of determining who are the people in whom sovereignty ultimately resides. To resolve the ambiguity of the term *popular sovereignty,* democracy is usually defined as the "will of the people" determined by a majority of votes in free and fair elections. In this way, the "majority rules" by periodically voting in the government. By extension, therefore, the minority is that group which is currently excluded from power.

More Than Numbers

The minority/majority relationship is often presented as a matter of numeric difference. Majorities outnumber minorities. For example, the leader of the political party with the most seats in the United States Senate is known as the *Majority Leader*; in contrast, the leader of the second-largest party is designated the *Minority Leader.* Indeed, at its most general, a minority can be any group of people (political party, club, family, etc.) that can be distinguished from the rest of society in some way (opinions, beliefs, associations, behavior, etc.). Thus, by counting the number of respondents on any given issue—the invasion of Iraq, political parties or candidates, or the latest movie releases from Hollywood—it is possible to identify both a majority and a minority. In this rendering, majority and minority are not so much competing interests, but rather aggregates of individuals in a certain arithmetical relationship.

The usual assumption of "majority rule" is that membership in government will change over time, so that majorities and minorities are fluid rather than fixed arrangements. But that assumption does not always hold true. Instead, the dynamics of political, economic, and social power may produce minority/majority cleavages of a more enduring nature—particularly when disparities in power follow ethnic, racial, religious, or linguistic divisions. Situations like this existed, for example, in the southern United States prior to the civil rights legislation of the 1960s and in apartheid South Africa; in both instances, they paralleled racial divisions, and in Northern Ireland during the "time of troubles," they paralleled sectarian divisions. If "majority rule" becomes fixed in this way, it is anything but democratic. Instead, it becomes a "tyranny of numbers."

For this reason, the idea of democracy has itself been reconsidered by liberals, who have come to recognize the need for social consensus that is more than just "majoritarian." In this rendering, democratic government involves not only making decisions by majority voting but also conceding political rights to minorities. Deny one, and the moral case for the other largely disappears. The contemporary "problem of minorities" thus emerges as a lack of consent or entitlement to full participation in political life such that the principle of democracy is compromised in some way. Minorities are in a position to claim special treatment from majorities precisely because they are not fully integrated into or do not exercise control over their own political community. They are thus "imperfectly" or "incompletely" self-determined.

Defining *Minority*

No universally agreed definition of *minority* exists at the present time precisely because the "problem of minorities" often manifests itself in efforts to distinguish between those who belong to a political community and those who do not. Nevertheless, the definition of *minority* advanced by United Nations Special Rapporteur Francesco Capotorti in his *Study on the Rights of Persons Belonging to Ethnic, Religious, and Linguistic Minorities* has emerged as the most widely cited among international lawyers and policymakers. It may therefore be reasonably considered the closest approximation to a universally accepted usage. Capotorti's definition emphasizes that a minority is a nondominant group numerically inferior to the rest of the population that possesses unique ethnic, religious, or linguistic characteristics and a desire to preserve these characteristics.

As the Capotorti definition makes clear, what makes minority status politically significant is not size, but belonging: Minorities are those who are denied or prevented from enjoying the full rights of membership within a political community because their religion, race, language, or ethnicity differs from that of the official public identity. For this reason, minorities are often described as being *nondominant*, that is, not in a position of control or authority within a political community. This emphasis on "nondominance" is an attempt to ensure that the term *minority* is not improperly applied to "dominant" numerical minorities, such as the White population of apartheid South Africa. In other words, it excludes those groups who exercise control or authority within a political community, even if in strict demographic terms such ruling communities are outnumbered.

Capotorti's characterization of the "problem of minorities" in terms of a "sense of solidarity directed towards preserving their culture" challenges the tendency to limit entitlements arising under self-determination to individual demands for equality. By restricting the application of self-determination in this way, the end result is to conflate otherwise distinct minority circumstances and corresponding claims. On one hand, there are those groups, such as non-Anglo-Saxon immigrant communities in the North American context, whose members seek and yet are denied incorporation into the larger community and therefore require antidiscrimination guarantees and equal civil liberties: minorities by force. The claims of individual members of these minority cultural communities do not entail any guarantees beyond those of equal citizenship.

On the other hand, there are minority cultural groups whose members want to preserve a separate collective existence but are prevented from doing so by the larger community. Such groups are often labeled *national minorities* or *stateless nations* to underscore their separate normative status. National minority claims arise because such groups possess that normative characteristic, namely, national identity within a historic territory, which has historically been recognized as the basis for political legitimacy, and yet, for various reasons, they are not members of a state that reflects their cultural characteristics (e.g., Kurds in the Middle East or Roma in Europe and North America).

In addition to the rights of equal citizenship, national minorities may also claim special provisions that would provide them with a measure of autonomous collective existence. Examples of such provisions include an appropriate share of public revenues in order to build and maintain schools, churches, and other community institutions and perhaps even self-government in those regions where such groups predominate.

Individual Autonomy

The fundamental value at stake in all endeavors to recognize minorities remains that essential liberal concern for the autonomy of the individual. Capotorti's definition discloses this presumption in favor of "autonomous" action on the part of individuals giving rise to "self-determined" cultural communities when it refers to the members of minority groups. In other words, the normative value accorded to cultural identity is derivative of the fundamental liberal belief in the individual.

From this perspective, humans are understood to possess wills, sentiments, beliefs, ideals, and ways of living peculiar to themselves and so crave room to "be themselves" and opportunities to express characteristics that define their individuality: the wish to be and do something of their own choosing and not simply that which another has compelled them to do or to become. Many choices an individual makes will concern his or her relationships with others: Humans are social animals. In totality, they desire and form an extremely diverse range of social relationships and associations that reflect their above-noted sentiments, beliefs, ideals, and ways of living. Included among these are social relationships and associations that reflect their identification with particular national, ethnic, religious, cultural, and linguistic groups, be these families, tribes, nations, states, or religions.

Accordingly, most people want to associate freely with other people like themselves, people with whom they can feel at home. They do not wish to be obliged to assume personas or form associations that are contrived for them by others, whether by the state, the party, or the nation or by any other agency that aims at reducing if not eliminating the recalcitrant individuality of human beings. For this reason, humans seek liberty of action and determination of their own lives, both collectively and individually, and are naturally resistant to paternalism, oppression, and assimilation.

Minority rights are thus intended to guarantee the individual's ability to make autonomous cultural choices. For this reason, minority status should not itself become a form of tyranny, either by the majority over the minority or by the minority over the individual member. On this basis, groups must respect the liberty of their members, including those who freely choose to dissent from majority opinions or ways of life. This line of reasoning currently applies to those traditional bearers of the right to self-determination—namely, states—and so one can only assume that it would also apply to other groups (i.e., national minorities or Indigenous Peoples) that might acquire rights under this principle.

This brief survey of the usage most commonly assigned to the concepts *majority* and *minority* is sufficient to make the point that political discourse on the subject reflects fundamental normative assumptions. The identity and culture of the population within a state is significant only because there is a presumption in favor of popular sovereignty and democratic government. Regardless of whether or not the people are defined in civic or in ethnic terms, their free associations and expressions and the identities and cultures these create are now matters of concern within both domestic and international politics, because legitimate rule is constructed in terms of self-determination.

This explains why cultural groups have a normative status distinct from that of other minorities and indeed why individuals belonging to such groups may have special entitlements beyond those accorded to them as human beings. In sum, minorities are normative outsiders whose very existence challenges prevailing assumptions with respect to political membership and legitimacy, and, for this reason, their claims for recognition require a public policy response. Whether that response is recognition in the form of special rights or denial in the form of oppression or assimilation may be debatable in instrumental terms. However, once prevailing norms with respect to individual autonomy and collective self-determination are taken into account, the latter become extremely difficult to defend or justify.

J. Jackson Preece

See also Apartheid; Assimilation; Citizenship; Cross-Frontier Contacts; Ethnonational Minorities; Identity Politics; Kurdish Americans; People of Color; Roma

Further Readings

Capotorti, Francesco. 1979. *Study on the Rights of Persons Belonging to Ethnic, Religious, and Linguistic Minorities.* New York: United Nations.

Claude, I. 1955. *National Minorities: An International Problem.* Cambridge, MA: Harvard University Press.

Jackson Preece, J. 1998. *National Minorities and the European Nation-States System.* Oxford, UK: Clarendon Press.

Jackson Preece, J. 2005. *Minority Rights: Between Diversity and Community.* Cambridge, UK: Polity Press.

Jennings, I. 1956. *The Approach to Self-Government.* Cambridge, UK: Cambridge University Press.

Laponce, J. 1960. *The Protection of Minorities.* Berkeley: University of California Press.

Minority Rights Group. 1991. *Minorities and Human Rights Law.* London: Minority Rights Group International.

Musgrave, T. 1997. *Self-Determination and National Minorities.* Oxford, UK: Clarendon Press.

Thornberry, P. 1993. *International Law and the Rights of Minorities.* Oxford, UK: Clarendon Press.

United Nations. 1949. *Definition and Classification of Minorities.* E/CN.4/SUB.2/83

Minority Rights

In culturally diverse societies, provisions and processes are needed to protect minority rights from the majority and from majoritarian processes. In this way, the cultural, political, and economic rights of nondominant groups can be protected from the tyranny of the majority.

Democracy, equality, and justice require that not even a single group's or person's political rights, civil liberties, and cultural rights should be constrained, including by a majority. This entry discusses the consequences of the majoritarian process in multicultural societies, ethnic conflicts, types of minorities, the evolution of minority rights and the norms of individual and group rights, the contributions of diversity, and mechanisms to protect minority rights.

Majoritarian Process, Exclusion, and Ethnic Conflicts

The majoritarian process is sound in principle but becomes problematic in practice in culturally diverse societies. It works in societies where cultural divisions are not salient bases of mobilization. People regularly change their political or economic preferences, and this facilitates alternation of power among different groups and political parties. However, in ethnically diverse societies, people's preferences on specific cultural issues may differ perennially. Such situations create permanent majorities and minorities. The ethnic minority groups may never form governments. Thus, the majoritarian process often leads to the exclusion of minorities. As the dominant group influences and defines the state and its institutions with their values and norms, the exclusion of minority groups becomes institutionalized. Political institutions rooted in dominant values do not equally address the aspirations of minorities in the society.

If their rights are not protected, minorities may not feel bound by the rules that exclude them. Exclusion has led to violent conflicts in many regions of the world. Most major conflicts around the globe in the post–cold war era are identity related and occur within and across states, not between states. Violent conflicts often occur in developing countries where identity differences coincide with resource inequalities. According to the Minorities at Risk (MAR) project at the University of Maryland, ethnic conflicts have been increasing since the Second World War and reached a peak in the mid-1990s. Since then, there has been a slight decline, but most major conflicts are still identity related.

Minority Groups

Ted Gurr and the MAR project classify minorities broadly into two categories, *national peoples* and *minority peoples,* and into three subgroups within each group. Ethnonationalists, national minorities, and Indigenous Peoples fall under national peoples. Ethnoclasses, communal contenders, and religious sects fall under minority peoples. Ethnonationalists are regionally concentrated groups with a history of autonomous governance. National minorities are groups who are a minority in the state of residence but whose kindred control an adjacent state. Indigenous Peoples are descendants of conquered native people. Ethnoclasses, on the other hand, consist of descendants of slaves or immigrants. Communal contenders are ethnoclasses that are politically organized. They could be disadvantaged, advantaged, or dominant groups. Religious sects are groups whose activities are centered on religious beliefs and cultural practices and their defense.

According to Ted Gurr, 17.5% of the world's population in 1998, or more than a billion people, were minorities. However, this count does not include numerous smaller minorities (fewer than 100,000 and minorities in countries of less than 500,000 population) and those that are not politically mobilized. Thus, the overall count of minorities would be much higher if the less mobilized and numerous smaller groups were counted.

Individual and Group Rights

Minority rights were protected by the League of Nations after World War I, but the concept was undermined when Germany used it as a pretext to attack neighboring countries with German minority populations during the Second World War. The international community and the modernizing and nationalist elite who controlled the state were reluctant to recognize the rights of diverse groups inside states' borders. The world largely emphasized individual rights for promoting modernization and democracy. However, it failed to provide equality to members of minority groups and in many instances led to their repression.

Individual rights alone cannot ensure equality and justice in culturally diverse societies. Political equality understood as equal treatment of everyone at an individual level can suppress differences. True equality requires not identical treatment, but rather differential treatment in order to accommodate different needs. Members of different communities, with varying worldviews and lifestyles, have different needs and aspirations. When major democratic institutions fail to take account of needs of different groups by ignoring their varied identities, those who are not recognized are hurt. Individuals whose languages and cultures are not protected cannot compete equally with those whose languages and cultures are promoted by the state. In culturally plural societies, equality can be achieved not by eliminating group differences, but rather by ensuring equality among different groups. Recognition of group identity and group rights, therefore, is essential for attending to the specific situations of social-cultural groups. Intergroup equality, then, can promote equality among members of different groups. Respecting minority rights is thus not only consistent with individual freedom, but can actually promote it.

Tension between collective and individual rights, however, could exist. Certain segments may control communities and impose their views in the name of the community. Women in general suffer from these tendencies in many societies. Will Kymlicka has resolved this tension by distinguishing between two types of claims ethnic or national groups might make. The first, called *internal restrictions,* involves the claim of a group against its own members; the second, called *external protection,* involves the claim of a group against the larger society. The first type is intended to protect the group from the destabilizing impact of internal dissent (e.g., the decision of individual members not to follow traditional practices or customs), whereas the second is intended to protect the group from the impact of external decisions. Internal restrictions raise the danger of individual oppression and so may not be compatible with liberal democratic theory. External protections, on the other hand, uphold liberal rights and democratic institutions by enhancing individual freedom of the members of the minority groups. These protections enable them to be on a more equal footing with members of the dominant group.

Benefits of Cultural Diversity

The protection of minority rights promotes diversity and enhances freedom. Freedom involves making choices among various options, and culture not only provides these options but also makes them meaningful. People understand and communicate better and make intelligent choices within their own cultural milieu. A shared vocabulary of everyday life, embodied in practices and institutions covering most areas of human activity, facilitates the process. It is important for promoting different cultures to enable members of those cultures to grow and develop. When a culture is decaying, options and opportunities available for the members of that culture will shrink and their pursuit is less likely to be successful.

Enabling different cultures to flourish benefits the society by making more choices available for everyone. Diversity enhances the quality of life by enriching our experience and expanding cultural resources. Hence, not only is it an obligation for the majority to protect minority rights in keeping with norms of justice and equality, but it is also in their self-interest to do so, since it offers them more resources and choices.

Mechanisms to Protect Minority Rights

In multiethnic and multicultural states, the state often has to make certain decisions that will favor one group and disadvantage others. In the areas of official languages, political boundaries, public holidays, and the division of powers, there is no way to avoid supporting one group over others by the state. In such circumstances, members of minority groups are disadvantaged because the dominant cultural elements are chosen by the state to conduct its business. To compensate for such disadvantages, minority cultural elements have to be somehow recognized, safeguarded, and promoted. Otherwise, minorities face injustice. Group-differentiated rights like territorial autonomy, nonterritorial federalism, veto powers, guaranteed representation in central institutions, land claims, affirmative actions, reservations, and language rights can help rectify this disadvantage. The protection of minority rights has to be incorporated in the national constitution, and the passing of constitutional amendments has to be made difficult. Arend Lijphart formulated the theory of consociationalism, which propounded power sharing among different groups. Major political institutions mentioned above are incorporated in it. The United Nations and the international community have also come forth with covenants, treaties, and declarations like the Minority Rights Declaration, the International Convention on the Elimination of All Forms of Racial Discrimination, the Declaration on the Rights of Indigenous Peoples, and others for protecting minority rights. Such protections ensure that members of the minority have the same opportunities to live and work in their own culture as do members of the majority, thus providing a more level ground between members of dominant and dominated groups.

Mahendra Lawoti

See also Civil Rights Movement; Cross-Frontier Contacts; Ethnic Group; Ethnonational Minorities; Identity Politics; International Convention on the Elimination of All Forms of Racial Discrimination; Minority/Majority; Multicultural Social Movements; Racism; Reservation System

Further Readings

Gurr, Ted Robert. 2000. *Peoples versus States: Minorities at Risk in the New Century.* Washington, DC: U.S. Institute of Peace.

Hannum, Hurst. 1998. *Autonomy, Sovereignty, and Self-Determination: The Adjudication of Conflicting Rights.* Philadelphia: University of Pennsylvania Press.

Horowitz, Donald. 1985. *Ethnic Groups in Conflict.* Berkeley: University of California Press.

Kymlicka, Will. 1995. *Multicultural Citizenship: A Liberal Theory of Minority Rights.* Oxford, UK: Clarendon Press.

Lijphart, Arend. 1977. *Democracy in Plural Societies: A Comparative Exploration.* New Haven, CT: Yale University Press.

MODEL MINORITY

The term *model minority* refers to a racial or ethnic minority that despite past prejudice and discrimination is able to achieve great success economically and socially. The minority subgroup emerges as the "main character of a success story" about how a disadvantaged group overcomes those disadvantages and achieves prosperity. Typically, the term *model minority* has been used in the United States to refer to Asian Americans generally or, more specifically, Japanese Americans, Asian Indians, and Korean Americans.

The alleged prosperity of the model minority is usually measured in terms of economic success, educational attainment, cultural contributions, political participation, and other forms of incorporation to the larger national community, such as exogamy or intermarriage. The minority group is a "model" because its members set an example for other groups to follow. The term has been put to controversial uses, particularly because it foists responsibility for a group's success, failure, and recovery from historical discrimination on the shoulders of the group itself, rather than the larger society. Credit for the term's coinage is usually attributed to a January 9, 1966, article in *New York Magazine*, titled, "Success Story: Japanese American Style."

An American Success Story

The concept of model minority is a product of competing visions of the social and cultural heterogeneity of the United States. Before the fairly recent ascendance of the ideal of a pluralistic multiculturalism, where differences are tolerated if not also celebrated, a single, common culture had been the desired product of cultural interactions, often referred to as a "melting pot." The melting-pot metaphor offered an image of viscous mixing. This conception was appealing because of the smoothness of both the mix and the mixing. Yet this smoothness did not account for myriad conditions that maintained differences, ranging from labor segmentation, ghettoization, and citizenship ineligibility to ethnic pride, linguistic diversity, and self-determination. "Salad bowls" and "mosaics" offered alternative explanatory power for making sense of the persistence of distinctions within a common social formation.

The model minority exists somewhere between the melting pot and the mosaic/salad bowl, because there is the simultaneous celebration of difference and sameness. This simultaneity is particularly evident when various features associated with the distinctness of a distinct group ironically serve as the basis for its commonality with an idealized larger whole. For example, a group's religious piety and strong emphasis on family and filial devotion, rather than setting it apart from the public sphere, turns out to promote a value system that encourages behavior seen as crucial to success, such as self-sacrifice, deferral of gratification, and communal distribution of resources, particularly in times of scarcity and crisis.

Model Minority Myth

Myth is often a term that accompanies the term *model minority*. The myth of the model minority concerns the questionable cause-and-effect relationship that is implied or at times explicitly articulated. A model minority's success, such as cultural assimilation and class mobility, is seen to be caused by characteristics that make that group a group in the first place. These characteristics can be and often are racial. For example, membership in a marked group may imply academic skills that test well or personality traits associated with compliance (or even independence) or highly valued physical attributes. Therefore, the failure of other minority groups, such as their cultural ostracism and persistent poverty, are seen to be caused by characteristics that make that group a group in the first place. These characteristics can be and often are racial as well. For example, membership in a marked group may imply lack of academic skills that test well or personality traits associated with antisocial behavior or physical attributes of little value.

The "effects" side of the cause and effect is controversial as well, as the terms of measuring success are held up to critical scrutiny. Questions arise over which numbers matter and what can and cannot be measured at all. Does one track individual or household income? Does one measure income or assets? Does visibility in the larger culture necessarily mean understanding and acceptance of differences?

The emergence and circulation of the model minority label or stereotype from the mid-1960s to today is also an important indication of the often heated debates around social justice legislation, such as affirmative action. Model minority is an implicit argument against the state playing an active role in redistributing wealth and opportunity, because model minority explicitly describes how a group picks itself up by its proverbial bootstraps and, in the spirit of the phrase famously used by Booker T. Washington in 1895, casts down its bucket where it is. That is, a group stops fighting for rights and the protection of those rights by the state and starts participating in the economic and perhaps social life of the larger community, even if their rights are curtailed and surrendered at that moment. A model minority is then counterrevolutionary. By contrast, the critical circulation of model minority as myth is a counter to that counterrevolutionary stance that emphasizes the contradictions to the actuality of model minority success. And, consequently, the critique of model minority can be a critique of arguments for the dismantling of social justice regulations.

Arguments for the existence of model minorities are also important for ideals of national culture, especially in times of war. Model minority can therefore be seen as a way of understanding social and cultural dynamics during the cold war. A minority is seen to be a model because of its steadfast allegiance to a country and its ideals, even when current and historical circumstances demonstrate the failure to realize those ideals. A model minority resists the appeal of a perceived enemy who offers the possibility of social, cultural, and economic transformations. Rather than espouse radical ideas, particularly from the Left, ideas that advocate an overthrow of existing systems of governance, the model minority adheres to the current system as a means for effecting social change. Rather than stridently protesting, a model minority quietly assimilates and, in choosing that path, putatively rejects outside agitators.

Recent History

With the rise of the neoconservatism generally associated with the 1980s, the model minority became an especially noteworthy site of ideological contestation. That era saw the rise of a backlash against the social justice measures that grew out of the Civil Rights Movement. Model minorities were used as evidence of the needlessness of affirmative action and the arrival of meritocracy. Indeed, affirmative action and welfare were seen as an affront to the ideals of meritocracy, which are seen as the core beliefs upon which U.S. civilization was built. Model minority, on the other hand, only seemed to make more dramatic the power of those core beliefs because a deserving group thrived in the face of adversity, with no apparent help—and in some cases outright harm—from the government and the larger society.

While assertions of the actual existence of model minorities may have become less feasible and more nakedly interested, the idea of model minorities lives on as neoconservatism has led to neoliberalism, particularly with the ascendance of globalization. Under cold war neoconservatism, subgroups have overcome historical discrimination to participate on the presumably level playing field of U.S. civilization. Under neoliberal globalization, the new world order is a leveled playing field—or at least one that can be leveled under existing forms of global management, such as free trade agreements.

Like the dominant group, model minorities under both neoconservatism and neoliberalism, by their example if not also their declarations, view the existing economic, social, cultural, and political order, that is, secular global capitalism, as the best possible way of life after the unsustainable détente of the cold war. For model minorities who embrace the terms of their inclusion by a majority, the current world order possesses the material and ideological resources suitable to the daunting task of managing the manifestations of difference across the globe.

Victor Bascara

See also Affirmative Action in Education; Asian Americans; Assimilation; Chin, Vincent; Chinese Americans; Cultural Capital; Indian Americans; Intermarriage; Internment Camps; Japanese Americans; Korean Americans; Labeling; Media and Race; Stereotypes; Washington, Booker T.

Further Readings

Lee, Stacey J. 1996. *Unraveling the Model Minority Stereotype: Listening to Asian American Youth.* New York: Teacher's College Press.

Osajima, Keith. 1988. "Asian Americans as the Model Minority: An Analysis of the Popular Press Image in the 1960s and 1980s." Pp. 165–174 in *Reflections on Shattered Windows,* edited by G. Y. Okihiro, S. Hune, A. A. Hansen, and J. M. Liu. Pullman: Washington State University Press.

Takagi, Dana. 1992. *The Retreat from Race: Asian American Admissions and Racial Politics.* New Brunswick, NJ: Rutgers University Press.

Mormons, Race and

The racial conceptions and policies of Mormonism can best be understood in four overlapping historical contexts: (1) European rationales for colonial expansion, including such concepts as Anglo-Saxon triumphalism and British Israelism; (2) the related American doctrine of Manifest Destiny; (3) the sectional conflicts in the early United States over the status of African American slaves and of Native Americans, along with the religious rationales used to justify the national policies toward those peoples; and (4) the growing preoccupation in popular religion with millennialism and the coming End Times. All four of these contexts generated emotional issues in the American consciousness as the new Church of Jesus Christ of Latter-day Saints (also "LDS" or "Mormon" Church) came into existence beginning in 1830 along the western frontier. Out of that political, cultural, and religious mix, plus their own religious ingenuity, the Mormons acquired specific doctrines about themselves as a people and about three other ethnic peoples in particular: Jews, Native Americans, and African Americans, or Blacks.

Starting in the mid-1830s, Mormons came increasingly to understand themselves as literal descendants of the Israelite tribe of Ephraim, called out of the world by the Holy Spirit in the End Times, as a kind of vanguard to prepare the world for the gathering of the rest of Israel. The Jews were to be gathered to Palestine and the rest of Israel to North America under the sponsorship of modern Ephraim (i.e., the Mormons). From this perspective, Jews came to be understood by Mormons as literal cousins. Mormon apostles made several trips to Jerusalem during the 19th century to dedicate that holy land for the return of the Jews and consistently supported international efforts to establish a new state of Israel in the ancient Jewish homeland. The modern Mormon Church then cultivated a special relationship with the modern state of Israel. Though the Israeli government has been vigilant in prohibiting Mormon proselytizing there, it has permitted the church to build a large Mormon Center for Near Eastern Studies on Mt. Scopus, in Jerusalem, under the auspices of Brigham Young University, where students come for a semester's study and various church-sponsored religious and cultural events are held.

Given such a Mormon posture toward Israel and the Jews, it is not surprising that anti-Semitism has always been absent in official Mormon discourse, public or private, and is rare among Mormon individuals. Philo-Semitism is far more apparent. Jews living among Mormons in the western states have often testified to warm relationships between the two peoples. The first two Jewish governors of any U.S. state were elected in Mormon country: Moses Alexander in Idaho (1914) and Simon Bamberger in Utah (1916), and systematic surveys have consistently shown comparatively low rates of anti-Semitism among Mormons. While the Mormons officially hold that Jews will eventually be brought to accept Christ as Messiah, Mormon proselytizing among Jews has historically been rare, somewhat halfhearted, and decidedly unproductive.

Where the Native Americans are concerned, Mormon conceptions have varied according to the responsiveness of the various American Aboriginal peoples to proselytizing. The first generation of Mormons, led by the founding prophet Joseph Smith, held a rather idealized view of the "Lamanites," as the Native Americans were called in Smith's *Book of Mormon.* They are portrayed there as a temporarily fallen and apostate Israelite race with a divine potential for redemption and destiny as a superior people, if only they will accept the gospel. However, once the

Mormons arrived in Utah (1847), the Natives among whom they lived (and skirmished) proved largely impervious to any but the most temporary conversion, although several serious missionary forays produced baptisms in the hundreds. As the century closed, the nomadic peoples of the Americas came to seem less like the redeemable Lamanites of the *Book of Mormon* and more like "plain old Indians."

For at least 3 decades in the mid-20th century, the Mormon Church, and many White Mormon families, supported thousands of high school and college students from various tribes with lodging and free education at both public schools and church-owned institutions such as Brigham Young University. Systematic evaluations of these efforts revealed that the "Indian" youth benefited greatly in secular and economic terms from these Mormon outreach efforts, but they were not much more likely to stay with the faith than their 19th-century ancestors had been. Accordingly, by about 1980, the official and unofficial Mormon characterization of the "Indians" had become quite ambivalent as far as their divine future was concerned, and the church redirected its proselytizing and educational efforts instead toward Latin America, where the various native peoples had been showing much more receptivity to the Mormon gospel. Indeed, at the time of this writing, more than a third of all Mormons (about 4 million) live in Latin America, leaving many Mormons with the conviction that the real Lamanites, or Israelitish peoples of the *Book of Mormon,* are now to be found in the southern part of the hemisphere, rather than among the tribes of North America. A thriving scholarly enterprise in the Maxwell Institute at Brigham Young University is devoted to collecting historical, ethnographic, and archaeological evidence to support Mormon claims about the *Book of Mormon* as an authentic record of ancient Meso-American peoples.

The LDS Church has been far better known, however, for its traditional doctrines and policies about African Americans than for those about Jews or Indians. Until a special revelation and proclamation in 1978, people of Black African ancestry could not hold the priesthood in the Mormon Church. This policy was not instituted by Joseph Smith, who, in fact, ordained at least one Black man in the 1830s. The policy apparently crept into church practice gradually in the late 1840s, after Smith had been succeeded by Brigham Young, and, in 1852, Young formally announced that Blacks were prohibited by divine command from holding the priesthood. The precise motives and theological basis for that announcement remain obscure. The occasion for Young's announcement, furthermore, was rather peculiar—namely, at the opening session of the Utah Territorial Legislature in his secular capacity as governor of the territory—the same legislature that passed an act permitting slavery.

Although Young, typical of much of White society in the United States at that time, believed in the inherent inferiority of Black people, he was not an advocate particularly of either slavery or its abolition, but he was prepared to tolerate slavery in the Utah territory for strategic reasons. In the so-called Compromise of 1850, Congress had adopted a policy of admitting new states to the federal union alternatively as slave or free states in roughly equal numbers. California had been admitted as a free state in 1850, and Young was exceedingly anxious to get Utah admitted next. He might have calculated that the chances would be better if Utah permitted slavery. That seems to be the political context in which he also barred the few Black Mormons from access to the priesthood. This was a more public and conspicuous restriction than it would have been in other religious denominations, for the LDS Church has always operated with a lay priesthood open in various ranks to all males of age 12 or older. Other denominations were able to restrict access to the priesthood simply by restricting entry to seminaries (as was also the case with access to medical and law schools).

During the ensuing decades, Mormon theological thought, at both official and grassroots levels, contrived a variety of explanations to justify the racial restriction. Much of this was simply borrowed from traditional Christian sources (e.g., stories about biblical curses on Cain or Ham, or both), but some of it was peculiarly Mormon (e.g., a notion about divine punishment for alleged past sins). Yet the racist Mormon policies and folklore were scarcely noticed in a nation permeated with Jim Crow practices until the age of civil rights in the 1960s. During those decades, the restriction created a public relations nightmare for the church, which usually responded to criticism by claiming the right to its own internal ecclesiastical policies, however unfashionable for the times, and invoked the necessity for a divine revelation in order to abolish the discriminatory policy. The revelation came in 1978, and since then, the church has reached out in many different ways to improve relationships with African Americans both inside and outside its membership. Africa has proved an astonishingly fruitful missionary field for the

Mormon Church, though the growth of its membership among African Americans has generally been much slower.

Armand L. Mauss

See also Danish Americans; Jim Crow; Native Americans; Religion; Social Darwinism

Further Readings

Bringhurst, Newell G. 1981. *Saints, Slaves, and Blacks: The Changing Place of Black People within Mormonism.* Westport, CT: Greenwood Press.

Bush, Lester E., Jr. and Armand L. Mauss, eds. 1984. *Neither White nor Black: Mormon Scholars Confront the Race Issue in a Universal Church.* Salt Lake City, UT: Signature Books. Also available from http://www.signaturebooks.com

Mauss, Armand L. 2003. *All Abraham's Children: Changing Mormon Conceptions of Race and Lineage.* Chicago: University of Illinois Press.

Multicultural Education

Carl Grant and Gloria Ladson-Billings, in the *Dictionary of Multicultural Education,* define *multicultural education* as a philosophical concept and educational process. They explicitly connect it to the ideas spelled out in the U.S. Constitution and Declaration of Independence and indicate that like the United States itself, multicultural education is based on principles of freedom, justice, equality, equity, and human dignity. A social movement created in response to the dominance of Eurocentric and patriarchal power and ideas in the United States and to the influence this dominance has had on the beliefs, values, attitudes, and public ethos of generations, multicultural education has evolved to become a primary deterrent to hegemony, sexism, homophobia, and other "isms" in our society.

Early Years

Multicultural education arose as the historical legacy of the movement that led to the 1954 *Brown v. Board of Education of Topeka* verdict. This case helped make public the inequities and inequality of the nation's school systems and society in general during the Jim Crow era. The process of integrating the nation's schools created a demand that teachers already in the field, as well as those in teacher preparation programs, think about and develop skills to address the needs of racially and ethnically different students.

Energized by President Lyndon Johnson's "war on poverty," the Congress passed legislation for programs such as Head Start, which began to address the needs of minority and low-income children. The release of the Coleman Report in 1967 significantly helped multicultural education reformers to address greater equity and equality and led to legislation such as Public Law 94-142, which expanded these concerns to include gay and lesbian people as well as students with disabilities.

Creating an Academic Discipline

The role of James Banks in this movement has been substantial. His *Teaching Ethnic Studies,* now in its eighth edition, is one of the most respected books in the field. With his wife, Cherry McGee Banks, he has authored numerous other publications, but none more important than the seminal 1999 anthology, *Handbook of Research on Multicultural Education.* The contributors to this text represent a "who's who" in the field and establish multicultural education as a significant discipline in education. The Bankses called upon scholars, including Amado Padilla, Shirley Brice Heath, and Carl Grant, to establish a research agenda. Carlos Cortes and Beverly Gordon laid the foundation for a construction of knowledge theory, while Sonia Nieto, Carol D. Lee, and Valerie Ooka Payne contributed chapters on specific ethnicities. The handbook took a stand on the achievement gap, with chapters by Linda Darling Hammond and John Ogbu, and on higher education, with work by Christine Bennett and Gloria Ladson-Billings. The handbook concluded with sections on intergroup education and with international perspectives on multicultural education, by Janet Ward Schofield, Robert Slavin, and Derald Wing Sue.

In addition to his publications, Banks helped establish the Center for Multicultural Education in the College of Education at the University of Washington, Seattle. The center has been able to attract some of the top scholars in the field, including Geneva Gay and Johnnella Butler. James Banks's ascension to the presidency of the American Educational Research Association was equally significant. This distinction, in essence, recognized the importance of his work in multicultural education as well as the movement that he helped to establish.

Organizations, Institutions, and Conferences

The National Organization of Multicultural Educators, the flagship organization in the field, was founded in 1990 and now has a membership of several thousand. Its quarterly journal, *Multicultural Perspectives,* features articles on contemporary research, curriculum transformation, and instructional strategies. A variety of other organizations with slightly different but overlapping themes now flourish.

The National Conference for Race and Ethnicity in American Higher Education (NCORE) has successfully promoted large national conferences dealing with multicultural education issues. NCORE held its first conference in 1988 and has evolved as one of the most important forums on diversity. Many regional and state organizations have also been developed. For example, the New Jersey Project, under the direction of Paula S. Rothenberg, has been a center for inclusive scholarship, curriculum, and teaching throughout New Jersey. The project's workshops and publications have been recognized as major contributions to the field of multicultural education. Similarly, the Dealing With Difference Summer Institute, sponsored by the Illinois Cultural Diversity Association (ICDA), was originally funded through a grant by the Illinois Board of Higher Education and has been providing annual conferences, workshops, publications, video media, and resources since 1989.

Related to these organizations and expanding multicultural education's initial focus on cultural diversity within the United States are those organizations promoting training in cross-cultural communication and social interaction. Among them are the Intercultural Communication Institute and the Society for Intercultural Education, Training, and Research, the world's largest interdisciplinary network of students and professionals working in the area of intercultural communication.

Contemporary Influences

The impact of multicultural education on education generally can be seen from the accreditation of education programs to policy considerations at the federal, state, and district levels. Multicultural education has created a consciousness that is present throughout the educational field, perhaps most noticeable in curriculum changes and in language that challenges those vocabularies demeaning to specific groups in society because of their physical characteristics, geographic origins, gender, or ability.

The official watchdog group for teacher preparation, the National Council for Accreditation of Teacher Education, ensures the quality of the basic standards governing the preparation of our nation's PK–12 educators. The fourth of six basic standards concentrates on issues of diversity and calls on schools of education to provide a diverse cohort of aspiring teachers with the knowledge and instructional skills to help all their students succeed academically. This standard clearly reflects the influence multicultural education has had on the skills that teacher preparation schools and teacher candidates are expected to demonstrate. This suggests teachers should be able to understand issues of diversity, develop and teach curriculum about issues of diversity, and create classroom and school climates that value diversity.

In the 1990s, to assist teachers in the field, organizations like the National Council for the Social Studies developed specific curriculum guidelines for reforming public schools through multicultural education. More recently, the Center for Multicultural Education produced a widely disseminated document called "Diversity Within Unity: Essential Principles for Teaching and Learning in a Multicultural Society," which has influenced hundreds of school districts that wrestle with the demands of multicultural education and the No Child Left Behind legislation that President George W. Bush made the center of his administration's educational reform efforts.

Critics of Multicultural Education

A number of critics over the years have expressed concern about multicultural education, asserting that it promotes divisiveness and leads to increased ethnic tensions reminiscent of conflicts in Eastern Europe and the Middle East. Conservatives such as Dinesh D'Souza and Arthur Schlesinger, Jr. and activists like David Duke have warned against balkanization resulting from immigrants maintaining their ethnic identities instead of fully assimilating into the mainstream culture. Duke, for instance, believes that integration has not successfully worked in the United States or in any other major society and cites examples of ethnic conflict in Brazil and Eastern Europe as proof.

Others, like Linda Chavez, promote immersion programs rather than English as a second language, bilingual, or dual-language programs that promote multicultural education perspectives. Changes in the law, such as California's Proposition 227 and Arizona's Proposition 203, have greatly influenced the education of English learners in both of these states. Still others, like affirmative action opponent Ward Connerly, have actively lobbied state legislators in California and Michigan to pass legislation that has influenced the criteria for admissions to colleges and universities based on race and ethnicity. All of these changes have greatly impacted the goals of multicultural education in the United States.

What the Future Holds

Given current demographic trends, the changing face of America will continue. The nation is "browning," but the economic and political clout is still in the hands of the White population. This country's ability to maintain a viable middle class and continue the pursuit of full equity and equality still needs to be one of the primary goals of the nation's educational system. Researchers Gary Orfield and Marcelo Suarez-Orozco have documented the increasing racial/ethnic residential segregation in local communities and the "hypersegregation" of African Americans, Hispanics, and members of the lower socioeconomic classes in the nation's schools.

Dr. Maulana Karenga, the creator of Kwanzaa, while strongly supporting multicultural education and asserting the importance of ethnic peoples being grounded in their own cultures, heritage, and histories, also recognizes the necessity for citizens of the United States and the world to know the many other cultures that exist. As increased globalization becomes the standard for the planet, multicultural education will be part of the new literacy required for living in an increasingly interdependent world. Lack of knowledge of other cultures is often evident in U.S. foreign policy decisions in the Middle East, Africa, and Asia, even though the advent of the Internet has created the means for connections between people never before thought possible. Whether this connectivity is used to bring greater knowledge and freedom to all people or to reinforce divisions remains to be seen. Multicultural education will play a key role in how this future unfolds.

J. Q. Adams

See also Affirmative Action in Education; Antiracist Education; *Brown v. Board of Education;* Globalization; Kwanzaa; Multicultural Social Movements; Pluralism; School Desegregation; Social Inequality

Further Readings

Adams, J. Q. and Pearlie M. Strother-Adams, eds. 2001. *Dealing with Diversity.* Dubuque, IA: Kendall/Hunt.

Banks, James A. 2005. *Teaching Strategies for Ethnic Studies.* 8th ed. Needham Heights, MA: Allyn & Bacon.

Banks, James A. and Cherry A. Banks, eds. 1995. *Handbook of Research on Multicultural Education.* Old Tappan, NJ: Macmillan.

Banks, James A., Peter Cookson, Geneva Gay, Willis D. Hawley, Jacqueline Jordan Irvine, Sonia Nieto, et al. 2001. *Diversity within Unity.* Seattle: University of Washington, Center for Multicultural Education, College of Education.

Coleman, James. 1967. *The Concept of Equality of Educational Opportunity.* Baltimore, MD: Johns Hopkins University Press.

Grant, Carl A. and Gloria Ladson-Billings, eds. 1997. *Dictionary of Multicultural Education.* Phoenix, AZ: Oryx.

MULTICULTURAL SOCIAL MOVEMENTS

Race and racial identities and ideologies critically affect social movements. Multicultural social movements theory addresses the connections between demands for the recognition of identity and the redistribution of resources. It also highlights the role of racialized systems of oppression and identities on social movement demands and outcomes. Building upon and synthesizing existing theories regarding "new" social movements, race, and multiculturalism, this theory posits that in social movements, race and racialized identities and group cultures play a pivotal role. Using examples from the Civil Rights Movement, this entry describes the resources on which these movements draw and the role racial identity has played in these movements in the United States.

During multicultural social movements, activists draw on their particular cultures and histories to articulate politics of difference and semblance, reflecting their cultural past and U.S. citizenship, respectively. Multicultural movements' trajectories of activism, mobilization, and success are shaped by race-related social, historical, and institutional contexts; characteristics of the group (such as networks of solidarity, access to various forms of resources, communities of support, oppositional consciousness, and traditions of activism); and the decisions and reactions of state agencies. Different racial constraints on mobilization and different group histories in particular times and places critically affect both short- and long-term outcomes.

Like identity movements, recognition struggles, and new social movements, the ultimate goal of multicultural movements is to rearticulate and recognize group-based identities such that they no longer retain connotations of inferiority. However, multicultural movements move beyond identity politics by seeking redistribution and equalization of resources. Similarly, multicultural movements theory recognizes that not all identities provide activists with equal resources to mobilize and sustain protest, nor do they result in similar constraints. Racialized groups enter protest cycles with unique culturally and historically based resources, while groups maintaining a White racial identity are considerably more advantaged than non-White activists in societies organized as a racial hierarchy, such as the United States.

By explicitly linking identity to resources, multicultural struggles seek to subvert the subjective reality of activists' political and racial status, question society's meanings of race and racial identities, challenge preexisting ideologies, and construct alternative oppositional frameworks of belonging within U.S. society. They not only destabilize the racial terrain through the reconstruction of identities and privileges using group cultures embedded within each racial community but also often attempt to rearticulate a larger national identity such that the formerly disadvantaged group is able to claim membership within the U.S. citizenry. These attempts to change the racial hierarchy result in the potential instability of racial meanings for all racial groups such that the system must either allow for change or further institutionalize racial difference.

Group Culture as a Mobilizable Resource

Racial activists have taken their cultures and identities to be not the basis of inequality, but a means to subvert the racial order, at the same time working to preserve those cultures and identities within a society that they demand recognize their rights and grant them resources as U.S. citizens. Thus, group-based knowledge and cultures act as mobilizable resources to inform the use of culturally and historically rooted tactics, strategies, and narratives. In the long term, these efforts often increase group cohesion, networks of solidarity, and critical and oppositional consciousness within minority communities and display the potential for political power embedded within each community. Civil rights activists mobilized resources and tactics deeply embedded in their communities, such as long-standing networks developed in the Black church and working-class communities.

Oppositional cultures inform the use of movement tactics deeply rooted within each community as well as group-specific political culture (and culturally based) objects. Racialized understandings of inequality embedded in each community as oppositional cultures and consciousness are deployed during multicultural movements as agency and resistance, using culturally stored transformative knowledge. To do this, racial groups draw on specific cultural histories of collective trauma and contemporary cultural conditions to shape both resource- and identity-related demands and translate group-based oppositional consciousness and political cultures into action. In this way, protest activities draw heavily on social movement tactics rooted in groups' histories and cultural repertoires.

Particular narratives embedded in group cultures feature prominently in multicultural movements as activists seek to enact change, mobilize a participation base from within communities, and gain support from those outside it, either from allied organizations or from the target of protest. Group culture provides activists with both a concrete language and a context for their desires for social change. Demands often link their racialized identities to their lack of access to social, economic, and political resources.

Speaking to members of the community using group-specific frames to create widespread mobilization, action, and activism, activists often develop a changing rhetoric that combines the dominant racial narrative of the time with concrete desires for social, political, and economic change. Organizational leaders and activists mobilize existing symbols and stories related to their distant and recent past, which are deeply rooted in group cultures and consciousnesses, resources to which only they have access. Collective action frames often draw directly on group cultures by engaging cultural artifacts, events, and experiences from the group's past and present. These frames strike responsive chords and resonate with existing cultural narratives, heritage, and traditions.

Racialized Contexts and Constraints

Resources, opportunities, and life chances are directly and critically linked to racial identities in racialized societies such as the United States. But social movements theories rarely take into consideration the specific role of race and White privilege, particularly privileges associated with citizenship, such as voting. During multicultural movements, existing opportunity structures based on histories of oppression and privilege impede racial minorities and critically influence the outcome of these racially based social movements. Specifically, White privilege and the social, political, and economic power embedded in different institutions impact racialized groups' abilities to change ideologies and gain access to privileges therein. Social movements involving racial minorities are deeply affected by existing racial identities, attitudes, and hierarchies. During the Civil Rights Movement, existing prejudices toward Blacks affected the types of protest that were acceptable and ultimately hindered their ability to achieve full equality.

The specific social, political, and economic historical context results in differential racialization of each racial group, resulting in different obstacles depending on the intensity of racial ideologies. Formal laws and informal sanctions often work in conjunction to maintain hegemonic claims to identities and resources that preclude the possibility for systemic change. Racial groups often lack power and representation in institutional bureaucracies. There may be a lack of legal precedent such that demands have no judicial backing. The media may contribute to racist ideologies that hinder support for social or political change. Actors may lack allies outside their communities that could create additional pressure for change. Perhaps most problematic, institutions and powerful individuals may outright deny that the problem articulated by activists exists, thereby making change nearly impossible. Activists are often able to use only existing frames to issue demands. Civil rights activists were most successful when they sought integration rather than Black empowerment.

Black activists during the Civil Rights Movement sought to rearticulate the meaning of Blackness from one associated with inferiority to one reflecting pride in an African American heritage. They also sought to redefine U.S. citizenship to extend to African Americans all the rights, resources, and protections to which citizens are entitled, such as access to quality education, public accommodations, and the ballot.

Institutional constraints, which vary over time, rarely allow for simultaneous recognition of racial equality in conjunction with substantive resource distribution. Hegemonic conceptions of race remain unaltered as movements and activists are absorbed into existing institutions and dispersed. By the end of the Civil Rights Movement, significant changes had been made, though these were constrained by existing stereotypes about Blacks. These attitudes and structures ultimately inhibited activists from gaining full access to equal resources. Instead, the government acceded to small demands without significantly altering the larger structure of racial inequality in America.

Melissa F. Weiner

See also Civil Rights Movement; Minority/Majority; Minority Rights; Multicultural Education; Racial Identity; Racialization; Social Inequality

Further Readings

Calhoun, Craig. 1994. *Social Theory and the Politics of Identity.* Malden, MA: Blackwell.

Hobson, Barbara, ed. 2003. *Recognition Struggles and Social Movements: Contested Identities, Agency, and Power.* New York: Cambridge University Press.

Lipsitz, George. 1998. *The Possessive Investment in Whiteness: How White People Profit from Identity Politics.* Philadelphia, PA: Temple University Press.

Moya, Paula M. 2002. *Learning from Experience: Minority Identity, Multicultural Struggles.* Berkeley, CA: University of California Press.

Omi, Michael and Howard Winant. 1994. *Racial Formation in the United States from the 1960s to the 1990s.* 2nd ed. New York: Routledge.

Willett, Cynthia. 1998. *Theorizing Multiculturalism: A Guide to the Current Debate.* Malden, MA: Blackwell.

Multiracial Identity

Multiracial (also biracial) identity is a concept of personal identity based on the physical mixing of biological racial essences. The assertion of a multiracial identity necessarily implies that the subject has parents or more distant ancestors of at least two different biological racial groups. Therefore, at the most fundamental level, the assertion of a multiracial identity requires a corresponding assent to belief in biological race. This entry briefly examines the tension between biological and social concepts of multiracial identity and its expression in North American culture and society during the late 20th and early 21st centuries.

Ideological Structure

Expressers of multiracial identity, as well as those who advocate its expression, make the basic argument that persons having parents (and sometimes ancestors farther back) who are members of two different racial groups are distinct racially from either of those parents (or more distant ancestors) and should be categorized as multiracial, as opposed to being categorized as monoracial (Black, White, Asian, Native American, etc.). Sometimes the argument includes the specific caveat that the races of those parents (or more distant ancestors) are socially, not biologically, determined. However, this caveat does not evade the problem of explaining why, logically, the child of parents from two different socially determined races should be categorized biologically instead of socially. In other words, it does not explain how the social designation of the parents or more distant ancestors is transferred biologically to the child, since the child could just as well be given a social designation herself or himself.

Beyond this necessary, albeit often disavowed, connection to biological race, adherents of multiracial identity have also struggled to define a criterion for inclusion that is not circular in nature. One popular criterion of inclusion is "having the experience of being multiracial," but beyond the logical circularity inherent in the qualification, that "experience" is often decidedly different for people of varying ancestral combinations. For example, persons of partial Japanese ancestry who express a multiracial identity often struggle for inclusion as full members within traditional Japanese American society, while persons of partial African American ancestry who express a multiracial identity are generally always accepted as full members by the American Black community as long as there is no perception that Black identity is thereby being rejected. It is thus unclear how "having the experience of being multiracial" would in a logically compelling way link the multiracially identifying individuals in these two hypothetical cases.

Nonetheless, these structural and logical difficulties have not prevented people from assuming and expressing a multiracial identity and arguing for its recognition as a racial identity alongside the existing set of biological races acknowledged in U.S. society. Local and regional multiracial support groups have grown in number, although the membership of such organizations is generally composed of parents of multiracially identified children, as opposed to people who themselves express a multiracial identity. College support groups have also grown, and the members of these organizations are usually individuals who personally identify as multiracial.

Contemporary History

Although multiracial identity has been an issue of varying emphasis and concern for British North America and the United States since the earliest days of population mixture on the North American continent, it has taken on a more enduring presence in contemporary times owing to a number of related phenomena that occurred in the late 20th century.

First, a movement dedicated to the assertion of multiracial identity began to surface in California in the late 1970s with the formation of I-Pride (Interracial/Intercultural Pride), which agitated for separate multiracial identification on local school forms. Following this effort, similar organizations arose across the country. These organizations included local support groups similar to I-Pride as well as a national umbrella organization, the Association of MultiEthnic Americans (AMEA). Under the coordination of AMEA, these various groups eventually engaged in a lobbying effort to revise the federal racial categories authorized by the Office of Management and Budget (OMB) in order to institute a separate federal multiracial category to be effective in time for the 1990 decennial census.

Although this effort was ultimately unsuccessful, it served to bring the notion of multiracial identity into limited national debate and set the stage for activists to make a subsequent and much more comprehensive and vigorous lobbying attempt timed for the 2000 census. This second attempt to institute a separate federal multiracial category, which, in addition to being backed by AMEA, was backed by another national organization, Project RACE (Reclassify All Children Equally), also failed, but it did result in a compromise modification by the OMB in 1997 that changed the federal standard for the collection of racial data from "Mark one only" to "Mark all that apply."

Second, the early to mid-1990s witnessed a significant increase in publications touching on multiracial identity. One such source was the publication of a number of book-length academic works on multiracial identity, primarily in the form of anthologies. Another was the proliferation of glossy newsmagazine articles that appeared during the public debate period established by the OMB prior to the 2000 census. These articles tended in a very uniform way to treat the subject of multiracial identity with maudlin sentimentality and overly affected appeals to "hipness," as opposed to the application of in-depth reporting and journalistic rigor. Finally, two relatively short-lived magazines devoted exclusively to multiracial identity, *Interrace* and *New People,* were available during this time. These magazines, both of which struggled with issues of basic journalistic quality, carried content ranging from poetry and advertisements for mixed-race dating services to personal testimonies and reports on the ongoing census debates. In various ways and for various audiences, these publications served to raise the national profile of the concept of multiracial identity at a time when the federal government was considering an official recognition of it.

Third, beginning in the late 1990s and in response to the debates surrounding the 2000 census and to the several kinds of publications mentioned above, a second wave of scholarly publishing ensued—this time featuring a larger number of single-authored books. The result of that continuing publishing boom, which includes anthologies as well, has been a richer and more nuanced intellectual dialogue that has begun to organize multiracial identity studies into a disciplinary subfield consisting of scholarly voices both in favor of and opposed to the concept of multiracial identity.

Rainier Spencer

See also Blood Quantum; Census, U.S.; *Hafu;* Media and Race; One-Drop Rule; Racial Formation; Racial Identity; Racial Identity Development

Further Readings

Brunsma, David, ed. 2006. *Mixed Messages: Multiracial Identities in the Color-Blind Era.* Boulder, CO: Lynne Rienner.
Dalmage, Heather M., ed. 2004. *The Politics of Multiracialism: Challenging Racial Thinking.* Albany: State University of New York Press.
Ifekwunigwe, Jayne O, ed. 2004. *"Mixed Race" Studies: A Reader.* London: Routledge.
Root, Maria P. P., ed. 1996. *The Multiracial Experience: Racial Borders as the New Frontier.* Thousand Oaks, CA: Sage.
Winters, Loretta and Herman DeBose, eds. 2003. *New Faces in a Changing America: Multiracial Identity in the 21st Century.* Thousand Oaks, CA: Sage.

Muslim Americans

Often referred to erroneously in the media as a homogeneous unit, Muslim Americans constitute a large population that is far from monolithic and is, in fact, extremely diverse. Although Muslims have been in the United States for centuries and have been studied by scholars interested in religion and new religious movements, the terrorist attacks in New York City and Washington, D.C., on September 11, 2001, have stimulated scholarship from a wider range of disciplines. A richer and more complex understanding of American Muslims and their varying rates of assimilation into U.S. society requires closer attention to differences in race, class, and ethnicity among the various American Muslim groups and the tensions and coalitions that exist between them. Indeed, American Muslims consist of many factions, such as Sunnis, Shi'as, and Sufis. Sunnis make up the largest numbers of American Muslims, followed by Shi'as, with Sufis in a small minority. This entry provides an overview of this diverse group and related issues.

African American Muslims

Muslims came to America from different parts of the world and at different times. The first accounts of Muslims in America were of those who came as slaves from Africa. One slave was eventually freed because of his literacy and knowledge of Islam. Many slaves were forced to convert to Christianity, but a few studies have shown that Islam played a role in encouraging rebellion of slaves against their masters.

There are two major types of African American Muslims in the United States today. The introduction of Islam to African Americans in the 1930s can be attributed to W. D. Fard and then later to Elijah Muhammad, who were both integral in increasing the size and popularity of the Nation of Islam among African Americans. Scholars claim that the Nation of Islam enjoyed the most conversions in the late 1950s, during the charismatic leadership of Malcolm X, at the very same time the Civil Rights Movement was gaining momentum. The type of Islam practiced by the Nation of Islam was far from orthodox, but it underwent a significant change that focused on the racial liberation of African Americans living under oppressive conditions in a racist society.

After the death of Elijah Muhammad, his son Warith Deen Muhammad took over the Nation of Islam and tried to move the teachings closer to the practices of orthodox Sunni Muslims while still retaining a focus on African American issues. Louis Farrakhan split from Warith Deen in order to bring the Nation back to the original teachings of Elijah Muhammad. The Nation of Islam under the leadership of Farrakhan organized two marches on Washington, the Million Man March in 1995 and the Millions More March in 2005, in an attempt to bring racism and the struggles of African Americans back into the consciousness of the American public.

Muslim Immigrants

Accounts of later groups of Muslims immigrating to America describe phases that have been divided by scholars in two different ways. The first divides Muslim immigration to the United States into five waves, with the first three waves (late 1800s to early 1900s) consisting primarily of Arab Muslim immigrants who were predominantly rural and uneducated. Immigrants who arrived during the fourth wave consisted of the elite and refugees and came from South Asia, the Soviet Union, the Middle East, and Eastern Europe. The fifth wave of Muslim immigrants came to the United States after immigration restrictions were lifted through the Immigration and Nationality Act of 1965. These Muslim immigrants contributed to the diversity of American Muslims that we see today, for there were a substantial number of immigrants from Asian, South Asian, and some African and Caribbean countries.

In a different view of Muslim immigration, the first wave occurred from the late 19th century until World War II and consisted primarily of Arab Muslims. In the second wave, between World War II and 1965, Muslims in America began to create religious institutions, reflecting the immigrants' desire to stay in America. The third wave accounted for all of the immigrants that migrated to America after the passage of the Immigration and Nationality Act of 1965.

Owing to the influx of Muslim immigrants to the United States, scholars have tried to better understand assimilation rates for this demographic. Although African American Muslims have been in the United States for centuries, the new immigrant Muslims have varied experiences. The first wave of immigrants from Islamic regions were mostly Arab (Syrian and Lebanese) and Christian, not Muslim. They came to America as sojourners, although many ended up staying. Between World War II and 1965, more Muslim immigrants migrated to the United States, and after the mass immigration of Muslims after 1965, religious institutions such as mosques appeared on the U.S. landscape.

Most scholarship on American Muslims focuses on "mosqued" Muslims (those who go to mosques and are considered somewhat religious) rather than "unmosqued" Muslims (those who do not attend mosques), because of their accessibility. Scholars identified two types of mosqued American Muslims who follow very different paths in terms of assimilation. The first are Muslim Isolationists, who see limitations to participation in the public sphere. These Muslims are more concerned with U.S. foreign policy and the Muslim world than with local issues. They feel that Muslims in the United States should avoid participation in anything that would compromise their religiosity. The second type, Muslim Democrats, are concerned with policies that affect Americans. According to scholars, they are interested in an interpretation of Islam that reflects the freedoms that American Muslims enjoy through their rights and privileges as citizens and is more compatible with American values. These Muslims are more active and participate in the public sphere. As a result of these Muslims' efforts to civically engage in the U.S. political system, many Muslim American organizations exist to help meet the needs of the growing American Muslim population.

American Muslims and Race, Class, and Ethnicity

American Muslims are divided on issues of race, ethnicity, and class. Because of the diversity among American Muslims, there has yet to be a unified Muslim coalition. Scholars note that racial tension between African American Muslims and the new immigrant Muslims divides American Muslims. Because Muslims are so diverse in racial and ethnic composition and class, their relationship with one another is complex.

Tensions With African Americans

The relationship between South Asians and African American Muslims is best understood by looking at a variety of factors. First, scholars of race and ethnicity note that the United States is heading toward a triracial society rather than a biracial one, owing to the increasing number of immigrants from non-European countries after the passage of the Immigration and Nationality Act of 1965. This new racial hierarchy helps to explain the racial tension that exists between South Asian Muslims and African American Muslims, who are treated differently in the United States because of their skin tone.

The context of immigration to America differs among the various ethnic groups. Many of the South Asian Muslims who immigrated after the passage of the 1965 law were professionals. As a result, the relatively affluent South Asian Muslims are less residentially segregated from Whites than are African American Muslims. A second reason for tension between African American Muslims and South Asian and Arab American Muslims involves the differences in their religious practices and beliefs. The Nation of Islam is not recognized by Sunni Muslims as a "real" Muslim religion because South Asian and Arab Sunni as well as Shi'a Muslims see it as a separatist religion based on race and not on the true teachings of the Koran.

Warith Deen Muhammad and his followers are recognized as practicing a valid Muslim religion because they follow orthodox Islam, even though issues of racial oppression are integral to them. *Khutbas* (religious sermons) in African American mosques find in Islam and the Koran a way to address racism, similar to Black liberation theology. The *khutbas* in South Asian American and Arab American mosques do not focus on issues of race, but rather preach the conventional tenets of Koranic scripture. Cultural differences between Arab American Muslims, South Asian Muslims, and African American Muslims have also had an effect on their relationships.

The Racialization of Muslims

The racialization of American Muslims is something that has been going on for decades in the United States. Scholars note that while "Muslim" is not a racial category, there has been a process in the United States and in European countries whereby Muslims have become racialized, that is, viewed by others as a distinct homogeneous group. They are then denied full access to opportunities because of their identity as Muslims. Citizenship historically is an example of a status that has been denied to people of color in the United States. Citizenship was granted to only free White men, as the U.S. Naturalization Act of 1790 limited the right to become a naturalized citizen to "free" White persons. Blacks, the poor, Native Americans, and women were denied the rights that citizenship guaranteed in the United States.

Several policies and acts precluded citizenship for immigrants who were not White. According to scholars in 1909 and 1914, Arabs were not seen as "free" White persons and were denied access to citizenship in the United States. In 1923, Asian Indians were denied citizenship as well because they were racially classified as Asiatic and "not White." A year later, the National Origins Act of 1924 made immigration of aliens who were not eligible for citizenship in the United States because of their race an illegal act, thereby preventing many Muslims from migrating to America. The passage of the Immigration and Nationality Act of 1965 changed the terrain of America by a reversal of racist policies such as the National Origins Act of 1924, opening up immigration to countries that were previously denied immigration to the United States and making legal the naturalization of immigrants who were previously denied citizenship on the basis of racial classification.

Impact of Terrorism

Since the attacks on the World Trade Center and the Pentagon on September 11, 2001, the reports of discrimination that American Muslims face have increased significantly. Studies have found that negative images of Muslims in the American media have often helped to fuel suspicion of Muslims in the United States. Recent policies, such as the USA PATRIOT Act, differentially impact U.S.-born and immigrant Muslims in the United States through increased surveillance by the government. Policies developed to curb terrorism in the United States and abroad have been viewed by many in the Muslim American community as resulting in the illegal incarceration and deportation of Muslim immigrants.

Consequently, many organizations, such as CAIR (Council on American-Islamic Relations), are taking on the responsibility of ensuring that the civil rights of American Muslims and Muslim immigrants are not violated in the United States. ISNA (Islamic Society of North America) is also encouraging its members to become citizens of the United States, if they are not already; to condemn terrorism; and to encourage Muslims in the United States to create a more positive image of themselves.

Further research is needed in the field of race and ethnicity of second- and third-generation Muslims, a population that is not only growing but also complex and often misunderstood.

Saher Farooq Selod

See Appendix B

See also Arab Americans; Immigration and Nationality Act of 1965; Islamophobia; Malcolm X; Muslims in Canada; Muslims in Europe; National Origins System; Nation of Islam; Orientalism; PATRIOT Act of 2001; Religion; "Us and Them"; Veil; Xenophobia

Further Readings

Allen, Ernest, Jr. 1998. "Identity and Destiny: The Formative Views of the Moorish Science Temple and the Nation of Islam." Pp. 201–266 in *Muslims on the Americanization Path?* edited by Y. Yazbeck Haddad and J. L. Esposito. Atlanta, GA: Scholars Press.

Curtis, Edward E. 2006. *Black Muslim Religion in the Nation of Islam, 1960–1975.* Chapel Hill: University of North Carolina Press.

Esposito, John L. 1998. "Muslims in America or American Muslims?" Pp. 3–17 in *Muslims on the Americanization Path?* edited by Y. Yazbeck Haddad and J. L. Esposito. Atlanta, GA: Scholars Press.

Haddad, Yvonne Yazbeck. 1998. "The Dynamics of Islamic Identity in North America." Pp. 19–46 in *Muslims on the Americanization Path?* edited by Y. Yazbeck Haddad and J. L. Esposito. Atlanta, GA: Scholars Press.

Haddad, Yvonne Yazbeck. 2004. *Not Quite American? The Shaping of Arab and Muslim Identity in the United States.* Waco, TX: Baylor University Press.

Leonard, Karen Isaksen. 2003. *Muslims in the United States: The State of Research.* New York: Russell Sage Foundation.

Nuruddin, Yusuf. 1998. "African American Muslims and the Question of Identity: Between Traditional Islam, African Heritage, and the American Way." Pp. 267–330 in *Muslims on the Americanization Path?* edited by Y. Yazbeck Haddad and J. L. Esposito. Atlanta, GA: Scholars Press.

Muslims in Canada

Even 10 years ago, an encyclopedia on race and ethnicity probably would not have included an entry on Muslims in Canada. It is a sign of the changing demographics of immigration to Canada that it is warranted and recognized now. Although the first Muslims came to Canada in the 1890s, the 1990s witnessed the greatest influx of immigrants adhering to Islam. Cities like Toronto and Montreal, which have the highest concentrations of Muslim Canadians, have been rapidly transformed from largely Christian enclaves to multiethnic and multireligious communities. While the much-heralded commitment to a multicultural Canada has mitigated some of the hostile response that has met Muslims elsewhere, it is still the case that this rapidly growing community has met with some resistance in Canada, especially in the aftermath of the September 11, 2001, terrorist attacks (9/11) in New York and Washington, D.C. This entry looks at the community of Muslim Canadians and their experiences of discrimination, especially since the advent of terrorism.

Muslim Canadians: Demographics

Muslims constitute approximately 2% of the Canadian population (579,600), as measured in the 2001 census. This is nearly double the 1991 figure of 253,300; in fact, over the 1990s, Muslims accounted for 15% of all new immigrants. Sixty-one percent of Canadian Muslims live in Ontario; 86% live in the major metropolitan areas; over 300,000 live in the Greater Toronto region; and over 150,000 live in Montreal. Vancouver, Ottawa, and Edmonton have smaller but nonetheless significant numbers of Muslims; the latter is the city in which the first Muslim immigrants to Canada settled.

By the opening years of the 21st century, there were more than eighty mosques across the country, most of which were located in those urban centers noted above. Roughly one-third of Canadian Muslims are of South Asian background, one-third of Arab background, and one-third of other backgrounds, including African and European.

Especially since 9/11, proportionately more Muslims have made their way to Canada than to the United States, over concerns of confronting racism and Islamophobia there. Most Muslim immigrants to Canada are highly skilled professionals; one-fourth of Muslims in Canada hold university degrees, including an elevated proportion of advanced degrees. They are trained as health professionals, engineers, and business professionals.

Yet Muslim integration into the fabric of Canadian society has not been without its limitations. As in other Western nations, the welcome mat has not been universally laid out for Muslims, and despite their credentials, they are overrepresented among the unemployed and underemployed.

Muslims in the Canadian Media

The apparent disparities in employment for Muslims can be explained in part by the widespread diffusion of negative images of Islam. In fact, many commentators have suggested that Arabs generally and Muslims specifically may represent the last "legitimate" subjects of negative stereotypes. The media are seen by many in the Muslim Canadian community as especially complicit in the dissemination of anti-Muslim imagery through the perpetuation of narrow caricatures of Muslims as terrorists and as rejecting Canadian values.

There is a widely held belief within the Muslim Canadian community that Muslims are not represented fairly in the mass media. In a 2002 nationwide survey of some 300 Canadian Muslims of South Asian, Arab, African, and European backgrounds, the Canadian Council on American-Islamic Relations (CAIR-CAN) found that 55% of respondents thought the Canadian media had become more biased since 9/11. Researchers single out the *National Post* as especially likely to engage in disparaging and inflammatory coverage of Islam, tending to emphasize extremist "tendencies."

While there is evidence of anti-Muslim bias in the Canadian news media, it is also important to note positive representations. Indeed, Denise Helly cites research suggesting that many Canadian media outlets offer relatively "balanced" or "objective" coverage of Islam. A recent case in point is newspaper coverage of the foiled terrorist attack in Toronto, in which seventeen suspects were arrested. Coverage in the *Toronto Star*, for example, has been rather sympathetic, taking pains to call for tolerance and pointing out that the suspects were fringe members of a marginal sect. Muslim leaders are cited liberally, in an apparent effort to present the peaceful side of Islam.

The Post–9/11 Environment

In the aftermath of the attacks of September 11, 2001, in the United States; October 12, 2002, in Bali; the London Underground in 2005; and the arrests of seventeen terror suspects in Toronto in 2006, reports of discriminatory treatment of those perceived to be Muslim have escalated dramatically, especially in Western nations like the United States, the United Kingdom, and Australia. Even in Canada, one of the few Western nations that did not initially support the U.S. military action in Iraq, anti-Muslim violence as well as anti-Muslim practices by the state mushroomed. These have included restrictions on immigration of young men from Muslim countries, racial profiling and detention of "Muslim-looking" individuals, and an increase in reports of hate violence against Arab, Muslim, and South Asian communities in the wake of 9/11.

For example, a survey of Canadian Muslims in 2002 by CAIR-CAN found that 56% of respondents had experienced at least one anti-Muslim incident in the 12 months since 9/11. The same percentage reported increased media bias against Muslims and Islam. Some 33% had experienced verbal abuse, 18% had experienced racial profiling, and 16% had experienced workplace discrimination. In 2003, the Canadian Islamic Congress (CIC) reported a 1,600% increase in the annual incidence of anti-Muslim hate crimes reported to them, from a low base of 11 cases in the year prior to 9/11 to 173 cases in the subsequent year. The CIC, for one, fears the possibility of more backlash violence following the arrests of seventeen young men arrested for their roles in a plotted terrorist attack in Toronto in June 2006. Indeed, within a day of the arrests, a major Toronto mosque was vandalized.

Interestingly, on one hand, Canadian politicians have been relatively temperate in their statements on Muslim involvement in terrorism. Yet, on the other hand, Canadian leaders have not been consistently quick to come to the defense of Muslims. Many in the Canadian Muslim community were critical of Prime Minister Jean Chrétien's failure to condemn the hate-motivated violence perpetrated against Canadian Muslims in the aftermath of 9/11. No public calls for peace and understanding were forthcoming; no strengthening reforms to hate crime legislation were ever considered (in contrast to rabid action on antiterrorist legislation; see below); nor were increased police or prosecutorial vigilance on the public agenda.

The 2004 CAIR-CAN report documents experiences in which law enforcement agents (Canadian Security Intelligence Services, Royal Canadian Mounted Police, municipal police) "approached" or "contacted" Arabs and Muslims, often with no explanation for the contact. In fact, of the 467 respondents, 8% had been contacted, the bulk of whom (84%) were Canadian citizens; among those who were not directly contacted, nearly half (43%) knew at least one other Canadian Muslim who had been.

According to the CAIR-CAN report, what was especially problematic about the contacts were the tactics used by law enforcement agents. Among the practices identified were discouraging legal or other third-party assistance; aggressive and threatening behavior; threats of arrest; problematic and suggestive questions about individuals' loyalty to Canada, as opposed to loyalty to their religious faith; improper identification; attempts to recruit participants as informants; and interrogation of minors. The ultimate result of these patterns has been to increase the alienation and mutual distrust between Muslims and law enforcement agents. In addition, it reinforces the public perception that Muslims are questionable with respect to their loyalty to Canada and with respect to their knowledge of, if not involvement in, terrorism. However unfounded or unjustified the police surveillance and racial profiling may be, it nonetheless leaves a lingering sense of doubt.

Patterns of anti-Muslim discrimination in Canada do not go unchecked. Formal Muslim organizations and associations across Canada have been very vocal in their resistance to both popular and political expressions of Islamophobia. Moreover, they have also been at the forefront of providing an array of services to the Muslim community. Some of the organizations, such as CAIR-CAN, are national in scope, with local contacts, and some (for example, the Ottawa Muslim Association) are local and specific to the communities in question. All are committed to serving the Muslim community, albeit in different ways. Local organizations tend to provide educational and religious services, while the national bodies tend to emphasize advocacy and community action. In the short term, at the very least, such agencies will be vital to empowering the growing Muslim community in Canada.

Barbara Perry

See also Canada; Hate Crimes in Canada; Islamophobia; Muslim Americans; Muslims in Europe; Racial Profiling; Xenophobia

Further Readings

Canadian Council on American-Islamic Relations. 2004. *Today's Media: Covering Islam and Canadian Muslims. Submission to Standing Committee on Transport and Communications, 26 February.* Available from http://www.caircan.ca/downloads/sctc-26022004.pdf

Canadian Council on American-Islamic Relations. 2005. *Presumption of Guilt: A National Survey on Security Visitations of Canadian Muslims.* Available from http://www.caircan.ca/downloads/POG-08062005.pdf

Canadian Islamic Congress. 2002. *Anti-Islam in the Media 2002.* Retrieved from http://www.canadianislamiccongress.com/rr/rr_2002_1.php

Helly, Denise. 2004. "Are Muslims Discriminated against in Canada since September 2001?" *Journal of Canadian Ethnic Studies* 36(1):24–47.

Ismael, T. Y. and John Measor. 2003. "Racism and the North American Media Following 11 September: The Canadian Setting." *Arab Studies Quarterly* 25(1/2):101–136.

Khouri, Raja. 2003. *Arabs in Canada—Post 9/11.* Toronto, Canada: Canadian Arab Federation/G7Books.

Web Sites

Canadian Islamic Congress: http://www.canadianislamiccongress.com

Muslims in Europe

An estimated 13 to 15 million Muslims are living in Europe today (not counting those living in the Russian Federation and the Balkan states). This number is difficult to determine more precisely because of illegal immigration and the lack of census data regarding a person's religious background; also, leaders of pro- and anti-Muslim causes inflate the numbers to advance their agendas. The majority of Muslims in Europe today came as labor migrants and their dependents to the prospering post–World War II economies of western Europe. More recently, with the arrival of asylum seekers, refugees, professionals, and students, the pool has diversified in both work background and country of origin.

Identification of Muslim immigrants primarily by their religion rather than by their ethnic and national origin is itself a relatively recent phenomenon, in both official debates and scholarly inquiry. Moreover, public discourse today often represents Muslims in Europe as a homogeneous group, when, in fact, the members of the community are rather diverse in terms of ethnicity, language, and culture, as well as individual adherence to Islam. While there has never been such a large number of Muslims in Europe, their presence in European history is not a new phenomenon, but rather started with Muslim rule in the Iberian Peninsula in medieval times; Muslims were also among colonial subjects in the context of European colonization of Africa, Asia, and the Caribbean. In the 20th century, a significant proportion of Muslim migrants to France, Great Britain, and the Netherlands came as a result of decolonization. Thus, these countries are home to some of the largest groups of Muslim communities today. Due to labor migration, significant numbers of Muslims (mostly from Turkey) have also settled in Germany, Belgium, Switzerland, Denmark, and Sweden. This entry traces the history of the Muslim population in Europe and discusses some current issues.

Early Muslim Presence

Sicily was under Arab Muslim leadership from 831 to 1072, but the best-known conquest of European territory by Muslims dates back to the 8th century. In 711, in the context of territorial expansion, "Moorish forces," as they were then called, attacked the Iberian Peninsula and within 8 years brought most of it under their control. Andalusia in Southern Spain became the center of Muslim rule, and a caliphate was established in 929. The history of Muslims in Spain is often told in one of two extreme versions: either as the golden age of religious tolerance or the total subjugation of *dhimmis* (non-Muslims in a Muslim state whose rights might be restricted but who are not enslaved).

A third interpretation presents a middle ground between the two. Muslim rulers placed some limitations on Jews and Christians, such as restrictions on clothing, construction of synagogues and churches, and marriage between Muslim women and non-Muslim men, and *dhimmis* had to acknowledge Muslim supremacy, but Muslim rulers largely practiced ethnic and religious tolerance and treated non-Muslims better than many other victorious powers treated subjects at the time. This rule of relative tolerance might be explained in a variety of ways: Judaism and Christianity were seen as fellow Abrahamic monotheistic religions; Christians outnumbered Muslims; and integrating *dhimmis* into the government provided loyal administrators not attached to any of the various Muslim groups.

Aided by both external forces and internal divisions among Muslims themselves, Muslim reign in Spain effectively ended 800 years later, in 1492. The *reconquista,* efforts of Spanish Christian forces to regain lands from the Muslims, had begun soon after the Muslim invasion and ended with the fall of Granada, the last Iberian Muslim state, in southern Spain. With the establishment of a united Roman Catholic kingdom, Muslims as well as Jews were forced to convert to Christianity or face expulsion. So-called *Moriscos,* nominal Christians who still secretly maintained their Muslim faith, faced persecution during the Spanish Inquisition, which was established to maintain Catholic orthodoxy in Spain. Finally, a decree to expel Moriscos was issued in 1609. Hundreds of thousands had to leave and resettle in North Africa.

Muslim Migration to Europe after World War II

Decolonization as well as labor migration in the post–World War II period brought a growing wave of immigrants to Europe, feeding the postwar economic boom from the 1950s onward. Among these immigrants were Muslims from various countries in Asia, Africa, and the Caribbean. Many former colonial subjects initially had legal advantages over other labor migrants, facilitating their immigration. In the case of Great Britain, for example, members of the Commonwealth were extended British citizenship and given equal rights to enter the country and the British job market. Similar legislation existed in France. This led to inhabitants of India, Pakistan, and the West Indies coming to Great Britain; Algerians, Moroccans, and Tunisians coming to France; and people from Indonesia, Surinam, and the Dutch Antilles coming to the Netherlands. Furthermore, throughout colonial times, many immigrants had become familiar with the culture and language of their former colonizers, further aiding the immigration process.

Other immigrants in this period were recruited by national governments and companies, Turks among them, coming in the context of so-called guest worker programs. While the majority of them settled in Germany, they also migrated to other European countries, such as France, the Netherlands, Austria, Belgium, and Switzerland. The 1970s marked a shift in the postwar migration regimes, as labor recruitment programs were halted in the wake of the oil crisis early in the decade. What followed was not an end of immigration, however, but an intensification of family unification, a pattern of migration that had already begun a decade earlier and increased as more migrants decided to settle in their host countries, leading to a continued rise in the number of Muslims in European countries.

More recently, immigration has diversified, with immigrants originating from a wide variety of countries and entering Europe as asylum seekers, refugees, professionals, and students. Especially since the end of the cold war, the war in Yugoslavia, and the conflict in the Middle East, the number of those seeking asylum in Europe has drastically increased, leading to tougher asylum policies in many receiving countries. These changes have contributed to the creation of the conception of a "Fortress Europe."

A variety of factors have led to singling out immigrants of Muslim background and identifying them by their religion rather than national origins. With some exceptions, major public concerns about the presence of immigrants did not surface until the 1970s, and by the 1980s, immigration and integration had become integral components of major party platforms across Europe. Initially, labor migration had been envisioned as temporary, and neither the host countries nor the majority of the foreign laborers themselves had planned on their permanent settlement. However, as their stay lengthened, the attitudes of immigrants about living in their host countries evolved, and they started to settle and bring their families. Moreover, labor migrants generally filled jobs as semi- or unskilled laborers, often disproportionately vulnerable to changes in the economy. Combined with prejudicial attitudes of employers, unemployment among this group became disproportionately high, especially from the 1970s onward. More recently, populist parties with anti-immigrant agendas, generally targeting especially those with Muslim backgrounds, have been able to gain a foothold in politics, among them the Front National in France, the Freedom Party in Austria, the People's Party in Denmark, and the National Democratic Party of Germany (NPD). Initially mainly supported by those on the right fringes, these parties are now increasingly buoyed by the center as well, gaining seats in local, regional, and national parliaments and becoming coalition partners of more moderate parties.

While Muslims have been singled out as migrants and ethnic minorities, scholars have recently argued that particular developments within and outside of Europe over the course of the last decades have aided in placing the focus on Muslim immigrants qua Muslims. An increasing turn toward fundamentalism within Islam and a growing series of violent events— among them conflicts in the Middle East, the kidnapping and murder of Israeli athletes at the 1972 Olympics in Munich by members of a Palestinian terrorist group, and the Iranian Revolution in 1979 leading to the establishment of an Islamic republic— converged with the phenomenon of immigrants within Europe speaking out as Muslims, as in the case of the publication of Salman Rushdie's *Satanic Verses* in 1988. Also drawing wide media attention was the 1989 incident in Creil, outside of Paris, when three Muslim girls were expelled from school for wearing headscarves.

The Integration Debate

Discussions about the possibility of integrating Muslims into European culture have become vociferous, and the intensity of debate has only been fanned by the attacks in the United States on September 11, 2001, and the bombings in Madrid on March 11, 2004, and in London on July 7, 2005. Also, an Islamic extremist killed the Dutch filmmaker Theo van Gogh on November 11, 2004, because he had become enraged by the Islam-critical film van Gogh had helped produce. One position, popularized by Samuel Huntington, supports the argument that Muslims are fundamentally different in their values and outlook and that religious background can explain Muslim discontent and lashing out in Europe, making the failure of integration a foregone conclusion. Other scholars have focused more on the socioeconomic context as well as national institutional barriers to integrating Islam, the interconnection of religion and public policies in Europe, and the novelty of religious pluralism within its borders.

States have responded to these developments by rethinking citizenship procedures and mechanisms of integration. The Netherlands, historically known for its openness and tolerance, has recently tightened its immigration controls and efforts to integrate ethnic minorities in an attempt to counter the trend of growing Turkish and Moroccan ghettos. Now, prospective immigrants to the Netherlands must pass a language test and prove their knowledge of Dutch history and society before their applications are considered. Once in the Netherlands, they are required to take classes on Dutch culture.

While Germany liberalized its citizenship law in 2000, allowing children born in Germany to foreign permanent residents to acquire German citizenship, the definition and preservation of Germany's core values and culture *(Leitkultur)* have been repeatedly debated among politicians. Since 2006, some states within the Federal Republic require Muslims who are applying for German citizenship to take a "naturalization test," in an effort to assess their attitudes toward basic German social, cultural, and political values.

In 2004, France, in an effort to maintain its republican principles of *laïcité*, or secularism, passed a law forbidding the wearing of the headscarf and other "ostentatious" religious symbols in school. Since 2001, Denmark has one of the strictest foreigner and refugee legislations in Europe, and its government has attempted to counteract what it considers the dangerous creation of parallel societies, especially among Muslims in Denmark, who are accused of refusing to integrate into the majority culture. As a countermeasure, in 2006, Denmark also introduced a mandatory Danish culture canon (containing eighty-four pieces of work in seven different categories, such as architecture, literature, film, and the fine arts) to be taught in school.

The situation in Denmark came to a head in 2005/2006, when the editor of a Danish newspaper, citing freedom of expression, invited cartoonists to draw images of Muhammed, after a children's book author had been unsuccessful in finding an illustrator for a book on the prophet. Such images are forbidden in the Muslim faith, and illustrators cited fear of retaliation after the murder of Theo van Gogh. After the cartoons were published, fundamentalist imams in Denmark declared them an affront to Muslims worldwide. Reactions to the cartoons expanded well beyond the borders of Denmark and Europe, ending in numerous demonstrations and riots.

Despite at times highly charged political rhetoric and often sensationalist news coverage to the contrary, most scholars agree and have pointed out repeatedly over the last few years that the majority of Muslims in Europe do want to integrate and that the attacks in Madrid, Amsterdam, and London are the deeds of a small number of extremists. Opinions differ, however, on how far the symptoms of alienation and lack of rootedness reach. Some argue that the violence of the few in the last several years is only a symptom of a much more far-reaching alienation among Muslim immigrants in Europe, which needs to be taken seriously.

Julia M. Woesthoff

See also Europe; France; Immigration and Race; Islamophobia; London Bombings (July 7, 2005); Muslim Americans; Muslims in Canada; Religion; Turkey; Xenophobia

Further Readings

Bleich, Erik. 2006. "Constructing Muslims as Ethno-racial Outsiders in Western Europe." *European Studies Newsletter* 26:1–7.

Buruma, Ian. 2006. *Murder in Amsterdam.* New York: Penguin.

Cramer, Jane. 2005. "Comment: Difference." *New Yorker,* November 2005. Retrieved from http://www.newyorker.com/archive/2005/11/21/051121ta_talk_kramer

Goody, Jack. 2004. *Islam in Europe.* Malden, UK: Polity Press.

Haddad, Y. Yazbeck and John L. Esposito, eds. 2002. *Muslim Minorities in the West: Visible and Invisible.* Lanham, MD: Alta Mira Press.

Huntington, Samuel. 1996. *The Clash of Civilizations and the Remaking of World Order.* New York: Simon & Schuster.

Klausen, Jytte. 2005. *The Islamic Challenge.* Oxford, UK: Oxford University Press.

Nielsen, Jørgen. 2004. *Muslims in Western Europe.* 3rd ed. Edinburgh, UK: Edinburgh University Press.

Shepard, Todd. 2006. *The Invention of Decolonization: The Algerian War and the Remaking of France.* Ithaca, NY: Cornell University Press.

Myanmarese Americans

Myanmarese Americans are immigrants and their descendants from Myanmar (formerly Burma), a country of 49.8 million as of 2007 estimates. According to the 2000 census, there were 32,590 people born in Myanmar resident in the United States, of whom 57.5% were citizens. There are more than 125 different ethnicities found in Myanmar. The majority of U.S. immigrants ethnically identify with the Burmans, Burmese, Arakese, Karens, Mons, Shans, and Nagas. This entry looks at the background of immigration from Myanmar to the United States and the contemporary picture of Myanmarese Americans.

Immigration Patterns

Myanmarese immigrants began to arrive during the 1960s. The year 1962 was significant because many Burmese (doctors, professors, and students) fled the country at the beginning of General Ne Win's rule, after a military coup d'état. In addition, when the quota cap of the Immigration Act of 1924 was lifted, many Asians began to immigrate to the United States looking for economic opportunities. Immigration during the past few decades has been quite small, especially in comparison to other Asian groups.

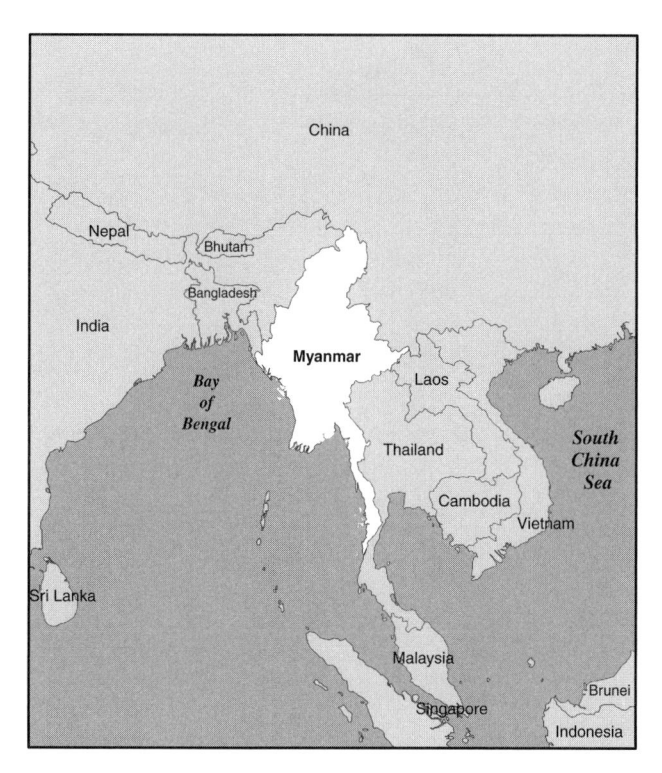

Contemporary Community

In recent years, people from Myanmar have sought permanent residency and refugee status and have completed the naturalization process to become citizens. From 1997 through 2004, about 1,300 Myanmarese immigrated to the United States annually, many of them arriving under immigration provisions that allowed for family reunification. During the years 2005 and 2006, about 6,600 Myanmarese were granted legal permanent status. About 300 refugees arrived annually between the years 1997 and 2004. The period 2004 through 2006 brought about 2,800 refugees. At least 10,000 Myanmarese Americans have become naturalized citizens since 1997.

According to the U.S. Census Bureau American Community Survey, there were 21,110 individuals of Myanmar national origin in the United States. Many have settled in large cities, such as Chicago, New York, Los Angeles, and Washington, D.C. In terms of geographic distribution, the top five states were California, New York, Indiana, Florida, and Washington.

As a result of their British colonial heritage and mandatory education in both the English and Burmese languages, many Myanmarese immigrants are bilingual and continue to speak Burmese at home, as well as at social gatherings. According to the 2000 census, 9% spoke a language other than English. Economic characteristics of the Myanmarese include occupations in management and professional sectors, as well as a significant portion working in the manufacturing, educational, and health industries. Myanmarese Americans' median family income was $61,725, compared with $50,890 for the nation as a whole.

Jennifer M. Klein

See Appendix A

See also Asian Americans; Assimilation; Immigrant Communities; Immigration, U.S.; Symbolic Ethnicity

Further Readings

Department of Homeland Security. 2007. *Yearbook of Immigration Statistics:* 2006. Washington, DC: Office of Immigration Statistics. Available from http://www.dhs.gov/ximgtn/statistics/publications/yearbook.shtm

Kyi, Aung San Suu. 1997. *Letters from Burma.* New York: Penguin Books.

Steinberg, David. 2006. *Turmoil in Burma: Contested Legitimacies in Myanmar.* Norwalk, CT: East Bridge.

U.S. Census Bureau. 2004. *Profile of Demographic and Social Characteristics: 2000. People Born in Myanmar.* Available from http://www.census.gov/population/928 www/socdemo/foreign/STP-159-2000tl.html

U.S. Census Bureau. 2006. *American Community Survey 2005.* Available from http://www.census.gov/acs/www

National Association for the Advancement of Colored People (NAACP)

The National Association for the Advancement of Colored People (NAACP) is one of the oldest civil rights organizations in the nation, focusing on improving the situation of African Americans. It has been criticized as both too radical and too conservative, but over the years, it has amassed an impressive record of achievements, which are summarized in this entry.

History

After the lynching of two Blacks in 1908, Mary White Ovington, a White woman and Brooklyn native, organized a conference in Springfield, Illinois, to discuss the growth of political and social equality of Blacks. The National Negro Committee was established shortly after, in 1909.

The second conference, in the following year, led to the formation of the National Association for the Advancement of Colored People (NAACP), a permanent body led by William E. B. Du Bois, Henry Moscowitz, Mary White Ovington, Oswald Garrison Villiard, William English Walling, and Ida Wells-Barnett. From its conception, the NAACP was composed largely of Black Americans, but many White members were actively involved. The ultimate goal of the NAACP was to strive for the end of racial discrimination and segregation. An early success arose for the organization as membership reached 90,000 within 10 years of its conception.

Du Bois served as director of publicity and research, a member of the board of directors, and editor of *The Crisis,* the NAACP's monthly magazine, from 1910 to 1934. After leaving the organization to pursue an anti-integration agenda of his own, Du Bois returned as director of special research from 1944 to 1948. During his second tenure, he was a consultant to the United Nations founding convention (1945) and wrote the famous "An Appeal to the World" in 1947.

Historically, the NAACP dealt with violence among its own ranks. In 1919, in Austin, Texas, John R. Shillady, executive secretary of the NAACP, was badly beaten; in 1951, Henry T. Moore, another executive secretary, was bombed in his house along with his wife; and, in 1963, Medgar Evers was murdered in Jackson, Mississippi.

Despite the violence directed toward individuals directly involved with the organization, the NAACP advocated nonviolent protests, litigation, and legislation to advance the rights of Blacks. Their methods often conflicted with the strategies of extremist Black groups, such as the Student Nonviolent Coordinating Committee (SNCC); the Black Panthers, in the 1960s and 1970s; the Congress of Racial Equality (CORE); and the Nation of Islam, in the 1980s and 1990s. The aforementioned groups often criticized the NAACP for being passive. However, the NAACP was also criticized for being outspoken with its condemnation of racist policies by such nonviolent advocates as Booker T. Washington.

The NAACP's nonviolent strategy was carried out in the late 1980s, when it organized silent marches in

Washington, D.C., as a form of protest against racial inequality. By the 1990s, the organization shifted its focus to the political arena on issues such as legislative redistricting, voter registration, and community activism through programs such as the Fair Share Program, Economic Reciprocity Program, and "Stop the Violence, Start the Love" campaign.

In the early 1990s, the organization encountered financial difficulties and weak leadership. By the late 1990s, it had weathered those difficulties through new leadership and played a prominent role in the 2000 national election. As of 2007, the NAACP is the nation's oldest and largest civil rights organization. There are about 500,000 members in 2,200 adult branches and 1,700 youth and college chapters. The NAACP remains the most influential civil rights organization in the United States.

Political Lobby

Initially, many of the efforts by the NAACP were geared against lynching, which virtually disappeared by the 1950s. However, the NAACP has worked on a number of social justice issues since its conception. In 1913, the NAACP launched a public protest against President Woodrow Wilson, who officially introduced segregation into the federal government. By 1918, the pressure from the NAACP led President Wilson to issue a statement against lynching.

The organization fought and won the battle to permit Blacks to be commissioned as officers in World War I in 1917. As a result, 600 Black officers were commissioned, and an additional 700,000 Blacks registered for the draft. This military achievement continued during World War II, as the NAACP led the effort against discrimination in war-related industries and federal employment through President Franklin Roosevelt's policies.

When Medgar Evers was turned away from the University of Mississippi Law School in February 1954, the NAACP launched a campaign to desegregate the school. Later that year, the U.S. Supreme Court ruling in the case of *Brown v. Board of Education* proclaimed that segregated schools were unconstitutional. In December of that year, Evers became the NAACP's first field officer in Mississippi. In February 1995, Myrlie Evers-Williams, the wife of Medgar Evers, became the first woman to be elected to the position of Chairman of the National Board of Directors of the NAACP.

In the 1960s, the NAACP played an instrumental role in the passage of two major acts, the Civil Rights Act of 1964 and the Voting Rights Act of 1965, which was extended in 1981 for another 25 years.

In 2001, George W. Bush became the first president since Herbert Hoover, during the Great Depression, not to address the NAACP, in what was seen as retaliation for the group's criticism of his leadership as the president. This friction lasted until 2006, when he addressed the NAACP at its convention for the first time.

Legal Battles

The NAACP has been involved in legal battles against segregation and racial discrimination in housing, education, employment, voting, and transportation. The NAACP Legal Defense and Education Fund, an independent legal aid group, argues in court on behalf of the NAACP and other civil rights groups. Along with the NAACP, this group was also instrumental in influencing the Supreme Court's ruling (1954) against segregated public education, in the landmark *Brown v. Board of Education of Topeka* case, under the leadership of Special Counsel Thurgood Marshall. The NAACP also won *Morgan v. Virginia* in 1946, which banned segregated facilities in interstate travel by train and bus.

Kiljoong Kim and Christina Diaz

See also Brown v. Board of Education; Death Penalty; Du Bois, William Edward Burghardt; Lynching; Marshall, Thurgood; Voting Rights

Further Readings

Hughes, Langston. 1962. *Fight for Freedom: The Story of the NAACP.* New York: Norton.

Jonas, Gilbert. 2007. *Freedom's Sword: The NAACP and the Struggle against Racism, 1909–1969.* New York: Routledge.

Mosnier, L. Joseph. 2005. *Crafting Law in the Second Reconstruction: Julius Chambers, the NAACP Legal Defense Fund, and Title VII.* Chapel Hill: University of North Carolina.

Tushnet, Mark V. 2005. *The NAACP's Legal Strategy against Segregated Education, 1925–1950.* Chapel Hill: University of North Carolina Press.

National Congress of American Indians

The National Congress of American Indians (NCAI) is the largest intertribal organization in the United States. Its membership is composed of American Indian tribal leaders from federally recognized tribes across the United States. Because of this diversity in membership, it is generally considered to be a politically moderate organization. Since its founding in 1944, NCAI has focused its efforts on preserving and protecting tribal sovereignty by bringing tribal leaders together to work toward this common goal. It strives to educate tribal leaders on federal policy that could impact tribal communities, and it serves as an international meeting place for tribal leaders.

NCAI was founded primarily by politically active American Indians who worked at the Bureau of Indian Affairs (BIA). They were concerned about the political tide in Washington at the time, as some congressmen were pushing for tribal termination. The U.S. Congress passed HR 108 in 1954, which over the next decade caused the termination of relations between the federal government and over 100 tribes. Proponents of the bill were hoping for a complete tribal dissolution and the assimilation of tribal people into mainstream society.

D'Arcy McNickle (Flathead Indian), Archie Phinney (Nez Perce), and Charles E. J. Heacock (Rosebud Sioux) were the original architects of the National Indian Education Association (NIEA). At first, Phinney wanted to create an Indian organization within the BIA, but McNickle believed it needed to operate independently from the BIA. He stressed that it was important to be seen as independent from the BIA and those policies. The organization began with 100 members from forty-two different American Indian tribes. These members were well educated and knew how to operate in tribal society as well as mainstream U.S. society. Most members were drawn from the American Indian elite: professionals, U.S. veterans, and boarding school graduates.

An early challenge for the young organization was finding a way to bring tribal people together in which discussions did not break down based on tribal or regional factionalism. It was successful in that it effectively demonstrated the power of working together on tribal sovereignty issues when dealing with the federal government. While many pan-Indian organizations have advocated for rights based on American Indians as an ethnic group within the larger U.S. society, NCAI has always recognized the sovereign political status of tribal governments and the unique cultural and emotional identities of their members.

Critics say NCAI has been too moderate in its politics by not advocating a more militant approach to social and political change. NCAI proponents argue that this was part of the plan. Members wanted to stay away from association with U.S. ethnic civil rights group tactics. By imitating tactics, it might have convoluted the differences between ethnicity and sovereign nation status. Tribal rights are rooted in sovereignty and the tribes' inherent rights to govern themselves on their homelands. Other groups were advocating for a different status in U.S. society. NCAI was concerned with protecting the sovereignty of tribal nations, not with changing Native people's position within the U.S. society.

Events of the day could not be completely ignored. It is believed that "Red Power" was first used by Vine Deloria, Jr. during the 1966 NCAI convention. This concept helped to spur an American Indian ethnic group movement, eventually leading Indians to demand equal treatment as U.S. citizens. NCAI supported these goals but remained true to its original mission of protecting tribal sovereignty.

The NCAI Policy Research Center opened in 2003, focusing on policy issues that directly affect tribal communities across the country. NCAI continues its work on strengthening tribal governance and the right to self determination through educating Indians and non-Indians about Native rights and tribal sovereignty. It is concerned with improving public safety in Indian Country and securing safe and affordable housing for Native Americans. It is addressing the health issues of tribal members, particularly the high rates of diabetes, and improving health care delivery in Native communities. It supports tribal economic development opportunities, including gaming, and the role of tribal members in steering community development.

Continuing from its highly educated membership roots, the NCAI remains a strong supporter of promoting educational opportunities for Native youth. It continues to address issues of Native religious freedoms and the protection of traditional cultural resources. A more recent policy issue has been advocating increased roles for tribes in the discussion of natural resources and the environment.

NCAI has been a supporter of young people interested in tribal government and leadership. The Miss NCAI Scholarship Pageant began in 1968, in which young women served as goodwill ambassadors in the American Indian community. This program was expanded to include young men in 2006 and was retitled the "NCAI Youth Ambassador Leadership Program." The NCAI Youth Commission was designed to introduce young people to government and leadership issues.

NCAI has proved to be a political powerhouse in Washington, D.C., and serves as the premiere national government organization. Today, it has 250 member tribes and is an extremely powerful lobbying organization on Capitol Hill. NCAI is currently raising capital to build an Embassy of Tribal Nations, which would solidify the international standing of American Indian tribes. As an intertribal, nonpartisan organization, NCAI remains one of the largest and most powerful Indian organizations in the United States. It influences decision making on federal policy regarding American Indians, and it affects how tribes implement programs and plan for their futures.

Elizabeth Arbuckle Wabindato

See Appendix B

See also Bureau of Indian Affairs; Deloria, Vine, Jr.; National Indian Youth Council; Native American Education; Native Americans; Pan-Indianism; Red Power

Further Readings

Cornell, Stephen. 1988. *The Return of the Native: American Indian Political Resurgence.* New York: Oxford University Press.

Cowger, Thomas W. 1999. *The National Congress of American Indians.* Lincoln: University of Nebraska Press.

Deloria, Vine, Jr. and Clifford M. Lytle. 1984. *The Nations Within: The Past and Future of American Indian Sovereignty.* Austin: University of Texas Press.

Nagel, Joane. 1997. *American Indian Ethnic Renewal: Red Power and the Resurgence of Identity and Culture.* New York: Oxford University Press.

Web Sites

National Congress of American Indians: http://www.ncai.org

NATIONAL COUNCIL OF LA RAZA

Recognized as the largest national organization in the United States advocating for Latinos and civil rights, the National Council of La Raza (NCLR) works with community-based organizations to improve opportunities for Latinos. The NCLR touches millions of Latinos annually throughout the United States and Puerto Rico, addressing quality-of-life influences such as poverty, discrimination, education, health, and housing.

Origins

The impetus for the NCLR was a small group of Mexican Americans in Washington, D.C., who in 1963 organized as the National Organization for Mexican American Services (NOMAS). This group of advocates, which included a young man from Texas named Raul Yzaguirre, approached the Ford Foundation for funding to establish an organization that could provide technical assistance and organizational structure for the Mexican American community. Although interested, the Ford Foundation confessed to a lack of understanding of the Mexican American community and its needs.

In 1966, the Ford Foundation hired three Mexican American leaders, Dr. Julian Samora, Dr. Ernesto Galarza, and Herman Gallegos, to travel the Southwest and identify how the foundation could help Mexican Americans. Within 9 months after the three consultants returned from their research travels, with a recommendation to establish an organization, the Southwest Council of La Raza (SWCLR) was incorporated in Arizona in 1968. Herman Gallegos was installed as the founding executive director, and Maclovio Barranza was the first chairperson of the board. In December 1972, SWCLR became a national organization and changed its name to National Council of La Raza; in 1973, the organization moved its headquarters to Washington, D.C.

The term *la raza* was introduced by a Mexican scholar and visionary by the name of José Vasconcelos, in his book *La Raza Cosmica*. Although the term has been mistranslated to mean "the race," a more accurate translation is "the people." Vasconcelos referred to the "cosmic people," those who share a mixture of races, cultures, and religions inherent in Latin America. *La raza* is an inclusive concept that is conducive to interaction and gathering of all peoples.

In 1974, Raul Yzaguirre became the national director for NCLR, marking the beginning of an enduring and stable leadership that would project the organization to the strong national status it holds today. Yzaguirre led the organization for 30 years, during which time the organization was influential in providing the Latino perspective on countless legislative issues. Upon Yzaguirre's retirement in 2004, Janet Murguía stepped into the role of president and chief executive officer of NCLR. With a degree in law and experience as former deputy director of legislative affairs and senior White House liaison to the Congress, Murguía was well prepared to be the official spokesperson for the NCLR and to lead the organization into the next era.

NCLR TODAY: Mission and Programs

NCLR is a nonprofit, private, nonpartisan advocacy organization with offices in Atlanta; Chicago; Los Angeles; New York; Phoenix; Sacramento; San Antonio; and San Juan, Puerto Rico. The organization is governed by a board that has been constructed for success, including representation from all Latino subgroups and all geographical regions of the United States, with approximate division by gender. According to its charter, 12 of the board members must represent affiliates. The organization is also guided by a corporate board of advisers (CBA), which is made up of senior executives from twenty-five major corporations. Originally conceived to address the needs of the Mexican American community, the board took a major step in 1979 to expand the scope of representation and assistance to all Latino subgroups.

The mission of NCLR is built on these cornerstones: capacity-building assistance to community-based organizations and public policy analysis and advocacy. Through these two complementary approaches, NCLR focuses on eight areas of concern for the Latino community, including advocacy and electoral empowerment, civil rights and justice, community and family wealth building, education, employment and economic opportunities, farmworkers, health and family support, and immigration.

In the area of advocacy and electoral empowerment, NCLR has been instrumental in providing input on policies regarding voting rights and racial profiling and the implementation of "LEAP to Action," a voter mobilization program. Latino homeownership has been increased and social security reform addressed through efforts in the community and family wealth-building programs.

Through the education arm of the strategic plan, NCLR sponsors Americorps, a program that provides educational and workforce development to increase the number of Latinos in national services; KIDS COUNT, a program in Puerto Rico that addresses the information gap concerning child-related issues such as poverty, education, health, abuse and neglect, adolescent drinking, teen pregnancy, and youth suicide and homicide; and the Early Care and Education (ECE) Program, focused on increasing the number of Latino children who are ready to enter school.

In the area of health and family support, NCLR has been active on issues of access to health insurance and language access and has partnered with California State University, Long Beach, to sponsor the NCLR/CSULB Center for Latino Community Health, Evaluation, and Leadership Training, a center that promotes health and disease prevention, provides technical assistance, information, and research, and works to increase the number of Latinos in the health professions.

Immigration and farmworkers pose many opportunities for NCLR, including being a force in policy debates regarding civil liberties after the attacks on September 11, 2001, and the DREAM Act, which proposes in-state college tuition for immigrant students, migrant education, and general immigration reform.

The NCLR Policy Analysis Center, in Washington, D.C., which serves as the hub for policy analysis and applied research, is recognized for its capacity to provide analysis and advocacy expertise. Covering a broad range of issues, work done at the center often leads to policy-oriented documents, fact sheets, training materials, congressional testimony, statistical analysis, selected speeches, and research papers, with a reputation for being a credible source of information and facts. NCLR also publishes a quarterly magazine, *Agenda*.

Advocating for Latinos in public policy issues relating to topics such as immigration, affordable housing, education, health, and tax reform, NCLR is the premier voice in Washington, D.C., and is often called on to testify in congressional hearings to provide a Latino perspective. NCLR played a major role in shaping the Immigration Reform and Control Act of 1986 (IRCA) and is credited with influencing the North American Free Trade Agreement (NAFTA).

Alma Alvarez-Smith

See Appendix B
See also La Raza; Mexican Americans; Minority Rights; Social Inequality; Voting Rights

Further Readings

Alvarez-Smith, Alma. 2004. "National Council of La Raza (NCLR)." Pp. 582–584 in *Encyclopedia of Latino Popular Culture,* edited by C. C., Candelaria, A. J. Aldama, and P. J. Garcia. Westport, CT: Greenwood Press.

Magaña, Lisa. 2005. *Mexican Americans and the Politics of Diversity.* Tucson: University of Arizona Press.

Web Sites

National Council of La Raza: http://www.nclr.org

NATIONAL INDIAN YOUTH COUNCIL

The National Indian Youth Council (NIYC) began as a militant American Indian civil rights organization in 1961 but has since evolved into a nonprofit charitable organization that focuses on global and regional indigenous issues.

NIYC was founded in Gallup, New Mexico, by college students and recent graduates, partly in reaction to young Indians feeling excluded from decision making at the American Indian Charter Convention in Chicago (AICCC) in 1961. Delegates attending AICCC created a Declaration of Purpose to present to President John F. Kennedy urging that he stop the federal policy of tribal terminations. The AICCC discussions were dominated by older, long-term tribal and urban Indian leaders, many currently affiliated with the National Congress of American Indians (NCAI).

After feeling shut out at AICCC, some young, well-educated, confident, defiant, and mostly urban American Indians formed their own organization, the NIYC. It was founded by ten youth from nine different tribes. Leaders Clyde Warrior (Ponca), Melvin Thom (Paiute), and Herbert Blatchford (Navajo) early on envisioned NIYC as starting a Red Power movement, with individuals who were grounded in their Indian heritage but still able to work within the White culture and education system. They saw themselves as remnants of a traditional warrior society, which fought any potential threat to the tribes. They were adamant their group would never allow political climbing or become complacent. Unlike NCAI, the NIYC was developed to represent young American Indian people, not tribes.

Melvin Thom coined the slogan "For a Greater Indian America," which rejected the values and capitalism of mainstream U.S. society. Clyde Warrior coined the term "Uncle Tomahawks" to describe tribal leaders of the day, whom he saw as too closely affiliated with the Bureau of Indian Affairs (BIA). NIYC leaders patterned their attitudes and organization after civil rights organizations of the day. NIYC had a confrontational style in their challenges of current tribal individuals and institutions designed to serve Indians. The well-educated members believed they could awaken an American Indian ethnic consciousness through efforts patterned after those of the Black Civil Rights Movement.

NIYC leaders found their first national target in the Pacific Northwest. Tribes in the state of Washington were fighting for the right to exercise fishing treaty rights. In the early 1960s, NIYC supported these efforts by staging "fish-ins," patterned after the effective Black civil rights "sit-ins." NIYC members watched from the shore as Washington tribal members fished. Eventually, thousands of Native Americans from over fifty different tribes around the country came to support treaty rights. There were arrests, protests at the state capitol building, marches, and canoe parades. NIYC member Hank Adams (Assiniboine and Sioux) was an instrumental leader during the fish-ins.

The fish-ins were designed to gain media and political attention for treaty rights violations. The most famous arrest came in 1964, on Puyallup River, when actor Marlon Brando was arrested for fishing without a state permit. The treaty rights issue was eventually settled in what came to be known as the Boldt decision. Federal Judge George Boldt ruled in 1974 that the treaties were valid and that the tribes were entitled to half of the salmon in Western Washington.

NIYC was one of eight American Indian organizations that participated in the Trail of Broken Treaties caravan in the fall of 1972. The caravan was designed to raise awareness of American Indian issues, including poor living conditions and treaty rights violations. The caravan began on the West Coast, traveling across country until it reached Washington, D.C. After lodging arrangements there turned out to be unsuitable for the protesters, some participants took over the BIA building. In a misguided attempt to protest the oppressive tactics of the BIA, several protesters vandalized the offices and destroyed important documents.

During the 1970s, NIYC expanded its scope to include a lawsuit-driven agenda in the fight to protect American Indian communities, particularly those trying to preserve their environments from exploitation. Efforts by the NIYC and others led to the halting of coal gasification plants worth $6 billion on the Navajo reservation.

Today, NIYC is a 501(c)(3) nonprofit organization and is overseen by a seven-member board of directors. It relies heavily on federal funding sources to maintain its operating costs and programs. The U.S. Department of Labor (DOL) is the primary funder, but private donations and grants supplement the NIYC budget as well. With DOL funds, NIYC operates a job training and placement program for off-reservation American Indians in the New Mexico cities of Albuquerque, Farmington, and Gallup.

As a nonpartisan organization, NIYC advocates increasing American Indian political participation in the U.S. political system. It holds voter registration drives in Native American communities and conducts its own political behavior poll. It has published an Indian Elections Directory and serves as a national resource for Indian political data. It has also filed lawsuits regarding unfair voting practices. Other domestic initiatives include litigation promoting the protection of treaty rights and sacred Native sites and efforts to educate the public about Native American concerns.

The international focus of NIYC is on raising awareness of problems faced by indigenous people in the Western Hemisphere. NIYC has nongovernmental organization (NGO) consultative status with the United Nations.

Elizabeth Arbuckle Wabindato

See Appendix B

See also American Indian Movement; Bureau of Indian Affairs; National Congress of American Indians; Native Americans; Pan-Indianism; Red Power; Trail of Broken Treaties

Further Readings

Shreve, Bradley Glenn. 2006. "Up against Giants: The National Indian Youth Council, the Navajo Nation, and Coal Gasification, 1974–1977." *American Indian Culture and Research Journal* 30(2): 17–34.

Steiner, Stan. 1968. *The New Indians.* New York: Dell.

Web Sites

National Indian Youth Council: http://www.niyc-alb.org

NATIONAL ORIGINS SYSTEM

The U.S. Immigration Act of 1924, which launched what has come to be known as the National Origins System, was the apex of a restrictionist movement 3 decades in the making. Also known as the Johnson-Reed Act, after its congressional sponsors, the National Origins Act replaced a hastily passed emergency immigration bill in 1921 that served as a stop-gap measure to an anticipated massive immigration from Europe following World War I. This emergency bill limited the number of immigrants to 3% of the foreign-born population of a given nationality resident in the United States based on the 1910 census. Viewed as insufficient in stemming the immigrant tide and as discriminatory toward the U.S. native-born population, the 1924 National Origins Act addressed these perceived deficiencies. Using the 1890 census, the bill restricted the number of entrants to 2% of the U.S. native-born White population as determined by their national origins—a nebulous concept that required a series of adjustments.

Historical Development

While efforts to restrict immigration to the United States extend to the 1830s, wholesale efforts to limit admissions did not begin until the latter part of the 19th century. Early efforts sought to exclude "undesirables"—such as convicts, sexual deviants, and the mentally ill—from the larger immigrant pool. As the flow of immigrants shifted from northern and western Europe to southern and eastern Europe, calls for immigration restrictions emerged. Seen largely as inferior to their northern and western European cousins, the often swarthier, olive-skinned newcomers (such as Slavs, Italians, and Jews) were of concern especially to the adherents of the newly emerging area of pseudoscientific inquiry known as *eugenics.* Concerns about their "poor racial stock" and the evils that could result by allowing them into the United States were voiced by Immigration Restriction League founder Prescott Hall, as well as by members of the American Breeders Association and the Eugenics Record Office, among others.

Opposition to immigration from southern and eastern Europe was heightened by economic recession, labor unrest, anti-Catholic sentiment, and events surrounding World War I. Fears that southern and eastern Europeans were unassimilable were intensified by persistent ties to the "old world" among even the earliest immigrant groups during World War I.

With the restrictionist sentiment building, efforts to restrict immigration ensued. Indeed, it became the main mission of the Immigration Restriction League. Formed in 1894 by Harvard graduates, the League had its political allies, including Senator Henry Cabot Lodge (later a member of the influential Dillingham Commission), who in 1896 introduced an immigration bill requiring all immigrants to read forty words in any language as a condition for entry. Although the bill passed Congress, it was vetoed by President Grover Cleveland in 1897 on the grounds that it contradicted traditional American values. This pattern was repeated three times—vetoed by President Taft and then by President Wilson (1915 and 1917). Yet Congress was able to successfully override Wilson's 1917 veto, making literacy requirements another provision of U.S. immigration law. Similarly, legislation containing quota restrictions was introduced over several legislative sessions before achieving success in 1921 and 1924.

Key Provisions

Writing shortly after passage of the 1924 National Origins Act, New York University sociology professor Henry Pratt Fairchild provided a summary of the key provisions of this law. The act specified that for 3 fiscal years, beginning July 1, 1924, immigration to the United States would be limited by quotas of 2% of the foreign-born individuals of each nationality resident in the United States as determined by the census of 1890. After July 1, 1927, the total quota was fixed at 150,000 annually, to be distributed among the different quota nationalities in the proportions according to the number of the original nationality as counted in the census of 1920. Determining national origin and national stock was left to a quota board under the jurisdictions of the secretaries of state, commerce, and labor, assisted by the U.S. Census Bureau.

The Immigration Act of 1924 also marked the beginning of the end for Ellis Island, which created American consular offices abroad to issue foreign visas. One of the negative consequences of the hastily passed immigration bill of 1921 and its assignment of quotas was that immigrants would make their passage across the Atlantic only to be denied entry into the United States because a particular quota had been filled. The creation of the visa system in the 1924 act and the assigning of counting responsibilities to the foreign consular office prevented such tragedies.

Consequences of the National Origins Act

The goal of the National Origins Act was to control both the quantity and quality of U.S. immigrants in an effort to prevent further erosion of the ethnic composition of U.S. society. The law accomplished this goal using three mechanisms: capping the overall number of immigrants allowed into the United States in a given month and year; favoring immigrants from certain countries; and screening out otherwise qualified immigrants as unsuitable to the United States during the visa screening process. The sorting mechanism heavily favored northern and western European countries. The temporary formula of 2% of the foreign-born of each nationality in the 1890 census gave 85% of the quotas to northern and western European nations. The national origins system fully implemented in 1929 continued the trend of both overall restriction and nation bias. Indeed, the act virtually halted all immigration from southern and eastern Europe. Thus, European immigration dropped from more than 800,000 in 1921 to less than 150,000 by the end of the decade.

In addition to controlling the volume of immigration from Europe, the National Origins Act also allowed a mechanism for selection of immigrants as well. In its creation of consular offices abroad, the act provided a frontline screening mechanism for selecting out those deemed unsuitable for the United States.

Lingering Effects of the National Origins Act

The National Origins Act racialized the world and its inhabitants. While the act differentiated Europeans according to nationality and then ranked them along a hierarchy of desirability, the very act of their inclusion for immigration conferred upon them a designation of assimilability and the right to U.S. citizenship. Given that the U.S. Supreme Court had already legally codified citizenship along two racial lines (White and Black), all Europeans—whether from northern, western, southern, or eastern Europe—were thusly categorized as White. In the act's delineation of groups ineligible for citizenship, these groups were placed into the non-White category and their immigration restricted.

The National Origins Act specified that quotas be based on nationalities in proportion to the original nationality of the White population of the United States in 1920. Non-European peoples residing in the country were omitted from the population universe governing the quotas, including (a) all Blacks and mulattoes; (b) residents of groups deemed ineligible for citizenship, including Chinese, Japanese, and South Asians; and (c) populations of Hawai'i, Puerto Rico, and Alaska. In effect, the National Origins System effectively ignored and indeed excluded all non-White, non-European peoples from the future vision of the United States.

In these designations and omissions, the act created variable ethnicities, while at the same time affixing a racial category of White onto European immigrants. For those not White, the law fixed both racial and ethnic designations. To be Asian, for example, is to occupy both the same racial and ethnic category along with the broader categories of "non-White" and "nonassimilable."

Nevertheless, American citizens, including those falling outside the official definition of "American" as conceptualized by the quota board, already had a long and established presence in the United States. Today, the same groups excluded by the Quota Board in the 1920s continue to occupy the second-class status prescribed for them in the National Origins Act. Racial and ethnic categories remain nebulously defined along a continuum between White and Black, with White remaining a fairly fixed and protected category, the benefits conferred by the designation going largely unacknowledged. The significant role the National Origins Act played in demarcating this color line also goes largely unacknowledged.

Karen Manges Douglas

See also Assimilation; Citizenship; Dillingham Flaw; Immigration, Economic Impact of; Immigration, U.S.; Immigration and Race; McCarran-Walter Act of 1952; Muslim Americans; Racialization; Xenophobia

Further Readings

Easterlin, Richard A., David Ward, William S. Bernard, and Reed Ueda. 1982. *Immigration: Dimensions of Ethnicity.* Cambridge, MA: Belknap Press of Harvard University Press.

Fairchild, Henry Pratt. 1917. "The Literacy Test and Its Making." *Quarterly Journal of Economics* 31:447–460.

Fairchild, Henry Pratt. 1924. "The Immigration Law of 1924." *Quarterly Journal of Economics* 38:653–665.

Hall, Prescott F. 1912. "Book Review of *The Immigration Problem* by Jeremiah W. Jencks and W. Jett Lauck." *American Economic Review* 2:675–667.

Hall, Prescott F. 1913. "The Recent History of Immigration and Immigration Restriction." *Journal of Political Economy* 21:735–751.

Jones, Maldwyn Allen. 1992. *American Immigration.* 2nd ed. Chicago, IL: University of Chicago Press.

Ngai, Mae M. 1999. "The Architecture of Race in American Immigration Law: A Reexamination of the Immigration Act of 1924." *Journal of American History* 86:167–192.

NATIONAL RAINBOW COALITION

Introduced in 1984 by social and political activist Jesse Jackson, the National Rainbow Coalition (NRC), based in Washington, D.C., was established as "a progressive, Black-led, multiracial, anti-corporate, and anti-imperialist movement that took an electoral form." As such, it became an informal subgroup within the Democratic Party that served as the vehicle of Jackson's 1984 and 1988 voter registration drives and presidential bids.

In 1983, during a climate of disenfranchisement of the politically underrepresented in the United States, Jackson formed a "rainbow coalition" to encourage millions of potential voters to register for and participate in the upcoming 1984 presidential election. As a result, he formally created the National Rainbow Coalition, which reached out to Blacks, Hispanics, Asian Americans, American Indians, homosexuals, poor Whites, females, those with family-run farms, and those living in poverty. The effort was both a success and a failure.

Despite the acquisition of parity for minorities gained with the passage of the Voting Rights Act of 1965, during that time there existed only a handful of organizations that represented the national political interests of Blacks, among them the National Association for the Advancement of Colored People (NAACP) and the Congressional Black Caucus. In 1972, the meeting of the National Black Political Convention discussed the formation of an independent political party; also during that year, Black congresswoman Shirley Chisholm ran for president. By 1984, a group of political leaders called the "Black Leadership Family" were again considering the pros and cons of affirming another Black presidential candidate. The advantages included national exposure to Black issues and encouraging voter registration in order to build a voting bloc within the Democratic Party; the main disadvantage was seen as the potential splintering of the party down racial lines. Present at the convention was Jackson, who made it clear that he was considering running with or without the group's endorsement; later that year, Jackson announced his candidacy on national television.

As an instrument for voter registration, Jackson's 1984 efforts were successful in accounting for 1 million new Black voters. In fact, during the primary elections, the increased voter turnout was considerable; the most notable was in New York State, where the Black vote increased by over 125%. Even more impressive, during his 1988 campaign, Jackson's candidacy encouraged an additional 2 million Blacks to register.

What proved most daunting to Jackson was the challenge of actually building a national "rainbow" coalition. First, even though he had recently gained prominence by securing the release of a U.S. serviceman from a Syrian jail as a "civilian diplomat," Jackson's lack of national alliances and political experience led some political leaders and the media not to take his candidacy seriously. Second, while the rhetoric of creating a rainbow coalition sounded plausible, Jackson found that his potential constituents were often competing for national attention and for the same scarce social, political, and economic resources. Issues such as housing, poverty, unemployment, wages, bilingual education, desegregation, immigration, affirmative action, welfare, and care for the elderly, when positioned on a race-neutral platform, actually weakened, rather than strengthened, the possibility of coalition building. Moreover, Jackson alienated two groups that might otherwise have joined his coalition: the Jewish community (whom he referred to as "Hymies" in a newspaper interview) and women's groups (who disagreed sharply with his 1972 antiabortion stance). Finally, Jackson may have underestimated the pervasive racism in the United States. In a 1988 poll, 25% of Whites said that they would automatically vote against any Black candidate; and while 85% and 95% of Blacks voted for Jackson in the 1984 and 1988 primaries, respectively, only 10% and 20% of Whites voted for him during those same two elections.

After the 1984 election, Jackson sought to create NRC affiliates throughout the United States; in 1986, he formally incorporated the organization, but as a result of his dictatorial management style and lack of follow-through, nothing came of it. After the 1988 election, Jackson returned to Chicago and merged the NRC with his previous civil rights organization, Operation PUSH (People United to Serve Humanity), forming the Rainbow/PUSH Coalition in 1989.

Glynis Christine

See Appendix B

See also African Americans; Jackson, Jesse, Sr.; Multicultural Social Movements; Operation PUSH; Race; Voting Rights

Further Readings

Smith, Robert Charles. 1996. *We Have No Leaders: African Americans in the Post Civil Rights Era.* Albany: State University of New York Press.

Walters, Ronald W. and Robert Charles Smith. 1999. *African American Leadership.* Albany: State University of New York Press.

Weir, Margaret. 1998. *The Social Divide: Political Parties and the Future of Activist Government.* New York: Brookings Institution Press.

Wilson, William J. 1999. *The Bridge over the Racial Divide: Rising Inequality and Coalition Politics.* Berkeley: University of California Press.

NATIONAL URBAN LEAGUE

The National Urban League, which traces its roots back to 1910, is the oldest national voluntary organization that seeks to empower African Americans socially and economically. Throughout its long history, its main focus has been on enabling economic self-reliance, parity, power, and civil rights of African Americans through series of community-based movements. This entry recounts its history and activities.

History

A series of events at the turn of the 20th century prompted rapid change for United States citizens, particularly for African Americans. Both the Emancipation Proclamation of 1863, which abolished slavery after the Civil War, and the *Plessy v. Ferguson* Supreme Court decision in 1896, which legally recognized segregation, prompted African Americans to move northward in hopes of finding robust economic opportunities. This period of the Great Migration dramatically shifted the African American population from the southern to northeastern and midwestern United States. Industrial cities like Chicago, Detroit, New York, and Cleveland gained a large African American population in just a few decades.

This massive transition was largely assisted by grassroots organizations and movements across many metropolitan areas. The Committee for the Improvement of Industrial Conditions Among Negroes in New York (established in 1906), the National League for the Protection of Colored Women (established in 1905), and the Committee on Urban Conditions Among Negroes merged to form the Urban League in 1910. The Urban League was renamed the National League on Urban Conditions Among Negroes, shortened to the National Urban League in 1920, by which it continues to be known today.

The National Urban League is the nation's oldest and largest community-based organization devoted to empowering African Americans to enter the economic and social mainstream. Led by George Edmund Haynes, the first African American to earn a PhD from Columbia University, and Ruth Standish Baldwin, a White New York City philanthropist, the Urban League was founded to provide social services, specifically housing and career opportunities, for thousands of African Americans who migrated north with hopes of building better lives for themselves and their families.

For the following century, the National Urban League conducted campaigns to enhance education and employment for African Americans, organized marches to protest against racial discrimination, actively participated in the Civil Rights Movement, and initiated alternative educational systems for dropout students. During the 1950s and 1960s, the Urban League, along with the National Association for the Advancement of Colored People (NAACP) and the Congress of Racial Equality (CORE), collaborated on many grassroots movements with the Southern Christian Leadership Conference (SCLC) and the Student Nonviolent Coordinating Committee (SNCC).

Today, the National Urban League, headquartered in New York City, spearheads the nonpartisan efforts of its local affiliates and aims to empower African Americans toward economic self-reliance, parity, power, and civil rights. There are over 100 local affiliates of the National Urban League located in thirty-five states and the District of Columbia. Nationally, more than 2 million people receive direct services through programs, advocacy, and research.

Activities

To implement the mission of the organization, the Urban League strives to tailor its activities to local needs in five areas: education, health, civic engagement, civil rights, and economic empowerment. The emphasis on education includes youth empowerment through college scholarships, early childhood literacy, and afterschool programs. Health issues are focused on eliminating health disparities by healthy food consumption, encouraging physical fitness, and access to affordable health care for all. Civic engagement encourages an active role in public policy and leadership in the communities through full participation as citizens and voters, as well as active community service. The area of civil rights is intended to promote and ensure equal participation in political, economic, social, educational, and cultural aspects of American life. The Urban League also advocates economic empowerment achieved through job training, well-paying jobs, homeownership, entrepreneurship, and wealth accumulation.

To monitor the progress of their mission, the National Urban League has produced annual reports since 1973. Using a measure called the "Equality Index," the reports compare the disparity between African Americans and Whites in the aforementioned five areas, in addition to the overall evaluation, referred to as "Total Equality." As of the 2007 report, the economic status of African Americans was 57% of that of Whites, while, in 2006, civic engagement was 5% higher for African Americans than it was for Whites. Focusing on African American men, the report stated that they are more than twice as likely to be unemployed, and those who work earn 75% of the annual income of White males. They are nearly seven times more likely to be incarcerated, and their average jail sentences are 10 months longer than those of White men. In addition, young Black males between the ages of 15 and 34 years are nine times more likely to die of homicide than their White counterparts and nearly seven times as likely to suffer from HIV/AIDS.

The National Urban League also has created auxiliary organizations in order to enhance specific areas that are considered deficient in the African American community. National Urban League Young Professionals

(NULYP) was created to develop leadership for the movement through corporate, social, and community activism by the younger generation (ages 21 to 40). The National Council of Urban League Guilds promotes volunteerism through supporting various programs and activities in the National Urban League.

Kiljoong Kim and Christina Diaz

See also Congress of Racial Equality (CORE); Emancipation Proclamation; National Association for the Advancement of Colored People (NAACP); *Plessy v. Ferguson;* Southern Christian Leadership Conference (SCLC); Student Nonviolent Coordinating Committee (SNCC)

Further Readings

Lubka, Lewis. 1973. *Toward Effective Citizen Participation in Urban Renewal: A Final Report of the National Urban League Urban Renewal Demonstration Project.* New York: National Urban League.

Moore, Jesse Thomas. 1981. *A Search for Equality: The National Urban League, 1910–1961.* College Park, PA: Pennsylvania State Press.

Parris, Guichard, ed. 1950. *National Urban League 40th Anniversary Year Book.* New York: National Urban League.

Weiss, Nancy. 1974. *National Urban League, 1910–40.* New York: Oxford University Press.

NATION OF ISLAM

The Nation of Islam (the Nation) had a very humble beginning but grew into an enormous organization of African Americans, devoted in large part to reconstituting their pride and self-sufficiency. This entry begins with the origin of the Nation, highlights relevant Nation philosophy, and concludes with a discussion of leadership in the Nation.

Origins of the Nation

Nation of Islam historians state that Master Wallace Fard Muhammad began teaching about Islam to Black Americans in 1931. The Nation's founder has been variously referred to as W. D. Fard, Mr. Muhammad, the son of man, the great Mahdi, and Master Fard Muhammad—a name more commonly used by the Nation today. His title, *master,* as explained by the Nation, refers to his ability to rehabilitate Black men and women from the wretched and debilitating experience of slavery. Black Americans, according to Mr. Muhammad, had to be reprogrammed about their life, their place in the world, and their place in the universe.

Mr. Muhammad's Islam included the study of biological science, including genetics, mathematics, and actual/factual measurements of the earth, in addition to traditional Islam. Mr. Muhammad's knowledge became a testament of who he was and why he came to America, according to the Nation. On the last page of every issue of the *Final Call,* under "What the Muslims Believe," No. 12 states that they believe that Master Fard Muhammad is God in Person and is the "Messiah" of the Christians and the "Mahdi" of the Muslims. The Nation proclaims that Mr. Muhammad is indeed the one prophesied in the *Holy Bible* and *Holy Koran.*

Basic Teachings

Mr. Muhammad instructed Elijah on how to use this knowledge to free the Black man's mind from mental and spiritual death and from the bondage of slavery and White society. Therefore, not only did Mr. Muhammad demonstrate that he possessed knowledge that identified him as superior; he also used his knowledge to bring about the liberation of Black Americans. The Nation considered these works as clear proof that Mr. Muhammad was the Mahdi or Messiah of the Black Americans. In many respects, this brand of Islam was the combination of Black spirituality and liberation theology that entailed powerful philosophical, spiritual, and psychological mechanisms combined with social, political, and economic thrust. Converts learned about traditional Islam, to live for the here and now, self-defense skills, knowledge of God and the devil, and cooperative economics.

The Nation reversed the negative tenets of White racism. The Nation claimed that the Black man is God and the White man is the devil. The Nation proposed that the United States give territory to Black Americans. The Nation challenged the racial identification and classification of Black Americans. These teachings attracted many African Americans and demanded that White America pay attention.

Furthermore, Nation of Islam historians contend that the Nation is not an offshoot of its predecessors, Noble Drew Ali's Moorish Science Temple or the Honorable Marcus Garvey's Universal Negro Improvement Association (UNIA). The significance of Islam in American history has long been underrated, a not uncommon dilemma. The faith of Islam persisted in

African American culture, since many Africans brought Islam with them to the New World and remained faithful to its teachings. Islam has emerged among Africans in America again and again, yet never more permanently and significantly than in the Nation of Islam.

New Leaders

Over the course of the 20th century, the Nation of Islam enjoyed the leadership of a number of eloquent and visionary people, among them Elijah Muhammad, his wife Clara, and his son Warith Deen; Malcolm X; and Louis Farrakhan, who remains in charge of the organization.

Mother Clara

Some writers and historians have claimed that it was Clara Muhammad, wife of the Honorable Elijah Muhammad, who first heard Mr. Muhammad's teachings and told her husband about them. Ajile' Rahman's dissertation "She Stood by His Side and at Times in His Stead: The Life and Legacy of Sister Clara Muhammad First Lady of the Nation of Islam" examines the role and responsibilities of Mother Clara Muhammad during the Nation's formative years. Rahman concludes that her role was in many instances so pivotal that when the Honorable Elijah Muhammad was incarcerated, Clara Muhammad was responsible for maintaining the Nation's programs, its school, and its membership.

Clara Muhammad's role in the Nation was very important and crucial to its initial development and maintenance. Her initial responsibility was to teach and train the women their roles and responsibilities in a class called "Muslim Girl Training and General Civilization Class" (MGT-GCC). She also wrote *Muhammad Speaks,* articles about the role of the woman in Islam. Mr. Muhammad gave clear instructions for womanhood training to the Honorable Elijah Muhammad and to Mother Clara Muhammad, as she is affectionately called today.

The Honorable Elijah Muhammad

Mr. Muhammad began teaching the man then called Elijah Poole in 1931, one-on-one. Elijah Poole's name was changed as his study increased, from Poole to Karriem to Muhammad. In 1934, the elder Mr. Muhammad disappeared, approximately 3½ years into the teaching of his successor. From 1934 to 1975, Elijah Muhammad led the Nation, and, eventually, he was given the title "Messenger of Allah." The Nation developed businesses, purchased a home mosque, began schools, and operated a printing press that produced the *Muhammad Speaks Newspaper.* The Nation experienced its largest period of growth from 1955 to 1965, a phenomenon that some historians attribute in part to the fiery national spokesman Malcolm X.

Malcolm X's assassination in 1965 marked a significant turning point for the Nation's growth. Members in the Nation were accused of assassinating Malcolm X, and the Nation received harsh criticism from the Black community, which had developed a strong association with the Nation and Malcolm. The Nation withstood this trial and continued to grow. By this time, the Nation was more than a "cult" with a few members; it was a nationally and even internationally known entity for the advancement of Black people in America and people of color in general. The Nation took a powerful stance against White America's injustices toward Black people and was a major mover in the Civil Rights Movement.

Wallace Dean Muhammad

The Honorable Elijah Muhammad died in 1975, although Nation historians assert that he did not physically die, but departed and is with Master Fard Muhammad. Leadership of the Nation was assumed by Minister Wallace Deen Muhammad (son of the Honorable Elijah Muhammad), whose extensive studies and travels throughout the Islamic world as well as his ability to articulate the ideology of Islam qualified him to take the Nation's mantle. Heading the Nation from 1975 until 1977, Minister Wallace Muhammad did not initially change the religious and organizational tenets established by his father. Later, he began to reorganize the Nation around orthodox Islam and renamed the Nation "American Muslim Mission."

At the same time, Minister Wallace Muhammad eliminated the manhood and womanhood training and the traditional Muslim style of dress instituted by the Honorable Elijah Muhammad. He sold most of the Nation's businesses and placed the responsibility of economic development in the hands of the members. He issued a proclamation about Mr. (Fard) Muhammad's identity, proclaiming that Master Fard Muhammad was not Allah or the embodiment of God, as the elder man had taught the Honorable Elijah Muhammad. Minister Wallace Muhammad declared that the brand of Islam practiced by his father and his father's teacher was deemed incorrect and unrepresentative of Islam's true purpose and meaning. Soon, Minister Wallace

Muhammad changed his name to reflect his embrace of orthodoxy and encouraged the members to do the same. Some members left the Nation, while others stayed.

Louis Farrakhan

In 1977, Minister Louis Farrakhan left the American Muslim Mission. One year later, he began reorganizing the Nation of Islam based on the original teachings of Mr. Muhammad and the Honorable Elijah Muhammad. In 1979, Minister Farrakhan began the *Final Call* newspaper, the only Black newspaper that is distributed across the entire United States.

As Minister Farrakhan's perspectives have evolved, so has the Nation. Farrakhan is considered more mainstream than both the Honorable Elijah Muhammad and Malcolm X. Although he was strongly repudiated in the beginning, even his harshest critics acknowledge that Farrakhan is one of the most influential Black men in America and the world today. In 1995, Farrakhan called for a million Black men to march to Washington to atone for their sins to each other and the Black community. The Million Man March is the largest gathering ever recorded in the United States.

Toni Sims

See also African Americans; Back to Africa Movement; Black Nationalism; Black Power; Malcolm X; Muslim Americans; Religion

Further Readings

Diouf, Sylviane. 1998. *Servants of Allah: African Muslims Enslaved in the Americas.* New York: New York University Press.
Karenga, Maulana. 1993. *Introduction to Black Studies.* 2nd ed. San Diego, CA: University of Sankore Press.
Lincoln, C. Eric. [1961] 1994. *The Black Muslims in America.* 3rd ed. Grand Rapids, MI: Eerdmans; Trenton, NJ: Africa World Press.
Muhammad, Elijah. 1965. *Message to the Blackman in America.* Chicago, IL: Muhammad Mosque of Islam No. 2.
Muhammad, Elijah. 1993. *History of the Nation of Islam.* Atlanta, GA: Secretarius Memps.

NATIVE AMERICAN EDUCATION

Native American education is a complex and unique topic, intricately interwoven with the social, political, and historical contexts that also make Native American tribes in the United States unique ethnically and politically. Formal schools are a relatively new way to educate Native American people. Precolonized Native American nations had, over thousands of years, developed successful means of educating members of their societies—transmitting tribal worldviews, philosophies, histories, knowledge, language, values, and life skills. Education, as defined by contemporary European American culture, was brought to indigenous nations during the process of European colonization. Historically, from a Native American standpoint, schools worked against the interests of the tribal community, with a focus on eliminating distinctive cultural and linguistic traditions. It has only been within the past generation that this has changed. Native American education has paralleled and reflected the political and social realities of Native American nations as colonized people who have now reclaimed sovereign status and self-determination. Thus, in many ways, Native American education has come full circle, from being a tool for systematic cultural extermination and assimilation to a means for preserving tribal worldview histories and culture.

Education, Colonialism, and Forced Assimilation

Mission Schools

The formal "education" of Native American people in North America began soon after European contact. Its pace and intensity paralleled the drive to colonize the continent. As early as 1611, formal education began, first, with mission schools opened by French Jesuit missionaries, followed by schools established by Dominicans and the Franciscans. The Spanish Jesuits, who had pioneered the creation of mission schools since 1609, continued their efforts, particularly on the West Coast, well into the 19th century. Often, priests were supported by military troops in removing Native American children from their homes and communities for "schooling," often for extended periods of time. Later, British Protestants followed much the same course as the Catholics; during the colonial era, conversion of Native Americans to Christianity, Eurocentric civilization, and learning were seen as inseparable and imperative to the goal of supplanting indigenous culture and furthering colonial settlement.

Immediately after the Revolutionary War, the newly formed U.S. government began appropriating funds

Carlisle Indian School physical education class. *Male Native American students are shown in a physical education class at Carlisle Indian School, Carlisle, Pennsylvania (early 1900s). The goal of the Carlisle School and its founder, U.S. Army officer Richard Henry Pratt, was total assimilation of Native Americans into White culture. The boarding school system, of which Carlisle was just one example, remained in some capacity until the 1950s and 1960s and had a far-reaching negative impact on Native American societies by separating children from their families and culture for extended periods.*

Source: Library of Congress, Prints & Photographs Division, LC-USZ62-120987.

for the education of American Indians. A high premium was initially placed on the arts of diplomacy and subversion for attaining U.S. objectives, thus creating the need for assimilated Indians educated in European American language and culture. In 1819, Congress established the Civilization Fund, for the purpose of "education of the frontier tribes." This was followed by acceptance of a proposal that future treaties with American Indian nations incorporate provisions for "education." For the delivery of these programs, the federal government relied heavily on missionaries. During the reservation era, it became mandatory for children age 6 through 16 to attend the mission day schools that were overseen by government Indian agents. After the creation of the Bureau of Indian Affairs (BIA), there was a transfer from religious control to civil control of Native American education.

Manual Labor Schools

In the early 19th century, Native American educational programs continued to expand and after 1825 included a new model that involved manual labor. The first of these schools was the Choctaw Academy, established by the Methodists in 1834. The Methodist Society soon opened a similar facility in Leavenworth, Kansas, in 1839. This "academy" imposed a rigid military-style work regimen, generating the revenues necessary to support itself and profit from the students' manual labor. This was considered to be so successful by both the church and the government that the Methodists were authorized to open more facilities. The notion of forced labor as a part of Native American education took hold as a means to "develop native character," and, by 1868, there were 109 manual labor schools, with enrollments of 4,600 students.

Boarding Schools

The manual labor schools eventually developed into government-sponsored boarding schools, the most infamous being the Carlisle Indian School. Despite forbidding the use of Native American languages and the federal law banning Native religious practices, it became apparent to governmental authorities that day schools afforded students too much interaction with their families and communities, and this interfered with the goals of deculturation and assimilation. It was in this context that the boarding school model was developed. After being removed from their families and communities for an extended period of time, often years, students returned to their communities with diffused identities—neither able to reenter their original culture nor able to assimilate into White America. The boarding school system, which remained in some capacity until the 1950s and 1960s, had a far-reaching negative impact on Native American societies. Despite heavy investment in the boarding school system, the federal government was reluctant to commit the resources necessary to create a universal educational system for all Native American students in the United States. Fortunately, this lack of funding and commitment prevented Native cultures and languages from being totally obliterated during this era.

Federal and State Public Schools

By 1906, the government was reluctant to broaden the boarding school system, and many Native American children began to be diverted into public schools. The termination and relocation legislation of the 1950s saw many more children being placed in public schools both off-reservation and in urban areas, where many families were relocating. While not as overtly brutal as the mission, manual labor, and boarding schools, the public school system failed to meet the needs of Native American students. Curricula that emphasized the superiority of the dominant culture and implied the inferiority of Native American people continued to be destructive to students' identities and development.

Reports on the experiences of Native American students as recently as the 1990s indicate that many still attend public schools with Eurocentric curriculums, subtle racism, and climates that fail to promote appropriate academic and social development. These factors may contribute to the high school drop-out rate of 36%, which is the highest of any minority group within the United States. With regard to higher education, a task force found that unsupportive institutional climates, inadequate academic preparation, insufficient financial support, few role models, and unaddressed cultural influences on student adjustment were identified as major causes for disenfranchisement of Native American students.

Resistance and Reform

The self-determination era of the 1960s and 1970s proved to be extremely important from the standpoint of both federal Indian policy and Indian educational reform—allowing Native Americans to gain greater control over their school systems and educational processes.

In 1969, the Senate Subcommittee on Indian Education issued its final report on the educational status of Native American people in a report, *Indian Education: A National Tragedy, A National Challenge.* This report documented the significant failure of U.S. public education to address the needs of Native American students. This failure was attributed to the federal government's policy of assimilation through education and attempts to eradicate indigenous languages and cultures. Congressional action as a response to this report occurred in 1972, when the Indian Education Act provided a means to meet the special needs of Native American students in public schools and to establish a National Advisory Council on Indian Education to train teachers, prioritize funding, and work with tribal community colleges.

In 1969, the first Native American community college was opened, followed by eight more by 1972. Today, there are over thirty tribally controlled colleges. Tribal colleges build important bridges for students seeking a college education. A task force found that students who completed study at a tribal community college and then transferred to a 4-year institution had a completion rate 75% greater than those who attended 4-year colleges or universities after high school.

Renaissance

Tribally controlled K–12 programs and community colleges are revitalizing Native American culture and philosophy, while facing many challenges, such as funding. In some communities, tribal schools and colleges provide the means for gathering, storing, and preserving language, art, oral history, and distinct aspects of culture. In addition, many academics are in the process of redefining their academic disciplines according to Native American epistemologies. As a result, Native American cultural forms of education contain seeds for new models of education that might serve to enliven education as a whole.

As in other areas of contemporary Native American life, a tension exists between preparing current and future generations for the demands of urban life while maintaining tribal values, culture, and traditions. A culturally sensitive and relevant education prepares students for participation in a culturally diverse, technological society. It also addresses the historical context and relationship between Native American cultures and the educational system. Moreover, it helps Native American students understand the nature of cultural identity itself and to identify ways in which educational strategies can build on, rather than destroy, cultural strengths.

Arieahn Matamonasa-Bennett

See Appendix B

See also American Indian Movement; Assimilation; Bureau of Indian Affairs; Higher Education; Higher Education: Racial Battle Fatigue; Native American Identity; Pipeline; Reservation System

Further Readings

Cajete, Gregory. 1994. *Look to the Mountain: An Ecology of Indigenous Education.* Durango, CO: Kivaki Press.

Cajete, Gregory. 2006. "It Is Time for Indian People to Define Indigenous Education on Our Own Terms." *Tribal College* 18(2):56–58.

Deloria, Vine, Jr. and Daniel R. Wildcat. 2001. *Power and Place: Indian Education in America.* Golden, CO: Fulcrum.

Noriega, Jorge. 1992. "Native American Education in the United States: Indoctrination for Subordination to Colonialism." Pp. 371–402 in *The State of Native America,* edited by M. A. Jaimes. Boston, MA: South End Press.

Reyhner, John and Jeanne Eder. 2006. *Native American Education: A History.* Norman: University of Oklahoma Press.

Szasz, Margaret. 1974. *Education of the Native American: The Road to Self-Determination, 1928–1973.* Albuquerque: University of New Mexico Press.

Szasz, Margaret. 1999. *Education and the Native American: The Road to Self-Determination since 1982.* Albuquerque: University of New Mexico.

Web Sites

Native American Higher Education Consortium (AIHEC) Virtual Library: http://www.aihecvl.org

NATIVE AMERICAN GRAVES PROTECTION AND REPATRIATION ACT OF 1990

On November 16, 1990, the U.S. Congress passed and President George W. Bush signed an act to provide for the protection of Native American graves. The public law was titled the Native American Graves Protection and Repatriation Act (NAGPRA) (104 Stat. 3048, Public Law 101-601, November 16, 1990). The act was designed not only to protect Native American graves but also to prevent illegal excavations on Federal and tribal lands, prohibit the illegal trafficking of indigenous human remains and cultural items obtained in violation of the act, and establish legal criteria for repatriating Native human remains, associated funerary objects, and artifacts of cultural patrimony. For federally recognized tribes and Native Hawaiian communities, the act represented an attempt to halt the illegal "grave robbing" and "pot hunting" related to the lucrative artifact collectors trade, as well as a mechanism to rectify past actions that created a need for a national law. This entry looks at the historical context and subsequent implementation of the law.

Historical Context of NAGPRA

Since the colonization of North America and the Hawaiian Islands, Indigenous Peoples have endured the desecration of gravesites and the theft of cultural objects. Initially, indigenous sites were destroyed to obtain natural resources and, later, to fill the cabinets of curiosities among the European elite. Regardless of the motives, European scholars and theologians argued that the Native peoples of the New World were barbaric, unreasoning, sunk in vice, incapable of learning, lacking a sophistication of language and cultural customs, and physically different from Europeans. Hence, Native Americans were viewed as lower on the scale of being, closer to a "natural" or "savage" state of humanness. Indigenous peoples were considered inferior and defective members of the human species.

By the 19th century, U.S. nation-building efforts under the policy of Manifest Destiny had led to the active collection of indigenous skeletal remains and artifacts, under the guise of promoting the racial sciences. American society required a science that would faithfully reflect societal inequities and reify the destiny of the nation-state to expand against neighboring "inferior," "primitive" peoples. This scientific tradition determined the future social and moral progress of the nation for many years.

National progress demanded a body of knowledge that would explain and determine the course, nature, and shape of society, including America's "racial" composition. A hallmark of 19th-century scientific racism was the development of craniometry, the measurement of skulls, to scientifically prove that the varieties of humankind, including Native Americans, were conceived of as separate species or degenerated races that possessed certain characteristics that were deeply rooted in their descent.

Soldiers, missionaries, physicians, explorers, Indian agents, and natural historians actively engaged in gathering indigenous remains and cultural objects. Using the largest Native American skull collection in the world, Philadelphia physician Dr. Samuel G. Morton published *Crania Americana* in 1839.

Drawing on the science of phrenology and craniometry, Morton asserted the inferiority of the American Indian, concluding that this race possessed a "deficiency of 'higher' mental powers" and an "inaptitude for civilization." In addition, the structure of an "Indian's" mind, Morton concluded, was quite different, making it impossible for European Americans and Native Americans to interact socially.

Morton's racial theories lent evidence to the proposition that Indigenous Peoples were a "vanishing race" that would become extinct as civilization progressed. The myth of the "vanishing race" prompted the science of ethnology to collect comparative data about indigenous life before its people disappeared or were radically altered by placement on reservations. Collecting cultural artifacts, along with indigenous remains, promoted the development of museum collections. To enhance the collection of the Army Medical Museum, for example, the surgeon general ordered army personnel in 1868 to collect Indian skulls from the western Indian wars. More than 4,000 skulls were collected under that order.

By the turn of the 20th century, after surviving Indigenous Peoples were either placed on reservations or confined to the margins of U.S. society, "salvage ethnology" and craniometry to ascertain racial characteristics had become an ingrained endeavor of the new science of anthropology. Along with members of several other disciplines, anthropologists attempted to gather firsthand data, including material artifacts that would simultaneously record traditional indigenous cultural practices and provide vital information that would assist the Indian Office in its forced assimilation of surviving Indian peoples.

It is no coincidence that on March 3, 1879, the Bureau of Ethnology (BAE) was created as an arm of the Smithsonian Institution to collect cultural and biological data about Native Americans, to break up the "habits of a savage" by introducing elements of civilization. Ethnocide, from 1880 to 1934, became officially sanctioned as government policy. With the emergence of tourism and the exotic art market, indigenous remains and artifacts became a commodity. Many items of cultural significance—among them medicine bundles, heraldic poles, altar objects, and mummies—found their way into the hands of private collectors.

A large amount of these materials were sold on the international market, leaving Native North America forever. Some of these artifacts were traded for or bought, sometimes from Native peoples. At the end of the 20th century, staggering amounts of cultural property was possessed by nonindigenous people for scientific or personal reasons. Human remains, grave contents, sacred objects, and objects of cultural patrimony lay stored or on display in museums, tourist attractions, art houses, private collections, and universities.

Implementation and Politics of NAGPRA

The passage of NAGPRA established legal mandates requiring museums and federal agencies to inventory improperly acquired human remains, funerary objects, sacred objects, and objects of cultural patrimony and return them to Native American claimants. Once an inventory is completed, submitted, and reviewed, the items must be returned to lineal descendants or culturally affiliated Indian tribes or Native Hawaiian groups under prescribed evidentiary and procedural guidelines.

In addition, NAGPRA prohibits trafficking in Native American body parts and the excavation of Native American graves found on federal or tribal land without tribal consent. When remains are accidentally discovered on such lands, affected tribes must be notified and consulted with about the disposition of the remains.

Initially, the passage of NAGPRA caused a backlash among segments of the scientific and museum community. A minority of physical anthropologists, museum curators, archaeologists, and private collectors openly opposed the act's implementation. Fearing a massive loss of valuable data and control, they charged that the law violated the First Amendment and interfered with their professional obligations to care for the past and to use empirical data to construct the truth; some claimed that indigenous people were distorting factual history to fit their present political needs.

Native peoples responded to the claims in a variety of ways. Some tribal representatives attempted to quell fears by working closely with the scientific community. Others, however, resorted to outright name-calling and using public forums to heighten tensions.

No case exemplified the legal tension concerning NAGPRA better than the Kennewick case. In 1996, on the shores of the Columbia River, human remains were discovered dated 7,000 to 9,000 years old. The find immediately raised legal, cultural, and scientific issues. Section 3 of NAGPRA states that human remains and associated funerary objects must be returned to the living descendants or descendant tribes. The find, however, was early prehistoric and could not be precisely assigned to any living tribal society.

Confounding the growing dispute were multiple tribal claims, a unique morphology that does not fit a Native American "skeletal type," and the desire to thoroughly study the remains before returning them. Through a series of trials, beginning in 1996, the Ninth Circuit Court of Appeals in February 2004 declared that the claimant tribes had demonstrated no direct kinship and the scientists could conduct further research. Since the Kennewick case, the federal government has refined the definitions in NAGPRA and added several technical amendments.

NAGPRA is still applied through a case-by-case process. The law will take years to fully implement as tribes, agencies, museums, and the courts clarify and apply the law. By 2004, about 30,261 indigenous human remains, 581,679 associated funerary objects, and 1,222 sacred objects had been repatriated to Native Hawaiian and Native American claimants. The 2007 Midyear Report indicates that there have been 360 Notices of Intent to Repatriate. The notices account for 118,442 funerary objects, 3,585 sacred objects, and 296 objects of cultural patrimony.

After nearly 2 decades, the mistrust and fears surrounding the implementation of the law among tribes, scientists, and museum professionals are being replaced with a growing trust and responsibility to do what is best for the materials in question. There is general agreement that the process has not harmed legitimate scientific inquiry but has instead led to a better understanding of Native American cultural history and closer collaboration between Native American tribes and scientists.

As is often the case with human and civil rights legislation, changes associated with the application of NAGPRA have not come without strife and challenges. Certainly, the law in the future will be occasionally tested in the legal arena. NAGPRA, however, is beginning to rectify past and present social injustices inflicted on Indigenous Peoples.

Gregory R. Campbell

See also Deloria, Vine, Jr.; Kennewick Man; Native Americans; Sacred Sites, Native American

Further Readings

Bieder, Robert E. 1990. *A Brief Historical Survey of the Expropriation of American Indian Remains.* Boulder, CO: Native American Rights Fund. Reprinted in Hearing before Select Committee on Indian Affairs on S. 1021 and S. 1980, 101 Cong., 2nd Sess. (May 14, 1990), pp. 278–362.

Echo-Hawk, Roger C. and Walter R. Echo-Hawk. 1994. *Battlefields and Burial Grounds: The Indian Struggle to Protect Ancestral Remains in the United States.* Minneapolis, MN: Lerner.

Gould, Stephen J. 1978. "Morton's Ranking of Races by Cranial Capacity: Unconscious Manipulation of the Data May Be the Scientific Norm." *Science* 200:503–509.

Gould, Stephen J. 1981. *The Mismeasure of Man.* New York: Norton.

Hinsley, Charles. 1981. *Savages and Scientists: The Smithsonian Institution and the Development of American Anthropology, 1846–1910.* Washington, DC: Smithsonian Institution Press.

Hoxie, Fredrick. 1984. *The Final Promise: The Campaign to Assimilate the Indians, 1880–1920.* Lincoln: University of Nebraska Press.

Pagden, Anthony. 1982. *The Fall of Natural Man: The American Indian and the Origins of Comparative Ethnology.* Cambridge, UK: Cambridge University Press.

Stuart, Paul. 1979. *The Indian Office: Growth and Development of an American Institution, 1865–1900.* Ann Arbor: University of Michigan Research Press.

Trigger, Bruce. 1989. *A History of Archaeological Thought.* Cambridge, UK: Cambridge University Press.

Trope, Jack F. and Walter R. Echo-Hawk. 1992. "The Native American Graves Protection and Repatriation Act: Background and Legislative History." *Arizona State Law Journal* 24(35):45–75.

NATIVE AMERICAN HEALTH CARE

From first European contact, the health status of Native American people changed dramatically as European infectious diseases, especially smallpox, ravaged Native communities. Beginning in the early 19th century and more or less continuously since then, the U.S. government has played a role in providing health care to American Indians. Under different names and different leadership, Native American health care has evolved from an organization devoted to missionizing Native American and Alaskan Native people in the "ways of civilization," through the introduction of Western medicine and a reactionary organization trying to control infectious diseases, and finally, into a service devoted to providing comprehensive health care and promoting health equity among Native American and Alaskan Native people.

Today, the primary responsibility of providing comprehensive health care for eligible Native Americans and Alaskan Natives is assigned to the Indian Health Service (IHS), one of eight agencies in the U.S. Public Health Service. The mission of the Indian Health Service is to achieve the highest attainable level of health for Native American and Alaskan Native people. The broad goals of the IHS are to ensure equity in health care delivery and to assist Native people in defining their health needs, establishing local health care priorities, and providing management for health programs.

During the 20th century, and especially since 1955, the health status of American Indians and Alaskan Natives has improved dramatically. Despite the tremendous gains in the level of health—and IHS efforts that have contributed to this outcome—American Indians and Alaskan Natives have not achieved an equitable level of health parallel to the general population. In a nine-IHS-Service-Area comparison of rates with the 1987 U.S. rates, American Indians and Alaskan Natives experienced a 400% greater rate of tuberculosis, a 663% greater rate for alcoholism, and a 295% greater rate for accidents than the U.S. general population. In addition, American Indians and Alaskan Natives suffer a 268% greater rate for diabetes mellitus, a 134% greater rate for homicide, and a 95% greater rate for suicide. Such statistics reveal how large the gap is in health equity between the non-Native population and our nation's Indigenous Peoples. This entry reviews the history of federal involvement in Native American health care, describes the operation of the IHS, and looks at the broader issue of Native American health status.

The Evolving Federal Role

Despite the rapid and acute periods of mortality among tribes, as well as the deterioration of health status in the early years of contact between American Indians and Whites, it was not until the early 1800s that federal health services for American Indians began under the auspices of the War Department, which administered Indian affairs.

19th Century

By 1819, legislation authorized $10,000 annually to instruct Indian people in the "arts of civilization." The Superintendent of Indian Trade initially distributed the monies, but after 1824, the Bureau of Indian Affairs (BIA), under the War Department, allocated the funds, primarily to missionary societies. Some minimal health care was delivered, largely targeting indigenous medical beliefs and practices. Linking health care to the process of "civilizing" American Indian people continued as official BIA policy until 1934.

The first legal commitment to provide a specific American Indian nation with health services was in 1832. The federal government negotiated a treaty with the Winnebago tribe stipulating that a physician would be provided as partial payment for ceded lands. Although the federal government had a legal mandate to deliver health care to select American Indian nations, health care remained sporadic and reactionary.

With the transfer of the BIA to the newly created Department of the Interior in 1849, a bureaucratic structure emerged to serve the growing health needs of Indian people under governmental control. By 1873, the BIA, under the Division of Education and Medicine, developed a rudimentary structure for health care delivery, the reporting of vital statistics from various Indian agencies, and the distribution of medical supplies.

In 1877, the Division of Education and Medicine was abolished and medical services were placed under the Civilization Division (which later evolved into the Education Division). During this period, a civilian corps of physicians was placed at some Indian agencies and reservations. By the 1880s, the permanent settlement of American Indian people on reservations allowed the Indian administration to construct a system of hospital-based care and to establish a nursing staff and a field matron corps in the 1890s. Although the availability of health care improved, inadequate facilities, a lack of medical supplies, transportation problems, and incompetent personnel as well as a general resistance by many Native American people toward Western medicine plagued the delivery of services. The rejection of Western medicine was related to the role of reservation medical practices in destroying Native American healing and religious beliefs.

Early 20th Century

The period between 1900 and 1955 saw revolutionary changes in the administration and practice of curative and preventive medicine. With regard to health organization, centralized medical supervision of Native American health care began in 1908, with the creation of the position of Chief Medical Supervisor. The supervisor position was strengthened in 1924 with the creation of the Health Division of the BIA. Two years later, the Indian Medical Service underwent a general reorganization.

The country was divided into four medical districts, each with a district medical director and a chief medical director. The reorganization of the Indian Medical Service was a response to the 1921 Snyder Act, which required the federal government to provide routine health care to American Indian people. As these bureaucratic changes took place, the practice of medicine among Native people also changed. These changes were largely prompted by major health surveys conducted by the Public Health Service in 1913 and the Meriam Commission report, published by the Brookings Institute in 1928. The quality of hospital facilities improved greatly.

Motivated by a 1922 American Red Cross report, public health nurses were added to the medical staff in 1924. Public health nurses reached a peak of 110 in 1939, but declined to 70 in 1955. Native American participation in the Indian Medical Service began in 1935, with the establishment of the Kiowa School of Practical Nursing. Through a 9-month course of study, Native American women were trained in practical nursing skills.

During this same period, BIA health officials instituted a number of specific disease control programs, especially for tuberculosis and trachoma, and health education programs on reservations. In 1911, the Indian Medical Service declared tuberculosis, trachoma, and infant mortality a national health tragedy. In response, the BIA between 1911 and 1940 created a system of boarding school tuberculosis sanatoria as well as a sanatoria system for non-school-age Native people. Concomitant with the expansion of sanatoria, as early as 1909, the BIA launched a medical education program and, by 1935, began a vaccination program.

Similarly, trachoma campaigns were carried out by medical doctors, especially at the boarding schools. Prior to 1930, Native American people had to undergo a painful 4- to 6-year procedure, but the discovery of sulfanilamide rapidly arrested the trachoma epidemic. Other disease control programs included smallpox vaccinations in 1901 and a 1935 venereal disease program in cooperation with the American Social Hygiene Association.

President Taft, in a message before Congress in 1912, declared that Indian mothers had a right to unmaimed births and healthy children. As part of a nationwide campaign, in 1916, the BIA launched the "Save the Babies" program on some Indian reservations. The health education program sent field nurses into homes to instruct women in the arts of proper sanitation and child care. From all indications, the program had little impact on infant mortality, but it demonstrated how health policy was tied still to assimilation.

Throughout this period, the Indian Medical Service attempted to improve reservation sanitation, promote health education and nutrition, solicit state and local cooperation on Native American health issues, begin medical social work, and hire more qualified personnel. These changes were reflected in the federal appropriations for Native American health services. In 1911, appropriations for general health care amounted to $40,000. By 1955, $17,754,555 was allocated for health services among Native people. Although the annual appropriations increased dramatically during this period, the success of the Indian Medical Service was marred by a lack of efforts to identify Native American health needs, a lack of qualified personnel, and chronic underfunding.

Postwar Changes

As the bureaucratic structure of health care delivery was undergoing changes, so was the makeup of the personnel who staffed the facilities. Health personnel employed by the BIA increased in number, qualifications, and occupational specialization. Beginning in 1926, physician-officers in the medical corps commissioned by the Public Health Service were detailed to hold health positions in the Indian Medical Service. The number of positions grew slowly until the 1950 Doctor-Dentist Draft Law, which permitted members to serve required duty in the Public Health Service. By 1955, over fifty physicians, twelve public health nurses, and a few dentists, pharmacists (organized in 1953), and sanitary engineers were working for the Indian Medical Service.

After World War II, a lack of qualified medical personnel, combined with a lack of funds, prompted the BIA in 1952 to adopt a policy of closing Native American health facilities and contracting health services to state or local non-Native hospitals. By 1955, the BIA had contracted with sixty-five community hospitals, sixteen tuberculosis sanatoria, and five mental institutions. It was argued that contract care was less expensive and allowed Indian patients to stay closer to home, but the closing of these health facilities paralleled the termination of Indian reservations. Although some of the hospital closings were partially offset by the construction of 24 health centers in local Native communities, the remaining hospitals were inadequate. By the mid-1950s, only sixteen Native American hospitals and sanatoria met accreditation requirements of the Joint Commission on Accreditation of Hospitals.

In 1949, the Association of State and Territorial Health Officers, the Governors' Interstate Council on Indian Affairs, the American Public Health Association, the American Medical Association, the National Tuberculosis Association, the Association on American Indian Affairs, and the 1949 Hoover Commission Task Force on Public Welfare lobbied heavily for the transfer of Native American health care to the U.S. Public Health Service (USPHS).

The Public Health Service

The transfer of federal responsibility for Native American health care delivery from the BIA to the Public Health Service was accomplished July 1, 1955 (42 U.S.C. 2004a), when the Indian Health Service took its present form. The USPHS Division of Indian Health, it was argued, would provide a firm bureaucratic foundation for direct and contract medical care for Native people. In reality, federal termination policy was behind the transfer. Thousands of American Indian people were denied their rights, including the right to health services, as a result of termination.

During the 1960s and into the early 1970s, Native American health care delivery and policy followed the general trajectory of Indian policy in other legal arenas. With regard to Native American health care, by 1962, the USPHS assumed full jurisdiction (Public Law 151; Public Law 121). Under USPHS management, Congress increased health appropriation monies dramatically. The goal was to achieve a level of health and well-being comparable to the general non-Native population. Despite the increase in appropriations, a report instituted by the Commission on the Rights, Liberties, and Responsibilities of the American Indian stated that a large disparity remained between the health status of American Indians and the general population. Most important, the report concluded that the health status of American Indians would improve only when their economic conditions were raised.

The watershed for American Indian health legislation came in the mid-1970s. In 1975, the Indian Self-Determination and Education Assistance Act (Public Law 93-638) permitted American Indian nations to directly administer programs managed by the BIA or the IHS. The following year, Congress passed the Indian Health Care Improvement Act (Public Law 94-437). The act clarified and reiterated federal health care responsibilities outlined in the 1921 Snyder Act. An amendment, Public Law 96-537, was passed in 1980 to clarify further federal responsibility in elevating the indigenous health status.

The 1980s, especially during the Reagan administration, saw declines in funding social services. With declining resources, new issues arose in health care delivery. The first issue regarded who was eligible for health care services. The Snyder Act includes no express statutory language on who is eligible for IHS services. Since the 1974 decision of *Morton v. Ruiz,* the IHS has attempted to limit eligibility of American Indians by residence, blood quantum, or other criteria. A second related issue is whether the Indian Health Service is a primary or residual health care provider for American Indian people. In 1986, in *McNabb v. Heckler, et al.,* the U.S. District Court for the District of Montana ruled that the federal government was responsible primarily for health care services. Since that ruling, the IHS has had to ensure reasonable health care for eligible American Indians and Alaskan Natives.

IHS Organization and Service Population

On January 4, 1988, the IHS was elevated to agency status, becoming the seventh agency of the Public Health Service. The IHS health delivery system is composed of two major systems: (1) a federal health care delivery system administered by federal personnel and (2) a tribally based health care system administered by American Indian nations. Both systems utilize contract health care services from over 2,000 private providers. In addition, there are thirty-five urban

Native American health projects located in major urban areas with concentrated Native populations.

The IHS comprises twelve regional administrative area offices. IHS headquarters are in Rockville, Maryland, although some headquarters functions are conducted in Phoenix, Tucson, and Albuquerque. The twelve area offices are located in Aberdeen, South Dakota; Anchorage, Alaska; Albuquerque, New Mexico; Bemidji, Minnesota; Billings, Montana; Nashville, Tennessee; Oklahoma City, Oklahoma; Phoenix, Arizona; Portland, Oregon; Sacramento, California; Tucson, Arizona; and Window Rock, Arizona. In 2006, there were 164 Indian Health Service and tribally managed service units.

As the Native American and Alaskan Native population grew, so did the service responsibility of the Indian Health Service. Today, the IHS serves over 1 million eligible Native American and Alaskan Native people. Within the continental United States, the service population comprises 561 federally recognized American Indian nations in thirty states. According to the 2000 census, the potential IHS user population was approximately 4.3 million people, of which approximately 2.4 million individuals reported only American Indian or Alaskan Native as their race. According to statistical data, approximately 1.8 million American Indians and Alaskan Natives are being served on or near reservations, with 600,000 individuals served by urban health facilities.

Current Demographics and Health Status

In 1890, there were approximately 273,607 American Indians and Alaskan Natives in the United States. For both groups, this represented a population nadir. Prior to this time, they were exposed to various infectious diseases and an oppressive colonial system. From this demographic nadir, their populations have made a remarkable recovery. To some degree, the health of American Indians and Alaskan Natives has also improved, but they have not as yet achieved the same level of health enjoyed by the majority of the non-Native population.

In a comparison of data between American Indians and Alaskan Natives with "U.S., All Races" statistics, the indigenous population was younger, less educated, underrepresented in management and professional positions, and poorer than the general U.S. population. The ratio of American Indians and Alaskan Natives living below the poverty level was over twice that reported for the U.S. total population. Although there is considerable variation between services areas, the data indicated a growing population with a wide range of health needs and a population that has not achieved health parity with the general U.S. population.

The birthrate for American Indians and Alaskan Natives residing in the IHS service area was 24.1 per 1,000. Although this figure is less than the rate recorded for 1955, it is 1.6 times the 1995 birthrate for the "U.S., All Races" population. In short, the Native American and Alaskan Native populations are growing faster than other segments of our society.

Although the birthrate is exceeding the rate of the general population, the 1994 through 1996 age-adjusted mortality rate (all causes) for the IHS Service Area was 699.3 per 100,000. This is 39% higher than the 1995 "U.S., All Races" rate of 503.9 per 100,000. As the IHS worked to control infectious diseases that plagued American Indian and Alaskan Native people well into the 20th century—and as sanitation improved, dietary patterns changed, and minimal economic gains were made—the causes of death shifted radically. In 1951 through 1953, for example, tuberculosis was the fourth leading cause of death. By 1972 through 1974, tuberculosis as an infectious disease had no appreciable impact on American Indian mortality.

Chronic diseases and behavioral diseases remain, however, in some instances in epidemic proportions. Compared with specific causes of death in the U.S. general population, death from alcoholism is 627% greater; tuberculosis is 533% greater; diabetes mellitus is 249% greater; and alcoholism, suicide, and homicide are, respectively, 204%, 72%, and 63% greater. Greater than one-third of patient demands at IHS facilities across American Indian country involve alcohol-, substance-abuse-, and mental-health-related issues.

A sensitive indicator of the health status of any population is infant mortality rates and life expectancy. Since 1955, the infant mortality rate among Native Americans has dropped considerably, but it remains higher than the rate for the general U.S. population. The infant mortality rate for American Indians and Alaskan Natives was 9.3 per 1,000 live births. This is 22% greater than in "U.S., All Races." Clearly, American Indian and Alaskan Native infants are dying in greater proportion than those in the general non-Native population.

Since 1940, the life expectancy of American Indian and Alaskan Native people has steadily risen, although it remains below the national rate. Life expectancy at birth for American Indians and Alaskan Natives, both sexes, is 4.7 years less than the 1994 to 1996 life expectancy for "U.S., All Races." In short, American Indian and Alaskan Native people remain a population at risk.

Current Issues

Despite legislative reinforcement of Public Law 94-437 through Public Law 101-630, surrounding federal responsibility for Native American health care, eligibility, and entitlement to services will remain in the forefront in health policy into the 21st century. Other issues will emerge regarding availability and adequacy of health resources, self-determination and tribal assumption of health services, the extent of congressional control of health care policies for American Indians and Alaskan Natives, and especially the future of urban health programs for these populations.

Census data indicate that approximately 64.1% of the Native American population resides outside tribal areas, especially in urban areas. Despite this profound shift in population geography, the appropriation for urban Native American health care has eroded steadily since 1980. The remaining programs emphasize increasing access to existing services funded by private and public sources, rather than the IHS paying for those services directly. Currently, there were programs providing a range of health services, from comprehensive health services to minimal community health and social services. Underlying all of these questions are concerns over increasing health care quality, accessibility, health care funding, and individual eligibility for services.

Gregory R. Campbell

See also Blood Quantum; Bureau of Indian Affairs; Health Disparities; Indian Child Welfare Act of 1978; Native Americans; Native Americans, Environment and

Further Readings

Brophy, William A. and Sophie D. Aberle, eds. 1966. *The Indian, America's Unfinished Business: Report of the Commission on the Rights, Liberties, and Responsibilities of the American Indian.* Norman: University of Oklahoma Press.

Campbell, Gregory R., ed. 1989. "Contemporary Issues in Native American Health." Special ed. *American Indian Culture and Research Journal* 1(3/4).

Office of Technology Assessment. 1986. *Indian Health Care.* Washington, DC: U.S. Government Printing Office.

Ogunwole, Stella U. 2006. *We the People: American Indians and Alaska Natives in the United States.* Washington, DC: U.S. Department of Commerce, U.S. Census Bureau.

Putney, Diane T. 1980. *Fighting the Scourge: American Indian Morbidity and Federal Indian Policy, 1897–1928.* Doctoral dissertation, Marquette University.

Stuart, Paul. 1987. *Nations within a Nation: Historical Statistics of American Indians.* Westport, CT: Greenwood Press.

U.S. Department of Health and Human Services. 1991. *Indian Health Service: Regional Differences in Indian Health.* Washington, DC: U.S. Government Printing Office.

U.S. Department of Health and Human Services. 2000. *Trends in Indian Health, 1998–99.* Washington, DC: U.S. Government Printing Office.

NATIVE AMERICAN IDENTITY

A simple definition of *identity* is "the name we call ourselves." Yet things are inevitably more complicated than that, for identity is both externally imposed and internally ascribed; identity claims involve individual agency yet exist within a larger sociohistorical context. Claiming a Native American identity, as with all racial/ethnic identities, is more contested, complex, and constrained by context than the claiming of a White ethnic identity. An analysis of Native American identity, in particular, emphasizes the role of external ascription in the process of identity construction. This entry reviews various ways in which Native identity claims can be challenged: along the lines of physical appearance or in terms of legal, biological, and cultural authenticity. Such contestation over identities emphasizes that while communities struggle to define their members, they do not always do so under conditions of their own choosing.

Sociological research on race and ethnicity has shifted in recent decades from a more structural analysis of race, ethnicity, and racial/ethnic relations to an analysis of racial/ethnic identity. For individuals designated as racial minorities, identity challenges and constraints are even greater than they are for individuals designated as White Americans, as legal proscriptions and physical appearance influence external ascription. For racial minorities, the dominant group exercises its power through government to define who belongs in which racial category. Historically, in the case of African Americans, we see the imposition of the so-called one-drop rule, where racially mixed individuals are classified as Black. For Native peoples, this manifests itself in the opposite direction, with the federal government insisting on a specific blood quantum, often inconsistent with tribal membership criteria, for determining whether or not one is Native American. Owing to the elaborate requirements for officially establishing one's blood quantum, this is a practice that manages to exclude many people of Native heritage from officially being recognized as such.

Whites, as the dominant racial group, play a significant role through legal and political maneuvering in determining who is and who is not "Native," in much the same way they determine who is and who is not "Black." Interaction between dominant and subordinate groups is an example of asymmetrical power relations, which play themselves out in terms of racial/ethnic identity assessment: In essence, certain groups exercise power over others to define group membership. Despite such structural constraints, it is imperative that we not disregard the notion of agency in claiming a racial/ethnic identity.

Is There a Native American Identity?

Questions concerning racial/ethnic identity remain highly contested territory. For Native Americans, one must ask, is there such a thing as a Native American identity? First, it is important to recognize that identities are relational; consequently, there was no such thing as a Native American identity prior to European colonization. Native identity, then, exists in opposition to a White identity. In addition, the vast diversity among Native tribes forces the question: Is there a Native American identity above and beyond a tribal identity? As culturally diverse as Native Americans are, research indicates that there is indeed such a thing as an "Indian" identity; Stephen Cornell refers to this as a "supratribal consciousness."

Additional complexities remain concerning identity construction for Native Americans, particularly regarding questions of legal and biological authenticity, the challenge of physical appearance, and questions surrounding cultural authenticity. Thus, claiming an Indian identity, while always a political act, is very much constrained by both legal and sociohistorical context. There is considerable contestation over who is a "real" American Indian, with self-designated "Indian police" enforcing somewhat arbitrary and fluctuating boundaries in efforts to weed out potential "wannabes," people who claim to be Indian yet have no legitimate claim to Indian culture. Individuals reclaiming an American Indian heritage—those who have spent most of their lives in the White, mainstream society yet choose to embrace this aspect of themselves later in life—are particularly susceptible to facing such identity challenges.

Native Identity and the Blood Quantum

Since the 19th century, the notion of "blood quantum" as a gauge of one's degree of Indianness fluctuates between scientific expertise and a "commonsense" criterion of authentic Indianness. Although the scientific community no longer claims a connection between cultural difference, physical differences, and blood type, blood quantum designations still hold legal significance. The federal government constrains the construction of Native identity by, for instance, establishing one-quarter blood quantum as a minimum requirement for federal recognition. Tribal governments establish their own criteria for membership, often in conflict with the federal blood quantum requirements.

There is considerable ambivalence surrounding the notion of blood quantum, for the idea falsely implies some level of racial purity. However, it is still used as a gauge of one's Indianness, both at the federal level and within Native communities, as the common expressions "full-blood" and "half-breed" make clear. It appears that what begins as a system of identification that works in favor of the federal government is being reinforced through its embrace by Native peoples. Tribes are compelled to accept this faulty authentication procedure because land allotments are tied to tribal enrollments. Individual American Indians embrace this concept because it is erroneously presumed to be an objective measure of Indianness and provides a legitimacy claim. Such legitimacy claims are particularly important for individuals raised outside of Native American communities, whose cultural heritage or physical appearance thus challenges their identity claims.

Determination of blood quantum, while offering a seemingly objective measure of Indianness, is often reliant on historical documents that are incomplete at best. Someone wishing to claim Nativeness has to "prove" his or her connection through finding an ancestor on tribal rolls. The problem with reliance on such documentation, however, is that not all Native peoples are recorded on these "official" government records. Names can be spelled numerous ways on different documents, whether due to census-taker errors, low levels of literacy, or name changes, in which some tribes routinely engage. Historically, many people intentionally hid their Native American heritage from census takers because of the threat of severe discrimination. Some tribes, such as the Cherokee, kept elaborate records, while others, such as the Apache, never kept records. Some Native people were able to avoid forced relocation; thus, for example, if one's ancestors did not make it to Oklahoma, they were not included on the official tribal rolls, so that, as a result, their descendants are unable to prove their ancestry, and their authenticity as Native Americans is challenged.

Other Criteria of Native Identity

Above and beyond reliance upon legal and biological claims to an authentic Native American identity, external ascription often depends on another rather arbitrary criterion: physical appearance. Research on racial/ethnic identity construction exposes a connection between physical appearance, race, and identity. Appearance plays a significant role in identity construction simply because it presents one's identity to others in social interaction, and thus it is partially through appearance that others ascribe a racial identity to an individual. Physical appearance is used by both insiders and outsiders to gauge whether or not a person belongs to a particular racial/ethnic group.

Certainly not all individuals claiming to be Native American "look Indian," meaning they may not hold the stereotypical Native features of dark hair, dark complexion, and high cheekbones. Physical appearance is somewhat associated with geographic location, and Native peoples spanned the American continents. Clearly, this alone would account for extreme physical differentiation among American Indians. Yet, despite this understanding, for individuals whose physical appearance contradicts widespread stereotypes of what Indians look like, more identity challenges are experienced. Their racial/ethnic identities are often questioned and are rarely reflected back to them, so that the external ascription aspect of identity construction is lacking.

Nativeness is often referred to as being about culture, about a way of being in the world, rather than simply being associated with physical appearance. Yet due to the aggressive federal termination policies in the 1950s and 1960s, almost half of Native Americans live in urban areas rather than on reservations. Lacking proximity to Native communities, these individuals often lack such cultural authenticity, and their identity claims are less likely to be affirmed. Thus, another measure of Nativeness, cultural knowledge, emphasizes a connection to Native communities, engaging in tribal practices, and exhibiting somewhat of a shared peoplehood and worldview with other Natives. Culture, almost by definition, is a lived experience. Thus, individuals making identity claims and lacking a cultural connection, the lived experience, are often challenged by Native peoples with such cultural capital.

Kathleen J. Fitzgerald

See also Identity Politics; Internalized Racism; Latin America, Indigenous People; Native American Education; Native American Identity, Legal Background; Native Americans; Pan-Indianism; Sovereignty, Native American

Further Readings

Cornell, Stephen. 1998. *Return of the Native: American Indian Political Resurgence.* New York: Oxford University Press.

Fitzgerald, Kathleen J. 2007. *Beyond White Ethnicity: Developing a Sociological Understanding of Native American Reclaiming.* Lexington, KY: Rowman & Littlefield.

Garroutte, Eva Marie. 2003. *Real Indians: Identity and the Survival of Native America.* Berkeley: University of California Press.

Nagel, Joane. 1996. *American Indian Ethnic Renewal: Red Power and the Resurgence of Identity and Culture.* New York: Oxford University Press.

Weaver, Hilary N. 2001. "Indigenous Identity: What It Is and Who Really Has It?" *American Indian Quarterly* 5:240–255.

NATIVE AMERICAN IDENTITY, LEGAL BACKGROUND

Before the European invasion of the Americas in 1492, there were no "Indians" and no "tribes." Both are terms Europeans imposed on Indigenous Peoples, as a way of translating them, first, into European epistemologies and, subsequently, as the balance of power shifted over time in favor of the invaders, into European colonial bureaucracies. Over time, the U.S. legal system and court decisions played a role in identifying who is and who is not a Native American, as discussed in this entry.

Colonial Era

The term *Indian* was coined by Columbus, who, as he wandered about the Caribbean, thought he had arrived on the shores of Asia, or the "Indies." The European association of the word *tribe* with Native American social and political organizations has no particular origin. But the earliest usage of the word *tribe* in English, going back to the 13th century, is associated with the twelve tribes of Israel, ten of which were conceptualized as "lost" after the Assyrians forced them into exile in the 8th century BC. At the beginning of English imperialism in the Americas, one strain of Protestant theological scholarship believed that American Indians were these lost tribes.

Beginning more or less at the same time, *tribe* was also associated with the political divisions of ancient Greece and Rome. Existing within and alongside these associations is the idea of tribe as an expansive patriarchal lineage, composed of various clans—hence the earliest notion of "race" as extended family or kinship; and embedded in this idea is that of the "primitive." In keeping with these associations, early modern Europeans, contradictorily enough, identified "Indians" with both ancient Western and Asian civilizations and with the "savage."

In fact, outside of Mayan, Aztec, and Incan city-state organizations, which were relatively short-lived because of their vulnerability to Western conquest, the social organizations of the Indigenous Peoples of the Americas were by and large formed through extended-family structures, based not in terms of "blood" relationships, but in terms of behavior: a set of cultural "rules" or obligations that one had to one's kin, which included not only the other human beings of one's kinship group but also the land and the inhabitants (the other animals and the plants) of the land on which one lived.

The Navajo *(Diné)* creation narratives, for example, describe the formation of this extended-kinship network from its beginnings in the "First World" to the present-day elaboration of it in the "clans" of the "Fifth World." These kinship-based social organizations could be matrilineal or patrilineal (not to be confused with *matriarchal* or *patriarchal*) or matrilocal or patrilocal; they could be organized into fixed villages, like the Pueblos, or mobile forms, as was the case with the Navajos. Typically, the governance structure of these groups was decentralized, based in consensual forms of governance, where all the adult members of the kinship community, male and female, were part of the decision-making process.

Until the late 18th century, then, when European colonization was well advanced, the Indigenous Peoples north of Mexico did not typically think of themselves as "Indians" or their social organizations as "tribes" or "nations," another term applied to and adopted by these communities in the United States once the treaty-making process had begun. Rather, they identified themselves according to the name of the kinship group or clan to which they belonged. Writing in 1829, the Pequot activist William Apess testifies in his autobiography, *A Son of the Forest*, to the alien origin of the word "Indian," even as he uses it to identify himself:

> I thought it disgraceful to be called an Indian; it was considered as a slur upon an oppressed and scattered nation, and I have often been led to inquire where the Whites received this word, which they so often threw as an opprobrious epithet at the sons of the forest.

Apess thought that his people should properly be called "Natives." Today, Indians in the United States have taken up both the words Indian and Native as their own; but, as Apess suggests, this process of translation was slow and painful, based as it is in the genocidal violence of European colonialism.

Because the basic indigenous social unit was not founded on biological identification but on complex cultural affiliations, outsiders could be adopted into the community as full-fledged members if they were willing to follow the social and cultural rules of kinship. The history of Europeans and others, including African Americans, being taken captive by or willingly joining Native communities witnesses this process of cultural conversion or adoption. The European American name *Jemison,* prominent in the Seneca nation today, marks the 1758 capture and adoption of 14-year-old Mary Jemison, whose descendants are full-fledged Senecas.

The Impact of Scientific Racism

The idea of race as a biological category begins to emerge in concert with the development of scientific racism in the United States in the first half of the 19th century. In this instance, the emerging science of physical anthropology was used to rationalize racial hierarchies grounded in the idea of White supremacy, the driving force behind the U.S. imperial policy of Manifest Destiny. During this period, the idea of *Indian* as a racial term enters the lexicon of federal Indian law, in the landmark Supreme Court case of *U.S. v. Rogers* (45 U.S. 567) in 1846.

In his decision in *Rogers,* which involved the killing of one White male citizen of the Cherokee nation by another White male Cherokee, Chief Justice Taney tried to distinguish between the political and social act of conferring membership in a Native community and the generalized notion of *Indian* as a racial category transcending specific cultural practices of incorporation. It is noteworthy that while Taney did not use the term *blood* in his definition of *Indian* and his definition remains ambiguously poised between a biological and a cultural notion of race, his decision has been used as a precedent in determining a modern racial definition of *Indian.*

So, for example, in *U.S. v. Broncheau* (597 F. 2d 1260), in 1979, a case in which the adequacy of the legal definition of *Indian* was called into question by the defendant, the Ninth Circuit Court of Appeals noted as follows:

> Unlike the term "Indian country," which has been defined in 18 U.S.C. § 1151, the term "Indian" has not been statutorily defined but instead has been judicially explicated over the years. The test, first suggested in *United States v. Rogers* . . . and generally followed by the courts, considers (1) the degree of Indian blood; and (2) tribal or governmental recognition as an Indian. (at 1263)

Broncheau points to two salient facts in the legal history of Indian identity. First, there is no single answer to the question, Who is an Indian? Rather, there are federal, state, tribal, and personal definitions (since 1960, the U.S. Census has allowed self-identification). Second, the federal definition of Indian combines a biological ("blood") and a political ("recognition") component, with emphasis being placed on one or the other, depending on the context. So, for example, in another landmark case, *Morton v. Mancari* (417 U.S. 535), in 1974, a class action suit by non-Native employees of the Bureau of Indian Affairs, under the Equal Employment Opportunities Act of 1972, challenging the bureau's employment preference for qualified Indians, the Supreme Court found that the Equal Employment Opportunities Act did not apply in this case because "the preference, as applied, is granted to Indians not as a discrete racial group, but, rather, as members of quasi-sovereign tribal entities whose lives and activities are governed by the BIA in a unique fashion" (at 554). Nevertheless, citing the BIA manual on the preference, the Court noted that the political component of federal recognition also entailed a racial component of blood quantum: "To be eligible for preference in appointment, promotion, and training, an individual must be one-fourth or more degree Indian blood and be a member of a Federally-recognized tribe" (at 554).

Blood Quantum and Policy

From the General Allotment or Dawes Act of 1887 forward, blood quantum became an increasingly important part of the federal policy identifying Indians. The act itself, in which Congress mandated the privatization of Indian communal lands, intensifying Native dispossession and poverty, required that agents of the Interior Department visit the tribes in order to officially determine who was and was not a tribal member. These agents used the legal fiction of "blood" to construct the tribal rolls: In her essay "Urban (Trans)Formations: Changes in the Use and Meaning of American Indian Identity," Angela Gonzales noted that although enumerators generally relied on their own judgment, self-reports, and the word of neighbors and relatives, their records were still used in decisions about whether a person was part of a tribe and eligible for government services to American Indians.

Sometime after 1934, when the Indian Reorganization Act mandated the end of allotment and "encouraged" the tribes to adopt Western-style constitutions, the federal government began to issue Certificates of Degree of Indian Blood (CDIBs), as a formal way of identifying those who had a specific degree of Indian blood in a recognized tribe and were therefore entitled to federal benefits.

While under U.S. federal Indian law the tribes themselves have autonomy in determining tribal membership, under the federal pressure of limited resources, they have by and large adopted to one degree or another the colonial apparatus of blood quantum in making these determinations. Needless to say, the colonial system of Indian identification, which creates arbitrary barriers between tribal, federal, state, and self-identified Indian persons, as well as barriers between those tribes that are federally recognized and those that are not, has proved divisive, inhibiting Native American communities and persons from organizing across these barriers in politically effective ways.

Eric Cheyfitz

See also Blood Quantum; Bureau of Indian Affairs; Colonialism; Dawes Act of 1887; Eugenics; Genocide; Identity Politics; Internal Colonialism; Native American Identity; Sovereignty, Native American

Further Readings

Cheyfitz, Eric. 2004. "'What Is An Indian?' Identity Politics in United States Federal Indian Law and American Indian Literatures." *Ariel: A Review of International English Literature* 35(1–2):59–80.

Gonzales, Angela A. 2001. "Urban (Trans)Formations: Changes in the Use and Meaning of American Indian Identity." Pp. 169–185 in *American Indians and the Urban Experience,* edited by S. Lobo and K. Peters. Walnut Creek, CA: Alta Mira Press.

O'Connell, Barry. 1992. *On Our Own Ground: The Complete Writings of William Apess, A Pequot.* Amherst, MA: University of Massachusetts Press.

Sturm, Circe. 2002. *Blood Politics: Race, Culture, and Identity in the Cherokee Nation of Oklahoma.* Berkeley: University of California Press.

NATIVE AMERICANS

There is no one single scientific, biological, cultural, or even legal definition for who is identified as an "American Indian" or "Native American" in the United States, although racial categorizations and definitions continue to impact those whose identities and heritages are tied to indigenous cultures. The idea that hundreds of different cultures with enormously diverse ways of life, social organizations, languages, and belief systems could be combined into a single racial or cultural category is an artifact of predominantly European colonization of the North American continent. This entry views American Indians through the lenses of race, nation, culture, and homeland.

Racial Definitions

Prior to the arrival of Europeans in the late 15th century, the Native peoples of both North and South America identified themselves primarily in relation to the particular people to whom they culturally belonged. European colonizers viewed Native peoples collectively as belonging to a single, inferior "race," based on the ideology that European cultures represented the pinnacle of social evolution. Particularly long-lasting effects resulted from racial definitions of "Indianness" that argued that the more "Indian blood" or blood quantum a person contained, the more "savage" or "uncivilized" he or she was.

Beginning in early U.S. colonial history, Indian blood quantum became a way of differentiating and excluding Native people from social, political, and economic participation in European American society. By the second half of the 19th century, this ideology was buttressed by a growing international body of social and biological sciences that claimed that this inferiority was scientifically demonstrable. This biological racism heavily influenced 19th-century U.S. policies toward Native peoples and its formal adoption into federal Indian policy with the passing of the General Allotment Act in 1887.

It was also during this time that the U.S. Census began to count Indians as a separate racial category (beginning in 1870). At that time, it was left up to census takers to determine whether an individual fit into the racial category of *Indian.* Today, assignment of individuals to the racial categories of *American Indian* or *Alaska Native* is based completely on self-identification at the time of filling out the census form. According to the 2000 census, the number of people who self-reported as only American Indian or Alaska Native was estimated at 2,475,956 people, or 0.9% of the total U.S. population. An additional 1,643,345 people self-reported as American Indian or Alaska Native in combination with one or more other races. Census self-identification is problematic since people can claim American Indian heritage regardless of whether they or their ancestors have ever actively practiced the cultures or been a part of the communities to which they claim their ancestry.

These estimates of the number of Native Americans are subject to variation. The 2004 American Community Survey placed the total number of self-reported American Indians or Alaska Natives at 2,151,322. The list of the largest tribal groups is shown in Table 1. While this represents a large difference from the 2000 census data, the table nonetheless offers a fairly accurate presentation of the larger tribal groups, led by the Cherokee and Navajo, both with over 200,000.

Table 1 American Indian and Alaska Native Household Population by Tribal Group, 2004

Tribal Group	Population	Percentage of American Indian and Alaska Native Alone Population
American Indian and Alaska Native alone[1,2]	2,151,322	100
American Indian tribal grouping, specified	1,729,574	80.4
Apache	66,048	3.1
Blackfeet	39,508	1.8
Cherokee	331,491	15.4
Cheyenne	15,715	0.7
Chickasaw	12,773	0.6
Chippewa	92,041	4.3
Choctaw	55,107	2.6
Creek	27,243	1.3
Iroquois	50,982	2.4
Lumbee	59,433	2.8
Navajo	230,401	10.7
Osage	13,982	0.6
Ottawa	12,824	0.6
Paiute	14,944	0.7
Pima	48,709	2.3
Potawatomi	14,952	0.7
Pueblo	69,203	3.2
Seminole	12,578	0.6
Sioux	67,666	3.1
Tohono O'Odham	20,577	1.0
Yaqui	16,169	0.8
Yuman	10,419	0.5
All other American Indian tribes[3]	446,809	20.8
American Indian tribes, not specified	45,736	2.1
Alaska Native tribes, specified	89,46	24.2
Alaska Athabascan	12,370	0.6
Aleut	11,037	0.5
Eskimo	35,951	1.7
Tlingit-Haida	18,677	0.9
All other Alaska Native tribes[4]	11,427	0.5
Alaska Native tribes, not specified	11,808	0.4
American Indian tribes or Alaska Native tribes, not specified[5]	274,742	12.8

Source: U.S. Census Bureau, 2004 *American Community Survey Report, Selected Population Profiles*, p. 2.

[1] Data based on sample limited to the household population and exclude the population living in institutions, college dormitories, and other group quarters.

[2] This category includes people who reported only *American Indian* or *Alaska Native,* either by specifying one or more American Indian or Alaska Native tribes or tribal groupings or by responding with a generic term such as *American Indian* or *Alaska Native.*

[3] This category includes people who reported one specified American Indian tribe or tribal grouping not shown above, as well as people who reported two or more specified American Indian tribes or tribal groupings but only reported as *American Indian* or *Alaska Native.*

[4] This category includes people who reported one specified Alaska Native tribe or tribal grouping not shown above, as well as people who reported two or more specified Alaska Native tribes or tribal groupings but reported only as *American Indian* or *Alaska Native.*

[5] This category includes respondents who checked the *American Indian* or *Alaska Native* response category or wrote in the generic term *American Indian* or *Alaska Native* or tribal entries not elsewhere classified.

The racial identification of "Indian" identity continues to negatively impact Native people today. The 1934 Indian Reorganization Act, which ended many abusive assimilationist policies and recognized the right of Native communities to be self-governing entities, forced tribes to continue to use blood quantum as the basis for determining tribal membership, using a standard of one-quarter Indian blood for tribal enrollment. Though the U.S. government has since recognized the right of tribes to define eligibility for enrollment according to their own criteria, nearly all tribes still use blood quantum as one of the requirements. To prove one's blood quantum is often an enormously time-consuming, expensive, and demoralizing process involving extensive archival research into one's ancestral lineage.

Those who, for a number of reasons, cannot prove the required blood quantum may be denied legal recognition of their identity by the tribe to which they and uncountable generations of their ancestors may have been members. They are also denied access to both tribal and federal services that are provided for enrolled members of federally recognized tribes. Blood quantum requirements also put pressure on Native people to avoid having children with non-Native or nontribal members, since they may lose these rights.

Thus, racial definitions of "Indian" identity are deeply problematic. Based historically on non-Native notions of racial inferiority, they reinforce racist ideologies and outside control over the destiny, opportunities, and everyday lives of Native people. They reinforce the colonial idea that Native people are racial minorities rather than members of sovereign nations. And they deny the legitimacy and importance of culture, community, and kinship structures that have been the basis for group identification in Native communities for millennia.

American Indians as Nations

A person's identity is formed and recognized in relation to other people. Most Native Americans define their identities in relation to one or more of the almost 800 tribal nations that exist within the territorial borders of the United States. Of these, 562 are "federally recognized" by the U.S. government to receive federal services, monies, and protections: 335 tribes in the lower forty-eight states and 227 in Alaska. There are at least an additional 220 tribes across thirty states, which have petitioned for but not received this federal recognition. Of these, between 45 and 65 (depending on the source) tribal nations are formally recognized by the states in which they are located.

The reasons for nonrecognition vary but generally are the result of historical U.S.-tribal relations and the ways in which the U.S. government sought to destroy tribal homelands and cultures. Like the racial definitions and classifications of Native people that continue to affect American Indian identity, the shared experiences of tribes as a result of U.S. policies and interventions in their lives continue to profoundly shape the consciousness, cultures, and material relations of Indian nations today.

All tribes have strong oral traditions recording their communities' histories, going back for hundreds of generations. Nearly all of them trace their people's origins to particular ancestral homelands on the North American continent. The master narrative taught to most non-Natives claims that Native people migrated to the continent from Asia across the Bering Straight during the last Ice Age. This narrative is substantiated primarily by linguistic and genetic studies that tie Native Americans to Asian and northern Russian ancestry. Well-respected scientists differ greatly on the details that are offered as evidence to support this theory. In addition, there is the issue of effectively denying the validity and cultural significance of Native people's own narratives about themselves and in implying that Native people are not truly indigenous to the soils of the Americas.

Oral histories record the past and lifeways of the thousands of Native communities that inhabited the continent and their interactions prior to European contact. Though there was, as there still is, extensive inter- and intracontinental trade, commerce, warfare, marriage, and movement before colonization, most communities were politically autonomous. Many communities, especially in the interior of the continent, had little contact with non-Native peoples until the middle of the 19th century. Of those groups that did have early contact with European and American colonizers, many were recognized by European nations and the U.S. government as sovereign nations with whom they signed hundreds of treaties. Others were faced with substantial violence, encroachment, and displacement.

U.S. Interventions

In the 1820s and 1830s, the federal government engaged in numerous wars with southeastern tribes and forcibly relocated thousands of Native people west of the Mississippi River to open their lands for settlement. During this same period, the Supreme Court, based on the "right of conquest," extinguished Indian title to their own lands and turned the property over to the trusteeship of the federal government to manage on their behalf. Tribes were thus officially labeled "domestic dependent nations" and wards of the federal government.

By the late 1840s, the U.S. government had consolidated its ocean-to-ocean continental empire, and, by the 1870s, railroads and settlers were penetrating its farthest reaches. Massive western migrations of U.S. settlers led to violence between colonizers and Native people. The U.S. government used its military forces to forcibly relocate Native people to federal lands called "reservations." In 1849, the Bureau of Indian Affairs was created within the Department of the Interior to oversee Indian affairs and the trusteeship of their lands.

By the 1870s, the federal government had abandoned treaty making with American Indian nations and declared unilateral authority to make decisions concerning Native people and their resources. Huge tracts of lands in the West were seized and redistributed to non-Native settlers. Meanwhile, the Bureau of Indian Affairs, along with support from congressional acts and executive orders, undertook large-scale attempts at dismantling tribes and assimilating American Indian people into the U.S. "mainstream." Among the tactics used were land reform and privatization of tribal lands, forced schooling of Native children in European American values and norms, and prohibitions against the practice of Native cultures and languages.

Native people were granted U.S. citizenship and voting rights in 1924, but openly assimilationist policies continued into the 1930s. In 1934, the Indian Reorganization Act recognized the right of Native people to continue practicing their own cultures and manage their own affairs. Tribes were given the opportunity to do so by adopting Western-style constitutional governments, which in some cases displaced traditional tribal governance structures and leadership. Despite these reforms, the secretary of the interior and the Bureau of Indian Affairs continued to have strong authority as federal trustees to oversee tribal decision making.

Federal policies again shifted toward assimilation of Native Americans after World War II in the 1940s. Known as the "Termination" era in federal Indian policy, the U.S. government sought to rapidly and permanently assimilate Native Americans into the mainstream by terminating federal recognition of tribal sovereignty, removing federal support services and funding for tribes, extending state jurisdiction over tribal lands, opening reservations to economic exploitation by private companies, and relocating over 100,000 Native people to urban areas.

Termination policies deepened reservation poverty and helped to galvanize what was already a growing pan-Indian civil rights movement in the late 1950s and 1960s. The Kennedy and Johnson administrations in the 1960s encouraged tribes to undertake economic development to overcome system poverty and provided some federal support to do so. However, it would not be until the 1970s that the federal government would officially end its termination and assimilationist policies. This "self-determination" era beginning in 1970 resulted in a proliferation of legislation and case law that recognized tribal sovereignty and the right to self-government, return of control over tribal affairs and resources to tribes themselves, and efforts to support tribal economic development, as well as support for cultural revitalization and religious freedom.

Recent Relations

This era of tribal self-determination continues today despite cutbacks in federal funding in the 1980s under the Reagan administration and continued federal authority over many tribal decision-making processes. This federal recognition of tribal sovereignty and self-determination has allowed many tribes to undertake vitally needed economic development and cultural revitalization programs. Tribes lacking federal recognition, however, have no legal mechanisms with which to leverage the protection, support, and enforcement of federal responsibilities and are unable to exercise true sovereign control over their affairs. They are denied access to federal programs and funding and are subject to often hostile local and state governments. Tribal members are without access to the vital support services that come with tribal membership in a federally recognized tribe. Thus, obtaining federal recognition as a tribal nation remains an extremely important part of obtaining true self-determination for many American Indian nations today.

Among the lasting legacies of federal Indian policies, racism, and interventions in Native Americans' lives is widespread poverty in many Native communities. This is evidenced by alarmingly high rates of poor health and nutrition and, morbidity, suicide, substance abuse, and unemployment, as well as poor sanitation, infrastructure, and housing conditions on many reservations. Many tribes hope that the opportunities opened up in the last 20 years to generate income through tribally owned casino gaming enterprises will assist them in overcoming this systemic poverty. Indeed, many tribes are using these revenues to expand and improve health care, education, infrastructure, and other social services. They are also using gaming revenues to gain access to and influence over the political and legal structures that have harmed them in the past in order to restore tribal control and protection over culturally important places and resources.

Shifts in the relationship between American Indian nations and European colonizers and the U.S. government continue to impact Native identity and communities, by shaping the constraints on and opportunities that are available to both individuals and their communities. Despite these constraints, tremendous diversity has been sustained among Native peoples in their cultures, their beliefs, and their ways of life. It is impossible to describe or categorize "Native Americans" as one ethnic or racial group, though outsiders have attempted to do so for several hundred years. As we have seen, these racial identifiers are extremely problematic and deeply rooted in racist and colonial ideologies that continue to impact Native people today.

On the other hand, a pan-Indian consciousness and identity has emerged as the result of these interventions and has since become an important part of American Indian social life and political mobilization in the United States. Most Native people, however, draw their sense of identity from the ties they maintain with the people, cultural practices, and homelands of their people. These include their sense of responsibility to their extended families, clans, and communities and the perpetuation of their languages and ways of life.

Native Cultures and Diversity

For many non-Native people in the United States, the only encounters they have with Native American cultures are through the Native language names given to places they live in or visit, through pop culture and media stereotypes, and through the often brief and misleading histories they learn about Native people in primary and secondary education. Images of painted warriors dressed in buckskins and feathers, riding horses, sleeping in tipis, and wielding bows and arrows and tomahawks have dominated contemporary mainstream stereotypes.

Stereotypes change with the times, and Native people have variously been typed at different times as "bloodthirsty" or "noble, nature-loving savages," living in an imagined "traditional" past. Others believe Native people have been fully assimilated into U.S. culture as impoverished racial minorities. In reality, there are a multitude of different Native communities in the United States, which actively practice and identify with hundreds of different Native cultures. Native people in the United States today live in the same modern world as non-Native Americans. Most live in European-American-style homes, dress in the same fashions as members of "mainstream" U.S. society, drive cars and pickup trucks, watch satellite TV, and live and work the same breadth of lifestyles and occupations as others do.

Changing Culture

Culture is not a static phenomenon. All people, everywhere on earth, creatively incorporate and reinterpret their inherited "traditional" cultures in the contexts of their contemporary needs, desires, and values. Most American Indian people have adopted many aspects of mainstream U.S. culture, pop culture, and the regional cultures where they are located (southern, southwestern Chicano, and northeastern French cultures, for example). In addition, many Native Americans have also adopted as part of their identities and cultural toolkits aspects of the pan-Indian music, art, imagery, political activism, powwows, and sacred and religious practices that have developed over the past century.

The continuing practice and revitalization of local traditional cultural practices specific to one's own people plays perhaps the largest part in defining the identity of most Native American people. Past U.S. policies and activities that aimed at destroying Native land bases and cultures, along with generations of reservation flight and the influences of U.S. culture, have all contributed to fears that traditional cultures, languages, and practices would disappear. Thus, American Indians struggle to maintain local traditional cultures despite these forces and to revitalize traditional arts, music, languages, healing practices, sacred rituals, and land use practices; this has always been and continues to be of the utmost importance in Native communities.

Because of the enormous variation among Native American cultures, it is impossible to adequately describe that diversity and complexity in this space. Historically, anthropologists attempted to describe and simplify this diversity in Native cultures by categorizing them into ten regional "culture areas," which are still used in many texts today. This taxonomy, however, is not meaningful to Native people themselves. Native groups have varied greatly in their subsistence strategies and social organization from small bands of people who ranged seasonally across widely different landscapes as hunters and gatherers, to those who were sedentary agriculturalists or fishermen, to those who maintained their subsistence through trade and commerce. These historic ways of living on the land shaped the particular cultural formations, community structures, and senses of identity that each community formed. Today, subsistence in most communities can be and usually is obtained in part through wage labor and purchase of needs from retail stores. Traditional lifeways, cultural practices, and community structures persist in forms that reinforce local identities and cultures.

Native peoples are equally diverse in their cosmological belief systems, religious practices, governance structures, languages, musical and artistic expressions, and myriad material objects that reproduce their cultures. These include foods, clothing, housing, and other objects of daily and ritual use. Among the clearest indications of this diversity is the large number of indigenous languages that are still spoken in the United States today. When Europeans first arrived in the Americas, it is estimated that around 300 Native languages, including 2,000 dialects, were spoken in the United States and Canada. Today, there are about 175 to 200 languages (depending on how dialects are counted) still spoken. A decline in the use of Native languages over the past century has led to renewed efforts in recent decades to revitalize their use through bilingual education programs and the encouragement of their use in tribal offices and homes. The continuation of Native languages is vital to the survival of Native cultures, histories (which are predominantly preserved through oral traditions), and identities.

Common Qualities

Granted this tremendous diversity among different Native American communities, a few general observations may be made about similarities between them. In most Native communities, kinship relations continue to dominate social organization. Male-headed, nuclear families are somewhat rare, though past U.S. policies and interventions in Native social life attempted to institute them as social norms. Extended families are common, often with many generations living in a single household or in close contact. Many Native communities are matrilocal, matrilineal, and matriarchal. In these communities, women control decision making, wealth, land use, and inheritance.

In most communities, people trace their lineages from and consider as part of their extended families those who belong to their clans. Clan lineage, often traced through one's mother, is important in the organization of social life and the everyday functioning of many communities. In many, specific clans are responsible for various cultural, religious, and infrastructural maintenance tasks, including such matters as caring for sacred objects, organizing hunting and gathering trips, and looking over the maintenance of the village, agricultural fields, or other important places.

In most Native American cultures, "religion" or spirituality is threaded throughout the social organization and everyday lives of people. Many members of a Native community may not explicitly learn the traditional spiritual ways and meanings of their people, though they may play an important role in organizing the ways in which they live and the yearly practices in which they participate. Spiritual and cultural practices are often tied to relationships with particular places and the yearly cycles of seasonal, climatological, and agricultural changes of their homelands. In many cultures, clan kinship and ancestry is also linked to the natural world.

Native Homelands and Reservations

Nearly universally, Native American groups' identities and cultures are tied to particular places. These places include sites of cosmological significance, such as those believed to be the location of their origins (places of emergence and creation); sites of communion with the holy, historic homelands, ancient villages, and burial grounds; places where they have collected foods, medicines, building and cultural materials, and holy objects for generations; and the reservations that their people now occupy. All of these specific places play important parts in the religions, cultures, and identities of Native people, and access to them is integral to their perpetuation as a people.

Even for the 66% of Native American people who now live away from reservations in urban areas in the United States, these places remain important to the orientation and perpetuation of their group identities. The struggle to maintain access to and control over these places continues today for nearly all tribes. Past U.S. violence and policies have significantly disrupted and fragmented Native homelands. In many cases, whole Native communities were forced from their lands and resettled elsewhere, especially in the 19th century. Many Indian lands were taken by the federal government and then given or leased to private citizens or kept as government lands, and, at various times, recognition of sovereign tribal authority to manage tribal lands and resources was denied.

The 2004 American Community Survey indicates that the American Indian and Alaska Native populations are not evenly distributed; just five states account for the majority of their populations: Arizona, California, New Mexico, Texas, and North Carolina. Their interactions with the U.S. government have resulted in a patchwork of 304 federal American Indian reservations and individual American-Indian-owned restricted fee lands, which make up the 55.7 million acres (225,410 km²), or 2.3%, of the area of the United States protected by the federal trust relationship today. The largest reservation in the United States is the Navajo Nation *(Diné Bikéyah)*, which is about the size of West Virginia, with 17 million acres and a resident population of nearly 200,000 people. Reservations vary in size from this extreme to the 100 or less acres of many California tribes, which may be inhabited by only a handful of people.

American Indian reservations include all the lands that a tribe reserved for itself and did not specifically cede to or have illegally seized by the U.S. government. These reservations were recognized historically by the United States through treaties, executive orders, administrative acts, and acts of Congress. On federal reservations, tribal governments are recognized by the federal government as having jurisdictional control over the management of those lands and as being responsible for the provisions of infrastructure and services. A small number of individual states have also recognized Indian reservation lands, even when the federal government has failed to do so.

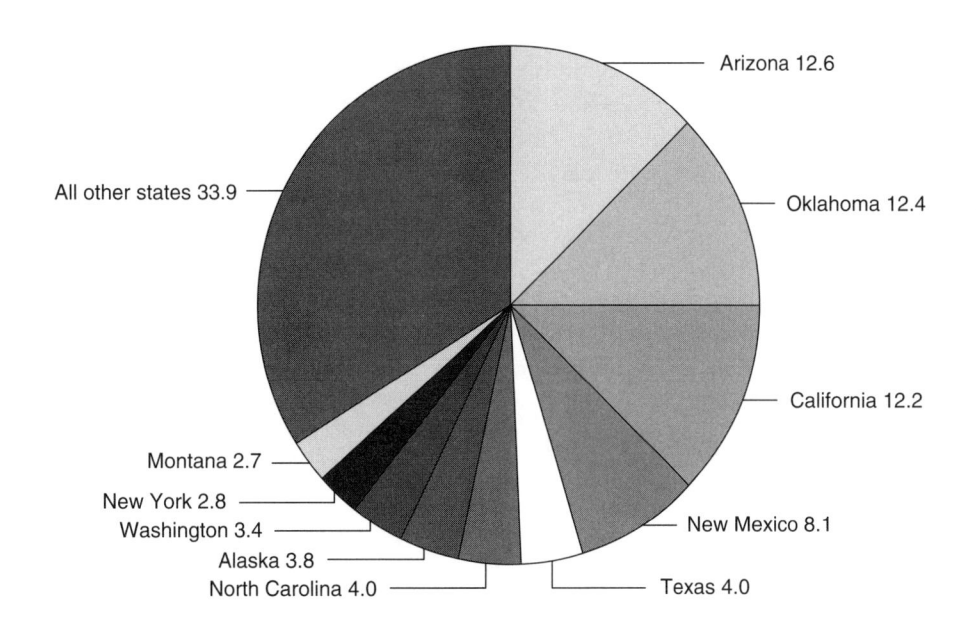

Figure 1 American Indian and Alaska Native Household Population by State, 2004

Source: U.S. Census, http://factfinder.census.gov

Note: Percent distribution of American Indian and Alaska Native population. Data based on sample limited to the household population and exclude the population living in institutions, college dormitories, and other group quarters. For information on confidentiality protection, sampling error, nonsampling error, and definitions, see http://factfinder.census.gov/home/en/datanotes/exp_acs2004.html

Of the reservation lands that have remained with or been restored to federally recognized tribes, many are highly fragmented in a checkerboard pattern of tribal ownership interspersed with non-Native private and government ownership. This makes it incredibly complicated both politically and legally for tribes, states, and the federal government to manage resources, work out jurisdictional disputes, and provide infrastructure and services to these communities. This is further complicated by the fact that many Native landholdings are located far from urban centers and in many cases are underdeveloped in terms of physical infrastructure, such as paved roads; power, water, and waste facilities; housing; and economic opportunities.

Maintaining and reclaiming tribal sovereignty over Native lands and supporting sustainable economic development and ecological restoration on them continues to be an ongoing struggle for many tribes. These struggles include regaining access to, ownership of, jurisdictional authority over, and federal trust protection of lands and resources that were taken from tribes in the past. Many tribes have also faced environmental degradation of their homelands due to federal interventions and leases of Native lands, abusive practices by extractive industries, and economic and political restrictions that have made it difficult to effectively manage and regulate pollution.

Changes in federal laws and funding available to tribes in the last 4 decades are making it possible for tribes to use their unique political and legal status to protect and restore their important places. In nearly all cases, tribes are working to socially and ecologically protect the places that are sacred and culturally important to them, as these places embody their histories, sense of identity, cultures, and spiritual relationships with nature.

Angela Ann Gonzales and Melanie Stansbury

See Appendix B

See also Aleuts; Black Elk; Blackfeet; Cherokee; Cheyenne; Choctaw; Deloria, Vine, Jr.; Hopi; Menominee; Navajo; Ojibwa; Peletier, Leonard; Pueblos; Sioux; Thorpe, Jim; Tlingit

Further Readings

Bataille, Gretchen M., ed. 1993. *Native American Women: A Biographical Dictionary.* New York: Garland.

Berkhofer, Robert F., Jr. 1979. *The White Man's Indian: Images of the American Indian from Columbus to the Present.* New York: Random House.

Bordewich, Fergus M. 1996. *Killing the White Man's Indian: Reinventing Native Americans at the End of the 20th Century.* New York: Doubleday.

Calloway, Colin G. 2004. *First People: A Documentary Survey of American Indian History.* 2nd ed. Boston, MA: Bedford/St.Martin's Press.

Clifton, J. A., ed. 1990. *The Invented Indian: Cultural Fictions and Government Policies.* New Brunswick, NJ: Transaction.

Cohen, Felix. 1971. *Handbook of Federal Indian Law.* Albuquerque: University of New Mexico Press.

Deloria, Philip J. 1998. *Playing Indian.* New Haven, CT: Yale University Press.

Deloria, Philip J. 2004. *Indians in Unexpected Places.* Lawrence: University Press of Kansas.

Deloria, Vine, Jr. 1988. *Custer Died for Your Sins: An Indian Manifesto.* Norman: University of Oklahoma Press.

Hauptman, Laurence M. 1995. *Tribes and Tribulations: Misconceptions about American Indians and Their Histories.* Albuquerque: University of New Mexico Press.

Hirschfelder, Arlene and Martha Kreipe de Montano. 1993. *The Native American Almanac: A Portrait of Native America Today.* New York: Prentice Hall General Reference.

Hoxie, Frederick E., ed. 1988. *Indians in American History: An Introduction.* Arlington Heights, IL: Harlan Davidson.

Knack, Martha C. and Alice Littlefield, eds. 1996. *Native Americans and Wage Labor: Ethnohistorical Perspectives.* Norman: University of Oklahoma Press.

Nabokov, Peter, ed. 1991. *Native American Testimony: A Chronicle of Indian-White Relations from Prophecy to the Present, 1492–1992.* New York: Penguin Books.

O'Neill, Colleen, ed. 2004. *Native Pathways: American Indian Culture and Economic Development in the 20th Century.* Boulder: University of Colorado Press.

Prucha, Francis Paul. 1984. *The Great Father: The United States Government and the American Indians.* Lincoln: University of Nebraska Press.

Riley, Patricia, ed. 1993. *Growing Up Native American.* New York: Avon Books.

U.S. Census Bureau. 2007. *The American Community—American Indians and Alaska Natives: 2004. American Community Survey Report.* Washington, DC: U.S. Government Printing Office.

Utter, Jack. 1993. *American Indians: Answers to Today's Questions.* Lake Ann, MI: National Woodlands.

NATIVE AMERICANS, ENVIRONMENT AND

Environmental issues are a central concern for Native North American peoples in several different ways that intertwine with what some have called a history of colonialist racism and genocide. These include the dispossession of land, the degradation of indigenous space, and the marginalization of Native American lifeways, which, it has been argued, are more sustainable than those of modern industrial and expansionist nation-states. Despite the great cultural diversity of Indigenous Peoples in the Americas and around the world who have faced similar experiences, a sustained global indigenous movement has emerged that emphasizes cultural survival and resistance to imperial history, learning, language, religion, and trade. Much of this resistance is embodied in guarding living ecologies where tribes have specific and ancestral bonds.

Tribalism

The indigenous people of the Americas have always encompassed a diverse set of cultures and societies, perhaps best understood as distinct tribes organized through kinship rules and institutions. Indeed, tribalism, as Vine Deloria, Jr. wrote in *Custer Died for Your Sins,* is a quintessential element of American Indian societies. Each tribe has many variations in practices (customs) and social structures (e.g., clans), as well as norms and expectations for tribal society and individuals within the respective tribe. Thus, each tribe has a unique political history and therefore unique relations with the earth, particularly because each tribe is place based: That is, it has developed within a specific ecological space.

Because tribes are place based, intimate knowledge about the nature of ecological systems and their dynamics is learned and recorded (usually) in oral histories and ceremonies passed down through elders in the tribes or other designated leaders. This place-based evolution of tribes, in addition to their egalitarian social structures, has limited the ways in which tribes have allowed themselves to change their landscapes and degrade the surrounding ecology. This is not to say that some tribes did not degrade their environments—some did so, which led to their own demise. However, the very fact that many tribes, such as the Yakima or the Hopi, may trace histories of thousands of years of living in a specific place indicates that they were able to maintain the integrity of the large ecological structure (e.g., hydrology, soils, game) without undermining their subsistence needs. Add this to the fact that most tribes saw and continue to see the world around them as a living family and that this worldview guided theocratic governance in tribes, and it becomes clear why tribes are considered relatively sustainable compared with Western cultures that have disposed of land as if it were a cog in a machine, much less a part of the family of life.

Dispossession

The dispossession of sacred and ancestral place-based tribal land is a critical element in Native American histories and in the histories of colonizing settlers who eventually established the nations of Canada and the United States. Seizure by European-based empires of land that had been under tribal tenure, sometimes for thousands of years, has been a consistent story in the last 500 years of Native American history. This dispossession was based on frankly racist attitudes toward Indigenous Peoples, whose societies were treated and viewed as less evolved than those of Europe. In fact, Europeans considered themselves to be at the center of civilization, which they believed was produced by controlling nature and centralizing political structure in European-type monarchies, and later republics. At the same time, European colonists saw Indigenous Peoples as "savage" and "uncivilized." Nature was something to be dominated, and Indigenous Peoples were seen as part of that untamed wilderness.

Under this premise of constructed racial superiority, partially empowered by church doctrine to convert Native peoples, Europeans and later the U.S. government waged wars against tribes, ostensibly to gain control over Native land. Not all of these wars were won by the government, and, according to the 1978 Indian Claims Commission Report (a federal government body), the U.S. government never attained legitimate title to more than one-third of land controlled by Native Americans in the United States. Thus, legally, this land still belongs to the tribes.

Altogether, Native American peoples have been maligned as having a supposedly less developed or less advanced social structure in part because tribes often see themselves as part of an organic and living world that deserves respect and reverence. For this reason, many tribes had strict rules about what kinds of changes to the surrounding environment were acceptable. For example, several tribes had sanctions against cutting into the earth, thereby prohibiting both farming and mining. Other tribes did farm and mine and continue to do so. Europeans and later the colonial U.S. governments would engage in wave after wave of policy initiatives meant to "civilize" the tribes and get them to take up farming (often on land that was not fertile or in climates that were inappropriate) or other Western practices, many of which were aimed at dismantling tribalism.

Key Policies

In contemporary times, the U.S. federal government has granted itself ultimate control over Native American environments through the doctrines of plenary power and the federal trust. *Plenary power* means that the U.S. government has complete power to decide the course of action for tribes, and the premise of *federal trust* is that the federal government is supposed to "take care of" tribes as a guardian would a child. Whereas tribes in the United States are considered "domestic dependent nations," with mitigated sovereignty to determine their own course of action, the 1902 Supreme Court case of *Lone Wolf v. Hitchcock* decided that the U.S. government had ultimate control to carry out the federal trust, even when the tribes disagree with the government. Thus, the doctrine asserts that as in ward-guardian relationships, the federal government knows the interest of tribes better than the tribes themselves. This belief stems from a history and practice of continued prejudice against Native people as "less than." More than that, however, when the *Lone Wolf* decision was written, it noted that the United States could be held to treaties or treaty promises if it was to carry out the federal trust doctrine.

Accordingly, while the United States has kept and honored some treaties or provisions in treaties, some of the most important elements of treaties have not been honored. For example, in many treaties, there is some reference to the permanent control of the reserved land ("reservations") agreed to in the treaties. These clauses, sometimes employing language such as "as long as the grass is green and the river flows," indicated that the tribe would control these lands in perpetuity. Nevertheless, the U.S. government has pursued policies such as *allotment,* as in the Dawes General Allotment Act of 1887, which disposed of tribal land, assigning some to individuals of the tribe and selling off the rest to homesteaders. Also, with plenary power, the control of Native lands rests ultimately not in the control of the tribes, but with the Department of the Interior, which can sign off on a lease (e.g., for mining) on tribal lands, in contradiction to tribal demands.

Degradation of Tribal Lands

Perhaps this loss of control over tribal lands accounts for some of the severe environmental degradation of tribal reservations over the last 100 years. In part, this degradation has involved deforestation, decline of game and fish populations, and pollution. Among the more profound losses on Native lands, however, has been the mining for radioactive materials on reservations. During the 1970s, all uranium was mined on Native American reservations, even though tribes controlled only about 60%. Thus, the decision to mine the vast majority of materials on Native land raises serious questions—and a lack of accountability for costly damage has been proposed as one reason. For example, the United Nuclear Corporation had a retention dam of radioactive water, which burst on *Diné* (Navajo) land, contaminating 100 miles of the Rio Puerco. This was the largest nuclear accident in U.S. history. *Diné* workers in uranium mines were lied to about the effects of radioactive exposure, and to this day there are hundreds of radioactive tailing (waste) piles that sit there unattended to, where children have been known to play.

Native American Lifeways

It should be clear from the preceding discussion that tribal lifeways continue to face serious threats. If a social group is land based, then dispossessing that group of its land is more than a disruption of economic subsistence. If a tribal group culturally identifies with a specific place and the ecological elements of that place, such as its wildlife, then undermining that lifeway also undermines an aspect of tribal identity, and some scholars have considered this an aspect of genocide. For example, there are places that are sacred to the Hopi people, but parts of that land are privately owned and currently being mined. Ceremonies tied to that place are now out of the question, and this element of Hopi culture and the aspect of "being in the world" that comes with paying respect through that ceremony are now lost. Indeed, through the erasure of places where ceremonies critical to Native American lifeways are performed and passed down, a part of that tribe is lost.

Despite these problems, some tribes have been mobilizing politically to fight for self-determination. Also, it is notable that one environmental policy, "Winter's Rights," declares that reservations have the right to enough water for tribal economic and agricultural functions—thereby reserving a powerful resource for tribes. Furthermore, many tribes have been resilient enough to maintain themselves in the face of 500 years of pressure. If Vine Deloria, Jr. is right, tribal structure will continue not only to provide a way for Native Americans but also to serve as an example to others.

Peter Jacques

See also Deloria, Vine, Jr.; Discrimination, Environmental Hazards; Environmental Justice; Native American Education; Native American Health Care; Native American Identity; Native Americans; Water Rights

Further Readings

Churchill, Ward. 2003. *Acts of Rebellion: The Ward Churchill Reader.* New York: Routledge.

Deloria, Vine, Jr. 1969. *Custer Died for Your Sins: An Indian Manifesto.* New York: Avon Books.

Greymorning, Stephen. 2004. *A Will to Survive: Indigenous Essays on the Politics of Culture, Language, and Identity.* Boston, MA: McGraw-Hill.

Johansen, Bruce. 2003. *Indigenous Peoples and Environmental Issues: An Encyclopedia.* Westport, CT: Greenwood Press.

NATIVISM

The term *nativism* refers to the beliefs and policies favoring native-born citizens over immigrants. Typically, it refers to political actions, but it has also been taken to refer to broader antiforeigner feelings. Virtually all nations that have attracted immigrants have, during different historical periods, developed anti-alien sentiments, especially when the immigrants are culturally different from the host society. This entry, however, focuses on nativism in the United States.

Nativism emerged in dramatic fashion in the mid-19th century as Europeans arrived in large numbers from countries other than Great Britain. In addition, these later immigrants were less likely to be of the Protestant faith. The relative absence of federal immigration legislation until the 1880s does not mean that all these new arrivals were welcomed. *Xenophobia,* the fear or hatred of strangers or foreigners, naturally led to nativism, which can be viewed as the institutionalization of xenophobia.

Roman Catholic settlers in general and the Irish in particular were among the first Europeans to experience nativism. Anti-Catholic feeling originated in Europe and was brought by the early Protestant immigrants. The Catholics of colonial America, although few, were subject to limits on their civil and religious rights. From independence until around 1820, little evidence appeared of the anti-Catholic sentiment of colonial days, but the cry against "popery" grew as the numbers of Irish immigrants, as well as German Catholics, increased.

One example of nativism was the political movement called the "American Republican Party," originating in 1843. Eventually, it became known as the "Know-Nothing Party" because of the semisecret nature of the group. When members were asked about its activities, they were supposed to reply "I know nothing." Levi Boone was elected mayor of Chicago on the Know-Nothing ticket in 1855. Reflecting nativism, he barred all immigrants from city jobs and created policies that significantly curtailed German- and Irish-owned taverns within the city. Revivals of anti-Catholicism continued well into the 20th century.

The most dramatic outbreak of nativism in the 19th century was aimed at the Chinese. If there had been any doubt by the mid-1800s that the United States could harmoniously accommodate all, debate on the Chinese Exclusion Act would negatively settle the question once and for all. Most Chinese were barred from immigrating; Chinese already in the United States were unable to bring their families to join them; and those who left the country, even if they had been born in the United States, might find reentry difficult or impossible. Still later, nativist sentiment would target Italian and Polish immigrants, Eastern European Jews after World War II, Vietnamese and other South Asian refugees of the 1970s, and the Cuban "Marielito" refugees of the 1980s.

While the term *nativism* has largely been used to describe 19th-century sentiments, anti-immigration views and organized movements have continued into the 21st century. Political scientist Samuel P. Huntington called continuing immigration a "clash of civilizations," which could only be remedied by significantly reducing legal immigration and closing the border to illegal arrivals. His view, which enjoys support, is that the fundamental world conflicts of the new century are cultural in nature rather than ideological or even economic.

Beginning in the 1990s and continuing through the present, recent immigrants and their descendants have been characterized by many as being responsible for a variety of social problems, or at least for making them worse. In 1994, Californians passed Proposition 187, which was aimed at denying access of illegal immigrants to social services, public education, and health care. Today's nativists point to low wages, overcrowded housing, unemployment, crime, overstretched health services, and burdened public schools as justifying their views. Concerns about terrorism have added a new emotional element to nativism in countries such as the United Kingdom and Spain, as well as the United States, which have experienced high-profile terrorist attacks in recent years.

Richard T. Schaefer

See also Americanization; Dillingham Flaw; Ethnocentrism; Immigration, U.S.; Immigration and Race; Irish Americans; Prejudice; Proposition 187; Racism; Stereotypes; Terrorism; "Us and Them"; Xenophobia

Further Readings

Billington, Ray A. [1938] 1964. *The Protestant Crusade, 1800–1860: A Study of the Origins of American Nativism.* New York: Quadrangle Books.

Duff, John B. 1971. *The Irish in the United States.* Belmont, CA: Wadsworth.

Gerber, David A. 1993. *Nativism, Anti-Catholicism, and Anti-Semitism.* New York: Scribner's.

Huntington, Samuel P. 1993. "The Clash of Civilizations?" *Foreign Affairs* 72(3):22–49.

Huntington, Samuel P. 1996. *The Clash of Civilizations and the Remaking of World Order.* New York: Simon & Schuster.

Morse, Samuel F. B. 1835. *Foreign Conspiracy against the Liberties of United States.* New York: Leavitt, Lord.

Warner, Sam Bass, Jr. 1968. *The Private City: Philadelphia in Three Periods of Its Growth.* Philadelphia, PA: University of Pennsylvania Press.

NAVAJO

The Navajo make up the largest single American Indian tribe and occupy the largest and most populated reservation. The Navajo Nation, or the *Diné* (meaning "the people"), has been a significant force in the Southwest and occupies a prominent role in most Native American issues and policymaking today. This entry includes an overview of Navajo history, the Navajo-Hopi dispute, contemporary Navajo education, and the contemporary life focusing on the Navajo reservation.

History

The earliest identifiable traces of the Navajo are the 500-year-old remains of *hogans,* rounded houses of poles and brush covered with earth that were, and still are in contemporary times, distinctively Navajo. Current thinking of archaeologists proposes that the Navajo and other Athapaskan (or Athabascan) people migrated from Canada as hunters and gatherers into what is now the U.S. Southwest by 1100 AD.

The *Diné* themselves describe their history as a series of worlds surviving surging floodwaters to form sacred mountains with holy people. The Navajo world is closely tied to the land, as each event of creation is linked to specific locations revered to this day.

When the Spanish entered New Mexico in 1540, the area north of the Pueblos was occupied by bands speaking an Athabascan language; they came to be called "Apaches." For 200 years, relations with the Pueblos varied from being hostile to more of a host-guest relationship. The Navajo emerged as more strongly influenced by the Pueblos, whereas the Athabascan-speaking Kiowa-Apache experienced a greater Plains influence. The Pueblo influence is seen in the Navajo's agricultural system, their matrilineal (mother-based) system of descent, and the practices of weaving and sand paintings.

Encounters between the Navajo and the United States began with the conclusion of the Mexican-American War, with the consequence that the Navajo people as of 1848 resided in U.S. territory. Early agreements with the first military expeditions led to misunderstandings, raids, retaliations, and still more treaties. These early treaties were virtually useless, since the Navajo hold no centralized authority and the federal government never grasped the autonomous nature of Navajo bands. Hostile engagements were numerous, in part because the Navajos raided Anglo settlements to find and free thousands of their people who had been enslaved.

Beginning in 1862, Colonel Kit Carson was charged with controlling the Navajos. His troops

Three Navajo women weaving (1914). The early Navajos were nomadic hunters and gatherers, and Navajo weaving tells a story of their encounters and adaptations with neighboring cultures over 300 years. Weaving continues to be an exciting expression of Navajo culture.

Source: Library of Congress, Prints & Photographs Division, LC-DIG-ppmsc-00135.

methodically destroyed fields and killed tribal people who resisted. Thousands were forced out by the threat of starvation and made to take the "Long Walk," over a 20-day period in 1863, of 300 miles across New Mexico to Fort Sumner in the eastern part of the state. The imprisoned Navajos were vulnerable to disease, especially to smallpox; those who survived were taught new farming techniques, the principles of Christianity, and the building of adobe houses. With the end of the Civil War, and of the perceived need to closely control the Navajos, a relaxation of government policy took place. The Navajos returned in 1868 to their former territory, straddling the Arizona-New Mexico state line, and returned to their accustomed practices of farming and raising small livestock, such as sheep and goats.

By the close of the 19th century, the Navajo culture had been influenced by continuing contact with different tribal groups, but particularly with the Pueblo, as already noted. In addition, as anthropologist Edward Spicer has observed, there had been significant aspects of Hispanicization, Mexicanization, and Anglicization.

The Navajo reservation came to be enlarged several times, from 3.5 million acres in 1868 to 15 million acres in 1934, eventually surrounding the area granted to the Hopi, leading to continuing tensions. Another major controversy developed over the population size of Navajo livestock, especially sheep. The Bureau of Indian Affairs (BIA) administrators beginning in 1934 argued that the Navajo had more livestock than the land could support. Most Navajo disagreed, but nonetheless the BIA killed nearly half the livestock, leading to generations of bitter feelings.

A celebrated aspect of 20th-century Navajo history is the participation of many *Diné* in the military. For example, Navajo soldiers served as "code talkers" during World War II. In this unique role, they utilized the Navajo language for coded messages, which Japan's military found impenetrable.

Navajo-Hopi Dispute

One long-term dispute illustrates the complexity of land claims when the federal government has tried to manage tribal people. In 1882, the United States declared an end to a century-long conflict over which tribe, the Hopi or Navajo, had the right to some lands in northeastern Arizona. The original inhabitants, the Hopi, were granted sole use of a group of mesas. These lands were surrounded by joint-use land to be used by both tribes, which was totally surrounded by the relatively populous Navajo reservation—about nine times the size of the Hopi land.

The original conflict was created when the Navajos fled the U.S. Cavalry in New Mexico and entered neighboring Arizona. Even after joint use was declared in the 1930s, the government began issuing grazing permits to Navajos in these areas. In 1993, a new agreement was proposed that would allow some Navajos to remain with their homes and livestock on Hopi land. In exchange, the Hopis would receive land and money from the government to resolve lawsuits. The compromise was attacked by both tribes and by White landowners in the disputed territory. As the dispute continued, Native Americans on these lands experienced extreme stress because their future was in limbo until 2006, when the final demarcation was determined.

Navajo Education

What leads to academic success? Often, the answer is a supportive family, but this has not always been said about Native Americans. Educators rooted in the European education traditions believed that children who were faithful to traditional Native culture could not succeed in schools. This assimilationist view argued that to succeed in the larger, White-dominated society, it was important to begin to shed the "old ways" as soon as possible. Interestingly, research done in the last 10 years questions the assimilationist view, concluding that American Indian students can improve their academic performance through educational programs that are less assimilationist and that use curricula building on what the Native American youth learn in their homes and communities.

Representative of this growing research is the study completed by sociologist Angela A. A. Willeto among her fellow Navajo tribal people. She studied a random sample of 451 Navajo high school students from eleven different Navajo Nation schools. She examined the impact on the students' performance of their orientation toward traditional Navajo culture. Willeto acknowledged that the prevailing view has been that all that is inherently Navajo in a child must be eliminated and replaced with mainstream, White-society beliefs and lifestyles.

In Willeto's study, the Navajo tradition was measured by a number of indicators, such as participating in Navajo dances, consulting a medicine man, entering a sweat bath to cleanse oneself spiritually, weaving rugs, having aspirations to attend a more traditional hogan, and using the Navajo language. School performance was measured by grades, commitment to school, and aspirations to attend college. Willeto found that the students who lived a more traditional life among the Navajo succeeded in school just as well and were just as committed to success in school and college as were high schoolers leading a more assimilated life.

These results are important because many Native Americans themselves accept an assimilationist view. Even within the Navajo Nation, where Navajo language *(Dinétah)* instruction has been mandated in all reservation schools since 1984, many Navajos still equate learning only with the mastery of White society's subject matter.

Contemporary Patterns

In the United States as of 2004, there were 230,401 Navajo, representing 10.7% of the tribal American Indian and Alaska Native population. According to the 2000 census, the Navajo are a young population, with a median age of 24.4, compared with 28.8 for all American Indians and 35.4 for the total U.S. population.

The Navajo household averages 3.66 members, compared with 2.59 for the United States as a whole. Only 6.9% of Navajos have college degrees, which is low even compared with all American Indians (12.1%). The poverty rate for the Navajo in 1999 was 37%, contrasted with 12.4% for the general population.

The most striking aspect of contemporary Navajo people is that as of 2000, 67.1% do not speak English at all in the home, compared with 60.4% of the Pueblo people (the next-highest group of non-English-speaking tribal people) and 27.9% of American Indians as a group. As of 2000, the Navajo reservation recorded 174,847 individuals, or about 63% of all Navajo people.

Hostilities between Navajo and non-Navajo did not end with the close of encounters with the cavalry or the army. The Navajo Nation Tribal Council (the legislative body of the reservation government) has often spoken out about racial discrimination and prejudice experienced by the Navajo in areas bordering the reservation. Another source of friction is past and future use of natural resources. The reservation has been the site of uranium processing and huge coal-firing plants. Disputes continue through the present about overpayment of past royalties and cleanup of closed facilities. The situation of the Navajo with respect to natural resources is not unusual for reservations, in terms of both non-Natives profiting and the tribal people experiencing environmental degradation.

Richard T. Schaefer

See Appendix A

See also Assimilation; Bureau of Indian Affairs; Environmental Justice; Hopi; Native American Education; Native American Health Care; Native Americans; Native Americans, Environment and; Pueblos; Treaty of Guadalupe Hidalgo (1848)

Further Readings

Alvord, Lori Arviso and Elizabeth Cohen Van Pelt. 1999. *The Scalpel and the Silver Bear.* New York: Bantam.

Barringer, Felicity. 2007. "Navajos Hope for Millions a Year from Power Plant." *New York Times,* July 27, p. A12.

Griffin-Pierce, Trady. 2000. *Native Peoples of the Southwest.* Albuquerque: University of New Mexico Press.

Kehoe, Alice B. 1992. *North American Indians: A Comprehensive Account.* 2nd ed. Upper Saddle River, NJ: Prentice Hall.

Ogunwole, Stella U. 2006. *We the People: American Indians and Alaska Natives in the United States.* Washington, DC: U.S. Government Printing Office.

Powers, Willow Roberts. 2001. *Navajo Trading: The End of an Era.* Albuquerque: University of New Mexico Press.

Reyhner, Jon. 2001. "Cultural Survival vs. Forced Assimilation." *Cultural Survival Quarterly* 25(2):22–25.

Spicer, Edward H. 1981. *Cycles of Conquest: The Impact of Spain, Mexico, and the United States on the Indians of the Southwest, 1533–1960.* Tucson: University of Arizona Press.

U.S. Census Bureau. 2007. *The American Community: American Indians and Alaska Natives 2004.* Washington, DC: U.S. Government Printing Office.

Wilkins, David E. 2003. *The Navajo Political Experience.* Rev. ed. Lanham, MD: Rowman & Littlefield.

Willeto, Angela A. A. 1999. "Navajo Culture and Female Influences on Academic Success: Traditional Is Not a Significant Predictor of Achievement among Young Navajos." *Journal of American Indian Education* 38(2):1–24.

NEGRO LEAGUE BASEBALL

When major league baseball retired uniform "number 42" in 1997, it was to honor Jackie Robinson, who broke the color barrier in 1947 with the Brooklyn Dodgers. Black baseball players had been barred from organized leagues through de facto exclusion from the late 1800s until 1946. At the annual convention in 1867, the National Association of Baseball Players (NABBP), the game's first league, decided that it was in their best interests to bar any person of African descent or any team that played a person of color. Such exclusion led to de facto segregation of players by race by the end of the century.

Nevertheless, Black teams were formed, and they played exhibition games on what was called the "barnstorming" circuit. These teams were particularly prominent starting in the 1890s, as they sometimes played against White teams, and all-Black teams would play in otherwise all-White leagues. This entry chronicles various attempts by Blacks and Whites to sustain America's pastime according to rapidly changing race relations in the early part of the 1900s.

The Early Years

A number of amateur teams, such as the Colored Union Club of Brooklyn and the Pythian Club of Philadelphia, were formed in the 1860s, and the New York Cuban Giants, the first salaried Black baseball team, was established in 1885. Beginning with this period, barnstorming was the way of life for Black baseball players. These early teams were located where players could find day jobs. Such industrial towns as Portsmouth, Virginia (Firefighters), and Baltimore, Maryland (Stars), were home to players who worked in railroad shops while playing for semipro teams. The Pittsburgh and Washington, D.C., area had the "Blue Ribbons" industrial league team, which eventually came to be known as the "Homestead Grays." The early days of barnstorming also included the "All-American Black Tourists," who traveled on their own railroad car; each of their games was preceded by an elaborate street parade.

While institutional-level measures were established for segregation in baseball, some individual players managed to integrate even in earlier days. For example, Bud Fowler, who is believed to be the first Black professional baseball player, first signed with a White team in New Castle, Pennsylvania, in 1872. By 1887,

Homestead Grays (1913). The Negro League champion Homestead Grays began as an industrial league team located in the mill town of Homestead, Pennsylvania. This team and others like it produced a number of players whose abilities were believed to be comparable to those of the White players in major-league baseball against whom they were prohibited from competing.

Source: Public domain.

twenty Black players were known to be playing with White teams. These were mostly in small leagues, but they included some historically significant figures. By and large, however, most White players did not feel comfortable playing together with Blacks.

At the time, the media praised these Black ballplayers, allowing them to gain some acceptance in organized baseball, while simultaneously blaming their miscues on the color of their skin. Some mainstream sports publications, like the *Sporting News,* recognized as early as 1889 the injustice in baseball toward Blacks and forecast a rough road ahead. In fact, by 1897, a year after *Plessy v. Ferguson* made separate-but-equal facilities constitutional, there were no Blacks in White baseball.

Most of the Negro ballplayers during this era had middle-class backgrounds, and practically all grew up in the North. Some, like Fleet Walker, attended college. Walker, the first Negro player with the International League, ended his career in 1889, when the league was closing its door to Blacks, and eventually became an author on race, including *Our Home Colony: A Treatise on the Past, Present, and Future of the Negro Race in America.* He is believed to be an originator of the modern militant Black movement because he rejected racial equality through education, religion, and enhancement of economic positions. Rather, he thought American Black citizens should emigrate to Africa.

The most prominent exceptions to the exclusion of Blacks in major-league baseball were Armando Marsans and Rafael Almeida, two light-skinned Cuban players who played for the Cincinnati Reds in 1911. While darker Cubans did not receive the same opportunities, these two players were clearly seen as "not Black," or "passing," due to their skin tone. In fact, during their playing days with the Reds, Marsans and Almeida denied that they had "Negro" blood in them, even though racial mixing was quite common in Cuba.

A League of Their Own

As the country as a whole experienced an economic boom in the late 1910s, the number of business opportunities for Blacks started to blossom. Andrew "Rube" Foster, who won 44 games in a row as a pitcher in 1902, collaborated with White interests, including John M. Schorling, Chicago White Sox owner Charles Comiskey's son-in-law, to play games in major-league ballparks. In exchange for permission to play in their ballparks, disproportionate amounts of revenue were taken away from Black owners, which eventually made their status meaningless. Gradually, these White owners decided to integrate the booking process and do away with the Black owners entirely.

This practice of undercutting profits from Black entrepreneurship was quite common across society at the time. Being frustrated by this exploitation and realizing the increasing interest in Black baseball among Whites, Foster formed the first organized league, the National Negro League, on February 13, 1920, based in Kansas City, Missouri. It included the Homestead Grays and later on the Newark Eagles, the first professional team owned and operated by a woman, Effa Manley. While Foster successfully fended off White stadium owners, he still had to answer to semi-silent White backers.

The league produced a number of players whose abilities were believed to be comparable to those of the White players in major-league baseball. Among them was Satchel Paige, who played for eight different teams in the National Negro League, beginning in 1926. He entered major-league baseball at age 42 with the Cleveland Indians, a year after Robinson's debut and the year the Indians won the American League pennant. Also entering the league was Josh Gibson, a catcher who was often compared to Babe Ruth for his ability to hit home runs, but with more humility and grace.

Many National Negro League players were compared with major-league baseball players. In some instances, such a comparison was acknowledged by the players themselves. For example, John Henry Lloyd, a legendary shortstop for the Philadelphia Cuban X Giants, Philadelphia Giants, New York Lincoln Giants, and Chicago American Giants, came to be known as the "Black Wagner," after legendary Hall-of-Famer Honus Wagner. In fact, Wagner himself was quoted as saying that it was a privilege to have been compared to Lloyd. While Wagner was elected into the baseball Hall of Fame as one of the first inductees in 1936, Lloyd was not recognized until 1977, when the Negro League Committee inducted him.

Although the National Negro League had regular schedules, fans often associated them with barnstorming, since promoters kept them busy on their days off with other teams outside the league, so that they routinely played over 200 games a year. These games not only provided opportunities for more exposure but were also financially rewarding for the players, who otherwise had to rely on jobs outside baseball to survive.

In addition to the National Negro League, a number of attempts were made to operate baseball leagues among Blacks in the early to mid-1900s. The formation of the Eastern Colored League in 1923 led to the first Negro World Series in 1924 with the National Negro League. In 1937, the Negro American League was formed in the South and the Midwest. The Negro American League and the National Negro League managed to coexist through the 1948 season. In 1949, the two leagues were merged, and the last Black major league was operated through 1960.

Social and Historical Context

Beginning with the Great Migration of Blacks from South to North, beginning in 1915, and despite subsequent race riots in twenty-six American cities, racial segregation continued to be a way of life at the beginning of the 20th century. However, some Whites in baseball spoke out on behalf of Black players who were being shut out. The *Baseball Weekly* in 1923 called the exclusion of Blacks a "hideous monster." While some managers and owners expressed interest in adding Black players to their teams, they inevitably ran into resistance from White players. By the late 1920s, the discussion of integration in baseball receded as the nation headed into the Great Depression, and the issue of social justice in general took a backseat to high unemployment rates. Given the circumstances, Foster and his league focused on building a competitive product of their own rather than integration, which created further cleavage. By 1931, the impact of economic hardship was too great for the league to survive. Though the second Negro League was established 2 years later, the league struggled to maintain a consistent number of participating teams, and, by 1936, the National Negro League was operating solely in the East.

The reasons for segregation in baseball did not deviate too far from societal reasons: the lack of travel accommodations for Black players, the fear of (White) public resistance, and the general belief that Black players were inferior. However, Robert Peterson, the author of *Only the Ball Was White*, suggests that the most prominent reason for segregation was the strong tradition in baseball that led many never to question how things have always been.

However, as the 1940s approached, more and more White reporters, scouts, and managers who had witnessed players like Paige and Gibson in person were convinced that a number of Negro League players belonged in the major leagues. Around the same time, increasing prominence and visibility of Blacks in education, the economy, and World War II military service had made the consideration of Blacks in major-league baseball more than an abstract discussion.

In 1941, President Franklin D. Roosevelt established the Fair Employment Practices Commission (FEPC) to monitor discriminatory hiring practices. Then, in August 1945, New York mayor Fiorello La Guardia formed a subcommittee on baseball of the Anti-Discrimination Committee. Mounting legal and political pressure was fully recognized by White owners, who already were short of talent due to World War II.

In the meantime, after 3 years in the army, UCLA alumnus Jack Roosevelt Robinson joined the Kansas City Monarchs in April 1945. Unaware that he had been carefully selected over other Negro League players and then monitored by Wesley Branch Rickey, president and general manager of the Brooklyn Dodgers, he was known to be a fierce competitor who did not hesitate to stand up for his rights and against Jim Crow.

Upon ferocious negotiation between Rickey and Robinson, Robinson spent the 1946 season in Montreal, the highest minor-league team for the Dodgers. While he readied himself for the major-league competition and media scrutiny, the Dodgers added six more Black players to its minor-league system, including Roy Campanella and Don Newcombe. Conversely, Eddie Klepp, a White pitcher, joined the Cleveland Buckeyes of the Negro American League in the same year. Just as Robinson's traveling arrangements were challenging, Klepp often had to be separated from his teammates, depending on local ordinances.

Robinson's arrival in Brooklyn in 1947 was carefully planned ahead for by Rickey and Black community leaders, who informally campaigned to appear subdued without gloating or special treatment, out of fear of resistance. Despite such efforts, Robinson endured hostility and death threats throughout his first year when the *Sporting News* named him the rookie of the year.

With much publicity generated by Robinson's signing with the major leagues, the Negro Leagues flourished during the same period. However, integration had taken top players out of the leagues and into major-league baseball. And even though the total number of Black players did not rise, the attendance for the 1948 season suggested the eventual demise of the Negro Leagues.

Recognition

Baseball among African Americans in various organized forms, whether local semipro leagues or Negro Leagues, persisted for nearly a half century without much institutional support, but often with a sizable fan base. The notable Negro League All-Star Game in Chicago's Comiskey Park attracted over 51,000 fans, watching such Hall-of-Famers as Paige and Gibson, names recognized by both Black and White fans. Traces of the Negro League live on in the names of a few minor-league teams, such as the Birmingham Barons and the Chattanooga Lookouts.

In 2006, the National Baseball Hall of Fame inducted twelve Negro League players and executives, including Cum Posey, the owner of the Homestead Grays; J. L. Wilkinson, the owner of the Kansas City Monarchs; and Effa Manley, co-owner and business manager of the Newark Eagles and the first woman to have her plaque hung in the Hall of Fame. They joined Rube Foster, who was inducted in 1981.

In his induction to the Hall of Fame in 2005, a baseball reporter from the *Boston Globe*, Peter Gammons, noted that Jackie Robinson was in the major league 7 years before the *Brown v. Board of Education* ruling that ended school segregation. Baseball's intimate ties to social and economic structure led those involved in the sport to think beyond societal constraints. During their existence, the Negro Leagues were a reflection of U.S. societal history and still remain very much a part of U.S. history. Though they no longer entertain and empower Blacks, who live under the shadow of White society, and though racial integration was finally achieved in baseball, the leagues provided an outlet to maintain an important tradition in the United States that eventually became a device for recognizing social inequality.

Kiljoong Kim and Jack Clarke

See also *Brown v. Board of Education;* Du Bois, William Edward Burghardt; Leisure; *Plessy v. Ferguson;* Robinson, Jackie; Segregation; Thorpe, Jim

Further Readings

Bak, Richard. 1995. *Turkey Stearnes and the Detroit Stars: The Negro Leagues in Detroit, 1919–1933.* Ventura, CA: Gospel Light Publications.

Hogan, Lawrence D. and Jules Tygiel. 2006. *Shades of Glory: The Negro Leagues and the Story of African-American Baseball.* Washington, DC: National Geographic.

Jacobson, Steve. 2007. *Carrying Jackie's Torch: The Players Who Integrated Baseball—and America.* New York: Lawrence Hill Books.

Lanctot, Neil. 2004. *Negro League Baseball: The Rise and Ruin of a Black Institution.* Philadelphia: University of Pennsylvania Press.

Peterson, Robert. 1970. *Only the Ball Was White: A History of Legendary Black Players and All-Black Professional Teams.* New York: Oxford University Press.

Ribowsky, Mark. 1996. *The Power and the Darkness: The Life of Josh Gibson in the Shadow of the Game.* New York: Simon & Schuster.

Tygiel, Jules. 1983. *Baseball's Great Experiment: Jackie Robinson and His Legacy.* New York: Oxford University Press.

Newton, Huey (1942–1989)

Huey Percy Newton is best known for his cofounding in 1966 of the Black Panther Party for Self-Defense, later known simply as the Black Panther Party (BPP). A complex and controversial figure, twice indicted for felony crimes and acquitted, Newton was a radical grassroots activist, public intellectual, writer, and political candidate who advocated for the rights of African Americans to self-determination and self-defense. Although critics such as Stanley Crouch, Tom Orloff of the *San Francisco Chronicle,* and author Hugh Pearson have labeled Newton as a "thug," "criminal," and "hoodlum," others, such as former Black Panther Donald Cox, have spoken of him as a messianic presence whose every word was revered as gospel by his followers and associates. A romantic figure to many on the political Left in the 1960s and 1970s, Newton was anathematized by the Right as an advocate of violent revolution.

Early Years

Born in Monroe, Louisiana, and named after the populist Louisiana governor Huey Long, Huey Newton was the seventh and youngest child of Armelia and Walter Newton, a sharecropper and Baptist minister. When he was a year old, his family moved to Oakland, California, where Huey grew up in poverty and later graduated from Oakland Technical High School, although functionally illiterate. He later taught himself to read, he said, by listening to audio recordings of poetry while following the written poems to correlate the sounds with how the words appeared. Newton attended Merritt College intermittently, ultimately earning an associate of arts degree, and later studied law at Oakland City College and San Francisco Law School. In 1980, he received a PhD degree in the history of consciousness from the University of California at Santa Cruz, where one of his professors was Edwin Meese III, future attorney general of the United States during the Reagan administration.

At Merritt and City College, Newton encountered the Black radical tradition. He formed a relationship with members of the Revolutionary Action Movement (RAM) at City College, who soon dismissed him as "bourgeois," while he dismissed them as "armchair olutionaries." Newton immersed himself in the racial and class politics of the San Francisco Bay area, joining the Afro-American Association and becoming a member of the African American fraternity Phi Beta Sigma. Newton also worked with others to demand the inclusion of Black History courses at City College. He began to study the life of Malcolm X and gained familiarity with organizations such as Negroes With Guns, the Lowndes County Freedom Party, the Soul Students Advisory Council, and the Deacons for Defense.

Radical Activism and Exile

A widely reported incident involving the harassment of motorist Marquette Frye and the beating of her three sons by officers of the Los Angeles Police Department in August 1965 sparked what became known as the Watts Riots. It was chiefly in response to such inflammatory events and other incidents of alleged police misconduct and brutality toward Black communities that Newton, in conjunction with fellow activist Bobby Seale, formed the BPP. Both men believed the BPP to be an extension of Malcolm X's ideology and considered themselves his heirs.

Against this background, Newton's philosophy of race and democracy was becoming solidified. From his earlier study of the law, Newton became versed in the California penal code and the state's laws concerning weapons. He convinced a number of African Americans to exercise their legal right to openly bear arms (concealed firearms were illegal). The resulting "Panther Patrols" were carloads of armed BPP members who patrolled areas where the Oakland police were alleged or known to have committed abuses against the community's Black citizens. This program was widely supported in the African American community for its efforts to deter racial abuse by local police. In addition to patrolling, Newton and Seale were responsible for writing the BPP platform and program, whose sources included the writings of Chinese premier Mao Tse-tung and the Nation of Islam's political format.

As civil and racial unrest and rioting spread across the United States in the summers of 1966, 1967, and 1968, the BPP mobilized local chapters to politicize the actions as urban rebellions. Grassroots responses included the development of "legal first aid" by Newton—booklets that included texts and explanations of statutes and bylaws to inform readers of their legal rights when confronted by police.

In October 1967, Newton and other BPP members were involved in a shootout with the Oakland police. Officer John Frey suffered four gunshot wounds and died shortly thereafter. Newton was also seriously wounded by gunfire; several hours later, he staggered into a hospital, where he was admitted and chained to a gurney. Accused of murdering Frey, Newton was convicted in September 1968 of voluntary manslaughter and was sentenced to 2 to 15 years in prison. In May 1970, the California Appellate Court reversed Newton's conviction and ordered a new trial. The State of California dropped its case against Newton after two subsequent mistrials.

In 1974, Newton was accused of murdering Kathleen Smith, a 17-year-old prostitute. When he failed to make his court appearance, his bail was revoked, a bench warrant was issued, and Newton's name was added to the Federal Bureau of Investigation's "Most Wanted" list. Newton jumped bail and escaped to Cuba, where he lived until he returned home in 1977 to face the murder charge. Because the evidence was largely circumstantial, Newton was acquitted after two trials were deadlocked.

Writings: The 1980s

As a writer, Newton attempted a synthesis of racial analysis with classic philosophy, merging the theories of Malcolm X with those of Karl Marx and those of Frantz Fanon with those of Thomas Hobbes. In a study of Newton, Judson L. Jefferies explored how the political suppositions of Newton's Durkheimian theory of "reactionary suicide" are connected to Dostoyevsky's ideas on poverty and beggary in *Crime and Punishment*. He also analyzed connections in Newton's thought to Nietzsche and psychological warfare, to Bakunin's fatalistic view of revolutionaries, to Plato's "cave" analogy, and to Marx's theories on existence and social consciousness. Newton's later writings considered both structural causations and personal responsibility as linchpins in the elimination of racism.

Newton's autobiography, *Revolutionary Suicide*, resembles *The Autobiography of Malcolm X* in its narrative account of human enlightenment and possibility. Newton's four other published books; *To Die for the People* (1972), *In Search of Common Ground* (1973), *Insights and Poems* (1975), and *War Against the Panthers* (his doctoral dissertation published posthumously, in 1996), illustrate his shift from Black Nationalism toward a synthesis he called "intercommunalism," in which he predicted an upcoming collapse of the nation-state and the rise of universal brotherhood.

During the last years of his life, Newton was involved with the African People's Socialist Party and the Uhuru House, headquartered in Oakland, California. Newton was also involved with the 1983 "Tent City" project for the homeless, the Oakland Summer Project that organized the Community Control of Housing Initiative, and the creation of the Bobby Hutton Freedom Clinic. On August 22, 1989, Newton was fatally shot on an Oakland street, allegedly over a drug deal gone wrong.

Matthew W. Hughey

See also Black Nationalism; Black Panther Party; Black Power; Carmichael, Stokely; Malcolm X; Nation of Islam

Further Readings

Cleaver, Kathleen and George Katsiaficas, eds. 2001. *Liberation, Imagination, and the Black Panther Party: A New Look at the Panthers and Their Legacy.* New York: Routledge Press.

Hilliard, David, with Keith Zimmerman and Kent Zimmerman. 2006. *Huey: Spirit of the Panther.* New York: Thunder's Mountain Press.

Hilliard, David and Lewis Cole. 1992. *This Side of Glory.* Boston, MA: Little, Brown.

Hughey, Matthew W. Forthcoming. "The Pedagogy of Huey P. Newton: Critical Reflections on Education in his Writings and Speeches." *Journal of Black Studies.*

Jeffries, Judson L. 2002. *Huey P. Newton: The Radical Theorist.* Jackson: University Press of Mississippi.

Jones, Charles E., ed. 1998. *The Black Panther Party Reconsidered.* Baltimore, MD: Black Classic Press.

Newton, Huey P. 1972. *To Die for the People.* New York: Writers and Readers Publishing.

Newton, Huey P. 1973. *Revolutionary Suicide.* New York: Writers and Readers Publishing.

Newton, Huey P. 1996. *War against the Panthers: A Study of Repression in America.* New York: Harlem River Press.

Newton, Huey P. and Erik H. Erikson. 1973. *In Search of Common Ground.* New York: Norton.

Newton, Huey P. and Ericka Huggins. 1975. *Insights and Poems.* San Francisco, CA: City Lights Books.

NICARAGUAN AMERICANS

Among U.S. society's large and growing population of immigrants are Nicaraguan Americans. In contemporary literature about immigrants, they often are labeled simply as *Hispanics,* a social construction that includes Mexicans, the largest and fastest-growing population, and the smaller and relatively prosperous population of Cubans. Although Nicaraguan Americans share some similarities with other Hispanic groups, they have a unique history of immigration as well as cultural and institutional adaptation. In this entry, the term *Nicaraguan Americans* refers to those who were born in Nicaragua and live in the

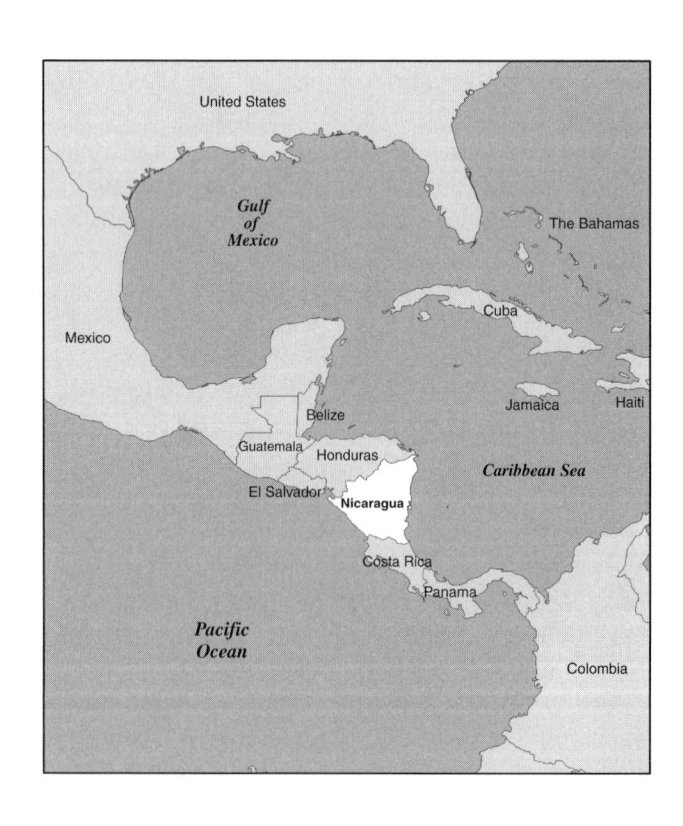

United States and also, when so noted, to people who were U.S.-born but whose parents were born in Nicaragua.

Nicaragua has an estimated population of 5.6 million as of 2007. According to the 2000 census, there were 228,346 people residing in the United States who came from Nicaragua. (This may be a low estimate. Immigration attorneys estimate, for example, at least 65,000 undocumented Nicaraguans in Miami.) That number represents less than 1% of the total foreign-born population (over 33 million in 2000) and 1.7% of foreign-born peoples from Mexico, Central and South America, and Spanish-speaking Caribbean nations. Although the number of Nicaraguan immigrants in the United States is small relative to all immigrants, they have a visible presence, especially in South Florida, where the majority of Nicaraguans live. Others have settled predominantly in large metropolitan areas, especially in California and Texas.

History of Nicaraguan Immigration to the United States

Nicaraguans who migrated to the United States during the last 30 years came initially in reaction to the political upheavals in Nicaragua that started with the Sandinista Revolution in the late 1970s, when the Frente Sandinista de Liberacion Nacional (FSLN) seized the home of dictator Anastasio Somoza Debayle and established socialist rule. As a result, the first wave of approximately 120,000 Nicaraguans entered the United States. They consisted of upper-class landholders, industrialists, and the exiled dictator and his family, who were among the South Florida elite.

The second wave, which began during the early 1980s, was made up of professionals and white-collar workers emigrating because of the civil war, led by U.S.-backed opponents ("contras") of the FSLN, and because of economic strife in Nicaragua. Another large wave of Nicaraguans entering the United States, consisting primarily of laborers, peaked in a large exodus in early 1989. Many in this third wave of immigrants settled in poor and deteriorating sections of Miami, where Mariel Cuban refugees had previously lived.

The influx of Nicaraguans between 1988 and 1990 had significantly diminished by 1991, with the defeat of the Sandinistas in the 1989 elections, and then rose again in 1993 because of extremely poor economic conditions in the homeland. Since then, people from Nicaragua have been coming to the United States steadily, seeking better opportunities for their children. Indeed, Nicaragua struggles economically. Figures in 2005 from the World Bank show a per capita income of $830, the lowest in the Western Hemisphere except for Haiti.

Socioeconomic Factors and Barriers

Compared with the total U.S. population, Nicaraguan immigrants have disproportionately low levels of education and employment. Of the 155,375 Nicaraguan foreign-born individuals between the ages of 15 and 64, 37% did not graduate from high school. This is slightly more than the percentage for the overall foreign-born population (36%) and significantly more than the percentage of U.S. citizens of the same age who have not completed high school. The median income of Nicaraguan Americans is $19,000 (about $5,000 lower than for the total immigrant population). Their jobs are predominately labor-intensive.

Disproportionate socioeconomic status of immigrants is often due to institutional and individual discrimination. Institutionally, Nicaraguan immigrants have faced struggles with legal citizenship. Once democratic elections in Nicaragua were held, the U.S. government classified Nicaraguans as economic, rather than political, refugees and thus refused many of them asylum on political grounds. Changes in immigration policy, like the 1996 Illegal Immigration Reform and Immigrant Responsibility Act (IIRIRA), and increased security measures since the attacks on America on September 11, 2001, make it tougher for Nicaraguans to obtain legal status in the United States.

Culture, Language, and Identity

While many scholars find that Nicaraguans have assimilated over the years, their homeland culture remains prominent in areas with high concentrations of Nicaraguan immigrants. For example, the Miami-Dade County municipality of Sweetwater is called "Little Managua" due to its large and visible presence of Nicaraguan Americans. The area possesses an array of Nicaraguan *fritangas,* open grills selling popular Nicaragua dishes such as tamales (cornmeal wrapped in banana leaves) and chorizo (a Nicaraguan sausage) and markets that sell embroidered cotton shirts and dresses. In December, churches with predominantly Nicaraguan membership (such as Our Lady of Divine Providence) enjoy the festivities of *Las Purisima,* which celebrates the *Virgen de la Asuncion* (the patroness of Nicaragua).

Most foreign-born Nicaraguan Americans speak Spanish in the home, but their children prefer English at school. Nicaraguan Spanish has several distinguishing characteristics: for example, instead of *tú* (for "you"), Nicaraguans use *vos,* which other Latin Americans rarely use. In Miami, Nicaraguan language usage reflects the context among other Hispanic groups. Some Nicaraguans, living and working among Cubans in Miami, have adopted the Cuban Spanish dialect, which locals and scholars refer to as *Cubonics.*

The perceived racial and ethnic identity of Nicaraguan Americans is also unique, as most of the population of Nicaragua is *mestizo* (a mix of European and indigenous ancestry). A study of Nicaraguan high school students in South Florida showed that second-generation Nicaraguans self-identify with panethnic labels more so than Cubans, who identify with their national label, *Cuban* or *Cuban American.* The ethnic label *Hispanic* used in the United States may very well represent self-assertion and a more inclusive solidarity. Over time, Nicaraguan Americans have successfully secured a certain degree of influence and, as a result, embrace their national identity.

Lisa Konczal

See Appendix A
See also Assimilation; Central Americans in the United States; Hispanics; *Hispanic* Versus *Latino;* Immigration, U.S.; "Marielitos"

Further Readings

Fernandez-Kelly, Patricia and Sarah Curran. 2001. "Nicaraguans: Voices Lost, Voices Found." Pp. 127–156 in *Ethnicities: Children of Immigrants in America,* edited by R. G. Rumbaut and A. Portes. Berkeley: University of California Press.

Fernandez-Kelly, Patricia and Lisa Konczal. 2005. "Murdering the Alphabet: Identity and Opposition among Second Generation Cubans, West Indians, and Central Americans." *Ethnic and Racial Studies* 28:1153–1181.

Portes, Alejandro and Ruben G. Rumbaut. 2006. *Immigrant America: A Portrait.* 3rd ed. Berkeley: University of California Press.

Portes, Alejandro and Alex Stepick. 1993. *City on the Edge: The Transformation of Miami.* Berkeley: University of California Press.

Suarez-Orozco, Marcelo. 1997. "Becoming Somebody: Central American Immigrants in U.S. Inner-City Schools." Pp. 115–129 in *Beyond Black and White: New Faces and Voices in U.S. Schools,* edited by M. Seller and L. Weis. New York: State University of New York Press.

NIGERIA

Nigeria is a country in West Africa with an estimated 2007 population of 144.4 million people. It is bordered by Benin on the east; Cameroon on the west; Chad and Niger to the north; and the Gulf of Guinea, the Bight of Benin, and the Bight of Biafra to the south. The country consists of thirty-six states and one capital district. The River Niger, the continent's third largest river, runs within Nigeria for almost 1,000 miles, terminating in an oil-rich delta providing about 40% of the country's gross domestic product. Nigeria is rich in natural resources, such as granite, salt, copper, and zinc, and roughly one-quarter of the current African population resides within its borders. This entry looks briefly at the history of Nigeria.

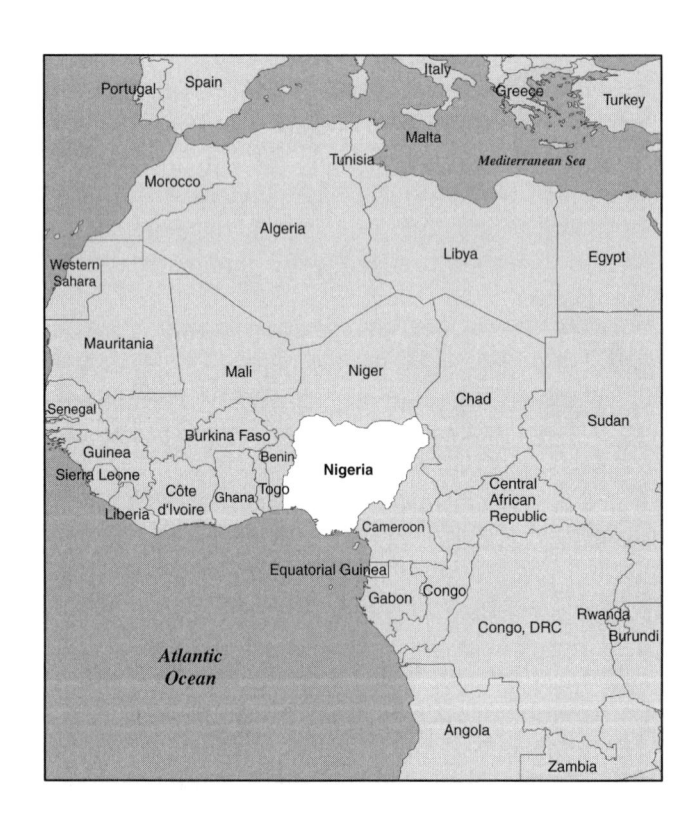

Early History and Empires

The people of Nigeria share an extensive history that can be traced back to as early as 12,000 BC, as shown by relics of the Stone Age found by archaeologists. Settlement patterns among the early Nigerians were dependent on the surrounding landscape and vegetation. In territories of high forestation, such as those occupied by early Yoruba, Ibibio, Igbo, and Edo tribes, agriculture was the main source of sustenance. In coastal areas inhabited by tribes such as Ijo and the Kalabari, goods such as fish and salt were traded as commerce.

Ethnic relations in present-day Nigeria come from a host of historic influences. The Kanem-Borno was an empire that ruled from about the 8th century until the 19th century, when it was subdued by the British. This northern empire became wealthy and powerful due to their familiarity with the trans-Sahara trade routes. These routes secured contact and strong diplomacy with the Middle East and northern African city-states, and, as a result, Islam became heavily practiced within the kingdom. The empire made it possible for other kingdoms to flourish.

The Hausa tribes were an ethnic group found in the northern savannas of precolonial Nigeria, located south of the Kanem-Borno Empire. Agriculture and security from their northern neighbors allowed the Hausa kingdoms to prosper. To the south, the tribes of the Yoruba, Nupe, Tiv, and Igala traded and held diplomatic relations with each other. The Niger delta was rich with city-states, such as the Bonny and the Calabar, which established trade with Europeans and controlled the sea and waterways.

The Empire of Benin was created by the Edo tribe and was one of the traders that also benefited from the European presence. Coming to power in the 14th century, the Benin Empire borrowed ideas and political tactics from those of the Oyo Empire to further its military ambitions. Contact with the Portuguese in the 15th century provided the empire with guns that were inevitably used to gather land and slaves, which ultimately were sold off in the transatlantic slave trade through the Bight of Benin.

The Yoruba, the strongest of the southern tribes, came into power with the Oyo Empire in the early 16th century. Using cavalry and an effectively functioning monarchy, the Oyo Empire dominated its neighbors. The military prowess of the empire continually subdued and conquered, allowing for expansion by the 17th century into one of the most formidable empires in Nigeria. The Oyo Empire, with its seat of power in Lagos, became the way of incursion for British trade, missionaries, and the eventual colonialization of the entire country.

European Involvement

The British eventually took control of Nigeria through a series of events that began with the annexation of Lagos. As economies changed and the use of slaves became less necessary, a cry in Britain to abolish slavery became more feverish due to Christian and other religious groups. The missionaries were instrumental in downplaying the importance of Islam and indigenous religions. They were also political, vocalizing their displeasure of laws and politicians they deemed "unfit" for ruling a country.

Such was the case in 1851, when the British attacked the city of Lagos. The slave trade, although officially abolished in the early part of the century, was still endorsed by King Kosoko of Lagos, who saw his city and empire profit greatly from the trade. Missionaries filed a formal complaint with England, which, in turn, accused Lagos of breaking a slave treaty. The British fleet attacked on December 26, 1851, causing Kosoko to flee. The British government and consul were then able to help install King Akitoye, who, in turn, provided preferential treatment, and granted entrance that would eventually result in Lagos becoming the first British colony of Nigeria. The British then worked to complete the subjugation of the Yoruba, the Igbo, the Kingdom of Benin, and the Hausa and unite them under one national flag. Nigeria would be considered a colony and protectorate from 1914 until 1960, when the country won its independence.

Ethnic Unification

Due to the large number of tribes that were united under British rule in the days of colonialism, Nigeria is a multiethnic, multilingual country, with 200 ethnicities speaking over 250 different languages. Of the ethnic languages, Hausa (21%), Yoruba (20%), and Igbo (17%) are the most prominent. English is the official language, spoken in conjunction and sometimes in combination with other languages. Three major political parties focus on the three major ethnic groups in Nigeria, and their struggle for power over the others has been the cause of numerous military coups, politically based ethnic massacres, and three republic installations.

C. Centae Richards

See Appendix A
See also Belize; Colonialism; Dominican Republic; Jamaica; Nigerian Americans

Further Readings

Falola, Toyin. 1999. *The History of Nigeria.* Westport, CT: Greenwood Press.

Rothchild, Donald. 1997. *Managing Ethnic Conflict in Africa: Pressures and Incentives for Cooperation.* Washington, DC: Brookings Institution.

Wright, Stephen. 1998. *Nigeria: The Struggle for Stability and Status.* Boulder, CO: Westview Press.

NIGERIAN AMERICANS

Nigerian Americans are the immigrants and their descendants from Nigeria, a country of 144.4 million as of 2007 estimates. According to the 2000 census, there 134,940 people born in Nigeria resident in the United States, of whom 37.1% were citizens. This entry will look at the background of immigration from Nigeria to the United States and the contemporary picture of Nigerian Americans.

Immigration Patterns

Nigerians have been arriving since about 1926, as students, travelers, or businessmen. Since then, the number of immigrants from Nigeria has slowly increased. Nigeria's oil boom and bust during the 1970s marked a significant period for Nigerian immigration to the United States. During this decade, the elite, the upwardly mobile working class, and students immigrated to the United States. Reasons included political instability and economic problems. While many return-migrated in the following decade, others obtained citizenship and sponsored their relatives to migrate to the United States.

According to Immigration and Naturalization statistics, about 35,000 Nigerians immigrated to the United States between 1981 and 1990. Nigerian immigrants during the 1990s arrived mostly as part of the Diversity Program (part of the 1990 Immigration Act that grants additional visas for immigrants who were underrepresented in the past) as well as family reunification programs.

Contemporary Community

In recent years, people from Nigeria have sought permanent residency and refugee status and completed the naturalization process to become citizens. From 1997 through 2006, about 8,700 Nigerians immigrated to the United States annually. The number of refugees arriving has varied greatly since 1997. One thousand two hundred twenty-four Nigerian refugees arrived from 1997 to 2006, with 625 refugees arriving in 1999 alone. Over 51,000 Nigerian Americans have become naturalized citizens since 1997.

Many Nigerian Americans are employed in management or professional occupations. In addition, according to the 2000 census, more than 30% reported working in the educational, health, and social services industry. Their median family income was $52,586, compared with $50,890 for the nation as a whole.

According to the U.S. Census Bureau American Community Survey, there were 188,076 people of Nigerian national origin in the United States. Nigerian communities can be found in New York City; Newark; Washington, D.C.; Chicago; Atlanta; and Los Angeles. In terms of geographic distribution, the top five states were Texas, New York, Maryland, California, and New Jersey.

Jennifer M. Klein

See Appendix A
See also Africans in the United States; Assimilation; Immigrant Communities; Immigration, U.S.; Muslim Americans; Nigeria; Refugees; Return Migration

Further Readings

Aprraku, K. K. 1991. *African Emigrés in the United States.* New York City: Praeger.

Department of Homeland Security. 2007. *Yearbook of Immigration Statistics:* 2006. Washington, DC: Office of Immigration Statistics. Available from http://www.dhs.gov/ximgtn/statistics/publications/yearbook.shtm

Linton, Cynthia, ed. 1996. *The Ethnic Handbook.* Schiller Park, IL: Business Press.

Offoha, Marcellina Ulunm. 1989. *Educated Nigerian Settlers in the United States: The Phenomenon of Brain Drain.* Philadelphia, PA: Temple University.

U.S. Census Bureau. 2004. *Profile of Demographic and Social Characteristics: 2000. People Born in Nigeria.* Available from http://www.census.gov/population/www/socdemo/foreign/STP-159-2000tl.html

U.S. Census Bureau. 2006. *American Community Survey 2005.* Avaialable from http://www.census.gov/acs/www

NIKKEIJIN

The term *Nikkeijin* refers to Japanese emigrants and their descendants, or "person of Japanese ancestry" in Japanese, although this usually does not include Japanese nationals in Japan. Until the 1990s, this term referred primarily to ethnic Japanese communities abroad, distinguishing between Japanese in Japan and ethnic Japanese outside of Japan. In the early 1990s, however, with the revision of Japan's Immigration Control and Refugee Recognition Act, large numbers of ethnic Japanese from Brazil and other South American countries began migrating to Japan. As a result, the Japanese/Nikkeijin distinction is no longer territorially or geographically definable and has begun to take on new meanings in societies such as the United States and Japan.

Usage in the United States

Nikkei literally means "of Japanese ancestry" in Japanese. Its meaning and connotations are different inside and outside of Japan. In the United States, the term *Nikkei* is increasingly used interchangeably with, and sometimes in place of, the term *Japanese American*. This semantic shift is largely due to the limited connotations of the latter. *Japanese American* has historically referred to pre–World War II immigrants and their descendants, who were predominantly monoracial.

Over the years, however, the population of Japanese Americans has significantly diversified. Now there are also people who trace their family histories to the post–World War II wave of migration. At the same time, the younger generations of Japanese Americans are predominantly of mixed ancestries (i.e., one parent has Japanese ancestry, and one parent does not) and mixed generations (e.g., one parent is *Issei*, or first generation, and one parent is *Sansei*, or third generation). Many "Japanese American" community leaders and organizations are identifying as *Nikkei* in an attempt to acknowledge and reflect this growing diversity. So *Nikkei* is more inclusive of diversity than *Japanese American*.

Within the American context, *Nikkei* is predominantly used as both a noun and an adjective; one rarely hears *Nikkeijin* in the United States, unless it is referring to ethnic Japanese populations in other countries or to those who have "return migrated" to Japan. In the United States, people tend to use *Nikkei* in two different ways: either including the original Japanese migrants along with their descendants or referring only to their American-born descendants. If Japanese migrants are included, they are referred to as "Issei"; if they are differentiated from Nikkei, they are referred to as "Japanese." This slippage is also common with the term *Japanese American*.

Usage in Japan

Meanwhile, in Japan, *Nikkeijin* is the more commonly used term. As in the United States, *Nikkeijin* always refers to the descendants of Japanese migrants, but it may or may not include the original migrants themselves. From a Japanese perspective, those who were born and socialized primarily in Japan, especially if they still have Japanese citizenship, would in most cases be considered "Japanese." At the same time, however, if these "Japanese" adapted to a different society and developed new communities and worldviews, and especially if they gave up their Japanese citizenship, they could also be seen as having become "Nikkeijin."

The term *Nikkeijin* is not country-specific: In Japan, it would be similar to saying "the Japanese diaspora." To be country-specific, one would say either "Brazilian Nikkeijin" or "Nikkei Brazilian." In Japanese and from a Japanese perspective, *Nikkeijin* is more commonly used without a country marker, not necessarily referencing people from any particular country. Rather, in Japan, it is more common to define *Nikkeijin* in contrast to *Nihonjin*, that is, majority Japanese. In this context, *Nikkeijin* references those who appear to be Japanese but may not behave like or speak Japanese (because they are the descendants of Japanese emigrants and were raised abroad).

Brazilian and Other Nikkeijin in Japan

Since the 1990s, there has been an influx of Nikkeijin from Brazil and other Latin American countries to

Japan due to the revision of the Immigration Control and Refugee Recognition Act. An estimated 280,000 Brazilian Nikkeijin and several thousand other Latin American Nikkeijin now live in Japan. Though Nikkeijin experiences previously referred only to a history of emigration and settlement outside of Japan, they now also include the "return migration" of Nikkeijin individuals from foreign countries who have gone to Japan to live and work.

Most Brazilian Nikkeijin work as "unskilled" laborers in Japanese factories, despite their middle-class, educated backgrounds in Brazil. This is because they can earn five to ten times more as unskilled factory workers in Japan than they can as white-collar workers in Brazil. How did this come to be? It all started with the coincidence of the Brazilian economic crisis and the rise of the Japanese "bubble" economy in the late 1980s. The instability of the Brazilian economy was leading many Brazilian residents to emigrate; those who had Japanese citizenship or had parents who were Japanese citizens could easily go to Japan. But many ethnic Japanese in Brazil were Sansei, or third generation, as well, and they could not readily obtain visas to Japan.

Meanwhile, the Japanese economy was growing so fast that Japanese companies could not fill their low-paid labor needs with domestic workers. Restrictive immigration laws, however, made it difficult for them to import unskilled labor; the official stance of the government was that Japanese society was homogeneous and the acceptance of too many foreigners would disrupt the social harmony and integrity of the nation.

Recognizing the limits of Japanese immigration policy and wanting to support businesses in their quest for unskilled labor, beginning in the 1990s, the Japanese government decided to revise the immigration law while maintaining the limitation on "foreigners." Rather than permit all "foreigners" or "unskilled laborers" to enter Japan in larger numbers, the new law included the euphemism of "Nikkeijin," with Brazilian labor in mind. In this way, the justification for allowing in this new category of migrants was not explicitly as labor—though their visas did allow them to work—but as descendants of Japanese. The justification was cultural, not economic or political; the effect was economic, however, as the labor shortage problem in Japan was solved, while the Japanese government continued to maintain its policy of limiting labor migration. The integrity of the nation was supposedly maintained because Nikkeijin, though raised abroad, were imagined to be culturally similar enough to Japanese that they would assimilate into Japanese society with relative ease.

Through the revision of immigration policy, the Japanese government reconstructed Nikkeijin as extensions of Japanese, emphasizing their shared lineage. From the perspective of policymakers representing Japan as an ancestral homeland, it was in their best interest to redefine Nikkeijin in this way to meet their objectives of accessing foreign labor without officially calling it such. However, the consequence of this policy decision was the institutionalization of a racial definition of Nikkeijin that emphasized their shared ancestry over their foreign citizenships or national identities. No matter where in the world they were, if someone could prove they had a grandparent who was a Japanese national, that person now could apply for a visa to Japan.

Recently, however, the Japanese government has suggested that it is changing its perspective. Over the decade since mass Brazilian Nikkeijin migration to Japan began, Nikkeijin communities have been forming, distinct from the Japanese majority. This development of culturally Brazilian communities was unanticipated by Japanese policymakers; most Nikkeijin who have "returned" to Japan do not speak much Japanese and are culturally foreign. As a way of salvaging some of their original intentions, at the end of 2006, government officials announced that they were considering the implementation of language tests to some groups of foreigners to ensure that they were integrating into Japanese society properly. If the foreign migrants were found to have an insufficient level of Japanese, their visas would not be renewed. Over the next decade, policymakers will need to carefully reevaluate the restrictive immigration policy, given that the Japanese population and birthrate continue to decline and increased immigration is one way that this crisis could be mitigated.

In addition, many migrants are bringing children to Japan or having children after they arrive. The Japanese school system is not structured to accommodate cultural diversity; thus, there is the added problem of how to educate and raise this younger generation. Despite perceived racial similarity, national and cultural differences between Japanese and Nikkeijin are becoming more and more salient and cannot be ignored any longer.

Most scholarly research on Nikkeijin has been conducted on the Brazilian population in Japan. This is because the term *Nikkeijin*, as mentioned earlier, tends to suggest Japan as a frame of reference, and Brazilians have the largest Nikkeijin presence in Japan. Other Nikkeijin populations in Japan are also becoming subjects of study. In addition, more comparative work on Nikkei communities around the world is also being done. Comparative histories of emigration and settlement in each country help to show what the social conditions were both in Japan and in the countries of settlement, and why migration occurred at the specific times and to the specific places that it did. This type of research reveals how Japanese migrant experiences in different sociopolitical contexts have led to the formation of very different Nikkei communities around the world.

Jane H. Yamashiro

See also *Brazil; Burakumin; Hafu;* Issei; Japan; Japanese Americans; Nisei; Return Migration; Sansei

Further Readings

Hirabayashi, Lane Ryo, Akemi Kikumura-Yano, and James A. Hirabayashi. 2002. *New Worlds, New Lives: Globalization and People of Japanese Descent in the Americas and from Latin America in Japan.* Stanford, CA: Stanford University Press.

Kikumura-Yano, Akemi. 2002. *Encyclopedia of Japanese Descendants in the Americas: An Illustrated History of the Nikkei.* Walnut Creek, CA: Alta Mira.

Lesser, Jeffrey. 2003. *Searching for Home Abroad: Japanese Brazilians and Transnationalism.* Durham, NC: Duke University Press.

Roth, Joshua H. 2002. *Brokered Homeland: Japanese Brazilian Migrants in Japan.* Ithaca, NY: Cornell University Press.

Tsuda, Takeyuki. 2003. *Strangers in the Ethnic Homeland: Japanese Brazilian Return Migration in Transnational Perspective.* New York: Columbia University Press.

Web Sites

Discover Nikkei: http://www.discovernikkei.org/en

Japanese American National Museum: http://www.janm.org/projects/inrp

Kaigai Nikkeijin Kyokai (The Association of Nikkei and Japanese Abroad), 1995–2005: http://www.jadesas.or.jp/EN/index.html

NISEI

The term *Nisei* (second-generation) refers to American-born children of Japanese immigrants. In the United States, this typically refers to the children of *Issei* (first-generation) migrants from Japan who entered Hawai'i and the U.S. mainland in the late 19th and early 20th centuries. Generations are counted from the people who migrated to the United States (not the first generation born in the United States). The children of post–World War II Japanese migrants to the United States are included as Nisei but are sometimes referred to more specifically as *Shin-Nisei*, that is, "new (postwar) second generation," to distinguish between the two major pre- and postwar waves of Japanese migration. Though American citizens by birth, Nisei loyalties to the United States were repeatedly questioned throughout the war era because of their Japanese ancestry. In response, most Nisei emphasized their American identities and discarded or downplayed Japanese ethnic identities. Nisei experiences have been greatly shaped by their shifting racial exclusion and inclusion in different periods.

Americanization as a Response to Racism

Before, during, and after World War II, Nisei were confronted with racist doubts about their national loyalties and had to decide how to respond to them. The mass internment of people of Japanese ancestry from the West Coast, the administration of a loyalty questionnaire to internees, and the question of whether or not to serve in the U.S. military while their civil rights were being violated sparked debates about what it meant to be an American of Japanese ancestry while the United States was at war with Japan. More specifically, the discussions centered on what rights Japanese Americans were entitled to and how to react once those rights were taken away. Opinions differed, and a spectrum of responses ensued, but the mainstream strategy was to cooperate with the U.S. government to demonstrate loyalty to the United States. Many felt they had no other option and trusted that the government was looking out for their best interests. In this way, most Japanese Americans adopted a tactic of Americanization and assimilation, and those who took on different approaches were often ostracized and marginalized by the larger community.

The Loyalty Questionnaire

In 1943, interned Japanese Americans were required to fill out what is now called the "loyalty questionnaire." The most infamous questions were #27 and #28, which respectively asked whether the individual was willing to serve in the U.S. armed forces on combat duty "wherever ordered" and whether the individual would swear "unqualified allegiance" to the United States and renounce any form of allegiance to the Japanese emperor or any other foreign group or power. Both the ambiguities of the questions and the insinuations of disloyalty caused much consternation among respondents. Those who rebelliously responded "no" and "no" were deemed "no-no boys" and seen as social outcasts for challenging the mainstream Japanese American tactic of demonstrating loyalty to the United States, regardless of the circumstances. These "no-no boys" were one of several groups who responded in a more confrontational way to the irony of a country illegally imprisoning its citizens based on racial and ethnic classifications and then questioning them about their national loyalties.

Nisei and the U.S. Military

Young Nisei men were faced with the dilemma of whether or not to serve in the U.S. military. Their decisions and rationalizations were highly politicized, and differences in perspectives led to clashes within the community. The majority of young Nisei men served in the U.S. military at some point, whether as volunteers or as draftees. Most volunteers came from Hawai'i, where Japanese Americans were not interned on a mass scale. Many men also volunteered from the U.S. mainland, while their families remained incarcerated behind barbed wire.

The 442nd Regimental Combat Team/100th Battalion is the most famous Nisei combat unit, fighting in Europe, receiving numerous medals, and becoming the most decorated unit in history. Apparently, this segregated unit was sent to Europe because it was thought that if they fought in the Pacific War anywhere that Japanese might be, they might be shot by their own countrymen, who might mistake them for Japanese soldiers because of their phenotype. In this way, even in military uniform, Nisei were still viewed as Japanese; their race was more salient than their uniform.

Meanwhile, some Japanese Americans did participate in the Pacific War, not in combat, but in intelligence, as linguists. Nisei in the Military Intelligence Service (MIS) were directly involved in the war with Japan, serving as interpreters and translators all over the Pacific. In particular, *Kibei Nisei,* those who had spent some time in Japan (and Okinawa), were able to use those experiences to help the U.S. military better understand their enemy and expedite an American victory.

In addition to those who served in the military (both voluntarily and via the draft), there were also some Nisei who resisted the draft, taking a stance that has remained controversial. Rather than aiming to demonstrate and prove their loyalty as Americans through military service, and in contrast to the attitudes of those who fought in the war, these individuals chose to question the premise of their being drafted out of internment camps. They challenged the idea that they should fight for a country that had illegally imprisoned them and violated their constitutional rights. Many of their contemporaries also questioned the appropriateness and legality of the camps but tried to avoid direct confrontation with the government and other authorities.

This small yet significant group believed that their incarceration was unconstitutional and that it violated their rights as U.S. citizens. With the passage of the Civil Liberties Act of 1988 and the government's acknowledgment that the internment was a violation of civil rights, the draft resisters' perspective has been validated on a larger scale. At the same time, however, it remains a controversial stance due to its diametric opposition to and invalidation of the military service of the majority of Nisei men, many of whom are now proud war veterans.

The Postwar Period

Japanese Americans have been called the "model minority," but this label overemphasizes culture and ethnicity as explanations for social and economic mobility. A better way to understand how Japanese Americans increased their status, income, and overall life chances in the 1950s and 1960s is to look at the convergence of structural factors, which provided them with new opportunities. According to sociologist Jere Takahashi, Japanese American access to higher education is one major factor that sets them apart from their Black and Latino counterparts. Because Japanese Americans were not excluded from the educational structure in the same ways, they were able to take advantage of opportunities that eventually arose for those with college degrees.

On the U.S. mainland, resettlement after leaving the camps meant starting over for most. The majority of families that were interned from the West Coast sold their property and belongings before evacuating and had little to return to. Moreover, the prewar ethnic economy that had provided jobs to many had been destroyed by the internment, and Japanese Americans were racially excluded from a number of professions.

The growing postwar economy in the 1950s and 1960s and the need for certain types of white-collar labor nonetheless led to the development of an American middle class. Japanese Americans had been racially excluded from U.S. society in various ways, though not in education. As a result, when the mainstream economy saw an increasing need for white-collar labor, educated Nisei were able to fill that growing labor niche in the professions that were open to Japanese Americans, professional, technical, clerical, and sales in particular. Many Nisei became a part of this expanding middle class of professionals, though limited to occupations in which they were not in direct competition with White labor.

In addition, Nisei politicians emerged at various levels of government, from local to national. The strategy of Americanization continued in the form of political participation. For the first time, Nisei from the U.S. mainland and Hawai'i became members of the U.S. Congress, as both representatives and senators. The efforts of these politicians at the national level were an indispensable part of the attainment of redress and reparations.

Nisei were an integral part of the redress and reparations movement that led to the passage of the Civil Liberties Act of 1988. The success of the movement is usually attributed to Sansei activism, including the persistent efforts of young Japanese American lawyers. However, it also depended largely on Nisei participation: Nisei testimonies of their wartime evacuation and internment were fundamental in illustrating how civil liberties were violated. Moreover, Nisei politicians sponsored the legislation and ensured its passage. Finally, on a social level, most Nisei had been silent about their internment experiences until then, and the process of gathering their oral histories and passing down those legacies was a crucial part of claiming their history for future generations.

Nisei Populations

Kibei Nisei

Kibei, meaning "returned to the United States," generally refers to American-born Nisei who spent a significant part of their formative years being educated or otherwise living in Japan. In the 1920s and 1930s, many Issei immigrants, especially those with larger families, struggled to make ends meet as they supported children and tried to earn and save money. For those who had the intention of returning to Japan as soon as they saved enough money to take back with them, it made sense to have their children educated in Japan until their eventual return. On the other hand, some who were planting roots in the United States saw that Nisei would face racial discrimination in the United States and believed that a Japanese education would give their children additional options should work and other opportunities in the United States become too limited. As a result, Kibei Nisei often have native or near-native Japanese language skills, in contrast to Nisei, who were raised primarily or entirely in the United States and have more limited Japanese language skills.

Kibei rejoined their families in the United States at various times; some returned to the United States before the war began, and others came back after experiencing the war in Japan. Many of those who returned before the war began served in military intelligence as linguists for the United States. Those who were in Japan during the war usually tried to hide their U.S. citizenship, English language skills, and foreign ways of thinking and acting to avoid discrimination in Japan. Some were drafted into the Japanese military. A well-known Kibei Nisei was Iva Toguri D'Aquino, a U.S.-born citizen accused of calling herself "Tokyo Rose" and broadcasting government anti-American propaganda over Japanese radio during World War II.

Thus, while many Nisei men and women fought in World War II as part of the U.S. military, some of their relatives who were in Japan when the war started were drafted into the Japanese military or otherwise experienced the war from the Japanese side, for example, in Hiroshima when the nuclear bomb was deployed. The case of Kibei Nisei is interesting and significant because, in many ways, they represented the polar opposite of what most Nisei aspired to be in Americanizing—they were more conspicuously Japanese.

Shin-Nisei

Shin-Nisei refers to Nisei whose Issei immigrant parents came to the United States in the postwar period. Specifically, while *Nisei* usually refers to people who experienced World War II and have been succeeded by *Sansei* (third generation), *Yonsei* (fourth generation), and *Gosei* (fifth generation), *Shin-Nisei* tends to refer younger Americans of Japanese ancestry whose parents migrated to the United States in more recent years and who have thus been able to maintain stronger ties to Japan because of less expensive transpacific travel and telecommunications and better access to foreign media. The term *Shin-Nisei* tends to be used more by academics and organizations to make a social cohort distinction than it does by individuals to refer to themselves. This categorization is significant in the U.S. context, to denote the two distinct waves of migration from Japan, but does not necessarily apply to ethnic Japanese populations in other countries.

Jane H. Yamashiro

See also Americanization; Assimilation; Internment Camps; Issei; Japanese American Citizens League; Japanese Americans; Military and Race; Model Minority; Sansei

Further Readings

Abe, Frank, producer. 2000. *Conscience and the Constitution* [Motion picture]. Ho-Ho-Kus, NJ: Transit Media.

Glenn, Evelyn Nakano. 1986. *Issei, Nisei, War Bride: Three Generations of Japanese American Women in Domestic Service.* Philadelphia, PA: Temple University Press.

Hawaii Nikkei History Editorial Board. 1998. *Japanese Eyes, American Heart: Personal Reflections of Hawaii's World War II Nisei Soldiers.* Honolulu, HI: Tendai Educational Foundation.

Takahashi, Jere. 1997. *Nisei/Sansei: Shifting Japanese American Identities and Politics.* Philadelphia, PA: Temple University Press.

Tamura, Eileen H. 1994. *Americanization, Acculturation, and Ethnic Identity: The Nisei Generation in Hawaii.* Urbana: University of Illinois Press.

Northern Ireland, Racism in

Northern Ireland is commonly portrayed as a society dominated by tensions between the majority Protestant community and the minority Catholic community. This emphasis tends to overshadow the historical relationship between people of color and the Irish (on both sides of the border) for more than a millennium. The Vikings traded North African slaves in Dublin in the 9th century, and later history records Irish peasants traveling with Norman lords on the crusades against Islam. The colonial era had a significant role in the Irish developing a sense of "the Other," for the British Empire could not have operated without the service of loyal Irish soldiers and administrators, all of whom were implicated directly or otherwise in the task of subjugating, ruling, and, indeed, sometimes slaughtering people of color.

The subject of racism in Northern Ireland, however, has only recently become topical, so the history of racism is largely contemporary. Nevertheless, over the past 30 years, it has become increasingly difficult to represent Northern Ireland as a society marked simply by two religiously defined communities. Recent immigrants have supplemented the older "Traveler" (gypsy or Roma) and Jewish populations; consequently, Northern Ireland is now a society with a host of different minority groups. This growing diversity creates challenges to the overwhelmingly White settled population. As a result, an overriding atmosphere of exclusion and a sense of not belonging have become prevalent within the minority ethnic population. This entry examines the various expressions of racism in Northern Ireland, including racist harassment, racial prejudice, and institutional racism.

A Persistent Problem

Northern Ireland has often been considered "a place apart," the product of a historical anomaly, which, at the turn of the 20th century, saw a Protestant majority in favor of union with Great Britain residing in the northeast corner of an overwhelmingly Catholic island that was demanding complete decolonization. This unhappy marriage resulted in the partition of the island and the foundation, in 1920, of Northern Ireland. When the ethnosectarian division and segregation endemic in Northern Irish society finally manifested itself in sustained political violence, from 1969 on, the outside world looked on in horror at what was perceived to be an aberration in the civilized West—White people fighting other White people. In an era before violent ethnic conflict erupted in the Balkans and long before the sectarian strife of present-day Iraq, the streets of Northern Ireland, and Belfast in particular, provided the most graphic evidence of the power of ethnonationalism.

Also evident is a persistent problem of racist harassment and violence toward members of minority ethnic communities. Whereas racism, racial discrimination, and inequality in Northern Ireland are certainly not new phenomena, the existence of minority ethnic communities and racism has received widespread attention only in recent years. The increased media interest in and reporting of racist attacks has led to Belfast's being dubbed the "Race Hate Capital of Europe."

Racist Harassment

A growing body of literature on the experiences of minority ethnic people in Northern Ireland makes clear that racist violence is a regular occurrence. All recent published research has acknowledged the ongoing presence of racist harassment in the lives of members of the minority community, and the number of racist attacks reported to the police in Northern Ireland has increased dramatically over the last 10 years.

Racist harassment does not manifest merely as verbal abuse at the street level. At the extreme end of direct individualized racism, members of minority ethnic communities have been pipe bombed, gasoline bombed, and brutally physically assaulted and left for dead. Some have been threatened and spat upon while going about their daily business; others have had their homes and workplaces daubed with racist graffiti. This has taken place in schools, housing, and the workplace and also in a range of places, such as in city centers, shops, train stations, buses, and the street. Furthermore, because of victims' fear of coming forward and their lack of confidence in the police tackling racist violence, the official statistics are likely to significantly underestimate the extent of the problem.

Recent harassment has been aimed at Eastern European, Filipino, and Portuguese migrant workers, some of whom have been badly beaten and their homes attacked. This group represents a new Other for the racist discourse, which blames such migrant workers for job losses, lack of housing, and all other problems working-class people are facing. Racial harassment continues to be a common experience for many minority ethnic people in Northern Ireland, who are twice as likely to face a racist incident as those in England or Wales.

Racist Prejudice

A number of attitudinal studies concerning race and ethnicity have been conducted in Northern Ireland. The most striking finding to emerge is that racist prejudice appears to be more strongly demonstrated than sectarian prejudice. Bearing in mind that sectarianism and racism are different processes that manifest themselves in very different ways, some authors warn it would be wrong to claim that racism "is worse than" or "more of a problem than" sectarianism in Northern Ireland. Nevertheless, a "suspicion of difference" is entrenched: One in three people were found to state that they would not willingly accept a Chinese or Indian or African Caribbean person as a colleague at work; or one in four would not willingly accept a member of the minority ethnic population as a resident in their local area.

Some scholars have found that people who support Unionist (associated with the Protestant population) political parties are more likely to say they were prejudiced than those who supported Nationalist (associated with the Catholic population) political parties. Or, in the case of national identity, people who self-identified as British or Ulster were more likely to declare they were prejudiced than those who identified themselves as Northern Irish or Irish. Media reports and some scholars have indicated that Loyalist paramilitaries are believed to be behind a significant proportion of the incidents. At the same time, there have been attacks in both Catholic and Protestant areas, usually perpetrated by organized criminals in working-class areas. Furthermore, this is just one type of racism that permeates Northern Irish society; still extant is institutional racism, which involves society as a whole and is not dominated by a particular ethnonational group. Consequently, there is a strong sentiment by many minority ethnic activists not to hold any one community culpable, but to work with all communities in the fight against racist prejudice.

Racist prejudice permeates all sections of Northern Irish society, from unashamedly fascist-style racist statements made by several politicians to the disregard by some teachers of racist bullying toward ethnic minority children in schools. Some authors who try to explain this sense of intolerance point to the political projects of Unionism and Nationalism. They are both racialized and founded upon a sense of Whiteness, and both continue to encourage a sense of identity that is essentially White and exclusionary. Furthermore, factors unique to the culture and history of Northern Ireland ("the Troubles") have given rise to a culture of violence.

Institutional Racism

It has been argued that as a consequence of "the Troubles," there has been a tendency to neglect, ignore, or minimize minority ethnic problems such as institutional racism, as the preoccupation with traditional sociopolitical matters has left scant room for other agendas. And although Northern Ireland has a relatively young and growing minority ethnic population, their experiences documented thus far have included marginalization, overt and covert forms of racism, and inequitable treatment.

More recently, however, academic and policy research within Northern Ireland appear to lend increasing weight to the existence of institutional racism. This has played an important role in drawing attention to the structure and routine nature of racial discrimination. Cultural diversity in Northern Ireland might not exist on a large scale, but there are diverse cultural and ethnic communities present, however small. By virtue of their small numbers and by making themselves invisible, minority ethnic groups are suffering from the institutional difference, complacency, and racism(s) evident in majority–minority relations.

As "invisibles," minority ethnic groups are devalued as subjects of policy and excluded from the issue of rights. This is most clearly evident, for example, in the fact that antidiscrimination legislation was applied just a decade ago via the implementation of the 1997 Race Relations (Northern Ireland) Order. Only since then have issues of racism and ethnicity begun to find their way onto the local political agenda. In addition, through recent legislation stemming from the Belfast Agreement of 1998, an obligation has been placed on all public organizations to address issues of race/ethnicity, as well as equality.

With the introduction of antiracist legislation and the new equality duty, recognition of differences is beginning to occur within various institutions, so that some institutional racism has lessened; however, it still remains an issue. While many government agencies and organizations have begun to acknowledge the problem of racism or at least begun to think about how they might respond to the problem, there has been little concrete activity that effectively responds to the current situation. This sentiment was reiterated in a report recently published by a local government body, which found a slow response to racism, institutional racism, and issues of inequality by organizations in all sectors of social, political, and economic life in Northern Ireland.

Minority ethnic people find themselves constantly struggling against two ethnonational groups for equality against a backdrop of widespread sectarian division and conflict in Northern Ireland. Thus, the more obvious presence of minority groups has presented a challenge to this bicultural status quo, and, as a result, it has become increasingly obvious that different minority groups face considerable discrimination and inequality.

The tensions between Catholics and Protestants in Northern Ireland have not gone away, but, since the signing of the Belfast Agreement in 1998, the conflict has stabilized. As confidence in the peace process has grown, the region has experienced a minor economic resurgence, and the number of people immigrating to Northern Ireland has increased substantially. Minority ethnic communities who were rendered invisible during "the Troubles" are becoming more vocal, and antiracism has emerged as a prominent discourse across the political spectrum as antiracist organizations and initiatives have developed in Northern Ireland. The pressure toward homogeneity of contemporary Northern Irish society is slowly beginning to disperse and make way for a more heterogeneous society.

Romana Khaoury

See Appendix A; Appendix B
See also Institutional Discrimination; Ireland; Irish Americans; United Kingdom; United Kingdom, Immigrants and Their Descendants in the United States

Further Readings

BBC News Online. 2004. *Race Hate on the Rise in NI.* Retrieved from http://news.bbc.co.uk/1/hi/northern_ireland/3390249.stm

Boal, Frederick W., ed. 2000. *Ethnicity and Housing: Accommodating Differences.* Aldershot, UK: Ashgate.

Connolly, Paul. 2005. "'It Goes Without Saying (Well Sometimes)': Racism, Whiteness, and Identity in Northern

Ireland." In *The New Countryside? Ethnicity, Nation, and Exclusion in Contemporary Rural Britain,* edited by J. Agyeman and S. Neal. Bristol, UK: Policy Press.

Coulter, Colin. 1999. *Contemporary Northern Irish Society: An Introduction.* London: Pluto Press.

Gilligan, Chris and Katrina Lloyd. 2006. *Racial Prejudice in Northern Ireland.* Available from http://www.ark.ac.uk/publications/updates/update44.pdf

Hainsworth, Paul, ed. 1998. *Divided Society: Ethnic Minorities and Racism in Northern Ireland.* London: Pluto Press.

Macpherson, William. 1999. *The Stephen Lawrence Inquiry.* London: The Stationery Office. Retrieved from http://www.archive.official-documents.co.uk/document/cm42/4262/4262.htm

McVeigh, Robbie. 2006. *The Next Stephen Lawrence: Racist Violence and Criminal Justice in Northern Ireland.* Belfast, UK: Northern Ireland Council for Ethnic Minorities.

Rolston, Bill and Michael Shannon. 2002. *Encounters: How Racism Came to Ireland.* Belfast, UK: Beyond the Pale.

NORWEGIAN AMERICANS

A high percentage of immigrants from Norway in the mid-1800s and afterward made the United States their primary destination, founding settlements that participated in U.S. culture, while contributing their own traditions to that culture. Today, elements of the culture of Norway, a country with an estimated population of 4.7 million people as of 2007, persist in the United States, while many contemporary Norwegian Americans continue to maintain an enthusiastic attachment to the traditions of their homeland. This entry will discuss the history and significance of Norwegian immigrants to the U.S.

Early Immigration

Although the reasons for emigration from Norway to the United States are varied and complex, the conditions in Norway were similar to those in Sweden: A dramatic and rapid increase in population strained the economic systems to the maximum; a period of famine exacerbated these effects; and the general lack of potential for social mobility caused many Norwegians to feel discontented with the quality of life in Norway. A lack of good farmland had made rural survival difficult, and overpopulation in the urban areas had made urban survival just as rough. In addition, Norway was as yet not fully independent when the strong waves of emigration began in the 1860s—it had passed from Danish control to Swedish control in 1814 and would not gain independence from Sweden until 1905.

Though the first major emigration from Norway began in 1825, the main waves followed those Sweden experienced in the 1860s, 1880s, and early 1900s and in World War I as a response to German occupation. Peter Munch pointed out that the waves in the 1860s and 1880s were also times of particular strain in the relationship between Norway and Sweden. The reasons the United States was attractive were mostly economical. The promise of steady, well-paying employment was a promise to be fulfilled not in Norway, but in America. The early emigrants wrote letters home to relatives and friends in Norway emphasizing the higher standard of living made available to them through their move. Emigration agents, who arranged passage for the emigrants, further confirmed this perspective of America in their advertisements.

Early Settlements

Norwegians settled chiefly in Minnesota, Wisconsin, and North Dakota, but they also settled in other areas with water access, such as New York City and Seattle, Washington. In New York and Seattle, the Norwegian men exercised their maritime skills on fishing vessels and in the shipyards. In the Midwest, many men found employment in factories and in industrial jobs, and many women and girls became domestic servants. The Lutheran state church continued its influence, and Norwegian Lutheran churches were built in the cities where Norwegians settled. In those communities, services were often conducted in the Norwegian language. This practice was questioned in the wake of World War I, when Americanness was foregrounded, and many churches at this time and in the coming decades ceased to provide services in Norwegian.

Community Developments

Norwegian American immigrant newspapers, such as *Skandanavien* and *Nordvesten,* encouraged the retention of the Norwegian language in the immigrant communities, particularly in the Chicago region. In addition, groups like the Norwegian American Historical Association (founded in 1925) and local associations and societies created ways for Norwegian Americans to commune and identify with others in similar ethnic positions. The immigrant children gained experiences with U.S. culture in their schooling, which was a controversial issue in the second half of the 1800s. The Norwegian Evangelical Lutheran Synod was a powerful organization, with distrust of U.S. schools from the early grades to postsecondary education. Through a series of items called the "Manitowoc Declarations," after the location of the meeting in Manitowoc, Wisconsin, the Synod planned to begin their own curriculum and schools, which presented such major challenges to finances and time that the primary emphasis on U.S. schools was eventually accepted by the 1880s.

A further problem arose as the Norwegian immigrants had trouble finding universities and colleges to attend, and, in answer to this call, in 1875, Rasmus Bjørn Anderson became the first professor of Scandinavian at the University of Wisconsin at Madison. Norwegian language classes had been offered at the university since 1870, but the hiring of Anderson resulted in the founding of one of the few remaining Scandinavian departments at a public university in the United States. Anderson was a strong proponent of the retention of Norwegian culture in the Norwegian American community and was convinced that this community contributed strongly through its involvement in the U.S. educational system. Though Anderson was instrumental in promoting the academic study of Scandinavia in America, the first professor of Scandinavian in the United States had been Paul C. Sinding, a Dane hired in 1858 to teach both Danish and Norwegian at New York University. A few other colleges that were founded by Norwegian immigrants or Norwegian American immigrant communities are Concordia College, in Moorhead, Minnesota; Luther College, in Decorah, Iowa; St. Olaf College, in Northfield, Minnesota; Pacific Lutheran College, in Parkland, Washington; and Augustana College, in Rock Island, Illinois. Universities and colleges as these often offer such courses as Norwegian language, the plays of Henrik Ibsen, and the music of Edvard Grieg and are instrumental in encouraging the study not only of Norway, but of the cultural position of Norwegian Americans.

Later Settlements and Festivals

Norwegian American communities, because of their desire to become active participants in their adopted country and the pervasiveness of U.S. culture, began to lose their language in favor of assimilation, though they retained many customs practiced by their parents and grandparents. During World War I, the questioning of ethnic heritage and the discouraging of non-American practices exacerbated an already diminishing Norwegian influence. Festivities held in the Twin Cities of Minneapolis and St. Paul, in Minnesota, to celebrate the centennial of Norwegian independence in 1914 generated controversy regarding demonstrations of pride and ethnic solidarity in a country other than the United States. In addition, foreign-language newspapers and religious services were strongly discouraged by the U.S. government during this period in favor of a unified U.S. identity. The celebration of the centennial of Norwegian immigration in 1925, also held in Minnesota but at the state fairgrounds, was a more complicated affair, advertising not only Norwegian heritage but also inclusion in U.S. culture.

Where large clusters of Norwegian immigrants settled, strong community heritage exists. Such cities as Mount Horeb and Stoughton, Wisconsin, are known for their representations of Norwegian heritage. Mount Horeb proclaims itself the "Troll Capital of the World," owing to the many statues and carvings around town, not to mention its shops and restaurants with similar references to Norwegian lore. Stoughton famously advertises its May 17 *(syttende mai)* festival in honor of Norwegian independence. A major industry in

Stoughton was a wagon factory owned by Norwegian immigrant T. G. Mandt, who hired his fellow countrymen and thus supported the growth of Norwegian American heritage in the area. A number of other towns in the vicinity celebrate their Norwegian American heritage, among them Blue Mounds, Springdale, and Blanchardville. In many of these locales, as in many other Norwegian American communities, traditional food such as *lutefisk* (whitefish, sometimes cod or haddock, soaked in lye) and *lefse* (potato flatbread) are served regularly. While variations of *lefse* are available in Norway, the version typically found in Norwegian American areas is a thin version somewhat resembling a tortilla. Some Norwegian Americans have preserved the art of making aquavit *(akvavit)*, potato liquor infused with caraway, or have been able to import the liquor from Norway and enjoy this drink with the *lutefisk* and *lefse*. This liquor is served ice-cold and sipped from stemmed glasses.

Norwegian American Folk Arts

Norwegian American folk arts are a primary means of upholding customs and confirming a sense of community. Music typically includes folk melodies played on the Hardanger fiddle *(hardingfele),* an instrument that originated in Hardanger province in Norway and consists of bowed strings (the fiddler usually plays two or three at a time) and sympathetic strings that resonate along with the bowed strings, providing a "drone." The Hardanger Fiddle Association of America, founded in 1983, is the most recent of various fiddling associations that had been founded, and later disbanded, throughout the 20th century. The association also encourages the continuation of traditions in folk dancing and singing, particularly because these art forms were often performed together during festivals and celebrations in the homeland. Folk dancing, particularly the polka, waltz, and schottische, is common in Norwegian American heritage arts groups and is often combined in performance with traditional Norwegian fiddle music. Norwegian American folk art may be viewed at galleries associated with Norwegian American universities and colleges as well as such venues as the Vesterheim Norwegian American Museum in Decorah, Iowa. Rosemaling, decorative folk painting, has enjoyed a nearly constant popularity among Norwegian Americans, who correctly identify this as a main form of folk art from their homeland.

Suzanne B. Martin

See Appendix A; Appendix B
See also Assimilation; Danish Americans; Ethnic Enclave, Economic Impact of; Ethnic Group; Finnish Americans; Icelandic Americans; Immigrant Communities; Sami; Swedish Americans; Symbolic Ethnicity

Further Readings

Jonassen, Christen T. 1986. "The Norwegian Heritage in Urban America: Conflict and Cooperation in a Norwegian Immigrant Community." *Norwegian-American Studies* 31:73–96. Retrieved from http://www.stolaf.edu/naha/pubs/nas/volume31/v0131_03.htm

Leary, James P., ed. 1998. *Wisconsin Folklore.* Madison: University of Wisconsin.

Nelsen, Frank C. 1974. "The School Controversy among Norwegian Immigrants." *Norwegian-American Studies* 26:206–219. Retrieved from http://www.stolaf.edu/naha/pubs/nas/volume26/v0126_10.htm

Web Sites

Hardanger Fiddle Association of America: http://www.hfaa.org
Norwegian American Historical Association: http://www.stolaf.edu/naha
Vesterheim Norwegian American Museum: http://www.vesterheim.org

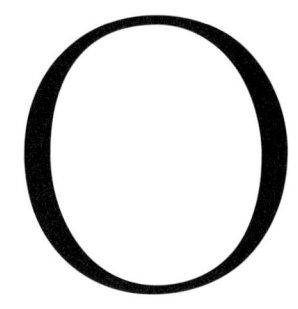

Ojibwa

The Ojibwa, also known as the Chippewa and the Aanishanabe, are an indigenous nation located primarily in Minnesota, Wisconsin, Michigan, and the Canadian province of Ontario. There are also Ojibwa reservations and communities in North Dakota, Montana, and the Canadian provinces of Alberta, Manitoba, and Saskatchewan, as well as significant Ojibwa populations in urban areas of both the United States and Canada. The U.S. federal government currently recognizes 23 Ojibwa reservations; the Canadian government recognizes 130 reserves of Ojibwa First Nations. When the population of all United States and Canadian Ojibwa are considered together, the Ojibwa make up one of the most populous indigenous nations in North America.

Indigenous populations in both the United States and Canada are difficult to determine because of the variety of definitions, criteria, and data-gathering methods used in both countries, and so wide variation exists in reports on the Ojibwa population. The most recent census figures in both countries place the total Ojibwa population at about 200,000. Some sources report that the Ojibwa population is about evenly divided between the United States and Canada, while others claim that up to two-thirds of the entire Ojibwa population resides in Canada, with about half of Canadian Ojibwa living in Ontario. In both countries, the Ojibwa population is about evenly divided between those who live on reserves (Canada) or reservations (United States) and those who live in urban centers, although those who live off reserves or reservations typically maintain strong ties to their homelands. Within the United States, the Ojibwa are the third most populous indigenous nation, surpassed only by the Navajo and the Cherokee.

There is significant variation in the tribal name and also no standardized English spelling for *Ojibwa,* with variations that include *Ojibway* and *Ojibwe.* *Chippewa,* the name most often used by the U.S. government, is an English corruption of the word *Ojibwa.* In Canada, the names *Salteaux* and *Bungi* also refer to Ojibwa who reside in the Plains regions. The Ojibwa refer to themselves as *Aanishinabe,* or "first or original people."

The Ojibwa are part of the Algonquian language family and maintain about four different dialects of the Ojibwa language. Regular and first usage of the Ojibwa language is much more common in Canada than in the United States, although the Ojibwa language is enjoying a contemporary renaissance in the United States. Language revitalization programs for children and adults are active on a number of Ojibwa reservations and in urban areas.

Traditionally, the Ojibwa have been a people who depended for their subsistence on hunting, fishing, and trading and moved seasonally in accordance with the maple sugar and wild rice harvests, while walleye fishing remained a year-round pursuit. Traditional Ojibwa society is clan based, with each clan named after a specific animal. Clans are inherited from the father, and marriage within clans is prohibited. Ojibwa spirituality centers around the *Midewiwin,* or Medicine Lodge Society. All of these traditional components of Ojibwa society remain active among Ojibwa people in both Canada and the United States today and often in tandem with Western and Christian practices.

Ojibwa Indian family in canoe (1913). *The Ojibwa are an indigenous nation located primarily in Minnesota, Wisconsin, Michigan, and the Canadian province of Ontario. Today, the Ojibwa are the third most populous indigenous nation in the United States, surpassed only by the Navajo and the Cherokee.*

Source: Library of Congress, Prints & Photographs Division, LC-USZ62-101332.

History

First contact between the Ojibwa and Europeans occurred in the early 17th century, when French fur trappers and missionaries entered the region. By the end of the 17th century, the Ojibwa were heavily involved in the fur trade. Early relations between the Ojibwa and the fur traders were generally congenial. Many trappers and traders intermarried with the Ojibwa, especially in Canada, where a new *Métis* culture and identity emerged that blended Native American and European cultures. The fur trade did, however, place pressure on the Ojibwa, who increasingly moved west and south, a scenario that led to occasional conflict with the neighboring tribes the Ojibwa were displacing. Some Ojibwa bands moved far west to the Plains region and adopted elements of the buffalo-hunting culture of the Dakota and Lakota but also retained many elements of their woodlands culture.

The first Ojibwa land cessions to Europeans took place by international nation-to-nation treaties with Great Britain in the late 1700s. After achieving independence from Great Britain, the Americans followed the British lead and also made international sovereign-to-sovereign treaties with the Ojibwa beginning in the early 1800s. In the United States, most treaties with the Ojibwa were signed and ratified between 1820 and 1860, with Ojibwa bands ceding land in return for retained land in reservation trust status, cash or annuity payments, and certain promises, including perpetual hunting, fishing, and gathering rights in the ceded territories. A number of court rulings during the 1980s and 1990s reaffirmed the perpetuity of Ojibwa rights to hunt, fish, and gather in these ceded lands. In 1998, the U.S. Supreme Court in *State of Minnesota v. Mille Lacs Band of Ojibwe* firmly upheld Ojibwa hunting and fishing rights in territories ceded in the 1837 treaty between the Ojibwa and the United States.

In Canada, the treaty process worked differently. In 1839, Great Britain unilaterally declared that all Indian land in Canada would be Crown land, while Indians living on Indian land were to be given wardship status, since they were considered to be in need of protection by the Crown. During the entire 19th and most of the 20th century, Canada's Indian policy was one of coercive civilization, and Canada began to experiment with individual land ownership schemes for Natives as a part of their "civilizing" policy. When land surrenders occurred and treaties were signed in Canada, reserves were intentionally small and set up close to White population centers in order to enhance the prospects for assimilation and Christianization of the Indians. By the mid-19th century, the Ojibwa in Canada were largely supportive of treaties, viewing them as a way to protect and retain their lands in the face of Canadian Indian policy. Crown ownership of Native land and the wardship status of the indigenous population produced a dispute in the 1850s, when mineral deposits were discovered on Ojibwa land. Ojibwa leaders pressed the Crown to turn over the lease payments paid by the mining companies, since the deposits were located on Ojibwa land, but these efforts were unsuccessful. The Crown claimed ownership of the land and therefore felt no obligation to turn over any monies from those leases to the Ojibwa.

In the United States, the federal government unilaterally ended treaty making with indigenous nations in 1871. Although existing treaties were to remain in force and the treaty making actually continued under the guise of agreements, the 1871 decision nevertheless represented a significant shift in the relationship between indigenous nations and the federal government from nation-to-nation status toward a federally directed policy of assimilation. In 1887, Congress passed the Dawes Act, which established the allotment policy that eventually led to the allotting of tribal lands in 160-acre parcels to individual Indians in an attempt to break up the reservations and force Indians to assimilate to the European American way of life. Unallotted tribal lands were sold off to non-Natives as "surplus." The result of this policy was massive land loss and fractionation of land throughout Indian country. The Ojibwa in the United States suffered gravely under Dawes Act policies. Nearly all Ojibwa reservations were allotted. The Red Lake Band in Minnesota, however, was one of the few reservations in the region to resist the allotment policy and maintain its own tribal government throughout this period. The remaining Ojibwa reservations suffered such severe land losses as a result of allotment that these reservations are today only a tiny proportion of their original size. Most Ojibwa reservations also remain highly fractionated today, with discontiguous parcels of trust land, allotted land, and non-Native owned land scattered in a checkerboard pattern throughout the reservations.

In the 1930s, following reports of the devastation wrought by allotment era policies, the U.S. federal government shifted its policy to one that favored some measure of self-rule for indigenous nations. The Indian Reorganization Act (IRA) of 1934 ended land allotment and renewed a government-to-government relationship between indigenous nations and the federal government. Tribes were encouraged to reestablish their own governments via the constitutional process. Historically, the Ojibwa have typically been among the first beneficiaries of any federal policy shift, and the IRA was no exception to this rule. Most Ojibwa reservations quickly adopted IRA constitutions after 1934. In Michigan, Wisconsin, North Dakota, and Montana, all federally recognized Ojibwa reservations have IRA constitutions. In Minnesota, six bands of Ojibwa (Bois Forte, Fond du Lac, Grand Portage, Leech Lake, Mille Lacs, and White Earth) adopted a single constitution in 1936 as the consolidated Minnesota Chippewa Tribe. The Red Lake Band maintains its own separate tribal government.

No Ojibwa reservation experienced termination during the mid-20th century, although the Ojibwa reservations did lose significant population during the post–World War II era as many reservation residents migrated to urban areas both in search of employment and as a result of federal relocation policies.

Contemporary Issues

Indigenous political activism surged in the late 1960s and 1970s, and many Ojibwa were active in the American Indian Movement (AIM) during that era. AIM also spread into Canada, due in part to Ojibwa connections that traverse the border. In both countries, activists sought land rights, restoration of treaty rights, and increased rights to self-government. As a result of this increased activism, federal policy in the United States shifted once again in the 1970s to one of tribal self-determination. In Canada, certain treaty rights and Aboriginal rights were entrenched with the passage of the Constitution Act of 1982.

In the contemporary period, Ojibwa in Canada and the United States struggle with a number of issues that are common among indigenous nations in both countries: poverty, lack of access to adequate health care, lack of quality education and job training, high levels of crime and discrimination in the criminal justice system, and limited economic development opportunities. Ojibwa in both countries also continue to struggle for recognition of their land and treaty rights, along with rights to increased self-government and self-determination. In the United States, Ojibwa reservations were among the first indigenous nations to establish casino gaming enterprises under provisions of the Indian Gaming Regulatory Act of 1988, an initiative intended to enhance reservation economic development and self-determination for tribal governments. While all Ojibwa tribes in Michigan, Wisconsin, Minnesota, and North Dakota currently operate casinos, Ojibwa reservations are located in remote areas and, as a result, casino gaming has not been the panacea of economic development for Ojibwa communities as has been the case for some other indigenous nations. Many serious economic and social problems remain present on Ojibwa reservations throughout Canada and the United States

Sheryl Lightfoot

See Appendix A

See also American Indian Movement; Canada, First Nations; Dawes Act of 1887; Gaming, Native American; Indian Gaming Regulatory Act of 1988; Native Americans; Native American Identity, Legal Background; Sovereignty, Native American

Further Readings

Deloria, Vine, Jr., ed. 1985. *American Indian Policy in the Twentieth Century.* Norman: University of Oklahoma.

Dickason, Olive Patricia. 2006. *A Concise History of Canada's First Nations.* Toronto, Canada: Oxford University.

Johnston, Basil. 1990. *The Ojibwe Heritage.* Lincoln: University of Nebraska.
Tanner, Helen Horbeck. 1992. *The Ojibwa.* New York: Chelsea House.
Vizenor, Gerald. 1984. *The People Named the Chippewa: Narrative Histories.* Minneapolis: University of Minnesota.
Warren, William W. 1984. *History of the Ojibwe People.* St. Paul, MN: Minnesota Historical Society.
Wilkins, David E. 2006. *American Indian Politics and the American Political System.* Lanham, MD: Rowman & Littlefield.

ONE-DROP RULE

The "one-drop rule" as it was applied in the United States dictated that any person with any amount of African ancestry be considered as Black regardless of their percentage of "Black blood." The standard was not applied to other races, such as Native Americans or Asian Americans. This entry considers the social significance of the one-drop rule, the legal history, the related concept of "passing," and, finally, multiracial designations and the legacy of the rule in contemporary times.

Social Significance

The one-drop rule was established during the slavery era in the United States. It had multiple aims or social purposes: to prevent interracial relationships, ensure the purity of the White race, and maintain the slave status of Black children born to White women as well as Black women. This meant children born to White women were considered Black if the father was Black, while all children born to Black women were considered Black even if the father was White. Thus, Black children often inherited their slavery status from their mothers.

The one-drop rule was adopted by different states at different periods of time. Both Louisiana and Tennessee adopted the rule in 1910, Texas and Arkansas in 1911, and Mississippi in 1917. By 1925, almost every state had some form of the one-drop rule. Many states maintained that false reporting of one's racial identity would result in legal penalty.

A group of citizens in Louisiana challenged the one-drop rule as applied in the state's Separate Car Act, which endorsed "separate but equal" seating in railroad cars. Because he was only one-eighth Black and appeared White, Homer Plessy was chosen to test the constitutionality of the act by attempting to sit in the White section of a railroad car. He was arrested and charged with violating the act. In the 1896 precedent-setting case of *Plessy v. Ferguson,* the U.S. Supreme Court upheld Plessy's conviction in the lower Louisiana courts. Without ruling directly on the definition of a Negro or a Black, the Supreme Court ruled that the Separate Car Act was constitutional.

In the case of *Loving vs. Virginia,* in 1967, the Supreme Court declared the one-drop rule unconstitutional by overturning state laws that forbid interracial marriages. However, the one-drop rule persisted in law. A law in Louisiana defining anyone with a "trace" of Black ancestry as Black withstood legal challenges during the civil rights era. In 1983, this law was repealed as a result of a legal challenge on behalf of a child who was 1/256 Black, whose parents wanted the option of selecting the race of their newborn as officially declared on the birth certificate. Finally, in 1986, the Supreme Court denied further appeals, establishing the end of the one-drop rule as a legal definition.

"Passing"

Legitimizing the one-drop rule was intended to prevent or minimize the social practice of "passing." "Passing as White" is the practice of a person or member of multiracial ancestry, typically including African American heritage, becoming accepted by others as White, which was undertaken by people desperate to escape the low social status of being Black in a racist society. Passing in a multiracial society can be very complex. Gunnar Myrdal noted that Black Americans who were not light skinned enough to pass as White would instead pass for Filipinos, Spaniards, Italians, or Mexicans to escape discrimination.

Sometimes passing as White was undertaken for convenience. For example, Walter White, chief executive from 1929 to 1955 of the National Association for the Advancement of Colored People (NAACP), was a light-skinned African American of mixed race, and he passed as White to investigate lynchings and other hate crimes. White's life and travels through the United States and abroad highlight the absurdity of the one-drop rule in practice. Most telling was the time his father was seriously injured in a traffic accident in Atlanta in 1931. Rushed to the hospital unconscious, he was taken to the nearest White hospital. When Walter White's brother first arrived on the scene, horrified hospital workers realized the gravely wounded man was in the wrong place. Despite his condition, White's father was immediately transferred in the rain to the overcrowded, inadequately equipped "colored' medical facility, where he died 17 days later. Even when one was near death, passing was not tolerated.

As noted earlier, the one-drop rule was applied uniquely to Blacks in the United States. For example, historically, a person who was one-fourth Filipino or Cherokee was considered White unless that person chose to openly declare his or her biracial or multiracial ancestry, as occurs frequently in contemporary times. During the Jim Crow era and for much of the 20th century, a person of Black ancestry who passed as White had to sever all family ties to the African American community and any public loyalties to the challenges faced by Black people.

In the 21st century, the notion of passing may seem "quaint" to some, while to others it smacks of being a "race traitor"; nonetheless, the act of passing underscores the historical social, economic, and psychological costs of "being Black" in the United States.

Multiracial Designations

The concept of mixed race is not new in the United States. Federal recognition of the category *mulatto* was used by census enumerators from 1840 through 1910, though people classified as such (or *quadroon* or *octoroon*) were considered socially and legally as Black.

When self-definition of race in the U.S. Census questionnaire began in 1960 (a person was asked to specify his or her race), only one race was to be selected. Even up to the present, efforts to allow *biracial* or *multiracial* as a distinct census (and hence legal) category have failed at the federal levels. However, quite in contrast to the legacy of the one-drop rule and practice of passing, as of the 2000 census, people can now publicly and legally identify for themselves or their children two or more racial categories.

As shown in the accompanying table, most people were content with identifying themselves in one of five racial categories offered in the 2000 census. Only 4.8% of African Americans identified themselves Black in combination with another racial group. (See Table 1.)

Table 1 Percent Reporting Two or More Races by Specified Race, 2000

Specified race	Alone or in combination[1]	Alone[2]	In combination[3]	Percent in combination[4]
White	216,930,975	211,460,626	5,470,349	2.5
Black or African and American	36,419,434	34,658,190	1,761,244	4.8
American Indian and Alaska Native	4,119,301	2,475,956	1,643,345	39.9
Asian	11,898,828	10,242,998	1,655,830	13.9
Native Hawaiian and Other Pacific Islander	874,414	398,835	475,579	54.4
Some other race	18,521,486	15,359,073	3,162,413	17.1

Source: U.S. Census Bureau, Census 2000 Redistricting Data (Public Law 94–171) Summary File, Table PL1.

Notes: For information on confidentiality protection, nonsampling error, and definitions, see http://www.census.gov/prod/cen2000/doc/pl94–171.pdf

[1] People who reported only one race, together with those who reported that same race plus one or more other races, are combined to create the race *alone* or *in combination* categories.

[2] People who reported only one race create the race *alone* categories.

[3] People who reported more than one of the six race categories create the race *in combination* categories.

[4] The "percent in combination" is the proportion that the *in combination* population represented of the *alone* or in *combination* population. This is the equivalent of the percent of people reporting a specified race who reported two or more races.

The U.S. Census Bureau, in response to the changing racial climate, changed its categorization to reflect more flexible racial categories. For example, in the 2000 census, more than 35,000 people who previously identified themselves as Black were allowed to indicate two or more racial categories. This change reflects the recognition by the federal government of a multiracial society in the United States.

Contemporary Times

As golfer Tiger Woods burst on the national scene in the 1990s, much was made of his multiracial heritage: a multiracial father (one-half Black, one-fourth Chinese, and one-fourth Native American) and a multiracial mother (one-half Thai, one-fourth Chinese, and one-fourth Dutch). While Woods coined the term *Cablinasia* to refer to himself, he is most often viewed as a pathbreaker for African Americans in professional golf.

In 2007, presidential candidate Barack Obama's racial identification provoked debates on the definition of Blackness. Obama self-identifies as Black. However, since his mother is White, many people consider him as biracial. Thus, the complexity of racial categorization continues in contemporary society in the United States.

Shu-Ju Ada Cheng and Richard T. Schaefer

See also African Americans; *American Dilemma, An;* Asian Americans; Blood Quantum; Census, U.S.; Color Line; Cuba; *Loving v. Virginia;* Multiracial Identity; *Plessy v. Ferguson;* Racial Formation; Racial Identity; Racial Identity Development; Racism

Further Readings

Davis, F. James. 2001. *Who Is Black? One Nation's Definition.* University Park: Pennsylvania State University Press.

Gittoes-Singh, Xennia. 2003. *One Drop: To Be the Color Black.* West Conshohocken, PA: Infinity Publishing.

Herring, Cedric, Verna M. Keith, and Hayward Derrick Horton, eds. 2004. *Skin Deep: How Race and Complexion Matter in the "Color-Blind" Era.* Chicago: University of Illinois Press.

Jones, Nicholas A. and Amy Symens Smith. 200. *The Two or More Races Population: 2000. Census 2000 Brief. C2KBR/01–6.* Washington, DC: U.S. Government Priority Office.

Myrdal, Gunner. 1944. *An American Dilemma: The Negro Problem and Modern Democracy.* New York: Harper.

Sweet, Frank W. 2005. *Legal History of the Color Line: The Rise and Triumph of the One-Drop Rule.* Palm Coast, FL: Backintyme.

White, William Francis. 1995. *A Man Called White: The Autobiography of William White.* Athens: University of Georgia Press.

Operation Bootstrap

Operation Bootstrap was a development plan implemented in the U.S. territory of Puerto Rico in the 1950s. Concerned about the growing independence movement, in 1942, the government established the Puerto Rican Development Corporation *(Fomento Industrial y Económico)*. The idea of transforming the island into an industrial center emerged as part of the government programs of Luis Muñoz Marín to lessen the problems of poverty, unemployment, and underemployment of workers. However, that idea was turned into a program by Teodoro Moscoso. Operation Bootstrap *(Operación Manos a la Obra)* presented a new economic model different from the previous agro-export model. The main objective of Operation Bootstrap was to promote economic growth by attracting U.S. industries. To do so, the program offered appealing tax exemptions, cheap labor, and low-cost infrastructure for outside investors interested in establishing their manufacturing on the island. For instance, the program offered no tariffs on trade between the United States and Puerto Rico.

One of the strongest criticisms of the implementation of Operation Bootstrap is that the agricultural sector was overlooked and no resources were allocated to advance the technology used in producing various agricultural goods. It has been argued that the economic growth experienced in the Caribbean island from 1950 to 1970 was more a consequence of the transformation from an agricultural to an industrial economy than a result of the integration of Puerto Ricans to the workforce. As a consequence of the decline of the agricultural sector, many employment opportunities were lost. The industrial sector was dramatically growing, but the number of jobs generated was not enough to compensate for those lost in agriculture. This has led to a chronic history of unemployment and underemployment.

The program experienced many changes over time. For instance, extending the U.S. minimum wage to

Puerto Rico increased the cost of labor. More important, Section 936, which offered tax reductions to U.S. industries, was eliminated. The full effects of the elimination of Section 936 are still unclear; however, numerous industries have left the island because of rising production costs. In fact, Mayaguez is among the U.S. metropolitan areas with the highest loss of employment in 2000. Furthermore, economic affairs in the government do not seem very encouraging. Because of the tax exemptions and other benefits granted to attract foreign investment, the government did not develop a tax-based economy. To support the construction and maintenance of the existing infrastructure and public services, the government went heavily into debt. This pattern of economic insolvency and the need to increment jobs in the public sector as a response to the constant decline in industrial jobs presents another problem generated by Operation Bootstrap. As of 1975, the public sector was the main employer in the island.

Evidence of the ineffectiveness of this program and a key indicator of the lack of economic resilience among Puerto Rico's population is the personal savings rate of island residents. Since 1940, the personal savings rate of island residents has reached zero only twice, while remaining most of the time in the negative digits. It is more striking to see how after 3 decades of the implementation of Operation Bootstrap, in 1985, the personal savings rate fell lower than ever. Although it seemed to be recovering in the 1990s, it started falling again and continues its negative pattern. One of the goals of Operation Bootstrap was to increase the amount of jobs and economic integration, but the persistent poverty, heavy reliance on federal nutrition assistance, unemployment, and the fact that the government employs the largest segment of the labor force testify to the problems of this development strategy.

Jennifer M. Santos-Hernández

See also East Harlem; Puerto Rican Americans; Puerto Rican Armed Forces of National Liberation (FALN); Puerto Rican Legal Defense and Education Fund; Puerto Rico

Further Readings

Bermán-Santana, D. 1996. *Kicking off the Bootstraps: Environment, Development, and Community Power in Puerto Rico.* Tucson: University of Arizona Press.

Colón-Reyes, L. 2005. *Pobreza en Puerto Rico: Radiografía del Proyecto Americano* [Poverty in Puerto Rico: Radiography of the American Project]. San Juan, Puerto Rico: Editorial Luna Nueva.

Dietz, James L. 2003. *Puerto Rico: Negotiating Development and Change.* Boulder, CO: Lynne Rienner.

Maldonado, Alex W. 1997. *Teodoro Moscoso and Puerto Rico's Operation Bootstrap.* Gainesville: University Press of Florida.

Santiago, Carlos E. 1992. *Labor in the Puerto Rican Economy: Postwar Development and Stagnation.* New York: Praeger.

Weisskoff, Richard. 1985. *Factories and Food Stamps: The Puerto Rico Model of Development.* Baltimore, MD: John Hopkins University Press.

OPERATION PUSH

With the passage of the Civil Rights Act of 1964 and the Voting Rights Act of 1965, civil rights leaders redirected their focus on securing economic parity for all minorities. Operation PUSH (People United to Save [later changed to "Serve"] Humanity) was established in Chicago, in 1971, by Reverend Jesse Jackson, Sr., after the dissolution of Operation Breadbasket, the economic arm of the Southern Christian Leadership Conference (SCLC).

In Chicago, Jackson worked as national director of Operation Breadbasket. In 1971, the SCLC Board of Directors suspended him for failing to incorporate the annual Black Business Expo in the name of the SCLC. Later that month, Jackson resigned and started Operation PUSH.

Jackson's new group focused on "economic colonialism" by White-owned businesses. Using his "kingdom theory," he described how Blacks could exert "the authority of kings" to control every aspect of the numerous economies that influence their lives. He argued that once control has been achieved, political involvement is essential if Blacks wish to protect these gains. As a result, he began negotiating "a Marshall Plan for African Americans" that would be financed by U.S. corporations and financial institutions.

The success of PUSH was due in large part to three factors. First, when Jackson resigned from the SCLC, all the organization's resources went with him; the most notable (and profitable) among them was Jackson himself. Because of his tremendous popularity, participants at the weekly meetings—along with their financial contributions—literally followed him to PUSH headquarters. Second, the "selective patronage" techniques employed by Jackson were effective, though sometimes considered economic intimidation. In an attempt to serve as a "corporate conscience" to large corporations that catered to African American consumers, Jackson would threaten to initiate a boycott if owners refused to adequately invest in the African American community. Finally, PUSH was successful because its goals were consistent with those of the government and corporations anxious to support affirmative action programs.

Corporate Covenants

The PUSH Covenant program used local ministers to deliver a "Diversity Questionnaire" to White-owned businesses that catered to the Black community; the purpose was to determine what percentage of their workforce and suppliers was Black. If the percentages were grossly inconsistent, the ministers would again meet with the owner (at a site in a more impoverished area of the Black community) and request that the company employ higher percentages of Blacks, especially in upper management, and transfer a portion of their banking to Black-owned banks. If the business owner refused, Jackson and other members of the clergy would call for a boycott; if the owner agreed and signed a "covenant," members of the organization would work to educate the owner and staff about the challenges of increased desegregation.

Over time, Jackson negotiated covenants with corporations such as Avon, Burger King, Coca-Cola, General Foods, Ford Motors, Kentucky Fried Chicken, Miller Brewing, Quaker Oats, and Revlon. While the covenants demonstrated PUSH's commitment to achieving economic parity for minorities, one major criticism was that once the covenant was signed, there was no system in place to ensure that the company would keep their promises—and often they did not.

Nike Boycott

In July 1990, Jackson (who had stepped down as the head of PUSH to focus on his two presidential bids, in 1984 and 1988) announced that PUSH would target the athletic shoe industry, renowned for generating high profits from its sales to African Americans. During the first meeting with Nike, PUSH Executive Director Reverend Tyrone Crider submitted a questionnaire to the head of Nike, hoping to call attention to the disparity in their hiring and supplier practices. Before the second meeting took place, Crider called for a national boycott of the shoemaker. Because the boycott did not obtain open support from political and religious leaders in the Portland, Oregon, area, where Nike's headquarters were located, or from several noted athletes, it was deemed a failure.

PUSH for Excellence

To help minority youth get the most out of their educational experiences, Jackson created the PUSH for Excellence (PUSH/Excel) Program in 1979. The goal of the program was to encourage greater student, parent, and community involvement in schools with high minority populations. The program, while ambitious, was harshly criticized because it was never theoretically articulated; the lack of a theoretical basis made it impossible to operationalize, duplicate, and quantitatively measure the effects of the program.

In 1988, possibly because Jackson ran for public office, the U.S. government audited the PUSH/Excel program and found that it failed to articulate its objectives. As a result, PUSH agreed to pay $550,000, or one-half of the $1.1 million that the Justice Department sought in civil claims. Again, Jackson's dogmatic leadership style and lack of follow-through were given as reasons for the program's failure. In addition, when the program was introduced to school districts across the country, it met with bureaucratic resistance because it was designed to decentralize the administration of schools.

Rainbow/PUSH Coalition

In 1996, Jackson merged Operation PUSH with the National Rainbow Coalition (NRC) to form the Rainbow/PUSH Coalition. The NRC was an organization that Jackson founded in 1984 to serve as the basis for his presidential bids.

Glynis Christine

See also Affirmative Action in the Workplace; Boycott; Civil Rights Movement; Discrimination; Jackson, Jesse, Sr.; National Rainbow Coalition; Southern Christian Leadership Conference (SCLC)

Further Readings

Frady, Marshall. 1996. *Jesse: The Life and Pilgrimage of Jesse Jackson*. New York: Random House.

House, Ernest R. 1988. *Jesse Jackson and the Politics of Charisma: The Rise and Fall of the PUSH/Excel Program.* Boulder, CO: Westview Press.

Jackson, Janice E. and W. T. Schantz. 1993. "Crisis Management Lessons: When PUSH Shoved Nike: Boycott of Nike by People United to Serve Humanity." *Business Horizons* 36(1):27–35.

Johnson, Ollie A., III, and Karin L. Stanford, ed. 2002. *Black Political Organizations in the Post–Civil Rights Era.* New Brunswick, NJ: Rutgers University Press.

Timmerman, Kenneth R. 2002. *Shakedown: Exposing the Real Jesse Jackson.* Washington, DC: Regnery.

Web Sites

Rainbow/PUSH Coalition: http://www.rainbowpush.org

ORIENTALISM

Orient, meaning "the East," is juxtaposed to *Occident,* "the West." Orientalism is a system of thoughts, beliefs, theories, and discourses propagated by Western scholars about the East, including Middle East as well as Asia. Orientalism describes the representation and the construction of the East in the imagination of the West. The East is the "other" to the West.

As a projection and a reflection of the West, Orientalism reflects the history of colonialism and imperialism. As the object of the Western imagination, the East is seen as "the uncivilized," "the savage," "the undeveloped," "the weak," and "the feminized," while the West is considered as "the superior," "the civilized," "the strong," and "the masculine." In this regard, Orientalism represents a simplistic labeling or stereotyping of people of the East. The simplicity can be seen in the traditional view of the Orient as a relatively unchanging people with few distinctions among them worthy of serious attention. Even today, the general public and some policymakers may be unaware of the complexity of Muslim and Arab peoples of the world.

Orientalism dates back to the 19th century, when Orientalists translated the writings of the Orient into English. These writings were deemed as necessary knowledge for the domination and the colonization of the East. It was thought that the knowledge about the Orient would assist the imperial and colonial project of the West. In this sense, the Orient was traditionally the passive object for study by Orientalists, while some scholars in the area attempted to offer a different voice.

The best-known scholar on this topic is Edward W. Said (1935–2003), whose seminal work, *Orientalism,* deconstructs the system of orientalism. Said earned a BA from Princeton University and an MA and PhD from Harvard University. He took a position at Columbia University in 1963 and served as a faculty in English and Comparative Literature for several decades. As a pro-Palestinian activist, Said campaigned for a creation of an independent Palestinian state. From 1977 to 1991, Said was an independent member of the Palestinian National Council. He supported a two-state solution. As a public intellectual, his work impacted the younger generations of scholars on colonialism, postcolonialism, cultural studies, and literary studies.

In *Orientalism,* Said argues that Western scholars, with Eurocentric prejudice, misrepresent the Middle East and Islam. Western thought sustained a history of false representation and romanticized the image of Arab-Islamic peoples and their culture. Until recently, this long history of romanticization and misrepresentation of the East justified the colonization and the domination of the East. The concept of Orientalism continues to be important in contemporary neocolonial and postcolonial context.

Shu-Ju Ada Cheng

See also Colonialism; Ethnocentrism; Islamophobia; Labeling; Stereotypes; "Us and Them"

Further Readings

Said, Edward. 1979. *Orientalism.* New York: Vintage Books.
Said, Edward. 1994. *Culture and Imperialism.* New York: Vintage.
Said, Edward, Moustafa Bayoumi, and Andrew Rubin, eds. 2001. *The Edward Said Reader.* London: Granta Books.

P

Pachucos/Pachucas

Pachucos were young Mexican American men and pachucas were young Mexican American women affiliated with *pachuquismo,* a youth subculture of the 1940s and 1950s. Many pachucos and pachucas were the children of immigrants from Mexico and hailed from the working class.

Identifying features of *pachuquismo* include the zoot suit and a vernacular known as pachuco slang or *caló*. The masculine version of the zoot suit often consisted of a long coat, billowing trousers that tapered at the ankle, a long watch chain that sometimes extended from the waist to the calves, and a pair of thick-soled shoes. Some pachucos combed their hair in a ducktail and punctuated their ensembles with a broad-brimmed hat. The feminine version of the zoot suit was usually composed of a skirt that fell to or above the knees and a sweater or long coat. Pachucas frequently wore dark lipstick and inserted foam "rats" into their hair to lift it into a high bouffant. Some also lightened their hair with peroxide. In addition, some pachucos and pachucas sported a tattoo between the thumb and index finger depicting a small cross with lines radiating above it. Both the masculine and feminine versions of the zoot look represented a distortion, if not a repudiation, of White and middle-class aesthetics.

The geographical origins of *pachuquismo* are not known precisely. Some claim that the subculture began in El Paso, Texas, and spread as Mexicans and Mexican Americans migrated from, or by way of, Texas to California and other parts of the U.S. Southwest during the first half of the 20th century. Likewise, the exact origin of the zoot suit is unclear, but the African American jazz vocalist Cab Calloway wore the ensemble at his performances during the 1930s. By the early 1940s, the masculine and feminine versions of the zoot suit were popular among young U.S. residents of various races and ethnicities and were associated with jazz and the jitterbug dance craze. Meanwhile, across the Atlantic, French youth known as *les zazous* adopted a look similar to that of U.S. zoot-suiters. After World War II, the look spread to youth in Britain.

During World War II, a period of social homogenization, enforced rationing, and increased class and physical mobility, the zoot suit emerged as a symbol of conspicuous consumption and working-class style in the United States. Its wearers, many of whom were young men and women of color, were accused of being unpatriotic for flaunting their newfound spending power and donning the flamboyant costume. In addition, the zoot suit became a hallmark of juvenile delinquency even though most of its wearers were not criminals or members of formal gangs. In particular, it came to be associated with Mexican American and African American juvenile delinquency.

The zoot suit was linked explicitly to Mexican American youth during the Sleepy Lagoon investigation and trial and the Zoot Suit Riots. Although Mexican American youth gangs were identified as a social problem as early as the 1920s, they began to receive national and international attention with these two events. The Sleepy Lagoon incident, which took place in August 1942, involved an alleged gang fight and murder at a swimming hole in Los Angeles. Twenty-one young Mexican American men and one young White man were tried and convicted en masse in what at the time was the largest criminal trial in California history. Meanwhile, several of their female companions were sentenced to the Ventura School for Girls, a reformatory. In the police investigation that led to the boys' trial, Captain Edward Duran Ayres of the Los Angeles County Sheriff's Department argued that Mexican Americans, by virtue of their Aztec blood, were intrinsically more violent than and, therefore, biologically inferior to White Americans. Ironically, as the United States combated biological racism overseas, the Ayres report blatantly espoused biological determinism. Furthermore, it equated Mexicans with "Orientals" and, by extension, the Japanese enemy. Like Japanese Americans, Mexican Americans transcended the putative Black–White binary of U.S. racial identity. As racial and cultural hybrids, they represented a threatening alien ambiguity during a period of heightened xenophobia, jingoism, and paranoia.

The Zoot Suit Riots occurred in Los Angeles in June 1943, nearly a year after the Sleepy Lagoon incident. During the riots, White servicemen hunted and attacked zoot-clad youth and young people of color, often regardless of their attire. When servicemen apprehended zoot-suiters, they sometimes stripped them of their clothing and cut their hair, thereby destroying what some U.S. residents regarded as un-American or even anti-American symbols.

Like the zoot suit, pachuco slang is a prominent and identifiable characteristic of *pachuquismo* and marker of racial and class difference. Some scholars maintain that it originated in medieval Spain among Gypsies. In both the Old World and New World, it has been linked to criminals and the underclass. Pachuco words and expressions are often associated with street smarts and *la vida loca* (the gang life, literally "the crazy life").

Frequently regarded as pachucos' and pachucas' heirs, cholos and cholas were late 20th-century Mexican American street youth or gang members. Well before the 20th century, the pejorative *cholo* referred to a poor Indian or mestizo, and during World War II mainstream newspapers in Los Angeles disparaged pachucas as *cholitas*. Although the style of clothing and hair of late 20th-century cholos and cholas differed from that of the pachucos and pachucas of the 1940s and 1950s, some remnants of the zoot look persisted. For example, some cholas teased their hair into high bouffants, lightened it with peroxide, and wore dark lipstick.

By and large, pachucos, pachucas, cholos, and cholas have been denigrated as hoodlums. Pachucas and cholas have also been vilified as both morally and sexually loose. However, during the Chicano movement of the 1960s, 1970s, and 1980s, various writers and artists transformed the pachuco and cholo into icons of Chicano pride and style. The pachuco, in particular, was upheld as a symbol of Chicano resistance, biculturality, and U.S. identity, as evidenced by the subtitle of Luis Valdez's celebrated 1978 play, *Zoot Suit: An American Play*. In the arts and social sciences, the pachuca and chola have received far less attention than have their male counterparts.

Catherine S. Ramírez

See also Deviance and Race; Drug Use; Gangs; Juvenile Justice; Mexican Americans; Zoot Suit Riots

Further Readings

Alvarez, Luis. 2005. "Zoot Violence on the Home Front: Race, Riots, and Youth Culture during World War II." Pp. 141–175 in *Mexican Americans and World War II*, edited by Maggie Rivas-Rodríguez. Austin: University of Texas Press.

Barajas, Frank. 2006. "The Defense Committees of Sleepy Lagoon: A Convergent Struggle against Fascism, 1942–1944." *Aztlán* 31(1):33–62.

Escobar, Edward J. 1999. *Race, Police, and the Making of a Political Identity: Mexican Americans and the Los Angeles Police Department, 1900–1945*. Berkeley: University of California Press.

Fregoso, Rosa Linda. 1999. "Re-imagining Chicana Urban Identities in the Public Sphere, Cool Chuca Style." Pp. 72–91 in *Between Women and Nation: Nationalisms, Transnationalisms, and the State*, edited by Caren Kaplan, Norma Alarcón, and Minoo Moallem. Durham; NC: Duke University Press.

Kelley, Robin D. G. 1992. "The Riddle of the Zoot: Malcolm Little and Black Cultural Politics during World War II." Pp. 155–182 in *Malcolm X: In Our Image*, edited by Joe Wood. New York: St. Martin's.

Mazón, Mauricio. 1984. *The Zoot Suit Riots: The Psychology of Symbolic Annihilation*. Austin: University of Texas Press.

Ramírez, Catherine S. 2002. "Crimes of Fashion: The Pachuca and Chicana Style Politics." *Meridians* 2(2):1–35.

Ramírez, Catherine S. 2007. "Saying 'Nothin': Pachucas and the Languages of Resistance." *Frontiers* 27(3).

Valdez, Luis. 1992. *Zoot Suit and Other Plays*. Houston, TX: Arte Público.

Pacific Islanders

The term *Pacific Islanders* includes individuals from a variety of origins. In the 2000 census, a number of racial categories could be checked: White, Black or African American, American Indian or Alaska Native, and several Asian groups, including Native Hawaiian, Guamanian or Chamorro, and Samoan. The Other Pacific Islanders category also could be checked. In addition, individuals were allowed to select one or more racial categories to indicate their racial identity. Thus, the Pacific Islanders category includes Native Hawaiians, Guamanians or Chamorro, Tongans, Marquesans, Maori, Tahitians, Fijians, and others from the smaller islands of the Pacific—altogether, a diverse grouping of languages and cultures. The largest of these groups, as shown in Table 1, are the Native Hawaiians and Samoans. This entry presents information and a brief review of these groups on both the mainland and Hawaiian Islands of the United States. It also briefly discusses the issues of out-marriage, language retention, and homelands.

For many census and governmental purposes, Pacific Islanders are often grouped with the larger Asian groups for analysis. However, they differ greatly from most Asians linguistically, culturally, and in area of origin. Asians as a whole do quite well in standard comparisons with the other residents of the United States—in educational levels, standard of living, occupational status, and poverty status. Pacific Islanders, however, are not doing as well on some of these indicators as are most Asian groups or Americans.

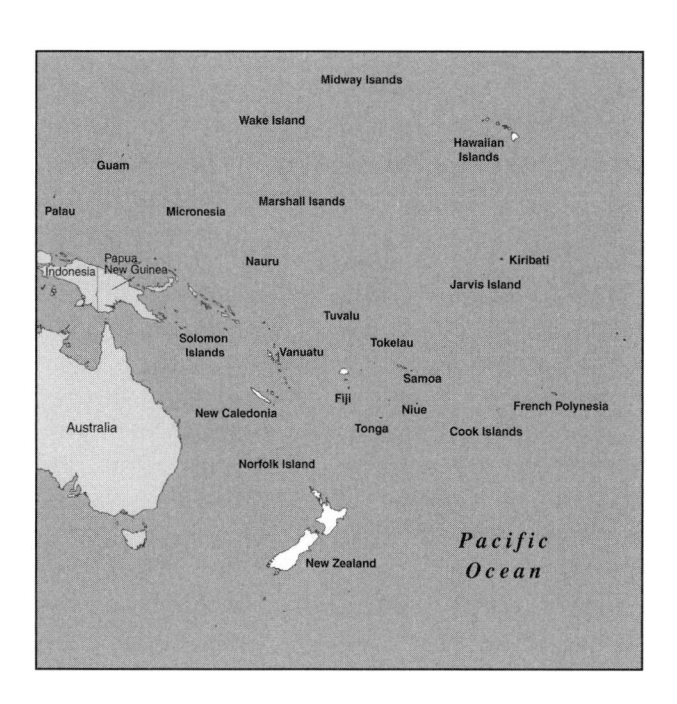

Origins of Pacific Islanders

Pacific Islanders trace their ancestry to numerous islands of the Pacific Ocean, an area collectively referred to as Oceania, which also includes Australia, New Zealand, and the islands of Indonesia and New Guinea. The islands east of New Guinea are referred to as Melanesia. Further east are two additional groupings: the Micronesian Islands (meaning small islands) and the Polynesian Islands (meaning many

Table 1 Native Hawaiian and Other Pacific Islander Household Population by Detailed Group: 2004

Detailed Group	Population	Percent of Pacific Islander-alone population
Native Hawaiian and Other Pacific Islander alone	403,832	100.0
Polynesian	256,406	63.5
Native Hawaiian	154,666	38.3
Samoan	60,520	15.0
Tongan	39,052	9.7
Other Polynesian	2,168	0.5
Micronesian	101,335	25.1
Guamanian or Chomorro	68,336	16.9
Other Micronesian	32,999	8.2
Melanesian	22,912	5.7
Fijian	22,840	5.7
Other Melanesian	72	—
Other Pacific Islander	23,179	5.7

Source: U.S. Census Bureau. 2004. *American Community Survey* (Detailed Tables, B02007). Washington, DC: U.S. Census Bureau.

Notes: Data are based on sample limited to the household population and exclude the population living in institutions, college dormitories, and other group quarters. For information on confidentiality protection, sampling error, nonsampling error, and definitions, see http://factfinder.census.gov/home/en/datanotes/exp_acs2004.html. In the table, a dash (–) indicates that the figure rounds to 0.0.

islands). Micronesia includes the Marianas, Guam, Wake Island, the Marshall Islands, and the Federated States of Micronesia. The Polynesian Islands are generally considered to be those east of New Zealand, stretching to the Hawaiian Islands; they include the Midway Atoll, Samoa, American Samoa, Tonga, Tuvalu, the Cook Islands, French Poloynesia, and Easter Island. Other islands, such as the Philippines, the islands of the South China Sea, and Indonesia, are usually identified with their nearest continent because these islands are not located in any of the three regions of Oceania.

Pacific Islanders in the United States

Most Pacific Islanders in the United States are from Polynesia, with the largest group being Native Hawaiians. The Hawaiian Islands were annexed by the United States, without consent of the native peoples and government, over the period from 1893 to 1898. Statehood was granted in 1959. The 2000 U.S. Census listed a total of 874,000 people who reported their "race" as Native Hawaiian or Pacific Islander. Pacific Islanders constitute 0.3% of the total population of the United States. The total number includes 398,835 who reported only Pacific Islander and 475,579 who reported Native Hawaiian or Other Pacific Islander as well as one or more other races. Those who reported mixed ancestry were most likely to have Asian (29%), White (24%), or both Asian and White (19%) ancestry.

Because of the changes in the way the U.S. Census Bureau classifies race, changes in size of the groups cannot be assessed directly. At a minimum, the census estimates the growth rate of Pacific Islanders to be at least 9% from 1990 to 2000. The growth rate likely is much higher, however, and may be as high as 140%.

Pacific Islanders in the United States are relatively young; their median age of 28 years is substantially lower than that of the total U.S. population (35 years). Among the Pacific Islanders, Samoans, Tongans, and Marshall Islanders are the youngest. Compared with the U.S. population as a whole, Pacific Islanders also have larger households (3.6 vs. 2.6 persons in 2000) and are more likely to be married (79% vs. 68%).

Although Pacific Islanders are as likely as other U.S. residents to have graduated from high school, they are less likely than others to have completed college (14% vs. 24%). Among Pacific Islanders, Native Hawaiians are most likely to have completed college, and Marshall Islanders are the least likely. Thus, Pacific Islanders are less likely than the total population to occupy management and professional jobs. Their median family income is approximately $4,100 lower than that of all families in the United States. During the 2002–2004 period, poverty rates for Pacific Islanders were 13.2% as compared with 8.6% for other Asians, 8.6% for non-Hispanic Whites, 21.9% for Hispanics, and 24.7% for Blacks. Although the wage scale of Pacific Islanders is lower than that of the general population, and although the poverty rates for Pacific Islanders are higher, most Pacific Islanders in the United States have a much higher standard of living than do those who live in their native lands. This accounts for the migration to the United States. Nevertheless, more than 80% of Pacific Islanders in the United States were born in the United States.

Most Pacific Islanders live in Hawai'i (282,667 in 2000) and California (221,458 in 2000). Smaller numbers live in Washington, Texas, New York, and Florida, although nearly three-quarters live in the western part of the United States. Hawai'i has the largest percentage of Pacific Islanders (23.0%, although the percentage there appears to be declining), followed by Utah (1.0%), Alaska (0.9%), Nevada (0.8%), and California and Washington (both 0.7%). The cities with the largest numbers of Pacific Islanders are Honolulu, New York, and Los Angeles. The cities with the highest proportions are Honolulu (15.6%); West Valley City, Utah, a lower-income suburb of Salt Lake City (3.5%); and Hayward, California (3.4%). As numerous groups have done before them, Pacific Islanders appear to practice chain migration, with new immigrants following friends and relatives who moved to the mainland earlier.

Two-thirds of Native Hawaiians live in Hawai'i, and the other third are split among mainland states. Nearly half of the mainland share of the Native Hawaiian population are in California. Native Hawaiians in Hawai'i fare poorly on most socioeconomic indicators; they have the state's worst health statistics, highest number of school dropouts, highest unemployment rate, and highest levels of incarceration.

Outmarriage, Language, and Homeland Issues

Three additional issues arise for Pacific Islanders: outmarriage, language retention, and homelands. Because the Pacific Islander category as a whole, as well as the specific groups within it, is relatively small, Pacific

Pacific Island census workers taking a break. *Special efforts were made to reach Pacific Islanders for the 2000 Census, and similar plans are underway for 2010. In 2000, an estimated 874,000 U.S. residents indicated that they are Native Hawaiian or Other Pacific Islander either alone or in combination with one or more other races. That was roughly one-third of 1% of the total U.S. population.*

Source: Photo by Norman Shapiro for the U.S. Census Bureau.

Islanders are more likely by chance to meet and marry out of their own group. This is of concern to some Pacific Islanders. Out-marriage has occurred in both Hawai'i and Guam as other groups have moved there. Furthermore, the contact in these two areas has longer historical roots than for many of the other groups. Racism also likely lowers the intermarriage rates. Nearly 65% of Native Hawaiians report mixed ancestry, as compared with 37% of Guamanians or Chamorroo, 32% of Samoans, 28% of Fijians, and 25% of Tongans. These figures likely reflect the amount of contact each group has had with other populations.

Language retention is a concern of many groups within the United States, especially small groups and those who are foreign born. The 2000 census reported that approximately 314,000 people in the United States speak a language from the Pacific Islands. Given that the total population (both mixed and lone Pacific Island ancestry) is more than 874,000, only roughly 36% speak their native language. Most native speakers live in Hawai'i (90,111) and California (113,432). Although Hawai'i has the highest percentage of native speakers and the second largest number of Pacific Islanders, fewer there speak their native language than in the nation as a whole. Instead, California has the highest percentage of Pacific Islanders who speak a home language (51%), followed by Utah (42%) and Washington (38%). After California and Hawai'i, Washington has the third largest number of speakers (more than 16,000). These differences likely reflect recency of migration, relative group size, and length of contact with the larger populations.

Native Hawaiians are also concerned about homelands within Hawai'i. Some tracts have been designated homelands as a result of the Hawaiian Homes Commission Act passed by the U.S. Congress in 1920. Less than 2% of the population of Hawai'i lives on the current homelands, but members of the Hawaiian community have pressed for more lands. Those living on these lands tend to have a higher percentage of Hawaiian ancestry than do other Hawaiians. Native Hawaiians represent 83% of those living on the homelands.

A Hawaiian sovereignty movement has emerged during recent decades, with efforts to teach the Hawaiian language and culture and to develop a government of Hawaiians for Hawaiians. Some feel that the islands were stolen from the Native Hawaiians by the United States. Some of the state's most powerful political leaders support versions of Hawaiian sovereignty. Advocates of sovereignty want Hawaiians to be recognized in the same way as American Indians are recognized on the mainland, that is, as a nation within a nation and with control of disputed lands.

Cardell K. Jacobson and Robyn J. Barrus

See Appendix A; Appendix B
See also Asian Americans; Hawaiians; Hawai'i, Race in; Peoplehood; Samoan Americans; Tongan Americans

Further Readings

U.S. Census Bureau. 2006. *American Community Survey 2005.* Available from http://www.census.gov/acs/www

Dougherty, Michael. 1992. *To Steal a Kingdom.* Waimanalo, Hawai'i: Island Style Press.

Harris, Philil M. and Nicholas A. Jones. 2005. *We the People: Pacific Islanders in the United States.* Available from http://www.census.gov/prod/2005pubs/censr-26.pdf

Tizon, Tomas Alex. 2005. "Rebuilding a Hawaiian Kingdom." *Los Angeles Times,* July 21.

PAKISTANI AMERICANS

Pakistani Americans are the immigrants and their descendants from Pakistan, a country of 169.3 million, as of 2007 estimates. Pakistani Americans represent the diverse groups of Pakistan, including the different linguistic, political, religious, and ethnic groups. The five major languages in Pakistan are Urdu, Punjabi, Singhi, Pashto (Pushtu), and Baluchi. The majority of Pakistani Americans are either Punjabi- or Urdu-speaking. Although a majority of Pakistani Americans are Muslims by religion, others identify themselves as Hindus, Christians, Parsis, Baha'is, or Sikhs. According to the 2000 Census, there were a total of 223,475 people resident in the United States who had been born in Pakistan, of whom 42.3 percent were U.S. citizens. This entry will look at the background of immigration from Pakistan to the United States and the contemporary picture of Pakistani Americans.

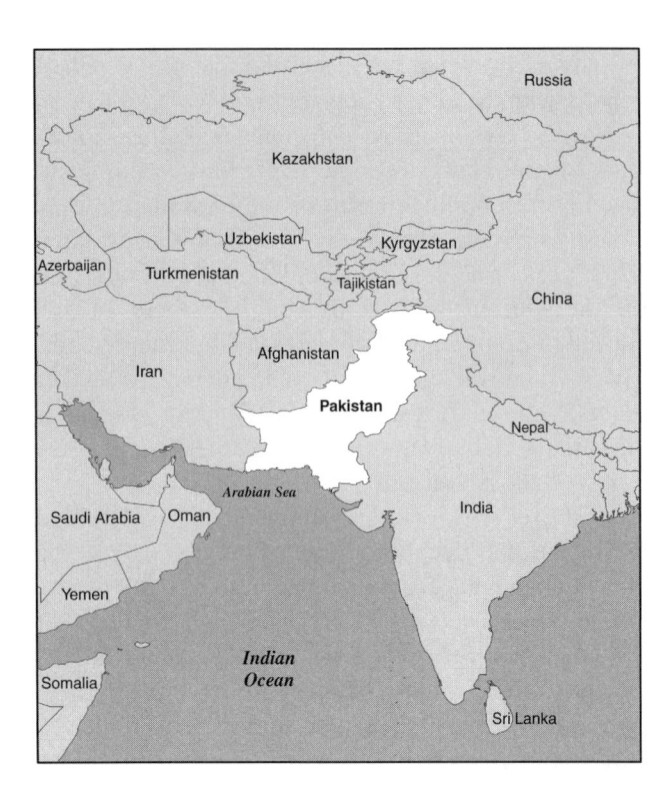

Immigration Patterns

Recordings of Pakistani immigration to the U.S. began in 1947 when Pakistan became an independent nation. Between the years of 1947 and 1965, about 2,500 Pakistanis immigrants arrived, according to data from the Immigration and Naturalization Service. The largest wave of immigrants arrived primarily after 1965, when the national immigration quota was lifted. The expired act allowed for a larger number of non-European immigrants; relatives of U.S. citizens; specialists with needed skills; and political, racial, and/or religious refugees. Many of the Pakistani immigrants were students and educated professionals, such as engineers, bankers, scientists, and pharmacists. Additionally, these immigrants came from urban areas; they tended to settle in areas similar to the cities they came from and thus found similar job opportunities.

The number of Pakistani immigrants swelled after 1970. This was due in part to the first wave of immigrants, who were now naturalized citizens and could serve as sponsors for the second immigration wave. The following decades continued to bring educated professionals; however, a significant number were less educated, middle-class immigrants.

Contemporary Community

Figures from the U.S. Census Bureau's American Community Survey indicate that there were 296,982 of Pakistan national origin in the United States in 2005. In terms of geographic distribution, the states with the highest number of Pakistani immigrants were: New York, Texas, California, Illinois, and Virginia. New York City has the largest Pakistani community. Other communities can be found in Chicago, Houston, and Washington, D.C.

In recent years, people from Pakistan have sought permanent residency and refugee status and completed the naturalization process to become citizens. From 1997 through 2006, about 1,400 Pakistanis immigrated to the United States annually. The number of refugees that arrived during these years was quite low, at 67. About 8,000 Pakistani Americans have become naturalized citizens annually, beginning in 1997.

While still being culturally distinct, Pakistani immigrants have assimilated to American culture quite easily. This is mainly due to the fact that they have few language barriers (due to the legacy of British colonization, most Pakistani Americans are fluent in English), are usually well educated, and come from a similar multi-ethnic society.

A significant segment of Pakistani Americans have achieved success in many fields, including medicine, engineering, finance, and information technology. However, another segment within the Pakistani American community is self-employed business people generating minimal profits in what has been termed the *hourglass economy*—that is, people engaged in work at either the higher end or lower end of the social class system. Therefore, according to the 2000 Census, the Pakistani American median family income was $45,590, as compared to $50,890 for the nation as a whole.

Like other immigrant groups, Pakistani Americans often organize their social lives around national holidays and religious festivals. Ties with the home country are acknowledged by Pakistan Day (March 23), Independence Day (August 14), and the Birthday of the Founder of the Nation (December 25). For example, August 14, 2007, marked the 60th anniversary of Pakistan's creation, and it was celebrated with fervor and enthusiasm while residents also recalled the struggle and sacrifices that led up to nationhood. Such ceremonies are characterized by recitation of verses from the Holy Quran and playing the national anthem. Religious festivals are those typical of the followers of Islam.

For Pakistani Americans, especially in the post–September 11, 2001, world, being Muslim may serve as just as important an identifier as being of Pakistani ancestry. What, if anything, is different for Pakistani Americans and other Muslims about Islam in the United States as opposed to in an Islamic country? The Muslim population in the United States numbers in the millions and reflects the diversity of the worldwide Islamic faith; it practices its rituals and beliefs, however, in a nation where the expression of Christianity dominates culturally.

Some scholars of Islam argue that the experience of democracy and the history of religious diversity and free expression in the United States have facilitated a stronger and even more correct Islamic practice—uninhibited by the more totalitarian regimes many find in their homelands. Certainly there is disagreement over what is correct, but there is little pressure outside the Muslim community in the United States about how to precisely follow the teachings of the Prophet Muhammad.

Other scholars contend that what makes the Pakistani American Muslim experience unique is that followers must place an even stronger focus on Islam in order to survive in a culture that is permissive and, indeed, encourages much behavior that is prohibited by either Islamic law or their cultural traditions. For many Pakistani American Muslims in the United States, pop culture resembles paganism, a cult that celebrates money and sex. In the United States, many Muslims experience both the freedom to be Muslim and the pressure to be Muslim.

Among famous Pakistani Americans are Mazhar Ali Khan Malik, professor of economics/engineering and founder of the Pakistan League of America (PLA); Dr. Muhammad Akhtar, commissioner of Public Health; Bapsi Sidhwa, novelist/playwright; and Saghir "Saggy" Tahir, politician.

Jennifer M. Klein

See Appendix A
See also Arab Americans; Asian Americans; Assimilation; Deficit Model of Ethnicity, Hourglass Economy; Immigrant Communities, Immigration, U.S.; Islamophobia; Muslim Americans; Rites of Passage; Symbolic Ethnicity

Further Readings

Associated Press of Pakistan. 2007. Pakistani Americans celebrate Independence Day, Ambassador unfurls flag at ceremony. August 14. Retrieved December 10, 2007, from http://www.app.com.pk/en/index.php?option=com_content&task=view&id=14811&Itemid=2

Belt, Don. 2002. "The World of Islam." *National Geographic*:76–85.

Department of Homeland Security. 2007. *Yearbook of Immigration Statistics*: 2006. Washington, DC: Office of Immigration Statistics. Available from http://www.dhs.gov/ximgtn/statistics/publications/yearbook.shtm

Kumar, Avitava. 2005. *Husband of a Fanatic: A Personal Journey through India, Pakistan, Love and Hate.* New York: The New Press.

Malik, Salahuddin. 1993. "Pakistanis in Rochester, New York: Establishing Islamic Identity in the American Melting Pot." *Islamic Studies* 63:461–475.

U.S. Census Bureau. 2004. *Profile of Demographic and Social Characteristics: 2000. People Born in Pakistan.* Available from http://www.census.gov/population/www/socdemo/foreign/STP-159-2000tl.html

U.S. Census Bureau. 2006. *American Community Survey 2005.* Available from http://www.census.gov/acs/www

Weaver, Mary Anne. 2002. *Pakistan: In the Shadow of Jihad and Afghanistan.* New York: Farrar, Straus and Giroux.

PALESTINIAN AMERICANS

Palestinian Americans, a division of Arab Americans who themselves or whose families originate from historic Palestine, constitute the largest Palestinian community outside the Arab world. While sharing many characteristics with other minority and immigrant groups as well as with other Arab communities in the

United States, the Palestinian American experience remains unique owing to political, historical, cultural, and social reasons. It is distinct in terms of the causes, dates, places, and conditions of Palestinians' immigration to the United States.

Although (as with other immigrants) both push and pull factors have affected Palestinian immigration, the political conditions in Palestine and the subsequent wars in the Middle East region since World War I have played a significant role. Thus, experts tend to divide Palestinian immigration to the United States into three waves, usually discerned as a matter of socioeconomic status of the immigrants and place of immigration but separated mainly by the major political events that befell the Middle East and Palestine: from the middle of the 19th century up to the 1948 Arab–Israeli war, from 1948 until the 1967 Arab–Israeli War, and from 1967 onward. Other political events, such as the 1975–1990 Lebanese civil war, the 1982 Israeli invasion of Lebanon, the 1987–1993 Palestinian Uprising, the 1991 Gulf War, and the 2000 Palestinian Uprising, all contributed to Palestinian immigration and influenced the composition and the variety of immigrants. The Palestinian Territory as defined in 2007 was estimated to have a population of 4 million people, although most Palestinian people live outside this area in Israel and neighboring Arab states. This entry examines their history of immigration, the current U.S. community, and their adaptation to life in the new land.

Waves of Immigration

Palestinian immigration to the United States began as early as the second half of the 19th century but intensified after World War I. Early immigrants (the pre-1948 war wave) were mainly poor and rural Palestinians, the majority of whom were Christians due to their contact with Christian missionaries and missionary educational institutions such as Bir Zeit College (now Bir Zeit University) and Society of Friends schools. Nonetheless, immigration from Palestine remained less than that from other neighboring Arab countries until World War I due to the relatively better economic conditions in Palestine.

Because immigrants from the Middle East were listed in the U.S. immigration records as "Asian" prior to 1899, and because Arabs generally were listed as "Turks in Asia" (between 1869 and 1898) and later Palestinians were listed as Syrians (between 1899 and 1932), it is difficult to know exactly how many Palestinians immigrated to the United States during the first wave (prior to 1948). It is, however, possible to estimate the number and to consider the reasons for immigration during the period leading up to the 1948 war.

Between 1920 and 1930, Palestinian immigrants to the United States constituted nearly one-third of all Arab immigration (2,933 of 8,553 Arabs), which included few Arab countries at that time. Following the famous three-year Great Arab Revolt in Palestine (1936–1939), as well as political disturbances in Palestine leading up to the 1948 war, the number increased to 7,047 during the 1940s, while Arab immigration diminished significantly owing to the Asian Exclusion Act of 1924 and the Johnson–Reed Immigration Act.

Unlike the case with other Arab immigrants, economic conditions could not have been the root cause and push factor underlying Palestinian immigration. Historians and political economists document a record high level of economic growth in Palestine during the early 1940s. At that time, Palestine was by far outdistancing neighboring Arab countries in nearly every economic indicator. The political events already mentioned played a significant role in Palestinian immigration. Unskilled workers found peddling—*Qasheesh* (carrier of wooden or leather cases or *qashsha*)—as a possible job, thereby attaining a sort of middleman ethnicity. This was also true of many poor and rural Palestinian inhabitants who immigrated to the United States during the interwar period (1948–1967) and thereafter.

Following the 1948 war (the wave of 1948–1967) and the expulsion of nearly 800,000 Palestinians by Israel, a second—and more significant—wave of Palestinian immigration to the United States took place. Although the period from 1948 to 1967 remains the only period documented by the U.S. Immigration and Naturalization Service following a separate category for "Palestine," U.S. immigration statistics show that only 4,385 Palestinian immigrants entered the country between 1948 and 1966. However, tens of thousands of Palestinian refugees entered the United States from the country of their first refuge (Jordan, Syria, or Lebanon). The second wave comprised predominantly Palestinian Muslims and included many professional, educated, and middle-class members in addition to poor and unskilled individuals. The McCarran-Walter Act of 1952, which relaxed the quota system established in 1924, enabled greater

Muslim immigration that continued after the 1965 revisions of the immigration law.

The third—and most significant—wave that began in the aftermath of the 1967 war and continues today has been fostered by subsequent political events that befell the Middle East (the 1967 Arab–Israeli war, the 1973 War, the 1975–1990 Lebanese civil war, the 1982 Israeli invasion of Lebanon, the 1987–1993 Palestinian Uprising, the 1991 Gulf War, and the 2000 Palestinian Uprising). Throughout this wave, the Immigration and Naturalization Service stopped recognizing the Palestine category, and most Palestinians entering from historic Palestine were listed under *Jordan* while other Palestinians were listed under the country of their earlier residence or their first or second refuge country (e.g., Israel, Lebanon, Syria, Kuwait, Iraq, Latin American countries). This wave included not only the Palestinian refugees of these wars but also many Palestinian students who came to U.S. universities and settled in the United States. This category included many professionals and educated people (e.g., lawyers, university professors, medical doctors, engineers), skilled workers, and investors. During this time, half of all Arab science and engineering PhD holders left the Arab world (the so-called Arab brain drain). Many of them were Palestinians, and a considerable number of them immigrated to the United States.

The Current Community

Estimating the number of Palestinian Americans has been a matter of speculation by experts due to the absence of accurate data sources. In addition to the fact that the Immigration and Naturalization Service does not recognize Palestinian nationality, Palestinians immigrate to the United States not only from historic Palestine but also from other countries to which they or their parents have been displaced. Usually, Palestinians emigrating from the West Bank have been listed as Jordanians; other immigrants arriving from the rest of historic Palestine have been listed under Israel, and the rest have been listed under other countries (usually their first country of refuge) from which they might have immigrated to the United States.

Beginning with the 1980 census, the first to provide the opportunity to list immigrants' ancestry, 21,288 individuals listed "Palestinian" as their ancestry; the *Statistical Abstract of Palestine* estimated the number of Palestinian Americans at 108,045 in 1983. In the 2000 U.S. Census, 72,112 people in twenty-seven states listed Palestinian as their ancestry; of these, 36,278 were born in the United States. However, given the number of Palestinians entering the country between 1948 and 2003 (133,929 from both Palestine and Jordan), and given the locations and numbers of Palestinian refugees in other parts of the world, experts' estimates range between 250,000 and 300,000 scattered throughout the country but concentrated, in twenty-seven states, mainly California (San Francisco and Los Angeles), Michigan (Detroit), New York (*New* York City, Brooklyn), New Jersey, Illinois (Chicago), Ohio (Cleveland and Youngstown), Florida (Jacksonville), Georgia (Atlanta), and Texas (Houston, Dallas, and Fort Worth).

Economic Status

Economic data provided by the 2000 U.S Census and estimates by specialists indicate that the Palestinian American median household income was $4,468 higher than that of the total population, the median family income was approximately $500 higher than that of the national average (the difference between the two seems to be due to the larger family size among Palestinians), and the per capita income was approximately $100 higher than the national average.

However, the Palestinian community and communities in the United States are sharply bifurcated and fragmented. In 2000, the reported proportion of Palestinian Americans living below the poverty line—approximately 16% or 11,339 individuals—was higher than the national rate of 12%, and some Palestinian communities reported slightly to significantly lower median household income, median family income, and per capita income than the average in eleven states (Illinois, New Jersey, New York, Ohio, North Carolina, Pennsylvania, Wisconsin, Alabama, Colorado, Massachusetts, and Missouri). In another twenty-seven states covered by the 2000 census, Palestinian communities were either close to the state's average, slightly higher, or significantly higher in all three economic indicators.

Within the Palestinian American communities themselves, economic well-being ranges between quite poor to fairly good, with the most recent immigrants being closer to quite poor. Certain studies presenting the Palestinian experience as a success story seem to focus only on a segment of the Palestinians, especially those who immigrated during the second wave or came from historic Palestine and managed to establish successful businesses or self-employment, whereas other studies presenting the negative side of the Palestinian experience seem to focus on a segment of the most recent immigrants.

Age and Education

Demographically, the Palestinian American community is relatively young, with a median age of 28 years, as compared with 35 years for the total U.S. population, coupled with a significantly low percentage of approximately 6% of members over 65 years of age. In addition, although both males and females immigrate to the United States, the Palestinian community has a higher percentage of males than females (56% vs. 44%), apparently due to cultural aspects that favor male immigration over female immigration. Moreover, in 2000, the average size of the Palestinian American family, four individuals, was higher than the U.S. average family size of three individuals.

Many Palestinians managed to establish self-employment or businesses that usually employ family members. Moreover, the Palestinian American community is relatively well educated. The percentage of Palestinian Americans with a bachelor's degree or higher (23%) is above the national average (16%), although the percentage of those identifying as a high school graduate or higher is slightly lower than the national average, apparently due to the relatively larger percentage of those under 5 years of age in the Palestinian communities.

Many Palestinian Americans, especially those who came during the first two waves, continue to maintain traditional values and ways of life similar to those dominant in Palestine prior to their immigration despite the significant changes that have taken place in Palestine itself since 1948. Aspects of the Palestinian social structures are visible in the Palestinian American community; there are divisions based on clan, village, region, social class, and even education. Thus, the Palestinian community in the United States tends to be fragmented in spite of the many characteristics such as language, religion, and cultural values that its members share, and they tend to be grouped in one form following the village, town, or region from which they originate (e.g., American Ramallah Federation, Nablus Club).

Politics

A more recent aspect of fragmentation within the Palestinian American community has been political and mirrors the political schisms that befell the Palestine Liberation Organization and Palestine since the 1982 Israeli invasion of Lebanon. Thus, social structural factors brought from Palestine and other Palestinian communities outside the United States continue to play a role in the organization of the Palestinian American community and affect the choice of the area of residency, type of work, and even social interaction. Concentrations of Palestinians originating from particular areas in Palestine have settled in certain states or cities in the United States; for example, Paterson, New Jersey, has a high concentration of residents from Beit Anan, a village in the Jerusalem/Ramallah district, and Chicago has a high concentration of residents from Beit Hanina, Sha'afat, and the Jerusalem district as well as from certain villages in the Ramallah district.

Alongside community organizations, Palestinian Americans have established several religious (mosques and churches), political, and civil rights organizations (e.g., Palestine Congress of North America) and are active and founding members of many Arab American organizations such as the National Association of Arab Americans (NAAA) and the Association of Arab American University Graduates (AAUG), which has had among its members and former presidents a number of nationally and globally prominent Palestinian American scholars such as Edward Said, who contributed greatly to the rise of postcolonial theory, and Hisham Sharabi, a noted Palestinian American sociologist. The AAUG publishes a reputable scholarly journal, *Arab Studies Quarterly*, that has become an important reference source about the Arab world and the Middle East.

Identity, Adaptation, and Assimilation

The adjustment of any immigrant group depends on more than the willingness of its members to integrate into the new society. It also depends on how the host country identifies them, how it treats them, and what it expects from them. This particular issue is at the heart of the Palestinian American uniqueness. Both the underlying political factors driving Palestinian immigration, including the nonneutral

U.S. involvement in the Palestine question, as well as the racial/ethnic conditions of the United States, including the ostensibly negative image that Arabs and Palestinians seem to have in the U.S. popular imagination, distinguish the Palestinian American experience and affect the community's attempts to adjust.

Although many Palestinians thought of their immigration to the United States as merely temporary intended for work, or until the resolution of the question of Palestine, the majority of them remained in the country and started a new life. Thus, the question of integration and assimilation of Palestinian Americans became an issue for both Palestinians and non-Palestinians.

Scholarship on Palestinian Americans shows that their adaptation to U.S. society ranges from total assimilation to total alienation, with the latter not being the norm but more likely to be the case with women than with men. Both assimilation and alienation are products of complex cultural, racial, and political conditions facing Palestinian Americans. In addition, the dual identity (Palestinian and American) seems to persist, especially among the most recent and first-generation immigrants. Dual identity does not mean resistance to assimilation or a rejection of the larger society. The best Palestinian nationalists are not by any means the least Americans, nor do the most assimilated lack any sense of being Palestinians, as one expert noted. Thus, many Palestinian Americans have a strong sense of Palestinian nationalism due to the ongoing regional conflict, but it does not seem to affect their sense of Americanism.

Many Palestinian Americans, especially the second generation, while maintaining some sense of Palestinianism (perhaps due more to domestic U.S. factors and racial conditions rather than attachment to the ancestral homeland), can hardly be distinguished from other U.S. groups. They eat the most typical U.S. food, join Rotary Clubs, vote on all sides of the political spectrum, serve in the military, and root for their local baseball teams. Palestinian Americans, a small and growing community, contribute to the cultural richness of the nation as do other minority and immigrant communities in the United States. They are active participants in all aspects of U.S. life, from military service to distinguished academic scholarship.

Seif Da'Na

See Appendix A
See also Arab Americans; Islamophobia; Israeli Americans; Muslim Americans; Turkey; Zionism

Further Readings

Barghouti, Iyad. 1997. "Palestinian Americans: Sociopolitical Attitudes of Palestinian Americans towards the Arab–Israeli Conflict." Occasional Paper No. 38, Center for Middle Eastern and Islamic Studies, University of Durham.

Christison, Kathleen. 1989. "The American Experience: Palestinians in the U.S." *Journal of Palestine Studies* 18(4):18–36.

Cohen, Yinon and Andrea Tyree. 1994. "Palestinian and Jewish Israeli-Born Immigrants in the United States." *International Migration Review* 28:243–255.

Mansur, Riyad. 1980. "The Palestinian Community in the United States: Motives for Immigration and Demographic Conditions." *Palestine Affairs* 99:84–106.

Orfalea, Gregory. 2006. *The Arab Americans.* Northampton, MA: Olive Branch Press.

Suleiman, Michael, ed. 1999. *Arabs in America: Building a New Future.* Philadelphia, PA: Temple University Press.

Panamanian Americans

Panamanian Americans are the immigrants and their descendants from Panama, a country with an estimated population of 3.3 million people as of 2007. Panama is ethnically diverse but can be divided into three general categories of people. More than two-thirds are mestizo, that is, a mix of American Indian and Spanish. Other categories include the Guaymi, Cuna, and Choco Indians and the Afro-Panamanians. According to the 2000 census, there were a total of 105,175 people born in Panama residing in the United States; of these, 58.2% were citizens. This entry looks at the background of immigration from Panama to the United States and at the contemporary picture of Panamanian Americans.

Immigration Patterns

Central and South American persons have migrated to the United States since the early 19th century. However, due to Panamanians being categorized with other Central and South American immigrants, early statistics of specifically Panamanian immigration are not available. Data indicate that after the Immigration Quota Act was lifted in 1965, the number of South American immigrants grew rapidly, and by 1970 Panamanians were one of the largest Central

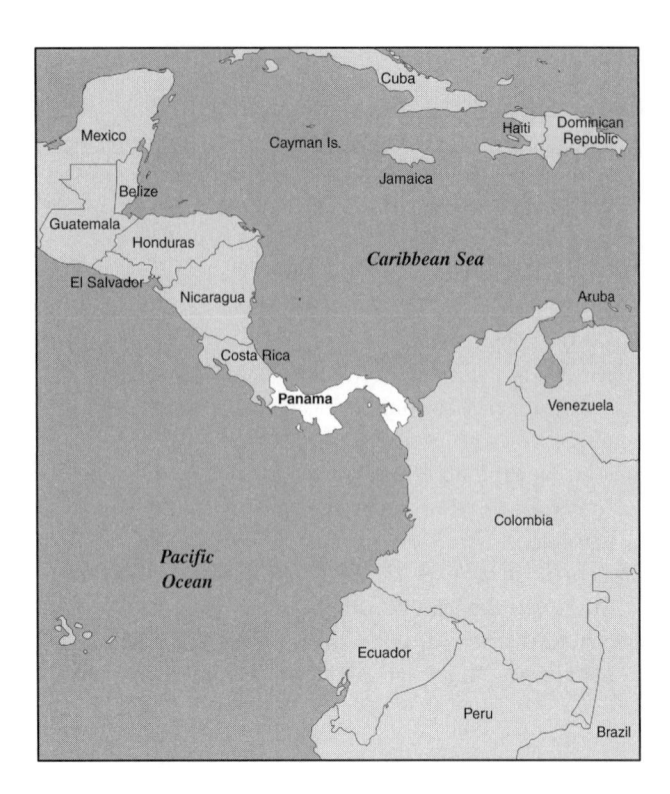

American groups in the United States. During the decades that followed, the number of Panamanian immigrants continued to increase due to family reunification programs.

Historically, the building of the Panama Canal led to a special and unique relationship between the United States and Panama. From 1903 to 1979, the territory was controlled by the United States; for the next 20 years, the operations switched to joint U.S.–Panamanian control. Since 1999, the canal has been in Panamanian hands, but the previous U.S.-managed enclave with its significant military presence was the cause of sporadic—and sometimes significant—tensions between the United States and Panama.

Contemporary Community

During recent years, people from Panama have sought permanent residency status and have completed the naturalization process to become citizens. From 1997 through 2006, approximately 1,700 Panamanians immigrated to the United States annually. At least 19,000 Panamanian Americans have become naturalized citizens since 1997. According to the U.S. Census Bureau's *American Community Survey 2005,* there were 129,128 people of Panamanian national origin in the United States. In terms of geographic distribution, the top five states were New York, California, Florida, Texas, and Georgia. Panamanian Americans' primary language is Spanish, although approximately 80% are bilingual, speaking English fluently as well. Their median family income was $44,302 as compared with $50,890 for the nation as a whole.

Jennifer M. Klein

See Appendix A

See also Assimilation; Central Americans in the United States; Immigrant Communities; Immigration, U.S.; Latin America, Indigenous People

Further Readings

Anderson, Jon Lee. 1999. "233,000 Acres, Ocean Views" [Letter from Panama]. *The New Yorker,* November 29, 50–61.

Barry, Tom, John Lindsay-Poland, Marco Gandasegui, and Peter Simonson. 1995. *Inside Panama.* Albuquerque, NM: Resource Center Press.

Conniff, Michael L. 1991. *Panama and the United States: The Forced Alliance.* Athens: University of Georgia Press.

Department of Homeland Security. 2007. *Yearbook of Immigration Statistics*: 2006. Washington, DC: Office of Immigration Statistics. Available from http://www.dhs.gov/ximgtn/statistics/publications/yearbook.shtm

U.S. Census Bureau. 2004. *Profile of Demographic and Social Characteristics: 2000. People Born in Panama.* Available from http://www.census.gov/population/www/socdemo/foreign/STP-159-2000tl.html

U.S. Census Bureau. 2006. *American Community Survey 2005.* Available from http://www.census.gov/acs/www

Pan-Asian Identity

Pan-Asian identity denotes a specific consciousness whereby individuals of Asian background identify primarily as Asian Americans owing to a shared experience of racism in the United States. The formation of pan-Asian identity is complicated by the socially constructed nature of the Asian American category that came into existence with the Immigration and Nationality Act of 1924. Once consigned to this category, migrants from various Asian nations were indefinitely prohibited from immigrating to the United States. The Immigration Reform and Control Act of 1965, which removed key barriers on immigration from Asia to the United States, also had the ironic effect of further solidifying the category. Thus, the Asian American category includes various groups of Asian origin whose relationships with each other are in fact not organic. Although the contributions of the Asian American movement of the 1960s to the development of a pan-Asian identity cannot be overlooked, the extent to which this consciousness is shared by all who are classified as Asian American is open to question. This entry highlights the main arguments on both sides of the pan-Asian issue and provides a map to navigate the debate.

Pan-Asianism: Challenges to Its Formation

An impediment to the formation of a pan-Asian American identity is created by the divergent cultural and political identities of those groups labeled as Asian American. The cultural and political identities of Filipino Americans, for example, are influenced by their history of U.S. colonization, as are their patterns of immigration to the United States. In contrast, the Japanese American experience has been shaped by Japan's position as an imperial power in East Asia, a position that led to different types of restrictions on immigration from Japan to the United States during the early 20th century as well as to Japanese Americans' detainment in internment camps during World War II. South Asian Americans, on the other hand, feel excluded from Asian America because their relationship with the United States has been qualitatively different from that of East Asians and Southeast Asians. The case of the Vietnamese refugee movement further illustrates the disparate experiences and interests that inform the lives of individuals defined as Asian American.

Consequently, the development of a pan-Asian American identity is difficult because each Asian group is likely to differ according to the type of racism it has experienced in the United States. During World War II, Japanese Americans, unlike other Asian American groups, were sent to internment camps because they were seen as a national security threat. Similarly, South Asian Americans are alone in their experience of hate crimes and racial profiling as terrorists following the events of September 11, 2001. The "Dotbusters" incident is another illustration; in this case, Indian Americans were subject to a series of hate crimes perpetrated against them in Jersey City, New Jersey.

In addition, hardships faced by Asian groups entering the United States as refugees are likely to be distinctive as well. Such experiences and the respective position of each Asian group vis-à-vis the U.S. nation-state produce different interests and, in turn, limit the possibility of a pan-Asian racial identity. In fact, some Asian groups have distanced themselves from those Asian groups who are subject to racism so as to avoid a similar fate: During the early 20th century, Japanese American leaders condoned the exclusion laws that prohibited Chinese immigration to the United States. Later, during World War II, Chinese Americans desired a distance from Japanese Americans so as to avert internment.

Increasing diversification since the 1970s in the socioeconomic backgrounds of immigrants from the various Asian nations is yet another obstacle to pan-Asianism. This diversity inevitably fractures the lived experiences of Asian Americans along class lines. Besides issues of economic survival, how each group chooses to express its struggle against racism can also vary with its socioeconomic position. When Indian Americans were the victims of the so-called Dotbusters during the mid-1980s, the middle-class organizations, unlike the working-class organizations, invoked the "model minority" stereotype of Asian Americans to assert their demands for justice—a strategy unavailable to working-class immigrants of the same group owing to their lower socioeconomic status. Research has also demonstrated that middle-class Asian Americans, given their economic success, are largely able to ignore racism. In general, such intra-Asian American differences only serve to divide Asian American interests and impede the formation of a pan-Asian consciousness.

Other factors have created fissures among Asian Americans, including gender divisions; intraregional differences in language, custom, and culture within a specific Asian nationality group; religious differences; and language diversity.

Pan-Asianism: The Possibilities

Some scholars remain optimistic about the possibility of pan-Asian American racial identity formation despite their recognition of issues that tend to fragment the community. One such possibility, as Yen Le Espiritu argued, lies in the development of a critical transnational framework that identifies the commonalities among various Asian American groups and facilitates pan-Asianism. According to Espiritu, this critical transnational framework must examine the history of U.S. involvement in various Asian countries that creates the conditions for emigration. Thus, the evolution of pan-Asianism is possible by way of the analysis of a shared history of imperialism among Asian Americans.

Furthermore, the development of pan-Asianism may be encouraged through the experiences shared by different Asian American groups in the United States. Because they are commonly racialized, all Asian American groups are subject to being perceived as "foreigners" who harm "American" interests. This inherently racist logic was present when Japanese Americans were sent to internment camps and again with the recent racial profiling of South Asian Americans as terrorists in the post-9/11 United States. Such patterns of bias direct Asian Americans' attention to shared experiences of racism as "foreigners" that has helped to establish the foundations of pan-Asianism.

In fact, pan-Asian goals have been expressed by the second and subsequent generations of Asian Americans born in the United States. It is this cohort who spearheaded the Asian American movement of the 1960s that, in turn, planted the seeds of pan-Asianism. As Asian Americans whose identities are influenced by the U.S. context, they seek to mobilize a broader Asian American identity so as to combat racism.

Moreover, Asian American advocacy-based organizations that operate as interest groups are an important space where pan-Asianism actually exists. Two examples of such organizations are the New York Taxi Workers Alliance, which advocates for all taxi drivers' rights (not just those for Asian Americans) in the New York metropolitan area, and the Asian American Legal Defense and Education Fund, which resists racist legal practices that limit opportunities for Asian Americans. Empirical evidence also shows that new immigrants from Asia have partnered with those born in the United States to form business organizations designed to collectively challenge the economic barriers faced by Asian Americans. Although relationships among the various Asian American groups might not be spontaneous because the category is a socially constructed one, organizations have formed and movements have developed to oppose the subordination of Asian Americans as a group.

Those scholars who are optimistic about pan-Asianism have argued that pan-Asianism is not necessarily where all Asian Americans present a united front toward all experiences of racial subordination. Rather, the optimists are in agreement with the skeptics, who question that kind of unity on the grounds that the experience of racism is not identical for all Asian American groups. The optimists maintain, however, that pan-Asian identity and subsequent mobilization around that identity can be issue specific. For example, whereas one group of Asian Americans may mobilize around worker rights, another may mobilize around refugee movements from Asia. Other Asian American groups may mobilize around racism experienced in the criminal justice system, and still other pan-Asian groups may form along generational lines. Researchers have in fact documented such types of pan-Asianism over time. Hence, the optimists envision a pan-Asianism that is plural.

Thus, although a pan-Asian American identity that is all-encompassing is perhaps unattainable because groups converge on certain issues and diverge on others, a more realistic possibility is the formation of pan-Asian American identities that are multiple and varied. Such patterns of pan-Asianism are evident in the extant literature on the topic.

Diditi Mitra

See also Asian Americans; Asian American Studies, Mixed-Heritage; Cambodian Americans; Chin, Vincent; Filipino Americans; Hate Crimes; Immigration Reform and Control Act of 1986; Indian Americans; Internment Camps; Japanese Americans; Model Minority; Panethnic Identity

Further Readings

Dhingra, Pawan. 2003. "The Second Generation in Big D: Korean American and Indian American Organizations in Dallas, Texas." *Sociological Spectrum* 23:247–279.

Espiritu, Yen Le. 1992. *Asian American Panethnicity: Bridging Institutions and Identities.* Philadelphia, PA: Temple University Press.

Espiritu, Yen Le. 1996. "Crossroads and Possibilities: Asian Americans on the Eve of the Twenty-First Century." *Amerasia Journal* 22(2):vii–xii.

Espiritu, Yen Le. 2004. "Asian American Panethnicity: Contemporary National and Transnational Possibilities." Pp. 217–234 in *Not Just Black and White: Historical and Contemporary Perspectives on Immigration, Race, and Ethnicity in the United States,* edited by Nancy Foner and George M. Fredrickson. New York: Russell Sage.

Espiritu, Yen Le. 2005. "Asian American Panethnicity: Contemporary National and Transnational Possibilities." Presented at the meeting of the American Sociological Association, Philadelphia, PA.

Kar, S. B., K. Campbell, A. Jimenez, and S. R. Gupta. 1996. "Invisible Americans: An Exploration of Indo-American Quality of Life." *Amerasia Journal* 21(3):25–52.

Kibria, Nazli. 1996. "Not Asian, Black, or White? Reflections on South Asian American Racial Identity." *Amerasia Journal* 22:77–86.

Kibria, Nazli. 1998. "The Contested Meanings of 'Asian American': Racial Dilemma in the Contemporary U.S." *Ethnic and Racial Studies* 21:939–958.

Misir, Deborah. 1996. "The Murder of Navroze Mody: Race, Violence, and the Search for Order." *Amerasia Journal* 22:55–76.

PANETHNIC IDENTITY

The development of panethnic identities is an increasingly important phenomenon in the multicultural and multiethnic context of the United States because it represents a new form of integration into U.S. society that immigration scholars did not predict. In addition, when ethnic group members are able to shift their ethnic identities upward to construct a new broader identity around which to organize collectively and create new institutions and organizations, this can translate into political power and social change. This entry deals with the factors that generate panethnic identities, the different types of panethnic identities, and the future of panethnicity.

Development of Panethnic Identities

Since the passage of the liberalized Immigration Reform and Control Act of 1965 and a consequent increase in immigration from Asia—as well as from Latin America and Africa—immigrants to the United States are experiencing new forms of adaptation. Immigration scholars once believed that the newcomers would assimilate into mainstream society over generations, much like European immigrants did at the turn of the 20th century, becoming fully integrated into the dominant society such that no distinct ethnic groups remained. However, new immigrants and the second generation have not yet assimilated into mainstream society; ethnic or national origin identities remain salient, and patterns of behavior and identification suggest that new panethnic identities have emerged. These broad identities, which transcend ethnic or national origin boundaries, have developed in response to the larger society's racialized view of immigrants and ethnic minorities and are often expressed as part of a larger social movement for change. For example, tribes in different regions of the United States formed a pan-Indian social movement and adopted a pantribal identity to organize for collective goods. Scholars have also documented how diverse groups such as Mexicans, Puerto Ricans, Dominicans, and Cubans have acted on a shared Latino identity to strengthen their communities. In addition, research has found that Chinese, Japanese, Korean, Filipino, Vietnamese, and South Asian Americans developed panethnic institutions and identities to form a cohesive Asian American community.

Ethnic groups tend to be distinct in terms of national origin, language, culture, religion, and collective history, so it has been a puzzle for scholars to understand how and why panethnic identities form. Even though panethnic identities are based on a shared culture and experience, scholars suggest that structural commonalities such as race are more likely to provide a basis for panethnic organizing and the development of panethnic identities. Most scholars agree that racialization, or the process through which ethnic groups are viewed and treated as racial categories, has led to the emergence of panethnic identities. Stephen Cornell pointed out that when societies are organized on the basis of race—when classification schemes, political and economic systems, and the public culture adopt racial boundaries as real—this provides the logic for the construction of panethnic identities. The process of racialization reinforces the belief that racial categories are significant. In a society where race is an important organizing principle, group members may respond to the constraints of racial boundaries by reasserting and reconstructing their identities to be based on a shared history and culture. This shared history is often characterized by common experiences of racial discrimination, stereotyping, and profiling, and the shared culture is composed of common experiences in terms of language use, values, norms, and family expectations. Panethnic identities are formed through the interaction between ascription by others in the larger society and assertions about a shared history made by the groups themselves. Such an understanding of panethnic identities recognizes the agency of ethnic groups and how racial categories are transformed and imbued with new meanings.

As already suggested, racialization can take many forms to influence group formation and identity. Scholars have documented how public policies and government programs use racial categories to distribute scarce resources, and this has led national origin groups to adopt panethnic identities. In particular, studies have demonstrated how the creation of civil rights laws, equal employment opportunities, and affirmative action increased the symbolic and material value of panethnic identities and facilitated organizing along a panethnic boundary. Even though many ethnic groups who belong to the same racial category have very different histories of immigration and patterns of adaptation that shape their group interests, they still have been able to come together to make claims for the larger collective. Organizing on such a basis not only allows for ethnic groups to benefit from race-based policies but also provides a visible platform for panethnic groups to publicize their concerns. Scholars report that the success of organizing on a panethnic basis often contributes to a panethnic political and personal consciousness among individual participants.

External threats, such as racial violence and discrimination, are another manifestation of racialization that can lead individuals to organize across cultural, linguistic, religious, and ethnic backgrounds. Scholars have found that if diverse ethnic groups experience racial threats, this can lead to the development of panethnic identities and organizing. Yen Le Espiritu explained how anti-Asian violence during the 1980s galvanized the Asian American community. Vincent Chin, a Chinese American man, was mistaken for a Japanese national and blamed for the auto industry layoffs in Detroit by two unemployed auto workers, who beat him to death with a baseball bat. Given that these perpetrators lumped all Asians together, making no distinctions based on ethnicity or nativity, this led the Asian American community to band together because all ethnic groups were under threat. In addition, given that the U.S. court system failed—the perpetrators received probation and a monetary fine for their crime—the Asian American community had a common enemy to fight against, engaged in public demonstrations to protest the verdict, and formed organizations to monitor and report anti-Asian violence.

It is clear that the structural commonality of race contributes to the development of panethnic identities. Scholars have suggested that other structural commonalities such as class, generation, and geography are important in facilitating the emergence of panethnicity. One study found that when Asians shared a geographic space segregated from other racial groups, this led to higher rates of collective action along panethnic lines. Conversely, the spatial separation of Asian ethnic groups from one another contributed to lower rates of panethnic collective activity, suggesting that shared race and geography are necessary for the emergence of panethnicity. Another study showed that preferences for affiliating with other ethnic group members within the same racial category differed by social class; middle-class ethnics were often tied into panethnic networks on college campuses and held preferences for dating and marrying ethnic others, whereas working-class ethnics did not have access to such networks and actually preferred to create intimate relationships across racial boundaries. These studies indicate that structural commonalities are important in understanding the conditions under which panethnic identities develop.

Political and Sociocultural Dimensions

Studies on panethnic identities focus primarily on organizing around a panethnic identity as an effective strategy in a political context where numbers and resources are essential in securing collective goods. In these instances, panethnic identities are formed and acted on because of common interests and political or material benefits. The formation of organizations, voting patterns, and instances of protests and demonstrations are examples of ethnic groups coming together and participating in panethnic behavior in the name of political and collective gain. Given the political basis of these identities, they are often viewed as short term, strategic, and even instrumental. As noted by many scholars, panethnicity as a political strategy can be fleeting once the external threat has been neutralized or once the resources have been secured. Group members no longer "need" one another, and panethnic associations, networks, and behavior may dissipate over time.

Scholars also focus on panethnic identity as personal—an identity that organizes daily life and is used when making important personal choices. Studies of individual panethnic identities are often based on interviews with the sons and daughters of immigrants from Asia and Latin America. These data reveal that panethnic identities represent a shared culture, worldview, and life experiences across ethnic or national origin boundaries. For these respondents, commonality with ethnic others in the same racial category is expressed in sociocultural terms rather than political terms. For some, the boundaries of the panethnic community include only second- and later-generation others given that there is a clear divide between native- and foreign-born individuals in terms of shared culture. This divide is heightened by the fact that panethnic identities are made in the United States. Using data from the Children of Immigrants Longitudinal Study, scholars found that the second generation adopted panethnic identities with greater frequency over time and that those who were native born were more likely to choose panethnic identities rather than ethnic identities. These findings strongly suggest that panethnic identities develop among those who spend more time in the United States and who, in turn, are more likely to have experiences with race and racism.

Research also shows that ethnic group members not only choose panethnic identities to signify who they are but also adopt identities to indicate who they are not. For example, scholars have found that ethnic group members identify in panethnic terms as Latino or Latina to actively reject the labels of Black and White. The respondents chose to identity as Latino or Latino because they viewed their experiences as separate from either racial category. Blacks are also considered to be a panethnic group; similar to Latinos, new immigrants from Africa and the Caribbean often choose their identities to indicate who they are not. Instead of adopting a panethnic Black identity, new immigrants often choose ethnic identities to distance themselves from Black Americans owing to the negative attitudes and stereotyping associated with native-born Blacks. Other ethnic group members also reject panethnic identities in favor of ethnic or national origin identities such as Mexican, Cuban, Pakistani, Vietnamese, and Korean. Studies suggest that some individuals view panethnic labels as artificial and unable to capture the complexity of those who fall under such labels. These individuals also tend to see panethnic labels as reifying racial categories and the system of race in the United States. Panethnic identities may also be problematic in the sense that not all ethnic groups are included in the larger panethnic community, nor do they have equal influence regarding the shared goals and interests that define the larger collective. Differences based on national origin, citizenship status, generation, and social class complicate the construction of an all-encompassing group where all group members have equal weight.

Scholars have suggested that to understand the uneven formation of panethnic identities, we must take a transnational approach that emphasizes global structures of inequality. Such structures are critical for understanding immigration and refugee flows because they produce different historical and material conditions that, in turn, affect whether and how different ethnic groups are incorporated, accepted, ignored, and resisted as part of a larger panethnic community. For example, U.S. military intervention in Vietnam during the mid-1970s led directly to the out-migration of more than 500,000 refugees who generally had low levels of education and lacked skills that could translate well into the U.S. economy. Even though panethnic identities are made in the U.S. context, U.S. engagement in foreign countries influences migration flows, indirectly affecting the process of group formation and the uneven adoption of panethnic identities among different ethnic groups.

The Future of Panethnic Identities

As institutions continue to adopt race as a central organizing principle, panethnic identities will likely continue to flourish. For the Latino community, the media are an important site for promoting panethnic identities. Newspapers, radio shows, television programs, and products directed at Latinos as a group are creating a new market, and this will likely result in the maintenance of a Latino or Latina identity. Other institutions, such as churches, schools, and foundations, have adopted and promoted panethnic labels that will influence how ethnic groups organize and come to see themselves. However, continuing waves of immigration from Asia, Latin America, Africa, and the Caribbean will challenge the viability of panethnic identities. With increasing diversity among immigrants, it will be of interest to find out how and whether panethnic identities will remain salient and whether organizing around such identities will continue to be an effective strategy for collective claims.

For many scholars, the option of panethnic identification is viewed as a widening of choices. Instead of simply identifying along village, regional, or ethnic lines, panethnic identities represent another basis on which groups can identify and organize. However, a number of scholars have argued that panethnic identities do not provide additional meaningful ethnic options for groups such as Latinos and Asians. In other words, Asians and Latinos do not have the same kind of ethnic options, nor do they have the same assimilation process as European immigrants, who eventually became part of the dominant group. Even though Italian and Polish immigrants who came to the United States between 1850 and 1920 were racialized by the larger society, their positioning changed during the post-1965 era; they not only became European Americans but also became White—part of the dominant group. Scholars suggest that the boundaries of the dominant group weakened to allow European Americans at a time when there were increasing numbers of immigrants from Asia, Africa, and Latin America. The expansion of dominant group boundaries was in response to these new populations; group boundaries were erected against the newer groups to ensure their differences. The question remains as to whether, how, and when the racial boundaries signifying Asians, Latinos, African Americans, Native Americans, and Whites will decline.

Dina G. Okamoto

See also Asian Americans; Assimilation; Caribbean; Civil Rights Movement; Discrimination; Hispanics; Immigration, U.S.; Pan-Asian Identity; Pan-Indianism; People of Color; Racialization; Segregation

Further Readings

Cornell, Stephen and Douglas Hartmann. 1998. *Ethnicity and Race: Making Identities in a Changing World.* Thousand Oaks, CA: Pine Forge.

Espiritu, Yen Le. 1992. *Asian American Panethnicity: Bridging Institutions and Identities.* Philadelphia, PA: Temple University Press.

Foner, Nancy and George M. Frederickson, eds. 2004. *Not Just Black and White: Historical and Contemporary Perspectives on Immigration, Race, and Ethnicity in the United States.* New York: Russell Sage.

Kibria, Nazli. 2002. *Becoming Asian American: Second-Generation Chinese and Korean American Identities.* Baltimore, MD: Johns Hopkins University Press.

Lao-Montes, Agustin and Arlene Davila, eds. 2001. *Mambo Montage: The Latinization of New York.* New York: Columbia University Press.

Nagel, Joane. 1996. *American Indian Ethnic Renewal: Red Power and the Resurgence of Identity and Culture.* Cambridge, UK: Oxford University Press.

Okamoto, Dina G. 2003. "Toward a Theory of Panethnicity: Explaining Collective Action among Asian Americans." *American Sociological Review* 68:811–842.

Padilla, Felix M. 1985. *Latino Ethnic Consciousness: The Case of Mexican Americans and Puerto Ricans in Chicago.* Notre Dame, IN: University of Notre Dame Press.

Rodriguez, Clara. 2000. *Changing Race: Latinos, the Census, and the History of Ethnicity in the United States.* New York: New York University Press.

Waters, Mary. 1999. *Black Identities: West Indian Immigrant Dreams and American Realities.* Cambridge, MA: Harvard University Press.

Pan-Indianism

Pan-Indianism and supratribalism, a social movement that began during the mid-20th century and found widespread acceptance among Native Americans during the decades that followed, emphasizes the commonalities among the many indigenous North American peoples rather than the cultural and ethnic distinctiveness of each tribe. In so doing, the movement has created an ideological and political tool for understanding "Indian" identity, one in contrast to an earlier notion of identity based on specific tribal cultures and customs (e.g., Choctaw, Atakapa, Creek, Sioux). It has also served a useful purpose in connecting displaced urban Indians of many tribes into a social, political, cultural, and economic entity, creating a basis for the revitalization and restoration of indigenous people's experiences in both urban and rural reservation settings. According to its critics, however, supratribal identity tends to reduce Indian ethnicity to a static, often stereotypic, and essentialist construction.

Racism and Response

Historically, White racism has excluded Americans of color, including Indigenous Peoples, from full participation in the U.S. economy, polity, and society. Although the legal framework supporting this centuries-old system has largely been dismantled, racial prejudices and ideologies still undergird and rationalize widespread racial discrimination. American Indians' response to such societal racism has been doubly challenged—not only by Indians' physical isolation on rural reservations but also by U.S. policies that, over time, have resulted in virtually the removal and erasure of indigenous people from the U.S. imagination.

During the early centuries of European colonization, Native Americans had their lands taken from them, sometimes by chicanery and sometimes by force. Subsequently, most Native Americans were not incorporated into the dominant culture but instead were driven westward, beyond the boundaries of White interest, and eventually were restricted to segregated enclaves known as "Indian reservations." Moreover, a great many Native Americans died, directly or indirectly, as a result of government actions and policies that many scholars have described as genocidal. Furthermore, the process by which people in the United States are categorized according to race has not allowed for an accurate count of Native Americans; according to Jack Forbes, thousands of Indians have been "lost" within other ethnic communities because of their misdesignation as Black, White, Latino, or some other race that excludes Indian in the definition or possible ethnic classification of the group.

From the 1960s to the 1990s, American Indian activism increased to an all-time high, especially between 1965 and 1980. Federal government policies during the 1940s and 1950s had led to the relocation of hundreds of thousands of Indians from rural reservations to urban areas, where they later organized important acts of resistance such as the occupation of Alcatraz Island in San Francisco from November 1969 to 1971; the occupation and takeover of the Bureau of Indian Affairs (BIA) building in Washington, D.C., in 1972; and the 1973 siege at Wounded Knee in South Dakota.

The American Indian Movement (AIM), in particular, was highly successful in restoring public attention to the plight of Indians living on reservations and in urban areas with little economic, educational, or social support for the many disenfranchised individuals and communities. Moreover, AIM sought to reassert specific aspects of Indian identity that were common to most tribes. The occupation of Alcatraz Island and the protest activism that spread across the country in its wake stirred more than Indian ethnic pride. The multithread, urban membership of many Red Power organizations, including AIM, the National Indian Youth Council (NIYC), and Indians of All Tribes, and the Indian nationalist agenda of the movement, which emphasized the rights of all tribes and all Indians, combined to legitimize and empower supratribal Indianness as an identity, a source of pride, and a basis for activism.

An issue of concern with the rise of supratribal identity, however, is that it may lead to deeper misunderstandings, both within the U.S. mainstream and among Native Americans themselves, about the diversity of Indian identities, especially with regard to cultural versus racial identity. Thus, the ethnic distinctiveness of, for example, the Apache, Navajo, and Seminole becomes conflated to simply "Indian." Although the construction of urban, diasporic, pan-Indian ethnic enclaves did much to restore the American Indian presence for both Indians and non-Indians around the world, the reemergence also fostered the notion that there was "one Indian community" rather than many communities and tribes with different looks, traditions, degrees of ancestry, and spiritual beliefs. For example, an "Indian tradition" of sweat lodges was in fact not common historically to every tribe in the nation. Under supratribal consciousness, however, this articulation of "Indian identity and tradition" gets normalized for all American Indians, thereby excluding those Natives who do not participate in this cultural ritual. In this way, the formation of "new Indians" and "new Indian identities" can lead to other stereotypes about indigenous people in North America.

Moreover, AIM itself, through the media, tended to focus on the stereotypical physical traits of American Indians, especially those from the Plains area—another example of how pan-Indian constructions placed limits on who could fit into the American Indian community (at least on a social level). Thus, important and useful as it has been as a catalyst for changes in government policies and funding for Indians, this form of political organization has also created a pan-Indian paradigm that, critics say, reduces Indian ethnicity to a static, often stereotypic, and essentialist construction. It has also been pointed out that, especially in the case of Native people of mixed descent, the all-encompassing *Indian* label does not always fit, hence the importance of retaining an emphasis on tribal or community/regionally specific cultural practices and affiliations. The coming decades will witness the ongoing evolution of the relationship between an emergent supratribal identity and the tribal identities that preceded it within both the American Indian community and the society at large.

Increased funding of the new Indian programs during the 1960s and 1970s, like the funding of assimilationist policies during an earlier era, inadvertently contributed to an American Indian ethnic resurgence in three ways. First, increased funding directly provided a material incentive for Indian self-identification as the number of programs, benefits, and opportunities available to Native Americans expanded. Second, the expansion of new, non-BIA sources of funding undermined the BIA's near total control over Indian tribes and its unchallenged neglect of urban Indian programs, creating alternative non-BIA resource bases on reservations and new urban Indian programs. Third, as Joane Nagel noted, increased funding promoted organizational formation and growth in cities and on reservations. These new economic benefits, however, were not necessarily directly beneficial to all mixed-race Indian populations because of historic misrepresentation and legal classification of American Indian people.

Andrew Jolivette

See also National Congress of American Indians; National Indian Youth Council; Native Americans; Panethnic Identity; Red Power; Reservation System; Trail of Broken Treaties; Water Rights; Wounded Knee (1890 and 1973)

Further Readings

Cornell, Stephen. 1988. *The Return of the Native: American Indian Political Resurgence.* New York: Oxford University Press.

Deloria, Vine. 1988. *Custer Died for Your Sins: An Indian Manifesto.* Norman: University of Oklahoma Press.

Forbes, Jack D. 1993. *Africans and Native Americans: The Language of Race and the Evolution of Red–Black Peoples.* 2nd ed. Urbana: University of Illinois Press.

Johnson, Troy, Joane Nagel, and Duane Champagne. 1997. *American Indian Activism: Alcatraz to the Longest Walk.* Urbana: University of Illinois Press.

Johnson, Troy. 1994. *Alcatraz: Indian Land Forever.* Berkeley: University of California Press.

Jolivette, Andrew. 2006. *Cultural Representation in Native America.* Lanham, MD: AltaMira.

Josephy, Alvin, Troy Johnson, and Joane Nagel. 1999. *Red Power: The American Indians' Fight for Freedom.* Norman, OK: Bison Books.

Nagel, Joane. 1996. *American Indian Ethnic Renewal: Red Power and the Resurgence of Identity and Culture.* New York: Oxford University Press.

Snipp, Matthew. 1989. *American Indians: First of This Land.* New York: Russell Sage.

Parenting

Parenting behaviors involve hundreds of activities that caregivers engage in either with or for their children. Although conditional on age of the children and outcome, parenting behaviors influence children's well-being, including their cognitive, social, emotional, and physical development. This entry addresses how researchers typically define and measure parenting, the universality of these behaviors, and how these behaviors affect children's well-being.

Dimensions of Parenting

Although parenting has been conceptualized in many ways and there is not always an agreement on how to define various dimensions, some consensus does exist on the general contours of parenting. Many researchers agree that parenting consists of three main roles: nurturer, teacher, and manager. How these roles are defined and operationalized, however, depends on many factors. Traditionally, parenting behaviors have been assessed by measures that are representative of middle-class families in the United States. Consequently, some parenting behaviors are probably not measured or, if so, are not measured well.

Much of the research that investigates parenting relies on schemes such as those developed by E. E. Maccoby and others that often distinguish between authoritative parenting (warm firm control) and authoritarian parenting (negative harsh control). Authoritative parenting is typically considered to be optimal. Psychologists such as Cynthia Garcia-Coll are beginning to examine how traditional theories of parenting and socialization "fit" when applied to research on immigrant families and families of color. It has been posited that the effect of parenting on child outcomes may differ across groups because parenting strategies are influenced by ethnic socioeconomic background and community characteristics. For example, Laurence Steinberg and Amanda S. Morris found that European American parents are more likely to engage in authoritative parenting emphasizing the growth of separation and autonomy, whereas Latino, Asian American, and African Americans are more likely to engage in authoritarian parenting with a greater emphasis on obedience and conformity.

Universal and Culturally Situated Behaviors

Researchers tend to agree that the domains of parenting are universal, meaning that many aspects of parenting are exhibited by parents in many societies. All parents have ways of nurturing, teaching, and managing children. Variation exists, however, in how these behaviors are expressed, what behaviors are emphasized, and what the actual functions of certain behaviors are. Differences in parenting may be a factor of what is valued in a given culture. For example, according to Sara Harkness and Charles M. Super, parents in eastern Africa focus on developing their toddlers' motor skills; not surprisingly, their children's motor skills are more advanced than those of U.S. children.

Cross-cultural differences in parenting behaviors may also influence the actual meaning of certain behaviors by culture. For example, recent research examining parenting behaviors among immigrant groups in the United States has suggested that parenting typologies need to be expanded because the general authoritative and authoritarian parenting types do not transfer neatly in cross-cultural research. To illustrate, Nancy E. Hill and colleagues examined the relationship between harsh parenting and negative child outcomes in Mexican American and European American mothers and their children and found that, among Spanish-speaking parents, hostile control co-occurred with acceptance—a result that is generally inconsistent with the traditional European American model of parenting.

Similarly, Ruth K. Chao argued that the traditional view of Chinese parents as authoritarian, restrictive, and controlling is misleading because these parenting behaviors are not relevant for describing the socialization styles of Chinese parents. Instead, the type of parenting style used by Chinese American mothers is better understood as *chiao shun,* a training orientation performed by parents who are deeply concerned with and involved in the lives of their children.

Recent research using African American mothers also found that the traditional parenting style might not account for the fact that parental control may have different meaning for different ethnic groups. Jeanne Brooks-Gunn and colleagues identified a "tough love" group of mothers who were high in both warm firm control and negative harsh control. The tough love group was composed of mostly older African American mothers with at least a high school education. Children of mothers in the tough love group had higher IQ and vocabulary scores than did children in the classic authoritarian group or in a "detached" group.

Cultural similarities and differences are also found in parent attachment research. Mary D. S. Ainsworth and colleagues studied the impact of early infant–mother attachments (secure or insecure) on children's development. She found that all children across cultures have a basic need for attachment and that the level of attachment (secure, insecure, or detached) is associated with a type of maternal care (e.g., affectionate). However, culture-related differences can be found in terms of how mothers express affection.

In terms of parenting and gender roles, Beatrice Blyth Whiting and Carolyn P. Edwards investigated "masculine" and "feminine" behavior in young children across six different cultures. They found that although there are some universal sex differences in the behaviors of these children (e.g., aggressiveness in boys), how children are socialized affects how children behave.

Racial/Ethnic Variations

Parenting behaviors also differ within groups. A prime example of this difference is language use. Language use is the parenting behavior most associated with children's academic success and cognitive development. Betty Hart and Todd R. Risley, after examining transcriptions of naturally occurring mother–child conversations, suggested that children's exposure to language and conversation varies significantly across social class groups. As these differences accumulate over the first years of life, children in families from high socioeconomic backgrounds engage in literally thousands more conversations than do children from lower socioeconomic backgrounds. The higher socioeconomic status children have larger vocabularies than do the children from middle and lower socioeconomic status families. This is evident as soon as the children start to talk, and this difference accelerates over time.

In addition to quantity of language, the quality of language is also a factor. Catherine E. Snow and other researchers found that the educated middle to upper middle classes use language differently. These parents tend to provide more language, more varied language, more language topics, more questions, and more conversation. They also vary in how they read to their children. These parents tend to engage in more nonimmediate talk (going beyond information in the story) and provide more contextual information to the reading experience. All of these behaviors are linked with toddlers' and preschoolers' vocabulary as well as to their speed of language acquisition.

Another example of how parenting behaviors can differ within a group was illustrated in Susan A. Brunelli and colleagues' study of adolescent mothers in New York City. These African American, Dominican, and Puerto Rican adolescent mothers were compared on measures of child-rearing attitudes. Although all of the women were urban minority mothers, the Hispanic mothers reported more negative child-rearing attitudes than did the African American mothers. Moreover, within the group of Hispanic mothers, those from the Dominican Republic were more likely than those from Puerto Rico to endorse attitudes reflecting strictness and irritation.

The degree of acculturation also highlights within-group differences. For example, a study looking at the differential influence of collectivist and individualist orientations among Asian American, Mexican American, and European American adolescents found a greater endorsement of familial obligation among youth in more collective cultures. Thus, Andrew J. Fuligni and others found that Asian American and Mexican American adolescents were more likely than their European American peers to believe that they should assist parents and siblings throughout the life span and should be willing to make sacrifices for the family. In addition, Susan E. Keefe and Amado M. Padilla found that this collectivist orientation is still evident in acculturated third-generation Mexican Americans, who do not have a direct parental link to Mexico and might not speak Spanish.

Influence on Child Well-Being

Literally thousands of studies show an association between parenting behavior and child well-being. Because many of these studies tend not to take selection into account, researchers typically look to animal and adoption studies to try to decipher the actual impact of parenting. The temperament of rhesus monkey mothers (high reactive or calm) affects their parenting behavior, which in turn influences how reactive macaque monkey offspring are (even when using a cross-fostering design where "reactive" mothers raise babies from a "calm" mothers and vice versa).

In addition, adoption studies show a link between parenting and behavior. These studies tend to look at children who were born "at risk" (where biological parents have a history of criminality, schizophrenia, alcoholism, and/or cocaine or other drug use) and who were adopted early in life. Results have found that when children are placed in adoptive homes with parents who are middle class, they are less likely to manifest certain antisocial behaviors even though they may have a genetic predisposition for certain behaviors.

Lisa B. Markman, R. Gabriela Barajas, and Jeanne Brooks-Gunn

See also Assimilation; Child Development; Domestic Violence; Family; Immigration, U.S.; Testing

Further Readings

Ainsworth, Mary D. S., Mary C. Blehar, Everett Waters, and Sally Wall. 1978. *Patterns of Attachment: A Psychological Study of the Strange Situation.* Hillsdale, NJ: Lawrence Erlbaum.

Bornstein, Marc H. 2002. *Handbook in Parenting.* Vols. 1–5. Mahwah, NJ: Lawrence Erlbaum.

Bornstein, Marc H. and Linda R. Cote. 2006. *Acculturation and Parent–Child Relationships.* Mahwah, NJ: Lawrence Erlbaum.

Brooks-Gunn, Jeanne and Lisa B. Markman. 2005. "The Contribution of Parenting to Ethnic and Racial Gaps in School Readiness." *Future of Children* 15(1):139–168.

Brunelli, Susan A., Gail A. Wasserman, Virginia A. Rauh, Luz E. Alvarado, and L. R. Caraballo. 1995. "Mothers' Reports of Paternal Support: Associations with Maternal Child-Rearing Attitudes." *Merrill–Palmer Quarterly* 41:152–171.

Chao, Ruth K. 2001. "Extending Research on the Consequences of Parenting Style for Chinese Americans and European Americans." *Child Development* 72:1832–1843.

Collins, W. Andrew, Eleanor E. Maccoby, Laurence Steinberg, E. Mavis Hetherington, and Marc H. Bornstein. 2000. "Contemporary Research on Parenting: The Case for Nature and Nurture." *American Psychologist* 55:218–232.

Fuligni, Andrew J. 1997. "The Academic Achievement of Adolescents from Immigrant Families: The Roles of Family Background, Attitudes, and Behavior." *Child Development* 68:351–363.

Harkness, Sara and Charles M. Super. 1987. "Fertility Change, Child Survival, and Child Development: Observations on a Rural Kenyan Community." Pp. 59–70 in *Child Treatment and Child Survival: Culture, Society, and the Value of Children,* edited by N. Scheper-Hughes. Boston, MA: D. Reidel.

Hart, Betty and Todd R. Risley. 1995. *Meaningful Differences in the Everyday Experience of Young American Children.* Baltimore, MD: Brookes.

Hill, Nancy E., Kevin R. Bush, and Mark W. Roosa. 2003. "Parenting and Family Socialization Strategies and Children's Mental Health: Low-Income Mexican-American and Euro-American Mothers and Children." *Child Development* 74:189–204.

Keefe, Susan E. and Amado M. Padilla. 1987. *Chicano Ethnicity.* Albuquerque: University of New Mexico Press.
Maccoby, Eym M. and John A. Martin. 1983. "Socialization in the Context of the Family: Parent–Child Interaction." Pp. 1–102 in *Handbook of Child Psychology,* vol. 4: *Socialization, Personality, and Social Development,* 4th ed., edited by E. Mavis Hetherington. New York: John Wiley.
Snow, Catherine E. 1972. "Mothers' Speech to Children Learning Language." *Child Development* 43:549–565.
Steinberg, Laurence and Amanda S. Morris. 2001. "Adolescent Development." *Annual Review of Psychology* 52:83–110.
Weizman, Zehava and Catherine E. Snow. 2001. "Lexical Input as Related to Children's Vocabulary Acquisition: Effects of Sophisticated Exposure and Support for Meaning." *Developmental Psychology* 37:265–279.
Whiting, Beatrice Blyth and Carolyn P. Edwards. 1988. *Children of Different Worlds: The Formation of Social Behavior.* Cambridge, MA: Harvard University Press.

PARK, ROBERT E. (1864–1944)

Robert E. Park is considered to be one of the most influential academics of early U.S. sociology. Throughout his life, Park was concerned with social issues, especially racial problems in urban settings. He is widely known for his focus on the city as a laboratory for social investigation and for his involvement in the development of the "Chicago School" of sociology. Park served as president of both the American Sociological Society and the Chicago Urban League. He was also a member of the Social Science Research Council.

Early Years

Park was born February 14, 1864, in rural Pennsylvania. His mother, Theodosia Warner, was a schoolteacher, and his father, Hiram Asa Park, fought as a soldier for the Union army. When the U.S. Civil War ended, the Parks moved to Red Wing, Minnesota, where Robert Park lived for the next 18 years. He did not excel in school, although he took an interest in the personal histories of his townspeople and studied the immigrant community of the family's household helper, Litza. Park graduated from high school in 1882 and left home against his father's wishes to begin college at the University of Minnesota. Hiram Park initially opposed the idea of Robert going to college but decided to finance his son's education after Robert passed all of his first-year courses. The elder Park even convinced Robert to enroll in the more reputable University of Michigan, where he studied under professors Calvin Thomas and John Dewey.

After graduating with a bachelor's degree in philology in 1887, Park turned down a position as a schoolteacher in Red Wing, Minnesota, and instead moved to Minneapolis in the hopes of landing a job as a reporter. Inspired by Goethe's *Faust,* Park wanted to see the world. He found work as a reporter and held positions in several metropolitan areas, including Detroit, Denver, and New York. At this time, Park continued to gain insight into the functioning of newspapers and made the acquaintance of Franklin Ford, a Wall Street reporter. Under Ford's guidance, Park came to believe that better reporting would revolutionize the progressive historical process and, in turn, would lead to the demise of depression and violence.

Ford and Park began planning an experimental newspaper, *The Thought News,* that would unite scholarship and journalism, but the newspaper was never published. While working on the project, Park met an artist named Clara Cahill, whom he married in 1894 and with whom he eventually had four children.

Park's interest in reporting led him to study philosophy at Harvard University. He wanted to describe the behavior of society in scientific language, which he considered to be precise and universal. After a year at Harvard, he went abroad to study at Friederich Wilhelm University in Germany, where he took his one and only formal class in sociology from Georg Simmel. Park later described Simmel as "the greatest of all sociologists."

While in Berlin, Park also discovered a book on the logic of the social sciences written by Bogdan Kistiakowski, a student of Wilhelm Windelband. Park soon left Berlin to study under Windelband and eventually followed him to Heidelberg, where Windelband was chair of the philosophy department. Park wrote most of his dissertation, "Masse und Publikum" (Crowd and Public), in Heidelberg and presented it to the faculty there, but he did not finish it until he returned to Harvard in 1903.

Professional Career

Although Park secured a job as an assistant in the Department of Philosophy at Harvard, he had grown weary of the academic world and, still inspired by Faust, longed to know human nature widely and intimately. He worked as a newspaper editor and as secretary of the Congo Reform Association. The latter job motivated Park to study inequality in the Congo. Believing that inequality was inherent in colonialism, Park decided to travel to Africa to study the effects of colonialism firsthand.

Before leaving for Africa, Park sought the advice of Booker T. Washington, who invited him to visit the Tuskegee Institute to begin his study of Africa in the southern states. Park never made it to Africa; instead, he accepted a job as publicity handler for the Institute. Over the next seven years, Park worked for Washington, did field research, and took courses. In 1910, he traveled to Europe with Washington to compare European poverty with U.S. poverty. Following that trip, Washington wrote *The Man Farthest Down* (1913) with the collaboration of Park. Later, Park claimed to have learned more about human nature and society while in the South working under Washington than he had in all of his previous studies. Park's primary interest was in the system that had evolved to define Black–White relations in the South.

In 1914, Park accepted a job at the University of Chicago, where he taught until 1932. During that time, he continued to study race relations and to advance his theory of human ecology. To further his study of race relations on the Pacific Coast, Park traveled to Hawai'i, Japan, and China, and in 1921 he and Ernest W. Burgess coauthored *Introduction to the Science of Sociology,* which became the standard textbook for the study of the discipline.

After retiring from the University of Chicago, Park and his wife took a trip around the world and then settled in Nashville, Tennessee, where he taught at Fisk University until his death in 1944. Park claimed that his biggest contribution to sociology was in giving it working concepts and a systematic basis. Park is better known today for his theories of assimilation, community structure, human ecology, natural areas, and racial mobility.

Duke W. Austin

See also Assimilation; Chicago School of Race Relations; Colonialism; Culture of Poverty; Immigration, U.S.; Social Mobility

Further Readings

Lyman, Stanford M. 1992. *Militarism, Imperialism, and Racial Accommodation: An Analysis and Interpretation of the Early Writings of Robert E. Park.* Fayetteville: University of Arkansas Press.

Park, Robert E. 1925. *The City.* Chicago, IL: University of Chicago Press.
Park, Robert E. 1950. *Race and Culture.* New York: Free Press.
Park, Robert E. 1952. *Human Communities: The City and Human Ecology.* New York: Free Press.

PARKS, ROSA (1913–2005)

Rosa Parks died October 24, 2005, at 92 years of age, just a little more than a month before the fiftieth anniversary of the event that came to define her life and make her the stuff of myth—her quiet refusal to give up her seat on a bus to a White man in Montgomery, Alabama, on December 1, 1955. Her arrest triggered the Montgomery Bus Boycott and led to a U.S. Supreme Court decision that struck down Jim Crow segregation laws in the South.

The Montgomery Bus Boycott propelled Martin Luther King, Jr., into a leadership position in the Civil Rights Movement, but Parks is often represented as the "mother" of the movement with King as the "father." Her arrest is reenacted again and again on elementary school stages and in classrooms across the country, most often during African American History Month. One of the reasons why Parks's story has received so much attention is that it can be condensed down to very basic elements of time (the afternoon of December 1, 1955), space (a bus in Montgomery), and affirmation of rights (Parks's refusal to give up her seat).

In 1999, Parks received the Presidential Medal of Freedom from President Bill Clinton. In introducing Parks, the president said, "For most of us alive today, in a very real sense the journey began 43 years ago." Parks has been transformed into a national hero for everyone, a member of the canon of heroes inaugurated into the newly revised multicultural history of the nation. The phrases "a seat on the bus" and "the back of the bus" have become metaphors used again and again by many social groups—from women, to gays and lesbians, to the physically challenged—as part of their struggle for equal rights.

Role in Civil Rights

At the time of her arrest, Parks was secretary of the Montgomery chapter of the National Association for the Advancement of Colored People (NAACP) and

Rosa Parks. In this often reproduced photograph, civil rights hero Rosa Parks is shown defying de jure segregation by sitting in the White section of the bus that launched the Montgomery, Alabama, bus boycott in 1955. Actually, while the event was very real, there were no journalists present at the time and this iconic photography was a re-creation with an Associated Press reporter seated behind Rosa Parks.

Source: Library of Congress, Prints & Photographs Division, LC-USZ62-109643.

had been active in the Civil Rights Movement in the city for more than a decade. By the early 1950s, the NAACP became committed to overthrowing Jim Crow segregation laws in the city through a combination of civil disobedience and legal challenges, and public busing was selected as a primary scene of the battle. Not only were Blacks required to sit in a special section in the back of the bus, they also were required to give up their seats to Whites when buses were crowded and there were not enough seats for everyone to sit. During the summer of 1955, Parks, along with King, visited Highlander Academy in Monteagle, Tennessee, where they met with both Black and White political activists under the leadership of Myles Horton to plan for civil disobedience.

Although Parks's arrest and the subsequent Montgomery Bus Boycott stirred the conscience of many White Americans, political leadership in the United States at the time was also motivated by less altruistic reasons to end segregation laws. A growing number of influential Whites came to believe that the images of Parks's arrest and other images of violent confrontations between Black protesters and Whites in the South, beamed by the mass media around the world, were adversely affecting the nation's image in the developing world. For example, the first editorial in *The New York Times* to mention Parks's arrest—on February 24, 1956—noted, "All over the world the communists, who hate democracy, will have this tragically true story to add to their existing assortment of lies."

Among social and political conservatives such as William Bennett, who included Parks's story in his *Book of Virtues,* the early Civil Rights Movement is associated with the establishment of a "color-blind" law in the United States—the realization of the "American dream" of equality of opportunity. From this perspective, affirmative action is an unfortunate subversion of what Parks stood for. From a liberal or progressive perspective, Parks's story is generally treated as one more small victory on a long road to freedom and justice for African Americans where the battle must be waged on a number of educational and cultural fronts as well as through law and the courts.

In both liberal and conservative narratives of the Civil Rights Movement, tolerance of those who are different is presented as a primary democratic virtue, and Parks spent much of her later life promoting tolerance. Most notably, she lent her name to a "Wall of Tolerance" monument in a museum in Montgomery sponsored the Southern Poverty Law Center. People visiting the monument are encouraged to make a "declaration of tolerance" that concludes, "I pledge to have respect for people whose abilities, beliefs, culture, race, sexual identity, or other characteristics are different from my own."

Later Accomplishments

Also during her later years, Parks began to assume more of a role in speaking to Black youth about "positive" values and lifestyles. In two books she wrote during the 1990s, *Quiet Strength* (1994) and *Dear Mrs. Parks* (1996), she wrote to Black youth in particular, and the message was clearly that for African American youth to succeed, they will need to avoid "bad" influences and role models and to keep on the straight and narrow path of "good" behavior. In *Quiet Strength,* she quoted from the Bible (Titus 2:7–8) to support her argument that to be a role model one must "show integrity, seriousness, and soundness of speech that cannot be condemned." The aims of Black Americans, she argued, should be to make White people ashamed because they have "nothing bad to say about us."

This emphasis on positive values and role models was consistent with Parks's story. Certainly, there is evidence that the NAACP in Montgomery decided to use Parks to test the city's segregated bus laws because she fit the White community's image of a "good" Black person. It is perhaps understandable, then, that as Parks was transformed into a symbol of self-discipline and "good manners," she began to lose favor with some Black Americans, including those identified with hip-hop culture.

This tension was exacerbated by Parks's much publicized lawsuit against the rap group *Outkast* during the last few years of her life, where she claimed that the group's song *Rosa Parks* defamed her good name. The group claimed that the song actually honored Parks by introducing her to a new generation of Black youth. But it also can be interpreted as suggesting that an older generation of timid and meek Black leaders, symbolized by Parks, needs to "move to the back of the bus" and let a younger, more assertive generation take over. As the stuff of legend, Parks has become a cultural icon open to different and even competing meanings. But as a person, she will be remembered for what she did on that fateful day she got on a bus in Montgomery and the events that followed.

Dennis Carlson

See also Boycott; Civil Rights Movement; Civil Rights Movement, Women and; Hip-Hop; King, Martin Luther, Jr.; National Association for the Advancement of Colored People (NAACP)

Further Readings

Bennett, William. 1993. *The Book of Virtues: A Treasure of Great Moral Stories.* New York: Simon & Schuster.

Carlson, Dennis. 2003. "Troubling Heroes: Of Rosa Parks, Multicultural Education, and Critical Pedagogy." *Cultural Studies/Critical Methodologies* 3(1):44–61.

Carlson, Dennis. 2004. "Narrating the Multicultural Nation: Rosa Parks and the White Mythology of the Civil Rights Movement." Pp. 302–314 in *Off White: Readings on Power, Privilege, and Resistance,* 2nd ed., edited by M. Fine, L. Weis, L. Pruitt, and A. Burns. New York: Routledge.

Kohl, Herbert. 1991. "The Politics of Children's Literature: The Story of Rosa Parks and the Montgomery Bus Boycott." *Journal of Education* 173:35–50.

Parks, Rosa. 1994. *Quiet Strength: The Faith, the Hope, and the Heart of a Woman Who Changed a Nation.* New York: Zondervan.

Parks, Rosa with Gregory Reed. 1996. *Dear Mrs. Parks: A Dialogue with Today's Youth.* New York: Lee & Low.

Parks, Rosa with Jim Haskins. 1992. *Rosa Parks: My Story.* New York: Dial Books.

Phillips, W. 1956. "Montgomery Is Stage for a Tense Drama." *The New York Times,* March 4, E6.

PATRIOT Act of 2001

Commonly referred to as the USA PATRIOT Act or simply the PATRIOT Act, the law signed on October 26, 2001, is titled the Uniting and Strengthening America by Providing Appropriate Tools Required to Intercept and Obstruct Terrorism Act of 2001 (or Public Law 107–56). In the immediate aftermath of the September 11, 2001, attacks, there was little congressional debate regarding many controversial provisions that expanded law enforcement authority and limited the civil liberties of citizens and noncitizens involved in terrorism investigations. Over time, considerable debate has arisen related to its implementation, but surveys suggest that most U.S. residents continue to support the act. This entry looks at the controversial provisions and enforcement strategies, the actual impact on prosecutions, and current differences of opinion as to whether it should be modified.

What the Act Does

The most controversial provisions increased access to all forms of electronic and nonelectronic communication and records, eliminated a need for probable cause in "sneak and peak" searches, gave the secretary of the treasury the authority to regulate financial transactions linked to terrorism, and gave the Federal Bureau of Investigation (FBI) (in concert with the Bureau of Immigration and Customs Enforcement [ICE]) broad discretion in questioning, detaining, and deporting immigrants relative to terrorism investigations.

The most negative racial/ethnic impact was the profiling and severe curtailment of the rights of certain temporary visitors, permanent resident aliens, and visa overstayers in the United States. The Department of Justice classified young male immigrants of certain national origins and Islamic religious affiliation as targets for interviews and special registration. National origins targeted included Afghanistan, Algeria, Bahrain, Bangladesh, Egypt, Eritrea, Indonesia, Iran, Iraq, Jordan, Kuwait, Lebanon, Libya, Morocco, North Korea, Oman, Qatar, Somalia, Tunisia, United

Arab Emirates, and Yemen. The FBI set out to interview 5,000 men between 18 and 33 years of age who had entered the United States from countries thought to harbor cells of Al Qaeda, the group responsible for the 9/11 attacks. These interviews were "voluntary," but if noncitizens did not appear it became an immigration violation and they could be deported.

The PATRIOT Act gives the attorney general unilateral authority regarding detainment. Detainees are not allowed to appeal any charge related to suspicion of terrorism. The law defined *terrorist suspect* so broadly that even a very remote contact or transaction could result in detention. Some suspects had connections to a humanitarian organization that the government believes had passed money for terrorists. ICE is allowed to keep a noncitizen suspect in detention even if an immigration judge orders that person to be released. ICE is routinely allowed to appeal a release order without any need to provide evidence that would change a judicial decision.

The PATRIOT Act may have been used for, or may have resulted in, a sweep to remove immigrants as a result of their national origin and religion. Visa overstayers who were "out of status" were identified and ordered to be deported regardless of any ties to terrorists. In addition, ICE detained many noncitizen men secretly with no access to their families or lawyers under the provision for "special interest cases" of the PATRIOT Act. Many became subject to indefinite detention during these lengthy investigations. Previously, the U.S. Supreme Court had found indefinite detention to be unconstitutional, but the PATRIOT Act again authorized it. In 2006, its use to combat terrorism was authorized by the Court. The wives and children of detained and deported men suffered both emotionally and financially. Immigrant advocates tried to provide legal assistance for detainees, but the ICE practice of moving them between detention facilities made this difficult.

Arrests and Prosecutions

It is known that 1,200 noncitizens were detained before the Department of Justice stopped the practice of providing an accounting of detainees. Zacarias Moussaoui, a French-born entrant, is the only person to be found guilty as a terrorist in relation to the 9/11 attacks but is not thought to be the 20th hijacker. Nonetheless, the federal government has repeatedly searched for terrorists among the immigrant and foreign entrant populations.

Transactional Records Access Clearinghouse (TRAC), a data collection organization affiliated with Syracuse University, indicates that 6,472 individuals were classified as "terrorists" or "antiterrorists" since the 9/11 attacks. Most of these cases were referred during the two years following the attacks. Four of five of these individuals have been considered for trial or tried, and the outcomes have been made known under the Freedom of Information Act. Prosecutors declined prosecution in 64% of these cases on the basis of insufficient evidence. For an additional 9% of individuals, the cases were dismissed or they were declared not guilty. Approximately one of four cases (27%) resulted in convictions.

The charges and sentencing of these individuals is also of interest. Among convicted individuals (1,329), 1% (14) received a sentence of 20 years or more, 5% (67) received a sentence of 5 years or more, 53% (704) received no prison time, and 25% (327) received sentences ranging from 1 day to 1 year. TRAC pointed out that convictions are seldom for terrorist activities. The top four charges were fraud or making false statements (14.5%), terrorism with criminal penalties (14.4%), providing material support to terrorists (11.6%), and release or detention of material witnesses. In looking at convictions, fraud and false statements accounted for more than one-half (56.8%); other convictions were based on fraud and related activity–ID documents (5.6%), fraud and misuse of visas or permits (4.7%), providing material support for terrorists (3.8%), and release or detention of material witnesses (3.3%). Two-thirds of all convictions for suspects in terrorism investigations involved a fraud or fraud-related charge. Approximately two-thirds of these arrests were made by the FBI (931, with 18% of the cases being prosecuted), whereas Customs and Border Protection and ICE made 161 arrests (with 49.3% of the cases being prosecuted). The Social Security Administration referrals had the highest conviction rate (84 arrests, with 92% of the cases being prosecuted).

The help of the affected immigrant communities might have been useful in combating terrorism, but the climate of suspicion seems to have encouraged alienation rather than cooperation. The national origin and religious profiling of immigrants has produced only 14 terrorist-related sentences of 20 years or more. It could be argued, then, that this surveillance has tended to exonerate the immigrant community at a significantly large cost in terms of taxpayers' money. TRAC pointed out that prosecutions have declined sharply during the years subsequent to 9/11, although some political leaders still talk about a substantial terrorist threat. During recent years, the turndown rate for referrals has been nine of ten. Finally, the low rate of cases with substantial sentences suggests that national origin and religion profiling of noncitizens in certain immigrant communities was unproductive, especially the use of FBI resources. Some argue that the PATRIOT Act's deprivation of civil liberties might not be justified by the results.

Continuing Debate

Although the most severe provisions of the act were due to end in 2005, it was reauthorized with few changes on March 2, 2006. In the interim, the PATRIOT Act has been strongly criticized for weakening civil liberties. The most strongly contested elements were renewal of indefinite detention of immigrants, sneak and peak searches without owner or occupant knowledge, FBI use of "national security letters" to search any type of communication or records, and increased access of law enforcement to government records, including library and financial ones. The provision for search of records was challenged successfully by the American Civil Liberties Union (ACLU), and the law has been changed to require more judicial oversight. Other provisions related to access to records, sneak and peek searches, and use of roving wiretaps were subject to twenty-seven new provisions providing for more judicial oversight of their use.

A 2006 national survey showed that most U.S. residents support the erosion of civil liberties caused by the PATRIOT Act because they consider fighting terrorism to be more important. The public believes that the act did not go too far, but it does object to the government's amassing a huge database of previously private records. Impacts have varied in kind and degree between citizens and noncitizens. Loss of privacy is a big concern to citizens because they can see that their records have been put in view of law enforcement. Noncitizens, including permanent resident aliens, have been much more affected by counterterrorist scrutiny. Only watchdog organizations such as the ACLU, Amnesty International, and immigrant organizations have reacted by filing lawsuits or protesting the immigrant profiling used in the "War on Terror" that were authorized by this act.

Another negative consequence of the PATRIOT Act is that it creates a two-tier society of citizens and noncitizens. A key issue is that immigrants who are not naturalized citizens are more likely to have lost civil and human rights, in practice, under the secrecy provision for special interest cases of the act. The Supreme Court has ruled that indefinite detention by ICE is unconstitutional, but even immigrants with paperwork in compliance with the law have been subject to indefinite detainment if they were profiled in the War on Terror.

Given the absence of terrorist incidents since 9/11, U.S. citizens may assume that the PATRIOT Act is a key component in this outcome. The law enforcement record, however, indicates that few substantial convictions have resulted from the harassment of profiled immigrants and foreign entrants.

Judith Ann Warner

See also Discrimination; Immigration, U.S.; Immigration and Race; London Bombings (July 7, 2005); Muslim Americans; Police; Racial Profiling; Refugees; Terrorism

Further Readings

Cole, David. 2003. *Enemy Aliens: Double Standards and Constitutional Freedoms in the War on Terrorism*. New York: New Press.

Dow, Mark. 2004. *American Gulag: Inside U.S. Immigration Prisons*. Berkeley: University of California Press.

Gallup Poll. 2006. *Gallup's Pulse of Democracy: The Patriot Act and Civil Liberties*. Retrieved from http://www.galluppoll.com/content/?ci=5263

TRAC Report. 2006. *Criminal Terrorism Enforcement in the United States in the Five Years since the 9/11/01 Attacks*. Retrieved from http://trac.syr.edu/tracreports/terrorism/169

PELTIER, LEONARD (1944–)

Leonard Peltier, a leading Native American activist and prominent member of the American Indian Movement (AIM), is currently serving two life sentences for the murder of two Federal Bureau of Investigation (FBI) agents. The case that led to his incarceration remains highly controversial. For many, Peltier is a symbol of the history of the violation of human rights of Indigenous Peoples, and he has been called the Nelson Mandela of the American Indian people. To others, he is a murderer who has been erroneously turned into a martyr. This entry looks at his life and impact.

Early Years

Peltier was born September 12, 1944, on the Anishinabe/Chippewa Turtle Mountain Reservation in Grand Forks, North Dakota, to Leo and Alvina Peltier. His bloodline is predominantly Ojibway (Chippewa) and Dakota Sioux. He was also adopted in the traditional Indian way by the Lakota Sioux. His parents separated when he was four years old, and he then lived with his paternal grandparents. From 1953 to 1956, he was forced to attend the Bureau of Indian Affairs' (BIA) Wahpeton Indian Boarding School. He returned to the Turtle Mountain Reservation in 1957.

While on the reservation in 1958, Peltier observed his first Sun Dance and attended a political meeting regarding the government's plans to "terminate" the reservation—ending its recognition of the tribe's sovereignty and withdrawing services. These two events inspired Peltier to work for justice on behalf of his people, to work toward eliminating the extreme poverty he saw among Indian peoples, and to preserve tribal customs. During the 1960s, he joined the fight for civil, human, and Indian rights. Peltier became involved in Indian fishing rights, which was a key impetus leading to the establishment of AIM, as were the government's termination and relocation programs.

The American Indian Movement

AIM was established in Minneapolis in 1968. The movement concentrated on achieving justice for American Indians by demanding that the U.S. government honor previously signed treaties. In 1969, AIM activists occupied the abandoned federal prison on Alcatraz Island in the San Francisco Bay area from November 1969 through June 1971 to bring attention to their plight. Although Peltier was not involved in this action, it inspired him and acted as a model for his future activism.

Early Experiences

Peltier's first experience involving AIM-style militancy was the 1970 occupation of the abandoned Fort Lawton military base outside of Seattle. Like Alcatraz, this was on "surplus" federal land; hence, the United Indians of All Tribes Foundation (UIATF) used this takeover to test an old federal law that gives Indians first rights to lands abandoned by federal agencies. As a result of this takeover, people were arrested, beaten, taken into custody, and beaten again in the stockade cells. When Peltier was released, he refused to leave until all of the others were released, encouraging the others to also refuse to leave until all had been freed. Peltier's insistence on the importance of solidarity led to his emergence as a leader in the fight for Indian rights.

Peltier traveled to Arizona and then on to Colorado, following the activities of AIM through media reports. He went to the AIM office in Denver, where he met Vernon Bellecourt, who took Peltier to an AIM meeting in Minnesota. Dennis Banks, one of the cofounders of AIM, spoke at this meeting, impressing on Peltier the importance of AIM and its actions in the fight for Native rights. In 1972, Peltier joined AIM and worked with Banks and other AIM leaders and activists.

In 1972, Peltier traveled with Banks to Hollywood to raise support for Indian causes among people involved in the movie industry, hoping to achieve positive media attention. Marlon Brando and Jane Fonda are perhaps the most famous Hollywood insiders who publicly supported Indian causes. Peltier, however, did not like Los Angeles, claiming that it seemed like a jungle to him. Consequently, he moved to Milwaukee to work with the local AIM office, working specifically on alcohol problems in the Indian community.

Trail of Broken Treaties

During the fall of 1972, Peltier helped to organize the "Trail of Broken Treaties" caravan to the White House. Along with Stanley Moore, Peltier was chosen to direct security in Washington, D.C. The caravan arrived just days before the presidential election, having notified the authorities of plans to bring a list of twenty grievances and a proposal to improve Indian relations with the U.S. government. It was the intent of AIM to set up a series of meetings with government agencies to discuss the grievances. Specifically, AIM wanted to put the BIA under Indian control and to establish a commission for the purpose of examining treaty violations.

What had been planned as a meeting turned into an impromptu sit-in when government officials refused to meet and discuss AIM's grievances. The sit-in escalated into a takeover of the BIA building just a few blocks from the White House. All employees were allowed to leave, and AIM occupied the BIA building for five days, causing substantial damage and taking a number of documents that it declared confirmed the biased position of the government against Indians. The leaders on the Trail of Broken Treaties were added to the FBI's list of "key extremists." Because Peltier was a security chief during the BIA takeover, he once again drew the attention of the FBI as an agitator who already had been arrested during the Fort Lawton takeover.

Peltier returned to Milwaukee, and a few weeks later he was arrested and charged with attempted murder. A fight broke out in a restaurant between Peltier, along with two of his Indian friends, and two plainclothes policemen. The police maintained that Peltier threatened them by firing a gun twice. Peltier denied this accusation, claiming that he had been set up by the police. Peltier spent five months in jail. During this time, AIM activists occupied Wounded Knee on the Pine Ridge Reservation in South Dakota during a 71-day standoff beginning February 27, 1973. In April, Peltier was released on bail and went underground, assuming that he would not get a fair trial. Eventually, in 1978, Peltier was acquitted following the state crime lab's conclusion that his gun was incapable of firing.

While still a fugitive from trial dates, Peltier joined the fishing rights struggle in Washington State and later took part in AIM protests in Arizona and Wisconsin. In March 1975, Peltier responded to a request from the Elders of the Oglala Pine Ridge Reservation summoning AIM for protection, and he moved there as a security expert for AIM.

The Pine Ridge Shootout

During the preceding months of the Wounded Knee occupation, tensions escalated between traditional Lakota, who wanted independence from the federal government, and the tribal government, which supported the actions of the federal government. The tribal government augmented the BIA police force by funding a private police force, known for its brutality, whose members referred to themselves as the Guardians of the Oglala Nation (GOONs). Violent confrontations between the two groups continued as an everyday occurrence during the three years following the siege at Wounded Knee. This was the atmosphere that Peltier encountered when he and other AIM members set up a "tent city" on the Jumping Bull compound near Oglala to protect the traditional Lakota from attacks by the GOONs.

On June 26, 1975, FBI agents Jack Coler and Ronald Williams, in unmarked cars, chased a red pickup truck onto the Jumping Bull property. Gunfire erupted among the agents, other law enforcement officers, GOONs, and AIM members. The firefight resulted in the deaths of Coler and Williams along with the death of AIM member Joe Stuntz. Peltier and more than two dozen others fled the property, leading to a massive FBI manhunt. On September 10, 1975, a car driven by Bob Robideau, who had also escaped Jumping Bull, exploded. The FBI recovered an AR-15 rifle and declared that it was the weapon that killed the agents and that it belonged to Peltier. FBI lab reports, not revealed until years later, disclosed that the pin in the AR-15 rifle was different from the pin in the rifle used at Jumping Bull.

On November 25, 1975, Peltier, Robideau, Dino Butler, and James Eagle were indicted in the deaths of the FBI agents. Robideau and Butler pleaded innocent by reason of self-defense and were given a full acquittal, and the charges were dropped against Eagle. Peltier, who had fled to Canada, was arrested by the Canadian police and was held in custody in Vancouver, British Columbia. In December 1976, Peltier was extradited to the United States.

Murderer or Martyr?

Peltier's trial on double murder charges began March 16, 1977, in Fargo, North Dakota. From the Indian perspective, this region was notorious for anti-Indian sentiment. Peltier was not allowed to claim self-defense or to introduce the evidence that led to the acquittal of Robideau and Butler by reason of self-defense. Essentially, the defense argued that all exculpatory evidence was ruled inadmissible. On April 18, 1977, Peltier was convicted of the murder of the two FBI agents, and on June 2 he was sentenced to two consecutive life terms in federal prison. Although there have been several appeals for a new trial, all appeals have been denied.

Several human rights organizations, most notably Amnesty International and the Leonard Peltier Defense Committee, have called for executive clemency and a pardon from the president of the United States. President Bill Clinton's failure to pardon Peltier is seen by many Indians as characteristic bias against Indians. Peltier's case has attracted national and international attention and continues to be controversial.

Diane Sandage

See also American Indian Movement; Bureau of Indian Affairs; Discrimination; Native Americans; Sioux; Trail of Broken Treaties

Further Readings

Matthiessen, Peter. 1991. *In the Spirit of Crazy Horse.* New York: Viking Penguin.

Page, Jake. 2003. *In the Hands of the Great Spirit: The 20,000-Year History of American Indians.* New York: Free Press.

Peltier, Leonard. 1999. *Prison Writings: My Life Is My Sun Dance.* New York: St. Martin's Griffin.

PEOPLEHOOD

Peoplehood refers to the inclusionary and involuntary identity of a territorially based group with a putatively distinct way of life. A general concept, it encompasses groups usually classified separately under the categories "race," "ethnicity," and "nation," thereby implying a grouping larger than kinship but smaller than humanity. Peoplehood is characterized by both common descent—a shared sense of genealogy and geography—and contemporary commonality such as language, religion, culture, and/or consciousness. As a self-reflexive identity or internal conviction of a group, it is distinct from a *population,* which connotes an aggregate or an analytical category with externally defined attributes. Peoplehood often supersedes religious, class, and local identity to become a fundamental mode of identity in modern life. The term appears in the work of several scholars working independently, including Immanuel Wallerstein, Rogers Smith, and John Lie.

Most discussions of race, ethnicity, and nation dispense considerable effort in analytically distinguishing among the three. Racial categorization frequently appeals to biological distinction (or perceptions to that effect), and ethnic differentiation often depends on social or cultural difference. Yet in fact, the dividing line between the natural and the social turns out to be spurious; racial groups rely on achieved characteristics, and ethnic groups rely on ascriptive features. Furthermore, racial characteristics are frequently conflated with both the national and the ethnic. These categorical distinctions also fail to make adequate sense of the historically contingent definitions and developments. The concept of peoplehood seeks to supersede these conceptual confusions by asserting unifying elements in the classification of humans. Thus, peoplehood is at once rooted in both the natural and the social.

The concept of peoplehood is fundamentally a modern phenomenon. In the premodern world, the major categories of social distinction were not racial, ethnic, or national; rather, status, religion, and locality (e.g., village, region) were the major modes of distinction and identification. For example, one identified as a peasant, a Christian, or a villager rather than as a White person or a French person. The classification of humans in terms of peoplehood arose in early modern Europe and spread to the rest of the world.

The Rise of Modern Peoplehood

Identity does not arise naturally; rather, it usually arises from institutional identification. Identity is learned, and institution has the capacity and the will to inculcate it. Most powerful identities in early modern Europe, therefore, followed from the most powerful institutions of the time such as status hierarchy and religious organization. With their decline arose the expansion and intensification of state power. Modern peoplehood is ultimately a product of the modern state.

Modern state formation achieved two forms of integration that made modern peoplehood possible. Horizontal (or cultural) integration incorporated and integrated disparate local and regional identifications. The growing infrastructural and institutional spread of the state inculcated state-based identity. That is, national education, mass conscription, and national systems of communication and transportation culturally transmitted the idea of modern peoplehood as personal identity. Outside of the state, war and international competition sealed the identification of "us"—our people—against "them."

Whereas horizontal integration geographically expanded the spread of peoplehood as a form of identity, vertical (or status) integration weakened the formal barriers of status hierarchy within a polity. Premodern distinctions between lords and peasants were often racialized as biological distinctions between, for example, "blue-blooded" aristocrats and "dark" peasants. The advances of political liberty and industrialization made possible the theoretical equality of citizenry or people.

These twin processes of integration reconfigured group identities on a much larger scale than had been possible previously; once stabilized, the boundaries separating these peoplehood identities became increasingly impermeable. Spurred by warfare and national industrialization, the modern state was the fundamental motor driving the emergence of peoplehood identity in delineating clear lines between "us" and "them." Premodern modes of identification declined; linguistic, religious, and cultural integration occurred in tandem with the rise of peoplehood identity within national boundaries.

The rise of the modern state is responsible not only for peoplehood identity but also for the ontology of modern scientific understanding of the nation-state itself and of society. Horizontal and vertical modes of integration were in fact preconditions of the modern social sciences' use of the nation-state or society as a principal unit of analysis. Symptomatically, the modern European terminology for society as a modern, liberal, inclusive, and equal polity (*Gesellschaft* and *société*) became popular during the 18th century. The premodern equivalents (*Sozietät* and *monde*) referred to an earlier meaning of "society" that implied the elite stratum rather than people at large. The infrastructure of the modern state made the ideas of modern society and modern peoplehood largely coeval.

Finally, the particular trajectories of national development generated distinct articulations of peoplehood. Some countries valorized citizenship, emphasizing the voluntary nature of peoplehood belonging. Others stressed birth and descent, stressing the hereditary characteristic of identity. Nonetheless, this distinction is far from fixed. Just as the United States, a country of immigrant citizenship par excellence, has often stressed racial and biological grounding of "Americanness" (whiteness), Germany and Japan, countries that have emphasized "blood" transmission, make possible "naturalization" into the ambit of German and Japanese peoplehood.

Racism and Genocide

Racism, according to Lie, is a consequence of incomplete integration of peoplehood. The making of modern peoplehood may remain incomplete in terms of both horizontal and vertical integration. That is, some regions or religious groups, or newly arrived immigrants, remain outside of the ambit of peoplehood identity (e.g., Irish in England, Jews in Germany). Simultaneously, low-status groups might not be adequately integrated into the body politic (e.g., Burakumin minority group in Japan). Political racism identifies the incompletely integrated groups so as to mobilize identification with and support for the majority group. Economic racism, in contrast, occurs in the labor market, whether to protect the privileges of the majority group or to disband the solidarity of the working class by dividing workers and co-opting their interests. These distinctions, to be sure, are frequently elided, and racism is most powerful when the two dimensions overlap. Thus, the strength of racism against African Americans in the early 20th-century United States depended on both horizontally and vertically incomplete integration.

Genocide is the extreme manifestation of racism. Just as the modern state contributed to the construction of modern peoplehood, its bureaucratic and technological centralization also has made possible categorical destruction of a minority peoplehood identified as an enemy within. In this line of thinking, it is not so much racism that generates genocide as the development of the apparatus of state power that accounts in large part for both racism and genocide.

The Future of Peoplehood

If the modern state is the proximate institutional factor behind modern peoplehood, a relative decline of the state should lead to the waning impact of peoplehood identity. However, one of the reasons why peoplehood identity is at once proliferating and ostensibly strengthening is the fracturing and fractal nature of peoplehood identity. Nonetheless, the waning of structural inequality (or greater horizontal and vertical integration) may leave symbolic racism intact. Countermobilization by excluded groups may, therefore, lead to a greater assertion of minority peoplehood.

Nonetheless, recent major trends around the world point to the decline of peoplehood identity. On the one hand, globalization and its attendant processes—with transnational migration being most important—are vitiating cultural integration. On the other hand, the weakening welfare state and neoliberal economic policies are generating greater inequalities that threaten vertical integration. Thus, the unraveling of modern peoplehood identities may very well occur as other modes of social classification and identification come to the fore.

Julia Chuang and John Lie

See also Citizenship; Ethnic Groups; Genocide; Race; Racism

Further Readings

Lie, John. 2004. *Modern Peoplehood.* Cambridge, MA: Harvard University Press.
Smith, Rogers. 2003. *Stories of Peoplehood: The Politics and Morals of Political Membership.* Cambridge, UK: Cambridge University Press.
Wallerstein, Immanuel. 1987. "The Construction of Peoplehood: Racism, Nationalism, Ethnicity." *Sociological Forum* 2:373–388.

PEOPLE OF COLOR

The phrase *people of color* (and *person of color*) refers to racial and ethnic minority groups. Although historically the term has been used elsewhere, the notion of people of color is much more localized in contemporary popular, activist, and academic debates, mostly in the United States. *People of color* explicitly suggests a social relationship among racial and ethnic minority groups. The use of the term also expands on and challenges empirical uses of categories such as "race," "(pan)ethnicity," and "national identity." *People of color* is a term most often used outside of traditional academic circles, often infused by activist frameworks, but it is slowly replacing terms such as *racial and ethnic minorities.*

First examined in this entry are the origins of the term *people of color,* how it has been used recently, and the debates surrounding its meaning by various groups. The first section includes a brief discussion on the politics of skin color, whiteness, and racialization discussions. Next, the coalitional uses and possibilities of this term and its potentially productive use in academia (especially when linked to sociological discussions on race and racialization, panethnicity, and national identity) are addressed. The final main section offers details about some significant changes in the term by newer racialization processes. Thus, the entry moves from biological notions of race to discussions of racism and racialization to best illustrate the notion of people of color.

Historical Use

In the past, the phrase *free people of color* was used to encode the experience of non-Whites after the abolition of slavery throughout Latin America and the United States. In some cases, however, the phrase did not imply all non-White people, for example, when Native Americans and other free people of color were portrayed as having owned their own slaves. In such instances, the term was a more stratified term that regulated the colonization of the seemingly less enslaved people, creating a buffer of sorts between (Black) slaves and (White) colonizers.

In the United States in particular, there is a trajectory to the term—from more derogatory terms such as *negroes,* to *colored,* to *people of color.* (The term *colored,* however, has a different meaning in other countries such as South Africa, but that discussion is beyond the scope of this entry.) Although in this genealogy the term refers predominantly to Blacks, at certain historical moments and in various regions Mexicans, among some of the oldest "immigrants," were excluded from "White"-only spaces under the nomenclature of "colored" along with Blacks. One of the developments of the term *people of color* is precisely its flexibility in accommodating various groups similarly disadvantaged, even if their disadvantages are based on different variables (e.g., access to education, housing, employment, immigration status, English proficiency). Furthermore, a comparative view of the United States with another country, such as Canada, can show that however the term *people of color* is conceptualized there (e.g., through the language of aboriginal peoples), there are similarities in crucial aspects of inequality such as the high percentage of people of color in prisons.

Because of its development, the term has a strong association to phenotype, skin color, and eye/hair/other physiological aspects that often defined Blacks in the United States. As a result, at times African Americans use *people of color* to refer only to those individuals who "look Black." Yet Black scholars in the humanities and social sciences have also underscored how the notion of "feeling Black" is as much an imposition of outside group definitions of Black communities. Similarly, the use of the terms *Brown, Yellow,* and *Red,* while having various connotations depending on who is talking (sometimes their use is perceived as offensive), have been used politically to mobilize communities of color throughout the United States during the latter part of the 20th century and the early 21st century.

The social construction debates about race during the past couple of decades have challenged a notion of seemingly distinctive "races." Centuries after the uses of *Caucasoid, Mongoloid,* and *Negroid* as terms through which the sciences attempted to reify racial difference, recent research illustrates that genetic commonalities between so-called racial groups may exceed commonalities within a group. For instance, two Asian individuals or two Black individuals may have less genetic makeup in common than each of them would have with a person considered to be "White." Thus, the politics of naming a person solely based on how that person is perceived, a significant part of the revolutionary Civil Rights Movement during the 1960s, is being reshaped by discussions that are not limited to skin color privilege and "colorism." The term *people of color* should be understood in the context of racialization, which offers a range of shifts and changes throughout modern history on how various racialized ethnoracial minority groups are conceived and treated by the state.

The term *people of color* has been contested because of its seemingly oppositional definition to Whites. Many people, notably U.S. Whites, critique the use of the term because it presumes that Whites have no color, effectively missing the point that whiteness studies has tried to bring forth during the past decade or so—that the invisibility of whiteness is marked, even if in very subtle ways, by the politicized use of the term *people of color*. The affect solicited in these accounts makes the production and effects of whiteness noticeable; that which has "no color" is made visible by such uttering. All in all, one of the ways in which these uses of *color* (or even the *Black, Brown, Yellow,* and *Red* terms) have formed and solidified the term *people of color* has been in its opposition to *White,* but an equally important way has been the recognition that a racial/social hierarchy continues to both privilege whiteness (and White supremacy) and degrade various groups of people of color.

Coalitional and Contemporary Uses

People of color can self-identify by their country of origin or their panethnic label (e.g., *Asian* or *Latino* or even all-encompassing labels such as *Native Americans* that effectively erase tribal differences) and can also identify as people of color. In this sense, the term *people of color* offers individuals a certain range of identity choices from the regional/tribal/national, panethnic, and coalitional. *People of color* is, however it is viewed, a political term, but it is also a term that allows for a more complex set of identity for the individual—a relational one that is in constant flux. Immigration, travel, and racial constructs—in general, people's social world—all have an impact on how changing these identifications may be. It is perhaps because of the flexibility in identification that the term has become significant in biracial and multiracial writings (and for individuals) as a term that better helps to identify people with multiple national origins, panethnic backgrounds, or so-called racial makeup.

Academically, the term *people of color* has yet to supplant *racial and ethnic minorities*. Critics of the latter term insist that the word *minorities* carries a charged connotation that pathologizes the various groups perceived to be members. *Minority,* in some people's view, implies the "putting down" of a group of people by self-categorization as "less than"—or so the argument goes. This critique is often based on the faulty assumption that the use of minorities literally implies numbers; in the historical–political sense, the term *ethnoracial minorities* has implied people without resources or institutional power—elements often missing for people of color even when people of color are the numerical majority in a given state or region.

Political or coalitional categories such as the term *people of color* tend to offer much room for commonalities, just as other (often unexplored) categories such as *panethnicity* do as well. Although *people of color* is an all-inclusive term that incorporates African Americans, Latinas/os, Asians and Pacific Islanders, and Native Americans, the term has possibilities of moving outside of the census-defined (and institutionally bound) racial and ethnic categories imposed by the state. It is here, in the dissolution of panethnic and top-down imposed categories, where the U.S.–"Third World" boundaries can be blurred. Likewise, where country of origin, region, or language commonalities are put aside for more political economic issues that affect these groups similarly (colonialism, militarization, and imposition of economic development demands), intraethnic relations are more easily visible against the panethnic impositions of the state.

Among the terms linked to or derived from *people of color* are *women of color, Third World women,* and *queer people of color*. Feminist theorizing has linked Third World women and women of color in their discussions as a way to develop coalitions and solidarity among various groups of people. Similarly, the term *queer people of color* has been developed as an identity refusing (in sociological language) a single "master status"; in so doing, it has privileged both sexual and racial marginalization as the core of such identity. Theoretically, a most recent "queer of color critique" loops back into the feminist of color critiques of the 1980s and a burgeoning queer theory that used whiteness as a normative (invisible) referent in its theorizing (like much of the 1970s–1980s feminisms critiqued by feminists of color).

Changes in U.S. Racialization

Racialization moves beyond the notion of "race" as biological traits. At the same time, racialization does not leave behind discussions about racism; it conceptualizes racism differently. Racial formations, and the racialization in these, imply the marking of groups of people previously unmarked; in so doing, racialization is not static. Historically, discussions of who immigrates to the United States and how they are perceived once they arrive have depended on elements such as notions of whiteness and blackness as well as panethnicity impositions.

Political–economic issues have been significantly implicated in the attacks on the United States, most notably the one on September 11, 2001. With the increasing demonization of Arabs, Middle Easterners, South Asians, and people who are Muslim (regardless of their country of origin), these groups are being racialized in ways that regroup Arabs, Middle Easterners, and South Asians—some previously labeled as *White* in the U.S. Census and some thought of as "model minorities"—on the bottom rungs of a racial ladder in U.S. society. In one report, Latinos and African Americans were portrayed in mainstream media as being "OK" with infringing on Middle Easterners' rights after 9/11, effectively showing that racialization takes place from more than the positions of power. Arabs, Muslims, Middle Easterners, and South Asians are continuously reracialized as terrorists and deficient citizens regardless of their political or religious belief system. Thus, the process of racialization of subgroups that could be considered as people of color by activist and popular standards, as well as by academic standards, is ongoing. This is a significant example of racialization as a process that continues to determine and redefine what *people of color* means in contemporary U.S. society.

Salvador Vidal-Ortiz

See also Critical Race Theory; Deviance and Race; Gender and Race, Intersection of; Identity Politics; Immigration and Race; Military and Race; Minority/Majority; Panethnic Identity; Racialization

Further Readings

Ahmad, Muneer. 2002. "Homeland Insecurities: Racial Violence the day after September 11." *Social Text* 72:101–115.

Alexander, Bryant K. 2004. "Racializing Identity: Performance, Pedagogy, and Regret." *Cultural Studies, Critical Methodologies* 4(1):12–27.

Almaguer, Tomás. 1994. *Racial Faultlines: The Historical Origins of White Supremacy in California.* Berkeley: University of California Press.

Anzaldúa, Gloria and Cherríe Moraga, eds. 1983. *This Bridge Called My Back: Radical Writings by Women of Color.* New York: Kitchen Table Press.

Ferguson, Roderick A. 2004. *Aberrations in Black: Toward a Queer of Color Critique.* Minneapolis: University of Minnesota Press.

Glenn, Evelyn N. 2002. *Unequal Freedom: How Race and Gender Shaped American Citizenship and Labor.* Cambridge, MA: Harvard University Press.

Omi, Michael and Howard Winant. 1986. *Racial Formation in the United States: From the 1960s to the 1980s.* New York: Routledge.

Vidal-Ortiz, Salvador. 2004. "On Being a White Person of Color: Using Autoethnography to Understand Puerto Ricans' Racialization." *Qualitative Sociology* 27:178–202.

Peru

Racial/Ethnic relations in Peru, a country with an estimated population of 27.9 million people in 2007, have experienced tremendous changes during the past 500 years but have always remained central to social and political life. Indigenous Peoples, while making up more than 40% of the current population, have been continually "othered," even as large-scale demographic and governing changes have altered the country. Whites (*criollos*) have always struggled (overtly and covertly) to maintain their privileged position at the top of the racial hierarchy. A small population of Blacks continue to suffer from obscurity. But the mestizo population has demonstrated the greatest flux, emerging out of marginality to both pioneer some of the greatest historical changes and reproduce some of the most repressive social relations.

Spanish Invasion

As with most of the Americas, contemporary race relations in Peru were born in the early 16th century with the Spanish invasion of the New World. In 1532,

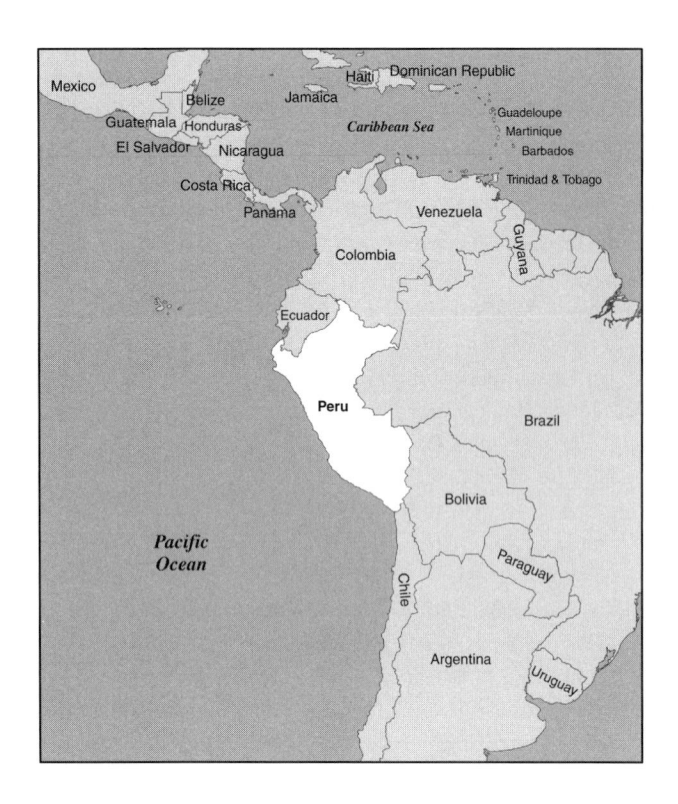

Francisco Pizarro, seeking the riches and fame discovered by Hernando Cortez in Mexico, led a small team of Spaniards, battle ready from the recent Iberian wars with the Moors, into the Tawantinsuyo or Incan Empire. A recently ended civil war, most likely precipitated by the death of the last king (Inca) by smallpox, made the "Empire of the Sun" particularly vulnerable, with many Incan nobles greeting the Spaniards as liberators.

After quickly capturing the current Inca (Atahualpa), holding him for ransom of a room full of gold, and eventually executing him, the gold-hungry Europeans soon established an "economy of plunder" through which the newly servile native populations supplied their new Spanish overlords with a tremendous flow of goods and labor. A strict racial division between the Europeans and native groups fueled this system of exploitation. Yet at the same time, Spanish rule weakened the multiple Incan-wrought ties between the myriad indigenous groups, resulting in populations reforming their previous, much more highly localized ethnic identities, although now largely dependent on the beneficence of a new Spanish overlord for protection against rivals and enemies in other areas. A class of noble elites, called *curacas,* served as intermediaries between the Spanish and natives, capitalizing on their privileged position while also attempting to soften Spanish demands and native unrest.

Throughout the next four centuries, as the European population grew, the central authorities created various means to extract more native labor. For example, the Toledo Reforms at the end of the 16th century relocated a large portion of the native populations onto small areas of marginal lands called *reducciones,* thereby heavily limiting native alternatives and concentrating the populations in more manageable areas. As the crown hauled the fantastic fortunes from the mines of Potosí in Upper Peru (contemporary Bolivia), demand for labor accelerated in the mining sector and the vast array of supporting services. Europeans even imported African slaves for the mines, adding another distinct racial group to the country.

Insurrection, Repression, and Reform

The draconian policies of the colonial period proved to be genocidal, with this "great dying" reducing native populations by at least 95%, a demographic collapse from which the country did not recover until the 1980s. Although indigenous groups sporadically acted against Spanish rule, the 18th century truly became known as the age of Andean insurrection, culminating in the rebellion led by the curaca José Gabriel Condorcanqui (a.k.a. Tupac Amaru, assuming the name of the last Inca). Inspired by Enlightenment ideals and a glorification of the Incan past, this rebellion encompassed much of the southern highlands and thousands of indigenous and other individuals until it was brutally put down and its leaders were executed in 1781. Postinsurrection, the colonial authorities intensified their rapacious policies, including eliminating the native aristocracy and executing every fifth male of sympathetic communities.

Throughout this period, colonial authorities had also attempted to maintain a strict racial hierarchy through means such as the Caste Law, which enumerated more than fifty different racial categories and their corresponding privileges and obligations. Miscegenation, however, made enforcement difficult, and the official categorization scheme did not survive independence in 1824. Nevertheless, a strong tripartite system emerged, with Whites maintaining the highest stratum, Indigenous Peoples maintaining the lowest stratum, and the vast majority of in-between categories collapsing into the rubric of mestizo. The Black category also survived independence, with its populations generally concentrated in coastal cities (particularly Lima). Blacks actually lost social standing from earlier assimilationist gains and have largely become landless laborers with few social connections or prospects of upward economic mobility.

Although Peruvian elites reluctantly accepted independence from Spain, the governing racial hierarchy actually became more acute in key ways. Elites generally accepted the new ideas about individual liberty, particularly when this applied to property regimes, but also reproduced the paternalistic aristocratic order in regard to native peoples, particularly the colonial Indian head tax (*contribución indígena*), which made up 40% of the national budget. Through "independence," then, native Andeans lost protections against land appropriation while still needing to pay taxes. Because of these changes, Whites who could successfully control large land areas—and consequently the native populations and their labor—became the major power holders, ushering in the era of the rural landlords, otherwise known as *hacendados* or *gamonales*.

Population recovery in Peru, however, occurred primarily through the ever-expanding numbers of mestizos. Although this term literally means "mixed," mestizos have enjoyed a rich and diverse cultural heritage for centuries. The hybridized label testifies significantly to their strength; nearly all peoples of the world are cultural hybrids, but only such mixed groups can successfully operate in multiple venues. By the beginning of the 20th century, mestizos began to successfully challenge the aristocratic order of White Peruvians, attempting to apply more universal notions of citizenship and thereby bring about Peruvian state formation.

Both ideologically and institutionally, however, mestizo inclusion depended on continued indigenous disenfranchisement. Indians represented the marginalized "other" against whom mestizos successfully contrasted themselves. Simultaneously, White discontent was allayed by leaving indigenous clientelism in place, with many mestizos increasingly inheriting the lucrative position of patron. The long-resisted inclusive project of nation building, then, shifted control of the countryside from the *criollo* Whites to the now enfranchised mestizos. But the native Andean populations remained caught in networks of patronage that alienated them from the larger political system.

The 1969 Agrarian Reform allegedly put an end to native dependence by redistributing the resource that fueled rural overlord power. A combination of factors, however, caused indigenous marginalization to continue. First, *gamonales* occupied crucial offices in the new government and other key links to the countryside, thereby retaining tight control over these areas. Second, the new progressive military government did not alter the clientelistic relations of the countryside but instead insinuated itself as the new patron. Despite the agrarian reform, then, from this point onward the government remained highly racialized, generally providing mestizo privilege at the cost of indigenous marginalization. As occurred in other countries such as the United States, most of the projects of this new "development" era were controlled by mestizos and used to further entrench their privileged positions.

Current Conditions and Trends

Development policies aimed at industrialization also spawned massive urbanization, particularly in Lima, which now contains a third of the national population. The White population generally lives behind high walls in exclusive neighborhoods such as Miraflores and San Isidro. Indigenous Peoples have also moved to the city in large numbers, mostly living in the shanties (*barrios jóvenes*) surrounding the city, making Lima the largest Quechua-speaking city in the world. As indigenous people proved to be the prime target of the horrible violence of the recent civil (or "internal") war, their movement to the cities accelerated. To migrate, indigenous people rely greatly on networks from their villages and largely reproduce the inequality of those home areas. But cities mostly represent a mestizo crucible, reproducing and redefining this culture through a multitude of inputs from Peru's principal geographic areas of coast, sierra, and jungle. Here terms such as *indigenous mestizos* emerge, emphasizing a connection to Peru's rich cultural heritage but largely stripped of the terrible subjugation readily associated with *Indian*.

Some pro-indigenous mobilizations, attempting to remove the derogatory connotations associated with *Indian* and assert indigenous enfranchisement in their place, exist to some degree in Peru but have never achieved a countrywide scale as they have in other Latin American countries such as neighboring Ecuador and Bolivia. In those other countries, a cultural negotiation facilitated the imposition of regressive neoliberal economic policies. Peru relied much more on a military authoritarianism that squelched most popular movements. It still relies on the 1993 constitution written by the authoritarian neoliberal government of Alberto Fujimori. A strong current of "Andean Utopia," which informed the Tupac Amaru rebellion as well as movements behind state formation, still charges the national imagination and is called on by diverse groups, including radical mestizo nationalists (*Caceristas*), coca growers, nongovernmental organizations, and internationally linked indigenous groups. In addition, many locally based groups concerned with resource extraction, environmental destruction, or even education have found some success through appealing to indigenous patrimonial rights.

Arthur Scarritt

See Appendix A

See also Latin America, Indigenous People; Peruvian Americans; South Americans in the United States

Further Readings

Cotler, Julio, ed. 1995. *Peru 1964–1994*. Lima, Peru: Instituto de Estudios Peruanos.

De la Cadena, Marisol. 2000. *Indigenous Mestizos*. Durham, NC: Duke University Press.

García, María Elena. 2005. *Making Indigenous Citizens*. Stanford, CA: Stanford University Press.

Klarén, Peter Flindell. 2000. *Peru: Society and Nationhood in the Andes*. New York: Oxford University Press.

Mallon, Florencia. 1995. *Peasant and Nation*. Berkeley: University of California Press.

Wade, Peter. 1997. *Race and Ethnicity in Latin America*. Chicago, IL: Pluto.

Peruvian Americans

The historical and contemporary experience of Peruvians in the United States is perhaps among the least known or documented of the Latina/o populations in the United States. Although most Peruvians arriving in the United States speak Spanish and are mestizos (of mixed indigenous and European descent), the Peruvian community in the country also includes those who, given their indigenous heritages and backgrounds, speak one of a number of indigenous languages such as Quechua and Aymara. Peruvian immigrants also include Afro-Peruvians, descendants of enslaved Africans, many of whom live in the coastal regions of Peru, accounting for 5% of Peru's total population of 27 million. Moreover, Asian Peruvians have also migrated to the United States and include not only Chinese Peruvians but also Peruvians of Japanese descent who, during World War II, were forcefully brought from Peru to internment camps in the United States and who chose to remain at the end of the war.

Peruvians in the United States: A Brief Historical Overview

Like other South Americans, Peruvians have been coming to the United States since the early 1800s as immigrants, exiles, refugees, temporary visitors, or permanent settlers. During the 1849 gold rush, for example, hundreds of Peruvians, primarily sailors and merchants, joined Mexicans and others in the gold mines of California, eventually marrying and settling permanently in the United States. The largest waves of Peruvians, however, began to arrive during the post–World War II period, when U.S. foreign policy, reinforcing the Peruvian governing elites' economic policies, played a significant role in shaping distinct waves of Peruvian immigration to the United States.

The first significant wave of Peruvian immigration began during the mid-1950s and lasted into the early 1970s. This wave, popularly known as the "brain drain," was a by-product of President John F. Kennedy's Alliance for Progress program and included a significant number of highly skilled middle- and upper-class professionals. The modernization of the Peruvian economy also pushed many other Peruvians, particularly youth from the lower social and economic sectors, to immigrate to the United States.

A second significant wave of Peruvians arrived during the 1980s, largely due to the country's economic turmoil as well as to the devastation of the 1980–1992 civil war waged between the Peruvian state and the Shining Path (*Sendero Luminoso*), first in Peru's Andean region and later in the capital city of Lima. Indeed, a 1989 article in *The New York Times*, describing the emigration from various Latin American countries to the United States, singled out the Peruvian case as the "most dramatic." The article title—"Starting Over, the Ex-Peruvian Way"—poignantly captured the despair and loss of a sense of national belonging that resulted from the downward spiral of poverty for growing numbers of people. Indeed, by the end of the 1980s, abandoning Peru was no longer limited to those who could afford it; rather, it came to be seen as a rational solution by whoever could find the barest means for doing so. By 1990, there were officially 175,035 Peruvians in the United States.

Since the mid-1990s, another significant wave of immigration has increased Peruvians' official numbers by 41.5% to 247,600. (Because of undocumented migration, the actual figure is likely much higher.) Made up chiefly, albeit not exclusively, of highly educated and wealthy professionals and upper-class Peruvians, these immigrants have settled primarily in South Florida.

Indeed, although concentrated primarily in the New York/New Jersey area, Peruvians today can be found throughout the United States, including California, Florida, Illinois, Texas, Georgia, Utah, Wyoming, and Washington, D.C.

What accounts for the differences between Peruvians arriving in the United States during the early 21st century and those who arrived during earlier waves is a marked change in the immigrants' relationship with Peru and their corresponding attitudes toward their host society. Peruvians arriving today are increasingly looking to the United States as a potential home. The expectation of returning to live in Peru one day is no longer the forgone conclusion that it once was. Moreover, the fact that the Peruvian government has recognized dual citizenship since 1980 has also contributed toward many Peruvians' decisions to establish permanent residence in the United States without forfeiting Peruvian nationality.

A number of Peruvian writers have been documenting the past and present experiences of Peruvians in the United States through autobiographical memoirs, poetry, novels, and documentary-style narratives. In 2001, Marie Arana explored the meaning of hybrid belonging in both the United States and the highlands of Peru in her autobiography *American Chica: Two Worlds, One Childhood.* Eduardo González Viaña described the experience of Peruvians and other Latinos in the United States in short story collections such as *American Dreams* (2005). Other Peruvian writers and poets living and writing in the United States include the award-winning Jewish Peruvian writer Isaac Goldenberg, Daniel Alarcón, Julio Ortega, Cecilia Bustamante, and Fredy Amilcar Roncalla.

Social, Cultural, and Economic Integration in U.S. Society

Peruvians are currently found at all occupational levels, both white- and blue-collar, in the United States. The time of arrival and the particular sociracial and class demographics of each immigrant wave have significantly affected the kinds of organizations Peruvians have created in the United States. Notwithstanding obstacles to community building such as the immigrants' anticipation of return, class differences, and overriding local and regional (rather than national) loyalties, the Peruvian anthropologist Teofilo Altamirano recorded at least forty registered Peruvian associations in various states during the late 1980s, particularly in California, Chicago, the New York/New Jersey area, and Washington, D.C. Events sponsored by Peruvian associations include religious processions such as the Señor de los Milagros procession, Independence Day celebrations, and other festivities. Peruvian food, crafts, music, and dance are always part of these events.

During the 1980s, wealthier Peruvians began to organize national conventions around the United States to discuss Peruvian national issues and matters related to the Peruvian community's experience in the country. Peruvian indigenous immigrants in the United States have also been creating associations to bridge the gap between the country and their homeland communities. They often re-create their traditional religious celebrations and festivities in various parts of the Northeast, and these events sometimes have included bringing religious icons from their villages in the Peruvian Andes.

More recently, Quechua Indians have also begun to forge stronger ties with various Native American nations in the United States, such as the Iroquois, Lakota, and Cheyenne, adopting a pan-American Indian identity and contributing toward the growing dialogue among Indians in the western hemisphere. Thus, while working toward integrating themselves in their new U.S. society, Peruvians of all ethnic and class backgrounds have also found various means of maintaining links to local, regional, and national Peruvian society.

Suzanne Oboler

See Appendix A

See also Hispanics; Immigrant Communities; Immigration, U.S.; Latin America, Indigenous People; Native Americans; Peru; South Americans in the United States; Transnational People

Further Readings

Altamirano, Teófilo. 1990. *Los que se fueron: Peruanos en Estados Unidos.* Lima, Peru: Pontificia Universidad Católica del Perú.

Berg, Ulla D. and Carla Tamagno. 2006. "El Quinto Suyo: Conceptualizing the 'Peruvian Diaspora' from above and below." *Latino Studies* 4(3):258.

Bourricaud, Francois. 1975. "Indian, Mestizo, and Cholo as Symbols in the Peruvian System of Stratification." Pp. 350–387 in *Ethnicity: Theory and Experience,* edited by Nathan Glazer and Daniel P. Moynihan. Cambridge, MA: Harvard University Press.

Higashide, Seiichi. 2000. *Adiós to Tears: The Memoirs of a Japanese-Peruvian Internee in U.S. Concentration Camps 2000* (with a foreword by C. Harvey Gardiner). Seattle: University of Washington Press.

Oboler, Suzanne. "South Americans." In *The Oxford Encyclopedia of Latinos and Latinas in the United States,* vol. 4, edited by Suzanne Oboler and Deena J. Gonzalez. New York: Oxford University Press.

Riding, Alan. 1989. "Starting Over, the Ex-Peruvian Way." *The New York Times,* January 19, A4.

Roncalla. Fredy Amilcar. "Indians, South American." In *The Oxford Encyclopedia of Latinos and Latinas in the United States,* vol. 2, edited by Suzanne Oboler and Deena J. Gonzalez. New York: Oxford University Press.

Sabogal, Elena. 2005. "*Viviendo en la Sombra:* The Immigration of Peruvian Professionals to South Florida." *Latino Studies* 3(1):113–131.

PEYOTE

Peyote is the name given to a small cactus that grows in the southwestern United States and the northern and central reaches of Mexico. The plant, which contains natural hallucinogenic substances, the most well known of which is mescaline, is very slow growing and is in danger of extinction in the wild because of demand caused by its growing use among Native American Church groups and natives in Mexico. This entry looks at its use and related legal issues.

Historical Background

When Spaniards first came to the New World, they found peyote being used by native groups throughout what is now central Mexico. Some scholars now think, based on archaeological evidence from Mexican and Texas sites, that peyote has been used in religious rituals for up to 3,000 years in the region. After the Europeans arrived, peyote use by natives became a major controversy in Spanish-occupied territories as the Catholic Church fought to suppress its use. However, given the strong traditions surrounding peyote use in native groups and its status as a sacrament, these efforts usually succeeded only in driving practitioners underground.

Use of peyote in religious rituals spread north from Mexico well over 100 years ago, with its use diffusing first to the Kiowa and Comanche tribes in the southwestern United States and later to other Native American groups in the United States and Canada. The spread of peyote use across North America led to considerable opposition from religious groups attempting to proselytize among Native Americans as well as from local government authorities. The liquor industry also opposed use of peyote, apparently preferring that natives use its product instead of naturally occurring peyote.

The opposition to peyote use prompted some Native American groups to formally organize the Native American Church so that their peyote rituals could gain some protection usually afforded religious groups in U.S. society. The church was organized in 1885, grew slowly, and now claims more than 250,000 participants from many different tribes across North America. Practitioners in North America seldom do their own gathering of peyote because of problems of distance and the increasing scarcity of the plant in the wild. Instead, peyote is now being cultivated by some individuals who sell it to church groups and do so legally given protections that have developed for its use by Native American Church groups over the years.

Legal Issues

Peyote use has played a significant role in defining the meaning of religious freedom in the United States, particularly for those participating in minority faiths. As it became increasingly used in religious rituals across North America beginning in the mid-1800s, a "crazy quilt" pattern developed where peyote use was legal among Native American Church members in some states but not in others. The problematic nature of this pattern was demonstrated in 1990 by the famous *Employment Division, State of Oregon v. Smith* decision deriving from developments in Oregon.

In *Smith,* two members of the Native American Church who worked as drug counselors for the State of Oregon were fired from their jobs for using peyote, which was illegal under Oregon's drug statutes. The two sought unemployment benefits and were denied by the state. They then sued and won at the trial court and Oregon Supreme Court levels on due process grounds because the law had never been enforced against members of the church. However, the State of Oregon appealed to the U.S. Supreme Court, which unexpectedly ruled against the plaintiffs and, in so doing, overturned decades of jurisprudence dealing with unemployment claims and religious freedom in the United States.

This controversial decision resulted in the formation of a massive coalition of religious groups to regain the privileged position for religion in U.S. society, and this in turn led to the eventual passage of the Religious Freedom Restoration Act of 1993, which sought to reinstate the "compelling interest" test that had prevailed before *Smith.* However, this act was itself declared unconstitutional in *City of Boerne v. Flores,* a 1998 case that dealt with land use, at least as applied to local and state governmental entities.

Congress again reacted and eventually passed the Religious Land Use and Institutionalized Persons Act of 2001 (RLUIPA). This act reinstated the compelling interest test in situations where religious groups were involved in land use disputes with governmental authorities, and the act also offered protections for the religious freedom of incarcerated persons. The religious freedom of prisoners gained considerably, as demonstrated in *Cutter v. Wilkerson,* a 2005 case that upheld RLUIPA as it pertains to prisoners and thereby granted considerable religious freedom to prisoners in the United States in both federal and state facilities. The Supreme Court found that a prison providing religious paraphernalia and access to religious leaders does not privilege religious practitioners over other prisoners and that prisons' accommodation of religious practice does not constitute a federal establishment of religion. However, it is worth noting that this decision does not allow use of peyote in prisons.

After the *Smith* decision, the State of Oregon amended its statutes in the area of drug use, legalizing the use of peyote in rituals of the Native American Church. Another development after *Smith* was the rapid passage of an amendment to the federal American Indian Religious Freedom Act that was originally passed in 1978. The 1994 amendment made it clear that federal law would allow the use of peyote in genuine religious ceremonies. Congress noted that "for many Indian people, the traditional ceremonial use of the peyote cactus as a religious sacrament has for centuries been integral to a way of life." Pointing out that state laws and Supreme Court decisions do not adequately protect this practice, Congress stated that "the use, possession, or transportation of peyote by an Indian for bona fide traditional ceremonial purposes in connection with the practice of a traditional Indian religion is lawful."

Thus, the use of peyote is now accepted by the federal government, and the states must abide by this statute as well. The use of peyote has changed and spread over the centuries in North America, but now its use seems secure for Native Americans engaged in the practice of their relatively new trans-Indian religion.

James T. Richardson

See also Native American Identity, Legal Background; Native Americans; Religion, Minority; Religious Freedom Restoration Act of 1993

Further Readings

Evans, Richard and Albert Hoffman. 1992. *Plants of the Gods: Their Sacred, Healing, and Hallucinogenic Powers.* Rochester, VT: Healing Arts Press.

Irwin, Lee. 2006. "Walking the Line: Pipe and Sweat Ceremonies in Prison." *Nova Religion* 3:39–60.

Slotkin, James S. 1975. "The Peyote Way." Pp. 96–103 in *Teachings from the Earth: Indian Religion and Philosophy,* edited by D. Tedlock and B. Tedlock. New York: Liveright Press.

Stewart, Omer Call. 1987. *Peyote Religion: A History.* Norman: University of Oklahoma Press.

PIPELINE

The term *pipeline* has been used over the past several decades in the education and career domain, and especially in higher education, to describe the process of training and preparing workers, professionals, and leaders in varied fields and industries. *Pipeline* refers to the route students follow from early childhood through postsecondary education and involves educational and socialization processes where intellectual potential and skills are maximized to provide career-building opportunities to future generations of experts in a particular field. The term can refer to all students and workers, but today it is often used in discussions of increasing opportunities for traditionally underrepresented groups, which during recent decades have included both women and members of racial/ethnic minority groups. This entry examines the pipeline in that context.

"Leaks" in the Pipeline

It is not always clear how to measure pipeline success, particularly for members of underrepresented racial/ethnic groups, and timely and accurate data collection and analysis can be challenging. Data are usually available on recruitment numbers such as new admissions, graduation or degree completion rates, attrition rates prior to completion, and (eventually) professional positions attained. Studies of pipeline success or failure generally also involve discussions of higher education expectations and/or aspirations on the part of individual students, levels of educational attainment, academic self-concept, and environmental factors that influence them such as family, school, and neighborhood resources. Because these factors are mitigated by class, race, and gender in the United States, the pipeline discussion involves a complex web of issues of interest to sociologists and other social scientists.

Race and ethnicity have been a common focus with regard to both building and reinforcing pipelines and overcoming historical barriers related to discrimination. There is little doubt that individuals most at risk for "leaking" from the pipeline are those from low-income households and racial/ethnic minority groups. Among the issues these students must address are financial constraints and family pressures, discrimination, and social isolation as well as documented gaps in expectations of academic achievement as well as the perceived adequacy of preparation for the next steps in education. Other common barriers to advancement and success for minority students and workers include stereotypes about roles and abilities, the development of talent and experience through formal processes, and a scarcity of mentors and personal networks.

Leakages, or cracks, in the educational and professional pipeline occur at every stage, beginning as early as primary education and continuing through high school, college, graduate school, and the hiring process for jobs. As the level of education goes up, the number of individuals who hold degrees decreases because of the requirements for entry, and the percentage of underrepresented minorities who finish with those degrees also drops.

Challenges to Success

Efforts to address leakages in the pipeline have sometimes been a source of controversy and political debate, particularly those involving affirmative action and other strategies that involve preferences for underrepresented people. Many of the affirmative action programs that addressed diversity in educational and employment opportunities initially took hold during the 1970s on the heels of the Civil Rights Movement of the 1950s and 1960s and increased public attention to past barriers.

In the field of education, those interested in greater representation of underrepresented groups and supporters of affirmative action believe that access to education has traditionally been the means for people to improve their life chances. They often focus on opportunities for racial/ethnic minorities in graduate school, although high school completion and college access and enrollment are obvious prerequisites to graduate study. Opponents of race-based programs argue that enough progress has been made over the past 30 years that special efforts at producing and maintaining diversity in the pipeline are no longer needed. Some also argue that remaining inequalities of opportunity are based on broader factors, such as family income and geography, and that these factors must be addressed first.

In recent related cases, the U.S. Supreme Court decided on two separate but parallel cases at the University of Michigan. At the university's law school, in 2003 the justices ruled in *Grutter v. Bollinger* that it is, in fact, admissible for academic institutions to use race as a criterion for admissions. This was seen as a victory for efforts to have numbers in fields and industries more accurately reflect the demographics of the nation at large. However, at the same time, in *Gratz v. Bollinger*, the justices struck down the affirmative action policy for undergraduate admissions that awarded extra points for being a member of a minority group on a larger rating scale used for student selection.

Overall, there continue to be a number of structural and individual challenges and barriers to pipeline success. On the legal front, statewide constitutional amendments opposing affirmative action, such as

Proposition 209 in California during the late 1990s and (more recently) Proposal 2 in Michigan, have won a majority of votes in their respective states and have added to the debate about the need for programs that preference race as a factor in school admissions on the grounds that such programs maintain a critical mass of minority students and, therefore, a fully diverse educational environment.

Another significant debate in pipeline discussions deals with issues of maintaining standards of entry and perceived qualifications necessary for success, such as test scores and other performance metrics, versus addressing the larger overall need to diversify fields and industries to keep pace with congruent demographic changes with regard to race and ethnicity in the U.S. population. According to projections from the 1996 U.S. Census, the White population, the largest of the five racial/ethnic groups, is projected to be the slowest growing during the 1995 to 2025 projection period, with the Black population being the second slowest growing, followed by the Native American population, the Hispanic population, and the Asian population.

Renewed Efforts in Educational Settings

Much of the attention to pipeline issues has focused on science and engineering (including computer science and medicine) along with the professoriate (particularly in the humanities and social sciences), teacher training, health care training, law education, and business schools (to address diversity and representation in corporate leadership).

The National Science Foundation's Alliance for Graduate Education and the Professoriate (AGEP) program is intended to significantly increase the number of students receiving doctoral degrees in the sciences, technology, engineering, and mathematics (STEM), with special emphasis on underrepresented populations. Its specific objectives are to develop and implement innovative models for recruiting, mentoring, and retaining minority students in STEM doctoral programs and to develop effective strategies for identifying and supporting underrepresented minorities who want to pursue academic careers. At the graduate school level, the Council of Graduate Schools, with financial support from the Pew Charitable Trusts, introduced the Preparing Future Faculty program during the 1990s to address preparedness for the range of academic careers—at research universities, liberal arts colleges, and community colleges.

In teacher education, schools are becoming more diverse, but there is concern that overall the teaching workforce is moving in the opposite direction. Some suggest opening the pipeline to students of color by introducing teaching as a career choice as early as possible. The academy and professoriate are unique settings in some ways because once someone has earned a terminal degree, the issues of success and retention may start to take on different meanings. Tenure and promotion become the eventual career goals, and although the official mechanisms take place at an arguably higher level, the challenges of discrimination, isolation, and other pressures remain.

In health care, increasing the number of minority health care providers is commonly proposed as one solution for eliminating health disparities between minority groups and the mainstream population. Increasing minority nursing research opportunities, for example, is seen as a possible way to increase patient–provider concordance and to improve the quality of care and level of patient satisfaction.

Particular efforts have been made by disciplinary associations, federal agencies, colleges and universities, individual workplaces, and higher education groups to address pipeline barriers for historically underrepresented groups. At the high school to college transition level, the Sloan Foundation, Ronald McNair Scholars, and Mellon Mays Undergraduate Fellows Program all have provided not only financial support but also mentoring and network-building opportunities to talented minority college students at institutions of higher learning across the United States. In addition, historically Black colleges and universities (HBCUs), Hispanic-serving institutions (HSIs), and Native American tribal colleges have played an important role since their inception in providing a unique environment for minority students where issues of inclusion and isolation are not as important as they would be in mainstream higher education settings. Although equality of (especially state-level) funding and equality of other institutional resources remain as challenges, there is little doubt that without these institutions a substantial number of minority students would not have had access to higher education historically and would not have access today.

Other federal agencies, such as those that comprise the National Institutes of Health, have developed pilot programs that support predoctoral and postdoctoral minority students in fields such as psychology, sociology, social work, nursing, and psychiatry. These programs house fellowships that provide both research training and mentorship from prominent researchers in the field and provide exposure to and an expanded awareness of research-intensive environments. Fellows also get exposed to successful minority researchers and scholars who can guide and help them to understand personal work patterns, career paths, and the importance of networks.

As the debate over the need for diversity-related programs continues into the 21st century, more careful attention will certainly be paid to federal legislation and the concept of affirmative action in political, legal, and educational circles. As the population of the United States grows and traditional definitions of race and ethnicity become challenged, this debate promises to manifest itself in a multitude of settings.

Jean H. Shin and Karina J. Havrilla

See also Affirmative Action in Education; Affirmative Action in the Workplace; *Bell Curve, The;* Discrimination; Educational Performance and Attainment; Educational Stratification; Glass Ceiling; *Grutter v. Bollinger;* Higher Education; Institutional Discrimination; Science Faculties, Women of Color on; Tracking

Further Readings

Allen, Walter R., Marguerite Bonous-Hammarth, and Robert Teranishi, eds. 2006. *Higher Education in a Global Society,* vol. 5: *Achieving Diversity, Equity, and Excellence.* San Diego, CA: Elsevier JAI.

Burgess, Robert G., ed. 1998. *Beyond the First Degree: Graduate Education, Lifelong Learning, and Careers.* Bristol, PA: Open University Press.

Glazer-Raymo, Judith. 2001. *Shattering Myths: Women in Academe.* Baltimore, MD: Johns Hopkins University Press.

Jones, Lee, ed. 2001. *Retaining African Americans in Higher Education: Challenging Paradigms for Retaining Students, Faculty, and Administrators.* Sterling, VA: Stylus.

Kolodny, Annette. 2000. *Failing the Future: A Dean Looks at Higher Education in the 21st Century.* Durham, NC: Duke University Press.

Lindsay, Beverly and Manuel J. Justiz, eds. 2001. *The Quest for Equity in Higher Education: Toward New Paradigms in an Evolving Affirmative Action Era.* Albany: State University of New York Press.

PLESSY V. FERGUSON

Plessy v. Ferguson (1896) is the notorious "separate but equal" case in which the U.S. Supreme Court upheld the Jim Crow segregation laws as constitutional. Although the phrase "separate but equal" does not appear in the decision itself, the doctrine it represents gave legal sanction to legalized segregation. In fact, "separate but equal" equals "Jim Crow affirmed." In *Plessy,* the Court held that "the enforced separation of the races, as applied to the internal commerce of the State, neither abridges the privileges or immunities of the colored man, deprives him of his property without due process of law, nor denies him the equal protection of the laws, within the meaning of the Fourteenth Amendment." In plain English—in black and white—Justice Henry Billings Brown kept Black from White.

This bad result was "good law" for nearly six decades. It would take the Supreme Court's decision in *Brown v. Board of Education* (1954) to overrule Justice Brown. To appreciate *Brown,* one must understand *Plessy.* If, as Justice John Marshall Harlan indicated in his dissent, *Plessy* is the worst Supreme Court ruling ever handed down (except for the *Dred Scott* decision), the *Brown* decision may rank as the greatest Supreme Court decision. This entry looks at the original facts of the *Plessy* case, traces its progress through the courts, and discusses its impact on U.S. society.

The Color Line

Although mollified by democratic language and reasoning, *Plessy* can be seen as an antidemocratic reaction to the democratic reforms of Reconstruction during the period from 1865 to 1877. As the nation's first experiment in economic emancipation and interracial democracy, Reconstruction produced three amendments to the U.S. Constitution—the Thirteenth, Fourteenth, and Fifteenth amendments (in 1865, 1868, and 1870, respectively)—which established (legally but not factually) civil rights for all U.S. residents. But the experiment failed—or, rather, the United States failed the experiment. Reconstruction was progressive, whereas *Plessy* was regressive. *Plessy,* in fact, was the ultimate deconstruction of Reconstruction. Far worse were its social and historical consequences. By reconciling White supremacy with the Reconstruction amendments of the 1860s, *Plessy* was a pact with the devil of Jim Crow, legitimizing the U.S. apartheid of systemic segregation.

The Railroad Line

In September 1891, the local activist Citizens Committee to Test the Constitutionality of the Separate Car Law (*Comité de Citoyens*) decided to challenge the constitutionality of the Louisiana Separate Car Act of 1890, which commanded that "all railway companies carrying passengers in their coaches in this State, shall provide equal but separate accommodations for the White, and colored races, by providing two or more passenger coaches for each passenger train, or by dividing the passenger coaches by a partition so as to secure separate accommodations." Violation of this act triggered a fine of $25 or imprisonment of not more than twenty days.

On June 7, 1892, Homer Adolph Plessy (1863–1925), a shoemaker in his late twenties, bought a first-class ticket at the Press Street Depot in New Orleans for passage on the East Louisiana Railroad to the city of Covington, which was in St. Tammany Parish in Louisiana. His ticket was for a seat in the first-class carriage on a train scheduled to depart at 4:15 PM. The trip was to have taken approximately two hours in its traverse to Covington, which was thirty miles to the north, on the other side of Lake Pontchartrain, near the Mississippi border. Plessy never reached his physical destination because he had a legal destination in mind. A dignified gentleman donning a suit and hat, this "Creole of color" quietly took his seat in a compartment reserved for Whites only. According to a story in the weekly *Crusader*, "As the train was moving out of the station, the conductor came up and asked if he was a White man. Plessy, who is as White as the average White Southerner, replied that he was a colored man. Then, said the conductor, 'you must go in the coach reserved for colored people.'" In effect, this scenario was staged; it was planned in advance.

Plessy could easily have passed as White. Phenotypically, Plessy exhibited none of the physical features associated with his race. Although there are no extant photographs of Plessy, the record is clear: "the mixture of colored blood was not discernible in him," as the Supreme Court acknowledged in its decision. To use the slang of the day, Plessy was an "octoroon" (a person of one-eighth Black blood)—an accident of "hypodescent" (a peculiar U.S. doctrine that classifies anyone with the least trace of African ancestry as "colored," with all of the legal and social stigmas that would attach to that classification). Facially, Plessy was White; racially, he was Black by the standards of that day. He was the perfect man to challenge the constitutionality of the Louisiana Separate Car Act. Plessy's racial ambiguity was useful as a legal strategy, providing a more poignant critique of White supremacy.

Conductor J. J. Dowling, pursuant to Louisiana law, informed Plessy that he needed to move from the "White car" to the "colored car." Typically hitched right behind the locomotive, this Jim Crow car would reek of soot and smoke. Whereas first-class seats were cushioned, colored seats were wooden. With dignified equipoise, Plessy refused. Law enforcement was summoned, and Detective Chris C. Cain asked Plessy to disembark from the train. Plessy complied with the officer of the law so as to challenge the law itself.

Drawing the Line

In Plessy's October 13 arraignment, John H. Ferguson, judge of Section A of the Criminal District Court, Parish of Orleans, presided. In the case filed as *State of Louisiana v. Homer Adolph Plessy*, Ferguson heard arguments by 55-year-old James Campbell Walker, a local Creole attorney, and Assistant District Attorney Lionel Adams, reputed to be a "crack trial lawyer." Walker agreed to defend Plessy for $1,000. Ironically, Plessy ("White as the average White Southerner") and Ferguson had the very same skin color.

After failing in his motion to have the case dismissed, Walker filed a motion to stay the proceedings so that arguments on the constitutionality of the Separate Car Act could be heard. Judge Ferguson then set a date for October 28. Meanwhile, in his October 14 brief, Walker argued that the Louisiana statute violated the Thirteenth and Fourteenth amendments. By requiring Plessy to sit in a Jim Crow car, the state was branding him with a "badge of slavery," which is proscribed by the Thirteenth Amendment (1865). The Separate Car Act also offended the Fourteenth Amendment (1868), which forbade any state's abridging the "privileges or immunities of citizens of the United States." The judge then congratulated Walker for the "great research, learning, and ability" that was evident in his brief. On November 18, Ferguson rendered his decision: "There is no pretense that he [Plessy] was not provided with equal accommodations with the White passengers. He was simply deprived of the liberty of doing as he pleased, and [is accused] of violating a penal statute with impunity." On November 22, Plessy appealed to the Louisiana Supreme Court.

Although Walker remained as part of Plessy's legal team, Albion Winegar Tourgée (1838–1905) took over as Plessy's lead attorney. After reviewing the statutory language of the Separate Car Act, the Louisiana Supreme Court in *Ex Parte Homer A. Plessy* (1893) noted a recent decision regarding the act's constitutionality: "We have had occasion very recently to consider the constitutionality of this act as applicable to interstate passengers and held that, if so applied, it would be unconstitutional because [it is] in violation of the exclusive right vested in Congress to regulate commerce between the States." However, because Plessy's destination was intrastate, the commerce clause (Article I, Section 8, Clause 3 of the U.S. Constitution) was not implicated: "It thus appears that the interstate commerce clause of the Constitution of the United States is not involved."

With Plessy's Thirteenth Amendment claim having failed, the Supreme Court then addressed his alternative pleading—his challenge of the Separate Car Act as a violation of the Fourteenth Amendment. The Court conceded that "no one has yet undertaken to submit the question to the final arbitrament of the Supreme Court of the United States." Then, in a prescient, almost prophetic pronouncement, the Court went on to say, "To hold that the requirement of separate, though equal, accommodations in public conveyances violated the [Fourteenth] Amendment would, on the same principles, necessarily entail the nullity of statutes establishing separate schools and of others existing in many States prohibiting intermarriage between the races. All are regulations based upon difference of race, and if such difference cannot furnish a basis for such legislation in one of these cases, it cannot in any."

The Bright Line

Three years later, the Supreme Court heard oral arguments on April 13, 1896, and handed down its decision on May 18. Tourgée continued to represent Plessy, with former Solicitor General Samuel F. Phillips serving as cocounsel. "The gist of our case," Tourgée declared in his opening statement, "is the unconstitutionality of the assortment [racial discrimination], *not* the question of equal accommodation." Space does not permit a detailed analysis of Tourgée's and Walker's constitutional arguments as laid out in their briefs.

In a 7 to 1 decision, Justice Brown delivered the opinion of the Supreme Court, which dismissed Plessy's Thirteenth Amendment and Fourteenth Amendment arguments in short order. On the issue of racial prejudice and the role of the law in promoting social equality beyond legal equality, Justice Brown stated, "Legislation is powerless to eradicate racial instincts or to abolish distinctions based upon physical differences, and the attempt to do so can only result in accentuating the difficulties of the present situation. If the civil and political rights of both races be equal, one cannot be inferior to the other civilly or politically. If one race be inferior to the other socially, the Constitution of the United States cannot put them upon the same plane."

A lone voice would beg to differ. Justice Harlan, in one of the most celebrated dissents in Supreme Court history, eloquently took his fellow justices to task for a fundamentally flawed decision: "But in view of the Constitution, in the eye of the law, there is in this country no superior, dominant, ruling class of citizens. There is no caste here. Our Constitution is color-blind, and neither knows nor tolerates classes among citizens. In respect of civil rights, all citizens are equal before the law." This dissent is all the more remarkable considering the fact that Justice Harlan was "a former slaveholder" from Kentucky. It is a little-known fact that he borrowed the metaphor of "color blindness" from the legal brief submitted by Plessy's lead counsel, Tourgée, who had first used the legal metaphor of color blindness as a Superior Court judge in North Carolina years earlier.

Converging racial and legal status, *Plessy*'s "separate but equal" doctrine was a "bright line" rule. First, the rule of hypodescence—that anyone with ancestry of color is automatically assigned to that color classification—sustains a binary opposition between Black and White and defines anyone with a perceptible trace of African ancestry as Black. On this basis, all Blacks must be segregated from Whites where Jim Crow laws demand it. Thus, Plessy was the perfect man to put the Separate Car Act to the test, for he exposed the absurdity of hypodescent biocentrism and its legal consequences. Although Plessy was Black by legal fiat, his skin color was as White as that of Judge Ferguson, who sat in initial judgment of him.

Hardening the Color Line

On January 11, 1897, more than four and a half years after his arrest, Plessy found himself before Orleans Parish Criminal District Court once more. On the charge of having violated Section 2 of Act 111 of the Separate Car Act, Plessy pleaded guilty. He duly paid his fine of $25. Nationally, his case was met with apathy; privately, Plessy faded into obscurity. On March 1, 1925, Plessy died. A local newspaper reported a two-line notice of his death. But Plessy is immortal as a symbol of the struggle for equality and racial justice.

In *The Souls of Black Folk* (1903), W. E. B. Du Bois wrote that "the problem of the Twentieth Century is the problem of the color line." The color line was drawn in bold by *Plessy v. Ferguson*. As Mark Elliott pointed out, *Plessy* marked the final effort by radical Republicans of the Civil War generation to establish an interracial democratic republic. By keeping the Jim Crow status quo, *Plessy* deepened the racial divide. Although the Louisiana courts differentiated between racial segregation and racial discrimination, the bottom line remains the same—race segregation is race subordination. Like cracks in glass, the "separate but equal" doctrine spread throughout the Jim Crow states as transportation segregation reinforced education segregation. Thus, it took 58 years before the *Brown* decision overruled Justice Brown's 1896 ruling to erase the color line legally, although not socially. Democracy is a process of progressive equalizing. This process is nowhere better illustrated than by the overturning of *Plessy* by *Brown*.

Christopher George Buck

See also African Americans; *Cisneros v. Corpus Christi School District;* Discrimination; Du Bois, William Edward Burghardt; Minority Rights; People of Color; Pluralism; Racism; Segregation

Further Readings

Aleinikoff, T. Alexander. 1992. "Symposium on Race Consciousness and Legal Scholarship: Re-reading Justice Harlan's Dissent in *Plessy v. Ferguson*—Freedom, Antiracism, and Citizenship." *University of Illinois Law Review* 1992:961–977.

Boxill, Bernard R. 1997. "Washington, Du Bois, and *Plessy v. Ferguson*." *Law and Philosophy* 16:299–330.

Brown v. Board of Education, 347 U.S. 483 (1954).

Dred Scott v. Sandford, 60 U.S. (19 How.) 393 (1857).

Elliott, Mark. 2001. "Race, Color Blindness, and the Democratic Public: Albion W. Tourgée's Radical Principles in *Plessy v. Ferguson*." *Journal of Southern History* 67:287–330.

Ex Parte Homer A. Plessy, 11 So. 948 (La. 1893).

Fireside, Harvey. 2004. *Separate and Unequal: Homer Plessy and the Supreme Court Decision that Legalized Racism.* New York: Carroll & Graf.

Golub, Mark. 2005. "*Plessy* as 'Passing': Judicial Responses to Ambiguously Raced Bodies in *Plessy v. Ferguson.*" *Law and Society Review* 39:563–600.

Harris, Cheryl I. 2004. "The Story of *Plessy v. Ferguson:* The Death and Resurrection of Racial Formalism." Pp. 181–222 in *Constitutional Law Stories,* edited by Michael C. Dorf. New York: Foundation Press.

Lofgren, Charles A. 1987. *The* Plessy *Case: A Legal–Historical Interpretation.* New York: Oxford University Press.

Medley, Keith Weldon. 2003. *We as Freedmen:* Plessy v. Ferguson. Gretna, LA: Pelican.

Plessy v. Ferguson, 163 U.S. 537 (1896).

Roback, Jennifer. 1986. "The Political Economy of Segregation: The Case of Segregated Streetcars." *Journal of Economic History* 46:893–917.

Wisdom, John Minor. 1996. "*Plessy v. Ferguson*—100 Years Later." *Washington and Lee Law Review* 53(1):9–20.

PLURALISM

Pluralism often implies the acceptance of social diversity as a positive cultural influence. Whereas diversity is a demographic fact, pluralism is more often an attitude about the positive value of diversity in a society that is informed by a democratic ideology of egalitarianism. Significantly, there are those who oppose it—some within the dominant culture because of fears of contamination and others within traditionally marginalized communities because of fears about the hegemonic power of the dominant culture in assimilating all peoples and eliminating cultural distinctiveness. This entry looks at the history and current status of pluralism in the United States.

Beginning With Religion

In the United States, pluralism was originally understood in religious terms and implied an acceptance of the variety of Protestant denominations. Even though the population of the early states was not homogeneous, that diversity had little impact on notions of pluralism; those from beyond the dominant culture were considered to be inferior and were excluded from society. This meant that nascent concepts of pluralism were informed by the diversity within a mostly Protestant male-dominant culture of European descent. Early political arrangements reinforced the status quo regardless of legal rhetoric and served as the gatekeepers of the right to participate in public culture.

Nonetheless, expanding religious diversity before and after the American Revolution—first and most noticeably within Protestantism, but later including Roman Catholicism and Judaism—led to increased demands for inclusion in the public sphere and the eventual transformation in the laws limiting participation. Religious diversity expanded dramatically during the two revival periods often identified as the Great Awakening (roughly the 1730s to the 1750s) and the Second Great Awakening (roughly the 1810s to the 1830s). The second revival period, in particular, coincided roughly with the presidency of Andrew Jackson and contributed significantly to the populist nature of U.S. religious diversity. Not surprisingly, this expansion represented a challenge to the dominant Protestant establishment that had been in place since before the American Revolution. The period only barely preceded a period of significant Roman Catholic immigration, and by the 1840s, although there were more Protestants than Catholics in the United States, the Roman Catholic Church had become the single largest religious denomination in the country.

The middle decades of the 19th century also marked a period of increased resistance to both diversity and pluralism on several fronts. Even before the Civil War, anti-immigration advocates sought to limit the ethnic definition of *American* to those of Anglo-Saxon descent and to increase restrictions on immigrants from other parts of the world. Initially, much of the energy was directed toward Irish immigrants, but by the end of the 19th century, the opposition would expand to include immigrants from Central, Eastern, and Southern Europe, resulting in a near cessation of immigration during the early years of the 20th century.

After the Civil War, segregation advocates fought to protect the privilege of Americans of European descent through "Jim Crow" laws such as gerrymandering and voting restrictions. Still others sought to protect the religious definition of *American* as Protestant, placing legal and then social restrictions on non-Protestants, particularly Catholics (who were kept out of elected office in some states into the 1890s) and Jews (who were barred from some hotels and other accommodations well into the 20th century).

An Expanded Scope

The acceptability of pluralism advanced significantly since the middle decades of the 20th century. The expanded scope of the First Amendment (made possible by broadened interpretations of the Fourteenth Amendment) meant that individuals could expect federal protection while pursuing their right to free speech, press, and association as well as religious liberty, bringing greater diversity (of identity as well as ideology) into the public sphere. Military service during World War II not only integrated soldiers from different ethnic and religious neighborhoods—often for the first time, Catholic, Protestant, and Jewish soldiers encountered each other in training or in combat—but also integrated those from different racial communities, thanks in large part to the integration of the army—de jure by President Harry S. Truman in 1948 and de facto by the early 1950s.

On the "homefront," the massive relocation of African Americans during the war—from southern rural areas to the northern and midwestern industrialized areas—and of the White American middle class after the war—from ethnic neighborhoods in the cities to generally economically determined suburbs—increased diversity and, with it, notions of pluralism in the country's metropolitan areas. By the 1970s, the various civil rights movements (for African Americans, gay men and lesbians, Latinas/os, Native Americans, and women) and the ubiquitous media (particularly television and film) increased the visibility of historically marginalized communities, slowly bringing them into the lives of the dominant culture. The reorganization of U.S. religion—first during the ecumenical period of the 1950s and 1960s and then into the ideologically polarized period since—facilitated increased interaction across traditional religious boundaries, enabling some Protestants, Roman Catholics, and Jews to build coalitions to oppose abortion rights, for example, or to support federal funding for parochial schooling.

Changes in immigration policy also increased diversity as it broadened the pool of countries of origin for those coming to the United States, with a noticeable shift from Western Europe (which had been the dominant source through most of the 19th century) through Central, Eastern, and Southern Europe (which had become a significant contributor before immigration shut down during the early decades of the 20th century) to South and East Asia (which became significant sources after 1965). By the 1990s, Los Angeles was home to more than 100 foreign language newspapers and contained ethnic populations larger than all but the capital cities of the countries of origin; that is, the only city in the world that had more Filipinos than Los Angeles was Manila, the only city that had more Israelis than Los Angeles was Tel Aviv, and so forth. Large urban areas, although often the sites of intercultural tension, continued to be the most fertile ground for intercultural dialogue and interaction into the 21st century and provided the strongest engines for expanded notions of pluralism.

Not all of those who resisted pluralism represented the dominant culture. Elements of various marginalized groups have often viewed pluralism as cultural hegemony and resisted it as a way of preserving community distinctiveness. Religious communities (e.g., Orthodox Jews, Fundamentalist Protestants, the Nation of Islam), as well as immigrant communities, have used this strategy to define the boundaries between their own particularistic worldviews and the universalizing worldviews of the dominant culture.

Eric Michael Mazur

See also Assimilation; Gerrymandering; Immigration, U.S.; Intergroup Relations, Surveying; Melting Pot; Multicultural Social Movements

Further Readings

Handy, Robert T. 1984. *A Christian America: Protestant Hopes and Historical Realities.* 2nd ed. New York: Oxford University Press.
Hatch, Nathan O. 1989. *The Democratization of American Christianity.* New Haven, CT: Yale University Press.
Moore, R. Laurence. 1986. *Religious Outsiders and the Making of Americans.* New York: Oxford University Press.
Wuthnow, Robert. 1988. *The Restructuring of American Religion: Society and Faith since World War II.* Princeton, NJ: Princeton University Press.

POLICE

The police have the unique authority to detain, arrest, employ physical force, and use deadly force in the commission of their jobs. As agents of social control, police are commonly associated with the motto "to protect and serve" in the communities where they work. From the origin of policing in the United States, themes of ethnicity/race have been dynamically intertwined with, and continue to shape, policing. Different racial/ethnic groups have different experiences with police that are shaped by the economic, political, and social conditions in particular historical periods. In considering police and racial/ethnic group relations, the important questions to ask are "Who are the police?" and "Who are policed?"

Colonial America Through the 19th Century

Some scholars have argued that policing in the United States was rooted in the slave patrols of Colonial America. As enslaved African labor became more indispensable to the colonial economy, the landed wealthy slave owners, primarily of English descent, sought to monitor and control enslaved African labor. Slave patrols were used to guard against slave revolts, capture runaway slaves, and deter runaways. As this system grew and became institutionalized, it came to resemble the modern police force. One example is the Charleston, South Carolina, police force, which became one of the nation's largest by the early 1800s.

Socially prominent Americans of English descent shaped the formation of major U.S. institutions, often turning to England for inspiration. Historians note that the model for the modern police force in the United States was the London Metropolitan Police, which was formed in 1829. The economic and social conditions of U.S. cities during the mid-19th century were frequently chaotic. Native-born Protestants, European immigrant groups (mostly from Ireland), and free African Americans battled for their place in the U.S. social and economic system. Northern cities experienced increased urban turmoil and draft riots just prior to and during the Civil War. The formation of police forces in many U.S. cities during the mid-1800s was demanded by powerful citizens to maintain public order and stop the rioting. During the draft riots, the racial/ethnic makeup of the police officers often determined which racial/ethnic groups received police protection. Members of African American communities, for example, could not rely on the police to protect them from violent attacks by members of "White" ethnic groups.

The United States expanded its territorial boundaries throughout the 19th century and absorbed members of multiple indigenous groups as well as Mexican citizens. Raw materials essential for industrial expansion were discovered on these lands, and immigrants from Asia and Europe worked in mining, the building of communication and transportation infrastructure, and industry. Policing agencies were seen as essential to supervise and control these groups. The Texas Rangers, one of the first statewide policing agencies, was created in 1835 in large part to police the border with Mexico. Chinese immigrants experienced disproportionate surveillance and control by police enforcing discriminatory laws. In both instances, officers from White ethnic groups policed members from "minority" ethnic groups—those without economic and political power. However, "tribal" police on reservations were often composed of members from both the indigenous ethnic groups and White groups. In industrialized areas, workers from White ethnic and African American groups fought for labor rights against the owners of industry and their private police forces such as the Pinkerton Agency and the Coal and Iron Police. Local police often were sympathetic to the workers from their racial/ethnic group but not to other workers. For example, although Irish policemen were generally sympathetic to Irish workers, they were hostile to African Americans and other competing groups.

Political machines were a force in numerous cities during the latter decades of the 19th century. Members of White ethnic groups used a variety of legal and illegal means to achieve political power and meet the economic and social needs of their constituents. Political patronage became part of this strategy as political leaders appointed loyal police officers from their ethnic group. The police who owed their jobs to political patronage were more sympathetic to members of their own racial/ethnic group. However, many racial/ethnic groups were denied access to political power and could not effectively shape the agencies that policed their communities.

The 20th Century

During the early decades of the 20th century, business leaders and public policymakers, mostly of English descent, argued that police who were sympathetic to labor or who owed their jobs to political patronage were impediments to the expansion of business and industry. Police reform was a component of the Progressive movement, which sought social justice and the elimination of corruption in government. The goal of police professionalism was to create a politically neutral police force and eliminate patronage. Police agencies were to be nonpolitical and serve the entire public with better educated supervisors and officers trained to fight crime with the latest techniques and tools. The ideal police officer was to be a professional who enforced the law, fought crime, and served all members of the public.

Some scholars argue, however, that because economic inequalities and differences between racial/ethnic groups persisted, the police represented the ethnic group with economic and political power and reflected their prejudices. Because laws were not neutral and tended to uphold the existing system of stratification, they argue, police officers could not be neutral and their actions advantaged the dominant White Anglo-Saxon Protestant (WASP) group. As the 20th century progressed, members of minority racial/ethnic groups increasingly became the objects of police authority and were unable to rely on the police for protection. Furthermore, members of these groups were unable to become police officers and provide safety and security for their communities.

African Americans in the South, for example, were largely prohibited from becoming police officers, were denied police protection from attacks by White mobs and criminals, and became (disproportionately) the targets of police activities. Moreover, it has been pointed out that those who terrorized African Americans were police or those who were allowed to act by the police. Similarly, indigenous ethnic group members have generally encountered high crime rates but have been historically underserved by inadequate numbers of poorly organized and underfunded police agencies. Latino ethnic groups are historically reluctant to call the police because of historically poor relations with them.

Minority ethnic group members clashed with police at various times throughout the 20th century, and many major riots, such as those during the 1910s and the 1940s, were in response to police actions. The late 1950s and 1960s were a time of great social upheaval as minority racial/ethnic groups fought for civil rights. Police agencies at various levels of government were used to quell social discontent through the use of force. Images of police attacking African American, Chicano, and other group activists became ingrained in the cultural imagination of the time. As more and more U.S. residents witnessed violent actions by police, government commissions were organized to study and solve the problem. All concluded that police actions were indeed the cause of many riots and that most minority racial/ethnic group members regarded the police as an occupying force rather than as a neutral professional agency that protected and served them.

Major changes had an impact on policing between the 1960s and the 1980s. The U.S. Supreme Court issued multiple rulings that shaped the daily activities of police officers, and politically appointed commissions recommended many solutions, including better training of officers and citizen oversight of agencies. The hiring of minority racial/ethnic group members by policing agencies was also recommended and was seen as vital to break the domination of White racial/ethnic groups over police agencies and reduce minority group distrust of the police. Affirmative action and Equal Employment Opportunity Commission (EEOC) guidelines were put in place to ensure that police departments became statistically representative of the communities they served. Despite some early growth, African Americans are still underrepresented on police forces, and the hiring of Latino and Asian ethnic group officers has been extremely slow. Many of the changes during earlier decades have been offset by crime control public policy since the 1980s, best exemplified by the so-called "War on Drugs" that has increased tensions between police and minority racial/ethnic group members.

Current Issues

During the first decade of the 21st century, two issues affecting relations between the police and racial/ethnic groups are illegal immigration and the so-called "War on Terror." Data from several recent studies demonstrated that minority racial/ethnic group members are disproportionately targeted for police stops. Continued police profiling of African Americans has been linked to the War on Drugs, and the expression "driving while Black" refers to profiling in traffic stops. Latino ethnics are profiled, stopped, and detained by police as a tactic to combat illegal immigration, and Arab and Muslim ethnic groups are profiled as part of antiterrorist activity.

Some research indicates that members of minority ethnic groups are more likely to be arrested or to encounter disproportionate use of physical or deadly force by police officers. Members of these groups further continue to encounter resistance to their inclusion in police agencies and, therefore, have a limited ability to shape the future direction of policing. Many scholars argue that until racial/ethnic group inequalities and tensions are addressed nationally, they will continue to affect and shape policing.

Kenneth Bolton, Jr.

See also Affirmative Action in the Workplace; Civil Rights Movement; Crime and Race; Ethnic Group; Immigration and Race; Minority/Majority; PATRIOT Act of 2001; Racial Profiling; Urban Riots; WASP

Further Readings

Bolton, Kenneth, Jr. and Joe Feagin. 2004. *Black in Blue: African-American Police Officers and Racism.* New York: Routledge.

Dulaney, W. Marvin. 1996. *Black Police in America.* Bloomington: Indiana University Press.

Mann, Coramae Richey. 1993. *Unequal Justice: A Question of Color.* Bloomington: Indiana University Press.

Walker, Samuel and Charles M. Katz. 2004. *The Police in America: An Introduction.* New York: McGraw-Hill.

Walker, Samuel, Cassia Spohn, and Miriam DeLone. 2006. *The Color of Justice: Race, Ethnicity, and Crime in America.* Belmont, CA: Wadsworth.

POLISH AMERICANS

Polish Americans, numbering nearly 9 million in the 2000 census, are one of the largest ethnic groups in the United States. Immigrants from Poland, a country with an estimated population of 38.1 million people in 2007, have had experiences similar to those of the Irish and Italians, but unlike these groups, Poles have immigrated to the United States primarily since World War II.

Polish migrants needed to overcome economic problems and personal hardships just to make the journey. Once in the United States, they often found themselves assigned to the jobs many citizens did not want to do. They needed to adjust to a new language and a familiar yet different culture. And they always were looking back to the family members left behind who either wanted to join them in the United States or, in contrast, never wanted them to leave in the first place.

Like other arrivals, many Poles sought improvement in their lives, the *Za Chlebem* (for bread) migration. The Poles who came were, at different times, more likely than many other European immigrants to see themselves as forced immigrants and were often described by, and often themselves adopted, the terminology directly reflecting this social role—*exiles, refugees, displaced persons,* or *émigrés.* The primary force for this exodus was the changing political status of Poland itself through most the 19th and 20th centuries, a period that was as turbulent as were the lives of the new arrivals. This entry reviews their history in the United States.

Early Immigration

Polish immigrants were among the settlers at Jamestown, Virginia, in 1608 to help develop the colony's timber industry, but it was the Poles who came later in that century who made a lasting mark. The successful exploits of Polish immigrants such as cavalry officer Casimir Pulaski and military engineer Thaddeus Kosciuszko are still commemorated today in communities with large Polish American populations. Polish immigration did not become significant in comparison with the arrival of European American nationals until much later. Admittedly, it is difficult to document the exact size of this immigration because at various historical periods Poland, or parts of the country, became part of Austria–Hungary, Germany (Prussia), and the Soviet Union, and so the migrants were not officially coming from a nation called "Poland."

Many of the Polish immigrants were adjusting not only to a new culture but also to a more urban way of life. Sociologists William I. Thomas and Florian Znaniecki, in their classic study *The Polish Peasant in Europe and America,* traced the path to the United States from rural Poland to urban America. Many of the peasants did not necessarily come directly to the United States but instead had traveled through other European countries. This pattern is not unique and reminds us that, even today, many immigrants have crossed several countries, sometimes establishing themselves for a period of time before finally settling in the United States.

Like other White ethnic groups, such as the Italians and Irish, Polish immigrants arrived at the large port cities of the East Coast, but unlike these other groups, Polish immigrants were more likely to settle in cities farther inland or to work in mines in Pennsylvania. In such areas, they would join kinfolk or acquaintances through the process of chain migration, a potent factor contributing to immigration anywhere in the world. In chain migration, one immigrant sponsors several other immigrants who, on their arrival, may sponsor still more immigrants. Immigration law in the United States favors people desiring to enter who already have relatives in the country; having others who can vouch for them financially may facilitate this sponsorship. But probably the most important aspect of chain migration is that it means the Polish arrivals anticipate knowing others already in the country who can help them to adjust to their new surroundings and find jobs, find places to live, and even find the kind of foods with which they are familiar.

The reference to coal mining as an occupation reflects the continuing tendency of immigrants to work in jobs avoided by U.S. citizens because they paid too little, were dangerous, or both. For example, in September 1897, a group of miners in Lattimer, Pennsylvania, marched to demand safer working conditions and an end to special taxes placed only on foreign-born workers. In the ensuing confrontation with local officials, police officers shot at the protesters, killing 19, most of whom were Polish; the others were Lithuanians and Slovaks.

Polonia

With growing numbers, the emergence of *Polonia* (meaning Polish America) communities became more common in cities throughout the Midwest. Male immigrants who came alone often took shelter through a system of inexpensive boarding houses called *tryzmanie bortnków* (meaning brother keeping) that allowed the new arrivals to save and send money back

Polish family working in the fields near Baltimore, Maryland (1909). Once in the United States, Polish migrants often assigned found themselves assigned to jobs that many U.S. citizens did not want to do. Today, Polish Americans are one of the largest ethnic groups in the United States.

Source: Library of Congress, Prints & Photographs Division, LC-DIG-nclc-05421.

to Poland to support their families and eventually provide the financial means necessary to bring them over. This added to the size of *Polonia* in cities such as Buffalo, Cleveland, Detroit, Milwaukee, Pittsburgh, and (above all) Chicago, where the population of Poles was second only to that of Warsaw, Poland.

Religion has played an important role among the Polish immigrants and their descendants. Most of the Polish immigrants who came to the United States prior to World War I were Roman Catholic. They quickly established their own parishes, where new arrivals could feel welcomed. Although religious services at that time were in the Latin language, as they had been in Poland, the many service organizations around the parish, not to mention the Catholic schools, kept the immigrants steeped in the Polish language and the latest happenings back home. Jewish Poles began immigrating during the first part of the 20th century to escape the growing hostility they faced in Europe, culminating with the Holocaust. Their numbers swelled greatly until movement from Poland stopped with the invasion of Poland by Germany in 1939, and then immigration resumed again after the war.

Although the Jewish–Catholic distinction may be the most obvious distinguishing factor among Polish Americans, there are other divisions as well. Regional subgroups such as the Kashubes, the Górali, and the Mazurians have often carried great significance. Some Poles emigrated from areas where German actually was the language of origin.

Feelings about Poland and its future have served to unify *Polonia* and at time reflect the political, economic, and cultural divisions of the ancestral homeland that they are able to follow through the dozens of Polish language local and national newspapers, magazines, radio stations, and cable television news shows.

Like other immigrant groups, Polish Americans could make use of a rich structure of self-help voluntary associations that were already well established by the 1890s. Besides providing economic assistance and social networks, they also directed attention to political and ideological controversies that swirled around back in Poland. Groups such as the Polish National Alliance and the Polish Roman Catholic Union, both based in Chicago, had well over 100,000 members for most of the 20th century.

Polish Americans were not distant bystanders to the rise of the Solidarity union and democratic opposition in Soviet-dominated Poland during the 1980s. Individual Polish Americans and U.S.-based organizations provided a variety of support. This included financial support to the independent movement, humanitarian assistance, lobbying efforts to influence the U.S. government's foreign policy, and economic support to open up the world market for Poland's exports. Poland-oriented actions were not coordinated and sometimes even worked at cross-purposes; nonetheless, *Polonia*'s efforts were felt back in Poland.

Like many other newcomers, Poles coming to the United States have been stigmatized as outsiders but also stereotyped as simple and uncultured—the typical biased view of working-class White ethnics. Their struggles in manual occupations placed them in direct competition with other White ethnics and African Americans, occasionally leading to labor disputes and longer term tense emotional rivalries. "Polish jokes" have had a remarkable shelf life in casual conversation well into the 21st century. Jewish Poles suffer the added indignities of anti-Semitism.

The Contemporary Picture

Today, *Polonia* numbers approximately 9 million. Although this might not seem significant in a country of more than 300 million, one should consider that Poland itself has a population of only approximately 39 million.

The largest urban concentration is in metropolitan Chicago, with nearly 900,000 Americans of Polish ancestry. New York State actually outnumbers Illinois in total number of Polish Americans, but Wisconsin has the highest proportion at 9.3%.

Whether to support the efforts of Lech Walesa, the Solidarity movement leader, in confronting the Soviet Union during the 1980s, or to celebrate the elevation of Karol Józef Wojtyla as Pope John Paul II in 1978, Polish Americans are a central part of the global Polish community.

A small interesting segment of more recent arrivals in the United States from Poland are young men training to be priests. Unlike in the United States, in Poland there is a surplus of young men wishing to become priests. Programs have developed to attract these young priests or seminarians to the United States to function in dioceses in North America. Because Poland today is 96% Roman Catholic, most of these young men have never interacted with Protestants, much less with Jews or Muslims, and because of their long religious schooling and training in Poland, they have had little informal contact with women. The programs developed by the Roman Catholic Church help the immigrants to adjust both to Catholicism and to everyday life in the United States.

Aging Polish American communities have received an influx of new arrivals since 1989 as elections in Poland marked the end of Soviet dominance, allowing Poles to join their relatives and facilitating immigration of entire households. Poland's entry into the North Atlantic Treaty Organization (NATO) in 1999 and into the European Union in 2004 further smoothed the way for Poles to migrate westward to Western Europe and on to the United States.

Many Polish Americans have retained little of their rich cultural traditions and may barely acknowledge even symbolic ethnicity. Others are still immersed in the *Polonia*, and their lives still revolve around many of the same religious and social institutions that were the center of *Polonia* a century ago. For example, as of 2006, fifty-four Roman Catholic churches in the metropolitan Chicago area still offered Polish language masses. Although in many of these parishes there may be only one service in Polish serving a declining number of celebrants, a few traditional "Polish" churches actually still have Polish-speaking priests in residence.

Polish core neighborhoods and strips of stores proudly proclaiming their Polish connections still abound, but Polish Americans increasingly have moved into suburban communities—first to inner-ring suburbs and then out to further reaches of metropolitan centers. This migration outward from the traditional ethnic enclaves is certain evidence of upward mobility but also of growing diversity in occupations and leisure time pursuits.

During the latter part of the 20th century, some of the voluntary associations relocated or built satellite centers to serve the outlying Polish American populations. These social organizations also reached out of central cities to tap into the financial resources of suburban Poles to sustain their activities financially. Yet people of Polish descent increasingly have now made their way into the same social networks populated by Irish, Italian, and other ethnic Americans.

Among the many Polish Americans well known or remembered today are actor Adrien Brody, home designer Martha (Kostyra) Stewart, comedian Jack Benny (Benjamin Kubelsky), guitarist Richie Sambora of the rock group Bon Jovi, actress Jane Kaczmarek of *Malcolm in the Middle*, entertainer Liberace, *Wheel of Fortune* host Pat Sajak, baseball star Stan Musial, football star Mike Ditka, Senator Barbara Mikulski, singer Bobby Vinton (Stanley Ventula, Jr.), polio vaccine pioneer Albert Sabin, and director Stanley Kubrick.

Richard T. Schaefer

See Appendix A; Appendix B
See also Ethnic Enclave, Economic Impact of; Holocaust; Immigration, U.S.; Jewish Americans; Labor Unions; Lithuanian Americans; Roman Catholics; Slovak Americans; Symbolic Ethnicity

Further Readings

Bukowcyk, John J. 1996. *Polish Americans and Their History: Community, Culture, and Politics*. Pittsburgh, PA: University of Pittsburgh Press.

Duszak, Thomas. 1997. "Lattimer Massacre Centennial Commemoration." *Polish American Journal*, August.

Erdmans, Mary Patrice. 1998. *Opposite Poles: Immigrants and Ethnics in Polish Chicago, 1976–1990*. University Park: Pennsylvania State University Press.

Erdmans, Mary Patrice. 2004. *The Grasinski Girls: The Choices They Had and the Choices They Made.* Athens: Ohio University Press.

Erdmans, Mary Patrice. 2006. "New Chicago *Polonia:* Urban and Suburban." Pp. 115–127 in *The New Chicago: A Social and Cultural Analysis,* edited by John Koval, Larry Bennett, Michael Bennett, Fassil Demissie, Roberta Garner, and Kiljoong Kim. Philadelphia, PA: Temple University Press.

Jaroszynska-Kirchman, Anna D. 1996. "Displaced Persons, Émigrés, Refugees, and Other Polish Immigrants: World War II through the Solidarity Era." Pp. 152–179 in *Polish Americans and Their History: Community, Culture, and Politics,* edited by John J. Bukowcyk. Pittsburgh, PA: University of Pittsburgh Press.

Lopata, Helena Znaniecki with Mary Patrice Erdmans. 1994. *Polish Americans.* 2nd rev. ed. New Brunswick, NJ: Transaction Books.

Mocha, Frank, ed. 1998. *American "Polonia" and Poland.* New York: Columbia University Press.

Polzin, Theresita. 1973. *The Polish Americans: Whence and Whither.* Pulaski, WI: Franciscan Publishers.

Radzilowski, John. 2005. *Poles in Minnesota* (foreword by Bill Holm). St. Paul: Minnesota Historical Press.

Thomas, William I. and Florian Znaniecki. [1918–1920] 1996. *The Polish Peasant in Europe and America,* edited by Eli Zaretsky. 5 vols. Urbana: University of Illinois Press.

POLITICAL ECONOMY

The term *economy* originates from the ancient Greek words *oikos* (house) and *nomos* (law). Political economy as an independent discipline is a modern phenomenon, although some ideas may be traced back to Aristotle in antiquity and to Thomas Aquinas during the Middle Ages. It is said that Antoine de Montchrétien was the first one to use the term *political economy* in the title of a book. In his book *Traité de l'Œconomie politique* (1615), he defined the object of political economy as the management of society. Jean-Jacques Rousseau followed this tradition in his classical essay on political economy in the French *Encyclopédie* (1755). But it was with James Steuart's book *An Inquiry Into the Principles of Political Economy* (1767) and more than so with Adam Smith's book *Inquiry Into the Nature and Causes of Nations* (1776) that political economy became an independent discipline asking the question: What is the best way to manage a society?

Important Theorists

Rousseau suggested that the grand object of political economy is to show the best way to administer property in a society. He thought that the aim of a government is to protect property. The right to property is the most sacred right, and it is even more important than freedom, he held. But government should also not allow a division of population into the rich and the poor, Rousseau said, and it must do this not taking away people's property. It should also take measures to fight against the symptoms of poverty not by building hospitals for the poor, for example, but rather by securing the citizens from becoming poor. And this can be achieved, according to Rousseau, only by keeping all humans from accumulating wealth.

The issues and problems that Rousseau raised in his article draw more or less accurately the framework of the object of political economy. What is wealth? How does it come into existence? Does the accumulation of wealth necessarily involve the division of society into the poor and the rich? What is the best way to manage the wealth of a given society? How does the distribution of wealth take place in a capitalist society? What is the best way to distribute wealth? What is property? What are the forms of property? One may differentiate among various schools in political economy by looking at how they respond to these questions.

There are two classical proposals to draw a demarcation line between various schools, both of which are still relevant. The first proposal is Smith's system of political economy, which he distinguishes from the mercantile system and Physiocratic theory. The second proposal came from Karl Marx, distinguishing between classical political economy and vulgar economy.

Smith made his distinction based on the question of how various schools reply to the question of what is wealth. Smith defined wealth in terms of the annual production of a given society produced by productive labor as distinct from unproductive labor. Smith's complicated concept defined as productive all sorts of labor that are involved immediately in the production of material wealth. But this is not to say that other sorts of labor are useless or not necessary. According to Smith, the work of a doctor or a teacher, for example, may be unproductive but necessary. He also saw some modes of labor as unproductive and not necessary, for example, the work of landlords. Following this line of thought, Marx and Frederich Engels defined the work of capitalists as unproductive and unnecessary labor.

Smith differentiated between his system and the mercantile system, which was the dominating theory of political economy between the 16th and 18th centuries in Europe. Unlike Smith, mercantilists define wealth in terms of the accumulation of precious metals and other forms of money. Smith's distinction of his system from Physiocrats referred to the question what is the cause of wealth. Smith pointed to annually employed productive labor in all areas of society. So, according to Smith, productive labor as such is the cause of wealth. Differing from this assessment, Physiocrats defined only one sort of labor as productive, namely that which is related to agriculture.

In Marx's distinction between classical political economy and vulgar economy, these questions play a central role as well. But his emphasis was on whether systems of political economy are scientific or not. According to Marx, classical political economy is scientific because its proponents, primarily Smith and David Ricardo, are interested in explaining economic phenomena. Vulgar economic thought, on the contrary, is merely interested in justifying capitalism. So, as Marx saw it, John Stuart Mill was a vulgar economist because, unlike classical political economists, he regarded production and distribution as entirely separate spheres and thought that distribution of wealth takes place in the market. In agreement with classical political economists, however, Marx thought that the question of distribution of wealth is already decided in the sphere of production in the sense that the owner of the means of production (capitalist) appropriates surplus value produced by laborers.

From Marx's point of view, to come to contemporary schools of political economy, monetarism, Keynesianism, and neoclassical schools are vulgar as well. Monetarism sees wealth as being produced in the exchange process rather than in the sphere of production. Keynesianism is concerned not so much with the production of wealth as with its redistribution by markets and by the state to correct some of the symptoms arising from the gap in the distribution of wealth between the rich and the poor. Neoclassical political economy is the critique of monetarism and Keynesianism. It aims to combine classical political economy with some elements of Marx's system of political economy.

Poverty and Racism

There is a close relationship between the political economy of poverty and the conceptual development of racism. Traditionally and generally subordinated classes and poor people (and foreign nations) are thought to be inferior races of humanity. The idea that subordinated classes and foreign people were lower classes of humankind by nature was formulated by Aristotle. He suggested, for example, that slaves were slaves by nature and that people other than Greeks were barbarians. Similar ideas were formulated in modern times in relation to the poor and cultures other than European. T. R. Malthus's Social Darwinist population theory, for example, may be qualified as a modern version of the Aristotelian approach. Similarly, all sorts of social Darwinist approaches to poverty and international relations, used to justify colonialism and imperialism, are now seen to be racist—taking for granted that there are inferior and superior people and cultures.

Contemporary racist theories about society and humanity refer to cultural differences more than to nature or biology. This is to say that the relationship between contemporary racist theories and the political economy of poverty is no longer as direct as it used to be. Nonetheless, there is still a close connection. Theories of the clash of civilizations may be placed within the cultural racists' theories.

Doğan Göçmen

See also Marxism and Racism; Social Darwinism; Wealth Distribution

Further Readings

Dennis, Rutledge and John Stone, eds. 2003. *Race and Ethnicity: Comparative and Theoretical Approaches*. London: Blackwell.

Meek, Ronald L. 1967. *Economics and Ideology and Other Essays: Studies in the Development of Economic Thought*. London: Chapman & Hall.

Meek, Ronald L. 1977. *Smith, Marx, and after: Ten Essays in the Development of Economic Thought*. London: Chapman & Hall.

Williams, Raymond. 2005. "Social Darwinism." Pp. 87–102 in *Culture and Materialism*, edited by Raymond Williams. London: Verso.

POPULAR CULTURE, RACISM AND

Race has taken on significant meaning in recent history. Beginning particularly during the eras of

European colonialism and imperialism, an ideology of White superiority was spread to rationalize Western conquest, exploitation, and domination over supposedly inferior-raced peoples. Since that time, popular culture has been one of the most important tools that Whites have used to communicate racist representations of "blackness" and "otherness," particularly in the United States. In this sense, and as research has documented, popular culture is more than entertainment; it is pedagogical. Through film, television, mass media, literature, and advertising, popular culture distorts, shapes, and socially constructs a racialized "reality." Although racial stereotypes are constructed, and thus not intrinsically "real," scholars demonstrate that they exact very real consequences, not only in terms of personal attitudes toward other races but also in the material structural inequalities they support and reproduce. From hyperviolent Black thugs and Asian Indian convenience store owners to amorous "Latin lovers" and Arab terrorists, society is replete with examples—both past and present—as this entry indicates.

Black Americans

Due to the centuries-old legacy of Black enslavement and segregation in the United States, anti-Black representations in popular culture are among the most numerous and deep-rooted. Indeed, as much research documents, popular culture was critical in spreading and reinforcing the racial ideology of White superiority and Black inferiority that undergirded both oppressive systems; some of this continues to circulate today.

Minstrel shows, often credited as the earliest form of U.S. popular culture, were wildly popular during the 19th century. The typical performance was put on by a troupe of White men in burnt cork blackface makeup acting out song, dance, and comedy claiming to be authentically "Negro." Such minstrels created extreme caricatures through heavy mocking dialect, bulging eyes, and gaping lips, easily reinforcing and popularizing beliefs among their almost exclusively White audiences that Blacks were inherently lazy, happy-go-lucky, dim-witted, and subhuman.

Aside from minstrel portrayals, blackfaced caricatures such as the "mammy," "coon," and "pickaninny" were mass produced on consumer goods, including postcards, lawn ornaments, kitchen items, and children's toys (e.g., noisemakers, dolls, costumes). Similarly, manufacturers plastered the insidious iconography on virtually every type of household product available, from coffee to detergents. Indeed, the wealth of research on the topic demonstrates that such images were truly ubiquitous and have not entirely left the U.S. consciousness even today. Consider the best-known "mammy" image, Aunt Jemima, who—although "updated"—continues to happily oversee pancakes and waffles today.

Birth of a Nation (1915) was a popular anti-Black, pro-Ku Klux Klan film that received unprecedented acclaim. Through the end of the 20th century, old racial stereotypes have occasionally resurfaced among contemporary characters in film and television, even in the face of seeming progress. Black women continue to be portrayed as "welfare queens," matriarchs, or jezebels in popular culture. In mass media, Black men are often portrayed as criminals or the "gangsta" figures in popular culture and music, only slightly updated from the older image of the "buck"—the supposed big, violent, and oversexed stereotype of Black men from the past. Overall, studies document that the recycling of anti-Black images has reached new heights of global commodification, circulating problematic ideas about race, class, gender, and sexuality not just domestically but also to a global audience.

American Indians

Popular images and film have reflected and fueled the fascination of White Americans with American Indians. Historical images of American Indians include essentializing portrayals that are often contradictory—the "noble savage" versus the bloodthirsty savage. As scholars note, mythical symbols, such as feathered headdresses, tepees, and tomahawks, have homogenized American Indian groups in the White mind, erasing nuances of individuality and group-specific cultures.

During U.S. western "expansion," images of American Indian men reflected White hysteria and racial fear as Whites attempted to obtain greater parcels of Indian land. During this time, the noble savage image found in newspapers was transformed into one of a brute red man who would sexually violate White women captives. In early films, common themes included Indian duplicity, the perils of miscegenation, and the impossibility of assimilation. Formulaic "Indian revenge" plots portrayed American Indians as dog-eating savages ready to attack "pioneers" unprovoked at any given time. Similar to blackface minstrelsy, for decades Indian roles were often played by Whites donning war paint.

Contemporary struggles have centered on the use of American Indian imagery for athletic team mascots such as football's Washington Redskins and baseball's Cleveland Indians. Some scholars have argued that Whites' stubborn refusal to give up such mythologized images reflects an "imperialist nostalgia"—a sense of entitlement to define and profit from their continued use. In addition, such images deny contemporary American Indians a meaningful sociopolitical identity, relegating them instead to the "mascot slot." Struggles against the mascots have been some of the most visible and successful examples of American Indian activism, suggesting the political importance of controlling popular cultural imagery.

Asians and Asian Americans

Anti-Asian sentiment abounded during the 19th century with the mass immigration of Chinese men hired to build the transcontinental railroad. "Yellow peril" stereotypes of cunning "Orientals" and "heathen Chinee," stealing jobs and White women, flourished in radio, theater, film, and books. One sinister fictional character introduced in 1913, Dr. Fu Manchu ("the yellow peril incarnate in one man"), excited readers for half a century with diabolical plots of world domination.

Asian men's portrayals began to shift during the later 19th century, from sexually violent, often "militarized" villains toward the weak, emasculated, more comedic characters that persist today. This has stood in particular contrast to the "dragon lady/lotus blossom dichotomy" film roles reserved for Asian women who are exotically portrayed and "fetishized" as submissive, childlike, and eager for sex.

Today, researchers have directed their attention toward the "model minority" myth, which is supported by roles for both Asian women and men as overachieving students (often "nerds") who excel in technical fields in film and television. Also common are stereotypical images of dim-witted South Asian food mart or gas station owners.

Latino and Hispanic Americans

Despite being the largest ethnic minority group in the United States, Latinos are vastly underrepresented in film and television. When cast, their roles are quite similar to the stereotypical portrayals found in early Hollywood. Similar to Asian and Asian American representations, which emphasize supposed "alien" characteristics, research documents that Latino and Hispanic Americans also have been targeted in popular culture representations as threatening to Anglo-American culture and society. Gendered stereotypes of *el bandido* (the clichéd Mexican bandit in countless westerns) and harlots ("hot mamas" lusty for Anglo men) continue today in a variety of forms—in both fictional portrayals and reality shows such as *Cops* as drug-related criminals.

One common reformulation, which took hold during the 1970s and continues today, is that of *los bandidos* transformed into modern-day criminal gang thugs and drug lords. The ever-popular movie *Scarface,* featuring (ironically) the White actor, Al Pacino, as a Cuban refugee-turned-cocaine lord, is one prominent example of this phenomenon. Other contemporary Latino caricatures include the stereotypical "Latin Lover"—seductive and sensuous, he adds a touch of danger to love—and the "*doméstica,*" a Latina or Chicana housekeeper or caregiver, as portrayed most recently and famously in the television comedy *Will & Grace* via the character of Karen's maid, Rosario.

White Americans

It is significant in an analysis of popular culture and racism not only to underscore the racial themes common to portrayals of people of color but also to position the roles of Whites, particularly when they relate to people of color in popular culture. Research documents the many ways in which White-produced products of popular culture, particularly those of film and television, often selectively represent or even rewrite oppressive racial history as a way of both reifying White goodness and misrepresenting or minimizing the racial divide. Indeed, even contemporary portrayals that attempt to expose ugly racial history (e.g., *Glory, Mississippi Burning*) typically feature White messianic protagonists. Here, the pedagogical lesson is that protagonists represent White goodness, with which White audience members identify, and create a contrasting distance from the accompanying portrayals of racist Whites, represented as anomalies and individual "bad apples."

Also prevalent in contemporary popular culture created by Whites are interracial "buddy" portrayals. Films such as *Men in Black* and the *Lethal Weapon* series feature idealized partnerships between Blacks and Whites where racism never intrudes. Such formulations reinforce the idea that the United States has appropriately achieved the color-blind ideal during the post–civil rights era—what some scholars have termed "virtual integration"—while simultaneously masking the reality of persistent systemic racism.

Conclusion

Through increasing globalization, Western popular culture, complete with its racist iconography and ideology, has helped to shape beliefs about different racial groups throughout much of the world. As argued elsewhere, although popular media cannot necessarily be implicated as the "cause" of racism, neither is it "value free"; rather, it influences the real life chances of individuals and groups. Segregation, domestically and globally, has limited real interpersonal experiences between racial groups, allowing popular culture to step in and dictate the way the populace "knows" people of color—as essentialized stereotypical "characters." And although most people can recognize the overt racism of past images, many are blind to the subtle yet equally egregious forms today. Indeed, contemporary images are often simply reformations of deeply rooted racist ideologies, making a historically contextual understanding of popular culture and racism crucial.

Danielle Dirks and Jennifer C. Mueller

See also African Americans; American Indian Movement; Asian Americans; *Birth of a Nation, The;* Black Cinema; Color Blindness; Film, Latino; Lee, Spike; Leisure; Media and Race; Racetalk; Racism; Whiteness; White Racism

Further Readings

Bogle, Donald. [1973] 2005. *Toms, Coons, Mulattoes, Mammies, and Bucks: An Interpretive History of Blacks in American Films.* New York: Continuum.
Guerrero, Ed. 1993. *Framing Blackness: The African American Image in Film.* Philadelphia, PA: Temple University Press.
hooks, bell. 1996. *Reel to Real: Race, Sex, and Class at the Movies.* New York: Routledge.
King, C. Richard and Charles F. Springwood. 2001. *Team Spirits: The Native American Mascots Controversy.* Lincoln: University of Nebraska Press.
Marchetti, Gina. 1994. *Romance and the "Yellow Peril": Race, Sex, and Discursive Strategies in Hollywood Fiction.* Berkeley: University of California Press.

Noriega, Chon A. 2000. *Shot in America: Television, the State, and the Rise of Chicano Cinema.* Minneapolis: University of Minnesota Press.
Pieterse, Jan Nederveen. 1992. *White on Black: Images of Africa and Blacks in Western Popular Culture.* New Haven, CT: Yale University Press.
Vera, Hernán and Andrew M. Gordon. 2003. *Screen Saviors: Hollywood Fictions of Whiteness.* Lanham, MD: Rowman & Littlefield.

Portuguese Americans

Portuguese Americans are immigrants and their descendants from Portugal, a country with an estimated population of 10.7 million people in 2007. Portugal is officially called the Portugal Republic and includes the Azores and Madeira Islands as well as Macao, a small territory on the coast of China. Portuguese Americans identify themselves with the terms *Portuguese Americans* (Azoreans, Maderians, continental Portuguese, and all of their descendants) and *Luso-Americans* (which serves to identify and differentiate the American-born descendants of the pre-1950 immigrants from the post-1950 immigrants). According to the 2000 census, there were a total of

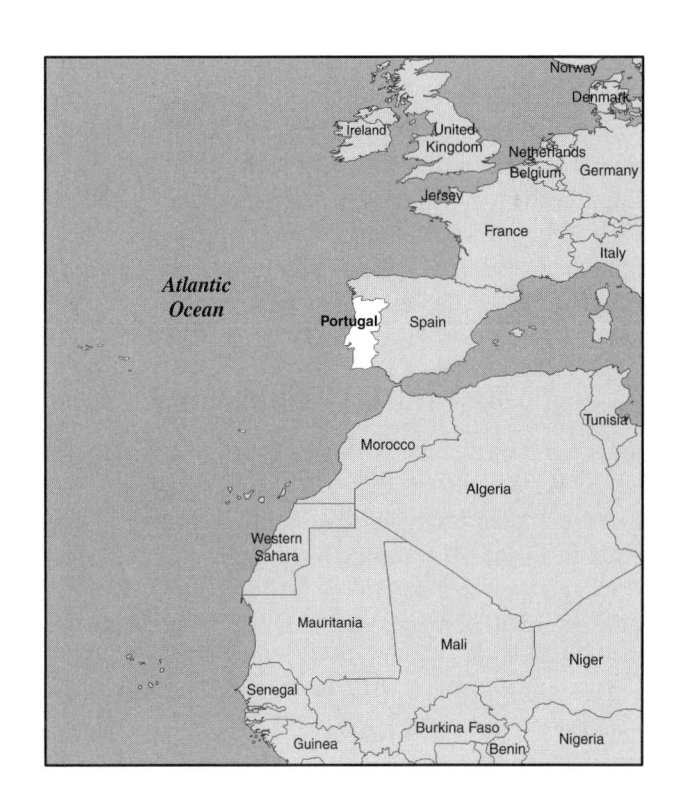

203,120 people born in Portugal residing in the United States; of these, 59.3% were citizens. This entry looks at the background of immigration from Portugal to the United States and the contemporary picture of Portuguese Americans.

Immigration Patterns

The Portuguese have a long history in the United States. Immigration and Naturalization Service (INS) data beginning in the 19th century indicate that approximately 5,200 Portuguese arrived between 1820 and 1860. A chain migration of Azorean families occurred between 1870 and 1900, bringing an estimated 63,000. This number rose significantly to 158,881 between 1900 and 1920. Many Portuguese immigrants came to United States to escape poverty and avoid military service. These immigrants settled in California and New England. Many immigrants also settled on sugar plantations in Hawai'i. They were brought by the Hawaiian Sugar Planters Association to work as contract laborers on the sugar plantations. In 1884, 11,000 Portuguese were in Hawai'i, making up 10% of the Hawaiian territorial population. After work contracts ended, many returned home, moved to California, or migrated to the cities to make their permanent homes. After 1914, immigration to Hawai'i ceased as the sugar planters recruited other immigrant groups for their source of labor.

The institution of a literacy test in 1917, the quota system of 1924, and the Great Depression slowed immigration between 1917 and 1958. However, in 1958 more than 4,800 refugees arrived in the United States because of natural disasters on the island of Faial. After the abolishment of the quota system in 1965, between 11,000 and 12,000 arrived annually until the 1980s.

Contemporary Community

During recent years, people from Portugal have sought permanent residency and refugee status and have completed the naturalization process to become citizens. From 1997 to 2006, approximately 1,300 Portuguese immigrated to the United States annually. At least 3,300 Portuguese Americans have become naturalized citizens annually beginning with 1997.

According to the U.S. Census Bureau's *American Community Survey*, there were 1,023,313 people of Portuguese national origin in the United States in 2005. In terms of geographic distribution, the top five states were Massachusetts, California, Rhode Island, New Jersey, and Florida. According to the 2000 census, 52.6% spoke English less than "very well." Their median family income was $53,500, as compared with $50,890 for the nation as a whole.

Among famous Americans with Portuguese heritage are the actor Tom Hanks, the chef Emeril Lagasse, the writer Danielle Steel, and singer/songwriter/producer Teena Marie or "Lady T" (born Mary Christine Brockert).

Jennifer M. Klein

See Appendix A
See also Acculturation; Assimilation; Deficit Model of Ethnicity; Immigrant Communities; Immigration, U.S.; Refugees

Further Readings

Anderson, James Maxwell. 2000. *The History of Portugal*. Westport, CT: Greenwood.
Department of Homeland Security. 2007. *Yearbook of Immigration Statistics*: 2006. Washington, DC: Office of Immigration Statistics. Available from http://www.dhs.gov/ximgtn/statistics/publications/yearbook.shtm
Ionnis, Maria and Benis Beganha. 1990. *Portuguese Emigration to the United States, 1820–1930*. New York: Garland.
Pap, Leo. 1981. *The Portuguese-Americans*. Boston, MA: Twayne.
U.S. Census Bureau. 2004. *Profile of Demographic and Social Characteristics: 2000. People Born in Portugal*. Available from http://www.census.gov/population/www/socdemo/foreign/STP-159-2000tl.html
U.S. Census Bureau. 2006. *American Community Survey 2005*. Available from http://www.census.gov/acs/www

PREJUDICE

Prejudice is a negative attitude toward an entire category of people. The two important components in this definition are attitude and entire category. Prejudice involves attitudes, thoughts, and beliefs—not actions. This entry provides an overview of elements of prejudice, a consideration of how prejudice relates to discrimination, a summary of theories that have been advanced to explain prejudice, and a description of the ways in which prejudice is measured.

Overview

A prejudiced belief leads to categorical rejection. Prejudice does not mean disliking a person one meets because one finds that person's behavior to be objectionable. It means disliking an entire racial/ethnic group even if one has had little or no contact with that group. A college student who requests a room change after three weeks of enduring his roommate's sleeping all day, playing loud music all night, and piling garbage on his desk is not prejudiced. However, he is displaying prejudice if he requests a change on arriving at school and learning that his new roommate is of a different nationality.

Prejudice often is expressed through the use of ethnophaulisms, or ethnic slurs, which include derisive nicknames such as "honky," "gook," and "wetback." Ethnophaulisms also include speaking about or to members of a particular group in a condescending way (e.g., "José does well in school for a Mexican American") or referring to a middle-aged woman as "one of the girls."

Prejudice and Discrimination

Prejudice and discrimination are related concepts but are not the same. Prejudice is a belief or an attitude, whereas discrimination is action. Discrimination involves behavior that excludes all members of a group from certain rights, opportunities, or privileges. Like prejudice, it must be categorical. If an employer refuses to hire as a typist an Italian American who is illiterate, it is not discrimination. If she refuses to hire any Italian Americans because she thinks that they are incompetent and does not make the effort to see whether an Italian American applicant is qualified, it is discrimination.

In exploring the relationship between negative attitudes (prejudice) and negative behavior (discrimination), sociologist Robert Merton identified four major categories. The label added to each of Merton's categories may more readily identify the type of person being described:

1. The unprejudiced nondiscriminator: all-weather liberal
2. The unprejudiced discriminator: reluctant liberal
3. The prejudiced nondiscriminator: timid bigot
4. The prejudiced discriminator: all-weather bigot

As the term is used in types 1 and 2, liberals are committed to equality among people. The all-weather liberal believes in equality and practices it. Merton was quick to observe that all-weather liberals may be far removed from any real competition with subordinate groups such as African Americans and women. Furthermore, such people may be content with their own behavior and may do little to change themselves. The reluctant liberal is not so committed to equality between groups. Social pressure may cause such a person to discriminate. Fear of losing employees may lead a manager to avoid promoting women to supervisory capacities. Equal opportunity legislation may be the best way to influence the reluctant liberal.

Types 3 and 4 do not believe in equal treatment for racial/ethnic groups, but they vary in their willingness to act. The timid bigot will not discriminate if discrimination costs money or reduces profits or if he or she is pressured not to discriminate by peers or the government. The all-weather bigot acts without hesitation on the prejudiced beliefs that he or she holds.

Merton's typology points out that prejudicial attitudes should not be confused with discriminatory behavior. People do not always act as they believe. More than 70 years ago, Richard LaPiere exposed the relationship between racial attitudes and social conduct. From 1930 to 1932, LaPiere traveled throughout the United States with a Chinese couple. Despite an alleged climate of intolerance of Asians, LaPiere observed that the couple was treated courteously at hotels, motels, and restaurants. He was puzzled by the good reception they received given that all of the conventional attitude surveys showed extreme prejudice by Whites toward Chinese.

Was it possible that LaPiere had been fortunate during his travels and consistently stopped at places operated by the tolerant members of the dominant group? To test this possibility, he sent questionnaires asking the very establishments at which they had been served whether each owner would "accept members of the Chinese race as guests in your establishment." More than 90% responded "no" even though LaPiere's Chinese couple had been treated politely at all of the establishments. How can this inconsistency be explained? People who returned questionnaires reflecting prejudice were unwilling to act based on those asserted beliefs; they were timid bigots.

The LaPiere study is not without flaws. First, he had no way of knowing whether each respondent to the questionnaire was the same person who had served him and the Chinese couple. Second, he accompanied the Chinese couple, but the questionnaire suggested that the arrival would be unescorted (and, in the minds of some, uncontrolled) and perhaps would consist of many Chinese people. Third, personnel may have changed between the time of the visit and the mailing of the questionnaire.

The LaPiere technique has been replicated with similar results. This technique raises the question of whether attitudes are important if they are not completely reflected in behavior. But even if attitudes are not important in small matters, they are important in other ways: Lawmakers legislate and courts may reach decisions based on what the public thinks.

This is not just a hypothetical possibility. Legislators in the United States often are persuaded to vote in a certain way, for example, by what they perceive as changed attitudes toward immigration, affirmative action, and prayer in public schools. Sociologists have enumerated some of prejudice's functions. For the majority group, it serves to maintain privileged occupations and more power for its members.

Theories of Prejudice

Prejudice is learned. Friends, relatives, newspapers, books, movies, television, and the Internet all teach it. At an early age, people become aware that there are differences between people that society judges to be important. Several theories have been advanced to explain the rejection of certain groups in a society, and four of them are examined here. The first two, scapegoating and authoritarian personality, tend to be psychological, emphasizing why a particular person harbors ill feelings. The second two theories, exploitation and normative, are more sociological, viewing prejudice in the context of people's interaction in a larger society.

Scapegoating Theory

Scapegoating theory states that prejudiced people believe they are society's victims. The term *scapegoat* comes from a biblical injunction telling the Hebrews to send a goat into the wilderness to symbolically carry away the people's sins. Similarly, the theory of scapegoating suggests that, rather than accepting guilt for some failure, a person transfers the responsibility for failure to some vulnerable group. In the major tragic 20th-century example, Adolf Hitler used the Jews as the scapegoat for all German social and economic ills during the 1930s. This premise led to the passage of laws restricting Jewish life in pre–World War II Germany and eventually escalated into the mass extermination of Europe's Jews.

Today in the United States, immigrants—whether legal or illegal—often are blamed by "real Americans" for their failure to get jobs or secure desirable housing. The immigrants become the scapegoat for people's own lack of skills, planning, and/or motivation. It is so much easier to blame someone else.

Like exploitation theory (discussed later), scapegoating theory enhances understanding of why prejudice exists but does not explain all of its facets. For example, scapegoating theory offers little explanation of why a specific group is selected or why frustration is not taken out on the real culprit whenever possible. Also, both the exploitation and scapegoating theories suggest that every person sharing the same general experiences in society would be equally prejudiced, but that is not the case. Prejudice varies between individuals who seem to benefit equally from the exploitation of a subordinate group or who have experienced equal frustration. In an effort to explain these personality differences, social scientists developed the concept of the authoritarian personality.

Authoritarian Personality Theory

A number of social scientists do not see prejudice as an isolated trait that anyone can have. Several efforts have been made to detail the prejudiced personality, but the most comprehensive effort culminated in a volume titled *The Authoritarian Personality*. Using a variety of tests and relying on more than 2,000 respondents ranging from middle-class Whites to inmates at San Quentin (California) State Prison, the authors claimed that they had isolated the characteristics of the authoritarian personality.

In these authors' view, the basic characteristics of the authoritarian personality are adherence to conventional values, uncritical acceptance of authority, and concern with power and toughness. With obvious relevance to the development of intolerance, the authoritarian personality was also characterized by aggressiveness toward people who did not conform to conventional norms or obey authority. According to the researchers, this personality type developed from an early childhood of harsh discipline. A child with an authoritarian upbringing obeyed and then later treated others as he or she had been raised.

Exploitation Theory

Racial prejudice often is used to justify keeping a group in a subordinate position such as a lower social class. Conflict theorists, in particular, stress the role of racial/ethnic hostility as a way for the dominant group to keep its position of status and power intact. Indeed, this approach maintains that even the less affluent White working class uses prejudice to minimize competition from upwardly mobile minorities.

Exploitation theory is clearly part of the Marxist tradition in sociological thought. Karl Marx emphasized exploitation of the lower class as an integral part of capitalism. Similarly, the exploitation or conflict approach explains how racism can stigmatize a group as inferior so that the exploitation of that group can be justified. As developed by Oliver Cox, exploitation theory saw prejudice against Blacks as an extension of the inequality faced by the entire lower class.

The exploitation theory of prejudice is persuasive. Japanese Americans were the object of little prejudice until they began to enter occupations that brought them into competition with Whites. The movement to keep Chinese out of the United States became strongest during the late 19th century when Chinese immigrants and Whites fought over dwindling numbers of jobs. Both the enslavement of African Americans and the removal westward of Native Americans were, to a significant degree, economically motivated.

Although many cases support the exploitation theory, it is too limited to explain prejudice in all of its forms. First, not all minority groups are exploited economically to the same extent. Second, many groups that have been the victims of prejudice have not been persecuted for economic reasons, including the Quakers and gays and lesbians. Nevertheless, as social psychologist Gordon Allport concluded, the exploitation theory correctly points a finger at one of the factors in prejudice, namely, the rationalized self-interest of the privileged.

Normative Approach

Although personality factors are important contributors to prejudice, normative or situational factors must also be given serious consideration. The normative approach takes the view that prejudice is influenced by societal norms and situations that encourage or discourage the tolerance of minorities.

Analysis reveals how societal influences shape a climate for tolerance or intolerance. Societies develop social norms that dictate not only what foods are desirable (or forbidden) but also what racial/ethnic groups are to be favored (or despised). Social forces operate in a society to encourage or discourage tolerance. The force may be widespread such as the pressure on White southerners to oppose racial equality while there was slavery or segregation. The influence of social norms may be limited such as when one man finds himself becoming more sexist as he competes with three women for a position in a prestigious law firm.

The four approaches to prejudice need not be mutually exclusive. Social circumstances provide cues for a person's attitudes; personality determines the extent to which people follow social cues and the likelihood that they will encourage others to do the same. Societal norms may promote or deter tolerance; personality traits suggest the degree to which people will conform to norms of intolerance. To understand prejudice, all four approaches are useful.

Measuring Prejudice

Prejudice is measured by identifying the stereotypes people use, levels of prejudice using the concept of social distance, trends in prejudice, and expressions of prejudice by members of the subordinate group.

Stereotypes

Stereotypes are unreliable generalizations about all members of a group that do not take individual differences into account. Numerous scientific studies have been made of these exaggerated images. This research has shown the willingness of people to assign positive and negative traits to entire groups of people and, in turn, to apply them to particular individuals. Stereotyping causes people to view Blacks as superstitious, Whites as uncaring, and Jews as shrewd. Over the past 70 years of such research, social scientists have found that people have become less willing to express such views openly, but prejudice persists.

If stereotypes are exaggerated generalizations, why are they so widely held and why are some traits more often assigned than others? Evidence for traits may arise out of real conditions. For example, more Puerto Ricans live in poverty than do Whites, and so the prejudiced mind associates Puerto Ricans with laziness. According to the New Testament, some Jews were responsible for the crucifixion of Jesus, and so the prejudiced mind views all Jews as Christ killers. Some activists in the women's movement are lesbians, and so the prejudiced mind sees all feminists as lesbians. From a kernel of fact, faulty generalization creates a stereotype.

Labels take on such strong significance that people often ignore facts that contradict their previously held beliefs. People who believe many Italian Americans to be members of the Mafia disregard law-abiding Italian Americans. Muslims are regularly portrayed in a violent, offensive manner that contributes to their being misunderstood and distrusted.

Do all stereotypes involve a dominant group holding ideas about subordinate groups? The answer is clearly no. White Americans even believe generalizations about themselves, although admittedly these are usually positive. Subordinate groups also hold exaggerated images of themselves. Studies before World War II showed a tendency for Blacks to assign to themselves many of the same negative traits assigned to them by Whites. Today, African Americans, Jews, Asians, and other minority groups largely reject stereotypes of themselves.

The Social Distance Scale

Robert Park and Ernest Burgess first defined social distance as the tendency to approach or withdraw from a racial group. Emory Bogardus conceptualized a scale that could measure social distance empirically. His social distance scale is so widely used that it is often called the Bogardus scale.

The scale asks people how willing they would be to interact with various racial/ethnic groups in specified social situations. The situations describe different degrees of social contact or social distance. The items used, with their corresponding distance scores, follow. People are asked whether they would be willing to work alongside, be a neighbor of, and (showing the least amount of social distance) be related through marriage. Over the 70-year period in which the tests were administered, certain patterns emerge. In the top third of the hierarchy are White Americans and Northern Europeans, held at greater social distance are Eastern and Southern Europeans, and generally near the bottom are racial minorities.

More recently, the concept of social distance has been applied to how people actually function—for example, with whom do they hang out? In 2004, sociologists Grace Kao and Kara Joyner released a study that considered the responses of more than 90,000 adolescents nationwide on an in-school survey. Among many questions, adolescents were asked to identify their best friend and later to identify that person's race and ethnicity. Most people have as their primary friendships someone of the same race or ethnicity. Whites are the numerical majority nationwide, and more than 81% of White respondents named as their best friend someone who was also White. Other racial/ethnic group members are more likely to venture outside of their groups' boundaries.

In general, the researchers also found that among the respondents whose best friend was of a different racial/ethnic origin, they were more likely to show greater social distance; that is, they were less likely to have been in each other's homes, shared in fewer activities, and were less likely to talk about their problems with each other.

Trends in Prejudice

People hold certain images or stereotypes of each other, and they also may be more prejudiced toward some groups of people than toward others. However, is there less prejudice than there used to be? The evidence is mixed, with some indications of willingness to give up some old prejudices while new negative attitudes emerge.

Over the years, nationwide surveys have consistently shown growing support by Whites for integration, even during the southern resistance and the northern turmoil of the 1960s. National opinion surveys conducted from the 1950s and into the 21st century, with few exceptions, show an increase in the number of Whites responding positively to hypothetical situations of increased contact with African Americans. For example, 30% of the Whites sampled in 1942 believed that Blacks should not attend separate schools, but 74% supported integrated schools by 1970—and fully 93% responded in that manner in 1991.

Attitudes are still important. A change of attitude may create a context in which legislative or behavioral change can occur. Such attitude changes leading to behavior changes did occur in some areas during the 1960s. Changes in intergroup behavior mandated by laws in housing, schools, public places of accommodation, and workplaces appear to be responsible for making some new kinds of interracial contact a social reality. Attitudes translate into votes, peer pressure, and political clout, each of which can facilitate efforts to undo racial inequality.

However, attitudes can work in the opposite direction. Surveys continue to show White Americans' resistance to affirmative action and aspects of immigration policy, including procedures that would allow illegal immigrants to become legal residents. Policymakers, while mindful of the support that such policies have for most African Americans and Latinos, are reluctant to alienate White American voters.

Looking at White attitudes toward African Americans, two conclusions are inescapable. First, attitudes are subject to change, and dramatic shifts can occur within one generation during periods of dramatic social upheaval. Second, less progress was made during the late 20th century than was made during the 1950s and 1960s. Researchers have variously called these subtle forms of prejudice *color-blind racism, modern racism,* or *laissez-faire racism.* People today might not be as openly racist or prejudiced as in the past in expressing the notion that they are inherently superior to others, yet much of the opposition to policies related to eradicating poverty or immigration is a smokescreen for those who dislike entire groups of racial/ethnic minorities.

The Mood of the Oppressed

Sociologist W. E. B. Du Bois related an experience from his childhood in a largely White community in Massachusetts. He described how, on one occasion, the boys and girls were exchanging cards and everyone was having a lot of fun. One girl, a newcomer, refused his card as soon as she saw that Du Bois was Black. He wrote of feeling as if he were shut out from the Whites' world by a vast veil. In using the image of a veil, Du Bois described how members of subordinate groups learn that they are being treated differently. In his case, and in the cases of many others, this leads to feelings of contempt toward all Whites that continues for a lifetime.

Opinion pollsters have been interested in White attitudes on racial issues longer than they have measured the views of subordinate groups. This neglect of minority attitudes reflects, in part, the bias of the White researchers. It also stems from the contention that the dominant group is more important to study because it is in a better position to act on its beliefs. National opinion surveys conducted during the 21st century have typically shown that African Americans are much less satisfied with the current situation than are White Americans and Hispanics.

The focus so far has been on one group hating another group, but there is another form of prejudice— a group may come to hate itself. Members of groups held in low esteem by society may, as a result, have low self-esteem themselves. Many social scientists once believed that members of subordinate groups hated themselves or at least had low self-esteem. Similarly, they argued that Whites had high self-esteem. High self-esteem means that individuals have fundamental respect for themselves, appreciates their own merits, and are aware of their personal faults and will strive to overcome them.

The research literature of the 1940s through the 1960s emphasized the low self-esteem of minorities. Usually, the subject was African Americans, but the argument has also been generalized to include any subordinate racial, ethnic, or nationality group. This view is no longer accepted. It should not be assumed that minority status influences personality traits in either a good way or a bad way. First, such assumptions may create a stereotype. A Black personality cannot be described any more accurately than can a White personality. Second, characteristics of minority group members are not entirely the result of subordinate racial status; they are also influenced by low incomes, poor neighborhoods, and so forth. Third, many studies of personality imply that certain values are normal or preferable, but the values chosen are those of dominant groups.

If assessments of a subordinate group's personality are so prone to misjudgments, why has the belief in low self-esteem been so widely held? Much of the research rests on studies with preschool-age Blacks who are asked to express preferences among dolls with different facial colors. Indeed, one such study, by psychologists Kenneth and Mamie Clark, was cited in the arguments before the U.S. Supreme Court in the landmark 1954 case *Brown v. Board of Education.* The Clarks' study showed that Black children preferred White dolls, a finding suggesting that the children had developed a negative self-image. Although subsequent doll studies have sometimes shown Black children's preference for white-faced dolls, other social scientists contend that this shows a realization of what most commercially sold dolls look like rather than documenting low self-esteem.

Because African American children, as well as children from other subordinate groups, can realistically see that Whites have more power and resources and so rate them higher does not mean that they personally feel inferior. Indeed, studies—even with children—show that when the self-images of middle-class or affluent African Americans are measured, their feelings of self-esteem are more positive than those of comparable Whites.

Because discrimination deals with actual efforts to deprive people of opportunities, it understandably receives more attention from policymakers. Reducing prejudice is important because it can lead to support for policy change.

Richard T. Schaefer

See Appendix B

See also Anti-Semitism: Authoritarian Personality; *Brown v. Board of Education;* Color Blindness; Contact Hypothesis; Discrimination; Du Bois, William Edward Burghardt; Eugenics; Intergroup Relations; Surveying Islamophobia; Labeling; Race, UNESCO Statements on; Racetalk; Racial Profiling; Racism; Racism, Aversive; Racism, Types of; Racism, Unintentional; Robbers Cave Experiment; Scapegoats; Social Distance; Stereotypes; Stereotype Threat; Sundown Towns; Victim Discounting; White Racism

Further Readings

Adorno, T. W., Else Frenkel-Brunswik, Daniel J. Levinson, and R. Nevitt Sanford. 1950. *The Authoritarian Personality.* New York: John Wiley.

Allport, Gordon W. 1979. *The Nature of Prejudice.* 25th anniversary ed. Reading, MA: Addison-Wesley.

Bloom, Leonard. 1971. *The Social Psychology of Race Relations.* Cambridge, MA: Schenkman.

Bogardus, Emory. 1968. "Comparing Racial Distance in Ethiopia, South Africa, and the United States." *Sociology and Social Research* 52:149–156.

Bonilla-Silva, Eduardo. 1996. "Rethinking Racism: Toward a Structural Interpretation." *American Sociological Review* 62:465–480.

Bonilla-Silva, Eduardo. 2006. *Racism without Racists.* 2nd ed. Lanham, MD: Rowman & Littlefield.

Clark, Kenneth B. and Mamie P. Clark. 1947. "Racial Identification and Preferences in Negro Children." Pp. 169–178 in *Readings in Social Psychology,* edited by Theodore M. Newcomb and Eugene L. Hartley. New York: Holt, Rinehart & Winston.

Cox, Oliver C. 1942. "The Modern Caste School of Social Relations." *Social Forces* 21:218–226.

Du Bois, W. E. B. [1903] 1961. *The Souls of Black Folks: Essays and Sketches.* New York: Facade.

Kao, Grace and Kara Joyner. 2004. "Do Race and Ethnicity Matter among Friends?" *Sociological Quarterly* 45:557–573.

LaPiere, Richard T. 1934. "Attitudes vs. Actions." *Social Forces* 13:230–237.

LaPiere, Richard T. 1969. "Comment of Irwin Deutscher's Looking Backward." *American Sociologist* 4:41–42.

MacRae, Neil C., Charles Stangor, and Miles Hewstone. 1996. *Stereotypes and Stereotyping.* New York: Guilford.

Merton, Robert. 1949. "Discrimination and the American Creed." Pp. 99–126 in *Discrimination and National Welfare,* edited by Robert M. MacIver. New York: Harper & Row.

Merton, Robert. 1968. *Social Theory and Social Structure.* New York: Free Press.

Park, Robert E. and Ernest W. Burgess. 1921. *Introduction to the Science of Sociology.* Chicago, IL: University of Chicago Press.

Powell-Hopson, Darlene and Derek Hopson. 1988. "Implications of Doll Color Preferences among Black Preschool Children and White Preschool Children." *Journal of Black Psychology* 14:57–63.

Schaefer, Richard T. 1986. "Racial Prejudice in a Capitalist State: What Has Happened to the American Creed?" *Phylon* 47:192–198.

Schaefer, Richard T. 1996. "Education and Prejudice: Unraveling the Relationship." *Sociological Quarterly* 37:1–16.

Schaefer, Richard T. 2008. *Racial and Ethnic Groups.* 11th ed. Upper Saddle River, NJ: Prentice Hall.

Prisons

By the turn of the 21st century, the United States had the highest incarceration rate of any industrialized nation in the world. Equally troublesome was the overrepresentation of Blacks and Hispanics in U.S. prisons. These concerns, as well as others, induced heated debate among scholars and politicians across a range of social problems associated with the U.S. criminal justice system. This entry briefly introduces some of most pressing dilemmas emerging from the U.S. penile system. In particular, it discusses the aims and effectiveness of prisons, demographic distinctions within the prison population, competing explanations of the sources of racial disparities in criminality, and policy prescriptions for reducing racial differences in imprisonment.

The Purpose of Prisons

The U.S. criminal justice system is an interacting system composed of law enforcement, criminal courts, and correctional facilities. Whereas these institutions and organizations all serve particular purposes, prisons seek to realize four specific goals: to act as a *deterrent* among individuals considering delinquent activity, to *isolate/incapacitate* offenders from the general public, to *rehabilitate* offenders so as to prevent future transgressions, and to *punish* offenders for prior offenses.

Research regarding the effectiveness of these goals has been beset by conceptual and methodological complications. For example, studies are inhibited by federal and state variations in criminal laws and procedures as well as by the fact that many crimes go unreported or do not lead to arrests. Moreover, the void of diverse data sources and measurement problems limit researchers' ability to assess motivations among nonoffenders, one-time offenders, and career offenders as well as other important assumptions about the sources of delinquent activity.

Nevertheless, existing studies provide limited support for the success of deterrence techniques. In particular, these approaches appear to be most successful when the certainty of arrest and incarceration is high. Rehabilitation techniques include mental health treatment (e.g., psychotherapy, psychotropic medication, vocational/educational training) and specific offender programs (e.g., violent, gang, sexual). In addition to variation in the quality and availability of such programs, studies are unable to determine why certain treatments are more or less effective for certain offenders than for others.

The death penalty is the most severe punishment used in the criminal justice system. Currently, more than two-thirds of all states have capital punishment statutes. Lethal injection is the most common method of execution, followed by electrocution and lethal gas. Hanging and firing squads remain permissible in some states. Overall, studies have shown that the death penalty fails to deter criminal activity; however, its supporters emphasize its effectiveness as a form of punishment and retribution.

The Prison Population

Data from the *Sourcebook of Criminal Justice Statistics* and U.S. Bureau of Prisons indicates that the total estimated corrections population is approaching 7 million. This number includes offenders in prisons (state and federal) and jails as well as those on probation or parole. In 2006, the racial composition of federal prisons was as follows: Whites (56.4%), Blacks (40.2%), Hispanics (31.5%, which can be of any race), Asians (1.7%), and Native Americans (1.7%). Women represented 6.7% of incarcerated offenders. It is important to note that the distribution of offenders in state prisons and local jails closely matched this distribution, although there are fewer Hispanics (15.0%) and more women (12.7%) in jails.

In 2006, drug offenders represented 53.6% of all federal prisoners, followed by offenders incarcerated for weapons/explosives/arson (14.1%) and immigration-related crimes (10.7%). Contrary to public opinion, offenders incarcerated for robbery (5.6%) and other violent offenses (including murder, assault, and sex) represent a relatively small percentage of the total prison population. So far as recidivism is concerned, in 1994 (this year contains the most recent and comprehensive data concerning this topic), many offenders with a prior arrest (93.1%), conviction (81.4%), or prison term (43.6%) completed their sentences in correctional facilities; of offenders released during this same year, 18.6% were likely to return to prison within 3 years.

There are high percentages of inmates with substance use and mental illness in the criminal justice system. In 2002, 66.0% of incarcerated offenders reported regular alcohol use and 34.5% reported drinking at the time of their offense. Approximately 57.6% reported using marijuana at least once a week for a month prior to their arrest, and 13.6% reported using it at the time of their offense. Approximately 30.5% of inmates reported using crack or powder cocaine regularly, and 10.6% reported using it at the time of their offense.

Regarding mental illness, in 2000, one in eight inmates in state prisons was enrolled in mental health therapy or counseling, and one in ten inmates in such facilities received psychotropic medications. For many criminal justice officials, these findings provide at least provisional support for the possibility that many inmates are improperly diagnosed or mistreated for mental health symptoms.

Racial Disproportionality

As stated earlier, Blacks and Hispanics are overrepresented across various aspects of the criminal justice system. Whereas some researchers maintain that racial discrimination explains these disparities, others conclude that differential offending patterns justify why minorities are disproportionately imprisoned. For example, in 2004, Blacks were involved in 53.6% of aggravated robberies, 47.7% of murders and nonnegligent manslaughters, and 32.2% of forcible rapes. (The U.S. Census Bureau does not keep data on Hispanics because this group is considered to be an ethnic group rather than a racial group.) For many scholars and politicians, these statistics suggest that the criminal justice system, irrespective of race, is correctly identifying and imprisoning the most dangerous criminals in our society.

Moreover, a majority of studies indicate that racial differences in offending disappear after statistical models account for an offender's previous criminal record. This finding suggests that racial discrimination does not drive the disparity in racial/ethnic incarceration rates. Consequently, many researchers have begun to question whether racism affects racial differences more *indirectly* in the criminal justice system.

For example, by the early 1980s, shifts in federal drug enforcement policy enacted a "War on Drugs" that affected minorities unevenly. In particular, the concerted attempt to purge crack cocaine from the country's central cities unduly focused on inner-city Black communities while largely overlooking drug use in predominantly White suburbs. This concentration on narcotics and street crimes was buttressed by the perception that government officials needed to be "tough on crime." Thus, during this time, there was an increase in state and federal funds for building prisons. The funds were necessary for accommodating the growing number of inmates receiving harsher penalties as well as the increasing number of juveniles being tried as adults. For many researchers, these events (as well as others) explain how racial discrimination fostered the differential enforcement of law that more circuitously explains why Blacks and Hispanics are overrepresented in the criminal justice system.

The implications of this racial discrepancy are severe. Blacks in particular are more likely to be arrested, charged, and convicted of capital crimes. Moreover, Blacks who murder Whites are more likely to be sentenced to death than are Blacks who murder other Blacks. Finally, because Blacks are less likely than Whites to have their death sentences commuted to life in prison, they are also overrepresented in both death sentences and executions.

Policy Prescriptions

Advocacy groups seeking to ameliorate these disparities advance a range of policies for reducing racial differences in the criminal justice system. First, many pundits call for racially balanced law enforcement. Examples consistent with this approach include the abolition of racial profiling and the establishment of national guidelines for establishing bail, criminal charges, jury selection, and sentencing. Second, social scientists in particular call for government policies aimed at reducing socioeconomic inequality. The results of many studies have demonstrated the link between criminality and low socioeconomic position. Thus, because Blacks and Hispanics suffer disproportionately from poverty, many scholars contend that access to viable employment, for example, can reduce delinquency among racial/ethnic minorities. Other reforms include supporting inmates' transition back into society (subsequent to their release) through placement in substance abuse, mental health, employment, and/or housing-related programs.

Jason Eugene Shelton and Sarah Spain

See also Crime and Race; Criminal Processing; Drug Use; Incarcerated Parents; Victimization

Further Readings

Beck, Allen and Laura Maruschak. 2001. *Mental Health Treatment in State Prisons, 2000.* Washington, DC: U.S. Department of Justice, Office of Justice Programs.

Pastore, Ann and Kathleen Maguire, eds. n.d. *Sourcebook of Criminal Justice Statistics.* 31st ed. Retrieved from http://www.albany.edu/sourcebook

Reiman, Jeffrey. 2004. *The Rich Get Richer and the Poor Get Prison.* Boston, MA: Allyn & Bacon.

Sampson, Robert and Janet Lauritsen. 1997. "Racial and Ethnic Disparities in Crime and Criminal Justice in the United States." Pp. 311–374 in *Ethnicity, Crime, and Immigration,* vol. 21, edited by Michael Tonry. Chicago, IL: University of Chicago Press.

Tonry, Michael. 1995. *Malign Neglect: Race, Crime, and Punishment in America.* New York: Oxford University Press.

Wilbanks, William. 1987. *The Myth of a Racist Criminal Justice System.* Monterey, CA: Brooks/Cole.

Web Sites

Federal Bureau of Prisons: http://www.bop.gov/news/quick.jsp

PRIVILEGE

In common parlance, *privilege* is defined as rights or immunities granted as a peculiar benefit, advantage, or favor. Although it retains that meaning, privilege has a more specific use in the recent literature, where it denotes the advantages held by a dominant group in society. In this view, privilege is the flip side of oppression. Whereas oppression confines and limits one's opportunities, privilege confers power, dominance, resources, and rewards. Contemporary scholarship argues that everyone is shaped by some combination of interacting social categories (e.g., race/ethnicity, gender, class, sexual orientation), and everyone experiences (on both the individual and collective levels) varying degrees of privilege and oppression depending on her or his social location or place in society. These scholars argue that examining oppression reveals only half of the picture; privilege and oppression operate hand in hand, and one cannot exist without the other. This entry reviews this area of research.

Although individuals benefit from privilege, some scholars say that the privilege is based on the person's group membership or social location rather than on anything he or she has done as an individual. In this view, privilege is not about people's qualities as individuals but instead about the ways in which social systems shape their lives regardless of their intentions. Privilege is systemic and systematic, they say, so even the most committed White antiracist activist receives privilege based on race; it is not something one can choose to relinquish. Although the United States is often assumed to be a meritocracy, this perspective challenges the idea that privilege is a reward for merit or achievement. Rather, it sees privilege as revealing that U.S. society has not achieved a level playing field and that inequality is still widespread.

Looking at White Privilege

Historically, most research on race has focused on the victims of racism. Courses on race have taken minority groups as their focus, and the field of ethnic studies arose to bring the lives of people of color out of the margins and to counter their exclusion from the disciplines of literature, history, and other fields. During recent years, the study of race and ethnicity has expanded, and there is now a growing field of research that examines whiteness and racial privilege. Just as men's lives are shaped by gender, White people's lives are shaped by their race.

In one of the first examinations of White privilege, Peggy McIntosh offered a long list of examples of the White privilege she experiences. She noted, for example, that White privilege includes being able to assume that most of the people one studies in school, or one's children study in school, will be of the same race; being able to go shopping without being followed; and never being called a credit to one's race or needing to represent one's entire race. It also includes simple details such as finding flesh-colored bandages to match one's skin color.

Other scholars have followed this lead and documented privileges based on gender, sexual orientation, and ability. For example, Allan Johnson observed that heterosexuals have the privilege to marry, to be openly intimate with their partners, and to know they will not be fired from their jobs based on their sexual orientation. Gender privilege ensures that men can assume their failures will not be attributed to their gender; that if they work hard and follow the rules, their merit will be rewarded; and that they will not be held to a higher standard on the job. The able-bodied can assume that they can travel freely without needing to worry about access and mobility issues and do not need to deal with others treating them like children.

McIntosh distinguished between two different forms of privilege. The first form is "unearned advantages"—things that everyone should have such as feeling valued and being safe. These are entitlements that should be extended to all but that are transformed into a form of privilege when some have them and others do not. The second form is "conferred dominance." This form of privilege contributes to giving one group power over another. These are privileges that no one should have in a society that values social justice and equity.

The Invisibility of Privilege

One of the most significant features of privilege, according to scholars in this area, is that those who experience privilege do not need to think about their race or other social location. They have the privilege of obliviousness. Although those who experience racism are faced with racism and racial inequality on a daily basis, those who experience racial privilege are often unaware of the workings of oppression and privilege and do not see how it affects their own lives.

It is common for those with privilege to be associated with the cultural norm. Our schools may teach about "Black inventors," but White inventors are simply referred to as "inventors." Their race becomes both invisible and assumed as the norm. Whites are seen as the average, normal, universal human.

Because privilege is invisible, privileged people often become angry when confronted by this perspective on social organization, having been taught to see their own accomplishments as based on their own efforts and hard work alone. Thus, whereas the oppressed quite often recognize the conditions of their oppression, the privileged rarely see the way privilege operates in their daily lives. Historically, it has been easier to talk about racism than to talk about privilege. Looking at privilege brings White people into the picture and expands the discussion of racism and racial inequality beyond the actions of "racists."

Because of the invisibility of privilege, these scholars would say, people of privilege often do not realize the extent to which inequality is still pervasive. Many scholars view color blindness as the predominant ideology of race today—one that sustains and justifies privilege. A color-blind perspective sees people only as individuals and assumes that institutionalized racism has been eliminated. According to the color-blind perspective, legal changes have already been made, discriminatory practices are now against the law, and all people have equal opportunity to succeed. Discrimination is seen as a thing of the past. Therefore, if anyone is not successful, it is a result of his or her own poor choices. Racial inequality is justified as naturally occurring rather than as the product of social forces. From this perspective, people simply *choose* to live near, work with, and marry people of the same race rather than doing so as a result of institutional discrimination.

To avoid responsibility, privileged people employ a number of strategies, according to Johnson. They deny that privilege exists or minimize its impact, they blame the victim, they call it something else or rationalize it as acceptable and natural, they excuse it because it is not purposeful, or they blame it on the actions of certain "racist" individuals.

A Theory of Domination

Sociologist Patricia Hill Collins has developed the concept of the matrix of domination to examine the ways in which race and other social statuses, such as gender and class, interact and intersect as part of a matrix of privilege and oppression. Because everyone is positioned by a number of intersecting social locations, individuals may experience privilege based on one status but experience oppression based on other aspects of one's identity. Thus, those who experience racial or gender oppression may nevertheless experience some form of privilege (perhaps based on class, ability, or sexual orientation). Examining privilege through an intersectional lens makes visible everyone's place in systems of inequality.

Understanding that everyone plays a role in the dynamics of privilege and oppression is a step toward beginning to work toward solutions, many scholars believe. To promote social change and social justice, individuals can work to create change in the ways in which systems are organized to perpetuate privilege. Once people begin to examine their own social locations and place within the matrix of domination, these scholars argue, they can begin to understand how their own individual actions and behavior can affect society as a whole in both positive and negative ways. This perspective enables people to see that everyone experiences varying degrees of privilege in some way or another. Exploring the ways in which each one is privileged potentially connects individuals and brings them together to work toward equality.

Abby L. Ferber

See also Collins, Patricia Hill; Whiteness; Whiteness and Masculinity; White Privilege; White Supremacy Movement

Further Readings

Bonilla-Silva, Eduardo. 2003. *Racism without Racists: Color-Blind Racism and the Persistence of Racial Inequality in the United States.* Lanham, MD: Rowman & Littlefield.

Collins, Patricia Hill. 2000. *Black Feminist Thought: Knowledge, Consciousness, and the Politics of Empowerment.* 2nd ed. New York: Routledge.

Feagin, Joe and Eileen O'Brien. 2003. *White Men on Race: Power, Privilege, and the Shaping of Cultural Consciousness.* Boston, MA: Beacon.

Johnson, Allan G. 2006. *Privilege, Power, and Difference.* 2nd ed. New York: McGraw-Hill.

Kimmel, Michael S. and Abby L. Ferber, eds. 2003. *Privilege: A Reader.* Boulder, CO: Westview.

McIntosh, Peggy. 1988. "White Privilege and Male Privilege: A Personal Account of Coming to See Correspondences through Work in Women's Studies." Working Paper 189, Center for Research on Women, Wellesley College.

Proposition 187

Proposition 187 was a ballot initiative, introduced in the 1994 California statewide elections, aimed at denying access to social services, public education, and health care for undocumented aliens or illegal immigrants. It was subtitled "Save Our State" and was seen by many as targeting California's burgeoning Latino population (and especially recent immigrants from Mexico). The campaign emerged mainly in the suburbs of Los Angeles and Orange counties and won a majority of voters (nearly 59%) in the entire state. The proposition was later overturned by federal courts, which deemed it unconstitutional. Since 1994, Proposition 187 has in many ways served as a benchmark for proposed legislation in other states aimed at limiting both legal and illegal immigration and at reducing the overall cost of social services for taxpayers. This entry describes Proposition 187, the legal battle it triggered, and its impact on similar efforts.

The Campaign

The worlds of immigration and politics have historically merged in the United States, and this was especially true as the face of immigration changed dramatically after around 1950. Although immigration has been part of the United States from its inception, the sources of this immigration after 1950 were primarily countries in Latin America and Asia, whereas prior to World War II these sources were primarily countries in Western and Eastern Europe. Thus, California was an environment ripe for such legislation in some ways.

Bordering Mexico and home to arguably the greatest melting pot of ethnicities and recent immigrants in the United States, California has the largest immigrant population of any state. During the early 1990s, economic conditions in California worsened and illegal immigrants became a target for Californians who believed they were paying too much in taxes for social services programs that were benefiting an ever-increasing number of these immigrants.

These concerns were addressed by the five major sections of Proposition 187. The first barred illegal aliens from the state's public education systems from kindergarten through college and required public educational institutions to begin verifying the legal status of both students and their parents. The second section required all providers of publicly paid, nonemergency health care services to verify the legal status of persons seeking services to be reimbursed by the state. The third section required that all persons seeking cash assistance and other benefits verify their legal status before receiving such benefits. The fourth section required all service providers to report suspected illegal aliens to the California attorney general and to the U.S. Immigration and Naturalization Service (INS). Finally, the fifth section made it a state felony to manufacture, distribute, or use false documents to obtain public benefits or employment by concealing one's legal status.

Public opinion on Proposition 187, not surprisingly, included vehement voices on both sides. Supporters of Proposition 187 backed their arguments by saying that the state would save a great deal of money and other resources on public services if these were not offered to illegal immigrants. However, opponents derided the legislation as racist and xenophobic and pointed out that it would cost more money to establish programs that would help to verify the residency status of all immigrants. In addition, health officials and doctors who opposed Proposition 187 feared that there would be a rise in health epidemics if illegal immigrants would not be permitted to receive immunizations or treatment for diseases or illnesses.

One special characteristic of Proposition 187 was that it offered incentives for public servants such as teachers, social workers, law enforcement officials, and health care workers to help curb illegal immigration by turning over suspected undocumented aliens to the police or other authorities such as the INS. This led to a fear of deportation among many undocumented aliens, fueled by the perception that any public servant they came into contact with could potentially turn them over to the INS.

The Legal Battle and Other Reactions

Once Proposition 187 passed its initial voter test in 1994, a bitter legal battle ensued between proponents of Proposition 187, many of whom were White and conservative, and its opponents, many of whom were Latino (and recently immigrated to the United States) and liberal. Legal action was almost immediate on the part of groups such as the American Civil Liberties Union, the Mexican American Legal Defense and Educational Fund, and the League of United Latin American Citizens. President Bill Clinton argued strongly against Proposition 187, urging citizens of

California to put the responsibility of dealing with illegal immigration on the federal government instead of on their own shoulders as state voters.

Ultimately, Proposition 187 was deemed unconstitutional by federal courts via interpretation of the Fourteenth Amendment, which contains an equal protection clause that protects everyone within a state's borders regardless of immigration status. The first blow against Proposition 187 was a temporary restraining order issued on November 11, 1994, and this was followed by a permanent injunction using the *Plyler v. Doe* (1982) Supreme Court case as evidence. After nearly an entire year of hearings and filings from both sides, protests against the legislation culminated in a protest march by between 70,000 and 250,000 people in downtown Los Angeles on October 15, 1995.

Two of California's governors, Pete Wilson and Gray Davis, were centrally involved in the Proposition 187 legal battle—on opposite sides. Wilson was the Republican governor of the state who backed the legislation while in office and was reelected with 55% of the vote in 1994. He remained a supporter throughout the aftermath of Proposition 187's introduction and worked with California Attorney General Dan Lungren (also reelected in 1994) to implement the legislation immediately. Wilson's logic was that denying public services to undocumented aliens would discourage them from coming to the United States and also encourage some of those already in the United States to leave.

Davis, who was elected in 1998, opposed Proposition 187 and the policy changes it contained. However, as the lengthy appeals process continued into his term as California governor, he eventually brought the issue before mediation and dropped the appeals process altogether. The only language stemming from Proposition 187 still in effect today makes it illegal to manufacture, distribute, or use false documents to obtain employment or public benefits.

Residual Effects

More than a decade later, the impact of Proposition 187 certainly remains alive and well. It was seen by many as the first significant attempt by state voters to "fight back" against the financial cost of providing social services to those deemed not to be contributing to the state tax base. Immigration reform proponents have used the language found in Proposition 187 to offer other arguments illustrating the financial burden on state and local government budgets brought about by large numbers of illegal immigrants. They have argued that stricter border controls are necessary to stem the tide of people coming to the United States, contending that immigrants will lower wages and produce crime in addition to being a burden on state and local social service agencies, hospitals, and public schools.

However, opponents of both Proposition 187 and immigration policy reform have used the movements against the legislation to branch out their protests within and beyond California. These protests have involved battling the continued use of racial/ethnic identity as a means of discrimination and the issue of "looking illegal" among Latinos and Asian Americans. This last issue highlights the visibility of physical trait differences as opposed to earlier immigrants from Europe and how this visibility allows for myths and assumptions to exist about particular groups. These myths and assumptions may cause problems for legal immigrants and native-born citizens from both ethnic groups if they become targets for the same kind of treatment as that directed toward illegal immigrants. For some opponents of Proposition 187, it is simply a question of human rights; they believe that the right of anyone living in the United States to an education and health care is beyond question.

Scholars studying race and ethnicity as well as immigration continue to debate the legacy of Proposition 187. It is seen as a significant effort to reduce both legal and illegal immigration but also as a largely symbolic (albeit controversial) expression of frustration with illegal immigration and the financial costs associated with it. Although it was unsuccessful at the federal level, the media attention surrounding it has continued to grow. Recently, a new surge of attention has been given to the issue of social services in California and other states, particularly border states such as Texas and Arizona. Elections in those states, as well as in other states with a significant number of recent immigrants, have highlighted this issue. Although border states do not necessarily make up the entire slate of states with large numbers of illegal immigrants (New York, Illinois, Florida, and New Jersey join the other three as the seven states with the largest numbers of illegal immigrants), they often serve as the most visible battlegrounds because of their proximity to Mexico in particular. The issue of illegal immigration promises to cause further political debate during the years to come, even within the

Latino population in the United States, as Latinos become the largest minority group.

Jean H. Shin and Karina J. Havrilla

See also Bilingual Education; Border Patrol; *Cisneros v. Corpus Christi School District;* Health, Immigrant; Hispanics; Illegal Immigration Reform and Responsibility Act of 1996; Immigration, Economic Impact of; Immigration, U.S.; Immigration and Naturalization Service (INS); Mexican American Legal Defense and Educational Fund (MALDEF); Mexican Americans; Nativism

Further Readings

Andreas, Peter. 2001. *Border Games: Policing the U.S.–Mexico Divide.* Ithaca, NY: Cornell University Press.

Gibbs, Jewelle Taylor and Teiahsha Bankhead. 2001. *Preserving Privilege: California Politics, Propositions, and People of Color.* Westport, CT: Praeger.

Long, Robert Emmet, ed. 1996. *Immigration.* New York: H. W. Wilson.

Nevins, Joseph. 2001. *Operation Gatekeeper: The Rise of the "Illegal Alien" and the Remaking of the U.S.–Mexico Boundary.* New York: Routledge.

Nicholson, Stephen P. 1995. *Voting the Election: Candidates, Elections, and Ballot Propositions.* Princeton, NJ: Princeton University Press.

Ono, Kent A. and John M. Sloop. 2002. *Shifting Borders: Rhetoric, Immigration, and California's Proposition 187.* Philadelphia, PA: Temple University Press.

PUBLIC HOUSING

Public housing in the United States may be thought to include a range of types of housing assistance. This entry focuses on dwellings that are funded by the national government and are owned and operated by local housing authorities. Public housing is a means-tested, non-cash transfer program available to households with incomes below specified levels. Although public housing has always been a controversial program, it provides low-cost housing to some 1.3 million needy households.

Much of the bad reputation of public housing has been the result of problems that have emerged during recent decades, including increasingly high proportions of extremely poor residents due to changes in legislation, deteriorating buildings due to a cut in annual appropriations for the Department of Housing and Urban Development (HUD) by nearly two-thirds between 1980 and 1998, a rapidly aging public housing stock with more than five-sixths of all units built before 1980, and the devastation wrought by the crack cocaine epidemic beginning in the mid-1980s. The problems of public housing disproportionately affect racial minority households, who comprise roughly two-thirds of the public housing population today.

Historical Background

Public housing in the United States was initially authorized by the (Wagner–Steagall) Housing Act of 1937. It was created in reaction to the economic crises of the Depression with the goals of creating employment opportunities and stimulating the economy while providing short-term housing for families who were temporarily poor as a result of the economy.

The Housing Act of 1949 declared the goal of "a decent home and suitable living environment for every American family"—a goal that remains unrealized today. It also established the urban renewal slum clearance program, which disproportionately displaced Black households and concentrated them in public housing projects accompanied by extreme poverty and social isolation.

During the following decades, the U.S. commitment to public housing declined steadily. During the Reagan and (George H.) Bush administrations, Congress appropriated funds for fewer than 5,000 new public housing units per year. Beginning in 1993, the Clinton administration significantly changed public housing with the HOPE VI program. To date, Congress has appropriated nearly $5 billion to this program to demolish large distressed projects and replace them with mixed-income, mixed-finance developments that, in keeping with the tenets of welfare reform, often require tenants to be employed. The majority of the low-income households displaced by this redevelopment are moved to other projects or given rent vouchers to use in the private market.

Characteristics of Units and Residents

There are approximately 1.3 million public housing units in the United States, with these units housing approximately 3.3 million people. More than three-quarters of these households are headed by single adults, typically elderly persons living alone, or single parents with children. Welfare is the largest source of income for half of all public housing tenants, with another 25% depending on social security or disability payments. For decades, public housing has largely been a "last resort" for the very poorest households. As of 2003, 76% of public housing residents earned less than 30% of the area median income. During recent years, average incomes of public housing residents have risen somewhat because of welfare reform and federal efforts to expand the range of incomes in public housing.

Although the stereotype of the public housing "project" in the United States is that of a superblock of high-density, low-quality, high-rise buildings, in fact only 28% of public housing developments have four or more stories, a share that is further receding under the HOPE VI program. In 1992, the National Commission for Severely Distressed Public Housing estimated that only 6% of public housing units were "severely distressed." Nonetheless, in the course of redeveloping these sites for mixed-income use, tens of thousands of subsidized units have been lost.

Patterns of Racial Discrimination in Public Housing

The structure of the public housing program, coupled with decades of lax federal oversight, often allowed racial discrimination to dictate the development of public housing projects. For example, municipal control over the location of public housing, granted by the Housing Act of 1937, often resulted in large projects being placed in poor and minority neighborhoods with weak political power. It was not until 1980 that HUD implemented "Site and Neighborhood Standards" to prevent negative economic and racial impacts from public housing location. However, 83% of the current public housing stock was already built by the time these standards were enacted. In 1990, the typical African American public housing resident lived in a project where 85% of the residents were also African American. The typical White public housing resident, on the other hand, lived in a project where only 27% of the residents were Black and 60% were White.

The decade-long lawsuit that culminated in the 1976 *Hills v. Gautreaux* decision by the U.S. Supreme Court established that specific aspects of public housing legislation had been racially discriminatory and led to unequal racial impacts. In 1966, a group of Black tenants filed a federal class action suit charging that the Chicago Housing Authority (CHA) racially segregated public housing projects and deliberately located them in Black neighborhoods. In September 1971, the U.S. Court of Appeals declared that HUD was "guilty of aiding and abetting racial segregation" in Chicago. The ultimate result of the lawsuit was that the CHA granted subsidy vouchers to 7,100 Black public housing residents over the next decade to enable them to move to other neighborhoods of their choice.

Although the recent focus of public housing has been on redevelopment of existing projects through HOPE VI, racial minorities have been disproportionately affected by that program's sweeping changes. For example, in fiscal year 2001, 95% of the families displaced by HOPE VI were minorities, of whom 79% were African American. These displaced households are both less likely to qualify to return to the redeveloped sites and more likely to face discrimination when they attempt to use housing vouchers in the private market. These outcomes violate the Fair Housing Act, which prohibits intentional discrimination as well as actions that have the effect of discriminating.

Despite its problems, public housing remains a critical source of shelter for millions of people who lack other options. Current trends toward scattered-site and mixed-income development, privatization of management and tenure, and demand-side subsidies rather than site-built projects are controversial attempts to rectify its previous inequities and deficiencies.

Willem van Vliet

See also African Americans; Discrimination; Discrimination in Housing; *Gautreaux* Decision; Housing Audits; Wealth Distribution

Further Readings

Carter, William H., Michael H. Schill, and Susan M. Wachter. 1998. "Polarisation, Public Housing, and Racial Minorities in U.S. Cities." *Urban Studies* 35:1889–1911.

Crump, Jeff. 2002. "Deconcentration by Demolition: Public Housing, Poverty, and Urban Policy." *Environment and Planning D* 20:581–596.

Goering, John, Ali Kamely, and Todd Richardson. 1994. *The Location and Composition of Public Housing in the United States.* Washington, DC: U.S. Department of Housing and Urban Development.

Keating, Larry. 2000. "Redeveloping Public Housing: Relearning Urban Renewal's Immutable Lessons." *Journal of the American Planning Association* 66:384–397.

Massey, Douglas S. and Nancy A. Denton. 1993. *American Apartheid: Segregation and the Making of the Underclass.* Cambridge, MA: Harvard University Press.

National Housing Law Project. 1999. "HUD's Fair Housing Duties and the Loss of Public and Assisted Housing." *Housing Law Bulletin,* January. Retrieved from http://www.nhlp.org/html/hlb/199/index.htm

Polikoff, Alexander. 2006. *Waiting for Gautreaux: A Story of Segregation, Housing, and the Black Ghetto.* Evanston, IL: Northwestern University Press.

Rainwater, Lee. 1970. *Behind Ghetto Walls: Black Families in a Federal Slum.* Chicago, IL: Aldine.

Schill, Michael H. and Susan M. Wachter. 1995. "The Spatial Bias of Federal Housing Law and Policy: Concentrated Poverty in Urban America." *University of Pennsylvania Law Review* 143:1285–1342.

Schnapper, Morris B., ed. 1939. *Public Housing in America.* New York: H. W. Wilson.

PUEBLOS

The term *Pueblo* refers both to a group of culturally related, but autonomous, Indian villages in the U.S. Southwest and to the people who live in these villages. When Spanish conquistadors entered the Rio Grande Valley during the 16th century, they found thousands of Indians living in compact villages along the river and westward into the mesa country of northeastern Arizona. They called these tribes *Indios de Pueblos* (literally village Indians) to distinguish them from their nomadic neighbors—hunters and gatherers such as the Apache and Navajo. Spanish settlers adopted the term as they developed different relations with their Puebloan and Apachean neighbors. The distinction was a legal one as Pueblo Indians were subject to being taxed, conscripted, and incorporated into the imperial system of Spain. When Americans entered the Santa Fe trade, they found the term *Pueblo* entrenched and embraced it.

The most conspicuous feature of Pueblo Indians' villages is the unique architecture. Their compact adobe villages have been described as "apartment-like" for the way in which the walls of one building abut the walls of the next building. Each subsequent story can be set back to create a terrace workspace. The room blocks surround a plaza that has a socioreligious role in the life of the village. Pueblo villages also have distinctive structures called *kivas* for the sacred activities of the religious societies. These secret ceremonies occur in conjunction with religious dances in the plazas. Kivas are often round or underground, but not always; they can be built into the room blocks or left freestanding. Although all Pueblo villages were originally built in this classic style, many modern pueblos are a simple single story; however, all maintain at least one plaza and one kiva for village use.

Pueblo Indians are an often misunderstood group in U.S. history. At one time, U.S. culture considered Pueblos to be Mexicans, not Indians at all. At another time, Pueblos were considered to be pagans, and at another time, they were romanticized as noble and peaceful. The reason for this waffling is that Pueblo Indians have been sedentary tribes with long established traditions since pre-Columbian times—traditions that are very different from those of the stereotypical "Indian." This entry, which uses the lowercase *pueblo* for the villages and the uppercase *Pueblo, Pueblo Indian,* or *Puebloan* for the various peoples, recalls the history of both as well as their presence in today's Southwest.

The Ancestral Puebloans

Although Puebloan peoples have different origin stories, archaeologists believe that they began as a nomadic people in the Southwest some 5,000 years ago. As big game grew scarce, they increasingly turned to smaller game and a wide variety of plants for sustenance. After corn found its way north from Mexico, the ancestral Puebloans added it to their lifestyle. The ability to grow corn provided a more secure subsistence, and as growing populations intensified pressure on the environment, they cached extra food in the dry alcoves of the canyons. Still, it was not until they began making pottery, which allowed them to use beans, that their agriculture led to a more settled lifestyle.

Puebloans' earliest villages were not pueblos but rather were composed of several pithouse structures. These were single-room semisubterranean homes with earthen roofs. They accessed these warm habitations by ladders through the roof or through an antechamber that served as a storeroom. Around 600 AD, when they began cultivating beans, domesticating turkeys, and using the bow and arrow, they replaced their pithouses with above-ground masonry rows of adjoining rooms. These surrounded a plaza with a stylized pithouse, or *proto-kiva,* which was probably built for ceremonies, meetings, and lodging during the winter months. By 800 AD, a large population of Puebloan people occupied the Four Corners region.

Scientific dating shows that by around 1000 AD, the pueblos had grown immense and achieved the configuration now associated with the term. At Chaco Canyon, Mesa Verde, Canyon de Chelly, and elsewhere, the population grew and the culture flourished. An elaborate ceremonial life based on true kivas appeared as systems of trade tied the people together over hundreds of miles and redistributed food throughout a land of unpredictable rainfall. Trade with Mexico and impressive scientific skills were other hallmarks of this "classic phase." The sandstone masonry was superb, and the architecture reached its zenith with the five-story, D-shaped, 800-room village of Pueblo Bonito in Chaco Canyon.

By the end of the 13th century, the ancestral Puebloans abandoned these centers and moved from the Four Corners region. Drought, depletion of resources, population growth, and cultural change probably precipitated the migration. Puebloan oral traditions state that each group needed to find its "Center Place"—the place where the spirit world meant them to live—and this contributed to a willingness to move on when these difficulties loomed.

The ancestral Puebloans moved to the south and southwest, to the Little Colorado and Zuni valleys, and to the southeast, to the valley of the Rio Grande. There they mixed with other Puebloan peoples, and as the population soared they established upward of 100 pueblo villages. Some of these villages, such as those at Bandelier National Monument, were subsequently abandoned, but most were occupied when Spanish explorers entered the region. The rich pueblo ceremonial life added a deep philosophical quality to the lives of Pueblo Indians, but the conquistadores did not understand it this way.

The Pueblo Indians and New Spain

Francisco Vasquez de Coronado's march from Mexico in 1540 effectively ended the isolation of the Puebloan world from the changes sweeping over Europe. The Spaniards came north in search of the fabled golden cities of *Cibola*—mythical cities reputed to rival those of the Aztecs. Coronado had dispatched a reconnaissance party the year before under Fray Marcos de Niza. He was guided by Estevanico, a Moor who wandered the Southwest with the Spanish party that first heard rumors of *Cibola*. De Niza and Estevanico made it to Zuni, but there Estevanico's indiscretions led the Zuni to kill him, and a terrified de Niza returned to Mexico.

Claiming that the reports of gold in New Mexico were true, de Niza led Coronado's army northward. There, Coronado waged war against the Zuni and sent expeditions to Hopi, Acoma, and the Rio Grande but found none of the riches that de Niza had reported. With winter approaching, Coronado settled among the Tiguex (or Tiwa) pueblos at the base of Sandia Mountain. Spanish demands for food and clothing, combined with their callous treatment of the tribes, led to a war that terrorized the Tiguex and compelled many to abandon their homes. Because the conquistadores could not accept the legitimacy of Pueblo religion, they sought to Christianize New Spain and believed that the Pueblo Indians should supply all of their needs in gratitude for bringing them the true faith.

The Indians did not understand the need to change religions, although their traditions of generosity mandated that they help strangers. However, they did not believe that they should supply the Spanish army by risking their own families' starving or freezing. The resulting war devastated the realm and served as a warning to other Pueblos. Therefore, the northern Pueblos plotted to escape the clutches of the Spanish army by leading them on a ruse of a richer city to the east called Quivira. When Coronado failed to find Quivira, his men convinced him to abandon their quest and return to Mexico.

Although Coronado did not stay long, he left a lasting legacy in the valley. His exotic nature and high-handed behavior left Pueblo Indians with contradictory feelings. His men had destroyed dozens of villages and killed hundreds of people. Yet the horses, sheep, and other Spanish goods left a desire for further trade. Their exposure to Christianity would be a future source of both conflict and solace. The Spaniards also brought new diseases, such as smallpox, that decimated the population, forcing the Pueblos to consolidate into fewer, more defensible villages.

In 1598, Juan de Oñate came to establish a permanent Spanish colony on the northern frontier of New Spain and built his capital near Ohkay Owingeh Pueblo. Oñate proved to be ruthless in demanding obedience and put down revolts among the Tompiro pueblos and at Taos. However, it was his destruction of Acoma and his judgment that every man over 25 years of age should have a foot cut off that won him eternal infamy. After his dismissal in 1608, the next governor established a new administrative center among the Tewa pueblos that was called *Santa Fe*.

Settling among the pueblos, the Spanish governors ingratiated themselves with other Spaniards by awarding *encomiendas* (tributes in food) and *repartimientos* (conscripted labor) to prestigious men—tributes that the Pueblo Indians resented being required to provide. At the same time, the Catholic Church claimed the same tribute to support its missions. The Franciscan priests who accompanied the Spanish army baptized many Puebloans, but the Indians continued to practice their traditional religion as well. This worried the missionaries and leaders of the Inquisition who came north with the governors. Although the church had troubles with the Spanish military and civil authorities, the army supported the missionary efforts to suppress native religion; officials filled kivas with sand, destroyed sacred objects, and antagonized Pueblo leaders. The missionaries encouraged the consolidation of smaller pueblos into larger pueblos. As the number of pueblos diminished, the Tompiro pueblos were abandoned.

Finally, in 1680, the Pueblo Indians had endured enough. United under the leadership of Po'pay from Ohkay Owingeh, they forced the Spaniards out in the Pueblo Revolt. It was the first successful native rebellion in the Americas against a European power. The Spanish army retreated to El Paso, taking along some Puebloan slaves. Fearing reprisal, consolidation continued. The Spanish army returned 12 years later under the direction of Diego de Vargas to secure the frontier and make the colony profitable.

Some Pueblos possibly welcomed the Spanish return, seeking their help to defend their towns against Apache and Comanche raids and desiring the renewal of trade. Others resented the Spanish return, believing that repression would begin anew. Many Indians recognized that they needed to reach an accord; the Spanish army was not going away. When de Vargas treated them more fairly than had earlier governors, many Puebloans changed their stance. The Spanish king had commissioned de Vargas to present land grants to the Pueblos, guaranteeing them their lands and nullifying the *encomiendas* and *repartimientos*. De Vargas showed greater tolerance for native religious beliefs, and the Spanish Inquisition did not return.

Still, there was resistance, and it was not until 1696 that all of the Rio Grande Pueblos had reconciled themselves to the Spanish presence. However, the Hopi in northeastern Arizona never accepted the Spaniards' return and were too far away for the governor to control. As it was, his control over the Zuni on the western boundary of New Mexico was tenuous. With time, many of the Rio Grande Pueblos adopted Catholicism—at least outwardly—and incorporated their dances into Spanish religious celebrations.

During the Mexican–American War, the Pueblo Indians were wary of the American forces, but resistance was curtailed until the main American army left. Then, during the winter of 1846–1847, the Taos Revolt alerted the Americans that they were seizing the territory of a semiautonomous people. The revolt ended with a siege of the pueblo, and in 1848 Mexico transferred the Rio Grande Valley to American control. The new government recognized the pueblo land grants and kept many of the Spanish compromises, preventing further war between Americans and Puebloans.

The Modern Pueblos

Whereas the Pueblos originally subsisted with fields of corn, beans, and squash, domesticated turkeys, game, and other wild foods, the Spaniards introduced wheat, peaches, sheep, and other commodities—leading to a cornucopia of agricultural produce. This improved the Puebloan lifestyle, and Spanish *hornos* (ovens) became commonplace in most pueblos.

The Spanish also introduced a new administrative system that the Pueblos judged to be useful. Each pueblo originally governed itself through a village chief who was assisted by a village council. Spain created another layer of government by requiring the pueblos to choose a governor, a lieutenant governor, and other officials to serve as intermediaries with the colonial government. This government has continued among the eastern pueblos because it has proven to be beneficial in keeping the White world at bay.

The Pueblos to the west, who resisted the Spanish reconquest, have strong matrilineal clans, whereas those to the east organize their villages with well-developed moiety systems that divide the pueblos into two parts, with everyone belonging to either moiety for ceremonial duties. Traditionally, each village is highly autonomous, although historically they formed strong intervillage alliances. Today, the New Mexico pueblos are confederated in the All Indian Pueblo Council, which coordinates responses to threats to their communities. The Hopi tribal council plays a similar role among the Hopi villages in Arizona.

When conflicts erupted with the state or federal government during the 20th century, these alliances fought for their rights through the U.S. legal system.

The distinctive pueblo architecture has remained intact in most villages, but in some villages government housing projects have added another dimension along with the U.S. educational system. Although Protestant missionaries have attempted to make inroads into the traditional life of the villages, most people retain their native religion while participating in Catholic traditions.

Today, there are nineteen pueblos in New Mexico and a dozen Hopi villages in Arizona, speaking four major languages: Tanoan, Keres, Hopi, and Zuni. The Tewa speak a Tanoan language and live in the villages of Ohkay Owingeh, Santa Clara, San Ildefonso, Pojoaque, Tesuque, and Nambe—all north of Santa Fe. The Tiwa speak a related language and live at Picuris and Taos, north of the Tewa, and at Sandia and Isleta, near Albuquerque. The Jemez Pueblo northwest of Albuquerque speak another variant, Towa. Between Santa Fe and Albuquerque are the five Keresan pueblos of Cochiti, Santo Domingo, San Felipe, Zia, and Tamaya. Between Albuquerque and Gallup are the two Keres villages of Acoma and Laguna as well as the Zuni. All nineteen pueblos are vibrant centers of Puebloan culture today.

Taos and Acoma maintain their original architecture and are often visited by tourists. The twelve Hopi villages are in northeastern Arizona. Because they have the least Spanish influence among the Puebloan tribes, they sometimes prefer to be identified as simply Hopi rather than as Pueblo. Finally, the Pueblo Indians who survived the trip to El Paso in 1680 established another village there known as Yselta del Sur. All of the modern pueblos still have their kivas and perform traditional dances during the year. Although the cities entice many Pueblo Indians into the wage economy each year, the villages still maintain the agricultural lifestyle of their ancestors.

Joseph Owen Weixelman

See Appendix A

See also Hispanics; Hopi; Mexican Americans; Native Americans; Navajo

Further Readings

Courlander, Harold. 1971. *The Fourth World of the Hopis.* Albuquerque: University of New Mexico Press.

Dozier, Edward P. 1970. *The Pueblo Indians of North America.* Prospect Heights, IL: Waveland.

Forbes, Jack D. 1960. *Apache, Navajo, and Spaniard.* Norman: University of Oklahoma Press.

Ortiz, Alfonso. 1969. *The Tewa World: Space, Time, Being, and Becoming in a Pueblo Society.* Chicago, IL: University of Chicago Press.

Ortiz, Alfonso. 1972. *New Perspectives on the Pueblos.* Albuquerque: University of New Mexico Press.

Ortiz, Alfonso and William C. Sturtevant, eds. 1979. *Handbook of North American Indians,* vol. 9: *Southwest.* Washington, DC: Smithsonian Institution.

Sando, Joe S. 1992. *Pueblo Nations: Eight Centuries of Pueblo Indian History.* Santa Fe, NM: Clear Light.

Stuart, David. 2000. *Anasazi America.* Albuquerque: University of New Mexico Press.

Talayesva, Don. 1942. *Sun Chief: The Autobiography of a Hopi Indian,* edited by Leo Simmons. New Haven, CT: Yale University Press.

PUERTO RICAN AMERICANS

As of 2003, there were more Puerto Ricans living in the United States than on the island of Puerto Rico—3.8 million on the mainland and 3.6 million in Puerto Rico—creating an unusual condition where the diaspora is greater than the country of origin's population. In addition, Puerto Ricans often migrate back and forth between the island and the mainland, giving them a foot in both places. This "divided nation" situation has been produced by the status of Puerto Rico as a "commonwealth," with its residents sharing some—but not all—of the benefits of U.S. citizens and its homeland economy dependent on the United States. The sense of nationalism is strong among Puerto Ricans living in the United States. One sign of this is the fact that few Puerto Ricans living in the United States would refer to themselves as Puerto Rican Americans. Most would simply identify as Puerto Rican or *Boricua,* which is a variation of the indigenous (Taino) word for the island of Puerto Rico, *Borinquen.* Latinos are now the largest minority population in the United States, and the Puerto Rican community accounts for 9% of that population—18% if island Puerto Ricans are included—making them the second largest national origin group among Latinos behind the Mexican origin population.

Migration to the United States

Puerto Ricans have been coming to the United States since the late 19th century, especially following the U.S. colonization of Puerto Rico in 1898. Puerto

Ricans were granted U.S. citizenship in 1917, and this greatly facilitated their ability to migrate to the country. However, the greatest migration of Puerto Ricans to the United States took place during the 1950s and 1960s. The governments of both the United States and Puerto Rico encouraged Puerto Ricans to come to the United States to ease unemployment on the island. To encourage and manage the emigration of Puerto Ricans to the United States, in 1947 the U.S. and Puerto Rican governments founded the Migration Division (or the Commonwealth Office), which eventually had offices in 115 U.S. cities and towns. By 1970, 1.5 million Puerto Ricans lived in the United States. Between 1990 and 2000, the Puerto Rican population in the United States grew by 24.9%—from 3.2 million to 3.6 million.

At first, most Puerto Ricans migrated to New York City or elsewhere on the East Coast. Now, Puerto Ricans are found across the nation. Once home to 80% of all stateside Puerto Ricans, New York City was home to only 23% of stateside Puerto Ricans by 2000. The states with the largest Puerto Rican populations in 2000 were New York, Florida, New Jersey, Pennsylvania, and Massachusetts. During the past 30 years, there has also been significant population growth in Connecticut, Illinois, California, Ohio, and Texas as well as in areas of the Midwest. Puerto Ricans are now found in most states, and a large community has migrated to Florida, where the population rose by 57.7% from 1990 to 2000. Although the cities that house the majority of Puerto Ricans continue to be located on the East Coast and in the Midwest (e.g., New York City, Chicago, Philadelphia, Newark, Hartford), the cities experiencing the fastest growth among Puerto Ricans from 1990 to 2000 were Orlando, Florida (142%); Allentown, Pennsylvania (83%); Tampa, Florida (78%); Reading, Pennsylvania (64%); and New Britain, Connecticut (52%).

Migration to the United States is affected by economic factors such as recessions and job booms on the island and in the United States. As U.S. citizens, Puerto Ricans have been able to migrate at will to and from the United States, and a circulatory migration pattern has emerged. For example, because of recession in the United States during the early 1970s, more Puerto Ricans returned to Puerto Rico than migrated to the country. Because of this transnational connection, Puerto Ricans have been referred to as a "commuter nation." Studies have shown that two of every three of Puerto Ricans who migrate to the United States have lived there previously and that most of those who move to Puerto Rico from the United States have also already lived on the island previously.

Discrimination and Resistance

Despite their U.S. citizenship, Puerto Ricans have experienced racial tensions, housing discrimination, linguistic barriers, police brutality, and other problems in New York, Chicago, Philadelphia, and other cities where they have settled. During the 1960s and 1970s, the Puerto Rican community became the site of many sociological studies that stigmatized it and blamed the Puerto Rican community, rather than racism and discrimination, for its poverty. Sociologists such as Oscar Lewis used a "culture of poverty" thesis and "blame the victim" paradigm to explain the situation of the community.

In New York City and Chicago, young people organized to defend and transform their communities. The Young Lords, a group that modeled itself after the Black Panther Party, emerged during the 1960s. The Young Lords had started out as a gang, but Cha Cha Jimenez and his associates in Chicago transformed the group into a direct action activist organization. A second Young Lords chapter followed in New York, and chapters in other cities were formed. The organization developed a Thirteen Point Manifesto stating its program; among other points, it advocated an end to discrimination toward Puerto Ricans and other people of color in the United States. Members also lobbied for the independence of Puerto Rico and declared their belief that capitalism was wrong and that sexism must be eliminated. At first, the group focused on educating the community, providing health services, and staging actions such as cleaning the streets neglected by the city. Gradually, as the response to the group's actions become more aggressive, its strategies also escalated. The Young Lords fought to secure the rights and needs of the Puerto Rican community that were being ignored by the city and state agencies. As a result of police infiltration, repression, and infighting, the group ceased to exist by 1976.

Puerto Ricans have created a series of important institutions to serve the community. These include ASPIRA, dedicated to promoting youth education and leadership, and Boricua College and the Center for Puerto Rican Studies of the City University of New York at Hunter College, focused on securing higher education for Puerto Ricans and other Latinos. Other organizations that concentrate on political issues include the National Puerto Rican Coalition, the

National Puerto Rican Forum, the Puerto Rican Legal Defense and Education Fund, and the National Conference of Puerto Rican Women.

Literary Contributions

Puerto Ricans have made important contributions to the literary world. Jesus Colón, who came to the United States in 1917, wrote expressive vignettes about the life and struggles of Puerto Ricans in New York during the first half of the 20th century. His sketches and articles were collected in a book, *A Puerto Rican in New York and Other Sketches*, published in 1961. It is the first English language book by a Puerto Rican describing the experiences of Puerto Ricans in New York City.

Another important writer is Piri Thomas. In *Down These Mean Streets* (1969), he chronicled his life growing up in New York as a young Black Puerto Rican. The autobiographical work vividly captures life in the ghetto and the saga of a young man caught within the Black–White U.S. racial paradigm and trying to discover where he fits. Nicholasa Mohr, in a series of novels and short story collections (*Nilda, Felita,* and *Going Home*), portrayed the lives of traditional Puerto Rican girls.

The 1970s saw the rise of a very strong Nuyorican poetry movement. Writers such as Pedro Pietri, Tato Laviera, Sandra Esteves, and Victor Cruz experimented with bilingual lyrical verses that captured the life of a bilingual and bicultural community. They documented the struggles with racism, poverty, and discrimination as well as the strength that the community derives from its culture. More recent authors, such as Esmeralda Santiago and Judith Ortiz Cofer, continue to describe the evolving situation of Puerto Ricans in the United States.

Lourdes Torres

See Appendix A; Appendix B
See also Culture of Poverty; Discrimination; East Harlem; Hispanics; Latina/o Studies; Puerto Rican Armed Forces of National Liberation (FALN); Puerto Rican Legal Defense and Education Fund; Puerto Rico

Further Readings

Acosta-Belén, Edna and Carlos Santiago. 2006. *Puerto Ricans in the United States: A Contemporary Portrait.* Boulder, CO: Lynne Rienner.

Duany, Jorge. 2002. *The Puerto Rican Nation on the Move: Identities on the Island and in the United States.* Chapel Hill: University of North Carolina Press.

Lewis, Oscar. 1966. *La Vida: A Puerto Rican Family in the Culture of Poverty—San Juan and New York.* New York: Random House.

Ramos-Zayas, Ana Y. 2003. *National Performances: The Politics of Class, Race, and Space in Puerto Rican Chicago.* Chicago, IL: University of Chicago Press.

Rodriguez, Clara E. 1989. *Puerto Ricans: Born in the U.S.A.* Boston, MA: Unwin Hyman.

Torres, Andrés and José E. Velázquez, eds. 1998. *The Puerto Rican Movement: Voices from the Diaspora.* Philadelphia, PA: Temple University Press.

Whalen Carmen Teresa and Victor Vazquez-Hernandez. 2005. *The Puerto Rican Diaspora: Historical Perspectives.* Philadelphia, PA: Temple University Press.

PUERTO RICAN ARMED FORCES OF NATIONAL LIBERATION (FALN)

The Puerto Rican Armed Forces of National Liberation—in Spanish, *Fuerzas Armadas de Liberacion Nacional* (FALN)—was a clandestine political organization and movement that emerged in Chicago and Spanish Harlem, well known as *El Barrio,* in New York City. The FALN demanded independence for the island and the liberation of Puerto Rican political prisoners Oscar Collazo-López, Lolita Lebrón, Rafael Cancel-Miranda, Andres Figueroa-Cordero, and Irving Flores-Rodríguez. The organization believed in the need for an armed struggle and in the education of the masses as the means through which political revolution and social justice could be accomplished. Furthermore, the organization believed that bringing about a social revolution would lead to the formation of an anti-imperialist Marxist–Leninist political party.

The movement was launched on October 26, 1974, when the FALN claimed responsibility for five attacks on banks and corporations in New York City resulting in approximately $1 million in damage. From 1974 to 1982, the organization claimed responsibility for more than 100 attacks in New York, Chicago, and Puerto Rico. However, the actions of this organization were concentrated in the United States, and the actions in Puerto Rico were organized by an analogous clandestine political organization, the Boricua Popular Army, well known as *Los Macheteros.* Filiberto Ojeda Ríos, the leader of the Boricua Popular Army, cofounder of the FALN, and one of the Federal Bureau of Investigation's (FBI) most wanted fugitives, died in a confrontation with the FBI on September 23, 2005, the date on which independence supporters commemorate the 1868 Puerto Rican revolt against Spain. The confrontation took place in his residence in Hormigueros, Puerto Rico, where the 72-year-old nationalist leader lived underground under the name of Don Luis. His death and the actions of the FBI in this case are currently under local and federal investigation.

The violent acts of the FALN were directed at law enforcement agencies, financial depositories, corporations, and individuals favoring or promoting capitalism or statehood for Puerto Rico. The organization's main argument was that before the Spanish–American War, Puerto Rico had obtained its autonomy through a bilateral pact signed by Spain and Puerto Rico. As a consequence, the Treaty of Paris through which Spain conceded Puerto Rico, Cuba, Guam, and the Philippines to the United States in 1898 constituted a violation of the aforementioned pact, the FALN argues. In addition, the movement denounced as racism the excessive use of force and abuses of the mostly White New York Police Department and the precarious living conditions of Puerto Ricans in urban areas of the United States.

The modus operandi of this leftist movement was to place homemade powder devices in the target sites and claim responsibility for the attacks using the mainstream media, leaving communiqués on the sites attacked, or mailing the communiqués to federal agencies. In fact, one member of the FALN, William Guillermo Morales, lost both hands and an eye as he fabricated a bomb. He was arrested and imprisoned and then later escaped from Bellevue Hospital, where he was receiving poor treatment for his injuries, the organization claimed. Morales currently resides in Cuba.

Several members of FALN were apprehended and imprisoned for criminal activities and their linkages with the Puerto Rican armed forces. In 1999, President Bill Clinton granted clemency to sixteen members of the organization; two of them, Oscar López-Rivera and Antonio Camacho-Negrón, rejected the offer. Two other prisoners, Carlos Alberto Torres and Marie Haydeé Beltrán-Torres, were not considered for clemency. Those who were freed continue to support and promote independence for Puerto Rico but have discontinued the use of violence in the quest for their ideals.

Jenniffer M. Santos-Hernández

See also Colonialism; Puerto Rican Americans; Puerto Rico

Further Readings

Gonzalez-Cruz, Michael. 2006. *Nacionalismo revolucionario puertorriqueño: Lucha armada, intelectuales y prisioneros políticos y de guerra* (Puerto Rican revolutionary nationalism: Armed struggle, intellectuals, and political and war prisoners). San Juan, Puerto Rico: Isla Negra Editores.

Latin American Studies Program. n.d. *Puerto Rican Separatists Fuerzas Armadas de Liberacion Nacional (FALN)*. Bloomington: Indiana University. Retrieved from http://www.latinamericanstudies.org/faln.htm

Maldonado-Denis, Manuel. 1976. "Prospects for Latin American Nationalism: The Case of Puerto Rico." *Latin American Perspectives* 3(3):36–45.

Ojeda-Ríos, Filiberto and Alicia Del Campo. 2002. "The Boricua Macheteros Popular Army: Origins, Program, and Struggle." *Latin American Perspectives* 29(6):104–116.

PUERTO RICAN LEGAL DEFENSE AND EDUCATION FUND

More than three decades of struggle to ensure and safeguard the civil and human rights of millions of Puerto Ricans and other Latinos has made the Puerto Rican Legal Defense and Education Fund one of the most valuable resources for Latinos in the United States. This entry describes the context in which the organization was formed and reviews some of its achievements.

Since the U.S. occupation of Puerto Rico in 1898, emigration to the U.S. mainland has been used as a mechanism to deal with the high unemployment and widespread poverty on the island and has produced economic dependency on the United States.

Between 1945 and 1970, roughly a third of the population of Puerto Rico migrated to the United States— mostly to the Northeast—because of the high demand for cheap industrial labor and government intervention to promote and facilitate emigration. In the United States, many Puerto Ricans continued to face poverty, poor housing conditions, inadequate health care, lack of access to quality education, abusive working conditions, lack of political power, and marginalization.

In this context, the pioneer lawyers Cesar A. Perales, Jorge Batista, and Victor Marrero founded the Puerto Rican Legal Defense and Education Fund to empower Puerto Ricans and serve as a tool to end inequalities. The organization is distinguished by its accomplishments in several areas of legal practice such as constitutional law, labor and employment law, immigration law, and education law.

A few years after its founding in 1972, the Puerto Rican Legal Defense and Education Fund achieved one of its biggest victories by representing ASPIRA, an organization dedicated to promoting youth education and leadership, in a lawsuit against the New York City Board of Education. As a result, hundreds of non-English-speaking children, residents of the city, were allowed to receive education in Spanish through the state school system. The organization also played an important role in the litigation against discriminatory hiring and employment policies.

The role of the Puerto Rican Legal Defense and Education Fund in granting access to symbolic forms of power to minority groups is also evident in its success in securing the voting rights of linguistic minorities, their housing rights, and the rights of undocumented immigrants. Furthermore, its solid commitment to the development and education of Latinos provides the foundation for an education division. Since its inception, the organization has advocated for the diversification of the legal system and has prepared numerous students for their law school admission tests, developed a variety of workshops, and provided funding for a number of law school minority students.

Jenniffer M. Santos-Hernández

See Appendix B

See also Hispanics; Puerto Rican Americans; Puerto Rican Armed Forces of National Liberation (FALN); Puerto Rico

Further Readings

Acosta-Belén, Edna and Carlos E. Santiago. 2006. *Puerto Ricans in the United States: A Contemporary Portrait.* Boulder, CO: Lynne Rienner.

Pérez y González, María E. 2000. *The New Americans: Puerto Ricans in the United States.* Westport, CT: Greenwood.

Rodríguez, Clara E. 1989. *Puerto Ricans: Born in the U.S.A.* Boston, MA: Unwin Hyman.

Web Sites

Puerto Rican Legal Defense and Education Fund: http://www.prldef.org

PUERTO RICO

Puerto Rico, a commonwealth or colony of the United States depending on one's political perspective, consists of the island of Puerto Rico plus the smaller islands of Vieques, Culebra, and Mona. Situated 1,000 miles southeast of Florida, the land area is 3,421 square miles. Puerto Rico's estimated population was more than 3.7 million people as of 2007; more Puerto Ricans live in the United States—3.9 million according to a 2004 estimate. Both Spanish and English are the official languages of Puerto Rico; Spanish is the primary spoken language, and English is taught as a second language in the schools. Most Puerto Ricans are Catholics, although Protestantism is increasing.

Once a Spanish colony, Puerto Rico has been part of the United States since 1898. Economically, socially, and politically, it is a hybrid creation dependent on the United States. This entry looks at its history and current situation.

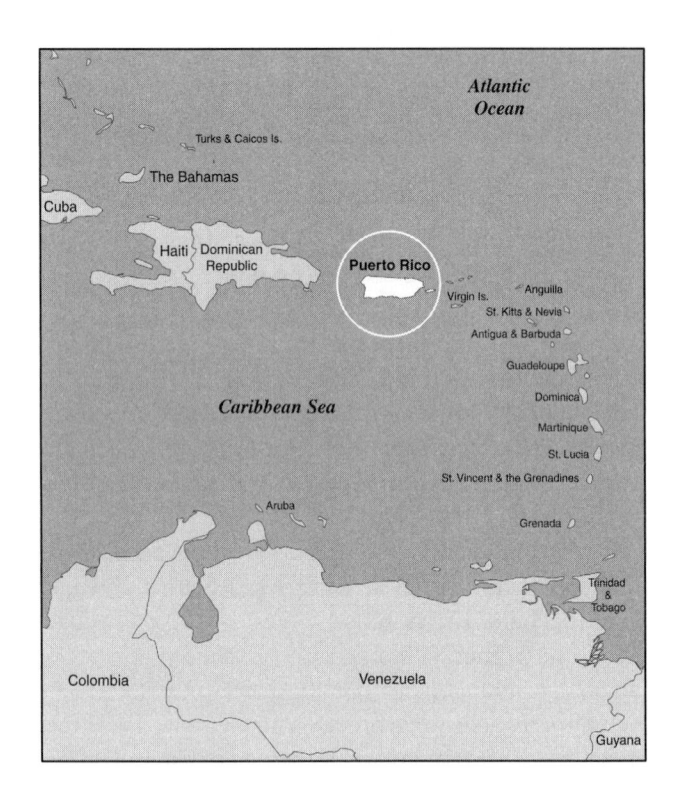

A History of Colonialism

To understand Puerto Rico's current situation, it is vital to examine its past. The history of Puerto Rico's colonial status predates the U.S. invasion in 1898. After 400 years as a colony of Spain, on November 25,

1897, the island of Puerto Rico achieved a measure of autonomy from a weakened Spanish crown. Puerto Ricans were granted an insular parliament that had vast powers over the laws concerning the business of the island. Although Spain retained power over most foreign matters, Puerto Ricans had the right to negotiate commercial treaties and import and export duties. The measure of self-government that Puerto Rico achieved was noteworthy and short-lived.

On April 25, 1898, the United States declared war on Spain. A few months later on July 25, 1898, the United States invaded Puerto Rico and soon established a military government on the island. Spain ceded Puerto Rico, along with Cuba and the Philippines and other territories, to the United States as part of the Treaty of Paris. Since that time, the status of Puerto Rico and its relationship to the United States has been unresolved. Although the terms of the relationship have shifted over the years, since 1898 Puerto Rico has been a territory of the United States.

Two organic laws determined the terms of this relationship. The Foraker Act of 1900 decreed that a governor appointed by the president of the United States would manage Puerto Rico. Presidential appointees would also head most established departments as well as the Supreme Court of Puerto Rico. All applicable U.S. laws were now enforceable in Puerto Rico. In essence, Puerto Rico lost many of the rights it had gained under the Spanish Autonomy Charter. The second organic law, the Jones Act of 1917, decreed that Puerto Ricans were citizens of the United States. They also gained a legislature elected by Puerto Ricans. However, this was a second-class citizenship given that the president of the United States and the U.S. Congress continued to have control of most important positions of power in the government. In addition, they had veto power over any laws enacted by the Puerto Rican legislative branch.

Puerto Ricans have continually lobbied for more rights from the United States. In 1947, Puerto Ricans were granted the right to elect their own governor. In 1952, Puerto Rico achieved commonwealth status. As part of this arrangement, Public Law 600 decreed that Puerto Rico could write and adopt its own constitution. However, the constitution was subject to approval by the U.S. Congress, which maintained sovereignty over the island. Today, Puerto Rico has a locally elected governor who serves a four-year term. There is a bicameral legislature consisting of a Senate (twenty-seven members) and a House of Representatives (fifty-one members). However, the U.S. Congress has the power to determine the constitutionality of the laws.

An Unusual Relationship

Although they are U.S. citizens, residents of Puerto Rico do not vote in national elections and have only a nonvoting representative in Congress. Residents of Puerto Rico do not pay federal income tax on their earnings, but they are eligible to receive social programs such as Social Security, Medicare, and Medicaid. Puerto Ricans can be drafted into the military service of the United States. Puerto Ricans have fought for the United States in World War I, World War II, the Korean War, the Vietnam War, and the Gulf War as well as in Kosovo, Afghanistan, and Iraq.

The United States controls the borders of Puerto Rico. The government of Puerto Rico cannot enter into commercial arrangements or any treaties or agreements with other countries. Therefore, Puerto Rico cannot independently develop economically and is a captive market to U.S. goods. The U.S. minimum wage system applies on the island. The United States controls all trade. It establishes restrictions to the market of Puerto Rican products to the mainland. The balance has always been that there are more goods imported than exported. U.S. maritime laws dictate that all goods traveling between ports within U.S. territory must be transported in ships of the U.S. merchant marine. Puerto Rico must abide by this law and, therefore, cannot avail itself of cheaper transportation costs that could be negotiated with other countries. The United States has power over the monetary system, nationality and citizenship, the legal system, and the communication system.

Resistance to U.S. control has always existed. Puerto Rican revolutionary actions have included an attempt to assassinate President Harry S. Truman on November 1, 1950, and an attack on the U.S. Capitol that wounded five congressmen on March 1, 1954. Between 1980 and 1983, fourteen alleged members of the Armed Forces of National Liberation (FALN) were arrested, accused of seditious conspiracy, and sentenced to prison terms of between 50 and 90 years for organizing to gain independence for their country. President Bill Clinton granted eleven Puerto Rican political prisoners clemency in 1999.

The Economy

Over the years following U.S. occupation of Puerto Rico, what was basically a rural agricultural society was transformed into an industrial society. In 1950, some 40% of the island's labor force worked on farms; today, the figure is less than 3%. This drastic transformation was enhanced greatly through Operation Bootstrap

Workers hoeing a tobacco slope in Puerto Rico (1938). *Puerto Rico's manufacturing sector has shifted from the original labor-intensive industries, such as the manufacturing of tobacco, food, and leather, to more capital-intensive industries, such as pharmaceuticals, chemicals, machinery, and electronics. In 1950, some 40% of the island's labor force worked on farms; today, the figure is less than 3%. This drastic transformation was enhanced greatly through Operation Bootstrap (Operación Manos a la Obra), an industrialization project that began during the 1940s. U.S. companies were encouraged to invest in Puerto Rico by the promise of cheap labor, access to U.S. markets without import duties, and other tax exemptions.*

Source: Library of Congress, Prints & Photographs Division, LC-DIG-fsa-8b30540.

(*Operación Manos a la Obra*), an industrialization project that began during the 1940s. U.S. companies were encouraged to invest in Puerto Rico by the promise of cheap labor, access to U.S. markets without import duties, and other tax exemptions. The program resulted in a major shift from agriculture to manufacturing and tourism. Capital-intensive industries, such as pharmaceuticals, chemical plants, and electronics factories, transferred operations to Puerto Rico in large numbers.

Although Operation Bootstrap was initially promoted as an economic miracle, by the 1960s it was clear that the project failed to create enough jobs to meet the demand. Many islanders moved to the urban areas in search of these opportunities. However, the demand for jobs greatly exceeded the availability of jobs, and many Puerto Ricans migrated to large cities on the mainland United States to escape unemployment. In time, with the elimination of tax incentives, many industries have left the island.

Personal income per capita in Puerto Rico in 2000 was $10,204. This was less than half that in Mississippi, the poorest state in the United States. Per capita income on the island was 34% of the U.S. national average. Officially, the unemployment rate was 12%; however, in 2004 only 66% of the working-age population was employed or actively looking for work. Puerto Rico's economy has been incapable of providing enough job opportunities for its working-age population, and so for decades many Puerto Ricans have migrated to the United States.

Education and Language

Education during that early U.S. occupation was focused primarily on turning Puerto Ricans into loyal U.S. subjects. English was the tool that U.S. leaders thought would lead most effectively to this desired imperative. When the United States arrived in Puerto Rico, less than 10% of all people were literate; therefore, policymakers decided that it would be appropriate to educate the few people who would have access to education using English rather than the Spanish vernacular of the population. Although this Americanization meant that more Puerto Ricans were being educated then ever before, the education these children received was inadequate because it focused mainly on the acquisition of the English language.

Over the first 40 years of colonization, at least five U.S. and Puerto Rican administrators tinkered with the educational system without any informed pedagogical insight on language acquisition and its connection to learning other content areas; the single-minded goal was the delivery of English as soon as possible. This unstable system, combined with a lack of qualified teachers and textbooks chosen more for ideological content than for appropriate content, doomed generations of students in the public schools to an inadequate education.

The first elected Puerto Rican governor, Luis Muñoz Marin, named Mariano Villaronga as secretary of education. Villaronga decreed in 1949 that all education from kindergarten to twelfth grade would be in Spanish. English would be taught in all grades as a second language every day for fifty minutes. This was an important milestone that put an end to the uniform use of English as the language of instruction; however, public education in Puerto Rico remains weak, and only those who can access private schools secure a quality education.

Contemporary Politics

Although other territories acquired by the United States, such as Hawai'i and Alaska, have achieved statehood, that has not happened for Puerto Rico. The three largest political parties continue to debate the island's relationship with the United States, with each party representing a different solution to the status question. The New Progressive Party of Puerto Rico (*Partido Nuevo Progresista de Puerto Rico* [PNP]) advocates for statehood for the island. The Popular Democratic Party of Puerto Rico (*Partido Popular Democrático de Puerto Rico* [PPD]) advocates for enhancement of the current commonwealth status. The Puerto Rican Independence Party (*Partido Independentista Puertorriqueño* [PIP]) advocates for the independence of Puerto Rico from the United States.

Since 1948 when Puerto Ricans began voting for governor, power has gone back and forth between the PNP and the PPD. The PIP has never won more than 5% of the vote. Although it is the U.S. Congress that will determine the fate of the island, residents of Puerto Rico have twice voted in nonbinding plebiscites to determine their political status. In 1967, the outcome was commonwealth 60%, statehood 39%, and independence 1%. In 1993, 48.6% of the population voted for commonwealth, 46.3% preferred statehood, and 4.4% voted for independence.

Another source of much debate on the island has been the presence of the U.S. Navy on the island of Vieques. After a struggle lasting more than six decades, the navy withdrew its base from the island in May 2003. The navy had been using the island as a bombing range since the 1940s. Residents of Vieques voted overwhelmingly to close the base in a referendum in 2001. Protests against the military presence grew after David Sanes, a resident of Vieques, was accidentally killed and four other people were injured during navy practice exercises on the island. Protests included civilians' occupying the bases.

Toxic pollution caused by explosives and radioactive-depleted uranium shells remain on the island. The people of Vieques have been found to have a cancer rate 26% higher than Puerto Rico's average. Many believe that this is another result of the navy's presence on the island. Activists continue to lobby for the cleanup of Vieques.

On December 14, 1960, the United Nations approved Resolution 1514-XV (Resolution on the Granting of Independence to Colonial Countries and Peoples), which condemned colonialism and recommended that superpowers liberate their colonies. Every year since the early 1970s, the Special Committee on the Granting of Independence to Colonial Countries and Peoples, which oversees the process of decolonization of the world's remaining colonies, issues resolutions calling for Puerto Rico's self-determination and independence.

During the past 10 years, there has been renewed lobbying for a final resolution to the status question. In 1998, the U.S. House of Representatives passed a bill that called for binding elections in Puerto Rico to decide the island's permanent political status. Since then, various presidential task forces under Presidents Bill Clinton and George W. Bush have studied the status question without resolution. In 2005, Bush's task force on Puerto Rico's status concluded that another vote by Puerto Ricans was the best next step. As of 2007, no progress had been made on this issue and Puerto Rico's future remained unresolved.

Lourdes Torres

See Appendix A

See also Americanization; Caribbean; Caribbean Americans; Colonialism; Culture of Poverty; Hispanics; Operation Bootstrap; Puerto Rican Americans; Puerto Rican Armed Forces of National Liberation (FALN); Puerto Rican Legal Defense and Education Fund

Further Readings

Briggs, Laura. 2002. *Reproducing Empire: Race, Sex, Science, and U.S. Imperialism in Puerto Rico.* Berkeley: University of California Press.

Duany, Jorge. 2002. *The Puerto Rican Nation on the Move: Identities on the Island and in the United States.* Chapel Hill: University of North Carolina Press.

Morris, Nancy. 1995. *Puerto Rico: Culture, Politics, and Identity.* Westport, CT: Praeger.

Trías Monge, José. 1997. *Puerto Rico: The Trials of the Oldest Colony in the World.* New Haven, CT: Yale University Press.